Collins

ESSENTIAL ROAD ATLAS

BRITAIN

Collins

Published by Collins
An imprint of HarperCollins Publishers
Westerhill Road, Bishopbriggs, Glasgow G64 2QT

www.harpercollins.co.uk

Copyright © HarperCollins Publishers Ltd 2015

Collins® is a registered trademark of HarperCollins Publishers Limited

Mapping generated from CollinsBartholomew digital databases

Contains Ordnance Survey data © Crown copyright and database right (2014)

The grid on this map is the National Grid taken from the Ordnance Survey map with the permission of the Controller of Her Majesty's Stationery Office.

Printed in China

ISBN 978 0 00 810230 2   ISBN 978 0 00 794773 7   10 9 8 7 6 5 4 3 2 1

e-mail: roadcheck@harpercollins.co.uk   facebook.com/collinsmaps   @collinsmaps

Information for the alignment of the Wales Coast Path provided by © Natural Resources Wales. All rights reserved. Contains Ordnance Survey Data. Ordnance Survey Licence number 100019741. Crown Copyright and Database Right (2013).

Information for the alignment of several Long Distance Trails in Scotland provided by © walkhighlands

Information on fixed speed camera locations provided by PocketGPSWorld.com

With thanks to the Wine Guild of the United Kingdom for help with researching vineyards.

Information regarding blue flag beach awards is current as of summer 2009. For latest information please visit www.blueflag.org.uk

Contents

Route planning

Route planning maps	ii-vii
Restricted motorway junctions	viii-ix
Motorway services information	x-xi
Orbital motorway maps - M25 & Birmingham	xii-xiii
Risk rating of Britain's motorways and A roads	xiv-xv
Distance chart	xvi

Urban approach maps (1 mile to 1 inch)   1-32

Symbols used on maps / Locator map	1
Plymouth	2
Bournemouth	3
Southampton & Portsmouth	4-5
Swansea	6
Cardiff & Newport	7
Bristol	8
Milton Keynes	9
London	10-13
West Midlands	14-15
Coventry	16
Leicester	17
Derby & Nottingham	18-19
Stoke-on-Trent	20
Sheffield	21
Merseyside	22-23
Greater Manchester	24-25
Leeds & Bradford	26-27
Newcastle upon Tyne & Sunderland	28
Middlesbrough	29
Glasgow	30-31
Edinburgh	32

Street maps   33-91

Symbols used on maps / Locator map	33	Hastings	75
		Hereford	75
Birmingham	34-35	Hull	76
Edinburgh	36-37	Inverness	76
Glasgow	38-39	Leicester	77
Leeds	40-41	Lincoln	77
Liverpool	42-43	Middlesbrough	78
London	44-45	Milton Keynes	78
Manchester	46-47	Newcastle upon Tyne	79
Birmingham index	48	Norwich	79
Edinburgh index	49	Nottingham	80
Glasgow index	51	Oxford	80
Leeds index	52	Perth	81
Liverpool index	54	Plymouth	81
London index	56	Portsmouth	82
Manchester index	60	Reading	82
Aberdeen	63	Salisbury	83
Bath	63	Scarborough	83
Blackpool	64	Sheffield	84
Bournemouth	64	Southampton	84
Bradford	65	Stoke-on-Trent	85
Brighton	65	Stratford-upon-Avon	85
Bristol	66	Sunderland	86
Cambridge	66	Swansea	86
Canterbury	67	Swindon	87
Cardiff	67	Torquay	87
Carlisle	68	Watford	88
Cheltenham	68	Weston-super-Mare	88
Chester	69	Winchester	89
Coventry	69	Windsor	89
Derby	70	Worcester	90
Dover	70	York	90
Dundee	71		
Durham	71	**Airport plans**	
Eastbourne	72	Birmingham International	91
Exeter	72	Gatwick	91
Folkestone	73	Glasgow	91
Gloucester	73	Heathrow	91
Guildford	74	Manchester	91
Harrogate	74	Stansted	91

Road maps   92-279

Symbols used on maps & key to map pages	92-93
England, Wales & Southern Scotland (3.2 miles to 1 inch)	94-253
Northern Scotland (4.2 miles to 1 inch)	254-279

Index   280-318

Legend

M62	Motorway
	Motorway junction with full / limited access
Tebay / Killington Lake	Motorway service area with full / limited access
A172	Primary route dual / single carriageway
A167	'A' road dual / single carriageway
	'B' road
	Toll
	Car ferry route
Newcastle International	Airport
	National boundary
Exmoor	National / Forest Park
147	Road map pages

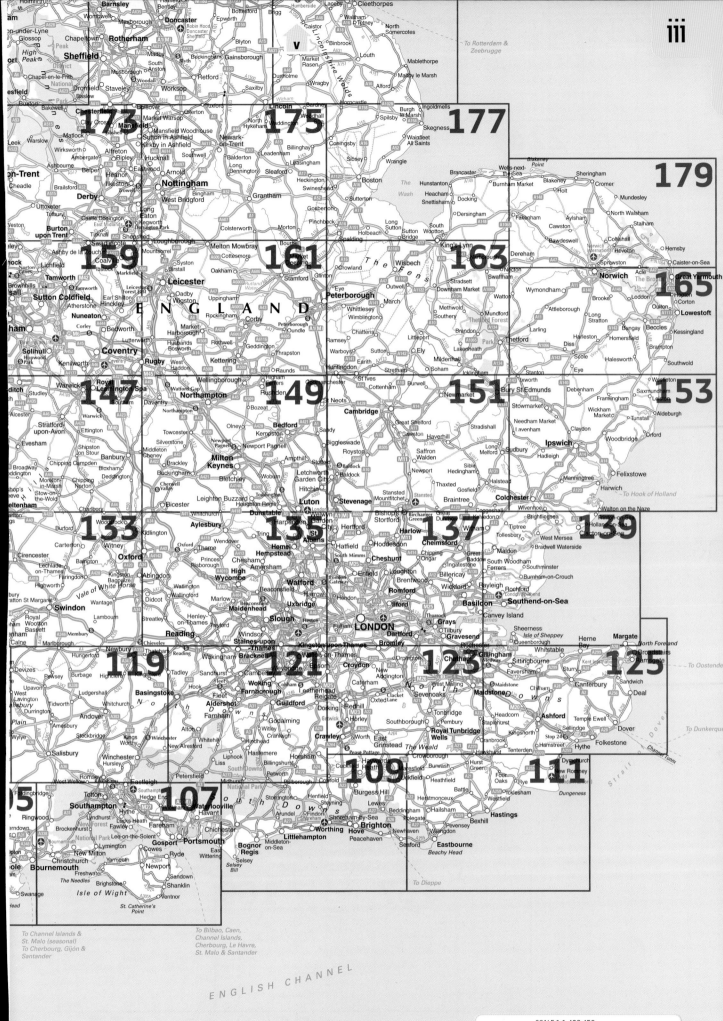

iii

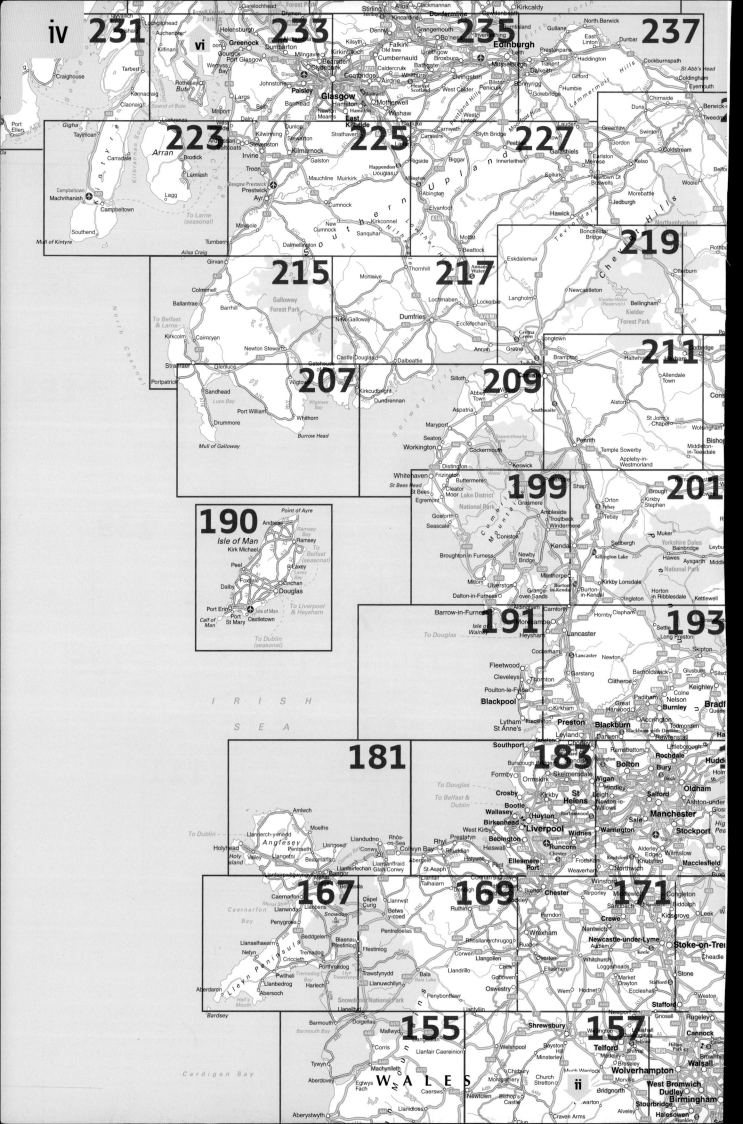

SCALE 1:1,408,450

0 · 10 · 20 · 30 · 40 miles
0 · 10 · 20 · 30 · 40 · 50 · 60 kilometres
22 miles to 1 inch / 14 km to 1 cm

M62	Motorway
	Motorway junction with full / limited access
Tebay ▣ Killington Lake	Motorway service area with full / limited access
A172	Primary route dual / single carriageway
A167	'A' road dual / single carriageway
	'B' road
⌐●⌐	Toll
	Car ferry route
✈ Newcastle International	Airport
	National boundary
Exmoor	National / Forest Park
147	Road map pages

229

Holy Island or Lindisfarne
Farne Islands
Bamburgh
North Sunderland
Alnwick
Longhoughton
Warkworth
Amble
Ashington
Newbiggin-by-the-Sea
Morpeth
Bedlington
Blyth
Cramlington
Whitley Bay
Gosforth
Whitley Bay
North Shields
Tynemouth
Newcastle upon Tyne
South Shields
Gateshead
Sunderland
Washington
Stanley
Houghton le Spring
Chester-le-Street
Easington
Durham
Peterlee
Crook
Spennymoor
Hartlepool
Shildon
Billingham
Redcar
Stockton-on-Tees
Middlesbrough
South Bank
Darlington
Yarm
Stokesley
Hinderwell
Sandsend
Whitby
Gilling West
Scotch Corner
Catterick
North York Moors
Robin Hood's Bay
Northallerton
Sleights
Burniston
Bedale
Leeming
Helmsley
Kirkbymoorside
Scalby
Scarborough
Masham
Thirsk
Pickering
Eastfield
Ripon
Oswaldkirk
Vale of Pickering
Snainton
Filey
Topcliffe
Malton · Norton
Hunmanby
Pateley Bridge
Easingwold
Bempton
Boroughbridge
Flamborough Head
Ripley
Langtoft
Bridlington
Knaresborough
Stamford Bridge
Driffield
Skipsea
Harrogate
Spofforth
Wetherby
York
Fulford
Bainton
Brandesburton
Leven
Hornsea
Otley
Tadcaster
Pocklington
Ilkley
Boston Spa
Holme-on-Spalding-Moor
Market Weighton
Skirlaugh
Aldbrough
Bingley
Leeds
Selby
Bubwith
North Cave
Beverley
Pudsey
Garforth
South Cave
Hessle
Hedon
Withernsea
Castleford
Ferrybridge
Goole
Kingston upon Hull
Knottingley
Barton-upon-Humber
Patrington
Wakefield
Pontefract
Winterton
Easington
Barnsley
Thorne
Scunthorpe
Immingham
Grimsby
Hemsworth
Doncaster North
Crowle
Bottesford
Brigg
Laceby
Cleethorpes
Wombwell
Bentley
Hatfield
Epworth
Caistor
Waltham · Tetney
Maxborough
Doncaster
North Somercotes
Chapeltown
Rotherham
Robin Hood Doncaster Sheffield
Blyton
Binbrook
Louth
Sheffield
Maltby
Gainsborough
Market Rasen
Mablethorpe
South Anston
Woodall
Beckingham
Mosborough
Dunholme
Maltby le Marsh
Staveley
Worksop
Retford
Saxilby
Wragby
Alford
Dronfield
Baslow
Lincoln
Horncastle
Burgh le Marsh
Ingoldmells
Chesterfield
Bolsover
Tuxford
Bardney
Spilsby
Skegness
Clay Cross
North Hykeham
Mansfield
Market Warsop
Mansfield Woodhouse
Waddington
Coningsby
Wainfleet All Saints
Matlock
Sutton in Ashfield
Newark-on-Trent
Leadenham
Billinghay
Wirksworth
Kirkby in Ashfield
Southwell
Sibsey
Wrangle
Alfreton
Hucknall
Balderton
Sleaford
Ambergate
Ripley
Long Bennington
Heckington
Swineshead
Brancaster
Wells-next-the-Sea
Blakeney Point
Sheringham
Belper
Eastwood
Arnold
Cromer
Heanor
Nottingham
Bingham
Grantham
Boston
Hunstanton
Burnham Market
Holt
Mundesley
Ilkeston
West Bridgford
Gosberton
Sutterton
Heacham
Docking
Fakenham
North Walsham
Derby
Long Eaton
Castle Donington
East Midlands
Pinchbeck
Long Sutton
Snettisham
Dersingham
Aylsham
Stalham
Ticknall
Kegworth
Donington Park
Colsterworth
Morton
Holbeach
Spalding
Sutton Bridge
South Wootton
King's Lynn
Dereham
Norwich
Hemsby
Burton on Trent
Swadlincote
Shepshed
Melton Mowbray
Bourne
Wisbech
Swaffham
Sprowston
Caister-on-Sea
Ashby de la Zouch
Coalville
Mountsorrel
Cottesmore
Crowland
Stradsett
Wymondham
Markfield
Oakham
Stamford
Downham Market
Norwich
Acle
Tamworth
Birstall
Syston
Rutland Water
Watton
The Broads
Leicester
Oadby
Wigston
Eye
Peterborough
Outwell
Methwold
Southery
Mundford
Brooke
Loddon
Lowestoft
Hinckley
Rockingham
Corby
Oundle
Whittlesey
Wimblington
Brandon
Thetford Forest Park
Larling
Long Stratton
Bungay
Beccles
Nuneaton
Corley
Bedworth
Market Harborough
Husbands Bosworth
Rothwell
Geddington
Ramsey
Chatteris
Littleport
Thetford
Harleston
Homersfield
Diss
Kessingland
Brampton

221

213

203

205

195

197

85

187

189

173

175

177

179

159

161

163

165

N O R T H   S E A

To Rotterdam & Zeebrugge

The Wash

The Fens

E N G L A N D

Yorkshire Wolds

Lincolnshire Wolds

Holderness

Mouth of the Humber

Vale of York

North York Moors National Park

Vale of Pickering

Peak District National Park

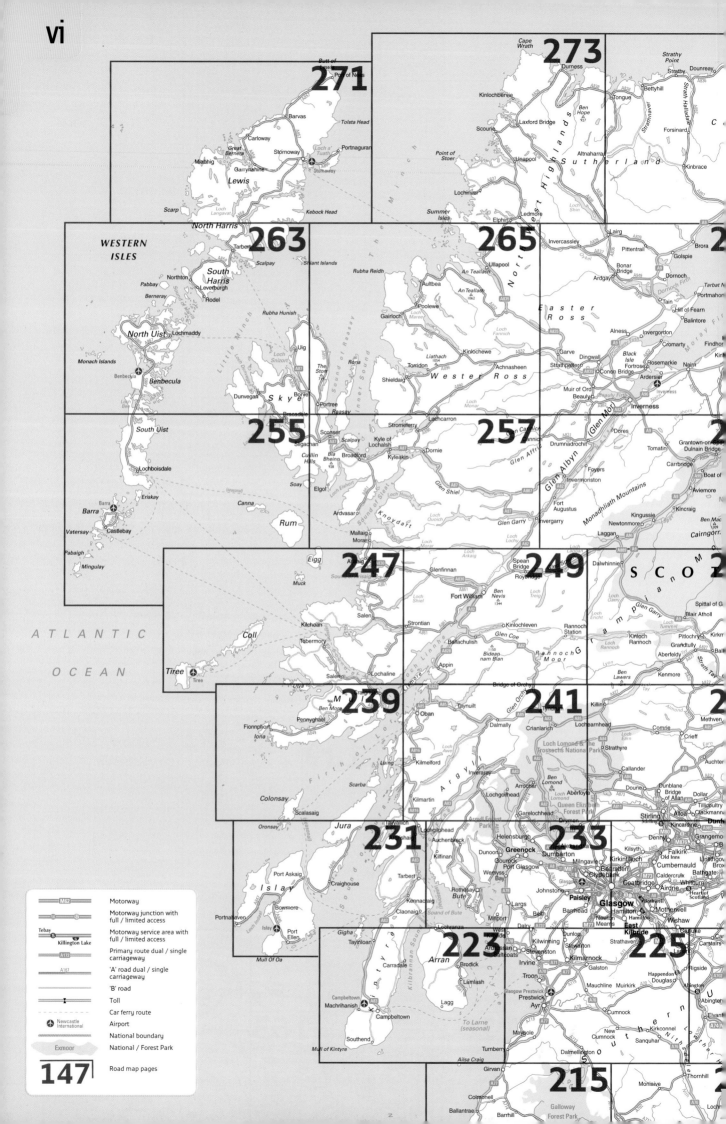

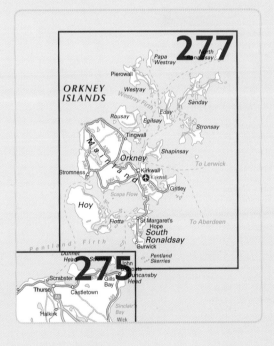

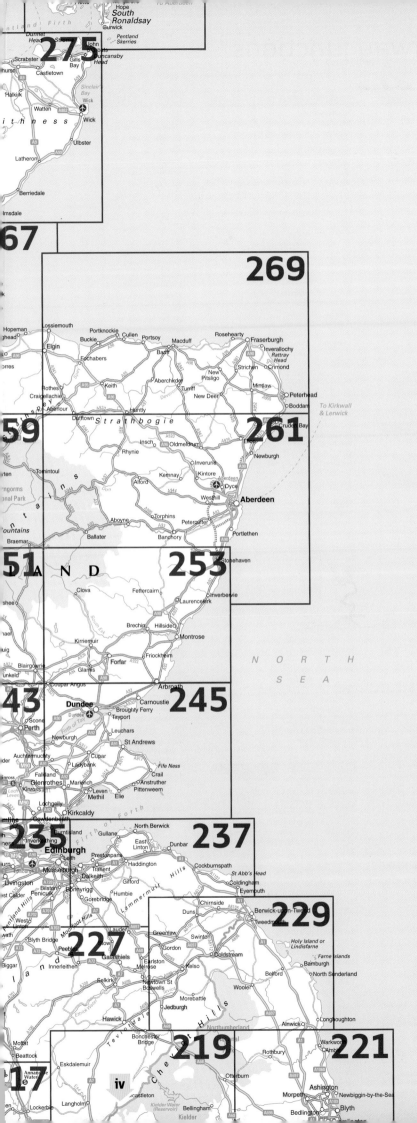

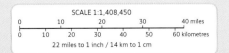

Restricted motorway junctions

A1(M) LONDON TO NEWCASTLE

②
Northbound : No access
Southbound : No exit

③
Southbound : No access

⑤
Northbound : No exit
Southbound : No access
: No exit

④1
Northbound : No exit to M62 Eastbound

④3
Northbound : No exit to M1 Westbound

Dishforth
Southbound : No access from A168 Eastbound

⑤7
Northbound : No access
: Exit only to A66(M) Northbound
Southbound : Access only from A66(M) Southbound
: No exit

⑥5
Northbound : No access from A1
Southbound : No exit to A1

A3(M) PORTSMOUTH

①
Northbound : No exit
Southbound : No access

④
Northbound : No access
Southbound : No exit

A38(M) BIRMINGHAM

Victoria Road
Northbound : No exit
Southbound : No access

A48(M) CARDIFF

Junction with M4
Westbound : No access from M4 ㉙ Eastbound
Eastbound : No exit to M4 ㉙ Westbound

29A
Westbound : No exit to A48 Eastbound
Eastbound : No access from A48 Westbound

A57(M) MANCHESTER

Brook Street
Westbound : No exit
Eastbound : No access

A58(M) LEEDS

Westgate
Southbound : No access
Woodhouse Lane
Westbound : No exit

A64(M) LEEDS

Claypit Lane
Eastbound : No access

A66(M) DARLINGTON

Junction with A1(M)
Northbound : No access from A1(M) Southbound
: No exit
Southbound : No access
: No exit to A1(M) Northbound

A74(M) LOCKERBIE

⑱
Northbound : No access
Southbound : No exit

A167(M) NEWCASTLE

Campden Street
Northbound : No exit
Southbound : No access
: No exit

M1 LONDON TO LEEDS

②
Northbound : No exit
Southbound : No access

④
Northbound : No exit
Southbound : No access

6A
Northbound : Access only from M25 ㉑
: No exit
Southbound : No access
: Exit only to M25 ㉑

⑦
Northbound : Access only from A414
: No exit
Southbound : No access
: Exit only to A414

M1 LONDON TO LEEDS (continued)

⑰
Northbound : No access
: Exit only to M45
Southbound : Access only from M45
: No exit

⑲
Northbound : Exit only to M6
Southbound : Access only from M6

21A
Northbound : No access
Southbound : No exit

23A
Northbound : No access from A453
Southbound : No exit to A453

24A
Northbound : No exit
Southbound : No access

35A
Northbound : No access
Southbound : No exit

④3
Northbound : No access
: Exit only to M621
Southbound : No exit
: Access only from M621

④8
Northbound : No exit to A1(M) Southbound
: Access only from A1(M) Northbound
Southbound : Exit only to A1(M) Southbound
: No access

M2 ROCHESTER TO CANTERBURY

①
Westbound : No exit to A2 Eastbound
Eastbound : No access from A2 Westbound

M3 LONDON TO WINCHESTER

⑧
Westbound : No access
Eastbound : No exit

⑩
Northbound : No access
Southbound : No exit

⑬
Southbound : No exit to A335 Eastbound
: No access

⑭
Westbound : No access
Eastbound : No exit

M4 LONDON TO SWANSEA

①
Westbound : No access from A4 Eastbound
Eastbound : No exit to A4 Westbound

②
Westbound : No access from A4 Eastbound
: No exit to A4 Eastbound
Eastbound : No access from A4 Westbound
: No exit to A4 Westbound

㉑
Westbound : No access from M48 Eastbound
Eastbound : No exit to M48 Westbound

㉓
Westbound : No exit to M48 Eastbound
Eastbound : No access from M48 Westbound

㉕
Westbound : No access
Eastbound : No exit

25A
Westbound : No access
Eastbound : No exit

㉙
Westbound : No access
: Exit only to A48(M)
Eastbound : Access only from A48(M) Eastbound
: No exit

㉚
Westbound : No access

㉛
Westbound : No exit
Eastbound : No access
: No exit

④1
Westbound : No exit
Eastbound : No access

④2
Westbound : No exit to A48
Eastbound : No access from A48

M5 BIRMINGHAM TO EXETER

⑩
Northbound : No exit
Southbound : No access

11A
Northbound : No access from A417 Eastbound
Southbound : No exit to A417 Westbound

M6 COVENTRY TO CARLISLE

Junction with M1
Northbound : No access from M1 ⑲ Southbound
Southbound : No exit to M1 ⑲ Northbound

3A
Northbound : No access from M6 Toll
Southbound : No exit to M6 Toll

④
Northbound : No exit to M42 Northbound
: No access from M42 Southbound
Southbound : No exit to M42
: No access from M42 Southbound

4A
Northbound : No access from M42 ⑧ Northbound
: No exit
Southbound : No access
: Exit only to M42 ⑧

⑤
Northbound : No access
Southbound : No exit

10A
Northbound : No access
: Exit only to M54
Southbound : Access only from M54
: No exit

11A
Northbound : No exit to M6 Toll
Southbound : No access from M6 Toll

㉔
Northbound : No exit
Southbound : No access

㉕
Northbound : No access
Southbound : No exit

㉚
Northbound : Access only from M61 Northbound
: No exit
Southbound : No access
: Exit only to M61 Southbound

31A
Northbound : No access
Southbound : No exit

M6 Toll BIRMINGHAM

T1
Northbound : Exit only to M42
: Access only from A4097
Southbound : No exit
: Access only from M42 Southbound

T2
Northbound : No exit
: No access
Southbound : No access

T5
Northbound : No exit
Southbound : No access

T7
Northbound : No access
Southbound : No exit

T8
Northbound : No access
Southbound : No exit

M8 EDINBURGH TO GLASGOW

⑧
Westbound : No access from M73 ② Southbound
: No access from A8 Eastbound
: No access from A89 Eastbound
Eastbound : No access from A89 Westbound
: No exit to M73 ② Northbound

⑨
Westbound : No exit
Eastbound : No access

⑬
Westbound : Access only from M80
Eastbound : Exit only to M80

⑭
Westbound : No exit
Eastbound : No access

⑯
Westbound : No access
Eastbound : No exit

⑰
Eastbound : Access only from A82,
not central Glasgow
: Exit only to A82,
not central Glasgow

⑱
Westbound : No access
Eastbound : No access

⑲
Westbound : Access only from A814 Eastbound
Eastbound : Exit only to A814 Westbound,
not central Glasgow

M8 EDINBURGH TO GLASGOW (cont)

⑳
Westbound : No access
Eastbound : No exit

㉑
Westbound : No exit
Eastbound : No access

㉒
Westbound : No access
: Exit only to M77 Southbound
Eastbound : Access only from M77 Northbound
: No exit

㉓
Westbound : No access
Eastbound : No exit

25A
Eastbound : No access
Westbound : No exit

㉘
Westbound : No access
Eastbound : No exit

28A
Westbound : No access
Eastbound : No exit

M9 EDINBURGH TO STIRLING

②
Westbound : No exit
Eastbound : No access

③
Westbound : No access
Eastbound : No exit

⑥
Westbound : No exit
Eastbound : No access

⑧
Westbound : No access
Eastbound : No exit

M11 LONDON TO CAMBRIDGE

④
Northbound : No access from A1400 Westbound
: No exit
Southbound : No access
: No exit to A1400 Eastbound

⑤
Northbound : No access
Southbound : No exit

8A
Northbound : No access
Southbound : No exit

⑨
Northbound : No access
Southbound : No exit

⑬
Northbound : No access
Southbound : No exit

⑭
Northbound : No access from A428 Eastbound
: No exit to A428 Westbound
: No exit to A1307
Southbound : No access from A428 Eastbound
: No access from A1307
: No exit

M20 LONDON TO FOLKESTONE

②
Westbound : No exit
Eastbound : No access

③
Westbound : No access
: Exit only to M26 Westbound
Eastbound : Access only from M26 Eastbound
: No exit

11A
Westbound : No exit
Eastbound : No access

M23 LONDON TO CRAWLEY

⑦
Northbound : No exit to A23 Southbound
Southbound : No access from A23 Northbound

10A
Southbound : No access from B2036
Northbound : No exit to B2036

Restricted motorway junctions are shown on the maps as:

M25 LONDON ORBITAL MOTORWAY
1B
Clockwise : No access
Anticlockwise : No exit
5
Clockwise : No exit to M26 Eastbound
Anticlockwise : No access from M26 Westbound
Spur of M25 5
Clockwise : No access from M26 Westbound
Anticlockwise : No exit to M26 Eastbound
19
Clockwise : No access
Anticlockwise : No exit
21
Clockwise : No access from M1 6A Northbound
: No exit to M1 6A Southbound
Anticlockwise : No access from M1 6A Northbound
: No exit to M1 6A Southbound
31
Clockwise : No exit
Anticlockwise : No access

M26 SEVENOAKS
Junction with M25 5
Westbound : No exit to M25 Anticlockwise
: No exit to M25 spur
Eastbound : No access from M25 Clockwise
: No access from M25 spur
Junction with M20
Westbound : No access from M20 3 Eastbound
Eastbound : No exit to M20 3 Westbound

M27 SOUTHAMPTON TO PORTSMOUTH
4 West
Westbound : No exit
Eastbound : No access
4 East
Westbound : No access
Eastbound : No exit
10
Westbound : No access
Eastbound : No exit
12 West
Westbound : No exit
Eastbound : No access
12 East
Westbound : No access from A3
Eastbound : No exit

M40 LONDON TO BIRMINGHAM
3
Westbound : No access
Eastbound : No exit
7
Eastbound : No exit
8
Northbound : No access
Southbound : No exit
13
Northbound : No access
Southbound : No exit
14
Northbound : No exit
Southbound : No access
16
Northbound : No exit
Southbound : No access

M42 BIRMINGHAM
1
Northbound : No exit
Southbound : No access
7
Northbound : No access
: Exit only to M6 Northbound
Southbound : Access only from M6 Northbound
: No exit
7A
Northbound : No access
: Exit only to M6 Eastbound
Southbound : No access
: No exit
8
Northbound : Access only from M6 Southbound
: No exit
Southbound : Access only from M6 Southbound
: Exit only to M6 Northbound

M45 COVENTRY
Junction with M1
Westbound : No access from M1 17 Southbound
Eastbound : No exit to M1 17 Northbound
Junction with A45
Westbound : No exit
Eastbound : No access

M48 CHEPSTOW
M4
Westbound : No exit to M4 Eastbound
Eastbound : No access from M4 Westbound

M49 BRISTOL
18A
Northbound : No access from M5 Southbound
Southbound : No access from M5 Northbound

M53 BIRKENHEAD TO CHESTER
11
Northbound : No access from M56 15 Eastbound
: No exit to M56 15 Westbound
Southbound : No access from M56 15 Eastbound
: No exit to M56 15 Westbound

M54 WOLVERHAMPTON TO TELFORD
Junction with M6
Westbound : No access from M6 10A Southbound
Eastbound : No exit to M6 10A Northbound

M56 STOCKPORT TO CHESTER
1
Westbound : No access from M60 Eastbound
: No access from A34 Northbound
Eastbound : No exit to M60 Westbound
: No exit to A34 Southbound
2
Westbound : No access
Eastbound : No exit
3
Westbound : No exit
Eastbound : No access
4
Westbound : No access
Eastbound : No exit
7
Westbound : No access
Eastbound : No exit
8
Westbound : No exit
Eastbound : No access
9
Westbound : No exit to M6 Southbound
Eastbound : No access from M6 Northbound
15
Westbound : No access
: No access from M53 11
Eastbound : No exit
: No exit to M53 11

M57 LIVERPOOL
3
Northbound : No exit
Southbound : No access
5
Northbound : Access only from A580 Westbound
: No exit
Southbound : No access
: Exit only to A580 Eastbound

M58 LIVERPOOL TO WIGAN
1
Westbound : No access
Eastbound : No exit

M60 MANCHESTER
2
Westbound : No exit
Eastbound : No access
3
Westbound : No access from M56 1
: No access from A34 Southbound
: No exit to A34 Northbound
Eastbound : No access from A34 Southbound
: No exit to M56 1
: No exit to A34 Northbound
4
Westbound : No access
Eastbound : No exit to M56

M60 MANCHESTER (continued)
5
Westbound : No access from A5103 Southbound
: No exit to A5103 Southbound
Eastbound : No access from A5103 Northbound
: No exit to A5103 Northbound
14
Westbound : No access from A580
: No exit to A580 Eastbound
Eastbound : No access from A580 Westbound
: No exit to A580
16
Westbound : No access
Eastbound : No exit
20
Westbound : No access
Eastbound : No exit
22
Westbound : No access
25
Westbound : No access
26
Eastbound : No access
: No exit
27
Westbound : No exit
Eastbound : No access

M61 MANCHESTER TO PRESTON
2
Northbound : No access from A580 Eastbound
: No access from A666
Southbound : No exit to A580 Westbound
3
Northbound : No access from A580 Eastbound
: No access from A666
Southbound : No exit to A580 Westbound
Junction with M6
Northbound : No exit to M6 30 Southbound
Southbound : No access from M6 30 Northbound

M62 LIVERPOOL TO HULL
23
Westbound : No exit
Eastbound : No access
32A
Westbound : No exit to A1(M) Southbound

M65 BURNLEY
9
Westbound : No exit
Eastbound : No access
11
Westbound : No access
Eastbound : No exit

M66 MANCHESTER TO EDENFIELD
1
Northbound : No access
Southbound : No exit
Junction with A56
Northbound : Exit only to A56 Northbound
Southbound : Access only from A56 Southbound

M67 MANCHESTER
1
Westbound : No exit
Eastbound : No access
2
Westbound : No access
Eastbound : No exit

M69 COVENTRY TO LEICESTER
2
Northbound : No exit
Southbound : No access

M73 GLASGOW
1
Northbound : No access from A721 Eastbound
Southbound : No exit to A721 Eastbound
2
Northbound : No access from M8 8 Eastbound
Southbound : No exit to M8 8 Westbound

M74 GLASGOW
1A
Westbound : No exit to M8 Kingston Bridge
Eastbound : No access from M8 Kingston Bridge
3
Westbound : No access
Eastbound : No exit
3A
Westbound : No exit
Eastbound : No access

M74 GLASGOW (continued)
7
Northbound : No exit
Southbound : No access
9
Northbound : No access
: No exit
Southbound : No access
10
Southbound : No access
11
Southbound : No access
12
Northbound : Access only from A70 Northbound
Southbound : Exit only to A70 Southbound

M77 GLASGOW
Junction with M8
Northbound : No exit to M8 22 Westbound
Southbound : No access from M8 22 Eastbound
4
Northbound : No exit
Southbound : No access
6
Northbound : No exit to A77
Southbound : No access from A77
7
Northbound : No access
: No exit
8
Northbound : No access
Southbound : No access

M80 STIRLING
4A
Northbound : No access
Southbound : No exit
6A
Northbound : No exit
Southbound : No access
8
Northbound : No access from M876
Southbound : No exit to M876

M90 EDINBURGH TO PERTH
2A
Northbound : No access
Southbound : No exit
7
Northbound : No exit
Southbound : No access
8
Northbound : No access
Southbound : No exit
10
Northbound : No access from A912
: No exit to A912 Southbound
Southbound : No access from A912 Northbound
: No exit to A912

M180 SCUNTHORPE
1
Westbound : No exit
Eastbound : No access

M606 BRADFORD
Straithgate Lane
Northbound : No access

M621 LEEDS
2A
Northbound : No exit
Southbound : No access
5
Northbound : No access
Southbound : No exit
6
Northbound : No exit
Southbound : No access

M876 FALKIRK
Junction with M80
Westbound : No exit to M80 8 Northbound
Eastbound : No access from M80 8 Southbound
Junction with M9
Westbound : No access
Eastbound : No exit

Motorway services information

All motorway service areas have fuel, food, toilets, disabled facilities and free short-term parking

For further information on motorway services providers:
Moto www.moto-way.com
Euro Garages www.eurogarages.com
RoadChef www.roadchef.com
Extra www.extraservices.co.uk
Welcome Break www.welcomebreak.co.uk
Westmorland www.westmorland.com

Motorway	Junction	Service provider	Service name	Fuel supplier	Information	Accommodation	Conference facilities	Showers	M&S Simply Food	Costa Coffee	Starbucks	Burger King	KFC	McDonalds	Wimpy
A1(M)	1	Welcome Break	South Mimms	BP	●	●	●	●				●	●		
	10	Extra	Baldock	Shell	●	●							●	●	
	17	Extra	Peterborough	Shell	●	●		●	●				●	●	
	34	Moto	Blyth	Esso	●	●		●	●	●	●				
	46	Moto	Wetherby	BP	●	●			●	●	●				
	61	RoadChef	Durham	Total	●	●	●		●				●		
	64	Moto	Washington	BP	●	●		●		●	●				
A74(M)	16	RoadChef	Annandale Water	BP	●	●			●						
	22	Welcome Break	Gretna Green	BP	●	●		●			●	●	●		
M1	2-4	Welcome Break	London Gateway	Shell	●	●	●	●			●	●			
	11-12	Moto	Toddington	BP		●		●	●	●	●				
	14-15	Welcome Break	Newport Pagnell	Shell	●	●		●			●	●	●		
	15A	RoadChef	Northampton	BP						●				●	
	16-17	RoadChef	Watford Gap	BP	●	●		●		●				●	
	21-21A	Welcome Break	Leicester Forest East	BP	●	●	●	●			●	●	●		
	22	Euro Garages	Markfield	BP	●	●		●		●					
	23A	Moto	Donington Park	BP	●	●	●	●	●	●	●				
	25-26	Moto	Trowell	BP	●	●		●	●	●	●				
	28-29	RoadChef	Tibshelf	Shell	●	●	●		●					●	
	30-31	Welcome Break	Woodall	Shell	●	●		●			●	●	●	●	
	38-39	Moto	Woolley Edge	BP	●	●		●	●	●	●				
M2	4-5	Moto	Medway	BP	●		●		●		●				
M3	4A-5	Welcome Break	Fleet	Shell	●	●	●	●			●	●	●		
	8-9	Moto	Winchester	Shell	●		●		●		●				
M4	3	Moto	Heston	BP	●	●	●	●	●		●				
	11-12	Moto	Reading	BP	●	●	●	●	●	●	●				
	13	Moto	Chieveley	BP		●			●	●					
	14-15	Welcome Break	Membury	BP	●	●		●			●	●	●		
	17-18	Moto	Leigh Delamere	BP	●	●	●	●	●	●	●				
	23A	RoadChef	Magor	Esso	●	●		●						●	
	30	Welcome Break	Cardiff Gate	Total		●		●			●	●			
	33	Moto	Cardiff West	Esso	●	●		●	●		●				
	36	Welcome Break	Sarn Park	Shell		●		●			●	●			
	47	Moto	Swansea	BP	●	●			●		●				
	49	RoadChef	Pont Abraham	Texaco	●				●						
M5	3-4	Moto	Frankley	BP		●		●	●	●	●				
	8	RoadChef	Strensham (South)	BP	●				●					●	
	8	RoadChef	Strensham (North)	Texaco	●	●	●		●					●	
	11-12	Westmorland	Gloucester	Texaco	●				●						
	13-14	Welcome Break	Michaelwood	BP	●	●		●			●	●	●		
	19	Welcome Break	Gordano	Shell	●	●	●	●			●	●	●		
	21-22	RoadChef	Sedgemoor (South)	Total	●				●						
	21-22	Welcome Break	Sedgemoor (North)	Shell	●	●	●	●			●	●	●		
	24	Moto	Bridgwater	BP	●		●		●	●	●				
	25-26	RoadChef	Taunton Deane	Shell	●	●			●						
	27	Moto	Tiverton	Shell	●	●			●		●				
	28	Extra	Cullompton	Shell						●				●	
	29-30	Moto	Exeter	BP	●	●		●	●	●	●				
M6 Toll	T6-T7	RoadChef	Norton Canes	BP	●	●		●	●						

Motorway	Junction	Service provider	Service name	Fuel supplier	Information	Accommodation	Conference facilities	Showers	M&S Simply Food	Costa Coffee	Starbucks	Burger King	KFC	McDonalds	Wimpy
M6	3-4	Welcome Break	Corley	Shell	●	●		●			●	●	●		
	10-11	Moto	Hilton Park	BP	●	●		●	●	●	●				
	14-15	RoadChef	Stafford (South)	Esso	●	●	●	●		●				●	
	14-15	Moto	Stafford (North)	BP	●	●		●	●	●	●				
	15-16	Welcome Break	Keele	Shell	●						●	●	●		
	16-17	RoadChef	Sandbach	Esso	●			●		●				●	
	18-19	Moto	Knutsford	BP	●	●		●	●	●	●				
	27-28	Welcome Break	Charnock Richard	Shell	●	●		●			●	●	●		
	32-33	Moto	Lancaster	BP	●	●		●	●	●	●				
	35A-36	Moto	Burton-in-Kendal (N)	BP	●	●			●	●					
	36-37	RoadChef	Killington Lake (S)	BP	●	●			●						
	38-39	Westmorland	Tebay	Total	●	●	●								
	41-42	Moto	Southwaite	BP	●	●		●	●	●	●				
	44-45	Moto	Todhills	BP/Shell	●				●		●				
M8	4-5	BP	Heart of Scotland	BP				●	●	●					
M9	9	Moto	Stirling	BP	●	●		●		●	●				
M11	8	Welcome Break	Birchanger Green	Shell	●	●	●	●			●	●	●		
M18	5	Moto	Doncaster North	BP	●	●	●	●		●	●				
M20	8	RoadChef	Maidstone	Esso	●	●		●					●	●	
	11	Stop 24	Stop 24	Shell	●			●		●				●	
M23	11	Moto	Pease Pottage	BP	●			●	●	●	●				
M25	5-6	RoadChef	Clacket Lane	Total	●	●		●						●	
	9-10	Extra	Cobham	Shell		●	●		●		●		●	●	
	23	Welcome Break	South Mimms	BP	●	●	●				●	●	●		
	30	Moto	Thurrock	Esso	●	●		●	●	●	●				
M27	3-4	RoadChef	Rownhams	Esso	●	●			●					●	
M40	2	Extra	Beaconsfield	Shell	●			●		●		●		●	
	8	Welcome Break	Oxford	BP	●	●		●			●	●	●		
	10	Moto	Cherwell Valley	Esso	●	●	●	●	●	●	●				
	12-13	Welcome Break	Warwick	BP	●	●	●	●			●	●	●		
M42	2	Welcome Break	Hopwood Park	Shell	●			●			●	●	●		
	10	Moto	Tamworth	Esso	●	●		●	●	●	●				
M48	1	Moto	Severn View	BP	●			●		●				●	
M54	4	Welcome Break	Telford	Shell	●	●			●		●			●	
M56	14	RoadChef	Chester	Shell	●	●			●					●	
M61	6-7	Euro Garages	Rivington	BP	●	●	●		●		●				
M62	7-9	Welcome Break	Burtonwood	Shell	●			●			●	●			
	18-19	Moto	Birch	BP	●	●	●	●	●	●	●				
	25-26	Welcome Break	Hartshead Moor	Shell	●	●		●			●	●			
	33	Moto	Ferrybridge	Esso	●	●		●	●	●	●				
M65	4	Extra	Blackburn with Darwen	Shell	●	●	●		●		●			●	
M74	4-5	RoadChef	Bothwell (South)	BP	●	●		●						●	
	5-6	RoadChef	Hamilton (North)	BP	●	●		●		●				●	
	11-12	Cairn Lodge	Happendon	Shell					●	●					
	12-13	Welcome Break	Abington	Shell	●	●		●			●	●			
M80	6-7	Shell	Old Inns	Shell											
M90	6	Moto	Kinross	BP	●	●		●	●	●	●				

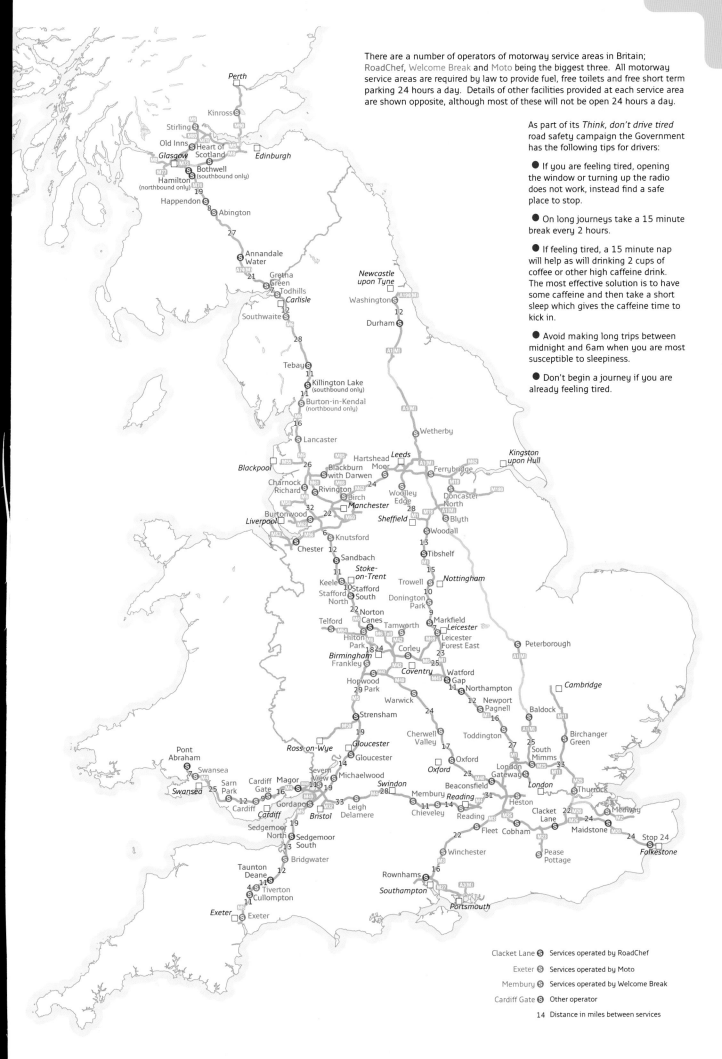

There are a number of operators of motorway service areas in Britain; RoadChef, Welcome Break and Moto being the biggest three. All motorway service areas are required by law to provide fuel, free toilets and free short term parking 24 hours a day. Details of other facilities provided at each service area are shown opposite, although most of these will not be open 24 hours a day.

As part of its *Think, don't drive tired* road safety campaign the Government has the following tips for drivers:

● If you are feeling tired, opening the window or turning up the radio does not work, instead find a safe place to stop.

● On long journeys take a 15 minute break every 2 hours.

● If feeling tired, a 15 minute nap will help as will drinking 2 cups of coffee or other high caffeine drink. The most effective solution is to have some caffeine and then take a short sleep which gives the caffeine time to kick in.

● Avoid making long trips between midnight and 6am when you are most susceptible to sleepiness.

● Don't begin a journey if you are already feeling tired.

Clacket Lane Ⓢ Services operated by RoadChef

Exeter Ⓢ Services operated by Moto

Membury Ⓢ Services operated by Welcome Break

Cardiff Gate Ⓢ Other operator

14 Distance in miles between services

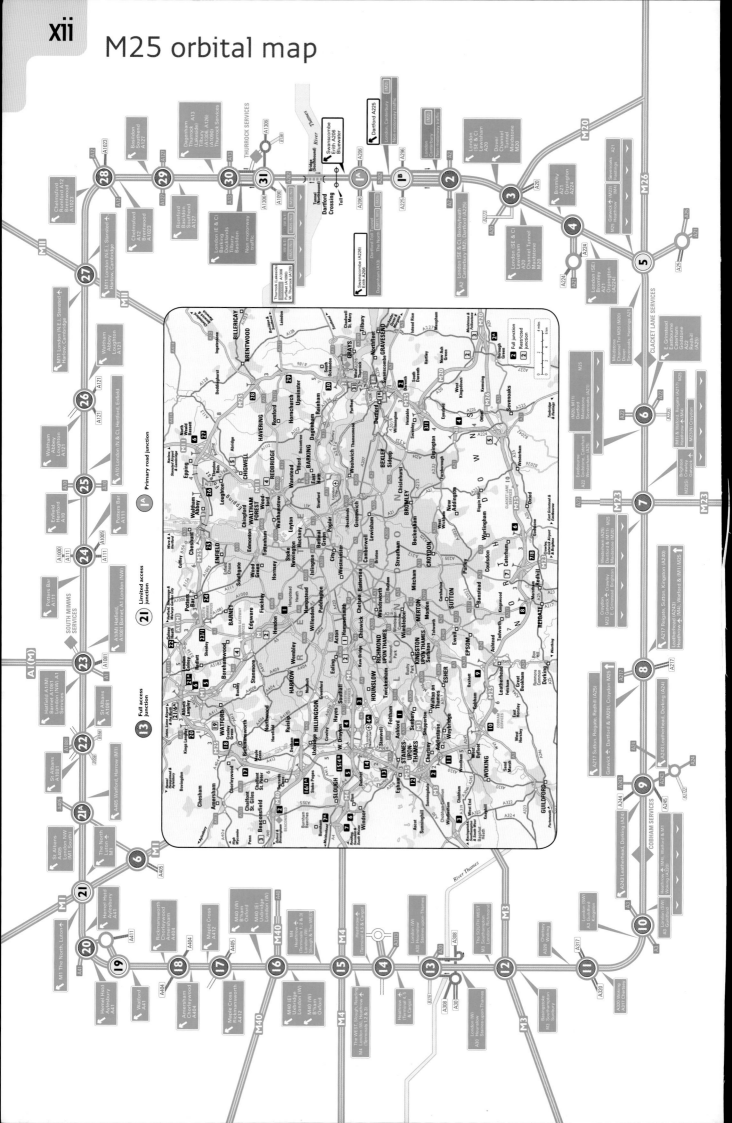

M6

Road sign labels (clockwise / top area):

- M6 The SOUTH, B'ham The S. WEST (M5)
- The SOUTH M6 Toll
- A4601
- A460
- A5148 Lichfield, (A38i) Burton
- The SOUTH, Tamworth M6 Toll
- A5148
- A5 Tamworth (M42 North)
- The SOUTH, Birmingham Sutton Coldfield M6 Toll
- A38
- A5195 Brownhills, Burntwood
- The SOUTH, Lichfield M6 Toll
- A34 A460
- A5

M6 Toll junctions: 11A — T8 — M6 Toll — T7 — Toll — T6 — Toll — T5 — Toll — T4

- NORTON CANES SERVICES
- A460 (M6 south) Wolverhampton
- The NORTH WEST (M6, North) Stafford, telford M6 Toll
- A34
- A34 Walsall, Cannock A460 Rugeley TOLLS
- A5195 Brownhills, Burntwood
- The NORTH WEST (M6 North), Cannock M6 Toll
- A38 Burton, Lichfield A5 Tamworth
- The NORTH WEST (M6 North), Cannock M6 Toll
- A38 Birmingham Sutton Coldfield
- M6 Toll London, Coventry, (M6, M42)
- A38
- Toll

11 — M6

- A460 Wolverhampton Cannock
- A460 Cannock
- HILTON PARK SERVICES

10A

- M54 NORTH (& MID) WALES Wolverhampton & Telford
- The NORTH WEST & Stafford M6
- A454 Walsall
- T3 Tolls
- A446 (M42 North) Coleshill
- M6 Toll London, Coventry, (M6, M42(S))
- A446

10

- A454
- A454 Walsall, W'hampton (Cent. & East)
- The North West, Telford (M54), W'hampton (N) M6
- A461 Wednesbury
- The SOUTH & Birmingham M6
- A38 Sutton Coldfield
- The NORTH WEST Cannock, Lichfield M6 Toll

9 — M6

- A4148
- A461
- A461 Wednesbury
- The NORTH WEST, Walsall & W'hampton M6
- London (M1 & M40) Birmingham (N. E. & Cen.) N.E.C. &
- The SOUTH WEST M5 Birmingham (W & S) West Bromwich
- M5 M6 M6

T2 — A4091 — A446

8

- A34 Birmingham (N)
- London (M1 & M40) Birmingham (S & Cen.) N.E.C. & M6
- A34
- T1 — A446 — M42 — 9
- A4097
- A446

- M6 London (M1 & M40) Birmingham (N & E)
- The NORTH WEST Walsall & Wolverhampton M6
- The SOUTH WEST M5 Birmingham (W & S) West Bromwich
- The NORTH WEST & Wolverhampton M6
- A34 Birmingham (N) & Walsall
- The NORTH WEST The SOUTH WEST B'ham (W & S) (M5) M6

8 — M6 — 7

- A34
- A38(Mi & A38 B'ham (E, Cen, & NE) & Lichfield
- London (M1 & M40) N.E.C. & B'ham M6
- A5127
- A452
- A4097 A446 M42 The N. EAST (M1), Tamworth
- The NORTH WEST Cannock, Lichfield M6 Toll
- M42

8

- M42 (N), The SOUTH (M40) N.E.C.
- M42 & M6
- M8 LONDON (M1) Coventry N.E.C.
- M6(N) Birmingham (Cen, E, N, & W)
- M42 The SOUTH WEST (M5), (M6, South M40) Birmingham (S) N.E.C. & London, Coventry

6 — 5 — M6 — 4A

- A38
- A452
- B4147
- A4540
- A38(M)
- Stay in lane through markings
- M6 & A38(M), A38 B'ham (Cen & NE) M6 M6
- A452 B'ham (E) & Sutton Coldfield
- The NORTH WEST & B'ham (Cen. N & W) M6
- A446
- M42 The SOUTH WEST (M5) B'ham (S), N.E.C. & London, (S & W) M6, Coventry (S & W)
- M6 Birmingham (N & E) (M1) London, & N. E. & E)

7A

- A4540
- A38 A4540
- M6 London (M1), Coventry
- The N. WEST (M6Toll) M42 The N. EAST (M1), Tamworth
- 7 — 4 — M6 — 3A

1 — A41

- A41
- A41 West Bromwich, Sandwell & B'ham (N & W)
- The SOUTH WEST & Birmingham (W & S) M5
- A41 West Bromwich & B'ham (NW)
- The NORTH (M1 & M6), Birmingham (N), N.E.C. & M5
- M6 The NORTH WEST, B'ham
- The NORTH EAST (M1) M42
- M42 B'ham (S.E.) N.E.C. Coventry
- M42 The SOUTH WEST (M5), LONDON (M40) Birmingham (SE), Solihull

M5

- A4123 Birmingham (W) & Dudley
- The SOUTH WEST & Birmingham (S) M5

2 — A4123

- A4123 Dudley, W'hampton & Sandwell
- The NORTH (M1 & M6), Birmingham (N) M5
- A45 B'ham (S.E.) N.E.C., Coventry (S & W)
- The NORTH, B'ham (E,N & Cen), Coventry (N & E) M42
- A45

6 — A45

- A456 Kidderminster
- The SOUTH WEST & Birmingham (S) M5
- A41 Solihull

3 — A456

- A456
- A456 Birmingham (W & Cen)
- FRANKLEY SERVICES
- A41 Solihull

5 — A4141

- A3400 Henley-in-Arden
- A38 B'ham (SW) Bromsgrove
- A34 Shirley

4 — A38

- A491
- A38
- A38 Birmingham (SW), A491 Stourbridge
- A34 — 4 — A3400
- M42 N.E.C. & M42 & M5 M5 The SOUTH WEST Worcester
- A40 London, Warwick, Stratford M40
- The NORTH M42 N.E.C. & M42 & M40 The SOUTH WEST (M5), Birmingham (S & W) M40

M5

- M42 The NORTH EAST (M1), London (M40) N.E.C. &
- M42 & M5
- M5 The NORTH WEST, B'ham (W, N & Cen)
- A441
- A38
- HOPWOOD PARK SERVICES
- A441 Birmingham (S)
- A435 B'ham (S), Redditch Evesham
- A435
- M40 London, Warwick, Stratford M40
- The SOUTH WEST (M5), Birmingham (S & W) M40

4A — M42 — 1 — 2 — 3 — M42 — 3A

- M5 The NORTH WEST B'ham (W, N & Cen) Stourbridge (M6)
- M5 The SOUTH WEST Worcester
- A38
- A38 Bromsgrove
- A441 Birmingham (S)
- A435 B'ham (S), Redditch Evesham
- M40

Legend:

- 3 Full access junction
- 4A Limited access junction
- T4 Full access junction M6 Toll
- T1 Limited access junction M6 Toll

Inset map labels: NORTON CANES, Burntwood, LICHFIELD, Cheslyn Hay, Great Wyrley, Brownhills, Shenstone, Hilton Park, Essington, Aldridge, WALSALL, SUTTON COLDFIELD, Fazeley, DUDLEY, WEST BROMWICH, Water Orton, Coleshill, BIRMINGHAM, HALESOWEN, BIRMINGHAM INTERNATIONAL, Curdworth, Bickenhill, SOLIHULL, Knowle, Wythall, Cofton Hackett, Bernt Green, Catshill, Marlbrook, Alvechurch, Romsley, Hopwood Park

Risk rating of Britain's motorways and A roads

EuroRAP

This map shows the statistical risk of death or serious injury occurring on Britain's motorway and A road network for 2010–2012. Covering 44,500km in total, the EuroRAP network represents just 11% of Britain's road length but carries 56% of the traffic and 50% of Britain's road fatalities.

The risk is calculated by comparing the frequency of road crashes resulting in death and serious injury on every stretch of road with how much traffic each road is carrying. For example, if there are 20 crashes on a road carrying 10,000 vehicles a day, the risk is 10 times higher than if the road has the same number of crashes but carries 100,000 vehicles.

Some of the roads shown have had improvements made to them recently, but during the survey period the risk of a fatal or serious injury crash on the black road sections was 24 times higher than on the safest (green) roads.

For more information on the Road Safety Foundation go to **www.roadsafetyfoundation.org.**

For more information on the statistical background to this research, visit the EuroRAP website at **www.eurorap.org.**

Road Assessment Programme Risk Rating

- Low risk (safest) roads
- Low–medium risk roads
- Medium risk roads
- Medium–high risk roads
- High risk roads

- Motorway
- Single and dual carriageway
- Unrated roads

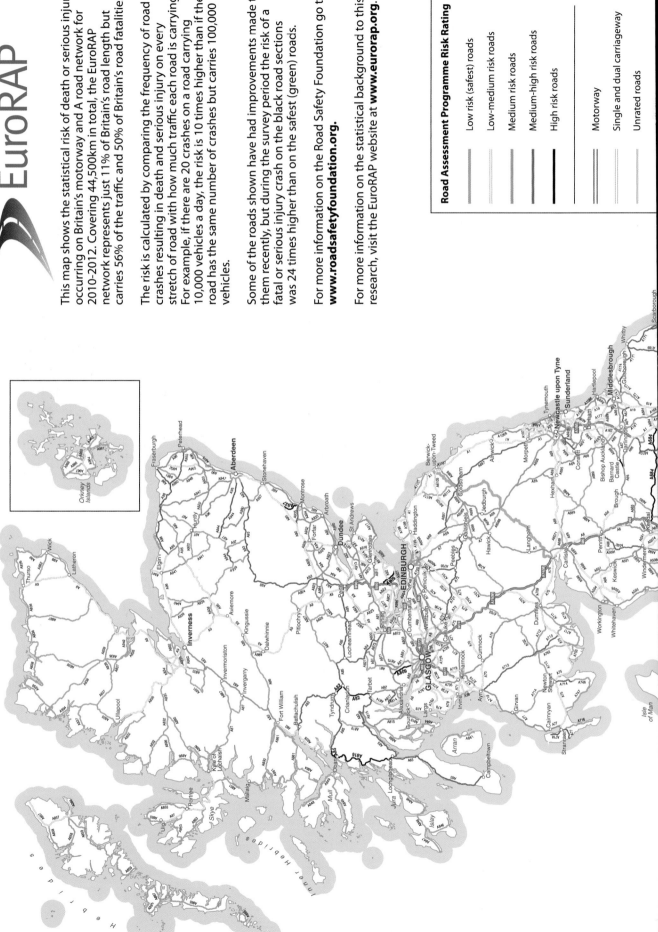

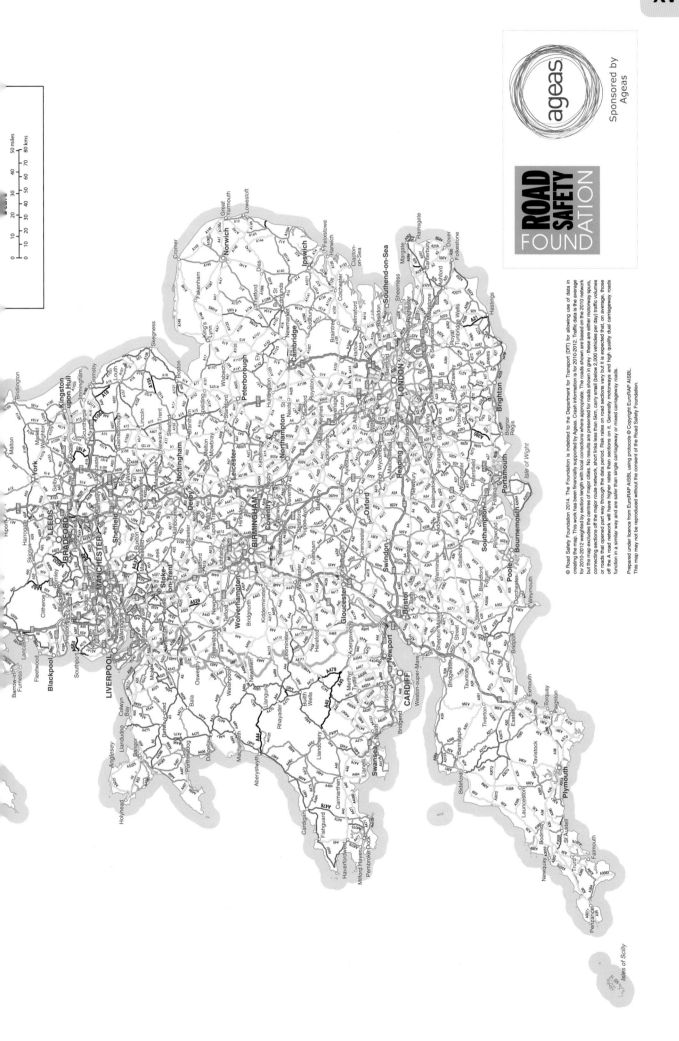

Distance chart

Distances between two selected towns in this table are shown in miles and kilometres.
In general, distances are based on the shortest routes by classified roads.

Distance in kilometres

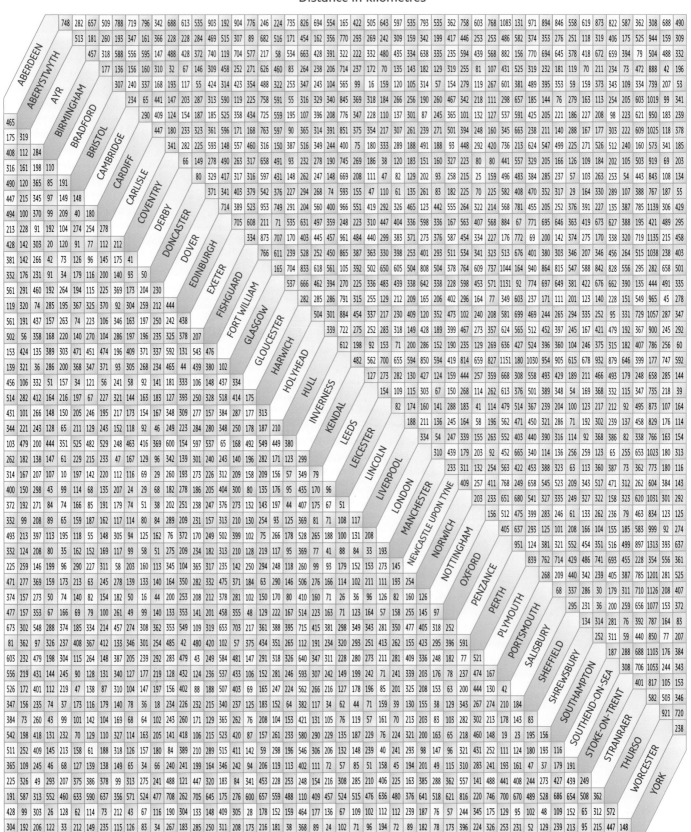

Distance in miles

Symbols used on the map

Blue place of interest symbols e.g ☆ are listed on page 93

Motorway junction with full / limited access	Level crossing	Notable building
Motorway service area	National Trail / Long Distance Route	Hospital
MARKFIELD SERVICES	Hadrian's Wall Path	
M6 Toll — Toll motorway	Fixed safety camera / fixed average-speed safety camera. Speed shown by number within camera, a V indicates a variable limit.	Spot height (in metres) / Lighthouse
A316 — Primary route dual / single carriageway / junction / service area	Park and Ride site operated by bus / rail (runs at least 5 days a week)	Built up area
A4054 'A' road dual / single carriageway	Car ferry with destination	Woodland / Park
B7078 'B' road dual / single carriageway	West Cowes ¾hr Foot ferry with destination	National Park
Minor road dual / single carriageway	Airport	Heritage Coast
Restricted access road	Railway line / Railway tunnel / Light railway line	BRISTOL County / Unitary Authority boundary and name
Road proposed or under construction	Railway station / Light rail station	SEE PAGE 68 Area covered by street map
Road tunnel	London Underground / London Overground stations	
Roundabout	Glasgow Subway station	
Toll / One way street	Extent of London congestion charging zone	

Locator map

Urban approach maps	
Birmingham	14-15
Bournemouth	3
Bradford	26-27
Bristol	8
Cardiff	7
Coventry	16
Derby	18-19
Edinburgh	32
Glasgow	30-31
Greater Manchester	24-25
Leeds	26-27
Leicester	17
Liverpool	22-23
London	10-13
Manchester	24-25
Merseyside	22-23
Middlesbrough	29
Milton Keynes	9
Newcastle upon Tyne	28-29
Newport	7
Nottingham	18-19
Plymouth	2
Portsmouth	4-5
Sheffield	21
Southampton	4-5
Stoke-on-Trent	20
Sunderland	28-29
Swansea	6
West Midlands	14-15

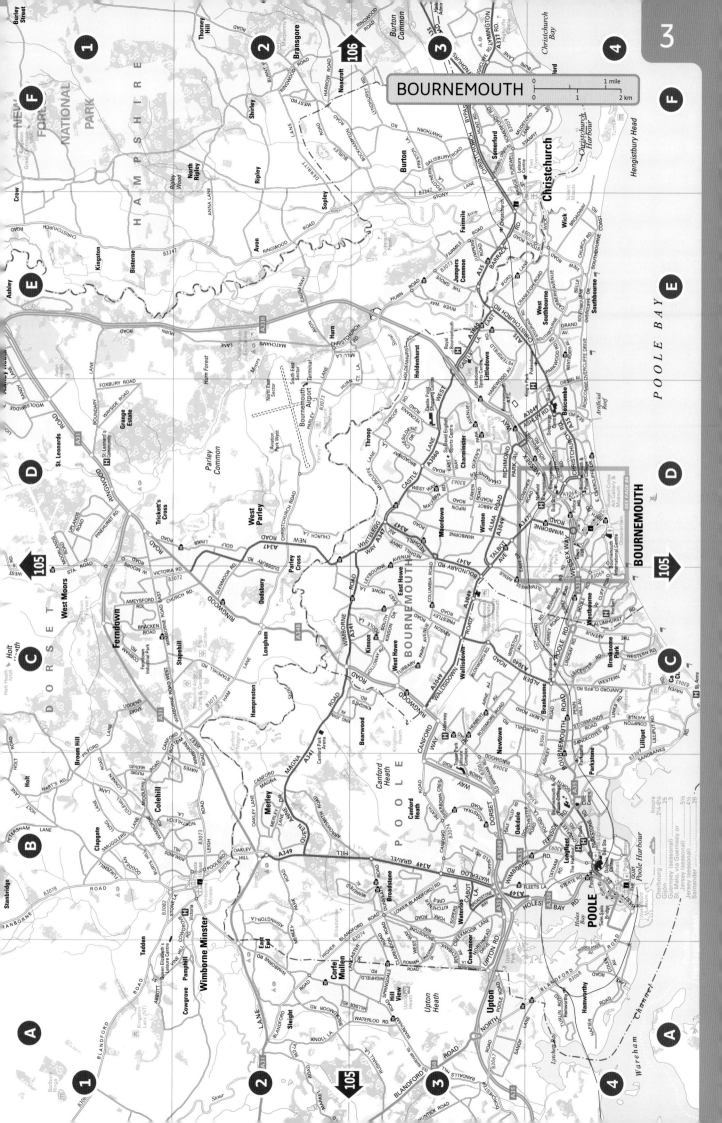

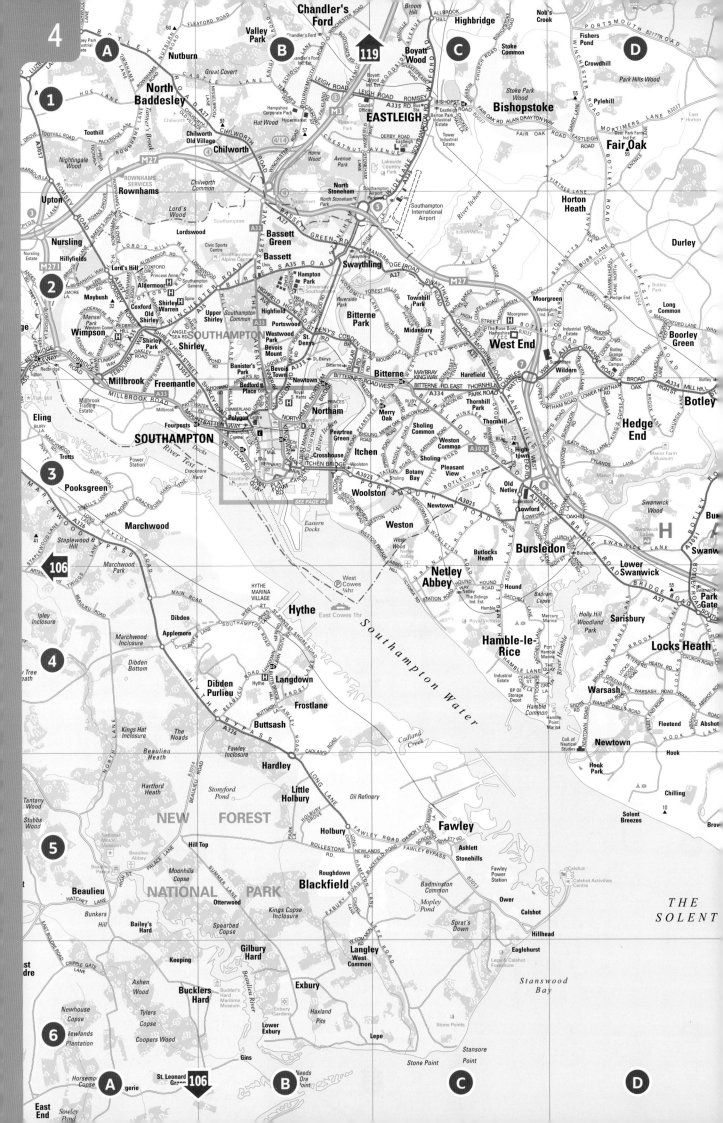

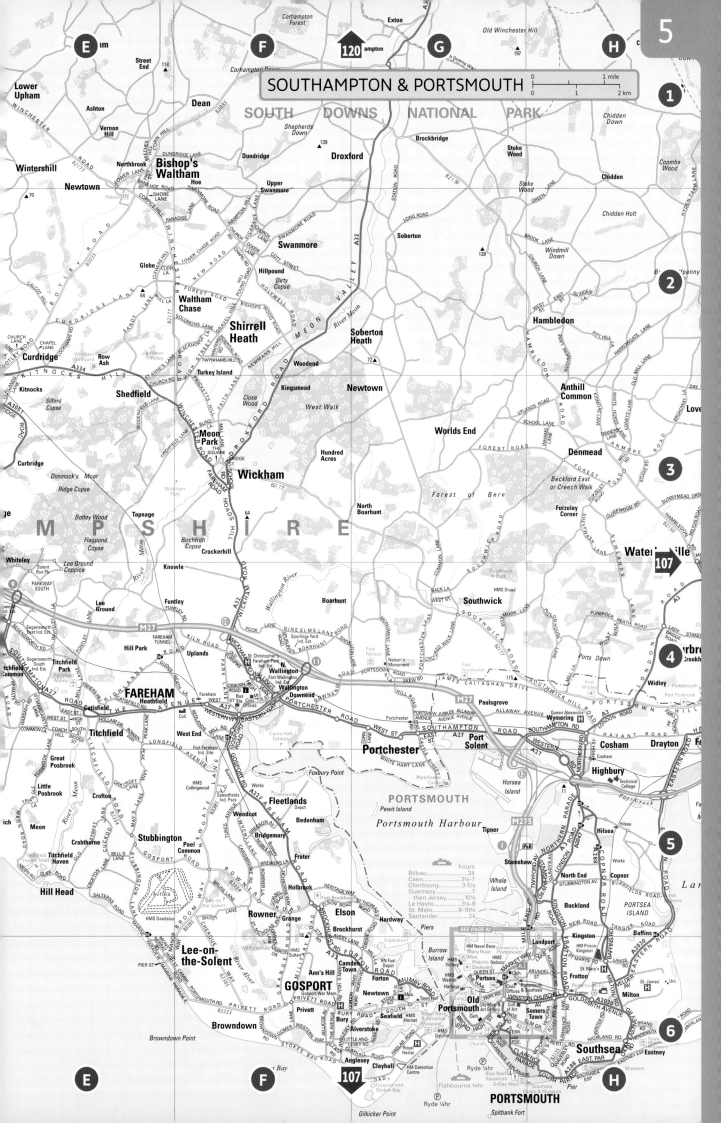

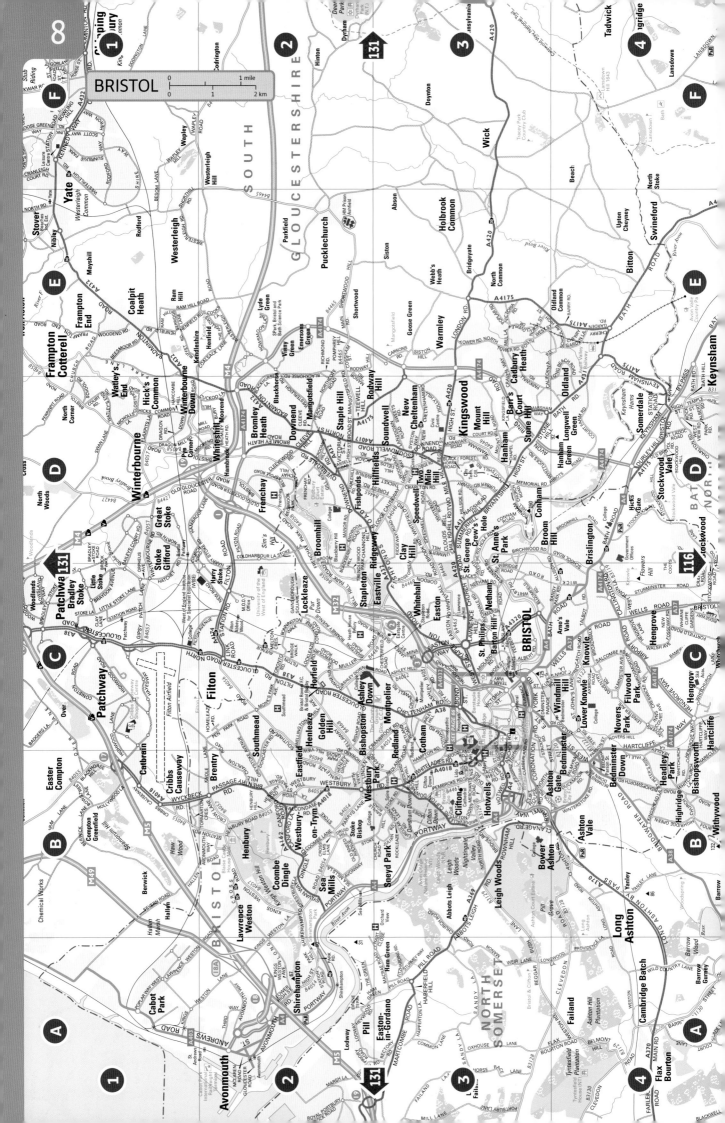

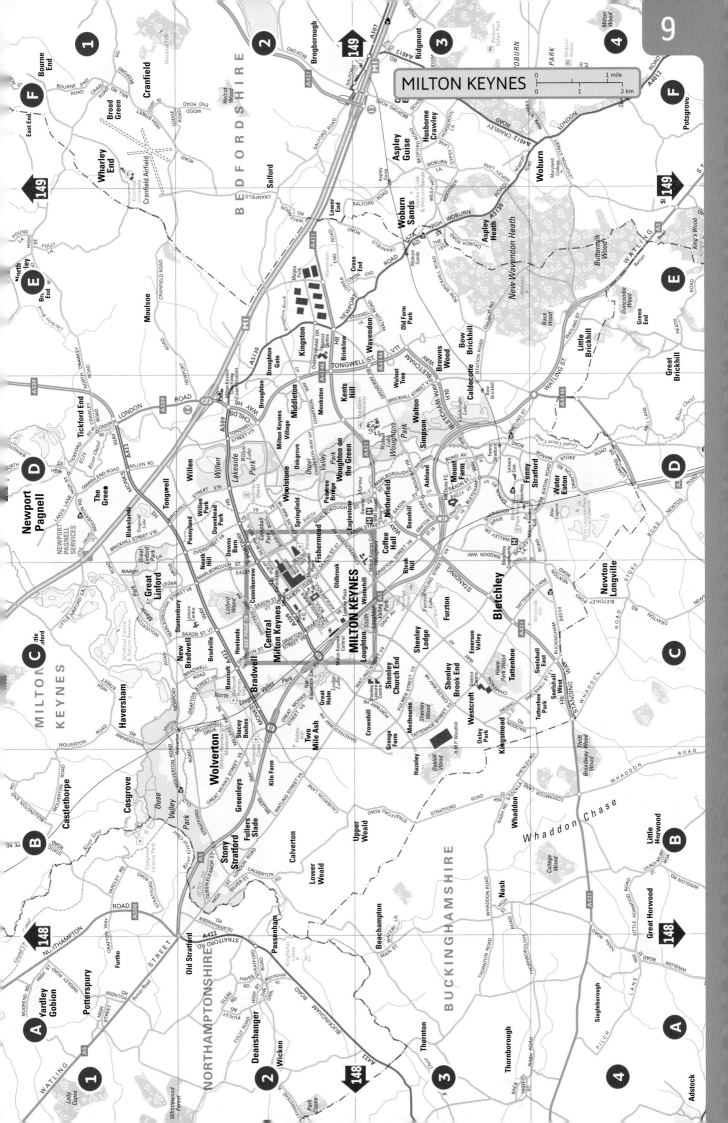

GREATER LONDON - WEST

GREATER LONDON - EAST

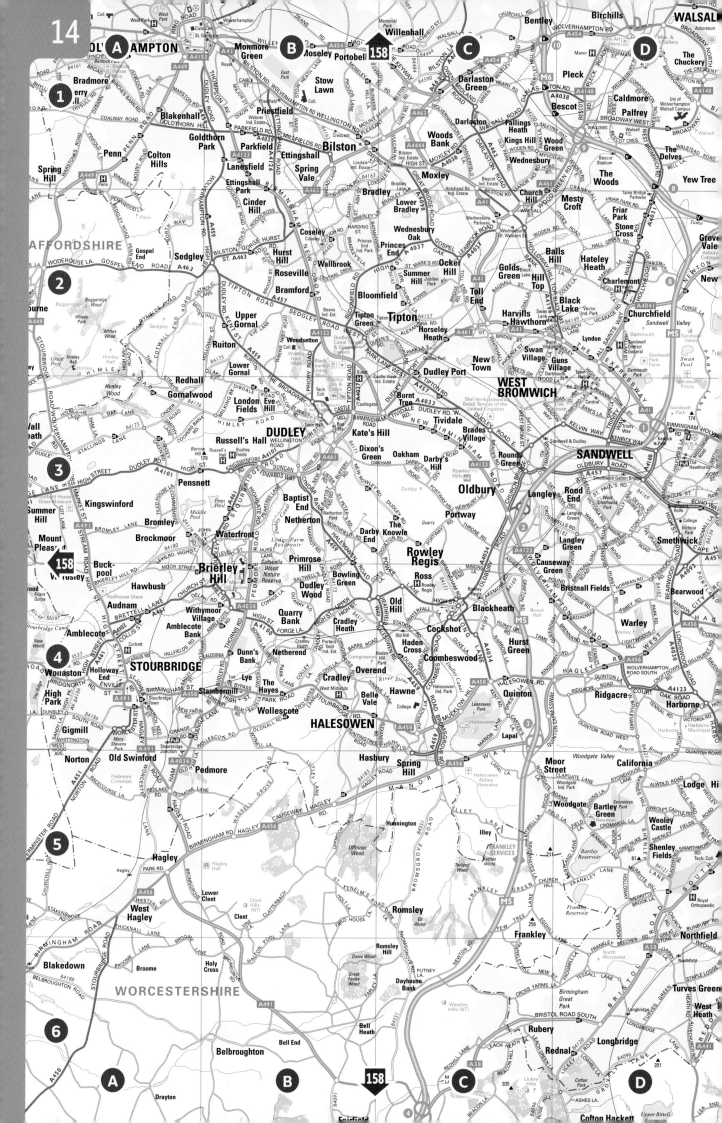

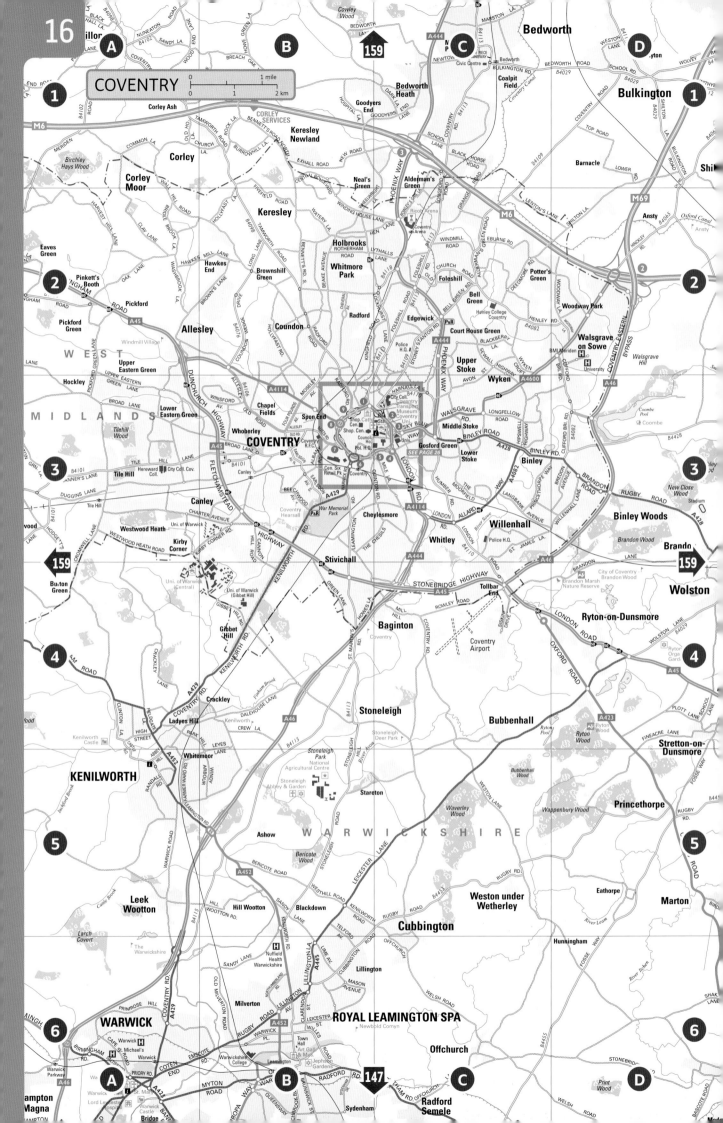

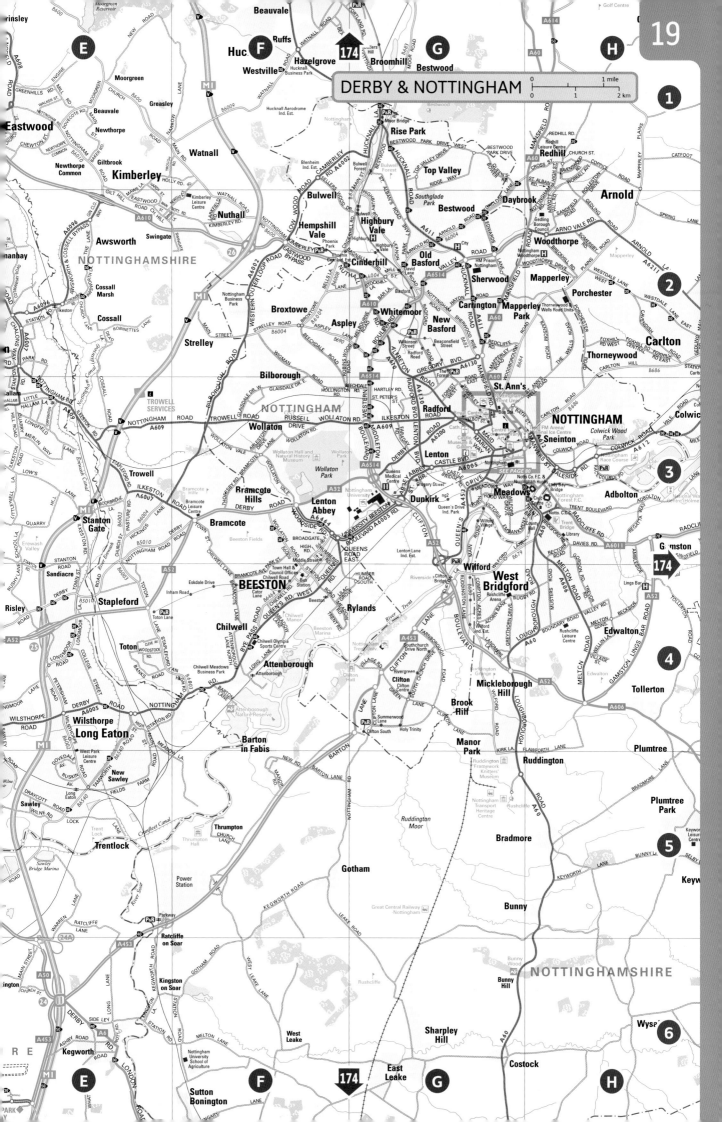

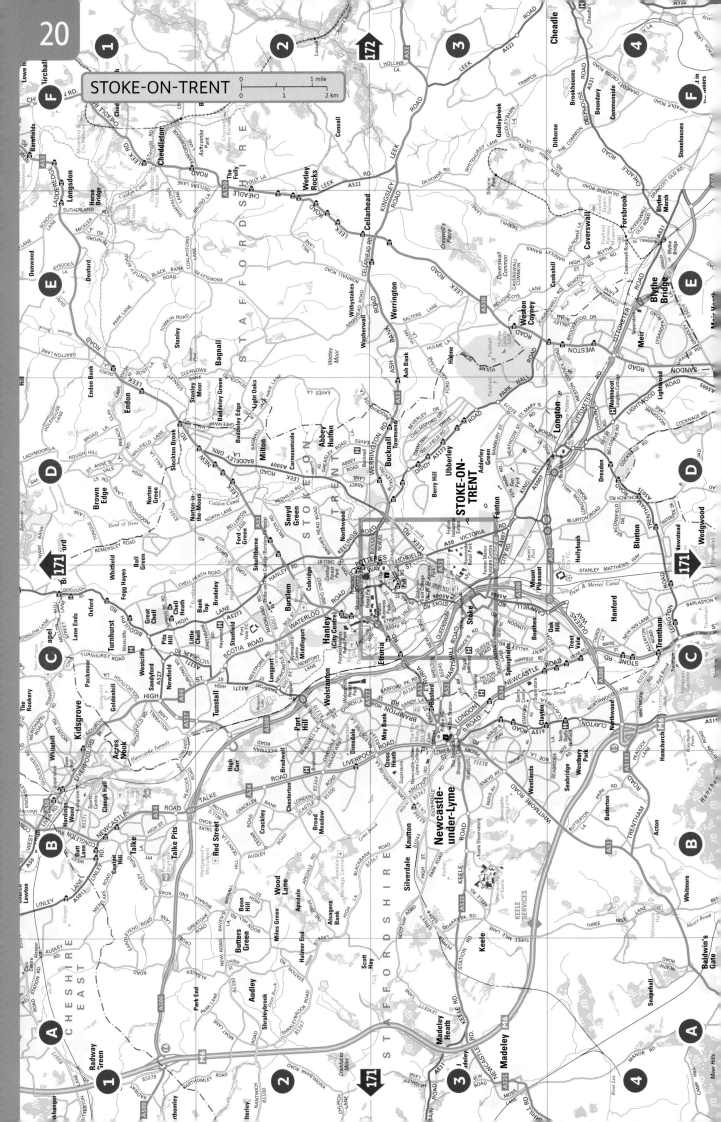

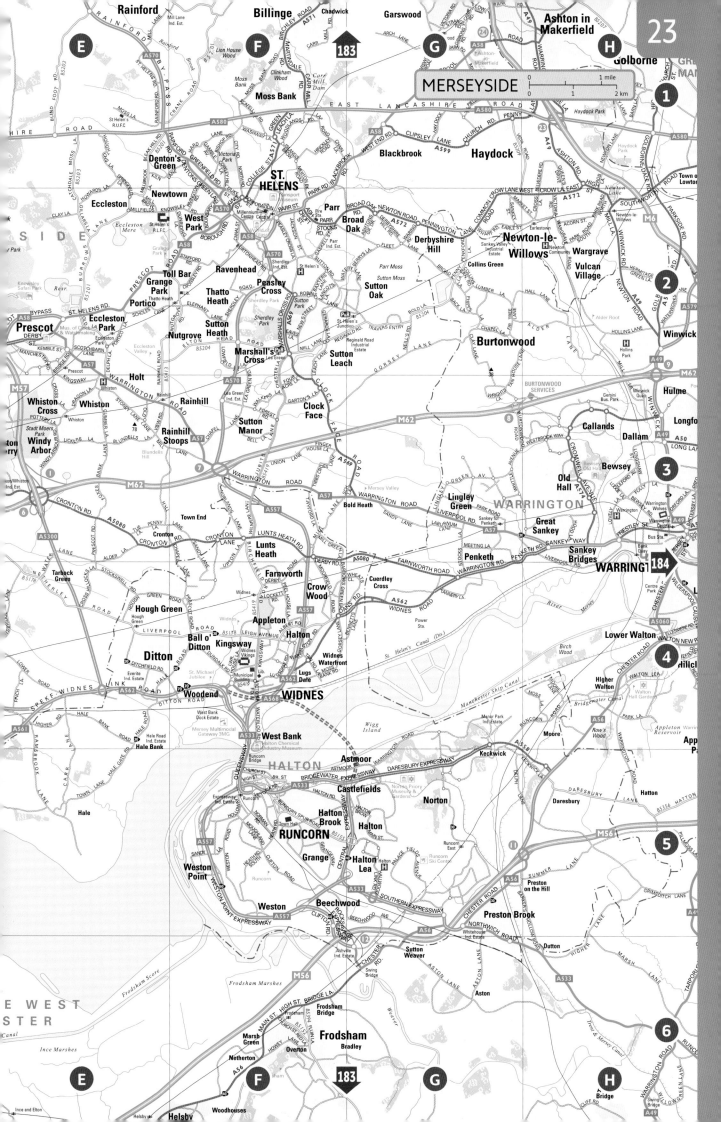

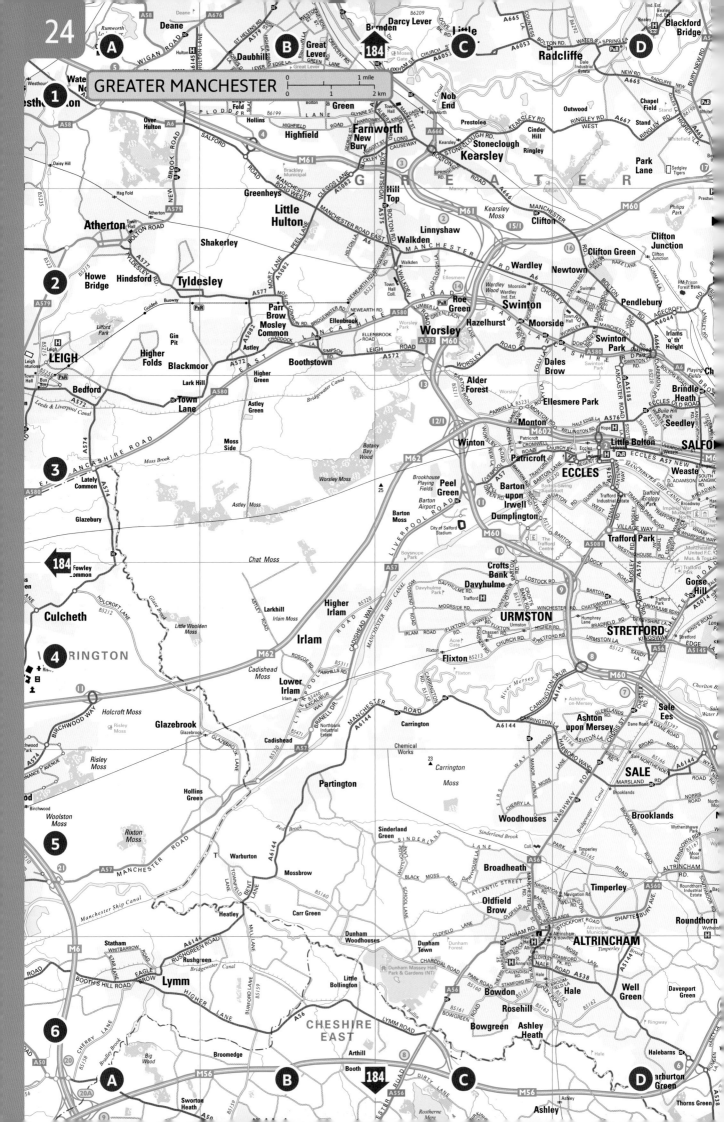

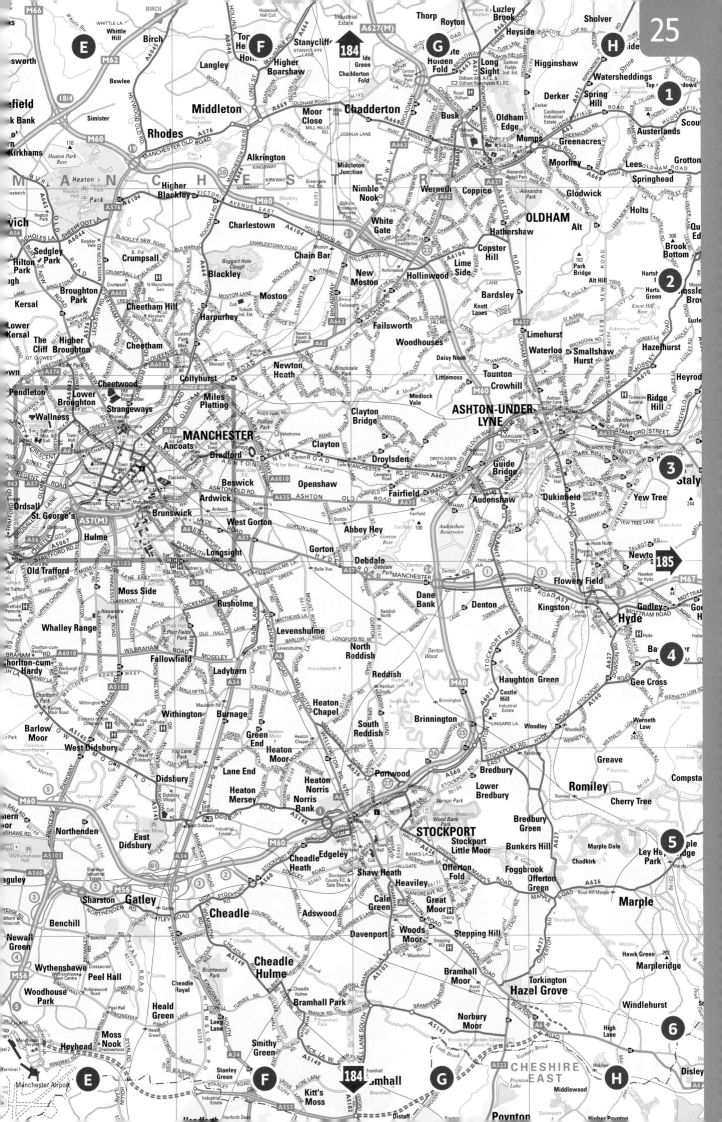

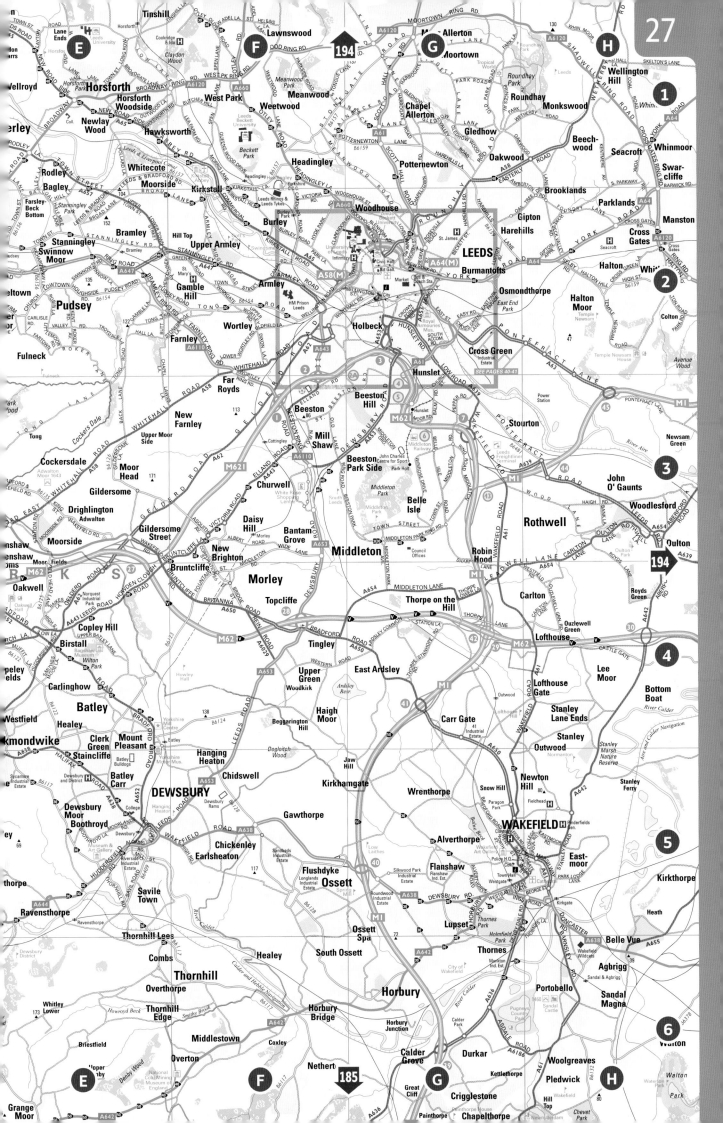

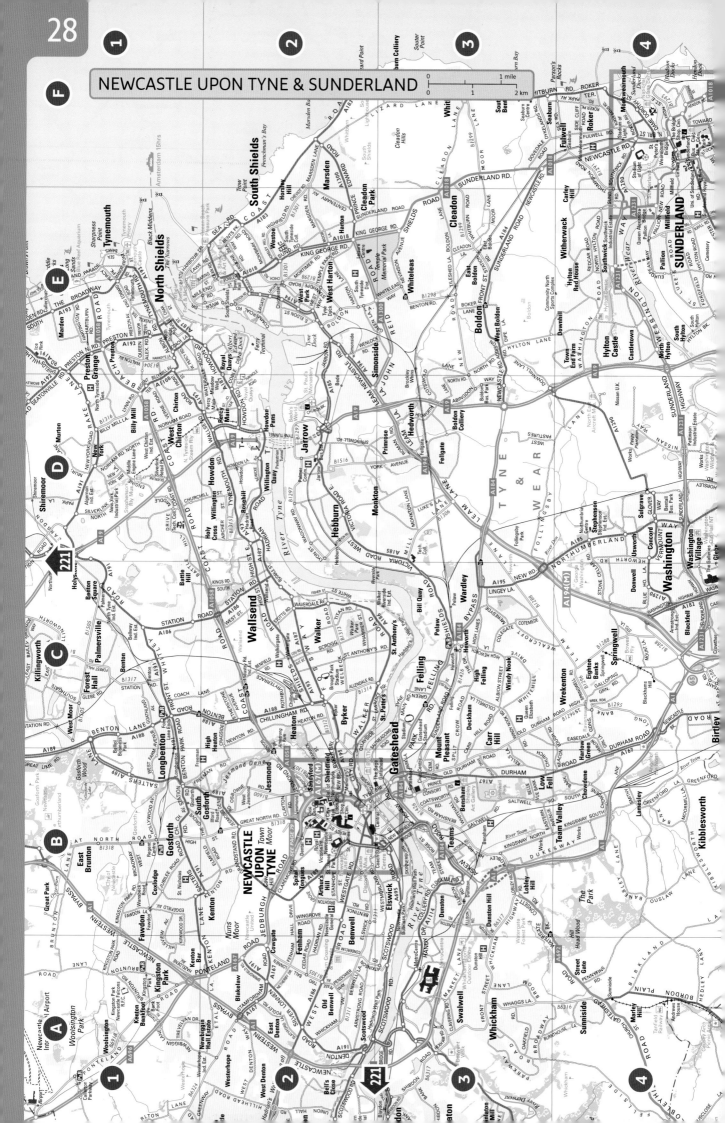

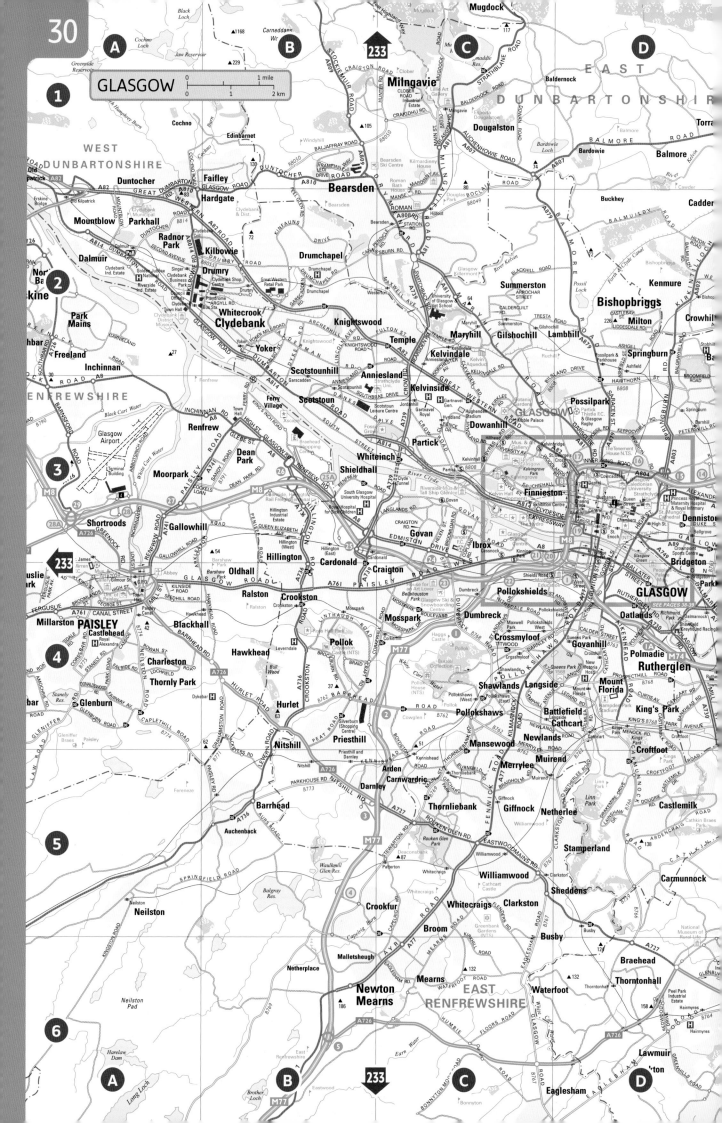

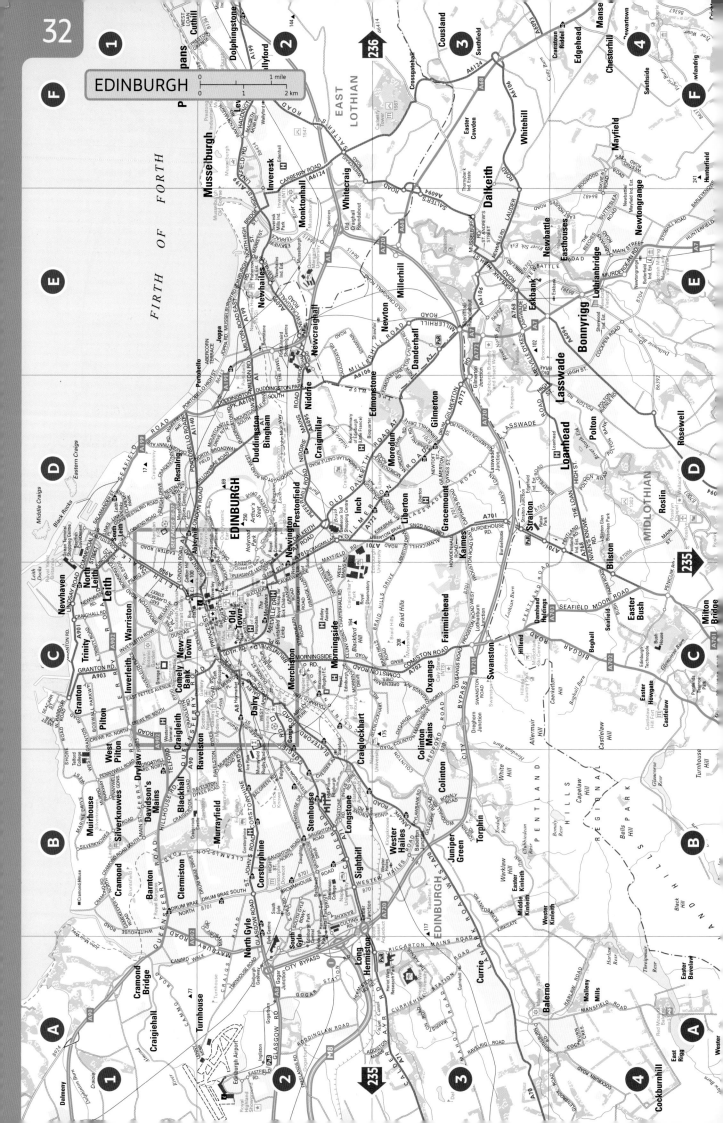

Symbols used on the map

M8	Motorway	Bus / Coach station		JAPAN	Embassy
A4 ①	Primary route dual / single carriageway / Junction	P&R	Park and Ride site - rail operated (runs at least 5 days a week)	Cinema
A40	'A' road dual / single carriageway		Extent of London congestion charging zone	Cathedral / Church
B507	'B' road dual / single carriageway	Dublin 8hrs	Vehicle / Pedestrian ferry	Mormon	Mosque / Synagogue / Other place of worship
Toll	Other road dual / single carriageway / Toll	P P	Car park		Leisure & tourism
→ ⑦	One way street / Orbital route	Theatre			Shopping
	Access restriction	Major hotel			Administration & law
	Pedestrian street	Public House			Health & welfare
	Street market	Pol	Police station		Education
	Minor road / Track	Lib	Library		Industry / Office
FB	Footpath / Footbridge	PO	Post Office		Other notable building
	Road under construction	i i	Visitor information centre (open all year / seasonally)		Park / Garden / Sports ground
	Main / other National Rail station		Toilet		Cemetery
	London Underground / Overground station				
	Light Rail / Station				

Locator map

Street maps

Aberdeen	63	Leeds index	52
Bath	63	Leicester	77
Birmingham	34-35	Lincoln	77
Birmingham index	48	Liverpool	42-43
Blackpool	64	Liverpool index	54
Bournemouth	64	London	44-45
Bradford	65	London index	56
Brighton	65	Manchester	46-47
Bristol	66	Manchester index	60
Cambridge	66	Middlesbrough	78
Canterbury	67	Milton Keynes	78
Cardiff	67	Newcastle upon Tyne	79
Carlisle	68	Norwich	79
Cheltenham	68	Nottingham	80
Chester	69	Oxford	80
Coventry	69	Perth	81
Derby	70	Plymouth	81
Dover	70	Portsmouth	82
Dundee	71	Reading	82
Durham	71	Salisbury	83
Eastbourne	72	Scarborough	83
Edinburgh	36-37	Sheffield	84
Edinburgh index	49	Southampton	84
Exeter	72	Stoke-on-Trent	85
Folkestone	73	Stratford-upon-Avon	85
Glasgow	38-39	Sunderland	86
Glasgow index	51	Swansea	86
Gloucester	73	Swindon	87
Guildford	74	Torquay	87
Harrogate	74	Watford	88
Hastings	75	Weston-super-Mare	88
Hereford	75	Winchester	89
Hull (Kingston upon Hull)	76	Windsor	89
Inverness	76	Worcester	90
Leeds	40-41	York	90

Airport plans

Birmingham International	91
Gatwick	91
Glasgow	91
Heathrow	91
Manchester	91
Stansted	91

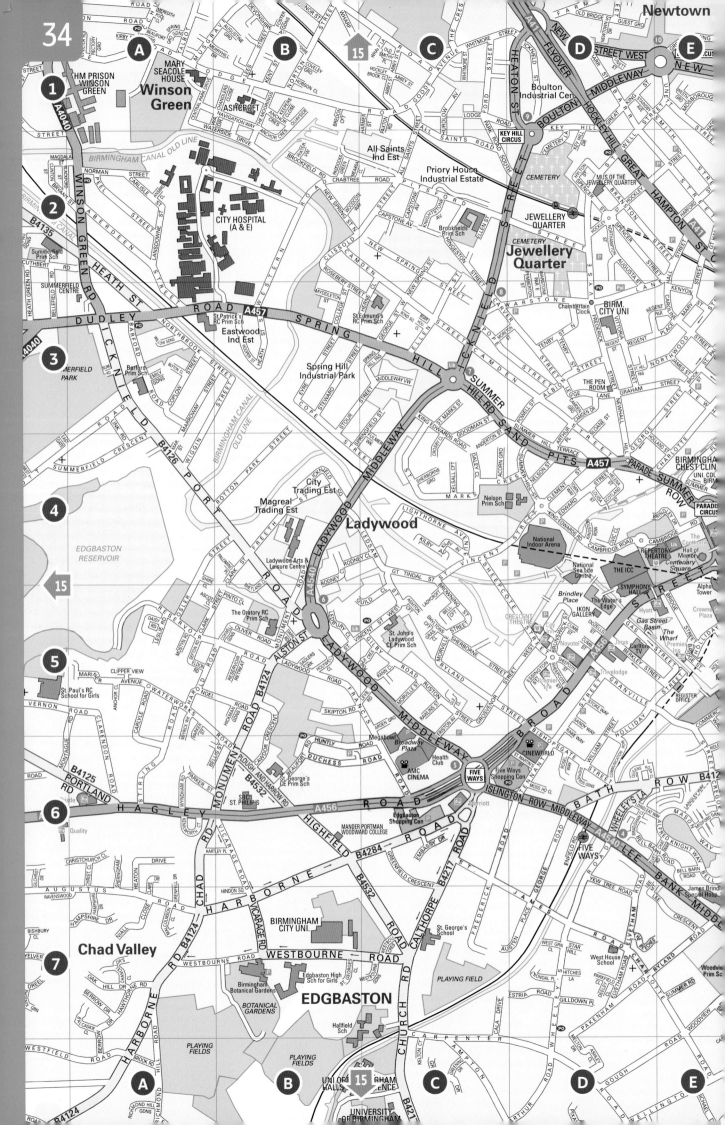

BIRMINGHAM
Birmingham street index is on page 48

0   0.25   0.5 km
0   1/4 mile

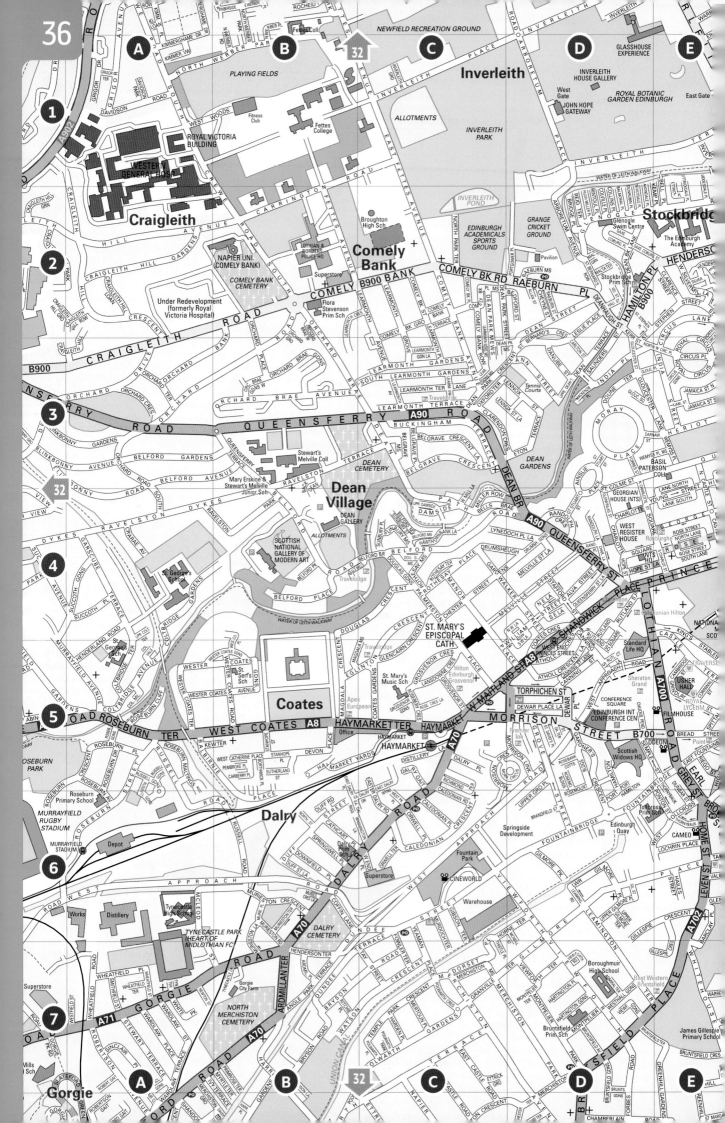

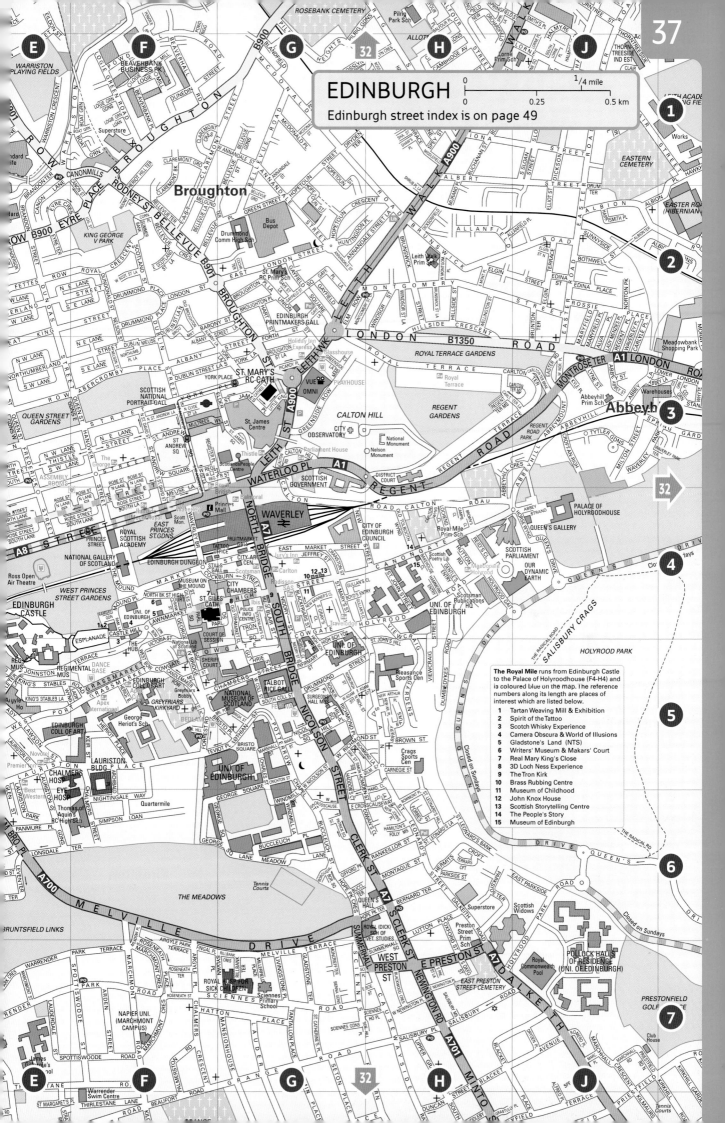

EDINBURGH

Edinburgh street index is on page 49

0   0.25   0.5 km

0   1/4 mile

The Royal Mile runs from Edinburgh Castle to the Palace of Holyroodhouse (F4-H4) and is coloured blue on the map. The reference numbers along its length are places of interest which are listed below.

1 Tartan Weaving Mill & Exhibition
2 Spirit of the Tattoo
3 Scotch Whisky Experience
4 Camera Obscura & World of Illusions
5 Gladstone's Land (NTS)
6 Writers' Museum & Makars' Court
7 Real Mary King's Close
8 3D Loch Ness Experience
9 The Tron Kirk
10 Brass Rubbing Centre
11 Museum of Childhood
12 John Knox House
13 Scottish Storytelling Centre
14 The People's Story
15 Museum of Edinburgh

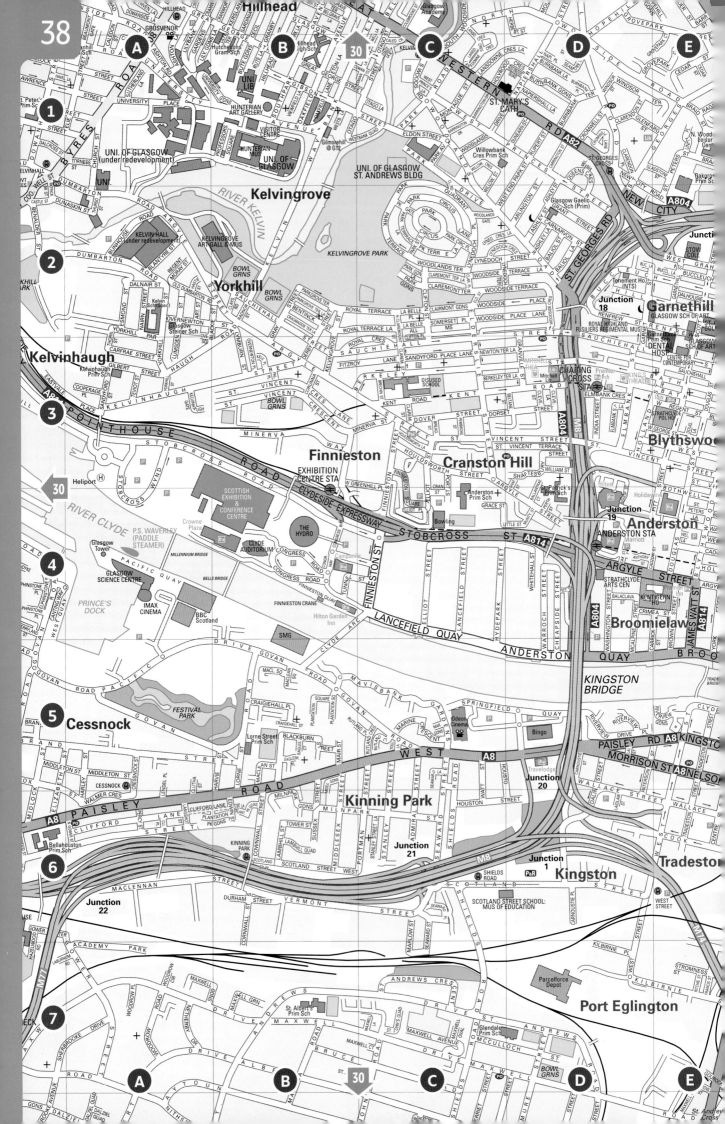

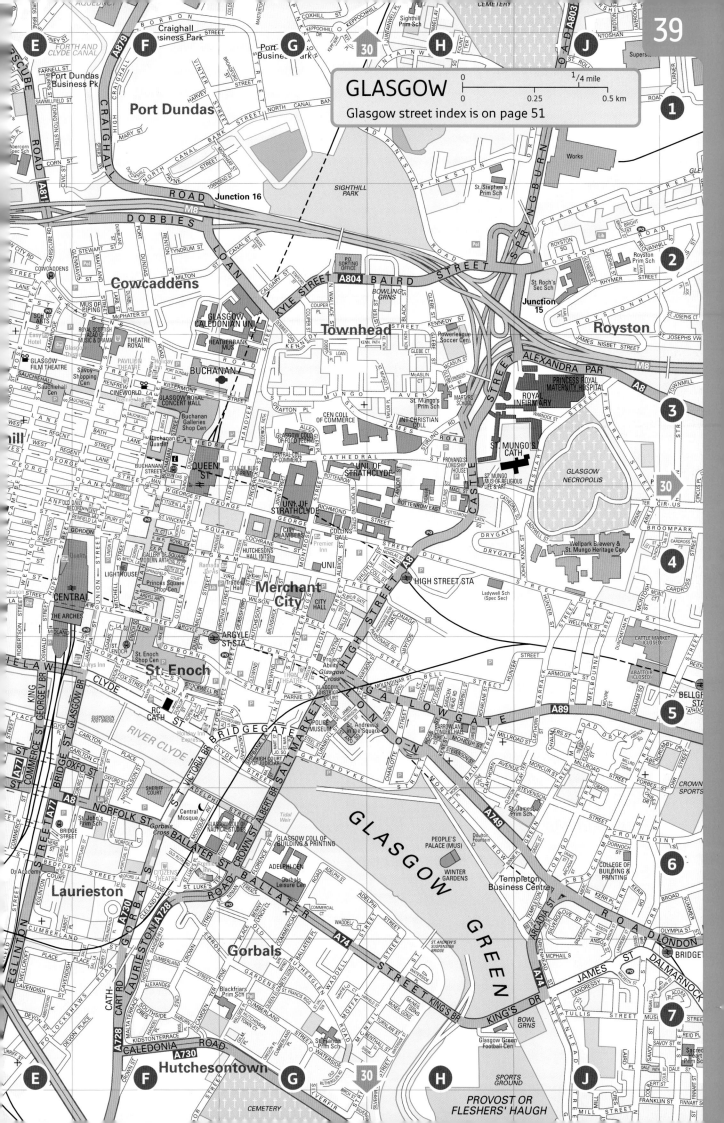

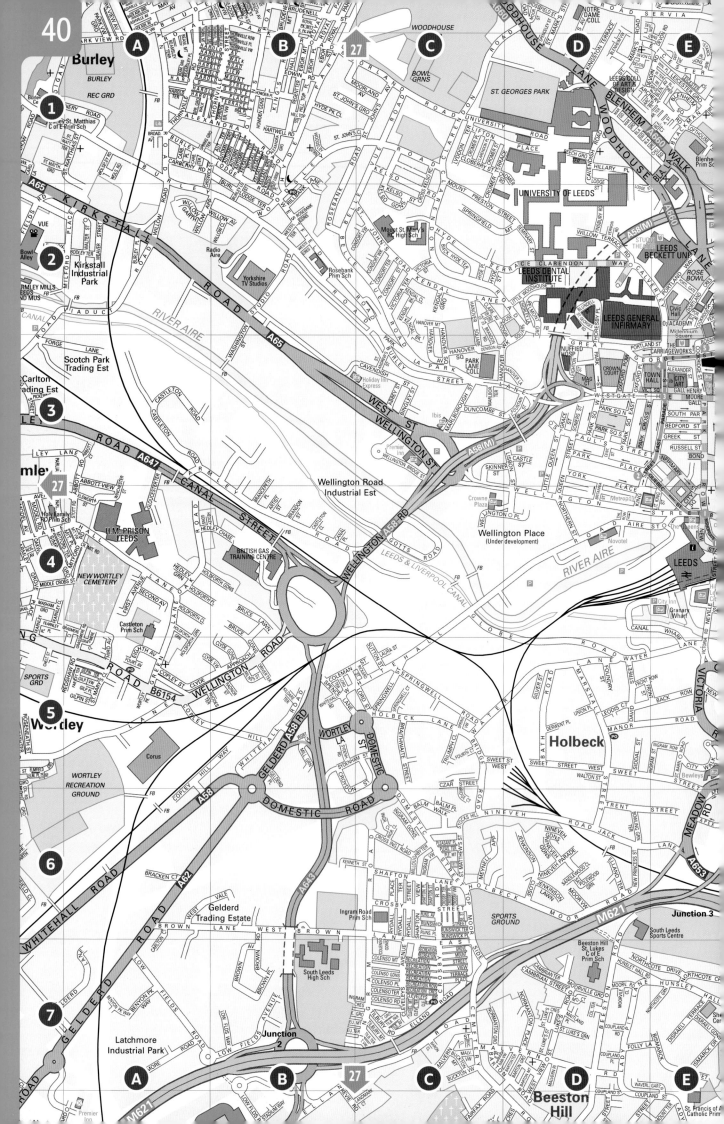

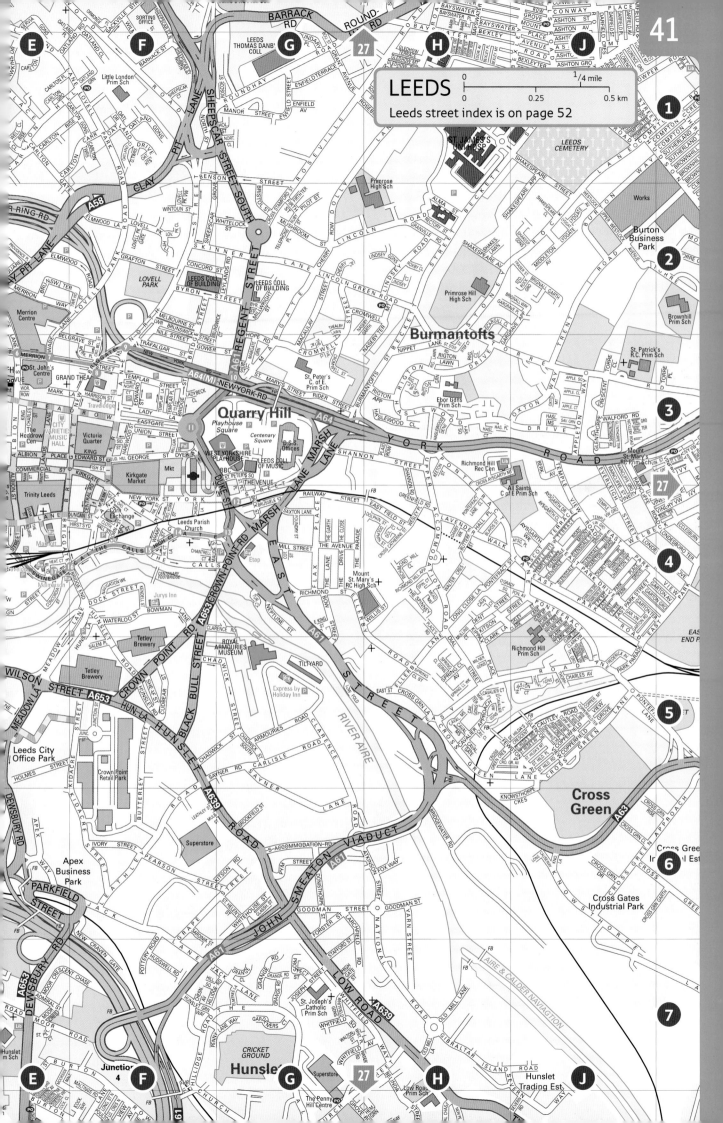

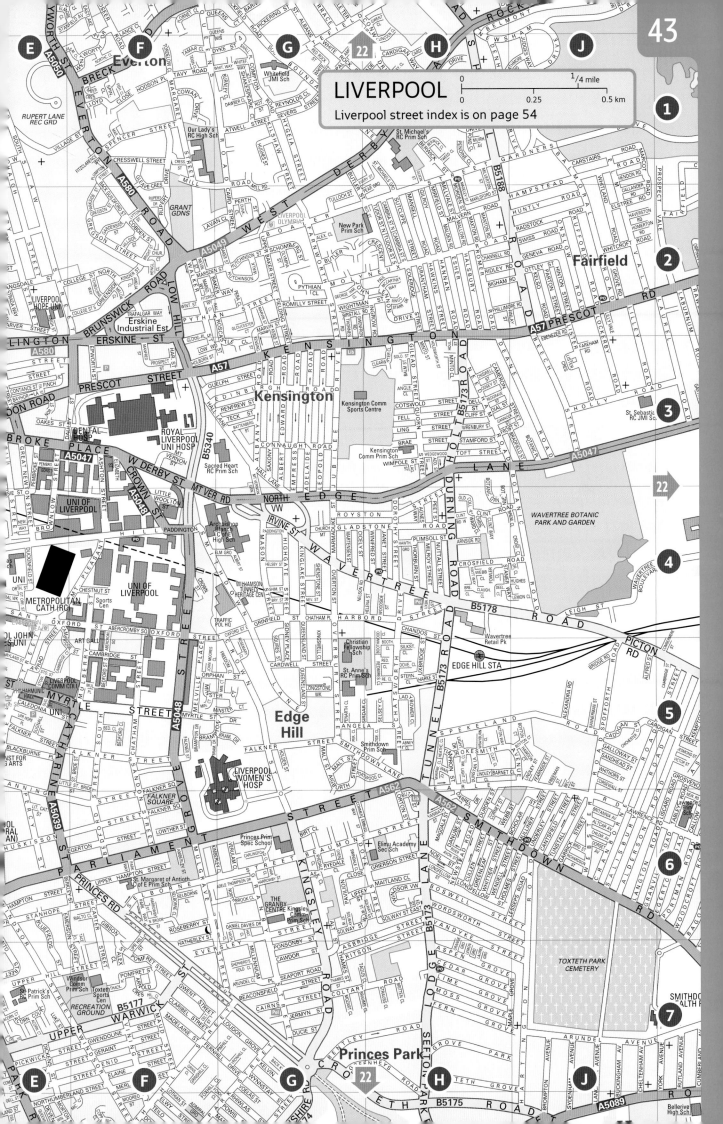

Indexes to street maps

General abbreviations

All	Alley	Chyd	Churchyard	Embk	Embankment	La	Lane	Pl	Place	W	West
App	Approach	Circ	Circus	Est	Estate	Lo	Lodge	Rd	Road	Wf	Wharf
Arc	Arcade	Clo	Close	Flds	Fields	Mans	Mansions	Ri	Rise	Wk	Walk
Av/Ave	Avenue	Cor	Corner	Gdn	Garden	Mkt/Mkts	Market/Markets	S	South	Yd	Yard
Bdy	Broadway	Cres	Crescent	Gdns	Gardens	Ms	Mews	Sq	Square		
Bldgs	Buildings	Ct	Court	Grd	Ground	N	North	St	Street		
Br/Bri	Bridge	Ctyd	Courtyard	Grn	Green	Par	Parade	St.	Saint		
Cen	Central, Centre	Dr	Drive	Gro	Grove	Pas	Passage	Ter	Terrace		
Ch	Church	E	East	Ho	House	Pk	Park	Twr	Tower		

Place names are shown in bold type

Birmingham street index

A
Abbey St **34** C1
Abbey St N **34** C1
Aberdeen St **34** A2
Acorn Gro **34** C4
Adams St **35** H2
Adderley St **35** H5
Adelaide St **35** G6
Albert St **35** G4
Albion St **34** D3
Alcester St **35** G7
Aldgate Gro **35** E2
Alfred Knight Way **34** E6
Allcock St **35** H5
Allesley St **35** G1
Allison St **35** G5
All Saints Rd **34** C1
All Saints St **34** C2
Alston St **34** B5
Anchor Cl **34** A5
Anchor Cres **34** B1
Anderton St **34** C4
Angelina St **35** G7
Ansbro Cl **34** A2
Arden Gro **34** C5
Arthur Pl **34** D4
Ascot Cl **34** A5
Ashted Lock **35** H3
Ashted Wk **35** J2
Ashton Cft **34** C5
Aston **35** H1
Aston Br **35** G1
Aston Brook St **35** G1
Aston Brook St E **35** H1
Aston Expressway **35** G2
Aston Rd **35** H1
Aston St **35** G3
Attenborough Cl **35** F1
Auckland Rd **35** J7
Augusta St **34** D2
Augustine Gro **34** B1
Austen Pl **34** C7
Autumn Gro **34** E1
Avenue Cl **35** J1
Avenue Rd **35** H1

B
Bacchus Rd **34** A1
Bagot St **35** G2
Balcaskie Cl **34** A7
Banbury St **35** G4
Barford Rd **34** A3
Barford St **35** G6
Barn St **35** H5
Barrack St **35** J3
Barrow Wk **35** F7
Barr St **34** D1
Bartholomew Row **35** G4
Bartholomew St **35** G4
Barwick St **35** F4
Bath Pas **35** F5
Bath Row **34** D6
Bath St **35** F3
Beak St **35** F5
Beaufort Gdns **34** A1
Beaufort Rd **34** B6
Bedford Rd **35** J6
Beeches, The **34** D7
Belgrave Middleway **35** F7
Bell Barn Rd **34** D6
Bellcroft **34** C5
Bellevue **35** F7
Bellis St **34** A6
Belmont Pas **35** J4
Belmont Row **35** H3
Benacre Dr **35** H4
Bennett's Hill **35** F4
Benson Rd **34** A1
Berkley St **34** D5
Berrington Wk **35** G7
Birchall St **35** G6
Bishopsgate St **34** D5
Bishop St **35** G7
Bissell St **35** G7
Blews St **35** G2
Bloomsbury St **35** J2
Blucher St **35** E5
Blyton Cl **34** A3
Boar Hound Cl **34** C3
Bodmin Gro **35** J1
Bolton St **35** J5
Bond Sq **34** C3
Bond St **35** E3
Bordesley **35** J5
Bordesley Circ **35** J6
Bordesley Middleway **35** J7
Bordesley Pk Rd **35** J6
Bordesley St **35** G4
Boulton Middleway **34** D1
Bow St **35** F6
Bowyer St **35** J6
Bracebridge St **35** G1
Bradburn Way **35** J2
Bradford St **35** G5
Branston St **34** D2
Brearley Cl **35** F2
Brearley St **35** F2
Bredon Cft **34** B1
Brewery St **35** G2
Bridge St **34** E5
Bridge St W **35** E1
Brindley Dr **34** D4
Brindley Pl **34** D5
Bristol St **35** F7
Broad St **34** D6
Broadway Plaza **34** C6
Bromley St **35** H5
Bromsgrove St **35** F6
Brookfield Rd **34** B2
Brook St **34** E3
Brook Vw Cl **34** E1
Broom St **35** H6
Brough Cl **35** J1
Browning St **34** C5
Brownsea Dr **35** E5
Brunel St **35** E5
Brunswick St **34** D5
Buckingham St **35** E2
Bullock St **35** H2
Bull St **35** F4

C
Cala Dr **34** C7
Calthorpe Rd **34** C7
Cambridge Rd **34** D4
Camden Dr **34** D3
Camden Gro **34** D3
Camden St **34** B2
Camp Hill **35** J7
Camp Hill Middleway **35** H7
Cannon St **35** F4
Capstone Av **34** C2
Cardigan St **35** H3
Carlisle St **34** A2
Carlyle Rd **34** A5
Caroline St **34** E3
Carpenter Rd **34** C7
Carrs La **35** G4
Carver St **34** C3
Cawdor Cres **34** B6
Cecil St **35** F2
Cemetery La **34** D2
Centenary Sq **34** E4
Central Pk Dr **34** A1
Central Sq **34** E5
Chad Rd **34** A7
Chadsmoor Ter **35** J1
Chad Valley **34** A7
Chamberlain Sq **35** E4
Chancellor's Cl **34** A7
Chandlers Cl **34** B1
Chapel Ho St **35** H5
Chapmans Pas **35** E5
Charles Henry St **35** G7
Charlotte Rd **34** D7
Charlotte St **34** E4
Chatsworth Way **34** E6
Cheapside **35** G6
Cherry St **35** F4
Chester St **35** H1
Chilwell Cft **35** F1
Christchurch Cl **34** A6
Church Rd **34** C7
Church St **35** F3
Civic Cl **34** D4
Clare Dr **34** A7
Clarendon Rd **34** A5
Clark St **34** A5
Claybrook St **35** F6
Clement St **34** D4
Clipper Vw **34** A5
Clissold Cl **35** G7
Clissold St **34** B2
Cliveland St **35** F3
Clyde St **35** H6
Colbrand Gro **35** E7
Coleshill St **35** G4
College St **34** B3
Colmore Circ **35** F3
Colmore Row **35** F4
Commercial St **34** E5
Communication Row **34** D6
Constitution Hill **34** E2
Conybere St **35** G7
Cope St **34** B3
Coplow St **34** A3
Cornwall St **35** E4
Corporation St **35** F4
Coveley Gro **34** B1
Coventry Rd **35** J6
Coventry St **35** G5
Cox St **35** E3
Coxwell Gdns **34** B5
Crabtree Rd **34** B2
Cregoe St **34** E6
Crescent, The **34** C1
Crescent Av **34** C1
Cromwell St **35** J1
Crondal Pl **34** D7
Crosby Cl **34** C4
Cumberland St **34** D5
Curzon Circ **35** H3
Curzon St **35** H4

D
Daisy Rd **34** A5
Dale End **35** G4
Daley Cl **34** C4
Dalton St **35** G4
Darnley Rd **34** B5
Dartmouth Circ **35** G1
Dartmouth Middleway **35** G2
Dart St **35** J6
Darwin St **35** G6
Dean St **35** G5
Deeley Cl **34** D7
Denby Cl **35** J2
Derby St **35** J4
Devonshire Av **34** B1
Devonshire St **34** B1
Digbeth **35** G6
Digbeth **35** G5
Dollman St **35** J3
Dover St **34** B1
Duchess Rd **34** B6
Duddeston Manor Rd **35** J2
Dudley St **35** F5
Dymoke Cl **35** G7

E
Edgbaston **34** B7
Edgbaston St **35** F5
Edmund St **35** E4
Edward St **34** D4
Eldon Rd **34** A5
Elkington St **35** G1
Ellen St **34** C3
Ellis St **35** E5
Elvetham Rd **34** D7
Embassy Dr **34** C6
Emily Gdns **34** A3
Emily St **35** G7
Enfield Rd **34** D6
Enterprise Way **35** G2
Ernest St **35** E6
Erskine St **35** J3
Essex St **35** F6
Essington St **34** D5
Estria Rd **34** C7
Ethel St **35** F4
Exeter Pas **35** F6
Exeter St **35** F6
Eyre St **34** B3
Eyton Cft **35** H7

F
Farmacre **35** J5
Farm Cft **34** D1
Farm St **34** D1
Fawdry St **35** J4
Fazeley St **35** G4
Felsted Way **35** J3
Ferndale Cres **35** H7
Finstall Cl **35** J3
Five Ways **34** C6
Fleet St **34** E4
Floodgate St **35** H5
Florence St **35** E6
Ford St **34** C1
Fore St **35** F4
Forster St **35** H3
Foster Gdns **34** B1
Fox St **35** G4
Francis Rd **34** B5
Francis St **35** J3
Frankfort St **35** F1
Frederick Rd **34** C7
Frederick St **34** D3
Freeman St **35** G4
Freeth St **34** B4
Friston Av **34** C6
Fulmer Wk **34** C4

G
Garrison Circ **35** J4
Garrison La **35** J4
Garrison St **35** J4
Gas St **34** D5
Gas St Basin **34** E5
Geach St **35** F1
Gee St **35** F1
George Rd **34** D7
George St **34** D4
George St W **34** C3
Gibb St **35** H5
Gilby Rd **34** C5
Gilldown Pl **34** D7
Glebeland Cl **34** C5
Gloucester St **35** F5
Glover St **35** J5
Gooch St **35** F7
Gooch St N **35** F6
Goode Av **34** C1
Goodman St **34** C4
Gopsal St **35** H3
Gough St **35** E5
Grafton Rd **35** J7
Graham St **34** D3
Grant St **35** E6
Granville St **34** D5
Graston Cl **34** C5
Great Barr St **35** H5
Great Brook St **35** H3
Great Charles St Queensway **35** E4
Great Colmore St **34** E6
Great Hampton Row **34** E2
Great Hampton St **34** D2
Great King St **34** D1
Great King St N **34** E1
Great Lister St **35** H2
Great Tindal St **34** C4
Greenfield Cres **34** C6
Green St **35** H6
Grenfell Dr **34** A7
Grosvenor St **35** G4
Grosvenor St W **34** C5
Guest Gro **34** D1
Guild Cl **34** B5
Guild Cft **35** F1
Guthrie Cl **35** E1

H
Hack St **35** H5
Hadfield Cft **34** E2
Hagley Rd **34** A6
Hall St **34** E3
Hampshire Dr **34** A7
Hampton St **35** E2
Hanley St **35** F2
Hanwood Cl **35** G7
Harborne Rd **34** A7
Harford St **34** E2
Harmer St **34** C2
Harold Rd **34** A5
Hartley Pl **34** A6
Hatchett St **35** F1
Hawthorn Cl **35** J5
Hawthorne Rd **34** A7
Heath Mill La **35** H5
Heath St S **34** B3
Heaton Dr **34** A7
Heaton St **34** D1
Helena St **34** D4
Heneage St **35** H2
Heneage St W **35** H3
Henley St **35** J7
Henrietta St **35** F3
Henstead St **35** F6
Herne Cl **34** C3
Hickman Gdns **34** B5
Highfield Rd **34** B6
Highgate **35** H7
Highgate St **35** G7
High St **35** G4
Hilden Rd **35** J3
Hill St **35** E4
Hinckley St **35** F5
Hindlow Cl **35** J3
Hindon Sq **34** B7
Hingeston St **34** C2
Hitches La **34** D7
Hobart Cft **35** J2
Hobson Cl **34** B1
Hockley Brook Cl **34** B1
Hockley Cl **35** F1
Hockley Hill **34** D1
Hockley St **34** D2
Holland St **34** D4
Holliday Pas **34** E5
Holliday St **34** E5
Holloway Circ **35** F5
Holloway Head **35** E6
Holt St **35** G2
Holywell Cl **34** B5
Hooper St **34** B3
Hope St **35** F7
Hospital St **35** F1
Howard St **35** E2
Howe St **35** H3
Howford Gro **35** J2
Hubert St **35** H1
Hunter's Vale **34** D1
Huntly Rd **34** B6
Hurdlow Av **34** C2
Hurst St **35** F5
Hylton St **34** D2
Hyssop Cl **35** J2

I
Icknield Port Rd **34** A3
Icknield Sq **34** B4
Icknield St **34** C3
Inge St **35** F6
Inkerman St **35** J3
Irving St **35** E6
Islington Row Middleway **34** C6
Ivy La **35** J4

J
Jackson Cl **35** J7
James St **34** E3
James Watt Queensway **35** G3
Jennens Rd **35** G4
Jewellery Quarter **34** D2
Jinnah Cl **35** G7
John Bright St **35** F5
John Kempe Way **35** H7

K
Keeley St **35** J5
Keepers Cl **34** B1
Kellett Rd **35** H2
Kelsall Cft **34** C4
Kelsey Cl **35** J2
Kemble Cft **35** F7
Kendal Rd **35** J7
Kenilworth Ct **34** A6
Kent St **35** F6
Kent St N **34** B1
Kenyon St **34** E3
Ketley Cft **35** G7
Key Hill **34** D2
Key Hill Dr **34** D2
Kilby Av **34** C4
King Edwards Rd **34** D4
Kingston Rd **35** J5
Kingston Row **34** D4
Kirby Rd **34** A1
Knightstone Av **34** C2
Kyotts Lake Rd **35** J7

L
Ladycroft **34** C5
Ladywell Wk **35** F5
Ladywood **34** C4
Ladywood Middleway **34** B5
Ladywood Rd **34** B5
Lancaster Circ **35** G3
Landor St **35** J4
Langdon St **35** J4
Lansdowne St **34** A2
Latimer Gdns **35** E7
Lawden Rd **35** J6
Lawford Cl **35** J3
Lawford Gro **35** G7
Lawley Middleway **35** H3
Ledbury Cl **34** B5
Ledsam St **34** C4
Lee Bk **35** E7
Lee Bk Middleway **34** D6
Lee Cres **34** D7
Lee Mt **34** D7
Lees St **34** B1
Legge La **34** D3
Legge St **35** G2
Lennox St **35** E1
Leopold St **35** G7
Leslie Rd **34** A5
Leyburn Rd **34** C5
Lighthorne Av **34** C4
Link Rd **34** A3
Lionel St **34** E4
Lister St **35** G3
Little Ann St **35** H5
Little Barr St **35** J4
Little Broom St **35** H6
Little Edward St **35** J5
Little Francis Grn **35** J2
Little Shadwell St **35** F3
Liverpool St **35** H5
Livery St **35** F3
Locke Pl **35** J4
Lodge Rd **34** A1
Lombard St **35** G6
Longleat Way **34** D6
Lord St **35** H2
Louisa St **34** D4
Loveday St **35** F3
Love La **35** G2
Lower Dartmouth St **35** J4
Lower Essex St **35** F6
Lower Loveday St **35** F2
Lower Severn St **35** F5
Lower Temple St **35** F4

Lower Twr St 35 F2
Lower Trinity St 35 H5
Lowe St 35 J6
Ludgate Hill 35 E3
Lytham Cft 35 E6

M
Macdonald St 35 G6
Malcolmson Cl 34 A7
Manchester St 35 F2
Margaret St 35 E4
Mariner Av 34 A5
Marroway St 34 A3
Marshall St 35 E5
Mary Ann St 35 E3
Mary St 34 E3
Mason Way 34 E6
Masshouse La 35 G4
Mearse Cl 34 C2
Melton Dr 34 D7
Meredith Pool Cl 34 A1
Meriden St 35 G5
Merryhill Dr 34 A1
Meyrick Wk 34 A6
Middleway Vw 34 C3
Midford Grn 34 E6
Milford Cft 35 E2
Milk St 35 H5
Miller St 35 F1
Mill La 35 G5
Mill St 35 G2
Milton St 35 F1
Moat La 35 G5
Moland St 35 G2
Montague St 35 J4
Monument Rd 34 B6
Moore's Row 35 H5
Moorings, The 34 B1
Moorsom St 35 F1
Moor St Queensway 35 G4
Moreton St 34 C3
Morville St 34 C5
Mosborough Cres 34 F1
Mosedale Way 35 E6
Moseley Rd 35 H6
Moseley St 35 G6
Moss Ho Cl 34 D6
Mostyn Rd 34 A5
Mott St 34 E2
Mowbray St 35 F7
Murrell Cl 35 F7
Musgrave Rd 34 A1
Myddleton St 34 B3

N
Navigation St 35 E5
Navigation Way 34 B1
Nechells Parkway 35 H3
Needless All 35 F4
Nelson St 34 D4
New Bartholomew St 35 G4
Newbold Cft 35 J1
New Bond St 35 J5

New Canal St 35 G4
Newhall Hill 34 D3
Newhall St 34 E3
Newhope Cl 35 F7
New John St 35 G2
New John St W 34 E1
New Mkt St 35 E4
New Moseley Rd 35 H7
New Spring St 34 C2
New Spring St N 34 B2
New St 35 F4
New Summer St 35 F2
Newton St 35 G4
Newtown 34 E1
Newtown Dr 34 D1
Newtown Middleway 35 F1
New Town Row 35 F1
Niall Cl 34 A7
Noel Rd 34 A5
Northampton St 34 D2
Northbrook St 34 A3
Northumberland St 35 J3
Northwood St 34 D3
Norton St 34 B1
Nova Scotia St 35 G4
Nursery Rd 34 D1

O
Oak Hill Dr 34 A7
Old Br St 34 D1
Old Camp Hill 35 J6
Old Smithy Pl 34 C1
Old Snow Hill 35 F3
Old Sq 35 F4
Oliver Rd 34 B5
Oliver St 35 J1
Oozells St 34 D5
Orchid Dr 35 E1
Orwell Pas 35 G5
Osler St 34 A5
Oxford St 35 G5

P
Paddocks Grn 34 B2
Pakenham Rd 34 D7
Palmer St 35 J5
Palomino Pl 34 B4
Pannel Cft 35 F1
Parade 34 D4
Paradise Circ 34 E4
Paradise St 34 E4
Parker St 34 A6
Parkfield Cl 34 D7
Park Rd 34 C1
Park Rd S 34 C1
Park St 35 G5
Paxton Rd 34 C2
Peel St 34 A2
Pemberton St 34 D2
Penn St 35 H3
Pershore St 35 F5
Pickford St 35 H5

Pinfold St 35 E4
Pinto Cl 34 B5
Pitsford St 34 C2
Pitt St 35 H3
Plough & Harrow Rd 34 B6
Pool St 35 G1
Pope St 34 C3
Port Hope Rd 35 J7
Powell St 34 D3
Power Cres 34 C5
Price St 35 F3
Princip St 35 F3
Printing Ho St 35 F3
Priory
  Queensway, The 35 G4
Pritchett St 35 F2
Proctor St 35 H2

Q
Quayside 34 B1
Queens Hosp Cl 34 D6
Quigley Av 35 J5

R
Radnor St 34 B1
Radshaw Cl 34 D6
Rake Way 34 D5
Rann Cl 34 C5
Ravenhurst St 35 H6
Rawlins St 34 C5
Rea St 35 G6
Rea St S 35 G6
Rea Ter 35 H5
Rectory Gro 34 A1
Regent Par 34 D3
Regent Pl 34 D3
Regent St 34 D3
Reservoir Retreat 34 B5
Reservoir Rd 34 A5
Richard St 35 H2
Rickman Dr 35 E7
Ridley St 34 E6
River St 35 H5
Rocky La 35 J1
Rodney Cl 34 B4
Roseberry St 34 B2
Roseland Way 34 D6
Rotton Pk St 34 B4
Rupert St 35 H2
Ruston St 34 C5
Ryland Rd 34 D7
Ryland St 34 C5

S
Sadlers Wk 34 B5
St. Andrew's Rd 35 J4
St. Chad's Queensway 35 F3
St. Georges Cl 34 B7
St. Georges St 35 E2
St. Helen's Pas 34 D3
St. James Pl 35 J3
St. James Rd 34 C6
St. Jude's Pas 35 F5

St. Lukes Rd 35 F7
St. Marks Cres 34 C4
St. Marks St 34 C3
St. Martin's Circ
  Queensway 35 F5
St. Martin's Sq 35 G5
St. Martin's St 34 D6
St. Mary's Row 35 F3
St. Paul's Sq 34 E3
St. Phillips Pl 35 F4
St. Stephen's St 35 F1
St. Vincent St 34 C4
St. Vincent St W 34 B5
Salop St 35 H7
Sampson Rd 35 J7
Sampson Rd N 35 J6
Sand Pits 34 C3
Sandy Way 34 D5
Scotland St 34 D4
Sefton Rd 34 A5
Severn St 35 E5
Shadwell St 35 F3
Shawbury Gro 35 H7
Shaw's Pas 35 G4
Sheepcote St 34 C4
Shefford Rd 35 G1
Shepherds Gdns 34 D6
Sherborne Gro 34 C4
Sherborne St 34 C5
Sheringham 34 A6
Sherlock St 35 F7
Shetland Rd 34 B5
Shillcock Gro 35 F2
Shire Cl 34 A4
Shyltons Cft 34 C5
Skinner La 35 G6
Skipton Rd 34 B5
Sloane St 34 D4
Smallbrook
  Queensway 35 F5
Smith St 34 E1
Snow Hill Queensway 35 F3
Soho Pool Way 35 B1
Southacre Av 35 F7
South Rd 35 J7
Spencer St 34 D2
Spooner Cft 35 F7
Springbank Rd 34 E7
Springfield St 34 B4
Spring Gro Gdns 34 A1
Spring Hill 34 B3
Spring Hill Pas 34 C3
Spring St 35 E7
Stainsby Av 34 D1
Stanhope Rd 35 G7
Staniforth St 35 G2
Star Hill 34 D7
Station St 35 F5
Steelhouse La 35 F3
Stephenson Pl 35 F5
Stephenson St 35 F4
Steward St 34 B3
Stirling Rd 34 A6

Stoke Way 34 D5
Stone Rd 35 E7
Stone Yd 35 H5
Stour St 34 B3
Stratford Pl 35 H7
Stratford Rd 35 J7
Stratford St N 35 J7
Suffolk St
  Queensway 35 E5
Sugden Gro 35 F6
Summer Cft 35 F1
Summerfield Rd 34 A3
Summer Hill Rd 34 C3
Summer Hill St 34 D4
Summer Hill Ter 34 D3
Summer La 35 F3
Summer Rd 34 E7
Summer Row 34 E4
Sutton St 35 E6
Swallow St 35 E5

T
Talbot St 34 A1
Temple Pas 35 F4
Temple Row 35 F4
Temple Row W 35 F4
Temple St 35 F4
Tenby St 34 D3
Tenby St N 34 D3
Tennant St 34 D6
Theatre App 35 F5
Theresa Rd 35 J7
Thomas St 35 G1
Thorp St 35 F6
Tower St 35 F2
Townsend Way 34 D4
Trent St 35 H5
Trinity Ter 35 J6

U
Unett St 34 E1
Union Pas 35 F4
Union St 35 F4
Upper Dean St 35 F5
Upper Gough St 35 E6
Upper Marshall St 35 E5
Upper Trinity St 35 H5
Uxbridge St 35 E1

V
Vaughton St 35 G7
Vaughton St S 35 G7
Vauxhall Gro 35 J3
Vauxhall Rd 35 J3
Venture Way 35 H2
Verbena Gdns 35 J2
Vere St 35 F7
Vernolds Cft 35 F6
Vesey St 35 F3
Viaduct St 35 J4
Vicarage Rd 34 B6
Victoria Sq 35 E4
Victor Rd 34 A1

Vittoria St 34 D3
Vyse St 34 D3

W
Walter St 35 J1
Wardlow Rd 35 J2
Ward St 35 H6
Warner St 35 H6
Warstone La 34 C3
Warstone Par E 34 D2
Warwick Pas 35 F4
Warwick St 35 H6
Washington St 34 E5
Waterloo St 35 E4
Waterside Dr 34 A1
Waterside Vw 34 B2
Water St 35 E3
Waterworks Rd 34 A5
Watery La Middleway 35 J4
Weaman St 35 F3
Well La 35 G5
Well St 34 D2
Westbourne Cres 34 C7
Westbourne Gdns 34 B7
Westbourne Rd 34 A7
Western Rd 34 B3
West Grn Cl 34 D7
Westhorpe Gro 34 E1
Westley St 35 J5
Wharf, The 34 E5
Wharf La 34 C1
Wharfside St 35 E5
Wharf St 34 B1
Wheeler St 35 E1
Wheeley's La 34 D6
Whitehouse St 35 H1
Whitmore St 34 C1
Whittall St 35 F3
Wiggin St 34 A4
William Booth La 35 F3
William Henry St 35 J1
William St 34 D6
William St N 35 F2
Willow Gdns 34 A3
Windmill St 35 F6
Windrush Way 35 E7
Windsor St 35 H2
Windsor St S 35 H3
Winson Grn 34 A1
Witton St 35 J4
Woodcock St 35 G3
Woodcote Way 34 B2
Woodview Dr 34 E7
Wrentham St 35 F6
Wrottesley St 35 F5
Wyndham Rd 34 A6
Wynn St 35 E6

Y
Yew Tree Rd 34 D6

Edinburgh street index

A
Abbeyhill 37 J3
Abbeyhill 37 J3
Abbeyhill Cres 37 H4
Abbey La 37 J3
Abbeymount 37 J3
Abbey Strand 37 J4
Abbey St 37 J3
Abercromby Pl 37 F3
Admiral Ter 36 D7
Ainslie Pl 36 D3
Albany La 37 F2
Albany St 37 F3
Albany St La 37 F3
Albert St 37 H1
Albion Gdns 37 J2
Albion Pl 37 J2
Albion Rd 37 J2
Albion Ter 37 J2
Alfred Pl 37 J7
Allanfield 37 H2
Allanfield Pl 37 H2
Allan St 36 D2
Alva Pl 37 J3
Alva St 36 D4
Angle Pk Ter 36 B7
Annandale St 37 G1
Annandale St La 37 G2
Ann St 36 D3
Arboretum Av 36 D2
Arboretum Pl 36 D1

Archibald Pl 37 F6
Arden St 37 F7
Ardmillan Pl 36 B7
Ardmillan Ter 36 B7
Argyle Pk Ter 37 F7
Argyle Pl 37 F7
Arthur St 37 H1
Arthur St La 37 H1
Atholl Cres 36 D5
Atholl Cres La 36 D5
Avondale Pl 36 D1

B
Back Dean 36 B4
Bakehouse Cl 37 H4
Balbirnie Pl 36 A5
Balmoral Pl 36 D2
Bank St 37 F4
Barclay Pl 36 E7
Barony St 37 F2
Beaverbank Pl 37 F1
Beaverhall Rd 37 F1
Bedford St 36 D2
Belford Av 36 A3
Belford Br 36 C4
Belford Gdns 36 A3
Belford Ms 36 C4
Belford Pk 36 A4
Belford Pl 36 B4
Belford Rd 36 B4
Belgrave Cres 36 C3

Belgrave Cres La 36 C3
Belgrave Ms 36 C3
Belgrave Pl 36 C3
Bellevue 37 F2
Bellevue Cres 37 F2
Bellevue Gdns 37 G1
Bellevue Gro 37 G2
Bellevue La 37 F2
Bellevue Pl 37 F2
Bellevue Rd 37 G2
Bellevue St 37 G2
Bellevue Ter 37 F2
Bell Pl 36 E1
Bells Brae 36 C4
Bell's Mills 36 B4
Bernard Ter 37 H6
Blacket Av 37 H7
Blacket Pl 37 H7
Blackfriars St 37 G4
Blackwood Cres 37 H7
Blair St 37 G4
Blandfield 37 G1
Boat Grn 37 F1
Boroughloch 37 G6
Boroughloch Sq 37 G6
Borthwick Pl 36 B5
Bothwell St 37 J2
Bowmont Pl 37 H6
Boyd's Entry 37 G4
Brandfield St 36 D6
Brandon St 37 E2

Brandon Ter 37 E2
Bread St 36 E5
Bridge Pl 36 D2
Briery Bauks 37 H5
Brighton St 37 G5
Bristo Pl 37 F5
Bristo Port 37 F5
Brougham Pl 37 E6
Brougham St 36 E6
Broughton 37 F1
Broughton Mkt 37 F3
Broughton Pl 37 G2
Broughton Pl La 37 G2
Broughton Rd 37 F1
Broughton St 37 G2
Broughton St La 37 G3
Brown's Cl 37 H4
Brown St 37 H5
Brunswick Rd 37 H2
Brunswick St 37 H2
Brunswick St La 37 H2
Bruntsfield Av 36 D7
Bruntsfield Cres 36 E7
Bruntsfield Gdns 36 D7
Bruntsfield Ter 36 D7
Bryson Rd 36 B7
Buccleuch Pl 37 G6
Buccleuch St 37 G6
Buccleuch Ter 37 G6
Buchanan St 37 H1

Brandon Ter 37 E2
Buckingham Ter 36 C3

C
Caledonian Cres 36 C6
Caledonian Pl 36 C6
Caledonian Rd 36 C6
Calton Hill 37 G3
Calton Rd 37 G3
Cambridge Av 37 H1
Cambridge Gdns 37 H1
Cambridge St 36 E5
Campbell's Cl 37 H4
Candlemaker Row 37 F5
Canning St 36 D5
Canning St La 36 D5
Canongate 37 G4
Canon La 37 E2
Canonmills 37 E1
Canon St 37 E1
Carberry Pl 36 B5
Carlton St 36 D3
Carlton Ter 37 H3
Carlton Ter Brae 37 J3
Carlton Ter La 37 H3
Carlton Ter Ms 37 H3
Carlton Wynd 37 H4
Carlyle Pl 37 J3
Carnegie St 37 H5
Carrington Rd 36 B2
Castle Hill 37 F4

Castle Ter 36 E4
Cathcart Pl 36 B6
Cathedral La 37 G3
Causewayside 37 H7
Chalmers Cres 37 F7
Chalmers St 37 F5
Chambers St 37 F5
Chapel St 37 G5
Charles St 37 G5
Charlotte La 36 D4
Charlotte Sq 36 D4
Chester St 36 C4
Cheyne St 36 D2
Chuckie Pend 36 D5
Circus Gdns 36 E3
Circus La 36 E3
Circus Pl 36 E3
Claremont Bk 37 F2
Claremont Cres 37 F1
Claremont Gro 37 F1
Clarence St 36 E2
Clarendon Cres 36 C3
Clerk St 37 G6
Coates 36 B5
Coates Cres 36 D5
Coates Gdns 36 C5
Cochran Ter 37 G2
Cockburn St 37 F4
Coffin La 36 B6
Collins Pl 36 D2
Coltbridge Av 36 A5

Name	Ref		Name	Ref		Name	Ref		Name	Ref		Name	Ref		Name	Ref
Coltbridge Gdns	36 A5		Dunedin St	37 F1		Green St	37 G2		King's Stables La	37 E5		Moncrieff Ter	37 G7		Polwarth Cres	36 C7
Coltbridge Millside	36 A5		Dunrobin Pl	36 D2		Greyfriars Pl	37 F5		King's Stables Rd	36 E4		Montague St	37 H6		Polwarth Gdns	36 C7
Coltbridge Ter	36 A5		**E**			Grigor Av	36 A1		Kirkhill Rd	37 J7		Montgomery St	37 G2		Polwarth Pk	36 C7
Coltbridge Vale	36 A5		Earl Grey St	36 E5		Grigor Dr	36 A1		Kyle Pl	37 J3		Montgomery St La	37 G2		Polwarth Pl	36 C7
Colville Pl	36 D2		East Adam St	37 G5		Grigor Gdns	36 A1					Montpelier	36 D7		Ponton St	36 D6
Comely Bk	36 C2		East Castle Rd	36 C7		Grindlay St	36 E5		**L**			Montpelier Pk	36 D7		Portgower Pl	36 D2
Comely Bk	36 B2		East Claremont St	37 F2		Grosvenor Cres	36 C5		Lady Lawson St	37 E5		Montpelier Ter	36 D7		Port Hamilton	36 D6
Comely Bk Av	36 C2		East			Grosvenor Gdns	36 C5		Lady Menzies Pl	37 J3		Montrose Ter	37 J3		Potterrow	37 G5
Comely Bk Gro	36 C3		Crosscauseway	37 G6		Grosvenor St	36 C5		Lady Wynd	37 F5		Moray Pl	36 D3		Powderhall Rd	37 F1
Comely Bk Pl	36 C2		Easter Dalry Dr	36 B6		Grove St	36 D5		Lamb's Cl	37 H6		Morrison Circ	36 C5		Priestfield Rd N	37 J7
Comely Bk Pl Ms	36 C2		Easter Dalry Pl	36 B5		Gullan's Cl	37 G4		Lansdowne Cres	36 C5		Morrison Cres	36 D5		Primrose Ter	36 C7
Comely Bk Rd	36 C2		Easter Dalry Rigg	36 B6		Guthrie St	37 G5		Lauderdale St	37 E7		Morrison Link	36 D5		Princes St	36 D4
Comely Bk Row	36 C2		Easter Dalry Rd	36 C5					Lauder Rd	37 G7		Morrison St	36 C5		
Comely Bk St	36 C2		Easter Dalry Wynd	36 C6		**H**			Lauriston Gdns	37 E5		Mound, The	37 F4		**Q**	
Comely Bk Ter	36 C2		Easter Rd	37 J3		Haddon's Ct	37 G5		Lauriston Pk	37 E5		Mound Pl	37 F4		Queen's Dr	37 H5
Conference Sq	36 D5		East Fettes Av	36 C1		Hailes St	36 E6		Lauriston Pl	36 E6		Mount Pl	37 F4		Queensferry Rd	36 B3
Cornwallis Pl	37 F2		East			Halmyre St	37 J1		Lauriston St	37 E5		Multrees Wk	37 F3		Queensferry St	36 D4
Cornwall St	36 E5		Fountainbridge	36 E5		Hamilton Pl	36 D2		Lauriston Pl	37 F4		Murano Pl	37 H2		Queensferry St La	36 D4
Cowan's Cl	37 G6		East London St	37 G2		Hamilton's Folly Ms	37 H6		Lawnmarket	37 F4		Murdoch Ter	36 C6		Queensferry Ter	36 B3
Cowgate	37 F5		East Mkt St	37 G4		Hammermen's Entry	37 H4		Leamington Rd	36 D6		Murieston Cres	36 B6		Queen St	36 E3
Cowgatehead	37 F5		East Montgomery Pl	37 H2		Hanover St	37 F3		Leamington Ter	36 D6		Murieston Cres La	36 B6		Queen St Gdns E	37 F3
Craigleith	36 A2		East Newington Pl	37 H7		Harden Pl	36 C7		Learmonth Av	36 B2		Murieston La	36 B7		Queen St Gdns W	37 E3
Craigleith Hill			East Parkside	37 H6		Hardwell Cl	37 H6		Learmonth Cres	36 B3		Murieston Pl	36 B6		
Cres	36 A2		East Preston St	37 H7		Harrismith Pl	37 J2		Learmonth Gdns	36 C3		Murieston Rd	36 B6		**R**	
Craigleith Hill			East Preston St La	37 H7		Harrison La	36 B7		Learmonth Gdn La	36 C3		Murieston Ter	36 B6		Raeburn Ms	36 D2
Gdns	36 A2		East Sciennes St	37 G7		Harrison Rd	36 B7		Learmonth Gdns Ms	36 C3		Myrtle Ter	36 B7		Raeburn Pl	36 D2
Craigleith Hill Ln	36 A2		East Scotland St La	37 F2		Hartington Gdns	36 D7		Learmonth Gro	36 C2					Raeburn St	36 D2
Craigleith Hill			East Silvermills La	37 E2		Hartington Pl	36 D7		Learmonth Pl	36 C2		**N**			Ramsay Gdn	37 F4
Row	36 A2		Edina Pl	37 J2		Hart St	37 G2		Learmonth Ter	36 C3		Napier Rd	36 C7		Ramsay La	37 F4
Cranston St	37 G4		Edina St	37 J2		Hatton Pl	37 F7		Learmonth Ter La	36 C3		Nelson St	37 F2		Randolph Cres	36 D4
Crarae Av	36 A4		Edinburgh Quay	36 D6		Haugh St	36 D2		Learmonth Vw	36 C3		New Arthur Pl	37 H5		Randolph La	36 D4
Crewe Rd S	36 A1		Eglinton Cres	36 B5		Hawthornbank La	36 C4		Leith St	37 G3		Newington Rd	37 H7		Randolph Pl	36 D4
Crichton St	37 G5		Eildon St	36 E1		Hawthornden Pl	37 H1		Leith Wk	37 G3		New John's Pl	37 H6		Rankeillor St	37 H6
Croft-an-Righ	37 J3		Eildon Ter	36 E1		Haymarket	36 C5		Lennox St	36 C3		New Skinner's Cl	37 G4		Ravelston Dykes	36 A4
Cumberland St	36 E2		Elder St	37 F3		Haymarket Ter	36 B5		Lennox St La	36 C3		New St	37 G4		Ravelston Pk	36 A4
Cumberland St			Elgin St	37 H2		Haymarket Yards	36 B5		Leslie Pl	36 D3		Newton St	36 A7		Ravelston Ter	36 B4
N E La	37 E2		Elgin St N	37 J2		Henderland Rd	36 A5		Leven St	36 E6		Nicolson Sq	37 G5		Regent Pl	37 J3
Cumberland St			Elgin Ter	37 J2		Henderson Pl	36 E2		Leven Ter	36 E6		Nicolson St	37 G5		Regent Rd	37 G3
N W La	37 E2		Elliot St	37 J2		Henderson Pl La	36 E2		Liddesdale Pl	36 E1		Niddry St	37 G4		Regent Ter	37 H3
Cumberland St			Elm Row	37 G2		Henderson Row	36 E2		Little King St	37 G3		Niddry St S	37 G5		Regent Ter Ms	37 H3
S E La	37 E2		Eton Ter	36 D3		Henderson Ter	36 B7		Livingstone Pl	37 G7		Nightingale Way	37 F6		Register Pl	37 F3
Cumberland St			Ettrickdale Pl	36 E1		Heriot Br	37 F5		Lochend Cl	37 H4		North Bk St	37 F4		Reid's Cl	37 H4
S W La	37 E2		Ettrick Gro	36 C7		Heriot Hill Ter	37 F2		Lochrin Pl	36 E6		North Br	37 G4		Reid Ter	36 D2
Cumin Pl	37 G7		Eyre Cres	37 E2		Heriot Pl	37 F5		Logan St	37 F2		North Castle St	36 E3		Richmond La	37 G5
			Eyre Pl	37 E2		Heriot Row	36 E3		Logie Grn Gdns	37 F1		North Charlotte St	36 D3		Richmond Pl	37 G5
D			Eyre Ter	37 E2		Hermits Cft	37 H6		Logie Grn Ln	37 F1		North Clyde St La	37 F3		Richmond Ter	36 C5
Dalkeith Rd	37 H6					High Riggs	36 E5		Logie Grn Rd	37 F1		Northcote St	36 B6		Riego St	36 E5
Dalmeny St	37 H1		**F**			High Sch Wynd	37 G4		Logie Mill	37 F1		North E Circ Pl	36 E3		Rillbank Cres	37 G7
Dalry	36 B6		Fettes Av	36 B2		High Sch Yards	37 G5		London Rd	37 J3		North Pk Ter	36 C2		Rillbank Ter	37 G7
Dalry Gait	36 C5		Fettes Row	37 E2		High St	37 F4		London St	37 F2		North Richmond St	37 G5		Rintoul Pl	36 D2
Dalry Pl	36 C5		Findhorn Pl	37 G7		Hill Pl	37 G5		Lonsdale Ter	37 E6		North St. Andrew La	37 F3		Ritchie Pl	36 B7
Dalry Rd	36 B7		Fingal Pl	37 F7		Hillside Cres	37 H2		Lorne Pl	37 J1		North St. Andrew St	37 F3		Robertson Av	36 A7
Damside	36 C4		Forbes St	37 H6		Hillside St	37 H2		Lorne Sq	37 J1		North St. David St	37 F3		Robertson Gait	36 A7
Danube St	36 D3		Forres St	36 D3		Hill Sq	37 G5		Lorne St	37 J1		Northumberland			Robertson's Cl	37 G5
Darnaway St	36 D3		Forrest Hill	37 F5		Hill St	36 E3		Lothian Rd	36 D4		Pl La	37 F3		Rodney Pl	37 F2
Davidson Pk	36 A1		Forrest Rd	37 F5		Hill St La N	36 E3		Lothian St	37 G5		Northumberland St	37 E3		Rodney St	37 F1
Davidson Rd	36 A1		Forth St	37 G3		Hill St La S	36 E4		Lower Gilmore Pl	36 D6		Northumberland			Romero Pl	37 J7
Davie St	37 G5		Fountainbridge	36 D6		Holyrood Gait	37 H4		Lower London Rd	37 J3		St N E La	37 F3		Rosebank Cotts	36 D5
Dean Bk La	36 D2		Fowler Ter	36 C6		Holyrood Pk Rd	37 H7		Lutton Pl	37 H6		Northumberland			Rosebery Cres	36 C5
Dean Br	36 C3		Frederick St	37 E3		Holyrood Rd	37 G4		Lynedoch Pl La	36 C4		St N W La	37 E3		Rosebery Cres La	36 C5
Deanhaugh St	36 D2					Home St	36 E6		Lyne St	37 J3		Northumberland			Roseburn Av	36 A5
Dean Pk Cres	36 C3		**G**			Hope Pk Cres	37 G6					St S E La	37 F3		Roseburn Cliff	36 A5
Dean Pk Ms	36 C2		Gardner's Cres	36 D5		Hope Pk Ter	37 G6		**M**			Northumberland			Roseburn Dr	36 A5
Dean Pk St	36 C2		Garscube Ter	36 A4		Hope St	36 D4		McDonald Pl	37 G1		St S W La	37 E3		Roseburn Gdns	36 A5
Dean Path	36 C3		Gayfield La	37 G2		Hope St La	36 D4		McDonald Rd	37 G1		North Werber Pk	36 A1		Roseburn Maltings	36 A5
Dean St	36 D3		Gayfield Pl La	37 G2		Hopetoun Cres	37 G2		McDonald St	37 G1		North Werber Pl	36 B1		Roseburn Pl	36 A5
Dean Ter	36 D3		Gayfield Sq	37 G2		Hopetoun St	37 G2		Mackenzie Pl	36 D3		North W Circ Pl	36 D3		Roseburn Ter	36 A5
Dean Village	36 B4		Gayfield St	37 G2		Horne Ter	36 C6		McLeod St	36 A6		Norton Pk	37 J2		Rosemount Bldgs	36 D6
Devon Pl	36 B5		Gayfield St La	37 G2		Horse Wynd	37 J4		McNeill St	36 D6					Roseneath Pl	37 F7
Dewar Pl	36 D5		Gentle's Entry	37 H4		Howden St	37 G5		Magdala Cres	36 B5		**O**			Roseneath St	37 F7
Dewar Pl La	36 D5		George IV Br	37 F4		Howe St	37 E3		Magdala Ms	36 B5		Old Broughton	37 F2		Roseneath Ter	37 F7
Dicksonfield	37 H2		George Sq	37 F6		Hugh Miller Pl	36 D2		Malta Grn	36 D2		Old Fishmarket Cl	37 G4		Rose St	36 E4
Dickson St	37 J1		George Sq La	37 F6		Hunter Sq	37 G4		Malta Ter	36 D2		Old Tolbooth Wynd	37 H4		Rose St N La	36 E4
Distillery La	36 C5		George St	36 E4		Huntingdon Pl	37 G2		Manor Pl	36 C4		Orchard Bk	36 A3		Rose St S La	36 E4
Dorset Pl	36 C7		Gibson Ter	36 C6		Hutton Rd	37 H4		Mansionhouse Rd	37 G7		Orchard Brae	36 B2		Rossie Pl	37 J2
Douglas Cres	36 B4		Gifford Pk	37 G6					Marchhall Cres	37 J7		Orchard Brae Av	36 B3		Rosslyn Cres	37 G1
Douglas Gdns	36 C4		Gillespie Cres	36 D6		**I**			Marchhall Pl	37 J7		Orchard Brae Gdns	36 B3		Rosslyn Ter	37 H1
Douglas Gdns Ms	36 C4		Gillespie St	36 D6		India Pl	36 D3		Marchhall Rd	37 J7		Orchard Brae			Rothesay Ms	36 C4
Doune Ter	36 D3		Gilmore Pk	36 D6		India St	36 E3		Marchmont Cres	37 F7		Gdns W	36 B3		Rothesay Pl	36 C4
Downfield Pl	36 B6		Gilmore Pl	36 D7		Infirmary St	37 G5		Marchmont Rd	37 F6		Orchard Brae W	36 B2		Rothesay Ter	36 C4
Drumdryan St	36 E6		Gilmour St	37 G5		**Inverleith**	36 C1		Marchmont St	37 E7		Orchard Cres	36 A3		Roxburgh Pl	37 G5
Drummond Pl	37 F2		Gladstone Ter	37 G7		Inverleith Gro	36 C1		Market St	37 F4		Orchard Dr	36 A3		Roxburgh St	37 G5
Drummond St	37 G5		Glencairn Cres	36 C5		Inverleith Pl	36 C1		Marshall's Ct	37 G3		Orchard Gro	36 B2		Royal Circ	36 E3
Drumsheugh			Glenfinlas St	36 D4		Inverleith Ter	36 D1		Marshall St	37 G5		Orchard Pl	36 B2		Royal Cres	37 F2
Gdns	36 C4		Glengyle Ter	36 E6		Inverleith Ter La	36 E1		Maryfield	37 J3		Orchard Rd	36 A3		Royal Ter	37 G3
Drum Ter	37 J2		Glenogle Rd	36 D2		Iona St	37 H1		Maryfield Pl	37 J3		Orchard Rd S	36 A3		Russell Gdns	36 A5
Dryden Gait	37 G1		Glen St	37 E5		Ivy Ter	36 A7		Meadow La	37 G6		Orchard Ter	36 A3		Russell Rd	36 A5
Dryden Gdns	37 G1		Gloucester La	36 D3					Meadow Pl	37 F7		Orwell Pl	36 C6		Rutland Ct La	36 D5
Dryden Pl	37 J7		Gloucester Pl	36 D3		**J**			Melgund Ter	37 F2		Orwell Ter	36 C6		Rutland Sq	36 D4
Dryden St	37 G1		Gloucester Sq	36 D3		Jamaica St	36 E3		Melville Dr	37 E6		Oxford St	37 H6		Rutland St	36 D4
Dryden Ter	37 G1		Gloucester St	36 D3		Jamaica St N La	36 E3		Melville St	36 C4		Oxford Ter	36 C3		
Dublin Meuse	37 F3		Gorgie Rd	36 A7		Jamaica St S La	36 E3		Melville St La	36 D4					**S**	
Dublin St	37 F2		Grange Rd	37 F7		Jameson Pl	37 H1		Melville Ter	37 G7		**P**			St. Andrew Sq	37 F3
Dublin St La N	37 F2		Granville Ter	36 C7		Jeffrey St	37 G4		Merchant St	37 F5		Palmerston Pl	36 C4		St. Bernard's Cres	36 D3
Dublin St La S	37 F3		Grassmarket	37 F5		Johnston Ter	37 E5		Merchiston Av	36 C7		Panmure Pl	37 E6		St. Bernard's Row	36 D2
Duff Rd	36 B6		Great King St	37 E3					Merchiston Gro	36 A7		Papermill Wynd	37 G1		St. Catherine's Pl	37 G7
Duff St	36 B6		Great Stuart St	36 D4		**K**			Merchiston Ms	36 C7		Parkside Pl	37 H6		St. Clair Av	37 J1
Duff St La	36 B6		Greenhill Ct	37 E7		Keir St	37 F5		Merchiston Pk	36 C7		Parkside Ter	37 H6		St. Clair Pl	37 J1
Dumbiedykes Rd	37 H5		Greenhill Gdns	36 E7		Kemp Pl	36 D1		Mertoun Pl	36 C7		Parliament Sq	37 F4		St. Clair Rd	37 J1
Dunbar St	36 E5		Greenhill Pl	36 E7		Kerr St	36 D2		Meuse La	37 F4		Pembroke Pl	36 B5		St. Clair St	37 J1
Dundas St	37 E2		Greenhill Ter	36 E7		Kew Ter	36 A5		Middlefield	37 H1		Perth St	36 E2		St. Colme St	36 D4
Dundee St	36 B7		Greenside La	37 G3		Kimmerghame Dr	36 A1		Millerfield Pl	37 G7		Picardy Pl	37 G3		St. David's Pl	36 D5
Dundee Ter	36 B7		Greenside Row	37 G3		Kimmerghame Vw	36 A1		Miller Row	36 C4		Pilrig Gdns	37 G1		St. David's Ter	36 D5
Dundonald St	37 F2								Milton St	37 J3		Pilrig Glebe	37 H1		St. Giles St	37 F4
									Minto St	37 H7		Pleasance	37 G5		

St. James Pl 37 G3
St. James Sq 37 G3
St. John's Hill 37 H5
St. John St 37 H4
St. Leonard's Bk 37 H6
St. Leonard's Hill 37 H6
St. Leonard's La 37 H6
St. Leonard's St 37 H6
St. Mary's St 37 G4
St. Patrick Sq 37 G6
St. Stephen Pl 36 D2
St. Stephen St 36 D3
St. Vincent St 36 E2
Salisbury Ms 37 H7
Salisbury Pl 37 H7
Salisbury Rd 37 H7
Saunders St 36 D3
Saxe Coburg Pl 36 D2
Saxe Coburg St 36 D2
Sciennes 37 G7
Sciennes Gdns 37 G7
Sciennes Hill Pl 37 G7
Sciennes Ho Pl 37 G7
Sciennes Pl 37 G7
Sciennes Rd 37 F7
Scotland St 37 F2
Semple St 36 D5
Seton Pl 37 G7
Shandwick Pl 36 D5
Shaw's Pl 37 H1
Shaw's St 37 H1
Shaw's Ter 37 H1
Shrub Pl La 37 H1
Sienna Gdns 37 G7

Silvermills 36 E2
Simon Sq 37 G5
Simpson Loan 37 F6
Sinclair Cl 36 A7
Sinclair Gdns 36 A7
Sinclair Pl 36 A7
Sloan St 37 J1
Smithfield St 36 A7
South Br 37 G4
South Charlotte St 36 E4
South Clerk St 37 H6
South Coll St 37 G5
South E Circ Pl 36 E3
South Gray's Cl 37 G4
South Learmonth Av 36 C3
South Learmonth Gdns 36 C3
South Lorne Pl 37 J1
South Oxford St 37 H7
South St. Andrew St 37 F3
South St. David St 37 F3
South Sloan St 37 J1
Spence St 37 J7
Spey St 37 H1
Spey St La 37 H1
Spey Ter 37 H1
Spittal St 36 E5
Spottiswoode Rd 37 E7
Spottiswoode St 37 F7
Spring Gdns 37 J3
Springwell Pl 36 B6
Stafford St 36 D4
Stanhope Pl 36 B5
Stanhope St 36 B5

Stevenlaw's Cl 37 G4
Stewart Ter 36 A7
Stockbridge 36 E2
Succoth Gdns 36 A4
Succoth Pl 36 A4
Summer Bk 37 F2
Summerhall 37 G6
Summerhall Sq 37 H7
Sunbury Ms 36 C4
Sunbury Pl 36 C4
Sunbury St 36 C4
Sunnyside 37 J2
Sutherland St 36 B5
Sylvan Pl 37 G7

T
Tantallon Pl 37 G7
Tarvit St 36 E6
Tay St 36 C7
Temple Pk Cres 36 C7
Terrars Cft 37 H6
Teviotdale Pl 36 D1
Teviot Pl 37 F5
Thirlestane Rd 37 E7
Thistle Pl 36 C7
Thistle St 37 E3
Thistle St N E La 37 F3
Thistle St N W La 37 E3
Thistle St S W La 37 E3
Thornybauk 36 E6
Torphichen St 36 D5
Tron Sq 37 G4
Tynecastle La 36 B7
Tynecastle Ter 36 A7

Tytler Gdns 37 J3
U
Union St 37 G2
Upper Bow 37 F4
Upper Coltbridge Ter 36 A4
Upper Damside 36 C4
Upper Dean Ter 36 D3
Upper Gilmore Pl 36 D6
Upper Gilmore Ter 36 D6
Upper Gray St 37 H7
Upper Gro Pl 36 D6
V
Valleyfield St 36 E6
Veitch's Sq 36 D2
Victoria St 37 F5
Viewcraig Gdns 37 H4
Viewcraig St 37 H5
Viewforth 36 C6
Viewforth Gdns 36 D7
Viewforth Sq 36 D7
Viewforth Ter 36 D7
W
Walker St 36 C4
Wardlaw Pl 36 A7
Wardlaw St 36 A7
Warrender Pk Cres 36 E7
Warrender Pk Rd 36 E7
Warrender Pk Ter 37 E7
Warriston Cres 37 E1
Warriston Rd 37 E1
Washington La 36 B6

Waterloo Pl 37 G3
Watson Cres 36 B7
Waverley Br 37 F4
Waverley Pk 37 J3
Waverley Pk Ter 37 J3
Waverley Pl 37 J3
Wellington St 37 H2
Wemyss Pl 36 E3
Wemyss Pl Ms 36 D3
West Adam St 37 G5
West Annandale St 37 F1
West App Rd 36 D5
West Bow 37 F5
West Bryson Rd 36 B7
West Castle Rd 36 C7
West Catherine Pl 36 B5
West Coates 36 A5
West Coll St 37 G5
West Crosscauseway 37 G6
West End Pl 36 C6
Wester Coates Av 36 A5
Wester Coates Gdns 36 A5
Wester Coates Pl 36 B5
Wester Coates Rd 36 B5
Wester Coates Ter 36 A5
Westfield St 36 A7
Westhall Gdns 36 D7
West Maitland St 36 C5
West Mill La 36 C4
West Montgomery Pl 37 H2
West Newington Pl 37 H7
West Nicolson St 37 G5
West Norton Pl 37 J3
West Pk Pl 36 C6

West Port 37 E5
West Preston St 37 H7
West Register St 37 F3
West Register St La 37 F3
West Richmond St 37 G5
West Scotland St La 37 F2
West Silvermills La 36 E2
West Tollcross 36 E6
West Wds 36 A1
Wheatfield Pl 36 A7
Wheatfield Rd 36 A7
Wheatfield St 36 A7
Wheatfield Ter 36 A7
Whitehouse Ln 36 E7
White Pk 36 A7
William St 36 C5
William St N E La 36 D4
William St N W La 36 D4
William St S E La 36 D4
William St S W La 36 D5
Windmill La 37 G6
Windmill St 37 G6
Windsor St 37 H2
Windsor St La 37 H2
Y
Yeaman Pl 36 C6
York La 37 G3
York Pl 37 F3
Young St 36 D4
Young St La N 36 E4
Young St La S 36 E4

Glasgow street index

A
Abbotsford Pl 39 E7
Abercromby Dr 39 J5
Abercromby Sq 39 J5
Abercromby St 39 J6
Academy Pk 38 A7
Adams Ct La 39 F5
Adelphi St 39 F6
Admiral St 38 C6
Aird's La 39 G5
Albert Br 39 G6
Albert Dr 38 B7
Albion Gate 39 G4
Albion St 39 G5
Alexander Cres 39 F7
Alexandra Par 39 J3
Allen Glen Pl 39 G3
Anchor La 39 F4
Anderston 38 E4
Anderston Quay 38 C5
Anson St 39 J7
Anthony St 38 D4
Arcadia Pl 39 J6
Arcadia St 39 J6
Argyle St 39 F4
Argyll Arc 39 F4
Ark La 39 J4
Arlington St 38 D2
Armour St 39 J5
Arthur St 38 A2
Ashley La 38 D2
Ashley St 38 D2
Ashton La 38 A1
Ashton Rd 38 A1
Auchentoshan Ter 39 J1

B
Bain St 39 H5
Baird St 39 H2
Balaclava St 38 D4
Baliol La 38 D2
Baliol St 38 D2
Ballantrae Ct 38 D4
Ballater Pl 39 G7
Ballater St 39 F6
Bank St 38 B1
Barrack St 39 J5
Barrington Dr 38 C1
Bath La 38 D3
Bath St 38 D3
Beaumont Gate 38 A1
Bedford La 39 F6
Bedford St 39 E6
Bell St 39 G4
Beltane St 38 D3
Benny Lynch Ct 39 G6
Benthall St 39 G7
Bentinck St 38 B2
Berkeley St 38 C3
Berkeley Ter La 38 C3

Binnie Pl 39 H6
Bishop St 38 D4
Blackburn St 38 B5
Blackfriars St 39 G4
Blackie St 38 B3
Black St 39 H2
Blantyre St 38 A2
Blythswoodhill 38 E3
Blythswood Sq 38 E3
Blythswood St 38 E4
Bothwell La 38 E4
Bothwell La (Hillhead) 38 C1
Bothwell St 38 E4
Braid Sq 38 E1
Braid St 38 E1
Breadalbane St 38 C3
Brechin St 38 C3
Bridgegate 39 F5
Bridge St 39 E6
Bridgeton Cross 39 J6
Bright St 39 J2
Broadford St 39 G1
Broomielaw 38 E5
Broompark Dr 39 J4
Brown St 38 E5
Bruce Rd 38 B7
Brunswick St 39 G4
Buccleuch La 38 E2
Buccleuch St 38 D2
Buchanan St 39 F4
Bunhouse Rd 38 A2
Burnbank Gdns 38 D1
Burnbank La 38 D1
Burnbank Pl 38 D1
Burnbank Ter 38 D1
Burns St 39 E1
Bute Gdns 38 B1
Bute La 38 B1

C
Cadogan St 38 E4
Cadzow St 38 D4
Caledonian Cres 38 C1
Caledonia Rd 39 F7
Caledon La 38 A1
Caledon St 38 A1
Calgary St 39 G2
Cambridge St 39 E3
Camden Ter 39 F7
Canal St 39 G2
Candleriggs 39 G5
Cardwell St 38 E7
Carfrae St 38 A3
Carlton Ct 39 E5
Carlton Pl 39 F5
Carnarvon St 38 D2
Carnoustie Pl 38 D6
Carnoustie St 38 D6
Carrick St 38 E5
Carrington St 38 D1

Castle St 39 H4
Cathcart Rd 39 F7
Cathedral Sq 39 H4
Cathedral St 39 F3
Cavendish Pl 39 E7
Cavendish St 39 E7
Cecil St 38 B1
Cedar Ct 38 E1
Cedar St 38 E1
Centre St 38 E6
Cessnock 38 A5
Chalmers St 39 J5
Charles St 39 J2
Charlotte St 39 H5
Cheapside St 38 D5
Chisolm St 39 G5
Church St 38 A2
Circus Dr 39 J4
Citizen La 39 F4
Civic St 39 E2
Clairmont Gdns 38 C2
Claremont Pl 38 C2
Claremont St 38 C3
Claremont Ter 38 C2
Claremont Ter La 38 C2
Clarendon Pl 38 D1
Clarendon St 38 D1
Clayslaps Rd 38 B2
Claythorn Av 39 H6
Claythorn Circ 39 H5
Claythorn Pk 39 H6
Claythorn St 39 J5
Claythorn Ter 39 J5
Cleland La 39 F6
Cleland St 39 F6
Cleveland La 38 D3
Cleveland St 38 D3
Clifford La 38 A6
Clifford Pl 38 A6
Clifford St 38 A6
Cliff Rd 38 C1
Clifton Pl 38 C3
Clifton St 38 C2
Clutha St 38 A6
Clyde Arc 38 B5
Clyde Pl 38 E5
Clydeside Expressway 38 B4
Clyde St 39 F5
Cobden Rd 39 J1
Coburg St 39 E6
Cochrane St 39 G4
College La 39 H4
College St 39 G4
Collins St 39 H4
Commerce St 39 E5
Commercial Ct 39 G6
Commercial Rd 39 G7
Congress Rd 38 B4
Congress Way 38 B4
Cook St 38 E6

Cooperage Pl 38 A3
Corn St 39 E1
Cornwall St S 38 B7
Corunna St 38 B3
Couper Pl 39 G2
Couper St 39 G2
Cowan La 38 C1
Cowan St 38 B1
Cowcaddens 39 F2
Cowcaddens Rd 39 E2
Cownwall St 38 A5
Cragmaddie Ter La 38 B2
Craighall Rd 39 F1
Craigiehall Pl 38 B5
Craigiehall St 38 B5
Cranston Hill 38 C3
Cranston St 38 C4
Cressnock St 38 A5
Crimea St 38 D4
Cromwell La 38 D1
Cromwell St 38 D1
Crownpoint Rd 39 J6
Crown St 39 F7
Cumberland Pl 38 D1
Cumberland St 39 E6

D
Dale Path 39 J7
Dalhouse St 38 E3
Dalhousie La 38 E2
Dalintober St 38 D6
Dalmarnock Rd 39 J7
Dalnair St 38 A2
Derby St 38 B3
Devon Pl 39 E7
Devon St 39 E7
Dixon St 39 F5
Dobbie's Ln 39 F2
Dobbie's Ln Pl 39 G3
Dornoch St 39 J6
Dorset St 38 C3
Douglas La 38 E3
Douglas St 38 E4
Dover St 38 C3
Drake St 39 J6
Drury St 39 F4
Drygate 39 H4
Duke St 39 H4
Dunblane St 39 F2
Dunchattan Pl 39 J5
Dunchattan St 39 J4
Dundashill 39 F1
Dundas La 39 F3
Dundas St 39 F3
Dunearn St 38 D1
Dunlop St 39 F5
Durham St 38 B6

E
Eaglesham Ct 38 B5

Eaglesham Pl 38 B5
Eagle St 39 F1
Earlston Av 39 J2
Earlston Pl 39 J2
East Bath La 39 F3
East Campbell St 39 H5
Edington St 39 E1
Edwin St 38 B6
Eglinton Ct 39 E6
Elcho St 39 J5
Elderslie St 38 C2
Eldon St 38 C1
Elie St 38 A1
Elliot Pl 38 C4
Elliot St 38 C4
Elmbank Cres 38 D3
Elmbank St 38 D3
Elmbank St La 38 D3
Errol Gdns 39 F6
Esmond St 38 A2
Eton La 38 B1
Exchange Pl 39 F4

F
Falfield St 38 E7
Farnell St 39 E1
Finnieston 38 B3
Finnieston Quay 38 B4
Finnieston Sq 38 C3
Finnieston St 38 C4
Firpark St 39 J3
Firpark Ter 39 J4
Fitzroy La 38 B3
Florence St 39 G6
Forbes Dr 39 J6
Forbes St 39 J5
Fountainwell Av 39 H1
Fountainwell Dr 39 H1
Fountainwell Pl 39 H1
Fountainwell Rd 39 H1
Fountainwell Sq 39 H1
Fountainwell Ter 39 H1
Fox St 39 F5
Francis St 38 E7

G
Gadshill St 39 J2
Gallowgate 39 H5
Garnethill 38 E2
Garnethill St 38 E2
Garnet St 38 D3
Garscube Rd 39 E2
Garth St 39 G4
George Sq 39 F4
George St 39 G4
Gibson St 39 H5
Gibson St (Hillhead) 38 B1
Gilbert St 38 A3
Gilmour Pl 39 G7
Gladstone St 38 D1

Glasgow Br 39 F5
Glassford St 39 G4
Glebe Ct 39 H3
Glebe St 39 H2
Glenbarr St 39 J2
Glenfarg St 38 D1
Glenmavis St 39 E2
Gloucester St 38 D6
Goosedubbs 39 G5
Gorbals 39 G7
Gorbals St 39 F7
Gordon La 39 F4
Gordon St 39 E4
Gourock St 38 E7
Govan Rd 38 A5
Grace St 38 C4
Grafton Pl 39 G3
Graham Sq 39 J5
Graignestock St 39 J6
Granby La 38 B1
Grant St 38 D2
Granville St 38 D3
Gray St 38 B3
Great Dovehill 39 H5
Great George St 38 B1
Green, The 39 J7
Greendyke St 39 G5
Greenhead St 39 J6
Green St 39 J6
Grovepark Ct 38 D1
Grovepark Gdns 38 D1

H
Hallside Pl 39 G7
Handel Pl 39 F7
Hanover St 39 F4
Harley St 38 A6
Harvey St 39 F1
Harvie St 38 B5
Hastie St 38 A2
Haugh Rd 38 A3
Hayfield Ct 39 G7
Hayfield St 39 G7
Herbertson St 39 E6
High Craighall Rd 39 F1
High St 39 G5
Hillhead St 38 B1
Hill St 38 D2
Holland St 38 D3
Holm St 38 E4
Holyrood Cres 38 C1
Holyrood Quad 38 D1
Hopehill Rd 38 D1
Hope St 38 E4
Houldsworth La 38 C3
Houldsworth St 38 C3
Houston Pl 38 C5
Houston St 38 C6
Howard St 39 F5
Hunter St 39 H5

Street	Ref
Huntingdon Rd	39 H1
Huntingdon Sq	39 H1
Hutcheson St	39 G5
Hutchesontown	39 G7
Hutchinson Town Ct	39 G7
Hydepark St	38 C5
I	
India St	38 D3
Ingram St	39 G4
J	
Jamaica St	39 F5
James Morrison St	39 G5
James Nisbet St	39 J3
James St	39 J7
James Watt St	38 E5
Jocelyn Sq	39 G5
John Knox St	39 J4
John St	39 G4
K	
Kelvingrove	38 B2
Kelvingrove St	38 B3
Kelvinhaugh	38 A3
Kelvinhaugh Gate	38 A3
Kelvinhaugh Pl	38 B3
Kelvinhaugh St	38 A3
Kelvin Way	38 B2
Kennedy Path	39 G3
Kennedy St	39 G3
Kent Rd	38 C3
Kent St	39 H5
Keppochhill Pl	39 G1
Keppochhill Way	39 G1
Kerr Dr	39 J6
Kerr Pl	39 J6
Kerr St	39 J6
Kidston Pl	39 F7
Kidston Ter	39 F7
Kilbarchan St	39 E6
Kilbirnie Pl	38 D7
Kilbirnie St	38 D7
Killermont St	39 F3
King George V Br	39 E5
King's Br	39 H7
King's Dr	39 H7
Kingston	38 D6
Kingston St	38 E5
King St	39 G5
Kinning Pk	38 B6
Kinning St	38 D6
Kyle St	39 G2
L	
La Belle Allee	38 C2
La Belle Pl	38 C2
Ladywell St	39 J4
Laidlaw St	38 D6
Laird Pl	39 J7
Lambhill Quad	38 B6
Lambhill St	38 B6
Lanark St	39 H5
Lancefield Quay	38 C4
Lancefield St	38 C4
Landressy Pl	39 J7
Landressy St	39 J7
Langshot St	38 A6
Lansdowne Cres	38 C1
Lansdowne Cres La	38 C1
Larbert St	39 F2
Laurieston	39 F6
Laurieston Rd	39 F7
Lendel Pl	38 A6
Lilybank Gdns	38 A1
Lilybank Gdns La	38 A1
Lilybank Ter	38 B1
Lister St	39 H2
Little Dovehill	39 H5
Little St	38 C4
London Rd	39 G5
Lorne St	38 B5
Lumsden St	38 A3
Lymburn St	38 B2
Lynedoch Cres	38 C2
Lynedoch Cres La	38 C2
Lynedoch Pl	38 C2
Lynedoch St	38 C2
Lynedoch Ter	38 D2
M	
Mcalpine St	38 D5
McAslin Ct	39 H3
Mcaslin St	39 H3
McCulloch St	38 C7
Mcfarlane St	39 H5
McIntosh Ct	39 J4
McIntosh St	39 J4
Mcintyre St	38 D4
MacKeith St	39 J7
MacKinlay St	39 E7
Maclean Sq	38 B5
Maclean St	38 B5
Maclennan St	38 A6
Macleod St	39 H4
McNeil Gdns	39 H7
McNeil St	39 G7
McPhail St	39 J7
McPhater St	39 F2
Mair St	38 B5
Maitland St	39 F2
Malta Ter	39 F7
Manresa Pl	39 E1
Marine Cres	38 C5
Marine Gdns	38 C5
Marlow St	38 C7
Martha St	39 G3
Mart St	39 G5
Mary St	39 F1
Mauchline St	38 E7
Mavisbank Gdns	38 B5
Maxwell Av	38 C7
Maxwell Ct	38 B7
Maxwell Dr	38 B7
Maxwell Gdns	38 A7
Maxwell Grn	38 B7
Maxwell La	38 C7
Maxwell Oval	38 C7
Maxwell Rd	38 C7
Maxwell St	39 F5
Megan Gate	39 J7
Megan St	39 J7
Melbourne St	39 J5
Melrose St	38 D1
Merchant City	39 G5
Merchant La	39 G5
Metropole La	39 F5
Middlesex Gdns	38 B6
Middlesex St	38 B6
Middleton St	38 A5
Midland St	39 E4
Midwharf St	39 F1
Miller St	39 F4
Millroad Dr	39 J5
Millroad Gdns	39 J5
Millroad St	39 H5
Milnpark Gdns	38 B6
Milnpark St	38 B6
Milton St	39 F2
Minerva St	38 B3
Minerva Way	38 B3
Mitchell La	39 F4
Mitchell St	39 F4
Moffat St	39 G7
Moir St	39 H5
Molendinar St	39 H5
Moncur St	39 H5
Montague St	38 C1
Monteith Pl	39 H6
Monteith Row	39 H5
Montrose St	39 G4
Moore St	39 J5
Morrison Ct	39 F4
Morrison St	38 D5
Mosque Av	39 F6
Muslin St	39 J7
N	
Naburn Gate	39 F7
Nairn St	38 A2
Napiershall La	38 D1
Napiershall Pl	38 D1
Napiershall St	38 C2
Nelson Mandela Pl	39 F4
Nelson St	38 E5
Netherby Dr	38 A7
New City Rd	38 D2
Newton St	38 D2
Newton Ter La	38 C3
New Wynd	39 G5
Nicholas St	39 H4
Nicholson St	39 F6
Norfolk Ct	39 F6
Norfolk St	39 F6
North Canal Bk	39 G1
North Canal Bk St	39 F1
North Claremount St	38 C2
North Ct	39 F4
North Ct La	39 F4
North Dr	39 F4
North Frederick Path	39 G3
North Frederick St	39 G4
North Gower St	38 A6
North Hanover St	39 G4
North Portland St	39 G4
North St	38 D2
North Wallace St	39 G2
O	
Oakfield Av	38 B1
Oakfield La	38 B1
Oak St	38 D4
Old Dumbarton Rd	38 A2
Old Rutherglen Rd	39 G6
Old Wynd	39 G5
Oregon Pl	39 G7
Orr St	39 J6
Osborne St	39 F5
Oswald St	39 E5
Otago La	38 C1
Otago La N	38 C1
Otago St	38 B1
Overnewton Pl	38 B3
Overnewton Sq	38 A3
Overnewton St	38 A2
Oxford La	39 F6
Oxford St	39 E5
P	
Pacific Dr	38 A5
Pacific Quay	38 A4
Paisley Rd	38 D5
Paisley Rd W	38 C5
Palmerston Pl	38 B3
Parnie St	39 G5
Park Av	38 C1
Park Circ	38 C2
Park Circ La	38 C2
Park Circ Pl	38 C2
Park Dr	38 C1
Park Gdns	38 C2
Park Gdns La	38 C2
Park Gate	38 C2
Parkgrove Ter	38 B2
Parkgrove Ter La	38 B2
Park Quad	38 C2
Park Rd	38 C1
Park St S	38 C2
Park Ter	38 C2
Park Ter E La	38 C2
Park Terrrace La	38 C2
Parsonage Row	39 H4
Parsonage Sq	39 H4
Parson St	39 H3
Paterson St	38 D6
Payne St	39 F1
Pembroke St	38 C3
Percy St	38 A6
Perth St	38 D4
Piccadilly St	38 D4
Pine Pl	39 G7
Pinkston Dr	39 H2
Pinkston Rd	39 H1
Pitt St	38 E4
Plantation Pk Gdns	38 A6
Plantation Sq	38 B5
Port Dundas	39 F1
Port Dundas La	38 D1
Port Dundas Rd	39 F2
Port Eglington	38 D7
Portman St	38 C6
Port St	38 C3
Portugal St	39 F6
Possil Rd	39 E1
Professors Sq	38 B1
Provanhill St	39 J2
Q	
Queen Elizabeth Gdns	39 G7
Queens Cres	38 D1
Queen St	39 F4
R	
Radnor St	38 B2
Raglan St	38 E1
Regent Moray St	38 A2
Renfield La	39 E4
Renfield St	39 F4
Renfrew Ct	39 F3
Renfrew La	39 F3
Renfrew St	38 D2
Renton St	39 F2
Rhymer St	39 J2
Richmond St	39 G4
Ritchie St	38 E7
Riverview Dr	38 D5
Riverview Gdns	38 E5
Riverview Pl	38 D5
Robertson La	38 E4
Robertson St	39 E5
Rodney St	39 E1
Ropework La	39 F5
Rose St	39 E3
Ross St	39 H5
Rottenrow	39 G3
Rottenrow E	39 H4
Royal Bk Pl	39 F4
Royal Cres	38 B3
Royal Ex Ct	39 F4
Royal Ex Sq	39 F4
Royal Ter	38 B2
Royal Ter La	38 B2
Royston	39 J2
Roystonhill	39 J2
Royston Rd	39 J2
Royston Sq	39 J2
Rupert St	38 D1
Rutland Ct	38 C5
Rutland Cres	38 C5
Rutland Pl	38 B5
S	
St. Andrews Cres	38 C7
St. Andrew's La	39 G5
St. Andrews Rd	38 C7
St. Andrews Sq	39 G5
St. Andrews St	39 G5
St. Clair St	38 D1
St. Enoch	39 F5
St. Enoch Sq	39 F4
St. Francis Rigg	39 G7
St. Georges Rd	38 D2
St. Georges Rd	38 D2
St. James Rd	39 G3
St. John's Ct	38 B7
St. John's Quad	38 C7
St. Josephs Vw	39 J2
St. Luke's Pl	39 F6
St. Luke's Ter	39 F6
St. Margaret's Pl	39 G5
St. Marys La	39 G5
St. Mungo Av	39 G3
St. Mungo Pl	39 H3
St. Ninian Ter	39 F6
St. Peters La	38 E4
St. Peters St	38 E2
St. Rollox Brae	39 J1
St. Valentine Ter	39 G7
St. Vincent Cres	38 B3
St. Vincent Cres La	38 B3
St. Vincent La	38 E3
St. Vincent Pl	39 F4
St. Vincent St	38 C3
St. Vincent Ter	38 C3
Salisbury La	39 F7
Salisbury St	39 F7
Salkeld St	38 E7
Saltmarket	39 G5
Sandiefield Rd	39 F7
Sandyford Pl La	38 C3
Sandyford St	38 A3
Saracen Head Rd	39 H5
Sauchiehall La	38 E3
Sauchiehall St	38 B2
Savoy St	39 J7
Sawmillfield St	39 E1
Scotland St	38 C6
Scotland St W	38 B6
Scott St	38 E3
Seamore St	38 D1
Seaward La	38 C5
Seaward Pl	38 C6
Seaward St	38 C6
Shaftesbury St	38 D3
Shamrock St	38 E2
Shields Rd	38 C6
Shipbank La	39 G5
Shuttle St	39 G4
Sighthill	39 H1
Silverfir St	39 G7
Silvergrove St	39 J6
Snowdon St	39 G7
Somerset Pl Ms	38 C2
South Ex Ct	39 F4
South Frederick St	39 G4
Southpark Av	38 B1
Southpark La	38 B1
South Portland St	39 F5
Southside Cres	39 F7
South Woodside Rd	38 C1
Spiers Wf	39 F1
Spoutmouth	39 H5
Springburn Rd	39 J2
Springfield Ct	39 F4
Springfield Quay	38 C5
Spring Wynd	39 G7
Stafford St	39 G2
Stanley St	38 C6
Stanley St La	38 C6
Steel St	39 G5
Stevenson St	39 J6
Stewart St	39 F2
Stirlingfauld Pl	39 F7
Stirling Rd	39 H3
Stobcross Rd	38 A3
Stobcross St	38 C4
Stobcross Wynd	38 A3
Stockwell Pl	39 F5
Stockwell St	39 F5
Stromness St	38 E7
Suffolk St	39 H5
Surrey St	39 F7
Sussex St	38 B6
Sutherland La	38 A1
Swan St	39 G2
Sydney St	39 J5
T	
Taylor Pl	39 H3
Taylor St	39 H4
Templeton St	39 J6
Teviot St	38 A3
Thistle St	39 G6
Thistle Ter	39 F7
Thornbank St	38 A3
Thurso St	38 A2
Tobago Pl	39 J5
Tobago St	39 J6
Toll La	38 C5
Tontine La	39 G5
Torness St	38 A1
Tower St	38 B6
Townhead	39 G2
Townsend St	39 F2
Tradeston	38 E6
Tradeston St	38 E6
Trongate	39 G5
Tullis Ct	39 J7
Tullis St	39 J7
Tunnel St	38 B4
Tureen St	39 J5
Turnbull St	39 G5
Turnlaw St	39 H7
Turriff St	39 E7
Tyndrum St	39 F2
U	
Union Pl	39 F4
Union St	39 F4
Unity Pl	38 E1
University Av	38 A1
University Gdns	38 A1
University Pl	38 A1
V	
Vermont St	38 B6
Victoria Br	39 F5
Viewfield La	38 B1
Vinter St	39 F1
Virginia Pl	39 G4
Virginia St	39 G4
W	
Waddell Ct	39 G6
Waddell St	39 G7
Wallace St	38 D5
Walls St	39 G4
Walmer Cres	38 A6
Warnock St	39 J3
Warroch St	38 D5
Washington St	38 D5
Waterloo La	39 E4
Waterloo St	38 E4
Waterside Pl	39 H7
Waterside St	39 G7
Watson St	39 G5
Watt St	38 C6
Weaver St	39 H4
Wellcroft Pl	39 E7
Wellington La	38 E4
Wellington St	38 E4
Wellpark St	39 J4
Westbank La	38 B1
Westbank Quad	38 B1
West Campbell St	38 E4
West End Pk St	38 C2
West George La	38 E3
West George St	38 E3
West Graham St	38 E2
West Greenhill Pl	38 B3
West Nile St	39 F4
West Prince's La	38 C1
West Princes St	38 C1
West Regent La	39 E3
West Regent St	39 E3
West St	38 D7
Whitehall St	38 D4
William St	38 D3
Willowbank Cres	38 C1
Willowbank St	38 C2
Wilson St	39 G4
Windsor St	38 D1
Windsor Ter	38 D1
Wishart St	39 J4
Woodlands Dr	38 C1
Woodlands Gate	38 C2
Woodlands Rd	38 C1
Woodlands Ter	38 C2
Woodrow Circ	38 A7
Woodrow Pl	38 A7
Woodrow Rd	38 A7
Woodside Cres	38 D2
Woodside Pl	38 C2
Woodside Pl La	38 C2
Woodside Ter	38 C2
Woodside Ter La	38 C2
Y	
Yorkhill	38 B2
Yorkhill Par	38 A2
Yorkhill St	38 A3
York St	38 E5

Leeds street index

Street	Ref
A	
Abbey St	40 C3
Abbott Ct	40 A3
Abbott Rd	40 A4
Abbott Vw	40 A3
Admiral St	41 E7
Aire St	40 D4
Albion Pl	41 E3
Albion St	41 E3
Alexander St	40 E3
Alexandra Gro	40 B1
Alexandra Rd	40 A1
Alma St	41 H2
Anderson Av	41 H1
Anderson Mt	41 H1
Apex Vw	40 E6
Apex Way	41 E6
Appleton Cl	41 J3
Appleton Ct	41 J3
Appleton Sq	41 J3
Appleton Way	41 J3
Archery Pl	40 D1
Archery Rd	40 D1
Archery St	40 E1
Archery Ter	40 E1
Armley Rd	40 A3
Armouries Rd	41 G5
Artist St	40 B4
Ascot Ter	41 J4
Ashley Av	41 J1
Ashley Rd	41 J1
Ashley Ter	41 J1
Ashton Av	41 J1
Ashton Gro	41 J1
Ashton Mt	41 J1
Ashton Pl	41 J1
Ashton Ter	41 J1
Ashton Vw	41 J1
Ashville Vw	40 A1
Assembly St	41 F4
Atkinson St	41 G6
Autumn Av	40 B1
Autumn Gro	40 B1
Autumn Pl	40 B1
Autumn St	40 B1
Autumn Ter	40 B1
Avenue, The	41 G4
Aysgarth Cl	41 J4

Aysgarth Dr 41 J4
Aysgarth Pl 41 J4
Aysgarth Wk 41 J4

B
Back Ashville Av 40 A1
Back Hyde Ter 40 C2
Back Row 40 E5
Balm Pl 40 C6
Balm Wk 40 C6
Bank St 41 E4
Baron Cl 40 C7
Barrack St 41 F1
Barran Ct 41 H1
Barton Gro 40 D7
Barton Mt 40 D7
Barton Pl 40 C7
Barton Rd 40 C7
Barton Ter 40 D7
Barton Vw 40 C7
Bath Rd 40 D5
Bayswater Vw 41 H1
Beamsley Gro 40 A1
Beamsley Mt 40 A1
Beamsley Pl 40 A1
Beamsley Ter 40 A1
Beckett St 41 H3
Bedford St 40 E3
Beech Gro Ter 40 D1
Belgrave St 41 E3
Belinda St 41 H7
Belle Vue Rd 40 B2
Bell St 41 G3
Belmont Gro 40 D2
Benson St 41 F1
Benyon Pk Way 40 A7
Berking Av 41 J3
Bertrand St 40 C6
Bexley Av 41 H1
Bexley Gro 41 J1
Bexley Mt 41 H1
Bexley Pl 41 H1
Bexley Rd 41 J1
Bexley Tcr 41 J1
Bingley St 40 C3
Bishopgate St 40 E4
Bismarck Dr 40 E7
Bismarck St 40 E7
Black Bull St 41 F5
Blackman La 40 E1
Blandford Gdns 40 D1
Blandford Gro 40 D1
Blayds St 41 H4
Blayd's Yd 41 E4
Blenheim Av 40 E1
Blenheim Ct 40 E1
Blenheim Cres 40 E1
Blenheim Gro 40 E1
Blenheim Sq 40 E1
Blenheim Vw 40 D1
Blenheim Wk 40 D1
Blundell St 40 D2
Boar La 40 E4
Bodley Ter 40 A2
Bond St 40 E3
Boundary Pl 41 G1
Boundary St 41 G1
Bourse, The 41 E4
Bowling Grn Ter 40 D6
Bowman La 41 F4
Bow St 41 G4
Bracken Ct 40 A6
Braithwaite St 40 C5
Brancepeth Pl 40 B4
Brandon Rd 40 C2
Brandon St 40 B4
Branksome Pl 40 B1
Brick St 41 G4
Bridge Ct 40 C5
Bridge End 41 E4
Bridge Rd 40 C5
Bridge St 41 F3
Bridgewater Rd 41 H6
Briggate 41 E4
Brignall Garth 41 J2
Brignall Way 41 H2
Bristol St 41 G2
Britannia St 40 D4
Broadway Av 40 A1
Brookfield St 41 G6
Brown Av 40 B7
Brown La E 40 B6
Brown La W 40 A6
Brown Pl 40 B7
Brown Rd 40 B7
Bruce Gdns 40 B4
Bruce Lawn 40 B4
Brunswick Ct 41 F3
Brunswick Ter 41 E2
Brussels St 41 G4
Buckton Cl 40 C7
Buckton Mt 40 C7
Buckton Vw 40 C7
Burley 40 A1

Burley Lo Pl 40 B2
Burley Lo Rd 40 A1
Burley Lo St 40 B2
Burley Lo Ter 40 B1
Burley Pl 40 A2
Burley Rd 40 A1
Burley St 40 C3
Burmantofts 41 H3
Burmantofts St 41 G3
Burton Row 41 E7
Burton St 41 E7
Burton Way 41 J2
Butterfield St 41 H4
Butterley St 41 F6
Butts Ct 41 E3
Byron St 41 F2

C
Cain Cl 41 H4
Call La 41 F4
Calls, The 41 F4
Calverley St 40 D2
Cambrian St 40 D7
Cambrian Ter 40 D7
Canal Pl 40 B4
Canal St 40 A3
Canal Wf 40 D4
Carberry Pl 40 A1
Carberry Rd 40 A1
Carberry Ter 40 A1
Carlisle Rd 41 G5
Carlton Carr 41 E1
Carlton Ct 40 A7
Carlton Gdns 41 E1
Carlton Gate 41 E1
Carlton Gro 41 E1
Carlton Hill 41 E1
Carlton Pl 41 E1
Carlton Ri 41 E1
Carlton Twrs 41 F1
Carlton Vw 41 E1
Castle St 40 D3
Castleton Cl 40 B4
Castleton Rd 40 A3
Cautley Rd 41 J5
Cavalier App 41 H5
Cavalier Cl 41 H5
Cavalier Ct 41 H5
Cavalier Gdns 41 H5
Cavalier Gate 41 H5
Cavalier Ms 41 H5
Cavalier Vw 41 H5
Cavendish Rd 40 D1
Cavendish St 40 C3
Cemetery Rd 40 C7
Central Rd 41 F4
Central St 40 D3
Chadwick St 41 F5
Chadwick St S 41 F5
Chantrell Ct 41 F4
Charles Av 41 J5
Charlton Gro 41 J4
Charlton Pl 41 J4
Charlton Rd 41 J4
Charlton St 41 J4
Cherry Pl 41 G2
Cherry Row 41 G2
Chesney Av 41 F7
Chiswick St 40 A2
Chorley La 40 D2
Churchill Gdns 40 E1
Church La 41 F4
City Sq 40 E4
City Wk 40 E5
Claremont Av 40 C2
Claremont Gro 40 C2
Claremont Vw 40 C2
Clarence Rd 41 G5
Clarendon Pl 40 C1
Clarendon Rd 40 C1
Clarendon Way 40 D2
Clark Av 41 J4
Clark Cres 41 J4
Clark Gro 41 J5
Clark La 41 H5
Clark Mt 41 J4
Clark Rd 41 J5
Clark Row 41 J5
Clark Ter 41 J4
Clark Vw 41 J5
Clay Pit La 41 E2
Cleveleys Av 40 C7
Cleveleys Mt 40 C7
Cleveleys Rd 40 C7
Cleveleys St 40 C7
Cleveleys Ter 40 C7
Cloberry St 40 C1
Close, The 41 G4
Cloth Hall St 41 F4
Clyde App 40 A5
Clyde Gdns 40 B5
Clyde Gro 40 A5
Coleman St 40 B5
Colenso Gdns 40 C7

Colenso Mt 40 C7
Colenso Pl 40 C7
Colenso Rd 40 C7
Colenso Ter 40 C7
Colville Ter 40 D7
Commercial St 41 E3
Compton Av 41 J1
Compton Cres 41 J1
Compton Gro 41 J1
Compton Mt 41 J1
Compton Pl 41 J1
Compton Rd 41 J1
Compton St 41 J1
Compton Ter 41 J1
Compton Vw 41 J1
Concordia St 41 E4
Concord St 41 F2
Consort St 40 C2
Consort Ter 40 C2
Consort Vw 40 B2
Consort Wk 40 C2
Constance Gdns 40 E1
Constance Way 40 E1
Cookridge St 40 E3
Copley Hill 40 A5
Copley Hill Way 40 A6
Copley St 40 A5
Copperfield Av 41 J5
Copperfield Cres 41 J5
Copperfield Gro 41 J5
Copperfield Mt 41 J5
Copperfield Pl 41 J5
Copperfield Row 41 J5
Copperfield Ter 41 J5
Copperfield Vw 41 J5
Copperfield Wk 41 J5
Copperfiield Dr 41 J5
Cotton St 41 G4
Coupland Pl 40 D7
Coupland Rd 40 D7
Cowper Av 41 J1
Cowper Cres 41 J1
Cowper Rd 41 J1
Cromer Pl 40 C1
Cromer Rd 40 C1
Cromer St 40 C1
Cromer Ter 40 C2
Cromwell Mt 41 G2
Cromwell St 41 G2
Crosby Pl 40 C6
Crosby Rd 40 C7
Crosby St 40 C6
Crosby Ter 40 C6
Crosby Vw 40 C6
Cross Aysgarth Mt 41 H4
Cross Belgrave St 41 F3
Cross Catherine St 41 H4
Cross Grn 41 J6
Cross Grn App 41 J6
Cross Grn Av 41 H5
Cross Grn Cl 41 J6
Cross Grn Cres 41 H5
Cross Grn Dr 41 J6
Cross Grn Garth 41 J6
Cross Grn La 41 H5
Cross Grn Ri 41 J6
Cross Grn Way 41 J6
Cross Ingram Rd 40 C6
Cross Kelso Rd 40 C2
Cross Mitford Rd 40 A4
Cross Stamford St 41 G2
Cross York St 41 F4
Crown Ct 41 F4
Crown Pt Rd 41 F5
Crown St 41 F4
Croydon St 40 B5
Cudbear St 41 F5
Czar St 40 C5

D
Danby Wk 41 H4
David St 40 D5
Dene Ho Ct 40 E1
Denison Rd 40 C3
Dent St 41 H4
Derwent Pl 40 D5
Devon Cl 40 D1
Devon Rd 40 D1
Dewsbury Rd 41 E6
Dial St 41 H5
Disraeli Gdns 40 E7
Disraeli Ter 40 E7
Dock St 41 F4
Dolly La 41 G2
Dolphin Ct 41 H4
Dolphin St 41 H4
Domestic Rd 40 B6
Domestic St 40 C5
Donisthorpe St 41 G6
Drive, The 41 G4
Driver Ter 40 B5
Dudley Way 40 A5
Duke St 41 F4
Duncan St 40 C7

Duncombe St 40 C7
Duxbury Ri 40 E1
Dyer St 41 F3

E
East Fld St 41 H4
Eastgate 41 F3
East King St 41 G4
East Par 40 E3
East Pk Dr 41 J4
East Pk Gro 41 J4
East Pk Mt 41 J4
East Pk Par 41 J4
East Pk Pl 41 J4
East Pk Rd 41 J4
East Pk St 41 J4
East Pk Ter 41 J4
East Pk Vw 41 J4
East St 41 G4
Easy Rd 41 H5
Ebor Mt 40 B1
Ebor Pl 40 B1
Ebor St 40 B1
Edgware Av 41 H1
Edgware Gro 41 H1
Edgware Mt 41 H1
Edgware Pl 41 H1
Edgware Row 41 H1
Edgware St 41 H1
Edgware Ter 41 H1
Edgware Vw 41 H1
Edward St 41 F3
Edwin Rd 40 B1
Eighth Av 40 A5
Elland Rd 40 C7
Elland Ter 40 D6
Ellerby La 41 H5
Ellerby Rd 41 G4
Elmtree La 41 G7
Elmwood La 41 F2
Elmwood Rd 41 E2
Elsworth St 40 A4
Einfield Av 41 G1
Enfield St 41 G1
Enfield Ter 41 G1
Euston Gro 40 B7
Euston Mt 40 B7
Euston Ter 40 B7
Everleigh St 41 J3

F
Far Cft Ter 40 A5
Fewston Av 41 H5
Fewston Ct 41 J5
Finsbury Rd 40 D2
First Av 40 A4
Firth St 41 G2
Firth Ter 41 G2
Fish St 41 F3
Flax Pl 41 G4
Florence Av 41 J1
Florence Gro 41 J1
Florence Mt 41 J1
Florence Pl 41 J1
Florence St 41 J1
Folly La 40 D7
Forster St 41 G6
Foundry St (Holbeck) 40 C2
Foundry St (Quarry Hill) 41 G4
Fountain St 40 D3
Fourteenth Av 40 A5
Fourth Ct 40 C5
Fox Way 41 H6
Fraser St 41 J2
Frederick Av 41 J5
Front Row 40 D5
Front St 40 D5

G
Gardeners Ct 41 G7
Gargrave App 41 H3
Gargrave Pl 41 H2
Garth, The 41 G4
Garton Av 41 J4
Garton Gro 41 J4
Garton Rd 41 J4
Garton Ter 41 J4
Garton Vw 41 J4
Gelderd Pl 40 B5
Gelderd Rd 40 A7
George St 41 F3
Gibraltar Island Rd 41 H7
Gilpin Pl 40 A5
Gilpin St 40 A5
Gilpin Ter 40 A5
Gilpin Vw 40 A5
Glasshouse St 41 G6
Gledhow Mt 41 H1
Gledhow Pl 41 H1
Gledhow Rd 41 H1
Gledhow Ter 41 H1

Glencoe Vw 41 J5
Glensdale Gro 41 J4
Glensdale Mt 41 J4
Glensdale Rd 41 J4
Glensdale St 41 J4
Glensdale Ter 41 J4
Glenthorpe Av 41 J3
Glenthorpe Cres 41 J3
Glenthorpe Ter 41 J3
Globe Rd 40 C4
Gloucester Ter 40 A4
Goodman St 41 G6
Gotts Rd 40 C4
Gower St 41 F3
Grace St 40 D3
Grafton St 41 F2
Grange Cl 41 G7
Grange Rd 41 G7
Grant Av 41 G1
Granville Rd 41 H2
Grape St 41 F7
Grasmere Cl 40 A5
Grasmere Rd 40 A5
Great George St 40 D3
Great Wilson St 40 E5
Greek St 40 E3
Greenfield Rd 41 H4
Green La 40 A5
Grosvenor Hill 41 E1

H
Hall Gro 40 B1
Hall La 40 A4
Hall Pl 41 H4
Hanover Av 40 C2
Hanover La 40 D3
Hanover Mt 40 C2
Hanover Sq 40 C2
Hanover Wk 40 C3
Harewood St 41 F3
Harold Av 40 A1
Harold Gro 40 A1
Harold Mt 40 A1
Harold Pl 40 A1
Harold Rd 40 A1
Harold St 40 A1
Harold Ter 40 A1
Harold Vw 40 A1
Harold Wk 40 A1
Harper St 41 F4
Harrison St 41 F3
Hartwell Rd 40 B1
Haslewood Cl 41 H3
Haslewood Ct 41 H3
Haslewood Dene 41 H3
Haslewood Dr 41 H3
Haslewood Ms 41 J3
Haslewood Pl 41 H3
Haslewood Sq 41 H3
Hawkins Dr 41 E1
Headrow, The 40 D3
Heaton's Ct 41 E4
Hedley Chase 40 A4
Hedley Gdns 40 A4
Hedley Grn 40 A4
High 41 G7
High Ct 41 F4
High Ct La 41 F4
Hillary Pl 40 D1
Hillidge Rd 41 F7
Hillidge Sq 41 F7
Hill Top Pl 40 B1
Hill Top St 40 B1
Hirst's Yd 41 F4
Holbeck 40 D5
Holbeck La 40 C5
Holbeck Moor Rd 40 C6
Holdforth Cl 40 A4
Holdforth Gdns 40 A4
Holdforth Grn 40 A4
Holdforth Pl 40 A4
Holmes St 41 E5
Holroyd St 41 G1
Hope Rd 41 G3
Howden Gdns 40 B1
Howden Pl 40 B1
Hudson Rd 41 J1
Hudswell Rd 41 F7
Hunslet 41 G7
Hunslet Grn Way 41 F7
Hunslet Hall Rd 40 E7
Hunslet La 41 F5
Hunslet Rd 41 F4
Hyde Pk Cl 41 H7
Hyde Pk Rd 40 B1
Hyde Pl 40 C2
Hyde St 40 C2
Hyde Ter 40 C2

I
Infirmary St 40 E3
Ingram Cl 40 C6
Ingram Cres 40 B7

Ingram Gdns 40 C6
Ingram Rd 40 C7
Ingram Row 40 E5
Ingram St 40 E5
Ingram Vw 40 C6
Inner Ring Rd 40 E2
Ivory St 41 F6

J
Jack La 40 D6
Jenkinson Cl 40 D6
Jenkinson Lawn 40 D6
John Smeaton Viaduct 41 G6
Joseph St 41 G7
Junction St 41 F5

K
Keeton St 41 H3
Kelsall Av 40 B1
Kelsall Gro 40 B2
Kelsall Pl 40 B1
Kelsall Rd 40 B1
Kelsall Ter 40 B1
Kelso Gdns 40 C1
Kelso Rd 40 C1
Kelso St 40 C2
Kendal Bk 40 C2
Kendal Cl 40 C2
Kendal Gro 40 C2
Kendal La 40 C2
Kendell St 41 F4
Kenneth St 40 B6
Kepler Gro 41 H1
Kepler Mt 41 H1
Kepler Ter 41 H1
Kidacre St 41 F5
Kildare Ter 40 B5
King Charles St 41 E3
King Edward St 41 F3
Kings Av 40 B2
King's Rd 40 B1
Kingston Ter 40 D1
King St 40 D4
Kippax Pl 41 H4
Kirkgate 41 F4
Kirkstall Rd 40 A2
Kitson Rd 41 G6
Kitson St 41 H4
Knowsthorpe Cres 41 H5
Knowsthorpe La 41 J6

L
Ladybeck Cl 41 F3
Lady La 41 F3
Lady Pit La 40 D7
Lands La 41 E3
Lane, The 41 G4
Larchfield Rd 41 G6
Latchmore Rd 40 A7
Laura St 40 C5
Lavender Wk 41 H4
Leathley Rd 41 F6
Leathley St 41 F6
Leicester Cl 40 E1
Leicester Gro 40 E1
Leicester Pl 40 D1
Leighton St 40 D3
Leodis Ct 40 D5
Leylands Rd 41 G2
Lifton Pl 40 C1
Lincoln Grn Rd 41 G2
Lincoln Rd 41 G2
Lindsey Ct 41 H2
Lindsey Gdns 41 H2
Lindsey Rd 41 H2
Lisbon St 40 D3
Little King St 40 E4
Little Queen St 40 D4
Little Woodhouse St 40 D2
Livinia Gro 40 E1
Lodge St 40 D1
Lofthouse Pl 40 E1
Londesboro Gro 41 J4
Long Causeway 41 H6
Long Cl La 41 H4
Lord St 40 C5
Lord Ter 40 B5
Lovell Pk Cl 41 F2
Lovell Pk Gate 41 F2
Lovell Pk Hill 41 F2
Lovell Pk Rd 41 F2
Lovell Pk Vw 41 F2
Lower Basinghall St 40 E3
Lower Brunswick St 41 F2
Low Flds Av 40 B7
Low Flds Rd 40 A7
Low Flds Way 40 B7
Low Fold 41 G5
Low Whitehouse Row 41 G6
Ludgate Hill 41 F3
Lyddon Ter 40 C1
Lydgate 41 J2

Lydia St 41 F3

M
Mabgate 41 G3
Mabgate Grn 41 G3
Macaulay St 41 G3
Maitland Pl 40 D7
Maltings Rd 41 F7
Malvern Gro 40 D7
Malvern Ri 40 D7
Malvern Rd 40 C7
Malvern St 40 C7
Malvern Vw 40 C7
Manor Rd 40 D5
Manor St 41 G1
Mark La 41 E3
Marlborough Gdns 40 D1
Marlborough Gro 40 D1
Marlborough St 40 C3
Marlborough Twrs 40 C3
Marshall St 40 D5
Marsh La 41 G4
Maude St 41 F4
May Ter 41 H5
Meadowcroft Ms 41 H4
Meadow La 41 E5
Meadow Rd 40 E6
Melbourne St 41 F2
Merrion Pl 41 F3
Merrion St 41 E3
Merrion Way 41 E2
Meynell App 40 C6
Middleton Av 41 J2
Milford Pl 40 A2
Millgarth St 41 F3
Mill Grn 40 B5
Mill Hill 41 E4
Mill St 41 G4
Millwright St 41 G2
Milner Gdns 41 H5
Milnes St 40 B5
Mitford Rd 40 A4
Mitford Vw 40 A4
Moor Cres 41 E7
Moor Cres Chase 41 E7
Moorland Av 40 B1
Moorland Rd 40 B1
Moor Rd 41 E7
Moorside Maltings 41 E7
Moor Vw 40 D6
Moorvile Cl 40 D7
Moorville Ct 40 D7
Moorville Gro 40 D7
Moorville Rd 40 D7
Mount Preston St 40 C2
Mulberry St 41 F6
Mullins Ct 41 H5
Mushroom St 41 G2

N
Naseby Garth 41 G2
Naseby Ter 41 H3
National Rd 41 H6
Navigation Wk 41 F4
Neptune St 41 G4
Neville St 40 E4
New Briggate 41 F3
New Craven Gate 41 F6
New La 40 E5
New Mkt St 41 F4
New Princess St 40 D6
New Sta St 40 E4
New York Rd 41 G3
New York St 41 F4
Nickleby Rd 41 J3

Nile St 41 F3
Nineveh Gdns 40 D6
Nineveh Par 40 D6
Nineveh Rd 40 C6
Nippet La 41 H3
Normanton Gro 40 C7
Normanton Pl 40 D7
Nortech Cl 41 G1
Northcote Cres 40 E7
Northcote Dr 40 D7
Northcote Grn 40 D7
North Ct 41 F3
Northern St 40 D4
North St 41 F3

O
Oak Rd 40 A4
Oatland Cl 41 F1
Oatland Ct 41 F1
Oatland Dr 41 F1
Oatland Gdns 41 F1
Oatland Grn 41 F1
Oatland Hts 41 F1
Oatland La 41 E1
Oatland Rd 41 E1
Oatland Twrs 41 F1
O'Grady Sq 41 H4
Old Mill La 41 H7
Oval, The 41 G7
Oxford Pl 40 D3
Oxford Row 40 D3
Oxley St 41 J4
Oxton Mt 41 J3
Oxton Way 41 J3

P
Parade, The 41 G4
Park Cross St 40 D3
Parkfield St 41 E6
Park La 40 C3
Park Par 41 J5
Park Pl 40 D3
Park Row 40 E4
Park Sq E 40 D3
Park Sq S 40 D3
Park Sq W 40 D3
Park St 40 D3
Park Vw Rd 40 A1
Pearson St 41 F6
Penny La Way 41 F7
Pilot St 41 G2
Pitt Row 41 E4
Place's Rd 41 H4
Plaid Row 41 H3
Playhouse Sq 41 G3
Pleasant Mt 40 C6
Pleasant Pl 40 C6
Pleasant Ter 40 C6
Pontefract Av 41 J4
Pontefract La 41 H3
Pontefract La Cl 41 H4
Pontefract St 41 H4
Portland Cres 40 E2
Portland Gate 40 E2
Portland St 40 D3
Portland Way 40 E2
Pottery Rd 41 F7
Prosper St 41 G7
Providence Pl 41 E2
Pym St 41 G6

Q
Quarry Hill 41 G3
Quebec St 40 D3

Queen Sq 41 E2
Queens Rd 40 B1
Queen St 40 D4

R
Radnor St 40 B5
Railway St 41 G4
Raincliffe Gro 41 J3
Raincliffe Rd 41 J3
Raincliffe St 41 J3
Recreation Cres 40 C7
Recreation Gro 40 C7
Recreation Mt 40 C7
Recreation Pl 40 C7
Recreation Row 40 C7
Recreation St 40 C7
Recreation Ter 40 C7
Recreation Vw 40 C7
Rectory St 41 H2
Redshaw Rd 40 A5
Regent St 41 G3
Regent Ter 40 B1
Rhodes Ter 40 A5
Richmond Hill App 41 H4
Richmond Hill Cl 41 H4
Richmond St 41 G4
Rickard St 40 C5
Rider St 41 G3
Rigton App 41 H3
Rigton Cl 41 H3
Rigton Dr 41 H3
Rigton Grn 41 H3
Rigton Lawn 41 H3
Rigton Ms 41 H3
Rillbank La 40 B2
Roscoe St 41 G1
Rosebank Gdns 40 B2
Rosebank Rd 40 B2
Rosebud Wk 41 G1
Roseville Rd 41 G1
Roseville St 41 H1
Rossington St 40 E3
Roundhay Rd 41 G1
Roxby Cl 41 H2
Royal Pk Av 40 B1
Royal Pk Gro 40 B1
Royal Pk Rd 40 A1
Royal Pk Ter 40 B1
Ruby St 41 G2
Runswick Av 40 C6
Runswick Pl 40 C6
Runswick St 40 C6
Runswick Ter 40 C6
Russell St 40 E3
Rydall Pl 40 C6
Rydall St 40 C6
Rydall Ter 40 C6

S
Sackville St 41 F1
St. Andrew's St 40 C3
St. Barnabas Rd 40 E5
St. Georges Rd 40 D2
St. Helen's St 41 G6
St. Hilda's Av 41 J5
St. Hilda's Cres 41 H5
St. Hilda's Gro 41 J5
St. Hilda's Mt 41 J5
St. Hilda's Pl 41 J5
St. Hilda's Rd 41 J5
St. John's Av 40 C1
St. John's Cl 40 B1
St. John's Gro 40 B1
St. John's Rd 40 B2
St. Luke's Cescent 40 D7

St. Luke's Cres 40 D7
St. Luke's Grn 40 D7
St. Luke's Rd 40 D7
St. Luke's St 40 D7
St. Mark's Av 40 D1
St. Mark's Rd 40 D1
St. Mark's St 40 D1
St. Mary's Cl 40 A5
St. Mary's St 41 G3
St. Matthew's St 40 C6
St. Matthias St 40 A1
St. Matthias Ter 40 A1
St. Paul's St 40 D3
St. Peter's Ct 41 E7
St. Peter's Pl 41 G3
St. Peter's Sq 41 G3
St. Stephen's Ct 41 H3
St. Stephen's Rd 41 H3
Salem Pl 41 F5
Sandlewood Cl 40 D6
Sandlewood Grn 40 D6
Sardinia St 41 F6
Saville Grn 41 J3
Saxton La 41 G4
Sayner La 41 G5
Sayner Rd 41 F5
Scargill Cl 41 H2
Scarth Av 41 J1
Second Av 40 A4
Seminary St 40 D2
Severn Way 41 H7
Shafton La 40 C6
Shafton Pl 40 C6
Shafton St 40 C6
Shafton Vw 40 C6
Shakespeare App 41 H2
Shakespeare Av 41 H2
Shakespeare Cl 41 J2
Shakespeare Gdns 41 J2
Shakespeare Lawn 41 H2
Shakespeare St 41 J1
Shannon Rd 41 H3
Shannon St 41 G3
Sheaf St 41 F5
Sheepscar Ct 41 F1
Sheepscar Gro 41 F2
Sheepscar St N 41 F1
Sheepscar St S 41 F1
Siddal St 40 D5
Sidney St 41 F3
Silver St 40 D5
Skinner La 41 F2
Skinner St 40 C3
Somers St 40 E3
South Accommodation Rd 41 G6
South Par 40 E3
Sovereign St 40 E4
Spence La 40 B5
Spenceley St 40 D1
Spinney, The 41 H4
Spinneyfield Ct 41 H4
Spring Cl Av 41 H5
Spring Cl Gdns 41 H5
Spring Cl St 41 H5
Spring Cl Wk 41 H5
Springfield Mt 40 C2
Spring Gro Ter 40 A1
Spring Gro Vw 40 B1
Spring Gro Wk 40 A1
Springwell Ct 40 C5
Springwell Rd 40 C5
Springwell St 40 C5
Springwell Vw 40 C5
Stafford St 41 G7

Stanley Av 41 J1
Stanley Pl 41 J1
Stanley Rd 41 J1
Stanley Ter 41 J1
Stocks Hill 40 C6
Stoney Rock Gro 41 J2
Stoney Rock La 41 H2
Stott Rd 40 A4
Studio Rd 40 B2
Sutton St 40 C5
Sweet St 40 D5
Sweet St W 40 C5
Swinegate 41 E4
Sydenham Rd 40 B5
Sydenham St 40 B5

T
Telephone Pl 41 G2
Templar La 41 F3
Templar Pl 41 F3
Templar St 41 F3
Temple Vw Gro 41 J4
Temple Vw Pl 41 J4
Temple Vw Rd 41 J3
Temple Vw Ter 41 J4
Thealby Cl 41 G3
Thealby Lawn 41 G2
Thealby Pl 41 G3
Third Av 40 A5
Thirsk Row 40 D4
Thoresby Pl 40 D3
Thornleigh Gdns 41 J5
Thornleigh Gro 41 J5
Thornleigh Mt 41 J5
Thornleigh St 41 J5
Thornleigh Vw 41 J5
Thornville Pl 40 B1
Thornville Rd 40 A1
Thornville Row 40 B1
Thornville St 40 B1
Thornville Vw 40 B1
Tilbury Av 40 C7
Tilbury Gro 40 C7
Tilbury Mt 40 C7
Tilbury Par 40 C7
Tilbury Rd 40 C7
Tilbury Ter 40 C7
Tilbury Vw 40 C7
Tong Rd 40 A5
Top Moor Side 40 C6
Torre Cl 41 J3
Torre Dr 41 J2
Torre Rd 41 H3
Tower Ho St 41 F2
Trafalgar St 41 F3
Trent Rd 41 J3
Trent St 40 D6
Trinity St 41 E3
Triumph Cl 40 C5
Turlow Ct 41 G4

U
Union Pl 40 D5
Union St 41 F3
University Rd 40 C1
Upper Accommodation Rd 41 H3
Upper Basinghall St 40 E3
Upper N St 40 E2
Upper Westlock Av 41 J2

V
Vernon Rd 40 D2
Vernon St 40 E2
Vicar La 41 F3

Victoria Rd 40 E5
Victoria Sq 40 D3
Victoria St 40 C2
Victoria Ter 40 C2
Village Ter 40 A1
Vinery Mt 41 J4
Vinery Pl 41 J4
Vinery St 41 J3
Vinery Ter 41 J4

W
Wade La 41 E3
Walford Gro 41 J3
Walford Rd 41 J3
Walford Ter 41 J3
Walter Cres 41 H4
Walter St 40 A2
Walton St 40 D5
Washington St 40 B3
Water La 40 C5
Waterloo Rd 41 G7
Waterloo St 41 F4
Waverley Garth 40 D7
Weaver St 40 A2
Welbeck Rd 41 J4
Well Cl Ri 41 E1
Wellington Br St 40 C3
Wellington Pl 40 C4
Wellington Rd 40 B4
Wellington St 40 D4
Wesley Pl 41 H4
Westfield Cres 40 B2
Westfield Rd 40 B2
Westfield Ter 40 B2
Westgate 40 D3
Westlock Av 41 J2
West St 40 C3
West Vale 40 A6
Wharf St 41 F4
Whitehall Rd 40 B5
Whitehouse St 41 G7
Whitelock St 41 F2
Whitfield Av 41 G7
Whitfield Gdns 41 G7
Whitfield Pl 41 G7
Whitfield Sq 41 G7
Whitfield Way 41 G7
Willis St 41 H4
Willoughby Ter 40 C6
Willow App 40 A2
Willow Av 40 A2
Willow Cl 40 B2
Willow Garth 40 A2
Willow Rd 40 A2
Willow Ter Rd 40 D2
Wilmington St 41 F1
Winchester St 40 A4
Winfield Gro 40 E1
Winfield Pl 40 E1
Winfield Ter 40 E1
Wintoun St 41 F2
Wolseley Rd 40 A1
Woodhouse La 40 D1
Woodhouse Sq 40 D3
Woodsley Grn 40 B1
Woodsley Rd 40 B2
Wormald Row 41 E3
Wortley La 40 B5
Wortley Pk 40 A5

Y
Yarn St 41 H6
York Pl 40 D3
York Rd 41 H3
York St 41 F4

Liverpool street index

A
Abercromby Sq 43 F4
Abney Cl 43 H5
Acorn Ct 43 E7
Acton Way 43 H5
Adderley St 43 H3
Addison St 42 C2
Addison Way 42 C2
Adelaide Pl 42 D1
Adelaide Rd 43 G4
Adele Thompson Dr 43 F6
Agnes Way 43 H4
Aigburth St 43 G5
Ainsworth St 42 E4
Albany Rd 43 G3
Albert Edward Rd 43 G3
Albert St 43 G4
Alderson Rd 43 J6
Alexandra Cl 43 G2

Alexandra Rd 43 J5
Alex Cl 43 F7
Alfred Ms 42 E6
Alfred St 43 J5
Altcar Av 43 J6
Alt St 43 G6
Amberley St 43 F6
Amelia Cl 43 F2
Amethyst Cl 43 G1
Anchorage, The 42 C7
Angela St 43 G5
Anglezark Cl 43 H3
Anglican Ct 42 E6
Archbishop Warlock Ct 42 B1
Argyle St 42 C5
Arley St 42 C1
Arnold Cres 43 F7
Arnside Rd 43 H4

Arrad St 43 E5
Arundel Av 43 J7
Arundel Cl 43 J7
Asbridge St 43 G7
Ashton St 43 F3
Ashwell St 42 D6
Askham Cl 43 G6
Aspen Gro 43 H7
Atlantic Pt 42 C2
Atwell St 43 G1

B
Back Colquitt St 42 D5
Back Guildford St 43 F1
Back Kelvin Gro 43 G7
Back Leeds St 42 B2
Baker St 43 G2
Baker Way 43 F2
Balmoral Rd 43 J1

Balm St 43 H3
Baltimore St 42 E5
Bannerman St 43 J5
Barnet Cl 43 H5
Basnett St 42 C4
Bath St 42 A3
Battenberg St 43 G3
Bayhorse La 42 C2
Beaconsfield St 43 G7
Beaufort St 42 D7
Beaumont St 43 G6
Beau St 42 D1
Beckwith St 42 C5
Bective St 43 J5
Bedford Cl 43 F5
Bedford St S 43 F6
Beech St 43 J3
Benson St 42 D4
Bentley Rd 43 G7

Beresford St 42 E1
Berington St 42 C1
Berkley St 43 E6
Berry St 42 D5
Berwick Cl 43 H1
Berwick St 43 H1
Bevington Bush 42 C2
Bevington Hill 42 C1
Bidder St 42 E2
Bigham Rd 43 H2
Birchfield St 42 E2
Bird St 43 J6
Birkett St 42 D2
Birstall Rd 43 G2
Birt Cl 43 G6
Bishop Sheppard Ct 42 B1
Bixteth St 42 B3
Blackburne Pl 43 E5

Blackstock St 42 C2
Blair St 42 E6
Blenheim St 42 C1
Bluefields St 43 E6
Blundell St 42 C6
Boaler St 43 G2
Bold Pl 42 D5
Bold St 42 D4
Bolton St 42 D4
Bond St 42 C1
Boothwood Cl 43 H5
Boswell St 43 H6
Botanic Grn 43 H3
Botanic Pl 43 J3
Botanic Rd 43 J3
Boundary La 43 G1
Boyton Ct 43 J5
Bradfield St 43 H3
Brae St 43 H3

Street	Ref	Street	Ref
Brahms Cl	43 G7	Claughton Cl	43 H4
Brampton Dr	43 F5	Claypole Cl	43 H5
Brassey St	42 D7	Clay St	42 B1
Breames Cl	43 H4	Clearwater Cl	43 H3
Breck Rd	43 F1	Clegg St	42 D1
Bremner Cl	43 H4	Clement Gdns	42 C1
Brick St	42 D6	Cleveland Sq	42 C5
Bridge Rd	43 J5	Clifford St	42 E3
Bridgewater St	42 C6	Clifton Gro	43 H3
Bridport St	42 D3	Clint Rd	43 H4
Bright St	43 F2	Clint Rd W	43 H4
Brindley St	42 D7	Clint Way	43 H4
Britannia Av	43 J6	Coal St	42 D3
Britten Cl	43 H7	Cobden St	43 F2
Bronte St	42 E3	Coburg Wf	42 C7
Brook St	42 B3	Cockspur St	42 C3
Brownlow Hill	42 D4	Coleridge St	43 H2
Brownlow St	43 E4	College La	42 C4
Brow Side	43 E1	College St N	43 E2
Brunswick Rd	43 F3	College St S	43 F2
Brunswick St	42 B4	Colquitt St	42 D5
Bryges St	43 G4	Coltart Rd	43 G7
Brythen St	42 C4	Comberme St	43 E7
Burlington St	42 C1	Commerce Way	43 G6
Burnley Cl	43 G1	Commutation Row	42 D3
Burroughs Gdns	42 C1	Compton Rd	43 G1
Burrows Ct	42 B1	Comus St	42 D2
Burton Cl	42 C5	Concert St	42 D5
Bute St	42 D2	Connaught Rd	43 G3
Bute St (Edge Hill)	43 H6	Contance St	42 E3
Butler Cres	43 G2	Cookson St	42 D6
Butler St	43 G1	Cook St	42 C4
Button St	42 C4	Copperas Hill	42 D4
Byrom St	42 D3	Corinto St	42 E6
		Corney St	43 H6
C		Cornhill	42 C5
Cadogan St	43 J5	Cornwallis St	42 D5
Caird St	43 G2	Corsewall St	43 J5
Cairns St	43 G7	Cotswold St	43 H3
Caledonia St	43 E5	Cotton St	42 A1
Callander Rd	43 J2	Covent Gdn	42 B3
Cambria St N	43 H2	Cowan Dr	43 F1
Cambria St S	43 H2	Cranborne Rd	43 J6
Cambridge Ct	43 E5	Craven St	42 E3
Cambridge St	43 E4	Cresswell St	43 F1
Camden St	42 D3	Cropper St	42 D4
Cameo Cl	43 G1	Crosfield Cl	43 J4
Cameron St	43 H3	Crosfield Rd	43 H4
Campbell St	42 C5	Crosshall St	42 C3
Canada Boul	42 B4	Crown St	43 F3
Canning Pl	42 C4	Croxteth Gro	43 H7
Canning St	43 E5	Croxteth Rd	43 G7
Canterbury St	42 E2	Crump St	42 D6
Canterbury Way	43 E2	Cullen St	43 H6
Cantsfield St	43 J6	Cumberland St	42 C3
Cardigan St	43 J5	Cunliffe St	42 C3
Cardigan Way	43 H1	Custom Ho Pl	42 C5
Cardwell St	43 G5		
Carlingford Cl	43 G6	**D**	
Carlton St	42 A1	Dale St	42 B4
Carmarthen Cres	42 D7	Daniel Davies Dr	43 G6
Carpenters Row	42 B2	Dansie St	43 E4
Carruthers St	42 B2	Darrel Dr	43 H6
Carstairs Rd	43 J1	Daulby St	43 F3
Carter St	43 F6	Davies St	42 C3
Carver St	43 E2	Dawber Cl	43 G1
Caryl St	42 D7	Dawson St	42 C4
Castle St	42 B4	Dean Dillistone Ct	42 D6
Catharine St	43 F5	Deane Rd	43 H3
Cathedral Cl	42 E6	Dean Patey Ct	42 D5
Cathedral Gate	42 E5	Deeley Cl	43 H4
Cathedral Wk	42 E4	Dell St	43 H3
Cawdor St	43 G7	Denham Dr	43 H1
Cazneau St	42 D1	Denham Way	43 H1
Cedar Gro	43 H7	Dentdale Dr	42 E1
Celtic St	43 F7	Devon St	42 E3
Chadwick St	42 B2	Dexter St	42 E7
Chaloner St	42 C6	Dial St	43 H3
Chandos St	43 H4	Diamond St	42 C1
Channell Rd	43 H2	Dickens St	42 E7
Chapel St	42 B4	Dickson St	42 A1
Chase Way	42 E1	Dombey St	43 E7
Chatham Pl	43 G4	Dorothy St	43 H4
Chatham St	43 F5	Dorrit St	43 E7
Chatsworth Dr	43 H5	Dorset Av	43 J6
Chaucer St	42 D2	Douro St	42 D1
Cheapside	42 C3	Dovestone Cl	43 H5
Chesney Cl	42 E7	Dove St	43 G6
Chesterfield St	42 E6	Drury La	42 B4
Chester St	42 E7	Dryden St	42 C1
Chestnut St	43 F4	Dublin St	42 A1
Chichester Cl	43 J5	Ducie St	43 G7
Childwall Av	43 J6	Duckinfield St	43 E4
Chisenhale St	42 B1	Duke St	42 C5
Chiswell St	43 H3	Duncan St	42 D6
Christian St	42 D2	Dunkeld Cl	43 G2
Chris Ward Cl	43 H4	Dunstan La	43 H5
Church All	42 C4	Durden St	43 H6
Church Mt	43 G4	Durning Rd	43 H3
Church St	42 C4		
Churton Ct	43 F2	Dwerryhouse St	43 H4
Cicely St	43 G4	Dyke St	43 H5
Clarence St	42 E4		
Claribel St	43 F7	**E**	
		Earle Rd	43 H6
		Earle St	42 B3
		East St	42 B3
		Eaton St	42 B2
		Ebenezer Rd	43 J3
		Eden St	43 H6
		Edgar St	42 C2
		Edge Hill	43 G5
		Edge La	43 G4
		Edinburgh Rd	43 G3
		Edmund St	42 B3
		Egerton St	43 E6
		Elaine St	43 F7
		Eldonian Way	42 B1
		Eldon Pl	42 C1
		Eldon St	42 C1
		Elizabeth St	43 F3
		Elliot St	42 D4
		Elm Gro	43 G5
		Elm Vale	43 G4
		Elstree Rd	43 F7
		Ember Cres	43 F1
		Embledon St	43 G6
		Emerson St	43 E6
		Empress Rd	43 G4
		Enid St	43 F7
		Epworth St	43 F3
		Erin Cl	42 E7
		Erskine St	43 F3
		Esher Rd	43 H2
		Eversley St	43 F7
		Everton Brow	42 E2
		Everton Rd	43 F1
		Every St	43 G1
		Exchange St E	42 B3
		Exchange St W	42 B3

Street	Ref	Street	Ref
F		Gloucester Ct	42 D7
Fairclough St	42 D4	Gloucester Pl	43 F1
Fairfield	43 J2	Gore St	42 D7
Falkland St	43 E3	Gower St	42 B5
Falkner Sq	43 F6	Gradwell St	43 H6
Falkner St	43 E5	Grafton Cres	42 B3
Fareham Rd	43 J3	Grafton St	42 B3
Farnworth St	43 G2	Granary Wf	42 B2
Fazakerley St	42 B3	Granby St	43 J3
Fearnside St	43 J5	Grantham St	43 H6
Fell St	43 H3	Granville Rd	43 H2
Fenwick St	42 B4	Grayson St	42 C2
Fern Gro	43 H7	Great Crosshall St	43 G5
Fernhill Dr	43 F7	Great George Pl	43 G3
Fielding St	43 G2	Great George St	42 B3
Field St	42 E2	Great Howard St	43 E6
Finch Pl	43 E3	Great Nelson St	43 F7
Finlay St	43 H2	Great Newton St	43 E3
Fishguard Cl	43 F1	Great Orford St	43 E4
Fitzclarence Way	43 F1	Great Richmond St	43 F3
Fitzpatrick Ct	42 B1	Greek St	42 D4
Fitzroy Way	43 F2	Greenheys Rd	43 G7
Fleet St	42 D4	Greenland St	42 D6
Fleming Ct	42 B1	Green La	42 E4
Flint St	42 D6	Greenleaf St	43 H6
Fontenoy St	42 C3	Greenside	43 F2
Ford St	42 C2	Green St	42 C1
Forrest St	42 C5	Gregson St	43 F2
Fowler Cl	43 H4	Grenville St S	42 D5
Foxhill Cl	43 F7	Gresley Cl	43 J4
Fox St	42 C4	Grierson St	43 F3
Fraser St	42 D3	Grinfield St	42 E7
Freedom Cl	43 G5	Grinshill Cl	43 F7
Freeman St	43 J5	Grosvenor St	43 H2
Freemasons' Row	42 C2	Grove Pk	43 F7
Frost St	43 H3	Grove Rd	43 E2
		Grove St	43 J2
G		Guelph St	43 G1
Galloway St	43 J5	Guion St	42 B3
Gannock St	43 H3	Gwendoline St	43 G7
Gardenside St	43 F2	Gwenfron Rd	43 G7
Gardners Dr	43 H1	Gwent St	43 F7
Gardner's Row	42 C2		
Garrick St	43 J6	**H**	
Gascoyne St	42 B2	Hackins Hey	42 B3
Geneva Rd	43 J2	Haigh St	43 E1
George Harrison Cl	43 H4	Hale St	42 C3
Georges Dockway	42 B4	Hall La	43 F3
George St	42 B3	Halsbury Rd	43 H2
Geraint St	43 F7	Hampstead Rd	43 J2
Gerard St	42 D3	Hampton St	43 J5
Gibraltar Row	42 B3	Hannan Rd	43 H2
Gibson St	43 F6	Hanover St	42 C5
Gilbert St	42 C5	Harbord St	43 H7
Gildarts Gdns	42 C1	Hardman St	43 F7
Gildart St	43 E3	Hardy St	43 G2
Gilead St	43 H3	Harewood St	42 E2
Gill St	43 E3	Harker St	43 E3
Gilroy Rd	43 H2	Harke St	43 H2
Gladstone Rd	43 G4	Harper St	43 F3
Gladstone St	42 C2	Harrington St	42 C4
Gleave Cres	43 F1	Harrowby Cl	43 F1
Glegg St	42 B1	Harrowby St	43 F6
		Hartley Quay	42 B5
		Hart St	43 E3
		Hatherley Cl	43 G6
		Hatherley St	43 G6
		Hatton Gdn	42 C3
		Haverston Rd	43 J5
		Hawdon Ct	42 D4
		Hawke St	42 E7
		Hawkins St	43 H4
		Hawthorn Gro	43 G5
		Head St	43 J5
		Heathcote Cl	43 J5
		Heathfield St	42 C2
		Helena St	43 H4
		Helsby St	43 G4
		Hendon Rd	43 J1
		Henglers Cl	43 F2
		Henry Edward St	42 C2
		Henry St	42 C5
		Hewitts Pl	42 C3
		Highfield St	42 B2
		Highgate St	43 G4
		High St	42 B3
		Hilbre St	42 D4
		Hillaby Cl	43 F7
		Hillside St	43 F2
		Hill St	42 D7
		Hinton St	43 J2
		Hockenhall All	42 C3
		Hodson Pl	43 F1
		Holborn St	43 F3
		Holden St	43 G5
		Holdsworth St	43 H3
		Holly Rd	43 J3
		Holmes St	43 H6
		Holt Rd	43 H3
		Holy Cross Cl	42 C2
		Homerton Rd	43 J2
		Hood St	42 C3
		Hope Pl	42 E5
		Hope St	43 E6

Street	Ref	Street	Ref
Hornby Wk	43 G2	Lindley St	43 J5
Hotham St	43 F3	Ling St	43 H3
Houghton St	42 D7	Lister Cres	43 J3
Houlton St	42 B5	Lister Rd	43 J2
Hughes Cl	42 C4	Little Catherine St	43 E6
Hughes St	42 D7	Little Ct	42 B1
Huntly Rd	42 D6	Little Hardman St	42 E5
Hurst St	42 C7	Little Howard St	42 B1
Huskisson St	43 G6	Little St. Bride St	43 E5
Hutchinson St	43 H2	Little Woolton St	43 F4
Hutchinson Wk	43 J6	Liver St	42 C5
Hygeia St	43 G5	Lloyd Cl	43 F1
Hyslop St	42 C3	Lockerby Rd	43 J2
		Lodge La	43 H7
I		London Rd	42 D3
Iliad St	42 B2	Longfellow St	43 H6
Ingrow Rd	42 D1	Longstone Wk	43 G5
Irvine St	43 E3	Lord Nelson St	42 D3
Irwell St	43 E4	Lord St	42 C4
Islington	42 D2	Lorton St	43 H6
Ivatt Way	42 E3	Lothian St	43 F7
		Loudon Gro	43 G7
J		Love La	42 B1
Jack McBain Ct	42 B1	Lower Castle St	42 B4
Jade Rd	43 H1	Low Hill	43 F2
Jamaica St	42 D6	Lowther St	43 F6
James Clarke St	42 C1	Low Wd St	43 F3
James St	42 B4	Luke St	43 E7
Janet St	43 H4	Lyceum Pl	42 D4
Jasmine Cl	43 E1	Lydia Ann St	42 C5
Jenkinson St	42 E2	Lytton St	43 F2
Jermyn St	43 G7		
Jet Cl	43 H1	**M**	
John Lennon Dr	43 G2	Maddrell St	42 B1
John Moores Cl	43 F5	Madelaine St	43 F7
Johnson St	42 E2	Madeley St	43 H1
John St	42 D6	Magdala St	43 H6
Jordan St	42 D6	Maitland Cl	43 H6
Jubilee Dr	43 G3	Malden Rd	43 H2
Judges Dr	43 J1	Mallow Rd	43 H2
Judges Way	43 J1	Malt St	43 G5
Juvenal Pl	42 D1	Malvern Rd	43 H2
Juvenal St	42 D2	Manchester St	42 C3
		Manesty's La	42 C4
K		Manfred St	43 F3
Keble St	43 G2	Mann Island	42 B4
Kelso Rd	43 J2	Mann St	42 D7
Kelvin Gro	43 G7	Mansell Rd	43 H2
Kempston St	42 E3	Mansfield St	42 D2
Kenley Cl	43 H1	Manton Rd	43 H2
Kensington	43 G3	Maple Gro	43 H7
Kensington	43 G3	Marathon Cl	43 F1
Kensington St	43 G2	Marcot Rd	43 J1
Kent St	42 D5	Margaret St	43 F1
Kilshaw St	43 G1	Mariners Wf	42 C7
Kimberley Cl	43 F6	Maritime Pl	42 E2
Kinder St	43 F2	Maritime Way	42 C5
King Edward St	42 B3	Marlborough St	42 C2
Kinglake St	43 G4	Marlsford St	43 H2
Kings Dock St	42 C6	Marmaduke St	43 G4
Kingsley Rd	43 G6	Marquis St	42 E3
Kings Par	42 B5	Marsden St	43 F2
Kingsway Ct	42 C1	Marsden Way	43 F2
Kingswell Cl	43 G4	Marshall Pl	42 C1
Kitchen St	42 C6	Martensen St	43 G4
Knight St	42 D5	Marvin St	43 G2
		Marybone	42 C3
L		Maryland St	43 E5
Lace St	42 C3	Mason St	43 G4
Ladybower Cl	43 H5	Mathew St	42 C4
Laggan St	43 H3	Maud St	43 F7
Lairds Pl	42 C1	Maxton Rd	43 H2
Lakeland Cl	42 C5	Mayfair Cl	43 H1
Lambert Way	42 E3	May Pl	42 E4
Lamport St	42 E7	May St	42 E4
Lance Cl	43 F1	Melda Cl	43 F2
Langley St	42 E7	Melville Pl	43 F5
Langsdale St	42 E2	Merlin St	43 F7
Langton Rd	43 J6	Michael Dragonette Ct	42 C1
Lanyork Rd	42 B2	Midghall St	42 C2
Laurel Gro	43 H7	Mile End	42 C1
Lavan Cl	42 E2	Millennium Pl	43 G7
Lawrence Rd	43 J6	Mill La	42 D3
Lawton St	42 D4	Mill Rd	43 F1
Laxey St	42 E7	Mill St	42 E7
Leece St	42 E5	Millvale St	43 H1
Leeds St	42 B2	Milroy St	43 H4
Leigh St	43 F7	Milverton St	43 H4
Leigh St (Edge Hill)	43 J4	Minshull St	43 F4
Lemon Cl	43 J2	Minster Ct	43 F5
Lemon Gro	43 H7	Minto Cl	43 H3
Leopold Rd	43 G4	Minto St	43 H3
Lesseps Rd	43 H6	Mirfield St	43 H2
Lestock St	42 E6	Molyneux Rd	43 G2
Liffey St	43 G5	Montgomery Way	43 H1
Lightwood Dr	43 H3	Moorfields	42 C3
Lightwood St	43 H3	Moor Pl	42 D3
Lilley Rd	43 J2	Moor St	42 B4
Lilly Vale	43 J2	Morden St	43 H1
Lime Gro	43 H7	Moss Gro	43 H7
Lime St	42 C3	Mount Pleasant	42 D4
Lincoln Cl	43 J2	Mount St	42 E5
Lindley Cl	43 H5		

Mount Vernon Grn 43 G3
Mount Vernon Rd 43 F4
Mount Vernon St 43 F3
Mozart Cl 43 G7
Muirhead Av 43 H1
Mulberry Pl 43 F5
Mulberry St 43 F5
Mulgrave St 43 F6
Mulliner St 43 J6
Myrtle St 43 E5

N
Navigation Wf 42 C7
Naylor St 42 C2
Needham Rd 43 H3
Nelson Rd 43 G4
Nelson St 42 D6
Netherfield Rd S 42 E1
Nevin St 43 F2
Nevison St 43 G4
New Bird St 42 D6
New Grey Rock Cl 43 G1
Newhall St 42 D6
New Henderson St 42 D7
Newington 42 D4
New Quay 42 B3
New Red Rock Vw 43 G1
Newsham Dr 43 H1
Newstead Rd 43 H6
Newton Way 43 E4
Noel St 43 H6
Norfolk St 42 C6
Norman St 43 E3
Northbrook Cl 43 G6
North Brook St 43 F6
Northcote Cl 43 F1
North John St 42 C3
North St 42 C3
North Vw 43 G4
Norton St 42 D3
Norwood Gro 43 H1
Nuttall St 43 H4

O
Oakes St 43 E3
Oakham St 42 D7
O'Connell Rd 42 C1
Odsey St 43 H3
Oil St 42 A1
Old Coll Pl 43 H4
Old Hall St 42 B3
Oldham St 42 D5
Old Leeds St 42 B3
Olympia St 43 G2
Onslow Rd 43 J2
Opal Cl 43 G1
Orange Gro 43 H7
O'Reilly Ct 42 B1
Oriel Steet 42 C2
Ormond St 42 B3
Orphan St 43 F5
Orthes St 43 E4
Ottley St 43 J2
Overbury St 43 G4
Overton St 43 G4
Oxendale Cl 43 G6
Oxford St 43 E4
Oxford St E 43 G4

P
Paddington 43 F4
Page Wk 42 E2
Paisley St 42 A2
Pall Mall 42 B2
Paradise St 42 C5

Parker St 42 D4
Park La 42 C5
Park Pl 42 E7
Park Rd 43 E7
Parkside St 43 F2
Park Way 43 F6
Parliament Cl 42 E6
Parliament St 42 D6
Parr St 42 D5
Parton St 43 J2
Paul McCartney Way 43 H2
Paul Orr Ct 42 B1
Paul St 42 C2
Pavilion Cl 43 G6
Pear Gro 43 H2
Pearl Way 43 G1
Peet St 43 H4
Pembroke Gdns 43 E3
Pembroke Pl 42 E3
Pembroke St 43 E4
Penarth Cl 43 G5
Pendine Cl 43 H1
Penlinken Dr 43 H1
Penvalley Cres 43 H1
Peover St 42 D2
Pera Cl 43 G2
Percy St 43 E6
Perrygate Cl 43 G5
Perry St 42 D7
Perth St 43 G2
Peter's Arcade 42 C4
Peter St 42 C3
Phillimore Rd 43 H2
Pickop St 42 C3
Pickwick St 43 E7
Picton Rd 43 J5
Pilgrim St 42 E5
Pimhill Cl 43 G7
Pine Ms 42 E6
Pinetop Cl 43 H1
Pitt St 42 D5
Pleasant St 42 E4
Plimsoll St 43 H4
Plumpton St 43 F1
Pomfret St 43 F7
Pomona St 42 E4
Pond Cl 43 H1
Ponsonby St 43 G7
Porter St 42 A1
Portland Pl 42 D1
Portwood Cl 43 G5
Pownall Sq 42 C3
Pownall St 42 C5
Prescot Rd 43 J2
Prescot St 43 F3
Preston St 42 C3
Price St 42 C5
Primrose Hill 42 C3
Prince Albert Ms 42 D6
Prince Edwin St 42 D1
Princes Av 43 F6
Princes Gdns 42 B2
Princes Par 42 A3
Princes Pk 43 G7
Princes Rd 43 F6
Princes St 42 C3
Prince William St 42 D7
Prospect St 43 F3
Providence Cres 42 D7
Prussia St 42 B3
Pudsey St 42 D3
Pumpfields Rd 42 B2
Pythian Cl 43 G2
Pythian St 43 F2

Q
Queen Anne St 42 D2
Queensland St 43 G4
Queens Sq 42 D3
Queens Wf 42 B6
Quorn St 43 H3

R
Rachel St 42 D1
Radstock Rd 43 J2
Raffles St 42 D6
Rainford Gdns 42 C4
Rainford Sq 42 C4
Ranelagh St 42 D4
Raven Cl 43 F2
Raymond Pl 42 C1
Red Cross St 42 B4
Redgrave St 43 H3
Redmires Cl 43 H5
Red Rock St 43 G1
Regent St 42 A1
Renfrew St 43 G3
Renshaw St 42 D4
Reservoir St 43 F1
Reynolds St 43 G1
Rialto Cl 43 F6
Rice St 42 E5
Richardson St 43 J6
Richmond Row 42 D2
Richmond St 42 C4
Ridley Rd 43 H2
Rigby St 42 B3
Ringo Starr Dr 43 H2
Ritson St 43 G7
River Avon St 43 H6
Roberts St 42 A2
Roderick St 42 E2
Rodney St 42 E5
Roe St 42 D3
Rokeby Cl 42 E2
Rokeby St 42 E2
Rokesmith Av 43 H5
Romer Rd 43 H2
Romilly St 43 G2
Roscastle Cl 43 G2
Roscoe La 42 D5
Roscoe St 42 E4
Roscommon St 42 D1
Roseberry St 43 F6
Rose Hill 42 D2
Rosemary Cl 43 G4
Rose Pl 42 D2
Rothsay Cl 42 E1
Rothwell St 43 G1
Royal Mail St 42 D4
Royston St 43 G4
Rufford Rd 43 J2
Rumford Pl 42 B3
Rumford St 42 B3
Rupert Dr 43 F2
Russel St 42 E3
Ryedale Cl 43 G6

S
St. Andrew St 42 E4
St. Anne St 42 D2
St. Bride St 43 F5
St. James Pl 42 D6
St. James Rd 42 E6
St. James St 42 D6
St. John's La 42 D3
St. Josephs Cres 42 D2
St. Martins Ms 42 D1
St. Michaels Gro 43 H1
St. Nicholas Pl 42 A4

St. Stephen's Pl 42 C2
Salisbury Rd 43 J6
Salisbury St 42 E1
Salthouse Quay 42 B5
Saltney St 42 A1
Sandhead St 43 J5
Sandino St 42 E7
Sandon St 43 F5
Saxon Cl 43 G1
Saxony Rd 43 G3
Scholar St 43 J6
Schomberg St 43 G2
School La 42 C4
Scotland Rd 42 D2
Seaport Rd 43 G7
Seddon St 42 C5
Seel St 42 C4
Sefton Pk Rd 43 H7
Sefton St 42 C6
Selborne Cl 43 F6
Selborne St 43 F6
Selsey Cl 43 H5
Severs St 43 G1
Seymour St 42 E3
Shakespeare Cl 43 G1
Shallcross St 43 G1
Shaws All 42 C5
Shaw St 43 E1
Sheil Rd 43 H1
Shenstone St 43 G4
Shepherd's Fold Cl 43 G7
Sherwood St 43 B1
Shimmin St 43 G4
Sidney Pl 43 G4
Silkstone Cl 43 H5
Simpson St 42 C6
Sim St 42 E2
Sirdar Cl 43 H5
Sir Thomas St 42 C3
Skelhorne St 42 D5
Slater St 42 D5
Smithdown La 43 F4
Smithdown Rd 43 H6
Smithfield St 42 C3
Soho Pl 42 E2
Soho St 42 E2
Solomon St 43 H3
Solway St E 43 H6
Solway St W 43 G6
South Chester St 42 E7
Southern Cres 42 D7
South Ferry Quay 42 C7
South Hunter St 43 E5
South John St 42 C4
Sparling St 42 C6
Spekeland Rd 43 H5
Spencer St 43 F1
Spindle Cl 43 F1
Spofforth Rd 43 J5
Sprainger St 42 B1
Springfield 42 D2
Squires St 43 G4
Stafford St 42 E3
Stamford St 43 H3
Standish St 42 C3
Stanhope St 42 D7
Stanier Way 43 H4
Stanley St 42 C3
Star St 42 D7
Steinberg Ct 42 B1
Sterndale Cl 43 H5
Stockdale Cl 42 C2
Stone St 42 B1
Stowell St 43 E5
Strada Way 43 E2
Strand, The 42 B4

Strand St 42 B4
Strathmore Rd 43 H1
Strauss Cl 43 H7
Suffolk St 42 D5
Sugnall St 43 E5
Summer Seat 42 C1
Surrey St 42 C5
Sutcliffe St 43 H2
Sweeting St 42 B4
Swindale Cl 43 G6
Swiss Rd 43 J2

T
Tabley St 42 C6
Tace Cl 43 F6
Tagus Cl 43 G7
Tamar Cl 43 F1
Tarleton St 42 C4
Tatlock St 42 C1
Tavy Rd 43 F1
Teck St 43 G3
Teign Cl 43 F1
Tempest Hey 42 B3
Temple Ct 42 C4
Temple La 42 C3
Temple St 42 C3
Tenterden St 42 C1
Thackeray Pl 43 F7
Thames St 43 G7
Thomas St Way 42 C5
Thorburn St 43 H4
Thornes Rd 43 G2
Tichbourne Way 43 F2
Tideswell Cl 43 H5
Timpron St 43 H5
Titchfield St 42 C1
Tithebarn St 42 B3
Tobin Cl 42 C1
Toft St 43 H3
Tom Mann Cl 42 D3
Tordelow Cl 43 F1
Tower Gdns 42 B4
Trafalgar Way 43 F2
Trowbridge St 42 E4
Trueman St 42 C3
Tudor St N 43 H2
Tudor St S 43 H2
Tulloch St 43 G2
Tunnel Rd 43 H5
Tunstall St 43 J6
Tweed Cl 43 H1
Twomey Cl 42 C1

U
Underley St 43 J6
Union Ct 42 C4
Union St 42 B3
Upper Baker St 43 G2
Upper Beau St 42 D1
Upper Bute St 42 E1
Upper Duke St 42 D5
Upper Frederick St 42 C5
Upper Hampton St 43 F6
Upper Harrington St 42 D7
Upper Hill St 43 E7
Upper Hope Pl 43 E5
Upper Mann St 42 D7
Upper Mason St 43 G4
Upper Newington 42 D4
Upper Parliament St 42 D6
Upper Pitt St 42 D6
Upper Pownall St 42 C5
Upper Stanhope St 43 E6
Upper Warwick St 43 E7
Upper William St 42 B1
Uxbridge St 43 H5

V
Vandries St 42 A1
Vandyke St 43 H6
Vauxhall Rd 42 C2
Vernon St 42 C3
Verulam Cl 43 G6
Victoria St 42 C4
Village St 43 E1
Vincent Ct 42 D5
Vining St 43 F7
Virgil St 42 D1
Voelas St 43 G7
Vronhill Cl 43 G7
Vulcan St 42 A1

W
Wainwright Cl 43 H5
Wakefield St 42 D2
Waldron Cl 42 C2
Walker St 43 F2
Wall St 42 C4
Walsh Cl 42 C1
Wapping 42 C5
Ward St 42 D3
Warwick St 42 E7
Waterloo Quay 42 A2
Water St 42 B4
Watkinson St 42 C6
Watmough St 42 E1
Wavertree Boul 43 J4
Wavertree Rd 43 G4
Webb Cl 43 H4
Webb St 43 H6
Webster Rd 43 J6
Webster St 42 C3
Wedgewood St 43 H3
Wendell St 43 H6
Wentworth Dr 43 F1
West Derby Rd 43 G2
West Derby St 43 F3
Westmorland Dr 42 C2
Whitcroft Rd 43 J2
Whitechapel 42 C4
Whitefield Rd 43 G1
Whitefield Way 43 G1
White Rock Ct 43 G1
White Rock St 43 G1
Whithorn St 43 J5
Whitland Rd 43 J1
Whitley St 42 B1
Whittier St 43 H6
Wightman St 43 G2
Wilde St 42 D3
Wilfer Cl 43 H5
William Brown St 42 D3
William Henry St 42 E2
Williamson St 42 C4
Wimpole St 43 H3
Windsor St 43 E6
Windsor Vw 43 H6
Winifred St 43 H4
Winter St 43 F2
Wolstenholme Sq 42 D5
Woodside St 43 H4
Wood St 42 D4
Wordsworth St 43 H6
Wrayburn Cl 43 H5
Wrenbury St 43 H3
Wynnstay St 43 G7

Y
Yanwath St 43 H6
York St 42 C5

London street index

A
Abbey Orchard St SW1 44 D6
Abingdon St SW1 44 E6
Achilles Way W1 44 A5
Adam & Eve Ct W1 44 C2
Adams Row W1 44 A4
Adam St WC2 45 E4
Addington St SE1 45 F6
Addle Hill EC4 45 H3
Adelaide St WC2 44 E4
Adeline Pl WC1 44 D2
Adelphi Ter WC2 45 E4
Agar St WC2 44 E4
Air St W1 44 C4
Alaska St SE1 45 G5
Albany W1 44 C4
Albany Ctyd W1 44 C4

Albemarle St W1 44 B4
Albemarle Way EC1 45 H1
Albert Barnes Ho SE1 45 J7
Albion Pl EC1 45 H1
Albion Way EC1 45 J2
Aldburgh Ms W1 44 A2
Aldermanbury EC2 45 J2
Aldermanbury Sq EC2 45 J2
Aldersgate St EC1 45 J2
Aldford St W1 44 A4
Aldwych WC2 45 F3
Alfred Ms W1 44 D1
Alfred Pl WC1 44 D1
Allington St SW1 44 C7
All Souls Pl W1 44 B2
Ambassador's Ct SW1 44 C5
Ambrosden Av SW1 44 C7
Amen Cor EC4 45 H3

Amen Ct EC4 45 H2
America St SE1 45 J5
Andrew Borde St WC2 44 D2
Andrewes Ho EC2 45 J2
Andrews Crosse WC2 45 G3
Angel Ct SW1 44 C5
Angel St EC1 45 J2
Apothecary St EC4 45 H3
Apple Tree Yd SW1 44 C4
Apsley Way W1 44 A5
Aquinas St SE1 45 G4
Archer St W1 44 D1
Arch St SE1 45 J7
Argyll St W1 44 C3
Aria Ho WC2 45 E2
Arlington St SW1 44 C4

Arne St WC2 45 E3
Arneway St SW1 44 D7
Arrol Ho SE1 45 J7
Artillery Mans SW1 44 D6
Artillery Pl SW1 44 D7
Artillery Row SW1 44 D7
Arundel Gt Ct WC2 45 F3
Arundel St WC2 45 F3
Ashenden SE17 45 J7
Ashentree Ct EC4 45 G3
Ashland Pl W1 44 A1
Ashley Gdns SW1 44 C7
Ashley Pl SW1 44 C7
Astbury Ho SE11 45 G7
Audley Sq W1 44 A4
Austral St SE11 45 H7
Ave Maria La EC4 45 H3
Avery Row W1 44 B3

Avonmouth St SE1 45 J6
Avon Pl SE1 45 J6
Aybrook St W1 44 A2
Aylesbury St EC1 45 H1
Ayres St SE1 45 J5

B
Babmaes St SW1 44 D4
Back Hill EC1 45 G1
Bainbridge St WC1 44 D2
Baker's Ms W1 44 A2
Baker's Row EC1 45 G1
Baker's Yd EC1 45 G1
Balderton St W1 44 A3
Baldwin's Gdns EC1 45 G1
Balfour Ms W1 44 A4
Balfour Pl W1 44 A4

Baltic St W EC1 45 J1
Banbury Ct WC2 44 E3
Bank End SE1 45 J4
Banks Ho SE1 45 J7
Bankside SE1 45 J4
Bankside Lofts SE1 45 H4
Banner St EC1 45 J1
Barbican EC2 45 J2
Barbican, The EC2 45 E1
Barge Ho St SE1 45 G4
Barkham Ter SE1 45 G6
Barley Mow Pas EC1 45 H1
Barlow Pl W1 44 B4
Barnard's Inn EC1 45 G2
Barons Pl SE1 45 G6
Barrett St W1 44 A3
Barter St WC1 45 E2

Bartholomew Cl EC1 **45** J2
Bartholomew Pl EC1 **45** J2
Bartlett Ct EC4 **45** G2
Bartletts Pas EC4 **45** G2
Barton St SW1 **44** E6
Bastion Highwalk EC2 **45** J2
Bateman's Bldgs W1 **44** D3
Bateman St W1 **44** D3
Bath Ct EC1 **45** G1
Bath Ter SE1 **45** J7
Bayley St WC1 **44** D2
Baylis Rd SE1 **45** G6
Beak St W1 **44** C3
Bear All EC4 **45** H2
Bear Gdns SE1 **45** J4
Bear La SE1 **45** H4
Bear St WC2 **44** D3
Beauchamp St EC1 **45** G2
Beaumont Ms W1 **44** A1
Beaumont St W1 **44** A1
Bedford Av WC1 **44** D2
Bedfordbury WC2 **44** E3
Bedford Ct WC2 **44** E4
Bedford Pl WC1 **44** E1
Bedford Row WC1 **45** F1
Bedford Sq WC1 **44** D2
Bedford St WC2 **44** E3
Bedford Way WC1 **44** D1
Bedlam Ms SE11 **45** G7
Beech St EC2 **45** J1
Beeston Pl SW1 **44** B7
Belgrave Ms N SW1 **44** A6
Belgrave Ms S SW1 **44** A6
Belgrave Ms W SW1 **44** A6
Belgrave Pl SW1 **44** A6
Belgrave Sq SW1 **44** A6
Belgrave Yd SW1 **44** B7
Belgravia SW1 **44** A7
Bell Wf La EC4 **45** J4
Bell Yd WC2 **45** G2
Belvedere Bldgs SE1 **45** H6
Belvedere Pl SE1 **45** H6
Belvedere Rd SE1 **45** F5
Benjamin St EC1 **45** H1
Bennet's Hill EC4 **45** H3
Bennet St SW1 **44** C4
Bennett St SW1 **44** C4
Bennetts Yd SW1 **44** D7
Bentinck Ms W1 **44** A2
Bentinck St W1 **44** A2
Berkeley Sq W1 **44** B4
Berkeley St W1 **44** B4
Bernard St WC1 **44** E1
Berners Ms W1 **44** C2
Berners Pl W1 **44** C2
Berners St W1 **44** C2
Berwick St W1 **44** D3
Betterton St WC2 **44** E3
Bingham Pl W1 **44** A1
Binney St W1 **44** A3
Birdcage Wk SW1 **44** C6
Bird St W1 **44** A3
Bishop's Ct EC4 **45** H2
Bishop's Ct WC2 **45** G2
Bishops Ter SE11 **45** G7
Bittern St SE1 **45** J6
Blackburne's Ms W1 **44** A3
Blackfriars Br EC4 **45** H3
Blackfriars Br SE1 **45** H3
Blackfriars Ct EC4 **45** H3
Black Friars La EC4 **45** H3
Blackfriars Pas EC4 **45** H3
Blackfriars Rd SE1 **45** H6
Bleeding Heart Yd EC1 **45** G2
Blenheim St W1 **44** B3
Bloomfield Pl W1 **44** B3
Bloomsbury WC1 **44** D2
Bloomsbury Ct WC1 **45** E2
Bloomsbury Pl WC1 **45** E1
Bloomsbury Sq WC1 **45** E2
Bloomsbury St WC1 **44** D2
Bloomsbury Way WC1 **44** E2
Blore Ct W1 **44** D3
Blue Ball Yd SW1 **44** C5
Bolsover St W1 **44** B1
Bolt Ct EC4 **45** G3
Bolton St W1 **44** B4
Book Ms WC2 **44** D3
Booth La EC4 **45** J3
Booth's Pl W1 **44** C2
Borough, The SE1 **45** J6
Borough High St SE1 **45** J6
Borough Rd SE1 **45** H6
Borough Sq SE1 **45** J6
Boscobel Pl SW1 **44** A7
Boswell Ct WC1 **45** E1
Boswell St WC1 **45** E1
Boundary Row SE1 **45** H5
Bourchier St W1 **44** D3
Bourdon Pl W1 **44** B3
Bourdon St W1 **44** B3
Bourlet Cl W1 **44** C2

Bourne Est EC1 **45** G1
Bouverie St EC4 **45** G3
Bow Chyd EC4 **45** J3
Bow La EC4 **45** J3
Bow St WC2 **45** E3
Boyce St SE1 **45** F5
Boyfield St SE1 **45** H6
Boyle St W1 **44** C3
Brackley St EC1 **45** J1
Brad St SE1 **45** G5
Bread St EC4 **45** J3
Bream's Bldgs EC4 **45** G2
Briant Est SE1 **45** G7
Briant Ho SE1 **45** F7
Brick Ct EC4 **45** G3
Brick St W1 **44** B5
Bride Ct EC4 **45** H3
Bride La EC4 **45** H3
Bridewell Pl EC4 **45** H3
Bridford Ms W1 **44** B1
Bridge Pl SW1 **44** B7
Bridge St SW1 **44** E6
Bridgewater Sq EC2 **45** J1
Bridgewater St EC2 **45** J1
Bridle La W1 **44** C3
Brinton Wk SE1 **45** H5
Briset St EC1 **45** H1
Britton St EC1 **45** H1
Broadbent St W1 **44** B3
Broad Ct WC2 **45** E3
Broad Sanctuary SW1 **44** D6
Broadstone Pl W1 **44** A2
Broad Wk W1 **44** A4
Broadwall SE1 **45** G4
Broadway SW1 **44** D6
Broadwick St W1 **44** C3
Broad Yd EC1 **45** H1
Broken Wf EC4 **45** J3
Bromley Pl W1 **44** C1
Brook Dr SE11 **45** G7
Brooke's Ct EC1 **45** G1
Brookes Mkt EC1 **45** G1
Brooke St EC1 **45** G2
Brook's Ms W1 **44** B3
Brook St W1 **44** A3
Brown Hart Gdns W1 **44** A3
Browning Ms W1 **44** B2
Brownlow Ms WC1 **45** F1
Brownlow St WC1 **45** F2
Brunswick Sq WC1 **45** E1
Bruton La W1 **44** B4
Bruton Pl W1 **44** B4
Bruton St W1 **44** B4
Brydges Pl WC2 **44** E4
Buckingham Arc WC2 **45** E4
Buckingham Gate SW1 **44** C6
Buckingham Ms SW1 **44** C6
Buckingham Pl SW1 **44** C6
Buckingham St WC2 **45** E4
Buckley St SE1 **45** G5
Bucknall St WC2 **44** D2
Bull Inn Ct WC2 **45** E4
Bulstrode Pl W1 **44** A2
Bulstrode St W1 **44** A2
Burdett St SE1 **45** G6
Burgon St EC4 **45** H3
Burleigh St WC2 **45** F3
Burlington Arc W1 **44** C4
Burlington Gdns W1 **44** C4
Burrell St SE1 **45** H4
Burrows Ms SE1 **45** H5
Bury Pl WC1 **45** E2
Bury St WC1 **44** C4
Butler Pl SW1 **44** D6
Byng Pl WC1 **44** D1
Byword Pl WC1 **44** C2

C

Cadogan La SW1 **44** A7
Cahill St EC1 **45** J1
Caleb St SE1 **45** J5
Cambridge Circ WC2 **44** D3
Candover St W1 **44** C2
Cannon St EC4 **45** J3
Canon Row SW1 **44** E6
Canterbury Ho SE1 **45** F6
Canvey St SE1 **45** H4
Capener's Cl SW1 **44** A6
Capper St WC1 **44** C1
Carburton St W1 **44** B1
Carey La EC2 **45** J2
Carey St WC2 **45** F3
Carlisle La SE1 **45** F7
Carlisle Pl SW1 **44** C7
Carlisle St W1 **44** D3
Carlos Pl W1 **44** A4
Carlton Gdns SW1 **44** D5

Carlton Ho Ter SW1 **44** D5
Carlton St SW1 **44** D4
Carmelite St EC4 **45** G3
Carnaby St W1 **44** C3
Carpenter St W1 **44** B4
Carrington St W1 **44** B5
Carteret St SW1 **44** D6
Carter La EC4 **45** H3
Carthusian St EC1 **45** J1
Carting La WC2 **45** E4
Castle Baynard St EC4 **45** H3
Castlebrook Cl SE11 **45** H7
Castle La SW1 **44** C6
Castle Yd SE1 **45** H4
Cathedral Piazza SW1 **44** C7
Cathedral Wk SW1 **44** C6
Catherine Pl SW1 **44** C6
Catherine St WC2 **45** F3
Catherine Wheel Yd SW1 **44** C5
Catton St WC1 **45** F2
Cavendish Ms N W1 **44** B1
Cavendish Ms S W1 **44** B2
Cavendish Pl W1 **44** B2
Cavendish Sq W1 **44** B2
Caxton St SW1 **44** C6
Cecil Ct WC2 **44** D4
Centaur St SE1 **45** F6
Centrepoint WC1 **44** D2
Chadwick St SW1 **44** D7
Chancel St SE1 **45** H4
Chancery La WC2 **45** G2
Chandos Pl WC2 **44** E4
Chandos St W1 **44** B2
Chapel Pl W1 **44** B3
Chapel St SW1 **44** A6
Chaplin Cl SE1 **45** G5
Chapone Pl W1 **44** D3
Chapter Ho Ct EC4 **45** J3
Charing Cross SW1 **44** D4
Charing Cross Rd WC2 **44** D2
Charles II St SW1 **44** D4
Charles St W1 **44** B4
Charlotte Ms W1 **44** C1
Charlotte Pl W1 **44** C2
Charlotte St W1 **44** C1
Charterhouse, The EC1 **45** H1
Charterhouse Bldgs EC1 **45** H1
Charterhouse Ms EC1 **45** H1
Charterhouse Sq EC1 **45** H1
Charterhouse St EC1 **45** G2
Cheapside EC2 **45** J3
Chenies Ms WC1 **44** D1
Chenies St WC1 **44** D1
Chequer St EC1 **45** J1
Cherry Tree Wk EC1 **45** J1
Chesham Cl SW1 **44** A7
Chesham Ms SW1 **44** A6
Chesham Pl SW1 **44** A7
Chesham St SW1 **44** A7
Cheshire Ct EC4 **45** G3
Chester Cl SW1 **44** A6
Chesterfield Gdns W1 **44** B4
Chesterfield Hill W1 **44** B4
Chesterfield St W1 **44** B4
Chester Ms SW1 **44** B6
Chester Sq SW1 **44** B7
Chester Sq Ms SW1 **44** B7
Chester St SW1 **44** A6
Chicheley St SE1 **45** F5
Chichester Rents WC2 **45** G2
Chiltern St W1 **44** A1
Ching Ct WC2 **44** E3
Chiswell St EC1 **45** J1
Chitty St W1 **44** C1
Christ Ch Pas EC1 **45** H2
Church Entry EC4 **45** H3
Church Pl SW1 **44** C4
Churchyard Row SE1 **45** H7
Clare Mkt WC2 **45** F3
Clarges Ms W1 **44** B4
Clarges St W1 **44** B4
Clarke's Ms W1 **44** A1
Clement's Inn WC2 **45** F3
Clement's Inn Pas WC2 **45** F3
Clennam St SE1 **45** J5
Clerkenwell EC1 **45** H1
Clerkenwell Grn EC1 **45** G1
Clerkenwell Rd EC1 **45** G1
Cleveland Ms W1 **44** C1
Cleveland Pl SW1 **44** C4
Cleveland Row SW1 **44** C5
Cleveland St W1 **44** C1
Clifford's Inn Pas EC4 **45** G3
Clifford St W1 **44** C4
Clink St SE1 **45** J4
Clipstone Ms W1 **44** C1

Clipstone St W1 **44** B1
Cliveden Pl SW1 **44** A7
Cloak La EC4 **45** J3
Cloth Ct EC1 **45** H2
Cloth Fair EC1 **45** H2
Cloth St EC1 **45** J1
Coach & Horses Yd W1 **44** B3
Coburg Cl SW1 **44** C7
Cock La EC1 **45** H2
Cockpit Steps SW1 **44** D6
Cockpit Yd WC1 **45** F1
Cockspur Ct SW1 **44** D4
Cockspur St SW1 **44** D4
Coin St SE1 **45** G4
Cole St SE1 **45** J6
Coley St WC1 **45** F1
College Hill EC4 **45** J3
College Ms SW1 **44** E6
College St EC4 **45** J3
Collinson St SE1 **45** J6
Collinson Wk SE1 **45** J6
Colnbrook St SE1 **45** H7
Colombo St SE1 **45** H5
Colonnade WC1 **44** E1
Colville Pl W1 **44** C2
Computer Pass EC2 **45** J2
Concert Hall App SE1 **45** F5
Conduit Ct WC2 **44** E3
Conduit St W1 **44** B3
Cons St SE1 **45** G5
Constitution Hill SW1 **44** B5
Conway Ms W1 **44** C1
Conway St W1 **44** C1
Cooper Cl SE1 **45** G6
Copeland Ho SE11 **45** F7
Copperfield St SE1 **45** H5
Coptic St WC1 **44** E2
Coral St SE1 **45** G6
Coram St WC1 **44** E1
Cork St W1 **44** C4
Cork St Ms W1 **44** C4
Corner Ho St WC2 **44** E4
Cornwall Rd SE1 **45** G4
Cosmo Pl WC1 **45** E1
Cosser St SE1 **45** G6
Cottesloe Ms SE1 **45** G6
County St SE1 **45** J7
Covent Gdn WC2 **45** E3
Covent Gdn Mkt WC2 **45** E3
Coventry St W1 **44** D4
Cowcross St EC1 **45** H1
Cowley St SW1 **44** E6
Craigs Ct SW1 **44** E4
Cramer St W1 **44** A2
Cranbourn St WC2 **44** D3
Crane Ct EC4 **45** G3
Cranfield Row SE1 **45** G6
Craven Pas WC2 **44** E4
Craven St WC2 **44** E4
Crawford Pas EC1 **45** G1
Creed La EC4 **45** H3
Crescent Row EC1 **45** J1
Cripplegate St EC2 **45** J1
Cromwell Twr EC2 **45** J1
Cross Keys Cl W1 **44** A2
Cross Keys Sq EC1 **45** J2
Crown Ct EC2 **45** J3
Crown Ct WC2 **45** E3
Crown Office Row EC4 **45** G3
Crown Pas SW1 **44** C5
Cubitts Yd WC2 **45** E3
Cuddington SE17 **45** J7
Culross St W1 **44** A4
Cursitor St EC4 **45** G2
Curzon Gate W1 **44** A5
Curzon Sq W1 **44** A5
Curzon St W1 **44** A5
Cut, The SE1 **45** G5
Cypress Pl W1 **44** C1

D

Dacre St SW1 **44** D6
Dane St WC1 **45** F2
Dansey Pl W1 **44** D3
Dante Pl SE11 **45** H7
Dante Rd SE11 **45** H7
D'Arblay St W1 **44** C3
Dartmouth St SW1 **44** D6
Davidge St SE1 **45** H6
Davies Ms W1 **44** B3
Davies St W1 **44** B3
Deacon Way SE17 **45** J7
Dean Bradley St SW1 **44** E7
Deanery Ms W1 **44** A4
Deanery St W1 **44** A4
Dean Farrar St SW1 **44** D6
Dean Ryle St SW1 **44** E7
Deans Ct EC4 **45** H3
Deans Ms W1 **44** B2
Dean Stanley St SW1 **44** E7
Dean St W1 **44** D2
Dean's Yd SW1 **44** D6

Dean Trench St SW1 **44** E7
Denman St W1 **44** D4
Denmark Pl WC2 **44** D2
Denmark St WC2 **44** D3
Derby Gate SW1 **44** E5
Derby St W1 **44** A5
Dering St W1 **44** B3
Devereux Ct WC2 **45** G3
Devonshire Cl W1 **44** B1
Devonshire Ms N W1 **44** B1
Devonshire Ms S W1 **44** B1
Devonshire Ms W W1 **44** B1
Devonshire Pl W1 **44** A1
Devonshire Pl Ms W1 **44** A1
Devonshire Row Ms W1 **44** B1
Devonshire St W1 **44** A1
De Walden St W1 **44** A2
Diadem Ct W1 **44** D3
Dickens Ms EC1 **45** H1
Dickens Sq SE1 **45** J6
Disney Pl SE1 **45** J5
Disney St SE1 **45** J5
Distaff La EC4 **45** J3
Doby Ct EC4 **45** J3
Dodson St SE1 **45** G6
Dolben St SE1 **45** H5
Dombey St WC1 **45** F1
Doon St SE1 **45** G5
Dorrington St EC1 **45** G1
Dorrit St SE1 **45** J5
Dorset Bldgs EC4 **45** H3
Dorset Ms SW1 **44** B6
Dorset Ri EC4 **45** H3
Doughty Ms WC1 **45** F1
Dover St W1 **44** B4
Dover Yd W1 **44** B4
Downing St SW1 **44** E5
Down St W1 **44** B5
Down St Ms W1 **44** B5
Doyce St SE1 **45** J5
D'Oyley St SW1 **44** A7
Drake St WC1 **45** F2
Draper Ho SE1 **45** H7
Drury La WC2 **45** E3
Dryden St WC2 **45** E3
Duchess Ms W1 **44** B2
Duchess St W1 **44** B2
Duchy Pl SE1 **45** G4
Duchy St SE1 **45** G4
Duck La W1 **44** D3
Dufferin St EC1 **45** J1
Dufour's Pl W1 **44** C3
Dugard Way SE11 **45** H7
Duke of Wellington Pl SW1 **44** A5
Duke of York St SW1 **44** C4
Duke's Ms W1 **44** A2
Duke St SW1 **44** C4
Duke St W1 **44** A2
Duke's Yd W1 **44** A3
Duncannon St WC2 **44** E4
Dunns Pas WC1 **45** E2
Dunstable Ms W1 **44** A1
Durham Ho St WC2 **45** E4
Dyer's Bldgs EC1 **45** G2
Dyott St WC1 **44** E2

E

Eagle Ct EC1 **45** H1
Eagle Pl SW1 **44** C4
Eagle St WC1 **45** F2
Earlham St WC2 **44** D3
Earnshaw St WC2 **44** D2
Easley's Ms W1 **44** A2
Eastcastle St W1 **44** C2
East Harding St EC4 **45** G2
East Pas EC1 **45** H1
East Poultry Av EC1 **44** H2
Eaton Gate SW1 **44** A7
Eaton La SW1 **44** B7
Eaton Ms N SW1 **44** A7
Eaton Ms S SW1 **44** A7
Eaton Ms W SW1 **44** A7
Eaton Pl SW1 **44** A7
Eaton Row SW1 **44** B6
Eaton Sq SW1 **44** B6
Eaton Ter SW1 **44** A7
Eaton Ter Ms SW1 **44** A7
Ebury Ms SW1 **44** B7
Ebury Ms E SW1 **44** B7
Ebury St SW1 **44** B7
Eccleston Br SW1 **44** B7
Eccleston Ms SW1 **44** A7
Eccleston Pl SW1 **44** B7
Eccleston St SW1 **44** B7
Edwards Ms W1 **44** A3
Elba Pl SE17 **45** J7
Elephant & Castle SE1 **45** H7
Elephant Rd SE17 **45** J7
Elizabeth Ct SW1 **44** D7
Elizabeth St SW1 **44** A7
Ellington Ho SE1 **45** J6

Elliotts Row SE11 **45** H7
Elm Ct EC4 **45** G3
Elm St WC1 **45** F1
Elverton St SW1 **44** D7
Ely Ct EC1 **45** G2
Ely Pl EC1 **45** G2
Embankment Pier WC2 **45** F4
Embankment Pl WC2 **45** E4
Emerald St WC1 **45** F1
Emerson St SE1 **45** J4
Emery Hill St SW1 **44** C7
Emery St SE1 **45** G6
Endell St WC2 **44** E2
Errol St EC1 **45** J1
Essex Ct EC4 **45** G3
Essex St WC2 **45** G3
Euston Rd NW1 **44** B1
Evelyn Yd W1 **44** D2
Ewer St SE1 **45** J5
Excel Ct WC2 **44** D4
Exchange Ct WC2 **45** E4
Exeter St WC2 **45** E3
Exton St SE1 **45** G5
Eyre St Hill EC1 **45** G1

F

Falconberg Ct W1 **44** D2
Falconberg Ms W1 **44** D2
Falcon Ct EC4 **45** G3
Falmouth Rd SE1 **45** J6
Fann St EC1 **45** J1
Fann St EC2 **45** J1
Fareham St W1 **44** D2
Farm St W1 **44** B4
Farnham Pl SE1 **45** H5
Farringdon La EC1 **45** G1
Farringdon St EC4 **45** H2
Faulkner's All EC1 **45** H1
Ferrybridge Ho SE11 **45** F7
Fetter La EC4 **45** G3
Field Ct WC1 **45** F2
Fisher St WC1 **45** E2
Fitzalan St SE11 **45** G7
Fitzhardinge St W1 **44** A2
Fitzmaurice Pl W1 **44** B4
Fitzroy Ct W1 **44** C1
Fitzroy Ms W1 **44** C1
Fitzroy Sq W1 **44** C1
Fitzroy St W1 **44** C1
Fives Ct SE11 **45** H7
Flaxman Ct W1 **44** D3
Fleet St EC4 **45** G3
Flitcroft St WC2 **44** D2
Floral St WC2 **44** E3
Florin Ct EC1 **45** J1
Foley St W1 **44** C2
Fore St EC2 **45** J2
Fortune St EC1 **45** J1
Forum Magnum Sq SE1 **45** F5
Foster La EC2 **45** J2
Foubert's Pl W1 **44** C3
Fountain Ct EC4 **45** G3
Fountain Sq SW1 **44** B7
Fox & Knot St EC1 **45** H1
Francis St SW1 **44** C7
Frazier St SE1 **45** G6
Friars Cl SE1 **45** H5
Friar St EC4 **45** H3
Friary Ct SW1 **44** C5
Friday St EC4 **45** J3
Frith St W1 **44** D3
Fulwood Pl WC1 **45** F2
Furnival St EC4 **45** G2
Fynes St SW1 **44** D7

G

Gabriel's Wf SE1 **45** G4
Gage St WC1 **45** E1
Galen Pl WC1 **45** E2
Gambia St SE1 **45** H5
Ganton St W1 **44** C3
Garbutt Pl W1 **44** A1
Garden Row SE1 **45** H7
Gardners La EC4 **45** J3
Garlick Hill EC4 **45** J3
Garrick St WC2 **45** E3
Garrick Yd WC2 **45** E3
Gate Ho Sq SE1 **45** J4
Gate St WC2 **45** F2
Gaunt St SE1 **45** H6
Gayfere St SW1 **44** E7
Gaywood Est SE1 **45** H7
Gaywood St SE1 **45** H7
Gees Ct W1 **44** A3
George Ct WC2 **45** E4
George Mathers Rd SE11 **45** H7
George Yd W1 **44** A3
Geraldine St SE11 **45** H7
Gerald Ms SW1 **44** A7
Gerald Rd SW1 **44** A7
Gerrard Pl W1 **44** D3

Gerrard St W1 44 D3
Gerridge St SE1 45 G6
Gilbert Pl WC1 44 E2
Gilbert St W1 44 A3
Gildea St W1 44 B2
Gillingham Row SW1 44 C7
Gillingham St SW1 44 B7
Giltspur St EC1 45 H2
Gladstone St SE1 45 H6
Glasshill St SE1 45 H5
Glasshouse St W1 44 C4
Glasshouse Yd EC1 45 J1
Globe St SE1 45 J6
Globe Yd W1 44 B3
Godliman St EC4 45 J3
Golden Jubilee Br SE1 45 F5
Golden Jubilee Br
  WC2 45 E4
Golden La EC1 45 J1
Golden La Est EC1 45 J1
Golden Sq W1 44 C3
Goldsmith St EC2 45 J2
Goodge Pl W1 44 C2
Goodge St W1 44 C2
Goodwins Ct WC2 44 E3
Gordon Sq WC1 44 D1
Gosfield St W1 44 C1
Goslett Yd WC2 44 D3
Goswell Rd EC1 45 J1
Gough Sq EC4 45 G2
Gower Ms WC1 44 C1
Grafton Ms W1 44 C1
Grafton St W1 44 B4
Grafton Way W1 44 C1
Grafton Way WC1 44 C1
Granby Pl SE1 45 G6
Grand Av EC1 45 H1
Grange Ct WC2 45 F3
Grantham Pl W1 44 B5
Granville Pl W1 44 A3
Grape St WC2 44 E2
Gray's Inn WC1 45 F1
Gray's Inn Pl WC1 45 F2
Gray's Inn Sq WC1 45 G1
Gray St SE1 45 G6
Gray's Yd W1 44 A3
Great Arthur Ho EC1 45 J1
Great Castle St W1 44 B2
Great Chapel St W1 44 D2
Great Coll St SW1 44 E6
Great Dover St SE1 45 J6
Great George St SW1 44 D6
Great Guildford St
  SE1 45 J4
Great James St WC1 45 F1
Great Marlborough St
  W1 44 C3
Great New St EC4 45 G2
Great Ormond St
  WC1 45 E1
Great Peter St SW1 44 D7
Great Portland St W1 44 B1
Great Pulteney St W1 44 C3
Great Queen St WC2 45 E3
Great Russell St WC1 44 D2
Great. St. Thomas
  Apostle EC4 45 J3
Great Scotland Yd
  SW1 44 E5
Great Smith St SW1 44 D6
Great Suffolk St SE1 45 H5
Great Sutton St EC1 45 H1
Great Titchfield St W1 44 C2
Great Trinity La EC4 45 J3
Great Turnstile WC1 45 F2
Great Windmill St W1 44 D3
Greek Ct W1 44 D3
Greek St W1 44 D3
Green Arbour Ct EC1 45 H2
Greencoat Pl SW1 44 C7
Greencoat Row SW1 44 C7
Greenham Cl SE1 45 G6
Green's Ct W1 44 D3
Greenwell St W1 44 B1
Greet St SE1 45 G5
Grenville St WC1 45 E1
Gresham St EC2 45 J2
Gresse St W1 44 D2
Greville St EC1 45 G2
Greycoat Pl SW1 44 D7
Greycoat St SW1 44 D7
Greyfriars Pas EC1 45 H2
Greystoke Pl EC4 45 G2
Grindal St SE1 45 G6
Groom Pl SW1 44 A6
Grosvenor Cotts SW1 44 A7
Grosvenor Cres SW1 44 A6
Grosvenor Cres Ms
  SW1 44 A6
Grosvenor Est SW1 44 D7
Grosvenor Gdns SW1 44 B6
Grosvenor Gdns Ms E
  SW1 44 B6

Grosvenor Gdns Ms N
  SW1 44 B7
Grosvenor Gdns Ms S
  SW1 44 B7
Grosvenor Hill W1 44 B3
Grosvenor Pl SW1 44 A6
Grosvenor Sq W1 44 A3
Grosvenor St W1 44 B3
Grotto Pas W1 44 A1
Groveland Ct EC4 45 J3
Guildhall Yd EC2 45 J2
Guildhouse St SW1 44 C7
Guilford Pl WC1 45 F1
Guilford St WC1 45 E1
Gunpowder Sq EC4 45 G2
Gutter La EC2 45 J2

H
Half Moon Ct EC1 45 J2
Half Moon St W1 44 B4
Halkin Arc SW1 44 A6
Halkin Ms SW1 44 A6
Halkin Pl SW1 44 A6
Halkin St SW1 44 A6
Hallam Ms W1 44 B1
Hallam St W1 44 B1
Hamilton Ms W1 44 B5
Hamilton Pl W1 44 A5
Ham Yd W1 44 D3
Hand Ct WC1 45 F2
Hanging Sword All
  EC4 45 G3
Hanover Pl WC2 45 E3
Hanover Sq W1 44 B3
Hanover St W1 44 B3
Hanson St W1 44 C1
Hanway Pl W1 44 D2
Hanway St W1 44 D2
Hare Ct EC4 45 G3
Hare Pl EC4 45 G3
Harewood Pl W1 44 B3
Harley Pl W1 44 B2
Harley St W1 44 B2
Harmsworth Ms SE11 45 H7
Harp All EC4 45 H2
Harper Rd SE1 45 J6
Harpur Ms WC1 45 F1
Harpur St WC1 45 F1
Hat & Mitre Ct EC1 45 H1
Hatfields SE1 45 G4
Hatton Gdn EC1 45 G1
Hatton Pl EC1 45 G1
Hatton Wall EC1 45 G1
Haunch of Venison Yd
  W1 44 B3
Hay Hill W1 44 B4
Hayles St SE11 45 H7
Haymarket SW1 44 D4
Haymarket Arc SW1 44 D4
Hayne St EC1 45 H1
Hay's Ms W1 44 B4
Hayward's Pl EC1 45 H1
Headfort Pl SW1 44 A6
Heddon St W1 44 C3
Hedger St SE11 45 H7
Hen & Chicken Ct
  EC4 45 G3
Henrietta Pl W1 44 B3
Henrietta St WC2 45 E3
Herald's Pl SE11 45 H7
Herbal Hill EC1 45 G1
Hercules Rd SE1 45 F7
Herrick St SW1 44 D7
Hertford St W1 44 B4
High Holborn WC1 45 E2
High Timber St EC4 45 J3
Hills Pl W1 44 C3
Hill St W1 44 A4
Hind Ct EC4 45 G3
Hinde St W1 44 A2
Hindon Ct SW1 44 C7
Hobart Pl SW1 44 B6
Holborn EC1 45 G2
Holborn WC2 45 F2
Holborn Circ EC1 45 G2
Holborn Pl WC1 45 F2
Holborn Viaduct EC1 45 G2
Holland St SE1 45 H4
Hollen St W1 44 D2
Holles St W1 44 B2
Holmes Ter SE1 45 G5
Holsworthy Sq WC1 45 F1
Holyoak Rd SE11 45 H7
Honey La EC2 45 J3
Hood Ct EC4 45 G3
Hop Gdns WC2 44 E4
Hopkins St W1 44 C3
Hopton's Gdns SE1 45 H4
Hopton St SE1 45 H4
Hornbeam Cl SE11 45 G7
Horse & Dolphin Yd
  W1 44 D3
Horseferry Rd SW1 44 D7
Horse Guards Av SW1 44 E5

Horse Guards Rd SW1 44 D5
Horsemongers Ms
  SE1 45 J6
Horse Ride SW1 44 D5
Hosier La EC1 45 H2
Houghton St WC2 45 F3
Howick Pl SW1 44 C7
Howland Ms E W1 44 C1
Howland St W1 44 C1
Hudson's Pl SW1 44 B7
Huggin Ct EC4 45 J3
Huggin Hill EC4 45 J3
Hulme Pl SE1 45 J6
Hungerford Br SE1 45 E4
Hungerford Br WC2 45 E4
Hungerford La WC2 44 E4
Huntley St WC1 44 C1
Hunt's Ct WC2 44 D4
Hutton St EC4 45 G3
Hyde Pk Cor W1 44 A5

I
India Pl WC2 45 F3
Ingestre Pl W1 44 C3
Ingram Cl SE11 45 F7
Inigo Pl WC2 44 E3
Inner Temple La EC4 45 G3
Invicta Plaza SE1 45 H4
Ireland Yd EC4 45 H3
Irving St WC2 44 D4
Isaac Way SE1 45 J5
Isabella St SE1 45 H5
Ivybridge La WC2 45 E4

J
Jacob's Well Ms W1 44 A2
James St W1 44 A2
James St WC2 45 E3
Jermyn St SW1 44 C4
Jerusalem Pas EC1 45 H1
Jervis Ct W1 44 B3
Joan St SE1 45 H5
Jockey's Flds WC1 45 F1
Johanna St SE1 45 G6
John Adam St WC2 45 E4
John Carpenter St
  EC4 45 H3
John Milton Pass EC2 45 J3
John Princes St W1 44 B2
John's Ms WC1 45 F1
John St WC1 45 F1
Jones St W1 44 B4
Jubilee Mkt Hall WC2 45 E3
Juxon St SE11 45 F7

K
Kean St WC2 45 F3
Keeley St WC2 45 F3
Kell St SE1 45 H6
Kemble St WC2 45 F3
Kemp's Ct W1 44 C3
Kendall Pl W1 44 A2
Kennet Wf La EC4 45 J3
Kennington Rd SE1 45 G6
Kennington Rd SE11 45 G7
Kenrick Pl W1 44 A1
Keppel Row SE1 45 J5
Keppel St WC1 44 D1
Keyworth Pl SE1 45 H6
Keyworth St SE1 45 H6
King Charles St SW1 44 D5
King Edward St EC1 45 J2
King Edward Wk SE1 45 G6
Kinghorn St EC1 45 J2
King James Ct SE1 45 H6
King James St SE1 45 H6
Kingly Ct W1 44 C3
Kingly St W1 44 C3
Kings Bench St SE1 45 H5
Kings Bench Wk EC4 45 G3
Kingscote St EC4 45 H3
King's Ms WC1 45 F1
Kings Pl SE1 45 J6
King's Reach Twr SE1 45 G4
King's Scholars' Pas
  SW1 44 C7
King St EC2 45 J3
King St SW1 44 C5
King St WC2 45 E3
Kingsway WC2 45 F2
Kinnerton St SW1 44 A6
Kirby St EC1 45 G1
Kirkman Pl W1 44 D2
Kirk St WC1 45 F1
Knightrider St EC4 45 J3

L
Lambeth SE1 45 F7
Lambeth Br SE1 45 E7
Lambeth Br SW1 45 E7
Lambeth Hill EC4 45 J3
Lambeth Palace Rd
  SE1 45 F7
Lambeth Pier SE1 45 E7

Lambeth Rd SE1 45 F7
Lambeth Rd SE11 45 F7
Lambeth Twrs SE11 45 G7
Lambeth Wk SE1 45 F7
Lambeth Wk SE11 45 F7
Lambs Conduit Pas
  WC1 45 F1
Lamb's Conduit St
  WC1 45 F1
Lamlash St SE11 45 H7
Lamp Office Ct WC1 45 F1
Lancashire Ct W1 44 B3
Lancaster Pl WC2 45 F3
Lancaster St SE1 45 H6
Lanesborough Pl
  SW1 44 A5
Langham Pl W1 44 B2
Langham St W1 44 B2
Langley Ct WC2 44 E3
Langley St WC2 44 E3
Lansdowne Row W1 44 B4
Lansdowne Ter WC1 45 E1
Lant St SE1 45 J5
Lauderdale Twr EC2 45 J1
Launcelot St SE1 45 G6
Lavington St SE1 45 H5
Lawrence La EC2 45 J3
Laystall St EC1 45 G1
Laytons Bldgs SE1 45 J5
Lazenby Ct WC2 44 E3
Leake St SE1 45 F5
Leather La EC1 45 G2
Lees Pl W1 44 A3
Leicester Ct WC2 44 D3
Leicester Pl WC2 44 D3
Leicester Sq WC2 44 D4
Leicester St WC2 44 D3
Leigh Hunt St SE1 45 J5
Leigh Pl EC1 45 G1
Leopards Ct EC1 45 G1
Leo Yd EC1 45 H1
Lewisham St SW1 44 D6
Lexington St W1 44 C3
Library St SE1 45 H6
Lily Pl EC1 45 G1
Limeburner La EC4 45 H3
Lincoln's Inn WC2 45 F2
Lincoln's Inn Flds
  WC2 45 F2
Lindsey St EC1 45 H1
Lisle St WC2 44 D3
Litchfield St WC2 44 D3
Little Argyll St W1 44 C3
Little Britain EC1 45 J2
Little Chester St SW1 44 A6
Little Coll St SW1 44 E6
Little Dean's Yd SW1 44 E6
Little Dorrit Ct SE1 45 J5
Little Essex St WC2 45 G3
Little George St SW1 44 E6
Little Newport St WC2 44 D3
Little New St EC4 45 G2
Little Portland St W1 44 C2
Little Russell St WC1 44 E2
Little St. James's St
  SW1 44 C5
Little Sanctuary SW1 44 D6
Little Smith St SW1 44 D6
Little Titchfield St W1 44 C2
Little Trinity La EC4 45 J3
Little Turnstile WC1 45 F2
Livonia St W1 44 C3
Lollard St SE11 45 F7
Loman St SE1 45 H5
Lombard La EC4 45 G3
London Cen Mkts
  EC1 45 H1
London Rd SE1 45 H6
London Silver Vaults
  WC2 45 G2
London Trocadero,
  The W1 44 D4
London Wall EC2 45 J2
Long Acre WC2 44 E3
Long La EC1 45 H1
Longridge Ho SE1 45 J7
Long's Ct WC2 44 D3
Longstone Ct SE1 45 J6
Longville Rd SE11 45 H7
Long Yd WC1 45 F1
Lord N St SW1 44 E7
Love La EC2 45 J2
Lover's Wk W1 44 A4
Lower Belgrave St
  SW1 44 B7
Lower Grosvenor Pl
  SW1 44 B6
Lower James St W1 44 C3
Lower John St W1 44 C3
Lower Marsh SE1 45 G6
Lower Rd SE1 45 G5
Lowndes Cl SW1 44 A7
Lowndes Ct W1 44 C3
Lowndes Pl SW1 44 A7

Ludgate Bdy EC4 45 H3
Ludgate Circ EC4 45 H3
Ludgate Hill EC4 45 H3
Ludgate Sq EC4 45 H3
Lumley Ct WC2 45 E4
Lumley St W1 44 A3
Luxborough St W1 44 A1
Lyall Ms SW1 44 A7
Lyall Ms W SW1 44 A7
Lyall St SW1 44 A7
Lygon Pl SW1 44 B7

M
McAuley Cl SE1 45 G6
Macclesfield St W1 44 D3
McCoid Way SE1 45 J6
Macfarren Pl NW1 44 A1
Macklin St WC2 45 E2
Mac's Pl EC4 45 G2
Maddox St W1 44 B3
Magpie All EC4 45 G3
Maiden La SE1 45 J4
Maiden La WC2 45 E4
Maidstone Bldgs Ms
  SE1 45 J5
Malet Pl WC1 44 D1
Malet St WC1 44 D1
Mall, The SW1 44 C5
Maltravers St WC2 45 F3
Manchester Ms W1 44 A2
Manchester Sq W1 44 A2
Manchester St W1 44 A2
Mandeville Pl W1 44 A2
Manette St W1 44 D3
Mansfield Ms W1 44 B2
Mansfield St W1 44 B2
Maple Pl W1 44 C1
Maple St W1 44 C1
Margaret Ct W1 44 C2
Margaret St W1 44 B2
Marigold All SE1 45 H4
Market Ct W1 44 C2
Market Ms W1 44 B5
Market Pl W1 44 C2
Marlborough Ct W1 44 C3
Marlborough Rd SW1 44 C5
Marshall St W1 44 C3
Marshalsea Rd SE1 45 J5
Marsham St SW1 44 D7
Martin Ho SE1 45 J7
Martlett Ct WC2 45 E3
Marylebone High St
  W1 44 A1
Marylebone La W1 44 B3
Marylebone Ms W1 44 B2
Marylebone Pas W1 44 C2
Marylebone St W1 44 A2
Masons Arms Ms W1 44 B3
Mason's Yd SW1 44 C4
Matthew Parker St
  SW1 44 D6
Matthews Yd WC2 44 E3
Maunsel St SW1 44 D7
Mayfair W1 44 B4
Mayfair Pl W1 44 B4
Mays Ct WC2 44 E4
Meadow Row SE1 45 J7
Mead Row SE1 45 G6
Meard St W1 44 D3
Medway St SW1 44 D7
Melbourne Pl WC2 45 F3
Memel Ct EC1 45 J1
Memel St EC1 45 J1
Mepham St SE1 45 F5
Mercer St WC2 44 E3
Merrick Sq SE1 45 J6
Metro Cen Hts SE1 45 J7
Meymott St SE1 45 H5
Middlesex Pas EC1 45 H2
Middle St EC1 45 J1
Middle Temple EC4 45 G3
Middle Temple La
  EC4 45 G3
Middleton Pl W1 44 C2
Midford Pl W1 44 C1
Milcote St SE1 45 H6
Milford La WC2 45 F3
Milk St EC2 45 J3
Millbank SW1 44 E7
Millbank Ct SW1 44 E7
Millennium Br EC4 45 J3
Millennium Br SE1 45 J3
Miller Wk SE1 45 G5
Millman Ms WC1 45 F1
Millman St WC1 45 F1
Mill St W1 44 B3
Milroy Wk SE1 45 H4
Minera Ms SW1 44 A7
Mins St SE1 45 J5
Mitre Ct EC2 45 J2
Mitre Rd SE1 45 G5
Monck St SW1 44 D7
Monkton St SE11 45 G7
Monkwell Sq EC2 45 J2

Monmouth St WC2 44 E3
Montague Pl WC1 44 D1
Montague St EC1 45 J2
Montague St WC1 44 E1
Montreal Pl WC2 45 F3
Montrose Pl SW1 44 A6
Moor St W1 44 D3
Morley St SE1 45 G6
Morpeth Ter SW1 44 C7
Mortimer Mkt WC1 44 C1
Mortimer St W1 44 C2
Morton Pl SE1 45 G7
Morwell St WC1 44 D2
Mount Pleasant WC1 45 F1
Mount Row W1 44 B4
Mount St W1 44 A4
Mount St Ms W1 44 B4
Moxon St W1 44 A2
Munton Rd SE17 45 J7
Murphy St SE1 45 G6
Museum St WC1 44 E2

N
Nag's Head Ct EC1 45 J1
Nassau St W1 44 C2
Neal St WC2 44 E3
Neal's Yd WC2 44 E3
Neathouse Pl SW1 44 C7
Nelson Sq SE1 45 H5
Newall Ho SE1 45 J6
New Bond St W1 44 B3
New Br St EC4 45 H3
Newburgh St W1 44 C3
New Burlington Ms
  W1 44 C3
New Burlington Pl
  W1 44 C3
New Burlington St
  W1 44 C3
Newbury St EC1 45 J2
Newcastle Cl EC4 45 H2
New Cavendish St W1 44 B1
New Change EC4 45 J3
New Compton St
  WC2 44 D3
New Fetter La EC4 45 G2
Newgate St EC1 45 H2
New Globe Wk SE1 45 J4
Newington SE1 45 J7
Newington Causeway
  SE1 45 H7
New Inn Pas WC2 45 F3
New Kent Rd SE1 45 J7
Newman Pas W1 44 C2
Newman's Row WC2 45 F2
Newman St W1 44 C2
Newman Yd W1 44 C2
Newnham Ter SE1 45 G6
New N St WC1 45 F1
New Oxford St WC1 44 D2
Newport Ct WC2 44 D3
Newport Pl WC2 44 D3
New Row WC2 44 E3
New Sq WC2 45 F2
New St Sq EC4 45 G2
Newton St WC2 45 E2
New Turnstile WC1 45 F2
Nicholson St SE1 45 H5
Nightingale Ms SE11 45 G7
Noble St EC2 45 J2
Noel St W1 44 C3
Norfolk Row SE1 45 F7
Norris St SW1 44 D4
North Audley St W1 44 A3
North Cres WC1 44 D1
Northington St WC1 45 F1
North Ms WC1 45 F1
Northumberland Av
  WC2 44 E4
Northumberland St
  WC2 44 E4
Norwich St EC4 45 G2
Nottingham Ct WC2 44 E3
Nottingham Pl W1 44 A1
Nottingham St W1 44 A1
Nottingham Ter NW1 44 A1

O
Oakden St SE11 45 G7
Oakey La SE1 45 G6
Oat La EC2 45 J2
Odhams Wk WC2 45 E3
Ogle St W1 44 C1
Old Bailey EC4 45 H3
Old Barrack Yd SW1 44 A5
Old Bond St W1 44 C4
Old Brewers Yd WC2 44 E3
Old Bldgs WC2 45 G2
Old Burlington St W1 44 C3
Oldbury Pl W1 44 A1
Old Cavendish St W1 44 B2
Old Compton St W1 44 D3
Old Fish St Hill EC4 45 J3
Old Fleet La EC4 45 H2

Old Gloucester St WC1 **45** E1
Old Mitre Ct EC4 **45** G3
Old N St WC1 **45** F1
Old Palace Yd SW1 **44** E6
Old Paradise St SE11 **45** F7
Old Pk La W1 **44** A5
Old Pye St SW1 **44** D6
Old Queen St SW1 **44** D6
Old Seacoal La EC4 **45** H2
Old Sq WC2 **45** F2
O'Meara St SE1 **45** J5
Onslow St EC1 **45** G1
Ontario St SE1 **45** H7
Orange St WC2 **44** D4
Orange Yd W1 **44** D3
Orchard St W1 **44** A3
Orde Hall St WC1 **45** F1
Orient St SE11 **45** H7
Ormond Cl WC1 **45** E1
Ormond Ms WC1 **45** E1
Ormond Yd SW1 **44** C4
Osnaburgh St NW1 **44** A1
Ossington Bldgs W1 **44** A1
Oswin St SE11 **45** H7
Outer Circle NW1 **44** A1
Oxendon St SW1 **44** D4
Oxford St W1 **44** C2
Oxo Twr Wf SE1 **45** G4

P

Paddington St W1 **44** A1
Pageantmaster Ct EC4 **45** H3
Page St SW1 **44** D7
Palace Pl SW1 **44** C6
Palace St SW1 **44** C6
Pall Mall SW1 **44** C5
Pall Mall E SW1 **44** D4
Palmer St SW1 **44** D6
Pancras La EC4 **45** J3
Panton St SW1 **44** D4
Panyer All EC4 **45** J3
Paris Gdn SE1 **45** H4
Park Cres W1 **44** B1
Park Cres Ms E W1 **44** B1
Park Cres Ms W W1 **44** B1
Parker Ms WC2 **45** E2
Parker St WC2 **45** E2
Park La W1 **44** A5
Park Pl SW1 **44** C5
Park Sq Ms NW1 **44** B1
Park St SE1 **45** J4
Park St W1 **44** A3
Parliament Sq SW1 **44** E6
Parliament St SW1 **44** E6
Parliament Vw Apts SE1 **45** F7
Passing All EC1 **45** H1
Pastor St SE11 **45** H7
Paternoster Row EC4 **45** J3
Paternoster Sq EC4 **45** H3
Paul's Wk EC4 **45** H3
Peabody Est EC1 **45** J1
Peabody Est SE1 **45** G5
Peabody Est SW1 **44** C7
Peabody Sq SE1 **45** H6
Peabody Trust SE1 **45** J5
Pearman St SE1 **45** G6
Pear Pl SE1 **45** G5
Pear Tree Ct EC1 **45** G1
Pemberton Row EC4 **45** G2
Pembroke Cl SW1 **44** A6
Penhurst Pl SE1 **45** F7
Pepper St SE1 **45** J5
Percy Ms W1 **44** D2
Percy Pas W1 **44** C2
Percy St W1 **44** D2
Perkin's Rents SW1 **44** D6
Perkins Sq SE1 **45** J4
Perrys Pl W1 **44** D2
Peters Hill EC4 **45** J3
Peter's La EC1 **45** H1
Peter St W1 **44** C3
Petty France SW1 **44** C6
Phipp's Ms SW1 **44** B7
Phoenix St WC2 **44** D3
Piccadilly W1 **44** B5
Piccadilly Arc SW1 **44** C4
Piccadilly Circ W1 **44** D4
Piccadilly Pl W1 **44** C4
Pickering Pl SW1 **44** C5
Pickwick St SE1 **45** J6
Picton Pl W1 **44** A3
Pilgrim St EC4 **45** H3
Pineapple Ct SW1 **44** C6
Pitt's Head Ms W1 **44** A5
Playhouse Yd EC4 **45** H3
Plaza Shop Cen, The W1 **44** C2
Pleydell Ct EC4 **45** G3
Pleydell St EC4 **45** G3
Plough Pl EC4 **45** G2

Plumtree Ct EC4 **45** G2
Pocock St SE1 **45** H5
Poland St W1 **44** C3
Pollen St W1 **44** B3
Polperro Ms SE11 **45** G7
Pontypool Pl SE1 **45** H5
Pooles Bldgs EC1 **45** G1
Poppins Ct EC4 **45** H3
Porter St SE1 **45** J4
Portland Ms W1 **44** C3
Portland Pl W1 **44** B1
Portman Ms S W1 **44** A3
Portman St W1 **44** A3
Portpool La EC1 **45** G1
Portsmouth St WC2 **45** F3
Portugal St WC2 **45** F3
Powis Pl WC1 **45** E1
Pratt Wk SE11 **45** F7
Price's St SE1 **45** H5
Priest Ct EC2 **45** J2
Primrose Hill EC4 **45** G3
Prince's Arc SW1 **44** C4
Princes Pl SW1 **44** C4
Princess St SE1 **45** H7
Princes St W1 **44** B3
Princeton St WC1 **45** F1
Printers Inn Ct EC4 **45** G2
Printer St EC4 **45** G2
Procter St WC1 **45** F2
Providence Ct W1 **44** A3
Prudent Pas EC2 **45** J2
Puddle Dock EC4 **45** H3

Q

Quadrant Arc W1 **44** C4
Quality Ct WC2 **45** G2
Queen Anne Ms W1 **44** B2
Queen Anne's Gate SW1 **44** D6
Queen Anne St W1 **44** B2
Queenhithe EC4 **45** J3
Queen's Head Pas EC4 **45** J2
Queen Sq WC1 **45** E1
Queen Sq Pl WC1 **45** E1
Queen St EC4 **45** J3
Queen St W1 **44** B4
Queen St Pl EC4 **45** J4
Queen's Wk SW1 **44** C5
Queen's Wk, The SE1 **45** F5
Queens Yd WC1 **44** C1
Queen Victoria St EC4 **45** H3
Quilp St SE1 **45** J5

R

Ramillies Pl W1 **44** C3
Ramillies St W1 **44** C3
Rathbone Pl W1 **44** D2
Rathbone St W1 **44** C2
Raymond Bldgs WC1 **45** F1
Ray St EC1 **45** G1
Ray St Br EC1 **45** G1
Redcross Way SE1 **45** J5
Red Lion Ct EC4 **45** G2
Red Lion Sq WC1 **45** F2
Red Lion St WC1 **45** F1
Red Lion Yd W1 **44** A4
Red Pl W1 **44** A3
Reeves Ms W1 **44** A4
Regency Pl SW1 **44** D7
Regent Pl W1 **44** C3
Regent St SW1 **44** D4
Regent St W1 **44** B2
Remnant St WC2 **45** F2
Renfrew Rd SE11 **45** H7
Rennie St SE1 **45** H4
Rex Pl W1 **44** A4
Richardson's Ms W1 **44** C1
Richbell Pl WC1 **45** F1
Richmond Bldgs W1 **44** D3
Richmond Ms W1 **44** D3
Richmond Ter SW1 **44** E5
Ridgmount Gdns WC1 **44** D1
Ridgmount Pl WC1 **44** D1
Ridgmount St WC1 **44** D1
Riding Ho St W1 **44** C2
Risborough St SE1 **45** H5
Rising Sun Ct EC1 **45** H2
River Ct SE1 **45** H4
Robert Adam St W1 **44** A2
Roberts Ms SW1 **44** A7
Robert St WC2 **45** E4
Rochester Row SW1 **44** C7
Rochester St SW1 **44** D7
Rockingham Est SE1 **45** J7
Rockingham St SE1 **45** J7
Rodney Pl SE17 **45** J7
Rodney Rd SE17 **45** J7
Roger St WC1 **45** F1
Rolls Bldgs EC4 **45** G2
Rolls Pas EC4 **45** G2
Romilly St W1 **44** D3

Romney Ms W1 **44** A1
Romney St SW1 **44** D7
Roscoe St EC1 **45** J1
Rose All SE1 **45** J4
Rose & Crown Ct EC2 **45** J2
Rose & Crown Yd SW1 **44** C4
Rosebery Av EC1 **45** G1
Rosebery Sq EC1 **45** G1
Rose St EC4 **45** H2
Rose St WC2 **44** E3
Rotary St SE1 **45** H6
Rotherham Wk SE1 **45** H5
Rotten Row SW1 **44** A5
Roupell St SE1 **45** G5
Royal Arc W1 **44** C4
Royal Ms, The SW1 **44** B6
Royal Opera Arc SW1 **44** D4
Royal St SE1 **45** F6
Royalty Ms W1 **44** D3
Royalty Ms W1 **44** D3
Rugby St WC1 **45** F1
Rupert Ct W1 **44** D3
Rupert St W1 **44** D3
Rushworth St SE1 **45** H5
Russell Ct SW1 **44** C5
Russell Sq WC1 **45** E1
Russell St WC2 **45** E3
Russia Row EC2 **45** J3
Rutherford St SW1 **44** D7
Rutland Pl EC1 **45** J1
Ryder Ct SW1 **44** C4
Ryder St SW1 **44** C4
Ryder Yd SW1 **44** C4

S

Sackville St W1 **44** C4
Saddle Yd W1 **44** B4
Saffron Hill EC1 **45** G1
Saffron St EC1 **45** G1
Sail St SE11 **45** F7
St. Albans Ct EC2 **45** J2
St. Albans St SW1 **44** D4
St. Alphage Gdns EC2 **45** J2
St. Andrew's Hill EC4 **45** H3
St. Andrew St EC4 **45** G2
St. Anne's Ct W1 **44** D3
St. Ann's La SW1 **44** D6
St. Ann's St SW1 **44** D6
St. Anselm's Pl W1 **44** B3
St. Brides Av EC4 **45** H3
St. Bride St EC4 **45** H2
St. Christopher's Pl W1 **44** A2
St. Clement's La WC2 **45** F3
St. Cross St EC1 **45** G1
St. Ermin's Hill SW1 **44** D6
St. Georges Circ SE1 **45** H6
St. Georges Ct EC4 **45** H2
St. Georges Ms SE1 **45** G6
St. Georges Rd SE1 **45** G6
St. George St W1 **44** B3
St. Giles High St WC2 **44** D2
St. Giles Pas WC2 **44** D3
St. James's SW1 **44** D5
St. James's St SW1 **44** C4
St. James's Mkt SW1 **44** D4
St. James's Palace SW1 **44** C5
St. James's Pk SW1 **44** D5
St. James's Pl SW1 **44** C5
St. James's Sq SW1 **44** C4
St. James's St SW1 **44** C4
St. John's La EC1 **45** H1
St. John's Path EC1 **45** H1
St. John's Pl EC1 **45** H1
St. John's Sq EC1 **45** H1
St. John St EC1 **45** H1
St. Margaret's Ct SE1 **45** J5
St. Margaret's St SW1 **44** E6
St. Martin's La WC2 **44** E3
St. Martin's-le-Grand EC1 **45** J2
St. Martin's Ms WC2 **44** E4
St. Martin's Pl WC2 **44** E4
St. Martin's St WC2 **44** D4
St. Mary's Gdns SE11 **45** G7
St. Mary's Wk SE11 **45** G7
St. Matthew St SW1 **44** D7
St. Olaves Gdns SE11 **45** G7
St. Paul's Chyd EC4 **45** H3
St. Vincent St W1 **44** A2
Salisbury Ct EC4 **45** H3
Salisbury Sq EC4 **45** G3
Sanctuary, The SW1 **44** D6
Sanctuary St SE1 **45** J6
Sandell St SE1 **45** G5
Sandland St WC1 **45** F2
Saperton Wk SE11 **45** F7
Sardinia St WC2 **45** F3
Savile Row W1 **44** C3
Savoy Bldgs WC2 **45** F4
Savoy Ct WC2 **45** E4
Savoy Hill WC2 **45** F4
Savoy Pl WC2 **45** E4

Savoy Row WC2 **45** F3
Savoy St WC2 **45** F3
Savoy Way WC2 **45** F4
Sawyer St SE1 **45** J5
Scala St W1 **44** C1
Scoresby St SE1 **45** H5
Scotland Pl SW1 **44** E4
Scovell Cres SE1 **45** J6
Scovell Rd SE1 **45** J6
Secker St SE1 **45** G5
Sedding St SW1 **44** A7
Sedley Pl W1 **44** B3
Sekforde St EC1 **45** H1
Serjeants Inn EC4 **45** G3
Serle St WC2 **45** F2
Sermon La EC4 **45** J3
Seymour Ms W1 **44** A2
Shaftesbury Av W1 **44** D3
Shaftesbury Av WC2 **44** D3
Shakespeare Twr EC2 **45** J1
Shavers Pl SW1 **44** D4
Sheffield St WC2 **45** F3
Shelton St WC2 **44** E3
Shepherd Mkt W1 **44** B4
Shepherd's Pl W1 **44** A3
Shepherd St W1 **44** B5
Sheraton St W1 **44** D3
Sherlock Ms W1 **44** A1
Sherwood St W1 **44** C3
Shoe La EC4 **45** G2
Shorts Gdns WC2 **44** E3
Short St SE1 **45** G5
Shropshire Pl WC1 **44** C1
Sicilian Av WC1 **45** E2
Sidford Pl SE1 **45** F7
Silex St SE1 **45** H6
Silk St EC2 **45** J1
Silver Pl W1 **44** C3
Sermon La EC1 **45** J6
Skinners La EC4 **45** J3
Slingsby Pl WC2 **44** E3
Smart's Pl WC2 **45** E2
Smeaton Ct SE1 **45** J7
Smithfield St EC1 **45** H2
Smith's Ct W1 **44** C3
Smith Sq SW1 **44** E7
Smokehouse Yd EC1 **45** H1
Snow Hill EC1 **45** H2
Snow Hill Ct EC1 **45** H2
Soho W1 **44** C3
Soho Sq W1 **44** D2
Soho St W1 **44** D2
Southampton Bldgs WC2 **45** G2
Southampton Pl WC1 **45** E2
Southampton Row WC1 **45** E1
Southampton St WC2 **45** E3
South Audley St W1 **44** A4
South Cres WC1 **44** D2
South Eaton Pl SW1 **44** A7
South Molton La W1 **44** B3
South Molton St W1 **44** B3
South Sq WC1 **45** G2
South St W1 **44** A4
Southwark SE1 **45** H5
Southwark Br EC4 **45** J4
Southwark Br SE1 **45** J4
Southwark Br Rd SE1 **45** H6
Southwark St SE1 **45** H4
Spanish Pl W1 **44** A2
Spenser St SW1 **44** C6
Spring Gdns SW1 **44** D4
Spur Rd SE1 **45** G5
Spur Rd SW1 **44** C6
Stable Yd SW1 **44** C5
Stable Yd Rd SW1 **44** C5
Stacey St WC2 **44** D3
Stafford Pl SW1 **44** C6
Stafford St W1 **44** C4
Staining La EC2 **45** J2
Stamford St SE1 **45** G5
Stangate SE1 **45** F6
Stanhope Gate W1 **44** A4
Stanhope Row W1 **44** B5
Staple Inn WC1 **45** G2
Staple Inn Bldgs WC1 **45** G2
Star Yd WC2 **45** G2
Station App SE1 **45** F5
Stedham Pl WC1 **44** E2
Stephen Ms W1 **44** D2
Stephen St W1 **44** D2
Stew La EC4 **45** J3
Stillington St SW1 **44** C7
Stone Bldgs WC2 **45** F2
Stonecutter St EC4 **45** H2
Stones End St SE1 **45** J6
Store St WC1 **44** D2
Storey's Gate SW1 **44** D6
Strand WC2 **44** E4
Strand La WC2 **45** F3
Stratford Pl W1 **44** B3

Stratton St W1 **44** B4
Streatham St WC1 **44** D2
Strutton Grd SW1 **44** D6
Stukeley St WC1 **45** E2
Stukeley St WC2 **45** E2
Sturge St SE1 **45** J5
Sudrey St SE1 **45** J6
Suffolk Pl SW1 **44** D4
Suffolk St SW1 **44** D4
Sullivan Rd SE11 **45** G7
Summers St EC1 **45** G1
Sumner St SE1 **45** H4
Surrey Row SE1 **45** H5
Surrey St WC2 **45** F3
Sutton La EC1 **45** H1
Sutton Row W1 **44** D2
Sutton's Way EC1 **45** J1
Sutton Wk SE1 **45** F5
Swallow Pl W1 **44** B3
Swallow St W1 **44** C4
Swan St SE1 **45** J6
Swiss Ct W1 **44** D4
Sycamore St EC1 **45** J1

T

Tachbrook Ms SW1 **44** C7
Tallis St EC4 **45** G3
Tanswell Est SE1 **45** G6
Tanswell St SE1 **45** G6
Tarn St SE1 **45** J7
Tavistock St WC2 **45** E3
Telford Ho SE1 **45** J7
Temple Av EC4 **45** G3
Temple La EC4 **45** G3
Temple Pl WC2 **45** F3
Temple W Ms SE11 **45** H7
Tenison Ct W1 **44** C3
Tenison Way SE1 **45** G5
Tenterden St W1 **44** B3
Terminus Pl SW1 **44** B7
Thavies Inn EC1 **45** G2
Thayer St W1 **44** A2
Theed St SE1 **45** G5
Theobald's Rd WC1 **45** F1
Thirleby Rd SW1 **44** C7
Thomas Doyle St SE1 **45** H6
Thorney St SW1 **44** E7
Thornhaugh Ms WC1 **44** D1
Thornhaugh St WC1 **44** D1
Thrale St SE1 **45** J5
Three Barrels Wk EC4 **45** J4
Three Cups Yd WC1 **45** F2
Three Kings Yd W1 **44** B3
Tilney St W1 **44** A4
Tiverton St SE1 **45** J7
Took's Ct EC4 **45** G2
Torrington Pl WC1 **44** C1
Torrington Sq WC1 **44** D1
Tothill St SW1 **44** D6
Tottenham Ct Rd W1 **44** C1
Tottenham Ms W1 **44** C1
Tottenham St W1 **44** C2
Toulmin St SE1 **45** J6
Tower Ct WC2 **44** E3
Tower Royal EC4 **45** J3
Tower St WC2 **44** D3
Trafalgar Sq SW1 **44** D4
Trafalgar Sq WC2 **44** D4
Trebeck St W1 **44** B4
Treveris St SE1 **45** H5
Trig La EC4 **45** J3
Trinity Ch Sq SE1 **45** J6
Trinity St SE1 **45** J6
Trio Pl SE1 **45** J6
Trump St EC2 **45** J3
Trundle St SE1 **45** J5
Tudor St EC4 **45** G3
Tufton St SW1 **44** E7
Turk's Head Yd EC1 **45** H1
Turnagain La EC4 **45** H2
Turnmill St EC1 **45** H1
Tweezer's All WC2 **45** G3
Twyford Pl WC2 **45** F2
Tyler's Ct W1 **44** D3

U

Ufford St SE1 **45** G5
Ulster Pl NW1 **44** B1
Ulster Ter NW1 **44** B1
Union Jack Club SE1 **45** G5
Union St SE1 **45** H5
University St WC1 **44** C1
Upper Belgrave St SW1 **44** A6
Upper Brook St W1 **44** A4
Upper Grosvenor St W1 **44** A4
Upper Grd SE1 **45** G4
Upper James St W1 **44** C3
Upper John St W1 **44** C3
Upper Marsh SE1 **45** F6
Upper St. Martin's La WC2 **44** E3

Upper Tachbrook St SW1 **44** C7
Upper Thames St EC4 **45** H3
Upper Wimpole St W1 **44** B1

V

Valentine Pl SE1 **45** H5
Valentine Row SE1 **45** H6
Vandon Pas SW1 **44** C6
Vandon St SW1 **44** C6
Vane St SW1 **44** C7
Vauxhall Br Rd SW1 **44** C7
Vere St W1 **44** B3
Vernon Pl WC1 **45** E2
Verulam Bldgs WC1 **45** F1
Verulam St WC1 **45** G1
Vesage Ct EC1 **45** G2
Victoria Embk EC4 **45** F4
Victoria Embk SW1 **45** E5
Victoria Embk WC2 **45** F4
Victoria Pl SW1 **44** B7
Victoria Sq SW1 **44** B6
Victoria Sta SW1 **44** B7
Victoria St SW1 **44** C7
Vigo St W1 **44** C4
Villiers St WC2 **44** E4
Vincent Sq SW1 **44** C7
Vincent St SW1 **44** D7
Vine Hill EC1 **45** G1
Vine St W1 **44** C4
Vine St Br EC1 **45** G1
Vine Yd SE1 **45** J5
Vintners Ct EC4 **45** J3
Virgil St SE1 **45** F6
Viscount St EC1 **45** J1

W

Waithman St EC4 **45** H3
Walcot Sq SE11 **45** G7
Walcott St SW1 **44** C7
Walkers Ct W1 **44** D3
Wallis All SE1 **45** J5
Wallside EC2 **45** J2
Walnut Tree Wk SE11 **45** G7
Walworth Rd SE1 **45** J7
Walworth Rd SE17 **45** J7
Wardens Gro SE1 **45** J5
Wardour Ms W1 **44** C3
Wardour St W1 **44** C3
Wardrobe Ter EC4 **45** H3
Warner St EC1 **45** G1
Warner Yd EC1 **45** G1
Warren Ms W1 **44** C1
Warren St W1 **44** B1
Warwick Ct WC1 **45** F2
Warwick Ho St SW1 **44** D4
Warwick La EC4 **45** H3
Warwick Pas EC4 **45** H2
Warwick Row SW1 **44** B6
Warwick Sq EC4 **45** H2
Warwick St W1 **44** C3
Warwick Yd EC1 **45** J1
Watergate EC4 **45** H3
Watergate Wk WC2 **45** E4
Waterhouse Sq EC1 **45** G2
Waterloo Br SE1 **45** F4
Waterloo Br WC2 **45** F4
Waterloo Pl SW1 **44** D4
Waterloo Rd SE1 **45** G5
Waterloo Sta SE1 **45** G5
Water St WC2 **45** F3
Watling Ct EC4 **45** J3
Watling St EC4 **45** J3
Waverton St W1 **44** A4
Webber Row SE1 **45** G6
Webber St SE1 **45** G5
Wedgwood Ho SE11 **45** G7
Wedgwood Ms W1 **44** D3
Weighhouse St W1 **44** A3
Welbeck St W1 **44** B2
Welbeck Way W1 **44** B2
Well Ct EC4 **45** J3
Weller St SE1 **45** J5
Wellington St WC2 **45** E3
Wells Ms W1 **44** C2
Wells St W1 **44** C2
Wesley St W1 **44** A2
West Cen St WC1 **44** E2
West Eaton Pl SW1 **44** A7
West Eaton Pl Ms SW1 **44** A7
West Halkin St SW1 **44** A6
West Harding St EC4 **45** G2
Westminster SW1 **44** C6
Westminster Br SE1 **45** E6
Westminster Br SW1 **45** E6
Westminster Br Rd SE1 **45** F6
Westminster Gdns SW1 **44** E7
Westmoreland St W1 **44** A2

West One Shop Cen W1 **44** A3
West Poultry Av EC1 **45** H2
West Smithfield EC1 **45** H2
West Sq SE11 **45** H7
West St WC2 **44** D3
Weymouth Ms W1 **44** B1
Weymouth St W1 **44** A2
Wheatley St W1 **44** A2
Whetstone Pk WC2 **45** F2
Whichcote St SE1 **45** G5
Whitcomb St WC2 **44** D4
Whitefriars St EC4 **45** G3

Whitehall SW1 **44** E4
Whitehall Ct SW1 **44** E5
Whitehall Gdns SW1 **44** E5
Whitehall Pl SW1 **44** E5
White Hart St EC4 **45** H2
White Horse All EC1 **45** H1
White Horse Ms SE1 **45** G6
White Horse St W1 **44** B5
White Lion Hill EC4 **45** H3
White Lyon Ct EC2 **45** J1
Whitfield Pl W1 **44** C1
Whitfield St W1 **44** D2
Whitgift St SE11 **45** F7

Whittlesey St SE1 **45** G5
Whitworth Ho SE1 **45** J7
Wickstead Ho SE1 **45** J7
Wigmore Pl W1 **44** B2
Wigmore St W1 **44** A3
Wilcox Pl SW1 **44** C7
Wild Ct WC2 **45** F2
Wild St WC2 **45** E3
Wilfred St SW1 **44** C6
William IV St WC2 **44** E4
Willoughby St WC1 **44** E2
Willow Pl SW1 **44** C7
Wilton Cres SW1 **44** A6

Wilton Ms SW1 **44** A6
Wilton Pl SW1 **44** A6
Wilton Rd SW1 **44** B7
Wilton Row SW1 **44** A6
Wilton St SW1 **44** B6
Wilton Ter SW1 **44** A6
Wimpole Ms W1 **44** B1
Wimpole St W1 **44** B2
Wincott St SE11 **45** G7
Windmill St W1 **44** D2
Windmill Wk SE1 **45** G5
Windsor Pl SW1 **44** C7
Wine Office Ct EC4 **45** G2

Winnett St W1 **44** D3
Winsley St W1 **44** C2
Woburn Sq WC1 **44** D1
Wollaston Cl SE1 **45** J7
Woodstock Ms W1 **44** A2
Woodstock St W1 **44** B3
Wood St EC2 **45** J3
Wootton St SE1 **45** G5

Y

Yarmouth Pl W1 **44** B5
York Bldgs WC2 **45** E4
York Gate NW1 **44** A1

York Pl WC2 **45** E4
York Rd SE1 **45** F5
Yorkshire Grey Yd WC1 **45** F2
York Ter E NW1 **44** A1
York Ter W NW1 **44** A1

Z

Zoar St SE1 **45** J4

Manchester street index

A

Abingdon St **47** E4
Academy Wk **46** D7
Ackers St **47** F7
Acton Sq **46** A3
Adair St **47** G4
Addington St **47** F2
Addison Cl **47** G7
Adelphi St **46** B3
Aden Cl **47** J4
Adlington St **47** H5
Adstone Cl **47** J3
Adswood St **47** J3
Airton Cl **47** J7
Aked Cl **47** J7
Albion Pl **46** A3
Albion St **46** D5
Albion Way **46** A3
Alderman Sq **47** J4
Aldred St **46** A3
Alexander Gdns **46** C1
Alexandra St **47** H2
Alfred James Cl **47** H2
Alker Rd **47** J2
Alley St **46** E3
Almond St **47** G1
Altair Pl **46** B1
Amory St **47** G5
Anaconda Dr **46** C2
Ancoats **47** G3
Ancoats Gro **47** H4
Ancroft St **46** C7
Angela St **46** C6
Angel St **47** F2
Angora Cl **46** B2
Angora Dr **46** B2
Anita St **47** G3
Anne Nuttall St **46** B6
Anscombe Cl **47** H1
Antares Av **46** B1
Apsley Gro **47** H6
Aquarius St **47** E7
Archway **46** D7
Ardwick **47** J5
Ardwick Grn N **47** G5
Ardwick Grn S **47** G5
Arlington St **46** C2
Arnott Cres **46** E7
Artillery St **46** D4
Arundel St **46** C5
Asgard Dr **46** B5
Asgard Grn **46** B5
Ashlar Dr **47** J4
Ashley St **47** F2
Ashton New Rd **47** J3
Ashton Old Rd **47** H5
Aspin La **47** F2
Atherton St **46** C4
Atkinson St **46** D4
Atwood St **47** E5
Auburn St **47** F4
Audlem Cl **47** J2
Augustus St **47** E1
Avenham Cl **46** D7
Aytoun St **47** F4

B

Back Acton St **47** F4
Back Ashley St **47** F2
Back Bk St **47** F1
Back Br St **46** D3
Back China La **47** F4
Back Coll Land **46** D3
Back George St **47** E4
Back Hampson St **47** H1
Back Hulme St **46** B3
Back Junct St **47** G4
Back Piccadilly **47** F3
Back Pool Fold **46** E3
Back Red Bk **47** F1
Back St. George's Rd **47** G2
Back S Par **46** D3
Back Thomas St **47** F3

Back Turner St **47** F3
Badby Cl **47** J3
Bainbridge Cl **47** J7
Baird St **47** G4
Bale St **46** E4
Balloon St **47** E2
Balmforth St **46** C5
Balsam Cl **47** G6
Bangor St **46** C7
Bankmill Cl **47** G6
Bank Pl **46** B3
Bank St **46** B3
Baptist St **47** F2
Barbeck Cl **47** J2
Baring St **47** G5
Barker St **46** D1
Barlow Pl **47** G6
Barlow's Cft **46** D3
Barnett Dr **46** C2
Barrack St **46** B6
Barrhill Cl **46** C6
Barrow St **46** B3
Barton St **46** D5
Basildon Cl **47** J7
Beamish Cl **47** G6
Beattock St **46** C6
Beaufort St **46** C5
Beaver St **47** E5
Beckhampton Cl **47** H7
Bednal Av **47** J1
Beechcroft Cl **47** H2
Belfort Dr **46** A5
Bendix St **47** F2
Bengal St **47** G2
Bennett St **47** J6
Bentinck St **46** B6
Bent St **47** E1
Berkshire Rd **47** J1
Berry St **47** G5
Beswick Row **47** E2
Beswick St **47** H3
Betley St **47** G4
Bevan Cl **47** J4
Bilbrook St **47** F1
Billing Av **47** G5
Binns Pl **47** G3
Birchin La **47** F3
Birchvale Cl **46** D6
Birt St **47** H1
Bishopsgate **46** E4
Blackburn Pl **46** A4
Blackburn St **46** B2
Blackfriars Rd **46** C2
Blackfriars St **46** D3
Blackhill Cl **47** G6
Blackley St **46** B7
Blacklock St **46** E1
Blantyre St **46** C5
Bletchley Cl **47** H7
Blind La **47** J5
Blisworth Cl **47** J3
Bloom St **47** F4
Blossom St **46** D2
Blossom St (Ancoats) **47** G3
Blucher St **46** A4
Blyton St **47** F7
Boad St **47** G4
Bollington Rd **47** H2
Bombay St **47** F5
Bond St **47** G5
Bonsall St **46** D7
Boond St **46** D2
Booth St **46** E4
Booth St (Salford) **46** D3
Booth St E **47** F6
Booth St W **47** E7
Bootle St **46** D4
Botham Cl **46** E7
Bothwell Rd **47** G2
Boundary La **47** E6
Boundary St E **47** F6
Boundary St W **47** E6
Bourdon St **47** J2

Bow La **46** E4
Bow St **46** D4
Brackley Av **46** B6
Bradford Rd **47** H3
Bradleys Ct **47** F3
Braley St **47** G5
Bramble Av **46** A5
Bramwell Dr **47** G6
Brancaster Rd **47** F5
Branson St **47** J3
Brazennose St **46** D4
Brazil St **47** F5
Brennan Cl **47** E7
Brewer St **47** F3
Brian Redhead Ct **46** C6
Brickley St **47** E1
Brick St **47** F3
Briddon St **46** D1
Bridgeford St **47** F7
Bridge St **46** D3
Bridge St W **46** D3
Bridgewater Pl **47** E3
Bridgewater St **46** D5
Bridgewater St (Salford) **46** C1
Bridgewater Viaduct **46** D5
Briggs St **46** C2
Brighton Pl **47** F7
Brighton St **47** F1
Brindle Pl **47** E7
Brocade Cl **46** B2
Brock St **47** G3
Bromley St **47** F1
Bronte St **47** E7
Brook St **47** F5
Brotherton Cl **46** B6
Brotherton Dr **46** C2
Browfield Av **46** A5
Brown Cross St **46** C3
Browning St **46** B7
Browning St (Salford) **46** C3
Brown St **46** E4
Brunel Av **46** A3
Brunswick **47** G7
Brunswick St **47** F7
Bryant Cl **47** H7
Brydon Av **47** H5
Buckfield Av **46** A5
Bugle St **46** D5
Bunsen St **47** F3
Burlington St **47** E7
Burnell Cl **47** H2
Burstock St **47** F1
Burton St **47** G1
Burton Wk **46** B2
Bury St **46** C2
Butler La **47** H2
Butler St **47** H2
Butter La **46** D3
Buxton St **47** G5
Byrcland Cl **47** J5
Byron St **46** D4

C

Cable St **47** F2
Cabot St **47** G6
Cakebread St **47** G5
Calder St **46** B5
Calico Cl **46** B2
Camberwell St **47** E1
Cambridge St **47** J2
Cambridge St **46** E5
Cambridge St (Salford) **46** D3
Camelford Cl **47** E7
Cameron St **46** D5
Canal St **47** F4
Cannon St **46** B2
Canon Ct **46** E3
Canon Grn Dr **46** C2
Carding Gro **46** C2
Cardroom Rd **47** G3
Carey Cl **46** C1

Carib St **46** D7
Carmel Av **46** A5
Carmel Cl **46** A5
Carnarvon St **46** E1
Caroline St **46** C1
Carpenters La **47** F3
Carriage St **46** C7
Carruthers St **47** H3
Cassidy Cl **47** G2
Castle St **46** C5
Caterham St **47** J4
Cathedral App **46** E2
Cathedral Gates **46** E3
Cathedral St **46** E3
Cathedral Yd **46** E3
Catlow La **47** F3
Catlow St **46** D1
Cavalier St **47** J3
Cavanagh Cl **47** H7
Cavell St **47** F3
Cavendish St **47** E6
Cawdor St **46** B6
Caxton St **46** D3
Caygill St **46** D2
Cedar Pl **46** B1
Central St **46** E4
Century St **46** D5
Chadderton St **47** F2
Chain St **47** E4
Chancel Av **46** A5
Chancellor La **47** H5
Chancery La **46** E4
Change Way **46** C2
Chapelfield Rd **47** H5
Chapel St **46** C3
Chapeltown St **47** G4
Chapel Walks **46** E3
Charles St **47** E5
Charley Av **46** B1
Charlotte St **47** E4
Charlton Pl **47** G5
Charnley Cl **47** J2
Charter St **46** D1
Chase St **47** F1
Chatford Cl **46** C1
Chatham St **47** F4
Chatley St **46** E1
Cheapside **46** E3
Cheetham Hill Rd **46** E1
Cheetwood St **46** D1
Chepstow St **47** E5
Cherryton Wk **47** H2
Chesshyre Av **47** J3
Chester Rd **46** B6
Chester St **46** E6
Chevassut St **46** C6
Cheviot St **46** E1
Chevril Cl **47** E6
Chichester Rd **46** D7
Chiffon Way **46** B2
China La **47** F4
Chippenham Rd **47** H3
Chorlton Rd **46** C7
Chorlton St **46** D6
Chorlton St **47** F4
Chorlton St (Old Trafford) **46** A7
Christchurch Av **46** A3
Churchgate Bldgs **47** G4
Church St **47** F3
Cinder St **47** G2
Cipher St **47** G2
City Rd **46** B7
City Rd E **46** D6
Clarence St **46** E4
Clarendon St **46** D6
Clare St **47** G5
Clarion St **47** G2
Clayburn Rd **46** D6
Cleminson St **46** B3
Cleworth St **46** B6
Clifford St **47** F6
Clifton Gro **46** B7
Clifton St **46** B7

Clive St **47** F2
Cloak St **47** F5
Cloughfield Av **46** A5
Clowes St **46** D3
Cobourg St **47** F4
Coburg Av **46** B1
Cockcroft Rd **46** A2
Cockspur St **46** D3
Coleshill St **47** J1
Colin Murphy Rd **46** C6
College Land **46** D3
Collier St **46** D5
Collier St (Salford) **46** D2
Collingham St **47** F1
Collyhurst Rd **47** G1
Colman Gdns **46** A5
Comet St **47** G4
Commercial St **46** D5
Comus St **46** A4
Concert La **47** E4
Congou St **47** G4
Cooper St **46** E4
Coop St **47** F3
Copeman Cl **47** G7
Copperas St **47** F3
Coral St **47** G6
Cork St **47** J4
Cornbrook **46** B6
Cornbrook **46** B6
Cornbrook Ct **46** B7
Cornbrook Gro **46** B7
Cornbrook Pk Rd **46** B6
Cornbrook St **46** B7
Cornell St **47** G2
Coronation Sq **47** H5
Coronation St **46** A4
Corporation St **46** E3
Cottenham La **46** C1
Cottenham St **47** G6
Cotter St **47** G5
Cottingham Rd **47** J7
Cotton St **47** G3
County St **46** E4
Coupland Cl **47** E7
Coupland St **47** E7
Coupland St E **47** F7
Coverdale Cres **47** H6
Cowan St **47** J3
Cowburn St **46** E1
Cow La **46** B4
Crabbe St **47** F1
Cranbourne St **46** A4
Crane St **47** H5
Cranfield Cl **47** J2
Craven St **46** B4
Crediton Cl **46** E7
Cresbury St **47** H5
Crescent, The **46** A2
Cross Keys St **47** F2
Crossley Ct **47** J3
Cross St **46** E4
Cross St (Salford) **46** D3
Crown La **47** F2
Crown St **46** C5
Crown St (Salford) **46** C2
Culmington Cl **46** C7
Cumberland St **46** B1
Cumbrian Cl **47** G6
Cunard Cl **47** G6
Cygnus Av **46** B1
Cyrus St **47** J3

D

Dainton St **47** J5
Daintry Cl **46** D6
Dalberg St **47** H6
Dale St **47** F3
Dalley Av **46** B1
Dalton Ct **47** G1
Dalton St **47** G1
Damask Av **46** B2
Danebank Wk **47** G6
Danecroft Cl **47** H7
Danson St **47** J2

Dantzic St **47** E3
Dark La **47** H5
Dartford Cl **47** J7
Darton Av **47** J2
Darwen St **46** A7
Davy St **47** G1
Dawson St **46** B5
Dean Rd **46** D2
Deansgate **46** D4
Dean St **47** F3
Deanwater Cl **47** G6
Dearden St **46** D6
Dearmans Pl **46** D3
Deer St **47** G4
Denewell Cl **47** H7
Denver Av **47** J1
Derby St **47** E1
Derwent St **46** B5
Devas St **47** F7
Devine Cl **46** B2
Devonshire St **47** H7
Devonshire St N **47** J6
Devonshire St S **47** H7
Dewhurst St **46** D1
Dickinson St **46** E4
Dilston Cl **47** H7
Dinsdale Cl **47** J2
Dinton St **46** B6
Dobson Cl **47** H7
Dolefield **46** D3
Dolphin Pl **47** H6
Dolphin St **47** H6
Donald St **47** F5
Dorsey St **47** F3
Dover St **47** F7
Downing St **47** G5
Downley Dr **47** H3
Drayton Wk **46** B7
Droitwich Rd **47** H1
Dryden St **47** G7
Dryhurst Wk **47** E7
Ducie St **47** F4
Duke Pl **46** C5
Duke St **46** C5
Duke St (Salford) **46** D2
Dulwich St **47** F1
Duncan St **46** A4
Dun Cl **46** B3
Dunham St **46** D7
Dunlop St **46** D3
Durant St **47** F2
Durling Av **47** H6
Dutton St **46** E1
Dyche St **47** F2
Dyer St **46** A5

E

Eagle St **47** F2
Eastburn Av **47** H1
Eastfield Av **47** J2
Eastleigh Dr **47** H1
East Mkt St **46** C3
East Newton St **47** H2
Eastnor Cl **46** B7
East Ordsall La **46** B4
Eastpark Cl **47** H6
East Philip St **46** D1
East Union St **46** B7
Ebden St **47** F4
Ebenezer St **46** E6
Echo St **47** F5
Eden Cl **46** E7
Edgehill St **47** F3
Edge St **47** F3
Edward St **46** D1
Egerton Rd **46** C5
Egerton St **46** C3
Elbe St **47** H5
Eliza St **46** C6
Ellesmere St **46** B6
Ellis St **46** D7
Elsworth St **47** E1
Elton St **46** C1

Elton's Yd 46 C1
Elverdon Cl 46 D7
Empire St 46 E1
Empress St 46 A7
Encombe Pl 46 B3
Epping St 46 E6
Epsley Cl 47 E7
Epworth St 47 H4
Errington Dr 46 B1
Erskine St 46 C7
Essex St 46 E4
Essex Way 46 C7
Etruria Cl 47 J7
Evans St 46 D2
Everard St 46 B5
Every St 47 H4
Exford Cl 47 H2
Eyre St 47 E7

Fairbrother St 46 A6
Fairfield St 47 G5
Fair St 47 G4
Falkland Av 47 J1
Faraday St 47 F3
Farnborough Rd 47 H1
Farrell St 46 C1
Farwood Cl 46 B7
Faulkner St 47 E4
Federation St 47 E2
Fennel St 46 E2
Fenn St 46 C7
Fenwick St 47 E6
Ferdinan St 47 H1
Fernie St 47 E1
Fernbrook Cl 47 J7
Fernleigh Dr 46 B7
Fern St 47 E1
Ferry St 47 J4
Filby Wk 47 J1
Firbeck Dr 47 H2
Firefly Cl 46 B3
Fire Sta Sq 46 A3
Fir St 47 H1
Fitzwilliam St 46 C1
Flatley Cl 47 E7
Flora Dr 46 C1
Ford St 47 H6
Ford St (Salford) 46 C3
Foundry La 47 F3
Fountain St 47 E4
Four Yards 46 E4
Frances St 47 G6
Francis St 46 D1
Frederick St 46 C3
Freeman Sq 47 E7
Freya Gro 46 A5
Frobisher Cl 47 J7
Frost St 47 J3
Fulmer Dr 47 H2

Gaitskell Cl 47 J4
Galgate Cl 46 C6
Garden La 46 D3
Garden St 46 D2
Garden Wall Cl 46 A5
Garforth Av 47 H2
Gartside St 46 D4
Garwood St 46 D6
Gateaton St 46 E3
Gaythorn St 46 B3
George Leigh St 47 F3
George Parr Rd 46 D7
George St 47 E4
Georgette Dr 46 D2
Gibbs St 46 B3
Gibson Pl 47 E1
Girton St 46 C1
Glasshouse St 47 G2
Gleden St 47 J2
Glenbarry Cl 47 G7
Glenbarry St 47 J5
Gloucester St 46 E5
Gloucester St (Salford) 46 A5
Goadsby St 47 F2
Gold St 47 F4
Gordon St 46 C1
Gore St 47 F4
Gore St (Salford) 46 C3
Gorton St 46 D2
Goulden St 47 F2
Gould St 47 F1
Grafton St 47 G7
Granby Row 47 F5
Granshaw St 47 J2
Gratrix Av 46 A6
Gravell La 46 D2
Grear Ducie St 46 D1
Great Ancoats St 47 F3
Great Bridgewater St 46 D5
Great Clowes St 46 C1
Great Ducie St 46 D1
Great George St 46 B3

Great Jackson St 46 C5
Great John St 46 C4
Great Marlborough St 47 E5
Greek St 47 F6
Green Gate 46 D2
Greengate W 46 C2
Grenham Av 46 B6
Griffiths Cl 46 C1
Groom St 47 F6
Grosvenor Gdns 46 C1
Grosvenor Sq 46 C1
Grosvenor St 47 F6
Guide Post Sq 47 H7
Gunson St 47 H2
Gun St 47 G3
Gurner Av 46 A6
Gurney St 47 J3

Hackleton Cl 47 J3
Hadfield St 46 B7
Half St 46 D2
Hall St 46 E4
Halmore Rd 47 H2
Halsbury Cl 47 J7
Halston St 46 D7
Hamerton Rd 47 G1
Hamilton Gro 46 B7
Hamilton St 46 B7
Hampson St 47 H1
Hamsell Rd 47 G6
Handsworth St 47 J5
Hanging Ditch 46 E3
Hanover St 47 E2
Hanworth Cl 47 G6
Harding St 47 J4
Harding St (Salford) 46 D2
Hardman Sq 46 D4
Hardman St 46 D4
Hardshaw Cl 47 G6
Harehill Cl 47 G5
Harold St 46 B7
Hargreave's St 47 F1
Harkness St 47 H6
Harold St 46 B7
Harriett St 47 H1
Harrison St 47 H4
Harris St (Salford) 46 C1
Harris St 46 D1
Harry Hall Gdns 46 B1
Harter St 47 E4
Hartfield Cl 47 G6
Hart St 47 F4
Hatter St 47 F2
Hatton Av 46 B1
Haverlock Dr 46 B1
Haymarket Cl 47 H7
Heath Av 46 B1
Helga St 47 H1
Hellidon Cl 47 H6
Helmet St 47 H5
Henry St 47 G3
Henry St (Old Trafford) 46 A7
Hewitt St 46 D5
Heyrod St 47 G4
Higher Ardwick 47 H6
Higher Cambridge St 47 E6
Higher Chatham St 47 E6
Higher Ormond St 47 F6
Higher Oswald St 47 F2
Higher York St 47 F6
High St 47 E3
Hillcourt St 47 F6
Hillfield Cl 47 J7
Hillkirk St 47 J3
Hilton St 47 F3
Hinton St 47 G2
Hodson St 46 C2
Holdgate Cl 46 D7
Holkham Cl 47 H3
Holland St 47 H2
Holly Bk Cl 46 B6
Holly St 47 J4
Holt Town 47 J3
Honey St 47 F1
Hood St 47 G3
Hooper St 47 J5
Hope St 47 F4
Hope St (Salford) 46 A3
Hornby St 46 D1
Hornchurch St 46 C7
Horne Dr 47 H3
Houldsworth St 47 F3
Hoyle St 47 H5
Huddart Cl 46 A5
Hughes St 47 J5
Hull Sq 46 B2
Hulme 46 D7
Hulme Ct 46 C6
Hulme Hall Rd 46 B5
Hulme Pl 46 B3
Hulme St 46 D6

Hulme St (Salford) 46 B3
Humberstone Av 46 D6
Hunmanby Av 46 D6
Hunt's Bk 46 E2
Hyde Gro 47 G7
Hyde Pl 47 H7
Hyde Rd 47 H6
Hyde St 46 C7

Inchley Rd 47 F6
Instow Cl 47 H7
Ionas St 46 C1
Irk St 47 F1
Iron St 47 J2
Irwell Pl 46 A3
Irwell St 46 D1
Irwell St (Salford) 46 C3
Islington Way 46 B3

Jackson Cres 46 C6
Jackson's Row 46 D4
James Henry Av 46 A4
James St 47 J1
James St (Salford) 46 B3
Jenkinson St 47 F6
Jersey St 47 G3
Jerusalem Pl 46 D4
Jessamine Av 46 B1
Jessel Cl 47 G6
Joddrell St 46 D4
John Clynes Av 47 H1
John Dalton St 46 D3
Johnson Sq 47 H1
Johnson St 46 B7
Johnson St (Salford) 46 C3
John St 47 F3
John St (Lower Broughton) 46 C1
John St (Salford) 46 D2
Joiner St 47 F3
Jordan St 46 D5
Joynson Av 46 B1
Julia St 46 D1
Jury St 46 D1
Justin Cl 47 F6
Jutland St 47 G4

Kale St 47 G6
Kays Gdns 46 C3
Keele St 47 H1
Kelling Wk 46 C6
Kelvin St 47 F3
Kennedy St 47 E4
Kenwright St 47 F2
Kincardine Rd 47 F6
King Edward St 46 A5
Kingham Dr 47 H2
Kingsfold Av 47 H1
Kingsland Cl 47 H1
King St 46 D3
King St (Salford) 46 D2
King St W 46 D3
Kirkgate Cl 47 H2
Kirkhaven Sq 47 J1
Kirkstall Sq 47 G7
Kirkwood Dr 47 H1

Lackford Dr 47 H1
Lamb La 46 C3
Lamport Cl 47 F5
Lanchester St 47 J2
Landos Rd 47 H2
Langholme Cl 46 C6
Langport Av 47 J7
Langston St 47 D1
Lanstead Dr 47 J2
Lauderdale Cres 47 H7
Laystall St 47 G3
Layton St 47 J2
Leaf St 46 D6
Leak St 46 B6
Ledburn Ct 46 C6
Left Bk 46 C4
Lena St 47 F4
Leslie Hough Way 46 A1
Lever St 47 F3
Lewis St 47 J1
Leycroft St 47 G4
Lidbrook Wk 47 J7
Lime Bk St 47 J5
Lime Gro 47 F7
Limekiln La 47 H5
Linby St 46 C6
Lind St 47 J3
Linen Ct 46 B2
Linsley St 46 D2
Linton Cl 47 H4
Litcham Cl 47 F5
Little Ancoats St 47 F3
Little Holme St 47 J3

Little John St 46 C4
Little Lever St 47 F3
Little Nelson St 47 F2
Little Peter St 46 D5
Little Pit St 47 G3
Little Quay St 46 D4
Liverpool Rd 46 C4
Livesey St 47 G1
Lizard St 47 F3
Lloyd St 46 D4
Lloyd St N 47 F7
Lockett St 46 D1
Lockton Cl 47 G5
Lomax St 47 G3
London Rd 47 F4
Longacre St 47 G4
Long Millgate 46 E2
Longworth St 46 D4
Loom St 47 G3
Lordsmead St 47 C6
Lord St 46 E1
Lostock St 47 H2
Lowcock St 46 C1
Lower Byrom St 46 C4
Lower Chatham St 47 E6
Lower Mosley St 46 D5
Lower Moss La 46 C6
Lower Ormond St 47 E5
Lower Vickers St 47 J2
Lowndes Wk 47 G6
Loxford St 46 E6
Lucy St 46 B7
Ludgate Hill 47 F2
Ludgate St 47 F2
Luna street 47 F3
Lund St 46 A7
Lupton St 46 C3
Lyceum Pl 47 E6

Maidford Cl 47 J3
Major St 47 E4
Makin St 47 E5
Mallard St 47 E5
Mallow St 46 C6
Malta St 47 H3
Malt St 46 B6
Malvern St 46 B7
Manchester St 46 A7
Mancunian Way 46 C6
Mangle St Street 47 F3
Manor St 47 G5
Manson Av 46 B6
Maplin Cl 47 G6
Marble St 47 E3
Marcer Rd 47 H2
Marchmont Cl 47 H7
Market St 46 E3
Markfield Av 47 J7
Markham Cl 47 J4
Marple St 46 C7
Marsden St 46 E3
Marshall St 47 F2
Marshall St (Ardwick) 47 H6
Marsworth Dr 47 H3
Mary France St 46 C6
Mary St 46 D1
Mason St 47 F2
Mason St (Salford) 46 C3
Massey St 46 B3
Mayan Av 46 B2
Mayes St 47 E2
Mayo St 47 H5
Mays St 47 F2
Meadow Rd 46 B1
Medlock St 46 D5
Melbourne St 46 C6
Mellor St 47 H2
Melville St 46 C3
Merrill St 47 H3
Middlewood St 46 B4
Midland St 47 J5
Miles Platting 47 J1
Milk St 47 E3
Millbank St 47 G4
Millbeck St 47 E6
Miller St 46 E2
Mill Grn St 47 H5
Millhall Cl 46 C7
Millhead Av 47 J2
Millow St 47 E2
Milnrow Cl 47 F2
Milton St 46 C1
Mincing St 47 F2
Minshull St 47 F4
Minshull St S 47 F4
Mistletoe Grn 46 C2
Moorhead St 47 G2
Morbourne Cl 47 J7
Mosley St 47 E4
Mosscott Wk 47 G5
Mosshall Cl 46 C7
Moulton St 46 D1
Mouncey St 47 E5

Mount Carmel Cres 46 A5
Mount St 46 E4
Mount St (Salford) 46 C2
Mozart Cl 47 H2
Mulberry St 46 D4
Munday St 47 H3
Munster St 47 E2
Murrey St 47 G3
Museum St 46 E4
Muslin St 46 B4
Myrtle Pl 46 A1

Nancy St 46 B6
Nansen St 47 J5
Naples St 47 F2
Nash St 46 C7
Nathan Dr 46 C2
Naval St 47 G3
Naylor St 47 H1
Neild St 47 G5
Neill St 46 C1
Nelson St 47 J1
Nether St 47 G5
New Allen St 47 G2
Newbeck St 47 F2
New Br St 46 D2
Newcastle St 46 E6
New Cath St 46 E3
Newcombe St 46 E1
New Elm St 46 C4
New Gartside St 46 D4
New Islington 47 H3
New Mkt 46 E3
New Mkt St 46 E3
New Mt St 47 F2
New Quay St 46 C4
Newton St 47 F3
New Union St 47 G3
New Vine St 46 D6
New Wakefield St 47 E5
New Welcome St 46 D6
New Windsor 46 A3
Nicholas St 47 E4
Nine Acre Dr 46 A6
Niven St 47 G5
North Bailey St 46 C3
Northdown Av 46 B6
North George St 46 B2
North Hill St 46 C2
North Phoebe St 46 A4
North Star Dr 46 B3
Northumberland Cl 46 A7
Northumberland Cres 46 A7
North Western St 47 G5
North W Services Rd 46 D3
Norton St 46 D2
Norway St 47 J4
Nuneaton Dr 47 H1
Nuttall St 46 A7

Oakford Av 47 G1
Oak St 47 F3
Old Bk St 46 E3
Old Birley St 46 D7
Oldbury Cl 47 H2
Old Elm St 47 G6
Oldfield Rd 46 A5
Oldham Rd 47 F3
Oldham St 47 F3
Old Medlock St 46 C4
Old Mill St 47 G3
Old Mt St 47 F2
Old Trafford 46 A7
Old York St 46 C6
Oliver St 47 F7
Ordsall Dr 46 A6
Ordsall La 46 A5
Oregon Cl 47 G6
Orion Pl 46 B1
Ormsgill St 46 D7
Orsett Cl 47 H1
Osborne St 47 G1
Oswald St 47 F2
Oswald St (Ancoats) 47 H4
Overbridge Rd 46 D1
Oxford Rd 47 E5
Oxford St 46 E4

Paddock St 47 G5
Palfrey Pl 47 H6
Pall Mall 46 E4
Palmerston St 47 H4
Parish Vw 46 A4
Parker St 47 F3
Park Pl 47 E1
Park St 46 E1
Park St (Salford) 46 B3
Parsonage 46 D3
Parsonage La 46 D3
Parsonage Way 46 A5

Paton St 47 F4
Pattishall Cl 47 J4
Peak St 47 G3
Peary St 47 G1
Peel Mt 46 A1
Pegasus Sq 46 B1
Pembroke Cl 47 H7
Pencroft Way 47 F7
Penfield Cl 47 F5
Percy Dr 46 A6
Percy St 46 C7
Peru St 46 B2
Peter St 46 D4
Phoenix St 47 E3
Phoenix Way 46 D7
Piccadilly 47 F3
Pickford St 47 G3
Picton Cl 46 C2
Picton St 46 C1
Piercy Av 46 B1
Piercy St 47 H3
Pigeon St 47 G3
Pimblett St 46 E1
Pine St 47 E4
Pin Mill Brow 47 H5
Pittbrook St 47 J5
Plymouth Gro 47 G7
Plymouth Vw 47 G7
Pochin St 47 J1
Poland St 47 G2
Polebrook Av 47 H7
Police St 46 D3
Pollard St 47 H4
Pollard St E 47 H3
Polygon Av 47 H7
Polygon St 47 G6
Pomona Strand 46 A6
Poplar St 47 J5
Poplin Dr 46 D2
Portland St 47 E5
Portsmouth St 47 G7
Port St 47 F3
Portugal St 47 G2
Portugal St E 47 G4
Postal St 47 G3
Postbridge Cl 47 H7
Potato Wf 46 C5
Poynton St 46 E6
Price St 47 J3
Primrose St 47 G2
Prince's Br 46 C4
Princess Rd 46 D6
Princess St 46 E4
Princess St (Cornbrook) 46 B6
Pritchard St 47 F5
Providence St 47 H4
Pryme St 46 C5
Purslow Cl 47 J3

Quay St 46 C4
Quay St (Salford) 46 D3
Queen St 46 D4
Queen St (Salford) 46 D2
Quenby St 46 C6
Quendon Av 46 C1

Rachel St 47 H5
Radium St 47 G2
Ralli Cts 46 C3
Randerson St 47 G5
Rankin Cl 46 D7
Raven St 47 H5
Reather Wk 47 H1
Red Bk 47 E2
Redfern St 47 E2
Redhill St 47 G3
Red Lion St 47 F3
Regent Sq 46 A5
Reilly St 46 D6
Reservoir St 46 D2
Reyner St 47 E4
Rial Pl 47 E7
Ribston St 46 C7
Rice St 46 C5
Richmond St 47 F4
Richmond St (Salford) 46 C2
Ridgefield 46 D3
Ridgeway St E 47 H3
Ridgway St 47 H3
Riga St 47 F2
Rigel Pl 46 B1
Rigel St 47 H2
Rimworth Dr 47 H1
Ringstead Dr 47 G1
Ripley Cl 47 H4
River Pl 46 D5
Riverside 46 B2
River St 46 D6
River St (Ardwick) 47 H5
Robert St 46 E1

Roby St 47 F4
Rochdale Rd 47 F2
Rockdove Av 46 D6
Rocket Way 46 C3
Rockingham Cl 47 J7
Rodney St 47 H2
Rodney St (Salford) 46 C3
Roe St 47 G2
Roger St 47 F1
Rolla St 46 D2
Rolleston Av 47 H2
Rolls Cres 46 C7
Roman St 47 F3
Rome Rd 47 G2
Rondin Cl 47 J5
Rondin Rd 47 J5
Rope Wk 46 D2
Rosamond Dr 46 C3
Rosamond St W 47 E6
Rosewell Cl 47 J1
Rostron Av 47 J6
Rowendale St 46 D5
Royce Rd 46 C6
Roydale St 47 J2
Royds Cl 47 J7
Ruby St 47 E7
Rudcroft Cl 47 G6
Rudman Dr 46 A5
Rugby St 46 D1
Runcorn St 46 B6

S

Sackville St 47 E4
Sagar St 46 D1
St. Andrew's Sq 47 H4
St. Andrew's St 47 G4
St. Ann's Sq 46 D3
St. Ann St 46 D3
St. Bartholomew's Dr 46 A4
St. Chad's St 47 E1
St. Clement's Dr 46 A5
St. George's 46 B6
St. Ignatius Wk 46 A5
St. James's Sq 46 E4
St. James St 47 E4
St. John St 46 D4
St. Mary's Gate 46 E3
St. Mary's
  Parsonage 46 D3
St. Mary's St 46 C3
St. Michael's Sq 47 F2
St. Nicholas Rd 46 C6
St. Philip's St 46 B3
St. Simon St 46 C1
St. Stephen's Cl 47 H7
St. Stephen St 46 C3
St. Thomas St 47 F1
St. Vincent St 47 H3
St. Wilfrids St 46 C6
Salford 46 A4
Salford App 46 D3
Salmon St 47 F3
Saltford Av 47 H3
Salutation St 46 E7
Samouth Cl 47 H2
Sam Swire St 46 D7
Samuel Ogden St 47 F5
Sanctuary, The 46 D7
Sandal St 47 J2
Sandford St 46 C1
Sand St 47 G1
Sawley Rd 47 J1
Scarsdale St 46 A1
School Ct 47 G3
School St 47 F2
School St (Salford) 46 C1
Scotland 47 E2
Scotporth Cl 46 C6
Sefton Cl 47 G6
Senior St 46 D2
Seymour Cl 46 A7
Sharp St 47 F2
Shaw Cres 46 E2
Shawgreen Cl 46 C6
Shawheath Cl 46 C6
Shearsby Cl 46 D7
Sheffield St 47 G4
Sherborne St 46 D1
Sherbourne St W 46 D1
Sherratt St 47 G2
Shetland Rd 47 H1
Shilford Dr 47 G2
Shortcroft St 46 D5
Short St 47 F3
Short St (Salford) 46 C1
Shrewsbury St 46 B7
Shudehill 47 F3
Sidney St 47 F6
Sidney St (Salford) 46 C3
Silkin Cl 47 F6
Silk St 47 G2
Silk St (Salford) 46 B2
Silvercroft St 46 C5
Silver St 47 F4

Simeon St 47 F2
Simms Cl 46 B3
Simpson St 47 F2
Sirius Pl 46 B1
Skerry Cl 47 G6
Skip Pl 47 E1
Slate Av 47 H3
Sleaford Cl 47 H1
Smallridge Cl 47 H2
Smith St 46 A6
Smithy La 46 D3
Snell St 47 H4
Soar St 47 F3
Sorrel St 46 C6
Southall St 46 D4
Southall St
  (Strangeways) 46 D1
Southend Av 46 B7
Southern St 46 D5
Southgate 46 D3
South Hall St 46 B5
South King St 46 D3
Southmill St 46 E4
South Pump St 47 F4
South W Services Rd 46 C4
Sparkle St 47 G4
Spa St 47 F7
Spaw St 46 C3
Spear St 47 F3
Spectator St 47 H3
Springfield La 46 D2
Springfield Sq 46 D4
Spring Gdns 47 E4
Spruce St 46 C7
Stalham Cl 47 H1
Stanley Rd 46 B7
Stanley St 47 F1
Stanley St (Salford) 46 C4
Stansby Gdns 47 J7
Station App (for
  Oxford Road
  Station) 47 E5
Station App (for
  Piccadilly Station) 47 F4
Staverton Cl 47 G6
Stephen St 46 E1
Stevenson Pl 47 F3
Stevenson Sq 47 F3
Stevenson St 46 B3
Stockland Cl 47 F6
Stockport Rd 47 H6
Stocks St 47 E1
Stocks St E 47 E1
Stonall Av 46 C6
Stonelow Cl 46 E6
Stone St 46 C5
Store St 47 F4
Stracey St 47 J2
Strawberry Hill 46 A1
Stretford Rd 46 B7
Style St 47 F2
Sudbury Cl 46 B7
Sudell St 47 G2
Sussex St 46 B1
Swan St 47 F2
Swiftsure Av 46 B3
Syndall Av 47 H6
Syndall St 47 H6

T

Talgarth Rd 47 G1
Tamar Ct 46 B7
Tame St 47 H4
Tariff St 47 F3
Tasle All 46 D4
Tatton St 46 B6
Tatton St (Salford) 46 A5
Taunton St 47 J3
Tavery Cl 47 H3
Tebutt St 47 G2
Teer St 47 J3
Temperance St 47 G5
Tewkesbury Rd 47 J2
Thirsk St 47 G5
Thomas St 47 F3
Thompson St 47 F2
Thompson St
  (Strangeways) 46 D1
Thomson St 47 H7
Thor Grn 46 B5
Thornage Dr 47 H1
Thorncross Cl 46 B6
Thornden Rd 47 J1
Thornley Brow 47 E2
Thornton St 47 H1
Tib La 46 E4
Tib St 47 F3
Tideswell Av 47 H2
Tidworth Av 47 H3
Tinsley Cl 47 J2
Tivoli St 46 D4
Todd St 47 E2
Tomlinson St 46 D7
Tonge St 47 J5

Tonman St 46 D4
Torquay Cl 47 H7
Towcester Cl 47 J3
Town Hall La 46 E3
Trafford Bk Rd 46 A7
Trafford Ct 46 C6
Trafford Pl 46 B7
Trafford St 46 D5
Travis St 47 G5
Trentham St 46 B6
Trinity Way 46 B5
Tristam Cl 47 G6
Troutbeck Av 47 H3
Trumpet St 46 D5
Tudbury Way 46 C2
Tuer St 47 F7
Turner St 47 F3
Turner St
  (Old Trafford) 46 A6
Tutbury St 47 H4
Twillbrook Dr 46 D2

U

Union St 47 F3
Union St (Ardwick) 47 H5
University Rd 46 A2
University Rd W 46 A2
Upper Brook St 47 F6
Upper Cyrus St 47 J3
Upper Helena St 47 J2
Upper Kirby St 47 H3
Upper Moss La 46 C7
Upper Wf St 46 B3

V

Varley St 47 J1
Vauxhall St 47 G1
Velour Cl 46 B1
Vesta St 47 H3
Viaduct St 47 J4
Viaduct St (Salford) 46 D2
Vickers St 47 J1
Victoria Br St 46 D3
Victoria Sta App 46 E2
Victoria St 46 E3
Victor St 47 G1
Victor St (Salford) 46 C3
Virgil St 46 B6

W

Wadeford Cl 47 G2
Wadeson Rd 47 G5
Wadlow Cl 46 C2
Walker's Cft 46 E2
Wallness 46 A1
Wallness La 46 A1
Warde St 46 C7
Wardle St 47 J2
Warford St 47 F1
Warmington Dr 47 J7
Warwick St 47 F3
Warwick St (Hulme) 46 D7
Waterloo St 47 E4
Water St 46 B5
Water St (Ardwick) 47 H5
Watkin Cl 47 G7
Watkin St 46 C1
Watson St 46 D5
Weald Cl 47 G6
Weir St 46 D7
Welland Cl 46 B7
Wellhead Cl 46 E7
Wellington Grn 46 C7
Wellington St 46 C2
Well St 47 E3
West Bk St 46 A4
West Charles St 46 A3
West Crown Av 46 A4
West Hope St 46 A3
West King St 46 C2
Westminster St 46 B6
West Mosley St 47 E4
Weston St 47 J3
West Pk St 46 A5
Weybridge Rd 47 H3
Whalley St 47 H2
Wheater's Cres 46 B1
Wheater's St 46 B1
Wheater's Ter 46 B1
Whimberry Cl 46 A5
Whitchurch St 46 D1
Whitekirk Cl 47 G6
White St 46 B7
Whitfield St 47 E1
Whittle's Cft 47 G4
Whittle St 47 F3
Whitworth St 47 F5
Whitworth St W 46 D5
Wilberforce Cl 46 D7
Wilfred St 46 D1
William Chadwick Cl 47 H1
Williamson St 47 F1
William St 47 H5
Wilmott St 46 E6

Wilson St 47 H7
Wilton Pl 46 B3
Wilton St 47 F6
Winder Dr 47 H3
Windmill Av 46 A5
Windmill St 46 D4
Winfell Dr 47 J2
Winscombe Dr 47 H1
Winser St 47 E5
Winstanley Rd 47 H2
Withy Gro 47 E3
Woden's Av 46 A5
Woden St 46 B5
Woodlark Cl 46 B3
Wood St 46 D4
Woodward Pl 47 H3
Woodward St 47 H3
Woollam Pl 46 C4
Worrall St 46 A5
Worsley St 46 B5
Worsley St (Salford) 46 D3
Wright St 46 A7
Wroe St 46 B3
Wyatt Av 46 A5
Wynne St 46 A1
Wyre St 47 G5

Y

Yew St 46 C7
Yorkshire St 46 D3
York St 47 E3
York St (Hulme) 46 C6
York St (off Charles
  Street) 47 E5
York St E 47 F6

Z

Zion Cres 46 D7

Aberdeen

Tourist Information Centre: 23 Union Street
Tel: 01224 288828

Albert Quay	C3	Hutcheon Street	B2
Albert Street	B2	Justice Mill Lane	B3
Albury Road	B3	King's Crescent	C1
Albyn Place	A3	King Street	C1
Argyll Place	A2	Langstane Place	B3
Ashgrove Road	A1	Leadside Road	B2
Ashgrove Road West	A1	Leslie Terrace	B1
Ash-hill Drive	A1	Links Road	C2
Ashley Road	A3	Linksfield Road	C1
Back Hilton Road	A1	Loch Street	B2
Baker Street	B2	Maberly Street	B2
Beach Boulevard	C2	Market Street	C3
Bedford Place	B1	Menzies Road	C3
Bedford Road	B1	Merkland Road East	C1
Beechgrove Terrace	A2	Mid Stocket Road	A2
Belgrave Terrace	A2	Mile-end Avenue	A2
Berryden Road	B1	Miller Street	C2
Blaikie's Quay	C3	Mount Street	B2
Bon-Accord Street	B3	Nelson Street	C2
Bonnymuir Place	A2	North Esplanade East	C3
Bridge Street	B2	North Esplanade West	C3
Brighton Place	A3	Orchard Street	C1
Cairncry Road	A1	Osborne Place	A3
Canal Road	B1	Palmerston Road	C3
Carden Place	A3	Park Road	C1
Carlton Place	A3	Park Street	C2
Cattofield Place	A1	Pittodrie Place	C1
Causewayend	B1	Pittodrie Street	C1
Chapel Street	B2	Powis Place	B1
Claremont Street	A3	Powis Terrace	B1
Clifton Road	A1	Queens Road	A3
College Bounds	B1	Queens Terrace	A3
College Street	C3	Regent Quay	C2
Commerce Street	C2	Rosehill Crescent	A1
Commercial Quay	C3	Rosehill Drive	A1
Constitution Street	C2	Rosemount Place	A2
Cornhill Drive	A1	Rose Street	B2
Cornhill Road	A1	Rubislaw Terrace	A3
Cornhill Terrace	A1	St. Swithin Street	A3
Cotton Street	C2	Schoolhill	B2
Cromwell Road	A3	Seaforth Road	C1
Desswood Place	A3	Sinclair Road	C3
Devonshire Road	A3	Skene Square	B2
Elmbank Terrace	B1	Skene Street	B2
Esslemont Avenue	B2	South Crown Street	B3
Ferryhill Road	B3	South Esplanade West	C3
Fonthill Road	B3	Spital	C1
Forest Road	A3	Springbank Terrace	B3
Forest Avenue	A3	Spring Gardens	B2
Fountainhall Road	A2	Stanley Street	A3
Froghall Terrace	B1	Sunnybank Road	B1
Gallowgate	C2	Sunnyside Road	B1
George Street	B1	Union Glen	B3
Gillespie Crescent	A1	Union Grove	A3
Gladstone Place	A3	Union Street	B3
Golf Road	C1	Urquhart Road	C2
Gordondale Road	A2	Victoria Bridge	C3
Great Southern Road	B3	Victoria Road	C3
Great Western Road	A3	Walker Road	C3
Guild Street	C3	Waterloo Quay	C2
Hamilton Place	A2	Waverley Place	B3
Hardgate	B3	Well Place	B3
Hilton Drive	A1	Westburn Drive	A1
Hilton Place	A1	Westburn Road	A2
Hilton Street	A1	West North Street	C2
Holburn Road	B3	Whitehall Place	A2
Holburn Street	B3	Whitehall Road	A2
Holland Street	B1	Willowbank Road	B3

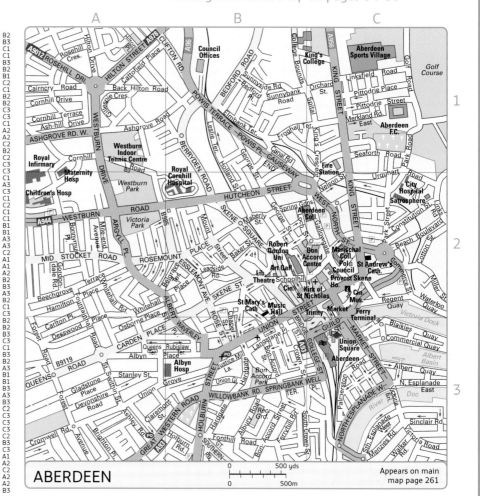

ABERDEEN   Appears on main map page 261

Bath

Tourist Information Centre: Abbey Chambers, Abbey Churchyard
Tel: 0906 711 2000

Ambury	A3	Pierrepont Street	B3
Archway Street	C3	Pulteney Gardens	C3
Argyle Street	B2	Pulteney Mews	C1
Avon Street	A2	Pulteney Road	C2
Barton Street	A2	Queen Street	A2
Bath Street	B2	Quiet Street	A1
Bathwick Hill	C1	Rossiter Road	B3
Beau Street	B2	Royal Crescent	A1
Bennett Street	A1	St. James's Parade	A2
Bridge Street	B2	St. John's Road	B1
Broad Quay	A3	St. Marks Road	B3
Broad Street	B1	Sawclose	A2
Broadway	C3	Southgate Street	B3
Brock Street	A1	Spring Crescent	C3
Chapel Row	A2	Stall Street	B2
Charles Street	A2	Sutton Street	C1
Charlotte Street	A1	Sydney Place	C1
Cheap Street	B2	The Circus	A1
Claverton Street	B3	Union Street	B2
Corn Street	A3	Upper Borough Walls	A2
Daniel Street	C1	Walcot Street	B1
Darlington Street	C1	Wells Road	A3
Dorchester Street	B3	Westgate Buildings	A2
Edward Street	C1	Westgate Street	A2
Excelsior Street	C3	Wood Street	A1
Ferry Lane	C2	York Street	B2
Gay Street	A1		
George Street	A1		
Grand Parade	B2		
Great Pulteney Street	C1		
Green Park Road	A2		
Green Street	B1		
Grove Street	B1		
Henrietta Gardens	C1		
Henrietta Mews	C1		
Henrietta Road	B1		
Henrietta Street	B1		
Henry Street	B2		
High Street	B2		
Holloway	A3		
James Street West	A2		
John Street	A1		
Kingsmead East	A2		
Kingsmead Square	A2		
Lansdown Road	B1		
Laura Place	B1		
Lime Grove	C2		
Lime Grove Gardens	C2		
Lower Borough Walls	B2		
Lower Bristol Road	A3		
Magdalen Avenue	A3		
Manvers Street	B3		
Milk Street	A2		
Milsom Street	B1		
Monmouth Place	A1		
Monmouth Street	A2		
Newark Street	B3		
New Bond Street	B2		
New King Street	A2		
New Orchard Street	B2		
New Street	A2		
North Parade	B2		
North Parade Road	C2		
Old King Street	A1		
Orange Grove	B2		
Paragon	B1		

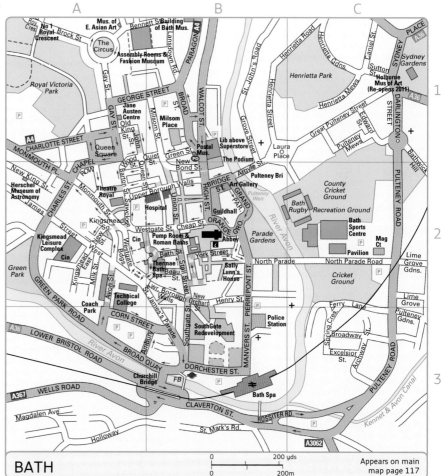

BATH   Appears on main map page 117

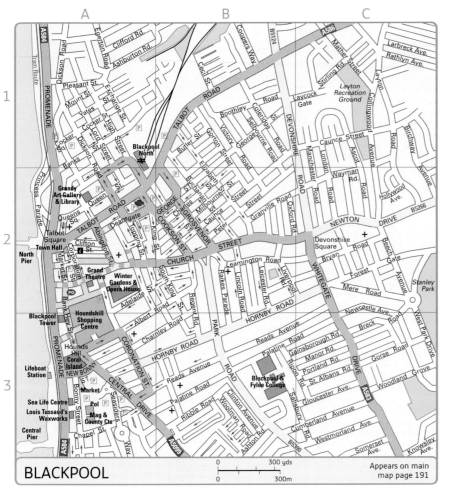

BLACKPOOL

0   300 yds
0   300m

Appears on main map page 191

Tourist Information Centre: 1 Clifton Street
Tel: 01253 478222

Abingdon Street	A2
Adelaide Street	A2
Albert Road	A3
Ascot Road	C1
Ashburton Road	A1
Ashton Road	B3
Bank Hey Street	A2
Banks Street	A1
Beech Avenue	C2
Birchway Avenue	C1
Bonny Street	A3
Boothley Road	B1
Breck Road	C3
Bryan Road	C2
Buchanan Street	B2
Butler Street	B1
Caunce Street	B2/C1
Cecil Street	B1
Central Drive	A3
Chapel Street	A3
Charles Street	B2
Charnley Road	A3
Church Street	B2
Clifford Road	A1
Clifton Street	A2
Clinton Avenue	B3
Cocker Square	A1
Cocker Street	A1
Coleridge Road	B1
Collingwood Avenue	C1
Cookson Street	B2
Coopers Way	B1
Coronation Street	A3
Corporation Street	A2
Cumberland Avenue	C3
Deansgate	A2
Devonshire Road	B1
Devonshire Square	C2
Dickson Road	A1
Egerton Road	A1
Elizabeth Street	B1
Exchange Street	A1
Forest Gate	C2
Gainsborough Road	B3
George Street	B2/B1
Gloucester Avenue	C3
Gorse Road	C3
Gorton Street	B1
Granville Road	B2
Grosvenor Street	B2
High Street	A1
Hollywood Avenue	C2
Hornby Road	A3
Hounds Hill	A3
King Street	A2
Knowsley Avenue	C3
Larbreck Avenue	C1
Laycock Gate	C1
Layton Road	C1
Leamington Road	B2
Leicester Road	B2
Lincoln Road	B2
Liverpool Road	B2
London Road	C1
Lord Street	A1
Manchester Road	C1

Manor Road	C3
Market Street	A2
Mather Street	C1
Mere Road	C2
Milbourne Street	B2
Mount Street	A1
New Bonny Street	A3
Newcastle Avenue	C2
Newton Drive	C2
Oxford Road	B3
Palatine Road	B3
Park Road	B3
Peter Street	B2
Pleasant Street	A1
Portland Road	C3
Princess Parade	A2
Promenade	A1
Queens Square	A1
Queen Street	A2
Rathlyn Avenue	C1
Reads Avenue	B3
Regent Road	B2
Ribble Road	B3
Ripon Road	B3
St. Albans Road	C3
Salisbury Road	C3
Seasiders Way	A3
Selbourne Road	B1
Somerset Avenue	C3
South King Street	B2
Stirling Road	C1
Talbot Road	A2/B1
Talbot Square	A2
Topping Street	A2
Victory Road	B1
Wayman Road	C2
Westmorland Avenue	C3
West Park Drive	C2
Whitegate Drive	C2/C3
Woodland Grove	C3
Woolman Road	B3
Yates Street	A1

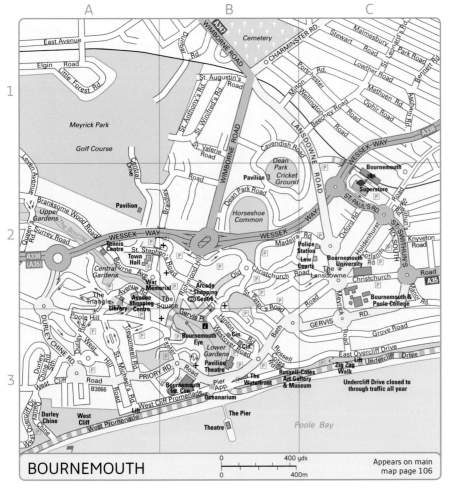

BOURNEMOUTH

0   400 yds
0   400m

Appears on main map page 106

Tourist Information Centre: Westover Road
Tel: 0845 05 11 700

Ascham Road	C1
Avenue Road	A2
Bath Road	B3
Beechey Road	C1
Bennett Road	C1
Bourne Avenue	A2
Braidley Road	B2
Branksome Wood Road	A2
Cavendish Road	B1
Central Drive	A1
Charminster Road	B1
Christchurch Road	C2
Cotlands	C2
Dean Park Road	B2
Dunbar Road	B1
Durley Chine	A3
Durley Chine Road	A3
Durley Chine Road South	A3
Durley Road	A3
East Avenue	A1
East Overcliff Drive	C3
Elgin Road	A1
Exeter Road	B3
Gervis Place	B3
Gervis Road	C3
Grove Road	C3
Hinton Road	B3
Holdenhurst Road	C2
Knyveton Road	C2
Lansdowne Road	B1
Leven Avenue	A1
Little Forest Road	A1
Lowther Road	C1
Madeira Road	B2
Malmesbury Park Road	C1
Manor Road	C2
Methuen Road	C1
Meyrick Road	C2
Milton Road	B1
Old Christchurch Road	B2
Ophir Road	C1
Oxford Road	C2
Pier Approach	B3
Poole Hill	A3
Portchester Road	C1
Priory Road	A3
Queen's Road	A2
Richmond Hill	B2
Russell Cotes Road	B3
St. Augustin's Road	B1
St. Anthony's Road	B1
St. Leonard's Road	C1
St. Michael's Road	A3
St. Pauls' Road	C2
St. Peter's Road	B2
St. Stephen's Road	A2
St. Swithun's Road	C2
St. Swithun's Road South	C2
St. Valerie Road	B1
St. Winifred's Road	B1
Stewart Road	C1
Surrey Road	A2
The Lansdowne	C2
The Square	B2
The Triangle	A2
Tregonwell Road	A3

Undercliff Drive	C3
Wellington Road	C1
Wessex Way	A2/C1
West Cliff Promenade	A3
West Cliff Road	A3
West Hill Road	A3
West Overcliff Drive	A3
West Promenade	A3
Westover Road	B3
Wimborne Road	B2

Tourist Information Centre: City Hall, Centenary Square
Tel: 01274 433678

Akam Road	A1	John Street	A2
Ann Place	A3	Kirkgate	B2
Ashgrove	A3	Leeds Road	C2
Balme Street	B1	Little Horton Lane	A3
Bank Street	B2	Lower Kirkgate	B2
Baptist Place	A1	Lumb Lane	A1
Barkerend Road	C1	Manchester Road	B3
Barry Street	A2	Manningham Lane	A1
Bolling Road	C3	Mannville Terrace	A3
Bolton Road	C1	Manor Row	B1
Brearton Street	A1	Melbourne Place	A3
Bridge Street	B2	Midland Road	B1
Britannia Street	B3	Moody Street	C3
Broadway	B2	Morley Street	A3
Burnett Street	C2	Neal Street	A3
Caledonia Street	B3	Nelson Street	B3
Canal Road	B1	North Parade	B1
Captain Street	C1	North Street	C1
Carlton Street	A2	North Wing	C1
Carter Street	C3	Nuttall Road	C1
Centenary Square	B2	Otley Road	A1
Chain Street	A1	Paradise Street	A1
Channing Way	B2	Park Road	B3
Chapel Street	C2	Peckover Street	C2
Charles Street	B2	Prince's Way	B2
Cheapside	B2	Prospect Street	C3
Chester Street	A3	Radwell Drive	A3
Churchbank	C2	Rawson Place	B1
Claremont	C1	Rawson Road	A1
Croft Street	B3	Rebecca Street	A1
Darfield Street	A1	Rouse Fold	C3
Darley Street	B1	Russell Street	A3
Drake Street	B2	Salem Street	B1
Drewton Road	A1	Sawrey Place	A3
Dryden Street	C3	Sedgwick Close	A1
Duke Street	B1	Sharpe Street	B3
Dyson Street	A1	Shipley Airedale Road	C1
East Parade	C2	Simes Street	A1
Edmund Street	A3	Snowden Street	A1
Edward Street	C3	Sunbridge Road	A1
Eldon Place	A1	Sylhet Close	A1
Fairfax Street	C3	Ternhill Grove	B3
Filey Street	C2	Tetley Street	A2
Fitzwilliam Street	C3	The Tyrls	B2
Fountain Street	A1	Thornton Road	A2
George Street	C2	Trafalgar Street	A1
Godwin Street	B2	Trinity Road	A3
Gracechurch Street	A1	Tumbling Hill Street	A2
Grafton Street	A3	Valley Road	B1
Grattan Road	A2	Vaughan Street	A1
Great Horton Road	A3	Vicar Lane	C2
Grove Terrace	A3	Vincent Street	A2
Guy Street	C3	Wakefield Road	C3
Hall Ings	B2	Wapping Road	C1
Hall Lane	C3	Water Lane	A2
Hallfield Road	A1	Westgate	A1
Hamm Strasse	B1	Wigan Street	A2
Hammerton Street	C2		
Hanover Square	A1		
Harris Street	C2		
Heap Lane	C1		
Houghton Place	A1		
Howard Street	A3		
Hustlergate	B2		
Ivegate	B2		
James Street	B2		

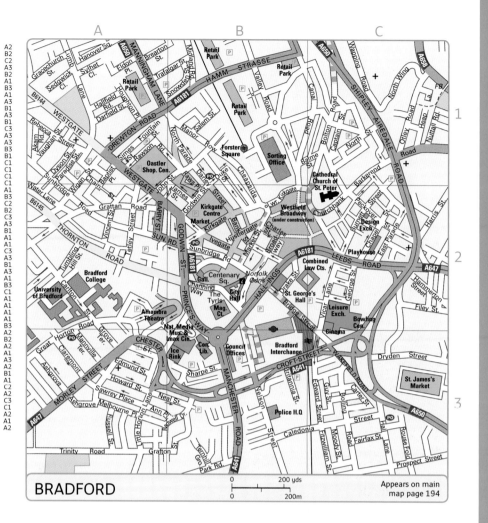

BRADFORD

0 ——— 200 yds
0 ——— 200m

Appears on main map page 194

Tourist Information Centre: Royal Pavilion Shop,
4-5 Pavilion Buildings Tel: 0300 3000088

Addison Road	A1	Southover Street	C2
Albion Hill	C2	Springfield Road	B1
Beaconsfield Road	B1	Stafford Road	A1
Brunswick Square	A2	Stanford Road	B1
Buckingham Place	B1	Sussex Street	C2
Buckingham Road	B2	Terminus Road	B2
Carlton Hill	C2	The Lanes	B3
Cheapside	B2	The Upper Drive	A1
Church Street	B2	Trafalgar Street	B2
Churchill Square	B3	Union Road	C1
Clifton Hill	A2	Upper Lewes Road	C1
Clyde Road	B1	Upper North Street	A2
Davigdor Road	A1	Upper Rock Gardens	C3
Ditchling Rise	B1	Viaduct Road	B1
Ditchling Road	C1	Victoria Road	A2
Dyke Road	B2	Waterloo Street	A2
Dyke Road Drive	B1	Wellington Road	C1
Eastern Road	C3	West Drive	C2
Edward Street	C3	West Street	B3
Elm Grove	C1	Western Road	A2
Fleet Street	B2	Wilbury Crescent	A1
Florence Road	B1	York Avenue	A2
Freshfield Road	C3	York Place	C2
Furze Hill	A2		
Gloucester Road	B2		
Grand Junction Road	B3		
Hamilton Road	B1		
Hanover Street	C2		
Highdown Road	A1		
Holland Road	A2		
Hollingdean Road	C1		
Howard Place	B1		
Islingword Road	C1		
John Street	C2		
King's Road	A3		
Lansdowne Road	A2		
Lewes Road	C1		
London Road	B1		
Lyndhurst Road	A1		
Madeira Drive	C3		
Marine Parade	C3		
Montefiore Road	A1		
Montpelier Road	A2		
New England Road	B1		
New England Street	B1		
Nizells Avenue	A1		
Norfolk Terrace	A2		
North Road	B2		
North Street	B2		
Old Shoreham Road	A1		
Old Steine	C3		
Park Crescent Terrace	C1		
Park Street	C2		
Port Hall Road	A1		
Preston Circus	B1		
Preston Road	B1		
Preston Street	A3		
Prince's Crescent	C2		
Queen's Park Road	C2		
Queen's Road	B2		
Richmond Place	C2		
Richmond Road	C1		
Richmond Street	C2		
Richmond Terrace	C2		
St. James's Street	C3		
Somerhill Road	A2		

BRIGHTON

0 ——— 200 yds
0 ——— 200m

Appears on main map page 109

BRISTOL

BRISTOL

200 yds / 200m

Appears on main map page 131

Tourist Information Centre: E Shed 1, Canons Road
Tel: 0906 711 2191

Alfred Hill	A1	Redcliffe Bridge	B3
Anchor Road	A3	Redcliffe Parade	B3
Avon Street	C2	Redcliff Hill	B3
Baldwin Street	A2	Redcliff Mead Lane	C3
Bath Road	C3	Redcliff Street	B2
Bond Street	B1	Redcross Street	C1
Bridge Street	B2	River Street	C1
Brigstowe Street	C1	Rupert Street	A1
Bristol Bridge	B2	St. James Barton	B1
Broadmead	B1	St. Matthias Park	C1
Broad Quay	A2	St. Michael's Hill	A1
Broad Street	B2	St. Nicholas Street	A2
Broad Weir	C1	St. Thomas Street	B2
Brunswick Square	B1	Small Street	A2
Cannon Street	B1	Somerset Street	C3
Canon's Road	A3	Southwell Street	A1
Canon's Way	A3	Station Approach Road	C3
Castle Street	C2	Straight Street	C2
Charles Street	B1	Surrey Street	C1
Cheese Lane	C2	Temple Back	C2
Christmas Steps	A1	Temple Gate	C3
Church Lane	C2	Temple Street	B2
College Green	A2	Temple Way	C3
Colston Avenue	A2	Terrell Street	A1
Colston Street	A1	The Grove	A3
Concorde Street	C1	The Haymarket	B1
Corn Street	C1	The Horsefair	B1
Countership	B2	Thomas Lane	B2
Eugene Street	A1	Trenchard Street	A2
Fairfax Street	B1	Tyndall Avenue	A1
Frogmore Street	A2	Union Street	B1
George White Street	C1	Unity Street	A2
High Street	B2	Unity Street	C2
Horfield Road	A1	Upper Maudlin Street	A1
Houlton Street	C1	Victoria Road	B2
John Street	B2	Wapping Road	A3
King Street	A2	Water Lane	C2
Lewins Mead	A1	Welsh Back	B2
Lower Castle Street	C1	Wilder Street	B1
Lower Maudlin Street	B1	Wine Street	B2
Marlborough Street	B1		
Marsh Street	A2		
Merchant Street	B1		
Nelson Street	B2		
Newfoundland Street	C1		
Newgate	B2		
New Street	C1		
North Street	B1		
Old Bread Street	C2		
Old Market Street	C2		
Park Row	A2		
Park Street	A2		
Passage Street	C2		
Penn Street	C1		
Pero's Bridge	A3		
Perry Road	A2		
Pipe Lane	A2		
Portwall Lane	B3		
Prewett Street	B3		
Prince Street	A3		
Prince Street Bridge	C1		
Quakers' Friars	B1		
Queen Charlotte Street	B2		
Queen Square	A3		
Queen Street	C2		
Redcliff Backs	B3		

CAMBRIDGE

CAMBRIDGE

400 yds / 400m

Appears on main map page 150

Tourist Information Centre: Wheeler Street
Tel: 0871 226 8006

Adam and Eve Street	C2	Tenison Road	C3
Alpha Road	B1	Tennis Court Road	B2
Aylestone Road	C1	Trinity Street	B2
Barton Road	A3	Trumpington Road	B3
Bateman Street	B3	Trumpington Street	B3
Belvoir Road	C1	Union Road	B3
Brookside	B3	Victoria Avenue	B1
Burleigh Street	C2	Victoria Road	B1
Carlyle Road	B1	West Road	A2
Castle Street	A1		
Chesterton Lane	B1		
Chesterton Road	B1		
Clarendon Street	C2		
De Freville Avenue	C1		
Devonshire Road	C3		
Downing Street	B2		
East Road	C2		
Eden Street	C2		
Elizabeth Way	C1		
Emmanuel Road	B2		
Fen Causeway, The	A3		
Glisson Road	C3		
Gonville Place	C3		
Granchester Street	A3		
Grange Road	A3		
Gresham Road	C3		
Hamilton Road	C1		
Harvey Road	C3		
Hills Road	C3		
Humberstone Road	C1		
Huntingdon Road	A1		
Jesus Lane	B2		
King's Parade	B2		
King Street	B2		
Lensfield Road	B3		
Madingley Road	A1		
Magdalene Bridge Street	B1		
Maids Causeway	B2		
Market Street	B2		
Mawson Road	C3		
Millington Road	A3		
Mill Road	C3		
Montague Road	C1		
Newmarket Road	C2		
Newnham Road	A3		
Norfolk Street	C2		
Panton Street	B3		
Parker Street	B2		
Park Parade	B1		
Parkside	C2		
Park Terrace	B2		
Pembroke Street	B2		
Queen's Road	A2		
Regent Street	B2		
Regent Terrace	B2		
St. Andrew's Street	B2		
St. Barnabas Road	C3		
St. John's Street	B2		
St. Matthew's Street	C2		
St. Paul's Road	C3		
Searce Street	A1		
Sidgwick Avenue	A3		
Sidney Street	B2		
Silver Street	A3		
Station Road	C3		
Storey's Way	A1		

Tourist Information Centre: 12-13 Sun Street, The Buttermarket
Tel: 01227 378100

Best Lane	B2	Watling Street	B2
Borough Northgate	B1	Whitehall Gardens	A2
Broad Street	C1	Whitehall Road	A2
Burgate	B2	Wincheap	A3
Castle Row	A3	York Road	A3
Castle Street	A3		
College Road	C1		
Cossington Road	C3		
Craddock Road	C1		
Dover Street	C2		
Edgar Road	C1		
Ersham Road	C3		
Forty Acres Road	A1		
Gordon Road	A3		
Havelock Street	C1		
Hawk's Lane	B2		
High Street	B2		
Ivy Lane	C2		
King Street	B1		
Kirby's Lane	A1		
Lansdown Road	B3		
Longport	C2		
Lower Bridge Street	C2		
Lower Chantry Lane	C2		
Marlowe Avenue	B3		
Martyrs' Field Road	A3		
Mead Way	A2		
Military Road	C1		
Monastery Street	C2		
New Dover Road	C3		
North Holmes Road	C1		
North Lane	A1		
Nunnery Fields	C3		
Oaten Hill	C3		
Old Dover Road	C3		
Orchard Street	A1		
Oxford Road	B3		
Palace Street	B2		
Pin Hill	A3		
Pound Lane	A1		
Puckle Lane	C3		
Rheims Way	A2		
Rhodaus Town	B3		
Roper Road	A1		
Rose Lane	B2		
St. Dunstan's Street	A1		
St. George's Lane	B2		
St. George's Place	C2		
St. George's Street	B2		
St. Gregory's Road	C1		
St. Margarets Street	B2		
St. Peter's Lane	B1		
St. Peter's Place	A2		
St. Peter's Street	A1		
St. Radigund's Street	B1		
St. Stephen's Road	B1		
Simmonds Road	A3		
Station Road East	A3		
Station Road West	A1		
Stour Street	A2		
The Causeway	B1		
The Friar's	B2		
Tourtel Road	C1		
Tudor Road	A3		
Union Street	C1		
Upper Bridge Street	B3		

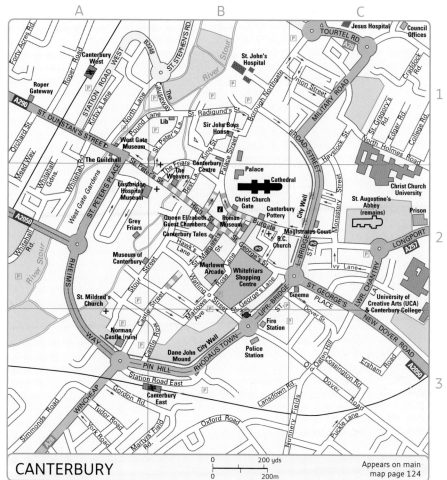

CANTERBURY

0 ———— 200 yds
0 ———— 200m

Appears on main map page 124

Tourist Information Centre: The Old Library, Trinity Street
Tel: 029 2087 3573

Adam Street	C3	Moira Terrace	C2
Albany Road	C1	Moy Road	C1
Allerton Street	A3	Museum Avenue	B1
Arran Place	C1	Neville Street	A2
Arran Street	C1	Newport Road	C2
Basil Place	B1	Newport Road Lane	C2
Bedford Street	C1	Ninian Park Road	A3
Boulevard de Nantes	B2	North Road	A1
Bridge Street	B3	Oxford Lane	C2
Brook Street	A3	Park Grove	B2
Bute Street	B3	Park Place	B1
Bute Terrace	B3	Park Street	B3
Castle Street	A2	Partridge Road	C1
Cathays Terrace	B1	Penarth Road	B3
Cathedral Road	A2	Pendyris Street	A3
Celerity Drive	C3	Pitman Street	A2
Central Link	C3	Planet Street	C2
Charles Street	B2	Queen Street	B2
Churchill Way	C2	Rhymney Street	B1
City Road	C1	Richard Street	B1
Clare Road	A3	Richmond Road	C1
Clare Street	A2	Ryder Street	A2
Claude Road	C1	St. Mary Street	B3
Coburn Street	B1	St. Peters Street	C2
College Road	B2	Salisbury Road	B1
Colum Road	A1	Schooner Way	C3
Corbett Road	B1	Senghennydd Road	B1
Cornwall Street	A3	Stafford Road	A3
Cottrell Road	C1	Strathnairn Street	C1
Cowbridge Road East	A2	Stuttgarter Strasse	B2
Craddock Street	A3	Taffs Mead Embankment	B3
Craiglee Drive	C3	Talbot Street	A2
Croft Street	C1	Thesiger Street	B1
Crwys Road	B1	The Parade	C2
Cyfartha Street	C1	The Walk	C1
De Burgh Street	A2	Tudor Street	A3
Despenser Street	A3	Tyndall Street	C3
Duke Street	B2	Wedmore Road	A3
Dumfries Place	C2	Wells Street	A3
Ellen Street	C3	West Grove	C2
Elm Street	C1	Westgate Street	B2
Fanny Street	B1	Windsor Place	B2
Fitzhamon Embankment	A3	Windsor Road	C2
Flora Street	B1	Wood Street	B3
Glossop Road	C2	Woodville Road	B1
Gordon Road	C1	Wordsworth Avenue	C2
Greyfriars Road	B2	Working Street	B2
Hamilton Street	A2	Wyeverne Road	B1
Harriet Street	B1		
Herbert Street	C3		
High Street	B2		
Hirwain Street	B1		
Keppoch Street	C1		
Kingsway	B2		
Lewis Street	A2		
Longcross Street	C2		
Maindy Road	A1		
Mardy Street	A3		
Mark Street	A2		
Merches Gardens	A3		
Merthyr Street	B1		
Meteor Street	C2		
Mill Lane	B3		
Minny Street	B1		
Miskin Street	B1		
Moira Place	C2		

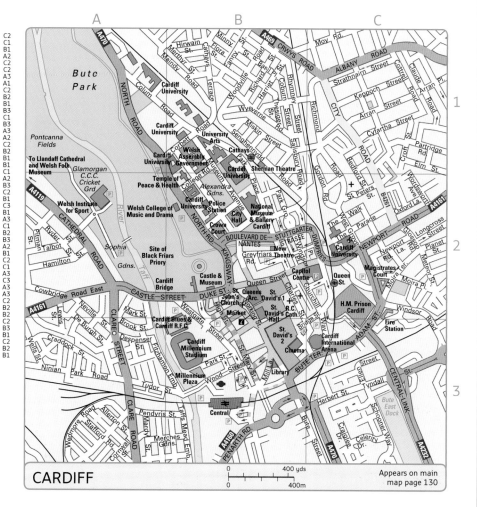

CARDIFF

0 ———— 400 yds
0 ———— 400m

Appears on main map page 130

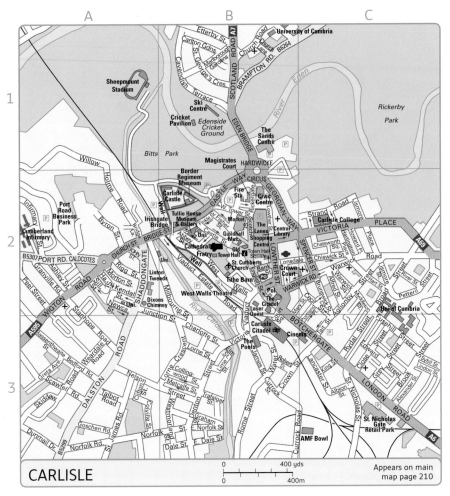

CARLISLE

0   400 yds
0   400m

Appears on main
map page 210

Tourist Information Centre: Old Town Hall, Green Market
Tel: 01228 625600

Abbey Street	B2	Lancaster Street	C3
Aglionby Street	C2	Lime Street	B3
Albion Street	C3	Lindon Street	C3
Alexander Street	C3	Lismore Place	C2
Alfred Street	C2	Lismore Street	C2
Ashley Street	A2	London Road	C3
Bank Street	B2	Lonsdale	B2
Bassenthwaite Street	A3	Lorne Crescent	B3
Bedford Road	A3	Lorne Street	B3
Botchergate	B3	Lowther Street	B2
Brampton Road	B1	Marlborough Gardens	B1
Bridge Lane	A2	Mary Street	B2
Bridge Street	A2	Metcalfe Street	B3
Broad Street	C2	Milbourne Street	A2
Brook Street	C2	Morton Street	A2
Brunswick Street	C2	Myddleton Street	C2
Byron Street	A2	Nelson Street	A3
Caldcotes	A2	Newcastle Street	A2
Carlton Gardens	B1	Norfolk Road	A3
Castle Street	B2	Norfolk Street	A3
Castle Way	B2	Peel Street	A2
Cavendish Terrace	B1	Petteril Street	C2
Cecil Street	C2	Port Road	A2
Charlotte Street	B3	Portland Place	C3
Chatsworth Square	C2	Rickergate	B2
Chiswick Street	C2	Rigg Street	A2
Church Lane	B1	River Street	C2
Church Road	B1	Robert Street	B3
Church Street	A2	Rome Street	B3
Clifton Street	A3	Rydal Street	C3
Close Street	C3	St. George's Crescent	B1
Collingwood Street	B3	St. James Road	A3
Colville Street	A3	St. Nicholas Street	C3
Crown Street	B3	Scawfell Road	A3
Currock Road	B3	Scotch Street	B2
Currock Street	B3	Scotland Road	B1
Dale Street	B3	Shaddongate	A2
Denton Street	B3	Silloth Street	A2
Dunmail Drive	A3	Skiddaw Road	A3
East Dale Street	B3	Spencer Street	C2
East Norfolk Street	B3	Stanhope Road	A2
Eden Bridge	B1	Strand Road	C2
Edward Street	C3	Sybil Street	C3
Elm Street	B3	Tait Street	C3
English Street	B2	Talbot Road	A3
Etterby Street	B1	Trafalgar Street	B3
Finkle Street	B2	Viaduct Estate Road	B2
Fisher Street	B2	Victoria Place	C2
Fusehill Street	C3	Victoria Viaduct	B3
Georgian Way	B2	Warwick Road	B2
Goschen Road	A3	Warwick Square	C2
Graham Street	B3	Water Street	B3
Granville Road	A2	Weardale Road	A3
Greta Avenue	A3	West Tower Street	B2
Grey Street	C3	West Walls	B2
Hardwicke Circus	B1	Westmorland Street	B3
Hart Street	C2	Wigton Road	A2
Hartington Place	C2	Willow Holme Road	A1
Hawick Street	A2		
Howard Place	C2		
Infirmary Street	A2		
James Street	B3		
John Street	A2		
Junction Street	A2		
Kendal Street	A2		
King Street	C3		

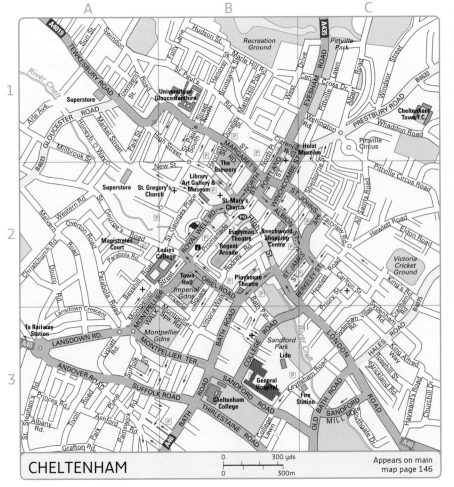

CHELTENHAM

0   300 yds
0   300m

Appears on main
map page 146

Tourist Information Centre: 77 Promenade
Tel: 01242 522878

Albany Road	A3	Portland Street	B2
Albert Road	C1	Prestbury Road	C1
Albion Street	B2	Princes Road	A3
All Saints Road	C2	Priory Street	C3
Andover Road	A3	Promenade	B2
Arle Avenue	A1	Rodney Road	B2
Ashford Road	A3	Rosehill Street	C3
Bath Parade	B2	Royal Well Road	B2
Bath Road	B3	St. George's Place	B2
Bayshill Road	A2	St. George's Road	A2
Berkeley Street	B2	St. James Street	B2
Brunswick Street	B1	St. Johns Avenue	B2
Carlton Street	C2	St. Margaret's Road	B1
Central Cross Drive	C1	St. Paul's Road	B1
Christchurch Road	A2	St. Paul's Street North	B1
Churchill Drive	C3	St. Paul's Street South	B1
Clarence Road	B1	St. Stephen's Road	A3
College Lawn	B3	Sandford Mill Road	C3
College Road	B3	Sandford Road	B3
Cranham Road	C3	Sherborne Street	C2
Douro Road	A2	Southgate Drive	C3
Dunalley Street	B1	Strickland Road	C3
Eldon Road	C2	Suffolk Road	A3
Evesham Road	C1	Suffolk Square	A3
Fairview Road	C2	Sun Street	A1
Folly Lane	B1	Swindon Road	A1
Gloucester Road	A2	Sydenham Road	C2
Grafton Road	A3	Sydenham Villas Road	C3
Hales Road	C3	Tewkesbury Road	A1
Hanover Street	B1	Thirlestaine Road	B3
Hayward's Road	C3	Tivoli Road	A3
Henrietta Street	B2	Townsend Street	A1
Hewlett Road	C2	Vittoria Walk	B3
High Street	B1	Wellington Road	C1
Honeybourne Way	A1	West Drive	B1
Hudson Street	B1	Western Road	A2
Imperial Square	B2	Whaddon Road	C1
Keynsham Road	B3	Winchcombe Street	B2
King Alfred Way	C3	Windsor Street	C1
King's Road	C2		
Lansdown Crescent	A3		
Lansdown Road	A3		
London Road	C3		
Lypiatt Road	A3		
Malvern Road	A2		
Market Street	A1		
Marle Hill Parade	B1		
Marle Hill Road	B1		
Millbrook Street	A1		
Montpellier Spa Road	B3		
Montpellier Street	A3		
Montpellier Terrace	A3		
Montpellier Walk	A3		
New Street	A2		
North Place	B2		
North Street	B2		
Old Bath Road	C3		
Oriel Road	B2		
Overton Road	A2		
Painswick Road	A3		
Parabola Road	A2		
Park Place	A3		
Park Street	A1		
Pittville Circus	C2		
Pittville Circus Road	C2		
Pittville Lawn	C1		

**Tourist Information Centre: Town Hall, Northgate Street
Tel: 01244 402111**

Bath Street	C2
Bedward Row	A2
Black Diamond Street	B1
Black Friars	A3
Bold Square	B2
Boughton	C2
Bouverie Street	A1
Bridge Street	B2
Brook Street	B1
Canal Street	A1
Castle Drive	A3
Charles Street	B1
Cheyney Road	A1
Chichester Street	A1
City Road	C2
City Walls Road	A2
Commonhall Street	A2
Cornwall Street	B1
Crewe Street	C1
Cuppin Street	A3
Dee Hills Park	C2
Dee Lane	C2
Deva Terrace	C2
Duke Street	B3
Eastgate Street	B2
Edinburgh Way	C3
Egerton Street	B1
Elizabeth Crescent	C3
Foregate Street	B2
Forest Street	B2
Francis Street	C1
Frodsham Street	B2
Garden Lane	A1
George Street	B1
Gloucester Street	B1
Grey Friars	A3
Grosvenor Park Terrace	C2
Grosvenor Road	A3
Grosvenor Street	A3
Handbridge	B3
Hoole Road	B1
Hoole Way	B1
Hunter Street	A2
King Street	A2
Leadworks Lane	C2
Lightfoot Street	C1
Louise Street	A1
Love Street	B2
Lower Bridge Street	B3
Lower Park Road	C3
Mill Street	C2
Milton Street	B1
Newgate Street	B2
Nicholas Street	A2
Nicholas Street Mews	A2
Northern Pathway	C3
Northgate Avenue	B1
Northgate Street	A2
Nun's Road	A3
Old Dee Bridge	B3
Pepper Street	B3
Phillip Street	C1
Prince's Avenue	C1
Princess Street	A2
Queen's Avenue	C1
Queen's Drive	C3
Queen's Park Road	B3
Queen's Road	C1
Queen Street	B2
Raymond Street	A1
Russel Street	C2
St. Anne Street	B1
St. George's Crescent	C3
St. John's Road	C3
St. John Street	B2
St. Martins Way	A1
St. Oswalds Way	B1
St. Werburgh Street	B2
Seller Street	C1
Sibell Street	C1
Souter's Lane	B3
Stanley Street	A2
Station Road	C1
Steam Mill Street	C2
Talbot Street	B1
The Bars	C2
The Groves	B3
Trafford Street	B1
Union Street	B2
Upper Northgate Street	A1
Vicar's Lane	B2
Victoria Crescent	C3
Victoria Place	B2
Victoria Road	A1
Walker Street	C1
Walpole Street	A1
Walter Street	B1
Watergate Street	A2
Water Tower Street	A2
Weaver Street	A2
White Friars	A3
York Street	B2

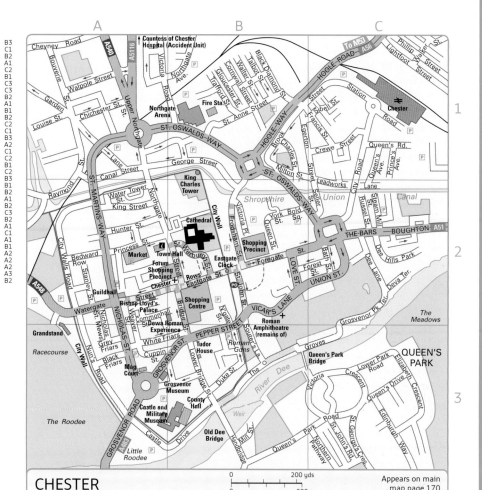

CHESTER

Appears on main map page 170

**Tourist Information Centre: St. Michael's Tower, Coventry
Cathedral   Tel: 024 7622 5616**

Abbott's Lane	A1
Acacia Avenue	C3
Albany Road	A3
Alma Street	C2
Asthill Grove	B3
Barker's Butts Lane	A1
Barras Lane	A2
Berry Street	C1
Bishop Street	B1
Blythe Road	C1
Bond Street	A2
Bramble Street	C2
Bretts Close	C1
Broadway	A3
Burges	B2
Butts Road	A2
Cambridge Street	C1
Canterbury Street	C1
Clifton Street	C1
Colchester Street	C1
Cornwall Road	C3
Corporation Street	B2
Coundon Road	A1
Coundon Street	A1
Cox Street	C2
Croft Road	A2
Drapers Fields	B1
Earl Street	B2
East Street	C2
Eaton Road	B3
Fairfax Street	B2
Far Gosford Street	C2
Foleshill Road	B1
Fowler Road	A1
Gordon Street	A3
Gosford Street	C2
Greyfriars Road	A2
Gulson Road	C2
Hales Street	B2
Harnall Lane East	C1
Harnall Lane West	B1
Harper Road	C2
Harper Street	B2
Hertford Street	B2
Hewitt Avenue	A1
High Street	B2
Hill Street	A2
Holyhead Road	A2
Hood Street	C2
Howard Street	B1
Jordan Well	B2
King William Street	C1
Lamb Street	B2
Leicester Row	B1
Leigh Street	C1
Little Park Street	B3
London Road	C3
Lower Ford Street	C2
Market Way	B2
Meadow Street	A2
Michaelmas Road	A3
Middleborough Road	A1
Mile Lane	B3
Mill Street	A1
Minster Road	A2
Much Park Street	B2
New Union Street	B2
Norfolk Street	A2
Oxford Street	C2
Park Road	B3
Parkside	B3
Primrose Hill Street	C1
Priory Street	B2
Puma Way	B3
Quarryfield Lane	C3
Queen's Road	A3
Queen Street	C1
Queen Victoria Road	A2
Quinton Road	B3
Radford Road	A1
Raglan Street	C2
Regent Street	A3
Ringway Hill Cross	A2
Ringway Queens	A2
Ringway Rudge	A2
Ringway St. Johns	B3
Ringway St. Nicholas	B1
Ringway St. Patricks	B3
Ringway Swanswell	B1
Ringway Whitefriars	C2
St. Nicholas Street	B1
Sandy Lane	B1
Seagrave Road	C3
Silver Street	B1
Sky Blue Way	C2
South Street	C2
Spencer Avenue	A3
Spon Street	A2
Srathmore Avenue	C3
Stoney Road	B3
Stoney Stanton Road	B1
Swanswell Street	B1
The Precinct	B2
Tomson Avenue	A1
Trinity Street	B2
Upper Hill Street	A2
Upper Well Street	B2
Vauxhall Street	C2
Vecqueray Street	C2
Victoria Street	C1
Vine Street	C1
Warwick Road	A3
Waveley Road	A2
Westminster Road	A3
White Street	B1
Windsor Street	A2
Wright Street	C1

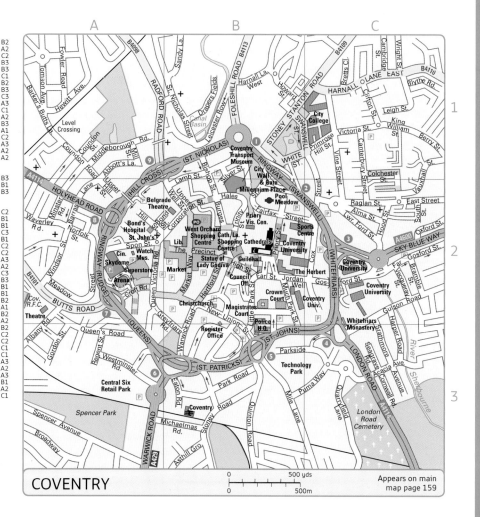

COVENTRY

Appears on main map page 159

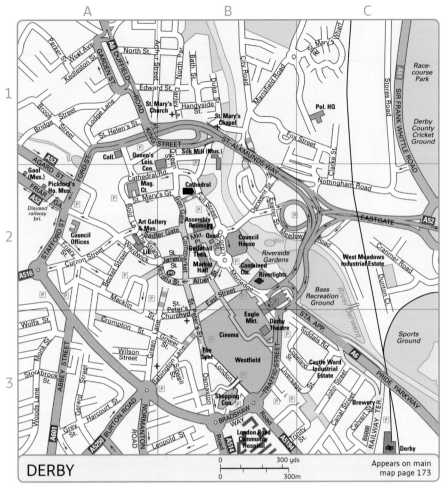

DERBY

Appears on main map page 173

Abbey Street	A3	Railway Terrace	C3
Agard Street	A1	Sadler Gate	B2
Albert Street	B2	St. Alkmunds Way	B1
Arthur Street	A1	St. Helen's Street	A1
Babington Lane	A3	St. James Street	B2
Bath Street	B1	St. Mary's Gate	A2
Becket Street	A2	St. Mary's Wharf Road	C1
Bold Lane	A2	St. Peter's Churchyard	B3
Bradshaw Way	B3	St. Peter's Street	B2
Bridge Street	A1	Siddals Road	C3
Brook Street	A1	Sir Frank Whittle Road	C1
Burton Road	A3	Sitwell Street	B3
Calvert Street	C3	Stafford Street	A2
Canal Street	C3	Station Approach	C2
Cathedral Road	A2	Stockbrook Street	A3
City Road	B1	Stores Road	C1
Clarke Street	C2	The Strand	A2
Copeland Street	B3	Traffic Street	B3
Cornmarket	B2	Trinity Street	B3
Corporation Street	B2	Victoria Street	A2
Cranmer Road	C2	Wardwick	A2
Crompton Street	A3	West Avenue	A1
Curzon Street	A2	Wilson Street	A3
Darley Lane	B1	Wolfa Street	A3
Derwent Street	B2	Woods Lane	A3
Duffield Road	A1		
Duke Street	B1		
Dunton Close	C2		
Eastgate	C2		
East Street	B2		
Edward Street	A1		
Exeter Street	B2		
Ford Street	A2		
Fox Street	B1		
Friar Gate	A2		
Friary Street	A2		
Full Street	B2		
Garden Street	A1		
Gerard Street	A3		
Gower Street	B3		
Green Lane	A3		
Grey Street	A3		
Handyside Street	B1		
Harcourt Street	A3		
Iron Gate	B2		
John Street	C3		
Kedleston Street	A1		
King Street	A1		
Leopold Street	A3		
Liversage Street	B3		
Lodge Lane	A1		
London Road	B3		
Macklin Street	A2		
Mansfield Road	B1		
Market Place	B2		
Meadow Road	B2		
Monk Street	A3		
Morledge	B2		
Normanton Road	A3		
North Parade	B1		
North Street	A1		
Nottingham Road	C2		
Osmaston Road	B3		
Parker Street	A1		
Pride Parkway	C3		
Queen Street	B1		

DOVER

Appears on main map page 125

Astor Avenue	A2
Barton Road	A1
Beaconsfield Avenue	A1
Beaconsfield Road	A1
Belgrave Road	A2
Biggin Street	B2
Bridge Street	B2
Brookfield Avenue	A1
Buckland Avenue	A1
Cannon Street	B2
Canons Gate Road	B2
Castle Avenue	B1
Castle Hill Road	B2
Castle Street	B2
Cherry Tree Avenue	A1
Citadel Road	A3
Clarendon Place	A2
Clarendon Street	A2
Connaught Road	B1
Coombe Valley Road	A2
Dover Road	C1
Durham Hill	B2
Eaton Road	A2
Edred Road	A2
Elms Vale Road	A2
Folkestone Road	A2
Frith Road	B1
Godwyne Road	B2
Green Lane	A1
Guston Road	B1
Heathfield Avenue	A1
High Street	B2
Hillside Road	A2
Jubilee Way	C1
Ladywell	B2
Limekiln Street	B3
London Road	A1
Longfield Road	A2
Maison Dieu Road	B2
Marine Parade	B2
Mayfield Avenue	A1
Military Road	B2
Mount Road	A3
Napier Road	A1
Noah's Ark Road	A2
Northbourne Avenue	A2
North Military Road	A2
Old Charlton Road	B1
Old Folkestone Road	A3
Oswald Road	A1
Park Avenue	B1
Pencester Road	B2
Priory Hill	A2
St. Radigund's Road	A1
Salisbury Road	B1
Snargate Street	B3
South Road	A2
Stanhope Road	B1
The Viaduct	B3
Tower Street	A2
Townwall Street	B2
Union Street	B3
Upper Road	C1
York Street	B2

Tourist Information Centre: 16 City Square
Tel: 01382 527527

Adelaide Place	A1	South Marketgait	B3
Albany Terrace	A1	South Tay Street	A3
Albert Street	C2	Strathmartine Road	B1
Alexander Street	B1	Tannadice Street	B1
Ann Street	B2	Tay Road Bridge	B3
Arbroath Road	C2	Trades Lane	B2
Arklay Street	C1	Upper Constitution Street	A1
Arklay Terrace	C1	Victoria Road	B2
Arthurstone Terrace	C2	Victoria Street	C2
Barrack Road	A2	Ward Road	A2
Blackness Road	A2	West Marketgait	A2
Blinshall Street	A2	West Port	A2
Brewery Lane	A2	William Street	C2
Brook Street	A2		
Broughty Ferry Road	C2		
Brown Street	A2		
Bruce Street	A1		
Byron Street	A1		
Canning Street	B1		
City Square	B3		
Clepington Road	C1		
Constitution Road	B2		
Constitution Street	B1		
Court Street	C1		
Cowgate Street	B2		
Dens Road	B1		
Douglas Street	A2		
Dudhope Street	A1		
Dudhope Terrace	C1		
Dundonald Street	C1		
Dura Street	C2		
East Dock Street	C2		
East Marketgait	B2		
Fairbairn Street	B1		
Greenmarket	B3		
Guthrie Street	A2		
Hawkhill	A2		
High Street	B3		
Hill Street	B1		
Hilltown	B1		
Kenmore Terrace	A1		
Killin Avenue	A1		
Kinghorne Road	A1		
King Street	B2		
Larch Street	A2		
Law Crescent	A1		
Lawside Avenue	A1		
Law Street	A1		
Leng Street	A1		
Lochee Road	A2		
Lower Princes Street	C2		
Mains Road	B1		
Main Street	B1		
Meadowside	B2		
Morgan Street	C2		
Murraygate	B2		
Nelson Street	B2		
Nethergate	A3		
North Marketgait	A2		
Perth Road	A3		
Polepark Road	A2		
Princes Street	C2		
Riverside Drive	A3		
Roseangle	A3		
Rosebank Road	B2		
Seagate	B2		

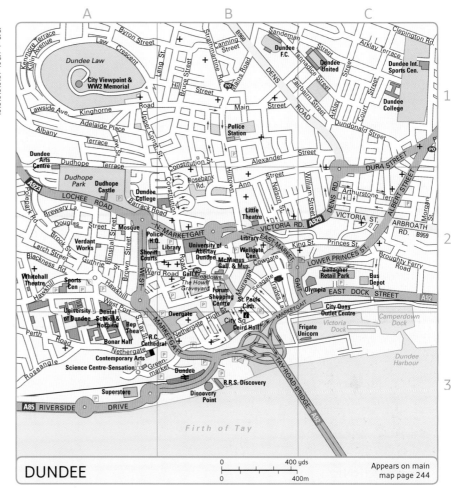

DUNDEE

Appears on main map page 244

Tourist Information Centre: 2 Millennium Place
Tel: 0191 384 3720

Aykley Heads	A1
Church Street	B3
Clay Lane	A3
Claypath	B2
Crossgate	B2
Crossgate Peth	A3
Darlington Road	A3
Dryburn Road	A1
Durham Road	A1
Fieldhouse Lane	A1
Framwelgate	B2
Framwelgate Peth	B1
Framwelgate Waterside	B2
Gilesgate	C2
Great North Road	A1
Green Lane	C2
Grove Street	B3
Hallgarth Street	C3
Hawthorn Terrace	A2
Leazes Road	B2
Margery Lane	B3
Market Place	B2
Millburngate Bridge	B2
Newcastle Road	A1
New Elvet	B2
North Bailey	B2
North End	A1
North Road	B2
Old Elvet	C2
Pity Me Bypass	A1
Potters Bank	A3
Quarryheads Lane	B3
Providence Row	B2
Redhills Lane	A2
St. Monica Grove	A2
Sidegate	B2
Silver Street	B2
South Bailey	B3
South Road	B3
South Street	B3
Southfield Way	A1
Stockton Road	B3
Sutton Street	B2
The Avenue	A3
Toll House Road	A2
Western Hill	A2
Whinney Hill	C3
Whitesmocks	A1

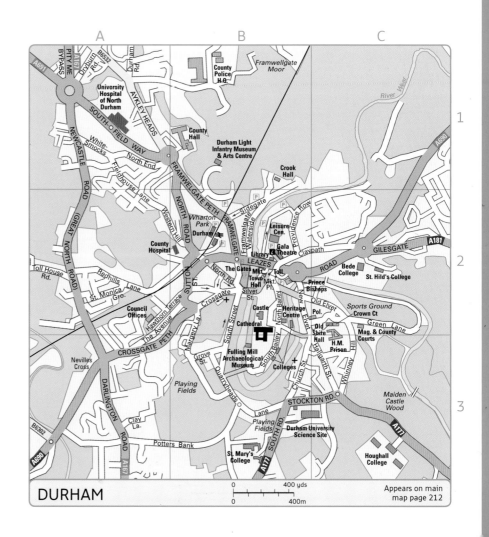

DURHAM

Appears on main map page 212

Eastbourne   Exeter

Edinburgh street map on pages 36-37

EASTBOURNE

Appears on main map page 110

Scale: 0 — 200 yds / 0 — 200m

Tourist Information Centre: 3 Cornfield Road
Tel: 0871 663 0031

Arlington Road	A2	The Avenue	B2
Arundel Road	B1	The Goffs	A1
Ashford Road	B2/C2	Trinity Trees	C2
Avondale Road	C1	Upper Avenue	B1
Bedfordwell Road	B1	Upperton Lane	B2
Belmore Road	C1	Upperton Road	A1
Blackwater Road	B3	Watts Lane	A1
Borough Lane	A1	Whitley Road	A1
Bourne Street	C2	Willingdon Road	A1
Carew Road	A1/B1	Winchcombe Road	C1
Carlisle Road	A3		
Cavendish Avenue	C1		
Cavendish Place	C2		
College Road	B3		
Commercial Road	B2		
Compton Place Road	A2		
Compton Street	B3		
Cornfield Terrace	B2		
Denton Road	A3		
Devonshire Place	B2		
Dittons Road	A2		
Dursley Road	C2		
Enys Road	B1		
Eversfield Road	B1		
Fairfield Road	A3		
Firle Road	C1		
Furness Road	B3		
Gaudick Road	A3		
Gilbert Road	C1		
Gildredge Road	B2		
Gorringe Road	A3		
Grand Parade	C3		
Grange Road	B3		
Grassington Road	B3		
Grove Road	B2		
Hartfield Road	B1		
Hartington Place	C2		
High Street	A1		
Hyde Gardens	B2		
King Edward's Parade	B3		
Langney Road	C2		
Lewes Road	B1		
Marine Parade	C2		
Mark Lane	B2		
Meads Road	A3		
Melbourne Road	C1		
Mill Gap Road	A1		
Mill Road	A1		
Moat Croft Road	A1		
Moy Avenue	C1		
Ratton Road	A1		
Royal Parade	C2		
Saffrons Park	A3		
Saffrons Road	A2		
St. Anne's Road	A1		
St. Leonard's Road	B2		
Seaside	C2		
Seaside Road	C2		
Selwyn Road	A1		
Silverdale Road	B3		
South Street	B2		
Southfields Road	A2		
Station Parade	B2		
Susan's Road	C2		
Sydney Road	C2		
Terminus Road	B2		

EXETER

Appears on main map page 102

Scale: 0 — 400 yds / 0 — 400m

Tourist Information Centre: Dix's Field
Tel: 01392 665700

Albion Street	A3	St. James' Road	C1
Alphington Street	A3	St. Leonard's Road	C3
Barnfield Road	B2	Sidwell Street	B2
Bartholomew Street West	A2	Southernhay East	B2
Bedford Street	B2	South Street	B2
Belmont Road	C1	Spicer Road	C2
Blackboy Road	C1	Station Road	A1
Blackall Road	B1	Streatham Drive	A1
Bonhay Road	A2	Streatham Rise	A1
Buller Road	A3	The Quay	B3
Church Road	A3	Thornton Hill	B1
Clifton Hill	C1	Topsham Road	B3
Clifton Road	C2	Velwell Road	A1
Clifton Street	C2	Victoria Street	C1
College Road	C2	Water Lane	B3
Commercial Road	B3	Well Street	C1
Cowick Street	A3	West Avenue	B1
Cowley Bridge Road	A1	Western Road	A2
Danes Road	B1	Western Way	C2
Denmark Road	C2	Wonford Road	C3
Devonshire Place	C1	York Road	B1
Dix's Field	B2		
East Grove Road	C3		
Elmside	C1		
Exe Street	A2		
Fore Street	B2		
Haldon Road	A2		
Haven Road	B3		
Heavitree Road	C2		
Hele Road	A1		
High Street	B2		
Holloway Street	B3		
Hoopern Street	B1		
Howell Road	B1		
Iddesleigh Road	C1		
Iron Bridge	A2		
Isca Road	B3		
Jesmond Road	C1		
Longbrook Street	B1		
Looe Road	A1		
Lyndhurst Road	C3		
Magdalen Road	C2		
Magdalen Street	B3		
Marlborough Road	C3		
Matford Avenue	C3		
Matford Lane	C3		
Mount Pleasant Road	C1		
New Bridge Street	A3		
New North Road	A1/B1		
North Street	B2		
Okehampton Road	A3		
Okehampton Street	A3		
Old Tiverton Road	C1		
Oxford Road	C1		
Paris Street	B2		
Paul Street	B2		
Pennsylvania Road	B1		
Portland Street	C1		
Prince of Wales Road	A1		
Princesshay	B2		
Prospect Park	C1		
Queen's Road	A3		
Queen Street	B2		
Radford Road	C3		
Richmond Road	A2		
St. David's Hill	A1		

**Tourist Information Centre: Discover Folkestone,
20 Bouverie Place. Tel: 01303 258594**

Alder Road	B2
Archer Road	C2
Bathurst Road	A2
Beatty Road	C1
Black Bull Road	B2
Bournemouth Road	B2
Bouverie Road West	A3
Bradstone Road	B2
Broadfield Road	A2
Broadmead Road	B2
Brockman Road	B2
Canterbury Road	C1
Castle Hill Avenue	B3
Cheriton Gardens	B3
Cheriton Road	A2/B2
Cherry Garden Avenue	A1
Christ Church Road	B3
Churchill Avenue	B1
Clifton Crescent	A3
Coniston Road	A1
Coolinge Road	B2
Cornwallis Avenue	A2
Dawson Road	B2
Dixwell Road	A3
Dolphins Road	B1
Dover Hill	C1
Dover Road	C1
Downs Road	B1
Earles Avenue	A3
Foord Road	B2
Godwyn Road	A3
Grimston Avenue	A3
Grimston Gardens	A3
Guildhall Street	B2
Guildhall Street North	B2
Harbour Way	C2
Hill Road	C1
Ivy Way	C1
Joyes Road	C1
Linden Crescent	B2
Links Way	A1
Lower Sandgate Road	A3
Lucy Avenue	A1
Manor Road	B3
Marine Parade	B3
Marshall Street	C1
Mead Road	B2
Old High Street	C3
Park Farm Road	B1
Pavilion Road	B2
Radnor Bridge Road	C2
Radnor Park Avenue	A2
Radnor Park Road	B2
Radnor Park West	A2
Sandgate Hill	A3
Sandgate Road	B3
Shorncliffe Road	A2
Sidney Street	C2
The Leas	B3
The Stade	C3
The Tram Road	C2
Tontine Street	C2
Turketel Road	A3
Tyson Road	C1
Wear Bay Crescent	C2
Wear Bay Road	C1

Westbourne Gardens	A3
Wingate Road	B1
Wood Avenue	C1
Wilton Road	A2

FOLKESTONE

0   200 yds
0   200m

Appears on main
map page 125

**Tourist Information Centre: 28 Southgate Street
Tel: 01452 396572**

Adelaide Street	B3
Alexandra Road	B1
Alfred Street	C2
Alma Place	A3
Alvin Street	B1
Archdeacon Street	A1
Argyll Road	C1
Askwith Road	C3
Barnwood Road	C1
Barton Street	B2
Black Dog Way	B1
Bristol Road	A3
Brunswick Road	B2
Bruton Way	B2
Calton Road	B3
Castle Meads Way	A1
Cecil Road	A3
Cheltenham Road	C1
Churchill Road	A3
Clifton Road	A3
Conduit Street	B3
Coney Hill Road	C3
Dean's Way	B1
Denmark Road	B1
Derby Road	B2
Estcourt Road	B1
Eastern Avenue	C3
Eastgate Street	B2
Frampton Road	A3
Gouda Way	A1
Great Western Road	B2
Greyfriars	B2
Hatherley Road	B3
Heathville Road	B1
Hempsted Lane	A2
Henry Road	B1
High Street	B3
Hopewell Street	B3
Horton Road	C2
Howard Street	B3
India Road	C2
King Edward's Avenue	B3
Kingsholm Road	B1
Lansdown Road	B1
Linden Road	A3
Llanthony Road	A2
London Road	B1
Lower Westgate Street	A1
Marlborough Road	C3
Merevale Road	C1
Metz Way	B2
Midland Road	B3
Millbrook Street	B2
Myers Road	C2
Northgate Street	B2
Oxford Road	B1
Oxstalls Lane	C1
Painswick Road	C3
Park Road	B2
Parkend Road	B3
Pitt Street	B1
Quay Street	A2
Regent Street	B3
Robinson Road	A3
Ryecroft Street	B3
St. Ann Way	A3

St. Oswald's Road	A1
Secunda Way	A3
Severn Road	A2
Seymour Road	A3
Southgate Street	A2
Spa Road	A2
Stanley Road	B3
Station Road	B2
Stroud Road	A3
The Quay	A2
Tredworth Road	B3
Trier Way	A3
Upton Street	B3
Vicarage Road	C3
Victoria Street	B2
Wellington Street	B2
Westgate Street	A1
Weston Road	A3
Wheatstone Road	B3
Willow Avenue	C3
Worcester Street	B1

GLOUCESTER

0   500 yds
0   500m

Appears on main
map page 132

GUILDFORD

0   200 yds
0   200m

Appears on main
map page 121

Tourist Information Centre: 14 Tunsgate
Tel: 01483 444333

Abbot Road	C3	Portsmouth Road	B3
Artillery Road	B1	Poyle Road	C3
Artillery Terrace	B1	Quarry Street	B2
Bedford Road	B1	Queens Road	C1
Bridge Street	B2	Rookwood Court	A3
Bright Hill	C2	Rupert Road	A2
Brodie Road	C2	Sand Terrace	B1
Bury Fields	B3	Semaphore Road	C3
Bury Street	B3	South Hill	C2
Castle Hill	C3	Springfield Road	C1
Castle Square	C2	Station Approach	C1
Castle Street	B2	Station View	A1
Chertsey Street	C1	Stoke Road	C1
Cheselden Road	C2	Swan Lane	B2
Commercial Road	B2	Sydenham Road	C2
Dapdune Court	B1	Testard Road	A2
Dapdune Road	B1	The Bars	B2
Dapdune Wharf	B1	The Mount	A3
Dene Road	C1	Tunsgate	C2
Denmark Road	C1	Upperton Road	A2
Denzil Road	A2	Victoria Road	C1
Drummond Road	B1	Walnut Tree Close	A1
Eagle Road	C1	Warwicks	C3
Eastgate Gardens	C1	Wharf Road	B1
Falcon Road	C1	Wherwell Road	A2
Farnham Road	A2	William Road	B1
Flower Walk	B3	Wodeland Avenue	A3
Fort Road	C3	Woodbridge Road	B1
Foxenden Road	C1	York Road	B1
Friary Bridge	B2		
Friary Street	B2		
Genyn Road	A2		
George Road	B1		
Great Quarry	C3		
Guildford Park Avenue	A1		
Guildford Park Road	A2		
Harvey Road	C2		
Haydon Place	B1		
High Pewley	C3		
High Street	B2/C2		
Laundry Road	B1		
Lawn Road	B3		
Leap Lane	B2		
Leas Road	B1		
Ludlow Road	A2		
Mareschal Road	A3		
Margaret Road	B1		
Market Street	B2		
Martyr Road	B2		
Mary Road	B1		
Millbrook	B3		
Millmead	B2		
Millmead Terrace	B3		
Mount Pleasant	A3		
Mountside	A3		
Nether Mount	A3		
Nightingale Road	C1		
North Place	B1		
North Street	B2		
Onslow Road	C1		
Onslow Street	B2		
Oxford Road	C2		
Pannells Court	C2		
Park Road	B1		
Park Street	B2		
Pewley Hill	C2		

HARROGATE

0   150 yds
0   150m

Appears on main
map page 194

Tourist Information Centre: Royal Baths, Crescent Road
Tel: 01423 537300

Ainsty Road	C1	Regent Grove	C1
Albert Street	B2	Regent Parade	C1
Alexandra Road	B1	Regent Street	C1
Arthington Avenue	B2	Regent Terrace	C1
Beech Grove	A3	Ripon Road	A1
Belford Road	B2	Robert Street	B3
Bower Road	B1	St. James Drive	C3
Bower Street	B2	St. Mary's Walk	A3
Cambridge Street	B2	Skipton Road	C1
Cavendish Avenue	C3	South Park Road	B3
Chelmsford Road	B2	Springfield Avenue	A1
Cheltenham Mount	B1	Spring Grove	A1
Chudleigh Road	C1	Spring Mount	A1
Clarence Drive	A2	Station Avenue	B2
Claro Road	C1	Station Parade	B2
Cold Bath Road	A3	Stray Rein	B3
Commercial Street	B1	Stray Walk	C3
Coppice Drive	A1	Studley Road	B1
Cornwall Road	A2	Swan Road	A2
Crescent Gardens	A2	The Grove	C1
Dragon Avenue	B1	Tower Street	B3
Dragon Parade	B1	Trinity Road	B3
Dragon Road	B1	Valley Drive	A2
Duchy Road	A1	Victoria Avenue	B2
East Parade	B2	Victoria Road	A3
East Park Road	B2	West End Avenue	A3
Franklin Mount	B1	West Park	B2
Franklin Road	B1	Woodside	B2
Gascoigne Crescent	C1	York Place	B3
Glebe Avenue	A2	York Road	A2
Glebe Road	A3		
Grove Park Terrace	C1		
Grove Road	B1		
Harcourt Drive	C2		
Harcourt Road	C1		
Heywood Road	A3		
Hollins Road	A1		
Homestead Road	B2		
James Street	B2		
Kent Road	A1		
King's Road	A2		
Knaresborough Road	C2		
Lancaster Road	A3		
Leeds Road	B3		
Lime Grove	C1		
Lime Street	C1		
Mayfield Grove	B1		
Montpellier Hill	A2		
Montpellier Street	A2		
Mowbray Square	C1		
North Park Road	C2		
Oatlands Drive	C3		
Otley Road	A3		
Oxford Street	B2		
Park Chase	C1		
Park Drive	B3		
Park Parade	C2		
Park Road	A3		
Park View	B2		
Parliament Street	A2		
Princes Villa Road	B2		
Providence Terrace	B1		
Queen Parade	C2		
Queen's Road	A3		
Raglan Street	B2		
Regent Avenue	C1		

Tourist Information Centre: Queens Square, Priory Meadow
Tel: 0845 274 1001

Albert Road	B3
All Saints Street	C2
Amherst Road	A2
Ashburnham Road	C2
Ashford Road	A1
Ashford Way	A1
Baldslow Road	B2
Beaconsfield Road	B1
Bembrook Road	C2
Bohemia Road	A2
Braybrooke Road	B2
Broomsgrove Road	C1
Cambridge Road	A3
Castle Hill Road	B3
Castle Street	B3
Chiltern Drive	C1
Church Road	A3
Collier Road	C2
Cornwallis Terrace	A3
Croft Road	C2
De Cham Road	A3
Denmark Place	B3
Downs Road	B1
East Parade	C3
Elphinstone Road	B1
Eversfield Place	A3
Falaise Road	A3
Farley Bank	C1
Fearon Road	B1
Fellows Road	C1
Frederick Road	C1
Freshwater Avenue	A1
George Street	C3
Harold Place	B3
Harold Road	C2
High Street	C2
Hillside Road	A1
Hoad's Wood Road	B1
Hughenden Road	B1
Laton Road	B1
Linley Drive	B1
Linton Road	A2
Lower Park Road	A2
Magdalen Road	A3
Malvern Way	C1
Marine Parade	C3
Milward Road	B2
Mount Pleasant Road	B1
Old London Road	C2
Park Avenue	A1
Park Crescent	A1
Park View	A1
Park Way	A1
Parker Road	B1
Parkstone Road	A1
Pelham Place	B3
Priory Avenue	B2
Priory Road	C2
Queen's Road	B2
Robertson Street	B3
Rock-a-Nore Road	C3
St. George's Road	C2
St. Helen's Down	B1
St. Helen's Park Road	B2
St. Helen's Road	A1
St. John's Road	A3

St. Margaret's Road	A3
St. Mary's Road	B2
St. Mary's Terrace	B2
St. Thomas's Road	C2
Thanet Way	A1
The Bourne	C2
Upper Park Road	A2
Vicarage Road	B2
Warrior Square	A3
Wellington Road	B2
White Rock	A3
Woodbrook Road	B1
Wykeham Road	A2

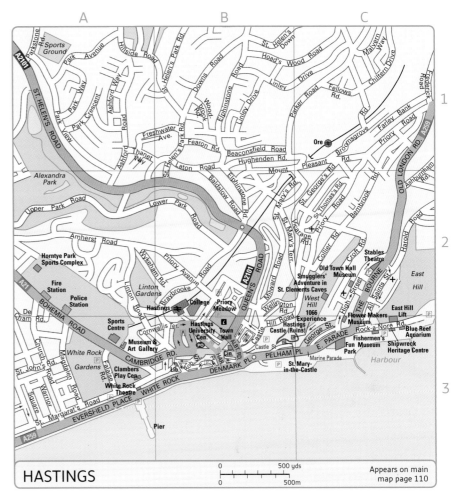

HASTINGS

0 ... 500 yds
0 ... 500m

Appears on main map page 110

Tourist Information Centre: 1 King Street
Tel: 01432 268430

Aubrey Street	B2
Barrs Court Road	C1
Barton Road	A2
Barton Yard	A2
Bath Street	C2
Belmont Avenue	A3
Berrington Street	B2
Bewell Street	B2
Blackfriars Street	B1
Blueschool Street	B1
Brewers Passage	B2
Bridge Street	B2
Broad Street	B2
Canonmoor Street	A1
Cantilupe Street	C2
Castle Street	B2
Catherine Street	B1
Central Avenue	C2
Church Street	B2
Commercial Road	C1
Commercial Street	B2
Coningsby Street	B1
East Street	B2
Edgar Street	B1
Eign Gate	B2
Eign Street	A2
Ferrers Street	B2
Friars Street	A2
Gaol Street	C2
Green Street	C3
Grenfell Road	C3
Greyfriars Avenue	A3
Greyfriars Bridge	B2
Grove Road	C3
Harold Street	C3
High Street	B2
High Town	B2
King Street	B2
Kyrle Street	C2
Maylord Street	B2
Mill Street	C3
Monkmoor Street	C1
Moorfield Street	A1
Moor Street	A1
Mostyn Street	A1
Nelson Street	C3
Newmarket Street	B1
Park Street	C3
Penhaligon Way	A1
Plough Lane	A1
Portland Street	A1
Quay Street	B2
Ryeland Street	A2
St. Guthiac Street	C2
St. James Road	C3
St. Martin's Avenue	B3
St. Martin's Street	B3
St. Owen Street	C2
Station Approach	C1
Station Road	A2
Stonebow Road	C1
Symonds Street	C2
The Atrium	B1
Turner Street	C3
Union Street	B2
Union Walk	C1

Vaughan Street	C2
Victoria Street	A2
West Street	B2
Widemarsh Street	B2
Wye Street	B3

HEREFORD

0 ... 250 yds
0 ... 250m

Appears on main map page 145

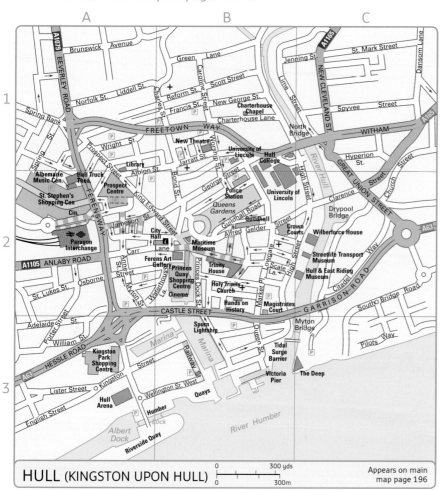

HULL (KINGSTON UPON HULL)

0   300 yds
0   300m

Appears on main map page 196

Tourist Information Centre: 1 Paragon Street
Tel: 0844 811 2070

Adelaide Street	A3
Albion Street	A2
Alfred Gelder Street	B2
Anlaby Road	A2
Anne Street	A2
Beverley Road	A1
Bond Street	B2
Brunswick Avenue	A1
Caroline Street	B1
Carr Lane	A2
Castle Street	B2
Charles Street	B1
Charterhouse Lane	B1
Church Street	C2
Citadel Way	C2
Clarence Street	C2
Cleveland Street	C1
Dansom Lane	C1
English Street	A3
Ferensway	A2
Francis Street	B1
Freetown Way	A1
Garrison Road	C2
George Street	B2
Great Union Street	C1
Green Lane	B1
Guildhall Road	B2
Hessle Road	A3
High Street	C1
Hyperion Street	C1
Jameson Street	A2
Jarratt Street	B1
Jenning Street	B1
King Edward Street	A2
Kingston Street	A3
Liddell Street	A1
Lime Street	B1
Lister Street	A3
Lowgate	B2
Market Place	B2
Myton Street	A2
New Cleveland Street	C1
New George Street	B1
Norfolk Street	A1
North Bridge	B1
Osborne Street	A2
Pilots Way	C3
Porter Street	A3
Princes Dock Street	B2
Prospect Street	A1
Queen Street	B3
Reform Street	B1
St. Lukes Street	A2
St. Mark Street	C1
Scale Lane	B2
Scott Street	B1
Scott Street Bridge	B1
South Bridge Road	C2
Spring Bank	A1
Spring Street	A2
Spyvee Street	C1
Waterhouse Lane	A2
Wellington Street West	A3
William Street	A3
Witham	C1
Worship Street	B1
Wright Street	A1

INVERNESS

0   300 yds
0   300m

Appears on main map page 266

Tourist Information Centre: Castle Wynd
Tel: 01463 252401

Abban Street	A1	Lochalsh Road	A1
Academy Street	B2	Longman Road	C1
Alexander Place	B2	Maxwell Drive	A3
Anderson Street	B1	Mayfield Road	B3
Ardconnel Street	B3	Midmills Road	C2
Ardconnel Terrace	C2	Millburn Road	C2
Ardross Place	B3	Montague Row	A2
Ardross Street	B3	Muirfield Road	C3
Argyle Street	C3	Nelson Street	A1
Argyle Terrace	C3	Ness Bank	B3
Attadale Road	A2	Ness Bridge	B2
Auldcastle Road	C2	Ness Walk	B3
Bank Street	B2	Old Edinburgh Road	B3
Baron Taylor's Street	B2	Park Road	A3
Benula Road	A1	Perceval Road	A2
Bishop's Road	A3	Planefield Road	A2
Bridge Street	B2	Queensgate	B2
Broadstone Park	C3	Rangemore Road	A2
Bruce Gardens	A3	Riverside Street	B1
Burnett Road	C1	Ross Avenue	A2
Carse Road	A1	Shore Street	B1
Castle Road	B2	Smith Avenue	A3
Castle Street	B2	Southside Place	C3
Castle Wynd	B2	Southside Road	C3
Cawdor Road	C2	Stephen's Brae	C2
Celt Street	A2	Strother's Lane	B2
Chapel Street	B1	Telford Road	A1
Charles Street	C2	Telford Street	A1
Church Street	B2	Tomnahurich Street	A3
Columba Road	A3	Union Road	C3
Crown Avenue	C2	Union Street	B2
Crown Circus	C2	View Place	B3
Crown Drive	C2	Walker Road	B1
Crown Road	C2	Waterloo Bridge	B1
Crown Street	C3	Wells Street	A2
Culduthel Road	B3	Young Street	B2
Denny Street	C3		
Dochfour Drive	A3		
Douglas Row	B1		
Duffy Drive	B3		
Duncraig Street	A2		
Eastgate	C2		
Fairfield Road	A2		
Falcon Square	B2		
Friars Bridge	A1		
Friars Lane	B2		
Friars Street	B2		
Gilbert Street	A1		
Glebe Street	B1		
Glen Urquhart Road	A3		
Gordon Terrace	B3		
Grant Street	A1		
Greig Street	A2		
Harbour Road	B1		
Harrowden Road	A2		
Haugh Road	B3		
High Street	B2		
Hill Street	C2		
Hontly Place	A1		
Huntly Street	A2		
Innes Street	B1		
Kenneth Street	A2		
Kingsmills Road	C2		
King Street	A2		
Leys Drive	C3		
Lindsay Avenue	A3		

Tourist Information Centre: 7-9 Every Street, Town Hall Square
Tel: 0844 888 5181

Abbey Street	B1	Market Place South	B2
Albion Street	B2	Market Street	B2
All Saints Road	A2	Mill Lane	A3
Aylestone Road	B3	Millstone Lane	B2
Bassett Street	A1	Montreal Road	C1
Bath Lane	A2	Morledge Street	C2
Bedford Street North	C1	Narborough Road	A3
Belgrave Gate	B1	Narborough Road North	A2
Bell Lane	C1	Nelson Street	C3
Belvoir Street	B2	Newarke Close	A3
Braunstone Gate	A2	Newarke Street	B2
Burgess Street	B1	Northgate Street	A1
Burleys Way	B1	Ottawa Road	C1
Byron Street	B1	Oxford Street	B2
Cank Street	B2	Pasture Lane	A1
Castle Street	A2	Peacock Lane	B2
Charles Street	C2	Pocklingtons Walk	B2
Christow Street	C1	Prebend Street	C3
Church Gate	B1	Princess Road East	C3
Clarence Street	B1	Pringle Street	A1
Clyde Street	C1	Queen Street	C2
College Street	C2	Regent Road	B3
Colton Street	C2	Regent Street	C3
Conduit Street	C2	Repton Street	A1
Crafton Street East	C1	Rutland Street	C2
Cravan Street	A1	Samuel Street	C2
De Montfort Street	C3	Sanvey Gate	A1
Deacon Street	B3	Saxby Street	C3
Dryden Street	B1	Slater Street	A1
Duns Lane	A2	Soar Lane	A1
Dunton Street	A1	South Albion Street	C2
Eastern Boulevard	A3	Southampton Street	C2
Friar Lane	B2	Sparkenhoe Street	C2
Friday Street	B1	St. George's Way	C2
Frog Island	A1	St. John's Street	B1
Gallowtree Gate	B2	St. Margaret's Way	A1
Gaul Street	A3	St. Matthew's Way	C1
Glebe Street	C2	St. Nicholas Circle	A2
Gotham Street	C3	Swain Street	C2
Granby Street	B2	Swan Street	A1
Grange Lane	B3	Taylor Road	C1
Grasmere Street	A3	Thames Street	B1
Great Central Street	A1	The Gateway	A3
Halford Street	B2	The Newarke	A2
Havelock Street	B3	Tigers Way	B3
Haymarket	B1	Tower Street	B3
High Street	B2	Tudor Road	A1
Highcross Street	A1	Ullswater Street	A3
Hobart Street	C2	University Road	C3
Horsfair Street	B2	Upperton Road	A3
Humberstone Gate	B2	Vaughan Way	A1
Humberstone Road	C1	Vestry Street	C2
Infirmary Road	B3	Walnut Street	A3
Jarrom Street	A3	Waterloo Way	C3
Jarvis Street	A2	Welford Road	B2
Kamloops Crescent	C1	Wellington Street	B2
Kent Street	C1	West Street	B3
King Richard's Road	A2	Western Boulevard	A3
Lancaster Road	B3	Western Road	A3
Lee Street	B1	Wharf Street North	C1
Lincoln Street	C2	Wharf Street South	C1
London Road	C3	Wilberforce Road	A3
Losebly Lane	B2	Windermere Street	A3
Lower Brown Street	B2	Woodboy Street	C1
Manitoba Road	C1	Yeoman Street	B2
Mansfield Street	B1	York Road	B2

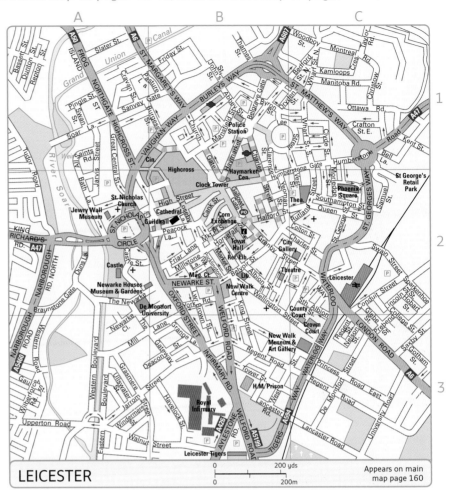

LEICESTER

| 0 | 200 yds |
| 0 | 200m |

Appears on main map page 160

Tourist Information Centre: 9 Castle Hill
Tel: 01522 873000

Alexandra Terrace	A2	Spa Road	C3
Baggholme Road	C2	St. Anne's Road	C2
Bailgate	B1	St. Giles Avenue	C1
Beaumont Fee	B2	St. Mark Street	B3
Beevor Street	A3	St. Mary's Street	B3
Brayford Way	A3	St. Rumbold Street	B2
Brayford Wharf North	A2	Stamp End	C3
Broadgate	B2	Steep Hill	B2
Broadway	B1	The Avenue	A2
Bruce Road	C1	Tritton Road	A3
Burton Road	A1	Union Row	B2
Canwick Road	B3	Upper Lindum Street	C2
Carholme Road	A2	Upper Long Leys Road	A1
Carline Road	A1	Vere Street	B1
Carr Street	A2	Vine Street	C2
Cheviot Street	C2	Waterside North	B3
Church Lane	B1	Waterside South	B3
Clasketgate	B2	West Parade	A2
Croft Street	B2	Westgate	B1
Cross Street	B3	Wigford Way	B2
Curle Avenue	C1	Wilson Street	A1
Drury Lane	B2	Winn Street	C2
East Gate	B2	Wragby Road	C2
Firth Road	A3	Yarborough Road	A1
George Street	C3		
Great Northern Terrace	B3		
Greetwell Close	C1		
Greetwell Road	C2		
Gresham Street	A2		
Hampton Street	A2		
Harvey Street	A2		
High Street	B3		
John Street	C2		
Langworthgate	B1		
Lee Road	C1		
Lindum Road	B2		
Lindum Terrace	C2		
Long Leys Road	A1		
Mainwaring Road	C1		
Mill Road	A1		
Milman Road	C2		
Monks Road	C2		
Monson Street	B3		
Moor Street	A2		
Mount Street	A1		
Nettleham Road	B1		
Newland	A2		
Newland Street West	A2		
Newport	B1		
Northgate	B1		
Orchard Street	A2		
Pelham Bridge	B3		
Portland Street	B3		
Portland Street	B3		
Pottergate	B2		
Queensway	C1		
Rasen Lane	B1		
Richmond Road	A2		
Ripon Street	B3		
Rope Walk	A3		
Rosemary Lane	B2		
Ruskin Avenue	C1		
Saltergate	B2		
Sewell Road	C2		
Silver Street	B2		
Sincil Bank	B3		

LINCOLN

| 0 | 200 yds |
| 0 | 200m |

Appears on main map page 187

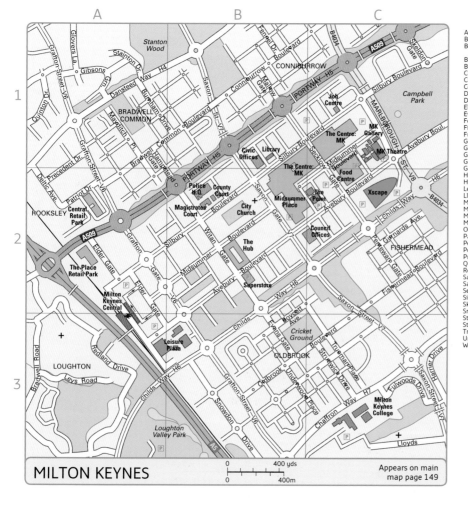

MIDDLESBROUGH

MILTON KEYNES

Newcastle upon Tyne

Tourist Information Centre: 8-9 Central Arcade
Tel: 0191 277 8000

Albert Street	C2	Pitt Street	A2
Ancrum Street	A1	Portland Road	C1
Argyle Street	C2	Portland Terrace	C1
Askew Road	C3	Pottery Lane	A3
Barrack Road	A1	Quarryfield Road	C3
Barras Bridge	B1	Quayside	C3
Bath Lane	A2	Queen Victoria Road	B1
Bigg Market	B2	Railway Street	A3
Blackett Street	B2	Redheugh Bridge	A3
Byron Street	C1	Richardson Road	A1
Chester Street	C1	Rye Hill	A3
City Road	C2	St. James Boulevard	A3
Claremont Road	B1	St. Mary's Place	B1
Clarence Street	C2	St. Thomas Street	B1
Clayton Street	B2	Sandyford Road	B1/C1
Clayton Street West	A3	Scotswood Road	A3
Corporation Street	A2	Skinnerburn Road	B3
Coulthards Lane	C3	South Shore Road	C3
Crawhall Road	C2	Stanhope Street	A2
Dean Street	B2	Starbeck Avenue	C1
Diana Street	A2	Stodart Street	C1
Elswick East Terrace	A3	Stowell Street	A2
Eskdale Terrace	C1	Strawberry Place	A2
Essex Close	A3	Summerhill Grove	A2
Falconar Street	C1	Swing Bridge	B3
Forth Banks	B3	The Close	B3
Forth Street	A3	Tyne Bridge	C3
Gallowgate	A2	Union Street	C2
Gateshead Highway	C3	Warwick Street	C1
George Street	A3	Wellington Street	A2
Gibson Street	C2	West Street	C3
Grainger Street	B2	Westgate Road	A2
Grantham Road	C1	Westmorland Road	A3
Grey Street	B2	Windsor Terrace	B1
Hanover Street	B3	York Street	A2
Hawks Road	C3		
Helmsley Road	C1		
High Street	C3		
Hillgate	C3		
Howard Street	C2		
Hunters Road	A1		
Ivy Close	A3		
Jesmond Road	C1		
Jesmond Road West	B1		
John Dobson Street	B2		
Kelvin Grove	C1		
Kyle Close	A3		
Lambton Street	C3		
Mansfield Street	A2		
Maple Street	A3		
Maple Terrace	A3		
Market Street	B2		
Melbourne Street	C2		
Mill Road	C3		
Neville Street	A3		
New Bridge Street	C2		
Newgate Street	B2		
Northumberland Road	B2		
Northumberland Street	B1		
Oakwellgate	C3		
Orchard Street	B3		
Oxnam Crescent	A1		
Park Terrace	B1		
Percy Street	B2		
Pilgrim Street	B2		
Pipewellgate	B3		

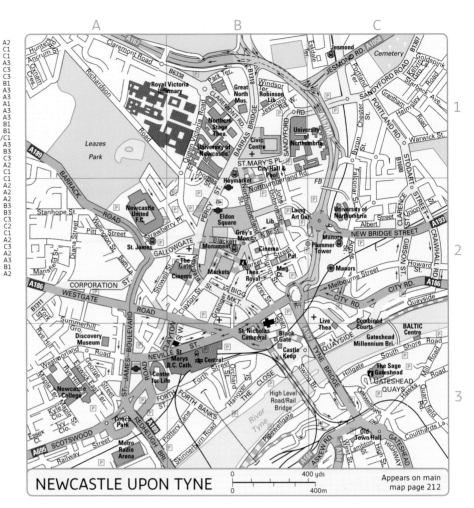

NEWCASTLE UPON TYNE

0   400 yds
0   400m

Appears on main map page 212

Norwich

Tourist Information Centre: The Forum, Millennium Plain
Tel: 01603 213999

Albion Way	C3	Queens Road	B3
All Saints Green	B3	Rampant Horse Street	B2
Ashby Street	B3	Recorder Road	C2
Bakers Road	A1	Red Lion Street	B2
Bank Plain	B2	Riverside	C3
Barker Street	A1	Riverside Road	C2
Barn Road	A2	Rosary Road	C2
Barrack Street	B1	Rose Lane	B2
Bedford Street	B2	Rouen Road	B3
Ber Street	B3	Rupert Street	A3
Bethel Street	A2	Russell Street	A1
Bishopbridge Road	C2	St. Andrew's Street	B2
Bishopgate	C2	St. Augustine's Street	A1
Botolph Street	B1	St. Benedict's Street	A2
Brazen Gate	B3	St. Crispin's Road	A1
Britannia Road	C1	St. Faiths Lane	B2
Brunswick Road	A3	St. George's Street	B1
Bullclose Road	B1	St. Giles Street	A2
Canary Way	C3	St. James Close	C1
Carrow Hill	C3	St. Leonards Road	C2
Carrow Road	C3	St. Martin's Road	A1
Castle Meadow	B2	St. Stephen's Road	A3
Chapel Field Road	A2	St. Stephen's Street	B3
Chapelfield North	A2	Silver Road	B1
City Road	B3	Silver Street	B1
Clarence Road	C3	Southwell Road	B3
Colegate	B1	Surrey Street	B3
Coslany Street	A2	Sussex Street	A1
Cowgate	B1	Theatre Street	A2
Dereham Road	A2	Thorn Lane	B3
Duke Street	B1	Thorpe Road	C2
Earlham Road	A2	Tombland	B2
Edward Street	B1	Trinity Street	A3
Elm Hill	B2	Trory Street	A2
Fishergate	B1	Union Street	A3
Gas Hill	C1	Unthank Road	A3
Grapes Hill	A2	Vauxhall Street	A3
Grove Avenue	A3	Victoria Street	A3
Grove Road	A3	Wensum Street	B1
Grove Walk	A3	Wessex Street	A3
Gurney Road	C1	Westwick Street	A1
Hall Road	B3	Wherry Road	C3
Hardy Road	C3	Whitefriars	B1
Heathgate	C1	Wodehouse Street	B1
Heigham Street	A1	York Street	A3
Horns Lane	B3		
Ipswich Road	A3		
Ketts Hill	C1		
King Street	B3		
Koblenz Avenue	C3		
Lothian Street	A1		
Lower Clarence Road	C2		
Magdalen Street	B1		
Magpie Road	B1		
Market Avenue	B2		
Marlborough Road	B1		
Mountergate	B2		
Mousehold Street	C1		
Newmarket Road	A3		
Newmarket Street	A3		
Oak Street	A1		
Orchard Street	A1		
Palace Street	B2		
Pitt Street	B1		
Pottergate	A2		
Prince of Wales Road	B2		

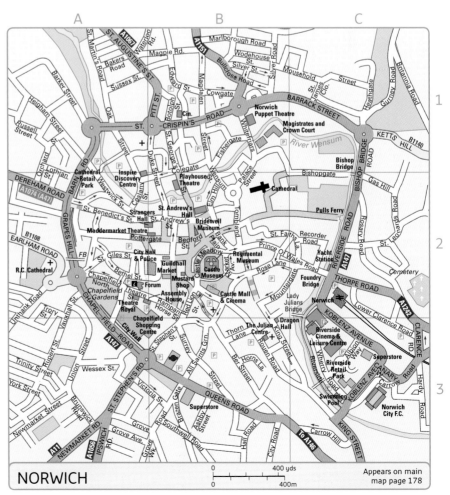

NORWICH

0   400 yds
0   400m

Appears on main map page 178

Tourist Information Centre: 1-4 Smithy Row
Tel: 08444 77 56 78

Abbotsford Drive	B1
Albert Street	B2
Angel Row	A2
Barker Gate	C2
Bath Street	C1
Beacon Hill Rise	C1
Bellar Gate	C2
Belward Street	C2
Bridlesmith Gate	B2
Broad Street	B2
Brook Street	C1
Burton Street	A1
Canal Street	B3
Carlton Street	B2
Carrington Street	B3
Castle Boulevard	A3
Castle Gate	B2
Castle Meadow Road	A3
Castle Road	A3
Chapel Bar	A2
Chaucer Street	A1
Cheapside	B2
City Link	C3
Clarendon Street	A1
Cliff Road	B3
Clumber Street	B2
College Street	A2
Collin Street	B3
Cranbrook Street	C2
Cromwell Street	A1
Curzon Street	B1
Derby Road	A2
Dryden Street	A1
Fisher Gate	C2
Fishpond Drive	A3
Fletcher Gate	B2
Forman Street	B2
Friar Lane	A2
Gedling Street	C2
George Street	B2
Gill Street	A1
Glasshouse Street	B1
Goldsmith Street	A1
Goose Gate	C2
Hamilton Drive	A3
Hampden Street	A1
Handel Street	C2
Heathcote Street	B2
High Pavement	B2
Hockley	C2
Hollowstone	C2
Hope Drive	A3
Huntingdon Drive	A2
Huntingdon Street	B1
Instow Rise	C1
Kent Street	B1
King Edward Street	B2
King Street	B2
Lamartine Street	C1
Lenton Road	A3
Lincoln Street	B2
Lister Gate	B3
London Road	C3
Long Row	B2
Low Pavement	B2
Lower Parliament Street	B2

Maid Marian Way	A2
Mansfield Road	B1
Manvers Street	C2
Market Street	B2
Middle Pavement	B2
Milton Street	B1
Mount Street	A2
North Church Street	B1
North Sherwood Street	B1
Park Row	A2
Park Terrace	A2
Park Valley	A2
Peel Street	A1
Pelham Street	B2
Pennyfoot Street	C2
Peveril Drive	A3
Pilcher Gate	B2
Plantagenet Street	C1
Popham Street	B3
Poplar Street	C2
Queens Road	B3
Queen Street	B2
Regent Street	A2
Robin Hood Street	C1
Roden Street	C1
St. Ann's Well Road	C1
St. James Street	A2
St. Mary's Gate	B2
St. Peter's Gate	B2
Shakespeare Street	A1
Shelton Street	B1
Sneinton Road	C2
South Parade	B2
South Sherwood Street	B1
Southwell Road	C2
Station Street	B3
Stoney Street	C2
Talbot Street	A1
The Great Northern Close	C3
The Rope Walk	A2
Union Road	B1
Upper Parliament Street	A2
Victoria Street	B2
Warser Gate	B2
Waverley Street	A1
Wheeler Gate	B2
Wilford Street	A3
Wollaton Street	A2
Woolpack Lane	C2

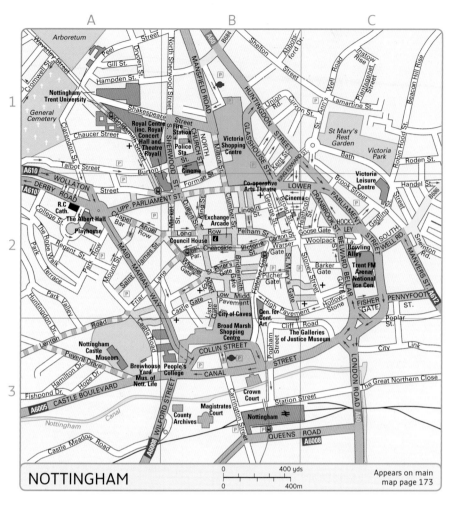

NOTTINGHAM

0	400 yds
0	400m

Appears on main
map page 173

Tourist Information Centre: 15-16 Broad Street
Tel: 01865 252200

Albert Street	A1
Banbury Road	B1
Beaumont Street	A2
Becket Street	A2
Blackhall Road	B1
Botley Road	A2
Broad Street	B2
Canal Street	A1
Cattle Street	B2
Cornmarket	B2
Cowley Place	C3
Folly Bridge	B3
George Street	A2
Great Clarendon Street	A1
Hart Street	A1
High Street	B2
Hollybush Row	A2
Holywell Street	B2
Hythe Bridge Street	A2
Iffley Road	C3
Juxon Street	A1
Keble Road	B1
Kingston Road	A1
Littlegate Street	B3
Longwall Street	C2
Magdalen Bridge	C2
Manor Road	C2
Mansfield Road	C1
Marlborough Road	B3
Merton Street	B3
Mill Street	A2
Museum Road	B1
Nelson Street	A2
New Road	A2
Norham Gardens	B1
Observatory Street	A1
Oxpens Road	A3
Paradise Street	A2
Park End Street	A2
Parks Road	B1
Plantation Road	A1
Queen Street	B2
Rewley Road	A2
Richmond Road	A2
Rose Place	B3
St. Aldate's	B3
St. Bernards Road	A1
St. Cross Road	C1
St. Ebbe's Street	B3
St. Giles	B1
St. Thomas' Street	A2
South Parks Road	B1
Speedwell Street	B3
Thames Street	B3
Trinity Street	A3
Turl Street	B2
Walton Crescent	A1
Walton Street	A1
Walton Well Road	A1
Woodstock Road	A1

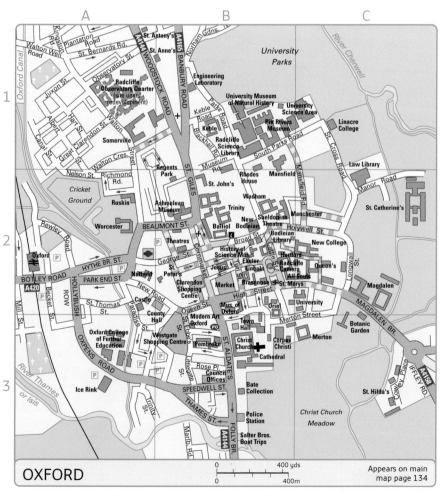

OXFORD

0	400 yds
0	400m

Appears on main
map page 134

Tourist Information Centre: Lower City Mills, West Mill Street
Tel: 01738 450600

Abbot Crescent	A3	Shore Road	C3
Abbot Street	A3	South Methven Street	B2
Albany Terrace	A1	South Street	B2
Atholl Street	B1	Strathmore Street	C1
Balhousie Street	B1	Stuart Avenue	A3
Barossa Place	B1	Tay Street	C2
Barossa Street	B1	Victoria Street	B2
Barrack Street	B1	Watergate	C2
Bowerswell Road	C2	Whitefriars Crescent	A2
Caledonian Road	B2	Whitefriars Street	A2
Canal Street	B2	William Street	B2
Cavendish Avenue	A3	Wilson Street	A3
Charlotte Street	B1	Young Street	A3
Clyde Place	A3	York Place	A2
Darnhall Drive	A3		
Dundee Road	C2		
Dunkeld Road	A1		
Edinburgh Road	B3		
Feus Road	A1		
Friar Street	A3		
George Street	C2		
Glasgow Road	A2		
Glover Street	A2		
Gowrie Street	C1		
Gray Street	A2		
Graybank Road	A2		
Hay Street	B1		
High Street	B2		
Isla Road	C1		
Jeanfield Road	A2		
King's Place	B3		
King James Place	B3		
King Street	B2		
Kinnoull Street	B1		
Kinnoull Terrace	C2		
Knowelea Place	A3		
Leonard Street	B2		
Lochie Brae	C1		
Long Causeway	A1		
Main Street	C1		
Manse Road	C2		
Marshall Place	B3		
Melville Street	B1		
Mill Street	B2		
Milne Street	B2		
Murray Crescent	A3		
Needless Road	A3		
New Row	B2		
North Methven Street	B1		
Park Place	A3		
Perth Bridge	C1		
Pickletullum Road	A2		
Pitcullen Terrace	C1		
Pitheavlis Crescent	A3		
Princes Street	C3		
Priory Place	B3		
Queen Street	A3		
Queens Bridge	C2		
Raeburn Park	A3		
Riggs Road	A2		
Rose Crescent	A2		
Rose Terrace	B1		
St. Catherines Road	A1		
St. John Street	C2		
St. Leonard's Bank	B3		
Scott Street	B2		

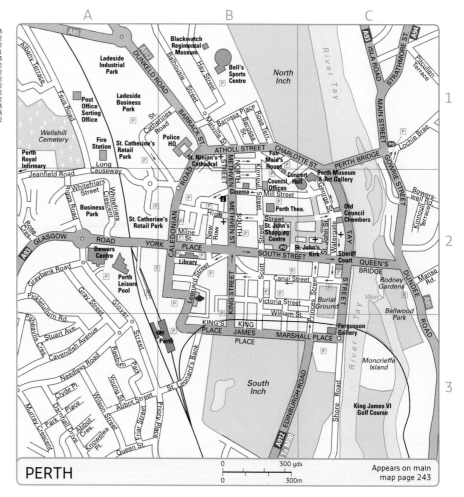

PERTH

0   300 yds
0   300m

Appears on main map page 243

Tourist Information Centre: Plymouth Mayflower Centre,
3-5 The Barbican   Tel: 01752 306330

Alexandra Road	C1	North Street	B2
Alma Road	A1	Notte Street	B3
Armada Street	B2	Oxford Street	A2
Armada Way	B2	Pentillie Road	B1
Ashford Road	C1	Ponsonby Road	A1
Barbican Approach	C3	Princess Street	B3
Beaumont Road	C2	Queen's Road	C1
Beechwood Avenue	B1	Royal Parade	B2
Belgrave Road	C1	Salisbury Road	C2
Bretonside	B2	Saltash Road	A1
Buckwell Street	B3	Seaton Avenue	B1
Camden Street	B2	Seymour Avenue	C2
Cattledown Road	C3	Southside Street	B3
Cecil Street	A2	Stoke Road	A2
Central Park Avenue	A1	Stuart Road	A1
Charles Street	B2	Sutton Road	C2
Citadel Road	A3	Sydney Street	A1
Clarence Place	A2	Teats Hill Road	C3
Cliff Road	A3	The Crescent	A3
Clifton Place	B1	Tothill Avenue	C2
Clovelly Road	C3	Tothill Road	C2
Cobourg Street	B2	Union Street	A2
Coleridge Road	C1	Vauxhall Street	B3
Connaught Avenue	C1	West Hoe Road	A3
Cornwall Street	B2	Western Approach	A2
Dale Road	B1	Whittington Street	A1
De-La-Hay Avenue	A1	Wilton Street	A2
Desborough Road	C2	Wyndham Street	A2
Drake Circus	B2		
East Street	A3		
Ebrington Street	B2		
Elliot Street	A3		
Embankment Road	C2		
Exeter Street	B2		
Ford Park Road	B1		
Furzehill Road	C1		
Gdynia Way	C3		
Glen Park Avenue	B1		
Grand Parade	A3		
Greenbank Avenue	C2		
Greenbank Road	C1		
Grenville Road	C2		
Harwell Street	A2		
Hill Park Crescent	B1		
Hoe Road	B3		
Houndiscombe Road	B1		
James Street	B2		
King Street	A2		
Knighton Road	C2		
Lipson Hill	C1		
Lipson Road	C2		
Lisson Grove	C1		
Lockyer Street	B3		
Looe Street	B2		
Madeira Road	B3		
Manor Road	A2		
Martin Street	A3		
Mayflower Street	B2		
Millbay Road	A3		
Mount Gould Road	C1		
Mutley Plain	B1		
New George Street	A2		
North Cross	B2		
North Hill	B2		
North Road East	B2		
North Road West	A2		

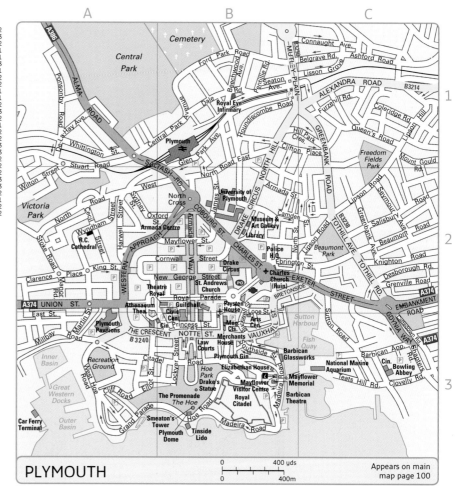

PLYMOUTH

0   400 yds
0   400m

Appears on main map page 100

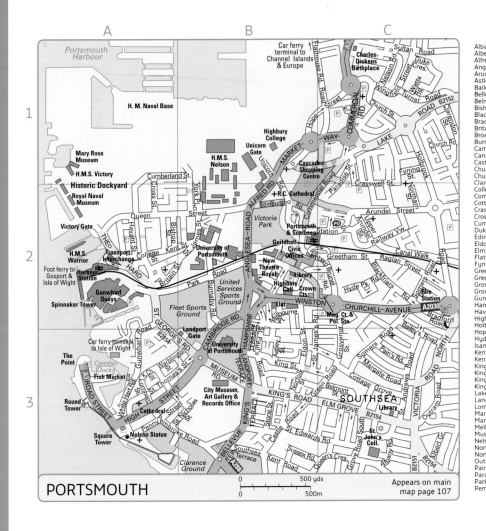

PORTSMOUTH

Albany Road	C3
Albert Grove	C3
Alfred Road	B2
Anglesea Road	B2
Arundel Street	C2
Astley Street	B3
Bailey's Road	C2
Bellevue Terrace	B3
Belmont Street	C3
Bishop Street	A1
Blackfriars Road	C2
Bradford Road	C2
Britain Street	A2
Broad Street	A3
Burnaby Road	B2
Cambridge Road	B3
Canal Walk	C2
Castle Road	B3
Church Road	C1
Church Street	C1
Clarendon Street	C1
College Street	A2
Commercial Road	B2
Cottage Grove	C3
Crasswell Street	C1
Cross Street	A1
Cumberland Street	A1
Duke Crescent	C1
Edinburgh Road	B2
Eldon Street	B3
Elm Grove	C3
Flathouse Road	C1
Fyning Street	C1
Green Road	B3
Greetham Street	C2
Grosvenor Street	C3
Grove Road South	C3
Gunwharf Road	A3
Hampshire Terrace	B3
Havant Street	A2
High Street	A3
Holbrook Road	C1
Hope Street	B1
Hyde Park Road	C2
Isambard Brunel Road	B2
Kent Road	B3
Kent Street	A1
King Charles Street	A3
King's Road	B3
King's Terrace	B3
King Street	B3
Lake Road	C1
Landport Terrace	B3
Lombard Street	A3
Margate Road	C3
Market Way	B1
Melbourne Place	B2
Museum Road	B3
Nelson Road	C1
Norfolk Street	B3
Northam Street	C2
Outram Road	C3
Pain's Road	C3
Paradise Street	C2
Park Road	B2
Pembroke Road	A3
Penny Street	A3
Queen's Crescent	C3
Queen Street	A2
Raglan Street	C2
Railway View	C2
St. Andrews Road	C3
St. Edward's Road	B3
St. George's Road	A2
St. James Road	B3
St. James Street	A2
St. Paul's Road	B3
St. Thomas's Street	A3
Somers Road	C2
Southsea Terrace	B3
Station Street	C2
Stone Street	B3
Sultan Road	C1
Sussex Street	B3
The Hard	A2
Turner Road	C1
Unicorn Road	B1
Upper Arundel Street	C2
Victoria Road North	C3
Warblington Street	A3
Watts Road	C1
White Hart Road	A3
Wingfield Street	C1
Winston Churchill Avenue	B2
York Place	B2

Appears on main map page 107

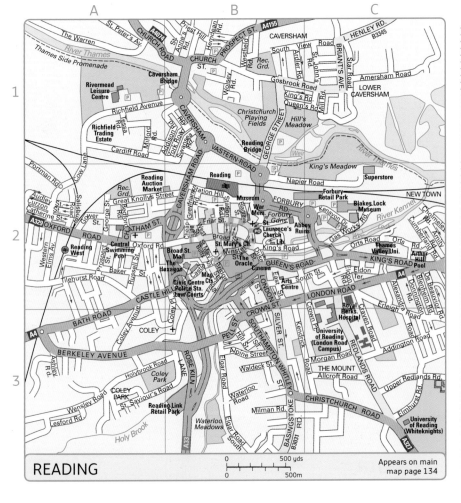

READING

Addington Road	C3
Addison Road	A1
Alexandra Road	C2
Allcroft Road	C3
Alpine Street	B3
Amersham Road	C1
Amity Road	A2
Ardler Road	B1
Ashley Road	A3
Audley Street	A2
Baker Street	A2
Basingstoke Road	B3
Bath Road	A3
Bedford Road	A2
Berkeley Avenue	A3
Blagrave Street	B2
Blenheim Road	C2
Briant's Avenue	C1
Bridge Street	B2
Broad Street	B2
Cardiff Road	A1
Castle Hill	A2
Castle Street	B2
Catherine Street	A2
Caversham Road	B2
Chatham Street	A2
Cheapside	B2
Cholmeley Road	C2
Christchurch Road	C3
Church Road	A1
Church Street	B1
Coley Avenue	A3
Coley Place	B2
Cow Lane	A2
Craven Road	C3
Crown Place	C2
Crown Street	B3
Cumberland Road	C2
Curzon Street	A2
De Beauvoir Road	C2
Donnington Road	C2
Duke Street	B2
East Street	B2
Eldon Road	B2
Eldon Terrace	C2
Elgar Road	B3
Elgar Road South	B3
Elmhurst Road	C3
Erleigh Road	C2
Fobney Street	B2
Forbury Road	B2
Friar Street	B2
Gas Work Road	C2
George Street *Caversham*	B1
George Street *Reading*	A2
Gosbrook Road	B1
Gower Street	A2
Great Knollys Street	A2
Greyfriars Road	B2
Hemdean Road	B1
Hill Street	B3
Holybrook Road	A3
Kenavon Drive	C2
Kendrick Road	B3
King's Road *Caversham*	B1
King's Road *Reading*	B2
Lesford Road	A3
London Road	C2
London Street	B2
Lower Henley Road	C1
Mill Road	C1
Mill Road	C1
Milford Road	A1
Milman Road	B3
Minster Street	B2
Morgan Road	C3
Napier Road	B2
Orts Road	C2
Oxford Road	A2
Pell Street	B3
Portman Road	A1
Priest Hill	B1
Prospect Street *Caversham*	B1
Prospect Street *Reading*	A2
Queen's Road *Caversham*	B1
Queen's Road *Reading*	B2
Richfield Avenue	A1
Rose Kiln Lane	B3
Russell Street	A2
St. Anne's Road	B1
St. John's Road	C1
St. Mary's Butts	B2
St. Peters Avenue	A1
St. Saviours Road	A3
Silver Street	B3
South Street	B2
Southampton Street	B3
South View Road	B1
Star Road	C1
Station Hill	B2
Station Road	B2
Swansea Road	B1
Tessa Road	A1
The Warren	A1
Tilehurst Road	A2
Upper Redlands Road	C3
Vastern Road	B1
Waldek Street	B3
Waterloo Road	B3
Wensley Road	A3
Western Elms Avenue	A3
Westfield Road	B1
West Street	B2
Whitley Street	B3
Wolsey Road	B1
York Road	B1

Appears on main map page 134

Albany Road	B1	Salt Lane	B2
Ashley Road	A1	Scots Lane	B2
Avon Terrace	A1	Silver Street	B2
Barnard Street	C2	Southampton Road	C3
Bedwin Street	B1	Swaynes Close	B1
Belle Vue Road	B1	Tollgate Road	C2
Bishops Walk	B3	Trinity Street	C2
Blackfriars Way	C3	Wain-a-long Road	C1
Blue Boar Row	B2	West Walk	B3
Bourne Avenue	C1	Wilton Road	A1
Bourne Hill	C1	Winchester Street	B2
Bridge Street	B2	Windsor Road	A1
Brown Street	B2	Wyndham Road	B1
Butcher Row	B2	York Road	A1
Carmelite Way	B3		
Castle Street	B1		
Catherine Street	B2		
Chipper Lane	B2		
Churchfields Road	A2		
Churchill Way East	C2		
Churchill Way North	B1		
Churchill Way South	C3		
Churchill Way West	A1		
Clifton Road	A1		
College Street	C1		
Crane Bridge Road	A2		
Crane Street	B2		
De Vaux Place	B3		
Devizes Road	A1		
Elm Grove Road	C2		
Endless Street	B1		
Estcourt Road	C1		
Exeter Street	B3		
Fairview Road	C1		
Fisherton Street	A2		
Fowlers Hill	C2		
Fowlers Road	C2		
Friary Lane	C3		
Gas Lane	A1		
Gigant Street	C2		
Greencroft Street	C1		
Hamilton Road	B1		
High Street	B2		
Ivy Street	B2		
Kelsey Road	C1		
Laverstock Road	C2		
Manor Road	C1		
Marsh Lane	A1		
Meadow Road	A1		
Milford Hill	C2		
Milford Street	B2		
Mill Road	A2		
Millstream Approach	B1		
Minster Street	B2		
New Canal	B2		
New Street	B2		
North Walk	B3		
Park Street	C1		
Pennyfarthing Street	B2		
Queens Road	B1		
Rampart Road	C2		
Rollestone Street	B1		
St. Ann Street	C3		
St. John's Street	B2		
St. Marks Road	C1		
St. Paul's Road	A1		

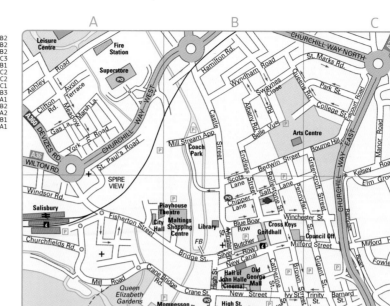

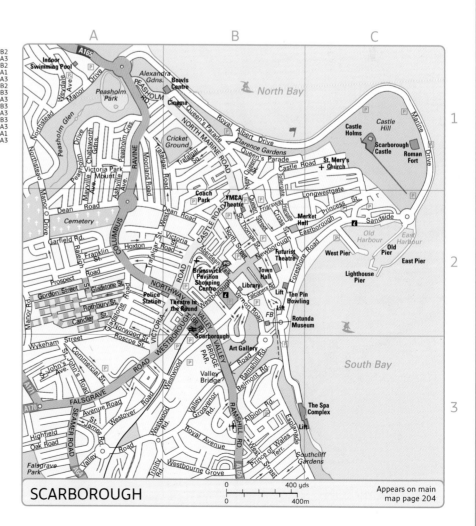

SALISBURY

0	200 yds
0	200m

Appears on main
map page 118

Aberdeen Walk	B2	Valley Bridge Road	B2
Albion Road	B3	Valley Road	A3
Ashville Avenue	A2	Vernon Road	B2
Avenue Road	A3	Victoria Park Mount	A1
Belmont Road	B3	Victoria Road	A3
Candler Street	A2	Victoria Street	B2
Castle Road	B2	West Street	B3
Chatsworth Gardens	A1	Westborough	A3
Columbus Ravine	A2	Westbourne Grove	B3
Commercial Street	A3	Westover Road	A3
Cross Street	B2	Westwood	B3
Dean Road	A2	Westwood Road	A3
Eastborough	B2	Weydale Avenue	A1
Esplanade	B3	Wykeham Street	A3
Falconers Rd	B2		
Falsgrave Road	A3		
Foreshore Road	B2		
Franklin Street	A2		
Friargate	B2		
Friarsway	B2		
Garfield Road	A2		
Gladstone Road	A2		
Gladstone Street	A2		
Gordon Street	A2		
Grosvenor Road	B3		
Highfield	A3		
Hoxton Road	A2		
Longwestgate	C2		
Manor Road	A2		
Marine Drive	C1		
Mayville Avenue	A2		
Moorland Road	A1		
New Queen Street	B1		
Newborough	B2		
North Marine Road	B1		
North Street	B2		
Northstead Manor Drive	A1		
Northway	A2		
Norwood Street	A2		
Oak Road	A3		
Peasholm Crescent	A1		
Peasholm Drive	A1		
Peasholm Road	A1		
Prince Of Wales Terrace	B3		
Princess Street	C2		
Prospect Road	A2		
Queen Street	B2		
Queen's Parade	B1		
Raleigh Street	A2		
Ramshill Road	B3		
Roscoe Street	A3		
Rothbury Street	A2		
Royal Albert Drive	B1		
Royal Avenue	B3		
Sandside	C2		
Seamer Road	A3		
St. James Road	A3		
St. John's Avenue	A3		
St. John's Road	A3		
St. Thomas Street	B2		
Tollergate	B1		
Trafalgar Road	A1		
Trafalgar Square	B1		
Trafalgar Street West	A2		
Trinity Road	A3		
Valley Bridge Parade	B3		

SCARBOROUGH

0	400 yds
0	400m

Appears on main
map page 204

SHEFFIELD

Tourist Information Centre: 14 Norfolk Row
Tel: 0114 221 1900

Allen Street	B1	Hanover Square	A3
Angel Street	C1	Hanover Street	A3
Arundel Gate	B2	Hanover Way	A3
Arundel Lane	C3	Harmer Lane	C2
Arundel Street	B3	Haymarket	C1
Bailey Lane	B1	Headford Street	A3
Bailey Street	B1	High Street	C1
Bank Street	C1	Hodgson Street	A3
Barker's Pool	B2	Hollis Croft	B1
Beet Street	A1	Howard Street	C2
Bellefield Street	A1	Hoyle Street	A1
Bishop Street	B3	Leadmill Road	C3
Blonk Street	C1	Leopold Street	B2
Boston Street	B3	Mappin Street	A2
Bower Street	B1	Margaret Street	B3
Bramwell Street	A1	Mary Street	B3
Bridge Street	C1	Matilda Street	C3
Broad Lane	A2	Meadow Street	A1
Broad Street	C1	Milton Street	A3
Broomhall Street	A3	Moore Street	A3
Broomhall Place	A3	Napier Street	A3
Broomspring Lane	A2	Netherthorpe Road	A1
Brown Street	C3	Norfolk Street	C2
Brunswick Street	A2	Nursery Street	C1
Campo Lane	B1	Pinstone Street	B2
Carver Street	B2	Pond Hill	C2
Castle Square	C1	Pond Hill	C2
Castle Street	C1	Pond Street	C2
Castlegate	C1	Portobello Lane	A2
Cavendish Street	A2	Queen Street	B1
Cemetery Road	A3	Queens Road	C3
Charles Street	B2/C2	Rockingham Street	B2
Charlotte Road	B3	St. Mary's Gate	B3
Charter Row	B3	St. Mary's Road	B3
Charter Square	B2	St. Philip's Road	A1
Church Street	B1	Scotland Street	B1
Clarke Street	A3	Sheaf Gardens	C3
Commercial Street	C1	Sheaf Square	C2
Copper Street	B1	Sheaf Street	C2
Corporation Street	B1	Shepherd Street	B1
Devonshire Street	A2	Shoreham Street	C3
Division Street	B2	Shrewsbury Road	C3
Dover Street	A1	Sidney Street	C3
Duchess Road	C3	Snig Hill	C1
Earl Street	B3	Snow Lane	B1
Earl Way	B3	Solly Street	A1
East Parade	C1	South Lane	B3
Ecclesall Road	A3	Spring Street	B1
Edmund Road	C3	Suffolk Road	C3
Edward Street	A1	Sunny Bank	A3
Eldon Street	B2	Surrey Street	B2
Exchange Street	C1	Tenter Street	B1
Exeter Drive	A3	The Moor	B3
Eyre Lane	C2	Thomas Street	A3
Eyre Street	B3	Townhead Street	B1
Farm Road	C3	Trafalgar Street	B2
Fawcett Street	A1	Trippet Lane	B2
Filey Street	A2	Upper Allen Street	A1
Fitzwilliam Street	A2	Upper Hanover Street	A2
Flat Street	C1	Victoria Street	A2
Furnace Hill	B1	Waingate	C1
Furnival Gate	B2	Wellington Street	B2
Furnival Square	B2	West Bar	B1
Furnival Street	B2	West Street	B2
Garden Street	A1	Westbar Green	A1
Gell Street	A2	Weston Street	A1
Gibraltar Street	B1	William Street	A3
Glossop Road	A2	Young Street	B3

Appears on main map page 186

SOUTHAMPTON

Tourist Information Centre: 9 Civic Centre Road
Tel: 023 8083 3333

Above Bar Street	B2	Queensway	B3
Albert Road North	C3	Radcliffe Road	C1
Argyle Road	B1	Roberts Road	A1
Bedford Place	A1	St. Andrews Road	B1
Belvidere Road	C2	St. Mary's Road	B1
Bernard Street	B3	St. Mary Street	B2
Brintons Road	B1	Shirley Road	A1
Britannia Road	C1	Solent Road	A2
Briton Street	B3	Southern Road	A2
Burlington Road	A1	South Front	B2
Canute Road	B3	Terminus Terrace	B3
Castle Way	B2	Town Quay	A3
Central Bridge	B3	Trafalgar Road	B3
Central Road	B3	West Quay Road	A2
Chapel Road	B2	West Road	B3
Civic Centre Road	A2	Western Esplanade	A2
Clovelly Road	B1	Wilton Avenue	A1
Commercial Road	A1		
Cranbury Avenue	A1		
Cumberland Place	A1		
Denzil Avenue	B1		
Derby Road	C1		
Devonshire Road	B1		
Dorset Street	B1		
East Park Terrace	B1		
East Street	B2		
Endle Street	C2		
European Way	B3		
Golden Grove	B2		
Graham Road	B1		
Harbour Parade	A2		
Hartington Road	C1		
Henstead Road	A1		
Herbert Walker Avenue	A2		
High Street	B2		
Hill Lane	A1		
Howard Road	A1		
James Street	B2		
Kent Street	C1		
Kingsway	B2		
Landguard Road	A1		
London Road	B1		
Lyon Street	B1		
Marine Parade	C2		
Marsh Lane	B2		
Melbourne Street	C2		
Millbank Street	C1		
Milton Road	A1		
Morris Road	A1		
Mount Pleasant Road	B1		
Newcombe Road	A1		
New Road	B2		
Northam Road	C1		
North Front	B2		
Northumberland Road	C1		
Ocean Way	B3		
Onslow Road	B1		
Orchard Lane	B3		
Oxford Avenue	B1		
Oxford Street	B3		
Palmerston Road	B2		
Peel Street	C1		
Platform Road	B3		
Portland Terrace	A2		
Pound Tree Road	B2		
Princes Street	C1		

Appears on main map page 106

Tourist Information Centre: Victoria Hall, Bagnall Street, Hanley Tel: 01782 236000

Albion Street	B1	Snow Hill	B2
Ashford Street	B2	Stafford Street	B1
Avenue Road	B2	Station Road	B3
Aynsley Road	B2	Stoke	B3
Bedford Road	B2	Stoke Road	B3
Bedford Street	A2	Stone Street	A3
Belmont Road	A1	Stuart Road	C2
Beresford Street	B2	Sun Street	B1
Berry Hill Road	C2	The Parkway	B2
Boon Avenue	A3	Trentmill Road	C2
Botteslow Street	C1	Victoria Road	C2
Boughey Road	B3	Warner Street	B1
Broad Street	B1	Waterloo Street	C1
Bucknall New Road	C1	Wellesley Street	B2
Bucknall Old Road	C1	Wellington Road	C1
Cauldon Road	B2	West Avenue	A3
Cemetery Road	A2	Westland Street	A3
Church Street	B3	Yoxall Avenue	A3
Clough Street	A1		
College Road	B2		
Commercial Road	C1		
Copeland Street	B3		
Dewsbury Road	C3		
Eagle Street	C1		
Eastwood Road	C1		
Elenora Street	B3		
Etruria Road	A1		
Etruria Vale Road	A1		
Etruscan Street	A2		
Festival Way	A1		
Forge Lane	A1		
Garner Street	A2		
Glebe Street	B3		
Greatbatch Avenue	A3		
Hanley	B1		
Hartshill Road	A3		
Hill Street	A3		
Honeywall	A3		
Howard Place	B2		
Ivy House Road	C1		
Leek Road	B3		
Lichfield Street	C1		
Liverpool Road	B3		
Lordship Lane	B3		
Lytton Street	B3		
Manor Street	C3		
Marsh Street	B1		
Newlands Street	B2		
North Street	A2		
Old Hall Street	B1		
Oxford Street	A3		
Parliament Row	B1		
Potteries Way	B1		
Potters Way	C1		
Prince's Road	A3		
Quarry Avenue	A3		
Quarry Road	A3		
Queen's Road	A3		
Queensway	A2		
Rectory Road	B2		
Regent Road	B2		
Richmond Street	A3		
Ridgway Road	B2		
Seaford Street	B2		
Shelton New Road	A2		
Shelton Old Road	A3		

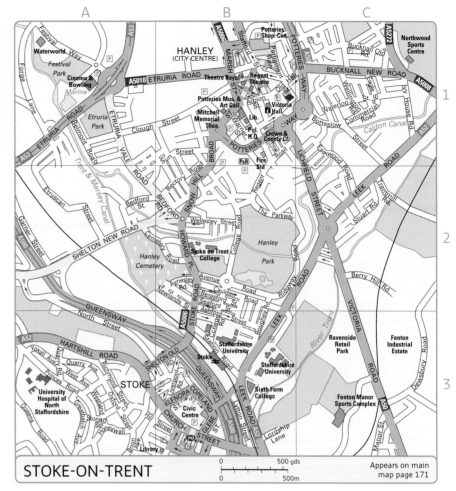

STOKE-ON-TRENT

0   500 yds
0   500m

Appears on main map page 171

Tourist Information Centre: Bridgefoot Tel: 01789 264293

Albany Road	A2	Swan's Nest Lane	C2
Alcester Road	A1	The Waterways	A1
Arden Street	A1	Tiddington Road	C2
Avonside	B3	Trinity Street	B3
Banbury Road	C2	Tyler Street	B1
Bancroft Place	C2	Union Street	B2
Birmingham Road	A1	Warwick Court	B1
Brewery Street	B1	Warwick Crescent	C1
Bridgefoot	C2	Warwick Road	C1
Bridge Street	B2	Waterside	B2
Bridgeway	C2	Welcome Road	C1
Bridgetown Road	C3	Westbourne Grove	A2
Broad Street	A3	Western Road	A1
Broad Walk	A3	West Street	A3
Bull Street	A3	Wharf Road	A1
Chapel Lane	B2	Windsor Street	B2
Chapel Street	B2	Wood Street	B2
Cherry Orchard	A3		
Chestnut Walk	A2		
Church Street	B2		
Clopton Bridge	C2		
Clopton Road	B1		
College Lane	B3		
College Street	B3		
Ely Street	B2		
Evesham Place	A3		
Evesham Road	A3		
Great William Street	B1		
Greenhill Street	A2		
Grove Road	A2		
Guild Street	B1		
Henley Street	B1		
High Street	B2		
Holtom Street	A3		
John Street	B1		
Kendall Avenue	B1		
Maidenhead Road	B1		
Mansell Street	A1		
Meer Street	B2		
Mill Lane	B3		
Mulberry Street	B1		
Narrow Lane	A3		
New Street	B3		
Old Town	B3		
Old Town Square	A3		
Old Tramway Walk	C3		
Orchard Way	A3		
Payton Street	B1		
Red Lion Court	B2		
Rother Street	A2		
Ryland Street	B3		
St. Andrews Crescent	A3		
St. Gregory's Road	B1		
Sanctus Drive	A3		
Sanctus Road	A3		
Sanctus Street	A3		
Sandfield Road	A3		
Scholar's Lane	A3		
Seven Meadow Road	A3		
Shakespeare Street	B1		
Sheep Street	B2		
Shipston Road	C3		
Shottery Road	A2		
Shrieve's Walk	B2		
Southern Lane	B3		
Station Road	A1		

STRATFORD-UPON-AVON

0   500 yds
0   500m

Appears on main map page 147

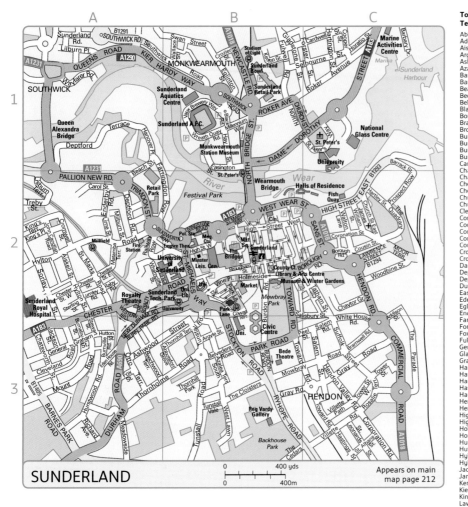

SUNDERLAND

0   400 yds
0   400m

Appears on main
map page 212

Tourist Information Centre: 50 Fawcett Street
Tel: 0191 553 2000

Abbotsford Grove	B3	Lime Street	A2
Addison Street	C3	Livingstone Road	B2
Aiskell Street	A2	Lumley Road	A2
Argyle Street	B3	Matamba Terrace	A2
Ashwood Street	A3	Milburn Street	A2
Azalea Terace South	B3	Millennium Way	B1
Barnes Park Road	A3	Moor Terrace	C2
Barrack Street	C1	Mount Road	A3
Beach Street	A2	Mowbray Road	B3
Beechwood Terrace	A3	New Durham Road	A3
Belvedere Road	B3	Newcastle Road	B1
Black Road	B1	North Bridge Street	B1
Borough Road	B2/C2	Otto Terrace	A3
Bramwell Road	C3	Pallion New Road	A2
Brougham Street	B2	Park Lane	B2
Burdon Road	B3	Park Road	B3
Burn Park Road	A3	Peel Street	B3
Burnaby Street	A3	Prospect Row	C2
Burnville Road	A3	Queens Road	A1
Carol Street	A2	Raby Road	A2
Chatsworth Street	A3	Railway Row	A3
Chaytor Grove	C2	Roker Avenue	B1/C1
Chester Road	A2	Rosalie Terrace	C3
Chester Street	A2	Ryhope Road	B3
Church Street East	C2	St. Albans Street	C3
Church Street North	B1	St. Leonards Street	C3
Cleveland Road	A3	St. Marks Road	A2
Commercial Road	C3	St. Mary's Way	B2
Cooper Street	C1	St. Michaels Way	B2
Coronation Street	C2	St. Peter's Way	C1
Corporation Road	C3	Salem Road	C3
Cousin Street	C2	Salem Street	C3
Cromwell Street	A2	Salisbury Street	B2
Crozier Street	B1	Sans Street	C2
Dame Dorothy Street	B1	Selbourne Street	A2
Deptford Road	A2	Silksworth Row	A2
Deptford Terrace	A1	Sorley Street	A2
Durham Road	A3	Southwick Road	A1
Easington Street	B1	Southwick Road	B1
Eden House Road	A3	Stewart Street	A3
Eglinton Street	B1	Stockton Road	B3
Enderby Road	A2	Suffolk Street	C3
Farringdon Row	A1	Sunderland Road	A1
Forster Street	C1	Swan Street	B1
Fox Street	A3	Tatham Street	C2
Fulwell Road	B1	The Cedars	B3
General Graham Street	A3	The Cloisters	B3
Gladstone Street	B1	The Parade	C3
Gray Road	B3/C3	The Quadrant	C2
Hanover Place	A1	The Royalty	A2
Hartington Street	C1	Thornhill Park	B3
Hartley Street	C2	Thornhill Terrace	B3
Hastings Street	C3	Thornholme Road	A3
Hay Street	B1	Toward Road	B2/C3
Hendon Road	C2	Tower Street	C3
Hendon Valley Road	C3	Tower Street West	C3
High Street East	C2	Trimdon Street	A2
High Street West	B2	Tunstall Road	B3
Holmeside	B2	Tunstall Vale	B3
Horatio Street	C1	Vaux Brewery Way	B1
Hurstwood Road	A3	Villette Road	C3
Hutton Street	A3	Vine Place	B2
Hylton Road	A2	Wallace Street	A2
Hylton Road	A2	West Lawn	B3
Jackson Street	A3	West Wear Street	B2
James William Street	C2	Western Hill	A2
Kenton Grove	B1	Wharncliffe Street	A2
Kier Hardy Way	A1	White House Road	C3
King's Place	A2	Woodbine Street	C2
Lawrence Street	C2	Wreath Quay Road	B1

SWANSEA

0   500 yds
0   500m

Appears on main
map page 128

Tourist Information Centre: Plymouth Street
Tel: 01792 468321

Aberdyberthi Street	C1	Mount Pleasant	B2
Albert Row	B3	Mumbles Road	A3
Alexandra Road	B2	Neath Road	C1
Argyle Street	A3	Nelson Street	B3
Baptist Well Place	B1	New Cut Road	C2
Baptist Well Street	B1	New Orchard Street	B1
Beach Street	A3	Nicander Parade	A2
Belgrave Lane	A3	Norfolk Street	A2
Belle Vue Way	B2	North Hill Road	B1
Berw Road	A1	Orchard Street	B2
Berwick Terrace	B1	Oxford Street	A3
Bond Street	A3	Oystermouth Road	A3
Brooklands Terrace	A2	Page Street	B2
Brunswick Street	A3	Pant-y-Celyn Road	A2
Brynymor Crescent	A3	Park Terrace	B1
Brynymor Road	A3	Pedrog Terrace	A1
Burrows Place	C3	Penlan Crescent	A2
Cambrian Place	C3	Pentre Guinea Road	C1
Carig Crescent	A1	Pen-y-Craig Road	A2
Carlton Terrace	B2	Picton Terrace	B2
Carmarthen Road	B1	Powys Avenue	A1
Castle Street	B2	Princess Way	B2
Clarence Terrace	B3	Quay Parade	C2
Colbourne Terrace	B1	Rhondda Street	A2
Constitution Hill	A2	Rose Hill	A2
Creidiol Road	A1	St. Elmo Avenue	C1
Cromwell Street	A2	St. Helen's Avenue	A3
Cwm Road	C1	St. Helen's Road	A3
De La Beche Street	B2	St. Mary Street	B2
Delhi Street	C2	Singleton Street	B3
Dillwyn Street	B3	Somerset Place	C3
Dyfatty Street	B1	South Guildhall Road	A3
Dyfed Avenue	A2	Strand	C2
Earl Street	C1	Taliesyn Road	A2
East Burrows Road	C3	Tan-y-Marian Road	A2
Eigen Crescent	A1	Tegid Road	A1
Emlyn Road	A1	Teilo Crescent	A1
Fabian Way	C2	Terrace Road	A2
Fairfield Terrace	A2	The Kingsway	B2
Ffynone Drive	A2	Townhill Road	A1
Ffynone Road	A2	Trawler Road	B3
Foxhole Road	C1	Villiers Street	C1
Glamorgan Street	B3	Vincent Street	A3
Gors Avenue	A1	Walter Road	A2
Granogwen Road	B1	Watkin Street	B2
Grove Place	C3	Waun-Wen Road	B1
Gwent Road	A1	Wellington Street	B3
Gwili Terrace	A1	West Way	B3
Hanover Street	A2	Westbury Street	A3
Heathfield	B2	Western Street	A3
Hewson Street	A2	William Street	B3
High Street	B2	Windmill Terrace	C1
High View	B1	York Street	C3
Islwyn Road	A1		
Kilvey Road	C1		
Kilvey Terrace	C2		
King Edward's Road	A3		
King's Road	C1		
Llangyfelach Road	B1		
Long Ridge	B1		
Mackworth Street	C2		
Maesteg Street	C1		
Mansel Street	A2		
Mayhill Road	A1		
Milton Terrace	B2		
Morris Lane	C2		

SWINDON

Tourist Information Centre: 37 Regent Street
Tel: 01793 530328

Albion Street	A3	Upham Road	C3
Bath Road	B3	Victoria Road	C2
Beatrice Street	B1	Westcott Place	A3
Beckhampton Street	C2	Western Street	A3
Birch Street	A2	William Street	A3
Bridge Street	B2	York Road	C2
Broad Street	C1		
Canal Walk	B2		
Caulfield Road	C1		
Church Place	A2		
Cirencester Way	C1		
Clifton Street	B3		
Commercial Road	B2		
County Road	C1		
Cricklade Street	C3		
Curtis Street	B2		
Dean Street	A2		
Drove Road	C3		
Eastcott Hill	B3		
Edmund Street	B2		
Elmina Road	C1		
Euclid Street	C2		
Faringdon Road	A2		
Farnsby Street	B2		
Fleet Street	B2		
Fleming Way	B2		
Gladstone Street	C1		
Goddard Avenue	B3		
Great Western Way	A1		
Grosvenor Road	A3		
Groundwell Road	C2		
Hawksworth Way	A1		
High Street	C3		
Holbrook Way	B2		
Hythe Road	B3		
Islington Street	B2		
Jennings Street	A2		
Kemble Drive	A1		
Kent Road	B3		
Kingshill Street	A3		
Lansdown Road	B3		
Manchester Road	B1		
Market Street	B2		
Milford Street	B2		
Milton Road	B2		
Morris Street	A1		
Newburn Crescent	A2		
Newcombe Drive	A1		
North Star Avenue	B1		
Ocotal Way	C1		
Okus Road	A3		
Park Lane	A2		
Penzance Drive	A2		
Plymouth Street	C2		
Princes Street	C2		
Queen Street	B2		
Radnor Street	A3		
Redcliffe Street	A2		
Regent Street	B2		
Rodbourne Road	A1		
Roseberry Street	C1		
Spring Gardens	C2		
Stafford Street	B3		
Station Road	B1		
Swindon Road	B3		
The Parade	B2		

TORQUAY

Tourist Information Centre: Vaughan Parade
Tel: 01803 211211

Abbey Road	B2	Thurlow Road	B1
Ash Hill Road	B1	Tor Hill Road	B2
Avenue Road	A2	Torbay Road	A3
Bampfylde Road	A2	Torwood Gardens Road	C3
Barton Road	A1	Torwood Street	C3
Belgrave Road	A2	Union Street	B2
Belmont Road	C1	Upton Hill	B1
Braddons Hill Road East	C2	Upton Road	A1
Bridge Road	A2	Vanehill Road	C3
Bronshill Road	B1	Victoria Parade	C3
Brunswick Square	B1	Walnut Road	A3
Carlton Road	C1	Warbro Road	C1
Cary Parade	C3	Warren Road	B2
Cedars Road	C2	Windsor Road	C1
Chestnut Avenue	A2		
Cockington Lane	A3		
Croft Road	B2		
Crownhill Park	A1		
Dunmere Road	C1		
East Street	A1		
Ellacombe Church Road	C1		
Ellacombe Road	B1		
Falkland Road	A2		
Falkland Road	A2		
Fleet Street	B2		
Forest Road	B1		
Goshen Road	A2		
Hatfield Road	B1		
Hennapyn Road	A3		
Higher Warberry Road	C2		
Hillesdon Road	C2		
Kenwyn Road	C1		
Lower Warberry Road	C2		
Lucius Street	A2		
Lymington Road	B1		
Mallock Road	A2		
Market Street	B2		
Marnham Road	C1		
Meadfoot Lane	C3		
Meadfoot Road	C3		
Middle Warberry Road	C2		
Mill Lane	A2		
Newton Road	A1		
Old Mill Road	A3		
Old Mill Road	A3		
Parkfield Road	B1		
Parkhill Road	C3		
Prince's Road	C2		
Princes Road East	C2		
Quinta Road	C1		
Rathmore Road	A3		
Reddenhill Road	C1		
Rosehill Road	C2		
Sanford Road	A2		
Seaway Lane	A3		
Shedden Hill	B2		
Sherwell Lane	A2		
Solsbro Road	A3		
South Street	A2		
St. Lukes Road	B2		
St. Marychurch Road	B2		
St. Michael's Road	A1		
Stitchill Road	C2		
Strand	C3		
Teignmouth Road	A1		
The King's Drive	A2		

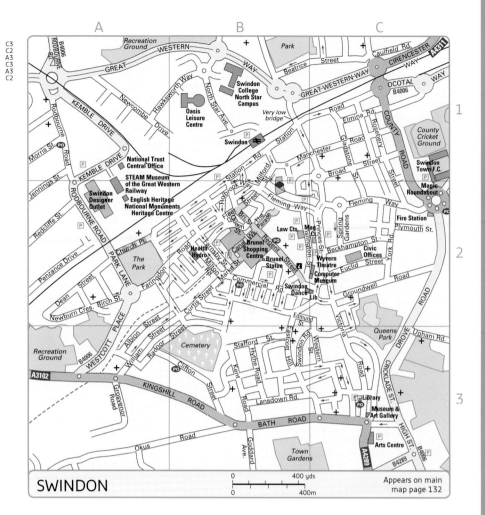

SWINDON

| 0 | 400 yds |
| 0 | 400m |

Appears on main map page 132

TORQUAY

| 0 | 400 yds |
| 0 | 400m |

Appears on main map page 101

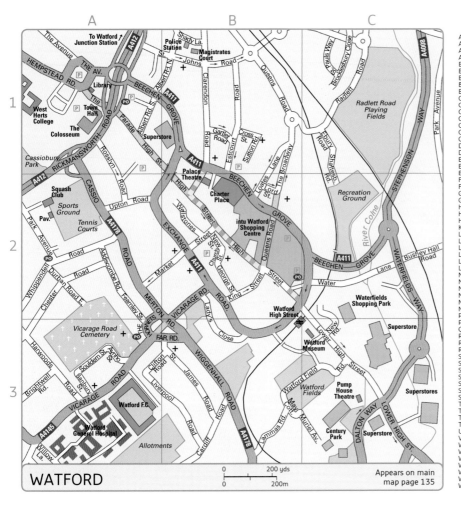

WATFORD

0 ——— 200 yds
0 ——— 200m

Appears on main
map page 135

Addiscombe Road	A2
Albert Road North	A1
Albert Road South	A1
Aynho Street	A3
Banbury Street	A3
Beechen Grove	A1/C2
Brightwell Road	A3
Brocklesbury Close	C1
Bushey Hall Road	C2
Cardiff Road	B3
Cassio Road	A2
Chester Road	A2
Church Street	B2
Clarendon Road	B1
Clifton Road	A3
Cross Street	B1
Dalton Way	C3
Durban Road East	A2
Ebury Road	C1
Estcourt Road	B1
Exchange Road	A2
Farraline Road	A3
Fearnley Street	A2
Garlet Road	B1
George Street	B2
Harwoods Road	A3
Hempsted Road	A1
High Street	A1/B2
King Street	B2
Lady's Close	B2
Lammas Road	B3
Liverpool Road	A3
Loates Lane	B2
Lord Street	B2
Lower High Street	C3
Market Street	A2
May Cottages	B3
Merton Road	A2
Muriel Avenue	B3
New Road	C3
New Street	B2
Park Avenue	C1
Park Avenue	A2
Queens Road	B1/B2
Radlett Road	C1
Rickmansworth Road	A2
Rosslyn Road	A1
Shaftesbury Road	C1
Souldern Street	A3
St. James Road	B3
St. Johns Road	A1
St. Pauls Way	C1
Stephenson Way	C2
Sutton Road	B1
The Avenue	A1
The Broadway	B2
The Hornets	A3
The Parade	A1
Upton Road	A2
Vicarage Road	A3/B2
Water Lane	C2
Waterfields Way	C2
Watford Field Road	B3
Wellstones	B2
Whippendell Road	A2
Wiggenhall Road	B3
Willow Lane	A3

WESTON-SUPER-MARE

0 ——— 400 yds
0 ——— 400m

Appears on main
map page 115

Tourist Information Centre: Winter Gardens, Royal Parade
Tel: 01934 417117

Addicott Road	B3	Stafford Road	C2
Albert Avenue	B3	Station Road	B2
Alexandra Parade	B2	Sunnyside Road	B3
Alfred Street	B2	Swiss Road	C2
All Saints Road	B1	The Centre	B2
Amberey Road	C3	Trewartha Park	C1
Arundell Road	B1	Upper Church Road	A1
Ashcombe Gardens	C1	Walliscote Road	B3
Ashcombe Road	C2	Waterloo Street	B2
Atlantic Road	A1	Whitecross Road	B3
Baker Street	B2	Winterstoke Road	C3
Beach Road	B3		
Beaconsfield Road	B2		
Birnbeck Road	A1		
Boulevard	B2		
Brendon Avenue	C1		
Bridge Road	C2		
Brighton Road	B3		
Bristol Road	B1		
Carlton Street	B2		
Cecil Road	B1		
Clarence Road North	B3		
Clarendon Road	C2		
Clevedon Road	B3		
Clifton Road	B3		
Drove Road	C3		
Earlham Grove	C2		
Ellenborough Park North	B3		
Ellenborough Park South	B3		
Exeter Road	B3		
George Street	B2		
Gerard Road	B1		
Grove Park Road	B1		
High Street	B2		
Highbury Road	A1		
Hildesheim Bridge	B2		
Hill Road	C1		
Jubilee Road	B2		
Kenn Close	C3		
Kensington Road	C3		
Knightstone Road	A1		
Langford Road	C3		
Lewisham Grove	C2		
Locking Road	C2		
Lower Bristol Road	C1		
Lower Church Road	C1		
Manor Road	C1		
Marchfields Way	C3		
Marine Parade	B3		
Meadow Street	B2		
Milton Road	C2		
Montpelier	B1		
Neva Road	B2		
Norfolk Road	C3		
Oxford Street	B2		
Queen's Road	B1		
Rectors Way	C3		
Regent Street	B2		
Ridgeway Avenue	B3		
Royal Crescent	A1		
St. Paul's Road	B3		
Sandford Road	C2		
Severn Road	B3		
Shrubbery Road	A1		
South Road	A1		
Southside	B1		

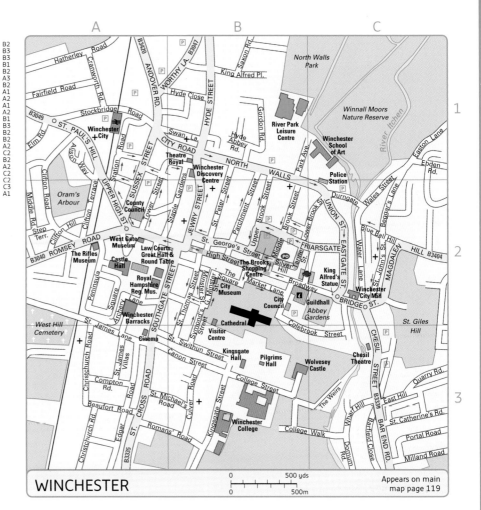

WINCHESTER

0   500 yds
0   500m

Appears on main
map page 119

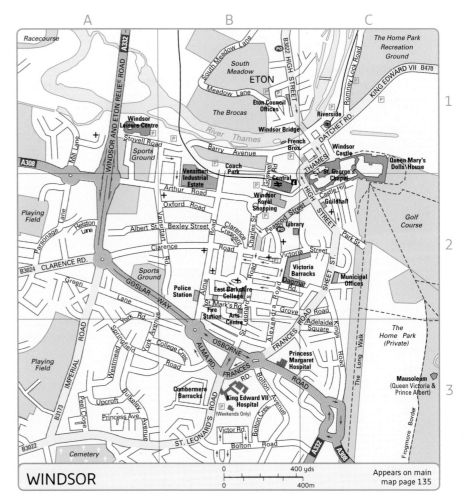

WINDSOR

0   400 yds
0   400m

Appears on main
map page 135

WORCESTER

A   B   C

1

2

3

Albany Terrace (map labels):

The Moors
Back Lane South
Britannia Square
Swan Theatre
Police Sta. & Meg. Court
Shire Hall
Crown Courts
Library Art Gallery & Museum
Vesta Tilley Centre
Swimming Pool
Chestnut Street
St. Oswalds Rd.
Foregate Street
City Council Offices
Shaw St.
Worcester Library & History Centre
Corn Market
Reindeer Court Shopping Centre
Crowngate Shopping Centre
Countess of Huntingdon Hall
Coll.
Guildhall
Copenhagen St.
College of Technology
The Greyfriars
Cathedral Plaza Shopping Centre
Cathedral
Commandery Museum
Royal Worcester Porcelain
Fort Royal Park
Racecourse
Coach & Lorry Park
Cripplegate Park
County Cricket Ground
Shrub Hill
Shrub Hill Retail Park
Shrub Hill Road
Worcestershire Royal Hospital
Tolladine Road

Roads: A4495, UPPER TYTHING, A443, HYLTON RD, A44, A449, NEW ROAD, CROFT ROAD, CASTLE STREET, DOLDAY, DEANSWAY, COLLEGE ST., CITY WALLS ROAD, LONDON RD, A4B, A44

| | 0 | 200 yds |
| 0 | | 200m |

Appears on main map page 146

Tourist Information Centre: The Guildhall, High Street
Tel: 01905 726311

Albany Terrace	A1	Sherriff Street	C1
Albert Road	C3	Shrub Hill	C2
Angel Place	A2	Shrub Hill Road	C2
Angel Street	B2	Sidbury	B3
Arboretum Road	B1	Southfield Street	B1
Back Lane South	A1	Spring Hill	C2
Bath Road	B3	Stanley Road	C3
Bridge Street	A2	Tallow Hill	C2
Britannia Road	A1	Tennis Walk	A1
Britannia Square	A1	The Butts	B2
Broad Street	A2	The Cross	B2
Carden Street	B3	The Moors	A1
Castle Street	A2	The Shambles	B2
Charles Street	B3	The Tything	A1
Chestnut Street	B1	Tolladine Road	C1
Chestnut Walk	B1	Trinity Street	B2
City Walls Road	B2	Upper Tything	A1
Cole Hill	C3	Vincent Road	C3
College Street	B3	Washington Street	B1
Compton Road	C3	Westbury Street	B1
Copenhagen Street	A3	Wyld's Lane	C3
Croft Road	A2		
Deansway	A2		
Dent Close	C3		
Dolday	A2		
Farrier Street	A2		
Foregate Street	B2		
Fort Royal Hill	C3		
Foundry Street	B3		
Friar Street	B3		
George Street	C2		
Grand Stand Road	A2		
High Street	B2		
Hill Street	C2		
Hylton Road	A2		
Infirmary Walk	A2		
Kleve Walk	B3		
Lansdowne Crescent	B1		
Lansdowne Walk	C1		
London Road	B3		
Loves Grove	A1		
Lowesmoor	B2		
Lowesmoor Place	B2		
Midland Road	C3		
Moor Street	A1		
Newport Street	A2		
New Road	A3		
New Street	B2		
Northfield Street	B1		
North Quay	A2		
Padmore Street	B2		
Park Street	B3		
Park Street	C3		
Pheasant Street	B2		
Pump Street	B3		
Rainbow Hill	B1		
Richmond Hill	C3		
St. Martin's Gate	B2		
St. Mary's Street	A1		
St. Oswalds Road	A1		
St. Paul's Street	B2		
Sansome Street	B2		
Sansome Walk	B1		
Severn Street	B3		
Severn Terrace	A1		
Shaw Street	A2		

YORK

A   B   C

1

2

3

(map labels):
York City A.F.C.
York District Hospital
Bootham Park Hospital
Playing Fields
Grosvenor Rd.
Yorkshire Museum & St. Mary's Abbey (Ruins)
Art Gallery
York St. John College
Dean's Park
Treasurer's House (NT)
City Wall
Richard III Mus.
Monk Bar
York Minster
Theatre Royal
Assembly Rooms
Museum Gardens
Barley Hall
War Mem. Gdns.
Mansion Ho.
Roman Bath Ho.
Guildhall
Cinema
Merchant Adventurers' Hall
Jorvik
DIG
Quilt Mus.
National Railway Museum
York
York Brewery
Grand Opera House
Glen Gardens
Red Tower
York Dungeon
Law Courts
Clifford's Tower
Crown Courts
Fairfax Ho.
Castle Mus.
Walmgate Bar
Bar Convent
Cinema
City Wall
Baile Hill
Rowntree Park
Cemetery
Charlotte St.

Roads: A19, A1036, A1237, MALTON RD, CLIFTON, BOOTHAM, MARYGATE, STATION RD., QUEEN ST., NUNNERY LANE, BLOSSOM ST., THE MOUNT, HOLGATE ROAD, MOUNT VALE, A59, MICKLEGATE, SKELDERGATE, TOWER ST., PARAGON ST., BISHOPGATE ST., FISHERGATE, BARBICAN RD., CEMETERY RD., LAWRENCE ST., A1079, HESLINGTON ROAD, FOSS ISLANDS ROAD, HEWORTH GREEN, WIGGINTON RD., River Ouse, River Foss

| | 0 | 400 yds |
| 0 | | 400m |

Appears on main map page 195

Tourist Information Centre: 1 Museum Street
Tel: 01904 550099

Abbey Street	A1	Paragon Street	B3
Albemarle Road	A3	Park Grove	B1
Aldwark	B2	Park Street	A3
Barbican Road	C3	Penley's Grove Street	B1
Bishopthorpe Road	B3	Petergate	B2
Bishopgate Street	B3	Piccadilly	B2
Blossom Street	A3	Queen Street	A2
Bootham	A1	Rougier Street	A2
Bootham Crescent	A1	St. Andrewgate	B2
Bridge Street	B2	St. John Street	B1
Bull Lane	C1/C2	St. Maurice's Road	B2
Burton Stone Lane	A1	St. Olave's Road	A1
Cemetery Road	C3	Scarcroft Hill	A3
Charlotte Street	C2	Scarcroft Road	A3
Church Street	B2	Shambles	B2
Clarence Street	B1	Sixth Avenue	C1
Clifford Street	B2	Skeldergate	B2
Clifton	A1	Southlands Road	A3
Coney Street	B2	Station Road	A2
Dale Street	A3	Terry Avenue	B3
Dalton Terrace	A3	The Avenue	A1
Dodsworth Avenue	C1	The Mount	A3
East Parade	C1	The Stonebow	B2
Eldon Street	B1	Thorpe Street	A3
Fairfax Street	B3	Tower Street	B2
Fifth Avenue	C1	Vine Street	B3
Fishergate	B3	Walmgate	B2
Foss Bank	C2	Water End	A1
Fossgate	B2	Watson Street	A3
Foss Islands Road	C2	Wellington Street	C3
Fourth Avenue	C2	Westminster Road	A1
Gillygate	B1	Wigginton Road	B1
Goodramgate	B2		
Grange Garth	B3		
Grosvenor Road	A1		
Grosvenor Terrace	A1		
Hallfield Road	C2		
Haxby Road	B1		
Heslington Road	C3		
Heworth Green	C1		
Holgate Road	A3		
Hope Street	B3		
Huntington Road	C1		
Irwin Avenue	C1		
James Street	B2		
Kent Street	C3		
Lawrence Street	C3		
Layerthorpe	C2		
Leeman Road	A2		
Lendal	B2		
Longfield Terrace	A2		
Lord Mayor's Walk	B1		
Lowther Street	B1		
Malton Road	C1		
Marygate	A2		
Maurices Road	B2		
Micklegate	A2		
Monkgate	B1		
Moss Street	A3		
Mount Vale	A3		
Museum Street	B2		
Navigation Road	C2		
North Street	B2		
Nunnery Lane	A3		
Nunthorpe Road	A3		
Ousegate	B2		

Key to map symbols

P Short stay car park   P Mid stay car park   P Long stay car park   P Other car park   ▨ Airport terminal building

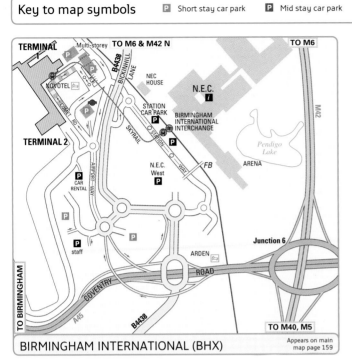

BIRMINGHAM INTERNATIONAL (BHX)

Appears on main map page 159

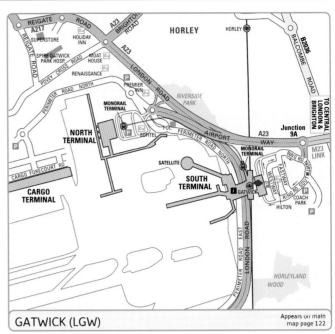

GATWICK (LGW)

Appears on main map page 122

GLASGOW (GLA)

Appears on main map page 233

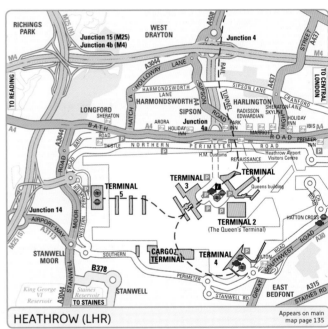

HEATHROW (LHR)

Appears on main map page 135

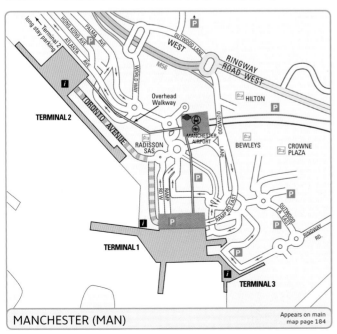

MANCHESTER (MAN)

Appears on main map page 184

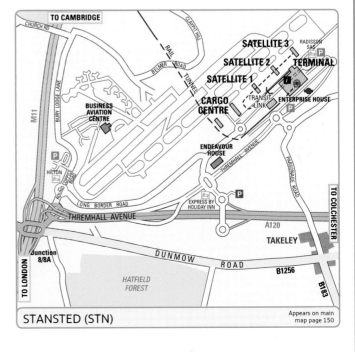

STANSTED (STN)

Appears on main map page 150

Symbols used on the map

M5 Motorway

M6Toll Toll motorway

8 **9** Motorway junction with full / limited access (in congested areas there is just a numbered symbol)

Maidstone / Birch / Sarn — Motorway service area with off road / full / limited access

A556 Primary route dual / single carriageway

S 24 hour service area on primary route

Peterhead Primary route destination
Primary route destinations are places of major traffic importance linked by the primary route network. They are shown on a green background on direction signs.

A30 'A' road dual / single carriageway

B1403 'B' road dual / single carriageway

Minor road

========== Road with restricted access

Roads with passing places

Road proposed or under construction

33 Multi-level junction with full / limited access (with junction number)

Roundabout

4 Road distance in miles between markers

Road tunnel

Steep hill (arrows point downhill)

Toll Level crossing / Toll

St. Malo 8hrs Car ferry route with journey times

Railway line / station / tunnel

Wales Coast Path National Trail / Long Distance Route

---

30 **V** Fixed safety camera
Speed limit shown by a number within the camera, a V indicates a variable limit.

30 **30** Fixed average-speed safety camera
Speed limit shown by a number within the camera.

✈ Airport with / without scheduled services

H Heliport

P&R **P&R** Park and Ride site operated by bus / rail (runs at least 5 days a week)

Built up area

□ □ ▫ Town / Village / Other settlement

Hythe Seaside destination

— ·· — ·· — National boundary

KENT County / Unitary Authority boundary and name

water	0	150	300	500	700	900	metres
0		490	985	1640	2295	2950	feet

Land height reference bar

Heritage Coast

National Park

Regional / Forest Park boundary

Woodland

Danger Zone Military range

•468 ▲941 Spot / Summit height (in metres)

Lake / Dam / River / Waterfall

Canal / Dry canal / Canal tunnel

Beach / Lighthouse

SEE PAGE 3 Area covered by urban area map

Reading our maps

Safety Camera
The number inside the camera shows the speed limit at the camera location.

Multi-level junctions
Non-motorway junctions where slip roads are used to access the main roads.

Distances
Blue numbers give distances in miles between junctions shown with a blue marker.

Park & Ride
Sites are shown that operate at least 5 days a week. Bus operated sites have a yellow symbol and rail operated sites a pink symbol.

Motorway service area

World Heritage site
Places of interest defined by UNESCO as special on a world scale.

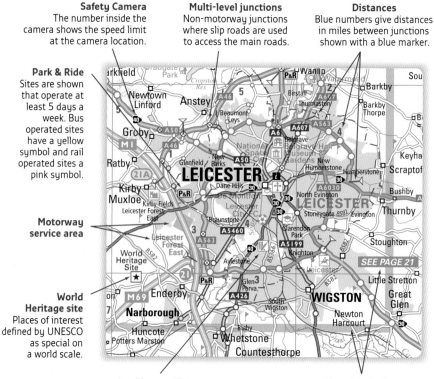

Places of interest
Blue symbols indicate places of interest. See the section to the right for the different types of feature represented on the map.

More detailed maps
Green boxes indicate busy built-up areas. More detailed mapping is available.

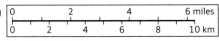

Places of interest

A selection of tourist detail is shown on the mapping. It is advisable to check with the local tourist information centre regarding opening times and facilities available.

Any of the following symbols may appear on the map in maroon ★ which indicates that the site has World Heritage status.

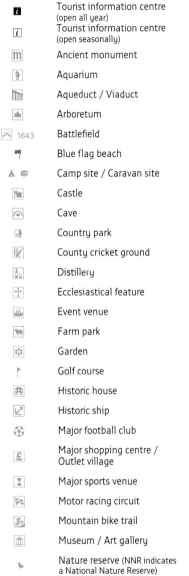

i	Tourist information centre (open all year)
i	Tourist information centre (open seasonally)
m	Ancient monument
?	Aquarium
	Aqueduct / Viaduct
	Arboretum
✕ 1643	Battlefield
⚑	Blue flag beach
▲ ⚏	Camp site / Caravan site
	Castle
	Cave
	Country park
	County cricket ground
	Distillery
✝	Ecclesiastical feature
	Event venue
	Farm park
✿	Garden
⚑	Golf course
	Historic house
	Historic ship
⚽	Major football club
£	Major shopping centre / Outlet village
	Major sports venue
	Motor racing circuit
	Mountain bike trail
	Museum / Art gallery
	Nature reserve (NNR indicates a National Nature Reserve)
	Racecourse
	Rail Freight Terminal
⛷ ⛷	Ski slope (artificial / natural)
	Spotlight nature reserve (Best sites for access to nature)
	Steam railway centre / preserved railway
	Surfing beach
	Theme park
	University
	Vineyard
	Wildlife park / Zoo
	Wildlife Trust nature reserve
★	Other interesting feature
(NT) (NTS)	National Trust / National Trust for Scotland property

Map scale

A scale bar appears at the bottom of every page to help with distances.

```
0          2          4        6 miles
0     2     4     6     8     10 km
```

England, Wales & Southern Scotland are at a scale of 1:200,000 or 3.2 miles to 1 inch
Northern Scotland is at a scale of 1:263,158 or 4.2 miles to 1 inch.

Map pages

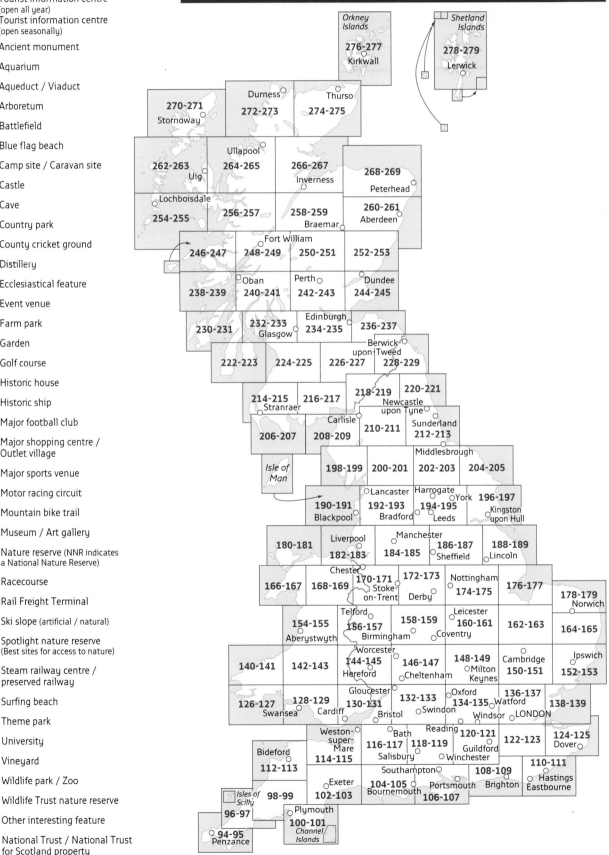

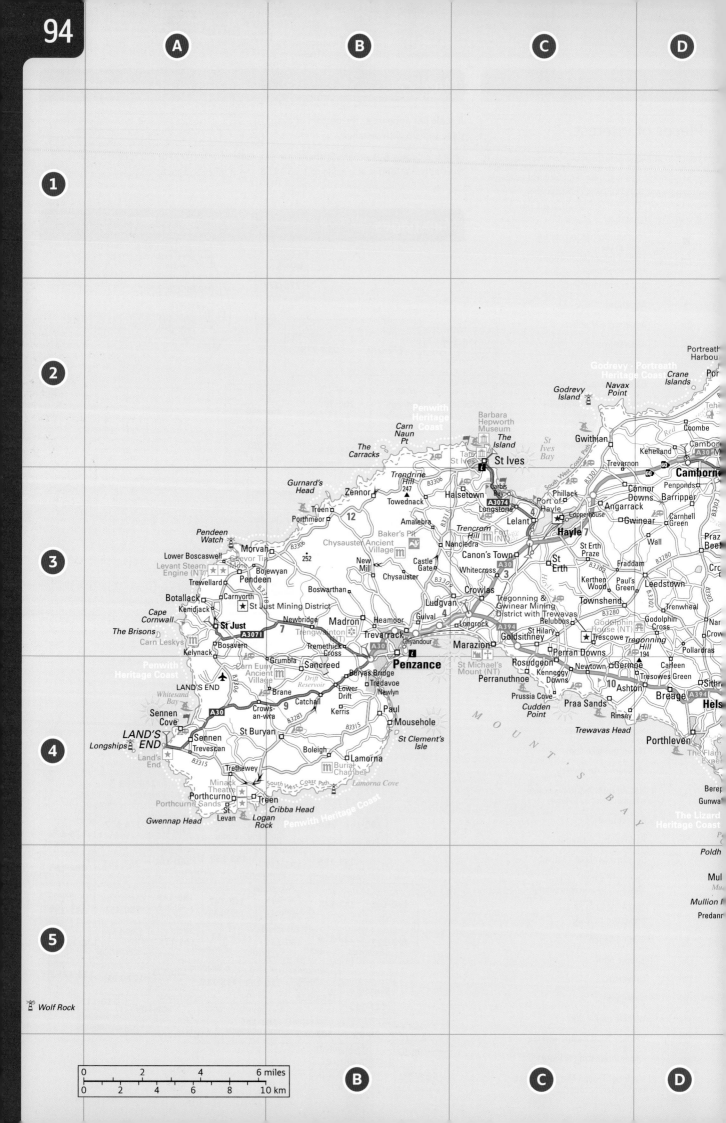

A   B   C   D

1

2

3

4

5

Portreath
Harbou
Godrevy - Portreath
Heritage Coast
Crane
Islands
Por
Godrevy
Island
Navax
Point
Tehi

Penwith
Heritage
Coast
Barbara
Hepworth
Museum
The
Island
St
Ives
Bay
Gwithian
Coombe
Kehelland
Cambor
A30
Carn
Naun
Pt
Tate
St Ives
St Ives
Trevarnon
Camborn
The
Carracks
Trendrine
Hill
247
B3306
Carbis
Bay
Phillack
Port of
Hayle
Connor
Downs
60
Penponds
Barripper
Gurnard's
Head
Zennor
Towednack
Halsetown
A3074
Longstone
4
Coppenhouse
Gwinear
Angarrack
Carnhell
Green
B3311
Praz
Beer
Treen
Porthmeor
12
Amalebra
Trencrom
Hill
Lelant
Hayle 7
St Erth
Praze
Wall
Cro
Pendeen
Watch
Baker's Pit
Chysauster Ancient
Village
Nancledra
(NT)
Port
(NT)
St
Erth
Fraddam
B3280
Kerthen
Wood
Paul's
Green
Leedstown
B3302
Nar
Morvah
B3306
252
New
Mill
Castle
Gate
Canon's Town
A30
Hale
3
B3303
Townshend
Trenwheal
Godolphin
Cross
Crow
Lower Boscaswell
Trevor Tin
Levant Steam
Engine (NT)
Bojewyan
Chysauster
Whitecross
Tregonning &
Gwinear Mining
District with Trewavas
Relubbus
B3280
Godolphin
House (NT)
Trewellard
Pendeen
Boswarthan
B3309
Crowlas
St
Hilary
Trescowe
Tregonning
Hill
194
Pollardras
Botallack
Carnyorth
Ludgvan
Guival
Longrock
A394
Goldsithney
Perran Downs
Carleen
Sithr
Cape
Cornwall
Kenidjack
St Just Mining District
Heamoor
4
Rosudgeon
Newtown
Germoe
Tresowes Green
The Brisons
Carn Leskys
St Just
Newbridge
7
Madron
Trengwainton
(NT)
Trevarrack
Gyandour
Marazion
St
Michael's
Mount (NT)
Kenneggy
Downs
10
Ashton
Breage
A394
Hels
Kelynack
Bosavern
Tremethick
Cross
Penzance
Prussia Cove
Praa Sands
Rinsay
Penwith
Heritage Coast
Grumbla
Sancreed
Buryas Bridge
Tredavoe
Lower
Drift
Newlyn
Cudden
Point
Trewavas Head
Porthleven
The Flam
Exper
Carn Euny
Ancient
Village
Drift
Reservoir
Catchall
Kerris
Paul
MOUNTS BAY
LAND'S
END
Brane
9
Mousehole
Whitesand
Bay
Crows-
an-wra
B3283
B3315
St Clement's
Isle
Bere
Gunwa
Sennen
Cove
A30
St Buryan
Boleigh
Lamorna
The Lizard
Heritage Coast
Pe
Sennen
Trevescan
Burial
Chamber
Lamorna Cove
LAND'S
END
Longships
Land's
End
Trethewey
South West Coast Path
Poldh
Mul
Mu
Minack
Theatre
Porthcurno
Treen
Mullion
B3315
St
Levan
Logan
Rock
Predann
Porthcurno Sands
Gwennap Head
Cribba Head
Penwith Heritage Coast

Wolf Rock

0   2   4   6 miles
0   2   4   6   8   10 km

B   C   D

A **B** **C** **D**

1

St Helen's
White Island
King Charles's
Tean
St Martin's
Isles of Scilly Heritage Coast
Cromwell's
Old Grimsby
Middle Town
Lower Town
Higher Town
New Grimsby
Blockhouse
Bryher
Tresco
Eastern Isles
Abbey & Gdns
Samson
Bant's Carn
Crow Sound
Chambered Cairns
The Road
A3110
Maypole
St Mary's
Hugh Town
Porth Hellick Down Burial Chamber
Star
ST. MARY'S
Garrison Walls
Old Town

North West Channel

2

Crim Rocks
St Mary's Sound
Annet
Broad Sound
Gugh
Bishop Rock
Western Rocks
St Agnes
Smith Sound

ISLES OF SCILLY

same scale as main map

Rumps Point *The*
Newland
Pentire Point
New Polzeath
Gulland Rock
Padstow Bay
Trebe
Trevose Head Heritage Coast
Gunver Head
Prideaux Place
Trevose Head
Harlyn Bay
Crugmeer
Pitym
Quies
Harlyn
Trevone
R
Constantine Bay
i **Padstow**
St Merryn
Constantine Bay
Treyarnon
Shop
A389
St Issey
Porthcothan Beach
Tregolds
Little Petherick
Porthcothan
Penrose
St Ervan
Rumford
Trenance
Park Head
Treburrick
St Eval
Tredinnick

3

Bedruthan Steps
15
Carnewas & Bedruthan Steps (NT)
Creely Adventure Park
Trenance
B3274
Mawgan Porth
8
Berryl's Point
Lanvean
The Fie
Trevarrian
St Mawgan
Talskiddy
Watergate Bay
Vale of Mawgan (Lanherne)
Winnard Perch
Tregurrian
Carloggas
NEWQUAY CORNWALL INTERNATIONAL
St Columb Major
Towan Head
Newquay
Reter
Fistral Bay
Blue Bay
Porth
Tregaswith
an-D
Newquay Blue Reef Aquarium
St Columb Minor
A3059
Porth Reservoir
A39
Newquay
30
Trebudannon
Colan
Black Cross
Newquay Zoo
Quintrell Downs
White
Ruthvoes
Kelsey Head
i
3
Mountjoy *5*
Cross
7
West Pentire
Pentire
Trencreek
Kestle Mill
St Columb Road
Trevarren
Crantock
Carines
A3058
Retyn
B3279
Holywell Bay
Tresean
Indian Queens
Penhale Point
Rosecliston
A3075
Trerice (NT)
Fraddon
St Denni
Holywell
Cubert
4
St Enoder
Blue Anchor
Ligger Pt
Mount
A3076
Retew
3
Holywell Bay Fun Park
St Newlyn East
Summercourt
Treviscoe
Penhale Sands
Rejerrah Lappa Valley Railway
A30
Meledor

4

Ligger Bay (Perran Bay)
Rose
Carland Cross
Brighton
Scarcewater
10
Newlyn Downs
Mitchell
3
10
Perranporth
Goonhavern
Miniatura Park
New Mills
St Stephen
Bawden Rocks (Man and his Man)
B3285
Truthan
Tregear
Coom
Bolingey
Zelah
St. Agnes Heritage Coast
Peranzabuloe
C O R N W A L
Ladock
Grampound Road
St Agnes Head
Penhallow
Healey's Cornish Cyder Farm
Trelassick
St Allen
Grampo
St Agnes Leisure Park
St Agnes
Mithian
8
Trispen
St Erme
Probus
Creed
St Agnes Mining District
Goonvrea
Goonbell
Truthan
6
Trewithen

5

Towan Cross
B3277
Allet Common
Shortlanesend
Idless
B275
Devoran - Portreath rtage Coast
Mount Hawke
Three Burrows
Tregavethan
Tresillian
Porthtowan
A30
Kenwyn
B3284
Portreath Harbour
Nancekuke
Blackwater
A390
P&R
Kenwyn
Merther
Crane Islands
Portreath
Bridge
Mawla Wheal Peevor
P&R
40
Gloweth
TRURO
Tregony
vy - Portreath age Coast
A3300
Cornish Gold & Treasure Park
Chacewater
Threemilestone
i
St Clement
Cavax Point
Illogan
Scorrier
Hugus
Baldhu
5
Truro Cathedral
Trewarthenick
A3078
Tehidy Heartlands
7
St Day
Gwennap Mining District
Cross Lanes
Royal Cornwall Museum
St Clement
Ruan Lanihorne
3
A393
Twelveheads
Kea
Malpas
Lamorran
Coombe
Mount Ambrose
Bissoe
Old Kea

Camborne
Camborne & Redruth Mining District
Redruth
Carharrack
Carnon Downs
Playing Place
St Michael Penkevil
Lamorran
12
Kehelland
A30
A3047
Cusgarne
Penelewey
Veryan Green
Trevarnon
Tuckingmill
Brea
Carn Brea Village
Pennance
Perranwell Sta
Coombe
Treworga
Veryan
Camborne
Carnkie
Lanner
7
A393
Gwennap
B3289
Trelissick
Philleigh
Port
Connor Downs
Penponds
Barripper
Four Lanes
95
Trewithian
Nare Head
Angarr
G
252
Praze-an-Beeble
Perranarworthal
A39
Devor
Peran
Angarrick
Feock
Gerrans Bay
Portscatho
le 7
Wall
B3280
B3297
Stithians
Kenwyn Pon
B
St Just in Roseland
Mylor Bridge
C
D
St Erth Praze
Stockdale
Carrick R
opperhouse
B
Gwithian
Feock
Trewithian
Trelissick

0   2   4   6 miles
0   2   4   6   8   10 km

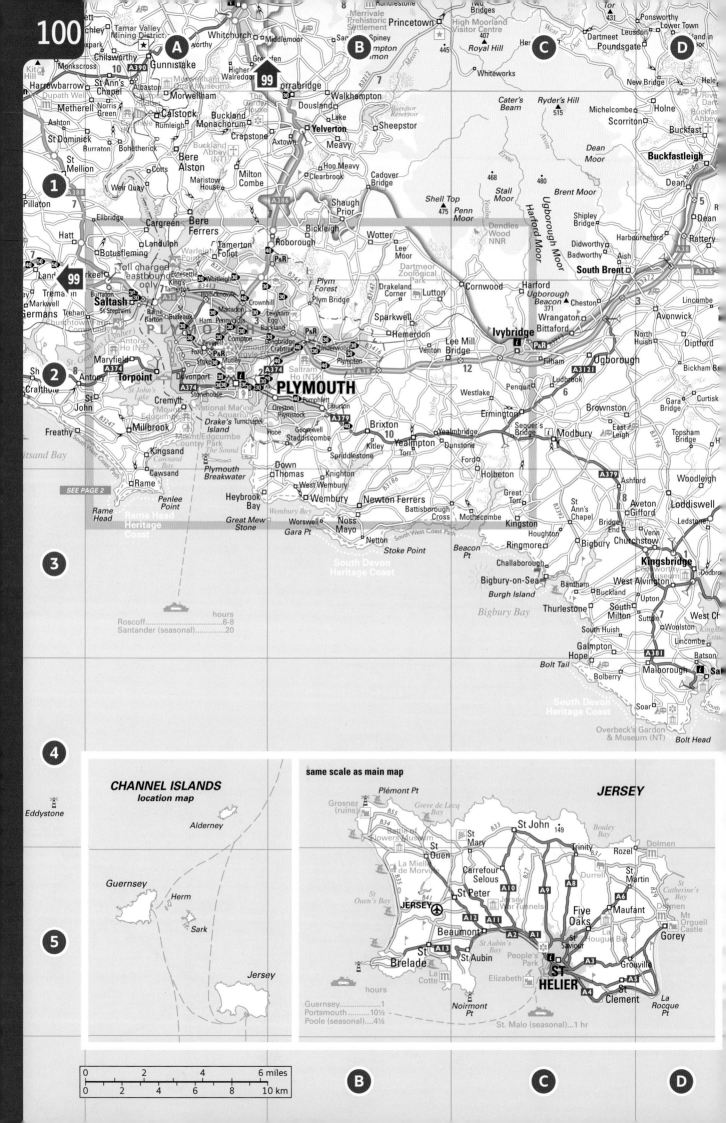

CHANNEL ISLANDS
location map

same scale as main map

JERSEY

SEE PAGE 2

Roscoff..................6-8
Santander (seasonal)............20

Guernsey...................1
Portsmouth.........10½
Poole (seasonal)............4½

St. Malo (seasonal)...1 hr

| 0 | | 2 | | 4 | | 6 miles |
| 0 | 2 | 4 | 6 | 8 | | 10 km |

102

D **E** **F** **G**

Sigford
Halford
Liverton
Nao Mills
Teigngrace
Bishopsteignton
40

ckington
South Knighton
A38
A382
Kingsteignton
Netherton
Shaldon
Ringmore
30 **Teignmouth**
Combe
Cross
Bradley
Manor (NT)
2
Combeinteignhead
Pier

Ashburton
Woodland
West Ogwell
East Ogwell
NEWTON ABBOT
30
Milber
Haccombe
Stokeinteignhead
A379
Babbacombe
Bay

Forder
Green
A381
Denbury
Abbotskerswell
Coffinswell
Daccombe
Lower Gabwell
Higher Gabwell
Maidencombe

Landscove
Woolston Green
Ipplepen
Kingskerswell
A380
Dainton
North
Whilborough
Wattcombe
Barton
Combe
Pafford
Babbacombe Model Village

Buckfast Butterfly &
Dartmoor Otter
Sanctuary
A381
Compton
Castle (NT)
Shiphay
Hele
St Marychurch
Kent's Cavern

A384
South Devon
Red Post
Compton
30
Torre
Abbey
30
Babbacombe

Staverton
Uphempston
Shorton
Cockington
30
TORQUAY

Dartington
Week
Littlehempston
Marldon
Berry
Pomeroy
Castle
Blagdon
A3022
Living
Coasts
Hope's Nose

Tigley
Cott
Motor
Museum
Totnes
30
Berry
Pomeroy
Preston
Holbeam
A380
Torbay
Mansion
Pier

Longcombe
Collaton
St Mary
TORBAY
A385
Paignton

Bowden
Sharpham
House
Aish
Yalberton
A379
Goodrington
Berry Head -
Sharkham Point
NNR

Ashprington
Stoke
Gabriel
Sandridge
Waddeton
Galmpton
Warborough
Brixham
Berry Head

Harbertonford
A381
Tuckenhay
East
Cornworthy
Galmpton
P&R
A3022
Churston
Ferrers
Berry Head
Wall Park
Holiday Centre
St Mary's Bay
Sharkham Point

Halwell
A3122
Washbourne
Allaleigh
Capton
Dittisham
Paignton &
Dartmouth
Steam Railway
Higher
Brixham
Hillhead
South Coast Path
South Devon
Heritage Coast

Woodlands
Leisure Park
Hemborough Post
A379
Woodhuish
Boohay
Scabbacombe Head

Weodford
Blackawton
Dartmouth
30
Coleton Fishacre (NT)

East
Allington
Millcombe
Eastdown
Bowden
P&R
Kingswear
Dartmouth Castle

Coombe
Cole's
Cross
Blackpool
River Link
Boat Cruises
Mew Stone

Merrifield
8
Strete
Stoke Fleming

Harleston
A379
South Devon
Heritage Coast
Start

Sherford
Slapton
Slapton
Ley
NNR
Bay

Frittiscombe
Stokenham
Slapton
Sands

Frogmore
A379
Chillington
Kernborough
Torcross

East
Charleton
Beeson
North Pool
Ford
Beesands

Kellaton
Bickerton
Hallsands

East Chivelstone
South
Allington
Start Point

ortlemouth
West Prawle
Lannacombe
Bay

Prawle
Point
East
Prawle
Coast Path

---

same scale as main map

Alderney

Fort Quesnard

ALDERNEY ✈ St
Anne
Alderney Rly

4

---

same scale as main map

Grande Havre
hours
Poole (seasonal)............3
Portsmouth..................7

GUERNSEY
Dolmen
Bordeaux

Grandes Rocques
L'Islet
Vale (ruins)
Herm
Shell
Beach

Albecq
Saumarez Park
& Folk Museum
St Sampson

Lihou
Dolmen
Vazon Bay
Kings
Mills
P&R
Guernsey
Museum
**St
Peter Port**
Jethou

Dolmen
German
Under
ground
Castle Cornet

Rocquaine Bay
St Saviour
Sark
La Seigneurie

Fort Grey
110
Saumarez
Manor
Brecqhou
Sark Dark Sky
Island

Pleinmont
Pt
GUERNSEY ✈
German
Occupation
Museum
**St
Martin**
hours
Jersey......................1
St. Malo (seasonal)......2½
Little Sark

Jerbourg Pt

5

2

3

D **E** **F** **G**

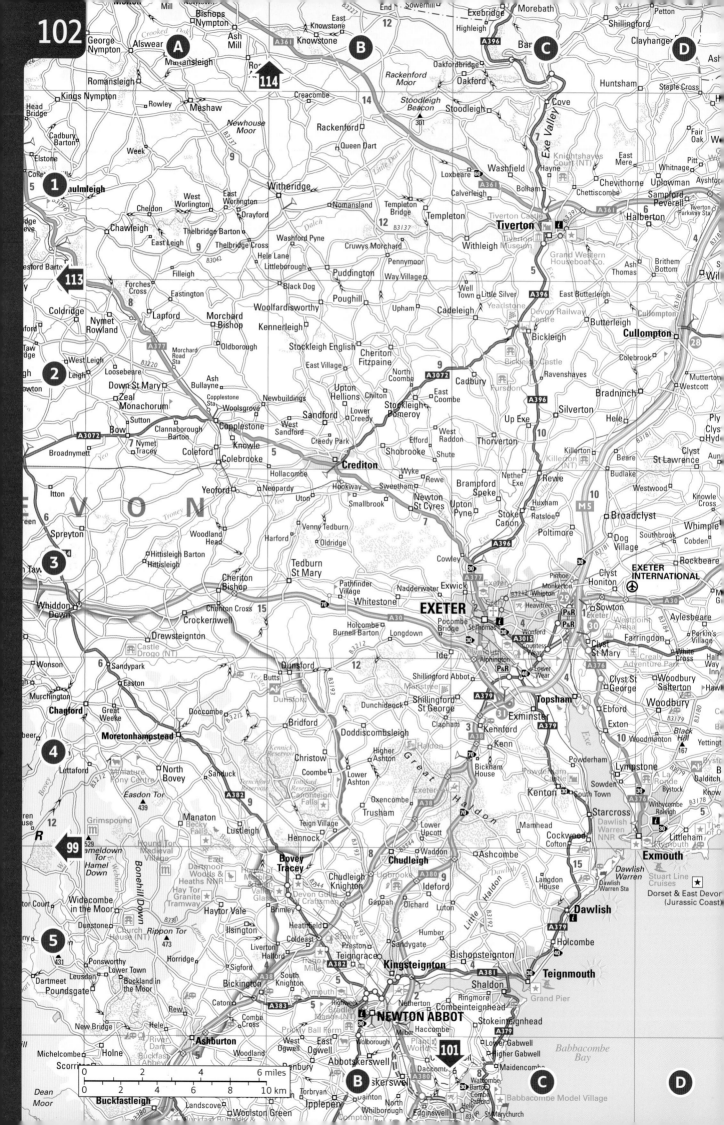

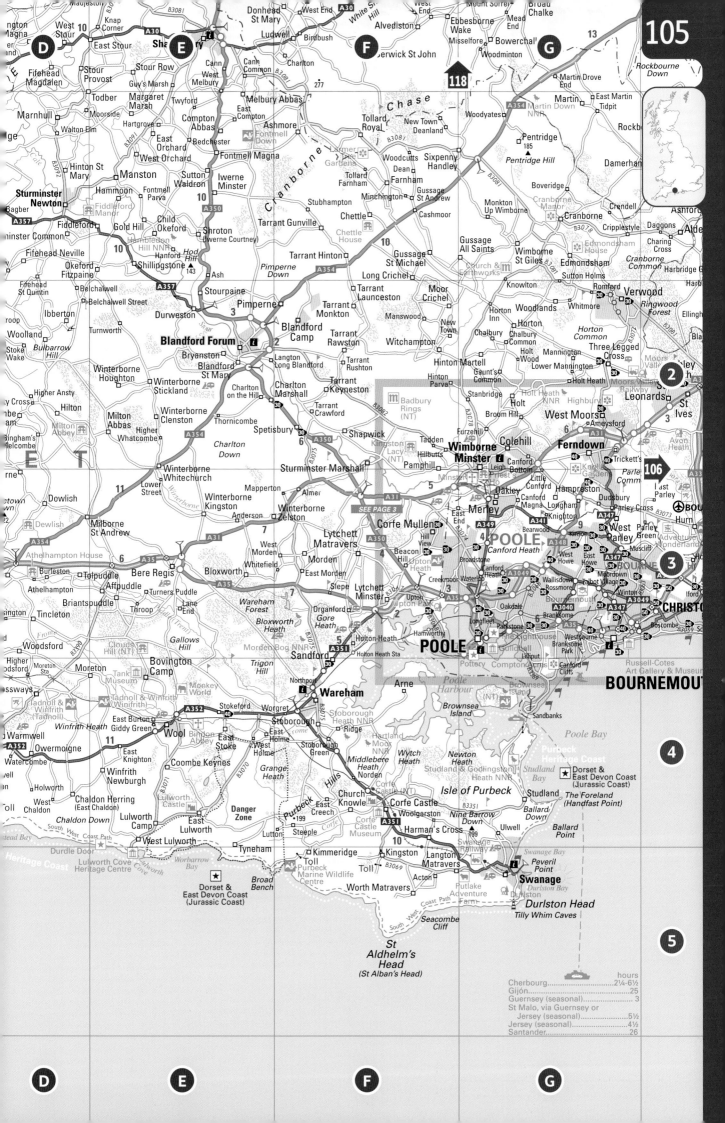

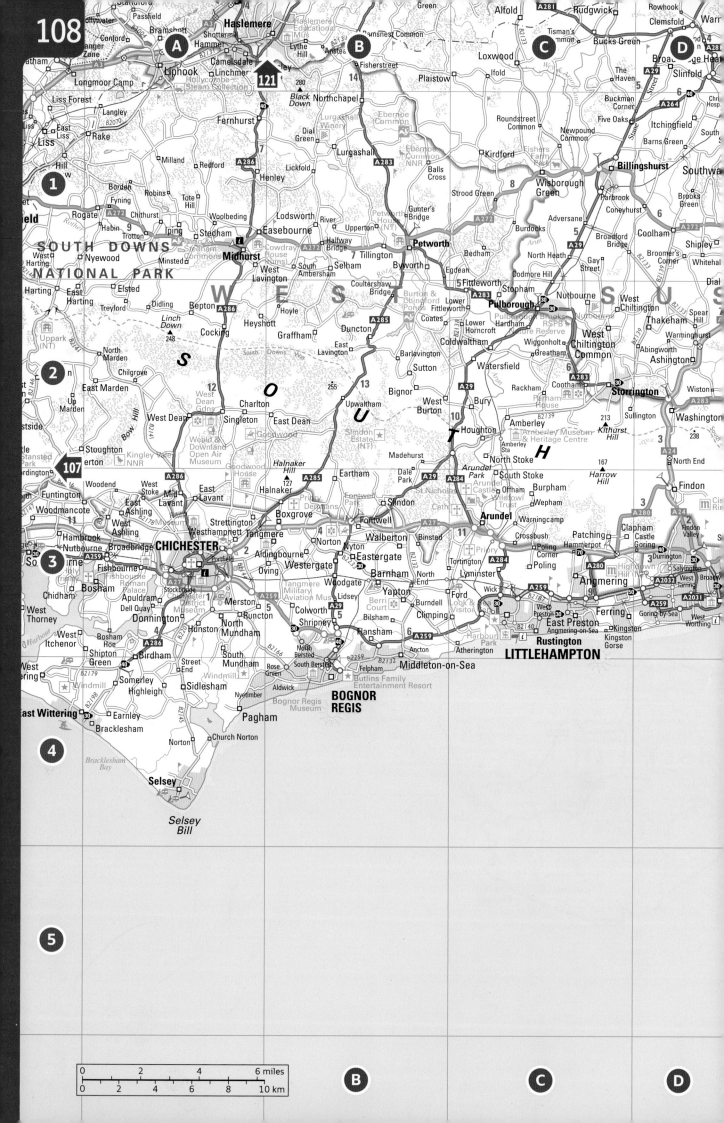

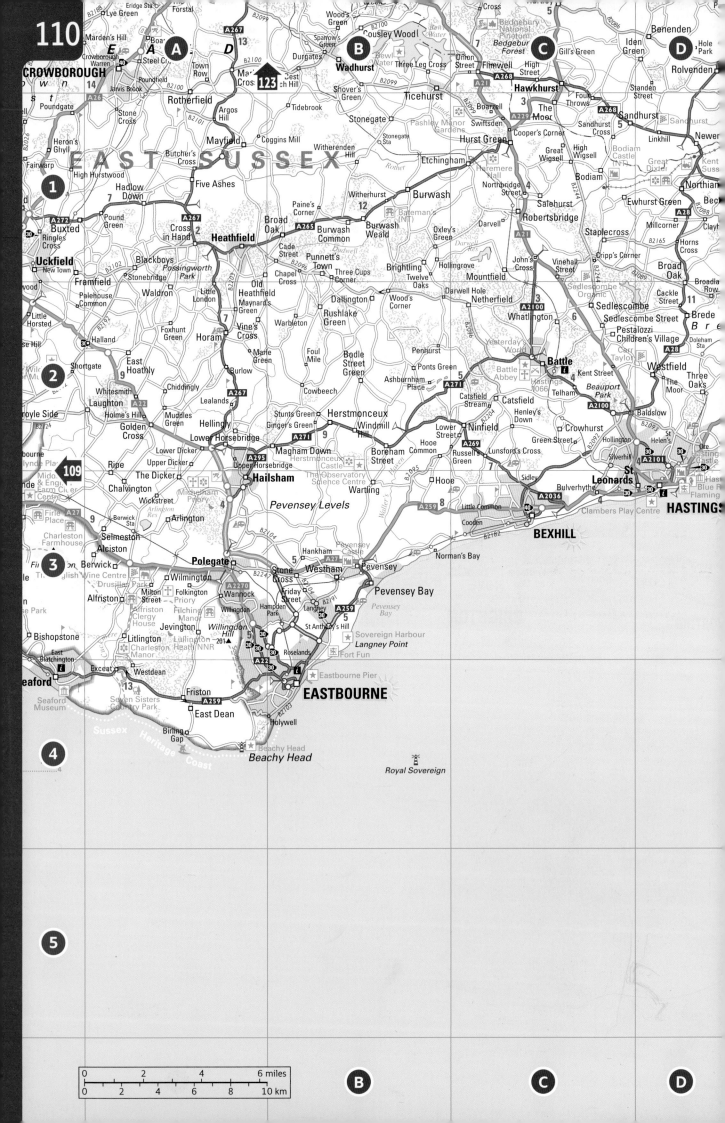

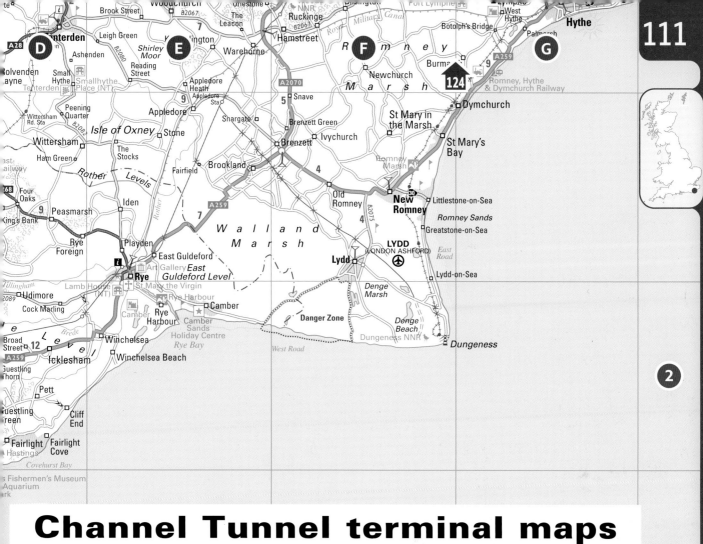

Channel Tunnel terminal maps

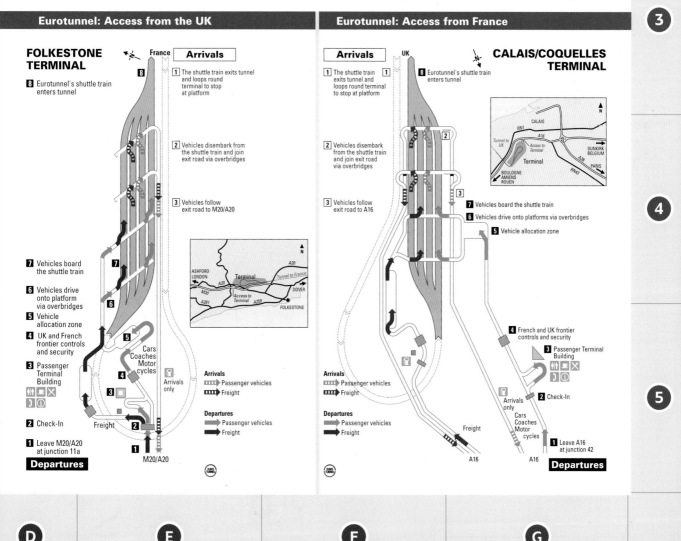

A   B   C   D

1

2

3

BARNS

B A

(B I D E

B A

North
West
Point
Lundy
Heritage Coast

LUNDY

Lundy Island
(NT)

Lundy
NNR

Shutter
Rock

Rat Island

Hartland
Point

Hartland
Heritage Coast

Titchberry

South   West   Coast   Path

Windbury
Point

Gallantry Bower

Hartland
Abbey

Hartland

Clovelly

Sierra

Clovelly
Bay

Hartland
Quay

Stoke

B3248

Dyke

Clovelly Cross

Milford

Edistone

Philham

Milky Way
Adventure Park

Elmscott

A39

Tosberry

Woolfardisworthy

South Hole

Almi

Knaps Longpeak

Welcombe

Ashmansworthy

Mead

Meddon

Torridge

Kis

Darracott

E

Woolley

Gooseham

Eastcott

14

East
Youlstone

Dinworthy

4

Morwenstow

West
Youlstone

Bradwort

Higher
Sharpnose
Point

Shop

Lower
Sharpnose
Point

Woodford

Taylors
Cross

Upper
Tamar Lake

Sutcomb

South   West   Coast

Coombe

Kilkhampton

Alfardisworthy

Soldon

Lower
Tamar Lake

Soldon Cross

Hartland
Heritage Coast

Stibb

A39

B3254

Thurdon

Youldonmoor
Cross

Dunsd
Farm NNR

Youldon

Dunsdo

Stratton
1643

Maer

Poughill

Hersham
Bush

Grimscott

Lana

Chilsworth

Bude
Haven

Flexbury

Stratton

Launcells
Cross

Pancrasweek

BUDE BAY

Bude

Lynstone

3

Launcells

Red
Post

5

Derril

Rydon

A

Upton

A3072

Derriton

Chasty

5

Helebridge

Marhamchurch

Bridgerule

Pyworthy

Widemouth Bay

Titson

Yeomadon

Pentire Point - Widemouth
Heritage Coast

Box's
Shop

Week Orchard

Tamar

B3254

Tinney

Dizzard Point

Coppathorne

Corfcott
Green

Poundst

98

reskinnick Cross

W

North Tamerton

D

St Genn

Tregole

Penlean

St I

Trebarrow

Tetcott

Cambeak

Trewint

Greena
Moor

C lo

0   2   4   6 miles
0   2   4   6   8   10 km

B

kington Haven

Rosecare

Jacobstow

19

15

A · B · C · D

1

2

Cowbridge
Llanblethian
Llansworney
Llandow
Llanmihangel
Wick
Broughton
Southerndown
Nash
Llandough
Sigingstone
The
Herberts
St Mary
Church
Tregurf
Llanmaes
Eglwys Brewis
Llanbethery
Llancadle
Marcross
Llantwit Major
Boverton
St Athan
Fonmo
Nash Point
St Donats
West Aberthaw
East
Aberthaw
Gileston
Breaksea
Pt

Tusker
Rock

Wales Coast Path

Glamorgan Heritage Coast

B R I S T O L

B

Coast
Woody
Bay
The Valley
of Rocks
Lynton &
Lynmouth
Cliff Railway
Lynmouth
Bay
Countisbury
Cove
Foreland Point
Toll
Lynton
Lynmouth
Barbrook
West
Lyn
East Lyn
Countisbury
Watersmeet Rd (NT)
Wilsham
387
Culbone Hill
A39
413
11
Culbone
Toll
Porlock
Weir
West
Porlock
Porlock
Bay
Exmoor Heritage Coast
South West Coast Path
**Selworthy
Beacon**
308
Holnicote Estate (NT)
South West Co
Minehead
Butlins Family
Entertainment Resort
Blue
Anchor
Bay
Lemacott
A39
Hillsford
Bridge
Cheriton
Tippacott
Brendon
Malmsmead
Oare
Brendon
Common
Hawkcombe
Woods NNR
Bossington
Lynch
Allerford
Selworthy
North Hill
Woodcombe
Bratton
Peiton
Alcombe
Dunster Sta
Marsh Street
Blue
Anchor
Furzehill
9
South Common
Exmoor International
Dark Sky Reserve
Luccombe
Stoke Pero
Horner
Holnicote
Hindon
8
Knowle
Dunster
Chap
Cleev
Shallowford
Hoaroak
Hill
473
E X M O O R
444
Dry
Hill
Dunkery Hill
Dunkery Beacon
Huntscott
Dunkery &
Horner Woods
NNR
Wootton
Courtenay
Ranscombe
7
Cowbridge
Dunster Castle
& Gardens (NT)
Carhampton
Old Cleeve
A39
7
Bilbrook
Challacombe
Common
480
Pinkworthy
Pond
Eve
559
Codsend
Moors
Quarme
Burrow
Timberscombe
Bickham
Croydon
Hill
365
Cleeve
Abbey
Beggearn Hi
Swincombe
Challacombe
113
Dure Down
B3358
9
EXMOOR
B3223
10
Edgcott
B3224
A396
Cutcombe
Wheddon
Cross
Luxborough
Rodhuish
Lower Roadwater
Roadwater
Torre
Shoulsbarrow
Common
Simonsbath
Exford
Luckwell
Bridge
Triscombe
Kingsbridge
Withycombe
Nettle
Leworthy
Fullaford
409
Great
Nurcot
North Quarme
Lype Hill
423
B R E N D O N H I L L S
Treborough
Leighland
Chapel
Span
Head
493
Long
Holcombe
436
NATIONAL
Blacklands
PARK
Eve
Withypool
Withiel
Florey
Lydcott
Whitefield
North
Radworthy
Withypool
Common
Winsford
Hill
426
Winsford
West Howetown
Gupworthy
High
Bray
ayford
Charles
East
Buckland
North Heasley
South Radworthy
Heasley Mill
Worth Hill
Dane's Brook
Knaplock
Tarr Steps
Woodland
NNR
Liscombe
Tarr
Steps
B3223
Exton
Bridgetown
Brompton
Regis
Woolcotts
S O M E R
Twitchen
Molland
Common
Hawkridge
Barle
Higher
Combe
Week
Clatworthy
Reservoir
Coombe
A361
A399
North
Molton
Molland
Dulverton
Battleton
Bury
Haddon
Hill
Hartford
Wimbleball
Lake
317
Upton
Huish Champflowe
Quince
Honey Farm
2
60
4
West Anstey
Yeo
B3222
Skilgate
Chipstable
Leigh
West
Anstey
East
Anstey
Nightcott
Brushford
Upcott
Timewell
Raddington
Waterr
**South
Molton**
B3227
Bish
Mill
Newtown
Yeo Mill
Oldways
End
Sowerhill
12
Exebridge
Morebath
Shillingford
Petton
Clayhanger
12
Bishops
Nympton
Ash
Mill
East
Knowstone
Knowstone
Highleigh
A396
Bampton
Clapworthy
George
Nympton
Alswear
Crooked Oak
A361
Mole
8
Mariansleigh
Rose
Ash
Rackenford
Moor
Oakfordbridge
Oakford
Huntsham
Staple Cross
Romansleigh
Creacombe
14
Stoodleigh
Beacon
301
102
Cove
ley
Kings Nympton
Rowley
Meshaw
B
C
D
Head
Bridge
Cadbury
Barton
Elstone
Rackenf
rt
Quc
rt
Washfield
Knightshayes
Court (NT)
Hayne
East
Mere
Pitt
Whitnage
Ash
ir

0   2   4   6 miles
0 2 4 6 8 10 km

129

3

10

4

11

5

8

102

2

14

9

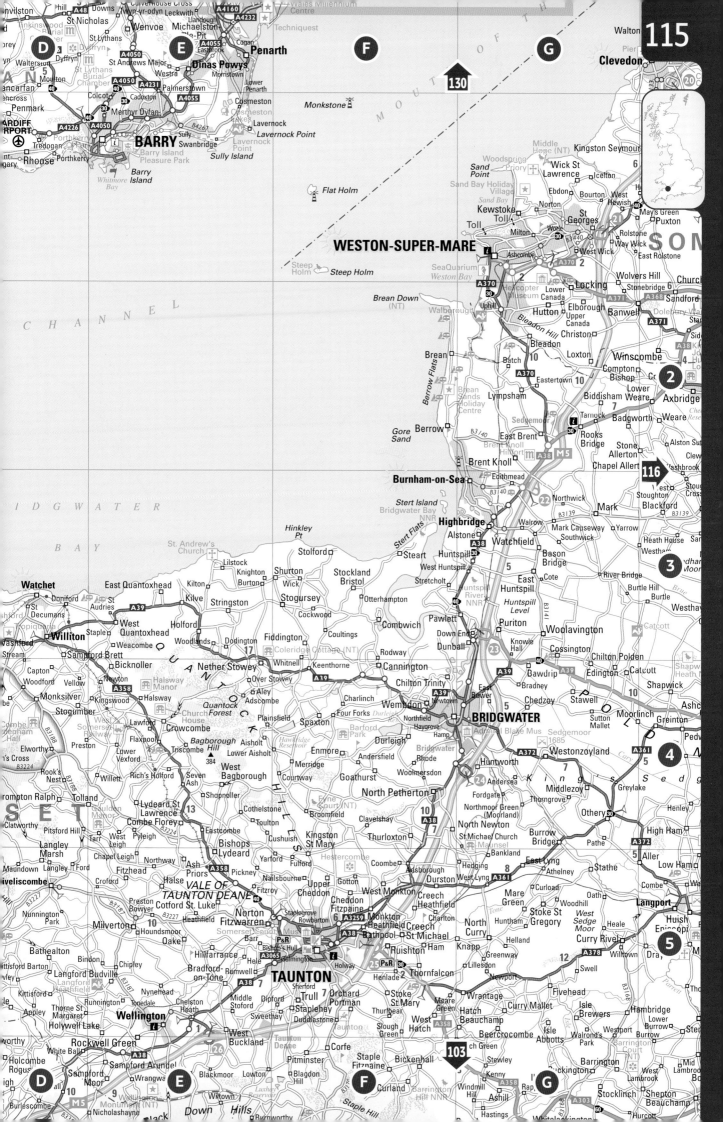

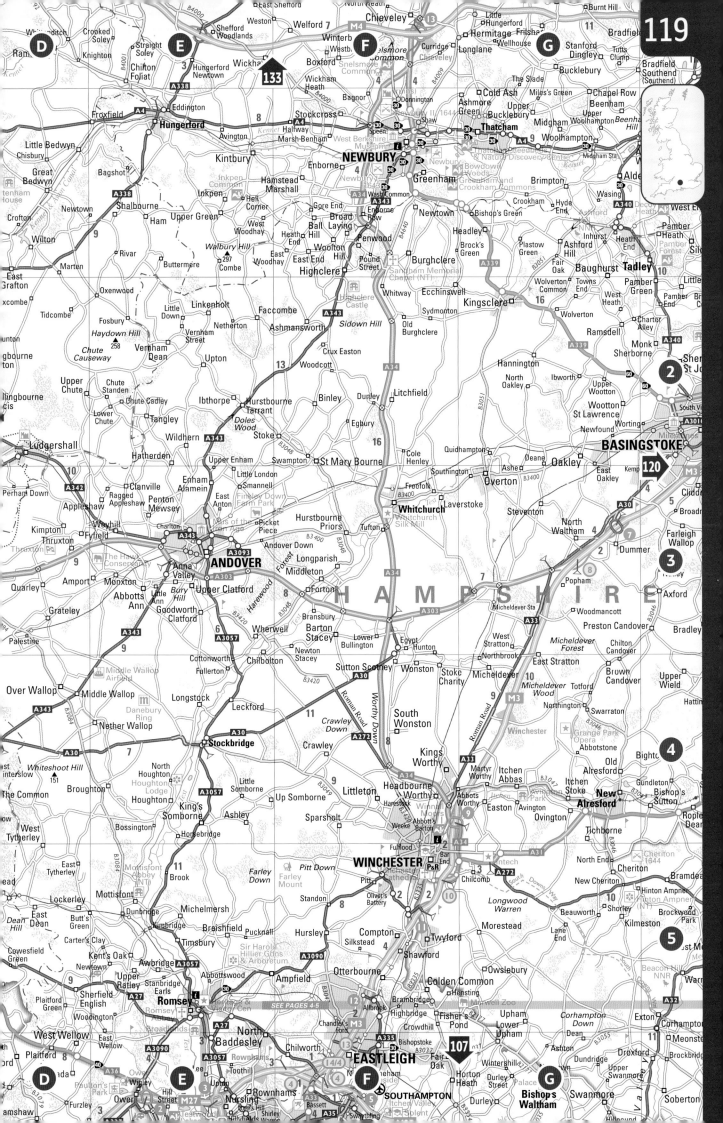

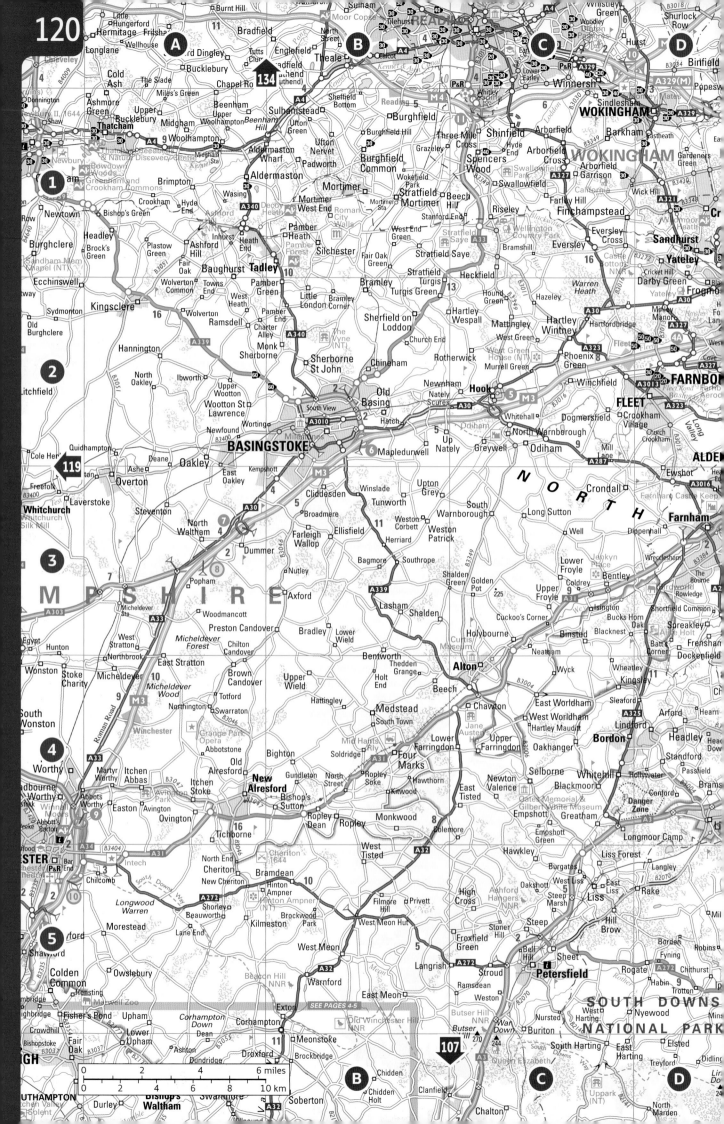

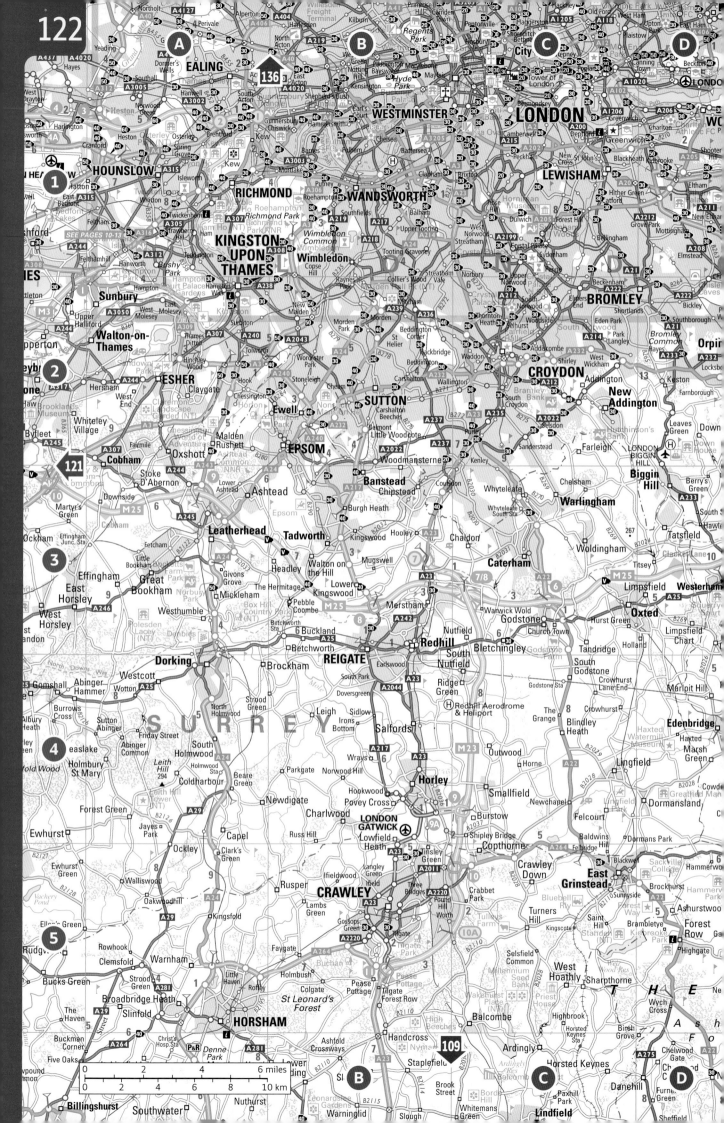

D · E · F · G

139

Long Nose Spit
South Channel
Foreness Point
White Ness
North Foreland
MARGATE
Tudor House
Cliftonville
Kingsgate
Westgate on Sea
Westbrook
Salmeston Grange
Quex House
& Gdns
A255
Birchington
Herne Bay
Reculver Country Park
Reculver
Towers & Roman Fort
Hillborough
Beltinge
Spitfire & Hurricane Memorial RAF Manston
A254
St Peter's
Broadstairs
Dickens House Museum
Bleak House
Acol
Haine
Hunters Forstal
Broomfield
St Nicholas at Wade
ISLE OF THANET
Northwood
Highstead
Herne Common
Boyden Gate
Sarre
KENT INTERNATIONAL
Manston
A256
A254
A255
West End
Maypole
Chislet
Gore Street
Minster
Abbey
Pegwell
A299
Hoath
Upstreet
Roman Road
Monkton
Cliffs End
St Augustine's Cross
Ramsgate
Calcott
Hersden
West Stourmouth
Plucks Gutter
Sandwich & Pegwell Bay NNR
Oostende........4hrs
Westbere
Grove
East Stourmouth
Pegwell Bay
Sturry
Stodmarsh
Preston
Westmarsh
Richborough Castle
Sandwich Flats
Fordwich
Stodmarsh NNR
Elmstone
Ware
Stonar Cut
Royal St. Georges
P&R
CANTERBURY
St Martin's Church
Wickhambreaux
Hoaden
Cop Street
Wingham Wildlife Park
Great Stonar
Sandwich Bay
St Augustine's Abbey
Littlebourne
Ickham
Shatterling
Roman Amphitheatre
Salutation Garden
Toll
Bramling
Wingham
Marshborough
Barnsole
Sandwich
Howletts Wild Animal Park
Wingham Well
Staple
Barnsole
Woodnesborough
Ham
Worth
Bekesbourne
Patrixbourne
Goodnestone Park
Staple
Worth
Hacklinge
Bridge
Adisham
Goodnestone
Eastry
Finglesham
Lower Hardres
Chillenden
Knowlton
Betteshanger
Sholden
Deal
Bishopsbourne
Aylesham
Nonington
Ratling
Northbourne
Great Mongeham
Deal Castle
Kingston
Elham
Womenswold
Easole Street
Tilmanstone
A256
Ripple
Walmer
Barham
Woolage Village
Barfrestone
Elvington
East Studdal
Sutton
Derringstone
Woolage Green
Lower Eythorne
Eythorne
Ashley
West Langdon
Walmer Castle & Garden
Kingsdown
Ringwould
Breach
Bladbean
Shepherdswell (Sibertswold)
North Downs Way
A258
Wingmore
Denton
Coldred
Martin Mill Sta.
East Langdon
West Cliffe
South Foreland Heritage Coast
Wootton
Lydden
A260
Lydden Temple Ewell NNR
Whitfield
Guston
St Margaret's at Cliffe
Selstead
Temple Ewell
River
St Margaret's Bay
Swingfield Minnis
Ewell Minnis
The Pines
Densole
Alkham
Buckland
South Foreland
South Foreland Lighthouse (NT)
Ottinge
South Alkham
St Radigund's Abbey
Women's Land Army Mus.
DOVER
Lyminge
Paddlesworth
Hawkinge
West Hougham
Maxton
Dover Castle
De Bradelei Wharf
Etchinghill
Capel le Ferne
Knights Templar Church
Calais..........1¼-1½
Dunkerque..............2
Channel Tunnel
Folkestone to Calais 35mins
Newington
Channel Tunnel Terminal
Cheriton
Samphire Hoe
East Wear Bay
Dover - Folkestone Heritage Coast
STRAIT OF DOVER
Saltwood
Sandgate
FOLKESTONE
Hythe

STRAIT OF DOVER

2 · 3 · 4 · 5

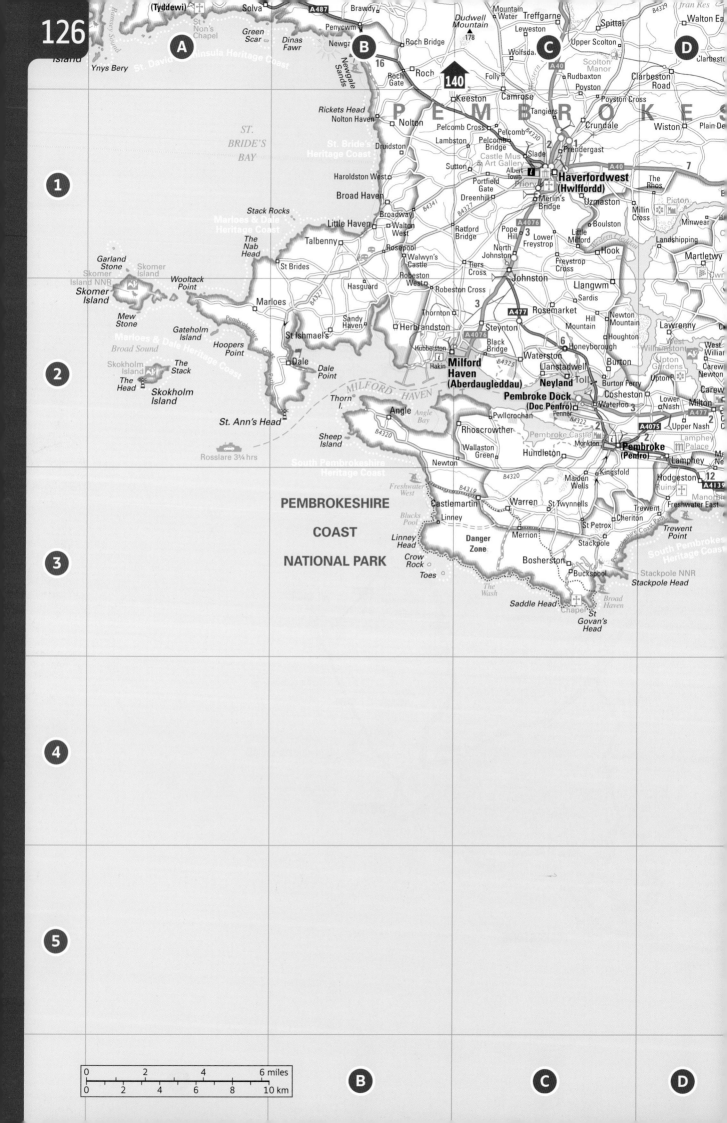

PEMBROKES

ST. BRIDE'S BAY

St. David's Peninsula Heritage Coast

St. Bride's Heritage Coast

Marloes & Dale Heritage Coast

Marloes & Dale Heritage Coast

Broad Sound

South Pembrokeshire Heritage Coast

South Pembrokeshire Heritage Coast

MILFORD HAVEN

PEMBROKESHIRE COAST NATIONAL PARK

(Tyddewi)
Solva
Brawdy
Dudwell Mountain
Mountain Water
Treffgarne
Spittal
Walton Ea
St Non's Chapel
Green Scar
Dinas Fawr
Penycwm
Newga
Roch Bridge
Leweston
Upper Scolton
Wolfsda
Clarbestor
Ynys Bery
Newgale Sands
16
Roch Gate
Roch
140
Keeston
Camrose
Folly
Rudbaxton
Poyston
Scolton Manor
Clarbeston Road
Poyston Cross
Plain De
Rickets Head
Nolton Haven
Nolton
Tangiers
Crundale
Wiston
7
Pelcomb Cross
Lambston
Pelcomb Bridge
Slade
Prendergast
The Rhos
Picton
Sutton
Portfield Gate
Albert Town
Prion
Haverfordwest (Hwlffordd)
Castle Mus & Art Gallery
Dreenhill
Merlin's Bridge
Uzmaston
Millin Cross
Minwear
Haroldston West
Broadway
Pope Hill
Lower Freystrop
Little Milford
Hook
Landshipping
Martletwy
Broad Haven
Walton West
Ratford Bridge
North Johnston
Freystrop Cross
Stack Rocks
Little Haven
Rosepool
Walwyn's Castle
Tiers Cross
Johnston
Llangwm
Cwr
The Nab Head
St Brides
Hasguard
Robeston West
Robeston Cross
Sardis
Newton Mountain
Lawrenny
Garland Stone
Skomer Island
Marloes
Sandy Haven
Thornton
Rosemarket
Hill Mountain
Houghton
West Willia
Skomer Island NNR
Wooltack Point
Herbrandston
Steynton
Honeyborough
Burton
Upton Gardens
West William
Carew Newton
Mew Stone
Gateholm Island
Hoopers Point
St Ishmael's
Black Bridge
Waterston
Llanstadwell
Burton Ferry
Upton
Carew
Broad Sound
Dale
Dale Point
Hubberston
Hakin
Milford Haven (Aberdaugleddau)
Neyland
Coshetton
Lower Nash
Milton
Skokholm Island
The Stack
Pembroke Dock (Doc Penfro)
Waterloo
Upper Nash
The Head
Skokholm Island
St. Ann's Head
Thorn I.
Angle
Angle Bay
Pwllcrochan
Pennar
Waterloo
Pembroke Castle
Monkton
Lower Nash
Rosslare 3¾ hrs
Sheep Island
Rhoscrowther
Wallaston Green
Hundleton
Pembroke (Penfro)
Lamphey Palace
Lamphey
Ma
Newton
Kingsfold
Hodgeston
Ne
Freshwater West
Castlemartin
Maiden Wells
Ruins
Manorbi
12
Bucks Pool
Linney
Warren
St Twynnells
Trewent
Freshwater East
Linney Head
Danger Zone
Merrion
Cheriton
Trewent Point
Crow Rock
Bosherston
St Petrox
Stackpole
Toes
Buckspool
Stackpole NNR
Stackpole Head
The Wash
Saddle Head
Chapel
St Govan's Head
Broad Haven
South Pembrokeshire Heritage Coast

0   2   4   6 miles
0 2 4 6 8 10 km

PEMBROKESHIRE COAST
NATIONAL PARK

CARMARTHEN
BAY

Carmarthen (Caerfyrddin)
Tre-vaughan
Johnstown

Meidrim
141

St Clears
(Sanclêr)

Whitland (Hendy-Gwyn)
Whitland Abbey
Hywel Dda Garden

Llanboidy
Login
Llandre
Llandissilio
Llangynin
Henllan Amgoed
Castell Gorfod
Gellywen
Mynach
Maesgwynne
Bronwydd
Abernant
Sarnau
Bron-y-gaer
Bancyfelin
Merthyr
Llanllwch
Gors Goch NNR

Llandewi Velfrey
Cwmfelin Boeth
Trevaughan
Llwyn-y-brain
Llanddewi Velfrey

Rhydywrach
Llanfallteg
Clunderwen
Gelly
Bethesda
Robeston Wathen
Redstone Bank
Canaston Bridge
Narberth (Arberth)
Crinow
Lampeter Velfrey
Princes Gate
Tavernspite

Oakwood Leisure Park
Camp Hill
Cold Blow
Red Roses
Crunwere Farm
Llanteg
Marros
Pendine (Pentywyn)
Llanmiloe
Pendine Sands
Laugharne Burrows
East Marsh
Ginst Point
Laugharne Sands
Laugharne (Lacharn)
Llansteffan
Llansteffan Castle
Wharley Point
Cliff
Broadlay
Ferryside (Glanyferi)
Broadway
Llansaint
St Ishmael
Cefn Sidan Sands
Welsh Motor Sports Centre
Pembrey Forest
Kidwelly (Cydweli)
Pembrey (Pen-bre)
Mynydd-y-Garreg
Mynyddygarreg

Llanddowror
Llandawke
Broadway
Brook
Plashett
Llansadurnen
Llandeilo Abercywyn
Llanybri
Cwmllyfri
Llangynog
Ffynnon
Llangain

Templeton
Ludchurch
Thomas Chapel
Begelly
Stepaside
Amroth
Colby Woodland Garden (NT)
Kilgetty
Pentlepoir
Cross Hands
Loveston
Reynalton
Jeffreyston
Broadmoor
Lanesend
Cresselly
East Williamston
Sageston
Redberth
Cold Inn
New Hedges
Saundersfoot
Saundersfoot Bay
Monkstone Point
Great Wedlock Dinosaur Experience
Heatherton Activity Park
St Florence
Gumfreston
Tenby (Dinbych-y-pysgod)
Tenby Roads
St Catherine's Island
Tudor Merchant's House (NT)
Penally
Manorbier Sta
Norchard
Lydstep
Manorbier
Giltar Point
Caldey Sound
St Margaret's Island
Monastery
Priory
Chapel Point
Caldey Island
Old Castle Head
South Pembrokeshire Heritage Coast

Burry Holms
Llanmadoc
Rhossili Bay
Rhossili Downs
Rhossili
Middleton
Pitton
Worms Head
Gower Coast NNR (NT)
Hillend

Pen-f
Bletherston
Llanycefn
Pen-y-fran
Robeston Wathen
Whaden
Bethesda
whaden
Cross Hands
Manorbier Castle
Lawrenny
Cross
Pwll-trap
Backe
Brandy Hill

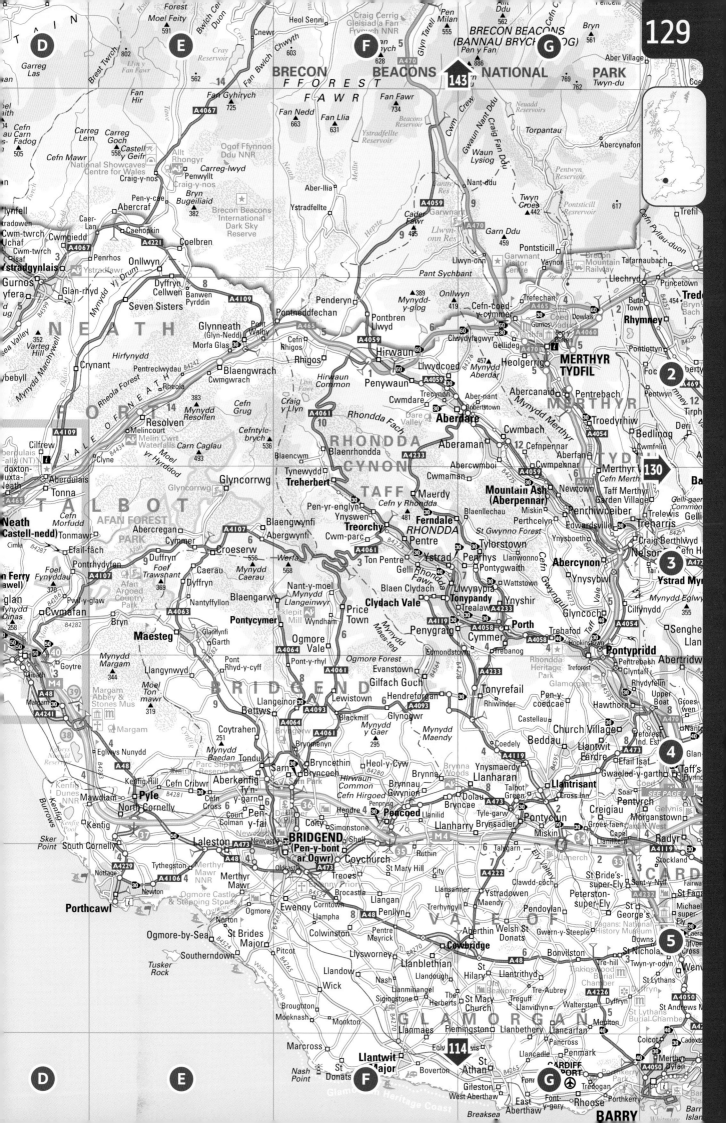

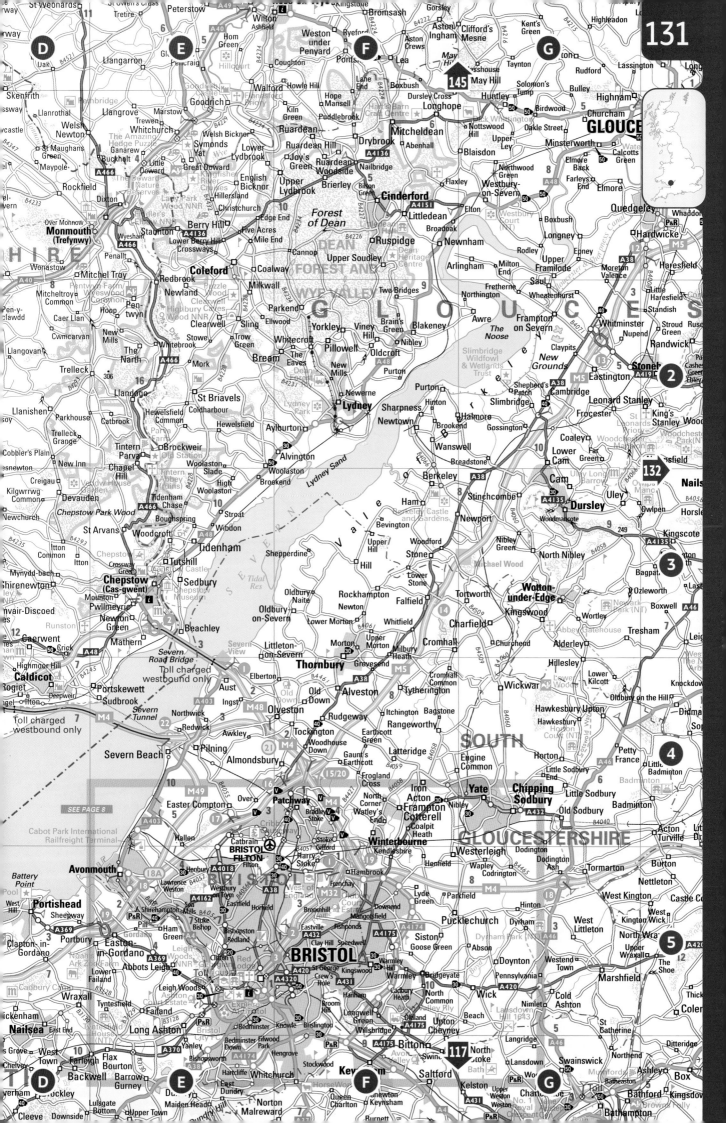

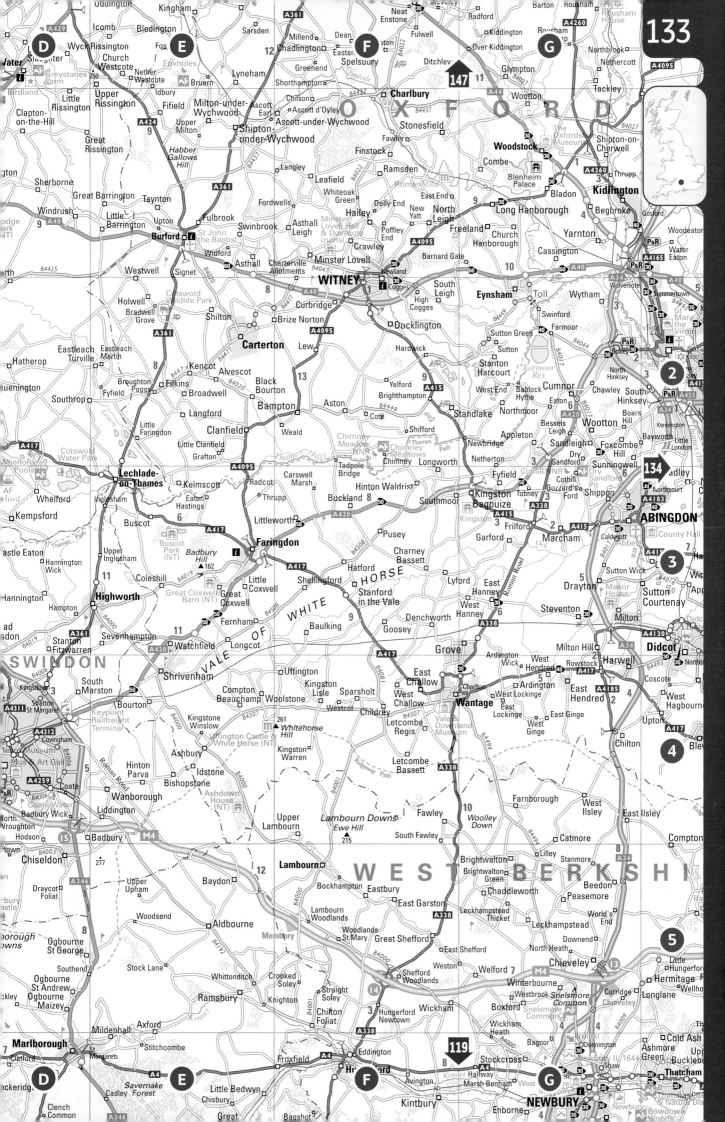

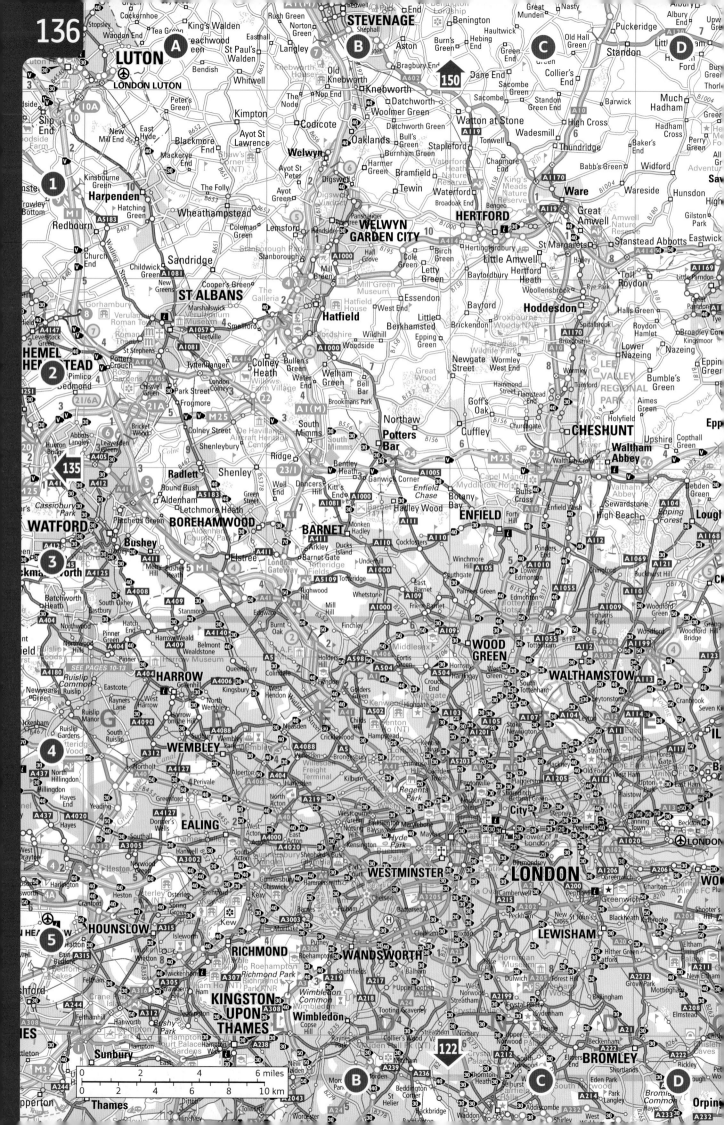

New Quay Head
New Quay Bay
New Quay (Ceinewydd)
Llwyn-onn
Llaingarreg
Maen-y-groes
Gilfachrheda
Cwmtudu
Cross Inn
Llanarth
Nanternis
A486
Ceredigion Heritage Coast
Pen-cae
Caerwedros
Ynys-Lochtyn
Llwyndafydd
Synod Inn (Post-mawr)
A487
2
Blaencelyn
A486
Llangrannog
Pontgarreg
Plwmp
Morfa
Wervil Grange
Pentregat
Talgarreg
Pencribach
Penbryn
A487
Aberporth
Tresaith
Sarnau
Brynhoffnant
Wstrws
Parcllyn
15
Glynarthen
142
Cardigan Island
Cardigan Island Coastal Farm Park
Tan-y-groes
8
Capel Cynon
Cemaes Head
Gwbert
Ferwig
Blaenannerch
Blaenporth
Betws Ifan
Rhydlewis
Ffostrasol
Pen-yr-afr
Penparc
Tremain
Falin-Wnda
Beulah
Pwllgranant
Cippyn
Noyadd Trefawr
Troedyraur
Penrhiw-pâl
Maesllyn
3
Tre-Rhys
Cardigan (Aberteifi)
Llangoedmor
Pantgwyn
Ponthirwaun
Brongest
Coed-y-bryn
Croes-lan
St Dogmaels (Llandudoch)
New Town
Teifi Marshes Nature Reserve
Llangynllo
Horeb
Ceibwr Bay
Abbey
Cardigan
Cwm-cou
Teifi Valley
Aberbanc
7
Penrhiw-llan
Moylgrove
Monington
Cilgerran (NT)
Capel Tygwydd
Llanfair-Orllwyn
A486
2
Glanrhyd
Cwm Plysgog
Manordeifi
Llandygwydd
Llandy
Llantood
Pen-y-bryn
10
Cenarth
A475
A484
6
Newcastle Emlyn (Castell Newydd Emlyn)
Llangeler
Pontwell
Berry Hill
Trewilym
Bridell
Carreg-wen
Abercych
Penrhiw
Pentrecagal
Henllan
Drefach
Pentre-cwrt
Nevern
Rhos-hill
Newchapel
Aber-Arad
National Wool Museum
3
Velindre
Clynfyw
Penrherber
Felindre
Saron
Bancyffordd
Newport (Trefdraeth)
Pengelli Forest
18
Eglwyswrw
Llanfair-Nant-Gwyn
Cilwendeg
Drefelin
Ty Canol NNR
Pentre Ifan Burial Chamber
Cwmhiraeth
5
Cwmpengraig
Penboyr
Bwlch-clawdd
257
Cilgwyn
Crosswell
Whitechurch
Boncath
Glaspant
Capel Iwan
Carningli Common
Brynberian
A478
Blaenffos
Moelfre 335
Rhos
4
Bwlch-y-groes
Cwmpengraig
Penboyr
Freni-fawr 395
Star
Clydey
Cilrhedyn
Cwm-Morgan
Gorllwyn
Hermon
Foel Eryr 468
MYNYDD PRESELI
Crymych
Taf
Tegryn
326
Cwmduad
Foel Cwmcerwyn 536
Glogue
Hermon
Llanpumsaint
Greenway
Mynachlog-ddu
368
Pentre Galar
Llanfyrnach
Trelech
Esgair
Llwyn-croes
Rosebush
Foel Drych
Dinas
Cynwyl Elfed
A484
Gwili
Glandwr
14
Maenclochog
Llanglydwen
Hebron
Blaenwaun
Pen-y-bont
Blaen-y-coed
6
Llangolman
A478
Talog
Bwlchnewydd
Newchurch
5
New Moat
Efailwen
Cefn-y-pant
Llanwinio
Cwmbach
Pemberton's Chocolate Farm
Cwmfelin Mynach
Gellywen
Bronwydd Arms
A48
wastad
Login
Maesgwynne
Llanboidy
Abernant
ys-y-frân
Llandre
Cwm-miles
Merthyr
Tre-vaughan
Tanerdy
Pen-ffordd
Llanycefn
Trinity
Bletherston
Llandissilio
Castell Gorfod
Carmarthen (Caerfyrddin)
A478
Henllan Amgoed
Meidrim
Johnstown
Rhydywrach
Bancyfelin
Llanllwch
Pensarn
Gelly
Clunderwen
Llanfallteg
10
Whitland Abbey
Sarnau
A40
H I R E
Bethesda
Cwmfelin Boeth
Whitland (Hendy-Gwyn)
Bron-y-gaer
127
30
Llangynin
Hywel Dda
Llangynog
Llanstephan
whaden
Robeston Wathen
4
Redstone Bank
Trevaughan
Llanddev Velfre
St Clears (Sanclêr)
Pwll-trap
Backe
Flynnon
Langain
Cwmffrwd
Croesyceiliog

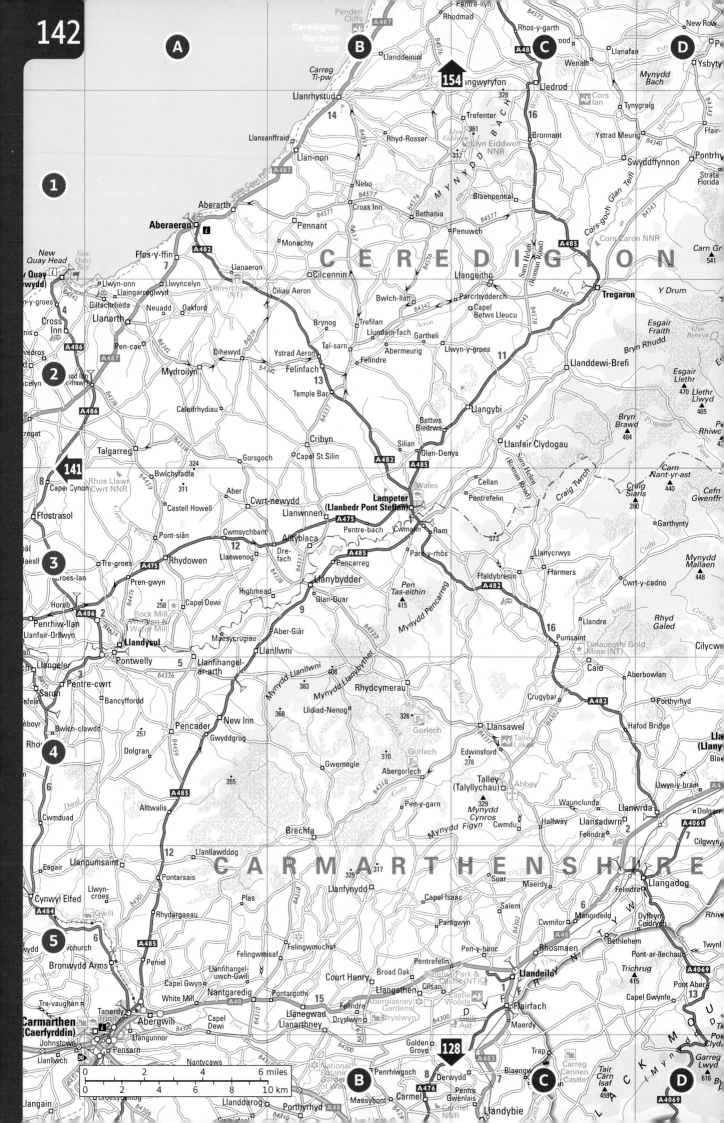

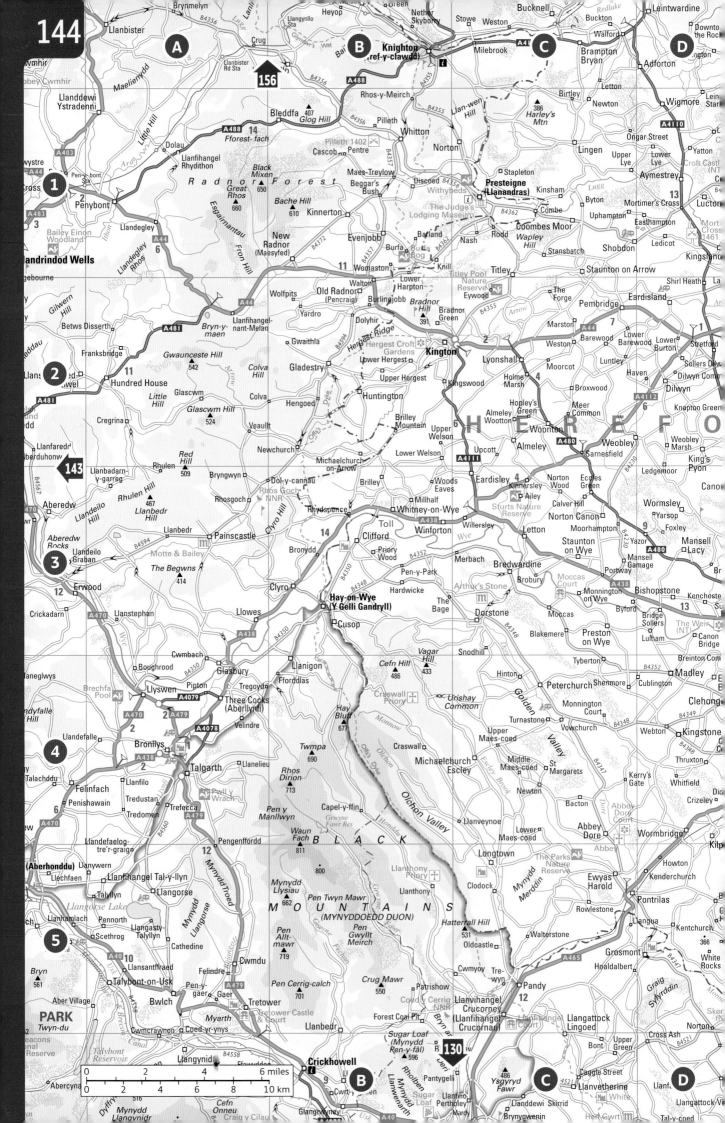

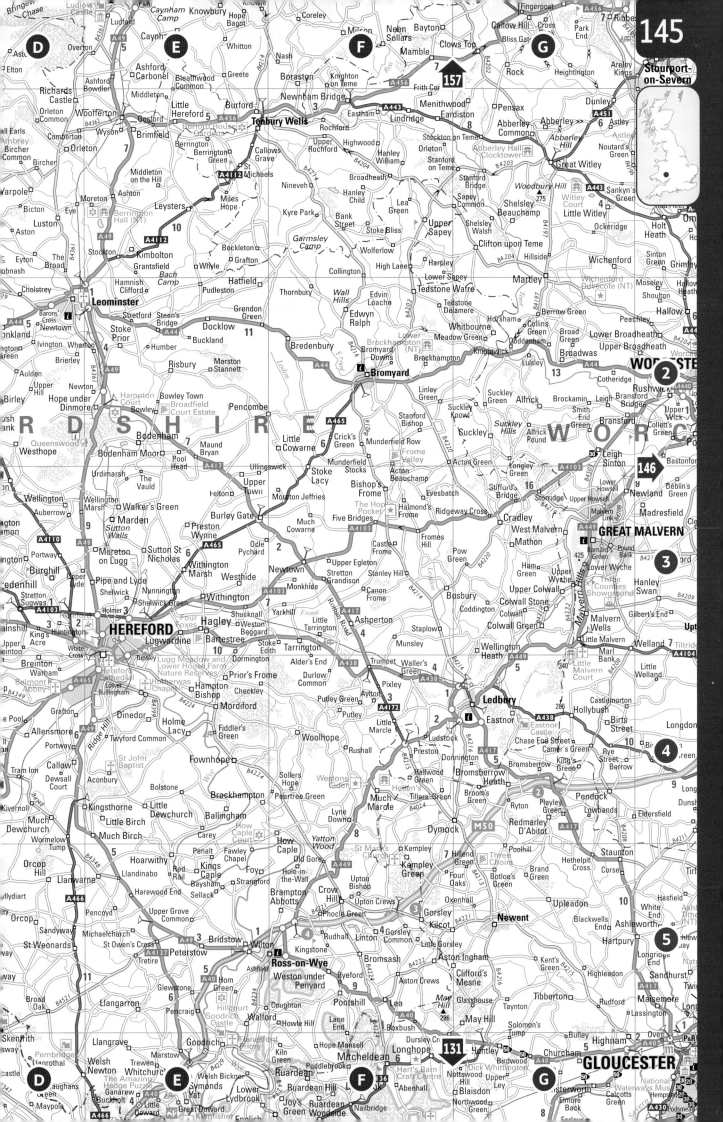

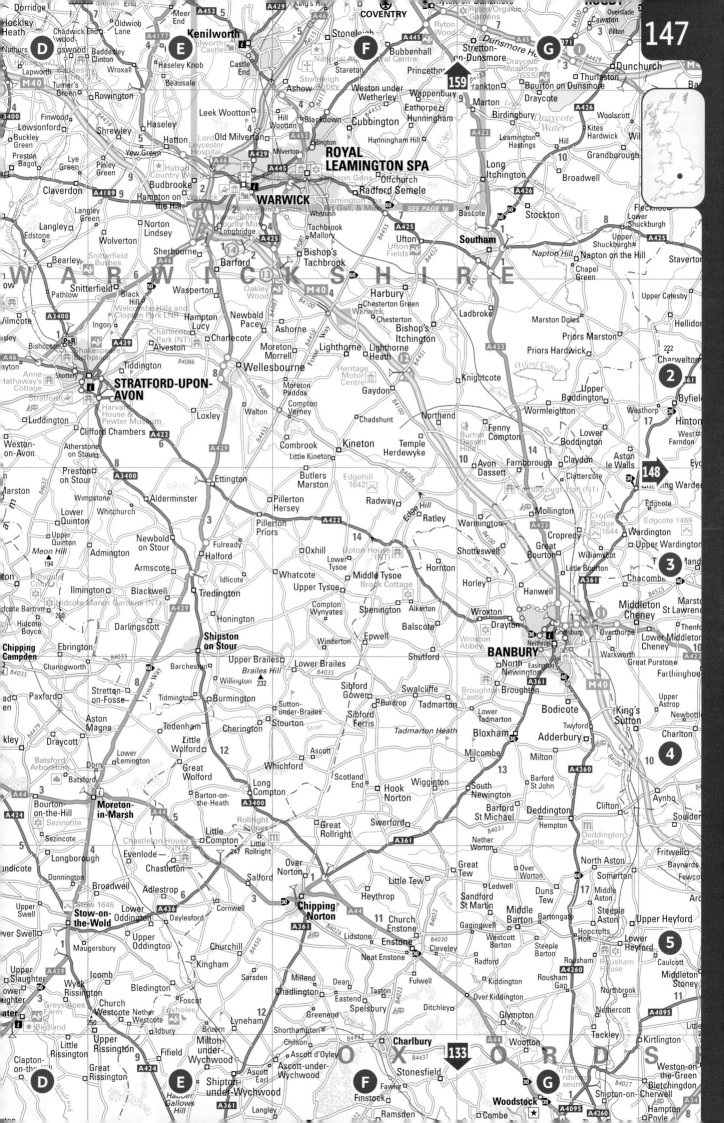

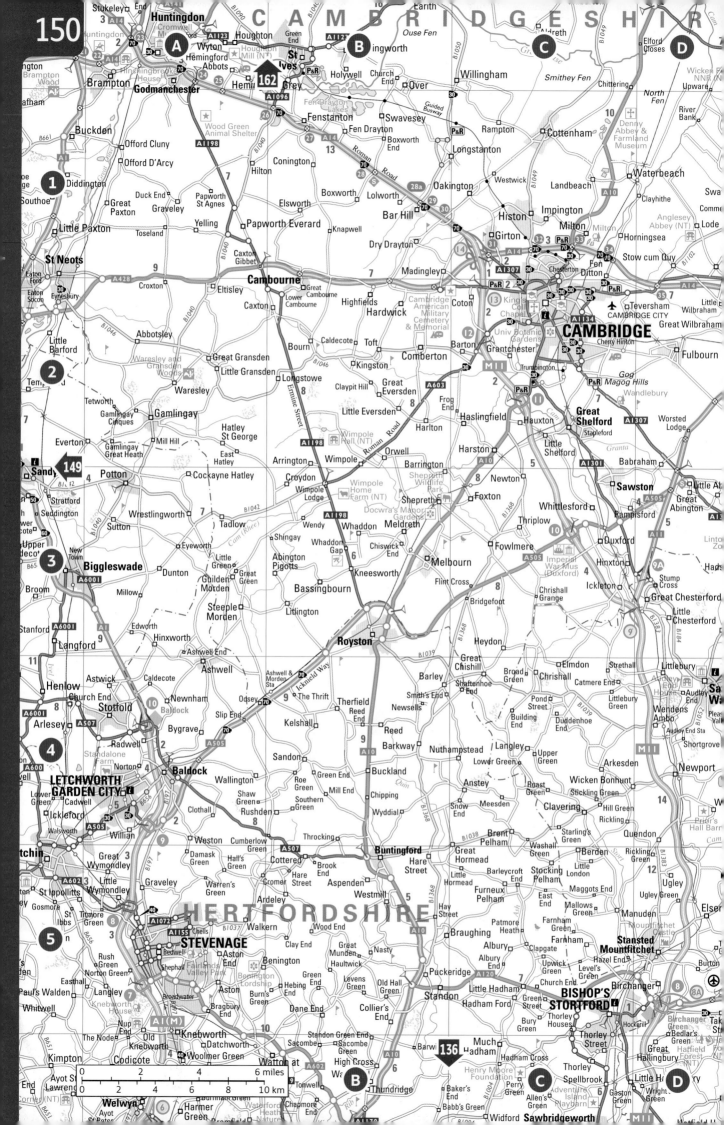

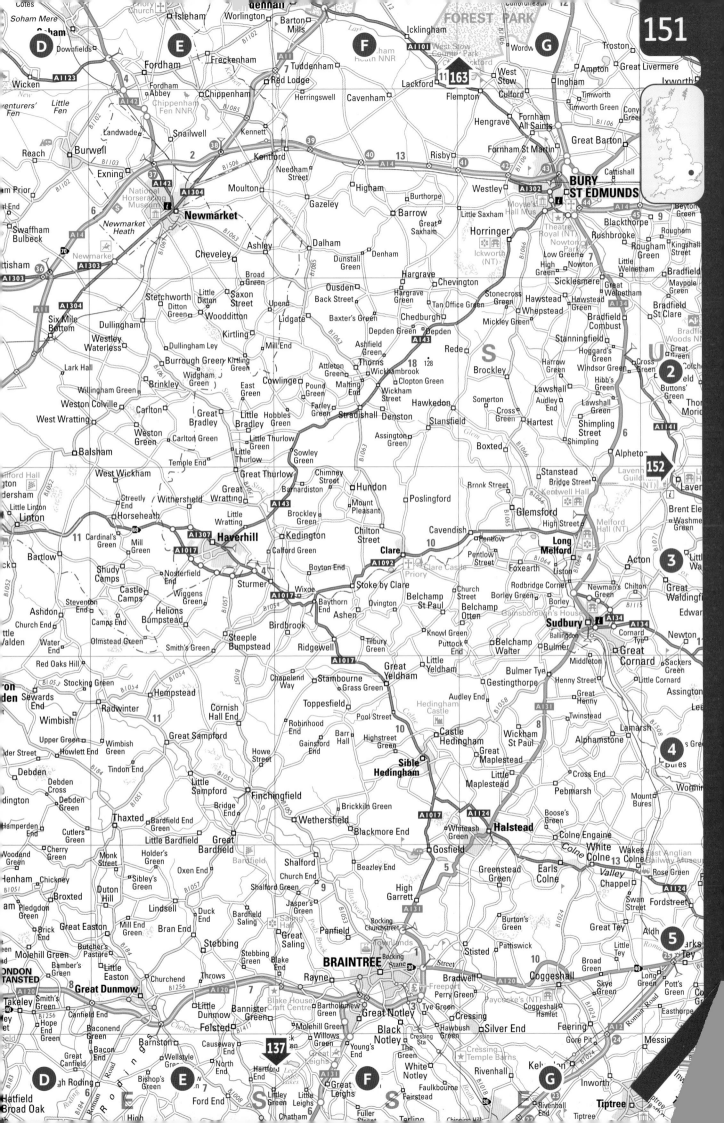

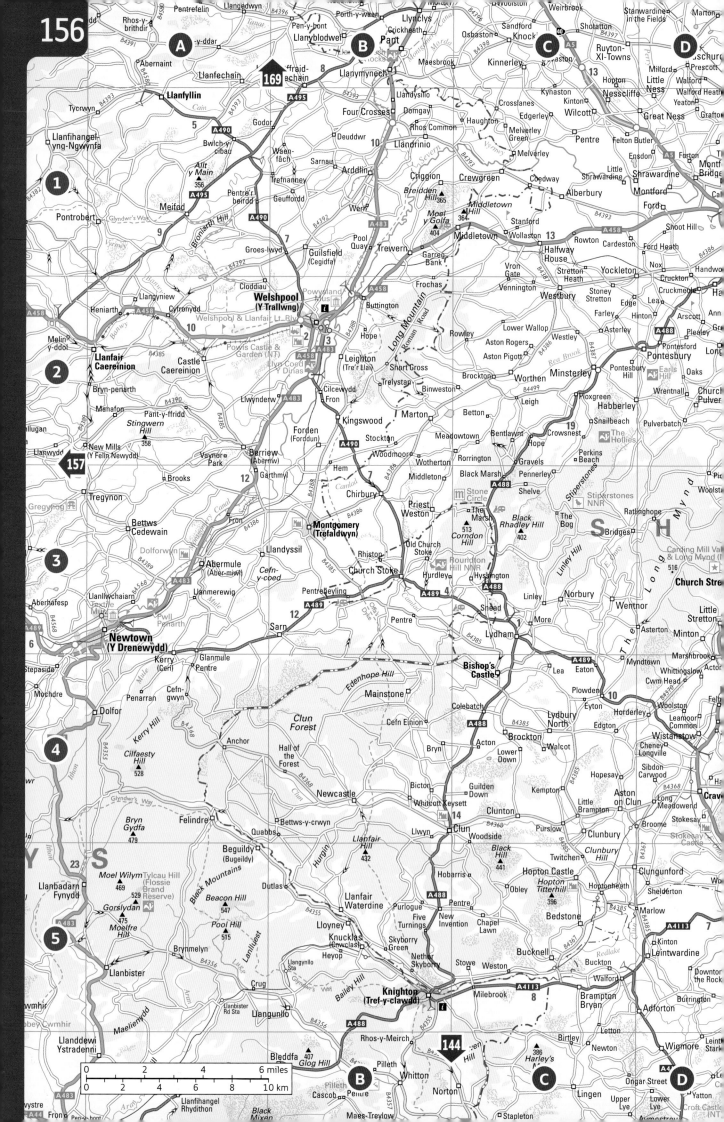

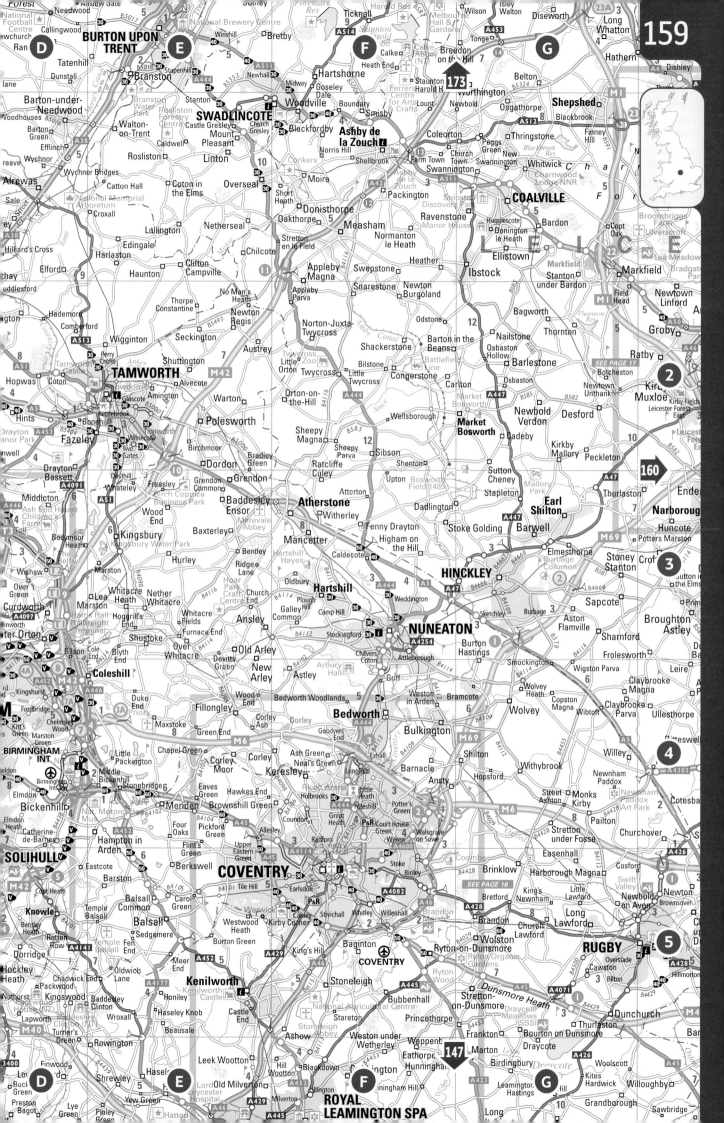

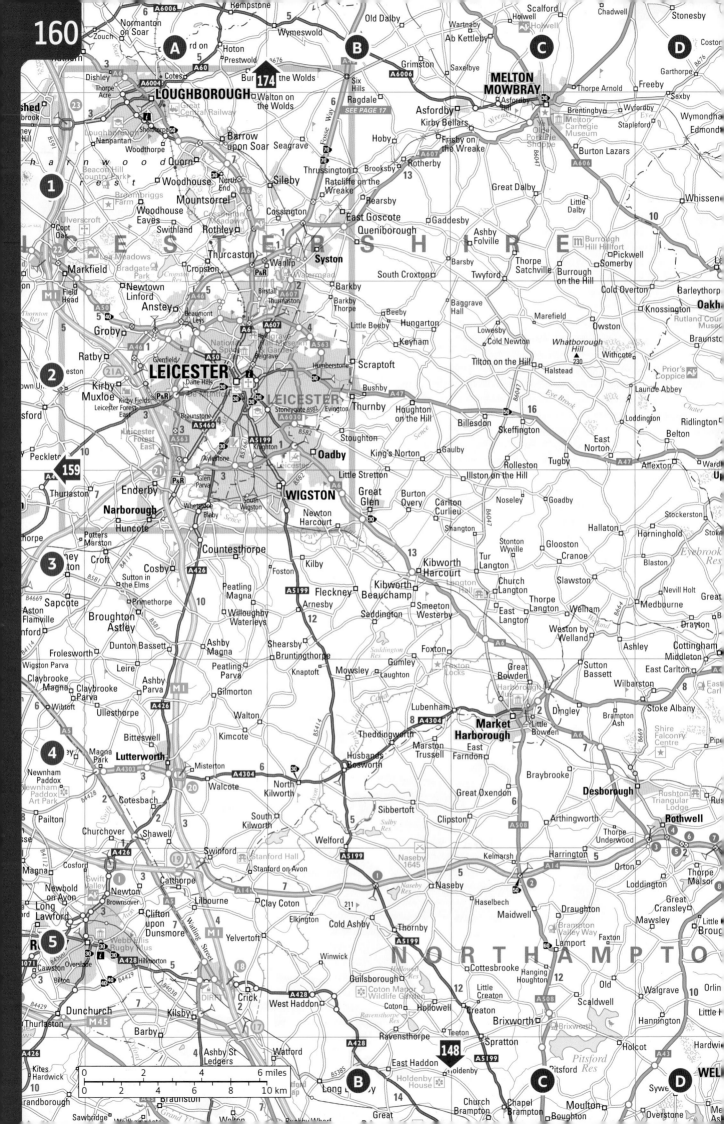

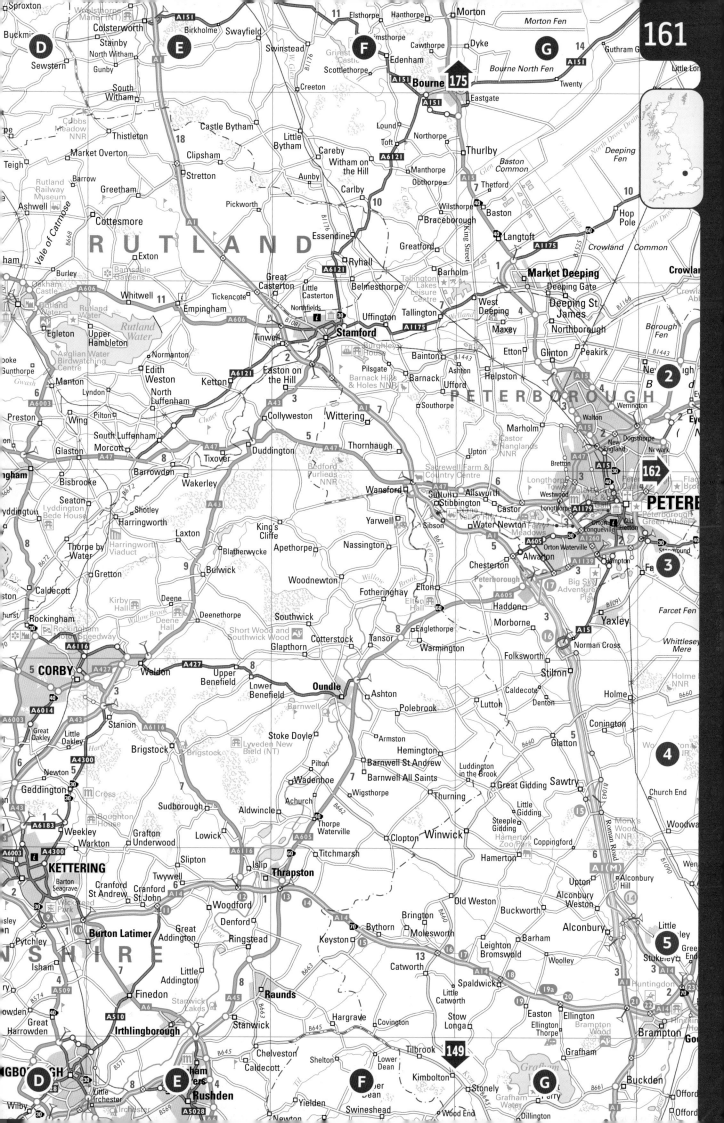

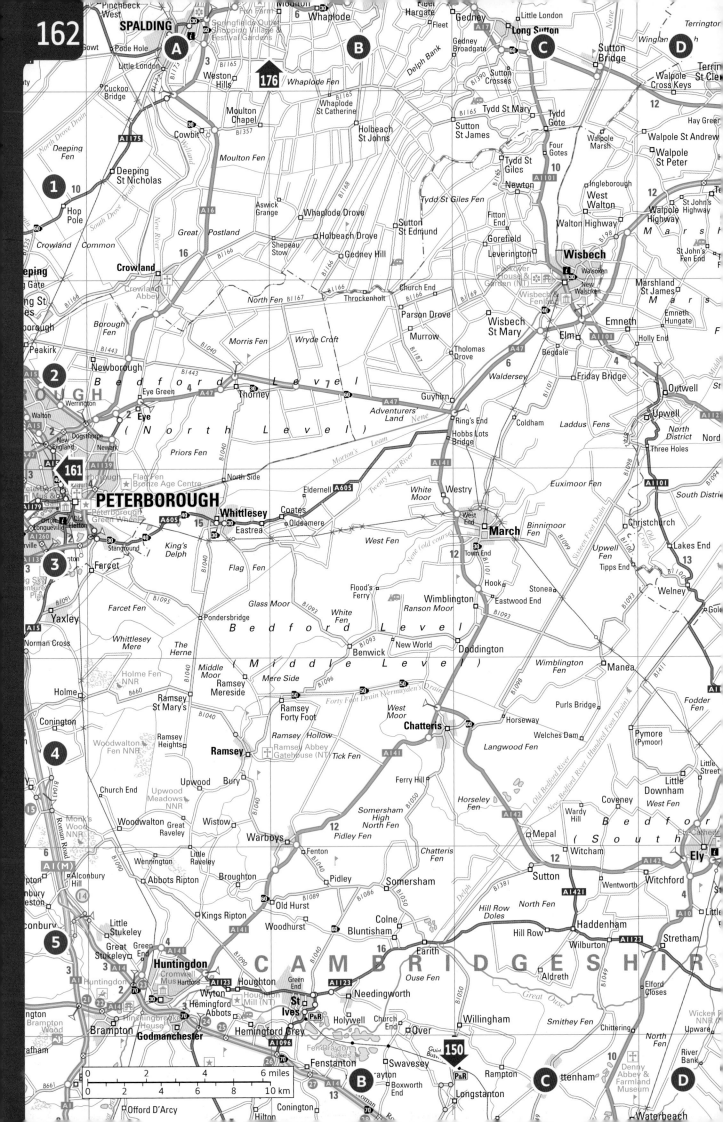

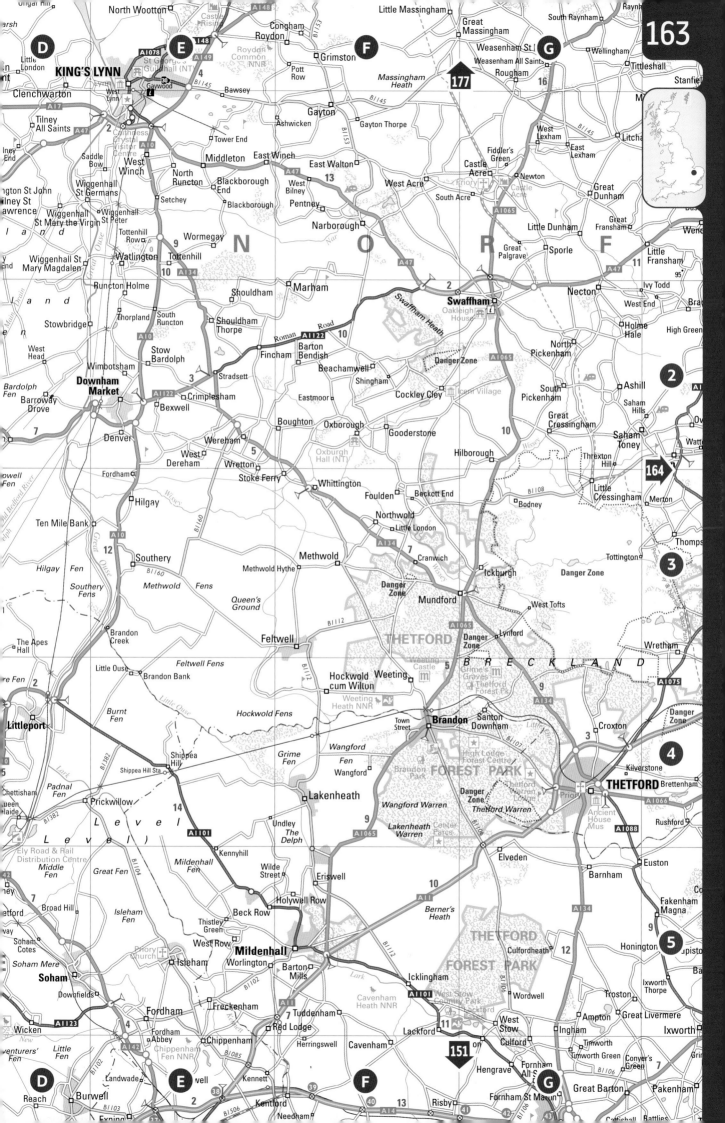

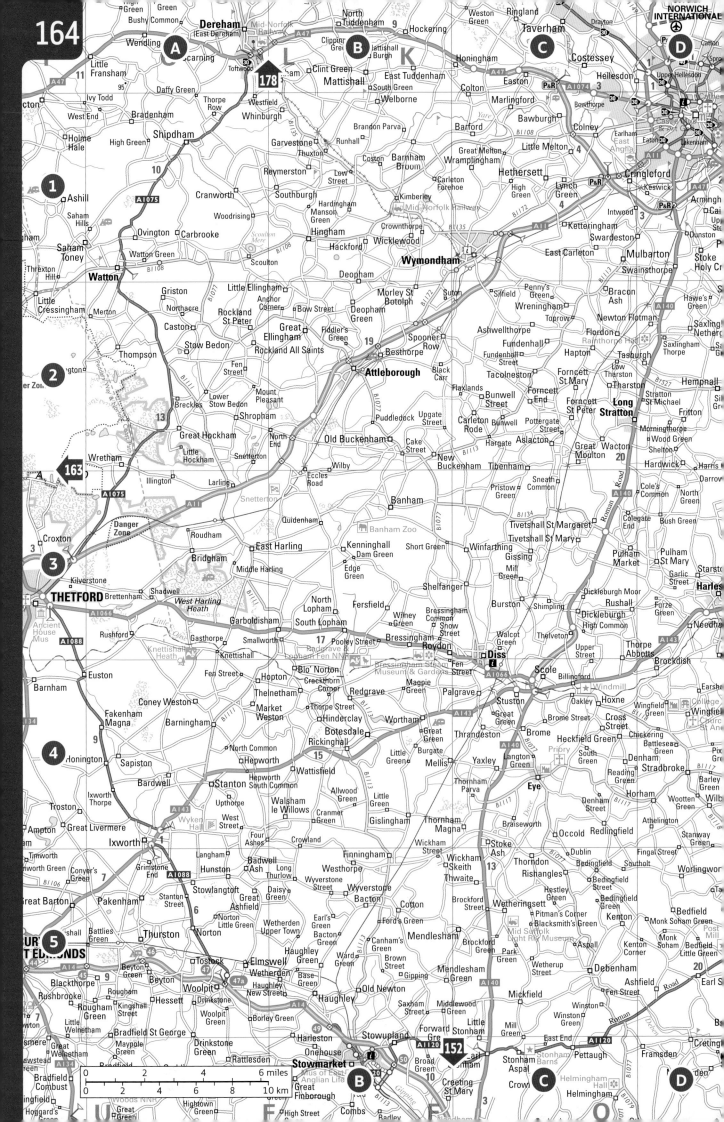

180

A B C D

C A E R N A R F O N

B A Y

Cymryan Bay

Burial Chamber

Rhosneigr

Llanfaelog

Pencarnisiog

A4080

Ty Croes Sta

Llanfaethlu

Cerrigceinwen

Langristi

Bethel

Trefdraeth

Barclodiad y Gawres Chambered Cairn

Aberffraw

Llangadwaladr

Hermon

Malltraeth

10

Bodorgan

A4080

Aberffraw Bay

Aberffraw Bay Heritage Coast

Malltraeth Sands

Newborough (Niwbwrch)

Pen-lôn

Dwyr

Malltraeth Bay

Llanddwyn Island

Llanddwyn Bay

Newborough Warren

Newborough Warren NNR

Regi

Abermenai Point

The Bar

Dinas Dinlle

Llandwrog

A499

Pontllyfni

Trwyn Maen Dylan

Aberdesach

10

Tai'n Lôn

Clynnog-fawr

Capeluchaf

Gyrn Goch

Bwlch Mawr 509

Bw de

Trefor

Gyrn Ddu 522

Llanaelhaearn

Pen-sarn

Trwyn y Gorlech

Yr Eifl 564

Carreg Ddu

Porth Dinllaen

Pistyll

Llithfaen

B4417

6

A499

Cefn-caer-Fe

St Cybi's Well

Morfa Nefyn

Nefyn

Llwyndyrys

Pencaenewydd

Llangybi

LLEYN PENINSULA

Groesffordd

Edern

B4412

Garn Boduan

Fron

B4354

Rhos-fawr

Llanarmon

Rhos-y-llan

Ceidio Fawr

Tan-y-graig

Hendre

7

Y Ffôr

B4354

Chwilo

Porth Ysgaden

Tudweiliog

Cors Geirch NNR

Bodfuan

A497

Llannor

Penarth Fawr Medieval

Afon

Dinas

Carn Fadryn

Efailnewydd

Abererch

Penchain S

Penllech

B4417

Garnfadryn 371

B4415

Denio

Wales Coast Path

Porth Colmon

Pen-y-Graig

Bryn-mawr

Llaniestyn

Rhyd-y-clafdy

1

Pwllheli

Pen-

Porth Colmon

Llangwnnadl

Sarn Meyllteyrn

Rhedyn

Penrhos

Carreg yr Imbill

T

Penrhyn Mawr

Ty-hen

Bryncroes

Botwnnog

B4413

Nanhoron

7

Y Gamlas

Lleyn Heritage Coast

Methlem

Llandegwning

Llanbedrog

Porth Oer

Rhydlios

Rhoshirwaun

Mynydd Rhiw 305

Plas-yn-Rhiw (NT)

Llangian

Mynytho

A499

Trwyn Llanbedrog

Capel Carmel

Rhiw

Llawr-y-dref

Abersoch

Braich Anelog

Mynydd Anelog 191

Anelog

B4413

Llanfaelrhys

Rhydolion

Llanengan

Sarn Bach

St Tudwal's Road

Lleyn Heritage Coast

Pwlldefaid

Aberdaron

Porth Neigwl (Hell's Mouth)

Bwlchtocyn

St Tudwal's Islands

Braich y Pwll

Uwchmynydd

Aberdaron Bay

Ynys Gwylan-fawr

Cilan Uchaf

Porth Ceiriad

Trwyn yr Wylfa

Pen y Cil

Bardsey Sound (Swnt Enlli)

Trwyn Cilan

Bardsey Island (Ynys Enlli)

St Mary's Abbey

Bardsey Island (Ynys Enlli) NNR

Lleyn Heritage Coast

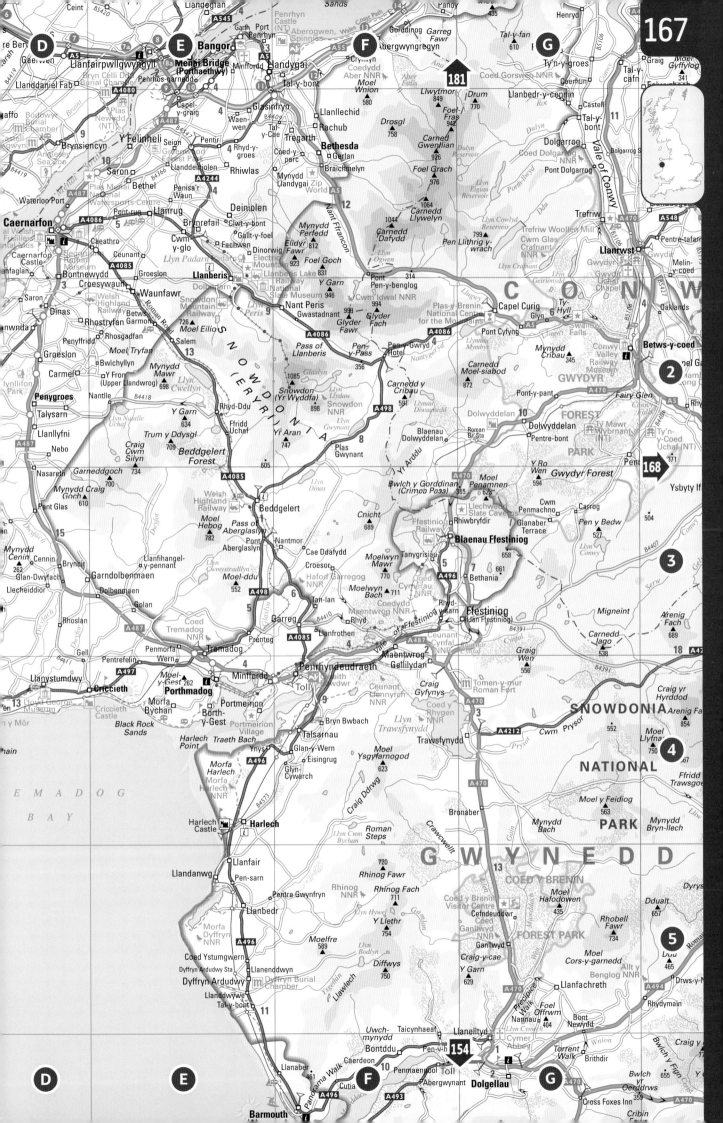

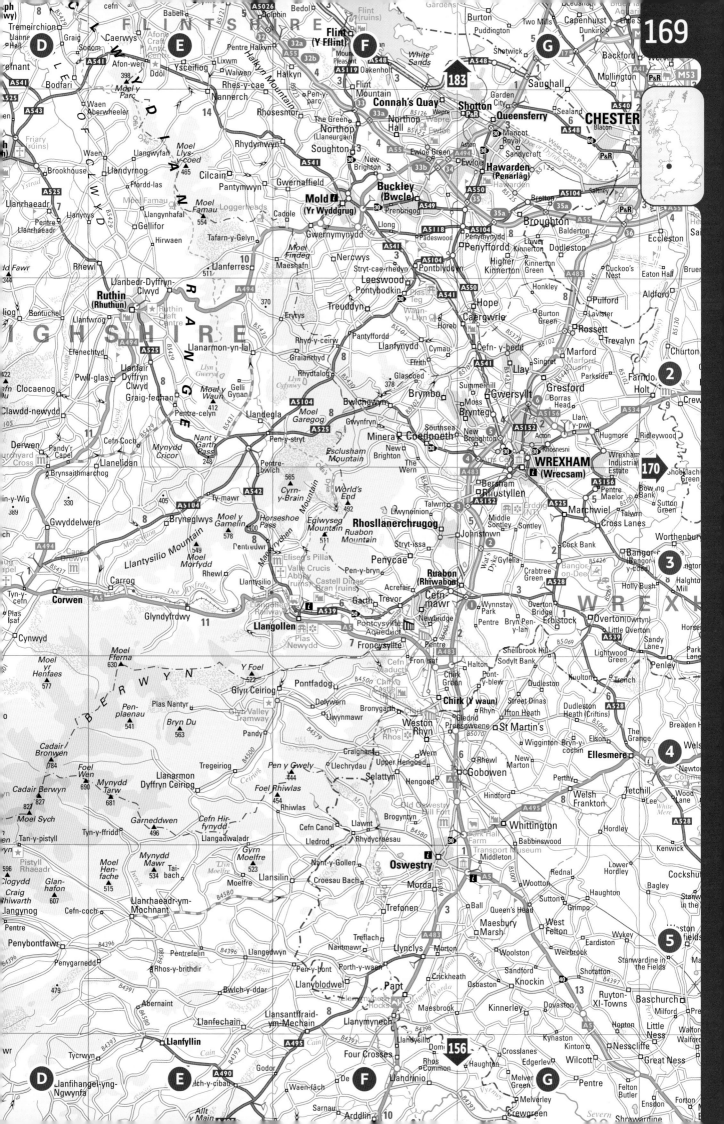

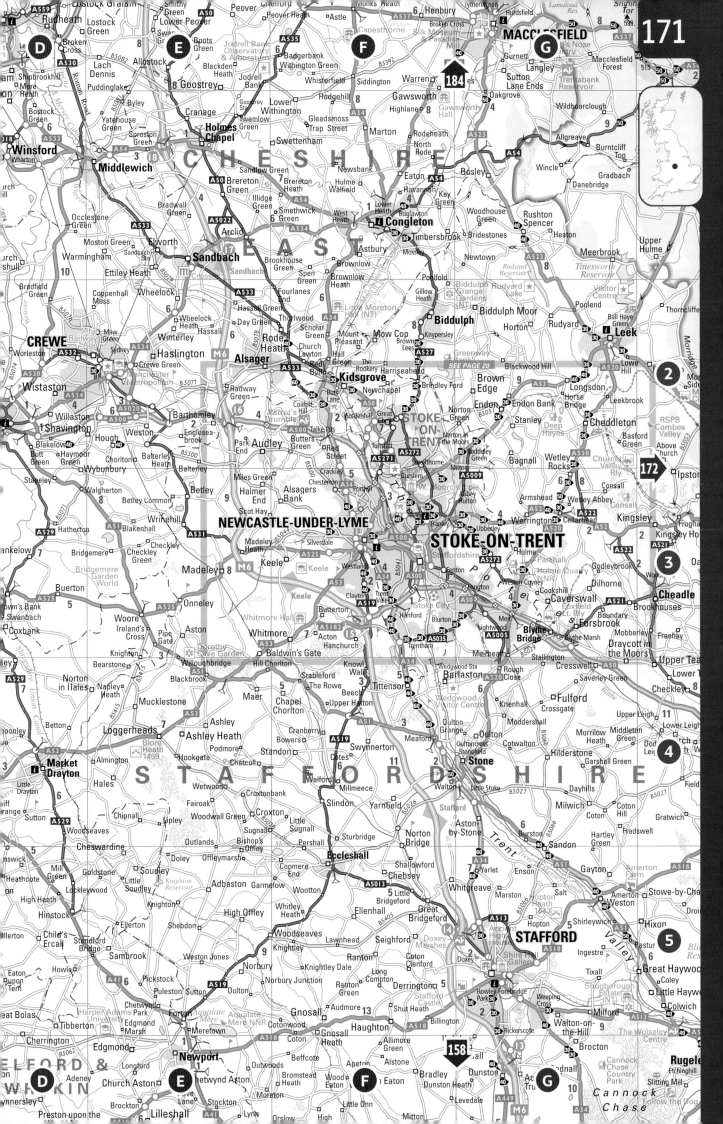

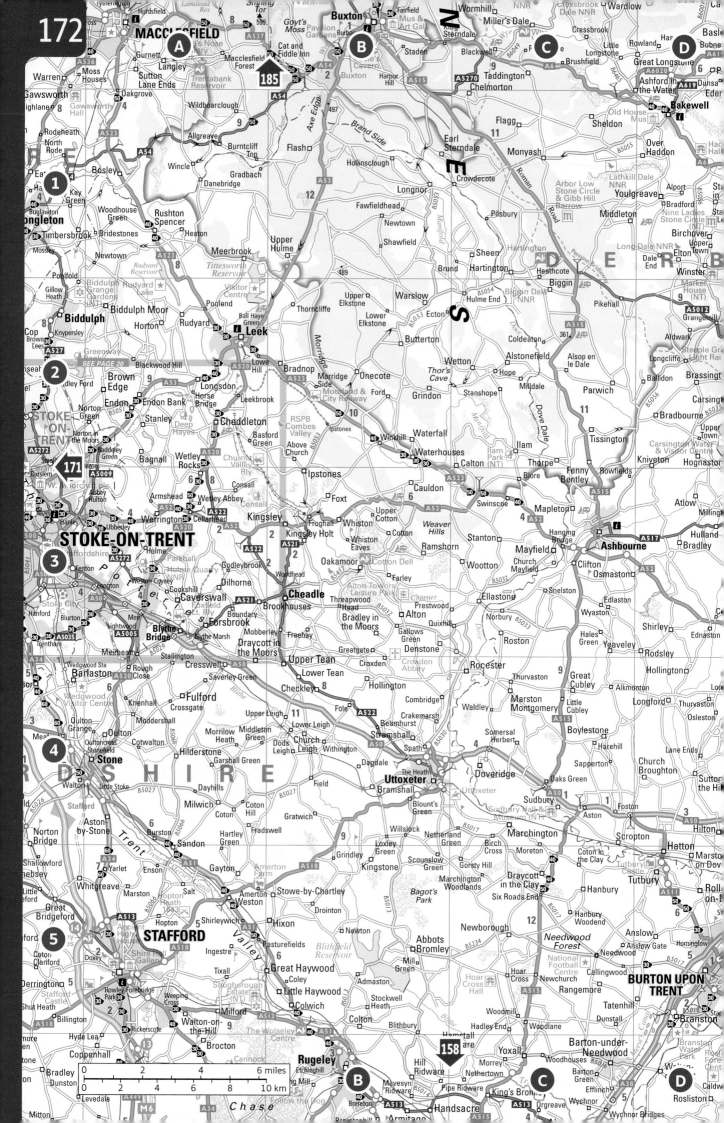

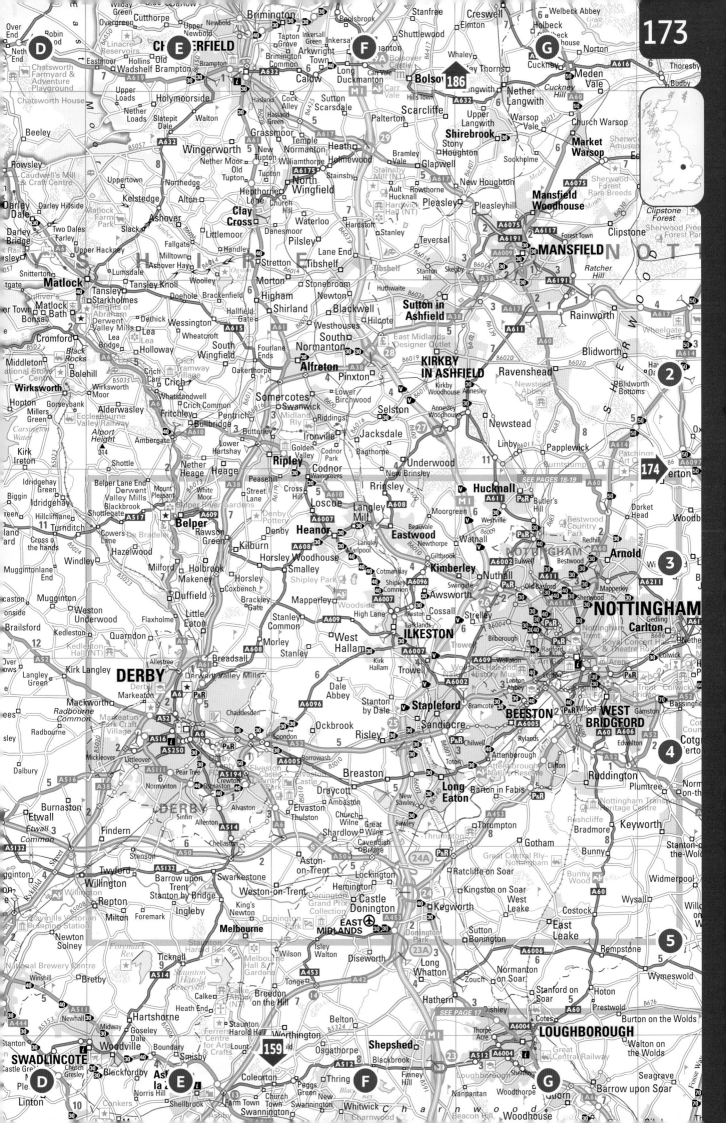

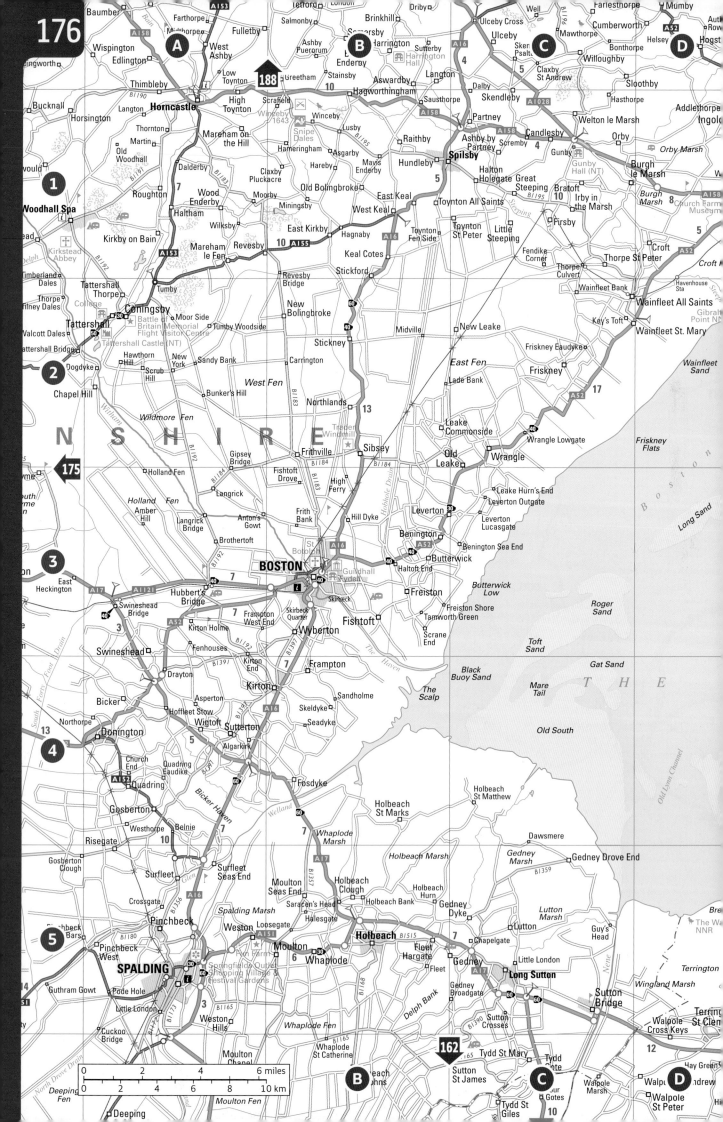

D Ct Leonards
189

E

F

G

2

Ingoldmells Point
Fantasy Island
Butlins Family Entertainment Resort
Skegness Water Leisure Park
Seathorne

Skegness
Natureland Seal Sanctuary

Seacroft

Gibraltar Point NNR
Gibraltar
Gibraltar Pt

Deeps

Lynn Deeps

WASH

Seal Sand

Peter Black Sand

Bulldog Sand

Sand

Little London
Clenchwarton

North Norfolk Heritage Coast
Scolt Head Island NNR
Holkham Bay

Brancaster Bay
Norton
Creek

Holme Dunes NNR

Brancaster Staithe
Burnham Deepdale
Burnham Norton
Burnham Overy Staithe
Burnham Overy Town

Holkham Bay NNR
Holkham

3
Wells-ne

Holme next the Sea
Thornham A149
Titchwell
Brancaster
17
Burnham Market
Burnham Thorpe

B1155
Holkham Hall

Wells & Walsingham Lt. Rly

B1105

Wight

Sea Life Centre
Hunstanton
Ringstead

Summerfield

Creake Abbey
North Creake

B1355

Egmere
Shireham Museum

Shrine of Our Lady of Walsingham

Norfolk Lavender

B1153

Stanhoe
South Creake

North Barsh
St Gil
East Barsham

4

Heacham
Eaton
Sedgeford

B1454
Docking

B1155

Barmer

Syderstone

West Barsham

Fring
Snettisham
13
Southgate

Bircham Newton
Great Bircham
Bircham Tofts
Bagthorpe

B1155

Sculthorpe

Langham Glass Ltd.

B1105

A149

Ingoldisthorpe
Shernborne

Tattersett
A148
Dunton
Shereford

178
Faken

Dersingham

Dersingham Bog NNR
Sandringham House

Anmer

Houghton Hall

Coxford
Tatterford

Hempton
Fakenl

Wolferton
Sandringham
West Newton

East Rudham

B1440

Trinity Hospital
St Mary Magdalene Chapel
Flitcham

New Houghton
West Rudham
17
Helhoughton
West Raynham

East Raynham

Colkirk

A1065

5

Castle Rising
Hillington

A148
Harpley
South Raynham

Whissonsett

North Wootton
Castle Rising

A148

Little Massingham
Great Massingham

West Raynham
South Raynham

Horningtoft
Godwick

Ongar Hill

Congham
Roydon

Roydon Common NNR

Weasenham St Peter
Wellingham
Tittleshall

A1078
South Wootton
A148
A149
St George's Guildhall (NT)

Grimston
Pott Row

Weasenham All Saints
Rougham
16

Stanfield

KING'S LYNN
90
Gaywood
4

Massingham Heath

163

Mileham

West Lynn

B1145
Bawsey

Gayton
Ashwicken
Thorpe

B1145

Litcham

Tilney
ints

Saddle Bow
West Winch
Middleton
East Winch
East Walton

B1153

Fiddler's Green

East Lexham

Castle Acre
Newton

A47

Bitterli

Longli

A17

Caithness Crystal Visitor Centre
2
A10

Tower End

A47

D

E

F

G

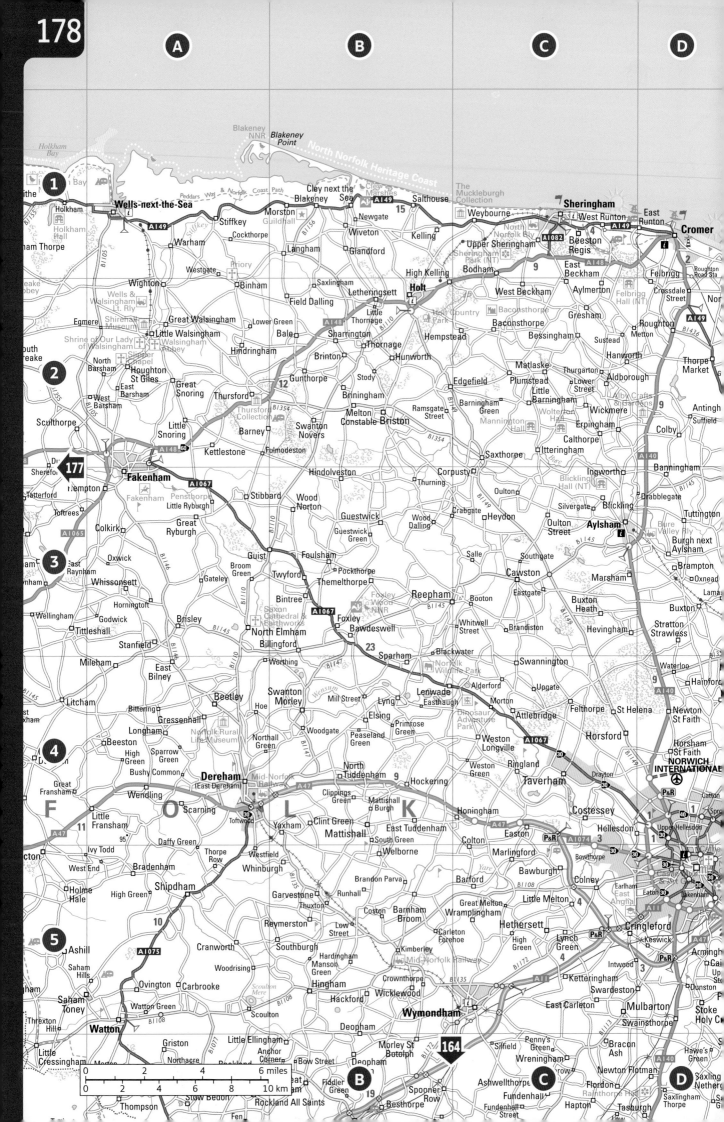

A   B   C   D

1

2

3

4

5

Holkham Bay   *Blakeney NNR* *Blakeney Point*   North Norfolk Heritage Coast

ithe   Bay   Holkham   Cley next the Sea   Salthouse   The Muckleburgh Collection   Sheringham   East Runton   Cromer

Wells-next-the-Sea   A149   Morston   Blakeney   Cley Marshes   15   Weybourne   West Runton   Beeston Regis

Holkham   Stiffkey   Newgate   Wiveton   Kelling   Upper Sheringham   East Beckham   Felbrigg

Holkham Hall   Warham   Cockthorpe   Langham   Glandford   High Kelling   Bodham   West Beckham   Aylmerton   Felbrigg Hall (NT)   Crossdale Street   Nor

ham Thorpe   Peddars Way & Norfolk Coast Path   A149   B1156   Saxlingham   Letheringsett   Holt   Bessingham   Gresham   Roughton   A149

Westgate   Binham   Field Dalling   Little Thornage   Holt Country Park   Baconsthorpe   Sustead   Metton   Thorpe Market

Priory   Lower Green   Bale   Sharrington   Thornage   Hempstead   Baconsthorpe   Matlaske   Thurgarton   Hanworth   Antingh   Suffield

Great Walsingham   Hindringham   Brinton   Hunworth   Edgefield   Barningham Green   Plumstead   Little Barningham   Lower Street   Aldborough   Colby

Little Walsingham   Houghton St Giles   Great Snoring   Thursford   12   Gunthorpe   Stody   Briston   Ramsgate Street   Mannington Hall   Wickmere   Erpingham   Colby   Suffield

Shrine of Our Lady of Walsingham   Slipper Chapel   Walsingham Abbey   Barney   Swanton Novers   Melton Constable   Briston   Barnham Green   Wolterton Hall   Calthorpe   Itteringham   Ingworth   Banningham

North Barsham   East Barsham   Little Snoring   Kettlestone   Fulmodeston   Hindolveston   Corpusty   Saxthorpe   Blickling Hall (NT)   Aylsham   Drabblegate   Tuttington   A140

Sculthorpe   West Barsham   177   Fakenham   A148   60   Thurning   Oulton   Heydon   Silvergate   Oulton Street   Blickling   Burgh next Aylsham   Oxnead   Lama

Dr   Shereford   Hempton   Fakenham   Penstborpe   Little Ryburgh   Stibbard   Wood Norton   Guestwick   Wood Dalling   Crabgate   Cawston   Southgate   Brampton

Tatterford   A1065   Colkirk   Great Ryburgh   A1067   Guist   Foulsham   Guestwick Green   Salle   Eastgate   Buxton   Marsham   Buxton

Toftrees   East Raynham   Oxwick   Gateley   Twyford   Pockthorpe   Themelthorpe   Reepham   Booton   Buxton Heath   Hevingham   Stratton Strawless

nham   A1065   Whissonsett   Horningtoft   Broom Green   Bintree   Foxley   Bawdeswell   B1145   Whitwell Street   Brandiston   Waterloo   Hainfor

Wellingham   Godwick   Brisley   Saxon Cathedral & Earthworks   23   Sparham   Blackwater   Swannington   Upgate   A140

Tittleshall   Stanfield   North Elmham   Billingford   Worthing   Mill Street   Lyng   Lenwade   Norfolk Wildlife Park   Alderford   Felthorpe   St Helena   Newton St Faith

Mileham   East Bilney   Beetley   Hoe   Swanton Morley   Elsing   Easthaugh   Morton   Attlebridge   Horsford   Horsham St Faith

Litcham   Bittering   Gressenhall   Northall Green   Woodgate   Peaseland Green   Primrose Green   Dinosaur Adventure Park   Weston Longville   Ringland   NORWICH INTERNATIONAL

Longham   Beeston   Sparrow Green   Norfolk Rural Life Museum   North Tuddenham   Weston Green   Taverham   Drayton   P&R   Catton

High Green   Bushy Common   Dereham (East Dereham)   Mid-Norfolk Railway   Clippings Green   Hockering   Honingham   Costessey   Hellesdon   Upper Hellesdon   Spr

Great Fransham   Wendling   Scarning   Toftwood   Mattishall Burgh   East Tuddenham   A47   Easton   P&R   A1074   Bowthorpe   40

11   Little Fransham   95   Yaxham   Clint Green   Mattishall   South Green   Colton   Marlingford   Colney   Earlham East Anglia   Eaton   Cringleford

ton   Ivy Todd   Daffy Green   Thorpe Row   Westfield   Whinburgh   Welborne   Bawburgh   A11   A

West End   Bradenham   Shipdham   Brandon Parva   Barford   Great Melton   Little Melton   Hethersett   Colney   Keswick   Arming

Holme Hale   High Green   Garveston   Runhall   Barnham Broom   Wramplingham   High Green   Lynch Green   Intwood   Cai   Up

10   Thuxton   Coston   Carleton Forehoe   Kimberley   Mid-Norfolk Railway   P&R   Swardeston   Dunston

Ashill   A1075   Cranworth   Reymerston   Low Street   Southburgh   Hardingham   Manson Green   Hingham   Wicklewood   Crownthorpe   A11   Ketteringham   East Carleton   Mulbarton   Stoke Holy

Saham Hills   Ovington   Woodrising   Hackford   Wymondham   Bracon Ash   Swainsthorpe

Saham Toney   Carbrooke   Scoulton Mere   Deopham   164   Silfield   Penny's Green   Wreningham   Newton Flotman   Hawe's Green

Threxton Hill   Watton Green   B1108   Griston   Little Ellingham   Anchor Corner   Bow Street   Morley St Botolph   Deopham   Ashwellthorpe   Flordon   Rainthorpe Hall   A140   Saxlingham Nether

Watton   Scoulton   Hingham   Fiddler's Green   Spooner Row   Fundenhall   Fundenhall Street   Hapton   Saxlingham Thorpe

Little Cressingham   Moro   Northacre   Rockland   19   Besthorpe   Row   Hapton   Tasburgh   D

Thompson   Stow Bedon   Rockland All Saints   Fen   Thompson   B   C   D

F   O   L   K

0   2   4   6 miles
0   2   4   6   8   10 km

Ⓐ   Ⓑ   Ⓒ   Ⓓ

1

2

3

The Skerries

Middle Mouse

West Mouse

North Anglesey Heritage Coast

Porth Wen Bay

Point Lynas

North Anglesey Heritage Coast

Carmel Head

Cemaes Bay

Llanbadrig
Llanbadrig

Bull Bay (Porth Llechog)

Ynys Dulas

Cemlyn Bay

Cemaes

Neuadd

Burwen

Amlwch
Amlwch Port

Llaneilian

Cemlyn

Tregele

Llanfechell

Bodewryd

Pengorffwysfa

Pen-y-sarn

Nebo

Llanfairynghornwy

Mynydd mechell

Parys Mountain

B5111

A5025

Dulas

Dulas Bay

Lligwy Bay

Capel Lligwy

Llanrhyddlad

Carreglefn

Rhos-goch

Rhos-y-bol

8

Llaneuddog

Rhyd-wyn

Llanflewyn

Llanbabo

City Dulas

Brynrefail

Din Lligwy

Rhoslligwy

Moelfre

4

HOLYHEAD BAY

Church Bay

17

Llanfaethlu

Gwredog

Ceidio

Capel Parc

Lligwy Burial Chamber

A5108

Llanallgo

Tyn-y-gongl

ISLE OF

A5025

Dublin .... hours 1¼-3¼

North Stack

Holyhead Mountain 220 ▲

Holyhead (Caergybi)

Roman Fort Salt Island

Llanddeusant

Windmill

Elim

Llannerch-y-medd

Bachau

Llandyfrydog

Maenaddwyn

Marian-glas

Benllech

South Stack

Llaingoch

Kingsland

Penrhos

Llanfwrog

Stryd y Facsen

Llanfigael

Llantrisant

ANGLESEY

Bryn-teg

Red Wharf (Traeth Co

Hut Circles

Standing Stones

Penrhyn Mawr

Burial Chambers

A5

Llanfachraeth

Llanynghenedl

Bodedern

B5109

Treewheler Standing Stone

Pen-llyn

Llyn Llywenan

Burial Chambers

Llechcynfarwy

ANGLESEY

Capel Coch

Carmel

Cors Erddreiniog NNR

Llanbedrgoch

Cors Goch

Myr Llwy

Holyhead Mountain Heritage Coast

Trearddur

Valley (Y Fali)

9

Caergeiliog

Trefor

Llangwyllog

Tregaian

Llanddyfnan

Pentreath

10

Four Mile Bridge

3

Bryngwran

B5112

(YNYS MÔN)

Llynfaes

A5025

HOLY ISLAND

Bodior

Llanfihangel-yn-Nhwyn

A5

Gwalchmai

Bodffordd

Rhosmeirch

Talwrn

Cors Bodeilio NNR

Rhoscolyn

Llanfair-yn-neubwll

Capel Gwyn

5

Heneglwys

Llangefni

Ceint

Penmynydd

Tywyn Trewan

6

A55

Rhostrehwfa

7

B5420

Cymyran Bay

A4080

3

Cerrigceinwen

Llangristiolus

8

Rhosneigr

Newydd Burial Chamber

Pencarnisiog

Burial Chamber

7

Llanfairpwllgwyngyll

5

Llanfaelog

Ty Croes

Capel Mawr

Pentre Berw

A5

7.5

Menai B (Porthaet

Barclodiad y Gawres Chambered Cairn

Ty Croes Sta

Bethel

B4422

Gaerwen

2

Trefdraeth

Cefni

Malltraeth Marsh

Llanddaniel Fab

Bryn Celli Burial Chamber

Plas Newydd (NT)

166

Aberffraw

Llangadwaladr

10

Heri

Malltraeth

Llangaffo

B4419

Bodowyr Burial Chamber

9

Y Felin

Greenwood Forest Park

Aberffraw Bay Heritage Coast

Aberffraw b

Bodorgan

A4080

Brynsiencyn

Anglesey Sea Zoo

Sej

Saron

Dwyran

Newborough

Y

Ⓑ   Ⓒ   Ⓓ

0 — 2 — 4 — 6 miles
0 — 2 — 4 — 6 — 8 — 10 km

D   E   F   G

182

2

3

4

Great Orme
Heritage Coast
Great Ormes Head   Great Orme
Cabin   Venue
Lift   Cymru
Great Orme
Country Park   Toll   Llandudno   Little Ormes Head
Gogarth   B5115   Penrhyn-side
Great Orme   Penrhyn Bay (Bae Penrhyn)
Tramway   A546   4   Rhos-on-Sea
Conwy   Glanwydden
St Seiriol's   Sands
Well   Degannwy   Colwyn Bay
Mariandyrys   CONWY   5   A470   20   (Bae Colwyn)   Abergele
Glan-yr-afon   Caim   Penmon   Aberconwy House (NT)   17   Llandudno   19   21   22   10   Roads
Denmon Priory   BAY   Junction   Mochdre   23
Llanddona   Llangoed   (ruins)   Dutchman   Conwy i   18   A547   Welsh   Llanddulas
Llan-faes   Bank   Dwygyfylchi   16a   Conwy Castle   Mountain Zoo   A547 Aber
Beaumaris   Penmaenmawr   16   Llansanffraid   Bryn-y-maen   Old   Penmaen-   Llysfaen
Castle   15a   Capelulo   Glan Conwy   Colwyn   Rhos   Rhyd-y-foe
Beaumaris   Penmaen   362   Suspension   Llanelian-
(Biwmares)   15   Foel Lus   Bridge (NT)   336   yn-Rhos   Dolwen
Llandegfan   4   A545   Llanfairfechan   Moelfre   Pentrefelin   Mynydd   324   Bet-
Lavan   14   Nant-y-Pandy   435   Henryd   B5106   Llanelian   Dawn   Moelfre Uchaf   yn-Rhos
Sands   Goroddinog   Garreg   Tal-y-fan   Rowen   Moel   Trofarth   396   5
Bangor   Garth Port   Fawr   610   Gyffylog   Mynydd
Penrhyn   Aberogwen   Abergwyngregyn   Ty'n-y-groes   Graig   341   Branar   Llanfair Talhaiarn
A5   Spinnies   Crymlyn   Caerhun   Tal-y-   Gell   A548
A4087   Llandygai   Coedydd   cafn   Eglwysbach   Pentre
Minffordd   12   Tal-y-bont   Aber   A470   Per   11   168   Mwdwl   Isaf
Penrhos-garnedd   Moel   NNR   Eithin   Rhos-
Glasinfryn   Wnion   Drum   Llanbedr-y-cennin   Castell   389   y-mawn
3   Llanllechid   580   Aber   770   Tal-y-bont   Gell   Wenlli
Waen   Rachub   Falls   849   Llwytmor   Dolgarrog Sta
Rhyd-   Tal-   Tregarth   Drosgl   Foel-Fras   -rrog   Vale of   B5382
Pentir   y-Cae   758   942   Pont Dolgarrog   12
Bethesda   Gerlan   Carned Gwenllian
Coed-y-parc   926   Coed Dolgarrog
Rhiwlas   Braichmelyn   Dulyn   SNOWDONIA
Res

Puffin Island
(Priestholm)

D   E   F   G
4   A4244
4

A5
A5

A   B   C   D

1

2

181

Birkenhead to   hours
Belfast.....8
Douglas.....4¼ (Nov-March)
Liverpool to   hours
Douglas......2¾ (March-Oct)
Dublin.....8

3

LIVERPOOL

BAY

West
Hoyle
Bank

East
Hoyle
Bank

Meols
Sta   A553

Hoylake
Royal
Liverpool   Manor Road Sta
Hoylake Sta
West
Red   Kirby
Rocks   Sta   Grange
Marsh
Frankby

Hilbre Island

West Kirby

Caldy   Ir
B5140
A540

Thurstaston

4

*Dawpool
Bank*

Point of
Ayr

Talacre   Llwyndy

Prestatyn
Sands
Holiday
Centre   *Welsh Channel*   *Mostyn Bank*

Prestatyn   Gronant   Gwespyr   Kynnongroyw
Sky   Efrith
Tower   A548   Pen-y-ffordd
Rhyl   A547   Llanasa   Gyrn
SeaQuarium   Sun Centre   Meliden   Gwaenysgor   Mostyn   *Mostyn Quay*
(Gallt Melyd)   A548
B5119   Tan-yr-   Trelogan   Glan-y-don   10
Kinmel Bay   allt   Gop   Mostyn
(Bae Cinmel)   Bodrhyddan   Hill 8   Axton
Hall   2   Trelawnyd   Whitford   Llannerch-y-Môr   40
A525   (Chwitffordd)   *Holywell Bank*
vyn Bay   *Abergele*   Wales Coast Path   Ochr-   Maen   Greenfield Valley
(Colwyn)   *Roads*   **Rhuddlan**   Dyserth   y-foel   Achwyfaen   Greenfield
22   10   Plas   5   A5151   Lloc   3   (Maes-Glas)
23   Towyn   6   Marian   Basingwerk
Llanddulas   Pensarn   Rhuddlan   3   Cwm   Roman   Gorsedd   A5026   Carmel   Abbey   Whelston
A547   Abergele   23a   A547   Roman   St Winefrid's Holy Well & Cha
Penmaen   24   A55   8   Road   Pantasaph   2   Walwen
Rhôs   Rhyd-y-foel   Pengwern   B5429   Pantasaph   Friary   Holywell (Treffynnon)   Bagillt
Llysfaen   St George   24a   A525   27a   28   Rhuallt   29   31   Pantasaph   A5026   Bagillt   Bank
Iwen   Bodelwyddan   25   26   27   Rhuallt   30   Calcoed   Brynford   Bedol
A548   6   **St Asaph**   Pen-y-   Babell   Dolphin   A548
Betws-   Moelfre Isaf   (Llanelwy)   cefn   Pentre Halkyn   32a   **Flint**
yn-Rhos   317   Tremeirchion   FLINTSHIRE   Lixwm   (Y Fflint)   A55
Dawn   Mynydd   Caerwys   Walwen   Mount Pleasant   32b
324   Bodrochwyn   Graig   Ddôl   Ysceifiog   Halkyn   A5119
Moelfre Uchaf   396   Llannerch   Afon-wen   Rhes-y-cae   4   3
Mynydd   Llannefydd   Hall   Sodom   A541   Moel   Nannerch   Pen-y-
Branar   Plas-yn-Cefn   Bodfari   y Parc   Afonwen   Rhosesmor   parc
Bont-newydd   398   Craft and   The Green
Trefnant   A541   Antique   14   thorp
Llanfair Talhaiarn   A525   Centre   A541
A548   Green   VALE OF CLWYD   168   Rhydymwyn   Soughton
Cefn   A543   Olds   A541
Berain   Henllan   Waen   Moel   Cilcain
A544   Llangwyfan   Llys-y-coed
B5382   Denbigh   Friary   465
Llansannan   (Dinbych)   (ruins)   Llandyrnog
A543

0   2   4   6 miles
0   2   4   6   8   10 km

B   C   D

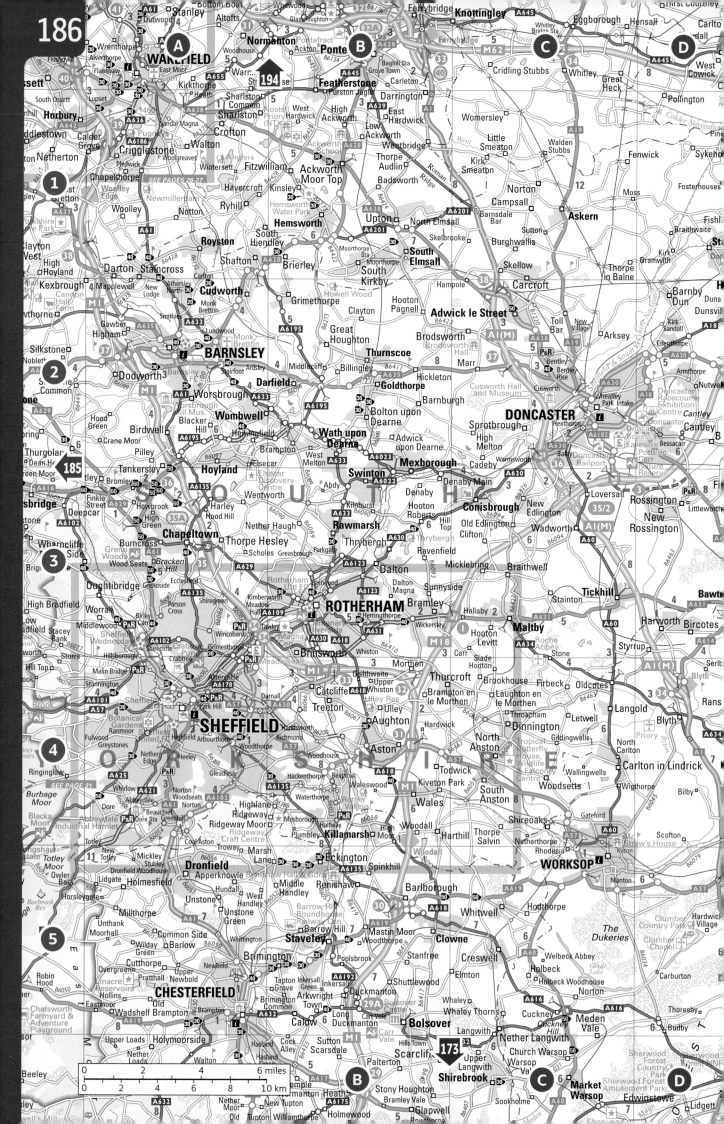

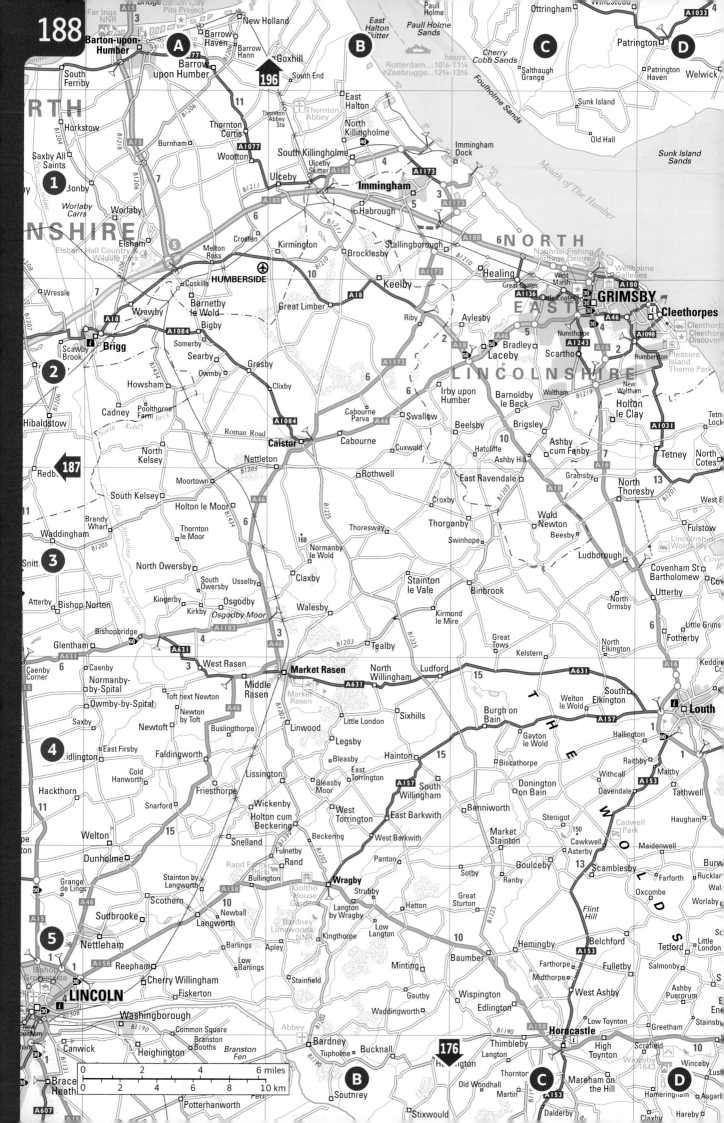

D **E** **F** **G**

Holmpton
Out Newton
197
Weeton
Skeffling
Easington

Skeffling
Clays

Kilnsea
Spurn Heritage
Coast

Kilnsea
Clays

Spurn NNR
Spurn Point
Nature Reserve

Spurn
Head
Spurn Head

Coast Light Rly
entre

2

Marshchapel
Donna Nook
Eskham
Donna Nook
Wragholme
Grainthorpe
Meals
North Somercotes
Donna Nook NNR
Ludney
Church End
Skidbrooke North End
Conisholme
South Somercotes
A1031
Saltfleet
ham St Mary
arburgh
South Somercotes Fen Houses
Skidbrooke
Alvingham
North Cockerington
Saltfleetby St Clements
ington
South Cockerington
Saltfleetby All Saints
12
Saltfleetby - Theddlethorpe NNR

3

Grimoldby
Manby
B1200
Saltfleetby St Peter
Theddlethorpe St Helen
newton
Little Carlton
Great Carlton
Theddlethorpe All Saints
37
Legbourne
North Reston
Gayton le Marsh
A1031
Little Cawthorpe
South Reston
Strubby
Mablethorpe
11
Withern
A157
Thorpe
4 Trusthorpe
Muckton
Authorpe
Tothill
3
A52
Woodthorpe
Maltby le Marsh
Sutton on Sea
Beesby
Belleau
Claythorpe
Hagnaby
Sutton le Marsh
Sandilands
White Pit
Saleby
6
Hannah
Ketsby
Swaby
Greenfield
Markby
A52
South Thoresby
A1104
A1111
Asserby
Ormsby
Aby
Ailby
Thoresthorpe
The Grange
5
Calceby
Rigsby
Bilsby
Thurlby
Huttoft
Anderby Creek
Driby
Haugh
Alford
B1449
Brinkhill
3
Bilsby Field
Anderby
ersby
Well
Farlesthorpe
Mumby
Harrington
A1104
Ulceby Cross
Cumberworth
Authorpe Row
Aswardby
Ulceby
Mawthorpe
Helsey
Hogsthorpe
Chapel St Leonards
gworthingham
4
Skendleby Psalter
Bonthorpe
Langton
Claxby St Andrew
Willoughby
Dalby
5
10
Sausthorpe
Skendleby
A1028
Welton le Marsh
Hasthorpe
Sloothby
Partney
A52
177
nby
Addlethorpe
Ingoldmells
Hundleby
1
A16
Ingoldmells Point
Fantasy Island
Spilsby
Scremby
Ashby by Partney
Gunby
Orby
Butlins Family Entertainment Resort
Halton
Gunby Hall (NT)
Orby Marsh
Skegness Water Leisure Park
nderby
Wintho
Seathorne

D **E** **F** **G**

4

5

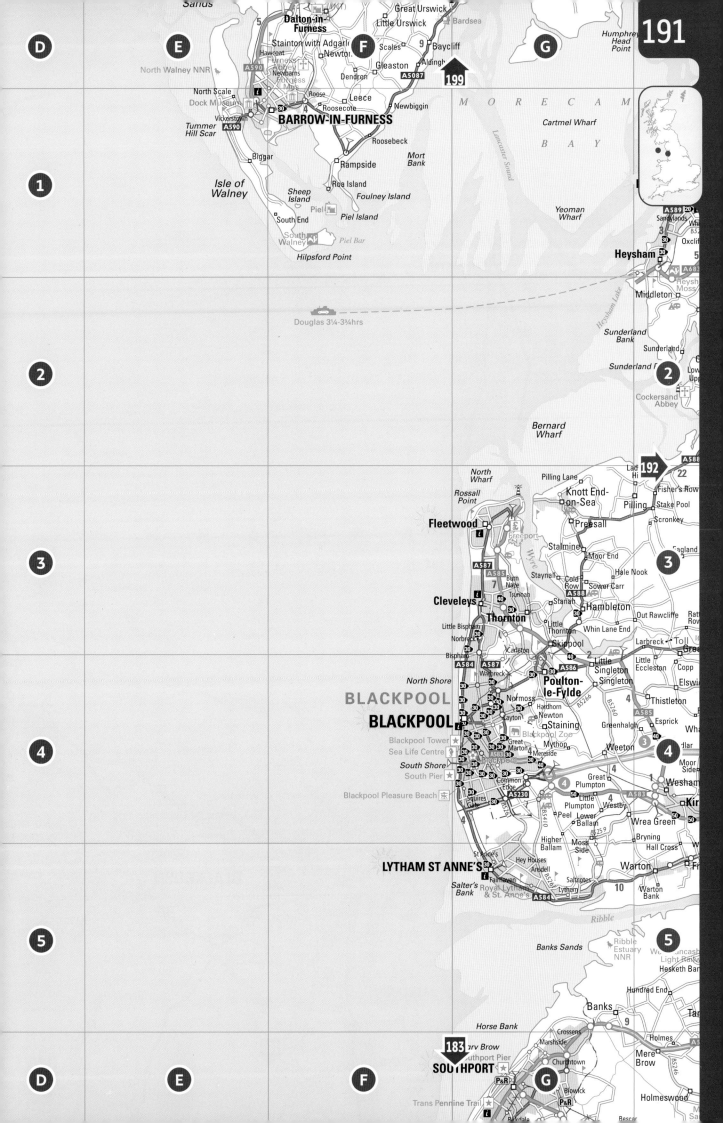

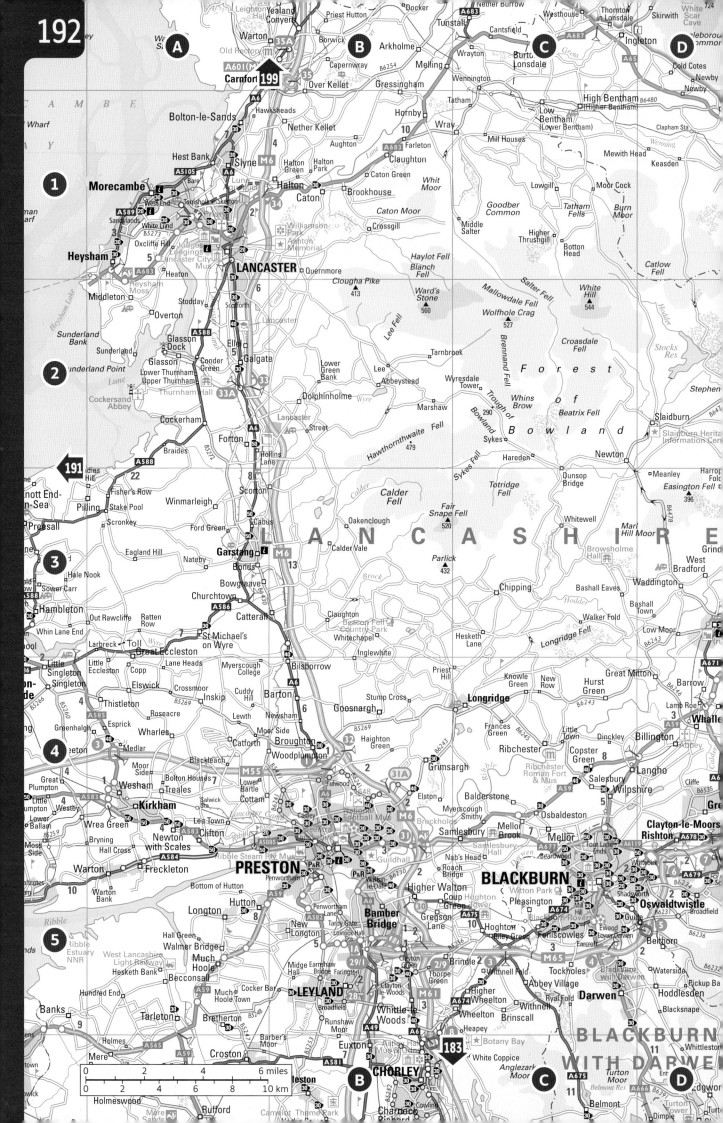

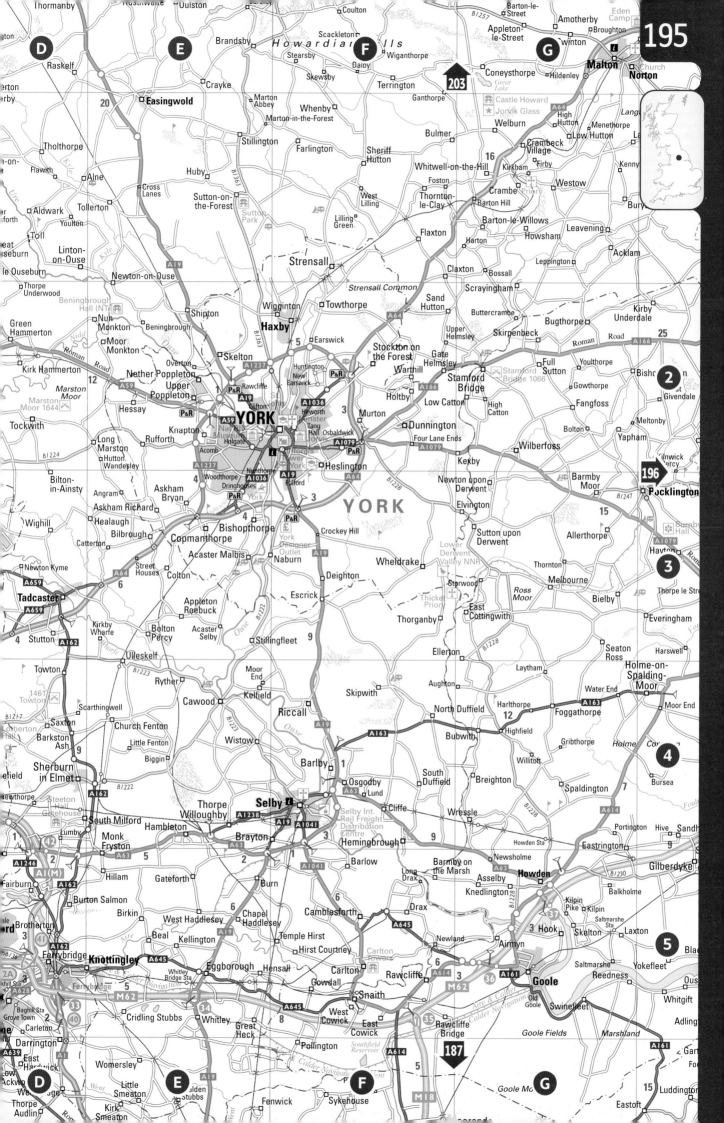

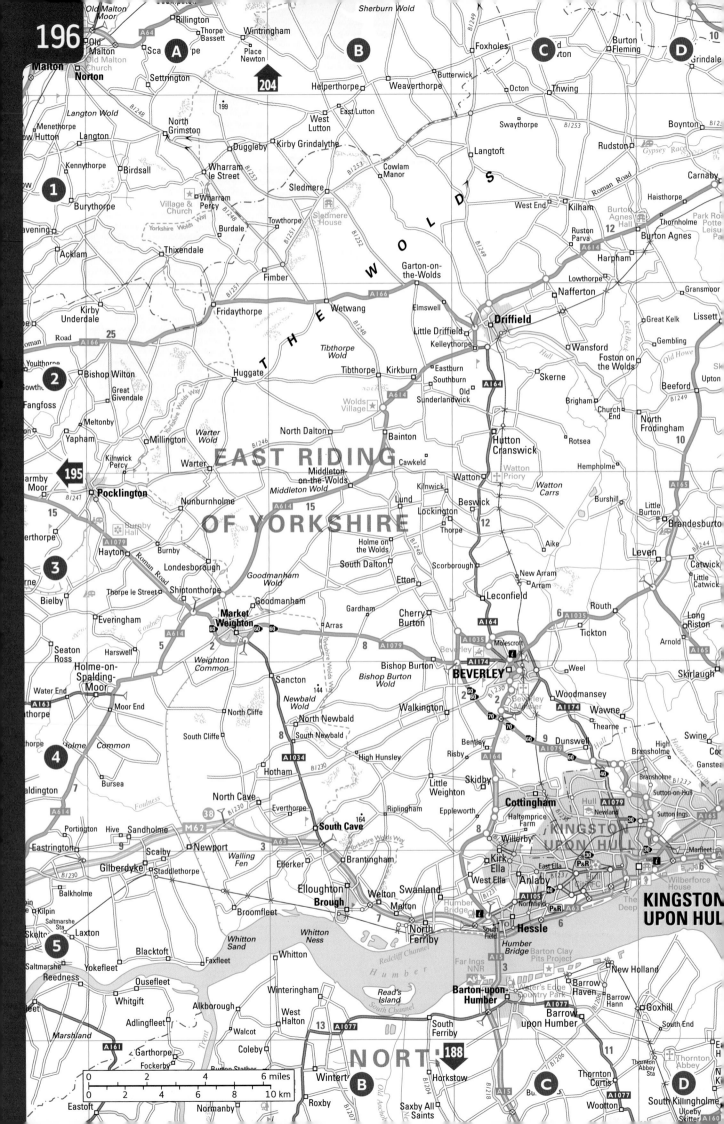

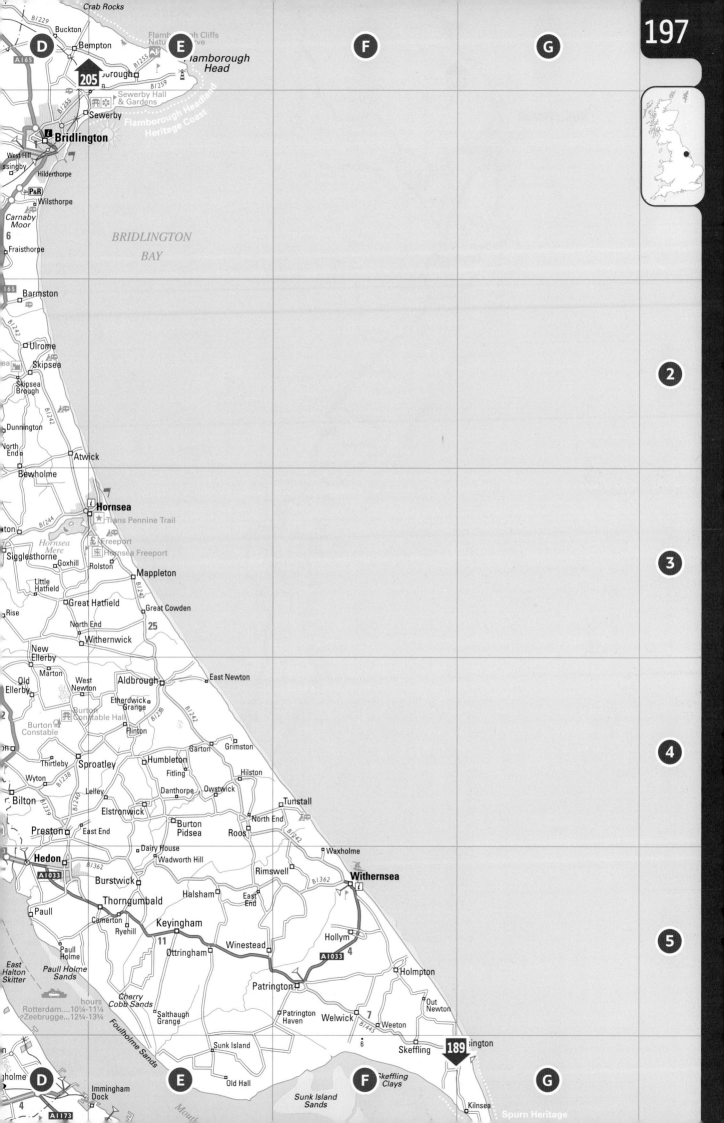

D **E** **F** **G**

Crab Rocks
B1229
Buckton
Bempton
Flamborough Cliffs
Nature Reserve
B1255
Flamborough
Head
borough
205
B1259
Sewerby Hall
& Gardens
B1255
Sewerby
Flamborough Headland
Heritage Coast
Bridlington
West Hill
ssingby
Hilderthorpe
P&R
Wilsthorpe
Carnaby
Moor
6
165
Fraisthorpe

BRIDLINGTON
BAY

Barmston
B1242
Ulrome
Skipsea
Skipsea
Brough
B1242
Dunnington
North
End
Atwick
Bewholme

Hornsea
Trans Pennine Trail
B1244
Hornsea
Mere
Freeport
Hornsea Freeport
Sigglesthorne
Goxhill
Rolston
Mappleton
Little
Hatfield
B1242
Great Hatfield
Great Cowden
Rise
North End
25
Withernwick
New
Ellerby
Marton
West
Newton
Aldbrough
East Newton
Old
Ellerby
Etherdwick
Grange
B1238
Burton
Constable Hall
B1242
Burton
Constable
Flinton
Thirtleby
Sproatley
Humbleton
Garton
Grimston
Wyton
B1238
Fitling
Hilston
Lelley
Danthorpe
Owstwick
Bilton
B1239
B1220
Elstronwick
Tunstall
Preston
East End
Burton
Pidsea
Roos
North End
B1242
Dairy House
Waxholme
Hedon
Wadworth Hill
B1362
Rimswell
A1033
Burstwick
B1362
Withernsea
Halsham
East
End
Paull
Thorngumbald
Hollym
Camerton
Keyingham
Ryehill
11
Winestead
A1033
4
Ottringham
Paull
Holme
East
Halton
Skitter
Holmpton
Paull Holme
Sands
hours
Patrington
Cherry
Cobb Sands
Salthaugh
Grange
Patrington
Haven
Welwick
7
Weeton
Rotterdam....10¼-11¼
Zeebrugge...12¾-13¾
Foulholme Sands
Sunk Island
B1445
6
Skeffling
189
ington
holme
Immingham
Dock
Old Hall
Skeffling
Clays
Sunk Island
Sands
Kilnsea
A1173
4
Mouth
Spurn Heritage

D **E** **F** **G**

2

3

4

5

A   B   C   D

208   209

1   2   3   4   5

WHITEHAVEN

The Beacon

Saltom Bay

St Bees Head

St. Bees Head Heritage Coast

Parton
Distington
Branthwaite
Ullock   A5086
Mockerkin
Gilgar
Pica
Moresby
Moresby Parks
Arlecdon
Asby
Lamplugh
Loweswater
Loweswater
Whinlatter Forest
Hopegill Head   790
Grisedale Pike
Braithwaite
Stair
Brandelhow
Causey Pike
Brackenthwaite Fell
Grasmoor   851

Rowrah
High Leys NNR
Kirkland
Croasdale
Blake Fell   572
Loweswater Fell
Crummock Water
B5289
Scale Force
Derwent Fells
Borro (N
Gran

Frizington
A5086
Henbury
Mirehouse
Hensingham
Sandwith
Cleator Moor
Moor Row
Wath Brow
Cleator
Bigrigg
Ennerdale Bridge
Ennerdale Water
Ennerdale Fell
Great Borne   616
Red Pike   755
Buttermere (NT)
High Stile   806
Scarth Gap Pass
Pillar
Robinson   737
Gatesgarth
Dale Head   754
Seatoller
Honister Pass
Little Town
C
Seathwaite
Honister Crag   358

St Bees
Rottington
St Bees Head
Egremont
How Man
Wilton
Lank Rigg   541
Hay Stacks
Haycock   797
Caw Fell   733
Steeple   892
Black Sail Pass   841
Kirk Fell   802
Great Gable   899
Green Gable   910
Allen Crags   785
Sty Head
Great End
Taylorgill Force
Glara
78

Snellings
Thornhill
Haile
Coulderton
Middletown
Nethertown
Beckermet
Braystones Sta
Sellafield Visitors Centre
Calder Bridge
Calder Abbey
Worm Gill
Calder
Nether
Seatallan   692
Wasdale Head
Lingmell
Scafell Pike   978
Esk Hause   759
Esk   902
Scafell   964
Bow
N
81
Crin
Cra

Ponsonby
Sellafield
Sellafield Sta
B5345
Gosforth
Wellington
Nether Wasdale
Copeland Forest
Wast Water
The Screes
Burnmoor Tarn
Eskdale Fell
Whin Rigg   535
Hardknott Roman Fort
Hardknott Pass

A595
Seascale
Holmrook
Drigg
Gubbergill
Santon Bridge
Eskdale Green
Beckfoot
Boot
Eskdale
Harter Fell   649
393
Seathw

Kokoarrah
Saltcoats
Ravenglass
Ravenglass & Eskdale Railway Mus
23
Ravenglass & Eskdale Railway
Roman Bath House
Devoke Water
Stanley Force

Waberthwaite
Broad Oak
Muncaster Castle World Owl Trust
Ulpha Fell
Woodend
Hall Dunnerdale
Caw   529
Seathwaite

Newbiggin
Lane End
Stainton Fell
Whitfell   573
Bigert Mire
Ulpha
Hoses

Stub Place
Corney
Prior Park
Ulpha Park
Broughton Mills
A59
6

Selker Bay
Hycemoor
Hyton
Bootle
Bootle Fell
Stoneside Hill   422
Bank End
Duddon Bridge
Lower Hawthw
Broughton in Fu
Ros

Annaside
A595
White Combe   417
The Green
Broadgate
Lady Hall
Hallthwaites
A595
5
Duddon Mo
Foxfield
Gri

Whitbeck
Black Combe   600
Black Combe   3
Arnaby
Green Road Sta
Strands
The Hill
Kirkby-in-Furness
4
Wall End
Beck Side

Whicham
A5093
Soutergate
8

Silecroft
Kirksanton
Millom
Millom Folk Mus
Millom
3
Borwick Rails
Steel Green
Moor Side
Askam in Furness
Ireleth
Marton
Pen
Lindal Furnes

Haverigg
Haverigg Point

Duddon Sands
Sandscale Haws NNR
South Lakes Wild Animal Park
Dalto Furne
Furness Abbey
Stainton with Adgarley
Hawcoat
Newton
5

North Walney NNR
A590
Newbarns
Furness Mus
North Scale
Dock Museum
BARROW-IN-FU
Tummer Hill Scar
A590
Roose
Roosecote
Vickerstown

Biggar

191

0   2   4   6 miles
0   2   4   6   8   10 km

B   C   D

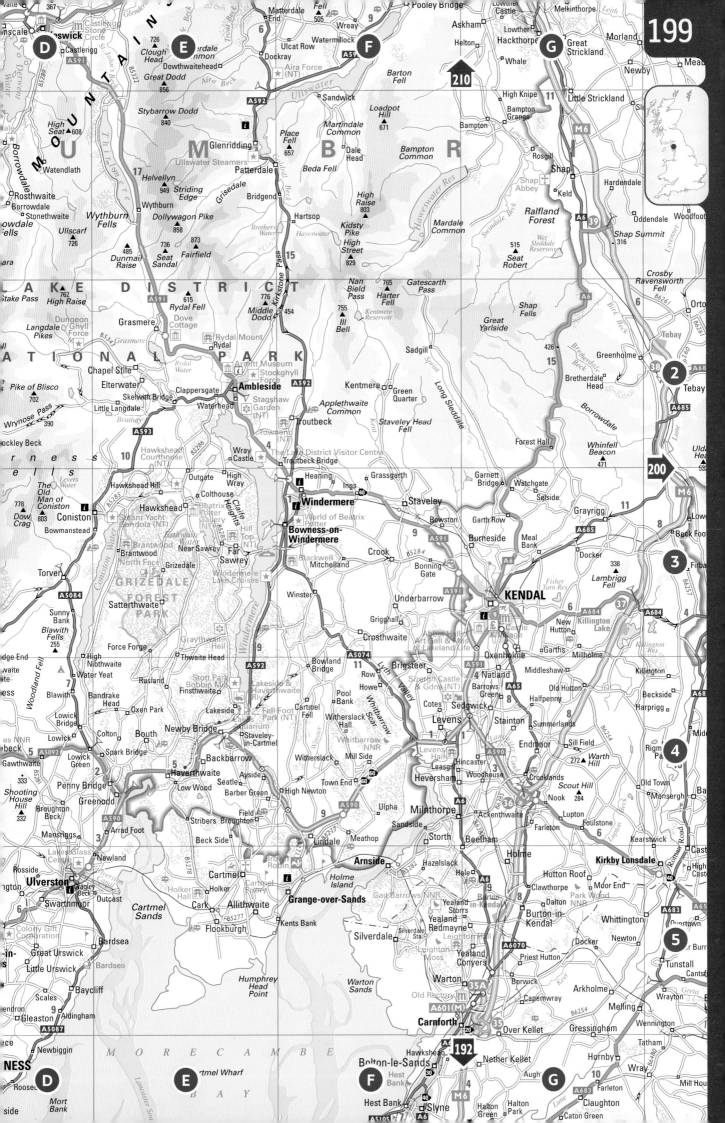

D   E   F   G

197

2

3

4

5

e & Cleveland

nt

ess Rocks
& Marine Sanctuary
North Bay
Miniature Railway

Scarborough Castle
SCARBOROUGH
rborough Art Gall
South Bay
Spa Complex
Black Rocks

&R
Osgodby
Cayton Bay
Cayton 7
Lebberston
Gristhorpe
Filey Brigg
The Wyke

Hertford
A165
Folkton 6   A1039   **Filey**
West   Muston
Flotmanby
Filey Bay

Hunmanby

Reighton Sands

Reighton
Speeton   *Crab Rocks*
B1229
Buckton   *Flamborough Cliffs*
Nature Reserve
Burton   Bempton
Fleming
ewton   A165   *Flamborough Head*
Grindale
Flamborough
old   Marton
Thwing   *Sewerby Hall & Gardens*
B1259
B1253   Sewerby
Boynton   B1253
Bridlington
udston   *Gypsey Race*   *Flamborough Headland*   *Heritage Coast*
West Hill
Bessingby
Carnaby

D   E   F   G

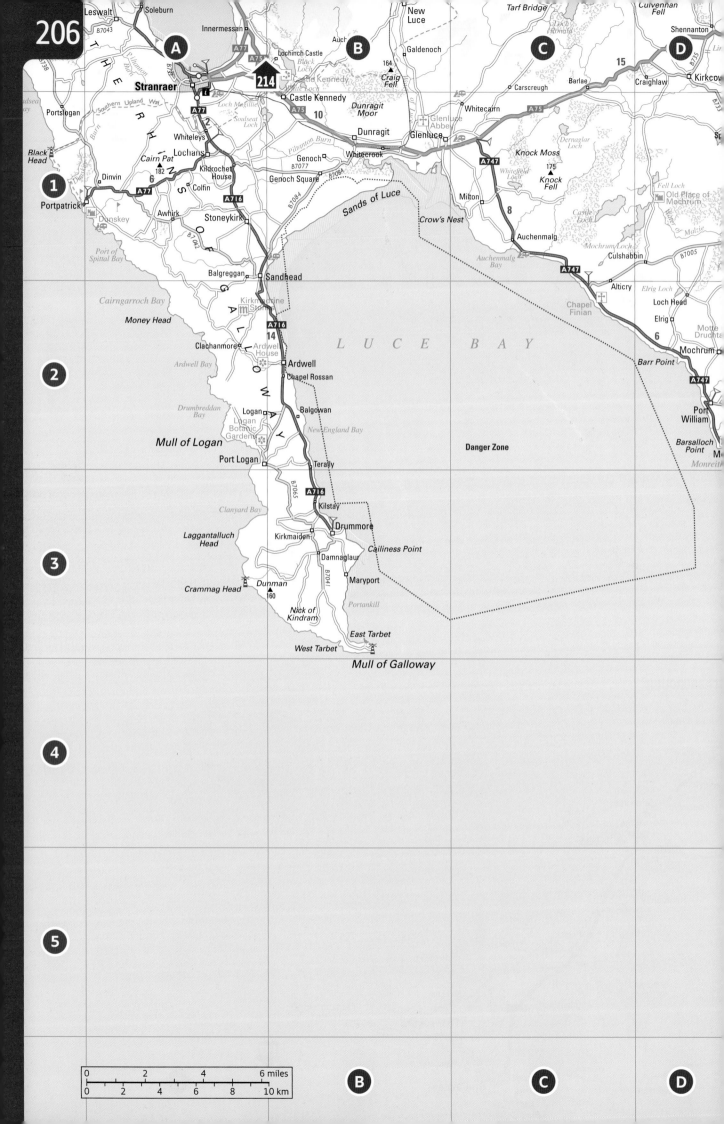

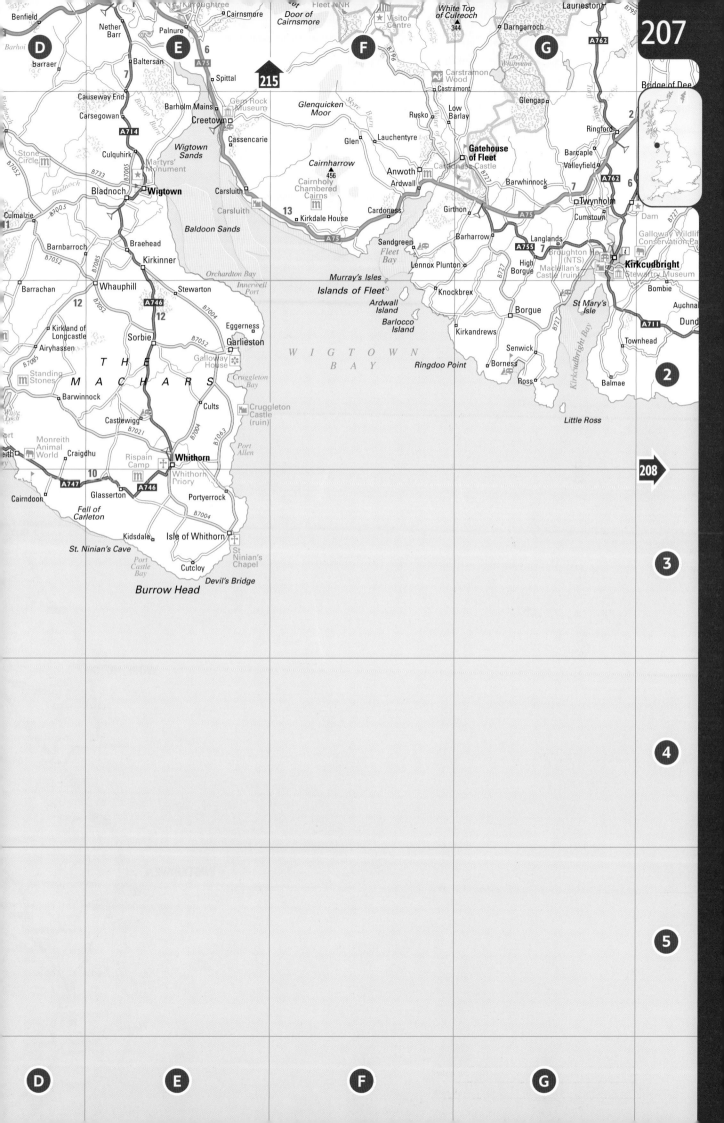

A713
A75
A711
A711
116

Motte
of Urr
94
Cuil
Hill
Loch Kindar
Mers
Black

Threave Castle
Hillowton
A
B
ifel
569
C
Carse
Bay
D

A
Castle Douglas
6
Craignair
Dalbeattie
Loch Fea
A710
Carsethorn
Kirkbean
Cavens

Buchan
216
Dalbeattie
Kirkbean
Borron Point

Bridge of Dee
Rhonehouse
(Kelton Hill)
Breoch
4
A711
Dalbeattie Forest
B793
Southwick
Caulkerbush
Mainsriddle

2
Dildawn
Gelston
Palnackie
Barnbarroch
Fairgirth
Southwick

Ringford
A711
Argrennan House
B736
Kippford
(Scaur)
A710
Preston Merse
Gillfoot
Bay

caple
1
Airieland
Screel Hill
343
Barnhourie
Sands
Southerness

eyfield
6
Netherthird
B727
391
Mote of
Mark (NTS)
White Loch
Sandyhills
10
Mersehead Sands
Southerness
Point

Cumstoun
Bengairn
Orchardton
Tower
Rough Firth
Colvend
Port o'Warren

Dam
Galloway Wildlife
Conservation Park
Rockcliffe

Kirkcudbright
Auchencairn
Castlehill Point

Stewartry Museum
Auchencairn
Bay
Almorness Point
Barnhourie
Sands

Bombie
Bankhead
Hazlefield
Hestan
Island

Mary's
Isle
Auchnabony
Rascarrel
Balcary Point

Dundrennan
Rascarrel
Bay

Townhead
A711
Orroland
Barlocco Bay

Abbey
Port Mary

mae
2
Abbey Head

Ross

Port Mary

FIRT

207

SOLWAY

Maryport
Lake District Coast Aquarium

3
Woodside
Flimby
5
A596
Seaton
Great Clifton
Ca

WORKINGTON
Stainburn
A66

Schoose
A597
A596
3
A595
Westfield
3
High Harrington
Salterbeck

Harrington
Brant

4
A595
Distington
Gilgar
5
Pica

40
Howgate
Low Moresby

Parton
Moresby
Parks

WHITEHAVEN
The Beacon

Hensingham
Frizin

Saltom Bay
Mirehouse
7
A5086

5
Sandwith
Cleator Moor

St Bees
Head
St Bees
Head
Moor Row
Wath Brow

St. Bees Head
Heritage Coast
Bigrigg
Cleator

Rottington
Wilton

St Bees
Egremont

How Man

Coulderton
Snellings
Thornhill

Middletown
Nethertown
Haile
Beckerme

Braystones
Sta
Selland
Visitors
Centre
Ca

0   2   4   6 miles
0 2 4 6 8 10 km

B
C
D

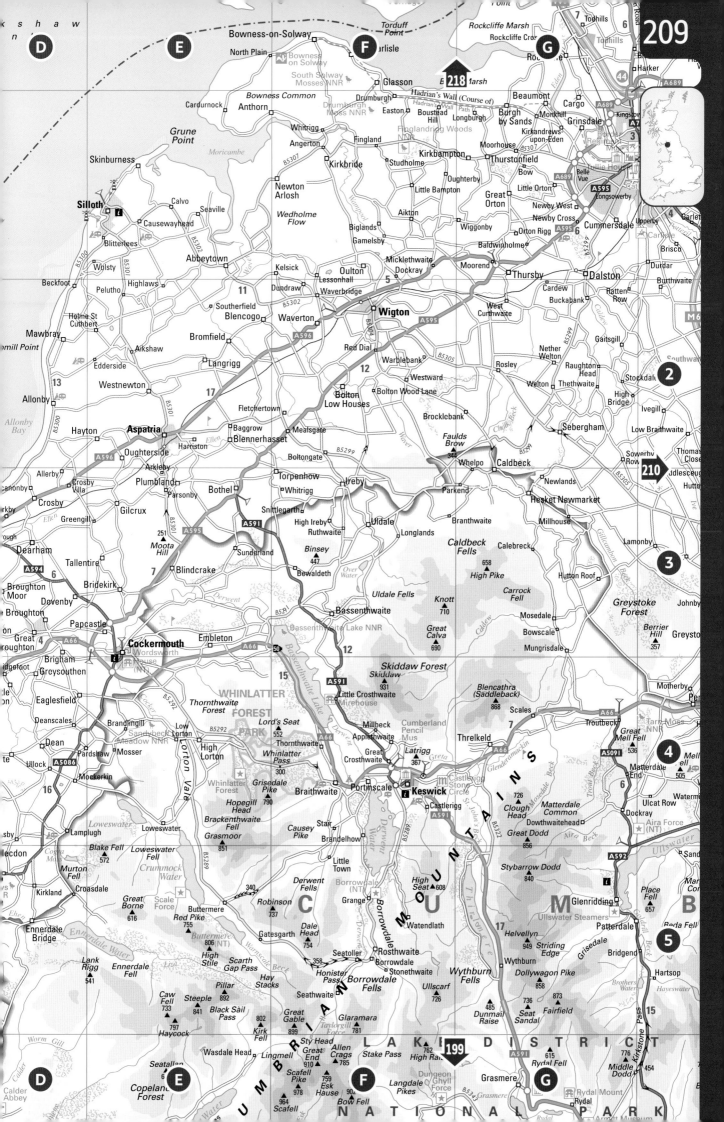

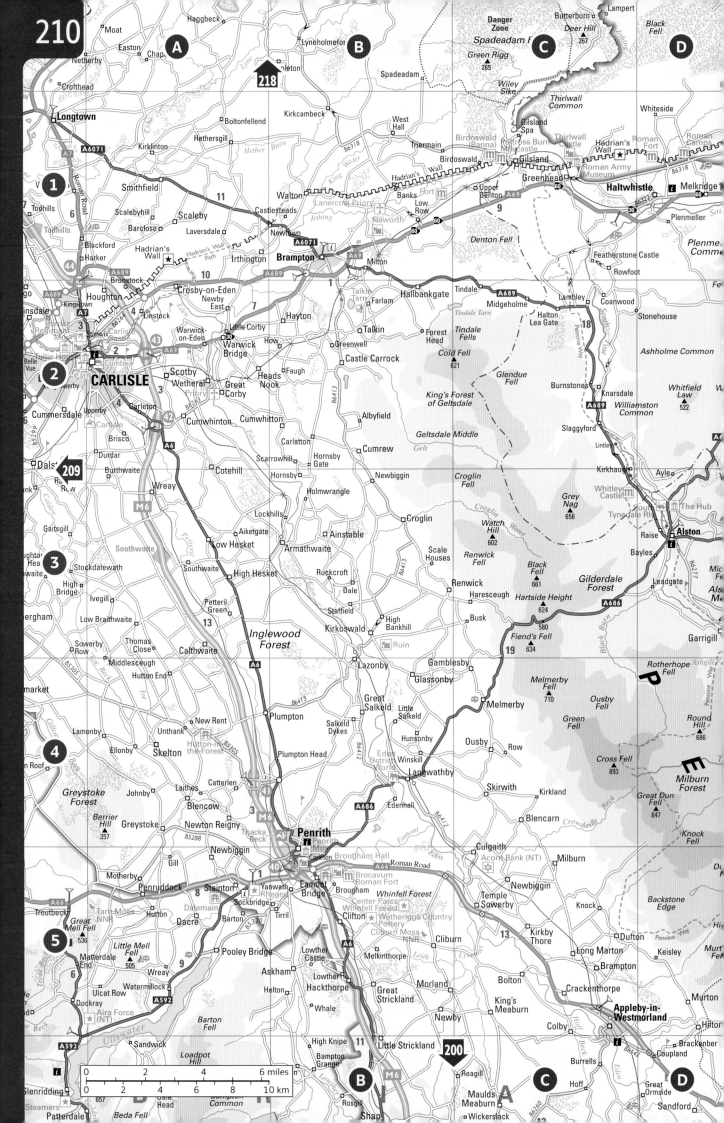

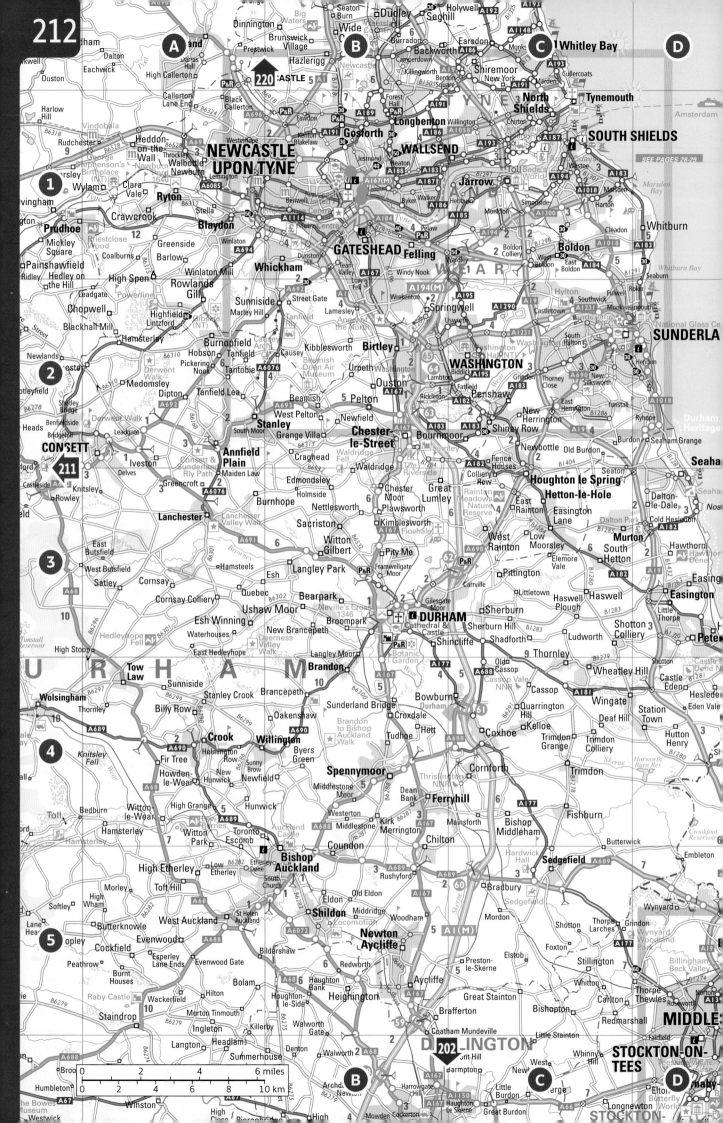

2

3

4

5

Harbour

's Point

Durham
Heritage Coast

on Colliery

orden
ee   *Dene Mouth*

Blackhall Colliery
Durham Coast NNR
Blackhall Rocks
High
Hesleden
Monk   Crimdon
Hesleden   Park
A1086
Durham Heritage Coast

Hart
aton   A1049
The Headland
Jackson's Landing
High   *Hartlepool Bay*
Throston   Hartlepool's Maritime Experience

Elwick
Dalton   Rift
Piercy   House
A178   **HARTLEPOOL**
HARTLEPOOL   *Tees*
Brierton   *Bay*
40   Seaton Carew

Claxton   6 A689
Grange
Greatham
Newton Bewley
9   *Seal*
Wolviston   *Sands*
A1185
illingham   A78   Warrenby Coatham
Cowpen   Coatham   r **Redcar**
Bewley   Marsh
Haverton   RSPB   A1042   SEE PAGE 29
Hill   Saltholm   A1085   **Marske-**
Ayrton   Kirkleatham   5   **by-the-Sea**   Saltburn Inclined
B1275 Salt   A1085   Railway
International Holme   Kirkleatham   **Saltburn-by-the-Sea**
Railway Port Clarence 4   Museum   Saltburn
Middlesbrough   **New**   Incline
Toll   Lazenby Yearby **Marske** Tramway Warsett 166
BROUGH   A66   Wilton   Upleatham   Gill Hill
South 5   B1269 Saltburn Brotton
Bank   **Skelton** Gill **203**
Grangetown   **(Skelton-in-Cleveland)** Tom Leonard **Loftus**
A1032 A172 A171 Normanby A174   North   Mining Museum   Boulby Staithes
3   Eston B1380 Dunsdale Skelton   Kilton
DDLESBROUGH **D** **E** **REDCAR** **F** Margrove **Boosbeck** Kilton Thorpe **G** Easin A174
n-Tees A1032 A172 A171 ham A173 2 Park   Liverton   Dalehouse
Marsh   Ormesby   atts Lane Woodland Priory Lingdale Charltons Roxby Port Mulgrave
Tollesby Marton Stewart Country Park Capt Cook Birthplace **AND** Runswick Bay Hinderwell
A19 Nature's Park Museum Guisborough
World

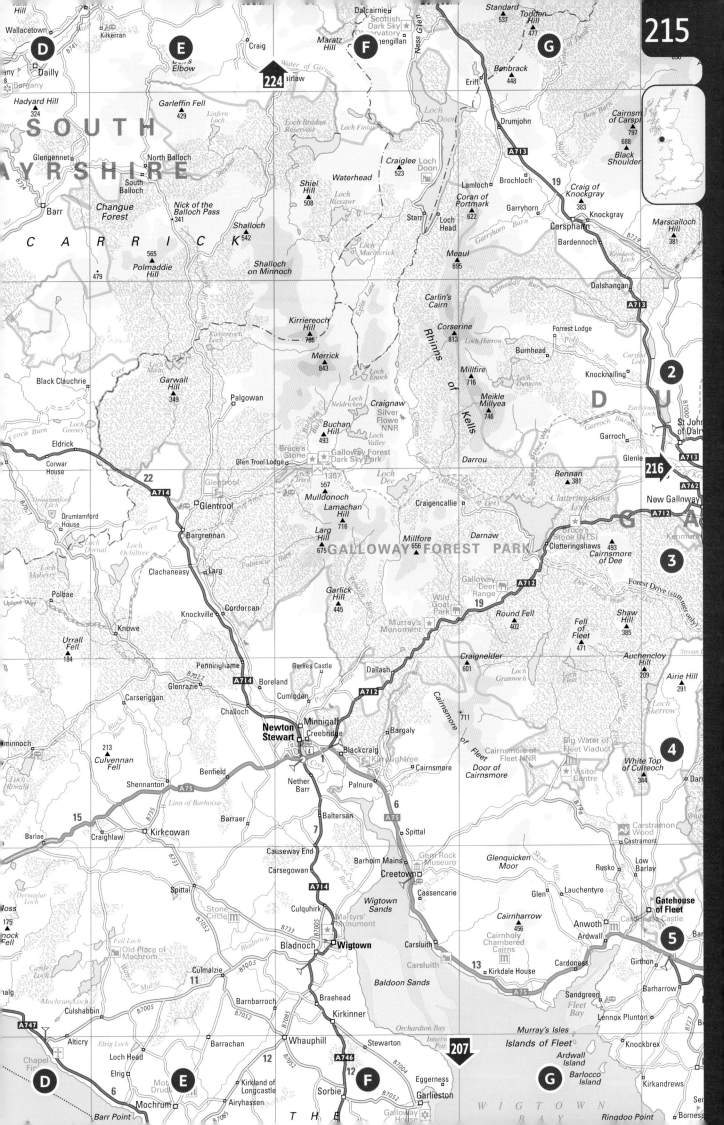

SOUTH

AYRSHIRE

CARRICK

Wallacetown
Kilkerran
Craig
Dailly
Bargany
Hadyard Hill
324
Garleffin Fell
429
Devil's Elbow
Dalcairnie
Maratz Hill
Gengillan
Scottish Dark Sky Observatory
Ness Glen

Standard
537
Todden Hill
477

Benbrack
448

Eriff

Drumjohn

Loch Doon

A713

Lamloch
Brochloch
19

Cairnsmore of Carsph
797

Black Shoulder
688

Craig of Knockgray
383

Knockgray

Carsphairn

Bardennoch

Marscalloch Hill
381

Glengennet
North Balloch
Sunchie
Craiglee
523
Loch Doon

Waterhead

Coran of Portmark
622

Garryhorn

Dalshangan

South Balloch

Barr
Changue Forest
Nick of the Balloch Pass
341
Shalloch
542
Shiel Hill
508
Loch Riecawr
Starr
Loch Head
Meaul
695
Garryhorn Burn
Polmaddy Burn
Bardennoch
A713

Polmaddie Hill
565
479
Shalloch on Minnoch
Loch Macaterick
Carlin's Cairn
Corserine
813
Loch Harrow
Forest Lodge
Burnhead
Knocknalling
Carsfad Loch
2

Black Clauchrie
Cree
Kirriereoch Hill
786
Merrick
843
Loch Enoch
Millfire
716
Rhinns of Kells
Meikle Millyea
746
Loch Dungeon
Garroch Burn
Earlstoun Loch
D U
St Joh of Dalr

Garwall Hill
349
Palgowan
Loch Neldricken
Craignaw
Silver Flowe NNR
Darrou
Garroch

Eldrick
Corwar House
Glentrool
22
A714
Buchan Hill
493
Loch Valley
Galloway Forest Dark Sky Park
Bruce's Stone
Glen Trool Lodge
Loch Trool
1307
Loch Dee
Craigencallie
of Dee
Black
Bennan
381
Glenlee
216
New Galloway
A762

Drumlamford Loch
Drumlamford House
Glentrool
Bargrennan
557
Mulldonoch
Lamachan Hill
716
Larg Hill
675
GALLOWAY FOREST PARK
Millfore
656
Darnaw
Clatteringshaws Loch
Bruce's Stone (NTS)
Clatteringshaws
493
Cairnsmore of Dee
A712
G
Kenmur

Clachaneasy
Larg
Knockville
Cordorcan
Garlick Hill
445
Galloway Deer Range
Wild Goat Park
A712
19
Round Fell
402
Fell of Fleet
471
Shaw Hill
385
Forest Drive (summer only)
3

Polbae
Upland Way
Loch Maberry
Knowe
Urrall Fell
184
Penninghame
Glenrazie
Garlies Castle
Dallash
Murray's Monument
Craignelder
601
Loch Grannoch
Loch Fleet
Auchencloy Hill
209
Airie Hill
291
Loch Skerrow
4

Carseriggan
Challoch
Boreland
Cumloden
A714
A712
Cairnsmore of Fleet
711

Culvennan Fell
213
Benfield
Newton Stewart
Minnigaff
Creebridge
Bargaly
Blackcraig
Kirroughtree
Cairnsmore
Cairnsmore of Fleet NNR
Door of Cairnsmore
Big Water of Fleet Viaduct
White Top of Culreoch
344
Visitor Centre

Shennanton
A75
Nether Barr
Palnure
6
A75

Barlae
15
Craighlaw
Kirkcowan
Barraer
Baltersan
7
Spittal
Carstramon Wood
Castramont

Linn of Barhoise
Causeway End
Carsegowan
Barholm Mains
Creetown
Gem Rock Museum
Glenquicken Moor
Rusko
Low Barlay
Glen
Lauchentyre
Gatehouse of Fleet
5

Spittal
B733
Stone Circle
A714
Culquhirk
Martyrs' Monument
Cassencarie
Cairnharrow
456
Anwoth
Ardwall
Cardoness Castle

Dernaglar Loch
Old Place of Mochrum
Bladnoch
Wigtown
Carsluith
Wigtown Sands
Cairnholy Chambered Cairns
Carsluith
13
Kirkdale House
Cardoness
Girthon
Barharrow

Culmalzie
11
Barnbarroch
Braehead
Kirkinner
Baldoon Sands
Sandgreen
Fleet Bay
Lennox Plunton

A747
Alticry
Elrig Loch
Loch Head
Culshabbin
Elrig
Barrachan
Whauphill
12
Stewarton
Eggerness
Orchardton Bay
Inner Por.
207
Murray's Isles
Islands of Fleet
Knockbrex

Chapel Fin
Mochrum
Barr Point
6
Mot Drud
Kirkland of Longcastle
Airyhassen
Sorbie
A746
12
Garlieston
Galloway House
B7004
WIGTOWN BAY
Ardwall Island
Barlocco Island
Kirkandrews
Ringdoon Point
Bornes

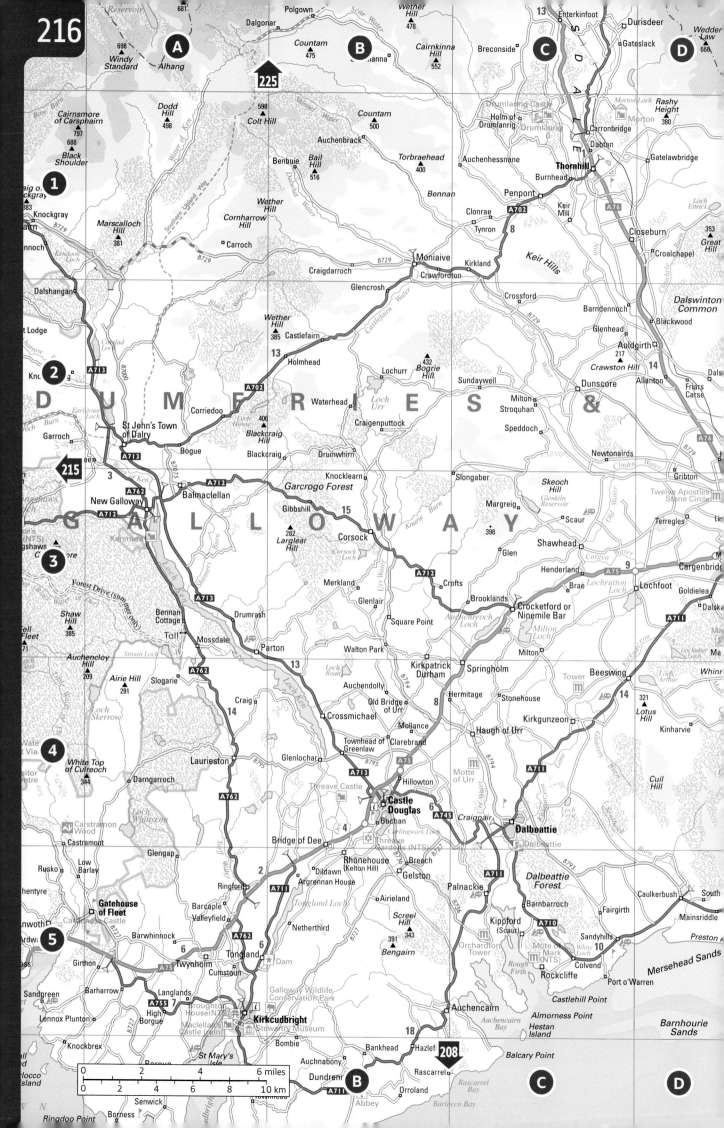

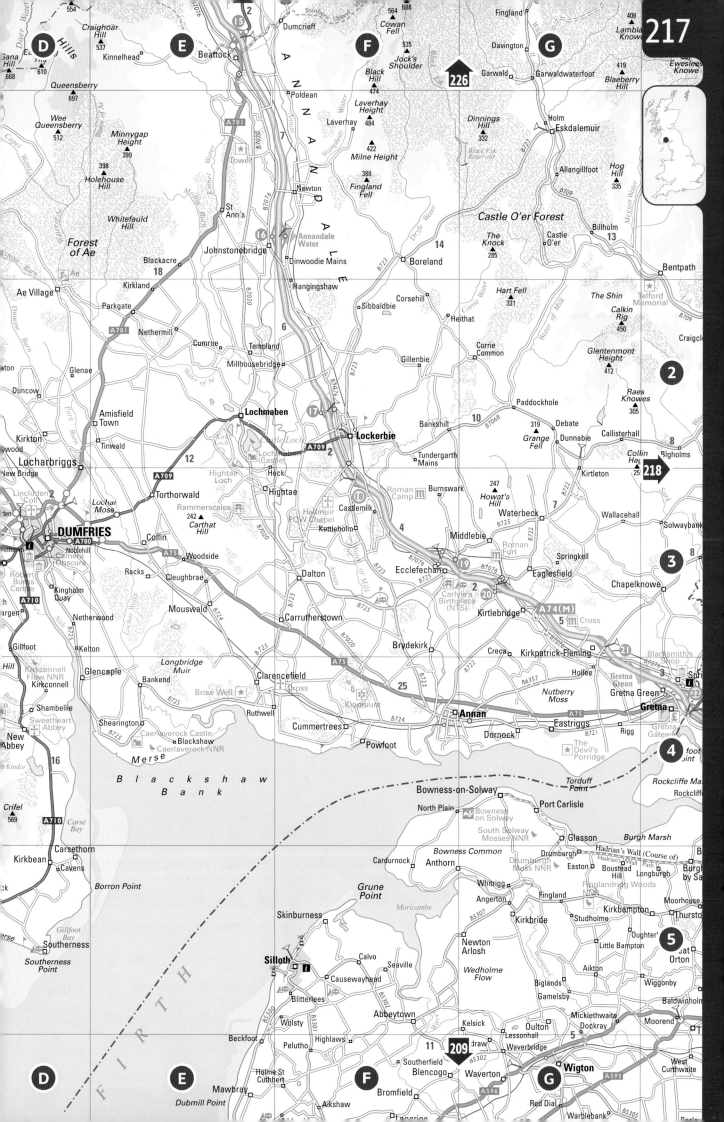

D

Gana Hill
668
Eack Hill
610

E
Beattock
15

F
Dumcrieff
Cowan Fell 564 688
Jock's Shoulder 535
Black Hill 474
Laverhay Height 484
Laverhay
Milne Height 422
Fingland Fell 388

226

G
Fingland
Davington
Garwald Garwaldwaterfoot
Lambla Knowe 406
Blaeberry Hill 419
Eweslees Knowe 440

Craighoar Hill
537
Kinnelhead

Queensberry 697
Wee Queensberry 512
Minnygap Height 399
398
Holehouse Hill
Whitefauld Hill

A701

B7020

Poldean
7
Newton

Annan Water
Wamphrey
Dryfe Water

Dinnings Hill 332
Black Esk Reservoir

Holm
Eskdalemuir
Allangillfoot
Hog Hill 335

B723
B709

Megget Water

Forest of Ae
Ae
Ae Village
Blackacre 18
Kirkland
Parkgate
Nethermill
A701

St Ann's
Johnstonebridge 16
Dinwoodie Mains
Hangingshaw

Annandale Water
B7076

Boreland
14

B723

Castle O'er Forest
The Knock 285
Castle O'er
Billholm
Bentpath 13

Telford Memorial
B709

The Shin

Glenae
Cumrue
Templand
Millhousebridge
6

Duncow
Amisfield Town
Tinwald

Kirkton
wood
Locharbriggs
New Bridge

12

A709

Lochmaben
Castle Loch
Lochmaben (Castle)
Kirk Loch
17
Lockerbie
A709 2
Heck
Hightae Loch
Hightae

Corsehill
Sibbaldie
Heithat
Gillenbie
Bankshill
10
B7068

Corrie Water
Hart Fell 331
Corrie Common
Paddockhole
Debate 319
Grange Fell
Dunnabie
Kirtleton

Calkin Rig 450
Glentenmont Height 412
Raes Knowes 305
Callisterhall
Collin Hag 25
Bigholms

Craigcl

2

8

218

Locharbriggs
Lincluden Coll
Lochar Moss
DUMFRIES
A780
Collin
A75
Woodside
Cleughbrae

Torthorwald
Rammerscales
242 Carthat Hill
B700

A709
Hightae
Hallmuir POW Chapel
Castlemilk
Kettleholm
4
Roman Camp

18

Burnswark
Howat's Hill 247
Middlebie
Roman Fort
Ecclefechan
19
B7076
Eaglesfield
B725
Springkell

Waterbeck
B725
B722

Wallacehall
Solwayban

7

8

3

Camera Obscura
Robert Burns Centre
A710
rgent
Gillfoot
Kelton

Noblehill
Racks
Mouswald
B724
Netherwood
B725

Carrutherstown
Dalton
B7020
Brydekirk

Carlyle's Birthplace (NTS)
2
Kirtlebridge
20
5
Cross
Creca
Kirkpatrick-Fleming
Hollee

Chapelknowe

Gretna Green
A74(M)
B7076
21
Blacksmith's Shop
Gretna
22

Kirkconnell Flow NNR
Kirkconnell
Shambellie
Sweetheart Abbey
New Abbey

Glencaple
Bankend
Longbridge Muir
B725
Shearington
Caerlaverock Castle
Blackshaw
Caerlaverock NNR

16

Clarencefield
Cross
Brow Well
Ruthwell
Cummertrees
Powfoot

25
B723
Kinmount

Annan
Dornock
Eastriggs
Rigg

A75
B721

Gretna Green
Gretna Gatewa
4
foot int

Crifel 569
A710
Carse Bay

Merse

Blackshaw Bank

The Devil's Porridge

Torduff Point
Rockcliffe Ma
Rockcliff

Carsethorn
Kirkbean
Cavens
Borron Point

Bowness-on-Solway
North Plain
Bowness on Solway
South Solway Mosses NNR
Port Carlisle
Glasson
Burgh Marsh

Hadrian's Wall (Course of)

Southerness
Southerness Point
Gillfoot Bay

Cardurnock
Anthorn
Bowness Common
Drumburgh
Drumburgh Moss NNR
Easton
Boustead Hill
Longburgh
Hadrian's Wall Path
Finglandrigg Woods NNR

Burgh by Sa

Grune Point
Moricambe
Skinburness

Whitrigg
Angerton
Fingland
Kirkbride
Studholme
Kirkbampton

Moorhouse
Thursto

FIRTH

Silloth
Causewayhead
Blitterlees

Calvo
Seaville
Newton Arlosh
Wedholme Flow

Biglands
Gamelsby
Aikton
Wiggonby
Oughter
Orton

5

Beckfoot
Peluthe
Highlaws

Wolsty
B5300
Abbeytown
B5302

Kelsick
Oulton
Lessonhall
Waverbridge
Dockray
5

Micklethwaite
Moorend
Baldwinhol

D

E
Dubmill Point

Mawbray

Holme St Cuthbert
Aikshaw

11
209

F
Southerfield
Blencogo
Waverton
Bromfield
B5302

Wigton
A595
A596
Red Dial

G
West Curthwaite
Warblebank
B5305

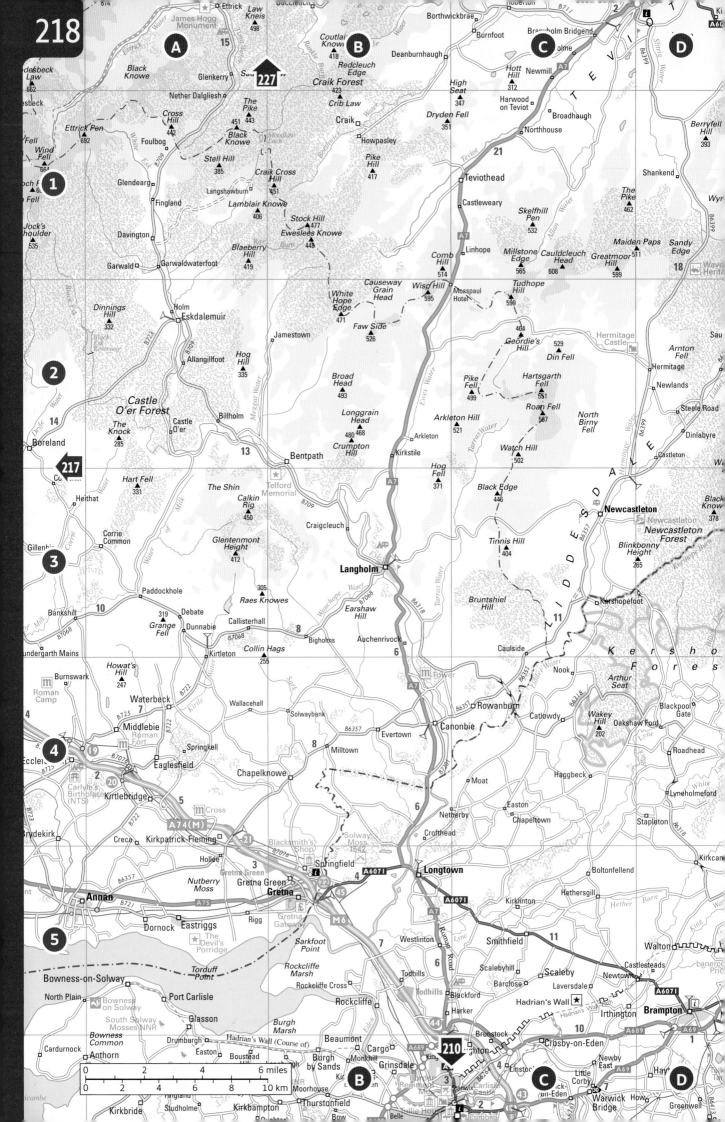

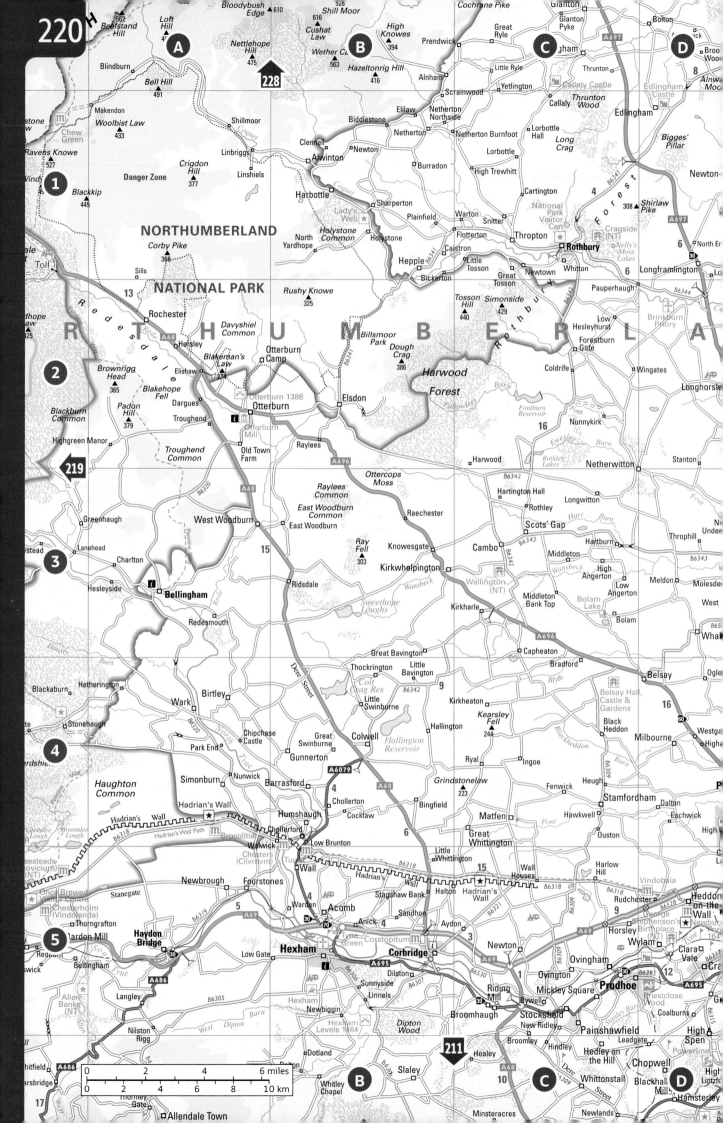

A   B   C   D

1

2

3

4

5

Ardmore
Point
Ardmore

Eilean
a' Chuirn

Eilean
Thride

2¼ hrs

West
Tarbert
Bay

East
Tarbert Bay

Tarbert

Bhan
Ardailly

Gigha

Ardminish

Craro
Island

Aghamore
Gardens

Ardminish
Bay

Druimyeon
Bay

231

100

Ronachan

Corriechrevie

Ballo

Auchinafaud

Loch
Ciaran

248

Cruach Mhic-
Gougain

Cnoc an t-
Samhlaidh

264

Loch Garasdale

Escart
Farm

Crossa

Cour

16

SOUND OF GIGHA

Rhunahaorine
Point

Grob Bagh

Cara Island

Mull
of Cara

Tayinloan

Killean

Beacharr

Muasdale

Achaglass

¼ hr

Rhunahaorine

285
Narachan
Hill

Cnoc
Reamhar
203

329
Deucheran Hill

Cruach Mhic-an-t- Saoir
364
Cruach nan Gabhar
354

Carradale
Forest

Diollaid
Mhòr
362

Beinn
Bhreac
426

Sunadale

Grogport

R

Whitefarla

33

Glenacardoch
Point

Belloch

Glenbarr

Arnicle

Barr Water

Beinn
an
Tuirc
454

T

Rhonadale

Carradale

Dippen

Torrisdale

Carradale
Garden

KILBRANNAN

Bellochantuy Bay

Bellochantuy

Killocraw

Corrylach

Lussa
Loch

Bord Mòr
408

Meall
Buidhe
374

N

Saddell Forest

Sgreadan Hill
397

Abbey
(ruins)

Saddell

Bunlarie

Whitestone

Carradale
Bay

Saddell Bay

13

Ugadale Point

Tangy
Loch

Tangy

Westport

Low Ballevain

Machrihanish Bay

Kilchenzie

East Darlochan

CAMPBELTOWN

Skeroblingarry

Drumgarve
Glen Lussa

Calliburn

Peninver

Ballochgair

Ardnacross
Bay

A83

I

Kilmichael

Drumore

Campbeltown
(Ceann Loch
Chille Chiarain)

Davaar Island

Ardrossan 2⅔ hrs
(seasonal)

Machrihanish

Machrihanish
Water

Dalivaddy

Witchburn

Mus

Davaar

Drumlemble

B843

6

Chiscan

Knocknaha

Kilchrist

Oatfield

Kilkerran

Glenramskill

New Orleans

Earadale Point

The
Slate
385

Conie

Killean

Beinn
Ghuilean
352

Cnoc
Moy
446

K

10

Cnoc
Odhar
277

Killellan

Chiscan Water

Arinarach
Hill
312

Feochaig

Ru Stafnish

Rubha
Dùin Bhàin

Largybaan

273
Cnoc
Reamhar

Glen Breackerie

Conie
Water

Conie Glen

Glen Kerran

Sheanachie

Brecklate

Strone Glen

Keprigan

Kildavie

Beinn
na Lice
428

South Point

Garveld

Feorlan

Carrine

Southend

Keil

Macharioch

Polliwilline Bay

Mull
of Kintyre

Borgadelmore Point

Carskey Bay

Sanda Sound

Sheep Island

Sanda
Island

½ hr (seasonal)

D **E** **F** **G**

St Blane's Church
Dunagoil Bay
Torr Mòr 146
Little Cumbrae
Millport Bay
Fairlie R.
Inner Brigurd Point
Hunterston
A78
Crosbie

Cock of Han
Newton
Loch Ranza
Lochranza
A841
Catacol
Catacol Bay
Isle of Arran Distillery
Garrochty
Garroch He
232
Gull Point
Portencross
Farland Head
B7048
Ardneil Bay
Seamill
12

Rubha Airigh Bheirg
Craw
Lenimore
Thundergay
Auchamore
Glen Catacol
Glen Chalmadale
North Glen Sannox
Glen Sannox
N O R T H   A Y R S
F I R T H
Horse Isle
Ardrossan
Salt

Pirnmill
Beinn Bhreac
554 573
Beinn Tarsuinn
523
Caisteal Abhail 859
Cir Mhòr 798
Cioch-na-h-Oighe 661
Sannox
Sannox Bay
14
Corrie
A841

Mullach Buidhe 711
Beinn Bhreac 715 721
Beinn Bharrain
Loch Tanna
Beinn Tarsuinn 825
792
Goat Fell 874

Point
Imachar
Balliekine
17
Beinn Nuis
Glen Rosa
Brodick (NTS)
Brodick Castle (NTS)
Brodick Bay
Merkland Point

Dougarie Point
Glen Iorsa
Iorsa Water
Dougarie
A R R A N
An Tunna 361
Chambered Cairn
Heritage Mus
Glencloy
Brodick
Strathwhillan
South Corriegills
Campbeltown 2⅓ hrs (seasonal)
1 hr

Machrie Bay
Auchgallon Stone Circle
Glaister
Machrie
Machrie Water
Tarrnacraig
Ard Bheinn 512
A'Chruach 512
11
B880
Glenkiln
Clauchlands Point

Tormore
King's Cave
Hut Circles
Ballymichael
Machrie Moor Stone Circles
Beinn Bhreac 503
Cnoc a' Chapuill 417
Benlister Glen
12
Margnaheglish
Lamlash
Lamlash Bay
Holy Island
Campbeltown 2½ hrs (seasonal Saturdays only)
224

Torbeg
Blackwaterfoot
Drumadoon Bay
Shiskine
Fort
Kilpatrick
Tighvein 458
Glen Scorrodale
Knockenkelly
A841
Kingscross Point
Kingscross
Whiting Bay
Kiscadale
Whiting Bay
Largymore

Brown Head
Corriecravie
Sliddery
Torr a' Chaisteal
13
Kilmory
Levencorroch
Glen Ashdale
Kilmory Water
Largybeg
Dippen
Largybeg Point
Dippin Head
3

Lagg
Chambered Cairns
Shannochie
Bennan Head
Sound of Pladda
Kildonan
4

Pladda

Ailsa Craig
214

Culzean Castle (N
Maidenhead Bay
Morristo
Maidens
Turnberry
Turnberry Bay
Turnberry
A77
Tu
60
Dowhill
Dipple
60
6
Low Craighead
Chapeldonan
Grangeston
60
G **Girvan**
Houdston
Saugh Hill 296
5
Glendoune
Black Neuk
Glendrissaig

D **E** **F** **G**

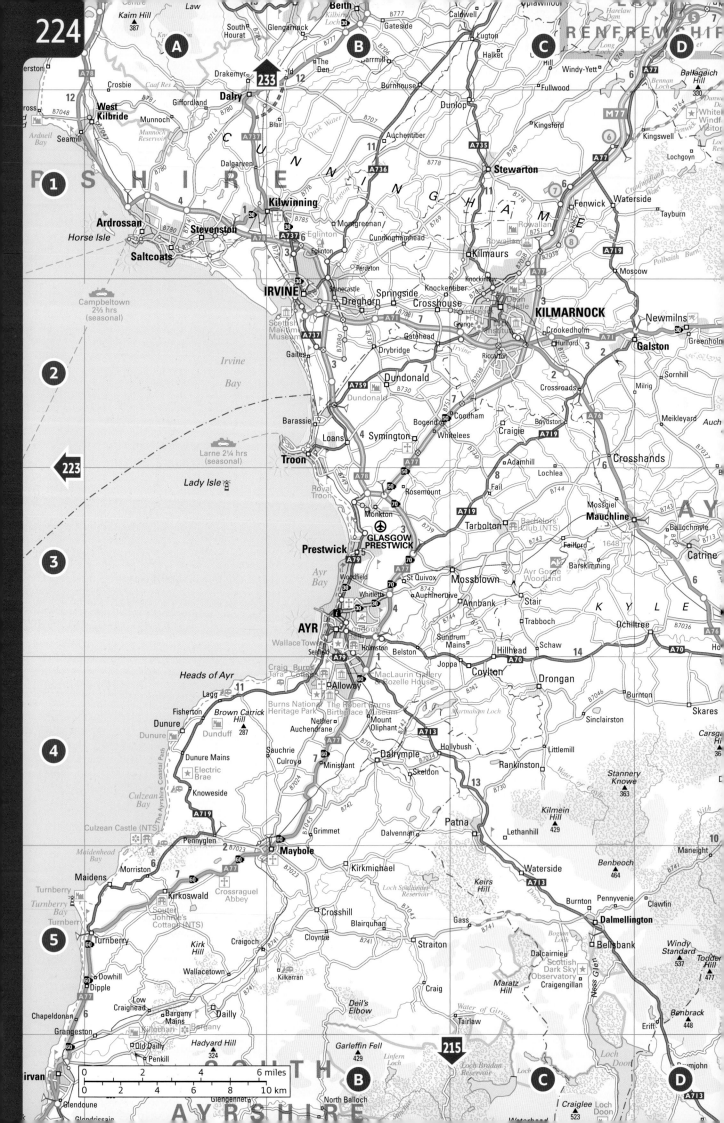

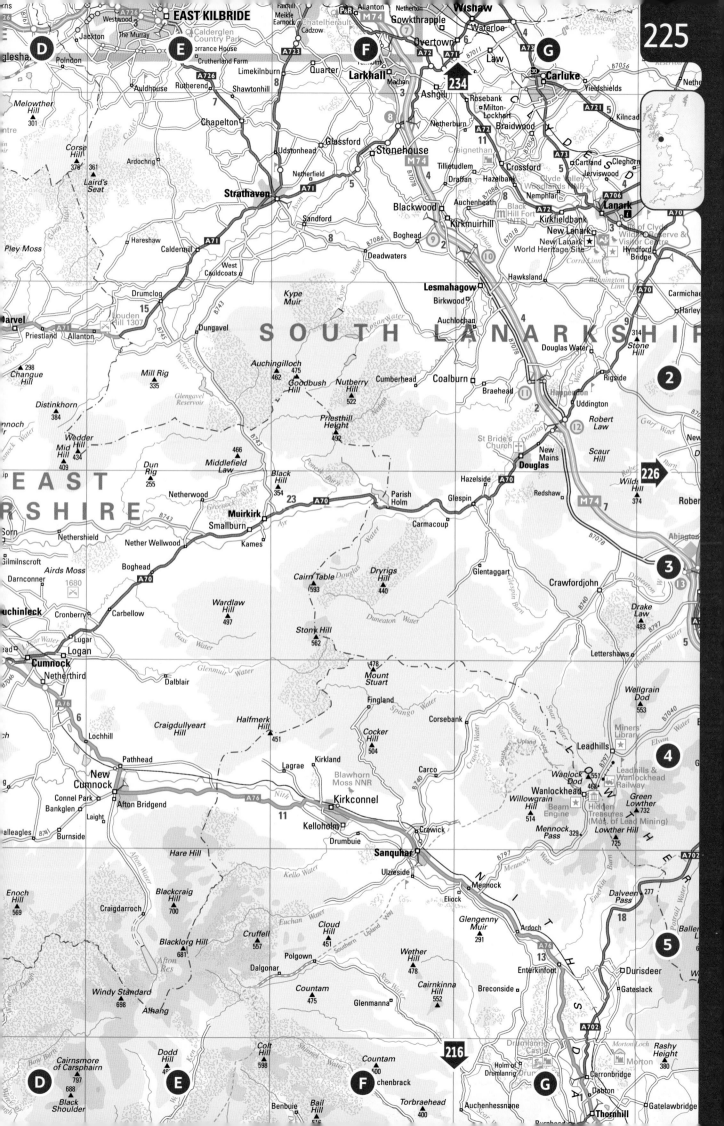

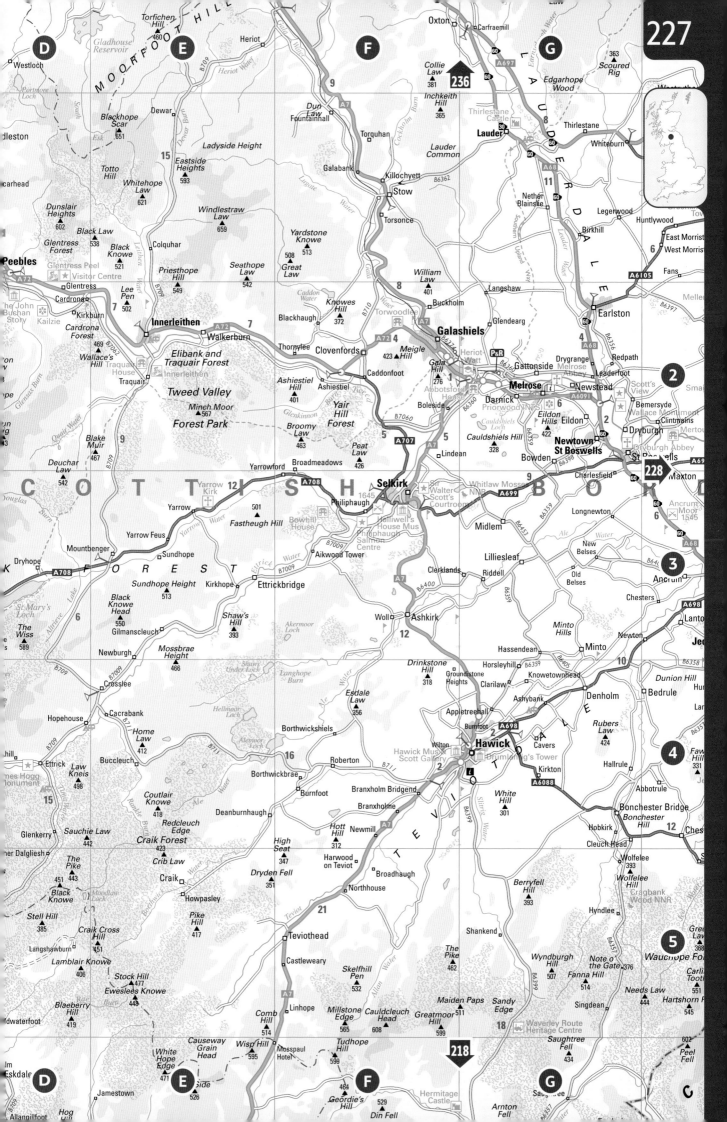

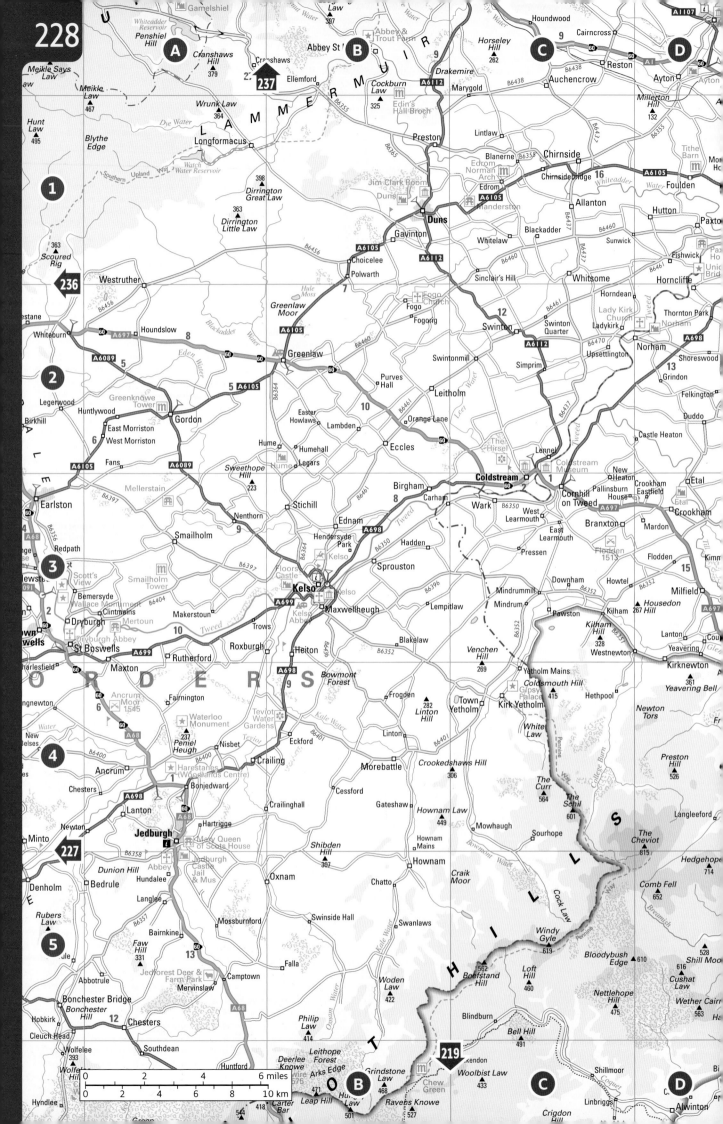

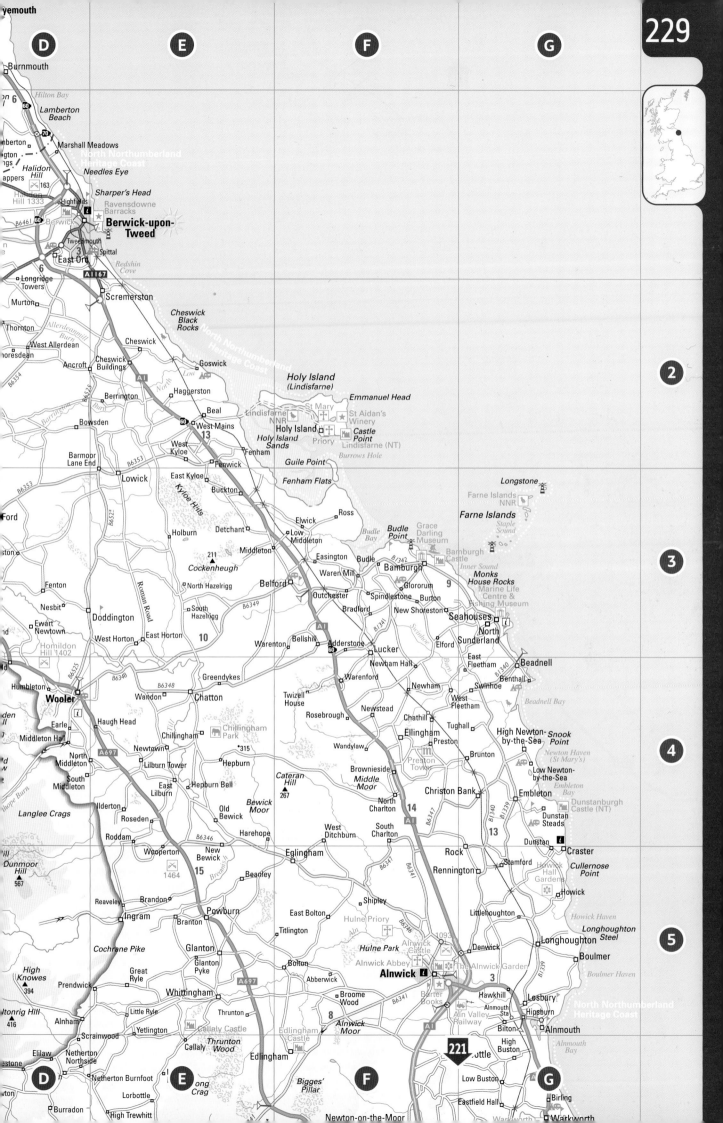

yemouth

D   E   F   G

Burnmouth
Hilton Bay
Lamberton Beach
60
erton
70
ington
ings
appers
Halidon Hill
163
Hill 1333
Highfields
B6461
60
Berwick
East Ord
A1167
6
Longridge Towers
Murton
Thornton
West Allerdean
oresdean
Ancroft
B6354
Bowsden
Barmoor Lane End
B6353
Lowick
B6353

Marshall Meadows
North Northumberland Heritage Coast
Needles Eye
Sharper's Head
Ravensdowne Barracks
Berwick-upon-Tweed
Tweedmouth
Spittal
Redshin Cove
Scremerston
Cheswick Black Rocks
North Northumberland Heritage Coast
Cheswick
Goswick
A1
Cheswick Buildings
Berrington
Haggerston
Beal
60
West Mains
13
West Kyloe
Penwick
East Kyloe
Buckton

Holy Island (Lindisfarne)
Emmanuel Head
St Mary
Lindisfarne NNR
St Aidan's Winery
Holy Island
Castle Point
Holy Island Sands
Priory
Lindisfarne (NT)
Fenham
Guile Point
Burrows Hole
Fenham Flats

2

Longstone
Farne Islands NNR
Farne Islands
Staple Sound

Ford
B6525
Barmoor
Kyloe Hills
Holburn
Detchant
211
Cockenheugh
North Hazelrigg
ston
Fenton
Nesbit
Ewart Newtown
Doddington
West Horton
East Horton
Homildon Hill 1402
B6555
Humbleton
Wooler
Earle
Haugh Head
Middleton Hall
North Middleton
South Middleton
A697
Chillingham
Newtown
Lilburn Tower
Hepburn
East Lilburn
Hepburn Bell
Langlee Crags
Ilderton
Roseden
Roddam
B6346
Wooperton
New Bewick
1464
Reaveley
Brandon
Branton
Ingram
Cochrane Pike
Glanton
Great Ryle
Glanton Pyke
A697
High Knowes
394
Prendwick
Whittingham
Little Ryle
Thrunton
ntonrig Hill
416
Alnham
Scrainwood
Yetlington
Elilaw
Netherton Northside
Callaly
Netherton Burnfoot
Lorbotton
Burradon
High Trewhitt

Elwick
Ross
Low Middleton
Middleton
South Hazelrigg
B6349
Belford
Outchester
Bradford
Warenton
Bellshill
60
Lucker
Newham Hall
Greendykes
Wandon
Chatton
Chillingham Park
*315
Twizell House
Roseborough
Newstead
Wandylaw
Cateran Hill
267
Brownieside
Middle Moor
North Charlton
14
Bewick Moor
Old Bewick
Harehope
Eglingham
West Ditchburn
South Charlton
A1
Beanley
B6346
Breamish
15
Powburn
Shipley
East Bolton
Titlington
Hulne Priory
Bolton
Abberwick
B6341
Broome Wood
8
Alnwick Moor
Edlingham Castle
Edlingham
Thrunton Wood
Callaly Castle
Biggers' Pillar

Budle Bay
Budle Point
Budle
Waren Mill
Easington
Spindlestone
Burton
New Shoreston
Adderstone
Warenford
Newham
Newton
West Fleetham
Chathill
Tughall
Ellingham
Preston
Brunton
Preston Tower
Christon Bank
B6347
Dunstan Steads
Dunstanburgh Castle (NT)
Embleton
Embleton Bay
Dunstan
Rock
B6341
Stamford
Rennington
Howick Hall Gardens
Howick
Littlehoughton
Alnwick Castle
1093
Hulne Park
Aln Valley Railway
Denwick
Hawkhill
Alnwick Abbey
Alnwick
Barter Books
The Alnwick Garden
3
Alnmouth Sta
Bilton
Lesbury
Hipsburn
Alnmouth
A1
221
ottle
High Buston
Low Buston
Eastfield Hall
Newton-on-the-Moor
Warkworth

Grace Darling Museum
Bamburgh Castle
Bamburgh
Glororum
9
Monks House Rocks
Seahouses
Marine Life Centre & Fishing Museum
North Sunderland
Inner Sound
East Fleetham
Beadnell
Benthall
Swinhoe
Beadnell Bay
High Newton-by-the-Sea
Snook Point
Newton Haven (St Mary's)
Low Newton-by-the-Sea

Cullernose Point
Craster
Howick Haven
Longhoughton
Longhoughton Steel
Boulmer
Boulmer Haven
Birling

North Northumberland Heritage Coast
Alnmouth Bay

3

4

5

D   E   F   G

239

232

222

D E F G

JURA

Corpach Bay
Beinn Bhreac 467
Dubh Bheinn
Lealt
365

Rainberg Mòr 453
Cruach Sganadail
Ardlussa
Lussagiven
Inverlussa
Lussa Point
Tramaig Bay

ARGYLL

Gleann Dorch
A846
Eilean an Rubha
Beinn Sgaillinish 190
Tarbert
Kilmory
Barrahormid
Taynish
Taynish NNR
Eilean Loain
Daltote

Creag Nam Fiadh Mòr 262
Tarbert Bay
Keillmore
New Ulva
Ulva Islands
Dunrostan

Rubha Barr
Ardnackaig
Gallchoille
Arinafad Beg
Scotnish
Tayvallich

Cnoc Reamhar 265
Ardnoe Point
Crinan
Crinan Ferry
Bellanoch
Arichonan
Knapdale Forest
Knapdale
Seafield
Achnamara
Kilmichael of Inverlussa
Ashfield

Kilmichael Glassary
Bridgend
Dunadd Fort
Môine Mhòr NNR
Cairnbaan
Craigglas
Badden
Auchindarroch
Brackley
Lochgilphead (Ceann Loch Gilb)
Achnaba
A83
Castleton
Ardrishaig

Carsaig Island
Carsaig Bay
Eilean Dubh
Turbiskill
Gariob
Cruach Breacain 360
Cam Loch
Beinn Bheag
331
Auchbraad
Inverneil

Lagg
Gate House
Achamore
Rubh' a' Chamais
Danna Island
Corr Eilean
Eilean Mòr
Kilmory
Chapel
Ellary
St Columba's Cave
Clachbreck
Achahoish
Loch Fuar Bheinne
Cruach a' Phubuill 477
Erines
Sròndoire
14

Rubha Beag
Kilfinan Bay
Port Leathan
Drum
2
Lower Auchalick
Auchalick Bay

24
Ardmenish
An Dùnan
Rubh' an Leim
Skervuile
Sròn Garbh
Point of Knap
Eilean Mòr St. Cormac's Chapel
Kilmory Bay
Ballyaurgan
Baile Boidheach
Ormsary
Druimdrishaig
Larach na Gaibhre
Cretshengan
Stob Odham 562
Meall Mòr
Cnoc a' Bharaille 471
Meall Reamhar 329
Duibhchladach
Loch Chaorunn
Ashens
Stonefield
Barfad
Tarbert
Barmore Island

Eilean Bhride
Meall Reamhar 477
Dubh Chreag 480
Loch nan Torran
Loch a' Chaoruinn
Meall Reamhar
Coulaghailtro
Kilberry
Crosses
Kilberry Head
Cruach Airde 213
Carse
Ardpatrick
West Tarbert
Escart
Corranbuie
Cruach an t-Sorchain 343
Achadacaie
Cruach Doire Leithe 377 422
Cnoc a' Bhaile-shios
334
Coire nan Capull
Kennacraig
Redhouse
Whitehouse

232
Mealdarroch Point
3

Rubha Cruitiridh
Achadhchoorrunn
Dunmore
Gartnagrenach
A83
Portachoillan
Ardpatrick Point
Quinhill
Clachan
Ronachan
Corriechrevie
Ballochroy
Auchinafaud
Ronachan Point

Glenrisdell
Skipness
Skipness
Claonaig
Auchameanach
Rockfield
Escart Farm
Port Fada
½ hr (seasonal)
Cruach nam Fiadh 269
5

Port Mòr
West Tarbert Bay
East Tarbert Bay
Creag Bhan 100
Tarbert
Ardailly
Druimyeon Bay
Rhunahaorine Point

Loch Ciaran
Crossaig
Lochranza
Catacol Bay
Loch Ranza
4

Gigha
Ardminish
Ardminish Bay
Achamore Gardens
¼ hr
Craro Island
Rhunahaorine
Cruach Mhic-Gougain 248
Cnoc an t-Samhlaidh 264
Cour Bay
Cour
16
Rubha Airigh Bheirg
Craw
Lenimore
Thundergay
Auchamore
Pirnmill

Grob Bagh
Cara Island
Mull of Cara
Tayinloan
Killean
Beacharr
Narachan Hill 285
Cnoc Reamhar 203
Cnoc Reamhar
Deucheran Hill 329
Cruach Mhic-an-t-Saoir 364
Cruach nan Gabhar
Sunadale
Grogport
Whitefarland Point
554
711
523
Beinn Bhreac
Mullach Buidhe 715 721
Beinn Bharrain
Imachar
Balliekine

CARRADALE FOREST
Diollaid Mhòr 362
Beinn Bhreac
Rhonadale
Carradale
Carradale Garden
Dougarie Point
Glen Iorsa
Glen Catacol
Isle of
5

33
Glenacardoch
Belloch
Barr Water
Arnicle
Beinn Tuirc 454
Muasdale
Achaglass
Dippen
Torrisdale
Carradale Bay
Dougarie
Auchgallon Stone Circle
Glenbarr

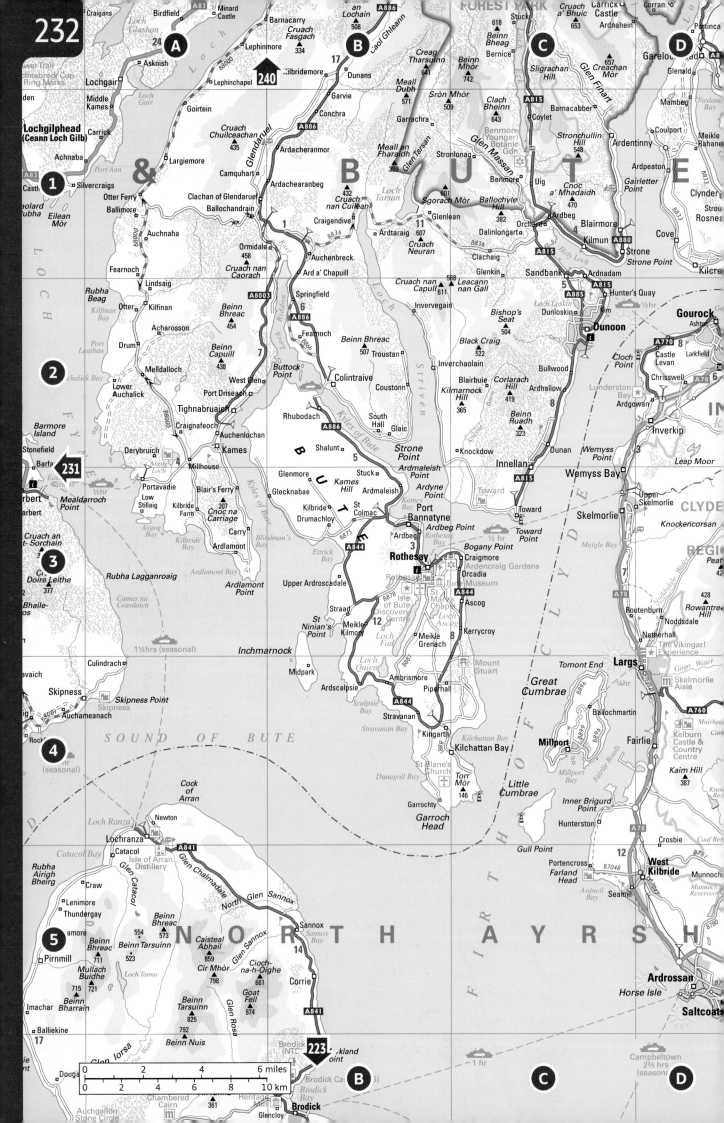

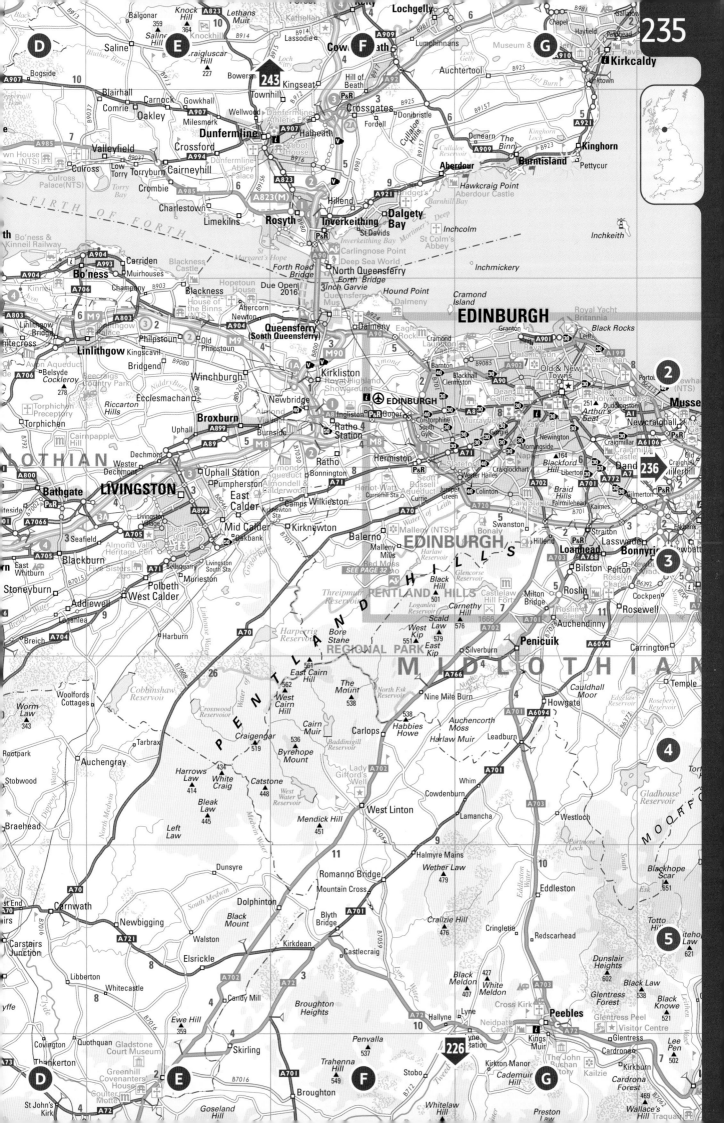

D   E   F   G

2

3

4

5

Dunbar
Belhaven
West Barns
A1087
Broxburn
Barns Ness
Dunbar 1650
70
Dunbar 1296
Spott
Doonhill Homestead
Brunt Hill 225
Innerwick
Skateraw
Skateraw Harbour
11
Thorntonloch
60
Reed Point
Halls
Dry Burn
Cocklaw Hill 319
Bilsdean
Cove   Pease Bay
Dunglass Church
Cockburnspath
60
Pease Dean
Siccar Point
Fast
Wheat Stack
Bransly Hill 397
Ecclaw
Oldhamstocks
Telegraph Hill 174
St. Abb's Head NNR (NTS)
St Abb's Head

H I L L S
Heart Law 391
Ecclaw Hill
277
245
Meikle Black Law
A1107
Coldingham Moor
Lumsdaine
Coldingham Loch
Northfield
St Abbs
Coldingham Bay

Monynut Edge
3
Southern Upland Way
Blackburn Rig
Grantshouse
60
Ale Water
13
Coldingham
Priory
Mus
A1107
Eyemouth

Bothwell Water
Laughing Law 307
Abbey & Trout Farm
Press
Houndwood
Gamelshiel
Monynut Water
Eye Water
9
Horseley Hill 262
9
Cairncross
Reston
A1
Ayton
Burnmouth

Cranshaws Hill 379
Cranshaws
Abbey St Bathans
Drakemire
Marygold
B6438
Auchencrow
Millerton Hill 132
Ayton
Hilton Bay
27
Ellemford
A6112
Cockburn Law 325
Edin's Hall Broch
60
Ayton Hill 199
6
60
Lamberton Beach

Wrunk Law 364
Longformacus
B6355
Preston
Lintlaw
B6437
Lamberton
70
Marshall Meadows
North Northumberland Heritage Coast
Needles Eye

398
Dirrington Great Law
Jim Clark Room
B6365
Blanerne
B6355
Chirnside
Edrom Norman Arch
Chirnsidebridge
16
A6105
Foulden
Whiteadder Water
Mordington Holdings
Clappers
Tithe Barn
Halidon Hill
163
Halidon Hill 1333
Highfields
Ravensdowne Barracks
Sha...Head

363
Dirrington Little Law
Duns
Edrom
Manderston
Allanton
Hutton
Paxton
B6461
60
Berwick
Tweedmouth
Berwick-u Tweed

Gavinton
Whitelaw
Blackadder
B6437
Sunwick
B6460
Fishwick
Paxton House
3
East Ord
Spittal

A6105
Choicelee
A6112
Sinclair's Hill
Whitsome
B6460
B6437
Horncliffe
Union Bridge
6
A1167
Redshin Cove

7
Polwarth
Hule Moss
Greenlaw Moor
A6105
Fogo Church
Fogo
Fogorig
12
Swinton
Swinton Quarter
A6112
Simprim
Whiteadder Water
Lady Kirk Church
Ladykirk
Norham
Horndean
Upsettlington
Thornton Park
A698
Thornton
West Allerdean
Allerdeanmill Burn
Longridge Towers
Murton
Screnwerston

Blackadder
Water
8
60
60
Greenlaw
5
A6105
B6364
Leitholm
10
B6461
Purves Hall
Lennel
The Hirsel
B6437
Swintonmill
B6470
Norham
13
Grindon
Felkington
B6354
Shoreswood
Shoresdean
Ancroft
Cheswick
Cheswick Buil...
5
A1
Berrington
B6525
Lowick

Easter Howlaws
Lambden
Orange Lane
Hume
Humehall
Legars
Eccles
60
Birgham
Carham
B6350
Wark
Coldstream
60
1
Coldstream Museum
New
Pallinsbu Hou...
228
...field
A697
Branxton
Mardon
Etal
B6353
Barmoor Lane End
B6353

Sweethope Hill 223
Stichill
B6461
Hendersyde Park
Hadden
Cornhill on Tweed
East Learmouth
Pressen
Flodden
Crookham
Kimmerston

D   E   F   G

A

B

C

D

1

2

3

4

5

Burgh Beg

Burg

Normann's Ruh

Fanmore

Ballyg

Loch Tuath

Ruh

Treshn' Isles

Sgeir a' Chaisteil

Fladda

Eile Dioghlu

C

Rubha Chulinish

Ballygo

D

Ki

Lunga

Gometra

Gometra House

Bearnus

306

Beinn nan Gall

Laggar Bay

Gometra

Rubha Maol na Mine

Beinn Chreagach

313

Beinn Eolasary

ULVA

Maisgeir

A'Chrannag

Bac Mòr (Dutchman's Cap)

Little Colonsay

Bac Beag

Sam Isle

Staffa

Eilean Dubh

Staffa NNR (NTS)

Chapel

Inch Kenneth

Fingal's Cave

Balmear

Erisgeir

Creach Bheinn

▲491

Aird na h-Iolaire

Ardmeanach

Bearraich

▲432

LO

Réidh Eilean

Eilean Chalbha

Rubha nan Cearc

Burg (NTS)

★

Carraig Mhic Thòmais

Port na Croise

Port an Duine Mhairbh

Dun I ▲100

Iona Abbey

Kintra

Beinn Chladan

Eorabus

Ardchrishnish

Maclean's Cross

Baile Mòr

Fionnphort

▲81

Ardtun

20

Ruanaich

Aridhglas

A849

Loch na Lathaich

Lee

Crua M

Stac an Aoineidh

IONA (NTS)

★

Fidden

Bunessan

37

Rubha na Carraig-gèire

Sound of Iona

Ross of Mull

Knockvologan

Ardalanish

Uisken

Soa Island

Erraid

87 ▲ Torr Fada

Ardchiavaig

Scoor

Eilean Dubh

Aird Mòr

Port Mòr

Rubha nan Bràithrean

Eilean a' Chalmain

▲89

Dearg Sgeir

Eilean Mòr

Rubh' Ardalanish

Torran Rocks

Na Torrain

Ruadh Sgeir

West Reef

McPhail's Anvil

Torran Sgoilte

Sgeir Ghobhlach

Otter Rock

Dubh Artach

Eilean Dubh

Balnahar

Balnahard

Rubh' a

Kiloran Bay

Kiloran Gardens

Loch an Sgoltaire

Colonsay House

Port Ceann a' Gharraidh

COLONSAY

Kiloran

Upper Kilchattan

B8086

Lower Kilchattan

B8087

Scalasaig

Port Mòr

Loch Fada

Machrins

B8086

Port Lotha

Loch Staosnaig

Baleromindubh

Sguide an Leanna

B8083

Rubha Dubh

Garvard

Balerominmore

Eilean Mhucaig

Rubha Bàn

Port Askaig 1¼ (seasonal)

Dubh Eilean

Priory

C

Oronsay

D

Eilean nan Ron

Eilean Ghaoideamal

Caolas Mòr

246

230

Beinn Bhuidhe an Fhiar Mhaim 387 309
Beinn na Croise
Beinn nan Carn 333
Lagganulva
Killiechronan
Kellan
B8073
Cruach Torran Lochain
Gruline
Beinn Bhuidhe 412
Na Binneinean 329
Beinn a' Ghraig 591
Knock
Gaodhail
M U L L
18
Monich
Clachandhu
Balnahard
Dhiseig
Beinn Fhada 702
Gortenbuie
Eorsa
Coirc Bheinn 561
Ben More 966
Cruachan Dearg 704
Guibean Uluvailt 328
Corra-bheinn 704
inn na eine
19
Balevulin
Maol na Coille Mòre 288
Dererach
Uluvalt
Cruach Choireadail 618
Craig
Creag na h-Iolaire 506
Loch Airdeglais
SCRIDAIN
Aird of Kinloch
Cruach nan Con 496
Beinn na Croise 503
Loch Fuaron
Ben Buie 717
Pennyghael
Maol nan Uan 274
A849
Killunaig
Brolass
Beinn Chreagach 376
Carsaig
Glenbyre
Leidle
Loch Uisg
Loch Buie
Nuns' Pass
Carsaig Bay
Rubha Dubh
Creachan Mòr 331
Malcolm's Point

Salen Bay
Salen
Pennygown
E
3
B8073
Killbeg
Killbeg
Glen Forsa
Beinn Chreagach Mhòr 579
Loch Ba
Beinn na Duatharach 455
Beinn Talaidh 761
Forsa
Beinn Chaisgidle 504
Glen More
A849
16
Ishriff
Creag na h-Iolaire
Creach Beinn 698
Beinn Fhada 501
Glas Bheinn 491
Fellonmore
Kinlochspelve
Creag nam Fitheach 314
Maol Bàn 338
Druim Fada 405
Beinn a' Bhainne 377
Port Ohirnie
Frank Lockwood's Island
FIRTH

Fishnish Bay
Fishnish
A849
7
Balmeanach
Garmony
Beinn Mheadhon 637
Dun da Ghaoithe 766
Salen Forest
5
Scallastle
Craignure
Maol nan Uan 429
Lochdon
Oakbank
Ardchoil
Ardnadrochit
Ardura
Cruach Ardura 216
Auchnacraig
Carn Bàn 248
Croggan
Dalnaha
Portfield
Rubha na Faoilinn
Loch Spelve
Sgurr Dearg 741

Lochaline (Loch Àlainn)
Inninbeg
Ardtornish Point
Inninmore Bay
Rubha an Ridire
Scallastle Bay
Craignure Bay
Duart Bay
Duart Castle
Duart Point
Grass Point
Port Donain
Barr-nam-boc Bay
Rubha na Lice
Loch Don
Gorten

Glais Bheinn 479
Mam a' Chullaich 462
An Sleaghach
513
481
Eignaig
Lynn of Morven
Bernera
Eilean Musdile
Lady's Rock
Maiden I
Rubh' a' Bhearna
Eilean nan Gamhna
Ardant
Ruba na Lice
Balliemore
Kerrera
Upper Gylen
Ardmore
Bach Island
Rubha Seanach
Dubh Sgeir
G
239

Lochboisdale
Tiere..........3½–4
Colonsay 2¼ hrs
Barnacarry Bay
Eilean Dùn
Rubha Garbh Airde
Barnacarry
Duachy
Kilninver
2
Minara Point
Lera
Galla
Ardentallan
Ardtri

240
Insh Island
Ardencaple House
Ardfad
Sound of Insh
An Cala Garden
Ellenabeich
Dùn-Mòr
Easdale Island Folk Museum
Easdale
Henderson's Rock
B8003
Clachan-Seil
Ardshellach
Seil
Balvicar
Caddleton
Cruach Kearna
3
Ardanstur

Cuan Sound
Cullipool
Garvellachs
Isles of the Sea
A'Chùli
Garbh Eileach
Belnahua
Glas Eilean
Eilean Dubh Mòr
Seil Sound
Torsay Island
Kilchoan
Degnish
Ardinamar
Degnish Point
Eilean Gamhna
Luing
Arduaine Garden (NTS)
Arduaine
Kames
Loch Melfort

Monastery
Eileach an Naoimh
Guirasdeal
Lunga
Black Mill Bay
Shuna Sound
Shuna
Shuna Point
Gemmil
Eilean Arsa
Lunga
Craobh Haven
Toberonochy
Asknish Bay
Barravu
4
Ardfern
Eilean Mhic Chrion
Corranmore
Eilean Righ
Tibertic
Carnassarie

Cruach Scarba 449
Scarba
Corryvreckan Whirlpool
Str. of Corryvreckan
Rubha Righinn
Bàgh Gleann a' Mhaoil
Bàgh Bàn
Reisa Mhic Phaidean
Craignish
Barrackan
Kirkton
Sculptured Stones
Old Poltalloch
Carnassarie
Kilmartin
Island Macaskin
Sculptured Stones
Stone Circle
Slockavullin
Ri Cruin Cairn
Poltalloch
Barsloisnoch
5

Beinn nan Capull 252
Cruach na Seilcheig 296
Kinuachdrach
Rèisa an t- Sruith
Kinuachdrachd Harbour
Craignish Point
Glengarrisdale Bay
Bàgh Gleann Speireig
Glengarrisdale
Glendebadel Bay
Ben Garrisdale 365
Corpach Bay
an 2¼ hrs
Lussa Burn
Lussa
Lealt
Ardnoe Point
Crinan
Crinan Ferry
Moine Mhòr
Crinan Loch
Rubha Garbh-ard
Dunn
NNR
Fort
Moine Mhòr
Cup
Kilmartin

JURA
Dubh Bheinn
Shian Bay
Rainberg Mòr 453
Loch Righ Mòr
Cruach Sganadail
Beinn Bhreac 467
Cruach Ionnastail 295
Eilean an Rubha
Ardlussa
Lussagiven
Lussa
Lussa Point
231
Tramaig Bay
Carsaig Island
Carsaig Bay
Eilean Dubh
Scotnish
Rubha nam Barr
Ardnackaig
Gallchoille
Arinafad Beg
Arichonan
Cnoc Reamhar 265
Bellanoch
B841
Knapdale Forest
Seafield
Achnamara
Kilmichael of Inverlussa
Turbiskill
Gariob
Craig
Cruach Breacain 360

A R G Y L L
D
E
F
G

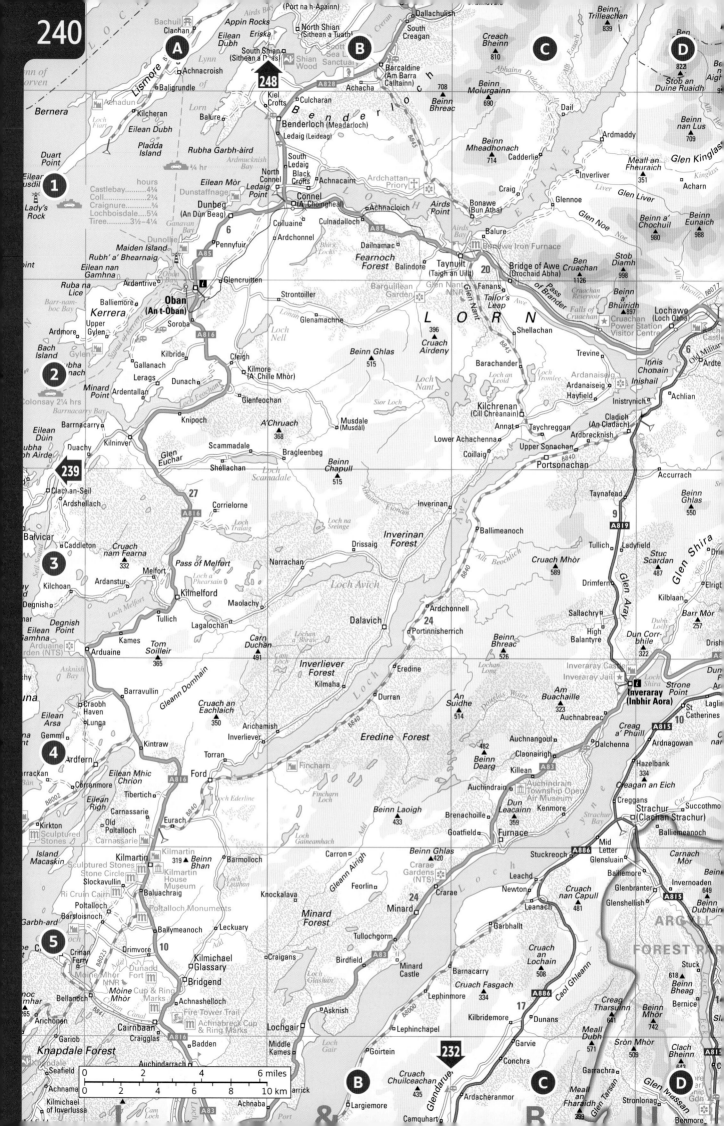

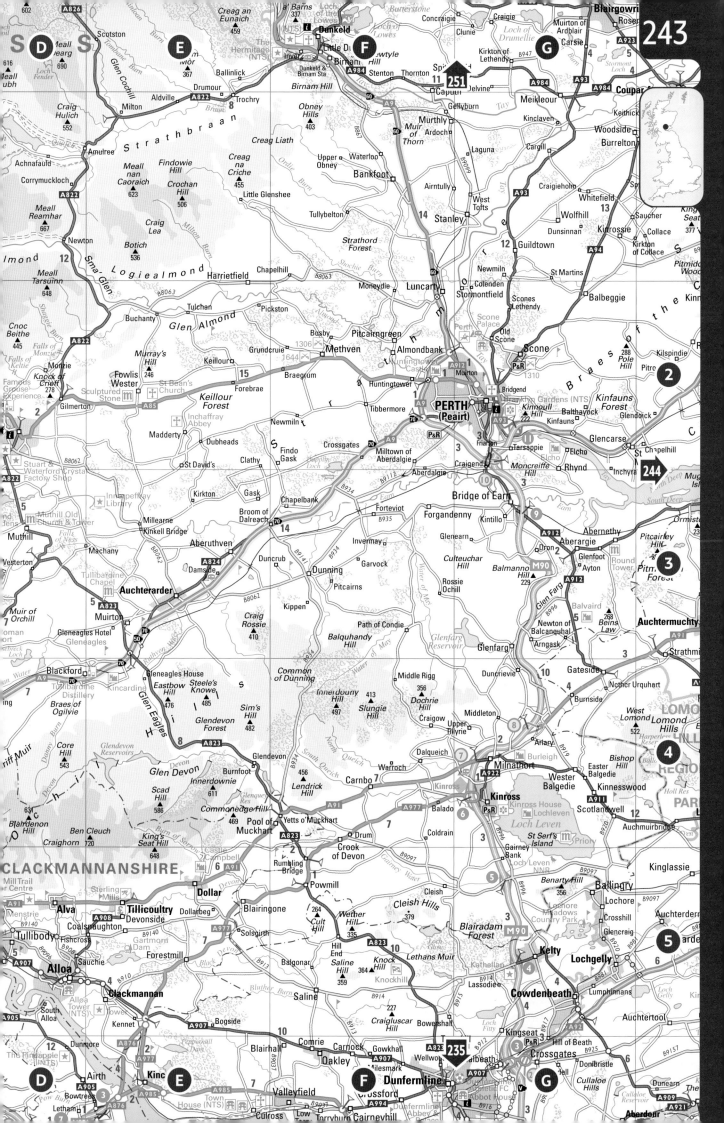

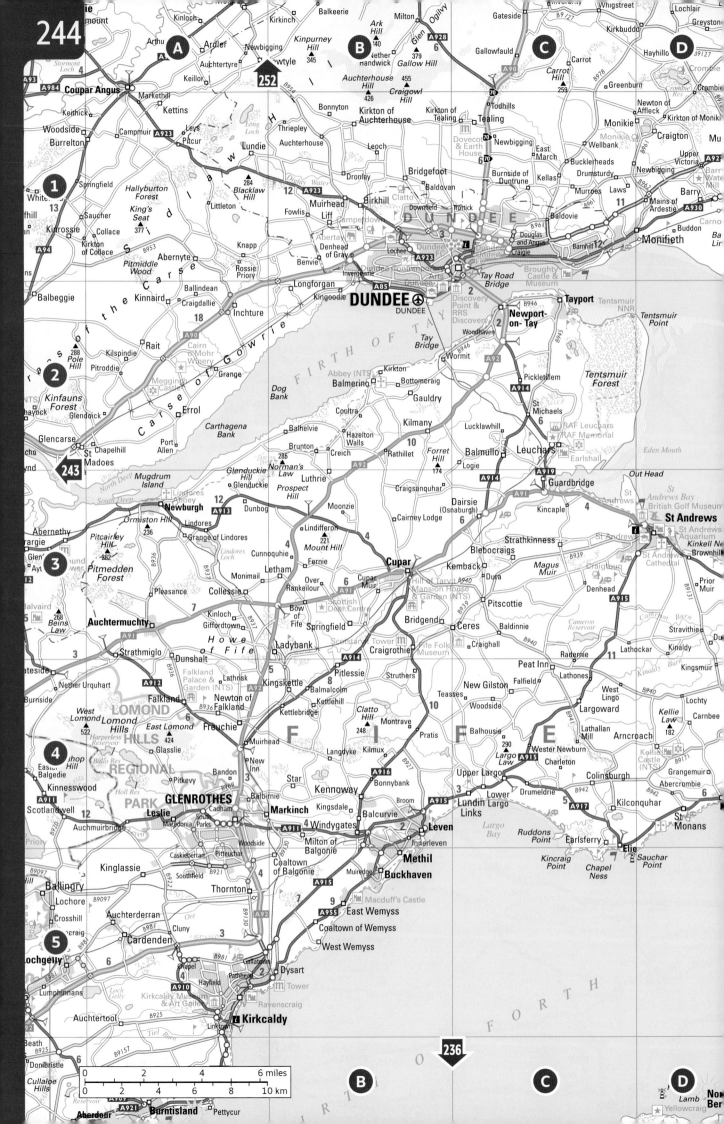

Redford
A933
Marywell
Meg's
Craig
A92
Carlingheugh
Bay
Denhead of
birlot
St Vigeans
Carmyll
E
The Deil's Heid
Guyr
B9127
Arbroath Abbey
Arbirlot
Arbroath
Bonnyton
Easter
Knox
A92
Elliot
um
6
Salmond's Muir
2
East Haven
Panbride
Carnoustie
e.
Buddon Ness

F
G

253

2

*Bell Rock
(Inchcape)*

3

Buddo Ness
arhills
Babbet Ness
10
A917
Cambo
Estate
Kingsbarns
*Cambo
Ness*
*North
Carr*
Wormiston
Tullybothy Craigs
Craighead
Fife Ness
Airdrie
B940
Crail
B9171
West Ness
A917
4
Spalefield
Innergellie
B9131
Kilrenny
Cellardyke
i
Anstruther
Scottish Fisheries Museum
enweem

4

North Ness
Isle of May NNR
Isle of May
Chapel
South Ness

5

237

D
E
F
G

Craig
Bass Rock
ck
Scottish
Seabird
Centre

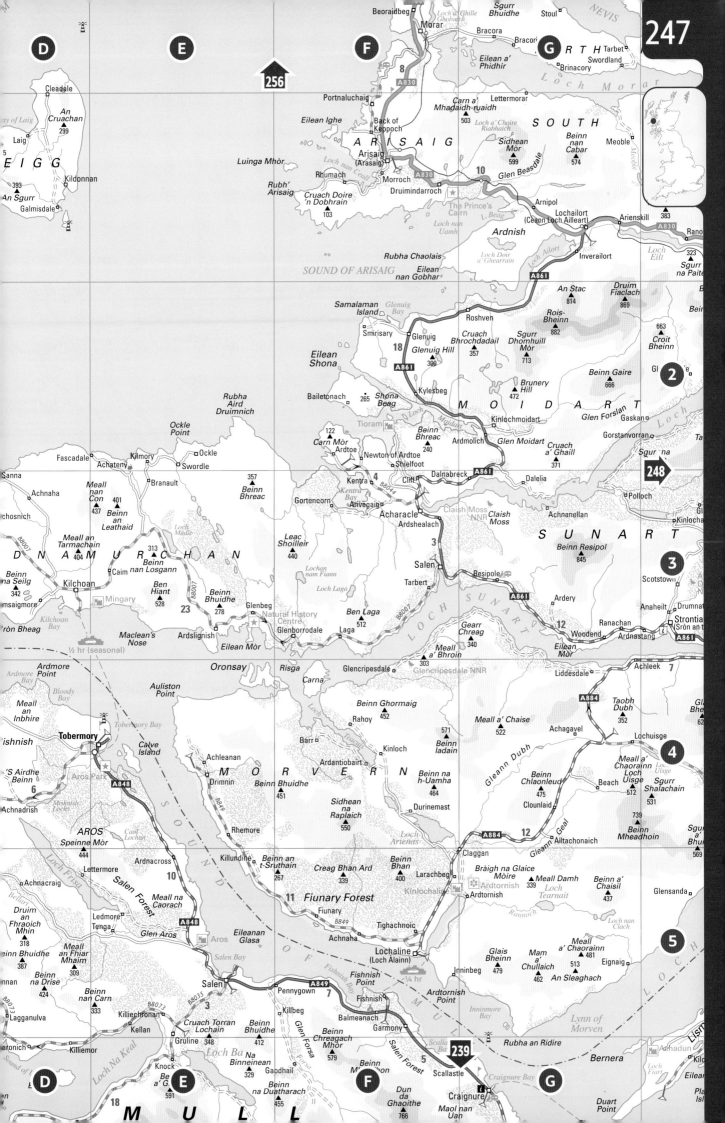

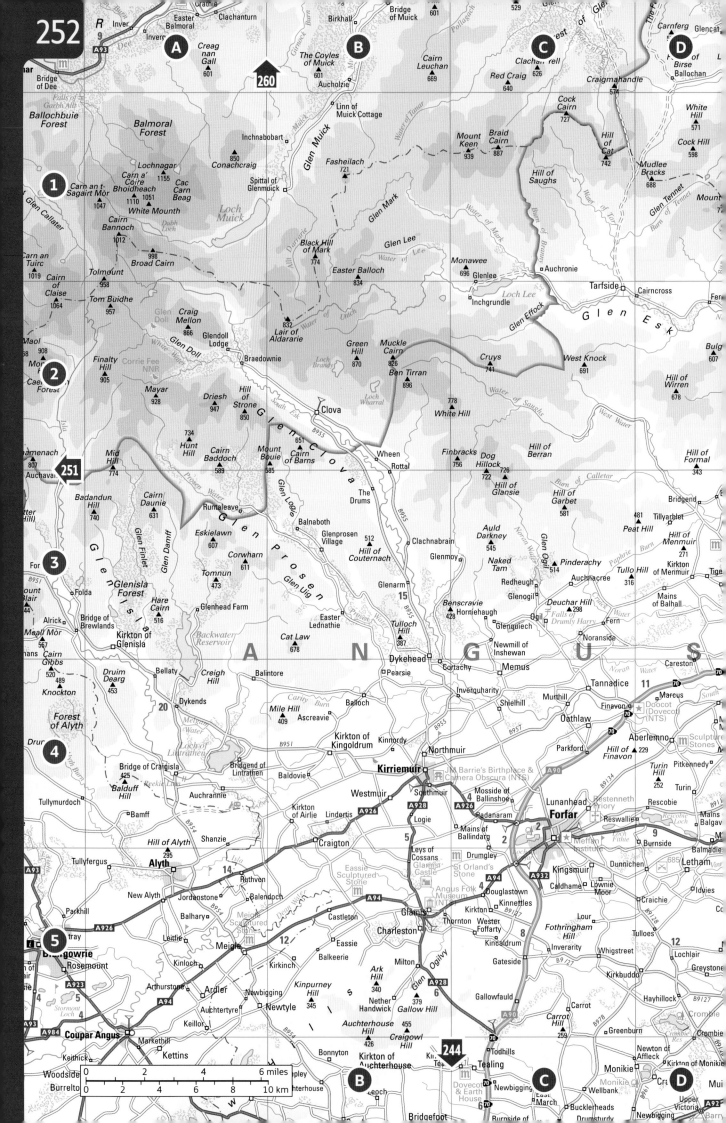

A   B   C   D   E

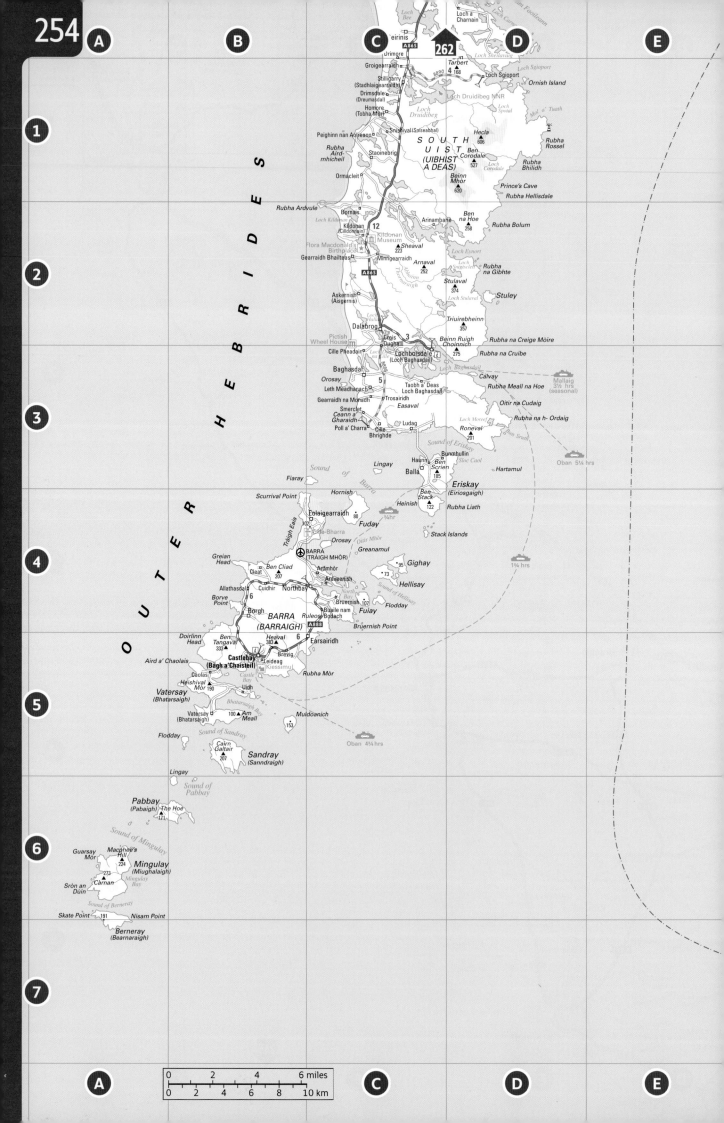

OUTER HEBRIDES

SOUTH UIST (UIBHIST A DEAS)

Loch Bee
Loch a Charnain
Loch Sgioport

262

Ceirinis
Orimore
Groigearraidh
Tarbert
4 168
Loch Sgioport
Ornish Island
Stilligarry
(Stadhlaigearraidh)
Drimsdale
(Dreumasdal)
Loch Shellavaig
Homore
(Tobha Mòr)
Loch Druidibeg NNR
Loch Druidibeg
Snishival (Snìseabhal)
Peighinn nan Aoireann
Loch Spotal
Hecla
606
Rubha Rossel
Rubha Àird mhicheil
Staoinebrig
Ben Corodale
527
Rubha Bhilidh
Ormacleit
Loch Corodale
Beinn Mhòr
620
Prince's Cave
Rubha Hellisdale

Rubha Ardvule
Bornais
Loch Kildonan
Kildonan (Cilldonnain)
12
Kildonan Museum
Flora Macdonald's Birthplace
Gearraidh Bhailteas
Ben na Hoe
258
Rubha Bolum
Arinambane
Sheaval
223
Minngearraidh
Arnaval
252
Askernish (Aisgernis)
Stulaval
374
Rubha na Gibhte
Stuley
Loch Eynort
Loch Snigisclett
Loch Stulaval

Dalabrog
Crois Dughall
Pictish Wheel House
Cille Pheadair
3
Lochboisdale (Loch Baghasdail)
Beinn Ruigh Choinnich
275
Triuirebheinn
357
Rubha na Creige Mòire
Rubha na Cruibe

Baghasdal
Orosay
Leth Meadhanach
5
Taobh a' Deas Loch Baghasdail
Calvay
Rubha Meall na Hoe
Gearraidh na Monadh
Trosairidh
Easaval
Oitir na Cudaig
Mallaig 3½ hrs (seasonal)
Smerclet
Ceann a' Gharaidh
Ludag
Roneval
201
Rubha na h-Ordaig
Poll a' Charra
Cille Bhrighde
Loch Moreal
Oban 5¼ hrs

Lingay
Bunmhullin
Haunn
Ben Scrien
185
Hartamul
Balla
Fiaray
Sound of Barra
Ben Stack
122
Eriskay (Eiriosgaigh)
Scurrival Point
Hornish
Heinish
Rubha Liath

Eolaigearraidh
Cille-Bharra
80
Fuday
¼ hr
Stack Islands

Orosay
Oitir Mhòr
Greanamul
BARRA (TRAIGH MHÒR)
Greian Head
Ben Cliad
207
Ardmhòr
Gighay
95
Ardveenish
73
Cleat
North Bay
Hellisay
1¼ hrs
Allathasdal
Cuidhir
Northbay
Bruernish
107
Floday
Fuiay
Borve Point
6
Borgh
BARRA (BARRAIGH)
Buaile nam Bodach
6
Bruernish Point

Doirlinn Head
Ben Tangaval
333
Heaval
383
6
Earsairidh
Aird a' Chaolais
Castlebay (Bàgh a' Chaisteil)
Leideag
Kiessimul
Brevig
Rubha Mòr
Caolas
Heishival Mòr
190
Uidh
Castle Bay

Vatersay (Bhatarsaigh)
Vatersay (Bhatarsaigh)
100
Am Meall
Muldoanich
153
Oban 4¼ hrs
Floday
Sound of Sandray
Cairn Galtair
207
Sandray (Sanndraigh)
Lingay
Sound of Pabbay

Pabbay (Pabaigh)
The Hoe
171

Sound of Mingulay
Guarsay Mòr
Macphee's Hill
224
Mingulay (Miughalaigh)
273
Carnan
Mingulay Bay
Sròn an Dùin
Sound of Berneray
Skate Point
191
Nisam Point
Berneray (Bearnaraigh)

0   2   4   6 miles
0   2   4   6   8   10 km

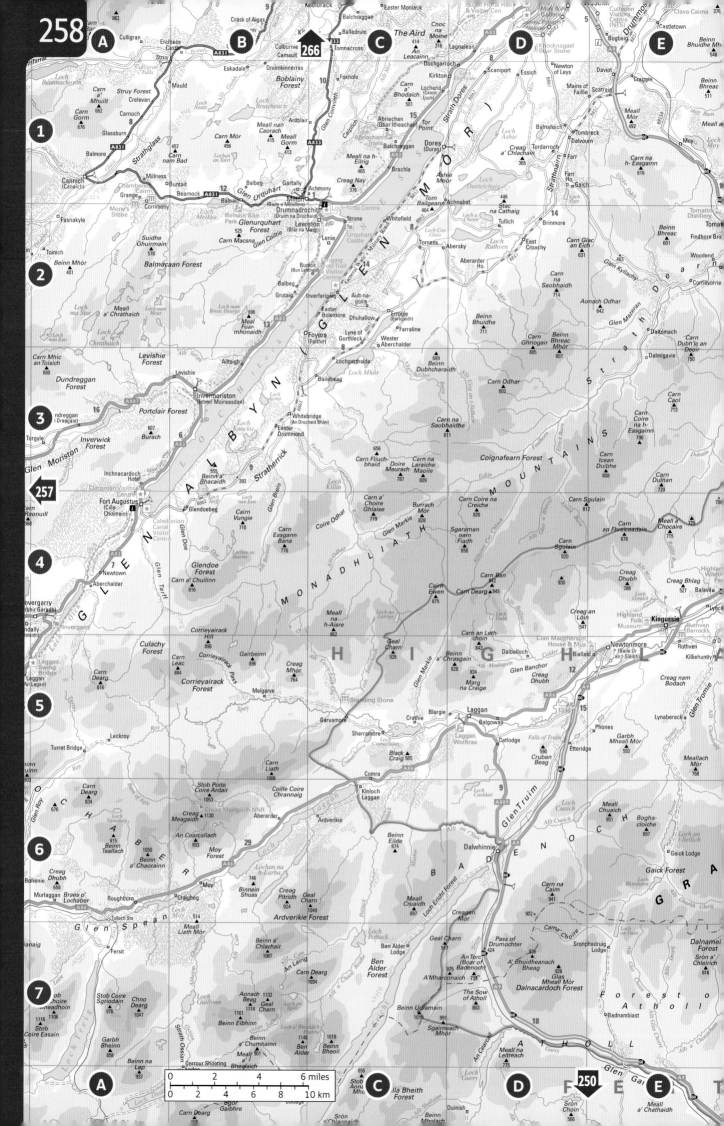

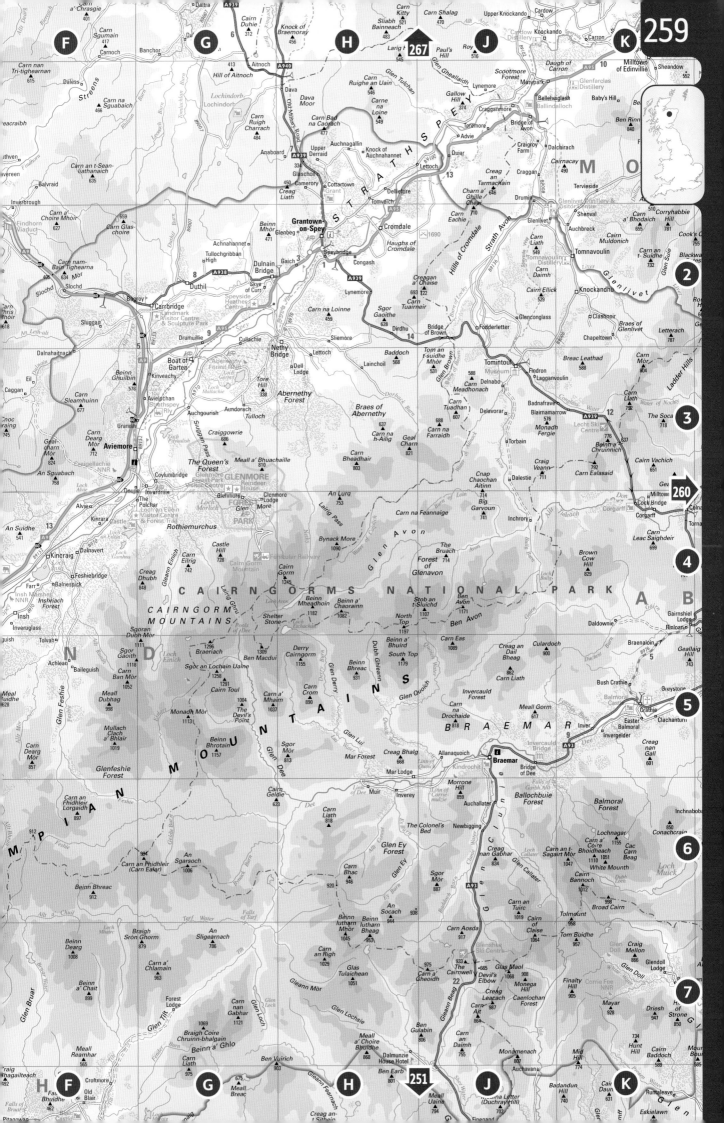

A   B   C   D   E

Gasker

Huisinis

Rubbha Point

Horsanis

1

Taransay Glorigs

Aird Vanish

Rubha Sgeirigin

2

Rubha Màs a' Chnui

Toe Head

339
Chaipaval
365

Tràigh na Cleavag

Shillay

Beinn a' Chàrnain
196

Pabbay

Northton
(Taobh Tuath)

Carminis
Island

Baile-na-Cill

Quinish

Ensay

3

Haskeir
Island

Haskeir
Eagach

NA H-EILEANAN SIAR
(WESTERN ISLES)

Borve
Hill
85

Ruisigearraidh

Berneray
(Eilean Bhearnaraigh)

Massacamber

Killegray

Borgh

Boreray

1 hr

Huilish Point

Otternish

Lingay

Groay

Veilish Point

Pòrt nan Long

Baile Mhic Phail

Aird Thormaid

HARRIS

Griminis
Point

Vallay

Oronsay

4

Scolpaig

Balelone
(Baile Lìon)

A865

Valley
Strand

Sollas
(Solas)

Granitote
(Greinetobht)

Trumaisgearraidh

Beinn Mhòr

Stromay

Hermetray

Baile Mhartainn

Malaclet

Middlequarter
(Ceathramh
Meadhanach)

Maari
180
171

Crogary
Mòr

A865

Keallasay
More

Loch
Aulasay

Leac
na Hoe

Tigh a' Gearraidh

Manish Point

Hosta

Loch nan
Geireann

Bhaltaisbhal

Keallasay
Beg

Lochportain

Scarts Rock

Hogha Gearraidh

NORTH UIST
(UIBHIST A TUATH)

Marrival
230

Loch
Skealtar

Causamul

Aird an
Rùnair

Baile Raghaill

Loch
Fada

Loch
Scadavay

Lochmaddy
(Loch na Madaidh)

Rubha Port Scolpaig

Ceann
a' Bhàigh

Cladach Chnoc a Lin

Loch
nan Eun

Loch na Madadh

Knocklntorran
(Cnoc an Torrain)

8

Batemore
(Baile Mòr)

Oitir
Mhòr

Cladach a' Chaolais

Loch a'
Bharpa

North
Lee

Deasker

Rubha Raouill

Cladach Chircebost

Loch
Huna

Langais

A867

South
Lee
281
250

5

Huskeiran

Sound of Monach

Kirkibost
Island

Clachan-a-Luib

Loch
Scadavay

Loch
Hunder

Rubha Mhic
Gille- mhicheil

Shillay

Ceann Iar

Hearnish

Stockay

Carnach

Samhla

A865

Cladach a Bhale Sheer

Saighdinis

Loch
Obisan

Eigneig Mhòr

Monach Islands
(Heisker Islands)

Ceann Ear

Teanamachar

Carinish
(Cairnis)

5

Eaval
347

Eigneig Bheag

Monach
Islands
NNR

Scrot Mòr

Baleshare
(Bhaleshear)

Teampull na
Trionaigh

Loch
Caravat

Floddaybeg

Loch
Euphoirt

Loch'port
(Locheuphort)

Floddaymore

Eachkamish

Oitir
Mhòr

Baile Glas

Grimsay
(Griomsaigh)

Beinn a'
Chàrnain
115

Ronay
(Ronaigh)

6

BENBECULA (BALIVANICH)

Uachdar

Eilean
Flodaigh

Bàgh Mòre

Ceann'ridh

Ceallan

Balivanich
(Baile a' Mhanaich)

Gramisdale
(Gramsdal)

Beinn
Rodagrich
99

Aird

Rubha na
Rodagrich

Baile nan Cailleach

Loch
Olavat

Rueval
124

Griminish
(Griminis)

BENBECULA
(BEINN NA FAOGHLA)

Loch Uisgebhagh

Torlum

Loch
Olavat

Uiskevagh
(Uisgebhagh)

Linaclate
(Lionacleit)

Gualann

Creagorry
(Creag Ghoraidh)

Hacklet
(Haclait)

Rubha Cam
nan Gall

Hornish Point

Baile
Gharbhaidh

Carnan

102

Ardivachar
Point

Clachan

Iochdar

Peters Port
(Port Pheadair)

Wiay

Aird a' Mhachair

Bualadubh

A865

Loch
Bee

Loch a' Charnain

Geirinis

Drimore

254

0   2   4   6 miles
0   2   4   6   8   10 km

Drimsdale
(Dreumasdal)

Loch
Sgioport

Ornish Island

Homore

Loch Druidibeg
NNR

Loch Druidbeg

A   B   C   D   E

263

OF SHIANT

1

2

Garbh
Eilean
161
Eilean Mhuire

Eilean an Tighe

nt Islands

Greenstone
Point

Leac Ba

Opinan

Rubha
Mòr
Mellon
Charles
Mellon
Udrigle
Achgarve

Slaggan Bay
Laic

Rubha
Reidh
Camas
Mòr

Eilean Furadh Mòr

LOCH EWE

Cove

Isle
of
Ewe
Aultbea
(An t-Allt Beithe)
Drumchor
A832

Loch an Draing

296
An Cuaidh

Ormiscaig
Bualnaluib

Melvaig

Aultgrishan

Inverasdale

9   Midtown

Loch a'
Bhaid
Luachraich

Loch Sgaod

Cnoc Breac
293

Naast

Tournaig
7

Peterburn

Boor

Loch Thurnaig

Inverewe Garde
(NTS)

North Erradale
10

Loch na Curra

Poolewe
Londubh
A832
5

Big Sand

Gairloch
Marine Life
Centre &
Cruises
Smithstown
Mial

Meall A'
Mhic
Craidh
349
Loch
Tollaidh

3   Rubha Hunish

Eilean Trodday

Rubha na h- Aiseig

Longa Island

Carn Dearg

Auchtercairn
Gairloch
(Gearrloch)

Gairloch Heritage Museum

Eilean
Ruaridh Me

4   The Aird
Kilmaluag
Balmaqueen

Kilmaluag Bay

A855

Galta Mòr

Sgeir Eirin

Port Henderson
B8056
Badachro

Charlestown
3

Loch Airigh
a' Phuill

Kerrysdale

Meall
Aundrary
329
A832

Slat

Rubha Hunish

re Bay
Hunglader
Duntulm
19

Flodigarry

Eilean Flodigarry

Opinan

Shieldaig

Loch
Clair

Loch Braigh
Horrisdale

Victoria Fall

Suidh'
a'
Mhinn
350
Loch Sneosdal

Quiraing
Meall
na Suiramach
543

The
Needle

Digg
Staffin Island

Rubha
Garbhaig

South Erradale

Loch
Bad
an Sgalaig

Mullach
nan Cadhaichean
294

Dubh Loch

Loch
Ghabhal

5   Bioda Buidhe
466

Staffin
Stenscholl

Maligar
Elishader

Red Point

Craig

Erradale

Meall
na
h-Uamha
288

Loch a'
Ghobhainn

Loch na
h-Oidhche
Baosbheinn
875

Ben
Gorm

Marishader
Garros

Rubha nam
Brathairean

Culnaknock

Red Point

Maol
Ruadh

Shieldaig Forest

Beinn Bhreac
624

Loch a'
Bhealaich

Balnaknock
Beinn Edra
611

Lealt

Rubha na Fearn

Loch a' Bhraige

Loch
Gaineamhach

An Ruadh-
mheallan
672

Sgurr Mhòr
985

Benn
Dea

Earlish

Trotternish

Glenuachdarach

Creag a'
Lain
608
Baca
Ruadh
637

A855

Leac
Tressirnish

Dry Harbour
125
RONA

Fearnmore

Fearnbeg

Lower
Diabaig

Upper
Diabaig

922

Beinn
Alligin

Peinlich

Beinn
a' Sga
452

Hartaval
668

Rigg

Loch
Diabaigas
Airde

Allt na h-Eirigh

Alligin
Shuas

Inveralligin

11

The
Aird

Romesdal

The
Storr
719

13

Bearreraig
Bay

Eilean Tigh
111

Arinacrinachd

Kenmore

Loch a'
Chracaich

Shieldaig
Island
(NTS)

Rubha na
Feola

Upper Loch Torridon

Balgy

6   Eyre
Carn
Liath

Kensaleyre
dale

Len Mòr

Haultin

Loch Leathan

Eilean
Fladday

Beinn na h-
Iolaire
254

Cuaig

Ardhestaig

Callakille

Lonbain

Inverbain

An
Garbh-
mheall
493

Loch
Gaineamhach

Shieldaig
516
Ben Shieldaig

Ben-damph
Forest

Beinn
Damh
902

Annat
Loch
Damh

Romesdal

Ben
Dearg
552

Loch Fada

Prince
Charles's
Cave

Manish
Point

Torran

Arnish

Brochel

Croic-
bheinn
493

Meall na
Fhuaid
518

An Fur
387

Glenshieldaig Forest

An Staonach
513

Meall na
Saobhaidhe
368

7   Skeabost
Carbost
A850

Borve

A855
392

Sithean
Bhealaich
Chumhaing

Hartfield

Applecross Forest

Loch
Lundie

646

Beinn Bhan
896

H

Sgurr
a' Gharaidh
730

Drumuie
4

Uigshader

A87

Glengrasco

B885

Portree
(Port Righ)

Torvaig

RAASAY

Glame
385

Applecross

Milton

Camusteel

Bealach
na
Ba
626

776

Sgurr a'
Chaorachain
792

Rassal Ashwood
NNR

18
A894

9

Am
Maol
212

Aros
Experience

Glenmore

400
Beinn
na
Greine

2

Penifiler

Ben
Tianavaig
413

Balachuirn

Camusterrach

Culduie

Bealach na Ba

Meall
Gorm
710

Russel

Ardarroch

Lochcarron
(Loch Carrann)

Duagrich
304

Mugear

K   A   E

(N T-EILEAN SGITHEANACH)

Beinn
Totaig

Meall an

Lower Ollach

Upper Ollach
Clachan

Beinn
na'Leac
319

a' Leac

Sròn na h-Airde Bh

C   D   E

Meall Loch Airigh
Alasdair

Ainrig-drishaig

Bad a'
Chreamha
395
Stromemore

0   2   4   6 miles
0   2   4   6   8   10 km

A   B   C   D   E

1

2

3

Halliman
Skerries
Stotfield Branderburgh
267 Lossiemouth
Oakenhead
Boar's
Head
Rock
Salterhill 6
New
Elgin
A941
ELGIN
Bishopmill
Palace
of Spynie
Loch
Spynie
Lossie Forest
Innes
Links
Spey Bay
Kingston
Garmouth
Nether
Dallachy
Spey
Mouth
Tugnet
Icehouse
Exhibition
Lochhill
Spey Bay
Portgordon
Mains of
Dallachy
Upper
Dallachy
Bogmoor
A990
Blackhead
Arradoul
Drybridge
Portknockie
A942
Findochty Scar Nose
Portessie
Ianstown
Bauds of
Cullen
Seatown
Cullen
Bin of
Cullen
320
Logie
Head
Cullen
Bay
Findlater
Castle
Redhythe
Point
Sandend
Sandend
Bay
Mains of
Glassaugh
A98
Portsoy
Boyne
Boyne
Bay
Knock
Head
Whitehills
B9139
Easter
Whyntie
Boyndie
A98 Blairshinnoch
Ban

4

Lhanbryde
9
Mosstodloch
A96
Fochabers
Muir of
Lochs
Brixton
Newlands of Tynet
Bridge
of Tynet
Clochan
Rathven
Buckie
Black
Hill
A98
Hill
of Maud
274
Slate
Haugh
Weston
Black
Hill
255
Shiel Muir
Craibstone
Deskford
Church
Milton
Clune
Fordyce
Durn
Hill
199
Fordyce
Hill
180
Kirktown of
Deskford
Ardiecow
Berryhillock
Hoggie
Canterbury
Cornhill
Oldtown
of Ord
Pattahead
9
B9025
Weachyburn
Greenlaw
The Pole of
Itlaw
135
Linhead
B9121
Kebholes
Hill of
Culbirnie
156
Wester
Culbeuchly
A97
Kirktown
of Alva
A95
Wood of
Barmuckity
Brackla
Longmorn
Blackhills
Clackmarras
Altonside
Orbliston
Dipple
Ordiequish
Inchberry
Chapel
Wood of
Ordiequish
Speymouth
Forest
250
Thief's
Hill
Whiteash
Hill
264
Braes
of Enzie
Millstone
Hill
301
Addie
Hill
272
Aultmore
Black Hill
262
Lurg Hill
313
Backies
Gordonstown
Knock
Hill
430
16
Glen Barry
Wether Hill
271
Park
Milbethill
Finnygaud
Knowes of
Elrick
Auchintoul
Gallow
Hill
Boghead
Cranna
Aberchirder
Bogton

5

Thomshill
Whitewreath
Coleburn
Teindland
Forest
Findlay's
Seat
262
Wood of
Dundurcas
Boat
o' Brig
Forgie
North Bogbain
Hill of
Mulderie
311
Broadrashes
Grange
Crossroads
Garralburn
Deerhill
Crannoch
Bracobrae
Sillyearn
Knock
A95
Drumnagorrach
Limehillock
Farmtown
Moss-side
Crombie
Old Crombie
Knabbygates
Mayen
Marnoch
Clunie
Carnousie
Laithers
Kirkto

6

Brylach
Hill
325
10
Glen of Rothes
Pikey
Hill
355
The
Kettles
Bardon
Auchinroath
Kirkhill
Mulben
Knock More
356
Ben
Aigan
471
12
Tauchers
Auchlunkart
Rosarie
Forest
Rosarie
Keith &
Dufftown Railway
Hill of
Towie
339
Fife
Keith
Keith
A95
Strathisla Distillery
Davoch
of Grange
Floors
Tower
Blackhillock
Meikle Balloch Hill
366
Balloch
Wood
The
Balloch
Haughs
B9022
Milltown
of Rothiemay
A97
Redhill
Yonder
Bognie
Hillbrae
Inverkeithny
Auchininna
Fortrie
Hill of
Carlincraig
192

7

Rothes
Hill
of Stob
308
Cairn
Cattoch
369
Hunt
Hill
365
Whiteacre
Telford
Bridge
Craigellachie
Robertstown
Ringorm
Dandaleith
Maggieknockater
Drummuir Castle
Drummuir
Braehead
B9014
Knockan
372
Towiemore
Edintore
Hillend
Glen of
Coachford
11
Coachford
Newton
Cairnie
Ruthven
Fourman
Hill
344
Cobairdy
B9001
Glendronach
Distillery
12
Conland
Cruichie
Largue
Drumblair
Feith-
hill
Denmoss
Auch
Nether
Lenshie

Carron
Speyview
Daugh of
Kinermony
Ringorm
Aberlour
(Charlestown
of Aberlour)
A941
5
Tullich
Aultnapaddock
Daugh
of
Invermarkie
Daugh of
Cairnborrow
Milton of
Cairnborrow
14
Huntly
A97
A920
Drumblade
Corse
Brideswell
Mosshead
Beggshill

Milltown of
Edinville
Balvenie
Glenfiddich
Distillery
Dufftown
Mortlach
Church
Auchindoun
Sheandow
552
Parkmore
Milltown of
Auchindoun
Keithmore
Bakebare
Haugh of Glass
Torry
Cairnargat
Clashmach
Hill
Strathbogie
Slioch
Thomastown
Ythanwells
Millburn
Logie Newton
Hill of
Tillymorgan
381

MORAY
Glenfarclas
Distillery
Baby's
Hill
Beatshach
Meikle
Conval
569
Laggan
The Scalp
Bridgehaugh
Backside
Succoth
Tillathrowie
Bridgend
Boldorney
Dumeath
Muckle
Long
Hill
391
Bailieswald
Coynachie
Kirkstile
Kirkney
Winds
Eye
314
Backburn
10
Bainshole
Skares
Kirton of
Culsalmond
Cairnhill

Carn an
t- Suidhe
Glenlivet Distillery &
Visitor Centre
Tomnavoulin
Tervieside
B9009
Hill of
Achmore
Glen Fiddich
Forest
Ardwell
Corryhabbie
Hill
781
Laird's
Seat
457
Carn Chrom
503
Glen Fiddich
365
Bridgend
Inverharroch
Farm
Black
Hill
505
Clashindarroch Forest
Quarry
Hill
Cransmill
Hill
440
Clashindarroch
Newnoth
Knockandy
Hill
434
Cults
Leith Hall,
Garden & Estate
(NTS)
Slack
Wardhouse
Picardy
Stone
Upper
Boddam
Wrangham
Largie

Auchbreck
Cairn
Muldonich
Carn an
t- Suidhe
755
Alldunie
571
18
Aldivalloch
Wheedlemont
Rhynie
260
Tap o'
Noth
563
Belhinnie
Cottown
Towie
Kennethm
Milton of
Noth
Kirkton of
Christ's
Kirk
Duncanston
Glanderston
Aulton
Rothney
Insch
Old Rayn
B9002
Bonnyton
Ardoyne
Westhall

A   C   **260**   D   E

0   2   4   6 miles
0   2   4   6   8   10 km

Macduff Marine Aquarium
Macduff
Melrose
Head of Garness
Longmanhill
Foulzie
Keithill
Balgreen
Gorrachie
Castleton
Plaidy
Fintry
Brackens
Wester Badentyre
Muiryfold
Turriff
Delgaty Forest
Bridgend
Gask
Darra
Braefoot
Birkenhills
Hatton Castle
Kingsford
Dykeside
Howe of Teuchar
Towie Barclay
Waggle Hill
Muirtack
South Redbriggs
Deer's Hill
Inverythan
Gourdas
Steinmanhill
Darnabo
Macterry
Kirktown of Auchterless
Gordonstoun
Rothiebrisbane
Tiffy
Backhill
Monkshill
Letheny
Cottown
Burnend
Cairnorrie
Brownhill
Monteach
Fyvie Castle (NTS)
Fyvie
Woodhead
Petty
Rothienorman
Crofts of Haddo
Methlick
Greenmyre
Collynie
St Katherines
Cromblet
Springleys
Core Hill
The Banking
Barthol Chapel
Hillbrae
Earlsfield Park
Craigie Brae
Newseat
Folla Rule
South Flobbets
Balgove
Silvermoss
Thornroan
Weddelfairs
Raxton
Cross of Jackston
Jackstown
South Blackbog
Tulloch
Meikle Wartle
Pitinnan
Tarves
Craigdam
Ythsie
Kinharrachie
Loanend
Newmill
Moss of Belnagoak
Knaven
Nethermuir
Crichie
Skelmuir
Skelmuir Hill
Stuartfield
Millbreck
Kinnadie
Clockhill
Bulwark
Backhill of Clackriach
Drymuir
New Deer
Maud
Mains of Culsh
Ironside
Oldwhat
Hill of Corsegight
Corsegight
Mains of Fedderate
Middlehill
West Cairncake
Cuminestown
Garmond
Balthangie
Adziel
Carnichal
Whitehill
Craigculter
Bonnykelly
New Byth
Knowhead
New Pitsligo
Cairnywhing
Turclossie
Craigmaud
Nether Glasslaw
Bogfold
Bracklamore
Hill of Fishrie
Netherbrae
Overbrae
Plaidy
Craigston
Milltown of Craigston
Minnonie
Cushnie
Dubford
Gamrie
Wester Greenskares
Gardenstown
Crovie
Crovie Head
Gamrie Bay
Troup Head
Northfield
Protstonhill
Pennan
Pennan Head
Aberdour Bay
New Aberdour
Upper Boyndlie
Lemnas
Windyheads Hill
Ladysford
Woodhead
Towie
Coburty
Quarry Head
Rosehearty
Pittulie
Sandhaven
Broadsea
Kinnairds Head
Museum of Scottish Lighthouses
Fraserburgh
Fraserburgh Bay
Peathill
Percyhorner
Pitblae
Cairnbulg Point
Cairnbulg
Inverallochy
Whitelinks Bay
Charlestown
St Combs
Inzie Head
South Inch
Mid Ardlaw
Cardno
Broomhead
Gowanhill
Tyrie
Memsie
Rathen
Cairness
Coralhill
Strathbeg Bay
Whitewell
Mensie Cairn
Craigellie
Whitebog
Hillhead of Auchentumb
Newburgh
Waughton Hill
Mormond Hill
Waughtonhill
Whitestripe
Strichen
New Leeds
Lonmay
Crimonmogate
Old Rattray
Seatown
Rattray Head
Loch of Strathbeg
Crimond
Dartfield
Blackhill
North Essie
Rattray Bay
Longhill
Upper Ridinghill
Gas Terminal
Leys
Backfolds
St Fergus Moss
Kirktown
St Fergus
Scotstown Head
Rora Moss
Cuttyhill
Rora
Kirkton Head
Denhead
Hythie
Fetterangus
Tortue
Mains of Pitfour
Forest of Deer
Deer Abbey
Aden
Old Deer
Mintlaw
Longside
Flushing
Thunderton
Inverquhomery
Millbank
Torterston
Inverugie
Lunderton
Craig Ewen
Arbuthnot Mus
Buchanhaven
Peterhead
Peterhead Maritime Heritage Centre
Keith Inch
Peterhead Bay
Burnhaven
Sandford Bay
Boddam
Buchan Ness
Clola
Nether Kinmundy
Little Dens
Blackhill
Stirling
Invernettie
Hillhead of Cocklaw
Sandfordhill
Aberdeenshire Farming Mus
Inverquhomery
Newton
Kinknockie
Smallburn
Carse of Balloch
Moss of Cruden
Aldie
Coldwells
Gask
Teuchan
Murdoch Head
North Haven
Bullers of Buchan
Auchiries
Errollston
Cruden Bay
Slains (ruins)
Port Erroll
Bay of Cruden
The Skares
Whinnyfold
The Veshels
Forvie Ness
Waterside
St Catherine's Dub
of Slains
Meikle Loch
Forvie NNR
Ellon
Esslemont
Kirktown
Logie
Meikle Tarty
Mounie Castle
Oldmeldrum
Cairnbrogie
Aberdeenshire Farming Mus
Whiteford
Fingask
Auquh
Tolquhon Castle
Pitmedden Garden (NTS)
Pitmedden
Cairnh
Mains of Glack
viot
Rayne
whiteford
Waterloo
Hatton
Bogbrae
Kiplaw Croft
Ardallie
Greenheads
Nether Kinmundy
Muirtack
Hill of Dudwick
Milton of Coldwells
Upper Hawkhillock
Ardallie
Chapel Hill
Arthrath
Mains of Dudwick
Toll of Birness
Bearnie
Leask
Artrochie
Auchmacoy
Clochtow
Inkhorn
Blindburn
Drumwhindle
Tanglandford
Inverebrie
Hilton Croft
Cookston
Broomfield
Auchnagatt
Mill of Elrick
Hill of Skilmafilly
Quilquox
Skelmonae
Ardo
B U C H A N
F O R M A R T I N E

A   B   C   D   E

1

2

3

4

5

6

7

OUTER

HEBRIDES

NA H-EILEANAN SIAR

(WESTERN ISLES)

NORTH HARRIS
(CEANN A TUATH NA HEARADH)

Aird Mhòr Bragair
Rinn
Druim
Tallig
Fibhig
Labost
Rubh' an Dùnain
Shawbost
(Siabost)
Siabost Bho Thu
Slabost
Bho Dheas
Pairc
Bagh
Dail Beag
Aird Mhòr
Dail Bean
Beinn
Bragar
261
Beinn
Choinnic
210
Gearrannan
Dail Mòr
Mullach
Charlabhaigh
248
Beinn
Rahacleit
Craigeam
Borghastan
Carloway (Carlabhagh)
Loch
Carlabhagh
Cirbhig
West
Loch Roag
Creag Mhòr
Carloway Broch
Little
Bernera
Crothair
Gallan Head
Pabaidh
Mòr
Tobson
Bostadh
Tolastadh a' Chaolais
Loch nam
Breac
Aird Uig
Bhaltos
Camas Sandig
Great
Breacleit
Geodha Nasavig
Vacsay
Breascleit
Flaivig Bàgh
Forsnaval
205
Miavaig
(Miabhaig)
Nisa
Mhòr
Reef (Riof)
Bernera
Kirkibost
(Circebost)
Calanais
Staldlàc
Stones
Cradhlastadh
Timsgearraidh
Uigen
Vuia
Mòr
Hacklete
(Tacleit)
Barraglom
Callanish (Calanais)
Camas
Uig
Loch an
Sgaslabhaig
Vuia
Beg
Iarsiadar
Crùlabhig
Eilean
Kearstay
Lundale
A858
Loch Airigh
nan Sloc
Aird Mhòr Mangurstadh
Cairisiadar
Floday
Geisiadar
Ben
Drovinish
185
Linsiadar
Garrynahine
(Gearraidh na h-Aibhne)
Mangurstadh
Eadar
dha
Fhadhail
Loch
Sgaslabhaig
5
B8011
Loch Cean
Tàbhaig
3
Aird Fenish
Suainaval
429
Teahaval
256
Ungisiadar
Griomarstaidh
Loch
Suainaval
Loch
Croistean
Einacleit
Loch
Tangavat
Loch Cleit
Steirmeis
Islibhig
Mealisval
574
Loch
Raonasgail
Loch
Croistean
B8011
Scealascro
Loch
Trealaval
Aird Breanais
Tahaval
515
Giosla
Calltraiseal
Bheag
Loch
Fadagoa
Breanais
Cracaval
514
Skeun
265
Kinlochroag
(Ceann Lochroag)
Beinn Mohal
207
Loch Airigh
na h-Airde
Loch
nam Falag
Mealasta
Tamanaisval
467
Beinn
Mheadhonach
241
Coduinn
16
Calltraiseal Bheag
226
Loch
Grunavat
397
228
Calltraiseal Mhòr
Maghannan
Roineval
281
Balallan
(Baile Aileir
Mealasta Island
Griomaval
Loch na
Craobhaig
Loch Morsgail
Scalaval
260
Loch
Coirigerod
Siidinis
Liongam
Aird
Bheag
Loch
Benisval
Sleiteachal
Mhòr
248
Loch Strandaval
Airidh a
Bhruaich
Kearstay
Gob na
h-Airde Mòire
Loch
Bodavat
Morsgail
Forest
Beinn a'
Bhoth
308
Kintarvie
Aird an
Troim
Ceann Loch
Shiphoir
Sgeir Moil Duinn
Sròn
Romul
308
Aird Mhòr
Mas
a Chnoic-
chuairtich
386
Kearnaval
378
A859
Sidhean
an
Airgid
381
Mòr
Mhonadh
401
Scarp
Sgianait
425
Mullach na
Reidheachd
295
Rapaire
453
Liuthaid
492
Beinn
a'
Mhuil
370
18
Beinn na
h-Uamha
389
Gasker
Huisinis
Husival Mòr
489
Tirga
Mòr
679
Stulaval
579
Mullach a' Ruisg
Ath Linne
Muaithabhal
424
Beann
Mòr
242
Hushinish Point
Ullaval
659
Oreval
662
Aird a'
Mhulaidh
Seaforth
Island
Arda
Beaga
Leosaval
412
Forest
of Harris
NORTH
HARRIS
Beinn Mhòr
572
Horsanish
Gobhaig
Cleiseval
511
Uisgnaval Mòr
729
Mulla-
fo-dheas
743
Clisham
799
Clett Ard
328
Maraig
(Maraig)
Kenmore
Abhainnsuidhe
Rubha
Bhuic
12
Caiteshal
449
Tathas
Mhòr
Crion
470
Taransay Glorigs
Soay Beg
Miabhag
Tolmachan
Bun Abhainn
Eadarra
Sgaoth
Aird
559
Straiaval
389
Toddun
528
Taransay
(Tarasaigh)
Soay Mòr
WEST
LOCH TARBERT
Ben
Raah
267
Aird Asaig
3
Straiaval
Rhenigidale
(Reinigeadal)
Beinn
Dhubh
506
Isle of Harris
Distillery
Tarbert
(Tairbeart)
Lasgdale
Lochs
Paible
Losgaintir
263
Beesdale
Taobh Siar
ann Reamhar
Urgha
Uieseval
334
Eilean Mòr
h-Eighea
Rubha Romagi
Seilebost
Carragrich
Sgeotasaigh
Kyles Scalpay
(Caolas Scalpay)
Sgeir F
Loch Ceann
Dibig
Miabhag
A859
Scalpay
Ben Scoravick
Scalpay

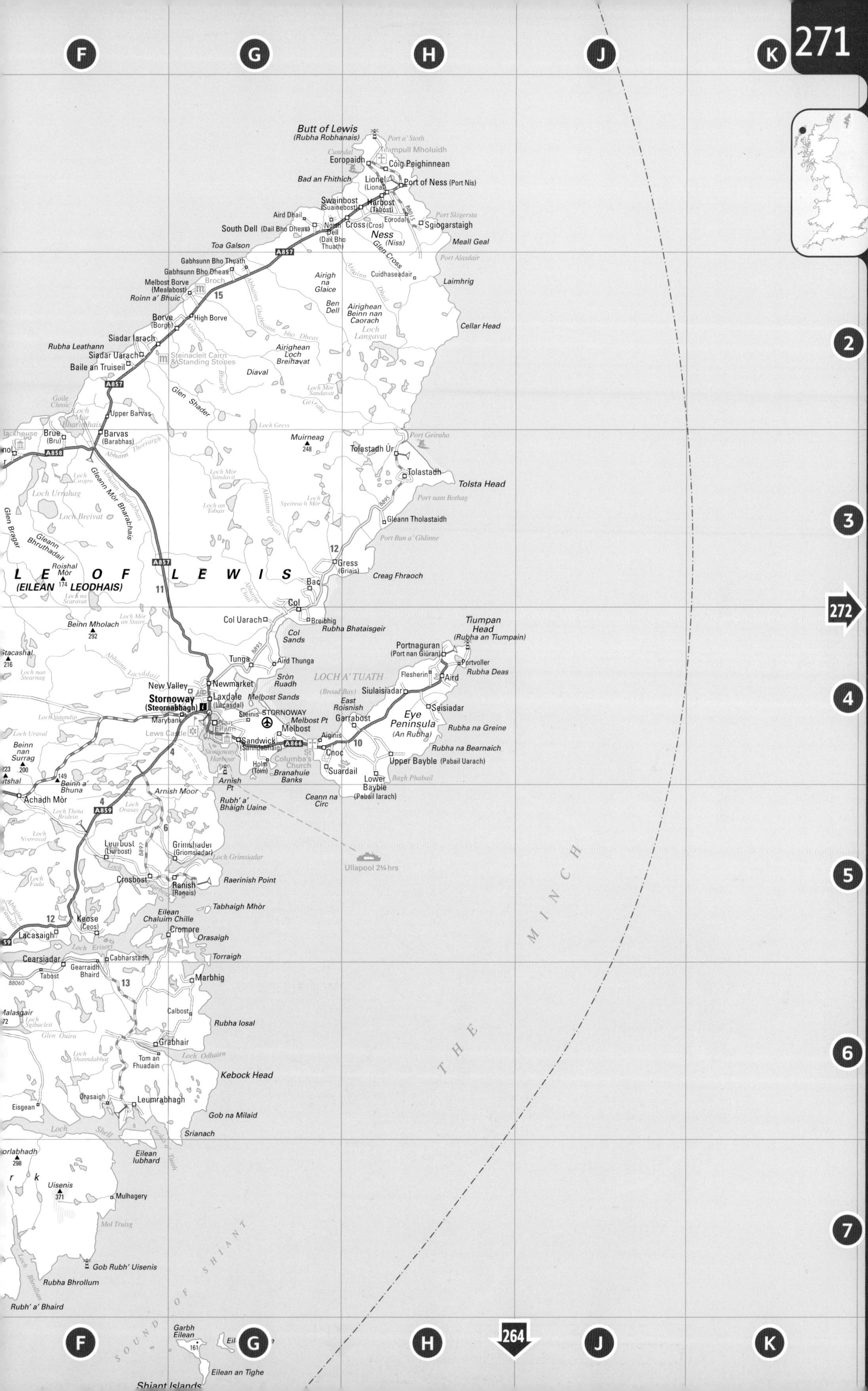

272 →

264 ↓

Butt of Lewis
(Rubha Robhanais)
Port a' Stoth
Cunndal
Teampull Mholuidh
Eoropaidh
Còig Peighinnean
Bad an Fhithich
Lionel
(Lional)
Port of Ness (Port Nis)
Swainbost
(Suainebost)
Harbost
(Tàbost)
Aird Dhail
Port Skigersta
South Dell (Dail Bho Dheas)
North
Dell
(Dail Bho
Thuath)
Cross (Cros)
Eorodal
Sgiogarstaigh
Ness
(Niss)
Toa Galson
Meall Geal
A857
Port Alasdair
Gabhsunn Bho Thuath
Airigh
na
Glaice
Cuidhaseadair
Laimhrig
Gabhsunn Bho Dheas
Melbost Borve
(Mealabost)
Broch
Airighean
Beinn nan
Caorach
Cellar Head
Roinn a' Bhuic
15
Ben
Dell
Borve
(Borgh)
High Borve
Loch
Langavat
Siadar Iarach
Rubha Leathann
Steinacleit Cairn
& Standing Stones
Airighean
Loch
Breihavat
Siadar Uarach
Baile an Truiseil
Diaval
A857
Glen Shader
Loch Mòr
Sandavat
Goile
Chnoc
Upper Barvas
Loch Mòr
Bharabhais
Loch Gress
Brue
(Brù)
Barvas
(Barabhas)
Muirneag
248
Tolastadh Ùr
Port Geiraha
A858
Loch
Casgro
Abhainn Thorraigh
Loch Mòr
Sandaval
Tolastadh
Loch
Sgeireach Mòr
Tolsta Head
Loch Urrahag
Gleann Mòr Bharabhais
Loch an
Tobair
Port nam Bothag
Loch Breivat
Gleann
Bhruthadail
Gleann Tholastaidh
LE OF LEWIS
(EILEAN LEODHAIS)
Roishal
Mòr
174
Port Bun a' Ghlinne
Creag Fhraoch
Beinn Mholach
292
A857
12
Gress
(Griais)
Loch Mòr
an Stairr
Loch nan
Scaravat
11
Bac
Stacashal
216
Col
Tiumpan
Head
(Rubha an Tiumpain)
Col Uarach
Breibhig
Rubha Bhataisgeir
Loch Vatandip
Col
Sands
Portnaguran
(Port nan Giùran)
Portvoller
Abhainn Lacsddail
Tunga
Aird Thunga
Rubha Deas
Sròn
Ruadh
LOCH A' TUATH
Flesherin
Aird
New Valley
Newmarket
Melbost Sands
(Broad Bay)
Siulaisiadar
Rubha na Greine
Stornoway
(Steornabhagh)
Laxdale
(Lacasdal)
East
Roisnish
Seisiadar
Melbost Pt
Melbost
Eye
Peninsula
(An Rubha)
Marybank
STORNOWAY
Garrabost
Rubha na Bearnaich
Beinn
nan
Surrag
200
Aiginis
10
4
Sandwick
(Sanndabhaig)
A866
St
Columba's
Church
Choc
Upper Bayble (Pabail Uarach)
149
Beinn a'
Bhuna
Holm
(Tom)
Suardail
223
Achadh Mòr
Arnish Moor
Branahuie
Banks
Lower
Bayble
(Pabail Iarach)
Bagh Phabail
itshal
A859
Loch Thota
Bridein
4
Arnish
Pt
Ceann na
Circ
Rubh' a'
Bhàigh Uaine
6
Loch
Orasay
Loch Nisreival
Loch
Fada
Leurbost
(Liurbost)
Grimshader
(Griomsiadar)
Ullapool 2¾ hrs
THE MINCH
Raerinish Point
Loch Grimsiadar
Crosbost
Ranish
(Ranais)
Tabhaigh Mhòr
12
Keose
(Ceos)
Eilean
Chaluim Chille
Lacasaigh
Cromore
Orasaigh
59
Cearsiadar
Gearraidh
Bhaird
Cabharstadh
Torraigh
Tabost
88060
13
Marbhig
Malasgair
72
Loch
Sgibacleit
Calbost
Glen Oùirn
Rubha Iosal
Grabhair
Loch
Shanndabhat
Tom an
Fhuadain
Loch Odhairn
6
Kebock Head
Orasaigh
Leumrabhagh
Gob na Milaid
Eisgean
Srianach
orlabhadh
298
Eilean
Iubhard
Loch Shell
THE SOUND OF SHIANT
Uisenis
371
Mulhagery
7
Mol Truisg
Gob Rubh' Uisenis
Rubha Bhrollum
Rubh' a' Bhaird
Garbh
Eilean
161
Eil
Eilean an Tighe
Shiant Islands

271

265

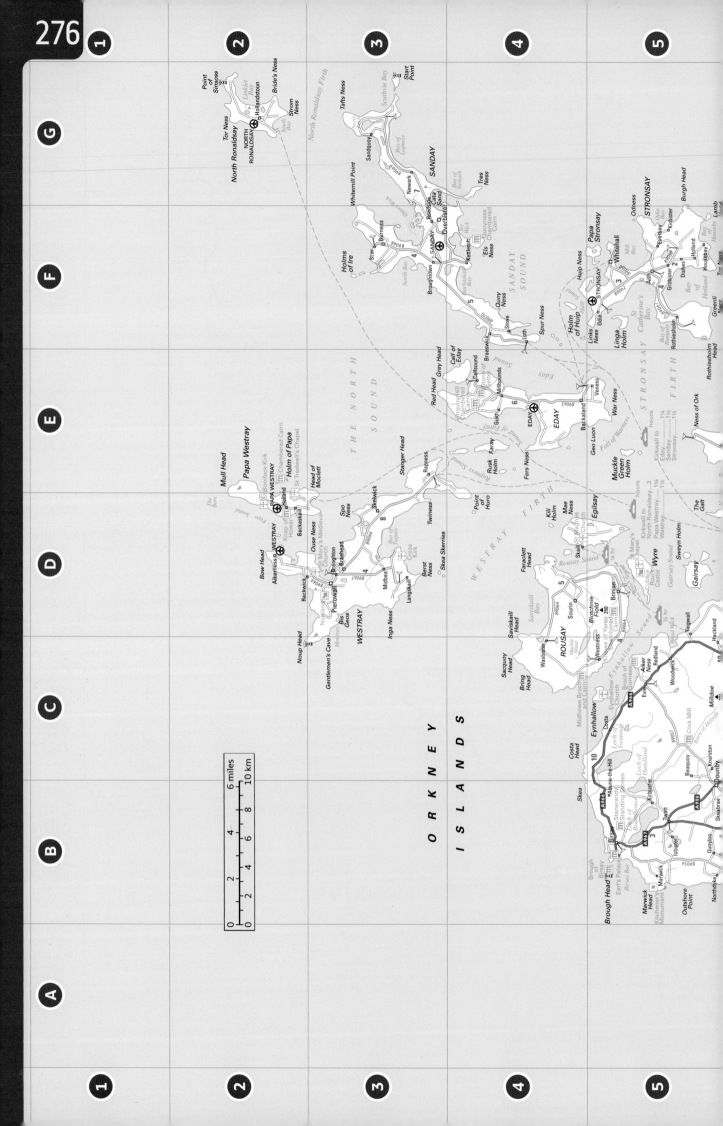

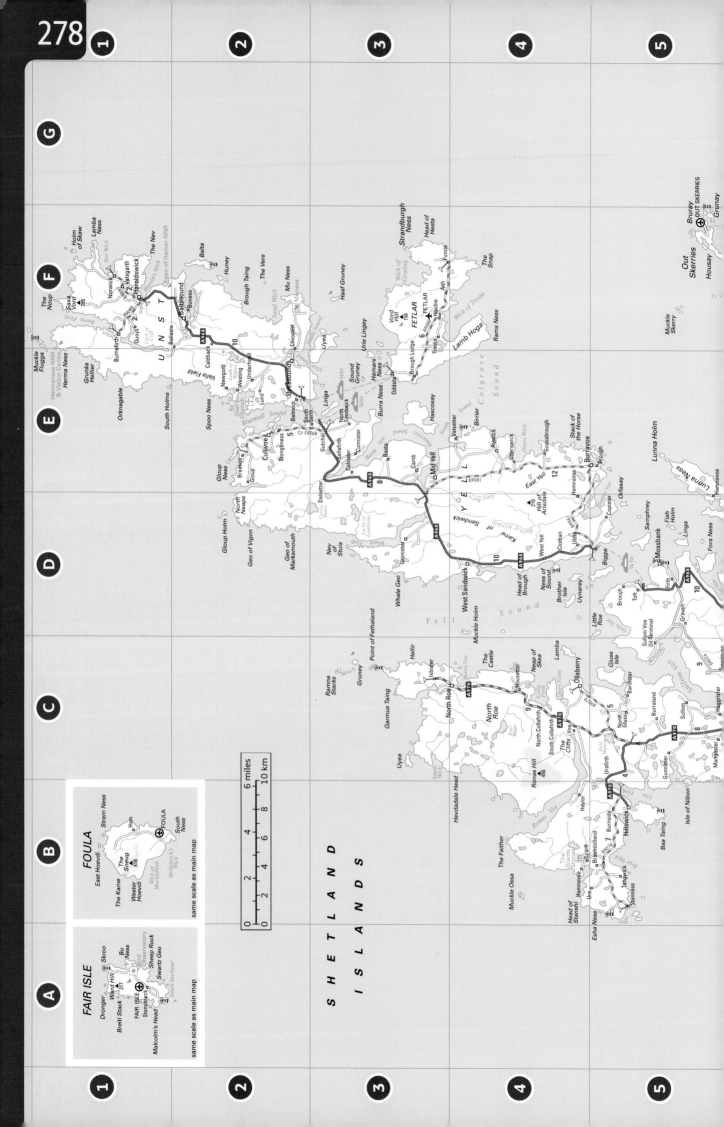

SHETLAND ISLANDS

FAIR ISLE

Dronger
Skroo
Ward Hill
217
Breiti Stack
Stonybreck
Malcolm's Head
Bu Ness
Bird Observatory
Sheep Rock
Swartz Geo
FAIR ISLE
South Harbour

same scale as main map

FOULA

Strem Ness
Ham
The Snaug
418
The Kame
East Hoevdi
FOULA
South Ness
Wester Hoevdi
Hedduwick's Wick
Wick of Mucklaberg

same scale as main map

6 miles

10 km

Place and place of interest names are followed by a **page number** and a grid reference in black type. The feature can be found on the map somewhere within the grid square shown.

Where two or more places have the same name the abbreviated county or unitary authority names are shown to distinguish between them. A list of these abbreviated names appears below.

The top 1000 most visited places of interest are shown within the index in blue type. Their postcode information is supplied after the county names to aid integration with satnav systems.

A&B	Argyll & Bute
Aber	Aberdeenshire
B&H	Brighton & Hove
B&NESom	Bath & North East Somerset
B'burn	Blackburn with Darwen
B'pool	Blackpool
BGwent	Blaenau Gwent
Bed	Bedford
Bourne	Bournemouth
BrackF	Bracknell Forest
Bucks	Buckinghamshire
Caerp	Caerphilly
Cambs	Cambridgeshire
Carmar	Carmarthenshire
CenBeds	Central Bedfordshire
Cere	Ceredigion
Chanl	Channel Islands
ChesE	Cheshire East
ChesW&C	Cheshire West & Chester
Corn	Cornwall
Cumb	Cumbria
D&G	Dumfries & Galloway
Darl	Darlington
Denb	Denbighshire
Derbys	Derbyshire
Dur	Durham
EAyr	East Ayrshire
EDun	East Dunbartonshire
ELoth	East Lothian
ERenf	East Renfrewshire
ERid	East Riding of Yorkshire
ESuss	East Sussex
Edin	Edinburgh
Falk	Falkirk
Flints	Flintshire
Glas	Glasgow
Glos	Gloucestershire
GtLon	Greater London
GtMan	Greater Manchester
Gwyn	Gwynedd
Hants	Hampshire
Hart	Hartlepool
Here	Herefordshire
Herts	Hertfordshire
High	Highland
Hull	Kingston upon Hull
Invcly	Inverclyde
IoA	Isle of Anglesey
IoM	Isle of Man
IoS	Isles of Scilly
IoW	Isle of Wight
Lancs	Lancashire
Leic	Leicester
Leics	Leicestershire
Lincs	Lincolnshire
MK	Milton Keynes
MTyd	Merthyr Tydfil
Med	Medway
Mersey	Merseyside
Middl	Middlesbrough
Midlo	Midlothian
Mon	Monmouthshire
Na H-ESiar	Na H-Eileanan Siar (Western Isles)
N'hants	Northamptonshire
N'umb	Northumberland
NAyr	North Ayrshire
NELincs	North East Lincolnshire
NLan	North Lanarkshire
NLincs	North Lincolnshire
NPT	Neath Port Talbot
NSom	North Somerset
NYorks	North Yorkshire
Norf	Norfolk
Nott	Nottingham
Notts	Nottinghamshire
Ork	Orkney
Oxon	Oxfordshire
P&K	Perth & Kinross
Pembs	Pembrokeshire
Peter	Peterborough
Plym	Plymouth
Ports	Portsmouth
R&C	Redcar & Cleveland
RCT	Rhondda Cynon Taff
Read	Reading
Renf	Renfrewshire
Rut	Rutland
S'end	Southend-on-Sea
SAyr	South Ayrshire
SGlos	South Gloucestershire
SLan	South Lanarkshire
SYorks	South Yorkshire
ScBord	Scottish Borders
Shet	Shetland
Shrop	Shropshire
Slo	Slough
Som	Somerset
Soton	Southampton
Staffs	Staffordshire
Stir	Stirling
Stock	Stockton-on-Tees
Stoke	Stoke-on-Trent
Suff	Suffolk
Surr	Surrey
Swan	Swansea
Swin	Swindon
T&W	Tyne & Wear
Tel&W	Telford & Wrekin
Thur	Thurrock
VGlam	Vale of Glamorgan
W&M	Windsor & Maidenhead
W'ham	Wokingham
WBerks	West Berkshire
WDun	West Dunbartonshire
WLoth	West Lothian
WMid	West Midlands
WSuss	West Sussex
WYorks	West Yorkshire
Warks	Warwickshire
Warr	Warrington
Wilts	Wiltshire
Worcs	Worcestershire
Wrex	Wrexham

1	Bath & North East Somerset
2	Blaenau Gwent
3	Bournemouth
4	Bracknell Forest
5	Bridgend
6	Bristol
7	Caerphilly
8	Cardiff
9	Clackmannanshire
10	Darlington
11	Dundee
12	East Dunbartonshire
13	East Renfrewshire
14	Glasgow
15	Halton
16	Hartlepool
17	Inverclyde
18	Luton
19	Merthyr Tydfil
20	Middlesbrough
21	Monmouthshire
22	Neath Port Talbot
23	Newport
24	North Lanarkshire
25	Plymouth
26	Poole
27	Portsmouth
28	Reading
29	Redcar And Cleveland
30	Renfrewshire
31	Rhondda Cynon Taff
32	Slough
33	South Gloucestershire
34	Southampton
35	Stockton-on-tees
36	Telford & Wrekin
37	Torfaen
38	Vale Of Glamorgan
39	Warrington
40	West Dunbartonshire
41	Windsor & Maidenhead
42	Wokingham

1853 Gallery *WYorks* BD18 3LA 26 C1

A

Ab Kettleby 174 C5
Ab Lench 146 C2
Abbas Combe 117 E5
Abberley 145 G1
Abberley Common 145 G1
Abberton *Essex* 138 D1
Abberton *Worcs* 146 B2
Abberwick 229 F5
Abbess Roding 137 E1
Abbey Dore 144 C4
Abbey Hulton 171 G3
Abbey St. Bathans 237 E3
Abbey Village 192 C5
Abbey Wood 137 D5
Abbeycwmhir 155 G5
Abbeydale 186 A4
Abbeystead 192 B2
Abbeytown 209 E1
Abbotrule 228 A5
Abbots Bickington 113 D4
Abbots Bromley 172 B5
Abbots Langley 135 F2
Abbots Leigh 131 E5
Abbots Morton 146 C2
Abbots Ripton 162 A5
Abbot's Salford 146 C2
Abbots Worthy 119 F4
Abbotsbury 104 B4
Abbotsbury Swannery, Subtropical Gardens & Children's Farm *Dorset* DT3 4JG 104 B4
Abbotsfield Farm 183 G3
Abbotsham 113 E3
Abbotskerswell 101 E1
Abbotsley 150 A2
Abbotstone 119 G4
Abbotts Ann 119 E3
Abbott's Barton 119 F4
Abbottswood 119 E5
Abdon 157 E4
Abdy 186 B3
Abenhall 131 F1
Aber 142 A3
Aber Village 144 A5
Aberaeron 142 A1
Aberaman 129 G2
Aberangell 155 E2
Aber-Arad 141 G3
Aberarder 249 G1
Aberarder House 258 D2
Aberargie 243 G3
Aberarth 142 A1
Aberavon 129 D3
Aber-banc 141 G3
Aberbargoed 130 A2
Aberbeeg 130 B2
Aberbowlan 142 C4
Aberbran 143 F5
Abercanaid 129 G2
Abercarn 130 B3
Abercastle 140 B4
Abercegir 155 E2
Aberchalder 257 K4
Aberchirder 268 E5
Abercorn 235 E2
Abercraf 129 E1
Abercregan 129 E3
Abercrombie 244 D4
Abercrychan 143 D4
Abercwmboi 129 G2
Abercych 141 F3
Abercynafon 129 G1
Abercynon 129 G3
Abercywarch 155 E1
Aberdalgie 243 F2
Aberdare 129 F2
Aberdaron 166 A5
Aberdeen (Obar Dheathain) 261 H4
Aberdeen Airport 261 G3
Aberdeen Art Gallery AB10 1FQ 63 Aberdeen
Aberdeen Exhibition & Conference Centre *Aberdeen* AB23 8BL 261 H3
Aberdesach 166 D2
Aberdour 235 F1
Aberdovey (Aberdyfi) 154 C3
Aberduhonw 143 G2
Aberdulais 129 D3
Aberedw 143 G3
Abereiddy 140 A4
Abererch 166 C4
Aberfan 129 G2
Aberfeldy 251 D5
Aberffraw 166 C1
Aberffrwd 154 C5
Aberford 194 D4
Aberfoyle 242 A4
Abergavenny (Y Fenni) 130 B1
Abergele 182 A5
Aber-Giâr 142 B3
Abergorlech 142 B4
Abergwesyn 143 E2
Abergwili 142 A5
Abergwydol 155 D2
Abergwynant 154 C1
Abergwynfi 129 E3
Abergwyngregyn 181 E5
Abergynolwyn 154 C2
Aberhafesp 155 G3
Aberhosan 155 E3
Aberkenfig 129 E4
Aberlady 236 B1
Aberlemno 252 D4
Aberllefenni 155 D2
Aber-Ilia 129 F1
Aberlour (Charlestown of Aberlour) 267 K7
Abermad 154 B5
Abermeurig 142 B2
Abermule (Aber-miwl) 156 A3
Abernaint 169 E5
Abernant *Carmar* 141 G5
Aber-nant *RCT* 129 G2
Abernethy 243 G3
Abernyte 244 A1
Aberporth 141 F2
Aberscross 266 E2
Abersky 258 C2
Abersoch 166 C5
Abersychan 130 B2
Aberthin 129 G5
Abertillery 130 B2
Abertridwr *Caerp* 130 A4
Abertridwr *Powys* 155 G1
Abertysswg 130 A2
Aberuthven 243 E3
Aberyscir 143 F5
Aberystwyth 154 B4
Aberystwyth Arts Centre *Cere* SY23 3DE 154 B4
Abhainnsuidhe 270 C7
Abingdon 133 G3
Abinger Common 121 G3
Abinger Hammer 121 F3
Abington 226 A3
Abington Pigotts 150 B3
Abingworth 108 D2
Ablington *Glos* 132 D2
Ablington *Wilts* 118 C3
Abney 185 F5
Above Church 172 B2
Aboyne 260 D5
Abram 184 A2
Abriachan (Obar Itheachan) 258 C1
Abridge 137 D3
Abronhill 234 B2
Abson 131 G5
Abthorpe 148 B3
Abune-the-Hill 276 B5
Aby 189 E5
Acaster Malbis 195 E3
Acaster Selby 195 E3
Accrington 193 D5
Accurrach 240 D2
Acha 246 A4
Achacha 248 B5
Achadacaie 231 G3
Achadh Mòr 271 F5
Achadh-chaorrunn 231 F4
Achadunan 241 E3
Achagavel 247 G4
Achaglass 231 F5
Achahoish 231 F2
Achalader 251 G5
Achallader 249 F5
Achamore 231 D2
Achandunie 266 D4
Achany 266 C1
Achaphubuil 248 C2
Acharacle 247 F3
Achargary 274 C3
Acharn *A&B* 240 D1
Acharn *P&K* 250 C5
Acharonich 239 D1
Acharosson 232 A2
Achateny 247 E2
Achath 261 F3
Achavanich 275 G4
Achddu 128 A2
Achduart 265 G1
Achentoul 274 D5
Achfary 272 E5
Achgarve 264 E2
Achiemore *High* 273 F2
Achiemore *High* 274 D3
Achies 275 G3
A'Chill 255 H4
Achiltibuie (Achd-'Ille-Bhuidhe) 265 G1
Achina 274 C2
Achindown 267 F7
Achinduich 266 C2
Achingills 275 G2
Achintee 265 F7
Achintee House (Achadh an t-Suidhe) 248 D2
Achintraid 256 E1
Achlean 259 F5
Achleanan 247 E4
Achleek 247 G4
Achlian 240 D2
Achlyness 272 E3
Achmelvich 272 C6
Achmony 258 C1
Achmore *High* 256 E1
Achmore *High* 265 G2
Achmore *Stir* 242 A1
Achnaba 232 A1
Achnabat 258 C1
Achnabourin 274 C3
Achnacairn 240 B1
Achnacarnin 272 C5
Achnacarry 249 D1
Achnaclerach 266 B5
Achnacloich *A&B* 240 B1
Achnacloich *High* 256 B4
Achnaclyth 275 F5
Achnacraig 247 D5
Achnacroish 248 A5
Achnadrish 246 D4
Achnafalnich 241 E2
Achnafauld 243 D1
Achnagairn 266 C7
Achnagarron 266 D4
Achnaha *High* 247 F5
Achnaha *High* 247 D3
Achnahanat 266 C2
Achnahannet 259 G2
Achnairn 273 H7
Achnalea 248 A3
Achnamara 231 F1
Achnanellan 247 G3
Achnasaul 249 D1
Achnasheen 265 H6
Achnashelloch 240 A5
Achnastank 259 K1
Achorn 275 G5
Achosnich *High* 266 E2
Achosnich *High* 246 D3
Achreamie 275 F2
Achriabhach 248 D3
Achriesgill 272 E3
Achtoty 273 J2
Achurch 161 F4
Achuvoldrach 273 H3
Achvaich 266 E2
Achvarasdal 274 E2
Achvlair 248 B4
Achvraie 265 G1
Ackenthwaite 199 G4
Ackergill 275 J3
Acklam *Middl* 203 D1
Acklam *NYorks* 195 G1
Ackleton 157 G3
Acklington 221 E1
Ackton 194 D5
Ackworth Moor Top 186 B1
Acle 179 F4
Acock's Green 158 D4
Acol 125 F2
Acomb *N'umb* 211 F1
Acomb *York* 195 E2
Aconbury 145 E4
Acre 193 D5
Acrefair 169 F3
Acrise Place 125 D4
Acton *ChesE* 170 D2
Acton *Dorset* 105 F5
Acton *GtLon* 136 A4
Acton *Shrop* 156 C4
Acton *Staffs* 171 F3
Acton *Suff* 151 G3
Acton *Worcs* 146 A1
Acton *Wrex* 170 A2
Acton Beauchamp 145 F2
Acton Bridge 183 G5
Acton Burnell 157 E2
Acton Green 145 F2
Acton Pigott 157 E2
Acton Round 157 F3
Acton Scott 157 D4
Acton Trussell 158 B1
Acton Turville 132 A4
Adamhill 224 C2
Adbaston 171 E5
Adber 116 C5
Adderbury 147 G4
Adderley 171 D4
Adderstone 229 F3
Addiewell 235 D3
Addingham 193 G3
Addington *Bucks* 148 C5
Addington *GtLon* 122 C2
Addington *Kent* 123 F3
Addiscombe 122 C2
Addlestone 121 F1
Addlethorpe 176 D1
Adel 194 B4
Aden Country Park *Aber* AB42 5FQ 269 H6
Adeney 157 G1
Adeyfield 135 F2
Adfa 155 G2
Adforton 156 D5
Adisham 125 E3
Adlestrop 147 E5
Adlingfleet 196 A5
Adlington *ChesE* 184 D4
Adlington *Lancs* 183 G1
Admaston *Staffs* 172 B5
Admaston *Tel&W* 157 F1
Admington 147 E3
Adsborough 115 F5
Adscombe 115 E4
Adstock 148 C4
Adstone 148 A2
Adventure Island *S'end* SS1 1EE 138 B4
Adventure Wonderland *Dorset* BH23 6BA 3 D2
Adversane 121 F5
Advie 259 J1
Adwalton 194 B5
Adwell 134 B3
Adwick le Street 186 C2
Adwick upon Dearne 186 B2
Adziel 269 H5
Ae Village 217 D2
Afan Argoed Country Park *NPT* SA13 3HG 129 E3
Affetside 184 B1
Affleck 261 G2
Affpuddle 105 E3
Afon Wen 166 D4
Afon-wen 182 C5
Afonwen Craft & Antique Centre *Flints* CH7 5UB 182 C5
Africa Alive! *Suff* NR33 7TF 165 G3
Afton 106 C4
Afton Bridgend 225 E4
Agglethorpe 201 F4
Aigburth 183 E4
Aiginis 271 G4
Aike 196 C3
Aikerness 276 D2
Aikers 277 D8
Aiketgate 210 A3
Aikshaw 209 E2
Aikton 209 F1
Aikwood Tower 227 F3
Ailby 189 E5
Ailey 144 C3
Ailsworth 161 G3
Aimes Green 136 D2
Aimster 275 G2
Ainderby Quernhow 202 C4
Ainderby Steeple 202 C3
Aingers Green 152 C5
Ainsdale 183 E1
Ainsdale-on-Sea 183 E1
Ainstable 210 B3
Ainsworth 184 B1
Ainthorpe 203 G2
Aintree 183 E3
Aird *Na H-ESiar* 262 C6
Aird *Na H-ESiar* 271 H4
Aird a' Mhachair 262 C7
Aird a' Mhulaidh 270 D6
Aird Asaig 270 D7
Aird Dhail 271 G1
Aird Leimhe 263 G3
Aird Mhige 263 G2
Aird Mhighe 263 F3
Aird of Sleat 256 B4
Aird Thunga 271 G4
Aird Uig 270 C4
Airdrie *Fife* 245 D4
Airdrie *NLan* 234 B3
Aire View 193 F3
Airidh a' Bhruaich 270 E6
Airieland 216 B5
Airies 214 A4
Airigh-drishaig 256 D1
Airmyn 195 G5
Airntully 243 F1
Airor 256 D4
Airth 234 C1
Airton 193 F2
Airyhassen 207 D2
Aisby *Lincs* 187 F3
Aisby *Lincs* 175 F4
Aisgill 200 C3
Aish *Devon* 100 C1
Aish *Devon* 101 E2
Aisholt 115 E4
Aiskew 202 B4
Aislaby *NYorks* 204 B2
Aislaby *NYorks* 203 G4
Aislaby *Stock* 202 D1
Aisthorpe 187 G4
Aith *Ork* 277 B6
Aith *Ork* 276 F5
Aith *Shet* 279 C7
Aith *Shet* 278 F3
Aithsetter 279 D9
Aitnoch 259 G1
Akeld 229 D4
Akeley 148 C4
Akenham 152 C3
Albaston 99 E3
Albecq 101 E5
Alberbury 156 C1
Albert Park *TS1 3LB* 78 Middlesbrough
Albert Town 126 C1
Albourne 109 E2
Albourne Green 109 E2
Albrighton *Shrop* 158 A2
Albrighton *Shrop* 157 D1
Alburgh 165 D3
Albury *Herts* 150 C5
Albury *Oxon* 134 B2
Albury *Surr* 121 F3
Albury End 150 C5
Albury Heath 121 F3
Albyfield 210 B2
Alcaig 266 C6
Alcaston 157 D4
Alcester 146 C2
Alciston 110 A3
Alcombe 114 C3
Alconbury 161 G5
Alconbury Hill 161 G5
Alconbury Weston 161 G5
Aldborough *Norf* 178 C2
Aldborough *NYorks* 194 D1
Aldbourne 133 E5
Aldbrough 197 E4
Aldbrough St. John 202 B1
Aldbury 135 E1
Aldclune 251 E3
Aldeburgh 153 F2
Aldeby 165 F2
Aldenham 136 A3
Aldenham Country Park *Herts* WD6 3AT 136 A3
Alderbury 118 C5
Alderford 178 C4
Alderholt 106 A1
Alderley 131 G3
Alderley Edge 184 C5
Aldermaston 119 G1
Aldermaston Wharf 120 B1
Alderminster 147 E3
Alderney 101 G4
Alderney Airport 101 F4
Alder's End 145 F4
Aldersey Green 170 B2
Aldershot 121 D2
Alderton *Glos* 146 B4
Alderton *N'hants* 148 C3
Alderton *Suff* 153 E3
Alderton *Wilts* 132 A4
Alderwasley 173 E2
Aldfield 194 B1
Aldford 170 B2
Aldham *Essex* 152 A5
Aldham *Suff* 152 B3
Aldie *Aber* 269 J6
Aldie *High* 266 E3
Aldingbourne 108 B3
Aldingham 199 D5
Aldington *Kent* 124 C5
Aldington *Worcs* 146 C3
Aldivalloch 260 B2
Aldochlay 241 F5
Aldons 214 C2
Aldous's Corner 165 E3
Aldreth 162 C5
Aldridge 158 C2
Aldringham 153 F1
Aldsworth *Glos* 133 D2
Aldsworth *WSuss* 107 G2
Aldunie 260 B2
Aldville 243 E1
Aldwark *Derbys* 172 D2
Aldwark *NYorks* 195 D1
Aldwick 108 B4
Aldwincle 161 F4
Aldworth 134 A5
Alexandra Palace *GtLon* N22 7AY 12 A1
Alexandria 233 E2
Aley 115 E4
Aley Green 135 F1
Alfardisworthy 112 C4
Alfington 103 E3
Alfold 121 F4
Alfold Crossways 121 F4
Alford *Aber* 260 D3
Alford *Lincs* 189 E5
Alford *Som* 116 D4
Alfreton 173 F2
Alfrick 145 G2
Alfrick Pound 145 G2
Alfriston 110 A3
Algarkirk 176 A4
Alhampton 116 D4
Alkborough 196 A5
Alkerton 147 F3
Alkham 125 E4
Alkington 170 C4
Alkmonton 172 C4
All Cannings 118 B1
All Saints South Elmham 165 E3
All Stretton 157 D3
Allaleigh 101 E2
Allanaquoich 259 J5
Allancreich 260 D5
Allanfearn 266 E7
Allangillfoot 218 A2
Allanton *D&G* 216 D2
Allanton *EAyr* 225 E2
Allanton *NLan* 234 C4
Allanton *ScBord* 237 F4
Allanton *SLan* 234 B4
Allardice 253 G2
Allathasdal 254 B4
Allbrook 119 F5
Allendale Town 211 E2
Allenheads 211 E3
Allen's Green 137 D1
Allensford 211 G2
Allensford Country Park *Dur* DH8 9BA 211 G2
Allensmore 145 D4
Allenton 173 E4
Aller 116 B5
Allerby 209 D3
Allercombe 102 D3
Allerford *Devon* 99 E2
Allerford *Som* 114 C3
Allerston 204 B4
Allerthorpe 195 G3
Allerton *Mersey* 183 F4
Allerton *WYorks* 194 A4
Allerton Bywater 194 D5
Allerton Mauleverer 194 D2
Allesley 159 E4
Allestree 173 E4
Allet Common 96 B5
Allexton 160 D2
Allgreave 171 G1
Allhallows 124 A1
Allhallows-on-Sea 124 A1
Alligin Shuas 264 E6
Allimore Green 158 A1
Allington *Dorset* 104 A3
Allington *Lincs* 175 D3
Allington *Wilts* 118 D4
Allington *Wilts* 118 B1
Allington *Wilts* 132 A5
Allithwaite 199 E5
Allnabad 273 G4
Alloa 243 D5
Allonby 209 D2
Allostock 184 B5
Alloway 224 B4
Allowenshay 103 G1
Allscot 157 G3
Allscott 157 F1
Allt na h-Airbhe 265 H2
Alltachonaich 247 G4
Alltbeithe 257 G2
Alltforgan 168 C5
Alltmawr 143 G3
Alltnacaillich 273 G4
Allt-nan-sùugh 257 F1
Alltsigh 258 B3
Alltwalis 142 A4
Alltwen 128 D2
Alltyblaca 142 B3
Allwood Green 164 B4
Almeley 144 C2
Almeley Wootton 144 C2
Almer 105 F3
Almington 171 E4
Almiston Cross 113 D3
Almondbank 243 F2
Almondbury 185 F1
Almondell & Calderwood Country Park *WLoth* EH52 5PE 235 E3
Almondsbury 131 F4
Alne 195 D1
Alness 266 D5
Alnham 229 D5
Alnmouth 229 G5
Alnwick 229 F5
Alnwick Garden, The *N'umb* NE66 1YU 229 F5
Alperton 136 A4
Alphamstone 151 G4
Alpheton 151 G2
Alphington 102 C3
Alport 172 D1
Alpraham 170 C2
Alresford 152 B5
Alrewas 159 D1
Alrick 251 G3
Alsager 171 E2
Alsagers Bank 171 F3
Alsop en le Dale 172 C2
Alston *Cumb* 210 D3
Alston *Devon* 103 G2
Alston Sutton 116 B2
Alstone *Glos* 146 B4
Alstone *Som* 116 A3
Alstone *Staffs* 158 A1
Alstonefield 172 C2
Alswear 114 A5
Alt 184 D2
Altandhu 272 B7
Altanduin 274 D6
Altarnun 97 G1
Altass 266 C1
Altens 261 H4
Alterwall 275 H2
Altham 193 D4
Althorne 138 C3
Althorp House *N'hants* NN7 4HQ 148 B1
Althorpe 187 F2
Alticry 215 D5
Altnafeadh 249 E4
Altnaharra 273 H5
Altofts 194 C5
Alton *Derbys* 173 E1
Alton *Hants* 120 C4
Alton *Staffs* 172 B3
Alton Barnes 118 C1
Alton Pancras 104 D2
Alton Priors 118 C1
Alton Towers Leisure Park *Staffs* ST10 4DB 172 B3
Alton Water Reservoir *Suff* IP9 2RY 152 C4
Altonside 267 K6
Altrincham 184 B4
Altura 257 J5
Alva 243 D5
Alvanley 183 F5
Alvaston 173 E4
Alvechurch 158 C5
Alvecote 159 E2
Alvediston 118 A5
Alveley 157 G4
Alverdiscott 113 F3
Alverstoke 107 F3
Alverstone 107 E4
Alverthorpe 194 C5
Alverton 174 C3
Alves 267 J5
Alvescot 133 E2
Alveston *SGlos* 131 F4
Alveston *Warks* 147 E2
Alvie 259 F4
Alvingham 189 D3
Alvington 131 F2
Alwalton 161 G3
Alweston 104 C1
Alwington 113 E3
Alwinton 220 B1
Alwoodley 194 C3
Alwoodley Gates 194 C3
Alyth 252 A5
Amalebra 94 B3
Ambaston 173 F4
Amber Hill 176 A3
Ambergate 173 E2
Amberley *Glos* 132 A2
Amberley *WSuss* 108 C2
Amble 221 E1
Amblecote 158 A4
Ambleside 199 E2
Ambleston 140 D5
Ambrismore 232 B4
Ambrosden 134 B1
Amcotts 187 F1
Amersham 135 E3
Amerton 171 G5
Amerton Farm *Staffs* ST18 0LA 171 G5
Amesbury 118 C3
Ameysford 105 G2
Amington 159 E2
Amisfield Town 217 E2
Amlwch 180 C3
Amlwch Port 180 C3
Ammanford (Rhydaman) 128 C1
Amotherby 203 G5
Ampfield 119 E5
Ampleforth 203 E5
Ampleforth College 203 E5
Ampney Crucis 132 C2
Ampney St. Mary 132 C2
Ampney St. Peter 132 C2
Amport 119 E3
Ampthill 149 F4
Ampton 163 G5
Amroth 127 E2
Amulree 243 D1
Anaboard 259 H1
Anaheilt 248 A3
Ancaster 175 E3
Anchor 156 A4
Anchor Corner 164 B2
Ancroft 237 G5
Ancrum 228 A4
Ancton 108 B3
Anderby 189 F5
Anderby Creek 189 F5
Andersea 116 A4
Andersfield 115 F4
Anderson 105 E3
Anderton 184 A5
Anderton Boat Lift *ChesW&C* CW9 6FW 184 A5
Andover 119 E3
Andover Down 119 E3
Andoversford 132 C1
Andreas 190 C2
Anelog 166 A5
Anfield 183 E3
Angarrack 94 C3
Angarrick 95 E3
Angelbank 157 E5
Angerton 209 F1
Angle 126 B2
Anglers Country Park *WYorks* WF4 2EB 186 A1
Angler's Retreat 154 D3
Anglesey (Ynys Môn) 180 B4
Anglesey Abbey *Cambs* CB25 9EJ 150 D1
Angmering 108 C3
Angmering-on-Sea 108 C3
Angram *NYorks* 195 E3
Angram *NYorks* 201 D3
Anick 211 F1
Anie 242 A3
Animal World & Butterfly House *GtMan* BL1 5UG 184 A1
Ankerville 267 F4
Anlaby 196 C5
Anmer 177 F5
Anmore 107 F1
Anna Valley 119 E3
Annan 217 F4
Annaside 198 B4
Annat *A&B* 240 C2
Annat *High* 264 E6
Annbank 224 C3
Anne Hathaway's Cottage *Warks* CV37 9HH 147 D2
Annesley 173 G2
Annesley Woodhouse 173 F2
Annfield Plain 212 A2
Anniesland 233 G3
Annscroft 157 D2
Ansdell 191 G5
Ansford 116 D4
Ansley 159 E3
Anslow 172 D5
Anslow Gate 172 C5
Ansteadbrook 121 E4
Anstey *Herts* 150 C4
Anstey *Leics* 160 A2
Anstruther 245 D4
Ansty *Warks* 159 F4
Ansty *Wilts* 118 A5
Ansty *WSuss* 109 E1
Ansty Coombe 118 A5
Ansty Cross 105 D2
Anthill Common 107 F1
Anthorn 209 E1
Antingham 179 D2
Anton's Gowt 176 A3
Antony 99 D5
Antrobus 184 A5
Anvil Corner 113 D5
Anvil Green 124 D4
Anwick 175 G2
Anwoth 215 G5
Aonach Mòr Mountain Gondola & Nevis Range Ski Centre *High* PH33 6SW 249 D2
Aoradh 230 A3
Apethorpe 161 F3
Apeton 158 A1
Apley 188 B5
Apperknowle 186 A5
Apperley 146 A5
Apperley Bridge 194 A4
Appersett 201 D3
Appin (An Apainn) 248 B5
Appin House 248 B5
Appleby 187 G1
Appleby Magna 159 F1
Appleby Parva 159 F2
Appleby-in-Westmorland 210 C5
Applecross 264 D7
Appledore *Devon* 113 E2
Appledore *Devon* 103 D1
Appledore *Kent* 111 E1
Appledore Heath 124 B5
Appleford 134 A3
Appleshaw 119 E3
Applethwaite 209 F4
Appleton *Halton* 183 G4
Appleton *Oxon* 133 G2
Appleton Roebuck 195 E3
Appleton Thorn 184 A4
Appleton Wiske 202 C2
Appleton-le-Moors 203 G4
Appleton-le-Street 203 G5
Appletreehall 227 G4
Appletreewick 193 G1
Appley 115 D5
Appley Bridge 183 G2
Apse Heath 107 E4
Apsey Green 153 D1
Apsley 135 F2
Apsley End 149 G4
Apuldram 108 A3
Arbeia Roman Fort & Museum *T&W* NE33 2BB 28 E1
Arbirlot 253 D5
Arborfield 120 C1
Arborfield Cross 120 C1
Arborfield Garrison 120 C1
Arbourthorne 186 A4
Arbroath 253 E5
Arbuthnott 253 F2
Archdeacon Newton 202 B1
Archiestown 267 K7
Arclid 171 F1
Ard a' Chapuill 232 B1
Ardachearanbeg 232 B1
Ardacheranmor 232 B1
Ardachoil 239 G1
Ardachu 266 D1
Ardailly 231 E4
Ardalanish 238 C3
Ardallie 261 J1
Ardanaiseig 240 C2
Ardaneaskan 256 E1
Ardanstur 240 A3
Ardantiobairt 247 F4
Ardantrive 240 A2
Ardarroch 264 E7
Ardbeg *A&B* 232 B3
Ardbeg *A&B* 230 C5
Ardbeg *A&B* 232 C1
Ardblair 258 C1
Ardbrecknish 240 C2
Ardcharnich 265 H3
Ardchiavaig 238 C3
Ardchonnel 240 B1
Ardchonnell 240 B3
Ardchrishnish 238 D2
Ardchronie 266 D3
Ardchuilk 257 J1
Ardchullarie More 242 A3
Ardchyle 242 A2
Arddlin 156 B1
Ardechvie 257 H5
Ardeley 150 B5
Ardelve 256 E2
Arden 233 E1
Ardencaple House 239 G3
Ardens Grafton 146 D2
Ardentallan 240 A2
Ardentinny 232 C1
Ardeonaig 242 B1
Ardersier 266 E6
Ardery 247 G3
Ardessie 265 G3
Ardfad 239 G3
Ardfern 240 A4
Ardfin 230 C3
Ardgartan 241 E4
Ardgay 266 D2
Ardgenavan 241 D3
Ardgour (Corran) 248 C3
Ardgowan 232 D2
Ardgowse 260 E3
Ardgye 267 J5
Ardhallow 232 C2
Ardheslaig 264 D6
Ardiecow 268 D4
Ardinamar 239 G3
Ardindrean 265 H3
Ardingly 109 F1
Ardington 133 G4
Ardington Wick 133 G4
Ardintoul 256 E2
Arkinglas House 241 D3
Ardlair 260 D2
Ardlamont 232 A3
Ardleigh 152 B5
Ardleigh Green 137 E4
Ardleigh Heath 152 B4
Ardeley 241 F3
Ardler 252 A5
Ardley 148 A5
Ardley End 137 E1
Ardlui (Àird Laoigh) 241 F3
Ardlussa 231 E1
Ardmaddy 240 C1
Ardmair 265 H2
Ardmaleish 232 B3
Ardmay 241 E4
Ardmenish 231 D2
Ardmhòr 254 C4
Ardminish 231 E5
Ardmolich 247 G2

Ardmore A&B 230 C4
Ardmore A&B 239 G2
Ardmore A&B 233 E2
Ardmore High 266 E3
Ardnackaig 239 G5
Ardnacross 247 E5
Ardnadam 232 C1
Ardnadrochit 239 G1
Ardnagoine 265 F1
Ardnagowan 240 D4
Ardnahein 241 D5
Ardnahoe 230 C2
Ardnarff 256 E1
Ardnastang 248 A3
Ardnave 230 A2
Ardno 241 D4
Ardo 261 G1
Ardoch D&G 225 G5
Ardoch Moray 267 J6
Ardoch P&K 243 F1
Ardochrig 234 A5
Ardoyne 260 E2
Ardpatrick 231 F3
Ardpeaton 232 D1
Ardradnaig 250 C5
Ardrishaig 231 G1
Ardroe 272 C6
Ardross 266 D4
Ardrossan 232 D5
Ardscalpsie 232 B4
Ardshave 266 E2
Ardshealach 247 F3
Ardshellach 239 G3
Ardsley 186 A2
Ardslignish 247 E3
Ardtalla 230 C4
Ardtalnaig 242 C1
Ardtaraig 232 B1
Ardteatle 240 D2
Ardtoe 247 F2
Ardtornish 247 G5
Ardtrostan 242 B2
Ardtur 248 B5
Arduaine 240 A3
Ardullie 266 C5
Ardura 239 F1
Ardvar 272 D5
Ardvasar 256 C4
Ardveenish 254 C4
Ardveich 242 B2
Ardverikie 250 A1
Ardvorlich A&B 241 F3
Ardvorlich P&K 242 B2
Ardwall 215 G5
Ardwell D&G 206 B2
Ardwell Moray 260 B1
Ardwell SAyr 214 C1
Ardwick 184 C3
Areley Kings 158 A5
Arford 120 D4
Argaty 242 C4
Argoed 130 A3
Argoed Mill 143 F1
Argos Hill 110 A1
Argrennan House 216 B5
Argyll & Sutherland Highlanders Museum Stir FK8 1EH 242 C5
Arichamish 240 B4
Arichastlich 241 E1
Arichonan 239 G5
Aridhglas 238 C2
Arienskill 247 G1
Arileod 246 A4
Arinacrinachd 264 D6
Arinafad Beg 231 F1
Arinagour 246 B4
Arinambane 254 C2
Arisaig (Àrasaig) 247 F1
Arivegaig 247 F3
Arkendale 194 C1
Arkesden 150 C4
Arkholme 199 G5
Arkle Town 201 F2
Arkleby 209 E3
Arkleside 201 F4
Arkleton 218 B2
Arkley 136 B3
Arksey 186 C2
Arkwright Town 186 B5
Arlary 243 G4
Arle 146 B5
Arlecdon 208 D5
Arlesey 149 G4
Arleston 157 F1
Arley 184 A4
Arlingham 131 G1
Arlington Devon 113 G1
Arlington ESuss 110 A3
Arlington Glos 132 D2
Arlington Beccott 113 G1
Armadale High 274 C2
Armadale High 256 C4
Armadale WLoth 234 D3
Armathwaite 210 B3
Arminghall 179 D5
Armitage 158 C1
Armitage Bridge 185 F1
Armley 194 B4
Armscote 147 E3
Armshead 171 G3
Armston 161 F4
Armthorpe 186 D2
Arnabost 246 B3
Arnaby 198 C4
Arncliffe 201 E5
Arncliffe Cote 201 E5
Arncroach 244 D4
Arne 105 F4
Arnesby 160 B3
Arngask 243 G3
Arngibbon 242 B5
Arngomery 242 B5
Arnhall 253 E3
Arnicle 222 C2
Arnipol 247 G1
Arnisdale (Arnasdal) 256 E3
Arnish 264 B7
Arniston Engine 236 A3
Arnol 271 F3
Arnold ERid 196 D3
Arnold Notts 173 G3
Arnolfini Gallery BS1 4QA 66 Bristol
Arnprior 242 B5
Arnside 199 F5
Aros Experience High IV51 9EU 263 K7
Arowry 170 B4
Arrad Foot 199 E4
Arradoul 268 C4
Arram 196 C3
Arran 223 E2
Arras 196 B3
Arrat 253 E4
Arrathorne 202 B3
Arreton 107 E4
Arrington 150 B2
Arrivain 241 E1
Arrochar 241 F4
Arrow 146 C2
Arscaig 273 H7
Arscott 156 D2
Arthington 194 B3
Arthingworth 160 C4
Arthog 154 C1
Arthrath 261 H1
Arthurstone 252 A5
Artrochie 261 J1
Aruadh 230 A3
Arundel 108 C3
Arundel Castle WSuss BN18 9AB 108 C3
Arundel Cathedral (R.C.) WSuss BN18 9AY 108 C3
Aryhoulan 248 C3
Asby 209 D4
Ascog 232 C3
Ascot 121 E1
Ascott 147 F4
Ascott d'Oyley 133 F1
Ascott Earl 133 E1
Ascott-under-Wychwood 133 F1
Ascreavie 252 B4
Asenby 202 D5
Asfordby 160 C1
Asfordby Hill 160 C1
Asgarby Lincs 176 B1
Asgarby Lincs 175 G3
Ash Dorset 105 E1
Ash Kent 125 E3
Ash Kent 123 F2
Ash Som 116 B5
Ash Surr 121 D2
Ash Barton 113 F5
Ash Bullayne 102 A2
Ash Green Surr 121 E3
Ash Green Warks 159 F4
Ash Magna 170 C4
Ash Mill 114 A5
Ash Parva 170 C4
Ash Priors 115 E5
Ash Street 152 B3
Ash Thomas 102 D1
Ash Vale 121 D2
Ashampstead 134 A5
Ashbocking 152 C2
Ashbourne 172 C3
Ashbrittle 115 D5
Ashburnham Place 110 B2
Ashburton 101 D1
Ashbury Devon 99 F1
Ashbury Oxon 133 E4
Ashby 187 F2
Ashby by Partney 176 C1
Ashby cum Fenby 188 C2
Ashby de la Launde 175 F2
Ashby de la Zouch 159 F1
Ashby Dell 165 F2
Ashby Folville 160 C1
Ashby Hill 188 C2
Ashby Magna 160 A3
Ashby Parva 160 A4
Ashby Puerorum 188 D5
Ashby St. Ledgers 148 A1
Ashby St. Mary 179 E5
Ashchurch 146 B4
Ashcombe Devon 102 C5
Ashcombe NSom 116 A1
Ashcott 116 B4
Ashdon 151 D3
Ashe 119 G3
Asheldham 138 C2
Ashen 151 F3
Ashenden 124 A5
Ashendon 134 C1
Ashens 231 G2
Ashfield A&B 231 F1
Ashfield Here 145 E5
Ashfield Stir 242 C4
Ashfield Suff 152 D1
Ashfield Green Suff 165 D4
Ashfield Green Suff 151 F2
Ashfold Crossways 109 E1
Ashford Devon 100 C3
Ashford Devon 113 F2
Ashford Hants 106 A1
Ashford Kent 124 C4
Ashford Surr 135 F5
Ashford Bowdler 157 E5
Ashford Carbonel 157 E5
Ashford Hill 119 G1
Ashford in the Water 185 F5
Ashgill 234 B4
Ashiestiel 227 F2
Ashill Devon 103 D1
Ashill Norf 163 G2
Ashill Som 103 G1
Ashingdon 138 B3
Ashington N'umb 221 E3
Ashington Som 116 C5
Ashington WSuss 108 D2
Ashkirk 227 F3
Ashlett 107 D2
Ashleworth 146 A5
Ashleworth Quay 146 A5
Ashley Cambs 151 E1
Ashley ChesE 184 B4
Ashley Devon 113 G4
Ashley Glos 132 B3
Ashley Hants 119 E4
Ashley Hants 106 B3
Ashley Kent 125 F4
Ashley N'hants 160 C3
Ashley Staffs 171 E4
Ashley Wilts 117 F1
Ashley Down 131 E5
Ashley Green 135 E2
Ashley Heath Dorset 106 A2
Ashley Heath Staffs 171 E4
Ashmanhaugh 179 E3
Ashmansworth 119 F2
Ashmansworthy 112 D4
Ashmolean Museum Oxon OX1 2PH 80 Oxford
Ashmore Dorset 105 F1
Ashmore P&K 251 G4
Ashmore Green 119 G1
Ashorne 147 F2
Ashover 173 E1
Ashover Hay 173 E1
Ashow 159 F5
Ashperton 145 F3
Ashprington 101 E2
Ashreigney 113 G4
Ashridge Estate Herts HP4 1LX 135 E1
Ashtead 121 G2
Ashton ChesW&C 170 C1
Ashton Corn 94 D4
Ashton Corn 99 D4
Ashton Hants 107 E1
Ashton Here 145 E1
Ashton Invcly 232 D2
Ashton N'hants 161 F4
Ashton N'hants 148 C3
Ashton Peter 161 G2
Ashton Common 117 F2
Ashton Court Estate NSom BS41 9JN 8 B3
Ashton Keynes 132 C3
Ashton under Hill 146 B4
Ashton upon Mersey 184 B3
Ashton-in-Makerfield 183 G3
Ashton-under-Lyne 184 D3
Ashurst Hants 106 C1
Ashurst Kent 123 E5
Ashurst WSuss 109 D2
Ashurst Bridge 106 C1
Ashurstwood 122 D5
Ashwater 99 D1
Ashwell Herts 150 A4
Ashwell Rut 161 D1
Ashwell End 150 A3
Ashwellthorpe 164 C2
Ashwick 116 D3
Ashwicken 163 F1
Ashybank 227 G4
Askam in Furness 198 D5
Askern 186 C1
Askernish (Aisgernis) 254 C2
Askerswell 104 B3
Askett 134 D2
Askham Cumb 210 B5
Askham Notts 187 E5
Askham Bryan 195 E3
Askham Richard 195 E3
Asknish 240 B5
Askrigg 201 E3
Askwith 194 A3
Aslackby 175 F4
Aslacton 164 C2
Aslockton 174 C3
Asloun 260 D3
Aspall 152 C1
Aspatria 209 E2
Aspenden 150 B5
Asperton 176 A4
Aspley Guise 149 E4
Aspley Heath 149 E4
Aspull 184 A2
Asselby 195 G5
Asserby 189 E5
Assington 152 A4
Assington Green 151 F2
Astbury 171 F1
Astcote 148 B2
Asterby 188 C5
Asterley 156 C2
Asterton 156 D3
Asthall 133 E1
Asthall Leigh 133 F1
Astle 184 C5
Astley GtMan 184 B2
Astley Shrop 157 E1
Astley Warks 159 F4
Astley Worcs 145 G1
Astley Abbotts 157 G3
Astley Bridge 184 B1
Astley Cross 146 A1
Astley Green 184 B3
Astley Lodge 157 E1
Aston ChesE 170 D3
Aston ChesW&C 183 G5
Aston Derbys 185 F4
Aston Derbys 172 C4
Aston Flints 170 A1
Aston Here 157 D5
Aston Here 145 D1
Aston Herts 150 A5
Aston Oxon 133 F2
Aston Shrop 170 C5
Aston Shrop 158 A3
Aston Staffs 171 E3
Aston SYorks 186 B4
Aston Tel&W 157 F2
Aston W'ham 134 C4
Aston WMid 158 C4
Aston Abbotts 148 D5
Aston Botterell 157 F4
Aston Cantlow 146 D2
Aston Clinton 135 D1
Aston Crews 145 F5
Aston Cross 146 B4
Aston End 150 A5
Aston Eyre 157 F3
Aston Fields 146 B1
Aston Flamville 159 G3
Aston Heath 183 G5
Aston Ingham 145 F5
Aston juxta Mondrum 171 D2
Aston le Walls 147 G2
Aston Magna 147 D4
Aston Munslow 157 E4
Aston on Carrant 146 B4
Aston on Clun 156 C4
Aston Pigott 156 C2
Aston Rogers 156 C2
Aston Rowant 134 C3
Aston Sandford 134 C2
Aston Somerville 146 C4
Aston Subedge 146 D3
Aston Tirrold 134 A4
Aston Upthorpe 134 A4
Aston-by-Stone 171 G4
Aston-on-Trent 173 F5
Astwick 150 A4
Astwood 149 E3
Astwood Bank 146 C1
Aswarby 175 F3
Aswardby 189 D5
Aswick Grange 162 B1
Atch Lench 146 C2
Atcham 157 E2
Ath Linne 270 D6
Athelhampton 105 D3
Athelington 164 D4
Athelney 116 A5
Athelstaneford 236 C2
Atherington Devon 113 F3
Atherington WSuss 108 C3
Athersley North 186 A2
Atherstone 159 F3
Atherstone on Stour 147 E2
Atherton 184 A2
Atlow 172 D3
Attadale 257 F1
Attenborough 173 G4
Atterby 187 G3
Attercliffe 186 A4
Atterley 157 F3
Atterton 159 F3
Attingham Park Shrop SY4 4TP 157 E1
Attleborough Norf 164 B2
Attleborough Warks 159 F3
Attlebridge 178 C4
Attleton Green 151 F2
Atwick 197 D2
Atworth 117 F1
Auberrow 145 D3
Aubourn 175 E1
Auch 241 F1
Auchairne 214 C2
Auchallater 251 G1
Auchameanach 231 G4
Auchamore 231 G5
Aucharnie 268 E6
Aucharrigill 266 B1
Auchattie 260 E5
Auchavan 251 G3
Auchbraad 231 G1
Auchbreck 259 K2
Auchenback 233 G4
Auchenblae 253 F2
Auchenbothie 233 E2
Auchenbrack 216 B1
Auchenbreck 232 B1
Auchencairn 216 B5
Auchencrow 237 F3
Auchendinny 235 G3
Auchendolly 216 B4
Auchenfoyle 233 E2
Auchengillan 233 G1
Auchengray 235 D4
Auchenhalrig 268 B4
Auchenheath 234 C5
Auchenhessnane 216 C1
Auchenlochan 232 A2
Auchenmalg 214 D5
Auchenrivock 218 B3
Auchentiber 233 E5
Auchenvennel 233 D1
Auchessan 241 G2
Auchgourish 259 G3
Auchinafaud 231 F4
Auchincruive 224 B3
Auchindarrach 231 G1
Auchindarroch 248 C4
Auchindrain 240 C4
Auchindrean 265 H3
Auchininna 268 E6
Auchinleck 224 D3
Auchinloch 234 A2
Auchinner 242 B3
Auchinroath 267 K6
Auchintoul Aber 260 D3
Auchintoul Aber 268 E5
Auchintoul High 266 C2
Auchiries 261 J1
Auchleven 260 E2
Auchlochan 225 G2
Auchlunachan 265 H3
Auchlunies 261 G5
Auchlunkart 268 B6
Auchlyne 242 A2
Auchmacoy 261 H1
Auchmair 260 B2
Auchmantle 214 C4
Auchmithie 253 E5
Auchmuirbridge 244 A4
Auchmull 253 D2
Auchnabony 208 A2
Auchnabreac 240 C4
Auchnacloich 242 D1
Auchnacraig 239 G1
Auchnacree 252 C3
Auchnafree 242 D1
Auchnagallin 259 H1
Auchnagatt 269 H6
Auchnaha 232 A1
Auchnangoul 240 C4
Aucholzie 260 B5
Auchorrie 260 E4
Auchrannie 252 A4
Auchraw 242 A2
Auchreoch 241 F2
Auchronie 252 C1
Auchterarder 243 E3
Auchtercairn 264 E4
Auchterderran 244 A5
Auchterhouse 244 B1
Auchtermuchty 244 A3
Auchterneed 266 B6
Auchtertool 244 A5
Auchtertyre Angus 252 A5
Auchtertyre (Uachdar Thìre) High 256 E2
Auchtertyre Moray 267 J6
Auchtertyre Stir 241 F2
Auchtubh 242 A2
Auckengill 275 J2
Auckley 186 D2
Audenshaw 184 D3
Audlem 171 D3
Audley 171 E2
Audley End Essex 150 D4
Audley End Essex 151 G4
Audley End Suff 151 G2
Audmore 171 F5
Auds 268 E4
Aughton ERid 195 G4
Aughton Lancs 183 E2
Aughton Lancs 192 B1
Aughton SYorks 186 B4
Aughton Wilts 118 D2
Aughton Park 183 F2
Auldearn 267 G6
Aulden 145 D2
Auldgirth 216 D2
Auldhame 236 C1
Auldhouse 234 A4
Aulich 250 B4
Ault a'chruinn 257 F2
Ault Hucknall 173 F1
Aultanrynie 273 F5
Aultbea (An t-Allt Beithe) 264 E3
Aultgrishan 264 D3
Aultguish Inn 265 K4
Aultibea 275 F6
Aultiphurst 274 D2
Aultmore 268 C5
Ault-na-goire 258 C2
Aultnamain Inn 266 D3
Aultnapaddock 268 B6
Aulton 260 E2
Aultvaich 266 C7
Aultvoulin 256 D4
Aunby 161 F1
Aundorach 259 G3
Aunk 102 D2
Aunsby 175 F4
Auquhorthies 261 G2
Aust 131 E4
Austerfield 187 D3
Austrey 159 E2
Austwick 193 D1
Authorpe 189 E4
Authorpe Row 189 F5
Avebury 132 D5
Avebury Trusloe 118 B1
Aveley 137 E4
Avening 132 A3
Averham 174 C2
Avery Hill 136 D5
Aveton Gifford 100 C3
Aviation Viewing Park GtMan M90 1QX 25 E6
Avielochan 259 G3
Aviemore 259 F3
Avington Hants 119 G4
Avington WBerks 119 E1
Avoch 266 D6
Avon 106 A3
Avon Dassett 147 G2
Avon Heath Country Park Dorset BH24 2DA 3 E1
Avon Valley Railway SGlos BS30 6HD 8 E4
Avonbridge 234 D2
Avoncliff 117 F2
Avonmouth 131 E5
Avonwick 100 D2
Awbridge 119 E5
Awhirk 214 B5
Awkley 131 E4
Awliscombe 103 E2
Awre 131 G2
Awsworth 173 F3
Axbridge 116 B2
Axford Hants 120 B3
Axford Wilts 133 E5
Axminster 103 F3
Axmouth 103 F3
Axton 182 C4
Axtown 100 B1
Aycliffe 212 B5
Aydon 211 G1
Aylburton 131 F2
Ayle 210 D3
Aylesbeare 102 D3
Aylesbury 134 D1
Aylesby 188 C2
Aylesford 123 G3
Aylesham 125 E3
Aylestone 160 A2
Aylmerton 178 C2
Aylsham 178 C3
Aylton 145 F4
Aymestrey 144 D1
Aynho 148 A4
Ayot Green 136 B1
Ayot St. Lawrence 136 A1
Ayot St. Peter 136 B1
Ayr 224 B3
Aysgarth 201 F4
Aysgarth Falls & National Park Centre NYorks DL8 3TH 201 F4
Ayshford 102 D1
Ayside 199 E4
Ayston 161 D2
Aythorpe Roding 137 E1
Ayton P&K 243 G3
Ayton ScBord 237 G3
Aywick 278 E4
Azerley 202 B5

B

Babbacombe 101 F1
Babbacombe Model Village Torbay TQ1 3LA 101 F1
Babbinswood 170 A4
Babb's Green 136 C1
Babcary 116 C5
Babel 143 E4
Babell 182 C5
Babeny 99 G3
Bablock Hythe 133 G2
Babraham 150 D2
Babworth 187 D4
Baby's Hill 259 K1
Bac 271 G3
Bachau 180 C4
Back of Keppoch 247 F1
Back Street 151 F2
Backaland 276 E4
Backaskaill 276 D2
Backbarrow 199 E4
Backburn 260 D1
Backe 127 F1
Backfolds 269 J5
Backford 183 F5
Backhill 261 F1
Backhill of Clackriach 269 H6
Backhill of Trustach 260 E5
Backies High 267 F1
Backies Moray 268 D5
Backlass 275 H3
Backside 260 C1
Backwell 116 B1
Backworth 221 E4
Bacon End 137 E1
Baconend Green 137 E1
Baconsthorpe 178 C2
Bacton Here 144 C4
Bacton Norf 179 E2
Bacton Suff 152 B1
Bacton Green 152 B1
Bacup 193 E5
Badachro 264 D4
Badanloch Lodge 274 C5
Badavanich 265 H6
Badbea 275 F7
Badbury 133 D4
Badbury Wick 133 D4
Badby 148 A2
Badcall High 272 D4
Badcall High 272 E3
Badcaul 265 G2
Baddeley Green 171 G2
Badden 231 G1
Baddesley Clinton 159 D5
Baddesley Clinton Warks B93 0DQ 159 D5
Baddesley Ensor 159 E3
Baddidarach 272 C6
Badenscoth 261 F1
Badenyon 260 B3
Badgall 97 G1
Badger 157 G3
Badgerbank 184 C5
Badgers Mount 123 D2
Badgeworth 132 B1
Badgworth 116 A2
Badicaul 256 D2
Badingham 153 E1
Badintagairt 273 G7
Badlesmere 124 C3
Badley 152 B2
Badlipster 275 H4
Badluarach 265 F2
Badminton 132 A4
Badnaban 272 C6
Badnabay 272 E4
Badnafrave 259 K3
Badnagie 275 G5
Badnambiast 250 C2
Badninish 266 E2
Badrallach 265 G2
Badsey 146 C3
Badshot Lea 121 D3
Badsworth 186 B1
Badwell Ash 152 A1
Badworthy 100 C1
Badyo 251 E3
Bag Enderby 189 D5
Bagber 105 D1
Bagby 203 D4
Bagendon 132 C2
Baggeridge Country Park Staffs DY3 4HB 14 A2
Bagginswood 157 F4
Baggrave Hall 160 B2
Baggrow 209 E2
Bàgh Mòr 262 D6
Baghasdal 254 C3
Bagillt 182 D5
Baginton 159 F5
Baglan 128 D3
Bagley Shrop 170 B5
Bagley Som 116 B3
Bagmore 120 B3
Bagnall 171 G2
Bagnor 119 F1
Bagpath 132 A3
Bagshot Surr 121 E1
Bagshot Wilts 119 E1
Bagstone 131 F4
Bagthorpe Norf 177 F4
Bagthorpe Notts 173 F2
Baguley 184 C4
Bagworth 159 G2
Bagwyllydiart 144 D5
Baildon 194 A4
Baile an Truiseil 271 F2
Baile Boidheach 231 F2
Baile Gharbhaidh 262 C7
Baile Glas 262 D6
Baile Mhartainn 262 C4
Baile Mhic Phail 262 D4
Baile Mòr 238 B2
Baile nan Cailleach 262 C6
Baile Raghaill 262 C5
Bailebeag 258 C3
Baileguish 259 F5
Baile-na-Cille 262 D3
Bailetonach 247 F2
Bailiesward 260 C1
Bailiff Bridge 194 A5
Baillieston 234 A3
Bainbridge 201 E3
Bainsford 234 C1
Bainshole 260 E1
Bainton ERid 196 B2
Bainton Oxon 148 A5
Bainton Peter 161 F2
Bairnkine 228 A5
Bakebare 260 B1
Baker Street 137 F4
Baker's End 136 C1
Bakewell 172 D1
Bala (Y Bala) 168 C4
Balachuirn 264 B7
Balado 243 F4
Balafark 242 B5
Balaldie 267 F4
Balallan (Baile Ailein) 270 E5
Balavil 258 E4
Balbeg High 258 B1
Balbeg High 258 B2
Balbeggie 243 G2
Balbirnie 244 A4
Balbithan 261 F3
Balblair High 266 E5
Balblair High 266 C2
Balblair High 266 E3
Balby 186 C2
Balcharn 266 C1
Balcherry 267 F3
Balchers 269 F5
Balchladich 272 C5
Balchraggan High 266 C7
Balchraggan High 258 C1
Balchrick 272 D3
Balcombe 122 C5
Balcurvie 244 B4
Baldernock 233 G2
Baldersby 202 C5
Baldersby St. James 202 C5
Balderstone GtMan 184 D1
Balderstone Lancs 192 C4
Balderton ChesW&C 170 A1
Balderton Notts 174 D2
Baldhu 96 B5
Baldinnie 244 C3
Baldock 150 A4
Baldon Row 134 A2
Baldovan 244 B1
Baldovie Angus 252 B4
Baldovie Dundee 244 C1
Baldrine 190 C3
Baldslow 110 C2
Baldwin 190 B3
Baldwinholme 209 G1
Baldwin's Gate 171 E3
Baldwins Hill 122 C5
Bale 178 B2
Balelone (Baile Lion) 262 C4
Balemartine 246 A2
Balemore (Baile Mòr) 262 C5
Balendoch 252 A5
Balephuil 246 A2
Balerno 235 F3
Balernock 233 D1
Baleromindubh 238 C5
Balerominmore 238 C5
Baleshare (Bhaleshear) 262 C5
Balevulin 239 D2
Balfield 252 D3
Balfour Aber 260 D5
Balfour Ork 277 D6
Balfron 233 G1
Balfron Station 233 G1
Balgonar 243 F5
Balgove 261 G1
Balgowan D&G 206 B2
Balgowan High 258 D5
Balgown 263 J5
Balgreen 269 F5
Balgreggan 214 B5
Balgy 264 E6
Balhaldie 242 D4
Balhalgardy 261 F2
Balham 136 B5
Balhary 252 A5
Balhelvie 244 B2
Balhousie 244 C4
Baliasta 278 F2
Baligill 274 D2
Baligrundle 248 A5
Balindore 240 B1
Balintore Angus 252 A4
Balintore High 267 F4
Balintraid 266 E4
Balintyre 250 B5
Balivanich (Baile a'Mhanaich) 262 C6
Balkeerie 252 B5
Balkholme 195 G5
Balkissock 214 C2
Ball 170 A5
Ball Haye Green 171 G2
Ball Hill 119 F1
Balla 254 C3
Ballabeg 190 A4
Ballacannell 190 C3
Ballacarnane Beg 190 A3
Ballachulish (Baile a' Chaolais) 248 C4
Balladoole 190 A5
Ballafesson 190 A4
Ballagyr 190 A3
Ballajora 190 C2
Ballakilpheric 190 A4
Ballamodha 190 A4
Ballantrae 214 B2
Ballards Gore 138 C3
Ballasalla IoM 190 A4
Ballasalla IoM 190 B2
Ballater 260 B5
Ballaterach 260 C5
Ballaugh 190 B2
Ballaveare 190 B4
Ballchraggan 266 E4
Ballechin 251 E4
Balleich 242 A4
Ballencrieff 236 B2
Ballidon 172 D2
Balliekine 231 G5
Balliemeanoch 240 D4
Balliemore A&B 240 D5
Balliemore A&B 240 A2
Ballig 190 A3
Ballimeanoch 240 C3
Ballimore A&B 232 A1
Ballimore Stir 242 A3
Ballinaby 230 A3
Ballindean 244 A2
Ballingdon 151 G3
Ballinger Common 135 E2
Ballingham 145 E4
Ballingry 243 G5
Ballinlick 251 E5
Ballinluig P&K 251 E4
Ballinluig P&K 251 F4
Ballintuim 251 G4
Balloch Angus 252 B4
Balloch High 266 E7
Balloch NLan 234 B2
Balloch WDun 233 E1
Ballochan 260 D5
Ballochandrain 232 A1
Ballochford 260 B1
Ballochgair 222 C3
Ballochmartin 232 C4
Ballochmorrie 214 D2
Ballochmyle 224 D3
Ballochroy 231 F4
Ballogie 260 D5
Balls Cross 121 E5
Balls Green Essex 152 B5

Ball's Green *Glos* **132** A3
Balls Hill **158** B3
Ballyaurgan **231** F2
Ballygown **246** D5
Ballygrant **230** B3
Ballyhaugh **246** A4
Ballymacneil **251** E4
Ballymichael **223** E2
Balmacara
(Baile Mac Ara) **256** E2
Balmaclellan **216** A3
Balmacneil **251** E4
Balmadies **253** D5
Balmae **207** G2
Balmalcolm **244** B4
Balmaha **241** G5
Balmalcolm **244** B4
Balmaqueen **263** K4
Balmeanach *A&B* **247** F5
Balmeanach *A&B* **238** D5
Balmeanach **240** A5
Balmedie **261** H3
Balmedie Country Park
Aber AB23 8XG **261** H3
Balmer Heath **170** B4
Balmerino **244** B2
Balmerlawn **106** C2
Balminnoch **215** D4
Balmore *EDun* **234** A2
Balmore *High* **267** F7
Balmore *High* **257** K1
Balmore *High* **263** H7
Balmore *P&K* **250** C4
Balmullo **244** C2
Balmungie **266** E6
Balmyle **251** F4
Balnaboth **252** B3
Balnabruaich **266** E4
Balnacra **265** F7
Balnafoich **258** D1
Balnagall **267** F3
Balnagown Castle **266** E4
Balnaguard **251** E4
Balnaguisich **266** D4
Balnahard *A&B* **238** D5
Balnahard *A&B* **239** D1
Balnain **258** B1
Balnakeil **273** F2
Balnaknock **263** K5
Balnamoon **252** D3
Balnapaling **266** E5
Balnespick **259** F4
Balquhidder **242** A2
Balsall **159** E5
Balsall Common **159** E5
Balscote **147** F3
Balsham **151** D2
Baltasound **278** F2
Balterley **171** E2
Balterley Heath **171** E2
Baltersan **215** F4
Balthangie **269** G5
Balthayock **243** G2
Baltonsborough **116** C4
Baluachraig **240** A5
Balulive **230** C3
Balure *A&B* **238** D5
Balure *A&B* **240** C1
Balvaird **266** C6
Balvarran **251** F3
Balvicar **239** G3
Balvraid *High* **256** E3
Balvraid *High* **259** F1
Bamber Bridge **192** B5
Bamber's Green **151** D5
Bamburgh **229** F3
Bamburgh Castle *N'umb*
NE69 7DF **229** F3
Bamff **252** A4
Bamford *Derbys* **185** G4
Bamford *GtMan* **184** C1
Bampton *Cumb* **199** G1
Bampton *Devon* **114** C5
Bampton *Oxon* **133** F2
Bampton Grange **199** G1
Banavie
(Banbhaidh) **248** D2
Banbury **147** G3
Banbury Museum *Oxon*
OX16 2PQ **147** G4
Bancffosfelen **128** A1
Banchor **267** G7
Banchory **261** F5
Banchory Devenick **261** H4
Bancycapel **128** A1
Bancyfelin **127** G1
Bancyffordd **142** A4
Bandon **244** A4
Bandrake Head **199** E4
Banff **268** E4
Bangor **181** D5
Bangor-on-Dee (Bangor-
is-y-coed) **170** A3
Bangor's Green **183** E2
Banham **164** B3
Banham Zoo *Norf*
NR16 2HE **164** B3
Bank **106** B2
Bank End **198** C4
Bank Newton **193** F2
Bank Street **145** F1
Bank Top *Lancs* **183** G2
Bank Top *WYorks* **194** A5
Bankend **217** E4
Bankfoot **243** F1
Bankglen **225** D4
Bankhead *Aber* **260** E4
Bankhead *Aber* **260** E4
Bankhead
Aberdeen **261** G3
Bankhead *D&G* **208** A2
Bankland **116** A5
Banknock **234** B2
Banks *Cumb* **210** B1
Banks *Lancs* **191** G5
Bankshill **217** F2
Banningham **178** D3
Bannister Green **151** E5
Bannockburn **242** D5
Banstead **122** B3
Bantham **100** C3
Banton **234** B2
Banwen Pyrddin **129** E2
Banyard's Green **165** E4
Bapchild **124** B2
Baptiston **233** G1
Bapton **118** A4

Bar End **119** F5
Bar Hill **150** B1
Barachander **240** C2
Barassie **224** B2
Barbaraville **266** E4
Barber Booth **185** F4
Barber Green **199** E4
Barber's Moor **183** F1
Barbican Arts & Conference
Centre *GtLon*
EC2Y 8DS **45** J1
Barbon **200** B4
Barbridge **170** D2
Barbrook **114** A3
Barby **160** A5
Barcaldine (Am Barra
Calltainn) **248** B5
Barcaple **216** A5
Barchester **147** E4
Barclose **210** A1
Barcombe **109** G2
Barcombe Cross **109** G2
Barden **202** A3
Barden Park **123** E4
Bardennoch **215** G1
Bardfield End Green **151** E5
Bardfield Saling **151** E5
Bardister **278** C5
Bardney **175** G1
Bardon *Leics* **159** G1
Bardon *Moray* **267** K6
Bardon Mill **211** D1
Bardowie **233** G2
Bardsea **199** D5
Bardsey **194** C3
Bardsey Island
(Ynys Enlli) **166** A5
Bardwell **164** A4
Bare **192** A1
Barewood **144** C2
Barfad **231** G3
Barford *Norf* **178** C5
Barford *Warks* **147** E1
Barford St. John **147** G4
Barford St. Martin **118** B4
Barford St. Michael **147** G4
Barfrestone **125** E3
Bargaly **215** F4
Bargany Mains **224** A5
Bargeddie **234** A3
Bargoed **130** A3
Bargrennan **215** E3
Barham *Cambs* **161** G5
Barham *Kent* **125** E3
Barham *Suff* **152** C2
Barharrow **216** A5
Barholm **161** F1
Barholm Mains **215** F5
Barkby **160** B2
Barkby Thorpe **160** B2
Barkers Green **170** C5
Barkestone-le-Vale **174** C4
Barkham **120** C1
Barking *GtLon* **136** D4
Barking *Suff* **152** B2
Barking Tye **152** B2
Barkisland **193** G5
Barkston **175** E3
Barkston Ash **195** D4
Barkway **150** B4
Barlae **215** E3
Barland **144** B1
Barlaston **171** F4
Barlavington **108** B2
Barlborough **186** B5
Barlby **195** F4
Barleston **159** G2
Barley *Herts* **150** B4
Barley *Lancs* **193** E4
Barley Green **164** D4
Barleycroft End **150** C5
Barleyhill **211** G2
Barleythorpe **160** D2
Barling **138** C4
Barlings **188** A5
Barlow *Derbys* **186** A5
Barlow *NYorks* **195** F5
Barlow *T&W* **212** A1
Barmby Moor **195** G3
Barmby on the
Marsh **195** F5
Barmer **177** G4
Barmolloch **240** A5
Barmoor Lane End **229** E3
Barmouth
(Abermaw) **154** C1
Barmpton **202** C1
Barmston **197** D2
Barnaby Green **165** F4
Barnacabber **232** C1
Barnacarry **240** B5
Barnack **161** F2
Barnacle **159** F4
Barnamuic **248** C5
Barnard Castle **201** F1
Barnard Gate **133** G1
Barnardiston **151** F3
Barnard's Green **145** G3
Barnbarroch *D&G* **215** E5
Barnbarroch *D&G* **216** C5
Barnburgh **186** B2
Barnby *Suff* **165** F3
Barnby Dun **186** D2
Barnby in
the Willows **175** D2
Barnby Moor **187** D4
Barndennoch **216** C2
Barne Barton **100** A2
Barnehurst **137** E5
Barnes **136** B5
Barnes Street **123** F4
Barnet **136** B3
Barnet Gate **136** B3
Barnetby le Wold **188** A2
Barney **178** B2
Barnham *Suff* **163** G5
Barnham *WSuss* **108** B3
Barnham Broom **178** B5
Barnhead **253** E4
Barnhill *ChesW&C* **170** B2
Barnhill *Dundee* **244** C1
Barnhill *Moray* **267** J6
Barnhills **214** A3
Barningham *Dur* **201** F1
Barningham *Suff* **164** A4
Barningham Green **178** C2
Barnoldby le Beck **188** C2
Barnoldswick **193** E3

Barns Green **121** G5
Barnsdale Bar **186** C1
Barnsley *Glos* **132** C2
Barnsley *SYorks* **186** A2
Barnsole **125** E3
Barnstaple **113** F2
Barnston *Essex* **137** F1
Barnston *Mersey* **183** D4
Barnstone **174** C4
Barnt Green **158** C5
Barnton *ChesW&C* **184** A5
Barnton *Edin* **235** F2
Barnwell All Saints **161** F4
Barnwell Country Park
N'hants
PE8 5PB **161** F4
Barnwell St. Andrew **161** F4
Barnwood **132** A1
Barons' Cross **145** D2
Barr *A&B* **230** B3
Barr *High* **247** E4
Barr *SAyr* **215** D1
Barr *Som* **115** F5
Barr Hall **151** F4
Barra (Barraigh) **254** B4
Barra (Tràigh Mhòr)
Airport **254** B4
Barrachan **207** D2
Barrackan **239** G4
Barraer **215** E4
Barraglom **270** D4
Barrahormid **231** F1
Barran **241** D2
Barrapoll **246** A2
Barrasford **220** B4
Barravullin **240** A4
Barregarrow **190** B3
Barrets Green **170** C2
Barrhead **233** F4
Barrhill **214** D2
Barrington *Cambs* **150** B3
Barrington *Som* **103** G1
Barripper **94** D3
Barrisdale **256** E3
Barrmill **233** E4
Barrnacarry **240** A2
Barrock **275** H1
Barrow *Glos* **146** A5
Barrow *Lancs* **192** D4
Barrow *Rut* **161** D1
Barrow *Shrop* **157** F2
Barrow *Som* **117** E4
Barrow *Som* **116** C3
Barrow *Suff* **151** F1
Barrow Gurney **116** C1
Barrow Hann **196** C5
Barrow Haven **196** C5
Barrow Hill **186** B5
Barrow Nook **183** F2
Barrow Street **117** F4
Barrow upon
Humber **196** C5
Barrow upon Soar **160** A1
Barrow upon Trent **173** E5
Barroway Drove **163** D2
Barrowby **175** D4
Barrowcliff **204** D4
Barrowden **161** E2
Barrowford **193** E4
Barrow-in-Furness **191** F1
Barrows Green **199** G4
Barry *Angus* **244** D1
Barry *VGlam* **115** E1
Barry Island Pleasure
Park *VGlam*
CF62 5TR **115** E1
Barsby **160** B1
Barsham **165** E3
Barskimming **224** C3
Barsloisnoch **240** A5
Barston **159** E5
Barter Books,
Alnwick *N'umb*
NE66 2NP **229** F5
Bartestree **145** E3
Barthol Chapel **261** G1
Bartholomew Green **151** F5
Bartholmey **171** E2
Bartley **106** C1
Bartley Green **158** C4
Bartlow **151** D3
Barton *Cambs* **150** C2
Barton *ChesW&C* **170** B2
Barton *Cumb* **210** A5
Barton *Glos* **146** C5
Barton *Lancs* **192** B4
Barton *Lancs* **183** E2
Barton *NYorks* **202** B3
Barton *Oxon* **134** A2
Barton *Torbay* **101** F1
Barton *Warks* **146** D2
Barton Bendish **163** F2
Barton End **132** A3
Barton Green **159** D1
Barton Hartshorn **148** B4
Barton Hill **195** G1
Barton in Fabis **173** G4
Barton in the Beans **159** F2
Barton Mills **163** F5
Barton on Sea **106** B3
Barton St. David **116** C4
Barton Seagrave **161** D5
Barton Stacey **119** F3
Barton Town **113** G1
Barton Turf **179** E3
Bartongate **147** G5
Barton-le-Clay **149** F4
Barton-le-Street **203** G5
Barton-le-Willows **195** G1
Barton-on-
the-Heath **147** E4
Barton-under-
Needwood **159** D1
Barton-upon-
Humber **196** C5
Barvas
(Barabhas) **271** F3
Barway **162** D5
Barwell **159** G3
Barwhinnock **216** A5
Barwick *Herts* **136** C1
Barwick *Som* **104** B1
Barwick in Elmet **194** C4
Barwinnock **207** D2
Baschurch **170** B5
Bascote **147** G1
Base Green **152** B1
Basford Green **171** G2

Bashall Eaves **192** C3
Bashall Town **192** D3
Bashley **106** B3
Basildon *Essex* **137** G4
Basildon *WBerks* **134** B5
Basingstoke **120** B2
Baslow **185** G5
Bason Bridge **116** A3
Bassaleg **130** B4
Bassenthwaite **209** F3
Basset's Cross **113** F5
Bassett **106** D1
Bassingbourn **150** B3
Bassingfield **174** B4
Bassingham **175** E2
Bassingthorpe **175** E5
Basta **278** E3
Baston **161** G1
Bastonford **146** A2
Bastwick **179** F4
Batavaime **241** G1
Batch **116** A2
Batchley **146** C1
Batchworth **135** F3
Batchworth Heath **135** F3
Batcombe
Dorset **104** C2
Batcombe *Som* **117** D4
Bate Heath **184** A5
Bath **117** E1
Bath Abbey *B&NESom*
BA1 1LT **63** Bath
Bathampton **117** E1
Bathealton **115** D5
Batheaston **117** E1
Bathford **117** E1
Bathgate **235** D3
Bathley **174** C2
Bathpool *Corn* **97** G2
Bathpool *Som* **115** F5
Bathway **116** C2
Batley **194** B5
Batsford **147** D4
Batson **100** D4
Battersby **203** E2
Battersea **136** B5
Battersea Cats & Dogs
Home *GtLon*
SW8 4AA **13** A5
Battersea Park Children's
Zoo *GtLon*
SW11 4NJ **13** A5
Battisborough
Cross **100** C3
Battisford **152** B2
Battisford Tye **152** B2
Battle *ESuss* **110** C2
Battle *Powys* **143** G4
Battle Abbey *ESuss*
TN33 0AD **110** C2
Battledown **146** B5
Battlefield **157** E1
Battlesbridge **137** G3
Battlesden **149** E5
Battlesea Green **164** D4
Battleton **114** C5
Battramsley **106** C3
Batt's Corner **120** D3
Bauds of Cullen **268** C4
Baugh **246** B2
Baughton **146** A3
Baughurst **119** G1
Baulds **260** E5
Baulking **133** F3
Baumber **188** C5
Baunton **132** C2
Baveney Wood **157** F5
Baverstock **118** B4
Bawburgh **178** C5
Bawdeswell **178** B3
Bawdrip **116** A4
Bawdsey **153** E3
Bawdsey Manor **153** E4
Bawsey **163** E1
Bawtry **187** D3
Baxenden **193** D5
Baxterley **159** E3
Baxter's Green **151** F2
Bay **117** F5
Baybridge **211** F3
Baycliff **199** D5
Baydon **133** E5
Bayford *Herts* **136** C2
Bayford *Som* **117** E5
Bayfordbury **136** C1
Bayham Abbey **123** F5
Bayles **210** C3
Baylham **152** C2
Baynards Green **148** A5
Bayston Hill **157** D2
Baythorn End **151** F3
Bayton **157** F5
Bayworth **134** A2
Beach *High* **247** G5
Beach *SGlos* **131** G5
Beachampton **148** C4
Beachamwell **163** F2
Beacharr **231** E5
Beachley **131** E3
Beacon *Devon* **103** E2
Beacon *Devon* **103** F3
Beacon Fell Country
Park *Lancs*
PR3 2NL **192** B3
Beacon Hill *Dorset* **105** F3
Beacon Hill *Essex* **138** C2
Beacon Hill *Surr* **121** D4
Beacon Hill Country Park
Leics LE12 8SR **17** A2
Beacon Park,
Up Holland *Lancs*
WN8 7RU **183** G2
Beacon's Bottom **134** C3
Beaconsfield **135** E3
Beacravik **263** G2
Beadlam **203** F4
Beadlow **149** G4
Beadnell **229** G4
Beaford **113** F4
Beal *N'umb* **229** E3
Beal *NYorks* **195** E5
Bealach **248** B4

Beale Park *WBerks*
RG8 9NH **134** B5
Bealsmill **99** D3
Beambridge **170** D2
Beamhurst **172** B4
Beaminster **104** A2
Beamish **212** B2
Beamish, North of England
Open Air Museum
Dur DH9 0RG **29** A1
Beamsley **193** G2
Bean **137** E5
Beanacre **118** A1
Beanley **229** E5
Beaquoy **276** C5
Beardon **99** F2
Beardwood **192** C5
Beare **102** C2
Beare Green **121** G3
Bearley **147** D1
Bearnie **261** H1
Bearnock **258** B1
Bearnus **246** C5
Bearpark **212** B3
Bearsbridge **211** D2
Bearsden **233** G2
Bearstone **171** E4
Bearsted **124** A3
Bearwood *Poole* **105** G3
Bearwood *WMid* **158** C4
Beattie Story
Mersey L3 4AD **42** M5
Beattock **226** B5
Beauchamp Roding **137** E1
Beauchief **186** A4
Beaudesert **147** D1
Beaufort **130** A1
Beaulieu **106** C2
Beaulieu: National Motor
Museum, Abbey & Palace
House *Hants*
SO42 7ZN **4** A5
Beauly (A' Mhanachainn)
266 C7
Beaumaris (Biwmares)
181 E5
Beaumont *Chanl* **100** C5
Beaumont *Cumb* **209** G1
Beaumont *Essex* **152** C5
Beaumont Hill **202** B1
Beaumont Leys **160** A2
Beausale **159** E5
Beauvale **173** F3
Beauworth **119** G5
Beaworthy **99** E1
Beazley End **151** F5
Bebington **183** E4
Bebside **221** E3
Beccles **165** F2
Beccles Heliport **165** F3
Becconsall **192** A5
Beck Foot **200** B3
Beck Hole **204** B2
Beck Row **163** E5
Beck Side *Cumb* **198** D4
Beck Side *Cumb* **199** E4
Beckbury **157** G2
Beckenham **122** C2
Beckering **188** B4
Beckermet **198** B2
Beckermonds **201** D4
Beckett End **163** F3
Beckfoot *Cumb* **198** C2
Beckfoot *Cumb* **209** D2
Beckford **146** B4
Beckhampton **118** B1
Beckingham *Lincs* **175** D2
Beckingham *Notts* **187** E4
Beckington **117** F2
Beckley *ESuss* **111** D1
Beckley *Oxon* **134** A1
Beck's Green **165** E3
Beckside **200** B4
Beckton **136** D4
Beckwithshaw **194** B3
Becontree **137** D4
Bedale **202** B4
Bedburn **211** G4
Bedchester **105** E1
Beddau **129** G4
Beddgelert **167** E3
Beddingham **109** G3
Beddington **122** B2
Beddington Corner **122** B2
Bedfield **152** D1
Bedfield Little
Green **152** D1
Bedford **149** F3
Bedgebury Cross **123** G5
Bedgrove **134** D1
Bedham **121** F5
Bedhampton **107** G2
Bedingfield **152** C1
Bedingfield Green **152** C1
Bedingham Green **165** D2
Bedlam *Lancs* **193** D5
Bedlam *NYorks* **194** B1
Bedlar's Green **150** D5
Bedlington **221** E3
Bedlinog **129** G2
Bedminster **131** E5
Bedmond **135** F2
Bednall **158** B1
Bedol **182** D5
Bedrule **228** A5
Bedstone **156** C5
Bedwas **130** A4
Bedwell **150** A5
Bedwellty **130** A2
Bedworth **159** F4
Bedworth
Woodlands **159** F4
Beeby **160** B2
Beech *Hants* **120** B4
Beech *Staffs* **171** F4
Beech Hill **120** B1
Beechingstoke **118** B2
Beechwood **183** G4
Beedon **133** G5
Beeford **196** D2
Beeley **173** D1
Beelsby **188** C2
Beenham **119** G1

Beeny **98** B1
Beer **103** F4
Beer Hackett **104** C1
Beercrocombe **116** A5
Beesands **101** E3
Beesby *Lincs* **189** E4
Beesby *NELincs* **188** C3
Beeson **101** E3
Beeston *CenBeds* **149** G3
Beeston *ChesW&C* **170** C2
Beeston *Norf* **178** A4
Beeston *Notts* **173** G4
Beeston *WYorks* **194** B4
Beeston Regis **178** C1
Beeston
St. Lawrence **179** E3
Beeswing **216** C4
Beetham *Cumb* **199** F5
Beetham *Som* **103** F1
Beetley **178** A4
Beffcote **158** A1
Began **130** B4
Begbroke **133** G1
Begdale **162** C2
Begelly **127** E2
Beggar's Bush **144** B1
Beggearn Huish **114** D4
Beggshill **260** D1
Beguildy (Bugeildy) **156** A5
Beighton *Norf* **179** E5
Beighton *SYorks* **186** B4
Beili-glas **130** C2
Beith **233** E4
Bekesbourne **125** D3
Bekonscot Model Village
Bucks HP9 2PL **135** E3
Belaugh **179** D4
Belbroughton **158** B5
Belchalwell **105** D2
Belchalwell Street **105** D2
Belchamp Otten **151** G3
Belchamp St. Paul **151** F3
Belchamp Walter **151** G3
Belchford **188** C5
Belford **229** F3
Belgrave **160** A2
Belhaven **237** D2
Belhelvie **261** H3
Belhinnie **260** C2
Bell Bar **136** B2
Bell Busk **193** F2
Bell End **158** B5
Bell Heath **158** B5
Bell Hill **120** C5
Bell o' th' Hill **170** C3
Bellabeg **260** B3
Belladrum **266** C7
Bellamore **240** A5
Bellanoch **240** A5
Bellaty **252** A4
Belle Isle **194** C5
Belle Vue **209** G1
Belleau **189** E5
Belleheiglash **259** J1
Bellerby **202** A3
Bellever **99** G3
Bellfields **121** E2
Belliehill **253** D3
Bellingdon **135** E2
Bellingham *GtLon* **136** C5
Bellingham *N'umb* **220** A3
Belloch **222** B2
Bellochantuy **222** B2
Bell's Cross **152** C2
Bells Yew Green **123** F5
Bellsbank **224** C5
Bellshill *N'umb* **229** F3
Bellshill *NLan* **234** B3
Bellside **234** C4
Bellsmyre **233** F2
Bellsquarry **235** E3
Belluton **116** D1
Belmaduthy **266** D6
Belmesthorpe **161** F1
Belmont *B'burn* **184** A1
Belmont *GtLon* **122** B2
Belmont *GtLon* **136** A3
Belmont *Shet* **278** E2
Belnie **176** A4
Belowda **97** D3
Belper **173** E3
Belper Lane End **173** E3
Belsay **220** D4
Belsford **101** D2
Belsize **135** F2
Belstead **152** C3
Belston **224** B3
Belstone **99** G1
Belstone Corner **99** G1
Belsyde **235** D2
Belthorn **192** D5
Beltinge **125** D2
Beltingham **211** D1
Beltoft **187** F2
Belton *Leics* **173** F5
Belton *Lincs* **175** E4
Belton *NLincs* **187** E2
Belton *Norf* **179** F5
Belton *Rut* **160** D2
Belton House *Lincs*
NG32 2LS **175** E4
Beltring **123** F4
Belvedere **137** D5
Belvoir **174** D4
Bembridge **107** F4
Bemersyde **227** G2
Bemerton **118** C4
Bempton **205** E5
Ben Alder Cottage **249** G3
Ben Alder Lodge **250** A2
Ben Rhydding **194** A3
Benacre **165** G3
Benbecula (Beinn na
Faoghla) **262** C6
Benbecula (Balivanich)
Airport **262** C6
Benbuie **216** B1
Bendish **149** G5
Benenden **124** A5
Benfield **215** E4
Benfieldside **211** G2
Bengate **179** E3
Bengeo **136** C1
Bengeworth **146** C3
Benhall Green **153** E1

Beeny **98** B1
Benhall Street **153** E1
Benholm **253** E2
Beningbrough **195** E2
Benington *Herts* **150** A5
Benington *Lincs* **176** B3
Benington Sea End **176** B3
Benllech **180** D4
Benmore *A&B* **232** C1
Benmore *Stir* **241** H2
Bennacott **98** C1
Bennan Cottage **216** A3
Bennett End **134** C3
Bennetts End **135** F2
Benniworth **188** C4
Benover **123** G4
Benson **134** B3
Benston **279** D7
Benthall *N'umb* **229** G4
Benthall *Shrop* **157** F2
Bentham **132** B1
Benthoul **261** G4
Bentlawnt **156** C2
Bentley *ERid* **196** C4
Bentley *Essex* **137** E3
Bentley *Hants* **120** C3
Bentley *Suff* **152** C4
Bentley *SYorks* **186** C2
Bentley *Warks* **159** E3
Bentley *WMid* **158** B3
Bentley *WYorks* **194** B4
Bentley Heath
Herts **136** B3
Bentley Heath
WMid **159** D5
Bentley Rise **186** C2
Benton **113** G2
Benton Square **221** E4
Bentpath **218** B2
Bentworth **120** B3
Benvie **244** B1
Benville Lane **104** B2
Benwell **221** E1
Benwick **162** B3
Beoley **146** C1
Beoraidbeg **256** C5
Bepton **108** A2
Berden **150** C5
Bere Alston **100** A1
Bere Ferrers **100** A1
Bere Regis **105** E3
Berea **140** A4
Berepper **95** D4
Bergh Apton **179** E5
Berinsfield **134** A3
Berkeley **131** F3
Berkhamsted **135** E2
Berkley **117** F3
Berkswell **159** E5
Bermondsey **136** C5
Bernera **256** E2
Berneray (Eilean
Bhearnaraigh) **262** E3
Berners Roding **137** F2
Bernice **240** D5
Bernisdale **263** K6
Berrick Prior **134** B3
Berrick Salome **134** B3
Berriedale **275** G6
Berriew (Aberriw) **156** A2
Berrington
N'umb **229** E2
Berrington *Shrop* **157** E2
Berrington *Worcs* **145** E1
Berrington Green **145** E1
Berriowbridge **97** G2
Berrow *Som* **115** F2
Berrow *Worcs* **145** G4
Berrow Green **145** G2
Berry Cross **113** E4
Berry Down Cross **113** F1
Berry Hill *Glos* **131** E1
Berry Hill *Pembs* **141** D3
Berry Pomeroy **101** E1
Berryhillock **268** C4
Berrynarbor **113** F1
Berry's Green **122** D3
Bersham **170** A3
Berstane **277** D6
Berthlŵyd **128** B3
Berwick **110** A3
Berwick Bassett **132** D5
Berwick Hill **221** D4
Berwick St. James **118** B4
Berwick St. John **118** A5
Berwick St. Leonard **118** A4
Berwick-upon-
Tweed **237** G4
Bescar **183** E1
Bescot **158** C3
Besford *Shrop* **170** C5
Besford *Worcs* **146** B3
Bessacarr **186** D2
Bessels Leigh **133** G2
Bessingby **197** D1
Bessingham **178** C2
Best Beech Hill **123** F5
Besthorpe *Norf* **164** B2
Besthorpe *Notts* **174** D1
Bestwood **173** G3
Bestwood Country Park
Notts NG6 8UF **19** G1
Beswick *ERid* **196** C3
Beswick *GtMan* **184** C3
Betchworth **122** B3
Bethania *Cere* **142** B1
Bethania *Gwyn* **167** E1
Bethania *Gwyn* **168** C4
Bethel *Gwyn* **167** E1
Bethel *Gwyn* **168** C4
Bethel *IoA* **180** B5
Bethersden **124** B5
Bethesda *Gwyn* **167** F1
Bethesda *Pembs* **127** D1
Bethlehem **142** C5
Bethnal Green **136** C4
Betley **171** E3
Betley Common **171** E3
Betsham **137** F5
Betteshanger **125** F3
Bettiscombe **103** G3
Bettisfield **170** B4
Betton *Shrop* **156** C2
Betton *Shrop* **171** D4
Betton Strange **157** E2
Bettws *Bridgend* **129** F4
Bettws *Newport* **130** B3
Bettws Bledrws **142** B2
Bettws Cedewain **156** A3

Bettws Gwerfil
  Goch 168 D3
Bettws Newydd 130 C2
Bettws-y-crwyn 156 B4
Bettyhill 274 C2
Betws 128 C1
Betws Disserth 144 A2
Betws Garmon 167 E2
Betws Ifan 141 G3
Betws-y-coed 168 A2
Betws-yn-Rhos 182 A5
Beulah Cere 141 F3
Beulah Powys 143 F2
Bevendean 109 F3
Bevercotes 187 D5
Beverley 196 C4
Beverston 132 A3
Bevington 131 F3
Bewaldeth 209 F3
Bewcastle 219 D4
Bewdley 157 G5
Bewerley 194 A1
Bewholme 197 D2
Bewl Water ESuss
  TN3 8JH 123 F5
Bewley Common 118 A1
Bexhill 110 C3
Bexley 137 D5
Bexleyheath 137 D5
Bexwell 163 E2
Beyton 152 A1
Beyton Green 152 A1
Bhalamus 270 E7
Bhaltos 270 C4
Biallaid 258 E5
Bibury 132 D2
Bicester 148 A5
Bickenhall 103 F1
Bickenhill 159 D4
Bicker 176 A4
Bickershaw 184 A2
Bickerstaffe 183 F2
Bickerton
  ChesW&C 170 C2
Bickerton Devon 101 E4
Bickerton N'umb 220 B1
Bickerton NYorks 195 D2
Bickford 158 A1
Bickham 114 C3
Bickham Bridge 100 D2
Bickham House 102 C4
Bickington Devon 113 F2
Bickington Devon 102 A5
Bickleigh Devon 100 D1
Bickleigh Devon 102 C2
Bickleton 113 F2
Bickley 122 D2
Bickley Moss 170 C3
Bickley Town 170 C3
Bicknacre 137 G2
Bicknoller 115 E4
Bicknor 124 A3
Bickton 106 A1
Bicton N'umb 145 D1
Bicton Shrop 156 D1
Bicton Shrop 156 B4
Bicton Heath 157 D1
Bicton Park Gardens
  Devon EX9 7BJ 103 D4
Bidborough 123 E4
Biddenden 124 A5
Biddenden Green 124 A4
Biddenham 149 F3
Biddestone 132 A5
Biddick 212 C2
Biddisham 116 A2
Biddlesden 148 B3
Biddlestone 220 B1
Biddulph 171 F2
Biddulph Moor 171 G2
Bideford 113 E3
Bidford-on-Avon 146 D2
Bidlake 99 E2
Bidston 183 D3
Bidwell 149 F5
Bielby 195 G3
Bieldside 261 G4
Bierley IoW 107 E5
Bierley WYorks 194 A4
Bierton 134 D1
Big Pit National Coal
  Museum Torfaen
  NP4 9XP 130 B2
Big Sand 264 D4
Big Sheep, The Devon
  EX39 5AP 113 E3
Big Sky Adventure Play
  Peter PE2 7BU 161 G3
Bigbury 100 C3
Bigbury-on-Sea 100 C3
Bigby 188 A2
Bigert Mire 198 C3
Biggar Cumb 191 E1
Biggar SLan 226 B2
Biggin Derbys 173 D3
Biggin Derbys 172 C2
Biggin NYorks 195 E4
Biggin Hill 122 D3
Biggin Hill Airport 122 D2
Biggings 279 A6
Biggleswade 149 G3
Bigholms 218 B3
Bighouse 274 D2
Bighton 120 B4
Biglands 209 F1
Bignor 108 B2
Bigrigg 208 D5
Bigton 279 C10
Bilberry 97 E4
Bilborough 173 F2
Bilbrook Som 114 D3
Bilbrook Staffs 158 A2
Bilbrough 195 E3
Bilbster 275 H3
Bilby 186 D4
Bildershaw 212 A5
Bildeston 152 A3
Billericay 137 F3
Billesdon 160 C2
Billesley 146 D2
Billholm 218 A2
Billingborough 175 F4
Billinge 183 G3
Billingford Norf 164 C4
Billingford Norf 178 B3
Billingham 213 D5
Billinghay 175 G2
Billingley 186 B2

Billingshurst 121 F5
Billingsley 157 G4
Billington CenBeds 149 E5
Billington Lancs 192 D4
Billington Staffs 171 F5
Billister 279 D6
Billockby 179 F4
Billy Row 212 A4
Bilsborrow 192 B4
Bilsby 189 E5
Bilsby Field 189 E5
Bilsdean 237 E2
Bilsham 108 B3
Bilsington 124 C5
Bilson Green 131 F1
Bilsthorpe 174 B1
Bilsthorpe Moor 174 B2
Bilston Midlo 235 G3
Bilston WMid 158 B3
Bilstone 159 F2
Bilting 124 C4
Bilton ERid 197 D4
Bilton N'umb 221 E2
Bilton NYorks 194 C2
Bilton Warks 159 G5
Bilton-in-Ainsty 195 D3
Bimbister 277 C6
Binbrook 188 C3
Bincombe 104 C4
Bindal 267 G2
Bindon 115 E5
Binegar 116 D3
Bines Green 109 D2
Binfield 134 D5
Binfield Heath 134 C5
Bingfield 220 B4
Bingham 174 C4
Bingham's
  Melcombe 105 D2
Bingley 194 A4
Bings Heath 157 E1
Binham 178 A2
Binley Hants 119 F2
Binley WMid 159 F5
Binniehill 234 C2
Binsoe 202 B5
Binstead 107 E3
Binsted Hants 120 C3
Binsted WSuss 108 B3
Binton 146 D2
Bintree 178 B3
Binweston 156 C2
Birch Essex 152 A5
Birch GtMan 184 C2
Birch Cross 172 C4
Birch Green Essex 138 C1
Birch Green Herts 136 B1
Birch Grove 109 G1
Birch Heath 170 C1
Birch Vale 185 E4
Birch Wood 103 F1
Bircham Newton 177 F4
Bircham Tofts 177 F4
Birchanger 150 D5
Bircher 145 E1
Bircher Common 145 D1
Birchfield 266 B2
Birchgrove Cardiff 130 A4
Birchgrove Swan 128 D3
Birchington 125 F2
Birchover 172 D1
Birchwood Lincs 175 E1
Birchwood Warr 184 A3
Bircotes 186 D3
Bird Street 152 B2
Birdbrook 151 F3
Birdbush 118 A5
Birdfield 240 B5
Birdforth 203 D5
Birdham 108 A3
Birdingbury 147 G1
Birdland, Bourton-on-
  the-Water Glos
  GL54 2BN 147 D5
Birdlip 132 B1
Birdoswald 210 C1
Birds Green 137 E2
Birdsall 196 A1
Birdsgreen 157 G4
Birdston 234 A2
Birdwell 186 A2
Birdwood 131 G1
Birdworld, Farnham Hants
  GU10 4LD 120 D3
Birgham 228 B3
Birichen 266 E2
Birkby Cumb 209 D3
Birkby NYorks 202 C2
Birkdale Mersey 183 E1
Birkdale NYorks 201 D2
Birkenhead 183 E4
Birkenhills 269 F6
Birkenshaw 194 B5
Birkhall 260 B5
Birkhill Angus 244 B1
Birkhill ScBord 236 C5
Birkhill ScBord 226 D4
Birkholme 175 E5
Birkin 195 E5
Birks 194 B5
Birkwood 225 G2
Birley 145 D2
Birley Carr 186 A3
Birling Kent 123 F2
Birling N'umb 221 E1
Birling Gap 110 A4
Birlingham 146 B3
Birmingham 158 C4
Birmingham Botanical
  Gardens WMid
  B15 3TR 34 B7
Birmingham City Museum
  & Art Gallery WMid
  B3 3DH 35 E4
Birmingham International
  Airport 159 D4
Birnam 251 F5
Birsay 276 B5 Birse
  260 D5
Birsemore 260 D5
Birstall 160 A2
Birstall Smithies 194 B5
Birstwith 194 B2
Birthorpe 175 G4
Birtle 184 C1
Birtley Here 144 C1

Birtley N'umb 220 A4
Birtley T&W 212 B2
Birts Street 145 G4
Birtsmorton 146 A4
Bisbrooke 161 D3
Biscathorpe 188 C4
Bish Mill 114 A5
Bisham 135 D4
Bishampton 146 B2
Bishop Auckland 212 B5
Bishop Burton 196 B3
Bishop Middleham 212 C4
Bishop Monkton 194 C1
Bishop Norton 187 G3
Bishop Sutton 116 C2
Bishop Thornton 194 B1
Bishop Wilton 195 G2
Bishopbridge 188 A3
Bishopbriggs 234 A2
Bishopmill 267 K5
Bishops Cannings 118 B1
Bishop's Castle 156 C4
Bishop's Caundle 104 C1
Bishop's Cleeve 146 B4
Bishop's Frome 145 F3
Bishops Gate 135 E5
Bishop's Green
  Essex 137 F1
Bishop's Green
  Hants 119 G1
Bishop's Hull 115 F1
Bishop's Itchington 147 F2
Bishops Lydeard 115 E5
Bishop's Norton 146 A5
Bishops Nympton 114 A5
Bishop's Offley 171 E5
Bishop's Sutton 120 B4
Bishop's Tachbrook 147 F1
Bishop's Tawton 113 F2
Bishopsbourne 125 D3
Bishopsteignton 102 C5
Bishopstoke 107 E1
Bishopston Bristol 131 E5
Bishopston Swan 128 B4
Bishopstone Bucks 134 D1
Bishopstone ESuss 109 G3
Bishopstone Here 144 D3
Bishopstone Swin 133 E4
Bishopstone Wilts 118 B5
Bishopstrow 117 F3
Bishopswood 103 F1
Bishopsworth 116 C1
Bishopthorpe 195 E3
Bishopton Darl 212 C5
Bishopton NYorks 202 B5
Bishopton Renf 233 F2
Bishopton Warks 147 D2
Bishton 130 C4
Bisley Glos 132 B2
Bisley Surr 121 E2
Bispham 191 G4
Bispham Green 183 F1
Bissoe 96 B5
Bisterne 106 A2
Bisterne Close 106 B2
Bitchet Green 123 E3
Bitchfield 175 E5
Bittadon 113 F1
Bittaford 100 C2
Bittering 178 A4
Bitterley 157 E5
Bitterne 107 E1
Bitteswell 160 A4
Bitton 117 D1
Bix 134 C4
Bixter 279 C7
Blaby 160 A3
Black Bourton 133 E2
Black Bridge 126 C2
Black Callerton 212 A1
Black Carr 164 B2
Black Clauchrie 215 D2
Black Corries Lodge 249 E4
Black Crofts 240 B1
Black Cross 96 C4
Black Dog 102 B2
Black Heddon 220 C4
Black Hill 147 E2
Black Marsh 156 C3
Black Moor 194 B3
Black Mount 249 E5
Black Notley 151 F5
Black Park Country
  Park Bucks
  SL3 6DR 135 F4
Black Pill 128 C3
Black Sheep Brewery
  Visitor Centre NYorks
  HG4 4EN 202 B4
Black Street 165 G3
Black Swan Guild,
  Frome Som
  BA11 1BB 117 E3
Black Torrington 113 E5
Blackaburn 219 F4
Blackacre 217 E1
Blackadder 237 F4
Blackawton 101 E2
Blackborough
  Devon 103 D2
Blackborough Norf 163 E1
Blackborough End 163 E1
Blackboys 110 A1
Blackbraes Aber 261 G3
Blackbraes Falk 234 D2
Blackbrook Derbys 173 E3
Blackbrook Leics 159 G1
Blackbrook Mersey 183 G3
Blackbrook Staffs 171 E4
Blackburn Aber 261 G3
Blackburn B'burn 192 C5
Blackburn WLoth 235 D3
Blackbushe 120 C2
Blackcastle 267 F6
Blackchambers 261 F3
Blackcraig D&G 215 F4
Blackcraig D&G 215 F4
Blackden Heath 184 B5
Blackdog 261 H3
Blackdown Devon 99 F3
Blackdown Dorset 103 G2
Blackdown Warks 147 F1

Blacker Hill 186 A2
Blackfen 137 D5
Blackfield 106 D2
Blackford Aber 261 G1
Blackford Cumb 218 B5
Blackford Som 117 D3
Blackford Som 116 B3
Blackfordby 159 F1
Blackgang 107 D5
Blackgang Chine
  IoW PO38 2HN 107 D5
Blackhall Edin 235 G2
Blackhall Renf 233 F3
Blackhall Colliery 213 D4
Blackhall Mill 212 A2
Blackhall Rocks 213 D4
Blackham 123 E5
Blackhaugh 227 F2
Blackhill Aber 269 J5
Blackhill Aber 269 J6
Blackhillock 268 C6
Blackhills 277 K6
Blackland 118 B1
Blacklands 114 B4
Blackleach 192 A4
Blackley 184 C2
Blacklunans 251 G3
Blackmill 129 F4
Blackmoor Hants 120 C4
Blackmoor Som 103 E1
Blackmoor Gate 113 G1
Blackmore 137 F2
Blackmore End
  Essex 151 F4
Blackmore End
  Herts 136 A1
Blackness Aber 260 E5
Blackness Falk 235 E2
Blackness High 275 H5
Blacknest 120 C3
Blackney 104 A3
Blacko 193 E3
Blackpole 146 A2
Blackpool B'pool 191 G4
Blackpool Devon 101 E3
Blackpool Bridge 127 D1
Blackpool Gate 218 C4
Blackpool Piers B'pool
  FY4 1BB 191 G4
Blackpool Pleasure
  Beach B'pool
  FY4 1PL 191 G4
Blackpool Tower
  FY1 4BJ 64 Blackpool
Blackpool Zoo
  B'pool FY3 8PP 191 G4
Blackridge 234 C3
Blackrock A&B 230 B3
Blackrock Mon 130 B1
Blackrod 184 A1
Blackshaw 217 E4
Blackshaw Head 193 F5
Blacksmith's Green 152 C1
Blacksnape 192 D5
Blackstone 109 E2
Blackthorn 134 B1
Blackthorpe 152 A1
Blacktoft 196 A5
Blacktop 261 G4
Blacktown 130 C4
Blackwater Corn 96 B5
Blackwater
  Hants 120 D2
Blackwater IoW 107 E4
Blackwater Norf 178 B3
Blackwater Som 103 F1
Blackwaterfoot 223 E3
Blackwell Darl 202 B1
Blackwell Derbys 185 F5
Blackwell Derbys 173 F2
Blackwell Warks 147 E3
Blackwell Worcs 158 B5
Blackwell WSuss 122 C5
Blackwells End 146 A5
Blackwood (Coed-duon)
  Caerp 130 A3
Blackwood D&G 216 D2
Blackwood SLan 234 B5
Blackwood Hill 171 G2
Blacon 170 A1
Bladbean 125 D4
Bladnoch 215 F5
Bladon 133 G1
Blaen Clydach 129 F3
Blaenannerch 141 F3
Blaenau
  Dolwyddelan 167 F2
Blaenavon 130 B2
Blaenawey 130 B1
Blaencelyn 141 G2
Blaencwm 129 F2
Blaendyryn 143 F4
Blaenffos 141 E4
Blaengarw 129 F3
Blaengeuffordd 154 C1
Blaengwrach 129 E2
Blaengwynfi 129 E3
Blaenllechau 129 G3
Blaenos 143 D4
Blaenpennal 142 C1
Blaenplwyf 154 B5
Blaenporth 141 F3
Blaenrhondda 129 F2
Blaenwaun 141 F5
Blaen-y-coed 141 G5
Blagdon NSom 116 C2
Blagdon Torbay 101 E1
Blagdon Hill 103 F1
Blaguegate 183 F2
Blaich 248 C2
Blain 247 F3
Blair 233 E5
Blair Atholl 251 D3
Blair Castle P&K
  PH18 5TL 251 D3
Blair Drummond 242 C5

Blair Drummond Safari &
  Adventure Park Stir
  FK9 4UR 242 C5
Blairannaich 241 F4
Blairbuie 232 C2
Blairgowrie 251 G5
Blairhall 235 E1
Blairhoyle 242 B4
Blairingone 243 E5
Blairkip 224 C2
Blairlogie 242 D5
Blairmore A&B 232 C1
Blairmore High 266 E1
Blairmore High 272 C4
Blairnairn 233 D1
Blairnamarrow 259 K3
Blairpark 232 D4
Blairquhan 224 B5
Blairquhosh 233 G1
Blair's Ferry 232 A3
Blairshinnoch 268 E4
Blairuskinmore 241 G4
Blairvadach 233 D1
Blairydryne 261 F5
Blairythan Cottage 261 H2
Blaisdon 131 G1
Blake End 151 F5
Blake House Craft
  Centre Essex
  CM77 6RA 151 F5
Blakebrook 158 A5
Blakedown 158 A5
Blakelaw ScBord 228 B3
Blakelaw T&W 212 B1
Blakeley 158 A4
Blakelow 171 D2
Blakemere 144 C3
Blakemere Shopping
  Experience ChesW&C
  CW8 2EB 183 G5
Blakeney Glos 131 F2
Blakeney Norf 178 B1
Blakenhall
  ChesE 171 E3
Blakenhall WMid 158 B3
Blakeshall 158 A4
Blakesley 148 B2
Blakelow 171 D2
Blanchland 211 F2
Bland Hill 194 B2
Blandford Camp 105 F2
Blandford Forum 105 F2
Blandford St. Mary 105 E2
Blanefield 233 G2
Blanerne 237 F4
Blankney 175 F1
Blantyre 234 A4
Blar a' Chaorainn 248 D3
Blargie 258 D5
Blarglas 233 E1
Blarmachfoldach 248 C3
Blarnalearoch 265 H2
Blashford 106 A2
Blaston 160 D3
Blathaisbhal 262 D4
Blatherwycke 161 E3
Blawith 199 D4
Blaxhall 153 E2
Blaxton 187 D2
Blaydon 212 A1
Bleadney 116 B3
Bleadon 116 A2
Bleak Hey Nook 185 E2
Blean 124 D2
Bleasby Lincs 188 B4
Bleasby Notts 174 C3
Bleasby Moor 188 B4
Bleatarn 200 C1
Bleathwood
  Common 145 E1
Blebocraigs 244 C3
Bleddfa 144 C1
Bledington 147 E5
Bledlow 134 C2
Bledlow Ridge 134 C3
Blencarn 210 C4
Blencogo 209 E2
Blencow 210 A4
Blendworth 107 G1
Blenheim Palace Oxon
  OX20 1PX 133 G1
Blennerhasset 209 E2
Blervie Castle 267 H6
Bletchingdon 134 A1
Bletchingley 122 C3
Bletchley MK 149 D4
Bletchley Shrop 170 D4
Bletherston 141 D5
Bletsoe 149 F2
Blewbury 134 A4
Blickling 178 C3
Blickling Hall Norf
  NR11 6NF 178 C3
Blidworth 173 G2
Blidworth Bottoms 173 G2
Blindburn Aber 261 H1
Blindburn N'umb 228 C5
Blindcrake 209 E3
Blindley Heath 122 C4
Blisland 97 E2
Bliss Gate 157 G5
Blissford 106 A1
Blisworth 148 C2
Blithbury 172 B5
Blitterlees 209 E1
Blo' Norton 164 B4
Blockley 147 D4
Blofield 179 E5
Blofield Heath 179 E4
Blore 172 C3
Blossomfield 158 D5
Blount's Green 172 B4
Blowick 183 E1
Bloxham 147 G4
Bloxholm 175 F2
Bloxwich 158 B2
Bloxworth 105 E3
Blubberhouses 194 A2
Blue Anchor Corn 96 D4
Blue Anchor Som 114 D3
Blue Bell Hill 123 G2
Blue Planet Aquarium,
  Ellesmere Port
  ChesW&C
  CH65 9LF 183 F5
Blue Reef Aquarium
  ESuss TN34 3DW
  75 Hastings

Blue Reef Aquarium,
  Newquay Corn
  TR7 1DU 96 C3
Blue Reef Aquarium,
  Southsea Ports
  PO5 3PB 5 G6
Blue Reef Aquarium,
  Tynemouth T&W
  NE30 4JF 28 E1
Bluebell Railway WSuss
  TN22 3QL 109 F1
Bluewater 137 E5
Blundellsands 183 E3
Blundeston 165 G2
Blunham 149 G2
Blunsdon
  St. Andrew 132 D4
Bluntington 158 A5
Bluntisham 162 B5
Blunts 98 D4
Blurton 171 F3
Blyborough 187 G3
Blyford 165 F4
Blymhill 158 A1
Blymhill Common 157 G1
Blymhill Lawn 158 A1
Blyth N'umb 221 F3
Blyth Notts 186 D4
Blyth Bridge 235 F5
Blyth Marsh 171 G3
Blyton 187 F3
Boarhills 245 D3
Boarhunt 107 F2
Boars Hill 133 G2
Boarsgreave 193 E5
Boarshead 123 E5
Boarstall 134 B1
Boarzell 110 C5
Boasley Cross 99 F1
Boat o' Brig 268 B5
Boat of Garten 259 G3
Boath 266 C4
Bobbing 124 A2
Bobbington 158 A3
Bobbingworth 137 E2
Bocaddon 97 F4
Bochastle 242 B4
Bocketts Farm Park
  Surr KT22 9BS 121 G2
Bockhampton 133 F5
Bocking 151 F5
Bocking
  Churchstreet 151 F5
Bockleton 145 E1
Boconnoc 97 F3
Boddam Aber 269 K6
Boddam Shet 279 F9
Bodden 116 D3
Boddington 146 A5
Bodedern 180 B4
Bodelwyddan 182 B5
Bodenham Here 145 E2
Bodenham Wilts 118 C5
Bodenham Moor 145 E2
Bodesbeck 226 C5
Bodewryd 180 C3
Bodfari 182 B5
Bodffordd 180 C5
Bodfuan 166 C4
Bodham 178 C1
Bodiam 110 C5
Bodicote 147 G4
Bodieve 97 E2
Bodinnick 97 F4
Bodior 180 A5
Bodle Street Green 110 B2
Bodmin 97 E3
Bodnant Garden Conwy
  LL28 5RE 181 G5
Bodney 163 G3
Bodorgan 166 C1
Bodrane 97 F3
Bodsham Green 124 C4
Bodwen 97 E3
Bodymoor Heath 159 D3
Bogallan 266 D6
Bogbain 266 E7
Bogbrae 261 J1
Bogbuie 266 C6
Bogend 224 B2
Bogfern 260 D4
Bogfields 260 D4
Bogfold 269 G5
Boghead Aber 268 D6
Boghead EAyr 225 E3
Boghead SLan 234 B5
Boghole Farm 267 G6
Bogmoor 268 B4
Bogniebrae 268 D6
Bognor Regis 108 B4
Bograxie 261 F3
Bogroy 259 G2
Bogside 243 E5
Bogston 260 B4
Bogton 268 E5
Bogue 216 A2
Bohemia 106 B1
Bohenie 249 E1
Bohetherick 100 A1
Bohortha 95 F3
Bohuntine 249 E1
Boirseam 263 F3
Bojewyan 94 A3
Bokiddick 97 E3
Bolam Dur 212 A5
Bolam N'umb 220 C3
Bolam Lake Country
  Park N'umb
  NE20 0HE 220 C3
Bolberry 100 C4
Bold Heath 183 G4
Bolderwood 106 B2
Boldon 212 C1
Boldon Colliery 212 C1
Boldre 106 C3
Boldron 201 F1
Bole 187 E4
Bolehill 173 D2
Boleigh 94 B4
Bolenowe 95 D3

Boleside 227 F2
Bolfracks 250 D5
Bolgoed 128 C2
Bolham Devon 102 C1
Bolham Notts 187 E4
Bolham Water 103 E1
Bolingey 96 B4
Bollington 184 D5
Bolney 109 E1
Bolnhurst 149 F2
Bolshan 253 E4
Bolsover 186 B5
Bolsterstone 185 G3
Bolstone 145 E4
Boltby 203 D4
Bolter End 134 C3
Bolton Cumb 210 C5
Bolton ELoth 236 C2
Bolton ERid 195 G2
Bolton GtMan 184 B2
Bolton N'umb 229 F5
Bolton Abbey 193 G2
Bolton Abbey Estate
  NYorks
  BD23 6EX 193 G2
Bolton Bridge 193 G2
Bolton by Bowland 193 D3
Bolton Houses 192 A4
Bolton Low Houses 209 F2
Bolton Museum &
  Art Gallery GtMan
  BL1 1SE 184 B2
Bolton Percy 195 E3
Bolton Priory NYorks
  BD23 6EX 193 G2
Bolton upon
  Dearne 186 B2
Bolton Wood Lane 209 F2
Boltonfellend 210 A1
Boltongate 209 F2
Bolton-le-Sands 192 A1
Bolton-on-Swale 202 B3
Bolventor 97 F2
Bombie 208 A2
Bomere Heath 157 D1
Bonar Bridge 266 D2
Bonawe (Bun Atha) 240 C1
Bonby 188 A1
Boncath 141 F4
Bonchester Bridge 227 G4
Bonchurch 107 E5
Bondleigh 113 G5
Bonds 192 A3
Bonehill 159 D2
Bo'ness 235 D1
Bonhill 233 E1
Boningale 158 A2
Bonjedward 228 A4
Bonkle 234 C4
Bonning Gate 199 F3
Bonnington Edin 235 F3
Bonnington Kent 124 C5
Bonnybank 244 B4
Bonnybridge 234 C1
Bonnykelly 269 G5
Bonnyrigg 236 A3
Bonnyton Aber 260 E1
Bonnyton Angus 245 D1
Bonnyton Angus 253 E5
Bonnyton Angus 244 B1
Bonsall 173 D2
Bont 130 C1
Bont Dolgadfan 155 E2
Bont Newydd 168 A5
Bontddu 154 C1
Bont-goch (Elerch) 154 C1
Bonthorpe 189 E5
Bont-newydd
  Conwy 182 B5
Bontnewydd Gwyn 167 D1
Bontuchel 169 D2
Bonvilston 129 G5
Bon-y-maen 128 C3
Boode 113 F2
Boohay 101 F2
Booker 134 D3
Booley 170 C5
Boor 264 E3
Boorley Green 107 E1
Boosbeck 203 F1
Boose's Green 151 G4
Boot 198 C2
Boot Street 152 D3
Booth 193 G5
Booth Bank 185 E1
Booth Green 184 D4
Booth Wood 185 E1
Boothby Graffoe 175 E2
Boothby Pagnell 175 E4
Boothstown 184 B2
Boothville 148 C1
Bootle Cumb 198 C4
Bootle Mersey 183 E3
Booton 178 C3
Boots Green 184 B5
Booze 201 F2
Boquhan 233 G1
Boraston 157 F5
Bordeaux 101 F4
Borden Kent 124 A2
Borden WSuss 120 D5
Bordley 193 F1
Bordon 120 C4
Boreham Essex 137 G2
Boreham Wilts 117 F3
Boreham Street 110 B2
Borehamwood 136 A3
Boreland D&G 217 F1
Boreland D&G 215 E4
Boreland Stir 242 A1
Boreley 146 A1
Boreraig 263 G6
Borgh Na H-E.Siar 262 C1
Borgh Na H-E.Siar 254 C4
Borghastan 270 D3
Borgie 273 J3
Borgue D&G 207 G2
Borgue High 275 G6
Borley 151 G3
Borley Green Essex 151 G3
Borley Green Suff 152 A1
Bornais 254 C2
Borness 207 G2
Bornisketaig 263 J4
Borough Green 123 F3
Boroughbridge 194 C1
Borras Head 170 A2
Borreraig 263 G6
Borrowash 173 F4

Borrowby NYorks 203 G1
Borrowby NYorks 202 D4
Borrowdale 209 F5
Borrowfield 261 G5
Borstal 123 G2
Borth 154 C4
Borthwick 236 A4
Borthwickbrae 227 F4
Borthwickshiels 227 F4
Borth-y-Gest 167 E4
Borve High 263 K7
Borve (Borgh) Na H-ESiar 271 G2
Borwick 199 G5
Borwick Rails 198 C5
Bosavern 94 A3
Bosbury 145 F3
Boscarne 97 E3
Boscastle 98 A1
Boscastle Pottery Corn PL35 0HE 98 B1
Boscombe Bourne 106 A3
Boscombe Wilts 118 D4
Bosham 108 A3
Bosham Hoe 108 A3
Bosherston 126 C3
Bosley 171 G1
Bossall 195 G1
Bossiney 97 E1
Bossingham 125 D4
Bossington Hants 119 E4
Bossington Som 114 B3
Bostadh 270 D4
Bostock Green 171 D1
Boston 176 B3
Boston Spa 194 D3
Boswarthan 94 B3
Boswinger 97 D5
Bosworth Battlefield Country Park Leics CV13 0AD 159 G2
Botallack 94 A3
Botanic Garden Oxon OX1 4AZ 80 Oxford
Botany Bay 136 C3
Botany Bay Lancs PR6 9AF 184 A1
Botcheston 159 G2
Botesdale 164 B4
Bothal 221 E3
Bothamsall 187 D5
Bothel 209 E3
Bothenhampton 104 A3
Bothwell 234 B4
Botley Bucks 135 E2
Botley Hants 107 E1
Botley Oxon 133 G2
Botloe's Green 145 G5
Botolph Claydon 148 C5
Botolphs 109 D3
Botolph's Bridge 124 D5
Bottacks 266 B5
Bottesford Leics 174 D4
Bottesford NLincs 187 F2
Bottisham 150 D1
Bottlesford 118 C2
Bottom Boat 194 C5
Bottom of Hutton 192 A5
Bottom o'th'Moor 184 A1
Bottomcraig 244 B2
Bottoms 193 F5
Botton Head 192 C1
Botusfleming 100 A1
Botwnnog 166 B4
Bough Beech 123 D4
Boughrood 144 A4
Boughspring 131 E3
Boughton N'hants 148 C1
Boughton Norf 163 F2
Boughton Notts 174 B1
Boughton Aluph 124 C4
Boughton Lees 124 C4
Boughton Malherbe 124 A4
Boughton Monchelsea 123 G3
Boughton Street 124 C3
Boulby 203 G1
Bouldnor 106 C4
Bouldon 157 E4
Boulge 153 D2
Boulmer 229 G5
Boulston 126 C1
Boultenstone Hotel 260 C3
Boultham 175 E1
Boundary Derbys 159 F1
Boundary Staffs 171 G3
Bourn 150 B2
Bourne 175 F5
Bourne End Bucks 135 D4
Bourne End CenBeds 149 E3
Bourne End Herts 135 F2
Bournebridge 137 E3
Bournemouth 105 G3
Bournemouth Airport 106 A3
Bournemouth International Centre BH2 5BH 64 Bournemouth
Bournheath 158 B5
Bournmoor 212 C2
Bournville 158 C4
Bourton Bucks 148 C4
Bourton Dorset 117 E4
Bourton NSom 116 A1
Bourton Oxon 133 E4
Bourton Shrop 157 E3
Bourton Wilts 118 B1
Bourton on Dunsmore 159 G5
Bourton-on-the-Hill 147 D4
Bourton-on-the-Water 147 D5
Bousd 246 B3
Boustead Hill 209 F1
Bouth 199 E4
Bouthwaite 202 A5
Bovain 242 A1
Boveney 135 E5
Boveridge 105 G1
Boverton 114 C1
Bovey Tracey 102 B5
Bovingdon 135 F2
Bovinger 137 E2
Bovington Camp 105 E4
Bow Cumb 209 G1
Bow Devon 102 A2
Bow Devon 101 E2
Bow Ork 277 C8
Bow Brickhill 149 E4
Bow of Fife 244 B3
Bow Street Cere 154 C4
Bow Street Norf 164 B2
Bowbank 211 F5
Bowburn 212 C4
Bowcombe 107 D4
Bowd 103 E3
Bowden Devon 101 E3
Bowden ScBord 227 G2
Bowden Hill 118 A1
Bowdon 184 B4
Bower 219 F3
Bower Hinton 104 A1
Bower House Tye 152 A3
Bowerchalke 118 B5
Bowerhill 118 A1
Bowermadden 275 H2
Bowers 171 F4
Bowers Gifford 137 G4
Bowershall 243 F5
Bowertower 275 H2
Bowes 201 E1
Bowgreave 192 A3
Bowhousebog 234 C4
Bowithick 97 F1
Bowker's Green 183 F2
Bowland Bridge 199 F4
Bowley 145 E2
Bowley Town 145 E2
Bowlhead Green 121 E4
Bowling WDun 233 F2
Bowling WYorks 194 A4
Bowling Bank 170 A3
Bowlish 116 D3
Bowmanstead 199 E3
Bowmore 230 B3
Bowness-on-Solway 218 A5
Bowness-on-Windermere 199 F3
Bowood House & Gardens Wilts SN11 0LZ 118 A1
Bowscale 209 G3
Bowsden 237 G5
Bowside Lodge 274 D2
Bowston 199 F3
Bowthorpe 178 C5
Bowtrees 234 D1
Box Glos 132 A2
Box Wilts 117 F1
Box End 149 F3
Boxbush Glos 131 G1
Boxbush Glos 145 F5
Boxford Suff 152 A3
Boxford WBerks 133 G5
Boxgrove 108 B3
Boxley 123 G3
Boxmoor 135 F2
Box's Shop 112 C5
Boxted Essex 152 A4
Boxted Suff 151 G2
Boxted Cross 152 A4
Boxwell 132 A3
Boxworth 150 B1
Boxworth End 150 B1
Boyden Gate 125 E2
Boydston 224 C2
Boylestone 172 C4
Boyndie 268 E4
Boynton 196 D1
Boys Hill 104 C2
Boysack 253 E5
Boyton Corn 98 D1
Boyton Suff 153 E3
Boyton Wilts 118 A4
Boyton Cross 137 F2
Boyton End 151 F3
Bozeat 149 E2
Braaid 190 B4
Braal Castle 275 G2
Brabling Green 153 D1
Brabourne 124 C4
Brabourne Lees 124 C4
Brabster 275 J2
Bracadale 255 J1
Braceborough 161 F1
Bracebridge Heath 175 E1
Braceby 175 F4
Bracewell 193 E3
Brachla 258 C1
Brackenber 200 C1
Brackenbottom 200 D5
Brackenfield 173 E2
Brackens 269 F5
Bracklach 260 B2
Bracklamore 269 G5
Bracklesham 108 A4
Brackletter (A' Bhreac-Leitir) 249 D1
Brackley A&B 231 G1
Brackley High 267 F6
Brackley N'hants 148 A4
Brackley Gate 173 E3
Brackley Hatch 148 B3
Bracknell 121 D1
Braco 242 D4
Bracobrae 268 D5
Bracon Ash 164 C2
Bracora 256 D5
Bracorina 256 D5
Bradbourne 172 D2
Bradbury 212 C5
Bradda 190 A4
Bradden 148 B3
Braddock 97 F3
Bradenham Bucks 134 D3
Bradenham Norf 178 A5
Bradenstoke 132 C5
Bradfield Devon 103 D2
Bradfield Essex 152 C4
Bradfield Norf 179 D2
Bradfield WBerks 134 B5
Bradfield Combust 151 G2
Bradfield Green 171 D2
Bradfield Heath 152 C5
Bradfield St. Clare 152 A2
Bradfield St. George 152 A1
Bradfield Southend (Southend) 134 A5
Bradford Corn 97 F2
Bradford Derbys 172 D1
Bradford Devon 113 E5
Bradford N'umb 229 F3
Bradford N'umb 220 C4
Bradford WYorks 194 A4
Bradford Abbas 104 B1
Bradford Cathedral Church of St. Peter WYorks BD1 4EH 65 Bradford
Bradford Leigh 117 F1
Bradford Peverell 104 C3
Bradford-on-Avon 117 F1
Bradford-on-Tone 115 E5
Bradgate Park Leics LE6 0HE 17 B3
Bradiford 113 F2
Brading 107 F4
Bradley ChesW&C 183 G5
Bradley Derbys 172 D3
Bradley Hants 120 B3
Bradley NELincs 188 C2
Bradley (Low Bradley) NYorks 193 G3
Bradley Staffs 158 A1
Bradley WMid 158 B3
Bradley Fold 184 B2
Bradley Green Warks 159 E2
Bradley Green Worcs 146 B1
Bradley in the Moors 172 B3
Bradley Mills 185 F1
Bradley Stoke 131 F4
Bradmore Notts 173 G4
Bradmore WMid 158 A3
Bradney 116 A4
Bradninch 102 D2
Bradnop 172 B2
Bradnor Green 144 B2
Bradpole 104 A3
Bradshaw GtMan 184 B1
Bradshaw WYorks 193 G4
Bradstone 99 D2
Bradwall Green 171 E1
Bradwell Derbys 185 F4
Bradwell Devon 113 E1
Bradwell Essex 151 G5
Bradwell MK 148 D4
Bradwell Norf 179 G5
Bradwell Grove 133 E2
Bradwell Waterside 138 C2
Bradwell-on-Sea 138 D2
Bradworthy 112 D4
Brae D&G 216 C3
Brae High 266 B1
Brae Shet 279 C6
Brae of Achnahaird 272 C7
Braeantra 266 C4
Braedownie 252 A2
Braefoot 269 F6
Braegrum 243 F2
Braehead D&G 215 F5
Braehead Glas 233 G3
Braehead Moray 268 B6
Braehead Ork 277 E7
Braehead Ork 276 D3
Braehead SLan 225 G2
Braehead SLan 235 D4
Braehead of Lunan 253 E4
Braehoulland 278 B5
Braeleny 242 B3
Braemar 259 J5
Braemore High 266 C1
Braemore High 275 F5
Braemore High 265 H4
Braenaloin 259 K5
Braes of Enzie 268 B5
Braes of Foss 250 C4
Braes of Ullapool (Bruthaicheann Ullapuil) 265 H2
Braeswick 276 F4
Braeval 242 A4
Braewick 279 C7
Brafferton Darl 212 B5
Brafferton NYorks 202 D5
Brafield-on-the-Green 148 D2
Bragar 270 E3
Bragbury End 150 A5
Bragenham 149 E5
Bragleenbeg 240 B2
Braichmelyn 167 F1
Braides 192 A2
Braidley 201 F4
Braidwood 234 C5
Braigo 230 A3
Brailsford 173 D3
Brain's Green 131 F2
Braintree 151 F5
Braiseworth 164 C4
Braishfield 119 E5
Braithwaite Cumb 209 F4
Braithwaite SYorks 186 D1
Braithwaite WYorks 193 G3
Braithwell 186 C3
Bramber 109 D2
Brambletye 122 D5
Brambridge 119 F5
Bramcote Notts 173 G4
Bramcote Warks 159 G4
Bramdean 120 B5
Bramerton 179 D5
Bramfield Herts 136 B1
Bramfield Suff 165 E4
Bramford 152 C3
Bramhall 184 C4
Bramham 194 D3
Bramhope 194 B3
Bramley Hants 120 B2
Bramley Surr 121 F3
Bramley SYorks 186 B3
Bramley Corner 120 B2
Bramley Head 194 A2
Bramley Vale 173 F1
Bramling 125 E3
Brampford Speke 102 C3
Brampton Cambs 162 A5
Brampton Cumb 210 B1
Brampton Cumb 210 C5
Brampton Derbys 186 A5
Brampton Lincs 187 F5
Brampton Norf 178 D3
Brampton Suff 165 F3
Brampton SYorks 186 B2
Brampton Abbotts 145 F5
Brampton Ash 160 C4
Brampton Bryan 156 C5
Brampton en le Morthen 186 B4
Brampton Street 165 F3
Brampton Valley Way Country Park N'hants NN6 9DG 160 C5
Bramshall 172 B4
Bramshaw 106 B1
Bramshill 120 C1
Bramshott 120 D4
Bramwell 116 B5
Bran End 151 E5
Branault 247 E3
Brancaster 177 F3
Brancaster Staithe 177 F3
Brancepeth 212 B4
Branchill 267 H6
Brand Green 145 G5
Brandelhow 209 F4
Branderburgh 267 K4
Brandesburton 196 D3
Brandeston 152 D1
Brandis Corner 113 E5
Brandiston 178 C3
Brandlingill 209 E4
Brandon Dur 212 B4
Brandon Lincs 175 E3
Brandon N'umb 229 E5
Brandon Suff 163 F4
Brandon Warks 159 G5
Brandon Bank 163 E4
Brandon Creek 163 E3
Brandon Park Suff IP27 0SU 163 F4
Brandon Parva 178 B5
Brandon to Bishop Auckland Walk Dur DH7 7RJ 212 B4
Brandsby 203 E5
Brandy Wharf 188 A3
Brane 94 B4
Branksome 105 G3
Branksome Park 105 G3
Bransbury 119 F3
Bransby 187 F5
Branscombe 103 E4
Bransford 145 G2
Bransford Bridge 146 A2
Bransgore 106 A3
Bransholme 196 D4
Branson's Cross 158 C5
Branston Leics 174 D5
Branston Lincs 175 F1
Branston Staffs 172 D5
Branston Booths 175 F1
Branston Water Park Staffs DE14 3EZ 172 D5
Brant Broughton 175 E2
Brantham 152 C4
Branthwaite Cumb 209 F3
Branthwaite Cumb 209 D4
Brantingham 196 B5
Branton N'umb 229 E5
Branton SYorks 186 D2
Brantwood 199 E3
Branxholm Bridgend 227 F4
Branxholme 227 F4
Branxton 228 C3
Brassey Green 170 C1
Brassington 172 D2
Brasted 123 D3
Brasted Chart 123 D3
Brathens 260 E5
Bratoft 176 C1
Brattleby 187 G4
Bratton Som 114 C3
Bratton Tel&W 157 F1
Bratton Wilts 118 A2
Bratton Clovelly 99 E1
Bratton Fleming 113 G2
Bratton Seymour 117 D5
Braughing 150 B5
Brauncewell 175 F2
Braunston N'hants 148 A1
Braunston Rut 160 D2
Braunstone 160 A2
Braunton 113 E2
Brawby 203 G5
Brawdy 140 B5
Brawith 203 E2
Brawl 274 D2
Brawlbin 275 F3
Bray 135 E5
Bray Shop 98 D3
Bray Wick 135 D5
Braybrooke 160 C4
Braydon Side 132 C4
Brayford 113 G2
Brayshaw 193 D2
Braythorn 194 B3
Brayton 195 F4
Braywoodside 135 D5
Brazacott 98 C1
Brea 96 A5
Breach Kent 125 D4
Breach Kent 124 A2
Breachwood Green 149 G5
Breacleit 270 D4
Breaden Heath 170 B4
Breadsall 173 E4
Breadstone 131 G2
Breage 94 D4
Breakon 278 E2
Bream 131 F2
Breamore 106 A1
Brean 115 F2
Breanais 270 B5
Brearton 194 C1
Breascleit 270 E4
Breaston 173 F4
Brechfa 142 B4
Brechin 253 E3
Brecklate 222 B4
Breckles 164 A2
Brecon (Aberhonddu) 143 G5
Brecon Beacons International Dark Sky Reserve Carmar./Powys 129 E1
Brecon Beacons Visitor Centre Powys LD3 8ER 143 F5
Breconside 225 G5
Bredbury 184 D3
Brede 110 D2
Bredenbury 145 F2
Bredfield 153 D2
Bredgar 124 A2
Bredhurst 123 G2
Bredon 146 B4
Bredon's Hardwick 146 B4
Bredon's Norton 146 B4
Bredwardine 144 C3
Breedon on the Hill 173 F5
Breibhig 271 G4
Breich 235 D3
Breightmet 184 B2
Breighton 195 G4
Breinton 145 D4
Breinton Common 145 D4
Bremhill 132 B5
Bremhill Wick 132 B5
Brenachoille 240 C4
Brenchley 123 F4
Brendon Devon 114 A3
Brendon Devon 113 D4
Brendon Devon 113 D5
Brenkley 221 E4
Brent Eleigh 152 A3
Brent Knoll 116 A2
Brent Pelham 150 C4
Brentford 136 A5
Brentingby 160 C1
Brentwood 137 E3
Brenzett 111 F1
Brenzett Green 111 F1
Breoch 216 B5
Brereton 158 C1
Brereton Green 171 E1
Brereton Heath 171 F1
Breretonhill 158 C1
Bressay 279 E8
Bressingham 164 B3
Bressingham Common 164 B3
Bressingham Steam Museum & Gardens Norf IP22 2AA 164 B3
Bretby 173 D5
Bretford 159 G5
Bretforton 146 C3
Bretherdale Head 199 G2
Bretherton 192 A5
Brettabister 279 D7
Brettenham Norf 164 A3
Brettenham Suff 152 A2
Bretton Derbys 185 F5
Bretton Flints 170 A1
Bretton Peter 161 G2
Brevig 254 B5
Brewood 158 A2
Briach 267 H6
Briantspuddle 105 E3
Brick End 151 D5
Brickendon 136 C2
Bricket Wood 136 A2
Brickfields Horse Country IoW PO33 3TH 107 E3
Brickkiln Green 151 F4
Bricklehampton 146 B3
Bride 190 C1
Bridekirk 209 E3
Bridell 141 E3
Bridestones 171 G1
Bridestowe 99 F2
Brideswell 260 D1
Bridford 102 B4
Bridge Corn 96 A5
Bridge Kent 125 D3
Bridge End Cumb 198 D4
Bridge End Devon 100 C3
Bridge End Essex 151 E4
Bridge End Lincs 175 G4
Bridge End Shet 279 C9
Bridge Hewick 202 C5
Bridge o'Ess 260 D5
Bridge of Alford 260 D3
Bridge of Allan 242 C5
Bridge of Avon 259 J1
Bridge of Awe (Drochaid Abha) 240 C1
Bridge of Balgie 250 A5
Bridge of Bogendreip 260 E5
Bridge of Brewlands 251 G3
Bridge of Brown 259 J2
Bridge of Cally 251 G4
Bridge of Canny 260 E5
Bridge of Craigisla 252 A4
Bridge of Dee Aber 259 J5
Bridge of Dee Aber 260 E5
Bridge of Dee D&G 216 B4
Bridge of Don 261 H4
Bridge of Dun 253 E4
Bridge of Dye 253 E1
Bridge of Earn 243 G3
Bridge of Ericht 250 A4
Bridge of Feugh 260 E5
Bridge of Forss 275 F2
Bridge of Gairn 260 B5
Bridge of Gaur 250 A4
Bridge of Muchalls 261 G5
Bridge of Muick 260 B5
Bridge of Orchy (Drochaid Urchaidh) 241 E1
Bridge of Tynet 268 B4
Bridge of Walls 279 B7
Bridge of Weir 233 E3
Bridge Reeve 113 G4
Bridge Sollers 144 D3
Bridge Street 151 G3
Bridge Trafford 183 F5
Bridgefoot Angus 244 B1
Bridgefoot Cambs 150 C3
Bridgefoot Cumb 209 D4
Bridgehampton 116 C5
Bridgehaugh 260 B1
Bridgehill 211 G2
Bridgemary 107 E2
Bridgemere 171 E3
Bridgend A&B 230 B3
Bridgend A&B 240 A5
Bridgend Aber 260 D1
Bridgend Aber 269 F6
Bridgend Angus 252 D3
Bridgend (Pen-y-bont ar Ogwr) Bridgend 129 F5
Bridgend Corn 97 F4
Bridgend Cumb 199 F1
Bridgend Fife 244 B3
Bridgend Moray 260 B1
Bridgend P&K 243 G2
Bridgend WLoth 235 E2
Bridgend of Lintrathen 252 A4
Bridgerule 112 C5
Bridges 156 C3
Bridgeton Aber 260 D3
Bridgeton Glas 234 A3
Bridgetown Corn 98 D2
Bridgetown Som 114 C4
Bridgewater Hall, Manchester GtMan M2 3WS 46 E5
Bridgeyate 131 F5
Bridgham 164 A3
Bridgnorth 157 G3
Bridgnorth Cliff Railway Shrop WV16 4AH 157 G3
Bridgtown 158 B2
Bridgwater 115 F4
Bridlington 197 D1
Bridport 104 A3
Bridstow 145 E5
Brierfield 193 E4
Brierley Glos 131 F1
Brierley Here 145 D2
Brierley SYorks 186 B1
Brierley Hill 158 B4
Brierton 213 D5
Briestfield 185 G1
Brig o'Turk 242 A4
Brigg 188 A2
Briggate 179 E3
Briggswath 204 B2
Brigham Cumb 209 D3
Brigham ERid 196 C2
Brighouse 194 A5
Brighstone 106 D4
Brightgate 173 D2
Brighthampton 133 F2
Brightholmlee 185 G3
Brightling 110 B1
Brightlingsea 139 D1
Brighton B&H 109 F3
Brighton Corn 96 D4
Brighton Centre, The B&H BN1 2GR 65 Brighton
Brighton Museum & Art Gallery B&H BN1 1EE 65 Brighton
Brighton Pier B&H BN2 1TW 65 Brighton
Brightons 234 D2
Brightwalton 133 G5
Brightwalton Green 133 G5
Brightwell 152 D3
Brightwell Baldwin 134 B3
Brightwell Upperton 134 B3
Brightwell-cum-Sotwell 134 A3
Brignall 201 F1
Brigsley 188 C2
Brigsteer 199 F4
Brigstock 161 E4
Brill Bucks 134 B1
Brill Corn 95 E4
Brilley 144 B3
Brilley Mountain 144 B2
Brimaston 140 C5
Brimfield 145 E1
Brimington 186 B5
Brimington Common 186 B5
Brimley 102 B5
Brimpsfield 132 B1
Brimpton 119 G1
Brims 277 B9
Brimscombe 132 A2
Brimstage 183 E4
Brinacory 256 D5
Brindham 116 C3
Brindister Shet 279 D9
Brindister Shet 279 B7
Brindle 192 B5
Brindley Ford 171 F2
Brineton 158 A1
Bringhurst 160 D3
Brington 161 F5
Brinian 276 D5
Briningham 178 B2
Brinkhill 189 D5
Brinkley Cambs 151 E2
Brinkley Notts 174 C2
Brinklow 159 G5
Brinkworth 132 C4
Brinmore 258 D2
Brinscall 192 C5
Brinsea 116 B1
Brinsley 173 F3
Brinsop 144 D3
Brinsworth 186 B3
Brinton 178 B2
Brisco 210 A2
Brisley 178 A3
Brislington 131 F5
Brissenden Green 124 B5
Bristol 131 E5
Bristol Cathedral BS1 5TJ 66 Bristol
Bristol City Museum & Art Gallery Bristol BS8 1RL 8 B3
Bristol Filton Airport 131 E4
Bristol International Airport 116 C1
Bristol Zoo Bristol BS8 3HA 8 B3
Briston 178 B2
Britain At War Experience GtLon SE1 2TF 12 C4
Britannia 193 E5
Britford 118 C5
Brithdir Caerp 130 A2
Brithdir Gwyn 155 D1
Brithem Bottom 102 D1
British Empire & Commonwealth Museum BS1 6QH 66 Bristol
British Library (St. Pancras) GtLon NW1 2DB 12 B4
British Museum GtLon WC1B 3DG 44 E2
Briton Ferry (Llansawel) 128 D3
Britwell 135 E4
Britwell Salome 134 B3
Brixham 101 F2
Brixton Devon 100 B2
Brixton GtLon 136 C5
Brixton Deverill 117 F4
Brixworth 160 C5
Brixworth Country Park N'hants NN6 9DG 160 C5
Brize Norton 133 E2
Broad Alley 146 A1
Broad Blunsdon 133 D3
Broad Campden 147 D4
Broad Carr 185 E1
Broad Chalke 118 B5
Broad Ford 123 G5
Broad Green Cambs 151 E2
Broad Green CenBeds 149 E3
Broad Green Essex 151 G5
Broad Green Essex 150 C4
Broad Green Mersey 183 F3
Broad Green Suff 152 B2
Broad Green Worcs 145 G2
Broad Haven 126 B1
Broad Hill 163 D5
Broad Hinton 132 D5
Broad Laying 119 F1
Broad Marston 146 D3
Broad Oak Carmar 142 B5
Broad Oak Cumb 198 C3
Broad Oak ESuss 110 D2
Broad Oak ESuss 110 B1
Broad Oak Here 145 D5
Broad Road 165 D4
Broad Street ESuss 111 D2
Broad Street Kent 124 A3
Broad Street Wilts 118 C2
Broad Street Green 138 B2
Broad Town 132 C5
Broadbottom 185 D3
Broadbridge 108 A3
Broadbridge Heath 121 G4
Broadclyst 102 C3
Broadfield Lancs 192 D5
Broadfield Lancs 192 B5
Broadford (An t-Ath Leathann) 256 C2
Broadford Airport 256 C2
Broadford Bridge 121 F5
Broadgate 198 C4
Broadhaugh 227 F5
Broadhaven 275 J3
Broadheath GtMan 184 B4
Broadheath Worcs 145 F1
Broadhembury 103 E2
Broadhempston 101 E1
Broadholme 187 F5
Broadland Row 110 D2
Broadlay 127 G2
Broadley Lancs 184 C1
Broadley Moray 268 B4
Broadley Common 136 D2
Broadmayne 104 D4
Broadmeadows 227 F2
Broadmere 120 B3
Broadmoor 127 D2
Broadnymett 102 A2
Broadoak Dorset 104 A3
Broadoak Glos 131 F1
Broadoak Kent 125 D2
Broadoak End 136 C1
Broadrashes 268 C5
Broad's Green 137 F1
Broadsea 269 H4
Broadstairs 125 F2
Broadstone Poole 105 G3
Broadstone Shrop 157 E4
Broadstreet Common 130 C4
Broadwas 145 G2
Broadwater Herts 150 A5
Broadwater WSuss 108 D3
Broadwater Down 123 E5
Broadwaters 158 A5
Broadway Carmar 127 G2
Broadway Carmar 127 F1
Broadway Pembs 126 B1
Broadway Som 103 G1
Broadway Suff 165 E4
Broadway Worcs 146 D4
Broadwell Glos 147 E5
Broadwell Oxon 133 E2
Broadwell Warks 147 G1
Broadwell House 211 F2
Broadwey 104 C4
Broadwindsor 104 A2
Broadwood Kelly 113 G5
Broadwoodwidger 99 E2
Brobury 144 C3
Brocastle 129 F5
Brochel 264 B7
Brochloch 215 G1
Brock 246 B2
Brockamin 145 G2
Brockbridge 107 F1
Brockdish 164 D4
Brockenhurst 106 B2
Brockford Green 152 C1
Brockford Street 152 C1
Brockhall 148 B1
Brockham 121 G3
Brockhampton Glos 146 C5
Brockhampton Glos 146 B5
Brockhampton Here 145 E4
Brockhampton Here 145 F2
Brockhampton Green 104 D2
Brockholes 185 F1
Brockhurst Hants 107 E2
Brockhurst WSuss 122 D5
Brocklebank 209 G2
Brocklesby 188 B1
Brockley NSom 116 B1
Brockley Suff 151 G2
Brockley Green 151 F3
Brock's Green 119 F1
Brockton Shrop 157 E3
Brockton Shrop 157 F2
Brockton Shrop 156 C2
Brockton Shrop 156 C4
Brockton Tel&W 157 G1
Brockweir 131 E2
Brockwood Park 120 B5

Brockworth 132 A1
Brocton 158 B1
Brodick 223 F2
Brodsworth 186 C2
Brogborough 149 E4
Brogden 193 E3
Brogyntyn 169 F4
Broken Cross
  ChesE 184 C5
Broken Cross
  ChesW&C 184 A5
Brokenborough 132 B4
Brokes 202 A3
Bromborough 183 E4
Brome 164 C4
Brome Street 164 C4
Bromeswell 153 E2
Bromfield Cumb 209 E2
Bromfield Shrop 157 D5
Bromham Bed 149 F2
Bromham Wilts 118 A1
Bromley GtLon 122 D2
Bromley SYorks 186 A3
Bromley Cross 184 B1
Bromley Green 124 B5
Brompton Med 123 G2
Brompton NYorks 202 C3
Brompton NYorks 204 C4
Brompton Shrop 157 E2
Brompton on Swale 202 B3
Brompton Ralph 115 D4
Brompton Regis 114 C4
Bromsash 145 F5
Bromsberrow 145 G4
Bromsberrow
  Heath 145 G4
Bromsgrove 158 B5
Bromstead Heath 158 A1
Bromyard 145 F2
Bromyard Downs 145 F2
Bronaber 168 A4
Brondesbury 136 B4
Brongest 141 G3
Bronington 170 B4
Bronllys 144 A4
Bronnant 142 C1
Brontë Weaving Shed
  WYorks
  BD22 8EP 193 G4
Bronwydd Arms 142 A5
Bronydd 144 B3
Bron-y-gaer 127 F2
Bronygarth 169 F4
Brook Carmar 127 F2
Brook Hants 106 B1
Brook Hants 119 E5
Brook IoW 106 C4
Brook Kent 124 C4
Brook Surr 121 E4
Brook Surr 121 F3
Brook Bottom 185 D2
Brook End Bed 149 F1
Brook End Herts 150 B5
Brook End MK 149 E2
Brook End Worcs 146 A3
Brook Hill 106 B1
Brook Street Essex 137 E3
Brook Street Kent 124 B5
Brook Street Suff 151 G3
Brook Street WSuss 109 F1
Brooke Norf 165 D2
Brooke Rut 160 D2
Brookend Glos 131 E3
Brookend Glos 131 F2
Brookfield 185 E3
Brookhampton 134 B3
Brookhouse ChesE 184 D5
Brookhouse Denb 169 D1
Brookhouse Lancs 192 B1
Brookhouse SYorks 186 C4
Brookhouse Green 171 F1
Brookhouses 171 G3
Brookland 111 E1
Brooklands D&G 216 C3
Brooklands Shrop 170 C3
Brooklands Museum Surr
  KT13 0QN 121 F1
Brookmans Park 136 B2
Brooks 156 A3
Brooks Green 121 G5
Brooksby 160 B1
Brookside Miniature
  Railway ChesE
  SK12 1BZ 25 G6
Brookthorpe 132 A1
Brookwood 121 E2
Broom CenBeds 149 G3
Broom Fife 244 B4
Broom Warks 146 C2
Broom Green 178 A3
Broom Hill Dorset 105 G2
Broom Hill Worcs 158 B5
Broom of Dalreach 243 F3
Broomcroft 157 E2
Broome Norf 165 E2
Broome Shrop 156 D4
Broome Worcs 158 B5
Broome Wood 229 F5
Broomedge 184 B4
Broomer's Corner 121 G5
Broomfield Aber 261 H1
Broomfield Essex 137 G1
Broomfield Kent 125 D2
Broomfield Kent 124 A3
Broomfield Som 115 F4
Broomfleet 196 B1
Broomhall Green 170 D3
Broomhaugh 211 G1
Broomhead 269 H4
Broomhill Bristol 131 F5
Broomhill N'umb 221 E1
Broomielaw 201 F1
Broompark 212 B3
Broom's Green 145 G4
Brora 267 G1
Broseley 157 F2
Brotherlee 211 F4
Brothertoft 176 A3
Brotherton 195 D5
Brotton 203 F1
Broubster 275 F2
Brough Cumb 200 C1
Brough Derbys 185 F4
Brough ERid 196 B5
Brough High 275 H1
Brough Notts 174 D2
Brough Ork 277 C6

Brough Shet 279 E8
Brough Shet 278 D5
Brough Shet 278 E6
Brough Shet 278 E5
Brough Lodge 278 E3
Brough Sowerby 200 C1
Broughall 170 C3
Brougham 210 B5
Brougham Hall Cumb
  CA10 2DE 210 B5
Broughton Bucks 134 D1
Broughton Cambs 162 A5
Broughton Flints 170 A1
Broughton Hants 119 E4
Broughton Lancs 192 B4
Broughton MK 149 D3
Broughton N'hants 160 D5
Broughton NLincs 187 G2
Broughton NYorks 203 G5
Broughton NYorks 193 F2
Broughton Ork 276 D3
Broughton Oxon 147 G4
Broughton ScBord 226 C2
Broughton VGlam 129 F5
Broughton Astley 160 A3
Broughton Beck 199 D4
Broughton Gifford 117 F1
Broughton Green 146 B1
Broughton Hackett 146 B2
Broughton in
  Furness 198 D4
Broughton Mills 198 D3
Broughton Moor 209 D3
Broughton Poggs 133 E2
Broughty Ferry 244 C1
Browland 279 B7
Brown Candover 119 G4
Brown Edge Lancs 183 E1
Brown Edge Staffs 171 G2
Brown Heath 170 B1
Brown Lees 171 F2
Brown Street 152 B1
Brownber 200 C2
Browndown 107 E3
Brownheath 170 B5
Brownhill 269 G6
Brownhills Fife 244 D3
Brownhills WMid 158 C2
Brownieside 229 F4
Brownlow 171 F1
Brownlow Heath 171 F1
Brown's Bank 170 D3
Brownsea Island Dorset
  BH13 7EE 105 G4
Brownshill 132 A2
Brownshill Green 159 F4
Brownsover 160 A5
Brownston 100 D2
Browston Green 179 F5
Broxa 204 C3
Broxbourne 136 C2
Broxburn ELoth 237 D2
Broxburn WLoth 235 E2
Broxholme 187 G5
Broxted 151 D5
Broxton 170 B2
Broxwood 144 C2
Broyle Side 109 G2
Bruachmary 267 F7
Bruan 275 J5
Brue (Brù) 271 F3
Bruera 170 B1
Bruern 147 E5
Bruernish 254 C4
Bruichladdich 230 A3
Bruisyard 153 E1
Bruisyard Street 153 E1
Brumby 187 G1
Brund 172 C1
Brundall 179 E4
Brundish Norf 165 E2
Brundish Suff 153 E1
Brundish Street 165 D4
Brunstock 210 A2
Brunswick Village 221 E4
Bruntingthorpe 160 B3
Bruntland 260 C2
Brunton Fife 244 B2
Brunton N'umb 229 F4
Brunton Wilts 118 D2
Brushfield 185 F5
Brushford Devon 113 G5
Brushford Som 114 C5
Bruton 117 D4
Bryanston 105 E2
Bryanton 170 B2
Bryant's Bottom 135 D3
Brydekirk 217 F3
Brymbo 169 F2
Brymor Ice Cream NYorks
  HG4 4PG 202 A4
Brympton 104 B1
Bryn Caerp 130 A3
Bryn Carmar 128 B2
Bryn ChesW&C 184 A5
Bryn GtMan 183 G2
Bryn NPT 129 E3
Bryn Shrop 156 B4
Bryn Bach Country
  Park BGwent
  NP22 3AY 130 A2
Bryn Bwbach 167 F4
Bryn Gates 183 G2
Bryn Pen-y-lan 170 A3
Brynamman 128 D1
Brynberian 141 E4
Bryncae 129 F4
Bryncethin 129 F4
Bryncir 167 D3
Bryncoch Bridgend 129 F4
Bryn-côch NPT 128 D3
Bryncroes 166 B4
Bryncrug 154 C2
Bryneglwys 169 E3
Brynford 182 C5
Bryngwran 180 B5
Bryngwyn Mon 130 C2
Bryngwyn Powys 144 A3
Bryn-henllan 140 D4
Brynhoffnant 141 G3
Bryning 192 A4
Brynithel 130 B2
Brynmawr BGwent 130 A1
Bryn-mawr Gwyn 166 B4
Brynmelyn 168 A5
Brynmenyn 129 F4
Brynna 129 F4
Brynnau Gwynion 129 F4

Brynog 142 B2
Bryn-penarth 156 A2
Brynrefail Gwyn 167 E1
Brynrefail IoA 180 C4
Brynsadler 129 G4
Brynsaithmarchog 169 D2
Brynsiencyn 167 D1
Bryn-teg IoA 180 C4
Bryn-teg Wrex 170 A2
Bryn-y-cochin 170 A1
Bryn-y-gwenin 130 C1
Bryn-y-maen 181 G5
Buaile nam Bodach 254 C4
Bualadubh 262 C7
Bualintur 255 K2
Bualnaluib 264 E2
Bubbenhall 159 F5
Bubnell 185 G5
Bubwith 195 G4
Buccleuch 227 E4
Buchan 216 B4
Buchanan Castle 233 F1
Buchanhaven 269 K6
Buchanty 243 E2
Buchlyvie 242 A5
Buckabank 209 G2
Buckby Wharf 148 B1
Buckden Cambs 149 G1
Buckden NYorks 201 E5
Buckenham 179 E5
Buckerell 103 E2
Buckfast 100 D1
Buckfast Abbey Devon
  TQ11 0EE 100 D1
Buckfastleigh 100 D1
Buckhaven 244 B5
Buckholm 227 F2
Buckholt 131 E1
Buckhorn Weston 117 E5
Buckhurst Hill 136 D3
Buckie 268 C4
Buckies 275 G2
Buckingham 148 B4
Buckingham Palace GtLon
  SW1A 1AA 44 B6
Buckland Bucks 135 D1
Buckland Devon 100 C3
Buckland Glos 146 C4
Buckland Hants 106 C3
Buckland Here 145 E2
Buckland Herts 150 B4
Buckland Kent 125 F4
Buckland Oxon 133 F3
Buckland Surr 122 B3
Buckland Brewer 113 E3
Buckland Common 135 E2
Buckland Dinham 117 E2
Buckland Filleigh 113 E5
Buckland in the
  Moor 102 A5
Buckland
  Monachorum 100 A1
Buckland Newton 104 C2
Buckland Ripers 104 C4
Buckland St. Mary 103 F1
Buckland-tout-
  Saints 101 D3
Bucklebury 134 A5
Bucklerheads 244 C1
Bucklers Hard 106 D3
Bucklesham 152 D3
Buckley (Bwcle) 169 F1
Buckley Green 147 D1
Bucklow Hill 184 B4
Buckman Corner 121 G5
Buckminster 175 D5
Bucknall Lincs 175 G1
Bucknall Stoke 171 G3
Bucknell Oxon 148 A5
Bucknell Shrop 156 C5
Buckridge 157 G5
Buck's Cross 112 D3
Bucks Green 121 F4
Bucks Hill 135 F2
Bucks Horn Oak 120 D3
Buck's Mills 113 D3
Bucksburn 261 G4
Buckspool 126 C3
Buckton ERid 205 E5
Buckton Here 156 C5
Buckton N'umb 229 E3
Buckton Vale 185 D2
Buckworth 161 G5
Budby 186 C5
Buddon 244 D1
Bude 112 C5
Budge's Shop 98 D5
Budlake 102 C2
Budle 229 F3
Budleigh Salterton 103 D4
Budock Water 95 E3
Budworth Heath 184 A5
Buerton 171 D3
Bugbrooke 148 B2
Buglawton 171 F1
Bugle 97 E4
Bugthorpe 195 G2
Building End 150 C4
Buildwas 157 F2
Builth Road 143 G2
Builth Wells (Llanfair-
  ym-Muallt) 143 G2
Bulby 175 F5
Bulcote 174 B3
Buldoo 274 E2
Bulford 118 C3
Bulford Camp 118 C3
Bulkeley 170 C2
Bulkington Warks 159 F4
Bulkington Wilts 118 A2
Bulkworthy 113 D4
Bull Bay
  (Porth Llechog) 180 C3
Bull Green 124 B5
Bullbridge 173 E2
Bullbrook 121 D1
Bullen's Green 136 B2
Bulley 131 G1
Bullington 188 A5
Bullpot Farm 200 B5
Bulls Cross 136 C3
Bull's Green Herts 136 B1
Bull's Green Norf 165 F2
Bullwood 232 C1
Bulmer Essex 151 G3
Bulmer NYorks 195 F1
Bulmer Tye 151 G4
Bulphan 137 F4

Bulstone 103 E4
Bulverhythe 110 C3
Bulwark 269 H6
Bulwell 173 G3
Bulwick 161 E3
Bumble's Green 136 D2
Bun Abhainn
  Eadarra 270 D7
Bun Loyne 257 J4
Bunarkaig 249 D1
Bunbury 170 C2
Bunbury Heath 170 C2
Bunchrew 266 D7
Bundalloch 256 E2
Buness 278 F2
Bunessan 238 C2
Bungay 165 E3
Bunker's Hill 176 A2
Bunlarie 222 C2
Bunloit
  (Bun Leothaid) 258 C2
Bunmhullin 254 C3
Bunnahabhain 230 C2
Bunny 173 G5
Buntait 257 K1
Buntingford 150 B5
Bunwell 164 C2
Bunwell Street 164 C2
Burbage Derbys 185 E5
Burbage Leics 159 G3
Burbage Wilts 118 D1
Burbage Common Leics
  LE10 3DD 159 G3
Burchett's Green 134 D4
Burcombe 118 B4
Burcot Oxon 134 A3
Burcot Worcs 158 B5
Burcott 149 D5
Burdale 196 A1
Burdocks 121 F5
Burdon 212 C2
Burdrop 147 F4
Bure Valley Railway Norf
  NR11 6BW 178 D3
Bures 152 A4
Bures Green 152 A4
Burfa 144 B1
Burford Oxon 133 E1
Burford Shrop 145 E1
Burg 246 C5
Burgate 164 B4
Burgates 120 C4
Burge End 149 G4
Burgess Hill 109 F2
Burgh 152 D2
Burgh by Sands 209 G1
Burgh Castle 179 F5
Burgh Heath 122 B3
Burgh le Marsh 176 C1
Burgh next
  Aylsham 178 D3
Burgh on Bain 188 C4
Burgh St. Margaret
  (Fleggburgh) 179 F4
Burgh St. Peter 165 F2
Burghclere 119 F1
Burghead 267 J5
Burghfield 120 B1
Burghfield
  Common 120 B1
Burghfield Hill 120 B1
Burghill 145 D3
Burghwallis 186 C1
Burham 123 G2
Buriton 120 C5
Burland 170 D2
Burlawn 97 D3
Burleigh 121 E1
Burlescombe 103 D1
Burleston 105 D3
Burley Hants 106 B2
Burley Rut 161 D1
Burley WYorks 194 B4
Burley Gate 145 E3
Burley in
  Wharfedale 194 A3
Burley Street 106 B2
Burley Woodhead 194 A3
Burleydam 170 D3
Burlingjobb 144 B2
Burlow 110 A2
Burlton 170 B5
Burmarsh 124 D5
Burmington 147 E4
Burn 195 E5
Burn Farm 253 E2
Burn Naze 191 G3
Burn of Cambus 242 C4
Burnage 184 C3
Burnaston 173 D4
Burnby 196 A3
Burncross 186 A3
Burndell 108 B3
Burnden 184 B1
Burnedge 184 D1
Burneside 199 G3
Burness 276 F3
Burneston 202 C4
Burnett 117 D1
Burnfoot High 274 D6
Burnfoot P&K 243 F4
Burnfoot ScBord 227 G4
Burnfoot ScBord 227 F4
Burnham Bucks 135 E4
Burnham NLincs 188 A1
Burnham Deepdale 177 G3
Burnham Green 136 B1
Burnham Market 177 G3
Burnham Norton 177 G3
Burnham Overy
  Staithe 177 G3
Burnham Overy
  Town 177 G3
Burnham Thorpe 177 G3
Burnham-on-
  Crouch 138 C2
Burnham-on-Sea 116 A3
Burnhaven 269 K6
Burnhead D&G 215 G2
Burnhead D&G 216 C1
Burnhervie 261 F3
Burnhill Green 157 G2
Burnhope 212 A3
Burnhouse 233 E4
Burniston 204 D3
Burnley 193 E4
Burnmouth 237 G3

Burnopfield 212 A2
Burn's Green 150 B5
Burns National Heritage
  Park SAyr
  KA7 4PQ 224 B4
Burnsall 193 G1
Burnside Aber 261 F3
Burnside Angus 252 D4
Burnside EAyr 225 D4
Burnside Fife 243 G4
Burnside Shet 278 B5
Burnside WLoth 235 E2
Burnside of
  Duntrune 244 C1
Burnstones 210 C2
Burnswark 217 F3
Burnt Hill 134 A5
Burnt Houses 212 A5
Burnt Oak 136 B3
Burnt Yates 194 B1
Burntcliff Top 171 G1
Burntisland 235 G1
Burnton EAyr 224 D5
Burntwood 158 C2
Burntwood Green 158 C2
Burnworthy 103 E1
Burpham Surr 121 F2
Burpham WSuss 108 C3
Burra 279 C9
Burradon N'umb 229 E1
Burradon T&W 221 E4
Burrafirth 278 F1
Burraland 278 C5
Burras 95 D3
Burravoe Shet 278 E5
Burravoe Shet 279 C6
Burray 277 D8
Burrell Collection
  Glas G43 1AT 30 C5
Burrells 200 B1
Burrelton 244 A1
Burridge Devon 103 G2
Burridge Hants 107 E1
Burrill 202 B4
Burringham 187 F2
Burrington Devon 113 G4
Burrington Here 156 D5
Burrington NSom 116 B2
Burrough Green 151 E2
Burrough on the
  Hill 160 C1
Burrow Som 114 C3
Burrow Som 104 A1
Burrow Bridge 116 A4
Burrowhill 121 E1
Burrows Cross 121 F3
Burry 128 A3
Burry Green 128 A3
Burry Port 128 A2
Burscough 183 F1
Burscough Bridge 183 F1
Bursea 196 A4
Burshill 196 C3
Bursledon 107 D2
Burslem 171 F3
Burstall 152 C3
Burstock 104 A2
Burston Norf 164 C3
Burston Staffs 171 G4
Burstow 122 C4
Burstwick 197 E5
Burtersett 201 D4
Burthorpe 151 F1
Burthwaite 210 A3
Burtle 116 B3
Burtle Hill 116 A3
Burton ChesW&C 183 E5
Burton ChesW&C 170 C1
Burton Dorset 106 A3
Burton Lincs 187 G5
Burton N'umb 229 F3
Burton Pembs 126 C2
Burton Som 115 E3
Burton Wilts 132 A5
Burton Wilts 117 F4
Burton Agnes 196 D1
Burton Bradstock 104 A4
Burton Coggles 175 E5
Burton End 150 D5
Burton Ferry 126 C2
Burton Fleming 205 D5
Burton Green
  Warks 159 E5
Burton Green Wrex 170 A2
Burton Hastings 159 G4
Burton in Lonsdale 200 B5
Burton Joyce 174 B3
Burton Latimer 161 E5
Burton Lazars 160 C1
Burton Leonard 194 C1
Burton on the
  Wolds 173 G5
Burton Overy 160 B3
Burton Pedwardine 175 G3
Burton Pidsea 197 E4
Burton Salmon 195 D5
Burton Stather 187 F1
Burton upon
  Stather 187 F1
Burton upon Trent 172 D5
Burton-in-Kendal 199 G5
Burton's Green 151 G5
Burtonwood 183 G3
Burwardsley 170 C2
Burwarton 157 F4
Burwash 110 B1
Burwash Common 110 B1
Burwash Weald 110 B1
Burwell Cambs 151 D1
Burwell Lincs 189 D5
Burwen 180 C3
Burwick Ork 277 D9
Burwick Shet 279 C8
Bury Cambs 162 A4
Bury GtMan 184 C1
Bury Som 114 C5
Bury WSuss 108 C2
Bury End 146 C4
Bury Green 150 C5
Bury St. Edmunds 151 G1
Buryas Bridge 94 B4
Burythorpe 195 G1
Busbridge 121 E3
Busby ERenf 233 G4
Busby P&K 243 F2

Buscot 133 E3
Bush 112 C5
Bush Bank 145 D2
Bush Crathie 259 K5
Bush Green 164 D3
Bushbury 158 B2
Bushby 160 B2
Bushey 136 A3
Bushey Heath 136 A3
Bushley 146 A4
Bushley Green 146 A4
Bushton 132 C5
Bushy Common 178 A4
Business Design Centre,
  Islington GtLon
  N1 0QH 12 B3
Busk 210 C2
Buslingthorpe 188 A4
Bussage 132 A2
Busta 279 C6
Butcher's Common 179 E3
Butcher's Cross 110 A1
Butcher's Pasture 151 E5
Butcombe 116 C1
Bute 232 B3
Bute Town 130 A2
Buthill 267 J5
Butleigh 116 C4
Butleigh Wootton 116 C4
Butler's Cross 134 C2
Butler's Hill 173 G3
Butlers Marston 147 F3
Butlersbank 170 C5
Butley 153 E2
Butley Abbey 153 E3
Butley Low Corner 153 E3
Butley Mills 153 E2
Butley Town 184 D5
Butt Green 171 D2
Butt Lane 171 F2
Butterburn 219 E4
Buttercrambe 195 G2
Butterknowle 212 A5
Butterleigh 102 C2
Butterley 173 F2
Buttermere Cumb 209 E5
Buttermere Wilts 119 E1
Butters Green 171 F2
Buttershaw 194 A4
Butterstone 251 F5
Butterton Staffs 172 B2
Butterton Staffs 171 F3
Butterwick Dur 212 C5
Butterwick Lincs 176 B3
Butterwick NYorks 204 C5
Butterwick NYorks 203 G5
Buttington 156 B2
Buttonbridge 157 G5
Buttonoak 157 G5
Buttons' Green 152 A2
Butts 102 B4
Butt's Green
  Hants 119 D5
Buttsash 106 D2
Buxhall 152 B2
Buxted 109 G1
Buxton Derbys 185 E5
Buxton Norf 178 D3
Buxton Heath 178 C3
Buxworth 185 E4
Bwlch 144 A5
Bwlch-clawdd 141 G4
Bwlch-derwin 167 D3
Bwlchgwyn 169 F2
Bwlch-llan 142 B2
Bwlchnewydd 141 G5
Bwlchtocyn 166 C5
Bwlch-y-cibau 156 A1
Bwlch-y-ddar 169 E5
Bwlchyfadfa 142 A3
Bwlch-y-ffridd 155 G3
Bwlch-y-groes 141 F4
Bwlchyllyn 167 E2
Bwlchymynydd 128 B3
Bwlch-y-sarnau 155 G5
Byers Green 212 B4
Byfield 148 A2
Byfleet 121 F1
Byford 144 C3
Bygrave 150 A4
Byker 212 B1
Byland Abbey 203 E5
Bylane End 97 G4
Bylchau 168 C1
Byley 171 E1
Bynea 128 B3
Byrness 219 F1
Bystock 102 D4
Bythorn 161 F5
Byton 144 C1
Bywell 211 G1
Byworth 121 E5

Cadmore End 134 C3
Cadnam 106 B1
Cadney 188 A2
Cadole 169 F1
Cadover Bridge 100 B1
Cadoxton 115 E1
Cadoxton-Juxta-
  Neath 129 D3
Cadwell 149 G4
Cadwst 168 D4
Cadzow 234 B4
Cae Ddafydd 167 F3
Caeathro 167 E1
Caehopkin 129 E1
Caen 275 F7
Caenby 188 A4
Caenby Corner 187 G4
Caer Llan 131 D2
Caerau Bridgend 129 E4
Caerau Cardiff 130 A5
Caerdeon 154 C1
Caerfarchell 140 A5
Caergeiliog 180 B5
Caergwrle 170 A2
Caerhun 181 F5
Caer-Lan 129 E1
Caerleon 130 C3
Caernarfon 167 D1
Caernarfon Castle Gwyn
  LL55 2AY 167 D1
Caerphilly 130 A4
Caersws 155 G3
Caerwedros 141 G2
Caerwent 131 D3
Caerwys 182 C5
Caethle Farm 154 C3
Caggan 259 F2
Caggle Street 130 C1
Caim High 247 F3
Caim IoA 181 E4
Caio 142 C4
Cairisiadar 270 C4
Cairminis 263 F3
Cairnargat 260 C1
Cairnbaan 240 A5
Cairnbeathie 260 D4
Cairnbrogie 261 G2
Cairnbulg 269 J4
Cairncross Angus 252 C2
Cairncross ScBord 237 F3
Cairncurran 233 E3
Cairndoon 207 D3
Cairndow 241 D3
Cairness 269 J4
Cairney Lodge 244 B3
Cairneyhill 235 E1
Cairngorm Mountain High
  PH22 1RB 259 G4
Cairnhill Aber 261 H2
Cairnhill Aber 260 E1
Cairnie Aber 261 G4
Cairnie Aber 268 C6
Cairnorrie 269 G6
Cairnryan 214 B4
Cairnsmore 215 F4
Caister-on-Sea 179 G4
Caistor 188 B3
Caistor St. Edmund 178 D5
Caistron 220 B1
Caithness Crystal Visitor
  Centre N'umb
  PE30 4NE 163 E1
Cake Street 164 B2
Cakebole 158 A5
Calbost 271 G6
Calbourne 106 C4
Calceby 189 D5
Calcoed 182 C5
Calcot 134 B5
Calcott Kent 125 D2
Calcott Shrop 156 D1
Calcotts Green 131 G1
Calcutt 132 D3
Caldarvan 233 F1
Caldback 278 F2
Caldbeck 209 G3
Caldbergh 201 F4
Caldecote Cambs 150 B2
Caldecote Cambs 161 G4
Caldecote Herts 150 A4
Caldecote N'hants 148 B2
Caldecote Warks 159 F3
Caldecott N'hants 149 E1
Caldecott Oxon 133 G3
Caldecott Rut 161 D3
Calder Bridge 198 B2
Calder Grove 186 A1
Calder Mains 275 F3
Calder Vale 192 B3
Calderbank 234 B3
Calderbrook 184 D1
Caldercruix 234 C3
Calderglen 234 A4
Calderglen Country Park
  SLan G75 0QZ 31 E6
Caldermill 234 A5
Caldey Island 127 E3
Caldhame 252 C5
Caldicot 131 D4
Caldwell Derbys 159 E1
Caldwell ERenf 233 F4
Caldwell NYorks 202 A1
Caldy 182 A4
Calebreck 209 G3
Caledrhydiau 142 A2
Calford Green 151 E3
Calfsound 276 E3
Calgary 246 C4
Califer 267 H6
California Falk 234 D2
California Norf 179 G4
California Suff 152 D3
California Country Park
  W'ham
  RG40 4HT 120 C1
Calke 173 E5
Calke Abbey Derbys
  DE73 7LE 173 E5
Callakille 264 C6
Callaly 220 C1
Callander 242 B4
Callanish (Calanais) 270 C4
Callaughton 157 F3
Callerton Lane End 212 A1
Calliburn 222 C3
Calligarry 256 C4
Callington 99 D4
Callingwood 172 C5

Callisterhall 218 A3
Callow 145 D4
Callow End 146 A3
Callow Hill Wilts 132 C4
Callow Hill Worcs 157 G5
Callow Hill Worcs 146 C1
Callows Grave 145 E1
Calmore 106 C1
Calmsden 132 C2
Calne 132 B5
Calow 186 B5
Calrossie 266 E4
Calshot 107 D2
Calstock 100 A1
Calstone Wellington 118 B1
Calthorpe 178 C2
Calthwaite 210 A3
Calton NYorks 193 F2
Calton Staffs 172 C2
Calveley 170 C2
Calver 185 G5
Calver Hill 144 C3
Calverhall 170 D4
Calverleigh 102 C1
Calverley 194 B4
Calvert 148 B5
Calverton MK 148 C4
Calverton Notts 174 B3
Calvine 250 C3
Calvo 209 E1
Cam 131 G3
Camasnacroise 248 A4
Camastianavaig 256 B1
Camasunary 256 B3
Camault Muir 266 C7
Camb 278 E3
Camber 111 E2
Camberley 121 D1
Camberwell 136 C5
Camblesforth 195 F5
Cambo 220 C3
Cambois 221 F3
Camborne 95 D3
Cambourne 150 B2
Cambridge Cambs 150 C2
Cambridge Glos 131 G2
Cambridge American Military Cemetery & Memorial Cambs CB23 7PH 150 B2
Cambridge City Airport 150 C2
Cambridge University Botanic Garden Cambs CB2 1JF 150 C2
Cambus 243 D5
Cambus o' May 260 C5
Cambusbarron 242 C5
Cambuskenneth 242 D5
Cambuslang 234 A3
Cambusnethan 234 C4
Camden Town 136 B4
Camel Hill 116 C5
Camel Trail Corn PL27 7AL 97 D2
Cameley 116 D2
Camelford 97 F1
Camelon 234 C1
Camelot Theme Park Lancs PR7 5LP 183 G1
Camelsdale 121 D4
Camer 123 F2
Cameron House 233 E1
Camerory 259 H1
Camer's Green 145 G4
Camerton B&NESom 117 D2
Camerton Cumb 208 D3
Camerton ERid 197 E5
Camghouran 250 A4
Camis Eskan 233 F1
Cammachmore 261 H5
Cammeringham 187 G4
Camore 266 E2
Camp Hill Pembs 127 E1
Camp Hill Warks 159 F3
Campbeltown (Ceann Loch Chille Chiarain) 222 C3
Campbeltown Airport 222 B3
Camperdown 221 E4
Camperdown Country Park Dundee DD2 4TF 244 B1
Campmuir 244 A1
Camps 235 F3
Camps End 151 E3
Camps Heath 165 G2
Campsall 186 C1
Campsea Ashe 153 E2
Campton 149 G4
Camptown 228 A5
Camquhart 232 A1
Camrose 140 C5
Camserney 250 D5
Camstraddan House 241 F5
Camus Croise 256 C3
Camus-luinie 257 F2
Camusnagaul High 248 C2
Camusnagaul High 265 G3
Camusrory 256 E5
Camusteel 264 D7
Camusterrach 264 D7
Camusurich 242 B1
Camusvrachan 250 B5
Canada 106 B1
Canaston Bridge 127 D1
Candacraig 260 B5
Candlesby 176 C1
Candy Mill 235 E5
Cane End 134 B5
Canewdon 138 B3
Canfield End 151 D5
Canford Bottom 105 G2
Canford Cliffs 105 G4
Canford Heath 105 G3
Canford Magna 105 G3
Canham's Green 152 B1
Canisbay 275 J1
Canley 159 F5
Cann 117 F5
Cann Common 117 F5
Canna 255 H4
Cannard's Grave 116 D3
Cannich (Canaich) 257 K1
Canning Town 136 D4
Cannington 115 F4
Cannock 158 B2
Cannock Wood 158 C1
Cannon Hall Country Park SYorks S75 4AT 185 G2
Cannon Hall Farm SYorks S75 4AT 185 G2
Cannon Hill Park WMid B13 8RD 15 E4
Cannop 131 F1
Canon Bridge 144 D3
Canon Frome 145 F3
Canon Pyon 145 D3
Canonbie 218 B4
Canons Ashby 148 A2
Canon's Town 94 C3
Canterbury Aber 268 D5
Canterbury Kent 124 D3
Canterbury Cathedral Kent CT1 2EH 67 Canterbury
Canterbury Tales, The Kent CT1 2TG 67 Canterbury
Cantley Norf 179 E5
Cantley SYorks 186 D2
Cantlop 157 E2
Canton 130 A5
Cantray 266 E7
Cantraydoune 266 E7
Cantraywood 266 E7
Cantsfield 200 B5
Canvey Island 137 G4
Canwell Hall 158 D2
Canwick 175 E1
Canworthy Water 98 C1
Caol 248 D2
Caolas A&B 246 B2
Caolas Na H-ESiar 254 B5
Caolasnacon 248 D3
Capel Kent 123 F4
Capel Surr 121 G3
Capel Bangor 154 C4
Capel Betws Lleucu 142 C2
Capel Carmel 166 A5
Capel Coch 168 B3
Capel Coch 180 C4
Capel Curig 168 A2
Capel Cynon 141 G3
Capel Dewi Carmar 142 A5
Capel Dewi Cere 154 C4
Capel Dewi Cere 142 A3
Capel Garmon 168 B2
Capel Gwyn Carmar 142 A5
Capel Gwyn IoA 180 B5
Capel Gwynfe 142 D5
Capel Hendre 128 B1
Capel Isaac 142 B5
Capel Iwan 141 F4
Capel le Ferne 125 E5
Capel Llanilltern 129 G4
Capel Mawr 180 C5
Capel Parc 180 C4
Capel St. Andrew 153 E3
Capel St. Mary 152 B4
Capel St. Silin 142 B2
Capel Seion 154 C5
Capel Tygwydd 141 F3
Capeluchaf 166 D3
Capelulo 181 F5
Capel-y-ffin 144 B4
Capel-y-graig 167 E1
Capenhurst 183 E5
Capernwray 199 G5
Capheaton 220 C3
Caplaw 233 F4
Capon's Green 153 D1
Cappercleuch 226 D3
Capplegill 226 C5
Capstone 123 G2
Capton Devon 101 E2
Capton Som 115 D4
Caputh 251 F5
Car Colston 174 C3
Caradon Town 97 G2
Carbellow 225 E3
Carbeth 233 G2
Carbis Bay 94 C3
Carbost High 263 K7
Carbost High 255 J1
Carbrain 234 B2
Carbrooke 178 A5
Carburton 186 D5
Carcary 253 E4
Carco 225 F4
Carcroft 186 C1
Cardenden 244 A5
Cardeston 156 C1
Cardew 209 G2
Cardiff (Caerdydd) 130 A5
Cardiff Bay Visitor Centre Cardiff CF10 4PA 7 C4
Cardiff Castle & Museum CF10 3RB 67 Cardiff
Cardiff Airport 115 D1
Cardiff Millennium Stadium CF10 1GE 67 Cardiff
Cardigan (Aberteifi) 141 E3
Cardinal's Green 151 E3
Cardington Bed 149 F3
Cardington Shrop 157 E3
Cardinham 97 F3
Cardno 269 H4
Cardonald 233 G3
Cardoness 215 G5
Cardow 267 J7
Cardrona 227 D2
Cardross 233 E2
Cardurnock 209 E1
Careby 161 F1
Careston 252 D4
Carew 126 D2
Carew Cheriton 126 D2
Carew Newton 126 D2
Carey 145 E4
Carfin 234 B4
Carfrae 236 C3
Carfraemill 236 C4
Cargate Green 179 E4
Cargen 217 D3
Cargenbridge 217 D3
Cargill 243 G1
Cargo 209 G1
Cargreen 100 A1
Carham 228 B3
Carhampton 114 D3
Carharrack 96 B5
Carie P&K 250 B4
Carie P&K 242 B1
Carines 96 B4
Carinish (Cairinis) 262 D5
Carisbrooke 107 D4
Carisbrooke Castle & Museum IoW PO30 1XY 107 D4
Cark 199 E5
Carkeel 100 A1
Carland Cross 96 C4
Carlatton 210 B2
Carlby 161 F1
Carlecotes 185 F2
Carleen 94 D4
Carleton Cumb 210 A2
Carleton Cumb 210 B5
Carleton Lancs 191 G3
Carleton NYorks 193 F3
Carleton WYorks 195 D5
Carleton Fishery 214 C2
Carleton Forehoe 178 B5
Carleton Rode 164 C2
Carleton St. Peter 179 E5
Carlin How 203 G1
Carlisle 210 A2
Carlisle Cathedral Cumb CA3 8TZ 68 Carlisle
Carlisle Park, Morpeth N'umb NE61 1YD 221 D3
Carloggas 96 C3
Carlops 235 F4
Carloway (Càrlabhagh) 270 E3
Carlton Bed 149 E2
Carlton Cambs 151 E2
Carlton Leics 159 F2
Carlton Notts 174 B3
Carlton NYorks 195 F5
Carlton NYorks 201 F4
Carlton NYorks 203 F4
Carlton Stock 212 C5
Carlton Suff 153 E1
Carlton SYorks 186 A1
Carlton WYorks 194 C5
Carlton Colville 165 G2
Carlton Curlieu 160 B3
Carlton Green 151 E2
Carlton Husthwaite 203 D5
Carlton in Lindrick 186 C4
Carlton Miniott 202 C4
Carlton Scroop 175 E3
Carlton-in-Cleveland 203 E2
Carlton-le-Moorland 175 E2
Carlton-on-Trent 174 D1
Carluke 234 C4
Carlyon Bay 97 E4
Carmacoup 225 F3
Carmarthen (Caerfyrddin) 142 A5
Carmel Carmar 128 B1
Carmel Flints 182 C5
Carmel Gwyn 167 D2
Carmel IoA 180 B4
Carmichael 226 A2
Carmont 253 G1
Carmunnock 233 G4
Carmyle 234 A3
Carmyllie 253 D5
Carn 230 A4
Carn Brea Village 96 A5
Carn Dearg 264 D4
Carnaby 196 D1
Carnach High 257 G2
Carnach High 265 G2
Carnach Na H-ESiar 262 D5
Carnan 262 C7
Carnassarie 240 A4
Carnbee 244 D4
Carnbo 243 F4
Carndu 256 E2
Carnduncan 230 A3
Carnforth 199 F5
Carnhedryn 140 B5
Carnhell Green 94 D3
Carnichal 269 H5
Carnkie Corn 95 D3
Carnkie Corn 95 E3
Carnmore 230 B5
Carno 155 F3
Carnoch High 257 K1
Carnoch High 265 J6
Carnoch High 267 F7
Carnock 235 E1
Carnon Downs 96 C5
Carnousie 268 E5
Carnoustie 245 D1
Carntyne 234 A3
Carnwath 235 D5
Carnyorth 94 A3
Carol Green 159 E5
Carperby 201 F4
Carr 186 C3
Carr Hill 187 D3
Carr Houses 183 E2
Carr Shield 211 E3
Carr Vale 186 B5
Carradale 222 D2
Carragrich 263 G2
Carrbridge 259 G2
Carrefour Selous 100 C5
Carreglefn 180 B4
Carreg-wen 141 F3
Carrhouse 187 E2
Carrick 232 A1
Carrick Castle 241 D5
Carriden 235 E1
Carrine 222 B5
Carrington GtMan 184 B3
Carrington Lincs 176 B2
Carrington Midlo 236 A3
Carroch 216 A1
Carrog Conwy 168 A3
Carrog Denb 169 E3
Carroglen 242 C2
Carrol 267 F1
Carron A&B 240 B5
Carron Falk 234 C1
Carron Moray 267 K7
Carron Bridge 234 B1
Carronbridge 216 C1
Carronshore 234 C1
Carrot 252 C5
Carrow Hill 130 D3
Carrutherstown 217 F3
Carruthmuir 233 E3
Carrville 212 C3
Carry 232 A3
Carsaig 239 E2
Carscreugh 214 D4
Carse 231 F3
Carse of Ardersier 267 F6
Carsegowan 215 F5
Carseriggan 215 E4
Carsethorn 217 D5
Carsgoe 275 G2
Carshalton 122 B2
Carshalton Beeches 122 B2
Carsie 251 G5
Carsington 173 D2
Carsington Water Derbys DE6 1ST 172 D2
Carsluith 215 F5
Carsphairn 215 G1
Carstairs 234 D5
Carstairs Junction 235 D5
Carswell Marsh 133 F3
Carter's Clay 119 E5
Carterton 133 E2
Carterway Heads 211 G2
Carthew 97 E4
Carthorpe 202 C4
Cartington 220 C1
Cartland 234 C5
Cartmel 199 E5
Cartmel Fell 199 F4
Cartworth 185 F2
Carway 128 A2
Cascades Adventure Pool Devon EX33 1NZ 113 E2
Cascob 144 B1
Cashel Farm 241 G5
Cashes Green 132 A2
Cashlie 249 G5
Cashmoor 105 F1
Caskieberran 244 A4
Cassencarie 215 F5
Cassington 133 G1
Cassop 212 C4
Castell 168 A1
Castell Gorfod 141 F5
Castell Howell 142 A3
Castellau 129 G4
Castell-y-bwch 130 B3
Casterton 200 B5
Castle Acre 163 G1
Castle Ashby 149 D2
Castle Bolton 201 F3
Castle Bromwich 158 D4
Castle Bytham 161 E1
Castle Caereinion 156 A2
Castle Camps 151 E3
Castle Carrock 210 B2
Castle Cary 116 D4
Castle Combe 132 A5
Castle Donington 173 F5
Castle Douglas 216 B4
Castle Drogo Devon EX6 6PB 102 A3
Castle Eaton 132 D3
Castle Eden 212 D4
Castle Eden Dene National Nature Reserve Dur SR8 1NJ 212 D4
Castle End 159 E5
Castle Frome 145 F3
Castle Gate 94 B3
Castle Goring 108 D3
Castle Green 121 E1
Castle Gresley 159 E1
Castle Heaton 237 G5
Castle Hedingham 151 F4
Castle Hill Kent 123 F4
Castle Hill Suff 152 C3
Castle Howard NYorks YO60 7DA 195 G1
Castle Kennedy 214 C5
Castle Leod 266 B6
Castle Levan 232 D2
Castle Madoc 143 G4
Castle Morris 140 C4
Castle O'er 218 A2
Castle Rising 177 E5
Castle Semple Water Country Park Renf PA12 4HJ 233 E4
Castle Stuart 266 E7
Castlebay (Bàgh a'Chaisteil) 254 B5
Castlebythe 140 D5
Castlecary 234 B2
Castlecraig High 267 F5
Castlecraig ScBord 235 F5
Castlefairn 216 B2
Castleford 194 D5
Castlemartin 126 C3
Castlemilk D&G 217 F3
Castlemilk Glas 234 A4
Castlemorton 145 G4
Castlerigg 209 F4
Castleside 211 G3
Castlesteads 210 B1
Castlethorpe 148 C3
Castleton A&B 231 G1
Castleton Aber 269 F5
Castleton Angus 252 B5
Castleton Derbys 185 F4
Castleton GtMan 184 C1
Castleton Newport 130 B4
Castleton NYorks 203 F2
Castleton ScBord 218 D2
Castletown Dorset 104 C5
Castletown High 275 G2
Castletown High 266 E7
Castletown IoM 190 A5
Castletown T&W 212 C2
Castleweary 227 F5
Castlewigg 207 E2
Castley 194 B3
Caston 164 A2
Castor 161 G3
Castramont 215 G4
Caswell 128 B4
Cat & Fiddle Inn 185 E5
Catacol 232 A5
Catbrain 131 E4
Catbrook 131 E2
Catchall 94 B4
Catcleugh 219 F1
Catcliffe 186 B4
Catcott 116 A4
Caterham 122 C3
Catfield 179 E3
Catfirth 279 D7
Catford 136 C5
Catforth 192 A4
Cathays 130 A5
Cathcart 233 G3
Cathedine 144 A5
Catherine-de-Barnes 159 D4
Catherington 107 F1
Catherston Leweston 103 G3
Catherton 157 F5
Cathkin 234 A4
Catisfield 107 E2
Catlodge 258 D5
Catlowdy 218 C4
Catmere End 150 C4
Catmore 133 G4
Caton Devon 102 A5
Caton Lancs 192 B1
Caton Green 192 B1
Cator Court 99 G3
Catrine 224 D3
Catsfield 110 C2
Catsfield Stream 110 C2
Catshaw 185 G2
Catshill 158 B5
Cattadale 230 B3
Cattal 194 D2
Cattawade 152 B4
Catterall 192 B3
Catterick 202 B3
Catterick Bridge 202 B3
Catterick Garrison 202 A3
Catterlen 210 A4
Catterline 253 G2
Catterton 195 E3
Catteshall 121 E3
Catthorpe 160 A5
Cattishall 151 G1
Cattistock 104 B3
Catton N'umb 211 E2
Catton Norf 178 D4
Catton NYorks 202 C5
Catton Hall 159 E1
Catwick 196 D3
Catworth 161 F5
Caudle Green 132 B1
Caudwell's Mill & Craft Centre Derbys DE4 2EB 173 D1
Caulcott CenBeds 149 F3
Caulcott Oxon 148 A5
Cauldcots 253 E5
Cauldhame Stir 242 B5
Cauldhame Stir 242 D4
Cauldon 172 B3
Caulkerbush 216 D5
Caulside 218 C3
Caundle Marsh 104 C1
Caunsall 158 A4
Caunton 174 C1
Causeway End D&G 215 F4
Causeway End Essex 137 F1
Causeway End Lancs 183 F1
Causewayhead Cumb 209 E1
Causewayhead Stir 242 D5
Causey 212 B2
Causey Arch Picnic Area Dur NE16 5EG 28 A4
Causey Park 221 D2
Causeyend 261 H3
Cautley 200 B3
Cavendish 151 G3
Cavendish Bridge 173 F5
Cavenham 151 F1
Cavens 217 D5
Cavers 227 G4
Caversfield 148 A5
Caversham 134 C5
Caverswall 171 G3
Cawdor 267 F6
Cawkeld 196 B2
Cawkwell 188 C4
Cawood 195 E4
Cawsand 100 A3
Cawston Norf 178 C3
Cawston Warks 159 G5
Cawthorn 203 G4
Cawthorne 185 G2
Cawthorpe 175 F5
Cawton 203 F5
Caxton 150 B2
Caxton Gibbet 150 A1
Caynham 157 E5
Caythorpe Lincs 175 E3
Caythorpe Notts 174 B3
Cayton 205 D4
CC2000 Pembs SA67 8DD 127 D1
Ceallan 262 D6
Ceann a' Bhàigh Na H-ESiar 262 C5
Ceann a' Bhàigh Na H-ESiar 263 F3
Ceann Loch Shiphoirt 270 E6
Ceannaridh 262 D6
Cearsiadar 271 F6
Cedig 168 C5
Cefn Berain 168 C1
Cefn Canol 169 F4
Cefn Cantref 143 G5
Cefn Coch Denb 169 E2
Cefn Coch Powys 155 G2
Cefn Cribwr 129 E4
Cefn Cross 129 E4
Cefn Einion 156 B4
Cefn Hengoed 130 A3
Cefn Llwyd 154 C4
Cefn Rhigos 129 F2
Cefn-brith 168 C2
Cefn-caer-Ferch 166 D3
Cefn-coch 169 E5
Cefn-coed-y-cymmer 129 G2
Cefn-ddwysarn 168 C4
Cefndeuddwr 168 A5
Cefneithin 128 B1
Cefn-gorwydd 143 F3
Cefn-gwyn 156 A4
Cefn-mawr 169 F3
Cefnpennar 129 G2
Cefn-y-bedd 170 A2
Cefn-y-pant 141 E5
Ceidio 180 C4
Ceidio Fawr 166 B4
Ceint 180 C5
Cellan 142 C3
Cellardyke 245 D4
Cellarhead 171 G3
Cemaes 180 B3
Cemmaes 155 E2
Cemmaes Road (Glantwymyn) 155 E2
Cenarth 141 F3
Cennin 167 D3
Centre for Life T&W NE1 4EP 79 Newcastle upon Tyne
Ceramica Stoke ST6 3DS 20 C2
Ceres 244 C3
Cerist 155 F4
Cerne Abbas 104 C2
Cerney Wick 132 C3
Cerrigceinwen 180 C5
Cerrigydrudion 168 C3
Cessford 228 B4
Ceunant 167 E1
Chaceley 146 A4
Chacewater 96 B5
Chackmore 148 B4
Chacombe 147 G3
Chad Valley 158 C4
Chadderton 184 D2
Chadderton Fold 184 C2
Chaddesden 173 E4
Chaddesley Corbett 158 A5
Chaddleworth 133 G5
Chadlington 147 F5
Chadshunt 147 F2
Chadstone 149 D2
Chadwell Leics 174 C5
Chadwell Shrop 157 G1
Chadwell St. Mary 137 F5
Chadwick End 159 E5
Chaffcombe 103 G1
Chafford Hundred 137 F5
Chagford 102 A4
Chailey 109 F2
Chainhurst 123 G4
Chalbury 105 G2
Chalbury Common 105 G2
Chaldon 122 C3
Chaldon Herring (East Chaldon) 105 D4
Chale 107 D5
Chale Green 107 D4
Chalfont Common 135 F3
Chalfont St. Giles 135 E3
Chalfont St. Peter 135 F3
Chalford Glos 132 A2
Chalford Wilts 117 F3
Chalgrove 134 B3
Chalk 137 F5
Chalk End 137 F1
Challaborough 100 C3
Challacombe 113 G1
Challister 279 E6
Challoch 215 E4
Challock 124 C3
Chalmington 104 B2
Chalton CenBeds 149 F5
Chalton Hants 107 G1
Chalvey 135 E5
Chalvington 110 A3
Champany 235 E2
Chancery 154 B5
Chandler's Cross 135 F3
Chandler's Ford 119 F5
Channel Islands 100 A5
Channel's End 149 G2
Channerwick 279 D10
Chantry Som 117 E3
Chantry Suff 152 C3
Chapel 244 A5
Chapel Allerton Som 116 B2
Chapel Allerton WYorks 194 C4
Chapel Amble 97 D2
Chapel Brampton 148 C1
Chapel Chorlton 171 F4
Chapel Cleeve 114 D3
Chapel Cross 110 B1
Chapel End 149 F3
Chapel Green Warks 159 E4
Chapel Green Warks 147 G1
Chapel Haddlesey 195 E5
Chapel Hill Aber 261 J1
Chapel Hill Lincs 176 A2
Chapel Hill Mon 131 E2
Chapel Hill NYorks 194 C3
Chapel Knapp 117 F1
Chapel Lawn 156 C5
Chapel Leigh 115 E5
Chapel Milton 185 E4
Chapel of Garioch 261 F2
Chapel Rossan 206 B2
Chapel Row Essex 137 G2
Chapel Row WBerks 119 G1
Chapel St. Leonards 189 F5
Chapel Stile 199 E2
Chapel Town 96 C4
Chapelbank 243 F3
Chapeldonan 223 G5
Chapelend Way 151 F4
Chapel-en-le-Frith 185 E4
Chapelgate 176 C5
Chapelhall 234 B3
Chapelhill High 267 F4
Chapelhill P&K 244 A2
Chapelhill P&K 243 F1
Chapelknowe 218 B4
Chapel-le-Dale 200 C5
Chapelthorpe 186 A1
Chapelton Aber 253 G1
Chapelton Angus 253 E5
Chapelton Devon 113 F3
Chapelton SLan 234 A5
Chapeltown B'burn 184 B1
Chapeltown Cumb 218 C4
Chapeltown Moray 259 K2
Chapeltown SYorks 186 A3
Chapmans Well 99 D1
Chapmanslade 117 F3
Chapmore End 136 C1
Chappel 151 G5
Charaton 98 D4
Chard 103 G2
Chard Junction 103 G2
Chardleigh Green 103 G1
Chardstock 103 G2
Charfield 131 G3
Charing 124 B4
Charing Cross 106 A1
Charing Heath 124 B4
Charingworth 147 D4
Charlbury 133 F1
Charlcombe 117 E1
Charlecote 147 E2
Charles 113 G2
Charles Tye 152 B2
Charlesfield 227 G3
Charleshill 121 D3
Charleston 252 B5
Charlestown Aber 269 J4
Charlestown Aberdeen 261 H4
Charlestown Corn 97 E4
Charlestown Derbys 185 E3
Charlestown Dorset 104 C5
Charlestown Fife 235 E1
Charlestown GtMan 184 C2
Charlestown High 264 E4
Charlestown High 266 D7
Charlestown WYorks 194 A4
Charlestown WYorks 193 F5
Charlestown of Aberlour (Aberlour) 267 K7
Charlesworth 185 E3
Charleton 244 C4
Charlinch 115 F4
Charlotteville 121 F3
Charlton GtLon 136 D5
Charlton Hants 119 E3
Charlton Herts 149 G5
Charlton N'hants 148 A4
Charlton N'umb 220 A3
Charlton Oxon 133 G4
Charlton Som 117 D2
Charlton Som 116 D3
Charlton Som 115 F5
Charlton Tel&W 157 E1
Charlton Wilts 118 A5
Charlton Wilts 132 B4
Charlton Wilts 118 C2
Charlton Worcs 146 C3
Charlton WSuss 108 A2
Charlton Abbots 146 C5
Charlton Adam 116 C5
Charlton Down 104 C3
Charlton Horethorne 117 D5
Charlton Kings 146 B5
Charlton Mackrell 116 C5
Charlton Marshall 105 E2
Charlton Musgrove 117 E5
Charlton on the Hill 105 E2
Charlton-All-Saints 118 C5
Charlton-on-Otmoor 134 A1
Charltons 203 F1
Charlwood 122 B4
Charminster 104 C3
Charmouth 103 G3
Charndon 148 B5
Charney Bassett 133 F3
Charnock Richard 183 G1
Charsfield 153 D2
Chart Corner 123 G4
Chart Sutton 124 A4
Charter Alley 119 G2
Charterhouse 116 B2
Charterville Allotments 133 F2
Chartham 124 D3
Chartham Hatch 124 D3
Chartridge 135 E2
Chartwell Kent TN16 1PS 123 D3
Charvil 134 C5
Charwelton 148 A2
Chase End Street 145 G4
Chase Terrace 158 C2
Chasetown 158 C2
Chastleton 147 E5
Chasty 112 D5
Chatburn 193 D3
Chatcull 171 E4
Chatelherault Country Park SLan ML3 7UE 31 G6
Chatham 123 G2
Chatham Green 137 G1
Chatham Historic Dockyard Med ME4 4TZ 123 G2
Chathill 229 F4
Chatsworth Farmyard & Adventure Playground Derbys DE45 1PP 185 G5
Chatsworth House Derbys DE45 1PP 185 G5
Chattenden 137 G5
Chatteris 162 B4
Chattisham 152 B3
Chatto 228 B5
Chatton 229 E4
Chaul End 149 F5
Chavey Down 121 D1
Chawleigh 102 A1
Chawley 133 G2
Chawston 149 G2
Chawton 120 C4
Chazey Heath 134 B5
Cheadle GtMan 184 C4
Cheadle Staffs 172 B3
Cheadle Heath 184 C4
Cheadle Hulme 184 C4
Cheam 122 B2
Cheapside 121 E1
Chearsley 134 C1
Chebsey 171 F5

Checkendon 134 B4
Checkley ChesE 171 E3
Checkley Here 145 E4
Checkley Staffs 172 B4
Chedburgh 151 F2
Cheddar 116 B2
Cheddar Caves & Gorge Som BS27 3QF 116 B2
Cheddington 135 E1
Cheddleton 171 G2
Cheddon Fitzpaine 115 F5
Chedglow 132 B3
Chedgrave 165 E2
Chedington 104 A2
Chediston 165 E4
Chediston Green 165 E4
Chedworth 132 C1
Chedzoy 116 A4
Cheesden 184 C1
Cheeseman's Green 124 C5
Cheetham Hill 184 C2
Cheglinch 113 F1
Cheldon 102 A1
Chelford 184 C5
Chellaston 173 E4
Chells 150 A5
Chelmarsh 157 G4
Chelmondiston 152 D4
Chelmorton 172 C1
Chelmsford 137 G2
Chelmsford Cathedral Essex CM1 1TY 137 G2
Chelmsley Wood 159 D4
Chelsea 136 B5
Chelsfield 123 D2
Chelsham 122 C3
Chelston Heath 115 E5
Chelsworth 152 A3
Cheltenham 146 B5
Chelveston 149 E1
Chelvey 116 B1
Chelwood 116 D1
Chelwood Common 109 G1
Chelwood Gate 109 G1
Chelworth 132 B3
Cheney Longville 156 D4
Chenies 135 F3
Chepstow (Cas-gwent) 131 E3
Cherhill 132 C5
Cherington Glos 132 B3
Cherington Warks 147 E4
Cheriton Devon 114 A1
Cheriton Hants 119 G5
Cheriton Kent 125 D5
Cheriton Pembs 126 C3
Cheriton Swan 128 A3
Cheriton Bishop 102 A2
Cheriton Cross 102 A3
Cheriton Fitzpaine 102 B2
Cherrington 171 D5
Cherry Burton 196 B3
Cherry Green 151 D5
Cherry Hinton 150 C2
Cherry Willingham 188 A3
Chertsey 121 F1
Cheselbourne 105 D3
Chesham 135 E2
Chesham Bois 135 E2
Cheshire Farm Ice Cream, Tattenhall ChesW&C CH3 9NE 170 B1
Cheshunt 136 C2
Cheslyn Hay 158 B2
Chessington 121 G1
Chessington World of Adventures GtLon KT9 2NE 121 G1
Chestall 158 C1
Chester 170 B1
Chester Cathedral ChesW&C CH1 2HU 69 Chester
Chester Moor 212 B3
Chester Zoo ChesW&C CH2 1LH 183 F5
Chesterblade 117 D3
Chesterfield Derbys 186 A5
Chesterfield Staffs 158 D2
Chester-le-Street 212 B2
Chesters ScBord 228 A5
Chesters ScBord 228 A4
Chesterton Cambs 150 C1
Chesterton Cambs 161 D3
Chesterton Oxon 148 A5
Chesterton Shrop 157 G3
Chesterton Staffs 171 F3
Chesterton Warks 147 F2
Chesterton Green 147 F2
Chestfield 124 D2
Cheston 100 C2
Cheswardine 171 E5
Cheswick 229 E2
Cheswick Buildings 229 E2
Cheswick Green 158 D5
Chetnole 104 C2
Chettiscombe 102 C1
Chettisham 162 D4
Chettle 105 F1
Chetton 157 F3
Chetwode 148 B5
Chetwynd Aston 157 G1
Chetwynd Park 171 E5
Cheveley 151 E1
Chevening 123 D3
Cheverell's Green 135 F1
Chevin Forest Park WYorks LS21 3JL 194 B3
Chevington 151 F2
Chevithorne 102 C1
Chew Magna 116 C1
Chew Moor 184 A2
Chew Stoke 116 C1
Chewton Keynsham 116 D1
Chewton Mendip 116 C2
Chicacote 99 G1
Chicheley 149 E3
Chichester 108 A3
Chichester Cathedral WSuss PO19 1PX 108 A3
Chickerell 104 C4
Chickering 164 D4
Chicklade 118 A4
Chickney 151 D5
Chicksands 149 G4

Chidden 107 F1
Chidden Holt 107 F1
Chiddingfold 121 E4
Chiddingly 110 A3
Chiddingstone 123 D4
Chiddingstone Causeway 123 E4
Chiddingstone Hoath 123 D4
Chideock 104 A3
Chidham 107 G2
Chidswell 194 B5
Chieveley 133 G5
Chignall St. James 137 F2
Chignall Smealy 137 F1
Chigwell 136 D3
Chigwell Row 137 D3
Chilbolton 119 E3
Chilcomb 119 G5
Chilcombe 104 B3
Chilcompton 117 D2
Chilcote 159 E1
Child Okeford 105 E1
Childer Thornton 183 E5
Childerditch 137 F4
Childrey 133 F4
Child's Ercall 171 D5
Childswickham 146 C4
Childwall 183 F4
Childwick Green 136 A1
Chilfrome 104 B3
Chilgrove 108 A2
Chilham 124 C3
Chilhampton 118 B4
Chilla 113 E5
Chillaton 99 E2
Chillenden 125 E3
Chillerton 107 D4
Chillesford 153 E2
Chilley 101 E2
Chillingham 229 E4
Chillington Devon 101 D3
Chillington Som 103 G1
Chilmark 118 A4
Chilson Oxon 133 F1
Chilson Som 103 G1
Chilsworthy Corn 99 E3
Chilsworthy Devon 112 D5
Chilthorne Domer 104 B1
Chilton Bucks 134 C1
Chilton Devon 102 B2
Chilton Dur 212 B5
Chilton Oxon 133 G4
Chilton Suff 151 G3
Chilton Candover 119 G4
Chilton Cantelo 116 C5
Chilton Foliat 133 F5
Chilton Polden 116 A4
Chilton Street 151 F3
Chilton Trinity 115 F4
Chilvers Coton 159 F3
Chilwell 173 G4
Chilworth Hants 106 D1
Chilworth Surr 121 F3
Chimney 133 F2
Chimney Street 151 F3
Chineham 120 B2
Chingford 136 C3
Chinley 185 E4
Chinley Head 185 E4
Chinnor 134 C2
Chipchase Castle 220 A4
Chipley 115 E5
Chipnall 171 E4
Chippenham Cambs 151 E1
Chipperfield 135 F2
Chipping Herts 150 B4
Chipping Lancs 192 C3
Chipping Campden 147 D4
Chipping Hill 138 B1
Chipping Norton 147 F5
Chipping Ongar 137 E2
Chipping Sodbury 131 G4
Chipping Warden 147 G3
Chipstable 114 D5
Chipstead Kent 123 D3
Chipstead Surr 122 B3
Chirbury 156 B3
Chirk (Y Waun) 169 F4
Chirk Green 169 F4
Chirmorrie 214 D3
Chirnside 237 F4
Chirnsidebridge 237 F4
Chirton T&W 212 C1
Chirton Wilts 118 B2
Chisbury 119 D1
Chiscan 222 B4
Chiselborough 104 A1
Chiseldon 133 D5
Chiserley 193 G5
Chislehampton 134 A3
Chislehurst 136 D5
Chislet 125 E2
Chiswell Green 136 A2
Chiswick 136 B5
Chiswick End 150 B3
Chisworth 185 D3
Chithurst 120 D5
Chittering 162 C5
Chitterne 118 A3
Chittlehamholt 113 G3
Chittlehampton 113 G3
Chittoe 118 A1
Chivelstone 101 D4
Chivenor 113 F2
Chobham 121 E1
Choicelee 237 E4
Cholderton 118 D3
Cholesbury 135 E2
Chollerford 220 B4
Chollerton 220 B4
Cholmondeston 170 D2
Cholsey 134 A4
Cholstrey 145 D2
Cholwell B&NESom 116 D2
Cholwell Devon 99 E3
Chop Gate 203 E3
Choppington 221 E3
Chopwell 212 A2
Chorley ChesE 170 C2
Chorley Lancs 183 G1
Chorley Shrop 157 F4
Chorley Staffs 158 C1
Chorleywood 135 F3

Chorlton 171 E2
Chorlton Lane 170 B3
Chorlton-cum-Hardy 184 C3
Chowley 170 B2
Chrishall 150 C4
Chrishall Grange 150 C3
Chrisswell 232 D2
Christ Church Oxon OX1 1DP 80 Oxford
Christchurch Cambs 162 C3
Christchurch Dorset 106 A3
Christchurch Newport 130 C4
Christian Malford 132 B5
Christleton 170 B1
Christmas Common 134 C3
Christon 116 A2
Christon Bank 229 G4
Christow 102 B4
Christskirk 260 E2
Chryston 234 A2
Chudleigh 102 B5
Chudleigh Knighton 102 B5
Chulmleigh 113 G4
Chunal 185 E3
Church 192 D5
Church Aston 157 G1
Church Brampton 148 C1
Church Brough 200 C1
Church Broughton 172 D4
Church Charwelton 148 A2
Church Common 153 E2
Church Crookham 120 D2
Church Eaton 158 A1
Church End Cambs 162 B2
Church End Cambs 162 B2
Church End Cambs 162 A4
Church End CenBeds 149 G4
Church End CenBeds 149 E5
Church End CenBeds 149 G2
Church End CenBeds 149 E4
Church End CenBeds 149 E4
Church End ERid 196 C2
Church End Essex 151 D3
Church End Essex 151 F5
Church End Glos 146 A4
Church End Hants 120 B3
Church End Herts 136 A1
Church End Herts 150 C5
Church End Lincs 176 A4
Church End Lincs 189 E3
Church End ESiar 196 E3
Church End Wilts 132 C5
Church Enstone 147 F5
Church Fenton 195 E4
Church Green 103 E3
Church Gresley 159 E1
Church Hanborough 133 G1
Church Hill ChesW&C 170 D1
Church Hill Derbys 173 F1
Church Houses 203 F3
Church Knowle 105 F4
Church Laneham 187 F5
Church Langton 160 C3
Church Lawford 159 G5
Church Lawton 171 F2
Church Leigh 172 B4
Church Lench 146 C2
Church Mayfield 172 C3
Church Minshull 171 D1
Church Norton 108 A4
Church Preen 157 E3
Church Pulverbatch 156 D2
Church Stoke 156 B3
Church Stowe 148 B2
Church Street Essex 151 F3
Church Street Kent 137 G5
Church Stretton 157 D3
Church Town Leics 159 F1
Church Town Surr 122 C3
Church Village 129 G4
Church Warsop 173 G1
Church Westcote 147 E5
Church Wilne 173 F4
Churcham 131 G1
Churchdown 132 A1
Churchend Essex 138 D3
Churchend Essex 151 D3
Churchend SGlos 131 G3
Churchfield 158 C3
Churchgate 136 C2
Churchgate Street 137 D1
Churchill Devon 113 F1
Churchill Devon 103 F3
Churchill NSom 116 B2
Churchill Oxon 147 E5
Churchill Worcs 146 B2
Churchill Worcs 158 A5
Churchinford 103 F1
Churchover 160 A4
Churchstanton 103 E1
Churchstow 100 D3
Churchtown Devon 113 G1
Churchtown IoM 190 C2
Churchtown Lancs 192 A3
Churchtown Mersey 183 E1
Churnsike Lodge 219 E3
Churston Ferrers 101 F2
Churt 121 D4
Churton 170 B2
Churwell 194 B5
Chute Cadley 119 E2
Chute Standen 119 E2
Chwilog 166 D2
Chyandour 94 B3
Chysauster 94 B3
Cilan Uchaf 166 B5
Cilcain 169 E1

Cilcennin 142 B1
Cilcewydd 156 B2
Cilfrew 129 D2
Cilfynydd 129 G3
Cilgerran 141 E3
Cilgwyn Carmar 142 D4
Cilgwyn Pembs 141 D4
Ciliau Aeron 142 B2
Cille Bhrighde 254 C3
Cille Pheadair 254 C3
Cilmaengwyn 128 D2
Cilmery 143 G2
Cilrhedyn 141 F4
Cilrhedyn Bridge 140 D4
Cilsan 142 B5
Ciltalgarth 168 B3
Cilwendeg 141 F4
Cilybebyll 128 D2
Cilycwm 143 D3
Cimla 129 D3
Cinderford 131 F1
Cippenham 135 E4
Cippyn 141 E3
Cirbhig 270 D3
Cirencester 132 C2
City GtLon 136 C4
City VGlam 129 F5
City Airport 136 D4
City Dulas 180 C4
City of Coventry Stadium (Coventry City F.C.) WMid CV6 6GE 16 C2
Clabhach 246 A4
Clachaig 232 C2
Clachan A&B 241 D3
Clachan A&B 248 A5
Clachan A&B 231 F4
Clachan High 256 B3
Clachan Na H-ESiar 262 C7
Clachan Mòr 246 A2
Clachan of Campsie 234 A2
Clachan of Glendaruel 232 A1
Clachan-a-Luib 262 D5
Clachandhu 239 D1
Clachaneasy 215 E3
Clachanmore 206 A2
Clachan-Seil 239 G3
Clachan-turn 259 K5
Clachbreck 231 F2
Clachnabrain 252 B3
Clachnaharry 266 D7
Clachtoll 272 C6
Clackmannan 243 E5
Clackmarras 267 K6
Clacton Pier Essex CO15 1QX 139 E1
Clacton-on-Sea 139 E1
Cladach a Bhale Shear 262 D5
Cladach a' Chaolais 262 C5
Cladach Chireboist 262 C5
Cladach Chnoc a Lin 262 C5
Cladich (An Cladach) 240 C2
Cladswell 146 C2
Claggan (An Claigeann) High 248 D2
Claggan High 247 G5
Claigan 263 H6
Claines 146 A2
Clambers Play Centre ESuss TN34 1LD 75 Hastings
Clandown 117 D2
Clanfield Hants 107 G1
Clanfield Oxon 133 E2
Clannaborough Barton 102 A2
Clanville 119 E3
Claonaig 231 G4
Claonairigh 240 C4
Claonel 266 C1
Clapgate 150 C5
Clapham Bed 149 F2
Clapham Devon 102 B4
Clapham GtLon 136 B5
Clapham NYorks 192 D1
Clapham WSuss 108 C3
Clapham Green 149 F2
Clapham Hill 124 D2
Clappers 237 G4
Clappersgate 199 E2
Clapton Som 104 A2
Clapton Som 116 D2
Clapton-in-Gordano 131 D5
Clapton-on-the-Hill 133 D1
Clapworthy 113 G3
Clara Vale 212 A1
Clarach 154 C4
Clarbeston 141 D5
Clarbeston Road 140 D5
Clarborough 187 E4
Clardon 275 G2
Clare 151 F3
Clare Castle Country Park Suff CO10 8NJ 151 F3
Clarebrand 216 B4
Clarencefield 217 E4
Clarilaw 227 E4
Clark's Green 121 G4
Clarkston 233 G4
Clashban 266 D2
Clashcoig 266 D2
Clashdorran 266 C7
Clashgour 249 E4
Clashindarroch 260 C1
Clashmore High 266 E3
Clashmore High 272 C5
Clashnessie 272 C5
Clashnoir 259 K2
Clatford 118 C1
Clathy 243 F2
Clatt 260 D2
Clatter 155 F3
Clattercote 147 G3
Clatterford 107 D4
Clatterford End 137 E2
Clatterin Brig 253 E2
Clatteringshaws 215 G3
Clatworthy 115 D4

Claughton Lancs 192 B1
Claughton Lancs 192 B3
Clavelshay 115 F4
Claverdon 147 D1
Claverham 116 B1
Clavering 150 C4
Claverley 157 G3
Claverton 117 E1
Claverton Down 117 E1
Clawdd-côch 129 G5
Clawdd-newydd 169 D2
Clawfin 224 D5
Clawthorpe 199 G5
Clawton 99 D1
Claxby 188 B3
Claxby Pluckacre 176 B1
Claxby St. Andrew 189 E5
Claxton Norf 179 E5
Claxton NYorks 195 F1
Clay Common 165 F3
Clay Coton 160 A5
Clay Cross 173 E1
Clay End 150 B5
Clay Hill 131 F5
Clay of Allan 267 F4
Claybrooke Magna 159 G4
Claybrooke Parva 159 G4
Claydene 123 D4
Claydon Oxon 147 G2
Claydon Suff 152 C3
Claygate Kent 123 G4
Claygate Surr 121 G1
Claygate Cross 123 F3
Clayhanger Devon 114 D5
Clayhanger WMid 158 C2
Clayhidon 103 E1
Clayhill ESuss 110 D1
Clayhill Hants 106 C2
Clayhithe 150 D1
Clayock 275 G3
Claypit Hill 150 B2
Claypits 131 G2
Claypole 174 D3
Claythorpe 189 E5
Clayton Staffs 171 F3
Clayton SYorks 186 B2
Clayton WSuss 109 E2
Clayton WYorks 194 A4
Clayton West 185 F1
Clayton Green 192 B5
Clayton-le-Moors 192 D4
Clayton-le-Woods 192 B5
Clayworth 187 E4
Cleadale 247 D1
Cleadon 212 C1
Clearbrook 100 B1
Clearwell 131 E2
Cleasby 202 B1
Cleat Ork 277 D9
Cleat Na H-ESiar 254 B4
Cleatlam 202 A1
Cleatop 193 E1
Cleator 208 D5
Cleator Moor 208 D5
Cleckheaton 194 A5
Clee St. Margaret 157 E4
Cleedownton 157 E4
Cleehill 157 E5
Cleestanton 157 E5
Cleethorpes 188 D2
Cleethorpes Discovery Centre NELincs DN35 0AG 188 D2
Cleeton St. Mary 157 F5
Cleeve NSom 116 B1
Cleeve Oxon 134 B4
Cleeve Hill 146 B5
Cleeve Prior 146 C3
C3 Cleghorn 234 C5
Clehonger 145 D4
Cleigh 240 A2
Cleish 243 F5
Cleland 234 B4
Clement's End 135 F1
Clemsfold 121 G4
Clench Common 118 C1
Clenchwarton 177 D5
Clennell 220 B1
Clent 158 B5
Clent Hills Worcs DY9 9JR 14 B5
Cleobury Mortimer 157 F5
Cleobury North 157 F4
Clephanton 267 F6
Clerklands 227 G3
Clermiston 235 F2
Clestrain 277 C7
Cleuch Head 227 G4
Cleughbrae 217 E3
Clevancy 132 C5
Clevedon 130 D5
Cleveland Tontine Inn 202 D2
Cleveley 147 F5
Cleveleys 191 G3
Clevelode 146 A3
Cleverton 132 B4
Clewer 116 B2
Clewer Green 135 E5
Clewer Village 135 E5
Cley next the Sea 178 B1
Cliburn 210 B5
Cliddesden 120 B3
Cliff Carmar 127 G2
Cliff High 247 F3
Cliff End 111 D2
Cliff Grange 170 D4
Cliffe Lancs 192 D4
Cliffe Med 137 G5
Cliffe NYorks 195 F4
Cliffe Woods 137 G5
Clifford Here 144 B3
Clifford WYorks 194 D3
Clifford Chambers 147 D2
Clifford's Mesne 145 F5
Clifford's Tower YO1 9SA 90 York
Cliffs End 125 F2
Clifton Bristol 131 E5
Clifton CenBeds 149 G4
Clifton Cumb 210 B5
Clifton Derbys 172 C3
Clifton Devon 113 F1
Clifton Lancs 192 A4
Clifton N'umb 221 E3
Clifton Nott 173 G4
Clifton NYorks 194 A3

Clifton Oxon 147 G4
Clifton Stir 241 F1
Clifton SYorks 186 C3
Clifton Worcs 146 A3
Clifton WYorks 194 A5
Clifton York 195 E2
Clifton Campville 159 E1
Clifton Hampden 134 A3
Clifton Maybank 104 B1
Clifton Park Museum SYorks S65 2AA 21 D1
Clifton Reynes 149 E2
Clifton upon Dunsmore 160 A5
Clifton upon Teme 145 G1
Cliftonville 125 F1
Climping 108 C3
Climpy 234 D4
Clink 117 E3
Clint 194 B2
Clint Green 178 B4
Clinterty 261 G3
Clintmains 228 A3
Clippesby 179 F4
Clippings Green 178 B4
Clipsham 161 E1
Clipston N'hants 160 C4
Clipston Notts 174 B4
Clipstone 173 G1
Clitheroe 192 D3
Clive 170 C5
Cliveden Garden & Maze Bucks SL6 0JA 135 E4
Clivocast 278 F2
Clixby 188 B2
Cloatley 132 B3
Clocaenog 169 D2
Clochan 268 C4
Clochtow 261 J1
Clock Face 183 G3
Clockhill 269 G6
Cloddach 267 J6
Cloddiau 156 A2
Clodock 144 C2
Cloford 117 E3
Cloichran 242 B1
Clola 269 J6
Clonrae 216 C1
Clophill 149 F4
Clopton 174 B3
Clopton Corner 152 C2
Clopton Green Suff 151 F2
Clopton Green Suff 152 D2
Close Clark 190 A4
Closeburn 216 C1
Closworth 104 B1
Clothall 150 A4
Clothan 278 D4
Clotton 170 C1
Clough Cumb 200 C3
Clough GtMan 184 D1
Clough GtMan 184 D2
Clough WYorks 185 E1
Clough Foot 193 F5
Clough Head 193 G5
Cloughfold 193 E5
Cloughton 204 D3
Cloughton Newlands 204 D3
Clounlaid 247 G4
Clousta 277 C7
Clouston 277 C6
Clova Aber 260 C2
Clova Angus 252 B2
Clove Lodge 201 E1
Clovelly 112 D3
Clovelly Cross 112 D3
Clovelly Village Devon EX39 5TA 112 D3
Clovenfords 227 F2
Clovenstone 261 F3
Cloves Aber 268 E5
Cloves P&K 251 J5
Clovullin 248 C3
Clow Bridge 193 E5
Clowne 186 B5
Clows Top 157 G5
Cloyntie 224 B5
Cluanach 230 B4
Clubworthy 98 C1
Cluddley 157 F1
Cluer (Cliuthar) 263 G2
Clumber Country Park Notts S80 3AZ 186 D5
Clun 156 C5
Clunas 267 F7
Clunbury 156 C4
Clunderwen 127 E1
Clune High 258 E2
Clune Moray 268 D4
Clunes 249 E1
Clungunford 156 C5
Clunie Aber 268 E5
Clunie P&K 251 G5
Clunton 156 C4
Cluny 244 A5
Clutton B&NESom 116 D2
Clutton ChesW&C 170 B2
Clwt-y-bont 167 E1
Clwydyfagwyr 129 G2
Clydach Mon 130 B1
Clydach Swan 128 C2
Clydach Terrace 130 A1
Clydach Vale 129 F3
Clydebank 233 F2
Clydey 141 F4
Clyffe Pypard 132 C5
Clynder 232 D1
Clyne 129 E2
Clynelish 267 F1
Clynfyw 141 F4
Clynnog-fawr 166 D2
Clyro 144 B3
Clyst Honiton 102 D3
Clyst Hydon 102 D2
Clyst St. George 102 C4
Clyst St. Lawrence 102 D2
Clyst St. Mary 102 C3
Clyst William 103 D2
Cnewr 143 E5
Cnoc 271 G4
Cnwch Coch 154 C5

Coaley 131 G2
Coalmoor 157 F2
Coalpit Heath 131 F4
Coalpit Hill 171 F2
Coalport 157 G2
Coalsnaughton 243 E5
Coaltown of Balgonie 244 B3
Coaltown of Wemyss 244 B5
Coalville 159 G1
Coalway 131 E1
Coanwood 210 C2
Coast 265 F2
Coat 116 B5
Coatbridge 234 B3
Coate Swin 133 D4
Coate Wilts 118 B1
Coates Cambs 162 B3
Coates Glos 132 B2
Coates Lincs 187 G4
Coates Notts 187 F4
Coates WSuss 108 B2
Coatham 213 E5
Coatham Mundeville 212 B5
Cobairdy 268 D6
Cobbaton 113 G3
Cobbler's Plain 131 D2
Cobby Syke 194 A2
Cobden 102 D3
Coberley 132 B1
Cobhall Common 145 D4
Cobham Kent 123 F2
Cobham Surr 121 G1
Cobleland 242 A5
Cobley Hill 158 C5
Cobnash 145 D1
Coburty 269 H4
Cochno 233 F2
Cock Alley 173 F1
Cock Bank 170 A3
Cock Bevington 146 C2
Cock Bridge 259 K4
Cock Clarks 138 B2
Cock Green 137 G1
Cock Marling 111 D2
Cockayne 203 F3
Cockayne Hatley 150 A3
Cockburnspath 237 E2
Cockenzie & Port Seton 236 B2
Cocker Bar 192 B5
Cockerham 192 A2
Cockermouth 209 E3
Cockernhoe 149 G5
Cockerton 202 B1
Cockett 128 C3
Cockfield Dur 212 A5
Cockfield Suff 152 A2
Cockfosters 136 B3
Cocking 108 A2
Cockington 101 E1
Cockington Country Park Torbay TQ2 6XA 101 E1
Cocklake 116 B3
Cocklaw 220 B4
Cockle Park 221 E2
Cockleford 132 B1
Cockpen 236 A3
Cockpole Green 134 C4
Cockshutt 170 B5
Cockthorpe 178 A1
Cockwood Devon 102 C4
Cockwood Som 115 F3
Cockyard 185 E4
Codda 97 F2
Coddenham 152 C2
Coddington ChesW&C 170 B2
Coddington Here 145 G3
Coddington Notts 174 D2
Codford St. Mary 118 A4
Codford St. Peter 118 A4
Codicote 136 B1
Codmore Hill 108 C2
Codnor 173 F3
Codnor Park 173 F3
Codrington 131 G5
Codsall 158 A2
Codsall Wood 158 A2
Coed Morgan 130 C1
Coed Ystumgwern 167 E5
Coedcae 130 B2
Coedely 129 G4
Coedkernew 130 B4
Coedpoeth 169 F2
Coedway 156 C1
Coed-y-bryn 141 G3
Coed-y-caerau 130 C3
Coed-y-paen 130 C3
Coed-y-parc 167 F1
Coed-yr-ynys 144 A5
Coelbren 129 E1
Coffinswell 101 E1
Cofton 102 C4
Cofton Hackett 158 C5
Cogan 130 A5
Cogenhoe 148 D1
Cogges 133 F2
Coggeshall 151 G5
Coggeshall Hamlet 151 G5
Coggins Mill 110 A1
Cóig Peighinnean 271 H1
Coilantogie 242 A4
Coileitir 248 D5
Coilessan 241 E4
Coillaig 240 C2
Coille Mhorgil 257 G4
Coille-righ 257 F2
Coillore 255 J1
Coity 129 F4
Col 271 G4
Col Uarach 271 G4
Colaboll 273 H7
Colan 96 C3
Colaton Raleigh 103 D4
Colbost 263 G7
Colburn 202 B3
Colbury 106 C1
Colby Cumb 210 C5
Colby IoM 190 A4
Colby Norf 178 D2
Colchester 152 A5

Colchester Castle Museum
Essex CO1 1TJ 152 A5
Colchester Green 152 A2
Colchester Zoo Essex
CO3 0SL 152 A5
Colcot 115 E1
Cold Ash 119 G1
Cold Ashby 160 B5
Cold Ashton 131 G5
Cold Aston 132 D1
Cold Blow 127 E1
Cold Brayfield 149 E2
Cold Chapel 226 A3
Cold Cotes 200 C5
Cold Hanworth 188 A4
Cold Harbour 134 B4
Cold Hatton 170 D5
Cold Hatton Heath 170 D5
Cold Hesledon 212 D3
Cold Higham 148 B2
Cold Inn 127 E2
Cold Kirby 203 E4
Cold Newton 160 C2
Cold Northcott 97 G1
Cold Norton 138 B2
Cold Overton 160 D2
Cold Row 191 G3
Coldbackie 273 J2
Coldblow 187 E5
Coldean 109 F3
Coldeast 102 B5
Coldeaton 172 C2
Colden Common 119 F5
Coldfair Green 153 F1
Coldham 162 C2
Coldharbour Glos 131 E2
Coldharbour Surr 121 G3
Coldingham 237 G3
Coldrain 243 F4
Coldred 125 E4
Coldrey 120 C3
Coldridge 113 G5
Coldrife 220 C2
Coldstream 228 C3
Coldwaltham 108 C2
Coldvreath 97 D4
Coldwells 269 K6
Cole 117 D4
Cole End 159 D4
Cole Green 136 B1
Cole Henley 119 F2
Colebatch 156 C4
Colebrook 102 D2
Colebrooke 102 A2
Coleburn 267 K6
Coleby Lincs 175 E2
Coleby NLincs 187 F1
Coleford Devon 102 A2
Coleford Glos 131 E1
Coleford Som 117 D3
Colegate End 164 C3
Colehill 105 G2
Coleman Green 136 A1
Coleman's Hatch 122 D5
Colemere 170 B4
Colemore 120 C4
Colemore Green 157 G3
Colenden 243 G2
Coleorton 159 G1
Colerne 132 A5
Cole's Common 164 D3
Cole's Cross 101 D3
Cole's Green 153 D1
Colesbourne 132 C1
Colesden 149 G2
Coleshill Bucks 135 E3
Coleshill Oxon 133 E3
Coleshill Warks 159 E4
Colestocks 103 D2
Coley B&NESom 116 C2
Coley Staffs 172 B5
Colfin 214 B5
Colgate 122 B5
Colgrain 233 E2
Colindale 136 B4
Colinton 235 G3
Colintraive 232 B2
Colkirk 178 A3
Coll 246 A4
Collace 244 A1
Collafirth 279 D6
Collamoor Head 98 B1
Collaton St. Mary 101 E1
Coll Dark Sky Island Argyll
& Bute 246 B4
Collessie 244 A3
Colleton Mills 113 G4
Collett's Green 146 A2
Collier Row 137 E3
Collier Street 123 G4
Collier's End 150 B5
Collier's Wood 136 B5
Colliery Row 212 C2
Collieston 261 J2
Collin 217 E3
Collingbourne
Ducis 118 D2
Collingbourne
Kingston 118 D2
Collingham Notts 174 D1
Collingham WYorks 194 C3
Collington 145 F1
Collingtree 148 C2
Collins End 134 B5
Collins Green
Warr 183 G3
Collins Green
Worcs 145 G2
Colliston 253 E5
Colliton 103 D2
Collmuir 260 D4
Collycroft 159 F4
Collyhurst 184 C2
Collynie 261 G1
Collyweston 161 E2
Colmonell 214 C2
Colmworth 149 G2
Coln Rogers 132 C2
Coln St. Aldwyns 132 D2
Coln St. Dennis 132 C1
Colnabaichin 259 K4
Colne Cambs 162 B5
Colne Lancs 193 E4
Colne Engaine 151 G4
Colney 178 C5
Colney Heath 136 B2

Colney Street 136 A2
Colonsay 238 C5
Colonsay House 238 C5
Colony Gift Corporation
Cumb LA12 0LD 199 D5
Colpy 260 E1
Colquhar 236 A5
Colsterdale 202 A4
Colsterworth 175 E5
Colston Bassett 174 B4
Colston Hall
BS1 5AR 66 Bristol
Coltfield 267 J5
Colthouse 199 E3
Coltishall 179 D4
Coltness 234 C4
Colton Cumb 199 E4
Colton Norf 178 C5
Colton NYorks 195 E3
Colton Staffs 172 B5
Colton WYorks 194 C4
Colva 144 B2
Colvend 216 C5
Colvister 278 E3
Colwall 145 G3
Colwall Green 145 G3
Colwall Stone 145 G3
Colwell 220 B4
Colwich 172 B5
Colwick 174 B3
Colwinston 129 F5
Colworth 108 B3
Colwyn Bay
(Bae Colwyn) 181 G5
Colyford 103 F3
Colyton 103 F3
Combe Here 144 C1
Combe Oxon 133 G1
Combe Som 116 B5
Combe WBerks 119 E1
Combe Common 121 E4
Combe Cross 102 A5
Combe Down 117 E1
Combe Florey 115 E4
Combe Hay 117 E2
Combe Martin 113 F1
Combe Martin Wildlife &
Dinosaur Park Devon
EX34 0NG 113 G1
Combe Pafford 101 F1
Combe Raleigh 103 E2
Combe St. Nicholas
103 G1
Combeinteignhead 102 B5
Comberbach 184 A5
Comberford 159 D2
Comberton Cambs 150 B2
Comberton Here 145 D1
Combpyne 103 F3
Combridge 172 B4
Combrook 147 F2
Combs Derbys 185 E5
Combs Suff 152 B2
Combs Ford 152 B2
Combwich 115 F3
Comer 241 F4
Comers 260 E4
Comhampton 146 A1
Comins Coch 154 C4
Commercial End 151 D1
Commins Coch 155 E2
Common Edge 191 G4
Common Moor 97 G2
Common Platt 132 D4
Common Side 186 A5
Common Square 188 A5
Commondale 203 F1
Commonside 172 D3
Compstall 185 D3
Compton Devon 101 E1
Compton Hants 119 F5
Compton Plym 100 A2
Compton Staffs 158 A4
Compton Surr 121 E3
Compton WBerks 134 A5
Compton Wilts 118 C2
Compton WSuss 107 G1
Compton WYorks 194 D3
Compton Abbas 105 E1
Compton Abdale 132 C1
Compton Bassett 132 C5
Compton
Beauchamp 133 E4
Compton Bishop 116 A2
Compton
Chamberlayne 118 B5
Compton Dando 116 D1
Compton Dundon 116 B4
Compton Martin 116 C2
Compton
Pauncefoot 116 D5
Compton Valence 104 B3
Compton Verney 147 F2
Compton Wynyates 147 F3
Comra 258 C5
Comrie Fife 244 A5
Comrie P&K 242 C2
Conchra A&B 232 B1
Conchra High 256 E2
Concraigie 251 G5
Conder Green 192 A2
Conderton 146 B4
Condicote 146 D5
Condorrat 234 B2
Condover 157 D2
Coney Weston 164 A4
Coneyhurst 121 G5
Coneysthorpe 203 G5
Coneythorpe 194 C2
Conford 120 D4
Congash 259 H2
Congdon's Shop 97 G2
Congerstone 159 F2
Congham 177 F5
Congleton 171 F1
Congresbury 116 B1
Congreve 158 B1
Conicavel 267 G6
Coningsby 176 A2
Conington Cambs 161 G4
Conington Cambs 150 B1
Conisbrough 186 C3
Conisby 230 A3
Conisholme 189 E3
Coniston Cumb 199 E3
Coniston ERid 197 D4
Coniston Cold 193 F2
Conistone 193 F1

Conkers, Swadlincote Leics
DE12 6GA 159 F1
Conland 268 E6
Connah's Quay 169 F1
Connel
(A' Choingheal) 240 B1
Connel Park 225 E4
Connor Downs 94 C3
Conon Bridge (Drochaid
Sgùideil) 266 C6
Cononish 241 F2
Cononley 193 F3
Cononsyth 253 D5
Consall 171 G3
Consett 212 A2
Constable Burton 202 A3
Constantine 95 E4
Constantine Bay 96 C3
Contin
(Cunndainn) 266 B6
Contlaw 261 G4
Contullich 266 D4
Conwy 181 F5
Conyer 124 B2
Conyer's Green 151 G1
Cooden 110 C3
Coodham 224 C2
Cooil 190 B4
Cookbury 113 E5
Cookbury Wick 113 D5
Cookham 135 D4
Cookham Dean 135 D4
Cookham Rise 135 D4
Cookhill 146 C2
Cookley Suff 165 E4
Cookley Worcs 158 A4
Cookley Green Oxon 134 B3
Cookley Green Suff 165 E4
Cookney 261 G5
Cook's Green 152 A2
Cooksbridge 109 F2
Cooksey Green 146 B1
Cookshill 171 G3
Cooksmill Green 137 F2
Cookston 261 H1
Coolham 121 G5
Cooling 137 G5
Cooling Street 137 G5
Coombe Corn 97 D4
Coombe Corn 112 C4
Coombe Corn 96 A5
Coombe Corn 96 C5
Coombe Devon 101 D3
Coombe Devon 96 B4
Coombe Devon 103 E3
Coombe Som 115 F5
Coombe Som 104 A2
Coombe Wilts 118 C2
Coombe Bissett 118 C5
Coombe Country Park
Warks CV3 2AB 16 D3
Coombe End 114 D5
Coombe Hill 146 A5
Coombe Keynes 105 E4
Coombes 109 D3
Coombes Moor 144 C1
Cooper's Corner
ESuss 110 C1
Cooper's Corner
Kent 123 D4
Cooper's Green 136 A2
Coopersale 137 E2
Coopersale Street 137 D2
Cootham 108 C2
Cop Street 125 E3
Copdock 152 C3
Copford Green 152 A5
Copgrove 194 C1
Copister 278 D5
Cople 149 G3
Copley Dur 211 G5
Copley WYorks 193 G5
Coplow Dale 185 F5
Copmanthorpe 195 E3
Copmere End 171 F5
Copp 192 A4
Coppathorne 112 C5
Coppenhall 158 B1
Coppenhall Moss 171 E2
Copperhouse 94 C3
Coppicegate 157 G4
Coppingford 161 G4
Coppleridge 117 F5
Copplestone 102 A2
Coppull 183 G1
Coppull Moor 183 G1
Copsale 121 G5
Copse Hill 122 B2
Copster Green 192 C4
Copston Magna 159 G4
Copt Heath 159 D5
Copt Hewick 202 C5
Copt Oak 159 G1
Copthall Green 136 D2
Copthorne 122 C5
Copy Lake 113 G4
Copythorne 106 C1
Coralhill 269 J4
Corbets Tey 137 E4
Corbiegoe 275 J4
Corbridge 211 F1
Corby 161 D4
Corby Glen 175 F5
Cordach 260 E5
Cordorcan 215 E3
Coreley 157 F5
Corfcott Green 98 D1
Corfe 103 F1
Corfe Castle Dorset
BH20 5EZ 105 F4
Corfe Mullen 105 F3
Corfton 157 D4
Corgarff 259 K4
Corhampton 120 B5
Corlae 216 A1
Corley 159 E4
Corley Ash 159 E4
Corley Moor 159 E4
Corn Exchange Cambs
CB2 3QB 66 Cambridge
Cornabus 230 B5
Cornard Tye 152 A3
Corndon 99 G2
Corney 198 C3
Cornforth 212 C4

Cornhill 268 D5
Cornhill on Tweed 228 C3
Cornholme 193 F5
Cornish Gold & Treasure
Park Corn
TR16 4HN 96 A5
Cornish Hall End 151 E4
Cornquoy 277 E7
Cornriggs 211 E3
Cornsay 212 A3
Cornsay Colliery 212 A3
Corntown High 266 C6
Corntown VGlam 129 F5
Cornwell 147 E5
Cornwood 100 C2
Cornworthy 101 E2
Corpach
(A' Chorpaich) 248 D2
Corpusty 178 C3
Corrachree 260 C4
Corran A&B 241 E5
Corran High 256 E4
Corran (Ardgour)
High 248 C1
Corranbuie 231 G3
Corrany 190 C3
Corribeg 248 B2
Corrie 232 B5
Corrie Common 218 A3
Corriecravie 223 E3
Corriedoo 216 A2
Corriekinloch 273 F6
Corrielorne 240 A3
Corrievorrie 258 E2
Corrimony 257 K1
Corringham
Lincs 187 F3
Corringham
Thur 137 G4
Corris 155 D2 Corris Uchaf
154 D2
Corrlarach 248 C3
Corrour Shooting
Lodge 249 G5
Corrow 241 D4
Corry 256 C2
Corrychurrachan 248 C1
Corrylach 222 C2
Corrymuckloch 243 D1
Corsback 275 H2
Corscombe 104 B2
Corse Aber 268 E6
Corse Glos 145 G5
Corse Lawn 146 A4
Corse of Kinnoir 268 D6
Corsebank 225 G4
Corsegight 269 G5
Corsehill 217 F2
Corsewall 214 B4
Corsham 132 A5
Corsindae 260 E4
Corsley 117 F3
Corsley Heath 117 F3
Corsock 216 B4
Corston B&NESom 117 D1
Corston Wilts 132 B4
Corstorphine 235 F2
Cortachy 252 A4
Corton Suff 165 G2
Corton Wilts 118 A3
Corton Denham 116 D5
Corwar House 215 D2
Coryton Devon 99 E2
Coryton Thur 137 G4
Cosby 160 A3
Coscote 134 A4
Coseley 158 B3
Cosford Shrop 157 G2
Cosford Warks 160 A5
Cosgrove 148 C3
Cosham 107 F2
Cosheston 127 D2
Coshieville 250 C5
Coskills 188 A2
Cosmeston 115 E1
Cosmeston Lakes Country
Park VGlam
CF64 5UY 115 E1
Cossall 173 F3
Cossington Leics 160 B1
Cossington Som 116 A3
Costa 276 C5
Costessey 178 C4
Costock 173 G5
Coston Leics 174 D5
Coston Norf 178 B5
Cote Oxon 133 F2
Cote Som 116 A3
Cotebrook 170 C1
Cotehill 210 A2
Cotes Cumb 199 F4
Cotes Leics 173 G5
Cotes Staffs 171 F4
Cotesbach 160 A4
Cotford St. Luke 115 E4
Cotgrave 174 B4
Cotham 174 C3
Cothelstone 115 E4
Cotheridge 145 G2
Cotherstone 201 F1
Cothill 133 G3
Cotleigh 103 F2
Cotmanhay 173 F3
Coton Cambs 150 C2
Coton N'hants 160 B5
Coton Staffs 171 G4
Coton Staffs 159 D2
Coton Staffs 171 F5
Coton Clanford 171 F5
Coton Hill 171 G4
Coton in the Clay 172 C5
Coton in the Elms 159 E1
Cotonwood Shrop 170 C4
Cotonwood Staffs 171 F5
Cott 101 D1
Cottam Lancs 192 A4
Cottam Notts 187 F4
Cottartown 259 H1
Cottenham 150 C1
Cotterdale 200 D3

Cottered 150 B5
Cotteridge 158 C5
Cotterstock 161 F3
Cottesbrooke 160 C5
Cottesmore 161 E1
Cottingham
ERid 196 C4
Cottingham
N'hants 160 D3
Cottingley 194 A4
Cottisford 148 A4
Cotton Staffs 172 B3
Cotton Suff 152 B1
Cotton End 149 F3
Cottonworth 119 E4
Cottown Aber 260 D2
Cottown Aber 269 G6
Cottown Aber 261 F4
Cotts 100 A1
Cottwood 113 G4
Cotwall 157 F1
Cotwalton 171 G4
Couch's Mill 97 F4
Coughton Here 145 E5
Coughton Warks 146 C1
Cougie 257 J2
Coulaghailtro 231 F3
Coulags 265 F7
Coulby Newham 203 E1
Coulderton 198 A2
Coull 260 D4
Coulport 232 D1
Coulsdon 122 B3
Coulston 118 A2
Coulter 226 B2
Coultershaw Bridge 108 B2
Coultings 115 F3
Coulton 203 F5
Coultra 244 B2
Cound 157 E2
Coundlane 157 E2
Coundon Dur 212 B5
Coundon WMid 159 F4
Countersett 201 E4
Countess Wear 102 C3
Countesthorpe 160 A3
Countisbury 114 A3
Coup Green 192 B5
Coupar Angus 252 A5
Coupland Cumb 200 C1
Coupland N'umb 228 D3
Cour 231 G5
Court Colman 129 E4
Court Henry 142 B5
Court House Green 159 F4
Court-at-Street 124 C5
Courtauld Institute of Art
Gallery GtLon
WC2R 0RN 45 F3
Courteenhall 148 C2
Courtsend 138 D3
Courtway 115 F4
Cousland 236 A3
Cousley Wood 123 F5
Coustonn 232 B2
Cove A&B 232 D1
Cove Devon 114 D5
Cove Hants 120 D2
Cove High 264 E2
Cove ScBord 237 E2
Cove Bay 261 H4
Cove Bottom 165 G3
Covehithe 165 G3
Coven 158 B2
Coveney 162 C4
Covenham
St. Bartholomew 188 D3
Covenham St. Mary 188 D3
Coventry 159 F5
Coventry Airport 159 F5
Coventry Cathedral WMid
CV1 5AB 69 Coventry
Coventry Transport Museum
WMid CV1 1JD
69 Coventry
Coverack 95 E5
Coverham 202 A4
Covesea 267 J4
Covingham 133 D4
Covington Cambs 161 F5
Covington SLan 226 A2
Cowan Bridge 200 B4
Cowbeech 110 B2
Cowbit 162 A1
Cowbridge Som 114 C3
Cowbridge VGlam 129 F5
Cowden 123 D4
Cowdenbeath 235 G5
Cowdenburn 235 G4
Cowers Lane 173 E3
Cowes 107 D3
Cowesby 203 D4
Cowesfield Green 119 D5
Cowey Green 152 B5
Cowfold 109 E1
Cowgill 200 C4
Cowie Aber 253 G1
Cowie Stir 234 C1
Cowlam Manor 196 B1
Cowley Devon 102 C3
Cowley Glos 132 B1
Cowley GtLon 135 E4
Cowley Oxon 134 A2
Cowling Lancs 183 G1
Cowling NYorks 193 F3
Cowling NYorks 202 B4
Cowlinge 151 F2
Cowmes 185 F1
Cowpe 193 E5
Cowpen 221 E3
Cowpen Bewley 213 D5
Cowplain 107 F1
Cowsden 146 B2
Cowshill 211 E3
Cowstrandburn 235 E5
Cowthorpe 194 D2
Cox Common 165 E3
Coxbank 171 D3
Coxbench 173 E3
Coxbridge 116 C4
Coxford 177 G5
Coxheath 123 G3
Coxhoe 212 C4
Coxley 116 C3
Coxley Wick 116 C3
Coxpark 99 E3
Coxtie Green 137 E3
Coxwold 203 E5
Coychurch 129 F5

Coylet 232 C1
Coylton 224 C4
Coylumbridge 259 G3
Coynach 260 C4
Coynachie 260 C1
Coytrahen 129 E4
Crabbet Park 122 C5
Crabgate 178 B3
Crabtree Plym 100 B2
Crabtree SYorks 186 A4
Crabtree WSuss 109 E1
Crabtree Green 170 A3
Crackaig 230 D3
Crackenthorpe 210 C5
Crackington 98 B1
Crackington Haven 98 B1
Crackley 171 F2
Crackleybank 157 G1
Crackpot 201 E3
Cracoe 193 F1
Craddock 103 D1
Cradhlastadh 270 C4
Cradley Here 145 G3
Cradley WMid 158 B4
Cradley Heath 158 B4
Crafthole 99 D5
Crafton 135 D1
Cragg 193 G5
Cragg Hill 194 B4
Craggan Moray 259 J1
Craggan High 258 E1
Craggan P&K 242 D3
Cragganmore 259 J1
Cragganruar 250 B5
Craggie High 258 E1
Craggie High 274 D7
Craghead 212 B2
Cragside N'umb
NE65 7PX 220 C1
Craibstone
Aberdeen 261 G3
Craibstone Moray 268 C5
Craichie 252 D5
Craig A&B 248 C3
Craig A&B 239 E1
Craig D&G 216 A4
Craig High 264 D5
Craig High 265 F7
Craig SAyr 224 B5
Craig Berthlŵyd 129 G3
Craigans 240 A5
Craigbeg 249 G1
Craig-cefn-parc 128 C2
Craigcleuch 218 B3
Craigculter 269 H5
Craigdallie 244 A2
Craigdam 261 F1
Craigdarroch D&G 216 B1
Craigdarroch EAyr 225 E5
Craigdhu D&G 207 E3
Craigdhu High 266 B7
Craigearn 261 F3
Craigellachie 267 K7
Craigellie 269 J4
Craigencallie 215 G3
Craigend Moray 267 J6
Craigend P&K 243 G2
Craigendive 232 B1
Craigendoran 233 E1
Craigengillan 224 C5
Craigens A&B 230 A3
Craigens EAyr 225 E4
Craighall 244 C3
Craighat 233 F1
Craighead Fife 245 E3
Craighead High 266 E5
Craighlaw 215 E4
Craighouse 230 D3
Craigie Aber 261 H3
Craigie Dundee 244 C1
Craigie P&K 251 G5
Craigie SAyr 224 C2
Craigie Brae 261 G1
Craigieburn 226 D5
Craigieholm 243 G1
Craigielaw 236 B2
Craiglockhart 235 G2
Craiglug 261 G5
Craigmaud 269 G5
Craigmillar 235 G2
Craigmore 232 C3
Craigmyle House 260 E4
Craignafeoch 232 A2
Craignant 169 F4
Craignavie 242 A1
Craigneil 214 C2
Craigneuk 234 B4
Craignure 239 G1
Craigo 253 E3
Craigow 243 F4
Craigrothie 244 B3
Craigroy Farm 259 J1
Craigruie 241 G2
Craigsanquhar 244 B3
Craigton Aberdeen 261 G4
Craigton Angus 244 D1
Craigton Angus 252 B4
Craigton High 266 D7
Craigton Stir 234 A1
Craigtown 274 D3
Craig-y-nos 129 E1
Craik Aber 260 C2
Craik ScBord 227 E5
Crail 245 E4
Crailing 228 A4
Crailinghall 228 A4
Crakehill 202 D5
Crakemarsh 172 B4
Crambe 195 G1
Cramlington 221 E4
Cramond 235 F2
Cranage 171 E1
Cranberry 171 F4
Cranborne 105 G1
Cranbourne 135 E5
Cranbrook
Common 123 G5
Cranbrook GtLon 136 D4
Cranbrook Kent 123 G5
Crane Moor 186 A2
Cranfield 149 E3
Cranford Devon 112 D3
Cranford GtLon 136 A5
Cranford St. Andrew 161 E5

Cranford St. John 161 E5
Cranham Glos 132 A1
Cranham GtLon 137 E4
Crank 183 G2
Cranleigh 121 F4
Cranmer Green 164 B4
Cranmore IoW 106 C3
Cranmore Som 117 D3
Cranna 268 E5
Crannoch 268 C5
Cranoe 160 C3
Cransford 153 E1
Cranshaws 237 D3
Cranstal 190 C1
Crantock 96 B3
Cranwell 175 F3
Cranwich 163 F3
Cranworth 178 A5
Craobh Haven 239 G4
Crapstone 100 B1
Crarae 240 C5
Crask Inn 273 H6
Crask of Aigas 266 B7
Craskins 260 D4
Craster 229 G5
Craswall 144 B4
Crateford 158 B2
Cratfield 165 E4
Crathes 261 F5
Crathie Aber 259 K5
Crathie High 258 C5
Crathorne 202 D2
Craven Arms 156 D4
Craw 231 F5
Crawcrook 212 A1
Crawford Lancs 183 F2
Crawford SLan 226 A3
Crawfordjohn 225 G3
Crawfordton 216 B1
Crawick 225 F4
Crawley Devon 103 F2
Crawley Hants 119 F4
Crawley Oxon 133 F1
Crawley WSuss 122 B5
Crawley Down 122 C5
Crawleyside 211 F3
Crawshawbooth 193 E5
Crawton 253 G2
Crawyn 190 B2
Cray NYorks 201 E5
Cray P&K 251 G3
Cray Powys 143 E5
Crayford 137 E5
Crayke 203 E5
Crays Hill 137 G3
Cray's Pond 134 B4
Crazies Hill 134 C4
Creacombe 102 B1
Creagbheitheachain 248 B3
Creagorry
(Creag Ghoraidh) 262 C7
Crealy Adventure
Park Devon
Devon EX5 1DR 102 C3
Creamore Bank 170 C4
Creaton 160 C5
Creca 218 A4
Credenhill 145 D3
Crediton 102 B2
Creebridge 215 F4
Creech Heathfield 115 F5
Creech St. Michael 115 F5
Creed 96 D5
Creedy Park 102 A2
Creekmoor 105 F3
Creekmouth 137 D4
Creeting St. Mary 152 B2
Creeton 175 F5
Creetown 215 F5
Creggans 240 C4
Cregneash 190 A5
Cregrina 144 A2
Creich 244 B2
Creigau 131 D4
Creigiau 129 G4
Crelevan 257 K1
Crelly 95 D3
Cremyll 100 A2
Crendell 105 G1
Cressage 157 E2
Cressbrook 185 F5
Cresselly 127 D2
Cressing 151 F5
Cresswell N'umb 221 E2
Cresswell Staffs 171 G4
Cresswell Quay 127 D2
Creswell 186 C5
Cretingham 152 D2
Cretshengan 231 F3
Crewe ChesE 171 E2
Crewe ChesW&C 170 B2
Crewe Green 171 E2
Crewgreen 156 C1
Crewkerne 104 A2
Crew's Hole 131 F5
Crewton 173 E4
Crianlarich (A' Chrion-
Làraich) 241 F2
Cribbs Causeway 131 E4
Cribyn 142 B2
Criccieth 167 D2
Crich 173 E2
Crich Carr 173 E2
Crich Common 173 E2
Crich Tramway Village
Derbys DE4 5DP 173 E2
Crichie 269 H6
Crichton 236 A3
Crick Mon 131 D3
Crick N'hants 160 A5
Crickadarn 143 G3
Cricket Hill 120 D1
Cricket St. Thomas 103 G2
Crickham 116 B3
Crickheath 169 F5
Crickhowell 130 B1
Cricklade 132 D3
Cricklewood 136 B4
Crickley Hill Country Park
Glos GL4 8JY 132 B1
Crick's Green 145 F2
Criddlestyle 106 A1
Cridling Stubbs 195 E5
Crieff 243 D2
Crieff Visitor Centre &
Caithness Glass P&K
PH7 4HQ 243 D2

Criftins (Dudleston Heath) 170 A4
Criggan 97 E3
Criggion 156 B1
Crigglestone 186 A1
Crimble 184 D4
Crimchard 103 G2
Crimdon Park 213 D4
Crimond 269 J5
Crimonmogate 269 J5
Crimplesham 163 E2
Crinan 239 G5
Crinan Ferry 239 G5
Cringleford 178 C5
Cringletie 235 G5
Crinow 171 E1
Cripplestyle 105 G1
Cripp's Corner 110 C1
Crix 137 G1
Crizeley 144 D4
Croalchapel 216 C3
Croasdale 209 D5
Crock Street 103 G1
Crockenhill 123 E2
Crocker End 134 C4
Crockerhill 107 E2
Crockernwell 102 A3
Crockerton 117 E3
Crockerton Green 117 E3
Crocketford (Ninemile Bar) 216 C3
Crockey Hill 195 F3
Crockham Hill 123 D3
Crockhurst Street 123 F4
Crockleford Heath 152 B5
Croes Hywel 130 C1
Croesau Bach 169 F5
Croeserw 129 E3
Croes-goch 140 B4
Croes-lan 141 G3
Croesor 167 F3
Croespenmaen 130 A3
Croesyceiliog Carmar 128 A1
Croesyceiliog Torfaen 130 B3
Croes-y-mwyalch 130 C3
Croes-y-pant 130 C2
Croesywaun 167 E2
Croford 115 E5
Croft Here 145 D1
Croft Leics 160 A3
Croft Lincs 176 D1
Croft Warr 184 A3
Croftamie 233 F1
Crofthead 218 B4
Croftmore 251 D3
Crofton Wilts 119 D1
Crofton WYorks 186 A1
Crofts 216 B3
Crofts of Benachielt 275 G5
Crofts of Buinach 267 J6
Crofts of Haddo 261 G1
Crofty 128 B3
Crogen 168 D4
Croggan 239 G2
Croglin 210 B3
Croick Here 266 D2
Croick High 274 D3
Croig 246 D4
Crois Dughaill 254 C3
Croit e Caley 190 A5
Cromarty (Cromba) 266 E5
Crombie 235 E1
Crombie Country Park Angus DD5 3QL 252 D5
Crombie Mill 244 D1
Cromblet 261 F1
Cromdale 259 H2
Cromer Herts 150 A5
Cromer Norf 178 D1
Cromford 173 D2
Cromhall 131 F4
Cromhall Common 131 F4
Cromore 271 G5
Crompton Fold 185 D1
Cromwell 174 C1
Cronberry 225 E3
Crondall 120 C2
Cronk-y-Voddy 190 B3
Cronton 183 F4
Crook Cumb 199 F3
Crook Dur 212 A4
Crook of Devon 243 F4
Crooked Soley 133 F5
Crookedholm 224 C2
Crookham N'umb 228 D3
Crookham WBerks 119 G1
Crookham Eastfield 228 D3
Crookham Village 120 C2
Crooklands 199 G4
Cropredy 147 G3
Cropston 160 A1
Cropthorne 146 B3
Cropton 203 G4
Cropwell Bishop 174 B4
Cropwell Butler 174 B4
Crosbie 232 D5
Crosbost 271 F5
Crosby Cumb 209 D3
Crosby IoM 190 B4
Crosby Mersey 183 E3
Crosby NLincs 187 F1
Crosby Court 202 C3
Crosby Ravensworth 200 B1
Crosby Villa 209 D3
Croscombe 116 C3
Crosland Hill 185 F1
Cross Som 116 B2
Cross (Cros) Na H-ESiar 271 H1
Cross Ash 130 C1
Cross Bank 157 G5
Cross End Bed 149 F2
Cross End Essex 151 G4
Cross Foxes Inn 155 D1
Cross Gates 142 C2
Cross Green Devon 99 D2
Cross Green Staffs 158 B2
Cross Green Suff 151 G2
Cross Green Suff 152 A2
Cross Green Suff 151 G2

Cross Hands Carmar 128 B1
Cross Hands Pembs 127 D1
Cross Hill 173 F3
Cross Hills 193 G3
Cross Houses 157 E2
Cross in Hand 110 A1
Cross Inn Cere 141 G2
Cross Inn Cere 142 B1
Cross Inn RCT 129 G4
Cross Keys 132 A5
Cross Lane 107 E3
Cross Lane Head 157 G3
Cross Lanes Corn 96 B5
Cross Lanes Corn 95 D4
Cross Lanes NYorks 195 E1
Cross Lanes Wrex 170 A3
Cross of Jackston 261 F1
Cross o'th'hands 173 D3
Cross Street 164 C3
Crossaig 231 G4
Crossapol 246 A4
Crossapoll 246 A2
Cross-at-Hand 123 G4
Crossbush 108 C3
Crosscanonby 209 D3
Crossdale Street 178 D2
Crossens 183 E1
Crossflatts 194 A3
Crossford D&G 216 C2
Crossford Fife 235 E1
Crossford SLan 234 C5
Crossgate Lincs 176 A5
Crossgate Staffs 171 G4
Crossgatehall 236 A3
Crossgates Fife 235 F1
Crossgates NYorks 204 D4
Crossgates P&K 243 F2
Crossgates Powys 143 G1
Crossgill 192 B1
Crosshands 224 C2
Crosshill Fife 243 G5
Crosshill SAyr 224 B5
Crosshouse 224 B2
Crosskeys 130 B3
Crosskirk 275 F1
Crosslanes 156 C1
Crosslee Renf 233 F3
Crosslee ScBord 227 E4
Crossmichael 216 B4
Crossmoor 192 A4
Crossroads Aber 261 F5
Crossroads EAyr 224 C2
Crossway Mon 130 D1
Crossway Powys 143 G2
Crossway Green Mon 131 E3
Crossway Green Worcs 146 A1
Crossways Dorset 105 D4
Crossways Glos 131 E1
Crosswell 141 E4
Crosthwaite 199 F3
Croston 183 F1
Crostwick 179 D4
Crostwight 179 E3
Crothair 270 D4
Crouch 123 F3
Crouch End 136 B4
Crouch Hill 104 D1
Croucheston 118 B5
Croughton 148 A4
Crovie 269 G4
Crow 106 A2
Crow Edge 185 F2
Crow Green 137 E3
Crow Hill 145 F4
Crowan 94 D3
Crowborough 123 E5
Crowborough Warren 123 E5
Crowcombe 115 E4
Crowdecote 172 C1
Crowden 185 E3
Crowdhill 119 F5
Crowell 134 C3
Crowfield N'hants 148 B3
Crowfield Suff 152 C2
Crowhurst ESuss 110 C2
Crowhurst Surr 122 C4
Crowhurst Lane End 122 C4
Crowland Lincs 162 A1
Crowland Suff 164 B4
Crowlas 94 C3
Crowle NLincs 187 E2
Crowle Worcs 146 B2
Crowle Green 146 B2
Crown Corner 165 D4
Crownhill 100 A2
Crownthorpe 178 B5
Crowntown 94 D3
Crow's Nest 97 G3
Crows-an-wra 94 A4
Crowsnest 156 C2
Crowthorne 120 D1
Crowton 183 G5
Croxall 159 E1
Croxby 188 B3
Croxdale 212 B4
Croxden 172 B4
Croxley Green 135 F3
Croxton Cambs 150 A2
Croxton NLincs 188 A1
Croxton Norf 163 G4
Croxton Staffs 171 E4
Croxtonbank 171 E4
Croy High 266 E7
Croy NLan 234 B2
Croyde 113 E2
Croyde Bay 113 E2
Croydon Cambs 150 B3
Croydon GtLon 122 C2
Cruach 268 D6
Cruchie 268 D6
Cruckmeole 156 D2
Cruckton 156 D1
Cruden Bay 261 J1
Crudgington 157 F1
Crudwell 132 B3
Crug 156 A5

Crugmeer 96 D2
Crugybar 142 C4
Crùlabhig 270 D4
Crumlin 130 B3
Crumpsall 184 C2
Crumpsbrook 157 F5
Crundale Kent 124 C4
Crundale Pembs 126 C1
Crunwere Farm 127 E1
Crux Easton 119 F2
Crwbin 128 A1
Cryers Hill 135 D3
Crymlyn 181 E5
Crymych 141 E4
Crynant 129 D2
Crystal Palace 136 C5
Crystal Palace Park GtLon SE20 8DT 13 C7
Cuaig 264 D6
Cubbington 147 F1
Cubert 96 B4
Cubley 185 G2
Cublington Bucks 148 D5
Cublington Here 144 D4
Cuckfield 109 F1
Cucklington 117 E5
Cuckney 186 C5
Cuckold's Green 165 F3
Cuckoo Bridge 176 A5
Cuckoo's Corner 120 C3
Cuckoo's Nest 170 A1
Cuddesdon 134 A2
Cuddington Bucks 134 C1
Cuddington ChesW&C 183 G5
Cuddington Heath 170 B3
Cuddy Hill 192 A4
Cudham 123 D2
Cudliptown 99 F3
Cudmore Grove Country Park Essex CO5 8UE 139 D1
Cudworth Som 103 G1
Cudworth SYorks 186 A2
Cuerdley Cross 183 G4
Cuffley 136 C2
Cuidhaseadair 271 H2
Cuidhir 254 B4
Cuidrach 263 J6
Cuilmuich 241 D5
Cuil-uaine 240 B1
Culag 241 D5
Culbo 266 D5
Culbone 114 B3
Culburnie 266 B7
Culcabock 266 D7
Culcharry 267 F6
Culcheth 184 A3
Culdrain 260 D1
Culduie 264 D7
Culford 151 G1
Culfordheath 163 G5
Culgaith 210 C5
Culgower 274 E7
Culham 134 A3
Culindrach 232 A4
Culkein 272 C5
Culkerton 132 B3
Cullachie 259 G2
Cullen 268 D4
Cullercoats 221 F4
Cullicudden 266 D5
Culligran 265 K7
Cullingworth 193 G4
Cullipool 239 G3
Cullivoe 278 E2
Culloch 242 C3
Culloden 266 E7
Cullompton 102 D2
Culmaily 267 F2
Culmalzie 215 E5
Culmington 157 D4
Culmstock 103 E1
Culnacraig 265 G1
Culnadalloch 240 B1
Culnaknock 264 B5
Culnamean 255 K2
Culpho 152 D3
Culquhirk 215 E5
Culrain 266 C2
Culross 235 D1
Culroy 224 B4
Culsh 260 B5
Culshabbin 215 E5
Culswick 279 B8
Culter Allers Farm 226 B2
Cultercullen 261 H2
Cults Aber 260 D1
Cults Aberdeen 261 G4
Cults D&G 207 E2
Cultybraggan Camp 242 C3
Culverhouse Cross 130 A5
Culverstone Green 123 F2
Culverthorpe 175 F3
Culvie 268 D5
Culworth 148 A3
Culzean Castle & Country Park SAyr KA19 8LE 224 A4
Cumberhead 225 F2
Cumberlow Green 150 B4
Cumbernauld 234 B2
Cumberworth 189 F5
Cuminestown 269 G6
Cumloden 215 E4
Cummersdale 209 G1
Cummertrees 217 F4
Cummingstown 267 J5
Cumnock 225 D3
Cumnor 133 G2
Cumrew 210 B2
Cumrue 216 D2
Cumstoun 216 A5
Cumwhinton 210 A2
Cumwhitton 210 B2
Cundall 202 D5
Cunninghamhead 233 E5
Cunningsburgh 279 D10
Cunnister 278 E3
Cunnoquhie 244 B3
Cupar 244 B3
Cupar Muir 244 B3

Curbar 185 G5
Curborough 158 D1
Curbridge Hants 107 E1
Curbridge Oxon 133 F2
Curdridge 107 E1
Curdworth 159 D3
Curland 103 F1
Curlew Green 153 E1
Curling Tye Green 138 B2
Curload 116 A5
Curridge 133 G5
Currie 235 F3
Curry Mallet 116 A5
Curry Rivel 116 A5
Curteis' Corner 124 A5
Curtisden Green 123 G4
Curtisknowle 100 D2
Cury 95 D4
Cusgarne 96 B5
Cushnie 269 F4
Cushuish 115 E4
Cusop 144 B3
Cusworth 186 C2
Cutcombe 114 C4
Cutgate 184 C1
Cuthill 266 E3
Cutiau 154 C1
Cutlers Green 151 D4
Cutnall Green 146 A1
Cutsdean 146 C4
Cutsyke 194 D5
Cutthorpe 186 A5
Cutts 279 D9
Cuttyhill 269 J5
Cuxham 134 B3
Cuxton 123 G2
Cuxwold 188 B2
Cwm BGwent 130 A2
Cwm Denb 182 B5
Cwm Ffrwd-oer 130 B2
Cwm Gwaun 140 D4
Cwm Head 156 D4
Cwm Irfon 143 E3
Cwm Penmachno 168 A3
Cwm Plysgog 141 E3
Cwmafan 129 D3
Cwmaman 129 G3
Cwmann 142 B3
Cwmbach Carmar 141 F5
Cwmbach Carmar 127 F1
Cwmbach Powys 144 A4
Cwmbach Powys 143 G2
Cwmbach RCT 129 G3
Cwmbelan 155 F4
Cwmbrân 130 B3
Cwmbrwyno 154 D4
Cwmcarn 130 B3
Cwmcarvan 131 D2
Cwm-Cewydd 155 E1
Cwm-cou 141 F3
Cwmcrawnon 130 A1
Cwmdare 129 F2
Cwmdu Carmar 142 C4
Cwmdu Powys 144 A5
Cwmduad 141 G4
Cwmerfyn 154 D4
Cwmfelin 129 G2
Cwmfelin Boeth 127 E1
Cwmfelin Mynach 141 F5
Cwmfelinfach 130 A3
Cwmffrwd 128 A1
Cwmgiedd 129 D1
Cwmgors 128 D1
Cwmgwili 128 B1
Cwmgwrach 129 E2
Cwmgwyn 128 C3
Cwmhiraeth 141 G4
Cwmifor 142 C5
Cwmisfael 128 A1
Cwm-Llinau 155 E2
Cwmllyfri 127 G1
Cwmllynfell 128 D1
Cwm-mawr 128 B1
Cwm-Morgan 141 F4
Cwm-parc 129 F3
Cwmpengraig 141 G4
Cwmpennar 129 G2
Cwmsychbant 142 A3
Cwmsymlog 154 C4
Cwmtillery 130 B2
Cwm-twrch Isaf 129 D1
Cwm-twrch Uchaf 129 D1
Cwm-y-glo 167 E1
Cwmyoy 144 C5
Cwm-yr-Eglwys 140 D3
Cwmyrhaiadr 155 D3
Cwmystwyth 155 D5
Cwrt 154 C2
Cwrt-newydd 142 A3
Cwrt-y-cadno 142 C3
Cwrt-y-gollen 130 B1
Cyffylliog 169 D2
Cyfronydd 156 A2
Cymau 169 F2
Cymmer NPT 129 E3
Cymmer RCT 129 G3
Cyncoed 130 A4
Cynghordy 143 E4
Cynheidre 128 A2
Cynwyd 169 D3
Cynwyl Elfed 141 G5

D

Dabton 216 C1
Daccombe 101 F1
Dacre NYorks 194 A1
Dacre Banks 194 A1
Daddry Shield 211 E4
Dadford 148 B4
Dadlington 159 G3
Dafen 128 B2
Daffy Green 178 A4
Dagdale 172 B4
Dagenham 137 D4
Daggons 106 A1
Daglingworth 132 B2
Dagnall 135 E2
Dail 240 C1
Dail Beag 270 E3
Dail Mòr 270 E3
Dailly 224 A5
Dailnamac 240 B1
Dainton 101 E1
Dairsie (Osnaburgh) 244 C3
Dairy House 197 E5
Daisy Bank 158 C3
Daisy Green 152 B1
Dalabrog 254 C2
Dalballoch 258 D5
Dalavich 240 B3
Dalblair 225 E4
Dalbog 253 D2
Dalbreck 274 C7
Dalbury 173 E4
Dalby IoM 190 A4
Dalby Lincs 176 C1
Dalby NYorks 203 F5
Dalby Forest Drive NYorks YO18 7LT 204 B4
Dalcairnie 224 C5
Dalchalloch 250 C3
Dalchalm 267 G1
Dalchenna 240 C4
Dalchirach 259 J1
Dalchork 273 H6
Dalchreichart 257 J3
Dalchruin 242 C2
Dalcross 266 E7
Dalderby 176 A1
Dalditch 102 D4
Daldownie 259 K4
Dale Cumb 210 B2
Dale GtMan 185 D2
Dale Pembs 126 B2
Dale Abbey 173 F4
Dale End Derbys 172 D1
Dale End NYorks 193 F3
Dale Head 199 F1
Dale of Walls 279 A7
Dale Park 108 B2
Dalehouse 203 G1
Dalelia 247 G3
Daless 259 F1
Dalestie 259 J3
Dalfad 260 B4
Dalganachan 275 F4
Dalgarven 233 D5
Dalgety Bay 235 F1
Dalgig 225 D4
Dalginross 242 C2
Dalgonar 225 F5
Dalguise 251 E5
Dalhalvaig 274 D3
Dalham 151 F1
Daligan 233 E1
Dalinlongart 232 C1
Dalivaddy 222 B3
Daljarrock 214 C2
Dalkeith 236 A3
Dallas 267 J6
Dallaschyle 267 F7
Dallash 215 F4
Dalleagles 225 D4
Dallinghoo 153 D2
Dallington ESuss 110 B2
Dallington N'hants 148 C1
Dallow 202 A5
Dalmadilly 261 F3
Dalmally (Dail Mhàilidh) 241 D2
Dalmarnock 234 A3
Dalmary 242 A5
Dalmellington 224 C5
Dalmeny 235 F2
Dalmichy 273 H7
Dalmigavie 258 E3
Dalmore 266 E5
Dalmuir 233 F2
Dalmunzie House Hotel 251 F2
Dalnabreck 247 G3
Dalnacarn 251 F3
Dalnaglar Castle 251 G3
Dalnaha 239 F2
Dalnahaitnach 259 F3
Dalnamain 266 E2
Dalnatrat (Dail na Tràghad) 248 B4
Dalnavert 259 F4
Dalnavie 266 D4
Dalness 249 D4
Dalnessie 273 J7
Dalnigap 214 C3
Dalqueich 243 F4
Dalreoch 214 C2
Dalriech 242 C1
Dalroy 266 E7
Dalrulzian 251 G4
Dalry 233 D5
Dalrymple 224 B4
Dalscote 148 B2
Dalserf 234 B5
Dalsetter 278 E3
Dalshangan 215 G2
Dalskairth 216 D3
Dalston 209 G1
Dalswinton 216 D2
Daltomach 258 E2
Dalton Cumb 199 G5
Dalton D&G 217 F3
Dalton Lancs 183 F2
Dalton N'umb 220 D4
Dalton N'umb 211 F2
Dalton NYorks 202 D5
Dalton NYorks 202 A2
Dalton SYorks 186 B3
Dalton Magna 186 B3
Dalton Piercy 213 D4
Dalton-in-Furness 198 D5
Dalton-le-Dale 212 D4
Dalton-on-Tees 202 B2
Daltote 231 F1
Daltra 267 G7
Dalveich 242 B1
Dalvennan 224 B4
Dalvourn 258 D1
Dalwhinnie 250 B1
Dalwood 103 F2
Dam Green 164 B3
Damask Green 150 A5
Damerham 106 A1
Damgate 179 F5
Damnaglaur 206 B3
Damside 243 F5
Danaway 124 A2
Danbury 137 G2
Danby 203 G2
Danby Wiske 202 C3
Dancers Hill 136 B3
Dandaleith 267 K7
Danderhall 236 A3

Dane Bank 184 D3
Dane End 150 B5
Dane Hills 160 A2
Danebridge 171 G1
Danehill 109 G1
Danesmoor 173 F1
Danestone 261 H3
Daniel's Water 124 B4
Danskine 236 C3
Danthorpe 197 E4
Danzey Green 146 D1
Darby End 158 B4
Darby Green 120 D1
Darenth 137 E5
Daresbury 183 G4
Darfield 186 B2
Dargate 124 C2
Darite 97 G3
Darland 123 G2
Darlaston 158 B3
Darley 194 B2
Darley Bridge 173 D1
Darley Dale 173 D1
Darley Head 194 A2
Darley Hillside 173 D1
Darlingscott 147 E3
Darlington 202 B1
Darliston 170 C4
Darlton 187 D5
Darnabo 269 F6
Darnall 186 A4
Darnconner 225 D3
Darnford 261 G5
Darngarroch 216 A4
Darnick 227 G2
Darowen 155 E2
Darra 269 F6
Darracott 112 C4
Darras Hall 221 D4
Darrington 186 B1
Darrow Green 165 D3
Darsham 153 F1
Dartfield 269 J5
Dartford 137 E5
Dartington 101 D1
Dartington Cider Press Centre Devon TQ9 6TQ 101 D1
Dartmeet 99 G3
Dartmouth 101 E2
Darton 186 A1
Darvel 225 D2
Darwell Hole 110 B2
Darwen 192 C5
Datchet 135 E5
Datchworth 136 B1
Datchworth Green 136 B1
Daubhill 184 A2
Daugh of Kinnermony 267 K7
Dauntsey 132 B4
Dauntsey Green 132 B4
Dauntsey Lock 132 B4
Dava 259 H1
Davaar 222 C4
Davan 260 C4
Davenham 184 A5
Davenport Green 184 B4
Daventry 148 A1
Daventry Country Park N'hants NN11 2JB 148 A1
David Marshall Lodge Stir FK8 3SX 242 A4
Davidstow 97 F1
Davington 216 D2
Daviot Aber 261 F2
Daviot High 258 E1
Davoch of Grange 268 C5
Davyhulme 184 B3
Dawley 157 F2
Dawlish 102 C4
Dawn 181 G5
Daws Heath 138 B4
Daw's House 98 D2
Dawsmere 176 C4
Day Green 171 E2
Dayhills 171 G4
Dayhouse Bank 158 B5
Daylesford 147 E5
Ddôl 182 C5
Deadman's Cross 149 G3
Deadwaters 234 B5
Deaf Hill 212 C4
Deal 125 F3
Deal Hall 138 D3
Dean Cumb 209 D4
Dean Devon 100 D1
Dean Dorset 105 F1
Dean Hants 107 F5
Dean Oxon 147 F5
Dean Som 117 D3
Dean Bank 212 B4
Dean Castle & Country Park EAyr KA3 1XB 224 C2
Dean Cross 113 F1
Dean Gallery Edin EH4 3DS 36 B4
Dean Head 185 G3
Dean Prior 100 D1
Dean Row 184 C4
Dean Street 123 G3
Deanburnhaugh 227 E4
Deane GtMan 184 A2
Deane Hants 119 G3
Deanland 105 F1
Deanlane End 107 G1
Deans Bottom 124 A2
Deanscales 209 D4
Deansgreen 184 A4
Deanshanger 148 C4
Deanston 242 C4
Debach 152 D2
Debate 217 F2
Debden 151 D4
Debden Essex 136 D3
Debden Green Essex 136 D3
Debenham 152 C1

Deblin's Green 146 A3
Dechmont 235 E2
Decker Hill 157 G1
Deddington 147 G4
Dedham 152 B4
Dedham Heath 152 B4
Dedworth 135 E5
Deecastle 260 C5
Deene 161 E3
Deenethorpe 161 E3
Deep, The HU1 4DP 76 Kingston upon Hull
Deep Sea World, North Queensferry Fife KY11 1JR 235 F1
Deepcar 185 G3
Deepcut 121 E2
Deepdale Cumb 200 C4
Deepdale NYorks 201 D5
Deeping Gate 161 G2
Deeping St. James 161 G2
Deeping St. Nicholas 162 A1
Deepweir 131 D3
Deerhill 268 C5
Deerhurst 146 A5
Deerhurst Walton 146 A5
Deerness Valley Walk Dur DH7 7RJ 212 A3
Deerton Street 124 C2
Defford 146 B3
Defynnog 143 F5
Deganwy 181 F5
Degnish 239 G3
Deighton NYorks 202 C2
Deighton WYorks 185 F1
Deighton York 195 F3
Deiniolen 167 E1
Delabole 97 E1
Delamere 170 C1
Delavorar 259 J3
Delfrigs 261 H2
Dell Lodge 259 H3
Dell Quay 108 A3
Delliefure 259 H1
Delly End 133 F1
Delnabo 259 J3
Delph 185 D2
Delphorie 260 C3
Delves 212 A3
Delvine 251 G5
Dembleby 175 F4
Denaby 186 B3
Denaby Main 186 B3
Denbies Wine Estate Surr RH5 6AA 121 G2
Denbigh (Dinbych) 168 D1
Denbury 101 E1
Denby 173 E3
Denby Dale 185 G2
Denby Pottery Derbys DE5 8NX 18 C1
Denchworth 133 F3
Dendron 198 D5
Denend 260 E1
Denford 161 E5
Dengie 138 C2
Denham Bucks 135 F4
Denham Suff 164 C4
Denham Suff 151 F1
Denham Green 135 F4
Denham Street 164 C4
Denhead Aber 261 F3
Denhead Aber 269 J5
Denhead Fife 244 C3
Denhead of Arbirlot 253 D5
Denhead of Gray 244 B1
Denholm 227 G4
Denholme 193 G4
Denholme Clough 193 G4
Denio 166 C4
Denmead 107 F1
Denmill 261 G3
Denmoss 268 E6
Dennington 153 D1
Denny 234 C1
Dennyloanhead 234 C1
Denshaw 185 D1
Denside 261 G5
Densole 125 E4
Denston 151 F2
Denstone 172 B3
Dent 200 C3
Denton Cambs 161 G4
Denton Darl 202 B1
Denton ESuss 109 G3
Denton GtMan 184 D3
Denton Kent 125 E4
Denton Kent 137 F5
Denton Lincs 175 D4
Denton N'hants 148 D2
Denton Norf 165 D3
Denton NYorks 194 A3
Denton Oxon 134 A2
Denton's Green 183 F3
Denver 163 E2
Denville 107 G2
Denwick 229 G5
Deopham 178 B5
Deopham Green 164 B2
Depden 151 F2
Depden Green 151 F2
Deptford GtLon 136 C5
Deptford Wilts 118 B4
Derby 173 E4
Derby City Museum & Art Gallery DE1 1BS 70 Derby
Derbyhaven 190 A5
Dereham (East Dereham) 178 A4
Dererach 239 E2
Deri 130 A2
Derril 112 D5
Derringstone 125 E4
Derrington 171 F5
Derriton 112 D5
Derry 242 B2
Derry Hill 132 B5
Derrythorpe 187 F2
Dersingham 177 E4
Dervaig 246 D4
Derwen 169 D2
Derwenlas 154 D3
Derwent Walk Country Park Dur NE16 3BN 28 A3

Derwydd 128 C1
Derybruich 232 A2
Desborough 160 D4
Desford 159 G2
Detchant 229 E3
Dethick 173 E2
Detling 123 G3
Deuddwr 156 B1
Deuxhill 157 F4
Devauden 131 D3
Devil's Bridge
(Pontarfynach) 154 D5
Devitts Green 159 E3
Devizes 118 B1
Devon Guild of Craftsmen
Devon
TQ13 9AF 102 B5
Devonport 100 A2
Devonside 243 E5
Devoran 95 E3
Dewar 236 A5
Dewlish 105 D2
Dewsall Court 145 D4
Dewsbury 194 B5
Dewsbury Moor 194 B5
Dhiseig 239 D1
Dhoon 190 C3
Dhoor 190 C2
Dhowin 190 C1
Dial Green 121 E5
Dial Post 109 D2
Dibden 106 D2
Dibden Hill 135 E3
Dibden Purlieu 106 D2
Dick Institute EAyr
KA1 3BU 224 C2
Dickleburgh 164 C3
Dickleburgh Moor 164 C3
Didbrook 146 C4
Didcot 134 A3
Diddington 149 G1
Diddlebury 157 E4
Didley 145 D4
Didling 108 A2
Didmarton 132 A4
Didsbury 184 C3
Didworthy 100 C1
Digby 175 F2
Digg 263 K5
Diggle 185 E2
Digmoor 183 F2
Digswell 136 B1
Dihewyd 142 B4
Dildawn 216 B5
Dilham 179 E3
Dilhorne 171 G3
Dillington 149 G1
Dilston 211 F1
Dilton Marsh 117 F3
Dilwyn 144 D2
Dilwyn Common 144 D2
Dimple 184 B1
Dinas Carmar 141 F4
Dinas Gwyn 167 D2
Dinas Gwyn 166 B4
Dinas Cross 140 D3
Dinas Dinlle 166 D2
Dinas Powys 130 A5
Dinas-Mawddwy 155 E1
Dinckley 192 C4
Dinder 116 C3
Dinedor 145 E4
Dingestow 131 D1
Dingley 160 C4
Dingwall (Inbhir
Pheofharain) 266 C6
Dinlabyre 218 D2
Dinnet 260 C5
Dinnington Som 104 A1
Dinnington SYorks 186 C4
Dinnington T&W 221 E4
Dinorwig 167 E1
Dinosaur Adventure Park
Norf NR9 5JW 178 C4
Dinosaur Museum,
Dorchester Dorset
DT1 1EW 104 C3
Dinton Bucks 134 C1
Dinton Wilts 118 B4
Dinton Pastures Country
Park W'ham
RG10 0TH 134 C5
Dinvin 214 B5
Dinwoodie Mains 217 F1
Dinworthy 112 D4
Dipford 115 F5
Dippen A&B 222 C2
Dippen NAyr 223 F3
Dippenhall 120 D3
Dipple Moray 268 B5
Dipple SAyr 224 A5
Diptford 100 D2
Dipton 212 A2
Dirdhu 259 H2
Dirleton 236 C1
Discoed 144 B1
Discovery Museum
T&W NE1 4JA
79 Newcastle upon Tyne
Diseworth 173 F5
Dishes 276 F5
Dishforth 202 C5
Dishley 173 G5
Disley 185 D4
Diss 164 C3
Disserth 143 G2
Distington 208 D4
Ditcheat 116 D4
Ditchingham 165 E2
Ditchley 147 F5
Ditchling 109 F2
Ditteridge 117 F1
Dittisham 101 E2
Ditton Halton 183 F4
Ditton Kent 123 G3
Ditton Green 151 E2
Ditton Priors 157 F4
Dixton Glos 146 B4
Dixton Mon 131 E1
Dobcross 185 D2
Dobwalls 97 G3
Doccombe 102 A4
Dochgarroch 258 C1
Dock Museum, Barrow-in-
Furness Cumb
LA14 2PW 191 E1

Dockenfield 120 D3
Docker Cumb 199 G3
Docker Lancs 199 G5
Docking 177 F4
Docklow 145 E2
Dockray Cumb 209 G4
Dockray Cumb 209 F1
Dodbrooke 100 D3
Doddenham 145 G2
Doddinghurst 137 E3
Doddington Cambs 162 C3
Doddington Kent 124 B3
Doddington Lincs 187 D5
Doddington
N'umb 229 D3
Doddington Shrop 157 F5
Doddiscombsleigh 102 B4
Doddycross 98 D4
Dodford N'hants 148 B1
Dodford Worcs 158 B5
Dodington SGlos 131 F5
Dodington Som 115 E3
Dodington Ash 131 G5
Dodleston 170 A1
Dods Leigh 172 B4
Dodscott 113 F4
Dodworth 186 A2
Doehole 173 E2
Doffcocker 184 A1
Dog Village 102 A3
Dogdyke 176 A2
Dogmersfield 120 C2
Dogsthorpe 162 A2
Dol Fawr 155 E2
Dolanog 155 G1
Dolau Powys 144 A1
Dolau RCT 129 G4
Dolbenmaen 167 E3
Doley 171 E5
Dolfach 155 F5
Dolfor 156 A4
Dolgarreg 142 D4
Dolgarrog 168 A1
Dolgellau 154 D1
Dolgoch 154 C2
Dolgran 142 A4
Doll 267 F1
Dollar 243 E5
Dollarbeg 243 E5
Dolphin 182 C5
Dolphinholme 192 B2
Dolphinton 235 F5
Dolton 113 F4
Dolwen Conwy 181 G5
Dolwen Powys 155 F2
Dolwyddelan 168 A2
Dol-y-bont 154 C4
Dol-y-cannau 144 A3
Dolyhir 144 B2
Dolywern 169 F4
Domgay 156 B1
Doncaster 186 C2
Doncaster Racecourse
Exhibition Centre
SYorks DN1 2BB 186 D2
Donhead
St. Andrew 118 A5
Donhead St. Mary 118 A5
Donibristle 235 F1
Doniford 115 D3
Donington Lincs 176 A4
Donington Shrop 158 A2
Donington le Heath 159 G1
Donington on Bain 188 C4
Donisthorpe 159 F1
Donkey Sanctuary,
Salcombe Regis Devon
EX10 0NU 103 E4
Donna Nook 189 E3
Donnington Glos 147 D5
Donnington Here 145 G4
Donnington Shrop 157 E2
Donnington Tel&W 157 G1
Donnington WBerks 119 F1
Donnington WSuss 108 A3
Donyatt 103 G1
Dorchester Dorset 104 C3
Dorchester Oxon 134 A3
Dorchester Abbey Oxon
OX10 7HH 134 A3
Dordon 159 E2
Dore 186 A4
Dores (Duras) 258 C1
Dorket Head 173 G3
Dorking 121 G3
Dorley's Corner 153 E1
Dormans Park 122 C4
Dormansland 122 D4
Dormanstown 213 E5
Dormer's Wells 136 A4
Dormington 145 E3
Dormston 146 B2
Dorn 147 E4
Dorney 135 E5
Dorney Reach 135 E5
Dornie
(An Dòrnaidh) 256 E2
Dornoch 266 E3
Dornock 218 A5
Dorrery 275 F3
Dorridge 159 D5
Dorrington Lincs 175 F2
Dorrington Shrop 157 D2
Dorsell 260 D3
Dorsington 146 D3
Dorstone 144 C3
Dorton 134 B1
Dorusduain 257 F2
Dosthill 159 E3
Dotland 211 F2
Dottery 104 A3
Doublebois 97 F3
Dougalston 233 G2
Dougarie 223 D2
Doughton 132 A3
Douglas IoM 190 B4
Douglas SLan 225 G3
Douglas & Angus 244 C1
Douglas Water 225 G2
Douglastown 252 C5
Doulting 116 D3
Dounby 276 B5
Doune A&B 241 F5
Doune A&B 241 F3
Doune High 259 F3
Doune High 266 B1
Doune Stir 242 C4
Dounepark 269 F4

Douneside 260 C4
Dounie High 266 D3
Dounie High 266 C2
Dounreay 274 E2
Dousland 100 B1
Dovaston 170 A5
Dove Holes 185 E5
Dovenby 209 D3
Dovendale 188 D3
Dover 125 F4
Dover Castle Kent
CT16 1HU 70 Dover
Dovercourt 152 D4
Doverdale 146 A1
Doveridge 172 C4
Doversgreen 122 B4
Dowally 251 E5
Dowdeswell 146 C5
Dowhill 224 A5
Dowland 113 F4
Dowlands 103 F3
Dowlais 129 G2
Dowland 113 F4
Dowlish Ford 103 G1
Dowlish Wake 103 G1
Down Ampney 132 D3
Down End 116 A3
Down Hatherley 146 A5
Down St. Mary 102 A2
Down Thomas 100 B3
Downderry 98 D5
Downe 122 D2
Downend IoW 107 E4
Downend SGlos 131 F5
Downend WBerks 133 G5
Downfield 244 B1
Downfields 163 E5
Downgate 99 D3
Downham Essex 137 G3
Downham Lancs 193 D3
Downham N'umb 228 C3
Downham Market 163 E2
Downhead Corn 97 G1
Downhead Som 117 D3
Downhead Som 116 C5
Downholland Cross 183 E2
Downholme 202 A3
Downies 261 H5
Downley 135 D3
Downs 130 A5
Downside NSom 116 B1
Downside Som 116 B1
Downside Som 116 D2
Downside Surr 121 G2
Downton Devon 99 F3
Downton Devon 101 E2
Downton Hants 106 B3
Downton Wilts 118 C5
Downton on the
Rock 156 D5
Dowsby 175 G5
Dowthwaitehead 209 G4
Doxey 171 G5
Doynton 131 G5
Drabblegate 178 D3
Draethen 130 B4
Draffan 234 B5
Dragley Beck 199 D5
Drakeland Corner 100 B2
Drakelow 158 A4
Drakemyre 233 D4
Drakes Broughton 146 B3
Drakes Cross 158 C5
Draughton N'hants 160 C5
Draughton NYorks 193 G2
Drax 195 F5
Draycot Foliat 133 D5
Draycote 147 G1
Draycott Derbys 173 F4
Draycott Glos 147 D4
Draycott Shrop 158 A3
Draycott Som 116 B2
Draycott Worcs 146 A3
Draycott in the
Clay 172 C5
Draycott in the
Moors 171 G4
Drayford 102 A1
Draynes 97 G3
Drayton Leics 160 D3
Drayton Lincs 176 A4
Drayton Norf 178 C4
Drayton Oxon 147 G3
Drayton Oxon 133 G3
Drayton Ports 107 F2
Drayton Som 116 B5
Drayton Warks 146 D2
Drayton Worcs 158 B5
Drayton Bassett 159 D2
Drayton Beauchamp
135 E1
Drayton Manor Park Staffs
B78 3TW 159 D2
Drayton Parslow 148 D5
Drayton
St. Leonard 134 A3
Drebley 193 G2
Dreemskerry 190 C2
Dreenhill 126 C1
Drefach Carmar 141 G4
Drefach Carmar 128 B1
Dre-fach Cere 142 B3
Drefelin 141 G4
Dreghorn 224 B2
Drem 236 C2
Drewsteignton 102 A3
Driby 189 D5
Driffield ERid 196 C2
Driffield Glos 132 C3
Drigg 198 B3
Drighlington 194 B5
Drimfern 240 C3
Drimlee 240 D3
Drimnin 247 E4
Drimore 262 C7
Drimpton 104 A2
Drimsdale
(Dreumasdal) 254 C1
Drimsynie 241 D4
Drimvore 240 A5
Drinan 256 B3
Dringhouses 195 E2
Drinisiadar 263 G2
Drinkstone 152 A1
Drinkstone Green 152 A1
Drishaig 241 D3
Drissaig 240 B3
Droitston 172 B5
Droitwich Spa 146 A1

Dron 243 G3
Dronfield 186 A5
Dronfield
Woodhouse 186 A5
Dronley 244 B1
Droop 105 D2
Dropmore 135 E4
Droxford 107 F1
Droylsden 184 D3
Druid 168 D3
Druidston 126 B1
Druimarbin 248 C2
Druimavuic 248 C5
Druimdrishaig 231 F2
Druimindarroch 247 F1
Druimkinnerras 258 B1
Drum A&B 231 G3
Drum P&K 243 F4
Drumachloy 232 B3
Drumbeg 272 D5
Drumblade 268 D6
Drumblair 268 E6
Drumbuie D&G 225 F4
Drumbuie High 256 D1
Drumburgh 209 F1
Drumchapel 233 G2
Drumchardine 266 C7
Drumchork 264 E3
Drumclog 225 D3
Drumdelgie 268 C6
Drumderfit 266 D6
Drumeldrie 244 C4
Drumelzier 226 C2
Drumfearn 256 C3
Drumfern 248 B2
Drumgarve 222 C3
Drumgley 252 C4
Drumguish 258 C5
Drumhead 260 E5
Drumin 259 J1
Drumlamford
House 215 D3
Drumlasie 260 E4
Drumlemble 222 B4
Drumlithie 253 F1
Drummond High 266 D5
Drummore 244 A3
Drummuir 268 B6
Drumnadrochit (Druim na
Drochaid) 258 C2
Drumnagorrach 268 D5
Drumnatorran 248 A3
Drumoak 261 F5
Drumore 222 C3
Drumour 243 E1
Drumrash 216 A3
Drumrunie 265 H1
Drums 261 H2
Drumsturdy 244 C1
Drumuie 263 K7
Drumuillie 259 G2
Drumvaich 242 B4
Drumwhindle 261 H1
Drumwhirn 216 B2
Drunkendub 253 E5
Druridge 221 E2
Drusillas Park ESuss
BN26 5QS 110 A3
Drws-y-nant 168 B5
Dry Doddington 174 D3
Dry Drayton 150 B1
Dry Harbour 264 C6
Dry Sandford 133 G2
Dry Street 137 F4
Drybeck 200 B1
Drybridge Moray 268 C4
Drybridge NAyr 224 B2
Drybrook 131 F1
Dryburgh 227 G2
Drygrange 227 G2
Dryhope 227 D3
Drymen 233 F1
Drymuir 269 H6
Drynoch 255 K1
Dryslwyn 142 B5
Dryton 157 E2
Duachy 240 A2
Dubford 269 F4
Dubhchladach 231 G3
Dubheads 243 E2
Dublin 152 C1
Dubton 253 D4
Duchally 273 F7
Duck Bay 233 E1
Duck End Bed 149 F3
Duck End Cambs 150 A1
Duck End Essex 151 E5
Duck Street 194 A1
Duckington 170 B2
Ducklington 133 F2
Duckmanton 186 B5
Duck's Cross 149 G2
Ducks Island 136 B3
Duddenhoe End 150 C4
Duddingston 235 G2
Duddington 161 E2
Duddlestone 115 F5
Duddleswell 109 G1
Duddo 237 G5
Duddon 170 C1
Duddon Bridge 198 C4
Dudleston 170 A4
Dudleston Heath
(Criftins) 170 A4
Dudley T&W 221 E4
Dudley WMid 158 B3
Dudley Port 158 B3
Dudley Zoo & Castle
WMid DY1 4QB 14 B3
Dudlow's Green 184 A4
Dudsbury 105 G3
Duffield 173 E3
Duffryn 129 E3
Dufftown 260 B1
Duffus 267 J5

Dufton 210 C5
Duggleby 196 A1
Duiar 259 J1
Duible 274 E6
Duiletter 241 D2
Duinish 250 B3
Duirinish 256 D1
Duisdealmor 256 D3
Duisky 248 C2
Duke End 159 E4
Duke Fd 159 E4
Dukestown 130 A1
Dukinfield 184 D3
Dulas 180 C4
Dulax 260 B3
Dulcote 116 C3
Dulford 103 D2
Dull 250 D5
Dullatur 234 B2
Dullingham 151 E2
Dullingham Ley 151 E2
Dulnain Bridge 259 G2
Duloe Bed 149 G1
Duloe Corn 97 G4
Dulsie 267 G7
Dulverton 114 C5
Dulwich 136 C5
Dulwich Picture Gallery
GtLon SE21 7AD 13 C7
Dumbarton 233 E2
Dumbleton 146 C4
Dumcrieff 226 C5
Dumeath 260 C1
Dumfin 233 E1
Dumfries 217 D3
Dumgoyne 233 G1
Dummer 119 G3
Dun 253 E4
Dunach 240 A2
Dunalastair 250 C4
Dunan A&B 232 C2
Dunan High 256 B2
Dunans 240 C5
Dunball 116 A3
Dunbar 237 D2
Dunbeath 275 G5
Dunbeg
(An Dùn Beag) 240 A1
Dunblane 242 C4
Dunbog 244 A3
Dunbridge 119 E5
Duncanston Aber 260 D2
Duncanston High 266 C6
Dunchideock 102 B4
Dunchurch 159 G5
Duncote 148 B2
Duncow 217 D2
Duncraggan 242 A4
Duncrievie 243 G4
Duncroist 242 A1
Duncton 108 B2
Dundee 244 C1
Dundee Airport 244 B2
Dundee Contemporary Arts
DD1 4DY 71 Dundee
Dundon 116 B4
Dundon Hayes 116 B4
Dundonald 224 B2
Dundonnell (Ach-Dà-
Dhòmhnaill) 265 G3
Dundraw 209 F2
Dundreggan
(Dul Dreagain) 257 K3
Dundrennan 208 A2
Dundridge 107 E1
Dundry 116 C1
Dunearn 235 G1
Dunecht 261 F4
Dunfermline 235 E1
Dunfield 132 D3
Dunford Bridge 185 F2
Dungate 124 B3
Dungworth 185 G3
Dunham 187 F3
Dunham Massey Hall,
Park & Gardens GtMan
WA14 4SJ 24 C6
Dunham Town 184 B4
Dunham
Woodhouses 184 B4
Dunham-on-the-
Hill 183 F5
Dunhampton 146 A1
Dunholme 188 A5
Dunino 244 A5
Dunipace 234 C1
Dunira 242 C2
Dunkeld 251 F5
Dunkerton 117 E2
Dunkeswell 103 E2
Dunkeswick 194 C3
Dunkirk ChesW&C 183 E5
Dunkirk Kent 124 C3
Dunk's Green 123 F3
Dunlappie 253 D3
Dunley Hants 119 F2
Dunley Worcs 145 G1
Dunlop 233 F5
Dunloskin 232 C2
Dunmere 97 E3
Dunmore A&B 231 F3
Dunmore Falk 234 C1
Dunn 275 G3
Dunn Street 123 G2
Dunnabie 218 A3
Dunnet 275 H1
Dunnichen 252 D5
Dunning 243 F3
Dunnington ERid 197 D2
Dunnington Warks 146 C2
Dunnington York 195 F2
Dunnockshaw 193 E5
Dunoon 232 C2
Dunragit 214 C5
Dunrostan 231 F1
Duns 237 E4
Duns Tew 147 G5
Dunsa 185 G5
Dunsby 175 G5
Dunscore 216 C2
Dunscroft 187 D2
Dunsdale 203 F1
Dunsden Green 134 C5
Dunsfold 121 F4
Dunsford 102 A4
Dunshalt 244 A3

Dunshill 146 A4
Dunsinnan 243 G1
Dunsland Cross 113 E5
Dunsley NYorks 204 B1
Dunsley Staffs 158 A4
Dunsmore 135 D2
Dunsop Bridge 192 C2
Dunstable 149 F5
Dunstable Downs CenBeds
LU6 2GY 149 F5
Dunstall 172 C5
Dunstall Green 151 F1
Dunstan 229 G5
Dunstan Steads 229 G4
Dunster 114 C3
Dunster Castle & Gardens
Som TA24 6SL 114 C3
Dunston Lincs 175 F1
Dunston Norf 178 D5
Dunston Staffs 158 B1
Dunston Heath 158 B1
Dunston Hill 212 B1
Dunstone Devon 102 A5
Dunstone Devon 100 B2
Dunsville 187 D2
Dunswell 196 C4
Dunsyre 235 E5
Dunterton 99 D3
Duntisbourne
Abbots 132 B2
Duntisbourne Leer 132 B2
Duntisbourne
Rouse 132 B2
Duntish 104 C2
Duntocher 233 F2
Dunton Bucks 148 D5
Dunton CenBeds 150 A3
Dunton Norf 177 G4
Dunton Bassett 160 A3
Dunton Green 123 E3
Dunton Wayletts 137 F3
Duntulm 263 K4
Dunure 224 A4
Dunure Mains 224 A4
Dunvant 128 B3
Dunvegan 263 H7
Dunvegan Castle High
IV55 8WF 263 H7
Dunwich 165 F3
Dura 244 C3
Durdar 210 A2
Durgan 95 E4
Durgates 123 F5
Durham 212 B3
Durham Cathedral
DH1 3EH 71 Durham
Durham Dales Centre Dur
DL13 2FJ 211 G4
Durham Tees Valley
Airport 202 C1
Durinemast 247 F4
Durisdeer 225 G5
Durleigh 115 F4
Durley Hants 107 E1
Durley Wilts 118 D1
Durley Street 107 E1
Durlow Common 145 F4
Durnamuck 265 G2
Durness 273 G2
Durno 261 F2
Duror 248 B4
Durran A&B 240 B4
Durran High 275 G2
Durrants 107 G2
Durrington Wilts 118 C3
Durrington WSuss 108 D3
Dursley 131 G3
Dursley Cross 131 F1
Durston 115 F5
Durweston 105 E2
Dury 279 D6
Duston 148 C1
Duthie Park & David Welch
Winter Gardens Aberdeen
AB11 7TH 261 H4
Duthil 259 G2
Dutlas 156 B5
Duton Hill 151 E5
Dutson 98 D2
Dutton 183 G5
Duxford 150 C3
Dwygyfylchi 181 F5
Dwyran 166 D1
Dyce 261 G3
Dyfatty 128 A2
Dyffryn Bridgend 129 E3
Dyffryn Pembs 140 C4
Dyffryn VGlam 129 G5
Dyffryn Ardudwy 167 E5
Dyffryn Castell 155 D4
Dyffryn Ceidrych 142 D5
Dyffryn Cellwen 129 E1
Dyke Devon 112 D3
Dyke Lincs 175 G5
Dyke Moray 267 G6
Dykehead Angus 252 B3
Dykehead NLan 234 C4
Dykehead Stir 242 A5
Dykelands 253 F3
Dykends 252 A4
Dykeside 269 F6
Dylan Thomas Centre
SA1 1RR 86 Swansea
Dylife 155 E3
Dymchurch 111 G1
Dymock 145 G4
Dyrham 131 G5
Dyrham Park SGlos
SN14 8ER 8 F2
Dysart 244 B5
Dyserth 182 B5

E

Eachwick 220 D4
Eadar dha Fhadhail 270 C4
Eagland Hill 192 A3
Eagle 175 D1
Eagle Barnsdale 175 D1
Eagle Moor 175 D1
Eaglescliffe 202 D1
Eaglesfield Cumb 209 D4
Eaglesfield D&G 218 A4
Eaglesham 233 G4
Eaglethorpe 161 F3
Eagley 184 B1

Eairy 190 A4
Eakley 148 D2
Eakring 174 B1
Ealand 187 E1
Ealing 136 A4
Eamont Bridge 210 B5
Earby 193 F3
Earcroft 192 C5
Eardington 157 G3
Eardisland 144 D2
Eardisley 144 C3
Eardiston Shrop 170 A5
Eardiston Worcs 145 F1
Earith 162 B5
Earl Shilton 159 G3
Earl Soham 152 D1
Earl Sterndale 172 B1
Earl Stonham 152 C2
Earle 229 D4
Earlestown 183 G3
Earley 134 C5
Earlham 178 C5
Earlish 263 J5
Earls Barton 149 D1
Earls Colne 151 G5
Earl's Common 146 B2
Earl's Court 136 B5
Earls Court Exhibition
Centre GtLon
SW5 9TA 11 E5
Earl's Croome 146 A3
Earl's Green 152 B1
Earlsdon 159 F5
Earlsferry 244 C4
Earlsford 261 G1
Earlsheaton 194 B5
Earlston 227 G2
Earlswood Mon 131 D3
Earlswood Surr 122 B4
Earlswood Warks 158 D5
Earnley 108 A3
Earnshaw Bridge 192 B5
Earsairidh 254 C5
Earsdon 221 F4
Earsdon Moor 221 D2
Earsham 165 E3
Earsham Street 164 D4
Earswick 195 F2
Eartham 108 B3
Earthcott Green 131 F4
Easby 203 E2
Easdale 239 G3
Easebourne 121 D5
Easenhall 159 G5
Eashing 121 E3
Easington Bucks 134 B1
Easington Dur 212 D3
Easington ERid 189 D1
Easington N'umb 229 F3
Easington Oxon 134 B3
Easington Oxon 147 G4
Easington R&C 203 G1
Easington Colliery 212 D3
Easington Lane 212 C3
Easingwold 195 E1
Easole Street 125 E3
Eassie 252 B5
East Aberthaw 114 D1
East Allington 101 D3
East Anstey 114 C5
East Anton 119 E3
East Appleton 202 B3
East Ardsley 194 C5
East Ashey 107 E4
East Ashling 108 A3
East Auchronie 261 G4
East Ayton 204 C4
East Barkwith 188 B4
East Barming 123 G3
East Barnby 204 B1
East Barnet 136 B3
East Barsham 178 A2
East Beckham 178 C2
East Bedfont 135 F5
East Bergholt 152 B4
East Bierley 194 A5
East Bilney 178 A4
East Blatchington 109 G4
East Boldon 212 C1
East Boldre 106 C2
East Bolton 229 F5
East Bower 116 A4
East Brent 116 A2
East Bridge 153 F1
East Bridgford 174 B3
East Brora 267 F1
East Buckland 113 G2
East Budleigh 103 D4
East Burnham 135 E4
East Burra 279 C9
East Burrafirth 279 C7
East Burton 105 E4
East Butsfield 212 A3
East Butterleigh 102 C2
East Butterwick 187 F2
East Cairnbeg 253 F2
East Calder 235 E3
East Carleton 178 C5
East Carlton
N'hants 160 D4
East Carlton
WYorks 194 B3
East Carlton Countryside
Park N'hants
LE16 8YF 160 D4
East Chaldon (Chaldon
Herring) 105 D4
East Challow 133 F4
East Charleton 101 D3
East Chelborough 104 B2
East Chiltington 109 F2
East Chinnock 104 A1
East Chisenbury 118 C2
East Clandon 121 F3
East Claydon 148 C5
East Clyne 267 G1
East Clyth 275 H5
East Compton
Dorset 105 E1
East Compton
Som 116 D3
East Coombe 102 B2
East Cornworthy 101 E2
East Cottingwith 195 G3
East Cowes 107 E3
East Cowick 195 F5

East Cowton 202 C2
East Cramlington 221 E4
East Cranmore 117 D3
East Creech 105 F4
East Croachy 258 D2
East Darlochan 222 B3
East Davoch 260 C4
East Dean ESuss 110 A4
East Dean Hants 119 D5
East Dean WSuss 108 B2
East Dereham (Dereham) 178 A4
East Down 113 F1
East Drayton 187 E5
East Dundry 116 C1
East Ella 196 C5
East End ERid 197 D4
East End ERid 197 E5
East End Essex 138 D2
East End Hants 119 F1
East End Hants 106 C3
East End Herts 150 C5
East End Kent 124 A5
East End Kent 124 B1
East End MK 149 E3
East End NSom 131 D5
East End Oxon 133 F1
East End Poole 105 F3
East End Som 116 C2
East End Suff 152 C4
East End Suff 152 C2
East Farleigh 123 G3
East Farndon 160 C4
East Ferry 187 F3
East Firsby 188 A4
East Fleetham 229 G4
East Fortune 236 C2
East Garston 133 F5
East Ginge 133 G4
East Goscote 160 B1
East Grafton 119 D1
East Green Suff 153 F1
East Green Suff 151 E2
East Grimstead 118 D5
East Grinstead 122 C5
East Guldeford 111 E1
East Haddon 148 B1
East Hagbourne 134 A4
East Halton 188 B1
East Ham 136 D4
East Hanney 133 G3
East Hanningfield 137 G2
East Hardwick 186 B1
East Harling 164 A3
East Harlsey 202 D3
East Harnham 118 C5
East Harptree 116 C2
East Hartford 221 E4
East Harting 107 G1
East Hatch 118 A5
East Hatley 150 A2
East Hauxwell 202 A3
East Haven 245 D1
East Heckington 175 G3
East Hedleyhope 212 A3
East Helmsdale 275 F7
East Hendred 133 G4
East Herrington 212 C2
East Heslerton 204 C5
East Hewish 116 B1
East Hoathly 110 A2
East Holme 105 E4
East Horndon 137 F4
East Horrington 116 C3
East Horsley 121 F2
East Horton 229 E3
East Howe 105 G3
East Huntspill 116 A3
East Hyde 136 A1
East Ilsley 133 G4
East Keal 176 B1
East Kennett 118 C1
East Keswick 194 C3
East Kilbride 234 A4
East Kimber 99 E1
East Kirkby 176 B1
East Knapton 204 B5
East Knighton 105 E4
East Knowstone 114 B5
East Knoyle 117 F4
East Kyloe 229 E3
East Lambrook 104 A1
East Lancashire Railway Lancs BL9 0EY 193 E5
East Langdon 125 F4
East Langton 160 C3
East Langwell 266 E1
East Lavant 108 A3
East Lavington 108 B2
East Layton 202 A1
East Leake 173 G5
East Learmouth 228 C3
East Learney 260 E4
East Leigh Devon 102 A2
East Leigh Devon 102 A1
East Leigh Devon 101 D2
East Leigh Devon 100 C2
East Lexham 163 G1
East Lilburn 229 E4
East Linton 236 C2
East Liss 120 C5
East Lockinge 133 G4
East Looe 97 G4
East Lound 187 E2
East Lulworth 105 E4
East Lutton 196 B1
East Lydford 116 C4
East Lyn 114 A3
East Lyng 116 A5
East Mains 260 E5
East Malling 123 G3
East Malling Heath 123 F3
East March 244 C1
East Marden 108 A2
East Markham 187 E5
East Martin 105 G1
East Marton 193 F2
East Meon 120 B5
East Mere 102 C1
East Mersea 139 D1
East Mey 275 J1
East Midlands Airport 173 F5
East Molesey 121 G1
East Moor 194 C5
East Morden 105 F3
East Morriston 236 D5
East Morton 194 A3
East Ness 203 F5
East Newton 197 E4
East Norton 160 C2
East Oakley 119 G2
East Ogwell 102 B5
East Orchard 105 E1
East Ord 237 G4
East Panson 99 D1
East Parley 106 A3
East Peckham 123 F4
East Pennard 116 C4
East Point Pavilion, Lowestoft Suff NR33 0AP 165 G2
East Portlemouth 100 D4
East Prawle 101 D4
East Preston 108 C3
East Pulham 104 D2
East Putford 113 D4
East Quantoxhead 115 E3
East Rainton 212 C3
East Ravendale 188 C3
East Raynham 177 G5
East Retford (Retford) 187 E4
East Rigton 194 C3
East Rolstone 116 A1
East Rounton 202 D2
East Row 204 B1
East Rudham 177 G5
East Runton 178 D1
East Ruston 179 E3
East Saltoun 236 B3
East Shefford 133 F5
East Sleekburn 221 E3
East Somerton 179 F4
East Stockwith 187 E3
East Stoke Dorset 105 E4
East Stoke Notts 174 C3
East Stour 117 F5
East Stourmouth 125 E2
East Stratton 119 G3
East Street 116 C4
East Studdal 125 F4
East Suisnish 256 B1
East Taphouse 97 F3
East Thirston 221 D2
East Tilbury 137 F5
East Tisted 120 C4
East Torrington 188 B4
East Town 116 D3
East Tuddenham 178 B4
East Tytherley 119 D5
East Tytherton 132 B5
East Village 102 B2
East Wall 157 E3
East Walton 163 F1
East Wellow 119 E5
East Wemyss 244 B5
East Whitburn 235 D3
East Wickham 137 D5
East Williamston 127 D2
East Winch 163 E1
East Winterslow 118 D4
East Wittering 107 G3
East Witton 202 A4
East Woodburn 220 B3
East Woodhay 119 F1
East Woodlands 117 E3
East Worldham 120 C4
East Worlington 102 A1
East Youlstone 112 C4
Eastacott 113 G3
Eastbourne 110 B4
Eastbourne Pier ESuss BN21 3EL 72 Eastbourne
Eastbrook 130 A5
Eastburn ERid 196 B2
Eastburn WYorks 193 G3
Eastbury Herts 136 A3
Eastbury WBerks 133 F5
Eastby 193 G2
Eastchurch 124 B1
Eastcombe Glos 132 A2
Eastcombe Som 115 E4
Eastcote GtLon 136 A4
Eastcote N'hants 148 B2
Eastcote WMid 159 D5
Eastcott Corn 112 C4
Eastcott Wilts 118 B2
Eastcourt 132 B3
Eastdown 101 E3
Eastend 147 F5
Easter Ardross 266 D4
Easter Balgedie 243 G4
Easter Balmoral 259 K5
Easter Boleskine 258 C2
Easter Borland 242 B4
Easter Brae 266 D5
Easter Buckieburn 234 B1
Easter Compton 131 E4
Easter Drummond 258 B3
Easter Dullater 242 B4
Easter Ellister 230 A4
Easter Fearn 266 D3
Easter Galcantray 267 F7
Easter Howlaws 237 E5
Easter Kinkell 266 C6
Easter Knox 253 D5
Easter Lednathie 252 B3
Easter Moniack 266 C7
Easter Ord 261 G4
Easter Poldar 242 B5
Easter Skeld (Skeld) 279 C8
Easter Suddie 266 D6
Easter Tulloch 253 F2
Easter Whyntie 268 E4
Eastergate 108 B3
Easterhouse 234 A3
Easterton 118 B2
Easterton Sands 118 B2
Eastertown 116 A2
Eastfield Bristol 131 E5
Eastfield NLan 234 C3
Eastfield NYorks 204 D4
Eastfield Hall 221 E1
Eastgate Dur 211 F4
Eastgate Lincs 161 G1
Eastgate Norf 178 C3
Easthall 150 A5
Eastham Mersey 183 E4
Eastham Worcs 145 F1
Easthampstead 121 D1
Easthampton 144 D1
Easthaugh 178 B4
Eastheath 120 D1
Easthope 157 E3
Easthorpe Essex 152 A5
Easthorpe Leics 174 D4
Easthorpe Notts 174 C2
Easthouses 236 A3
Eastington Devon 102 A2
Eastington Glos 132 D1
Eastington Glos 131 G2
Eastleach Martin 133 E2
Eastleach Turville 133 E2
Eastleigh Devon 113 E3
Eastleigh Hants 106 D1
Eastling 124 B3
Eastmoor Derbys 186 A5
Eastmoor Norf 163 F2
Eastnor 145 G4
Eastoft 187 F1
Eastoke 107 G3
Easton Cambs 161 G5
Easton Cumb 218 C4
Easton Cumb 209 F1
Easton Devon 102 A4
Easton Dorset 104 C5
Easton Hants 119 G4
Easton IoW 106 C4
Easton Lincs 175 E5
Easton Norf 178 C4
Easton Som 116 C3
Easton Suff 153 D2
Easton Wilts 132 A5
Easton Grey 132 A4
Easton Maudit 149 D2
Easton on the Hill 161 F2
Easton Royal 118 D1
Easton-in-Gordano 131 E5
Eastrea 162 A3
Eastriggs 218 A5
Eastrington 195 G4
Eastry 125 F3
Eastside 277 D8
East-the-Water 113 E3
Eastville 131 F5
Eastwell 174 C5
Eastwick 136 D1
Eastwood Notts 173 F3
Eastwood S'end 138 B4
Eastwood SYorks 186 B3
Eastwood WYorks 193 F5
Eastwood End 162 C3
Eathorpe 147 F1
Eaton ChesE 171 F1
Eaton ChesW&C 170 C1
Eaton Leics 174 C5
Eaton Norf 178 D5
Eaton Norf 177 E4
Eaton Notts 187 E5
Eaton Oxon 133 G2
Eaton Shrop 157 E3
Eaton Shrop 156 C4
Eaton Bishop 144 D4
Eaton Bray 149 E5
Eaton Constantine 157 F2
Eaton Ford 149 G2
Eaton Hall 170 B1
Eaton Hastings 133 E3
Eaton Socon 149 G2
Eaton upon Tern 171 D5
Eaves Green 159 E4
Eavestone 194 B1
Ebberston 204 B4
Ebbesborne Wake 118 A5
Ebbw Vale (Glynebwy) 130 A2
Ebchester 212 A2
Ebdon 116 A1
Ebford 102 C4
Ebley 132 A2
Ebnal 170 B3
Ebost 255 J1
Ebrington 147 D3
Ebsworthy Town 99 F1
Ecchinswell 119 F2
Ecclaw 237 E3
Ecclefechan 217 F3
Eccles GtMan 184 B3
Eccles Kent 123 G2
Eccles ScBord 237 E5
Eccles Green 144 C3
Eccles Road 164 B2
Ecclesfield 186 A3
Ecclesgreig 253 F3
Eccleshall 171 F5
Eccleshill 194 A4
Ecclesmachan 235 E2
Eccles-on-Sea 179 F3
Eccleston ChesW&C 170 B1
Eccleston Lancs 183 G1
Eccleston Mersey 183 F3
Eccup 194 B3
Echt 261 F4
Eckford 228 B4
Eckington Derbys 186 B5
Eckington Worcs 146 B3
Ecton N'hants 148 D1
Ecton Staffs 172 B2
Edale 185 F4
Eday 276 E4
Eday Airfield 276 E4
Edburton 109 E2
Edderside 209 E2
Edderton 266 E3
Eddington 119 E1
Eddleston 235 G5
Eden Camp NYorks YO17 6RT 204 B5
Eden Park 122 C2
Eden Project Corn PL24 2SG 97 E4
Eden Vale 212 D4
Edenbridge 122 D4
Edendonich 241 D2
Edenfield 184 B1
Edenhall 210 B4
Edenham 175 F5
Edensor 185 G5
Edentaggart 241 F5
Edenthorpe 186 D2
Edern 166 B4
Edgarley 116 C4
Edgbaston 158 C4
Edgcote 148 A3
Edgcott Bucks 148 B5
Edgcott Som 114 B4
Edgcumbe 95 E3
Edge Glos 132 A2
Edge Shrop 156 C2
Edge End 131 E1
Edge Green ChesW&C 170 B2
Edge Green GtMan 183 G3
Edge Green Norf 164 B3
Edgebolton 170 C5
Edgefield 178 B2
Edgehead 236 A3
Edgeley 170 C3
Edgerley 156 C1
Edgerton 185 F1
Edgeworth 132 B2
Edginswell 101 E1
Edgmond 157 G1
Edgmond Marsh 171 E5
Edgton 156 C4
Edgware 136 B3
Edgworth 184 B1
Edinample 242 B2
Edinbanchory 260 C3
Edinbane 263 J6
Edinbarnet 233 G2
Edinburgh 235 G2
Edinburgh Airport 235 F2
Edinburgh Castle Edin EH1 2NG 37 E4
Edinburgh Zoo Edin EH12 6TS 32 B2
Edinchip 242 A2
Edingale 159 E1
Edingley 174 B2
Edingthorpe 179 E2
Edingthorpe Green 179 E2
Edington Som 116 A4
Edington Wilts 118 A2
Edintore 268 C6
Edinvale 267 J6
Edistone 112 C3
Edith Weston 161 E2
Edithmead 116 A3
Edlaston 172 C3
Edlesborough 135 E1
Edlingham 220 D1
Edlington 188 C5
Edmondsham 105 G1
Edmondsley 212 B3
Edmondstown 129 G3
Edmondthorpe 161 D1
Edmonstone 276 E5
Edmonton Corn 97 D2
Edmonton GtLon 136 C3
Edmundbyers 211 G2
Ednam 228 B3
Ednaston 172 D3
Edney Common 137 F2
Edra 241 G3
Edradynate 251 D4
Edrom 237 F4
Edstaston 170 C4
Edstone 147 D1
Edvin Loach 145 F2
Edwalton 173 G4
Edwardstone 152 A3
Edwardsville 129 G3
Edwinsford 142 C4
Edwinstowe 174 B1
Edworth 150 A3
Edwyn Ralph 145 F2
Edzell 253 E3
Efail Isaf 129 G4
Efail-fâch 129 D3
Efailnewydd 166 C4
Efailwen 141 E5
Efenechtyd 169 E2
Effingham 121 G2
Effirth 279 C7
Efflinch 159 D1
Efford 102 B2
Egbury 119 F2
Egdean 121 E5
Egdon 146 B2
Egerton GtMan 184 B1
Egerton Kent 124 B4
Egerton Forstal 124 A4
Egerton Green 170 C2
Egg Buckland 100 A2
Eggborough 195 E5
Eggerness 207 E2
Eggesford Barton 113 G4
Eggington 149 E5
Egginton 173 D5
Egglescliffe 202 D1
Eggleston 211 F5
Egham 135 F5
Egham Wick 135 E5
Egilsay 276 D5
Egleton 161 D2
Eglingham 229 F5
Eglinton 233 D5
Egloshayle 97 E2
Egloskerry 97 G1
Eglwys Cross 170 B3
Eglwys Fach 154 C3
Eglwys Nunydd 129 E4
Eglwysbach 181 G5
Eglwys-Brewis 114 D1
Eglwyswrw 141 E4
Egmanton 174 C1
Egmere 178 A2
Egremont 208 D5
Egton 204 B2
Egton Bridge 204 B2
Egypt 119 F3
Eigg 247 D1
Eight Ash Green 152 A5
Eignaig 247 G5
Eil 259 F3
Eilanreach 256 E3
Eildon 227 G2
Eilean Darach 265 H3
Eilean Donan Castle High IV40 8DX 256 E2
Eilean Shona 247 F2
Einacleit 270 D5
Eisgean 271 F6
Eisingrug 167 F4
Eisteddfa Gurig 155 D4
Elan Valley Visitor Centre Powys LD6 5HP 143 F1
Elan Village 143 F1
Elberton 131 F4
Elborough 116 A2
Elburton 100 B2
Elcho 243 G2
Elcombe 132 D4
Elder Street 151 D4
Eldernell 162 B3
Eldersfield 145 G4
Elderslie 233 F3
Eldon 212 B5
Eldrick 215 D2
Eldroth 193 D1
Eldwick 194 A3
Elemore Vale 212 C3
Elford N'umb 229 F3
Elford Staffs 159 D1
Elford Closes 162 D5
Elgin 267 K5
Elgol 256 B3
Elham 125 D4
Elie 244 C4
Elilaw 220 B1
Elim 180 B4
Eling Hants 106 C1
Eling WBerks 134 A5
Eling Tide Mill Hants SO40 9HF 4 A3
Eliock 225 G5
Elishader 263 K5
Elishaw 220 A2
Elkesley 187 D5
Elkington 160 B5
Elkstone 132 B1
Elland 194 A5
Elland Upper Edge 194 A5
Ellary 231 F2
Ellastone 172 C3
Ellbridge 100 A1
Ellel 192 A2
Ellemford 237 E3
Ellenabeich 239 G3
Ellenborough 208 D3
Ellenhall 171 F5
Ellen's Green 121 F4
Ellerbeck 202 D3
Ellerby 203 G1
Ellerdine 170 D5
Ellerdine Heath 170 D5
Elleric (Eileirig) 248 C5
Ellerker 196 B5
Ellerton ERid 195 G3
Ellerton NYorks 202 B3
Ellerton Shrop 171 E5
Ellerton Abbey 201 F3
Ellesborough 134 D2
Ellesmere 170 A4
Ellesmere Park 184 B3
Ellesmere Port 183 F5
Ellingham Hants 106 A2
Ellingham N'umb 229 F4
Ellingham Norf 165 E2
Ellingstring 202 A4
Ellington Cambs 161 G5
Ellington N'umb 221 E2
Ellington Thorpe 161 G5
Elliot 245 E1
Elliot's Green 117 E3
Ellisfield 120 B3
Ellistown 159 G1
Ellon 261 H1
Ellonby 210 A4
Ellough 165 F3
Ellough Moor 165 F3
Elloughton 196 B5
Ellwood 131 E2
Elm 162 C2
Elm Park 137 E4
Elmbridge 146 B1
Elmdon Essex 150 C4
Elmdon WMid 159 D4
Elmdon Heath 159 D4
Elmers End 122 C2
Elmer's Green 183 F2
Elmesthorpe 159 G3
Elmhurst 158 D1
Elmley Castle 146 B3
Elmley Lovett 146 A1
Elmore 131 G1
Elmore Back 131 G1
Elmscott 112 C3
Elmsett 152 B3
Elmstead Essex 152 B5
Elmstead GtLon 136 D5
Elmstead Market 152 B5
Elmstone 125 E2
Elmstone Hardwicke 146 B5
Elmswell ERid 196 B2
Elmswell Suff 152 A1
Elmton 186 C5
Elphin 272 E7
Elphinstone 236 A2
Elrick Aber 261 G4
Elrick Moray 260 C2
Elrig 206 D2
Elrigbeag 240 D3
Elsdon 220 B2
Elsecar 186 A2
Elsecar Heritage Centre SYorks S74 8HJ 186 A3
Elsenham 150 D5
Elsfield 134 A1
Elsham 188 A1
Elsing 178 B4
Elslack 193 F3
Elson Hants 107 F2
Elson Shrop 170 A4
Elsrickle 235 E5
Elstead 121 E3
Elsted 108 A2
Elsthorpe 175 F5
Elstob 212 C5
Elston Lancs 192 B4
Elston Notts 174 C3
Elstone 113 G4
Elstow 149 F3
Elstree 136 A3
Elstronwick 197 E4
Elswick 192 A4
Elsworth 150 B1
Elterwater 199 E2
Eltham 136 D5
Eltisley 150 A2
Elton Cambs 161 F3
Elton ChesW&C 183 F5
Elton Derbys 172 D1
Elton Glos 131 G1
Elton GtMan 184 B1
Elton Here 157 D5
Elton Notts 174 C4
Elton Stock 202 D1
Elton Green 183 F5
Elvanfoot 226 A4
Elvaston 173 F4
Elvaston Castle Country Park Derbys DE72 3EP 18 C4
Elveden 163 G5
Elvingston 236 B2
Elvington Kent 125 E3
Elvington York 195 G3
Elwick Hart 213 D4
Elwick N'umb 229 F3
Elworth 171 E1
Elworthy 115 D4
Ely Cambs 162 D5
Ely Cardiff 130 A5
Emberton 149 D3
Emberton Country Park MK MK46 5FJ 149 D2
Embleton Cumb 209 E3
Embleton Hart 212 D5
Embleton N'umb 229 G4
Embo 267 F2
Embo Street 267 F2
Emborough 116 D2
Embsay 193 G2
Embsay Steam Railway NYorks BD23 6AF 193 G2
Emerson Park 137 E4
Emery Down 106 B2
Emley 185 G1
Emmington 134 C2
Emneth 162 C2
Emneth Hungate 162 D2
Empingham 161 E2
Empshott 120 C4
Empshott Green 120 C4
Emsworth 107 G2
Enborne 119 F1
Enborne Row 119 F1
Enchmarsh 157 E3
Enderby 160 A3
Endmoor 199 G4
Endon 171 G2
Endon Bank 171 G2
Enfield 136 C3
Enfield Wash 136 C3
Enford 118 C2
Engine Common 131 F4
Englefield 134 B5
Englefield Green 135 E5
Englesea-brook 171 E2
English Bicknor 131 E1
English Frankton 170 B5
Englishcombe 117 E1
Enham Alamein 119 E3
Enmore 115 F4
Ennerdale Bridge 209 D5
Enniscaven 97 D4
Ennochdhu 251 F3
Ensay 246 C5
Ensdon 156 D1
Ensis 113 F3
Enson 171 G5
Enstone 147 F5
Enterkinfoot 225 G5
Enterpen 203 D2
Enton Green 121 E3
Enville 158 A4
Eolaigearraidh 254 C4
Eorabus 238 C2
Eorodal 271 H1
Eoropaidh 271 H1
Epney 131 G1
Epperstone 174 B3
Epping 137 D2
Epping Green Essex 136 D2
Epping Green Herts 136 B2
Epping Upland 136 D2
Eppleby 202 A1
Eppleworth 196 C4
Epsom 122 B2
Epwell 147 F3
Epworth 187 E2
Epworth Turbary 187 E2
Erbistock 170 A3
Erbusaig 256 D2
Erchless Castle 266 B7
Erdington 158 D3
Eredine 240 B4
Eriboll 273 G3
Ericstane 226 B4
Eridge Green 123 E5
Eriff 224 D5
Erines 231 G2
Erisey Barton 95 E5
Eriskay (Eiriosgaigh) 254 C3
Eriswell 163 F5
Erith 137 E5
Erlestoke 118 A2
Ermington 100 C2
Ernesettle 100 A1
Erpingham 178 C2
Erringden Grange 193 F5
Errogie (Earagaidh) 258 C2
Errol 244 A2
Errollston 261 J1
Erskine 233 F2
Ervie 214 A4
Erwarton 152 D4
Erwood 143 G3
Eryholme 202 C2
Eryrys 169 F2
Escart 231 G3
Escart Farm 231 G4
Escomb 212 A5
Escrick 195 F3
Esgair 141 G5
Esgairgeiliog 155 D2
Esgyryn 181 G5
Esh 212 A3
Esh Winning 212 A3
Esher 121 G1
Eshott 221 E2
Eshton 193 F2
Eskadale 258 B1
Eskbank 236 A3
Eskdale Green 198 C2
Eskdalemuir 218 A2
Eskham 189 D3
Esknish 230 B3
Esperley Lane Ends 212 A5
Espley Hall 221 D2
Esprick 192 A4
Essendine 161 F1
Essendon 136 B2
Essich 258 D1
Essington 158 B2
Esslemont 261 H2
Eston 203 E1
Eswick 279 D7
Etal 228 D3
Etchilhampton 118 B1
Etchingham 110 C1
Etchinghill Kent 125 D5
Etchinghill Staffs 158 C1
Etherdwick Grange 197 E4
Etherley Dene 212 A5
Etherow Country Park GtMan SK6 5JQ 25 H5
Ethie Mains 253 E5
Eton 135 E5
Eton Wick 135 E5
Etteridge 258 D5
Ettiley Heath 171 E1
Ettington 147 E3
Etton ERid 196 B3
Etton Peter 161 G2
Ettrick 227 D4
Ettrickbridge 227 E3
Ettrickhill 227 D4
Etwall 173 D4
Eudon George 157 F4
Eurach 240 A4
Eureka! Museum for Children WYorks HX1 2NE 26 B4
Euston 163 G5
Euxton 183 G1
Evanstown 129 F4
Evanton 266 D5
Evedon 175 F3
Evelix 266 E2
Evenjobb 144 B1
Evenley 148 A4
Evenlode 147 E5
Evenwood 212 A5
Evenwood Gate 212 A5
Everbay 276 F5
Evercreech 116 D4
Everdon 148 A2
Everingham 196 A3
Everleigh 118 D2
Everley High 275 J2
Everley NYorks 204 C4
Eversholt 149 E4
Evershot 104 B2
Eversley 120 C1
Eversley Cross 120 C1
Everthorpe 196 B4
Everton CenBeds 150 A2
Everton Hants 106 B3
Everton Mersey 183 E3
Everton Notts 187 D3
Evertown 218 B4
Eves Corner 138 C3
Evesbatch 145 F3
Evesham 146 C3
Evesham Country Park Shopping & Garden Centre Worcs WR11 4TP 146 C3
Evie 276 C5
Evington 160 B2
Ewart Newtown 229 D3
Ewden Village 185 G3
Ewell 122 B2
Ewell Minnis 125 E4
Ewelme 134 B3
Ewen 132 C3
Ewenny 129 F5
Ewerby 175 G3
Ewerby Thorpe 175 G3
Ewhurst 121 F3
Ewhurst Green ESuss 110 C1
Ewhurst Green Surr 121 F4
Ewloe 170 A1
Ewloe Green 169 F1
Ewood 192 C5
Ewood Bridge 193 D5
Eworthy 99 E1
Ewshot 120 D3
Ewyas Harold 144 C5
Exbourne 113 G5
Exbury 106 D2
Exbury Gardens Hants SO45 1AZ 4 B6
Exceat 110 A4
Exebridge 114 C5
Exelby 202 B4
Exeter 102 C3
Exeter Cathedral Devon EX1 1HS 72 Exeter
Exeter International Airport 102 C3
Exford 114 B4
Exfords Green 157 D2
Exhall Warks 146 D2
Exhall Warks 159 F4
Exlade Street 134 B4
Exminster 102 C4
Exmoor International Dark Sky Reserve Devon/Som. 114 A3
Exmouth 102 D4
Exnaboe 279 F9
Exning 151 E1
Explore-At-Bristol BS1 5DB 66 Bristol
Exton Devon 102 C4
Exton Hants 120 B5
Exton Rut 161 E1
Exton Som 114 C4
Exwick 102 C3
Eyam 185 G5
Eydon 148 A3
Eye Here 145 D1
Eye Peter 162 A2
Eye Suff 164 C4
Eye Green 162 A2
Eyemouth 237 G3
Eyeworth 150 A3
Eyhorne Street 124 A3
Eyke 153 E2
Eynesbury 149 G2
Eynort 255 J2
Eynsford 123 E2
Eynsham 133 G2
Eype 104 A3
Eyre 263 K6
Eythorne 125 E4
Eyton Here 145 D1
Eyton Shrop 156 C4
Eyton on Severn 157 E2
Eyton upon the Weald Moors 157 F1
Eywood 144 C2

F

Faccombe **119** E2
Faceby **203** D2
Fachwen **167** E1
Facit **184** C1
Faddiley **170** C2
Fadmoor **203** F4
Faebait **266** B6
Faifley **233** G2
Fail **224** C3
Failand **131** E5
Failford **224** C3
Failsworth **184** C2
Fain **265** H4
Fair Isle **278** A1
Fair Isle Airstrip **278** A1
Fair Oak *Devon* **102** D1
Fair Oak *Hants* **107** D1
Fair Oak *Hants* **119** G1
Fair Oak Green **120** B1
Fairbourne **154** C1
Fairburn **195** D5
Fairfield *Derbys* **185** E5
Fairfield *GtMan* **184** D3
Fairfield *Kent* **111** E1
Fairfield *Mersey* **183** D4
Fairfield *Stock* **202** D1
Fairfield *Worcs* **158** B5
Fairfield Halls, Croydon *GtLon* CR9 1DG **122** C2
Fairford **132** D2
Fairgirth **216** C5
Fairhaven **191** G5
Fairhill **234** B4
Fairholm **234** B4
Fairlands Valley Park *Herts* SG2 0BL **150** A5
Fairley **261** G4
Fairlie **232** D4
Fairlight **111** D2
Fairlight Cove **111** D2
Fairmile *Devon* **103** D3
Fairmile *Surr* **121** G1
Fairmilehead **235** G3
Fairnington **228** A4
Fairoak **171** E4
Fairseat **123** F2
Fairstead **137** G1
Fairwarp **109** G1
Fairwater **130** A5
Fairy Cross **113** E3
Fairyhill **128** A3
Fakenham **178** A3
Fakenham Magna **164** A4
Fala **236** B3
Fala Dam **236** B3
Falahill **236** A4
Faldingworth **188** A4
Falfield *Fife* **244** C4
Falfield *SGlos* **131** F3
Falin-Wnda **141** G3
Falkenham **153** D4
Falkirk **234** C2
Falkirk Wheel *Falk* FK1 4RS **234** C1
Falkland **244** A4
Falla **228** B5
Fallgate **173** E1
Fallin **242** D5
Falmer **109** F3
Falmouth **95** F3
Falsgrave **204** D4
Falstone **219** F3
Famous Grouse Experience, Glenturret Distillery *P&K* PH7 4HA **243** D2
Fanagmore **272** D4
Fanans **240** C2
Fancott **149** F5
Fangdale Beck **203** E3
Fangfoss **195** G2
Fankerton **234** B1
Fanmore **246** D5
Fanner's Green **137** F1
Fans **236** D5
Fantasy Island *Lincs* PE25 1RH **177** D1
Far Cotton **148** C2
Far Forest **157** G5
Far Gearstones **200** C4
Far Green **131** G2
Far Moor **183** G2
Far Oakridge **132** B2
Far Royds **194** B4
Far Sawrey **199** E3
Farcet **162** A3
Farden **157** E5
Fareham **107** E2
Farewell **158** C1
Farforth **188** D5
Faringdon **133** E3
Farington **192** B5
Farlam **210** B2
Farlary **266** E1
Farleigh *NSom* **116** C1
Farleigh *Surr* **122** C2
Farleigh Hungerford **117** F2
Farleigh Wallop **120** B3
Farlesthorpe **189** E5
Farleton *Cumb* **199** G4
Farleton *Lancs* **192** B1
Farley *Derbys* **173** D1
Farley *Shrop* **156** C2
Farley *Staffs* **172** B3
Farley *Wilts* **118** D5
Farley Green *Suff* **151** F2
Farley Green *Surr* **121** F3
Farley Hill **120** C1
Farleys End **131** G1
Farlington **195** F1
Farlow **157** F4
Farm Town **159** F1
Farmborough **117** D1
Farmcote **146** C5
Farmington **132** D1
Farmoor **133** G2
Farmtown **268** D5
Farnborough *GtLon* **122** D2
Farnborough *Hants* **121** D2
Farnborough *Warks* **147** G3
Farnborough *WBerks* **133** G4
Farnborough Street **121** D2
Farncombe **121** E3
Farndish **149** E1
Farndon *ChesW&C* **170** B2
Farndon *Notts* **174** C2
Farne Islands **229** G3
Farnell **253** E4
Farnham *Dorset* **105** F1
Farnham *Essex* **150** C5
Farnham *NYorks* **194** C1
Farnham *Suff* **153** E1
Farnham *Surr* **120** D3
Farnham Common **135** E4
Farnham Green **150** C5
Farnham Royal **135** E4
Farningham **123** E2
Farnley *NYorks* **194** B3
Farnley *WYorks* **194** B4
Farnley Tyas **185** F1
Farnsfield **174** B2
Farnworth *GtMan* **184** B2
Farnworth *Halton* **183** G4
Farr *High* **274** C2
Farr *High* **258** D1
Farr *High* **259** F4
Farr House **258** D1
Farraline **258** C2
Farringdon **102** D3
Farrington Gurney **116** D2
Farsley **194** B4
Farthing Corner **124** A2
Farthing Green **124** A4
Farthinghoe **148** A4
Farthingstone **148** B2
Farthorpe **188** C5
Fartown **185** F1
Farway **103** E3
Fasag **264** E6
Fasagrianach **265** H3
Fascadale **247** E2
Fashion Museum *B&NESom* BA1 2QH **63** Bath
Faslane **232** D1
Fasnacloich **248** C5
Fasnakyle **257** K2
Fassfern **248** C2
Fatfield **212** C2
Fattahead **268** E5
Faugh **210** B2
Fauldhouse **234** D3
Faulkbourne **137** G1
Faulkland **117** E2
Fauls **170** C4
Faulston **118** B5
Faversham **124** C2
Favillar **259** K1
Fawdington **202** D5
Fawdon **212** B1
Fawfieldhead **172** B1
Fawkham Green **123** E2
Fawler **133** F1
Fawley *Bucks* **134** C4
Fawley *Hants* **107** D2
Fawley *WBerks* **133** F4
Fawley Chapel **145** E5
Fawsyde **253** G2
Faxfleet **196** A5
Faxton **160** C5
Faygate **122** B5
Fazakerley **183** E3
Fazeley **159** E2
Fearby **202** A4
Fearn **267** F4
Fearnan **250** C5
Fearnbeg **264** D6
Fearnhead **184** A3
Fearnmore **264** D5
Fearnoch *A&B* **232** B2
Fearnoch *A&B* **232** A1
Featherstone *Staffs* **158** B2
Featherstone *WYorks* **194** D5
Featherstone Castle **210** C1
Feckenham **146** C1
Feering **151** G5
Feetham **201** E3
Feith-hill **268** E6
Feizor **193** D1
Felbridge **122** C5
Felbrigg **178** D2
Felcourt **122** C4
Felden **135** F2
Felhampton **156** D4
Felindre *Carmar* **142** D5
Felindre *Carmar* **142** B5
Felindre *Carmar* **141** G4
Felindre *Carmar* **142** C4
Felindre *Cere* **142** B2
Felindre *Powys* **156** A4
Felindre *Powys* **144** A5
Felindre *Swan* **128** C2
Felinfach *Cere* **142** B2
Felinfach *Powys* **143** G4
Felinfoel **128** B2
Felingwmisaf **142** B5
Felingwmuchaf **142** B5
Felixkirk **203** D4
Felixstowe **153** E4
Felixstowe Ferry **153** E4
Felkington **237** G5
Felldownhead **99** D2
Felling **212** B1
Fellonmore **239** F2
Felmersham **149** E2
Felmingham **179** D3
Felpham **108** B4
Felsham **152** A2
Felsted **151** E5
Feltham **136** A5
Felthamhill **136** A5
Felthorpe **178** C4
Felton *Here* **145** E3
Felton *N'umb* **221** D1
Felton *NSom* **116** C1
Felton Butler **156** C1
Feltwell **163** F3
Fen Ditton **150** C1
Fen Drayton **150** B1
Fen End **159** E5
Fen Street *Norf* **164** A2
Fen Street *Norf* **164** B4
Fen Street *Suff* **164** A4
Fen Street *Suff* **152** C1
Fenay Bridge **185** F1
Fence **193** E4
Fence Houses **212** C2
Fencott **134** A1
Fendike Corner **176** C1
Fenham **229** E2
Fenhouses **176** A3
Feniscowles **192** C5
Feniton **103** E3
Fenn Street **137** G5
Fenni-fach **143** G5
Fenny Bentley **172** C2
Fenny Bridges **103** E3
Fenny Compton **147** G2
Fenny Drayton **159** F3
Fenny Stratford **149** D4
Fenrother **221** D2
Fenstanton **150** B1
Fenton *Cambs* **162** B5
Fenton *Lincs* **187** F5
Fenton *Lincs* **175** D2
Fenton *N'umb* **229** D3
Fenton *Notts* **187** E4
Fenton *Stoke* **171** F3
Fenton Barns **236** C1
Fenwick *EAyr* **233** F5
Fenwick *N'umb* **220** C4
Fenwick *N'umb* **229** E2
Fenwick *SYorks* **186** C1
Feochaig **222** C4
Feock **95** F3
Feolin **230** D3
Feolin Ferry **230** C3
Feorlan **222** B5
Feorlin **240** B5
Ferens Art Gallery HU1 3RA **76** Kingston upon Hull
Ferguslie Park **233** F3
Feriniquarrie **263** G6
Fern **252** C3
Ferndale **129** F3
Ferndown **105** G2
Ferness **267** G7
Fernham **133** E3
Fernhill Heath **146** A2
Fernhurst **121** D5
Fernie **244** B3
Fernilea **255** J1
Fernilee **185** E5
Fernybank **252** D2
Ferrensby **194** C1
Ferrers Centre for Arts & Crafts *Leics* LE65 1RU **173** E5
Ferrindonald **256** C4
Ferring **108** C3
Ferry Hill **162** B4
Ferrybridge **195** D5
Ferryden **253** F4
Ferryhill **212** B4
Ferryside (Glanyferi) **127** G1
Fersfield **164** B3
Fersit **249** F2
Ferwig **141** E3
Feshiebridge **259** F4
Festival Park *BGwent* NP23 8FP **130** A2
Fetcham **121** G2
Fetlar **278** F3
Fetlar Airport **278** F3
Fetterangus **269** H5
Fettercairn **253** E2
Fetternear House **261** F3
Feus of Caldhame **253** E3
Fewcott **148** A5
Fewston **194** A2
Ffairfach **142** C5
Ffair-Rhos **142** D1
Ffaldybrenin **142** C3
Ffarmers **142** C3
Ffawyddog **130** B1
Ffestiniog (Llan Ffestiniog) **168** A3
Ffestiniog Railway *Gwyn* LL49 9NF **167** F3
Ffordd-las *Denb* **169** E1
Fforddlas *Powys* **144** B4
Fforest **128** B2
Fforest-fach **128** C3
Ffostrasol **141** G3
Ffos-y-ffin **142** A1
Ffridd Uchaf **167** E2
Ffrith *Denb* **182** B4
Ffrith *Flints* **169** F2
Ffrwdgrech **143** G5
Ffynnon **127** G1
Ffynnongroyw **182** C4
Fibhig **270** E3
Fichlie **260** C3
Fidden **238** C2
Fiddington *Glos* **146** B4
Fiddington *Som* **115** F3
Fiddleford **105** E1
Fiddler's Green *Glos* **146** B5
Fiddler's Green *Here* **145** E4
Fiddler's Green *Norf* **163** G1
Fiddler's Green *Norf* **164** B2
Fiddlers Hamlet **137** D2
Field **172** B4
Field Broughton **199** E4
Field Dalling **178** B2
Field Head **159** G2
Fife Keith **268** C5
Fifehead Magdalen **117** E5
Fifehead Neville **105** D1
Fifehead St. Quintin **105** D1
Fifield *Oxon* **133** E1
Fifield *W&M* **135** E5
Fifield Bavant **118** B5
Figheldean **118** C3
Filby **179** F4
Filey **205** E4
Filgrave **149** D3
Filham **100** C2
Filkins **133** E2
Filleigh *Devon* **113** G3
Filleigh *Devon* **102** A1
Fillingham **187** G4
Fillongley **159** E4
Filmore Hill **120** B5
Filton **131** F5
Fimber **196** A1
Finavon **252** C4
Fincham **163** E2
Finchampstead **120** C1
Finchdean **107** G1
Finchingfield **151** E4
Finchley **136** B3
Findern **173** E4
Findhorn **267** H5
Findhorn Bridge **259** F2
Findhuglen **242** C3
Findo Gask **243** F2
Findochty **268** C4
Findon *Aber* **261** H5
Findon *WSuss* **108** D3
Findon Mains **266** D5
Findon Valley **108** D3
Findrassie **267** J5
Findron **259** J3
Finedon **161** E5
Finegand **251** G3
Fingal Street **164** D4
Fingask **261** F2
Fingerpost **157** G5
Fingest **134** C3
Finghall **202** A4
Fingland *Cumb* **209** F1
Fingland *D&G* **226** D5
Fingland *D&G* **225** F4
Finglesham **125** F3
Fingringhoe **152** B5
Finkle Street **186** A3
Finlarig **242** A1
Finmere **148** B4
Finnart *A&B* **241** E5
Finnart *P&K* **250** A4
Finney Hill **159** G1
Finningham **152** B1
Finningley **187** D3
Finnygaud **268** E5
Finsbay (Fionnsbhagh) **263** F3
Finsbury **136** C4
Finstall **158** B5
Finsthwaite **199** E4
Finstock **133** F1
Finstown **277** C6
Fintry *Aber* **269** F5
Fintry *Stir* **234** A1
Finwood **147** D1
Finzean **260** D5
Fionnphort **238** B2
Fir Tree **212** A4
Firbank **200** B3
Firbeck **186** C4
Firby *NYorks* **202** B4
Firby *NYorks* **195** G1
Firgrove **184** D1
Firs Lane **184** A2
Firsby **176** C1
Firsdown **118** D4
Firth **278** D5
Fishbourne *IoW* **107** E3
Fishbourne *WSuss* **108** A3
Fishburn **212** C4
Fishcross **243** E5
Fisherford **260** E1
Fishers Farm Park *WSuss* RH14 0EG **121** F5
Fisher's Pond **119** F5
Fisher's Row **192** A3
Fishersgate **109** E3
Fisherstreet **121** E4
Fisherton *High* **266** E6
Fisherton *SAyr* **224** A4
Fisherton de la Mere **118** A4
Fishguard (Abergwaun) **140** C4
Fishlake **187** D1
Fishleigh Barton **113** F3
Fishley **179** F4
Fishnish **247** F5
Fishpond Bottom **103** G3
Fishponds **131** F5
Fishpool **184** C2
Fishtoft **176** B3
Fishtoft Drove **176** B3
Fishtown of Usan **253** F4
Fishwick **237** G4
Fiskerton *Lincs* **188** A5
Fiskerton *Notts* **174** C2
Fitling **197** E4
Fittleton **118** C3
Fittleworth **108** C2
Fitton End **162** C1
Fitz **156** D1
Fitzhead **115** E5
Fitzroy **115** E5
Fitzwilliam **186** B1
Fitzwilliam Museum *Cambs* CB2 1RB **66** Cambridge
Fiunary **247** F5
Five Acres **131** E1
Five Ash Down **109** G1
Five Ashes **110** A1
Five Bridges **145** F3
Five Houses **106** D4
Five Lanes **130** D3
Five Oak Green **123** F4
Five Oaks *Chanl* **100** C5
Five Oaks *WSuss* **121** F5
Five Roads **128** A2
Five Turnings **156** B5
Five Wents **124** A3
Fivehead **116** A5
Fivelanes **97** G1
Flack's Green **137** G1
Flackwell Heath **135** D4
Fladbury **146** B3
Fladdabister **279** D9
Flagg **172** C1
Flambards Experience, The *Corn* TR13 0QA **95** D4
Flamborough **205** F5
Flamingo Land Theme Park *NYorks* YO17 6UX **203** G4
Flamingo Park, Hastings *ESuss* TN34 3AR **110** D3
Flamstead **135** F1
Flamstead End **136** C2
Flansham **108** B3
Flanshaw **194** C5
Flasby **193** F2
Flash **172** B1
Flashader **263** J6
Flask Inn **204** C2
Flatts Lane Woodland Country Park *R&C* TS6 0NN **29** D4
Flaunden **135** F2
Flawborough **174** C3
Flawith **195** D1
Flax Bourton **116** C1
Flax Moss **193** D5
Flaxby **194** C2
Flaxholme **173** E3
Flaxlands **164** C2
Flaxley **131** F1
Flaxpool **115** E4
Flaxton **195** F1
Fleckney **160** B3
Flecknoe **148** A1
Fledborough **187** F5
Fleet *Hants* **120** D2
Fleet *Hants* **107** G2
Fleet *Lincs* **176** B5
Fleet Air Arm Museum *Som* BA22 8HT **116** C5
Fleet Hargate **176** B5
Fleetville **136** A2
Fleetwood **191** G3
Flegburgh (Burgh St. Margaret) **179** F4
Flemingston **129** G5
Flemington **234** A4
Flempton **151** G1
Fleoideabhagh **263** F3
Flesherin **271** H4
Fletchersbridge **97** F3
Fletchertown **209** F2
Fletching **109** G1
Fleuchats **260** B4
Fleur-de-lis **130** A3
Flexbury **112** C5
Flexford **121** E2
Flimby **208** D3
Flimwell **123** G5
Flint (Y Fflint) **182** D5
Flint Cross **150** C3
Flint Mountain **182** D5
Flintham **174** C3
Flinton **197** E4
Flint's Green **159** E4
Flishinghurst **123** G5
Flitcham **177** F5
Flitholme **200** C1
Flitton **149** F4
Flitwick **149** F4
Flixborough **187** F1
Flixton *GtMan* **184** B3
Flixton *NYorks* **204** D5
Flixton *Suff* **165** E3
Flockton **185** G1
Flockton Green **185** G1
Flodden **228** D3
Flodigarry **263** K4
Flood's Ferry **162** B3
Flookburgh **199** E5
Floors **268** C5
Flordon **164** C2
Flore **148** B1
Flotta **277** C8
Flotterton **220** C1
Flowton **152** B3
Flushdyke **194** B5
Flushing *Aber* **269** J6
Flushing *Corn* **95** F3
Flushing *Corn* **95** E4
Fluxton **103** D3
Flyford Flavell **146** B2
Foals Green **165** D4
Fobbing **137** G4
Fochabers **268** B5
Fochriw **130** A2
Fockerby **187** F1
Fodderletter **259** J2
Fodderty **266** C6
Foddington **116** C5
Foel **155** F1
Foelgastell **128** B1
Foggathorpe **195** G4
Fogo **237** E5
Fogorig **237** E5
Fogwatt **267** K6
Foindle **272** D4
Folda **251** G3
Fole **172** B4
Foleshill **159** F4
Folke **104** C1
Folkestone **125** E5
Folkingham **175** F4
Folkington **110** A3
Folksworth **161** G4
Folkton **205** D5
Folla Rule **261** F1
Follifoot **194** C2
Folly *Dorset* **104** D2
Folly *Pembs* **140** C5
Folly Farm, Begelly *Pembs* SA68 0XA **127** E2
Folly Gate **99** F1
Fonmon **115** D1
Fonthill Bishop **118** A4
Fonthill Gifford **118** A4
Fontmell Magna **105** E1
Fontmell Parva **105** E1
Fontwell **108** B3
Font-y-gary **115** D1
Foolow **185** F5
Footherley **158** D2
Foots Cray **137** D5
Forbestown **260** B3
Force Forge **199** E3
Force Green **122** D3
Forcett **202** A1
Forches Cross **102** A2
Ford *A&B* **240** A4
Ford *Bucks* **134** C2
Ford *Devon* **100** C2
Ford *Devon* **113** E3
Ford *Devon* **101** D3
Ford *Glos* **146** C5
Ford *Mersey* **183** E3
Ford *Midlo* **236** A3
Ford *N'umb* **229** D3
Ford *Pembs* **140** C5
Ford *Plym* **100** A2
Ford *Shrop* **156** D1
Ford *Som* **115** D5
Ford *Staffs* **172** B2
Ford *Wilts* **132** A5
Ford *WSuss* **108** B3
Ford End **137** F1
Ford Green **192** A3
Ford Heath **156** D1
Ford Street **103** E1
Forda **99** F1
Fordbridge **159** D4
Fordcombe **123** E4
Fordell **235** F1
Forden (Fordun) **156** B2
Forder Green **101** D1
Fordgate **116** A4
Fordham *Cambs* **163** E5
Fordham *Essex* **152** A5
Fordham *Norf* **163** E3
Fordham Abbey **151** E1
Fordham Heath **152** A5
Fordhouses **158** B2
Fordingbridge **106** A1
Fordon **205** D5
Fordoun **253** F2
Ford's Green **152** B1
Fordstreet **152** A5
Fordwells **133** F1
Fordwich **125** D3
Fordyce **268** D4
Forebrae **243** E2
Forebridge **171** G5
Foredale **193** E1
Foreland **230** A3
Foremark **173** E5
Foremark Reservoir *Derbys* DE65 6EG **173** E5
Forest **202** B2
Forest Coal Pit **144** B5
Forest Gate **136** D4
Forest Green **121** G3
Forest Hall *Cumb* **199** G2
Forest Hall *T&W* **212** B1
Forest Head **210** B2
Forest Hill *GtLon* **136** C5
Forest Hill *Oxon* **134** A2
Forest Lane Head **194** C2
Forest Lodge (Taigh na Frithe) *A&B* **249** E5
Forest Lodge *P&K* **251** E2
Forest Row **122** D5
Forest Side **107** D4
Forest Town **173** G1
Forestburn Gate **220** C2
Forest-in-Teesdale **211** E5
Forestmill **243** E5
Forestside **107** G1
Forfar **252** C4
Forfar Loch Country Park *Angus* DD8 1BT **252** C4
Forgandenny **243** F3
Forge **155** D3
Forgie **268** B5
Forhill **158** C5
Formby **183** D2
Forncett End **164** C2
Forncett St. Mary **164** C2
Forncett St. Peter **164** C2
Forneth **251** F5
Fornham All Saints **151** G1
Fornham St. Martin **151** G1
Fornighty **267** G6
Forres **267** H6
Forrest **234** C3
Forrest Lodge **215** G2
Forsbrook **171** G3
Forse **275** H5
Forsie **275** F2
Forsinain **274** E4
Forsinard **274** D4
Forston **104** C3
Fort Augustus (Cille Chuimein) **257** K4
Fort Fun, Eastbourne *ESuss* BN22 7LQ **110** B3
Fort George **266** E6
Fort William (An Gearasdan) **248** D2
Forter **251** G3
Forteviot **243** F3
Forth **234** D4
Forthampton **146** A4
Fortingall **250** C5
Fortis Green **136** B4
Forton *Hants* **119** F3
Forton *Lancs* **192** A2
Forton *Shrop* **156** D1
Forton *Som* **103** G2
Forton *Staffs* **171** E5
Fortrie **268** E6
Fortrose (A'Chananaich) **266** E6
Fortuneswell **104** C5
Forty Green **135** E3
Forty Hill **136** C3
Forward Green **152** B2
Fosbury **119** E2
Foscot **147** E5
Fosdyke **176** B4
Foss **250** C4
Foss Cross **132** C2
Fossdale **201** D3
Fossebridge **132** C1
Foster Street **137** D2
Fosterhouses **186** D1
Foster's Booth **148** B2
Foston *Derbys* **172** C4
Foston *Leics* **160** B3
Foston *Lincs* **175** D3
Foston *NYorks* **195** F1
Foston on the Wolds **196** D2
Fotherby **188** D3
Fotheringhay **161** F3
Foubister **277** E7
Foul Mile **110** B2
Foula **278** B1
Foula Airstrip **278** B1
Foulbog **226** D5
Foulden *Norf* **163** F3
Foulden *ScBord* **237** G4
Foulness Island **138** D3
Foulridge **193** E3
Foulsham **178** B3
Foulstone **199** G4
Foulzie **269** F4
Fountainhall **236** B5
Four Ashes *Staffs* **158** B2
Four Ashes *Staffs* **158** A4
Four Ashes *Suff* **164** A4
Four Crosses *Denb* **168** D3
Four Crosses *Powys* **156** B1
Four Crosses *Powys* **155** G2
Four Crosses *Staffs* **158** B2
Four Elms **123** D4
Four Forks **115** F4
Four Gotes **162** C1
Four Lane Ends *B'burn* **192** C5
Four Lane Ends *ChesW&C* **170** C1
Four Lane Ends *York* **195** F2
Four Lanes **95** D3
Four Marks **120** B4
Four Mile Bridge **180** A5
Four Oaks *ESuss* **111** D1
Four Oaks *Glos* **145** F5
Four Oaks *WMid* **159** E4
Four Oaks *WMid* **158** D3
Four Oaks Park **158** D3
Four Roads **128** A2
Four Throws **110** C1
Fourlane Ends **173** E2
Fourlanes End **171** F2
Fourpenny **267** F2
Fourstones **211** E1
Fovant **118** B5
Foveran House **261** H2
Fowey **97** F4
Fowlis **244** B1
Fowlis Wester **243** E2
Fowlmere **150** C3
Fownhope **145** E4
Fox Hatch **137** E3
Fox Lane **121** D2
Fox Street **152** B5
Fox Up **201** D5
Foxbar **233** F3
Foxcombe Hill **133** G2
Foxcote *Glos* **132** C1
Foxcote *Som* **117** E2
Foxdale **190** A4
Foxearth **151** G3
Foxfield **198** D4
Foxham **132** B5
Foxhole *Corn* **97** D4
Foxhole *High* **258** C1
Foxholes **204** D5
Foxhunt Green **110** A2
Foxley *Here* **144** D3
Foxley *N'hants* **148** B2
Foxley *Norf* **178** B3
Foxley *Wilts* **132** A4
Foxt **172** B3
Foxton *Cambs* **150** C3
Foxton *Dur* **212** C5
Foxton *Leics* **160** B3
Foxton Locks *Leics* LE16 7RA **160** B4
Foxwist Green **170** D1
Foy **145** E5
Foyers (Foithir) **258** B2
Frachadil **246** C4
Fraddam **94** C3
Fraddon **96** D4
Fradley **159** D1
Fradswell **171** G4
Fraisthorpe **197** D1
Framfield **109** G1
Framingham Earl **179** D5
Framingham Pigot **179** D5
Framlingham **153** D1
Frampton *Dorset* **104** C3
Frampton *Lincs* **176** B4
Frampton Cotterell **131** F4
Frampton Mansell **132** B2
Frampton on Severn **131** G2
Frampton West End **176** A3
Framsden **152** D2
Framwellgate Moor **212** B3
France Lynch **132** B2
Frances Green **192** C4
Franche **158** A5
Frandley **184** A5
Frankby **182** D4
Frankfort **179** E3
Frankley **158** B4
Franksbridge **144** A2
Frankton **159** G5
Frant **123** E5
Fraserburgh **269** H4
Frating **152** B5
Fratton **107** F2
Freasley **159** E3
Freathy **99** D5
Freckenham **163** E5
Freckleton **192** A5
Freeby **174** D5
Freefolk **119** F3
Freehay **172** B3
Freeland **133** G1
Freester **279** D7
Freethorpe **179** F5
Freethorpe Common **179** F5
Freiston **176** B3
Freiston Shore **176** B3
Fremington *Devon* **113** F2
Fremington *NYorks* **201** F3
French Brothers Cruises *W&M* SL4 5JH **135** E5
Frenchay **131** F5
Frenchbeer **99** G2
Frendraught **268** E6
Frenich **241** G4
Frensham **120** D3
Fresgoe **274** E2
Freshbrook **132** D4
Freshfield **183** D2
Freshford **117** E1
Freshwater **106** C4
Freshwater Bay **106** C4
Freshwater East **126** D3
Fressingfield **165** D4
Freston **152** C4
Freswick **275** J2
Fretherne **131** G2
Frettenham **178** D4
Freuchie **244** A4
Freystrop Cross **126** C1
Friars, The, Aylesford *Kent* ME20 7BX **123** G3
Friars Carse **216** D2
Friar's Gate **123** D5
Friarton **243** G2

Friday Bridge 162 C2
Friday Street ESuss 110 B3
Friday Street Suff 152 D2
Friday Street Suff 153 E2
Friday Street Surr 121 G3
Fridaythorpe 196 A4
Friern Barnet 136 B3
Friesthorpe 188 A4
Frieston 175 E3
Frieth 134 C3
Frilford 133 G3
Frilsham 134 A5
Frimley 121 D2
Frimley Green 121 D2
Frindsbury 123 G2
Fring 177 F4
Fringford 148 B5
Friningham 124 A3
Frinsted 124 A3
Frinton-on-Sea 139 F1
Friockheim 253 D5
Friog 154 C1
Frisby on the
   Wreake 160 B1
Friskney 176 C2
Friskney
   Eaudyke 176 C2
Friston ESuss 110 A4
Friston Suff 153 F1
Fritchley 173 E2
Frith 124 B3
Frith Bank 176 B3
Frith Common 145 F1
Fritham 106 B1
Frithelstock 113 E4
Frithelstock
   Stone 113 E4
Frithville 176 B2
Frittenden 124 A4
Frittiscombe 101 E3
Fritton Norf 164 D2
Fritton Norf 179 F5
Fritwell 148 A5
Frizinghall 194 A4
Frizington 208 D5
Frocester 131 G2
Frochas 156 B2
Frodesley 157 E2
Frodesley Lane 157 E2
Frodingham 187 F1
Frodsham 183 G5
Frog End 150 C2
Frog Pool 145 G1
Frogden 228 B4
Froggatt 185 G5
Froghall 172 B3
Frogham 106 A1
Frogland Cross 131 F4
Frogmore Devon 101 D3
Frogmore Hants 120 D2
Frogmore Herts 136 A2
Frogwell 98 D4
Frolesworth 160 A3
Frome 117 E3
Frome Market 117 F2
Frome St. Quintin 104 B2
Frome Whitfield 104 C3
Fromes Hill 145 F3
Fron Gwyn 166 C4
Fron Powys 156 B2
Fron Powys 143 E2
Fron Powys 156 A3
Fron Isaf 169 F4
Froncysyllte 169 F3
Fron-goch 166 A2
Frostenden 165 F3
Frosterley 211 G4
Froxfield 119 E1
Froxfield Green 120 C5
Fruitmarket Gallery Edin
   EH1 1DF 37 G4
Fryerning 137 F2
Fugglestone
   St. Peter 118 C4
Fulbeck 175 E2
Fulbourn 150 D2
Fulbrook 133 E1
Fulflood 119 F5
Fulford Som 115 F5
Fulford Staffs 171 G4
Fulford York 195 F3
Fulham 136 B5
Fulking 109 E2
Full Sutton 195 G2
Fullaford 113 G2
Fuller Street 137 G1
Fuller's Moor 170 B2
Fullerton 119 E4
Fulletby 188 C5
Fullwood 233 F4
Fulmer 135 F4
Fulmodeston 178 A2
Fulnetby 188 B5
Fulready 147 E3
Fulstone 185 F2
Fulstow 188 D3
Fulwell Oxon 147 F5
Fulwell T&W 212 C2
Fulwood Lancs 192 B4
Fulwood SYorks 186 A4
Fun Farm, Spalding Lincs
   PE12 6JU 176 A5
Fundenhall 164 C2
Fundenhall
   Street 164 C2
Funtington 108 A3
Funtley 107 E2
Funzie 278 F3
Furley 103 F2
Furnace A&B 240 C4
Furnace Carmar 128 B2
Furnace Cere 154 C3
Furnace High 265 F4
Furnace End 159 E3
Furner's Green 109 G1
Furness Vale 185 E4
Furneux Pelham 150 C5
Furnham 103 G2
Further Quarter 124 A5
Furtho 148 C3
Furze Green 164 D3
Furze Platt 135 D4
Furzehill Devon 114 A3
Furzehill Dorset 105 G2
Furzeley Corner 107 F1
Furzey Lodge 106 C2
Furzley 106 B1
Fyfett 103 F1

Fyfield Essex 137 E2
Fyfield Glos 133 E2
Fyfield Hants 119 D3
Fyfield Oxon 133 G3
Fyfield Wilts 118 C1
Fyfield Wilts 118 C1
Fylingthorpe 204 C2
Fyning 120 D5
Fyvie 261 F1

G
Gabalfa 130 A5
Gabhsunn Bho
   Dheas 271 G2
Gabhsunn Bho
   Thuath 271 G2
Gablon 266 E2
Gabroc Hill 233 F4
Gaddesby 160 B1
Gaddesden Row 135 F1
Gadebridge 135 F2
Gadshill 137 G5
Gaer Newport 130 B4
Gaer Powys 144 A5
Gaer-fawr 130 D3
Gaerllwyd 130 D3
Gaerwen 180 C5
Gagingwell 147 G5
Gaich High 259 H2
Gaich High 258 C1
Gailes 224 B2
Gailey 158 B1
Gainford 202 A1
Gainsborough 187 F3
Gainsford End 151 F4
Gairloch
   (Geàrrloch) 264 D4
Gairlochy (Geàrr
   Lòchaidh) 249 D1
Gairney Bank 243 G5
Gairnshiel Lodge 259 K4
Gaitsgill 209 G2
Galabank 236 B5
Galashiels 227 F2
Galdenoch 214 C4
Gale 184 D1
Galgate 192 A3
Galhampton 116 D5
Gallanach 240 A2
Gallantry Bank 170 C2
Gallatown 244 A5
Gallchoille 239 G5
Gallery 253 E5
Gallery of Modern Art,
   Glasgow Glas
   G1 3AH 39 F4
Galley Common 159 F3
Galleyend 137 G2
Galleywood 137 G2
Galloway Forest Dark Sky
   Park D&G 215 F2
Gallowfauld 252 C5
Gallowhill 233 F3
Gallows Green 172 B3
Gallowstree
   Common 134 B4
Gallowstree Elm 158 A4
Galltair 256 E2
Gallt-y-foel 167 E1
Gallypot Street 123 E5
Galmington 115 F5
Galmisdale 247 D1
Galmpton Devon 100 C3
Galmpton Torbay 101 E2
Galmpton
   Warborough 101 E2
Galphay 202 B5
Galston 224 C2
Galtrigill 263 G6
Gamble's Green 137 G1
Gamblesby 210 C4
Gamelsby 209 F1
Gamesley 185 E3
Gamlingay 150 A2
Gamlingay Cinques 150 A2
Gamlingay Great
   Heath 150 A2
Gammaton 113 E3
Gammaton Moor 113 E3
Gammersgill 201 F4
Gamrie 269 F4
Gamston Notts 187 E5
Gamston Notts 174 B4
Ganarew 131 E1
Gang 98 D4
Ganllwyd 168 A5
Gannochy 253 D3
Ganstead 197 D4
Ganthorpe 203 F5
Ganton 204 C5
Ganwick Corner 136 B3
Gaodhail 239 F1
Gappah 102 B5
Gara Bridge 100 D2
Garabal 241 F3
Garadheancal 265 F1
Garbat 266 B5
Garbhallt 240 C5
Garboldisham 164 B3
Garden 242 A5
Garden City 170 A1
Garden Village 185 G3
Gardenstown 269 F4
Garderhouse 279 C8
Gardham 196 B3
Gare Hill 117 E3
Garelochhead 241 E5
Garford 133 G3
Garforth 194 D4
Gargrave 193 F2
Gargunnock 242 C5
Gariob 231 F1
Garlic Street 164 D3
Garlies Castle 215 F4
Garlieston 207 E2
Garlinge Green 124 D3
Garlogie 261 F4
Garmelow 171 F5
Garmond 269 G5
Garmony 247 F5
Garmouth 268 B4
Garmston 157 F2
Garnant 128 C1
Garndolbenmaen 167 D3
Garneddwen 155 D2

Garnett Bridge 199 G3
Garnfadryn 166 B4
Garnswllt 128 C2
Garrabost 271 H4
Garrachra 232 B1
Garralburn 268 C5
Garras 95 E4
Garreg 167 F3
Garreg Bank 156 B1
Garrett's Green 159 D4
Garrick 242 D1
Garrigill 210 D3
Garriston 202 A3
Garroch 215 G2
Garrochty 232 B4
Garros 263 K5
Garrow 251 G1
Garryhorn 215 G1
Garrynahine (Gearraidh na
   h-Aibhne) 270 E4
Garsdale 200 C4
Garsdale Head 200 C3
Garsdon 132 B4
Garshall Green 171 G4
Garsington 134 A2
Garstang 192 A3
Garston 183 F4
Garswood 183 G3
Gartachoil 242 A5
Gartally 258 B1
Gartavaich 231 G4
Gartbreck 230 A4
Gartcosh 234 A3
Garth Bridgend 129 E3
Garth Cere 154 C4
Garth Gwyn 181 D5
Garth IoM 190 B4
Garth Powys 143 F3
Garth Shet 279 B7
Garth Wrex 169 F3
Garth Row 199 G3
Garthbrengy 143 G4
Garthdee 261 H4
Gartheli 142 B2
Garthmyl 156 A3
Garthorpe Leics 174 D5
Garthorpe NLincs 187 F1
Garths 199 G3
Garthynty 142 D3
Gartincaber 242 B4
Gartly 260 D1
Gartmore 242 A5
Gartnagrenach 231 F4
Gartnatra 230 B3
Gartness 233 G1
Gartocharn 233 F1
Garton 197 E4
Garton-on-the-
   Wolds 196 B1
Gartymore 275 F7
Garvald 236 C2
Garvamore 258 C5
Garvan 248 B2
Garvard 238 C5
Garve (Clachan
   Ghairbh) 265 K5
Garveld 222 B5
Garvestone 178 B5
Garvie 232 B1
Garvock Aber 253 F2
Garvock Incly 233 E2
Garwald 226 D5
Garwaldwaterfoot 226 D5
Garway 145 D5
Garway Hill 144 D5
Gask Aber 269 J6
Gask Aber 269 F5
Gask P&K 243 E3
Gaskan 248 A2
Gass 224 C5
Gastard 117 F1
Gasthorpe 164 A3
Gaston Green 137 E1
Gatcombe 107 D4
Gate Burton 187 F4
Gate Helmsley 195 F2
Gateacre 183 F4
Gateford 186 C4
Gateforth 195 E5
Gatehead 224 B2
Gatehouse 251 D5
Gatehouse of Fleet 216 A5
Gatelawbridge 216 D1
Gateley 178 A3
Gatenby 202 C4
Gatesgarth 209 E5
Gateshaw 228 B4
Gateshead 212 B1
Gatesheath 170 B1
Gateside Aber 260 E3
Gateside Angus 252 C5
Gateside Fife 243 G4
Gateside NAyr 233 E4
Gateside Fife 243 G4
Gateslack 225 G5
Gathurst 183 G2
Gatley 184 C4
Gattonside 227 G2
Gatwick Airport 122 B4
Gaufron 143 F1
Gaulby 160 B2
Gauldry 244 B3
Gaunt's Common 105 G2
Gaunt's Earthcott 131 F4
Gautby 188 B5
Gavinton 237 E4
Gawber 186 A2
Gawcott 148 B4
Gawsworth 184 C5
Gawthrop 200 B4
Gawthwaite 199 D4
Gay Bowers 137 G2
Gay Street 121 F5
Gaydon 147 F2
Gayhurst 148 D3
Gayle 201 D4
Gayles 202 A2
Gayton Mersey 183 D4
Gayton N'hants 148 C2
Gayton Norf 163 F1
Gayton Staffs 171 G5
Gayton le Marsh 189 E4
Gayton le Wold 188 C4
Gayton Thorpe 163 F1
Gaywood 177 E5
Gazeley 151 F1

Geanies House 267 F4
Gearach 230 A4
Gearnsary 274 C5
Gearradh 248 B3
Gearrachra 232 B1
Gearraidh Bhailteas 254 C2
Gearraidh Bhaird 271 F5
Gearraidh na
   Monadh 254 C3
Gearrannan 270 D3
Geary 263 H5
Gedding 152 A2
Geddington 161 D4
Gedgrave Hall 153 F3
Gedintailor 256 B2
Gedling 174 B3
Gedney 176 C5
Gedney Broadgate 176 C5
Gedney Drove End 176 C5
Gedney Dyke 176 C5
Gedney Hill 162 B1
Gee Cross 185 D3
Geilston 233 E2
Geirinis 262 C7
Geisiadar 270 D4
Geldeston 165 E2
Gell Conwy 168 B1
Gell Gwyn 167 D4
Gelli 129 F3
Gelli Aur Country
   Park Carmar
   SA32 8LR 142 C5
Gelli Gynan 169 E2
Gellideg 129 G2
Gellifor 169 E1
Gelligaer 130 A3
Gellilydan 167 F3
Gellioedd 168 C3
Gelly 127 D1
Gellyburn 243 F1
Gellywen 141 F5
Gelston D&G 216 B5
Gelston Lincs 175 E3
Gembling 196 D2
Gemmil 239 G4
Genoch 214 C5
Genoch Square 214 C5
Gentleshaw 158 C1
Geocrab 263 G2
George Green 135 F4
George Nympton 114 A5
Georgeham 113 E2
Georgetown 233 F3
Gerlan 167 F1
Germansweek 99 E1
Germoe 94 C4
Gerrans 95 F3
Gerrards Cross 135 F4
Gerston 275 G3
Gestingthorpe 151 G4
Geuffordd 156 B1
Geufron 155 E4
Gibbet Hill 117 E3
Gibbshill 216 B3
Gibraltar Lincs 177 D2
Gibraltar Suff 152 C2
Gibraltar Point National
   Nature Reserve Lincs
   PE24 4SU 177 D2
Giddeahall 132 A5
Giddy Green 105 E4
Gidea Park 137 E4
Gidleigh 99 G1
Giffnock 233 G4
Gifford 236 C3
Giffordland 233 D5
Giffordtown 244 A3
Giggleswick 193 E1
Gigha 231 E5
Gilberdyke 196 A5
Gilbert's End 146 A3
Gilchriston 236 B3
Gilcrux 209 E3
Gildersome 194 B5
Gildingwells 186 C4
Gileston 114 D1
Gilfach 130 A3
Gilfach Goch 129 F4
Gilfachrheda 142 A2
Gilgarran 208 D4
Gill 210 A5
Gillamoor 203 F4
Gillen 263 H5
Gillenbie 217 F2
Gillfoot 217 D3
Gilling East 203 F5
Gilling West 202 A2
Gillingham Dorset 117 F5
Gillingham Med 123 G2
Gillingham Norf 165 F2
Gillivoan 275 G5
Gillock 275 H3
Gillow Heath 171 F2
Gills 275 J1
Gill's Green 123 G5
Gilmanscleuch 227 E3
Gilmerton Edin 235 G3
Gilmerton P&K 243 D2
Gilmilnscroft 225 D3
Gilmonby 201 E1
Gilmorton 160 A4
Gilsland 210 C1
Gilsland Spa 210 C1
Gilson 159 D3
Gilston 236 B4
Gilston Park 136 D1
Giltbrook 173 F3
Gilwern 130 B1
Gimingham 179 D2
Gin Pit 184 A2
Ginclough 185 D5
Ginger's Green 110 B2
Giosla 270 D5
Gipping 152 B1
Gipsey Bridge 176 A3
Girlsta 279 D7
Girsby 202 C2
Girtford 149 G3
Girthon 216 A5
Girton Cambs 150 C1
Girton Notts 174 D1
Girvan 214 C1
Gisburn 193 E3
Gisburn Cotes 193 E3
Gisleham 165 G3

Gislingham 164 B4
Gissing 164 C3
Gittisham 103 E3
Givons Grove 121 G2
Glackour 265 H3
Gladestry 144 B2
Gladsmuir 236 B2
Glaic 232 B2
Glais 128 C2
Glaisdale 203 G2
Glaister 223 E2
Glame 264 B7
Glamis 252 B5
Glamis Castle Angus
   DD8 1QJ 252 B5
Glan Conwy 168 B2
Glanaber Terrace 168 A3
Glanaman 128 C1
Glanbran 143 E4
Glan-Denys 142 B2
Glanderston 260 D2
Glandford 178 B1
Glan-Duar 142 B3
Glandwr 141 E5
Glan-Dwyfach 167 D3
Glangrwyney 130 B1
Glanllynfi 129 E3
Glan-rhyd NPT 129 D2
Glanrhyd Pembs 141 E3
Glanton 229 E5
Glanton Pyke 229 E5
Glanvilles Wootton 104 C2
Glanwern 154 C4
Glanwydden 181 G4
Glan-y-don 182 C5
Glan-y-llyn 130 A4
Glan-y-nant 155 F4
Glan-yr-afon
   Gwyn 168 C3
Glan-yr-afon
   Gwyn 168 B3
Glan-yr-afon IoA 181 E4
Glan-y-Wern 167 F4
Glapthorn 161 F3
Glapwell 173 F5
Glasahoile 241 G4
Glasbury 144 A4
Glaschoil 259 H1
Glascoed Mon 130 C2
Glascoed Wrex 169 F2
Glascorrie 260 D5
Glascote 159 E2
Glascwm 144 A2
Glasdrum 248 C5
Glasfryn 168 C2
Glasgow (Glaschu) 233 G3
Glasgow Airport 233 F3
Glasgow Botanic
   Garden Glas
   G12 0UE 30 C3
Glasgow Prestwick
   Airport 224 B3
Glasgow Royal Concert Hall
   Glas G2 3NY 39 F4
Glasgow Science Centre
   Glas G51 1EA 38 C4
Glashmore 261 F4
Glasinfryn 167 E1
Glasnacardoch 256 C5
Glasnakille 256 B3
Glaspant 141 F4
Glaspwll 154 D3
Glass Studio, Eastbourne
   Pier ESuss
   BN21 3EL 110 B4
Glassburn 257 K1
Glassel 260 E5
Glassenbury 123 G5
Glasserton 207 E3
Glassford 234 B5
Glasshouse 145 G5
Glasshouses 194 A1
Glassingall 242 C4
Glasslie 244 A4
Glasson Cumb 218 A5
Glasson Lancs 192 A3
Glasson Dock 192 A3
Glassonby 210 B4
Glasterlaw 253 D4
Glaston 161 D2
Glastonbury 116 B4
Glastonbury Abbey Som
   BA6 9EL 116 C4
Glatton 161 G4
Glazebrook 184 A3
Glazebury 184 A3
Glazeley 157 G4
Gleadless 186 A4
Gleadsmoss 171 F1
Gleann Tholastaidh 271 H3
Gleaston 199 D5
Glecknabae 232 B3
Gledhow 194 C4
Gledrid 169 F4
Glemsford 151 G3
Glen D&G 216 C3
Glen D&G 215 G5
Glen Auldyn 190 C2
Glen Mona 190 C3
Glen Parva 160 A3
Glen Trool Lodge 215 F2
Glen Village 234 C2
Glen Vine 190 B4
Glenae 217 D2
Glenaladale 248 A2
Glenald 241 E4
Glenamachrie 240 B2
Glenapp Castle 214 B2
Glenarm 252 B3
Glenbarr 222 B2
Glenbatrick 230 D2
Glenbeg High 265 K3
Glenbeg High 259 H2
Glenbeg High 247 E5
Glenbeich 242 B2
Glenbervie Aber 253 F1
Glenbervie Falk 234 C1
Glenboig 234 B3
Glenborrodale 247 F5
Glenbranter 240 D5
Glenbreck 226 B3
Glenbrittle 255 K2
Glenburn 233 F3
Glenbyre 239 E2
Glencaird 215 F3
Glencaple 217 D4
Glencarse 243 G2
Glencat 260 D5

Glenceitlein 248 D5
Glencloy 223 F2
Glencoe
   (A' Chàrnaich) 248 D4
Glencoe Visitor Centre
   High PH49 4LA 248 D4
Glenconglass 259 J2
Glencraig 243 G5
Glencripesdale 247 F4
Glencrosh 216 B2
Glencruitten 240 A2
Glencuie 260 D3
Glendearg D&G 226 D5
Glendearg ScBord 227 G2
Glendessary 257 F5
Glendevon 243 E4
Glendoebeg 258 B4
Glendoick 244 A2
Glendoll Lodge 252 A2
Glendoune 214 C1
Glendrissaig 214 C1
Glenduckie 244 A3
Glenduisk 214 D2
Glendye Lodge 253 E1
Gleneagles Hotel 243 E3
Gleneagles House 243 E3
Glenearn 243 G3
Glenegedale 230 B4
Glenelg
   (Gleann Eilg) 256 E3
Glenfarg 243 G3
Glenfeochan 240 A2
Glenfield 160 A2
Glenfinnan (Gleann
   Fhionnain) 248 B1
Glenfoot 243 G3
Glengalmadale 248 C4
Glengap 216 A5
Glengarnock 233 E4
Glengarrisdale 239 F5
Glengennet 215 D2
Glengolly 275 G2
Glengrasco 263 K7
Glenhead Farm 252 A3
Glenhurich 248 A3
Gleniffer Braes Country Park
   Renf PA2 8TE 30 A4
Glenkerry 227 D3
Glenkiln 223 F2
Glenkin 232 C1
Glenkindie 260 C3
Glenlair 216 B3
Glenlatterach 267 K6
Glenlean 232 B1
Glenlee Angus 252 C2
Glenlee D&G 216 A2
Glenlichorn 242 C3
Glenlivet 259 J2
Glenlochar 216 B4
Glenloig 223 E2
Glenluce 214 C5
Glenmallan 241 E5
Glenmanna 225 F5
Glenmavis 234 B3
Glenmaye 190 A4
Glenmeanie 265 J6
Glenmore A&B 232 B3
Glenmore High 263 K7
Glenmore High 259 G4
Glenmore Forest Park
   Visitor Centre High
   PH22 1QY 259 G3
Glenmore Lodge 259 G4
Glenmoy 252 C3
Glenmuick 273 F7
Glennoe 240 C1
Glenochar 226 A4
Glenogil 252 C3
Glenprosen
   Village 252 B3
Glenquiech 252 C3
Glenramskill 222 C4
Glenrazie 215 E4
Glenridding 209 G5
Glenrisdell 231 G4
Glenrossal 266 B1
Glenrothes 244 A4
Glensanda 248 A5
Glensaugh 253 E2
Glensgaich 266 B5
Glenshalg 260 D4
Glenshellish 240 D5
Glensluain 240 C5
Glentaggart 225 G3
Glentham 188 A3
Glenton 260 E2
Glentress 227 D2
Glentress ScBord
   EH45 8NB 235 G5
Glentrool 215 E3
Glentruan 190 C1
Glentworth 187 G4
Glenuachdarach 263 K6
Glenuig 247 F2
Glenure 248 C5
Glenurquhart 266 E5
Glenwhilly 214 C3
Glespin 225 G3
Gletness 279 D7
Glewstone 145 E5
Glodryd 141 F4
Glogue 141 E4
Glororum 229 F3
Glossop 185 E3
Gloster Hill 221 E1
Gloucester 132 A1
Gloucester Cathedral
   Glos GL1 2LR
   73 Gloucester
Gloucester Historic
   Docks Glos GL1 2ER
   73 Gloucester
Gloucestershire
   Airport 146 A5
Gloucestershire &
   Warwickshire Railway
   Glos GL54 5DT 146 B5
Gloup 278 E2
Gloweth 96 B5
Glusburn 193 G3
Glympton 147 G5
Glyn 168 A2
Glyn Ceiriog 169 F4
Glynarthen 141 G3
Glyncoch 129 G3
Glyncorrwg 129 E3

Glyn-Cywarch 167 F4
Glynde 109 G3
Glyndebourne 109 G2
Glyndyfrdwy 169 E3
Glynneath
   (Glyn-Nedd) 129 E2
Glynogwr 129 F4
Glyntaff 129 G4
Gnosall 171 F5
Gnosall Heath 171 F5
Go Bananas, Colchester
   Essex CO1 1BX 152 A5
Goadby 160 C3
Goadby Marwood 174 C5
Goatacre 132 C4
Goatfield 240 C4
Goathill 104 C1
Goathland 204 B2
Goathurst 115 F4
Gobernuisgeach 274 E5
Gobhaig 270 C7
Gobowen 170 A4
Godalming 121 E3
Goddard's Corner 153 D1
Goddards Green 109 E1
Godden Green 123 E3
Goddington 123 D2
Godford Cross 103 E2
Godington 148 B5
Godleybrook 171 G3
Godmanchester 162 A5
Godmanstone 104 C3
Godmersham 124 C3
Godney 116 B3
Godolphin Cross 94 D3
Godor 156 B1
Godre'r-graig 129 D2
Godshill Hants 106 A1
Godshill IoW 107 E4
Godstone 122 C3
Godstone Farm Surr
   RH9 8LX 122 C3
Godwick 178 A3
Goetre 130 C2
Goff's Oak 136 C2
Gogar 235 F2
Gogarth 181 F4
Goginan 154 C4
Goirtean a'
   Chladaich 248 C2
Goirtein 232 A1
Golan 167 E3
Golant 97 F4
Golberdon 98 D3
Golborne 184 A3
Golcar 185 F1
Gold Hill Cambs 162 D3
Gold Hill Dorset 105 E1
Goldcliff 130 C4
Golden Acre Park
   WYorks
   LS16 8BQ 194 B3
Golden Cross 110 A2
Golden Green 123 F4
Golden Grove 128 B1
Golden Pot 120 C3
Golden Valley
   Derbys 173 F2
Golden Valley Glos 146 B5
Goldenhill 171 F2
Golders Green 136 B4
Goldhanger 138 C2
Goldielea 216 D3
Golding 157 E2
Goldington 149 F2
Goldsborough
   NYorks 204 B1
Goldsborough
   NYorks 194 C2
Goldsithney 94 C3
Goldstone 171 E5
Goldthorn Park 158 B3
Goldthorpe 186 B2
Goldworthy 113 D3
Goleulong 2000 Lightship,
   Cardiff Cardiff
   CF10 4PA 7 C4
Golford 123 G5
Gollanfield 267 F6
Gollinglith Foot 202 A4
Golspie 267 F2
Golval 274 D2
Gomeldon 118 C4
Gomersal 194 B5
Gometra 246 C5
Gometra House 246 C5
Gomshall 121 F3
Gonachan Cottage 234 A1
Gonalston 174 B3
Gonerby Hill Foot 175 E4
Gonfirth 279 C6
Good Easter 137 F1
Gooderstone 163 F2
Goodleigh 113 G2
Goodmanham 196 A3
Goodmayes 137 D4
Goodnestone Kent 125 E3
Goodnestone Kent 124 C2
Goodrich 131 E1
Goodrington 101 E2
Goodshaw 193 E5
Goodshaw Fold 193 E5
Goodwick (Wdig) 140 C4
Goodworth Clatford 119 E3
Goodyers End 159 F4
Goole 195 G5
Goom's Hill 146 C2
Goonbell 96 B5
Goonhavern 96 C4
Goose Green Essex 152 C5
Goose Green Essex 152 C5
Goose Green
   GtMan 183 G2
Goose Green Kent 123 F3
Goose Green SGlos 131 F5
Goose Pool 145 D4
Gooseham 112 C4
Goosehill Green 146 B1
Goosewell 100 B3
Goosey 133 F3
Goosnargh 192 B4
Goostrey 184 B5
Gorcott Hill 146 C1
Gorddinog 181 E5
Gordon 236 D5
Gordonbush 267 F1
Gordonstoun 267 J5

Gordonstown *Aber* **268** D5
Gordonstown *Aber* **261** F1
Gore Cross **118** B2
Gore End **119** F1
Gore Pit **138** B1
Gore Street **125** E2
Gorebridge **236** A3
Gorefield **162** C1
Gorey **100** D5
Gorgie **235** G2
Gorgie City Farm *Edin*
EH11 2LA **36** B7
Goring **134** B4
Goring Heath **134** B5
Goring-by-Sea **108** D3
Gorleston-on-Sea **179** G5
Gorllwyn **141** G4
Gornalwood **158** B3
Gorrachie **269** F5
Gorran Churchtown **97** D5
Gorran Haven **97** E5
Gors **154** C5
Gorsedd **182** C5
Gorseinon **128** B3
Gorseness **277** D6
Gorseybank **173** D2
Gorsgoch **142** A2
Gorslas **128** B1
Gorsley **145** F5
Gorsley Common **145** F5
Gorstage **184** A5
Gorstan **265** K5
Gorstanvorran **248** A2
Gorsty Hill **172** C5
Gorten **239** G1
Gortenbuie **239** E1
Gorteneorn **247** F3
Gorton *A&B* **246** A4
Gorton *GtMan* **184** C3
Gosbeck **152** C2
Gosberton **176** A4
Gosberton Clough **175** G5
Goseley Dale **173** E5
Gosfield **151** F5
Gosford *Here* **145** E1
Gosford *Oxon* **134** A1
Gosforth *Cumb* **198** B2
Gosforth *T&W* **212** B1
Gosland Green **170** C2
Gosmore **149** G5
Gospel End **158** A3
Gosport **107** F3
Gossabrough **278** E4
Gossington **131** G2
Gossops Green **122** B5
Goswick **229** E2
Gotham **173** G4
Gotherington **146** B5
Gothers **97** D4
Gott **279** D8
Gotton **115** F5
Goudhurst **123** G5
Goulceby **188** C5
Gourdas **269** F6
Gourdon **253** G2
Gourock **232** D3
Govan **233** G3
Goverton **174** C2
Goveton **101** D3
Govilon **130** B1
Gowanhill **269** J4
Gowdall **195** F5
Gowerton **128** B3
Gowkhall **235** E1
Gowkthrapple **234** B4
Gowthorpe **195** G2
Goxhill *ERid* **197** D3
Goxhill *NLincs* **196** D5
Goytre **129** D4
Gozzard's Ford **133** G3
Grabhair **271** F6
Graby **175** F2
Gradbach **171** G1
Grade **95** E5
Gradeley Green **170** C2
Graffham **108** B2
Grafham *Cambs* **149** G1
Grafham *Surr* **121** F3
Grafham Water *Cambs*
PE28 0BH **149** G1
Grafton *Here* **145** D4
Grafton *NYorks* **194** D1
Grafton *Oxon* **133** E2
Grafton *Shrop* **156** D1
Grafton *Worcs* **145** E1
Grafton *Worcs* **146** B4
Grafton Flyford **146** B2
Grafton Regis **148** C3
Grafton Underwood **161** E4
Grafty Green **124** A4
Graianrhyd **169** F2
Graig *Carmar* **128** A2
Graig *Conwy* **181** G5
Graig *Denb* **182** B5
Graig-fechan **169** E2
Grain **124** A1
Grainel **230** A3
Grainhow **269** G6
Grains Bar **185** D2
Grainsby **188** C3
Grainthorpe **189** D3
Graizelound **187** E3
Gramisdale
(Gramsdal) **262** D6
Grampound **96** D5
Grampound Road **96** D4
Granborough **148** C5
Granby **174** C4
Grand Pier, Teignmouth
Devon
TQ14 8BB **102** C5
Grandborough **147** G1
Grandes Rocques **101** F4
Grandtully **251** E4
Grange *Cumb* **209** F5
Grange *EAyr* **224** C2
Grange *High* **257** K1
Grange *Med* **123** G2
Grange *Mersey* **182** D4
Grange *P&K* **244** A2
Grange Crossroads **268** C5
Grange de Lings **187** G5
Grange Hall **267** H5
Grange Hill **136** D3
Grange Moor **185** G1
Grange of Lindores **244** A3
Grange Villa **212** B2
Grangemill **172** D2

Grangemouth **234** D1
Grangemuir **244** D4
Grange-over-Sands **199** F5
Grangeston **214** D1
Grangetown
Cardiff **130** A5
Grangetown *R&C* **213** E5
Granish **259** G3
Gransmoor **196** D2
Granston **140** B4
Grantchester **150** C2
Grantham **175** E4
Grantley **202** B3
Grantlodge **261** F3
Granton **235** G2
Granton House **226** B5
Grantown-on-Spey **259** H2
Grantsfield **145** E1
Grantshouse **237** F3
Grappenhall **184** A4
Grasby **188** A3
Grasmere **199** E2
Grass Green **151** E4
Grasscroft **185** D2
Grassendale **183** E4
Grassgarth **199** F3
Grassholme **211** F5
Grassington **193** G1
Grassmoor **173** F1
Grassthorpe **174** C2
Grateley **119** D3
Gratwich **172** B4
Gravel Hill **135** F3
Graveley *Cambs* **150** A1
Graveley *Herts* **150** A5
Gravelly Hill **158** D3
Gravels **156** C2
Graven **278** D5
Graveney **124** C2
Gravesend **137** F5
Grayingham **187** G3
Grayrigg **199** G3
Grays **137** F5
Grayshott **121** D4
Grayswood **121** E4
Grazeley **120** B1
Greasbrough **186** B3
Greasby **183** D4

Great Aberystwyth Camera
Obscura *Cere*
SY23 2DN **154** B4
Great Abington **150** D3
Great Addington **161** E5
Great Alne **146** C2
Great Altcar **183** E2
Great Amwell **136** C1
Great Asby **200** B1
Great Ashfield **152** A1
Great Ayton **203** E1
Great Baddow **137** G2
Great Bardfield **151** E4
Great Barford **149** G2
Great Barr **158** C3
Great Barrington **133** E1
Great Barrow **170** B1
Great Barton **151** G1
Great Barugh **203** G5
Great Bavington **220** B3
Great Bealings **152** D3
Great Bedwyn **119** D1
Great Bentley **152** C5
Great Bernera **270** D4
Great Billing **148** D1
Great Bircham **177** F4
Great Blakenham **152** C2
Great Bolas **170** D3
Great Bookham **121** G2
Great Bourton **147** G3
Great Bowden **160** C4
Great Bradley **151** E2
Great Braxted **138** B1
Great Bricett **152** B2
Great Brickhill **149** E4
Great Bridgeford **171** F5
Great Brington **148** B1
Great Bromley **152** B5
Great Broughton
Cumb **209** D3
Great Broughton
NYorks **203** E2
Great Buckland **123** F2
Great Budworth **184** A5
Great Burdon **202** C1
Great Burstead **137** F3
Great Busby **203** E2
Great Cambourne **150** B2
Great Canfield **137** E1
Great Canney **138** B2
Great Carlton **189** E4
Great Casterton **161** F2
Great Chalfield **117** F1
Great Chart **124** B4
Great Chatwell **157** G1
Great Chell **171** F2
Great Chesterford **150** D3
Great Cheverell **118** A2
Great Chishill **150** C4
Great Clacton **139** E1
Great Clifton **208** D4
Great Coates **188** C2
Great Comberton **146** B3
Great Corby **210** A2
Great Cornard **151** G3
Great Cowden **197** E3
Great Coxwell **133** E3
Great Crakehall **202** B4
Great Cransley **160** D5
Great
Cressingham **163** G2
Great Crosby **183** E2
Great Crosthwaite **209** F4
Great Cubley **172** C4
Great Cumbrae **232** C4
Great Dalby **160** C1
Great Doddington **149** D1
Great Doward **131** E1
Great Dunham **163** G1
Great Dunmow **151** E5
Great Durnford **118** C4
Great Easton
Essex **151** E5
Great Easton *Leics* **160** D3
Great Eccleston **192** A4
Great Edstone **203** G4
Great Ellingham **164** B2
Great Elm **117** E3
Great Eversden **150** B2
Great Fencote **202** B3

Great Finborough **152** B2
Great Fransham **163** G1
Great Gaddesden **135** F1
Great Gidding **161** G4
Great Givendale **196** A2
Great Glemham **153** E1
Great Glen **160** B3
Great Gonerby **175** D4
Great Gransden **150** A2
Great Green
Cambs **150** A3
Great Green *Norf* **165** D3
Great Green *Suff* **152** A2
Great Green *Suff* **164** C4
Great Green *Suff* **164** B5
Great Habton **203** G5
Great Hale **175** G4
Great Hallingbury **137** E1
Great Hampden **134** D2
Great Harrowden **161** D5
Great Harwood **192** D4
Great Haseley **134** B2
Great Hatfield **197** D3
Great Haywood **172** B5
Great Heath **159** F4
Great Heck **195** E5
Great Henny **151** G4
Great Hinton **118** A2
Great Hockham **164** A2
Great Holland **139** F1
Great Horkesley **152** A4
Great Hormead **150** C4
Great Horton **194** A4
Great Horwood **148** C4
Great Houghton
N'hants **148** C2
Great Houghton
SYorks **186** B2
Great Hucklow **185** F5
Great Kelk **196** D2
Great Kimble **134** D2
Great Kingshill **135** D3
Great Langton **202** B3
Great Leighs **137** G1
Great Limber **188** B2
Great Linford **148** D3
Great Livermere **163** G5
Great Longstone **185** G5
Great Lumley **212** B3
Great Lyth **157** D2
Great Malvern **145** G3
Great Maplestead **151** G4
Great Marton **191** G4
Great Massingham **177** F5
Great Melton **178** C5
Great Milton **134** B2
Great Missenden **135** D2
Great Mitton **192** D3
Great Mongeham **125** F3
Great Moulton **164** C2
Great Munden **150** B5
Great Musgrave **200** C1
Great Ness **156** D1
Great Notley **151** F5
Great Oak **130** C2
Great Oakley *Essex* **152** C5
Great Oakley
N'hants **161** D4
Great Offley **149** G5
Great Ormside **200** C1
Great Orton **209** G1
Great Ouseburn **194** D1
Great Oxendon **160** C4
Great Oxney Green **137** F2
Great Parndon **136** D2
Great Paxton **150** A1
Great Plumpton **191** G4
Great Plumstead **179** E5
Great Ponton **175** E4
Great Potheridge **113** F4
Great Preston **194** C5
Great Purston **148** A4
Great Raveley **162** A4
Great Rissington **133** D1
Great Rollright **147** F4
Great Ryburgh **178** A3
Great Ryle **229** E5
Great Ryton **157** D2
Great St. Mary's Church
Cambs CB2 3PQ
66 Cambridge
Great Saling **151** F5
Great Salkeld **210** B4
Great Sampford **151** E4
Great Saredon **158** B2
Great Saxham **151** F1
Great Shefford **133** F5
Great Shelford **150** C2
Great Smeaton **202** C2
Great Snoring **178** A2
Great Somerford **132** B4
Great Stainton **212** C5
Great Stambridge **138** C3
Great Staughton **149** G1
Great Steeping **176** C1
Great Stonar **125** F3
Great Strickland **210** B5
Great Stukeley **162** A5
Great Sturton **188** C5
Great Sutton
ChesW&C **183** E5
Great Sutton *Shrop* **157** E4
Great Swinburne **220** B4
Great Tew **147** F5
Great Tey **151** G5
Great Thorness **107** D3
Great Thurlow **151** E3
Great Torr **100** C3
Great Torrington **113** E4
Great Tosson **220** C1
Great Totham
Essex **138** B1
Great Totham
Essex **138** B1
Great Tows **188** C3
Great Urswick **199** D5
Great Wakering **138** C4
Great Waldingfield **152** A3
Great Walsingham **178** A2

Great Waltham **137** F1
Great Warley **137** E3
Great Washbourne **146** B4
Great Weeke **102** A4
Great Welnetham **151** G2
Great Wenham **152** B4
Great Whittington **220** C4
Great Wigborough **138** C1
Great Wigsell **110** C1
Great Wilbraham **150** D2
Great Wilne **173** F4
Great Wishford **118** B4
Great Witcombe **132** B1
Great Witley **145** G1
Great Wolford **147** E4
Great Wratting **151** E3
Great Wymondley **150** A5
Great Wyrley **158** B2
Great Wytheford **157** E1
Great Yarmouth **179** G5
Great Yeldham **151** F4
Greatford **161** F1
Greatgate **172** B3
Greatham *Hants* **120** C4
Greatham *Hart* **213** D5
Greatham *WSuss* **108** C2
Greatness **123** E3
Greatstone-on-Sea **111** F1
Greatworth **148** A3
Green **169** D1
Green Cross **121** D4
Green End *Bed* **149** G1
Green End *Bucks* **149** E4
Green End *Cambs* **162** A5
Green End *Cambs* **162** B5
Green End *Herts* **150** B5
Green End *Herts* **150** B4
Green End *Warks* **159** E4
Green Hammerton **195** D2
Green Hill **132** C4
Green Lane **146** C1
Green Moor **185** G3
Green Ore **116** C2
Green Quarter **199** G2
Green Street *ESuss* **110** C2
Green Street *Herts* **136** B3
Green Street *Herts* **150** C5
Green Street *Worcs* **146** A3
Green Street
WSuss **121** G5
Green Street Green
GtLon **123** D2
Green Street Green
Kent **137** E5
Green Tye **136** D1
Greenburn **252** C5
Greencroft **212** A3
Greendams **253** E1
Greendykes **229** E4
Greenend **147** F5
Greenfield *CenBeds* **149** F4
Greenfield (Maes-Glas)
Flints **182** C5
Greenfield *GtMan* **185** E2
Greenfield *High* **257** J4
Greenfield *Lincs* **189** E5
Greenfield *Oxon* **134** C3
Greenford **136** A4
Greengairs **234** B2
Greengates **194** A4
Greengill **209** E3
Greenhalgh **192** A4
Greenhall **260** E2
Greenham **119** F1
Greenhaugh **219** F3
Greenhead **210** C1
Greenheads **261** J1
Greenheys **184** B2
Greenhill *GtLon* **136** A4
Greenhill *High* **267** G1
Greenhill *SYorks* **186** A4
Greenhithe **137** E5
Greenholm **224** D2
Greenholme **199** G2
Greenhow Hill **194** A1
Greenigo **277** D7
Greenland **275** H2
Greenlands **134** C4
Greenlaw *Aber* **268** C5
Greenlaw *ScBord* **237** D5
Greenloaning **242** B4
Greenmeadow **130** B3
Greenmoor Hill **134** B4
Greenmount **184** B1
Greenmyre **261** G1
Greenock **233** E1
Greenodd **199** E4
Greens Norton **148** B3
Greenscares **242** C3
Greenside *T&W* **212** A1
Greenside *WYorks* **185** F1
Greenstead **152** B5
Greenstead Green **151** G5
Greensted **137** E2
Greensted Green **137** E2
Greenway *Pembs* **141** D4
Greenway *Som* **116** A5
Greenwell **210** B2
Greenwich **136** C5
Greenwood Forest Park,
Y Felinheli *Gwyn*
LL56 4QN **167** E1
Greet **146** C4
Greete **157** E5
Greetham *Lincs* **188** D5
Greetham *Rut* **161** E2
Greetland **193** G5
Gregson Lane **192** B5
Greinton **116** B4
Grenaby **190** A4
Grendon *N'hants* **149** D1
Grendon *Warks* **159** E3
Grendon Common **159** E3
Grendon Green **145** E2
Grendon
Underwood **148** B5
Grenitote
(Greinetobht) **262** D4
Grenofen **99** E3
Grenoside **186** A3
Greosabhagh **263** G2
Gresford **170** A2
Gresham **178** C2
Greshornish **263** J6
Gress (Griais) **271** G4
Gressenhall **178** A4
Gressingham **192** B1

Greta Bridge **201** F1
Gretna **218** B5
Gretna Green **218** B5
Gretton *Glos* **146** C4
Gretton *N'hants* **161** E3
Gretton *Shrop* **157** E3
Grewelthorpe **202** B5
Greygarth **202** A5
Greylake **116** A4
Greys Green **134** C4
Greysouthen **209** D4
Greystead **219** F3
Greystoke **210** A4
Greystone *Aber* **259** K5
Greystone *Angus* **252** D5
Greystone *Lancs* **193** E3
Greystones **186** A4
Greywell **120** C2
Gribthorpe **195** G4
Gribton **216** D2
Griff **159** F4
Griffithstown **130** B3
Grigadale **246** D3
Grigghall **199** F3
Grimeford Village **184** A1
Grimesthorpe **186** A3
Grimethorpe **186** B2
Griminish (Griminis) **262** C6
Grimister **278** D3
Grimley **146** A1
Grimmet **224** B4
Grimness **277** D8
Grimoldby **189** D4
Grimpo **170** A4
Grimsargh **192** B4
Grimsay
(Griomsaigh) **262** D6
Grimsbury **147** G3
Grimsby **188** C2
Grimscote **148** B2
Grimscott **112** C5
Grimshader
(Griomsiadar) **271** G5
Grimsthorpe **175** F5
Grimston *ERid* **197** E4
Grimston *Leics* **174** B5
Grimston *Norf* **177** F5
Grimstone **104** C3
Grimstone End **152** A1
Grindale **205** E5
Grindiscol **279** D9
Grindle **157** G2
Grindleford **185** G5
Grindleton **193** D3
Grindley **172** B5
Grindley Brook **170** C3
Grindlow **185** F5
Grindon *N'umb* **237** G5
Grindon *Staffs* **172** B2
Grindon *Stock* **212** C5
Grindon *T&W* **212** C1
Gringley on the Hill **187** E3
Grinsdale **209** G1
Grinshill **170** C5
Grinton **201** F3
Griomarstaidh **270** E4
Grisdale **200** C3
Grishipoll **246** A4
Gristhorpe **205** D4
Griston **164** A2
Gritley **277** E7
Grittenham **132** C4
Grittleton **132** A5
Grizebeck **198** D4
Grizedale **199** E3
Grizedale Forest Park
Cumb LA22 0QJ **199** E3
Grobister **276** F5
Groby **160** A2
Groes **168** C1
Groes-faen **129** G4
Groesffordd **166** B4
Groesffordd Marli **182** B5
Groeslon *Gwyn* **167** D2
Groeslon *Gwyn* **167** E1
Groes-lwyd **156** B1
Groes-wen **130** A4
Grogport **231** G5
Groigearraidh **254** C1
Gromford **153** E2
Gronant **182** C4
Groombridge **123** E5
Groombridge Place Gardens
Kent TN3 9QG **123** E5
Grosmont *Mon* **144** D5
Grosmont *NYorks* **204** B2
Grotaig **258** B2
Groton **152** A3
Groundistone
Heights **227** F4
Grouville **100** C5
Grove *Bucks* **149** E5
Grove *Dorset* **104** C5
Grove *Kent* **125** E2
Grove *Notts* **187** E5
Grove *Oxon* **133** G3
Grove End **123** G2
Grove Green **123** G3
Grove Park **136** D5
Grove Town **195** D5
Grovehill **135** F2
Grovesend *SGlos* **131** F4
Grovesend *Swan* **128** B2
Gruids **266** C1
Gruinard House **265** F3
Grula **255** J2
Gruline **247** E5
Grumbla **94** B4
Grundcruie **243** F2
Grundisburgh **152** D2
Gruting **279** B8
Grutness **279** G10
Gualachulain **248** D5
Guardbridge **244** C3
Guarlford **146** A3
Guay **251** F5
Gubbergill **198** B3
Gubblecote **135** E1
Guernsey **101** F5
Guernsey Airport **101** E5
Guestling Green **111** D2
Guestling Thorn **111** D2
Guestwick **178** B3
Guestwick Green **178** B3
Guide **192** D5
Guide Post **221** E3
Guilden Down **156** C4
Guilden Morden **150** A3
Guilden Sutton **170** B1

Guildford **121** E3
Guildford House Gallery
Surr GU1 3AJ
74 Guildford
Guildtown **243** G1
Guilsborough **160** B5
Guilsfield (Cegidfa) **156** B1
Guilthwaite **186** B4
Guisborough **203** F1
Guiseley **194** A3
Guist **178** B3
Guith **276** E4
Guiting Power **146** C5
Gulberwick **279** D9
Gullane **236** B1
Gullane Bents *ELoth*
EH31 2AZ **236** B1
Gulval **94** B3
Gulworthy **99** E3
Gumfreston **127** E2
Gumley **160** B3
Gunby *Lincs* **175** E5
Gunby *Lincs* **176** C1
Gundleton **120** B4
Gunn **113** G2
Gunnersbury **136** A5
Gunnerside **201** E3
Gunnerton **220** B4
Gunness **187** F1
Gunnislake **99** D4
Gunnista **279** E8
Gunnister **278** C5
Gunstone **158** A2
Gunter's Bridge **121** E5
Gunthorpe *Norf* **178** B2
Gunthorpe *Notts* **174** B3
Gunthorpe *Rut* **161** D2
Gunville **107** D4
Gunwalloe **95** D4
Gupworthy **114** C4
Gurnard **107** D3
Gurnett **184** D5
Gurney Slade **116** D3
Gurnos *MTyd* **129** G2
Gurnos *Powys* **129** D2
Gushmere **124** C3
Gussage All Saints **105** G1
Gussage St. Andrew **105** F1
Gussage St. Michael **105** F1
Guston **125** F4
Gutcher **278** E3
Guthram Gowt **175** G5
Guthrie **253** D4
Guyhirn **162** B2
Guy's Head **176** C5
Guy's Marsh **117** F5
Guyzance **221** E1
Gwaelod-y-garth **130** A4
Gwaenysgor **182** C4
Gwaithla **144** B2
Gwalchmai **180** B5
Gwaun-Cae-Gurwen **128** D1
Gwaynynog **168** D1
Gwbert **141** E3
Gweek **95** E4
Gwehelog **130** C2
Gwenddwr **143** G3
Gwendreath **95** E5
Gwennap **96** B5
Gwenter **95** E5
Gwernaffield **169** F1
Gwernesney **130** D2
Gwernogle **142** B4
Gwernymynydd **169** F1
Gwern-y-Steeple **129** G5
Gwersyllt **170** A2
Gwespyr **182** C4
Gwinear **94** C3
Gwithian **94** C3
Gwredog **180** C4
Gwrhay **130** A3
Gwyddelwern **169** D3
Gwyddgrug **142** A4
Gwynfryn **169** F2
Gwystre **143** G1
Gwytherin **168** B1
Gyfelia **170** A3
Gyre **277** C7
Gyrn Goch **166** D3

H

H.M.S. Belfast *GtLon*
SE1 2JH **12** C4
H.M.S. Victory PO1 3PX
82 Portsmouth
H.M.S. Warrior PO1 3QX
82 Portsmouth
Habberley **156** C2
Habin **120** D5
Habrough **188** B1
Haccombe **102** B5
Hacconby **175** G5
Haceby **175** F4
Hacheston **153** E2
Hackbridge **122** B2
Hackenthorpe **186** B4
Hackford **178** B5
Hackforth **202** B3
Hackland **276** C5
Hackleton **148** D2
Hacklete (Haclait) **262** D7
Hacklete (Taclait) **270** D4
Hackleton **148** D2
Hacklinge **125** F3
Hackness *NYorks* **204** C3
Hackness *Ork* **277** C8
Hackney **136** C4
Hackthorn **187** G4
Hackthorpe **210** B5
Hacton **137** E4
Hadden **228** B3
Haddenham *Bucks* **134** C2
Haddenham
Cambs **162** C5
Haddington *ELoth* **236** C2
Haddington *Lincs* **175** E1
Haddiscoe **165** F2
Haddo Country Park *Aber*
AB41 7EQ **261** G1
Haddon **161** G3
Hade Edge **185** F2
Hademore **159** D2
Hadfield **185** E3
Hadham Cross **136** D1
Hadham Ford **150** C5
Hadleigh *Essex* **138** B4

Hadleigh *Suff* **152** B3
Hadleigh Castle Country
Park *Essex*
SS7 2PP **138** B4
Hadleigh Farm *Essex*
SS7 2AP **138** B4
Hadleigh Heath **152** A3
Hadley *Tel&W* **157** F2
Hadley *Worcs* **146** A1
Hadley End **172** C5
Hadley Wood **136** B3
Hadlow **123** F4
Hadlow Down **110** A1
Hadnall **170** C5
Hadspen **117** D4
Hadstock **151** D3
Hadston **221** E2
Hadzor **146** B1
Haffenden Quarter **124** A4
Hafod Bridge **142** C4
Hafod-Dinbych **168** B2
Hafodunos **168** B1
Hafod-y-rynys **130** B3
Haggate **193** E4
Haggbeck **218** C4
Haggersta **279** C8
Haggerston *GtLon* **136** C4
Haggerston *N'umb* **229** E2
Haggrister **278** C5
Haggs **234** B2
Hagley *Here* **145** E3
Hagley *Worcs* **158** B4
Hagnaby *Lincs* **176** B1
Hagnaby *Lincs* **189** E5
Hague Bar **185** D4
Hagworthingham **176** B1
Haigh **184** A2
Haigh Hall Country Park
GtMan
WN2 1PE **183** G2
Haighton Green **192** B4
Hail Weston **149** G1
Haile **198** B3
Hailes **146** C4
Hailey *Herts* **136** C1
Hailey *Oxon* **134** B4
Hailey *Oxon* **133** F1
Hailsham **110** A3
Haimer **275** G2
Hainault **137** D3
Hainault Forest Country
Park *Essex*
IG7 4QN **137** D3
Haine **125** F2
Hainford **178** D4
Hainton **188** B5
Haisthorpe **196** D1
Hakin **126** B2
Halam **174** B2
Halbeath **235** F1
Halberton **102** D1
Halcro **275** H2
Hale *Cumb* **199** G5
Hale *GtMan* **184** B4
Hale *Halton* **183** F4
Hale *Hants* **106** A1
Hale *Surr* **120** D3
Hale Bank **183** F4
Hale Barns **184** B4
Hale Nook **191** G3
Hale Street **123** F4
Hales *Norf* **165** E2
Hales *Staffs* **171** E4
Hales Green **172** C3
Hales Place **124** D3
Halesgate **176** B5
Halesowen **158** B4
Halesworth **165** E4
Halewood **183** F4
Half Way Inn **102** D3
Halford *Devon* **102** B5
Halford *Shrop* **156** D4
Halford *Warks* **147** E3
Halfpenny **199** G4
Halfpenny Green **158** A3
Halfway *Carmar* **142** C4
Halfway *Carmar* **128** B2
Halfway *Powys* **143** E4
Halfway *SYorks* **186** B4
Halfway *WBerks* **119** F1
Halfway Bridge **121** E5
Halfway House **156** C1
Halfway Houses
Kent **124** B1
Halfway Houses
Lincs **175** D1
Halghton Mill **170** B3
Halifax **193** G5
Halistra **263** H6
Halket **233** F4
Halkyn **182** D5
Hall **233** F4
Hall Cross **192** B5
Hall Dunnerdale **198** D3
Hall Green *ChesE* **171** F2
Hall Green *Lancs* **192** A5
Hall Green *WMid* **158** D4
Hall Grove **136** B1
Hall of the Forest **156** B4
Halland **110** A2
Hallaton **160** C3
Hallatrow **116** D2
Hallbankgate **210** B2
Hallen **131** E4
Hallfield Gate **173** E2
Halliglen **234** C2
Hallin **263** H6
Halling **123** G2
Hallington *Lincs* **188** D4
Hallington *N'umb* **220** B4
Halliwell **184** A1
Halloughton **174** C2
Hallow **146** A2
Hallow Heath **146** A2
Hallrule **227** G4
Halls **237** D2
Halls Green *Essex* **136** D2
Hall's Green *Herts* **150** A5
Hallsands **101** E4
Hallthwaites **198** C4
Hallwood Green **145** F4
Hallworthy **97** F1
Hallyne **235** F5
Halmer End **171** E3
Halmond's Frome **145** F3
Halmore **131** F2
Halmyre Mains **235** F5

Halnaker 108 B3
Halsall 183 E1
Halse N'hants 148 A3
Halse Som 115 E5
Halsetown 94 C3
Halstead Essex 151 G4
Halstead Kent 123 D2
Halstead Leics 160 C2
Halstock 104 B2
Halsway 115 E4
Haltemprice Farm 196 C4
Haltham 176 A1
Haltoft End 176 B3
Halton Bucks 135 D1
Halton Halton 183 G4
Halton Lancs 192 B1
Halton N'umb 211 F1
Halton Wrex 170 A4
Halton Gill 201 D5
Halton Green 192 B1
Halton Holegate 176 C1
Halton Lea Gate 210 C2
Halton Park 192 B1
Halton West 193 E2
Haltwhistle 210 D1
Halvergate 179 F5
Halwill 99 E1
Halwell 101 D2
Halwill Junction 99 E1
Ham Devon 103 F2
Ham Glos 131 F3
Ham Glos 146 B5
Ham GtLon 136 C5
Ham High 275 H1
Ham Kent 125 F3
Ham Plym 100 A2
Ham Shet 278 B1
Ham Som 115 F5
Ham Som 103 F1
Ham Wilts 119 E1
Ham Common 117 F5
Ham Green Here 145 G3
Ham Green Kent 124 C4
Ham Green Kent 111 D1
Ham Green NSom 131 E5
Ham Green Worcs 146 C1
Ham Hill 123 F2
Ham Hill Country Park
  Som TA13 6RW 104 A1
Ham Street 116 A5
Hambleden 134 C4
Hambledon Hants 107 F1
Hambledon Surr 121 E4
Hamble-le-Rice 107 D2
Hambleton Lancs 191 G3
Hambleton NYorks 195 E4
Hambridge 116 A5
Hambrook SGlos 131 F5
Hambrook WSuss 107 G3
Hameringham 176 B1
Hamerton 161 G1
Hamilton 234 B4
Hamlet Devon 103 E3
Hamlet Dorset 104 B2
Hammer 121 D4
Hammerpot 108 C3
Hammersmith 136 B5
Hammersmith Apollo
  GtLon W6 9QH 11 E5
Hammerwich 158 C2
Hammerwood 122 D5
Hammond Street 136 C2
Hammoon 105 E1
Hamnavoe Shet 279 C9
Hamnavoe Shet 278 B4
Hamnavoe Shet 278 D4
Hamnavoe Shet 278 D5
Hamnish Clifford 145 E2
Hamp 115 F4
Hampden Park 110 B3
Hampden Park Stadium
  Glas G42 9BA 30 D4
Hamperden End 151 E4
Hampnett 132 D1
Hampole 186 C2
Hampreston 105 G3
Hampstead 136 B4
Hampstead
  Norreys 134 A5
Hampsthwaite 194 B2
Hampton Devon 103 F2
Hampton GtLon 121 G1
Hampton Kent 125 D2
Hampton Shrop 157 G4
Hampton Swin 133 D3
Hampton Worcs 146 C3
Hampton Bishop 145 E4
Hampton Court Palace &
  Garden GtLon
  KT8 9AU 11 A2
Hampton Fields 132 A3
Hampton Heath 170 B3
Hampton in Arden 159 E4
Hampton Loade 157 G4
Hampton Lovett 146 A1
Hampton Lucy 147 E2
Hampton on the
  Hill 147 D1
Hampton Poyle 134 A1
Hampton Wick 121 G1
Hamptworth 106 B1
Hamsey 109 G2
Hamstall Ridware 158 D1
Hamstead 106 C3
Hamstead Marshall 119 F1
Hamsteels 212 A3
Hamsterley Dur 212 A4
Hamsterley Dur 212 A2
Hamsterley Forest Dur
  DL13 3NL 211 G5
Hamstreet 124 C5
Hamworthy 105 F3
Hanbury Staffs 172 C5
Hanbury Worcs 146 B1
Hanbury Woodend 172 C5
Hanby 175 F4
Hanchurch 171 F3
Handa Island 272 D4
Handbridge 170 B1
Handcross 122 B5
Handforth 184 C4
Handley ChesW&C 170 B2
Handley Derbys 173 E1

Handley Green 137 F2
Handsacre 158 C1
Handside 136 B1
Handsworth SYorks 186 B4
Handsworth WMid 158 C3
Handwoodbank 156 D1
Handy Cross 135 D3
Hanford Dorset 105 D1
Hanford Stoke 171 F3
Hanging Bridge 172 C3
Hanging Houghton 160 C5
Hanging Langford 118 B4
Hangingshaw 217 F2
Hanham 131 F5
Hankelow 171 D3
Hankerton 132 B3
Hankham 110 B3
Hanley 171 F3
Hanley Castle 146 A3
Hanley Child 145 F1
Hanley Swan 146 A3
Hanley William 145 F1
Hanlith 193 F1
Hanmer 170 B4
Hannah 189 E5
Hannington Hants 119 G2
Hannington
  N'hants 160 D5
Hannington Swin 133 D3
Hannington Wick 133 D3
Hanslope 148 D3
Hanthorpe 175 F5
Hanwell GtLon 136 A4
Hanwell Oxon 147 G3
Hanwood 156 D2
Hanworth GtLon 136 A5
Hanworth Norf 178 C2
Happisburgh 179 E2
Happisburgh
  Common 179 E3
Hapsford 183 F5
Hapton Lancs 193 D4
Hapton Norf 164 C2
Harberton 101 D2
Harbertonford 101 D2
Harbledown 124 C3
Harborne 158 C4
Harborough Magna 159 G5
Harbost (Tabost) 271 H1
Harbottle 220 B1
Harbour Park Amusements,
  Littlehampton WSuss
  BN17 5LL 108 C3
Harbridge 106 A1
Harbridge Green 106 A1
Harburn 235 E3
Harbury 147 F2
Harby Leics 174 C4
Harby Notts 187 F5
Harcombe 103 E3
Harcombe Bottom 103 G3
Harden WMid 158 C2
Harden WYorks 193 G4
Hardendale 199 G1
Hardenhuish 132 B5
Hardgate Aber 261 F4
Hardgate NYorks 194 B1
Hardham 108 C2
Hardhorn 191 G4
Hardingham 178 B5
Hardingstone 148 C2
Hardington 117 E2
Hardington
  Mandeville 104 B1
Hardington Marsh 104 B2
Hardington Moor 104 B1
Hardley 106 D2
Hardley Street 179 E5
Hardmead 149 E3
Hardraw 201 D3
Hardstoft 173 F1
Hardway Hants 107 F2
Hardway Som 117 E4
Hardwick Bucks 134 D1
Hardwick Cambs 150 B2
Hardwick Lincs 187 F5
Hardwick N'hants 149 D1
Hardwick Norf 164 D2
Hardwick Oxon 133 F2
Hardwick Oxon 148 A5
Hardwick SYorks 186 B5
Hardwick WMid 158 C3
Hardwick Hall Derbys
  S44 5QJ 173 F1
Hardwick Hall Country Park,
  Sedgefield Dur
  TS21 2EH 212 C5
Hardwicke Glos 131 G1
Hardwicke Glos 146 B5
Hardwicke Here 144 B3
Hardy's Green 152 A5
Hare Green 152 B5
Hare Hatch 134 D5
Hare Street Herts 150 B5
Hare Street Herts 150 B5
Hareby 176 B1
Harecroft 193 G4
Hareden 192 C3
Harefield 135 F3
Harehill 172 C4
Harehills 194 C4
Harehope 229 E4
Harelaw 234 D5
Hareplain 124 A5
Haresceugh 210 C3
Harescombe 132 A1
Haresfield 132 A1
Hareshaw NLan 234 C4
Hareshaw SLan 234 A5
Harestock 119 F4
Harewood 194 C3
Harewood End 145 E5
Harewood House WYorks
  LS17 9LG 194 C3
Harford Devon 100 C2
Harford Devon 102 B3
Hargate 164 C2
Hargatewall 185 F5
Hargrave ChesW&C 170 B1
Hargrave N'hants 161 F5
Hargrave Suff 151 F2
Hargrave Green 151 F2

Harle Syke 193 E4
Harlech 167 E4
Harlech Castle Gwyn
  LL46 2YH 167 E4
Harlequin 174 B4
Harlescott 157 E1
Harlesden 136 B4
Harleston Devon 101 D3
Harleston Norf 164 D3
Harleston Suff 152 B1
Harlestone 148 C1
Harley Shrop 157 E2
Harley SYorks 186 A3
Harleyholm 226 A2
Harlington
  CenBeds 149 F4
Harlington GtLon 135 F5
Harlosh 263 H7
Harlow 136 D2
Harlow Hill 211 G1
Harlthorpe 195 G4
Harlton 150 B2
Harlyn 96 C2
Harman's Cross 105 F4
Harmby 202 A4
Harmer Green 136 B1
Harmer Hill 170 B5
Harmondsworth 135 F5
Harmston 175 E1
Harnage 157 E2
Harnham 148 B1
Harnhill 132 C2
Harold Hill 137 E3
Harold Park 137 E3
Harold Wood 137 E3
Haroldston West 126 B1
Haroldswick 278 F1
Harome 203 F4
Harpenden 136 A1
Harpford 103 D3
Harpham 196 C1
Harpley Norf 177 F5
Harpley Worcs 145 F1
Harpole 148 B1
Harpsdale 275 G3
Harpsden 134 C4
Harpswell 187 G4
Harpur Hill 185 E5
Harpurhey 184 C2
Harracott 113 F3
Harrapool 256 C2
Harrietfield 243 E2
Harrietsham 124 A3
Harringay 136 C4
Harrington Cumb 208 C4
Harrington Lincs 189 D5
Harrington N'hants 160 C5
Harringworth 161 E3
Harris 255 J5
Harris Green 164 C2
Harris Museum & Art
  Gallery, Preston Lancs
  PR1 2PP 192 B5
Harriseahead 171 F2
Harriston 209 E2
Harrogate 194 C2
Harrogate International
  Centre NYorks HG1 5LA
  74 Harrogate
Harrold 149 E2
Harrold-Odell Country Park
  Bed MK43 7DS 149 E2
Harrop Fold 192 D3
Harrow GtLon 136 A4
Harrow High 275 H1
Harrow Green 151 G2
Harrow Museum GtLon
  HA2 6PX 10 B1
Harrow on the Hill 136 A4
Harrow Weald 136 A3
Harrowbarrow 99 E3
Harrowden 149 F3
Harrowgate Hill 202 B1
Harry Stoke 131 F5
Harston Cambs 150 C2
Harston Leics 174 D4
Harswell 196 A3
Hart 213 D4
Hartburn 220 C3
Hartest 151 G2
Hartfield ESuss 123 D5
Hartfield High 264 D7
Hartford Cambs 162 A5
Hartford
  ChesW&C 184 A5
Hartford Som 114 C5
Hartford End 137 F1
Hartfordbridge 120 C2
Hartforth 202 A2
Hartgrove 105 E1
Harthill ChesW&C 170 C2
Harthill NLan 234 D3
Harthill SYorks 186 B4
Hartington 172 C1
Hartington Hall 220 C3
Hartland 112 C3
Hartland Quay 112 C3
Hartlebury 158 A5
Hartlepool 213 E4
Hartlepool's Maritime
  Experience Hart
  TS24 0XZ 213 E4
Hartley Cumb 200 C3
Hartley Kent 123 F2
Hartley Kent 123 G5
Hartley N'umb 221 F4
Hartley Green 171 G5
Hartley Mauditt 120 C4
Hartley Wespall 120 B2
Hartley Wintney 120 C2
Hartlip 124 A2
Hartoft End 203 G3
Harton NYorks 195 G1
Harton Shrop 157 D4
Harton T&W 212 C1
Hartpury 146 A5
Hartridge 228 A4
Hartshead 194 A5
Hartshill 159 F3
Hartshorne 173 E5
Hartsop 199 F1
Hartwell Bucks 134 C1
Hartwell ESuss 123 D5
Hartwell N'hants 148 C2

Hartwith 194 B1
Hartwood 234 C4
Harvel 123 F2
Harvington Worcs 146 C3
Harvington Worcs 158 A5
Harwell Notts 187 D3
Harwell Oxon 133 G4
Harwich 152 D4
Harwood Dur 211 E4
Harwood GtMan 184 B1
Harwood N'umb 220 C2
Harwood Dale 204 C3
Harwood on
  Teviot 227 F5
Harworth 186 D3
Hasbury 158 B4
Hascombe 121 F3
Haselbech 160 C5
Haselbury
  Plucknett 104 A1
Haseley 147 E1
Haseley Knob 159 E5
Haselor 146 D2
Hasfield 146 A5
Hasguard 126 B2
Haskayne 183 E2
Hasketon 153 D2
Hasland 173 E1
Hasland Green 173 E1
Haslemere 121 E4
Haslingden 193 D5
Haslingden Grane 193 D5
Haslingfield 150 C2
Haslington 171 E2
Hassall 171 E2
Hassall Green 171 E2
Hassall Street 124 C4
Hassendean 227 G3
Hassingham 179 E5
Hassocks 109 F2
Hassop 185 G5
Haster 275 J3
Hasthorpe 176 C1
Hastigrow 275 H2
Hastingleigh 124 C4
Hastings ESuss 110 D3
Hastings Som 103 G1
Hastings Fishermen's
  Museum ESuss
  TN34 3DW 75 Hastings
Hastingwood 137 D2
Hastoe 135 E2
Haswell 212 C3
Haswell Plough 212 C3
Hatch CenBeds 149 G3
Hatch Hants 120 B2
Hatch Beauchamp 116 A5
Hatch End 136 A3
Hatch Green 103 G1
Hatching Green 136 A1
Hatchmere 183 G5
Hatcliffe 188 C2
Hatfield Here 145 E2
Hatfield Herts 136 B2
Hatfield SYorks 187 D2
Hatfield Broad Oak 137 E1
Hatfield Heath 137 E1
Hatfield House Herts
  AL9 5NF 136 B2
Hatfield Peverel 137 G1
Hatfield
  Woodhouse 187 D2
Hatford 133 F3
Hatherden 119 E2
Hatherleigh 113 F5
Hathern 173 F5
Hatherop 133 D2
Hathersage 185 G4
Hathersage Booths 185 G4
Hathershaw 184 D2
Hatherton ChesE 171 D3
Hatherton Staffs 158 B1
Hatley St. George 150 A2
Hatt 99 D4
Hattingley 120 B4
Hatton Aber 261 J1
Hatton Derbys 172 D5
Hatton GtLon 136 A5
Hatton Lincs 188 B5
Hatton Shrop 157 D3
Hatton Warks 147 E1
Hatton Warr 183 G4
Hatton Castle 269 F6
Hatton Country World
  Warks
  CV35 8XA 147 E1
Hatton Heath 170 B1
Hatton of Fintray 261 G3
Hattoncrook 261 G2
Haugh 189 E5
Haugh Head 229 E4
Haugh of Glass 260 C1
Haugh of Urr 216 C4
Haugham 188 D4
Haughhead 234 A2
Haughley 152 B1
Haughley Green 152 B1
Haughley New
  Street 152 B1
Haughs 268 D6
Haughton ChesE 170 C2
Haughton Notts 187 D5
Haughton Powys 156 C1
Haughton Shrop 157 F3
Haughton Shrop 157 E1
Haughton Shrop 170 A5
Haughton Staffs 171 F5
Haughton Green 184 D3
Haughton Le Skerne 202 C1
Haultwick 150 B5
Haunn 254 C3
Haunton 159 E1
Hauxton 150 C2
Havannah 171 F1
Havant 107 G2
Haven 144 D2
Havenstreet 107 E3
Havercroft 186 A1
Haverfordwest
  (Hwlffordd) 126 C1
Haverhill 151 E3
Haverigg 198 C5
Havering Park 137 D3
Havering-atte-
  Bower 137 E3
Haversham 148 D3
Haverthwaite 199 E4
Haverton Hill 213 D5

Haviker Street 123 G4
Havyat 116 C4
Hawarden
  (Penarlâg) 170 A1
Hawbridge 146 B3
Hawbush Green 151 F5
Hawcoat 198 D5
Hawes 201 D4
Hawe's Green 164 D2
Hawick 227 G4
Hawkchurch 103 G2
Hawkedon 151 F2
Hawkenbury Kent 123 E5
Hawkenbury Kent 124 A4
Hawkeridge 117 F2
Hawkerland 103 D4
Hawkes End 159 E4
Hawkesbury 131 G4
Hawkesbury
  Upton 131 G4
Hawkhill 229 G5
Hawkhurst 123 G5
Hawkinge 125 E4
Hawkley 120 C5
Hawkridge 114 B4
Hawkshead 199 E3
Hawkshead Hill 199 E3
Hawksheads 192 A1
Hawkswick 201 E5
Hawksworth
  Notts 174 C3
Hawksworth
  WYorks 194 A3
Hawksworth
  WYorks 194 B4
Hawkwell Essex 138 B3
Hawkwell N'umb 220 D4
Hawley Hants 121 D2
Hawley Kent 137 E5
Hawley's Corner 122 D3
Hawling 146 C5
Hawnby 203 E4
Haworth 193 G4
Hawstead 151 G2
Hawstead Green 151 G2
Hawthorn Dur 212 D3
Hawthorn Hants 120 B4
Hawthorn RCT 129 G4
Hawthorn Wilts 117 F1
Hawthorn Hill
  BrackF 135 D5
Hawthorn Hill
  Lincs 176 A2
Hawthorpe 175 F5
Hawton 174 C2
Haxby 195 F2
Haxey 187 E2
Haxted 122 D4
Haxton 118 C3
Hay Green 162 D1
Hay Mills 158 D4
Hay Street 150 B5
Haydock 183 G3
Haydon Dorset 104 C1
Haydon Swin 132 D4
Haydon Bridge 211 E1
Haydon Wick 132 D4
Hayes GtLon 135 F4
Hayes GtLon 122 D2
Hayes End 135 F4
Hayfield Derbys 185 E4
Hayfield Fife 244 A5
Hayfield High 275 G2
Haygrove 115 F4
Hayhillock 252 D5
Hayle 94 C3
Hayling Island 107 G2
Haymoor Green 171 D2
Hayne 102 C1
Haynes 149 G3
Haynes Church End 149 F3
Haynes West End 149 F3
Hay-on-Wye (Y Gelli
  Gandryll) 144 B3
Hayscastle 140 B5
Hayscastle Cross 140 C5
Hayton Cumb 210 B2
Hayton Cumb 209 E2
Hayton ERid 196 A3
Hayton Notts 187 E4
Hayton's Bent 157 E4
Haytor Vale 102 A5
Haytown 113 D4
Haywards Heath 109 F1
Haywood Oaks 174 B2
Hazel End 150 C5
Hazel Grove 184 D4
Hazel Street 123 F5
Hazelbank A&B 240 C4
Hazelbank SLan 234 C5
Hazelbury Bryan 104 D2
Hazeleigh 138 B2
Hazeley 120 C2
Hazelhurst 184 B1
Hazelside 225 G3
Hazelslack 199 F5
Hazelslade 158 C1
Hazelton Walls 244 B2
Hazelwood Derbys 173 E3
Hazelwood GtLon 122 D2
Hazlefield 208 A2
Hazlehead
  Aberdeen 261 G4
Hazlehead SYorks 185 F2
Hazlerigg 221 E4
Hazleton 132 C1
Hazon 221 D1
Heacham 177 E4
Head Bridge 113 G4
Headbourne
  Worthy 119 F4
Headcorn 124 A4
Headingley 194 B4
Headington 134 A2
Headlam 202 A1
Headless Cross 146 C1
Headley Hants 120 D4
Headley Hants 119 G1
Headley Surr 122 B3
Headley Down 120 D4
Headley Heath 158 C5
Headon 187 E5
Heads Nook 210 A2

Heady Hill 184 C1
Heage 173 E2
Healaugh NYorks 201 F3
Healaugh NYorks 195 E3
Heald Green 184 C4
Heale Devon 113 G1
Heale Som 116 A5
Healey Lancs 184 C1
Healey N'umb 211 G2
Healey NYorks 202 A4
Healey WYorks 194 B5
Healeyfield 211 G3
Healing 188 C1
Heamoor 94 B3
Heaning 199 F3
Heanish 246 B2
Heanor 173 F3
Heanton
  Punchardon 113 F2
Heanton Satchville 113 F4
Heap Bridge 184 C1
Heapey 192 C5
Heapham 187 F4
Hearn 120 D4
Heart of the Country
  Centre Staffs
  WS14 9QR 158 D2
Hearthstade 226 C3
Heasley Mill 114 A4
Heast 256 C3
Heath Cardiff 130 A4
Heath Derbys 173 F1
Heath WYorks 186 A1
Heath & Reach 149 E5
Heath End Derbys 173 E5
Heath End Hants 119 G1
Heath End Hants 119 F1
Heath End Surr 120 D3
Heath Hayes 158 C1
Heath Hill 157 G1
Heath House 116 B3
Heath Town 158 B3
Heathbrook 170 D5
Heathcot 261 G4
Heathcote Derbys 172 C1
Heathcote Shrop 171 D5
Heathencote 148 C3
Heather 159 F1
Heatherton Activity Park
  Pembs
  SA70 8RJ 127 D2
Heathfield Devon 102 B5
Heathfield ESuss 110 A1
Heathfield NYorks 194 A1
Heathfield Som 115 E5
Heathrow Airport 135 F5
Heathstone 158 A3
Heatley 184 B4
Heaton Lancs 192 A1
Heaton Staffs 171 G1
Heaton T&W 212 B1
Heaton WYorks 194 A4
Heaton Moor 184 C3
Heaton's Bridge 183 F1
Heaverham 123 E3
Heaviley 184 D4
Heavitree 102 C3
Hebburn 212 C1
Hebden 193 G1
Hebden Bridge 193 F5
Hebden Green 170 D1
Hebing End 150 B5
Hebron Carmar 141 E5
Hebron N'umb 221 D3
Heck 217 E2
Heckfield 120 C1
Heckfield Green 164 C4
Heckfordbridge 152 A5
Heckingham 165 E2
Heckington 175 G3
Heckmondwike 194 B5
Heddington 118 A1
Heddle 277 C6
Heddon-on-the-
  Wall 212 A1
Hedenham 165 E2
Hedge End 107 D1
Hedgerley 135 E4
Hedging 116 A5
Hedley on the Hill 211 G2
Hednesford 158 C1
Hedon 197 D5
Hedsor 135 E4
Heeley 186 A4
Heglibister 279 C7
Heighington Darl 212 B5
Heighington Lincs 175 F1
Heightington 157 G5
Heights of Brae 266 C5
Heilam 273 G3
Heiton 228 B3
Hele Devon 113 F1
Hele Devon 102 C2
Hele Devon 98 D1
Hele Devon 102 A5
Hele Som 115 E5
Hele Torbay 101 F1
Hele Bridge 113 F5
Hele Lane 102 A1
Helebridge 112 C5
Helensburgh 233 D1
Helford 95 E4
Helhoughton 177 G5
Helions Bumpstead 151 E3
Hell Corner 119 E1
Hellaby 186 C3
Helland Corn 97 E2
Helland Som 116 A5
Hellandbridge 97 E2
Hellesdon 178 D4
Hellidon 148 A2
Hellifield 193 E2
Hellingly 110 A2
Hellington 179 E5
Hellister 279 C8
Helmdon 148 A3
Helmingham 152 C2
Helmington Row 212 A4
Helmsdale 275 F7
Helmshore 193 D5
Helmsley 203 F4

Helperby 194 D1
Helperthorpe 204 C5
Helpringham 175 G3
Helpston 161 G2
Helsby 183 F5
Helsey 189 F5
Helston 95 D4
Helstone 97 E1
Helton 210 B2
Helwith 201 F2
Helwith Bridge 193 E1
Hem 156 B2
Hemborough Post 101 E2
Hemel Hempstead 135 F2
Hemerdon 100 B2
Hemingbrough 195 F4
Hemingby 188 B5
Hemingfield 186 A2
Hemingford Abbots 162 A5
Hemingford Grey 162 A5
Hemingstone 152 C2
Hemington Leics 173 F5
Hemington
  N'hants 161 F4
Hemington Som 117 E2
Hemley 153 D3
Hemlington 203 D1
Hemp Green 153 E1
Hempholme 196 C2
Hempnall 164 D2
Hempnall Green 164 D2
Hempriggs 267 J5
Hempriggs House 275 J4
Hempstead Essex 151 E4
Hempstead Med 123 G2
Hempstead Norf 179 F3
Hempstead Norf 178 C2
Hempsted 132 A1
Hempton Norf 178 A3
Hempton Oxon 147 G4
Hemsby 179 F4
Hemswell 187 G3
Hemswell Cliff 187 G4
Hemsworth 186 B1
Hemyock 103 E1
Henbury Bristol 131 E5
Henbury ChesE 184 C5
Henderland 216 C3
Hendersyde Park 228 B3
Hendham 100 D2
Hendon T&W 212 C2
Hendra 97 F1
Hendre Bridgend 129 F4
Hendre Gwyn 166 C4
Hendreforgan 129 F4
Hendy 128 B2
Heneglwys 180 C5
Henfield SGlos 131 F5
Henfield WSuss 109 E2
Henford 99 E1
Hengherst 124 B5
Hengoed Caerp 130 A3
Hengoed Powys 144 B2
Hengoed Shrop 169 F4
Hengrave 151 G1
Henham 150 D5
Heniarth 156 A2
Henlade 115 F5
Henley Dorset 104 C2
Henley Shrop 157 E5
Henley Som 116 B4
Henley Som 104 A2
Henley Suff 152 C2
Henley WSuss 121 D5
Henley Corner 116 B4
Henley Park 121 E2
Henley-in-Arden 147 D1
Henley-on-Thames 134 C4
Henley's Down 110 C2
Henllan Carmar 141 G3
Henllan Denb 168 C1
Henllan Amgoed 141 E5
Henllys 130 B3
Henlow 149 G4
Hennock 102 B4
Henny Street 151 G4
Henryd 181 F5
Henry's Moat 140 D5
Hensall 195 E5
Henshaw 211 D1
Hensingham 208 C5
Henstead 165 F3
Hensting 119 F5
Henstridge 104 D1
Henstridge Ash 104 D1
Henstridge Bowden 117 D5
Henstridge Marsh 117 E5
Henton Oxon 134 C2
Henton Som 116 B3
Henwood 97 G2
Heogan 279 D8
Heol Senni 143 F5
Heol-y-Cyw 129 F4
Heolgerrig 129 G2
Hepburn 229 E4
Hepburn Bell 229 E4
Hepple 220 B1
Hepscott 221 E3
Hepthorne Lane 173 F1
Heptonstall 193 F5
Hepworth Suff 164 A4
Hepworth WYorks 185 F2
Hepworth South
  Common 164 A4
Herbrandston 126 B2
Hereford 145 E3
Hereford Cathedral
  Here HR1 2NG
  75 Hereford
Heriot 236 A4
Heritage Motor Centre,
  Gaydon Warks
  CV35 0BJ 147 F2
Herm 101 G5
Hermiston 235 F2
Hermitage D&G 216 B4
Hermitage Dorset 104 C2
Hermitage ScBord 218 D2
Hermitage WBerks 134 A5
Hermitage WSuss 107 G2
Hermitage Green 184 A3
Hermon Carmar 141 G4
Hermon IoA 166 C1
Hermon Pembs 141 F4
Herne 125 D2
Herne Bay 125 D2
Herne Common 125 D2

Her - Hou

Herne Pound 123 F3
Herner 113 F3
Hernhill 124 C2
Herodsfoot 97 G3
Herongate 137 F3
Heron's Ghyll 109 G1
Heronsgate 135 F3
Herriard 120 B3
Herringfleet 165 F2
Herring's Green 149 F3
Herringswell 151 F1
Herringthorpe 186 B3
Hersden 125 D2
Hersham Corn 112 C5
Hersham Surr 121 G1
Herstmonceux 110 B2
Herston 277 D8
Hertford 136 C1
Hertford Heath 136 C1
Hertingfordbury 136 C1
Hesket Newmarket 209 G3
Hesketh Bank 192 A5
Hesketh Lane 192 C3
Heskin Green 183 G1
Hesleden 212 D4
Hesleyside 220 A3
Heslington 195 F2
Hessay 195 E2
Hessenford 98 D5
Hessett 152 A1
Hessle 196 C5
Hest Bank 192 A1
Hester's Way 146 B5
Hestley Green 152 C1
Heston 136 A5
Heswall 183 D4
Hethe 148 A5
Hethelpit Cross 145 G5
Hetherington 220 A4
Hethersett 178 C5
Hethersgill 210 A1
Hethpool 228 C4
Hett 212 B4
Hetton 193 F2
Hetton-le-Hole 212 C3
Heugh 220 C4
Heugh-head Aber 260 B3
Heugh-head Aber 260 D5
Heveningham 165 E4
Hever 123 D4
Hever Castle & Gardens Kent TN8 7NG 123 D4
Heversham 199 F4
Hevingham 178 C3
Hewas Water 97 D5
Hewell Grange 146 C1
Hewell Lane 146 C1
Hewelsfield 131 E2
Hewelsfield Common 131 E2
Hewish NSom 116 B1
Hewish Som 104 A2
Hewood 103 G2
Heworth 195 F2
Hewton 99 F1
Hexham 211 F1
Hexham Abbey N'umb NE46 3NB 211 F1
Hextable 137 E5
Hexthorpe 186 C2
Hexton 149 G4
Hexworthy 99 G3
Hey 193 E3
Hey Houses 191 G5
Heybridge Essex 137 F3
Heybridge Essex 138 B2
Heybridge Basin 138 B2
Heybrook Bay 100 A3
Heydon Cambs 150 C3
Heydon Norf 178 C3
Heydour 175 F4
Heylipoll 246 A2
Heylor 278 B4
Heyop 156 B5
Heysham 192 A1
Heyshaw 194 A1
Heyshott 108 A2
Heyside 184 D2
Heytesbury 118 A3
Heythrop 147 F5
Heywood GtMan 184 C1
Heywood Wilts 117 F2
Hibaldstow 187 G2
Hibb's Green 151 G2
Hickleton 186 B2
Hickling Norf 179 F3
Hickling Notts 174 B5
Hickling Green 179 F3
Hickling Heath 179 F3
Hickstead 109 E1
Hidcote Bartrim 147 D3
Hidcote Boyce 147 D3
Hidcote Manor Garden Glos GL55 6LR 147 D3
High Ackworth 186 B1
High Angerton 220 C3
High Balantyre 240 C3
High Bankhill 210 B3
High Beach 136 D3
High Bentham (Higher Bentham) 192 C1
High Bickington 113 F3
High Birkwith 200 C5
High Blantyre 234 A4
High Bonnybridge 234 C2
High Borgue 216 A5
High Borve 271 G2
High Bradfield 185 G3
High Bradley 193 G3
High Bransholme 196 D4
High Bray 113 G2
High Bridge 209 G2
High Brooms 123 E4
High Bullen 113 F3
High Burton 202 B4
High Buston 221 E1
High Callerton 221 D4
High Casterton 200 B5
High Catton 195 G2
High Close 202 A1
High Cogges 133 F2
High Common 164 C3
High Coniscliffe 202 B1
High Crompton 184 D2
High Cross Hants 120 C5
High Cross Herts 136 C1
High Cross WSuss 109 E2
High Easter 137 F1
High Ellington 202 A4
High Entercommon 202 C2
High Ercall 157 E1
High Etherley 212 A5
High Ferry 176 B3
High Flatts 185 G2
High Garrett 151 F5
High Gate 193 F5
High Grange 212 A4
High Green Norf 178 C5
High Green Norf 178 A4
High Green Norf 178 A5
High Green Suff 151 G1
High Green SYorks 186 A3
High Green Worcs 146 A3
High Halden 124 A5
High Halstow 137 G5
High Ham 116 B4
High Harrington 208 D4
High Harrogate 194 C2
High Hatton 170 D5
High Hauxley 221 E1
High Hawsker 204 C2
High Heath Shrop 171 D5
High Heath WMid 158 C2
High Hesket 210 A3
High Hesleden 213 D4
High Hoyland 185 G1
High Hunsley 196 B4
High Hurstwood 109 G1
High Hutton 195 G1
High Ireby 209 F3
High Kelling 178 B2
High Kilburn 203 E5
High Kingthorpe 204 B4
High Knipe 199 G1
High Lane Derbys 173 F3
High Lane GtMan 185 D4
High Lane Worcs 145 F1
High Laver 137 E2
High Legh 184 B4
High Leven 203 D1
High Littleton 116 D2
High Lodge Forest Centre Suff IP27 0AF 163 G4
High Lorton 209 E4
High Marishes 204 B5
High Marnham 187 F5
High Melton 186 C2
High Moor 186 B4
High Moorland Visitor Centre, Princetown Devon PL20 6QF 99 F3
High Newton 199 F4
High Newton-by-the-Sea 229 G4
High Nibthwaite 199 D3
High Offley 171 E5
High Ongar 137 E2
High Onn 158 A1
High Park Corner 152 B5
High Roding 137 F1
High Shaw 201 D3
High Spen 212 A1
High Stoop 212 A3
High Street Corn 97 D4
High Street Kent 123 G5
High Street Suff 153 F2
High Street Suff 165 E3
High Street Suff 165 F4
High Street Suff 151 G3
High Street Green 152 B2
High Throston 213 D4
High Town 158 B1
High Toynton 176 A1
High Trewhitt 220 C1
High Wham 212 A5
High Wigsell 110 C1
High Woods Country Park Essex CO4 5JR 152 B5
High Woolaston 131 E3
High Worsall 202 C2
High Wray 199 E3
High Wych 137 D1
High Wycombe 135 D3
Higham Derbys 173 E2
Higham Kent 137 G5
Higham Lancs 193 E4
Higham Suff 151 F1
Higham Suff 152 B4
Higham SYorks 186 A2
Higham Dykes 220 D4
Higham Ferrers 149 E1
Higham Gobian 149 G4
Higham on the Hill 159 F3
Higham Wood 123 F4
Highampton 113 E5
Highams Park 136 C3
Highbridge Hants 119 F5
Highbridge Som 116 A3
Highbrook 122 C5
Highburton 185 F1
Highbury 117 D3
Highclere 119 F1
Highcliffe 106 B3
Higher Alham 117 D3
Higher Ansty 105 D2
Higher Ashton 102 B4
Higher Ballam 191 G4
Higher Bentham (High Bentham) 192 C1
Higher Blackley 184 C2
Higher Brixham 101 F2
Higher Cheriton 103 E2
Higher Combe 114 C4
Higher Folds 184 A2
Higher Gabwell 101 F1
Higher Green 184 B3
Higher Halstock Leigh 104 B2
Higher Kingcombe 104 B3
Higher Kinnerton 170 A1
Higher Muddiford 113 F2
Higher Nyland 117 E5
Higher Prestacott 99 D1
Higher Standen 193 D3
Higher Tale 103 D2
Higher Thrushgill 192 C1
Higher Town Corn 97 E3
Higher Town IoS 96 B1
Higher Walreddon 99 E3
Higher Walton Lancs 192 B5
Higher Walton Warr 183 G4
Higher Wambrook 103 F2
Higher Whatcombe 105 E2
Higher Wheelton 192 C5
Higher Whiteleigh 98 C1
Higher Whitley 184 A4
Higher Wincham 184 A5
Higher Woodhill 184 B1
Higher Woodsford 105 D4
Higher Wraxall 104 B2
Higher Wych 170 B3
Highfield ERid 195 G4
Highfield NAyr 233 E4
Highfield Oxon 148 A5
Highfield SYorks 186 A4
Highfield T&W 212 A2
Highfields Cambs 150 B2
Highfields N'umb 237 G4
Highgate ESuss 122 D5
Highgate GtLon 136 B4
Highgreen Manor 220 A2
Highlane ChesE 171 F1
Highlane Derbys 186 B4
Highlaws 209 E2
Highleadon 145 G5
Highleigh Devon 114 C5
Highleigh WSuss 108 A4
Highley 157 G4
Highmead 142 B3
Highmoor Cross 134 B4
Highmoor Hill 131 D4
Highnam 131 G1
Highstead 125 E2
Highsted 124 B2
Highstreet 124 C2
Highstreet Green Essex 151 F4
Highstreet Green Surr 121 E4
Hightae 217 E3
Highter's Heath 158 C5
Hightown Hants 106 A2
Hightown Mersey 183 D2
Hightown Green 152 A2
Highway 132 C5
Highweek 102 B5
Highwood 145 F1
Highwood Hill 136 B3
Highworth 133 E3
Hilborough 163 G2
Hilcote 173 F2
Hilcott 118 C2
Hilden Park 123 E4
Hildenborough 123 E4
Hildenley 203 G5
Hildersham 150 D3
Hilderstone 171 G4
Hilderthorpe 197 D1
Hilfield 104 C2
Hilgay 163 E3
Hill SGlos 131 F3
Hill Warks 147 G1
Hill Worcs 146 B3
Hill Brow 120 C5
Hill Chorlton 171 E4
Hill Common 179 F3
Hill Cottages 203 G3
Hill Croome 146 A3
Hill Deverill 117 F3
Hill Dyke 176 B3
Hill End Dur 211 G4
Hill End Fife 243 F5
Hill End Glos 146 A4
Hill End GtLon 135 F3
Hill End NYorks 193 G2
Hill Green 150 C4
Hill Head 107 E2
Hill Houses 157 F5
Hill Mountain 126 C2
Hill of Beath 235 F1
Hill of Fearn 267 F4
Hill Ridware 158 C1
Hill Row 162 C5
Hill Side 185 F1
Hill Street 106 C1
Hill Top Hants 106 D2
Hill Top SYorks 186 B3
Hill Top SYorks 185 G4
Hill View 105 F3
Hill Wootton 147 F1
Hillam 195 E5
Hillbeck 200 C1
Hillberry 190 B4
Hillborough 125 E2
Hillbrae Aber 268 E6
Hillbrae Aber 261 F2
Hillbrae Aber 261 G1
Hillbutts 105 F2
Hillclifflane 173 D3
Hillend Aber 268 C6
Hillend Fife 235 F1
Hillend Midlo 235 G3
Hillend NLan 234 C3
Hillend Swan 128 A3
Hillend Green 145 G5
Hillersland 131 E1
Hillesden 148 B5
Hillesley 131 G4
Hillfarrance 115 E5
Hillfoot End 149 G4
Hillhead Devon 101 F2
Hillhead SAyr 224 C3
Hillhead of Auchentumb 269 H5
Hillhead of Cocklaw 269 J6
Hilliard's Cross 159 D1
Hilliclay 275 G2
Hillingdon 135 F4
Hillington Glas 233 G3
Hillington Norf 177 F5
Hillmorton 160 A5
Hillockhead Aber 260 B4
Hillockhead Aber 260 C3
Hillowton 216 B4
Hillpound 107 E1
Hill's End 149 E4
Hills Town 173 F1
Hillsborough 186 A3
Hillsford Bridge 114 A3
Hillside Aber 261 H5
Hillside Angus 253 F3
Hillside Moray 267 J5
Hillside Shet 279 D6
Hillside Worcs 145 G1
Hillswick 278 B5
Hillway 107 F4
Hillwell 279 F9
Hillyfields 106 C1
Hilmarton 132 C5
Hilperton 117 F2
Hilsea 107 F2
Hilston 197 E4
Hilton Cambs 150 A1
Hilton Cumb 210 D5
Hilton Derbys 172 D4
Hilton Dorset 105 D2
Hilton Dur 212 A5
Hilton High 267 G3
Hilton Shrop 157 G3
Hilton Staffs 158 C2
Hilton Stock 203 D1
Hilton Croft 261 H1
Hilton of Cadboll 267 F4
Hilton of Delnies 267 F6
Himbleton 146 B2
Himley 158 A3
Himley Hall & Park WMid DY3 4DF 14 A2
Hincaster 199 G4
Hinchley Wood 121 G1
Hinckley 159 G3
Hinderclay 164 B4
Hinderton 183 E5
Hinderwell 203 G1
Hindford 170 A4
Hindhead 121 D4
Hindley GtMan 184 A2
Hindley N'umb 211 G2
Hindley Green 184 A2
Hindlip 146 A2
Hindolveston 178 B3
Hindon Som 114 C3
Hindon Wilts 118 A4
Hindringham 178 A2
Hingham 178 B5
Hinksford 158 A4
Hinstock 171 D5
Hintlesham 152 B3
Hinton Glos 131 F2
Hinton Hants 106 B3
Hinton Here 144 C4
Hinton N'hants 148 A2
Hinton SGlos 131 G5
Hinton Shrop 156 D2
Hinton Admiral 106 B3
Hinton Ampner 119 G5
Hinton Blewett 116 C2
Hinton Charterhouse 117 E2
Hinton Martell 105 G2
Hinton on the Green 146 C3
Hinton Parva Dorset 105 F2
Hinton Parva Swin 133 E4
Hinton St. George 104 A1
Hinton St. Mary 105 D1
Hinton Waldrist 133 F3
Hinton-in-the-Hedges 148 A4
Hints Shrop 157 F5
Hints Staffs 159 D2
Hinwick 149 E1
Hinxhill 124 C4
Hinxton 150 C3
Hinxworth 150 A3
Hipperholme 194 A5
Hipsburn 229 G5
Hipswell 202 A3
Hirn 261 F4
Hirnant 169 D5
Hirst 221 E3
Hirst Courtney 195 F5
Hirwaen 169 E1
Hirwaun 129 F2
Hiscott 113 F3
Histon 150 C1
Hitcham Bucks 135 E4
Hitcham Suff 152 A2
Hitchin 149 G5
Hither Green 136 C5
Hittisleigh 102 A3
Hittisleigh Barton 102 A3
Hive 196 A4
Hixon 172 B5
Hoaden 125 E3
Hoaldalbert 144 C5
Hoar Cross 172 C5
Hoar Park Craft Centre Warks CV10 0QU 159 E3
Hoarwithy 145 E5
Hoath 125 E2
Hobarris 156 C5
Hobbister 277 C7
Hobbles Green 151 F2
Hobbs Cross 137 D3
Hobbs Lots Bridge 162 B2
Hobkirk 227 G4
Hobland Hall 179 G5
Hobson 212 A2
Hoby 160 B1
Hockerill 150 C5
Hockering 178 B4
Hockerton 174 C2
Hockley 138 B3
Hockley Heath 159 D5
Hockliffe 149 E5
Hockwold cum Wilton 163 F4
Hockworthy 102 D1
Hoddesdon 136 C2
Hoddlesden 192 D5
Hodgehill 171 F1
Hodgeston 126 D3
Hodnet 170 D5
Hodnetheath 170 D5
Hodsoll Street 123 F2
Hodson 133 D4
Hodthorpe 186 C5
Hoe 178 A4
Hoe Gate 107 F1
Hoff 200 B1
Hoffleet Stow 176 A4
Hoggard's Green 151 G2
Hoggeston 148 D5
Hoggie 268 D5
Hoggrill's End 159 E3
Hogha Gearraidh 262 C4
Hoghton 192 C5
Hognaston 172 D2
Hogsthorpe 189 F5
Holbeach 176 B5
Holbeach Bank 176 B5
Holbeach Clough 176 B5
Holbeach Drove 162 B1
Holbeach Hurn 176 B5
Holbeach St. Johns 162 B1
Holbeach St. Marks 176 B4
Holbeach St. Matthew 176 C4
Holbeck 186 C5
Holbeck Woodhouse 186 C5
Holberrow Green 146 C2
Holbeton 100 C2
Holborough 123 G2
Holbrook Derbys 173 E3
Holbrook Suff 152 C4
Holbrooks 159 F4
Holburn 229 E3
Holbury 106 D2
Holcombe Devon 102 C5
Holcombe GtMan 184 B1
Holcombe Som 117 D3
Holcombe Burnell Barton 102 B3
Holcombe Rogus 103 D1
Holcot 148 C1
Holden 193 D3
Holden Gate 193 E5
Holdenby 148 B1
Holdenhurst 106 A3
Holder's Green 151 E5
Holders Hill 136 B4
Holdgate 157 E4
Holdingham 175 F3
Holditch 103 G2
Hole 103 E1
Hole Park 124 A5
Holehouse 185 E3
Hole-in-the-Wall 145 F5
Holford 115 E3
Holgate 195 E2
Holker 199 E5
Holkham 177 G3
Hollacombe Devon 113 D5
Hollacombe Devon 102 B2
Hollacombe Town 113 G4
Holland Ork 276 D2
Holland Ork 276 F5
Holland Surr 122 D3
Holland Fen 176 A3
Holland-on-Sea 139 E1
Hollandstoun 276 G2
Hollee 218 A5
Hollesley 153 E3
Hollicombe 101 F1
Hollingbourne 124 A3
Hollingbury 109 F3
Hollingrove 110 B1
Hollington Derbys 172 D4
Hollington ESuss 110 C2
Hollington Staffs 172 B4
Hollingworth 185 E3
Hollins 186 A5
Hollins Green 184 A3
Hollins Lane 192 A2
Hollinsclough 172 D1
Hollinwood GtMan 184 D2
Hollinwood Shrop 170 C4
Hollocombe 113 G4
Hollow Meadows 185 G4
Holloway 173 E2
Hollowell 160 B5
Holly Bush 170 B3
Holly End 162 C2
Holly Green 134 C2
Hollybush Caerp 130 A2
Hollybush EAyr 224 B4
Hollybush Worcs 145 G4
Hollyhurst 170 C3
Hollym 197 F5
Hollywater 120 D4
Hollywood 158 C5
Holm D&G 218 A2
Holm (Tolm) Na H-Esiar 271 G4
Holm of Drumlanrig 216 C1
Holmbridge 185 F2
Holmbury St. Mary 121 G3
Holmbush 122 B5
Holme Cambs 161 G4
Holme Cumb 199 G5
Holme NLincs 187 G2
Holme Notts 174 D2
Holme NYorks 202 C4
Holme WYorks 185 F2
Holme Chapel 193 E5
Holme Hale 163 G2
Holme Lacy 145 E4
Holme Marsh 144 C2
Holme next the Sea 177 F3
Holme on the Wolds 196 B3
Holme Pierrepont 174 B4
Holme St. Cuthbert 209 E2
Holme-on-Spalding-Moor 196 A4
Holmer 145 E3
Holmer Green 135 E3
Holmes 183 F1
Holmes Chapel 171 E1
Holme's Hill 110 A2
Holmesfield 186 A5
Holmeswood 183 F1
Holmewood 173 F1
Holmfield 193 G5
Holmfirth 185 F2
Holmhead D&G 216 B2
Holmhead EAyr 225 D3
Holmpton 197 F5
Holmrook 198 B2
Holmsgarth 279 D8
Holmside 212 B3
Holmsleigh Green 103 F2
Holmston 224 B3
Holmwrangle 210 B3
Holne 100 D1
Holnest 104 C2
Holnicote 114 C3
Holsworthy 112 D5
Holsworthy Beacon 113 D5
Holt Dorset 105 G2
Holt Norf 178 B2
Holt Wilts 117 F1
Holt Worcs 146 A1
Holt Wrex 170 B2
Holt End Hants 120 B4
Holt End Worcs 146 C1
Holt Fleet 146 A1
Holt Heath Dorset 105 G2
Holt Heath Worcs 146 A1
Holt Wood 105 G2
Holtby 195 F2
Holton Oxon 134 B2
Holton Som 117 D5
Holton Suff 165 F4
Holton cum Beckering 188 B4
Holton Heath 105 F3
Holton le Clay 188 C2
Holton le Moor 188 A3
Holton St. Mary 152 B4
Holtspur 135 E4
Holtye 123 D5
Holtye Common 123 D5
Holway 115 F5
Holwell Dorset 104 C1
Holwell Herts 149 G4
Holwell Leics 174 C5
Holwell Oxon 133 E2
Holwell Som 117 E3
Holwick 211 F5
Holworth 105 D4
Holy Cross 158 B5
Holy Island IoA 180 A5
Holy Island (Lindisfarne) N'umb 229 F2
Holy Trinity Church, Skipton NYorks BD23 1NJ 193 F2
Holy Trinity Church, Stratford-upon-Avon Warks CV37 6BG 85 Stratford-upon-Avon
Holybourne 120 C3
Holyfield 136 C2
Holyhead (Caergybi) 180 A4
Holymoorside 173 E1
Holyport 135 D5
Holystone 220 B1
Holytown 234 B3
Holywell Cambs 162 B5
Holywell Corn 96 B4
Holywell Dorset 104 B2
Holywell ESuss 110 B4
Holywell (Treffynnon) Flints 182 C5
Holywell N'umb 221 F4
Holywell Bay Fun Park Corn TR8 5PW 96 B4
Holywell Green 185 E1
Holywell Lake 115 E5
Holywell Row 163 F5
Holywood 216 D2
Hom Green 145 E5
Homer 157 F2
Homersfield 165 D3
Homington 118 C5
Homore (Tobha Mòr) 254 C1
Honey Hill 124 D2
Honey Street 118 C1
Honey Tye 152 A4
Honeyborough 126 C2
Honeybourne 146 D3
Honeychurch 113 G5
Honicknowle 100 A2
Honiley 159 E5
Honing 179 E3
Honingham 178 C4
Honington Lincs 175 E3
Honington Suff 164 A4
Honington Warks 147 E3
Honiton 103 E2
Honkley 170 A2
Honley 185 F1
Hoo Med 137 G5
Hoo Suff 153 D2
Hoo Green 184 B4
Hoo Meavy 100 B1
Hood Green 186 A2
Hood Hill 186 A3
Hooe ESuss 110 B3
Hooe Plym 100 B2
Hooe Common 110 B2
Hook Cambs 162 C3
Hook ERid 195 G5
Hook GtLon 121 G1
Hook Hants 120 C2
Hook Hants 107 E2
Hook Pembs 126 C1
Hook Wilts 132 C4
Hook Green Kent 123 F5
Hook Green Kent 123 F2
Hook Green Kent 137 F5
Hook Green Kent 137 E5
Hook Norton 147 F4
Hook-a-Gate 157 D2
Hooke 104 B2
Hookgate 171 E4
Hookway 102 B3
Hookwood 122 B4
Hoole 170 B1
Hooley 122 B3
Hoop 131 E2
Hooton 183 E5
Hooton Levitt 186 C3
Hooton Pagnell 186 B2
Hooton Roberts 186 B3
Hop Farm, The Kent TN12 6PY 123 F4
Hop Pocket, The Here WR6 5BT 145 F3
Hop Pole 161 G1
Hopcrofts Holt 147 G5
Hope Derbys 185 F4
Hope Devon 100 C4
Hope Flints 170 A2
Hope Powys 156 B2
Hope Shrop 156 C2
Hope Staffs 172 C2
Hope Bagot 157 E5
Hope Bowdler 157 D3
Hope End Green 151 D5
Hope Mansell 131 F1
Hope under Dinmore 145 E2
Hopehouse 227 D4
Hopeman 267 J5
Hope's Green 137 G4
Hopesay 156 C4
Hopkinstown 129 G3
Hopley's Green 144 C2
Hopperton 194 D2
Hopsford 159 G4
Hopstone 157 G3
Hopton Derbys 173 D2
Hopton Norf 165 G2
Hopton Shrop 170 C5
Hopton Shrop 170 A5
Hopton Staffs 171 G5
Hopton Suff 164 A4
Hopton Cangeford 157 E4
Hopton Castle 156 C5
Hopton Wafers 157 F5
Hoptonheath 156 C5
Hopwas 159 D2
Hopwood 158 C5
Horam 110 A2
Horbling 175 G4
Horbury 185 G1
Horden 212 D3
Horderley 156 D4
Hordle 106 B3
Hordley 170 A4
Horeb Carmar 128 A2
Horeb Cere 141 G3
Horeb Flints 169 F2
Horfield 131 E5
Horham 164 D4
Horkesley Heath 152 A5
Horkstow 187 G1
Horley Oxon 147 G3
Horley Surr 122 B4
Horn Hill 135 F3
Hornblotton 116 C4
Hornblotton Green 116 C4
Hornby Lancs 192 B1
Hornby NYorks 202 B3
Hornby NYorks 202 C2
Horncastle 176 A1
Hornchurch 137 E4
Horncliffe 237 G5
Horndean Hants 107 G1
Horndean ScBord 237 G5
Horndon 99 F2
Horndon on the Hill 137 F4
Horne 122 C4
Horne Row 137 G2
Horner 114 B3
Horniehaugh 252 C3
Horniman Museum GtLon SE23 3PQ 13 C7
Horning 179 E4
Horninghold 160 D3
Horninglow 172 D5
Horningsea 150 C1
Horningsham 117 F3
Horningtoft 178 A3
Horningtops 97 G3
Horns Cross Devon 113 D3
Horns Cross ESuss 110 D1
Horns Green 123 D3
Hornsbury 103 G1
Hornsby 210 B3
Hornsby Gate 210 B2
Hornsea 197 E3
Hornsea Freeport ERid HU18 1UT 197 E3
Hornsey 136 C4
Hornton 147 F3
Horrabridge 100 B1
Horridge 102 A5
Horringer 151 G1
Horrocks Fold 184 B1
Horse Bridge 171 G2
Horsebridge Devon 99 E3
Horsebridge Hants 119 E4
Horsebrook 158 A1
Horsecastle 116 B1
Horsehay 157 F2
Horseheath 151 E3
Horsehouse 201 F4
Horsell 121 E2
Horseman's Green 170 B3
Horsenden 134 C2
Horseshoe Green 123 D4
Horseway 162 C4
Horsey 179 F3
Horsey Corner 179 F3
Horsford 178 C4
Horsforth 194 B4
Horsham Worcs 145 G2
Horsham WSuss 121 G4
Horsham St. Faith 178 D4
Horsington Lincs 175 G1
Horsington Som 117 E5
Horsington Marsh 117 E5
Horsley Derbys 173 E3
Horsley Glos 132 A3
Horsley N'umb 211 G1
Horsley N'umb 220 A2
Horsley Cross 152 C5
Horsley Woodhouse 173 E3
Horsleycross Street 152 C5
Horsleygate 186 A5
Horsleyhill 227 G4
Horsmonden 123 F4
Horspath 134 A2
Horstead 179 D4
Horsted Keynes 109 F1
Horton Bucks 135 E1
Horton Dorset 105 G2
Horton Lancs 193 E2
Horton N'hants 148 D2
Horton SGlos 131 G4
Horton Shrop 170 B5
Horton Som 103 G1
Horton Staffs 171 G2
Horton Swan 128 A4
Horton Tel&W 157 F1
Horton W&M 135 F5
Horton Wilts 118 B1
Horton Cross 103 G1
Horton Grange 221 E4
Horton Green 170 B3
Horton Heath 107 D1
Horton in Ribblesdale 200 D5
Horton Inn 105 G2
Horton Kirby 123 E2
Horton Park Farm Surr KT19 8PT 121 G1
Horton-cum-Studley 134 B1
Horwich 184 A1
Horwich End 185 E4
Horwood 113 F3
Hoscar 183 F1
Hose 174 C5
Hoses 198 D3
Hosh 243 D2
Hosta 262 C4
Hoswick 279 D10
Hotham 196 A4
Hothfield 124 B4
Hoton 173 G5
Houbie 278 F3
Houdston 214 C1
Hough 171 E2
Hough Green 183 F4

Hou - Ken

Hougham **175** D3
Hough-on-the-Hill **175** E3
Houghton *Cambs* **162** A5
Houghton *Cumb* **210** D4
Houghton *Devon* **100** C3
Houghton *Hants* **119** E4
Houghton *Pembs* **126** C2
Houghton **108** C2
Houghton Bank **212** B5
Houghton Conquest **149** F3
Houghton le Spring **212** C3
Houghton on the
    Hill **160** B2
Houghton Regis **149** F5
Houghton St. Giles **178** A2
Houghton-le-Side **212** B5
Houlsyke **203** G2
Hound **107** D2
Hound Green **120** C2
Houndslow **236** D5
Houndsmoor **115** E5
Houndwood **237** F3
Hounsdown **106** C1
Hounslow **136** A5
House of Marbles & Teign
    Valley Glass *Devon*
    TQ13 9DS **102** B5
Housebay **276** F5
Househill **267** F6
Houses Hill **185** F1
Housesteads Roman
    Fort *N'umb*
    NE47 6NN **211** D1
Houstter **278** C4
Housham Tye **137** E1
Houss **279** C9
Houston **233** F3
Houstry **275** G5
Houstry of Dunn **275** H3
Houton **277** C7
Hove **109** E3
Hove Edge **194** A5
Hoveringham **174** B3
Hoveton **179** E4
Hovingham **203** F5
How **210** B2
How Caple **145** F4
How End **149** F3
How Green **123** D4
How Man **208** C5
Howbrook **186** A3
Howden **195** G5
Howden Clough **194** B5
Howden-le-Wear **212** A4
Howe *Cumb* **208** C4
Howe *High* **275** J2
Howe *Norf* **165** D2
Howe *NYorks* **202** C4
Howe Green **137** G2
Howe of Teuchar **269** F6
Howe Street *Essex* **137** F1
Howe Street *Essex* **151** E4
Howegreen **138** B2
Howell **175** G3
Howey **143** G2
Howgate *Cumb* **208** C4
Howgate *Midlo* **235** G4
Howgill *Lancs* **193** E3
Howgill *NYorks* **193** G2
Howick **229** G5
Howle **171** D5
Howle Hill **145** F4
Howlett End **151** D4
Howletts Wild Animal Park
    Kent CT4 5EL **125** D3
Howley **103** F2
Hownam **228** B5
Hownam Mains **228** B4
Howpasley **227** E5
Howsham *NLincs* **188** A2
Howsham *NYorks* **195** G1
Howt Green **124** A2
Howtel **228** C3
Howton **144** D5
Howwood **233** F3
Hoxa **277** D8
Hoxne **164** C4
Hoy *High* **275** H2
Hoy *Ork* **277** B8
Hoylake **182** D4
Hoyland **186** A2
Hoylandswaine **185** G2
Hoyle **108** B2
Hubberholme **201** E5
Hubberston **126** B2
Hubbert's Bridge **176** A3
Huby *NYorks* **195** E1
Huby *NYorks* **194** B3
Hucclecote **132** A1
Hucking **124** A2
Hucknall **173** G3
Huddersfield **185** F1
Huddington **146** B2
Huddlesford **158** D2
Hudnall **135** F1
Hudscott **113** G3
Hudswell **202** A3
Huggate **196** A2
Hugglescote **159** G1
Hugh Town **96** B1
Hughenden Valley **135** D3
Hughley **157** E2
Hugmore **170** A2
Hugus **96** B5
Huish *Devon* **113** F4
Huish *Wilts* **118** C1
Huish Champflower **114** D5
Huish Episcopi **116** B5
Huisinis **270** B6
Hulcote **149** E4
Hulcott **135** D1
Hull **196** D5
Hulland **172** D3
Hulland Ward **173** D3
Hullavington **132** A4
Hullbridge **138** B3
Hulme **171** G4
Hulme End **172** C2
Hulme Walfield **171** F1
Hulverstone **106** C4
Humber *Devon* **102** B5
Humber *Here* **145** E2
Humber Bridge Country
    Park *ERid*
    HU13 0LN **196** C5
Humberside Airport **188** A1
Humberston **188** D2

Humberstone **160** B2
Humberton **194** D1
Humbie **236** B3
Humbleton *Dur* **201** F1
Humbleton *ERid* **197** E4
Humbleton *N'umb* **229** D4
Humby **175** F4
Hume **237** E5
Humehall **237** E5
Humshaugh **220** B4
Huna **275** J1
Huncoat **193** D4
Huncote **160** A3
Hundalee **228** A5
Hundall **186** A5
Hunderthwaite **211** F5
Hundleby **176** B1
Hundleton **126** C2
Hundon **151** F2
Hundred Acres **107** E1
Hundred End **192** A5
Hundred House **144** A2
Hungarton **160** B2
Hungate End **148** C3
Hungerford *Hants* **106** A1
Hungerford *Shrop* **157** E4
Hungerford *WBerks* **119** E1
Hungerford
    Newtown **133** F5
Hungerton **175** D5
Hunglader **263** J4
Hunmanby **205** D5
Hunningham **147** F1
Hunningham Hill **147** F1
Hunny Hill **107** D4
Hunsingore **194** D2
Hunslet **194** C4
Hunsonby **210** B4
Hunspow **275** H1
Hunstanton **177** E3
Hunstanworth **211** F3
Hunston *Suff* **152** A1
Hunston *WSuss* **108** A3
Hunsworth **194** A5
Hunt End **146** C1
Hunt House **204** B3
Huntercombe End **134** B4
Hunters Forstal **125** D2
Hunter's Inn **113** G1
Hunter's Quay **232** C2
Hunterston **232** C4
Huntford **219** E1
Huntham **116** A5
Huntingdon **162** A5
Huntingfield **165** E4
Huntingford **117** F4
Huntington *Here* **144** B2
Huntington *Here* **145** D3
Huntington *Staffs* **158** B1
Huntington *Tel&W* **157** F2
Huntington *York* **195** F2
Huntingtower **243** F2
Huntley **131** G1
Huntly **260** D1
Huntlywood **236** D5
Hunton *Hants* **119** F3
Hunton *Kent* **123** G4
Hunton *NYorks* **202** A3
Hunton Bridge **135** F2
Hunt's Cross **183** F4
Huntscott **114** C3
Huntsham **114** D5
Huntshaw **113** F3
Huntshaw Cross **113** F3
Huntshaw Water **113** F3
Huntspill **116** A3
Huntworth **116** A4
Hunworth **178** B2
Hurcott *Som* **116** C5
Hurcott *Som* **103** G1
Hurdley **156** B2
Hurdsfield **184** D5
Hurley *W&M* **134** D4
Hurley *Warks* **159** E3
Hurley Bottom **134** D4
Hurlford **224** C2
Hurliness **277** B9
Hurlston Green **183** E1
Hurn **106** A3
Hursley **119** F5
Hurst *NYorks* **201** F2
Hurst *W'ham* **134** C5
Hurst Green *Essex* **139** D1
Hurst Green *ESuss* **110** C1
Hurst Green *Lancs* **192** C4
Hurst Green *Surr* **122** C3
Hurst Wickham **109** E2
Hurstbourne Priors **119** F3
Hurstbourne
    Tarrant **119** E2
Hurstpierpoint **109** E2
Hurstwood **193** E4
Hurtmore **121** E3
Hurworth-on-Tees **202** C1
Hury **211** F5
Husabost **263** G6
Husbands
    Bosworth **160** B4
Husborne Crawley **149** E4
Husthwaite **203** E5
Hutcherleigh **101** D2
Huthwaite **173** F2
Huttoft **189** F5
Hutton *Cumb* **210** A5
Hutton *Essex* **137** F3
Hutton *Lancs* **192** A5
Hutton *NSom* **116** A2
Hutton *ScBord* **237** G4
Hutton Bonville **202** C2
Hutton Buscel **204** C4
Hutton Conyers **202** C5
Hutton Cranswick **196** C3
Hutton End **210** A4
Hutton Hang **202** A4
Hutton Henry **212** D4
Hutton Magna **202** A1
Hutton Mount **137** F3
Hutton Mulgrave **204** B2
Hutton Roof *Cumb* **199** G5
Hutton Roof *Cumb* **209** G3
Hutton Rudby **203** D2
Hutton Sessay **203** D5
Hutton Wandesley **195** E2
Hutton-le-Hole **203** G3
Huxham **102** C3

Huxham Green **116** C4
Huxley **170** C1
Huxter *Shet* **279** C7
Huxter *Shet* **279** E6
Huyton **244** A2
Hycemoor **198** B4
Hyde *GtMan* **184** D3
Hyde *Glos* **132** A2
Hyde End *W'ham* **120** C1
Hyde End *WBerks* **119** G1
Hyde Heath **135** E2
Hyde Lea **158** A1
Hydestile **121** E3
Hylands Park *Essex*
    CM2 8WQ **137** F2
Hyndford Bridge **234** D5
Hyndlee **227** G5
Hynish **246** A3
Hyssington **156** C3
Hythe *Hants* **106** D2
Hythe *Kent* **125** D5
Hythe End **135** F5
Hythie **269** J5
Hyton **198** B4

I

Ianstown **268** C4
Iarsiadar **270** D4
Ibberton **105** D2
Ible **172** D2
Ibsley **106** A2
Ibstock **159** G1
Ibstone **134** C3
Ibthorpe **119** E2
Iburndale **204** B2
Ibworth **119** G2
Icelton **116** A1
Ickenham **135** F4
Ickford **134** B2
Ickham **125** E3
Ickleford **149** G4
Icklesham **111** D2
Ickleton **150** C3
Icklingham **163** F5
Ickwell Green **149** G3
Icomb **147** E5
Idbury **147** E5
Iddesleigh **113** F5
Ide **102** C3
Ide Hill **123** D3
Ideford **102** B5
Iden **111** E1
Iden Green *Kent* **123** G5
Iden Green *Kent* **124** A5
Idle **194** A4
Idless **96** C5
Idlicote **147** E3
Idmiston **118** C4
Idridgehay **173** D3
Idridgehay Green **173** D3
Idstone **133** E4
Idvies **252** D5
Iffley **134** A2
Ifield **122** B5
Ifieldwood **122** B5
Ifold **121** F4
Iford *Bourne* **106** A3
Iford *ESuss* **109** G3
Ifton **133** G3
Ifton Heath **170** A4
Ightfield **170** C4
Ightham **123** E3
Ightham Mote *Kent*
    TN15 0NT **123** E3
Iken **153** F2
Ilam **172** C2
Ilchester **116** C5
Ilderton **229** E4
Ilford **136** D4
Ilfracombe **113** F1
Ilkeston **173** F3
Ilketshall
    St. Andrew **165** E3
Ilketshall
    St. Lawrence **165** E3
Ilketshall
    St. Margaret **165** E3
Ilkley **194** A3
Illey **158** B4
Illidge Green **171** F1
Illington **164** A3
Illingworth **193** G5
Illogan **96** A5
Illston on the Hill **160** C3
Ilmer **134** C2
Ilmington **147** E3
Ilminster **103** G1
Ilsington *Devon* **102** A5
Ilton *Som* **103** G1
Imachar **231** G5
Imber **118** A3
Immeroin **242** A3
Immingham **188** C1
Immingham Dock **188** C1
Imperial War Museum,
    Duxford *Cambs*
    CB22 4QR **150** C3
Imperial War Museum,
    London *GtLon*
    SE1 6HZ **45** G7
Imperial War Museum
    North *GtMan*
    M17 1TZ **24** D7
Impington **150** C1
Ince **183** F5
Ince Blundell **183** E2
Ince-in-Makerfield **183** G2
Inch Kenneth **238** D1
Inchbae Lodge **266** B5
Inchbare **253** E3
Inchberry **268** B5
Inchbraoch **253** F4
Inchgrundle **252** C2
Inchindown **266** D4
Inchinnan **233** F3
Inchkinloch **273** J4
Inchlaggan **257** H4
Inchlumpie **266** D4
Inchmarlo **260** E5
Inchmarnock **232** B4
Inchnabobart **252** B2
Inchnacardoch
    Hotel **257** K3

Inchnadamph **272** E6
Inchock **253** E5
Inchree **248** C3
Inchrory **259** J4
Inchture **244** A2
Inchvuilt **257** J1
Inchyra **243** G2
Indian Queens **96** D4
Inerval **230** B5
Ingatestone **137** F3
Ingbirchworth **185** G2
Ingerthorpe **194** B1
Ingestre **171** G5
Ingham *Lincs* **187** G4
Ingham *Norf* **179** E3
Ingham *Suff* **163** G5
Ingham Corner **179** E3
Ingleborough **162** C1
Ingleby *Derbys* **173** E5
Ingleby *Lincs* **187** F5
Ingleby Arncliffe **202** D2
Ingleby Barwick **202** D1
Ingleby Cross **202** D2
Ingleby Greenhow **203** E2
Inglesbatch **117** E1
Inglesham **133** E3
Ingleton *Dur* **212** A5
Ingleton *NYorks* **200** B5
Inglewhite **192** B4
Ingliston **235** F2
Ingmire Hall **200** B3
Ingoe **220** C4
Ingoldisthorpe **177** E4
Ingoldmells **177** D1
Ingoldsby **175** F4
Ingon **147** E2
Ingram **229** E5
Ingrave **137** F3
Ingrow **193** G4
Ings **199** F3
Ingst **131** E4
Ingworth **178** C3
Inhurst **119** G1
Inistrynich **240** C2
Injebreck **190** B3
Inkberrow **146** C2
Inkersall **186** B5
Inkersall Green **186** B5
Inkhorn **261** H1
Inkpen **119** E1
Inkstack **275** H1
Inmarsh **118** A1
Innellan **232** C3
Innergellie **245** D4
Innerhadden **250** B4
Innerleithen **227** E2
Innerleven **244** B4
Innermessan **214** B4
Innerwick *ELoth* **237** E2
Innerwick *P&K* **250** A5
Innibeg **247** F5
Innsworth **146** A5
Insch **260** E2
Inshore **273** F2
Inskip **192** A4
Instow **113** E2
Intake **186** C2
Intech, Winchester *Hants*
    SO21 1HX **119** G5
International Centre, The,
    Telford *Tel&W*
    TF3 4JH **157** G2
Intwood **178** C5
Inver *A&B* **248** B5
Inver *Aber* **259** K5
Inver *High* **267** F3
Inver *High* **275** G5
Inver *P&K* **251** F4
Inver Mallie **248** D1
Inverailort **247** G1
Inveralligin **264** E6
Inverallochy **269** J4
Inveran **266** C2
Inveraray
    (Inbhir Aora) **240** C4
Inverardoch Mains **242** C4
Inverardran **241** F2
Inverarish **256** B2
Inverarity **252** C5
Inverarnan
    (Inbhir Àirnein) **241** F3
Inverasdale **264** D6
Inverbain **264** D6
Inverberg **241** F5
Inverbervie **253** F2
Inverbroom **265** H3
Inverbrough **259** F2
Invercassley **266** B1
Inverchaolain **232** B2
Invercharnan **248** D5
Inverchoran **265** J6
Invercreran **248** C5
Inverdruie **259** G3
Inverebrie **261** H1
Invereen **258** E1
Inverernie **266** H5
Inveresk **236** A2
Inverey **251** G2
Inverfarigaig **258** C2
Invergarry
    (Inbhir Garadh) **257** K4
Invergelder **259** K5
Invergeldie **242** C2
Invergloy **249** E1
Invergordon **266** E5
Invergowrie **244** B1
Inverguseran **256** D4
Inverhadden **241** F2
Inverherive **241** F2
Inverhope **273** G2
Inverie **256** D4
Inverinan **240** B3
Inverinate **257** F2
Inverkeilor **253** E5
Inverkeithing **235** F1
Inverkeithny **268** E6
Inverkip **232** D2
Inverkirkaig **272** C7
Inverlael **265** H3
Inverlauren **233** E1
Inverliever **240** A4
Inverliver **240** C1
Inverlochlarig **241** G3
Inverlochy **241** D1
Inverlussa **231** E1

Invermay **243** F3
Invermoriston (Inbhir
    Moireasdan) **258** B3
Invernaver **274** C2
Inverneil **231** G1
Inverness
    (Inbhir Nis) **266** D7
Inverness Airport **266** E6
Invernettie **269** K6
Invernoaden **240** D5
Inveroran Hotel (Inbhir
    Orain) **249** E5
Inverquharity **252** C4
Inverquhomery **269** J6
Inverroy **249** E1
Inversanda **248** B4
Invershiel **257** F3
Invershore **275** H5
Inversnaid Hotel **241** F4
Invertrossachs **242** A4
Inveruglas (Inbhir
    Dhubhghlais) **241** F4
Inveruglass **259** F4
Inverurie **261** F2
Invervar **250** B5
Invervegain **232** B2
Invery House **260** E5
Inverythan **269** F6
Inwardleigh **99** F1
Inworth **138** C1
Iochdar **262** C7
Iona **238** B2
Iping **121** D5
Ipplepen **101** E1
Ipsden **134** B4
Ipstones **172** B3
Ipswich **152** C3
Irby **183** E4
Irby Hill **183** D4
Irby in the Marsh **176** C1
Irby upon Humber **188** B2
Irchester **149** E1
Ireby *Cumb* **209** F3
Ireby *Lancs* **200** B5
Ireland *Ork* **277** C7
Ireland *Shet* **279** C10
Ireland's Cross **171** E3
Ireleth **198** D5
Ireshopeburn **211** E4
Irlam **184** B3
Irnham **175** F5
Iron Acton **131** F4
Iron Cross **146** C2
Ironbridge **157** F2
Ironbridge Gorge *Tel&W*
    TF8 7DQ **157** F2
Irons Bottom **122** B4
Ironside **269** G5
Ironville **173** F2
Irstead **179** E3
Irthington **210** A1
Irthlingborough **161** E5
Irton **204** D4
Irvine **224** B2
Isauld **274** E2
Isbister *Ork* **277** C6
Isbister *Ork* **276** B5
Isbister *Shet* **279** E6
Isbister *Shet* **278** C3
Isfield **109** G2
Isham **161** D5
Ishriff **239** F1
Isington **120** C3
Island of Stroma **275** J1
Islawr-dref **154** C1
Islay **230** A3
Islay Airport **230** B4
Islay House **230** B3
Isle Abbotts **116** A5
Isle Brewers **116** A5
Isle of Bute Discovery Centre
    A&B PA20 0AH **232** B3
Isle of Lewis (Eilean
    Leodhais) **271** F3
Isle of Man **190** B3
Isle of Man Airport **190** A5
Isle of May **245** E5
Isle of Noss **279** E8
Isle of Sheppey **124** B1
Isle of Walney **191** E1
Isle of Whithorn **207** E3
Isle of Wight **107** D4
Isle of Wight Pearl *IoW*
    PO30 4DD **106** D4
Isle of Wight (Sandown)
    Airport **107** E4
Isle of Wight Zoo *IoW*
    PO36 8QB **107** F4
Isleham **163** E5
Isleornsay (Eilean
    Iarmain) **256** C3
Isles of Scilly
    (Scilly Isles) **96** B1
Islesburgh **279** C6
Isleworth **136** A5
Isley Walton **173** F5
Islibhig **270** B5
Islip *N'hants* **161** E5
Islip *Oxon* **134** A1
Isombridge **157** F1
Istead Rise **123** F4
Itchen **106** D1
Itchen Abbas **119** G4
Itchen Stoke **119** G4
Itchen Valley Country Park
    Hants SO30 3HQ **119** G5
Itchingfield **121** G5
Itchington **131** F4
Itteringham **178** C2
Itton *Devon* **99** G1
Itton *Mon* **131** D3
Itton Common **131** D3
Ivegill **210** A3
Ivelet **201** E3
Iver **135** F4
Iver Heath **135** F4
Iveston **212** A2
Ivetsey Bank **158** A1
Ivinghoe **135** E1
Ivinghoe Aston **135** E1
Ivington **145** D2
Ivington Green **145** D2
Ivy Hatch **123** E3
Ivy Todd **163** G2
Ivybridge **100** C2

Invermay **243** F3
Ivychurch **111** F1
Iwade **124** B2
Iwerne Courtney
    (Shroton) **105** E1
Iwerne Minster **105** E1
Ixworth **164** A4
Ixworth Thorpe **164** A4

J

Jack Hill **194** A2
Jackfield **157** F2
Jacksdale **173** F2
Jackstown **261** F1
Jackton **233** G4
Jacobstow **98** B1
Jacobstowe **99** F1
Jacobswell **121** E2
James Hamilton
    Heritage Park *SLan*
    G74 5LB **31** M5
James Pringle Weavers
    of Inverness *High*
    IV2 4RB **266** D7
Jameston **127** D3
Jamestown *D&G* **218** B2
Jamestown *High* **266** B6
Jamestown *WDun* **233** E1
Janefield **266** E6
Janetstown *High* **275** F2
Janetstown *High* **275** J3
Jarrow **212** C1
Jarvis Brook **123** E5
Jasper's Green **151** F5
Jawcraig **234** C2
Jayes Park **121** G3
Jaywick **139** E1
Jealott's Hill **135** D5
Jeater Houses **202** D3
Jedburgh **228** A4
Jeffreyston **127** D2
Jemimaville **266** E5
Jephson Gardens *Warks*
    CV32 4ER **16** B6
Jericho **184** C1
Jersay **234** C3
Jersey **100** C5
Jersey Airport **100** B5
Jersey Marine **128** D3
Jerviswood **234** C5
Jesmond **212** B1
Jevington **110** A3
Jinney Ring Craft Centre,
    The *Worcs*
    B60 4BU **146** B1
Jockey End **135** F1
Jodrell Bank **184** B5
Jodrell Bank Observatory &
    Arboretum *ChesE*
    SK11 9DL **184** B5
John Muir Country Park
    ELoth
    EH42 1UW **236** D2
John o' Groats **275** J1
Johnby **210** A4
John's Cross **110** C1
Johnshaven **253** F3
Johnson Street **179** E4
Johnston **126** C1
Johnstone **233** F3
Johnstone Castle **233** F3
Johnstonebridge **217** E1
Johnstown *Carmar* **127** G3
Johnstown *Wrex* **170** A3
Joppa **224** C4
Jordans **135** E3
Jordanston **140** C4
Jordanstone **252** A5
Jorvik *YO1 9WT* **90** York
Jorvik Glass *NYorks*
    YO60 7DA **195** G1
Joy's Green **131** F1
Jumpers Common **106** A3
Juniper Green **235** F2
Juniper Hill **148** A4
Jura **231** F1
Jura House **230** C3
Jurby East **190** B2
Jurby West **190** B2

K

Kaber **200** C1
Kaimes **235** G3
Kames *A&B* **232** A2
Kames *A&B* **240** A3
Kames *EAyr* **225** F3
Kathellan *Fife*
    KY4 0JR **243** G1
Kea **96** C5
Keadby **187** F1
Keal Cotes **176** B1
Kearsley **184** B2
Kearstwick **200** B5
Kearton **201** F3
Kearvaig **272** E1
Keasden **192** D1
Kebholes **268** E5
Keckwick **183** G4
Keddington **188** D4
Keddington Corner **189** D4
Kedington **151** F3
Kedleston **173** E3
Keelby **188** B1
Keele **171** F3
Keeley Green **149** F3
Keelham **193** G4
Keenthorne **115** F4
Keeres Green **137** E1
Keeston **126** B1
Keevil **118** A2
Kegworth **173** F5
Kehelland **96** A5
Keig **260** E3
Keighley **193** G3
Keighley & Worth Valley
    Railway *WYorks*
    BD22 8NJ **193** G4
Keil *A&B* **222** B5
Keil *High* **248** B4
Keilhill **269** F5
Keillmore **231** E1
Keillor **243** G5
Keillour **243** F2
Keills **230** C3

Keils **230** D3
Keinton Mandeville **116** C4
Keir House **242** C5
Keir Mill **216** C1
Keisby **175** F5
Keisley **210** D5
Keiss **275** J2
Keith **268** C5
Keithick **244** A1
Keithmore **260** B1
Keithock **253** E3
Kelbrook **193** F3
Kelby **175** F3
Keld *Cumb* **199** G1
Keld *NYorks* **201** D3
Keldholme **203** G4
Keldy Castle **203** G3
Kelfield *NLincs* **187** F2
Kelfield *NYorks* **195** E4
Kelham **174** C2
Kella **190** B2
Kellacott **99** E2
Kellan **247** E5
Kellas *Angus* **244** C1
Kellas *Moray* **267** J6
Kellaton **101** D4
Kellaways **132** B5
Kelleth **200** B2
Kellethorpe **196** C2
Kelling **178** B1
Kellington **195** E5
Kelloe **212** C4
Kelloholm **225** F4
Kelly *Corn* **97** E2
Kelly *Devon* **99** D2
Kelly Bray **99** D3
Kelmarsh **160** C5
Kelmscott **133** E3
Kelsale **153** E1
Kelsall **170** C1
Kelsay **230** A4
Kelshall **150** B4
Kelsick **209** E1
Kelso **228** B3
Kelstedge **173** E1
Kelstern **188** C3
Kelston **117** E1
Keltneyburn **250** C5
Kelton **217** D3
Kelton Hill
    (Rhonehouse) **216** B5
Kelty **243** G1
Kelvedon **138** B1
Kelvedon Hatch **137** E3
Kelvingrove Art Gallery &
    Museum *Glas*
    G3 8AG **38** A3
Kelvinside **233** G3
Kelynack **94** A4
Kemacott **113** G1
Kemback **244** C3
Kemberton **157** G2
Kemble **132** B2
Kemerton **146** B4
Kemeys
    Commander **130** C2
Kemeys Inferior **130** C3
Kemnay **261** F3
Kemp Town **109** F3
Kempe's Corner **124** C4
Kempley **145** F5
Kempley Green **145** F5
Kemps Green **158** D5
Kempsey **146** A3
Kempsford **133** D3
Kempshott **119** G3
Kempston **149** F3
Kempston Hardwick **149** F3
Kempston West End **149** E3
Kempton **156** C4
Kemsing **123** E3
Kemsley **124** B2
Kenardington **124** B5
Kenchester **144** D3
Kencot **133** E2
Kendal **199** G3
Kenderchurch **144** D5
Kendleshire **131** F5
Kenfig **129** E5
Kenfig Hill **129** E5
Kenidjack **94** A4
Kenilworth **159** E5
Kenilworth Castle *Warks*
    CV8 1NE **16** A4
Kenknock *P&K* **250** A5
Kenknock *Stir* **241** G1
Kenley *GtLon* **122** C2
Kenley *Shrop* **157** E2
Kenmore *A&B* **240** C4
Kenmore *High* **264** D6
Kenmore *P&K* **250** C5
Kenmore *Na H-ESiar*
    270 E7
Kenn *Devon* **102** C4
Kenn *NSom* **116** B1
Kennacley **263** G2
Kennacraig **231** G3
Kennavay **263** H2
Kenneggy Downs **94** C4
Kennerleigh **102** B2
Kennerty **260** E5
Kennet **243** E5
Kennethmont **260** D2
Kennett **151** E1
Kennford **102** C4
Kenninghall **164** B3
Kennington *Kent* **124** C4
Kennington *Oxon* **134** A2
Kennoway **244** B4
Kenny **103** G1
Kennyhill **163** E5
Kennythorpe **195** G1
Kenovay **246** A2
Kensaleyre **263** K6
Kensington **136** B4
Kensington Palace *GtLon*
    W8 4PX **10** F5
Kenstone **170** C5
Kensworth **135** F1
Kent & East Sussex Railway
    Kent TN30 6HE **124** A5
Kent International
    Airport **125** F2
Kent Street *ESuss* **110** C2
Kent Street *Kent* **123** F3
Kentallen (Ceann an t-
    Sàilein) **248** C4

Kentchurch 144 D5
Kentford 151 F1
Kentisbeare 103 D2
Kentisbury 113 G1
Kentisbury Ford 113 G1
Kentish Town 136 B4
Kentmere 199 F2
Kenton Devon 102 C4
Kenton Suff 152 C1
Kenton T&W 212 B1
Kenton Corner 152 D1
Kentra 247 F3
Kents Bank 199 E5
Kent's Green 145 G5
Kent's Oak 119 E5
Kenwick 170 B4
Kenwood House GtLon NW3 7JR 10 F2
Kenwyn 96 C5
Kenyon 184 A3
Keoldale 273 F2
Keose (Ceòs) 271 F5
Keppanach 248 C3
Keppoch A&B 233 E2
Keppoch High 256 E2
Keprigan 222 B4
Kepwick 203 D3
Keresley 159 F4
Kernborough 101 D3
Kerrera 240 A2
Kerridge 184 D5
Kerris 94 B4
Kerry (Ceri) 156 A3
Kerrycroy 232 C3
Kerry's Gate 144 C4
Kerrysdale 264 E4
Kersall 174 C1
Kersey 152 B3
Kersey Vale 152 B3
Kershopefoot 218 C3
Kerswell 103 D2
Kerswell Green 146 A3
Kerthen Wood 94 C3
Kesgrave 152 D3
Kessingland 165 G3
Kessingland Beach 165 G3
Kestle 97 D5
Kestle Mill 96 C4
Keston 122 D2
Keswick Cumb 209 F4
Keswick Norf 178 D5
Keswick Norf 179 E2
Ketley Bank 157 F1
Ketsby 189 D5
Kettering 161 D5
Ketteringham 178 C5
Kettins 244 A1
Kettle Corner 123 G3
Kettlebaston 152 A2
Kettlebridge 244 B4
Kettlebrook 159 E2
Kettleburgh 153 D1
Kettlehill 244 B4
Kettleholm 217 F3
Kettleness 204 B1
Kettleshulme 185 D5
Kettlesing 194 B2
Kettlesing Bottom 194 B2
Kettlesing Head 194 B2
Kettlestone 178 A2
Kettlethorpe 187 F5
Kettletoft 276 F4
Kettlewell 201 E5
Ketton 161 E2
Kevingtown 123 D2
Kew 136 A5
Kewstoke 116 A1
Kexbrough 186 A2
Kexby Lincs 187 F4
Kexby York 195 G2
Key Green 171 F1
Keyham 160 B2
Keyhaven 106 C3
Keyingham 197 E5
Keymer 109 F2
Keynsham 117 D1
Key's Toft 176 C2
Keysoe 149 F1
Keysoe Row 149 F1
Keyston 161 F5
Keyworth 174 B4
Kibblesworth 212 B2
Kibworth Beauchamp 160 B3
Kibworth Harcourt 160 B3
Kidbrooke 136 D5
Kiddemore Green 158 A2
Kidderminster 158 A5
Kiddington 147 G5
Kidlington 133 G1
Kidmore End 134 B5
Kidnal 170 B3
Kidsdale 207 E3
Kidsgrove 171 F2
Kidstones 201 E4
Kidwelly (Cydweli) 128 A2
Kiel Crofts 240 A1
Kielder 219 E2
Kielder Forest N'umb NE48 1ER 219 E2
Kielder Water N'umb NE48 1BX 219 F3
Kilbarchan 233 F3
Kilbeg 256 C4
Kilberry 231 F3
Kilbirnie 233 E4
Kilblaan 240 D3
Kilbraur 274 D7
Kilbrennan 246 D5
Kilbride A&B 240 A2
Kilbride A&B 232 B3
Kilbride High 256 B2
Kilbride Farm 232 A3
Kilbridemore 240 C5
Kilburn Derbys 173 E3
Kilburn GtLon 136 B4
Kilburn NYorks 203 E5
Kilby 160 B3
Kilchattan Bay 232 C4
Kilchenzie 222 B3
Kilcheran 240 A1
Kilchiaran 230 A3
Kilchoan A&B 239 G3
Kilchoan High 247 D3
Kilchoman 230 A3
Kilchrenan (Cill Chrèanain) 240 C2
Kilchrist 222 B4
Kilconquhar 244 C4
Kilcot 145 F5
Kilcoy 266 C6
Kilcreggan 232 D1
Kildale 203 F2
Kildary 266 E4
Kildavie 222 C4
Kildermorie Lodge 266 C4
Kildonan NAyr 223 F3
Kildonan (Cilldonnain) Na H-ESiar 254 C2
Kildonan Lodge 274 E6
Kildonnan 247 D1
Kildrochet House 214 B5
Kildrummy 260 C3
Kildwick 193 G3
Kilfinan 232 A2
Kilfinnan 257 J5
Kilgetty 127 E2
Kilgwrrwg Common 131 D3
Kilham ERid 196 C1
Kilham N'umb 228 C3
Kilkenneth 246 A2
Kilkenny 132 C1
Kilkerran A&B 222 C4
Kilkerran SAyr 224 B5
Kilkhampton 112 C4
Killamarsh 186 B4
Killay 128 C3
Killbeg 247 F5
Killean A&B 231 E5
Killean A&B 240 C4
Killearn 233 G1
Killellan 222 B4
Killen 266 D6
Killerby 212 A5
Killerton 102 C2
Killerton Devon EX5 3LE 102 C2
Killichonan 250 A4
Killiechonate 249 E1
Killiechronan 247 E5
Killiecrankie 251 E3
Killiehuntly 258 E5
Killiemor 239 D1
Killilan 257 F1
Killimster 275 J3
Killin High 267 F1
Killin Stir 242 A1
Killinallan 230 B2
Killinghall 194 B2
Killington Cumb 200 B4
Killington Devon 113 G1
Killingworth 221 E4
Killochyett 236 B5
Killocraw 222 B2
Killunaig 239 D2
Killundine 247 E5
Kilmacolm 233 E3
Kilmaha 240 B4
Kilmahog 242 B4
Kilmalieu 248 A4
Kilmaluag 263 K4
Kilmany 244 B2
Kilmarie 256 B3
Kilmarnock 224 C2
Kilmartin 240 A5
Kilmaurs 233 F5
Kilmelford 240 A3
Kilmeny 230 B3
Kilmersdon 117 D2
Kilmeston 119 G5
Kilmichael 222 B3
Kilmichael Glassary 240 A5
Kilmichael of Inverlussa 231 F1
Kilmington Devon 103 F3
Kilmington Wilts 117 E4
Kilmington Common 117 E4
Kilmorack 266 B7
Kilmore (A' Chille Mhòr) A&B 240 A2
Kilmore High 256 C4
Kilmory A&B 231 F1
Kilmory A&B 231 F2
Kilmory High 255 J4
Kilmory High 247 E2
Kilmory NAyr 223 E3
Kilmote 274 E7
Kilmuir High 263 H7
Kilmuir High 266 D7
Kilmuir High 266 E4
Kilmuir High 263 J4
Kilmun 232 C1
Kilmux 244 B4
Kiln Green Here 131 F1
Kiln Green W'ham 134 D5
Kiln Pit Hill 211 G2
Kilnave 230 A2
Kilncadzow 234 C5
Kilndown 123 G5
Kilnhurst 186 B3
Kilninian 246 D5
Kilninver 240 A2
Kilnsea 189 E1
Kilnsey 193 F1
Kilnwick 196 B3
Kilnwick Percy 196 A2
Kiloran 238 C5
Kilpatrick 223 E3
Kilpeck 144 D4
Kilphedir 274 E7
Kilpin 195 G5
Kilpin Pike 195 G5
Kilrenny 245 D4
Kilsby 160 A5
Kilspindie 244 A2
Kilstay 206 B3
Kilsyth 234 B2
Kiltarlity 266 C7
Kilton Notts 186 C5
Kilton R&C 203 F1
Kilton Som 115 E3
Kilton Thorpe 203 F1
Kiltyrie 242 B1
Kilvaxter 263 J5
Kilve 115 E3
Kilverstone 163 G4
Kilvington 174 D3
Kilwinning 233 E5
Kimberley Norf 178 B5
Kimberley Notts 173 G3
Kimberworth 186 B3
Kimble Wick 134 D2
Kimblesworth 212 B3
Kimbolton Cambs 149 F1
Kimbolton Here 145 E1
Kimbridge 119 E5
Kimcote 160 A4
Kimmeridge 105 F5
Kimmerston 229 D3
Kimpton Hants 119 D3
Kimpton Herts 136 A1
Kinaldy 244 D3
Kinblethmont 253 E5
Kinbrace 274 D5
Kinbreack 257 G5
Kinbuck 242 C4
Kincaldrum 252 C5
Kincaple 244 C3
Kincardine Fife 234 D1
Kincardine High 266 D3
Kincardine O'Neil 260 D5
Kinclaven 243 G1
Kincorth 261 H4
Kincraig Aber 261 H2
Kincraig High 259 F4
Kincraigie 251 E5
Kindallachan 251 E4
Kindrogan Field Centre 251 F3
Kinellar 261 G3
Kineton Glos 146 C5
Kineton Warks 147 F2
Kineton Green 158 D4
Kinfauns 243 G2
King Sterndale 185 E5
Kingarth 232 B4
Kingcoed 130 D2
Kingerby 188 A3
Kingham 147 E5
Kingholm Quay 217 D3
Kinghorn 235 G1
Kinglassie 244 A5
Kingoodie 244 B2
King's Acre 145 D3
King's Bank 111 D1
King's Bromley 158 D1
Kings Caple 145 E5
King's Cliffe 161 F3
King's College Chapel, Cambridge Cambs CB2 1ST 150 C2
King's Coughton 146 C2
King's Green 145 G4
King's Heath 158 C4
Kings Hill Kent 123 F3
King's Hill Warks 159 F5
King's Hill WMid 158 B3
Kings Langley 135 F2
King's Lynn 177 E5
King's Meaburn 210 C5
Kings Mills 101 E5
King's Moss 183 G2
Kings Muir 227 D2
King's Newnham 159 G5
King's Newton 173 E5
King's Norton Leics 160 B2
King's Norton WMid 158 C5
Kings Nympton 113 G4
King's Pyon 144 D2
Kings Ripton 162 A5
King's Somborne 119 E4
King's Stag 104 D1
King's Stanley 132 A2
King's Sutton 147 G4
King's Tamerton 100 A2
King's Walden 149 G5
Kings Worthy 119 F4
Kingsand 100 A2
Kingsbarns 245 D3
Kingsbridge Devon 100 D3
Kingsbridge Som 114 C4
Kingsburgh 263 J6
Kingsbury GtLon 136 A4
Kingsbury Warks 159 E3
Kingsbury Episcopi 116 B5
Kingsbury Water Park Warks B76 0DY 159 E3
Kingscavil 235 E2
Kingsclere 119 G2
Kingscote 132 A3
Kingscott 113 F4
Kingscross 223 F3
Kingsdale 244 B4
Kingsdon 116 C5
Kingsdown Kent 125 F4
Kingsdown Swin 133 D4
Kingsdown Wilts 117 F1
Kingseat 243 G5
Kingsey 134 C2
Kingsfold Pembs 126 C3
Kingsfold WSuss 121 G4
Kingsford Aber 269 F6
Kingsford Aber 260 D3
Kingsford Aberdeen 261 G4
Kingsford EAyr 233 F5
Kingsford Worcs 158 A4
Kingsgate 125 F1
Kingshall Street 152 A1
Kingsheanton 113 F2
Kingshouse 242 A2
Kingshouse Hotel 249 E4
Kingshurst 159 D4
Kingskerswell 101 E1
Kingskettle 244 B4
Kingsland Here 144 D1
Kingsland IoA 180 A4
Kingsley ChesW&C 183 G5
Kingsley Hants 120 C4
Kingsley Staffs 172 B3
Kingsley Green 121 D4
Kingsley Holt 172 B3
Kingslow 157 G3
Kingsmoor 136 D2
Kingsmuir Angus 252 C5
Kingsmuir Fife 244 D4
Kingsnorth 124 C5
Kingsnorth Power Station 124 A1
Kingstanding 158 C3
Kingsteignton 102 B5
Kingsteps 267 G6
Kingsthorne 145 D4
Kingsthorpe 148 C1
Kingston Cambs 150 B2
Kingston Corn 99 D3
Kingston Devon 100 C3
Kingston Devon 103 D4
Kingston Dorset 104 D2
Kingston Dorset 105 F5
Kingston ELoth 236 C1
Kingston GtMan 184 D3
Kingston Hants 106 A2
Kingston IoW 107 D4
Kingston Kent 125 D3
Kingston MK 149 E4
Kingston Moray 268 B4
Kingston WSuss 108 C3
Kingston Bagpuize 133 G3
Kingston Blount 134 C3
Kingston by Sea 109 E3
Kingston Deverill 117 F4
Kingston Gorse 108 C3
Kingston Lacy Dorset BH21 4EA 3 A1
Kingston Lisle 133 F4
Kingston Maurward 104 D3
Kingston near Lewes 109 F3
Kingston on Soar 173 G5
Kingston Russell 104 B3
Kingston St. Mary 115 F5
Kingston Seymour 116 B1
Kingston Stert 134 C2
Kingston upon Hull 196 D5
Kingston upon Thames 121 G1
Kingston Warren 133 F4
Kingstone Here 144 D4
Kingstone Here 145 F5
Kingstone Som 103 G1
Kingstone Staffs 172 B5
Kingstone Winslow 133 E4
Kingstown 209 G1
Kingswear 101 E2
Kingswell 233 G5
Kingswells 261 G4
Kingswinford 158 A4
Kingswood Bucks 134 B1
Kingswood Glos 131 G3
Kingswood Here 144 B2
Kingswood Kent 124 A3
Kingswood Powys 156 B2
Kingswood SGlos 131 F5
Kingswood Som 115 E4
Kingswood Surr 122 B3
Kingswood Warks 159 D5
Kingthorpe 188 B5
Kington Here 144 B2
Kington Worcs 146 B2
Kington Langley 132 B5
Kington Magna 117 E5
Kington St. Michael 132 B5
Kingussie 258 E4
Kingweston 116 C4
Kinharrachie 261 H1
Kinharvie 216 D4
Kinkell 234 A2
Kinkell Bridge 243 E3
Kinknockie 269 J6
Kinlet 157 G4
Kinloch Fife 244 A3
Kinloch High 273 F5
Kinloch High 247 F4
Kinloch High 255 K5
Kinloch High 266 C4
Kinloch P&K 252 A5
Kinloch P&K 251 G5
Kinloch Hourn (Ceann Loch Shubhairne) 257 F4
Kinloch Laggan 250 A1
Kinloch Rannoch 250 B4
Kinlochan 248 A3
Kinlochard 241 G4
Kinlocharkaig 257 F5
Kinlochbeoraid 248 A1
Kinlochbervie 272 E3
Kinlocheil 248 B2
Kinlochetive 248 D5
Kinlochewe 265 G5
Kinlochlaich 248 B5
Kinlochleven (Ceann Loch Liobhann) 249 D3
Kinlochmoidart 247 G2
Kinlochmorar 256 E5
Kinlochmore 249 D3
Kinlochroag (Ceann Lochroag) 270 D5
Kinlochspelve 239 F2
Kinloss 267 H5
Kinmel Bay (Bae Cinmel) 182 A4
Kinmuck 261 G3
Kinnaber 253 F3
Kinnadie 269 H6
Kinnaird 244 A2
Kinneff 253 G2
Kinnelhead 226 B5
Kinnell Angus 253 E4
Kinnell Stir 242 A1
Kinnerley 170 A5
Kinnersley Here 144 C3
Kinnersley Worcs 146 A3
Kinnerton 144 B1
Kinnerton Green 170 A1
Kinnesswood 243 G4
Kinnettles 252 C5
Kinninvie 211 G5
Kinnordy 252 B4
Kinoulton 174 B4
Kinrara 259 F4
Kinross 243 G4
Kinrossie 243 G1
Kinsbourne Green 136 A1
Kinsham Here 144 C1
Kinsham Worcs 146 B4
Kinsley 186 B1
Kinson 105 G3
Kintarvie 270 E6
Kintbury 119 E1
Kintessack 267 G5
Kintillo 243 G3
Kintocher 260 D4
Kinton Here 156 D5
Kinton Shrop 156 C1
Kintore 261 F3
Kintour 230 C4
Kintra A&B 230 B5
Kintra A&B 238 C2
Kintradwell 267 G1
Kintraw 240 A4
Kinuachdrachd 239 G5
Kinveachy 259 G3
Kinver 158 A4
Kinwarton 146 D2
Kiplaw Croft 261 J1
Kipp 242 A3
Kippax 194 D4
Kippen P&K 243 F3
Kippen Stir 242 B5
Kippenross House 242 C4
Kippford (Scaur) 216 C5
Kipping's Cross 123 F4
Kippington 123 E3
Kirbister Ork 277 C7
Kirbister Ork 276 F5
Kirbuster 276 B5
Kirby Bedon 179 D5
Kirby Bellars 160 C1
Kirby Cane 165 E2
Kirby Corner 159 E5
Kirby Cross 152 D5
Kirby Fields 160 A2
Kirby Green 165 E2
Kirby Grindalythe 196 B1
Kirby Hill NYorks 202 A2
Kirby Hill NYorks 194 C1
Kirby Knowle 203 D4
Kirby le Soken 152 D5
Kirby Misperton 203 G5
Kirby Muxloe 160 A2
Kirby Row 165 E2
Kirby Sigston 202 D3
Kirby Underdale 196 A2
Kirby Wiske 202 C4
Kirdford 121 F5
Kirk 275 H3
Kirk Bramwith 186 D1
Kirk Deighton 194 C2
Kirk Ella 196 C5
Kirk Hallam 173 F3
Kirk Hammerton 195 D2
Kirk Ireton 173 D2
Kirk Langley 173 D4
Kirk Merrington 212 B4
Kirk Michael 190 B2
Kirk of Shotts 234 C3
Kirk Sandall 186 D2
Kirk Smeaton 186 C1
Kirk Yetholm 228 C4
Kirkabister 279 D9
Kirkandrews 207 G2
Kirkandrews-upon-Eden 209 G1
Kirkbampton 209 G1
Kirkbean 217 D5
Kirkbride 209 F1
Kirkbuddo 252 D5
Kirkburn ERid 196 B2
Kirkburn ScBord 227 D2
Kirkburton 185 F1
Kirkby Lincs 188 A3
Kirkby Mersey 183 F3
Kirkby NYorks 203 E2
Kirkby Fleetham 202 B3
Kirkby Green 175 F2
Kirkby in Ashfield 173 F2
Kirkby la Thorpe 175 F3
Kirkby Lonsdale 200 B5
Kirkby Malham 193 E1
Kirkby Mallory 159 G2
Kirkby Malzeard 202 B5
Kirkby on Bain 176 A1
Kirkby Overblow 194 C3
Kirkby Stephen 200 C2
Kirkby Thore 210 C5
Kirkby Underwood 175 F5
Kirkby Wharfe 195 E3
Kirkby Woodhouse 173 F2
Kirkby-in-Furness 198 D4
Kirkbymoorside 203 F4
Kirkcaldy 244 A5
Kirkcambeck 210 B1
Kirkcolm 214 B4
Kirkconnel 225 F4
Kirkconnell 217 D4
Kirkcowan 215 E4
Kirkcudbright 216 A5
Kirkdale House 215 G5
Kirkdean 235 F5
Kirkfieldbank 234 C5
Kirkgunzeon 216 C4
Kirkham Lancs 192 A4
Kirkham NYorks 195 G1
Kirkhamgate 194 C5
Kirkharle 220 C3
Kirkhaugh 210 C3
Kirkheaton N'umb 220 C4
Kirkheaton WYorks 185 F1
Kirkhill Angus 253 E3
Kirkhill High 266 C7
Kirkhill Moray 268 B5
Kirkhope 227 E3
Kirkibost High 256 B3
Kirkibost (Circebost) Na H-ESiar 270 D4
Kirkinch 252 B5
Kirkinner 215 F5
Kirkintilloch 234 A2
Kirkland Cumb 210 C4
Kirkland Cumb 209 D5
Kirkland D&G 216 C1
Kirkland D&G 225 F4
Kirkland D&G 217 E2
Kirkland of Longcastle 207 D2
Kirkleatham 213 E5
Kirklevington 202 D1
Kirkley 165 G2
Kirklington Notts 174 B2
Kirklington NYorks 202 C4
Kirklinton 210 A1
Kirkliston 235 F2
Kirkmaiden 206 B3
Kirkmichael P&K 251 F3
Kirkmichael SAyr 224 B5
Kirkmuirhill 234 B5
Kirknewton N'umb 228 D3
Kirknewton WLoth 235 F3
Kirkney 260 D1
Kirkoswald Cumb 210 B3
Kirkoswald SAyr 224 A5
Kirkpatrick Durham 216 B3
Kirkpatrick-Fleming 218 A4
Kirksanton 198 C4
Kirkstall 194 B4
Kirkstead 175 G1
Kirkstile Aber 260 D1
Kirkstile D&G 218 B2
Kirkstyle 275 J1
Kirkthorpe 194 C5
Kirkton A&B 239 G4
Kirkton Aber 260 E2
Kirkton Aber 268 E5
Kirkton Aber 260 E3
Kirkton Angus 252 C5
Kirkton D&G 217 D2
Kirkton Fife 244 B2
Kirkton High 258 D1
Kirkton High 266 E2
Kirkton High 266 E4
Kirkton High 274 D2
Kirkton High 256 E2
Kirkton P&K 243 E3
Kirkton ScBord 227 G4
Kirkton Manor 226 D2
Kirkton of Airlie 252 B4
Kirkton of Auchterhouse 244 B1
Kirkton of Barevan 267 F7
Kirkton of Bourtie 261 G2
Kirkton of Collace 243 G1
Kirkton of Craig 253 F4
Kirkton of Culsalmond 260 E1
Kirkton of Durris 261 F5
Kirkton of Glenbuchat 260 B3
Kirkton of Glenisla 252 A3
Kirkton of Kingoldrum 252 B4
Kirkton of Lethendy 251 G5
Kirkton of Logie Buchan 261 H2
Kirkton of Maryculter 261 G5
Kirkton of Menmuir 252 D3
Kirkton of Monikie 244 D1
Kirkton of Rayne 260 E1
Kirkton of Skene 261 G4
Kirkton of Tealing 244 C1
Kirktonhill Aber 253 E3
Kirktonhill WDun 233 E2
Kirktown 269 J5
Kirktown of Alvah 268 E4
Kirktown of Auchterless 269 F6
Kirktown of Deskford 268 D4
Kirktown of Fetteresso 253 G1
Kirktown of Slains 261 J2
Kirkwall 277 D6
Kirkwall Airport 277 D7
Kirkwhelpington 220 B3
Kirmington 188 B1
Kirmond le Mire 188 B3
Kirn 232 C2
Kirriemuir 252 B4
Kirstead Green 165 D2
Kirtlebridge 218 A4
Kirtleton 218 A3
Kirtling 151 E2
Kirtling Green 151 E2
Kirtlington 134 A1
Kirtomy 274 C2
Kirton Lincs 176 B4
Kirton Notts 174 B1
Kirton Suff 153 D4
Kirton End 176 A3
Kirton Holme 176 A3
Kirton in Lindsey 187 G3
Kiscadale 223 F3
Kislingbury 148 B2
Kismeldon Bridge 113 D4
Kit Hill Country Park Corn PL17 8AX 99 D3
Kites Hardwick 147 G1
Kitley 100 B2
Kittisford 115 D5
Kittisford Barton 115 D5
Kittle 128 B4
Kitt's End 136 B3
Kitt's Green 159 D4
Kitwood 120 B4
Kivernoll 145 D4
Kiveton Park 186 B4
Klibreck 273 H5
Knabbygates 268 D5
Knaith 187 F4
Knaith Park 187 F4
Knap Corner 117 F5
Knaphill 121 E2
Knaplock 114 B4
Knapp P&K 244 A1
Knapp Som 116 A5
Knapthorpe 174 C2
Knaptoft 160 B4
Knapton Norf 179 E2
Knapton York 195 E2
Knapton Green 144 D2
Knapwell 150 B1
Knaresborough 194 C2
Knarsdale 210 C2
Knarston 276 C5
Knaven 269 G6
Knayton 202 D4
Knebworth 150 A5
Knebworth House Herts SG3 6PY 150 A5
Knedlington 195 G5
Kneesall 174 C1
Kneesworth 150 B3
Kneeton 174 C3
Knelston 128 A4
Knenhall 171 G4
Knettishall 164 A3
Knettishall Heath Country Park Suff IP22 2TQ 164 A3
Knightacott 113 G2
Knightcote 147 G2
Knightley 171 F5
Knightley Dale 171 F5
Knighton Devon 100 B3
Knighton Dorset 104 C1
Knighton Leic 160 A2
Knighton Poole 105 G3
Knighton (Tref-y-clawdd) Powys 156 B5
Knighton Som 115 E3
Knighton Staffs 171 E5
Knighton Staffs 171 E3
Knighton Wilts 133 E5
Knighton on Teme 157 F5
Knightswood 233 G3
Knightwick 145 G2
Knill 144 B1
Knipoch 240 A2
Knipton 174 D4
Knitsley 212 A3
Kniveton 172 D2
Knock A&B 239 E1
Knock Cumb 210 C5
Knock High 256 C4
Knock Moray 268 D5
Knock of Auchnahannet 259 H1
Knockalava 240 B5
Knockally 275 G6
Knockaloe Moar 190 A3
Knockan 272 E7
Knockandhu 259 K2
Knockando 267 J7
Knockarthur 266 E1
Knockbain 266 D6
Knockban 265 J5
Knockbreck 266 E3
Knockbrex 207 F2
Knockdamph 265 J2
Knockdee 275 G2
Knockdow 232 C2
Knockdown 132 A4
Knockenkelly 223 F3
Knockentiber 224 B2
Knockfin 257 K2
Knockgray 215 G1
Knockholt 123 D3
Knockholt Pound 123 D3
Knockin 170 A5
Knockinlaw 224 C2
Knockintorran (Cnoc an Torrain) 262 C5
Knocklearn 216 B3
Knockmill 123 E2
Knocknaha 222 B4
Knocknain 214 A4
Knocknalling 215 G2
Knockrome 231 D2
Knocksharry 190 A3
Knockville 215 E3
Knockvologan 238 C3
Knodishall 153 F1
Knodishall Common 153 F1
Knodishall Green 153 F1
Knole 116 B5
Knolls Green 184 C5
Knolton 170 A4
Knook 118 A3
Knossington 160 D2
Knott End-on-Sea 191 G3
Knotting 149 F1
Knotting Green 149 F1
Knottingley 195 E5
Knotts 193 D2
Knotty Green 135 E3
Knowbury 157 E5
Knowe 215 E3
Knowes of Elrick 268 E5
Knowesgate 220 B3
Knoweside 224 A4
Knowetownhead 227 G4
Knowhead 269 H5
Knowl Green 151 F3
Knowl Hill 134 D5
Knowl Wall 171 F4
Knowle Bristol 131 F5
Knowle Devon 102 A2
Knowle Devon 113 E2
Knowle Devon 103 D4
Knowle Shrop 157 E5
Knowle Som 114 C3
Knowle WMid 159 D5
Knowle Cross 102 D3
Knowle Green 192 C4
Knowle Hall 116 A3
Knowle St. Giles 103 G1
Knowlton Dorset 105 G1
Knowlton Kent 125 E3
Knowsley 183 F3
Knowsley Safari Park Mersey L34 4AN 23 E2
Knowstone 114 B5
Knox Bridge 123 G4
Knucklas (Cnwclas) 156 B5
Knutsford 184 B5
Knypersley 171 F2
Krumlin 185 E1
Kuggar 95 E5
Kyle of Lochalsh (Caol Loch Aillse) 256 D2
Kyleakin (Caol Acain) 256 D2
Kylerhea (Ceol Reatha) 256 D2
Kyles Scalpay (Caolas Scalpaigh) 263 H2
Kylesbeg 247 F2
Kylesknoydart 256 E5
Kylesku 272 E5
Kylesmorar 256 E5
Kylestrome 272 E5
Kyloag 266 D2
Kynaston 170 A5
Kynnersley 157 F1
Kyre Park 145 F1

L

Labost 270 E3
Lacasaigh 271 F5
Lace Market Centre NG1 1HF 80 Nottingham
Laceby 188 C2
Lacey Green 134 D2
Lach Dennis 184 B5
Lackford 163 F5
Lacklee (Leac a' Li) 263 G2
Lacock 118 A1
Ladbroke 147 G2
Laddingford 123 F4
Lade Bank 176 B2
Ladies Hill 192 A3
Ladock 96 C4
Lady Hall 198 C4
Lady Lever Art Gallery Mersey CH62 5EQ 22 B4
Ladybank 244 B3
Ladycross 98 D2
Ladyfield 240 C3
Ladykirk 237 F5
Ladysford 269 H4
Ladywood 146 A1
Laga 247 F3
Lagalochan 240 A3
Lagavulin 230 C5
Lagg A&B 231 D2
Lagg NAyr 223 E3
Lagg SAyr 224 A4
Laggan A&B 230 A4

Laggan (An Lagan)
  High 257 J5
Laggan High 258 D5
Laggan Moray 260 B1
Laggan Stir 242 A3
Lagganulva 247 D5
Lagganvoulin 259 J3
Laglingarten 240 D4
Lagnalean 266 D7
Lagrae 225 F4
Laguna 243 G1
Laid 273 G3
Laide 265 F2
Laig 247 D1
Laight 225 E4
Lainchoil 259 H3
Laindon 137 F4
Laing Art Gallery T&W
  NE1 8AG
  79 Newcastle upon Tyne
Lair 251 G3
Lairg 266 C1
Lairg Lodge 266 C1
Lairigmor 248 D3
Laisterdyke 194 A4
Laithes 210 A4
Lake Devon 113 F2
Lake Devon 100 B1
Lake IoW 107 E4
Lake Wilts 118 C5
Lake District Visitor Centre
  at Brockhole Cumb
  LA23 1LJ 199 E2
Lakenham 178 D5
Lakenheath 163 F4
Lakes Aquarium Cumb
  LA12 8AS 199 E4
Lakes End 162 D3
Lakes Glass Centre,
  Ulverston Cumb
  LA12 7LY 199 D5
Lakeside Cumb 199 E4
Lakeside Thur 137 F4
Lakeside & Haverthwaite
  Railway Cumb
  LA12 8AL 199 E4
Laleham 121 F1
Laleston 129 E5
Lamancha 235 G4
Lamarsh 152 A4
Lamas 178 D3
Lamb Corner 152 B4
Lamb Roe 192 B4
Lambden 237 E5
Lamberhurst
  Quarter 123 F5
Lamberton 237 G4
Lambfell Moar 190 A3
Lambley N'umb 210 C2
Lambley Notts 174 B3
Lambourn 133 F5
Lambourn
  Woodlands 133 F5
Lambourne End 137 D3
Lambs Green 122 B5
Lambston 126 C1
Lamellion 97 G3
Lamerton 99 E3
Lamesley 212 B2
Lamington High 266 E4
Lamington SLan 226 A2
Lamlash 223 F2
Lamloch 215 G1
Lamonby 210 A4
Lamorna 94 B4
Lamorran 96 C5
Lampert 219 E4
Lampeter (Llanbedr Pont
  Steffan) 142 B3
Lampeter Velfrey 127 E1
Lamphey 126 D2
Lamplugh 209 D4
Lamport 160 C5
Lamyatt 117 D4
Lana Devon 98 C1
Lana Devon 112 D5
Lanark 234 C5
Lanarth 95 E4
Lancaster 192 A1
Lancaster Leisure Park
  Lancs LA1 3LA 192 A1
Lancaster Priory Lancs
  LA1 1YZ 192 A1
Lanchester 212 A3
Lancing 109 D3
Landbeach 150 C4
Landcross 113 E3
Landerberry 261 F4
Landford 106 B1
Landhallow 275 G5
Landican 183 D4
Landimore 128 A3
Landkey 113 F2
Landmoth 202 D3
Landore 128 C3
Landrake 99 D4
Land's End Corn
  TR19 7AA 94 A4
Land's End Airport 94 A4
Landscove 101 D1
Landshipping 126 D1
Landulph 100 A1
Landwade 151 E1
Landywood 158 B2
Lane Bottom 193 E4
Lane End Bucks 134 D3
Lane End Cumb 198 C3
Lane End Derbys 173 F1
Lane End Dorset 105 E3
Lane End Hants 119 G5
Lane End Here 131 F1
Lane End Kent 138 C5
Lane End Wilts 117 F3
Lane Ends Derbys 172 D4
Lane Ends GtMan 185 D3
Lane Ends Lancs 193 D5
Lane Ends NYorks 193 F3
Lane Green 158 A2
Lane Head Dur 202 A1
Lane Head Dur 211 G5
Lane Head GtMan 184 B3
Lane Head WYorks 185 F2
Lane Heads 192 A4
Lane Side 193 D5

Laneast 97 G1
Lane-end 97 E3
Laneham 187 F5
Lanehead Dur 211 E3
Lanehead N'umb 219 F3
Lanesend 127 D2
Lanesfield 158 B3
Laneshawbridge 193 F3
Langais 262 D5
Langamull 246 C4
Langar 174 C4
Langbank 233 E2
Langbar 193 G2
Langbaurgh 203 E1
Langcliffe 193 E1
Langdale End 204 C3
Langdon Corn 98 C1
Langdon Corn 98 D2
Langdon Beck 211 E4
Langdon Hills 137 F4
Langdon Hills Country Park
  Essex SS17 9NH 137 F4
Langdon House 102 C5
Langdyke 244 B4
Langford CenBeds 149 G3
Langford Essex 138 B2
Langford Notts 174 D2
Langford Oxon 133 E2
Langford Budville 115 E5
Langham Essex 152 B4
Langham Norf 178 B1
Langham Rut 160 D1
Langham Suff 152 A1
Langham Moor 152 B4
Langho 192 C4
Langholm 218 B3
Langland 128 C4
Langlands 216 A5
Langlee 228 A5
Langleeford 228 D4
Langley ChesE 184 D5
Langley Derbys 173 F3
Langley Essex 150 C4
Langley Glos 146 C5
Langley GtMan 184 C4
Langley Hants 106 D2
Langley Herts 150 A5
Langley Kent 123 G3
Langley N'umb 211 E1
Langley Oxon 133 F1
Langley Slo 135 F5
Langley Som 115 D5
Langley Warks 147 D1
Langley WSuss 120 D5
Langley Burrell 132 B5
Langley Corner 135 F4
Langley Green
  Derbys 173 D4
Langley Green
  Warks 147 E1
Langley Green
  WSuss 122 B5
Langley Heath 124 A3
Langley Marsh 115 D5
Langley Mill 173 F3
Langley Moor 212 B3
Langley Park 212 B3
Langley Park Bucks
  SL3 6DW 135 F4
Langley Street 179 E5
Langney 110 B3
Langold 186 C4
Langore 97 G1
Langport 116 B5
Langrick 176 A3
Langrick Bridge 176 A3
Langridge
  B&NESom 117 E1
Langridge Devon 113 F3
Langridgeford 113 F3
Langrigg 209 E2
Langrish 120 C5
Langsett 185 G2
Langshaw 227 G2
Langshawburn 227 D5
Langside Glas 233 G3
Langside P&K 242 C3
Langskaill 276 D3
Langstone
  Newport 130 C3
Langstone Hants 107 G2
Langthorne 202 B3
Langthorpe 194 C1
Langthwaite 201 F3
Langtoft ERid 196 C1
Langtoft Lincs 161 G1
Langton Dur 202 A1
Langton Lincs 189 D5
Langton Lincs 176 A1
Langton NYorks 195 G1
Langton by Wragby 188 B5
Langton Green Kent 123 E5
Langton Green Suff 164 C4
Langton Herring 104 C4
Langton Long
  Blandford 105 E2
Langton Matravers 105 F5
Langtree 113 E4
Langtree Week 113 E4
Langwathby 210 B4
Langwell 266 B1
Langwell House 275 G6
Langwith 186 C5
Langworth 188 A5
Lanhydrock Corn
  PL30 5AD 97 E3
Lanivet 97 E3
Lank 97 E2
Lanlivery 97 E4
Lanner 96 B5
Lanoy 97 G2
Lanreath 97 F4
Lansallos 97 F4
Lansdown 117 E1
Lanteglos 97 E1
Lanteglos Highway 97 F4
Lanton N'umb 228 D3
Lanton ScBord 228 A4
Lanvean 96 C3
Lapford 102 A2
Laphroaig 230 B5
Lapley 158 A1
Lapworth 159 E5
Larach na Gaibhre 231 F2
Larachbeg 247 F5
Larbert 234 C1
Larbreck 192 A4
Larden Green 170 C2

Larg 215 E3
Largie 260 E1
Largiemore 232 A1
Largoward 244 C4
Largs 232 D4
Largue 268 E6
Larguybaan 222 B4
Largybeg 223 F3
Largymore 223 F3
Lark Hall 151 D2
Larkfield 232 D2
Larkhall 234 B4
Larkhill 118 C3
Larklands 173 F3
Larling 164 A3
Larriston 218 D2
Lartington 201 F1
Lary 260 B4
Lasborough 132 A3
Lasham 120 B3
Lashbrook 113 E5
Lashenden 124 A4
Lassington 145 G5
Lassodie 243 G5
Lastingham 203 G3
Latchford 184 A4
Latchingdon 138 B2
Latchley 99 E3
Lately Common 184 A3
Lathallan Mill 244 C4
Lathbury 149 D3
Latheron 275 G5
Latheronwheel 275 G5
Lathockar 244 C3
Lathones 244 C4
Lathrisk 244 A4
Latimer 135 F3
Latteridge 131 F4
Lattiford 117 D5
Latton 132 C3
Lauchentyre 215 G3
Lauchintilly 261 F3
Lauder 236 C5
Laugharne
  (Lacharn) 127 G1
Laughterton 187 F5
Laughton ESuss 110 A2
Laughton Leics 160 B4
Laughton Lincs 175 F4
Laughton Lincs 187 F3
Laughton en le
  Morthen 186 C4
Launcells 112 C5
Launcells Cross 112 C5
Launceston 98 D2
Launde Abbey 160 C2
Launton 148 B5
Laurencekirk 253 F2
Laurieston D&G 216 A4
Laurieston Falk 234 D2
Lavendon 149 E2
Lavenham 152 A3
Laverhay 217 F1
Lavernock 115 E1
Laversdale 210 A1
Laverstock 118 C4
Laverstoke 119 F3
Laverton Glos 146 C4
Laverton NYorks 202 B5
Laverton Som 117 E2
Lavister 170 A2
Law 234 C4
Lawers P&K 242 C2
Lawers P&K 242 B1
Lawford Essex 152 B4
Lawford Som 115 E4
Lawhitton 99 D2
Lawkland 193 D1
Lawkland Green 193 D1
Lawley 157 F2
Lawnhead 171 F5
Lawrence Weston 131 E5
Lawrenny 126 D2
Laws 244 C1
Lawshall 151 G2
Lawshall Green 151 G2
Lawton 144 D2
Laxdale (Lacasdal) 271 G4
Laxey 190 C3
Laxfield 165 D4
Laxfirth Shet 279 D7
Laxfirth Shet 279 D8
Laxford Bridge 272 E4
Laxo 278 D6
Laxton ERid 195 G5
Laxton N'hants 161 E3
Laxton Notts 174 C1
Laycock 193 G3
Layer Breton 138 C1
Layer de la Haye 138 C1
Layer Marney 138 C1
Layham 152 B3
Laymore 103 G2
Layter's Green 135 E3
Laytham 195 G4
Layton 191 G4
Lazenby 213 E5
Lazonby 210 B4
Lea Derbys 173 E2
Lea Here 145 F5
Lea Lincs 187 F4
Lea Shrop 156 D2
Lea Shrop 156 D2
Lea Wilts 132 B4
Lea Bridge 173 E2
Lea Green 145 F1
Lea Marston 159 E3
Lea Town 192 A4
Lea Yeat 200 C4
Leachd 240 C5
Leachkin
  (An Leacainn) 266 D7
Leadburn 235 G4
Leaden Roding 137 E1
Leadenham 175 E2
Leaderfoot 227 G2
Leadgate Cumb 210 D3
Leadgate Dur 212 A2
Leadhills 225 G4
Leadingcross Green 124 A3
Leafield 133 F1
Leagrave 149 F5
Leake Commonside 176 B2
Leake Hurn's End 176 C3
Lealands 110 A2

Lealholm 203 G2
Lealt A&B 239 F5
Lealt High 264 B5
Leam 185 G5
Leamington
  Hastings 147 G1
Leamington Spa 147 F1
Leamington Spa Art Gallery
  & Museum Warks
  CV32 4AA 16 B6
Leamoor Common 156 D4
Leanach A&B 240 C5
Leanach High 266 E7
Leanaig 266 C6
Leanoch 267 J6
Leargybreck 230 D2
Leasgill 199 F4
Leasingham 175 F3
Leask 261 J1
Leason 128 A3
Leasowe 183 D3
Leat 98 D2
Leatherhead 121 G2
Leathley 194 B3
Leaton Shrop 157 D1
Leaton Tel&W 157 F1
Leaveland 124 C3
Leavenheath 152 A4
Leavening 195 G1
Leaves Green 122 C2
Leavesden Green 136 A2
Lebberston 205 D4
Lechlade-on-
  Thames 133 E3
Leck 200 B5
Leckford 119 E4
Leckfurin 274 C3
Leckgruinart 230 A3
Leckhampstead
  Bucks 148 C4
Leckhampstead
  WBerks 133 G5
Leckhampstead
  Thicket 133 G5
Leckhampton 132 B1
Leckie High 265 G5
Leckie Stir 242 B5
Leckmelm
  (Leac Mailm) 265 H3
Leckroy 257 K5
Leckuary 244 B1
Leckwith 130 A5
Leconfield 196 C3
Ledaig (Leideag) 240 B1
Ledard 241 G4
Ledbeg 272 E7
Ledburn 149 D5
Ledbury 145 G4
Ledcharrie 242 A2
Ledgemoor 144 D2
Ledicot 144 D1
Ledmore A&B 247 E5
Ledmore High 272 E7
Lednagullin 274 C2
Ledsham ChesW&C
  183 E5
Ledsham WYorks 195 D5
Ledston 194 D5
Ledstone 100 D3
Ledwell 147 G5
Lee A&B 238 D5
Lee Devon 113 E1
Lee Hants 106 C1
Lee Lancs 192 B2
Lee Shrop 170 B4
Lee Brockhurst 170 C5
Lee Chapel 137 F4
Lee Clump 135 E2
Lee Mill Bridge 100 B2
Lee Moor 100 B1
Lee Valley Park Essex
  EN9 1XQ 136 C3
Leebotten 279 D10
Leebotwood 157 D3
Leece 191 F1
Leeds Kent 124 A3
Leeds WYorks 194 B4
Leeds Art Gallery WYorks
  LS1 3AA 40 E3
Leeds Bradford International
  Airport 194 B3
Leeds Castle & Gardens
  Kent ME17 1PL 124 A3
Leedstown 94 D3
Leegomery 157 F1
Leek 171 G2
Leek Wootton 147 E1
Leekbrook 171 G2
Leeming NYorks 202 B4
Leeming WYorks 193 G4
Leeming Bar 202 B4
Lee-on-the-Solent 107 E2
Lees Derbys 173 D4
Lees GtMan 185 D2
Leeswood 169 F2
Leftwich 184 A5
Legars 237 E5
Legbourne 189 D4
Legerwood 236 C5
Legoland Windsor W&M
  SL4 4AY 135 E5
Legsby 188 B4
Leicester 160 A2
Leicester Forest
  East 160 A2
Leideag 254 B5
Leigh Dorset 104 C2
Leigh Dorset 105 G3
Leigh GtMan 184 A2
Leigh Kent 123 E4
Leigh Shrop 156 C2
Leigh Surr 122 B4
Leigh Wilts 132 C3
Leigh Worcs 145 G2
Leigh Beck 138 B4
Leigh Common 117 E5
Leigh Delamere 132 A5
Leigh Green 124 B5
Leigh Park 107 G2
Leigh Sinton 145 G2
Leigh upon
  Mendip 117 D3
Leigh Woods 131 E5
Leigham 100 B2
Leighland Chapel 114 D4
Leigh-on-Sea 138 B4
Leighterton 132 A3
Leighton NYorks 202 A5

Leighton (Tre'r Llai)
  Powys 156 B2
Leighton Shrop 157 F2
Leighton Som 117 E3
Leighton
  Bromswold 161 G5
Leighton Buzzard 149 E5
Leinthall Earls 144 D1
Leinthall Starkes 144 D1
Leintwardine 156 D5
Leire 160 A4
Leirinmore 273 G2
Leiston 153 F1
Leitfie 252 A5
Leith 235 G2
Leitholm 237 E5
Lelant 94 C3
Lelley 197 E4
Lemington 212 A1
Lemnas 269 G4
Lempitlaw 228 B3
Lemreway 271 G6
Lemsford 136 B1
Lenchwick 146 C3
Lendalfoot 214 C1
Lendrick Lodge 242 A4
Lenham 124 A3
Lenham Heath 124 B4
Lenie 258 C2
Lenimore 223 E2
Lennel 237 F5
Lennox Plunton 216 A5
Lennoxtown 234 A2
Lent Rise 135 E4
Lenton Lincs 175 F4
Lenton Nott 173 G4
Lenton Abbey 173 G4
Lenwade 178 B4
Lenzie 234 A2
Leoch 244 B1
Leochel-Cushnie 260 D3
Leominster 145 D2
Leonard Stanley 132 A2
Leorin 230 B5
Lepe 106 D3
Lephin 263 G7
Lephinchapel 240 B5
Lephinmore 240 B5
Leppington 195 G1
Lepton 185 G1
Lerags 240 A2
Lerryn 97 F4
Lerwick 279 D8
Lesbury 229 G5
Leschangie 261 F3
Leslie Aber 260 D2
Leslie Fife 244 A4
Lesmahagow 225 G2
Lesnewth 98 B1
Lessendrum 268 D6
Lessingham 179 E3
Lessness Heath 137 D5
Lessonhall 209 F1
Leswalt 214 B4
Letchmore Heath 136 A3
Letchworth Garden
  City 150 A4
Letcombe Bassett 133 F4
Letcombe Regis 133 F4
Leth Meadhanach 254 C3
Letham Angus 252 D5
Letham Falk 234 D1
Letham Fife 244 B3
Lethanhill 224 C4
Lethenty 269 G6
Letheringham 153 D2
Letheringsett 178 B2
Lettaford 102 A4
Letter Finlay 257 J5
Letterewe 265 F4
Letterfearn
  (Leitir Fhearna) 256 E2
Lettermorar 247 G1
Lettermore A&B 247 D5
Lettermore High 273 J4
Letters 265 H3
Letterston 140 C5
Lettoch High 259 H3
Lettoch High 259 J1
Letton Here 156 C5
Letton Here 144 C3
Letty Green 136 B1
Letwell 186 C4
Leuchars 244 C2
Leumrabhagh 271 F6
Leurbost (Liurbost) 271 F5
Leusdon 102 A5
Levedale 158 A1
Level's Green 150 C5
Leven ERid 196 D3
Leven Fife 244 B4
Levencorroch 223 F3
Levenhall 236 A2
Levens 199 F4
Levens Green 150 B5
Levenshulme 184 C3
Levenwick 279 D10
Leverburgh
  (An T-Òb) 263 F3
Leverington 162 C1
Leverstock Green 135 F2
Leverton 176 B3
Leverton Lucasgate 176 C3
Leverton Outgate 176 C3
Levington 152 D4
Levisham 203 G3
Levishie 258 B3
Lew 133 F2
Lewannick 97 G1
Lewcombe 104 B2
Lewdown 99 E2
Lewes 109 G2
Leweston 140 C5
Lewisham 136 C5
Lewiston
  (Blàr na Maigh) 258 C2
Lewistown 129 F4
Lewknor 134 C3
Leworthy 113 G2
Lewson Street 124 B2
Lewth 192 A4
Lewtrenchard 99 E2
Ley Aber 260 D3
Ley Corn 97 F3
Ley Green 149 G5
Leybourne 123 F3
Leyburn 202 A3
Leyland 192 B5

Leylodge 261 F3
Leymoor 185 F1
Leys Aber 269 J5
Leys Aber 260 C4
Leys P&K 244 A1
Leys of Cossans 252 B5
Leysdown-on-Sea 124 C1
Leysmill 253 E5
Leysters 145 E1
Leyton 136 C4
Leytonstone 136 C4
Lezant 98 D3
Lezerea 95 D3
Lhanbryde 267 K5
Liatrie 257 J1
Libanus 143 F5
Libberton 235 D5
Libbery 146 B2
Liberton 235 G3
Liceasto 263 G2
Lichfield 158 D2
Lichfield Cathedral Staffs
  WS13 7LD 158 D2
Lickey 158 B5
Lickey End 158 B5
Lickey Hills Country Park
  Worcs B45 8ER 14 C6
Lickfold 121 E5
Liddaton Green 99 E2
Liddel 277 D9
Liddesdale 247 G4
Liddington 133 E4
Lidgate Derbys 186 A5
Lidgate Suff 151 F2
Lidget 174 B1
Lidgett 174 B1
Lidlington 149 E4
Lidsey 108 B3
Lidsing 123 G2
Lidstone 147 F5
Lienassie 257 F2
Lieurary 275 F2
Liff 244 B1
Lifton 99 D2
Liftondown 99 D2
Lightcliffe 194 A5
Lighthorne 147 F2
Lighthorne Heath 147 F2
Lighthouse, The, Glasgow
  Glas G1 3NU 39 F4
Lighthouse, The - Poole's
  Centre for the Arts
  Poole BH15 1UG 3 B4
Lightwater 121 E1
Lightwater Valley Park
  NYorks
  HG4 3HT 202 B5
Lightwood 171 G3
Lightwood Green
  ChesE 170 D3
Lightwood Green
  Wrex 170 A3
Lilbourne 160 A5
Lilburn Tower 229 E4
Lillesden 116 A5
Lilleshall 157 G1
Lilley Herts 149 G5
Lilley WBerks 133 G5
Lilliesleaf 227 G3
Lilling Green 195 F1
Lillingstone Dayrell 148 C4
Lillingstone Lovell 148 C3
Lillington Dorset 104 C1
Lillington Warks 147 F1
Lilliput 105 G3
Lilly 113 F2
Lilstock 115 E3
Lilyhurst 157 G1
Limbury 149 F5
Lime Side 184 D2
Limefield 184 C1
Limehillock 268 D5
Limehurst 184 D2
Limekilnburn 234 B4
Limekilns 235 E1
Limerigg 234 C2
Limerstone 106 D4
Limington 116 C5
Limpenhoe 179 E5
Limpley Stoke 117 E1
Limpsfield 122 D3
Limpsfield Chart 122 D3
Linaclate
  (Lionacleit) 262 C7
Linacre Reservoirs Derbys
  S42 7JW 186 A5
Linbriggs 220 A1
Linby 173 G2
Linchmere 121 D4
Lincluden 217 D3
Lincoln 187 G5
Lincoln Castle Lincs
  LN1 3AA 77 Lincoln
Lincoln Cathedral Lincs
  LN2 1PL 77 Lincoln
Lincomb 146 A1
Lincombe Devon 100 D2
Lincombe Devon 100 D2
Lindal in Furness 199 D5
Lindale 199 F4
Lindean 227 F2
Lindertis 252 B4
Lindfield 109 F1
Lindford 120 D4
Lindifferon 244 B3
Lindisfarne
  (Holy Island) 229 F2
Lindley 194 B3
Lindores 244 A3
Lindow End 184 C5
Lindridge 145 F1
Lindsaig 232 A2
Lindsell 151 E5
Lindsey 152 A3
Lindsey Tye 152 A3
Linfitts 185 D2
Linford Hants 106 A2
Linford Thur 137 F5
Linford Wood 148 D3
Lingague 190 A4
Lingards Wood 185 E1
Lingdale 203 F1
Lingen 144 C1
Lingfield 122 C4
Lingwood 179 E5
Linhead 268 E5
Linhope 227 F5
Linicro 263 J5

Linkend 146 A4
Linkenholt 119 E2
Linkhill 110 D1
Linkinhorne 98 D3
Linklater 277 D9
Linksness Ork 277 B7
Linksness Ork 277 E6
Linktown 244 A5
Linley Shrop 156 C3
Linley Shrop 157 F3
Linley Green 145 F2
Linlithgow 235 E2
Linlithgow Bridge 235 D2
Linn of Muick
  Cottage 252 B1
Linnels 211 F1
Linney 126 B3
Linshiels 220 A1
Linsiadar 270 E4
Linsidemore 266 C2
Linslade 149 E5
Linstead Parva 165 E4
Linstock 210 A2
Linthwaite 185 F1
Lintlaw 237 F4
Lintmill 268 D4
Linton Cambs 151 D3
Linton Derbys 159 E1
Linton Here 145 F5
Linton Kent 123 G3
Linton NYorks 193 F1
Linton ScBord 228 B4
Linton WYorks 194 C3
Linton-on-Ouse 195 D1
Lintzford 212 A2
Linwood Hants 106 A2
Linwood Lincs 188 B4
Linwood Renf 233 F3
Lionel (Lional) 271 H1
Liphook 120 D4
Lipley 171 E4
Liscard 183 E3
Liscombe 114 B4
Liskeard 97 G3
L'Islet 101 F4
Lismore 240 A1
Liss 120 C5
Liss Forest 120 C5
Lissett 196 D2
Lissington 188 B4
Liston 151 G3
Lisvane 130 A4
Liswerry 130 C4
Litcham 163 G1
Litchborough 148 B2
Litchfield 119 F2
Litherland 183 E3
Litlington Cambs 150 B3
Litlington ESuss 110 A3
Little Abington 150 D3
Little Addington 161 E5
Little Alne 146 D1
Little Altcar 183 E2
Little Amwell 136 C1
Little Ann 119 E3
Little Asby 200 B2
Little Assynt 272 D6
Little Aston 158 C3
Little Atherfield 107 D5
Little Ayton 203 E1
Little Baddow 137 G2
Little Badminton 132 A4
Little Ballinluig 251 E4
Little Bampton 209 F1
Little Bardfield 151 E4
Little Barford 149 G2
Little Barningham 178 C2
Little Barrington 133 E1
Little Barrow 170 B1
Little Barugh 203 G5
Little Bavington 220 B4
Little Bealings 152 D3
Little Bedwyn 119 D1
Little Beeby 160 B2
Little Bentley 152 C5
Little Berkhamsted 136 B2
Little Billing 148 D1
Little Birch 145 E4
Little Bispham 191 G3
Little Blakenham 152 C3
Little Bloxwich 158 C2
Little Bollington 184 B4
Little Bookham 121 G2
Little Bourton 147 G3
Little Bowden 160 C4
Little Bradley 151 E2
Little Brampton 156 C4
Little Braxted 138 B1
Little Brechin 253 D3
Little Brickhill 149 E4
Little Bridgeford 171 F5
Little Brington 148 B1
Little Bromley 152 B5
Little Broughton 209 D3
Little Budworth 170 C1
Little Burdon 202 C1
Little Burstead 137 F3
Little Burton 196 D3
Little Bytham 161 F1
Little Canford 105 G3
Little Carlton Lincs 189 D4
Little Carlton Notts 174 C2
Little Casterton 161 F2
Little Catwick 196 D3
Little Catworth 161 F5
Little Cawthorpe 189 D4
Little Chalfield 117 F1
Little Chalfont 135 E3
Little Chart 124 B4
Little Chesterford 150 D3
Little Chesterton 148 A5
Little Cheverell 118 A3
Little Clacton 139 E1
Little Clanfield 133 E2
Little Clifton 209 D4
Little Coates 188 C2
Little Comberton 146 B3
Little Common 110 C3
Little Compton 147 E4
Little Cornard 151 G4
Little Cowarne 145 F2
Little Coxwell 133 E3
Little Crakehall 202 B3
Little Cransley 160 D5
Little Crawley 149 E3
Little Creaton 160 C5
Little Creich 266 D3

Little Cressingham **163** G3
Little Crosby **183** E2
Little Crosthwaite **209** F4
Little Cubley **172** C4
Little Dalby **160** C1
Little Dens **269** J6
Little Dewchurch **145** E4
Little Ditton **151** E2
Little Down **119** E2
Little Downham **162** D4
Little Drayton **171** D4
Little Driffield **196** C2
Little Dunham **163** G1
Little Dunkeld **251** F5
Little Dunmow **151** E5
Little Durnford **118** C4
Little Easton **151** E5
Little Eaton **173** E1
Little Eccleston **192** A4
Little Ellingham **164** B2
Little Everdon **148** A2
Little Eversden **150** B2
Little Faringdon **133** E2
Little Fencote **202** B3
Little Fenton **195** E4
Little Finborough **152** B2
Little Fransham **178** A4
Little Gaddesden **135** E1
Little Garway **144** D5
Little Gidding **161** G4
Little Glemham **153** E2
Little Glenshee **243** E1
Little Gorsley **145** F5
Little Gransden **150** A3
Little Green *Cambs* **150** A3
Little Green *Notts* **174** C3
Little Green *Suff* **164** B4
Little Green *Suff* **164** B4
Little Grimsby **188** D3
Little Gringley **187** F4
Little Gruinard **265** F3
Little Habton **203** G5
Little Hadham **150** C4
Little Hale **175** G3
Little Hallingbury **137** D1
Little Hampden **135** D2
Little Haresfield **132** A2
Little Harrowden **161** D5
Little Haseley **134** B4
Little Hatfield **197** D3
Little Hautbois **179** D3
Little Haven
  Pembs **126** B1
Little Haven *WSuss* **121** G4
Little Hay **158** D2
Little Hayfield **185** E4
Little Haywood **172** B5
Little Heath **159** F4
Little Hereford **145** E1
Little Hockham **164** A2
Little Horkesley **152** A4
Little Hormead **150** C5
Little Horsted **109** G2
Little Horton **118** B1
Little Horwood **148** C4
Little Houghton **148** D2
Little Hucklow **185** F5
Little Hulton **184** B2
Little Hungerford **134** A5
Little Hutton **203** D5
Little Irchester **149** E1
Little Keyford **117** E3
Little Kimble **134** D2
Little Kineton **147** F2
Little Kingshill **135** D3
Little Langdale **199** E2
Little Langford **118** B4
Little Laver **137** E2
Little Lawford **159** G5
Little Leigh **184** A5
Little Leighs **137** G1
Little Lever **184** B2
Little Ley **260** E3
Little Linford **148** D3
Little Linton **151** D3
Little London
  Bucks **134** B1
Little London
  Essex **150** C5
Little London
  ESuss **110** A2
Little London
  Hants **119** E3
Little London
  Hants **120** B2
Little London *IoM* **190** B3
Little London *Lincs* **176** C5
Little London *Lincs* **175** A5
Little London *Lincs* **188** D5
Little London *Lincs* **188** B4
Little London *Norf* **177** D5
Little London *Norf* **163** F3
Little London *Oxon* **134** A2
Little London
  Powys **155** G4
Little London *Suff* **152** B2
Little London
  WYorks **194** B4
Little Longstone **185** F5
Little Lyth **157** E2
Little Malvern **145** G3
Little Maplestead **151** G4
Little Marcle **145** F4
Little Marland **113** F4
Little Marlow **135** D4
Little Marsden **193** E4
Little Massingham **177** F5
Little Melton **178** C5
Little Milford **126** C1
Little Mill **130** C2
Little Milton **134** B2
Little Missenden **135** E3
Little Musgrave **200** C1
Little Ness **156** D1
Little Neston **183** D5
Little Newcastle **140** C5
Little Newsham **202** A1
Little Oakley *Essex* **152** D5
Little Oakley
  N'hants **161** E2
Little Odell **149** E2
Little Offley **149** G5
Little Onn **158** A1
Little Orton *Cumb* **209** G1
Little Orton *Leics* **159** F2

Little Ouse **163** E4
Little Ouseburn **194** D1
Little Overton **170** A3
Little Packington **159** E4
Little Parndon **136** D1
Little Paxton **149** G1
Little Petherick **96** D2
Little Plumpton **191** G4
Little Plumstead **179** E4
Little Ponton **175** E4
Little Posbrook **107** E2
Little Potheridge **113** F4
Little Preston **148** A2
Little Raveley **162** A4
Little Ribston **194** C2
Little Rissington **133** D1
Little Rogart **266** C2
Little Rollright **147** E4
Little Ryburgh **178** A3
Little Ryle **229** E5
Little Ryton **157** D2
Little Salkeld **210** B4
Little Sampford **151** E4
Little Saxham **151** G1
Little Scatwell **265** K6
Little Shelford **150** C2
Little Shrawardine **156** C1
Little Silver **102** C2
Little Singleton **191** G4
Little Smeaton
  NYorks **186** C1
Little Smeaton
  NYorks **202** C2
Little Snoring **178** A2
Little Sodbury **131** G4
Little Sodbury End **131** G4
Little Somborne **119** E4
Little Somerford **132** B4
Little Soudley **171** E5
Little Stainforth **193** E1
Little Stainton **202** C1
Little Stanney **183** F5
Little Staughton **149** G1
Little Steeping **176** C1
Little Stoke **171** G4
Little Stonham **152** C2
Little Street **162** D4
Little Stretton *Leics* **160** B2
Little Stretton
  Shrop **156** D3
Little Strickland **199** G1
Little Stukeley **162** A5
Little Sugnall **171** F4
Little Sutton **183** E5
Little Swinburne **220** B4
Little Tarrington **145** F3
Little Tey **151** G5
Little Thetford **162** D5
Little Thornage **178** B2
Little Thornton **191** G3
Little Thorpe **212** D3
Little Thurlow **151** E2
Little Thurlow
  Green **151** E2
Little Thurrock **137** F5
Little Torboll **266** E2
Little Torrington **113** E4
Little Tosson **220** C1
Little Totham **138** B1
Little Town *Cumb* **209** F5
Little Town *Lancs* **192** C4
Little Town *Warr* **184** A3
Little Twycross **159** F2
Little Urswick **199** D5
Little Wakering **138** C4
Little Walden **150** D3
Little Waldingfield **152** A3
Little Walsingham **178** A2
Little Waltham **137** G1
Little Warley **137** F3
Little Washbourne **146** B4
Little Weighton **196** B4
Little Welland **146** A4
Little Welnetham **151** G1
Little Wenham **152** B4
Little Wenlock **157** F2
Little Whittington **211** F1
Little Wilbraham **150** D2
Little Wishford **118** B4
Little Witcombe **132** B1
Little Witley **145** G1
Little Wittenham **134** A3
Little Wittingham
  Green **165** D4
Little Wolford **147** E4
Little Woodcote **122** B2
Little Wratting **151** E3
Little Wymington **149** E1
Little
  Wymondley **150** A5
Little Wyrley **158** C2
Little Wytheford **157** E1
Little Yeldham **151** F4
Littlebeck **204** B2
Littleborough
  Devon **102** B1
Littleborough
  GtMan **184** D1
Littleborough
  Notts **187** F4
Littlebourne **125** E3
Littlebredy **104** B4
Littlebury **150** D4
Littlebury Green **150** C4
Littledean **131** F1
Littleferry **267** F2
Littleham *Devon* **113** E3
Littleham *Devon* **102** D4
Littlehampton **108** C3
Littlehempston **101** E1
Littlehoughton **229** G5
Littlemill *EAyr* **224** C4
Littlemill *High* **267** G6
Littlemoor *Derbys* **173** E1
Littlemoor *Dorset* **104** C4
Littlemore **134** A2
Littlemoss **184** D3
Littleover **173** E4
Littleport **163** D4
Littlestead Green **134** C5
Littlestone-on-Sea **111** F1
Littlethorpe **194** C1
Littleton *ChesW&C* **170** B1
Littleton *Hants* **119** F4
Littleton *P&K* **244** A1
Littleton *Som* **116** B4
Littleton *Surr* **121** F1

Littleton Drew **132** A4
Littleton Panell **118** B2
Littleton-on-Severn **131** E3
Littletown *Dur* **212** C3
Littletown *IoW* **107** E3
Littlewick Green **134** D5
Littleworth *Glos* **146** B1
Littleworth *Oxon* **133** F3
Littleworth *Staffs* **158** C1
Littleworth *SYorks* **186** D3
Littleworth *Worcs* **146** A3
Littley Green **137** F1
Litton *Derbys* **185** F5
Litton *NYorks* **201** E5
Litton *Som* **116** C2
Litton Cheney **104** B3
Liverpool **183** E3
Liverpool Cathedral
  Mersey L1 7AZ **42** E6
Liverpool John Lennon
  Airport **183** F4
Liverpool Metropolitan
  Cathedral (RC) *Mersey*
  L3 5TQ **43** E4
Liversedge **194** B5
Liverton *Devon* **102** B5
Liverton *R&C* **203** G1
Liverton Street **124** A4
Living Coasts, Torquay
  Torbay TQ1 2BG **101** F1
Livingston **235** E3
Livingston Village **235** E3
Lixwm **182** C5
Lizard **95** E5
Llaingarreglwyd **142** A2
Llaingoch **180** A4
Llaithddu **155** G4
Llampha **129** F5
Llan **155** E2
Llanaber **154** C1
Llanaelhaearn **166** C3
Llanaeron **142** A1
Llanafan **154** C5
Llanafan-fawr **143** F2
Llanafan-fechan **143** F2
Llanallgo **180** C4
Llanarmon **166** D4
Llanarmon Dyffryn
  Ceiriog **169** E4
Llanarmon-yn-Ial **169** E2
Llanarth *Cere* **142** A2
Llanarth *Mon* **130** C1
Llanarthney **142** B5
Llanasa **182** C4
Llanbabo **180** B4
Llanbadarn Fawr **154** B4
Llanbadarn Fynydd **155** G5
Llanbadarn-y-
  garreg **144** A3
Llanbadoc **130** C2
Llanbadrig **180** B3
Llanbeder **130** C3
Llanbedr *Gwyn* **167** E5
Llanbedr *Powys* **144** B5
Llanbedr *Powys* **144** A3
Llanbedr-Dyffryn-
  Clwyd **169** E2
Llanbedrgoch **180** D4
Llanbedrog **166** C4
Llanbedr-y-cennin **168** A1
Llanberis **167** E1
Llanbethery **114** D1
Llanbister **156** A5
Llanblethian **129** F5
Llanboidy **141** F5
Llanbradach **130** A3
Llanbryn-mair **155** E2
Llancadle **114** D1
Llancarfan **129** G5
Llancayo **130** C2
Llancynfelyn **154** C3
Llandafal **130** A3
Llandaff **130** A5
Llandaff North **130** A5
Llandanwg **167** E5
Llandawke **127** F1
Llanddaniel Fab **180** C5
Llanddarog **128** A1
Llanddeiniol **154** B5
Llanddeiniolen **167** E1
Llandderfel **168** C4
Llanddeusant
  Carmar **143** E5
Llanddeusant *IoA* **180** B4
Llanddew **143** G4
Llanddewi **128** A4
Llanddewi
  Rhydderch **130** C1
Llanddewi
  Skirrid **130** C1
Llanddewi Velfrey **127** E1
Llanddewi
  Ystradenni **144** A1
Llanddewi-Brefi **142** C2
Llanddewi'r Cwm **143** G3
Llanddoged **168** B1
Llanddona **181** D5
Llanddowror **127** F1
Llanddulas **182** A5
Llanddwywe **167** E5
Llanddyfnan **180** D5
Llandefaelog Fach **143** G3
Llandefaelog-
  tre'r-graig **144** A5
Llandefalle **144** A3
Llandegai **181** D5
Llandegfan **181** D5
Llandegla **169** E2
Llandegley **144** A1
Llandegveth **130** C3
Llandegwning **166** B4
Llandeilo **142** C5
Llandeilo
  Abercywyn **127** G1
Llandeilo Graban **143** G3
Llandeilo'r-Fan **143** E4
Llandeloy **140** B5
Llandenny **130** C2
Llandevaud **130** D3
Llandevenny **130** D4
Llandinabo **145** E5
Llandinam **155** G4
Llandissilio **141** E5
Llandogo **131** E2
Llandough *VGlam* **130** A5
Llandough *VGlam* **129** F5
Llandovery
  (Llanymddyfri) **143** D4
Llandow **129** F5
Llandre *Carmar* **142** C3
Llandre *Carmar* **141** E5
Llandre *Cere* **154** C4
Llandrillo **168** D4
Llandrindod Wells **143** G1
Llandrinio **156** B1
Llandudno **181** F4
Llandudno Junction **181** F5
Llandwrog **167** D2
Llandybie **128** C1
Llandyfaelog **128** A1
Llandyfan **128** C1
Llandyfriog **141** G3
Llandyfrydog **180** C4
Llandygai **181** D5
Llandygwydd **141** F3
Llandynog **169** E1
Llandyry **128** A2
Llandysilio **156** B1
Llandyssil **156** A2
Llandysul **142** A3
Llanedeyrn **130** B4
Llanedy **128** B2
Llaneglwys **143** G4
Llanegryn **154** C2
Llanegwad **142** B5
Llaneilian **180** C3
Llanelian-yn-Rhos **181** G5
Llanelidan **169** E1
Llanelieu **144** A4
Llanellen **130** C1
Llanelli **128** B2
Llanelli Millennium Coastal
  Park *Carmar*
  SA15 2LF **128** A3
Llanelltyd **154** D1
Llanelly **130** B1
Llanelly Hill **130** B1
Llanelwedd **143** G2
Llanenddwyn **167** E5
Llanengan **166** B5
Llanerfyl **155** G2
Llaneuddog **180** C4
Llanfachraeth **180** B4
Llanfachreth **168** A5
Llanfaelog **180** B5
Llanfaelrhys **166** B5
Llanfaenor **130** D1
Llanfaes *IoA* **181** E5
Llanfaes *Powys* **143** G5
Llanfaethlu **180** B4
Llanfaglan **167** D1
Llanfair **167** E5
Llanfair Caereinion **156** A2
Llanfair Clydogau **142** C2
Llanfair Dyffryn
  Clwyd **169** E2
Llanfair Talhaiarn **182** A5
Llanfair Waterdine **156** B5
Llanfair-Nant-Gwyn **141** E4
Llanfair-Orllwyn **141** E4
Llanfairpwllgwyngyll **180** D5
Llanfairynghornwy **180** B3
Llanfair-yn-neubwll **180** B5
Llanfallteg **127** E1
Llanfaredd **143** G2
Llanfarian **154** B5
Llanfechain **156** B1
Llanfechell **180** B3
Llanfendigaid **154** B2
Llanferres **169** E1
Llanfflewyn **180** B4
Llanfigael **180** B4
Llanfihangel Glyn
  Myfyr **168** C2
Llanfihangel Nant
  Bran **143** F4
Llanfihangel
  Rhydithon **144** A1
Llanfihangel Rogiet **130** D4
Llanfihangel
  Tal-y-llyn **144** A4
Llanfihangel-
  ar-arth **142** A3
Llanfihangel-nant-
  Melan **144** A2
Llanfihangel-uwch-
  Gwili **142** A5
Llanfihangel-y-
  Creuddyn **154** C5
Llanfihangel-yng-
  Ngwynfa **155** G1
Llanfihangel-yn-
  Nhwyn **180** B5
Llanfihangel-y-pennant
  Gwyn **167** E2
Llanfihangel-y-pennant
  Gwyn **154** C2
Llanfilo **144** A4
Llanfoist **130** B1
Llanfor **168** C4
Llanfrechfa **130** C3
Llanfrothen **167** F3
Llanfrynach **143** G5
Llanfwrog *Denb* **169** E2
Llanfwrog *IoA* **180** B4
Llanfyllin **156** A1
Llanfynydd *Carmar* **142** B5
Llanfynydd *Flints* **169** F2
Llanfyrnach **141** F4
Llangadfan **155** G1
Llangadog **142** D5
Llangadwaladr *IoA* **166** C1
Llangadwaladr
  Powys **169** E4
Llangaffo **166** D1
Llangain **127** G1
Llangammarch
  Wells **143** F3
Llangan **129** F5
Llangarron **145** E5
Llangasty-Talyllyn **144** A5
Llangathen **142** B5
Llangattock **130** B1
Llangattock
  Lingoed **130** C1
Llangattock-Vibon-
  Avel **130** D1
Llangedwyn **169** E5
Llangefni **180** C5
Llangeinor **129** F4
Llangeitho **142** C2
Llangeler **141** G4

Llangelynin **154** B2
Llangendeirne **128** A1
Llangennech **128** B2
Llangennith **128** A3
Llangenny **130** B1
Llangenyw **168** B5
Llangian **166** B5
Llangiwg **128** D2
Llangloffan **140** C4
Llanglydwen **141** E5
Llangoed **181** E5
Llangoedmor **141** E3
Llangollen **169** F4
Llangollen Railway *Denb*
  LL20 8SN **169** F4
Llangolman **141** E5
Llangorse **144** A5
Llangorwen **154** C4
Llangovan **131** D2
Llangower **168** C4
Llangrannog **141** G2
Llangristiolus **180** C5
Llangrove **131** E1
Llangua **144** C5
Llangunllo **156** B5
Llangunnor **142** A5
Llangurig **155** F5
Llangwm *Conwy* **168** C3
Llangwm *Mon* **130** D2
Llangwm *Pembs* **126** C2
Llangwnnadl **166** B4
Llangwyfan **169** E1
Llangwyllog **180** C5
Llangwyryfon **154** B5
Llangybi *Cere* **142** C2
Llangybi *Gwyn* **166** D3
Llangybi *Mon* **130** C2
Llangyfelach **128** C2
Llangynhafal **169** E1
Llangynidr **130** A1
Llangyniew **156** A1
Llangynin **127** F1
Llangynllo **141** G3
Llangynog *Carmar* **127** G1
Llangynog *Powys* **169** D5
Llangynwyd **129** E4
Llanhamlach **143** G5
Llanharan **129** F4
Llanharry **129** G4
Llanhennock **130** C3
Llanhilleth **130** B2
Llanidloes **155** F4
Llaniestyn **166** B4
Llanigon **144** B4
Llanilar **154** C5
Llanilid **129** F4
Llanishen *Cardiff* **130** A4
Llanishen *Mon* **131** D2
Llanllawddog **142** A5
Llanllechid **167** E1
Llanlleonfel **143** F2
Llanllugan **155** G2
Llanllwch **127** G1
Llanllwchaiarn **156** A3
Llanllwni **142** A4
Llanllyfni **167** D2
Llanllywel **130** C3
Llanmadoc **128** A3
Llanmaes **114** C1
Llanmartin **130** C4
Llanmerewig **156** A3
Llanmihangel **129** F5
Llanmiloe **127** F2
Llanmorlais **128** B3
Llannefydd **182** A5
Llannerch Hall **182** B5
Llannerch-y-medd **180** C4
Llannerch-y-Môr **182** C5
Llannon *Carmar* **128** B2
Llan-non *Cere* **142** B1
Llannor **166** C4
Llanover **130** C2
Llanpumsaint **142** A5
Llanreithan **140** B5
Llanrhaeadr **169** D1
Llanrhaeadr-ym-
  Mochnant **169** E5
Llanrhian **140** B4
Llanrhidian **128** A3
Llanrhyddlad **180** B4
Llanrhystud **142** B1
Llanrothal **131** D1
Llanrug **167** E1
Llanrumney **130** B4
Llanrwst **168** A1
Llansadurnen **127** F1
Llansadwrn *Carmar*
  142 C4
Llansadwrn *IoA* **181** D5
Llansaint **127** G2
Llansamlet **128** C2
Llansanffraid **142** B1
Llansanffraid Glan
  Conwy **181** G5
Llansannan **168** C1
Llansannor **129** F5
Llansantffraed **144** A5
Llansantffraed-
  Cwmdeuddwr **143** F1
Llansantffraed-in-
  Elwel **143** G2
Llansantffraid-ym-
  Mechain **169** F5
Llansawel **142** C4
Llansilin **169** F5
Llansoy **130** D2
Llanspyddid **143** G5
Llanstadwell **126** C2
Llansteffan **127** G1
Llanstephan **144** A3
Llantarnam **130** C3
Llanteg **127** E1
Llanthony **144** B5
Llantilio Crossenny **130** C1
Llantilio Pertholey **130** C1
Llantood **141** E3
Llantrisant *IoA* **180** B4
Llantrisant *Mon* **130** C3
Llantrisant *RCT* **129** G4
Llantrithyd **129** G5
Llantwit Fardre **129** G4
Llantwit Major **114** C1
Llantysilio **169** E3
Llanuwchllyn **168** B5
Llanvaches **130** D3
Llanvair-Discoed **130** D3
Llanvapley **130** C1

Llanvetherine **130** C1
Llanveynoe **144** C4
Llanvihangel Crucorney
  (Llanfihangel Crucornau)
  144 C5
Llanvihangel
  Gobion **130** C2
Llanvihangel-Ystern-
  Llewern **130** D1
Llanvithyn **129** G5
Llanwarne **145** E5
Llanwddyn **155** G1
Llanwenog **142** A3
Llanwern **130** C4
Llanwinio **141** F5
Llanwnda *Gwyn* **167** D2
Llanwnda *Pembs* **140** C4
Llanwnnen **142** B3
Llanwnog **155** G3
Llanwonno **129** G3
Llanwrda **143** D4
Llanwrin **155** D2
Llanwrthwl **143** F1
Llanwrtyd **143** F2
Llanwrtyd Wells **143** E2
Llanwyddelan **155** G2
Llanyblodwel **169** F5
Llanybri **127** G1
Llanybydder **142** B3
Llanycefn **141** E5
Llanychaer
  Bridge **140** C4
Llanycil **168** C4
Llanycrwys **142** C3
Llanymawddwy **155** E1
Llanymynech **169** F5
Llanynghenedl **180** B4
Llanynys **169** E1
Llan-y-pwll **170** A2
Llanyre **143** G1
Llanystumdwy **167** D3
Llanywern **144** A5
Llawhaden **127** D1
Llawndy **182** C4
Llawnt **169** F4
Llawr-y-dref **166** B5
Llawryglyn **155** F3
Llay **170** A2
Llechcynfarwy **180** B4
Llecheiddior **167** D3
Llechfaen **143** G5
Llechryd *Caerp* **130** A2
Llechryd *Cere* **141** E3
Llechrydau **169** F4
Llechwedd Slate Caverns
  Gwyn LL41 3NB **168** A3
Lledrod *Cere* **154** C5
Lledrod *Powys* **169** F5
Llethryd **128** B3
Llidiad-Nenog **142** B4
Llidiardau **168** B4
Llithfaen **166** C3
Lloc **182** C5
Llong **169** F1
Llowes **144** A3
Lloyney **156** B5
Llundain-fach **142** B2
Llwydcoed **129** F2
Llwydiarth **155** G1
Llwyn **156** B2
Llwyncelyn **142** A2
Llwyn-croes **142** A5
Llwyndafydd **141** G2
Llwynderw **156** B2
Llwyndyrus **166** C3
Llwyneinion **169** F3
Llwyngwril **154** B2
Llwynhendy **128** B3
Llwyn-Madoc **143** F2
Llwynmawr **169** F4
Llwyn-onn *Cere* **142** A2
Llwyn-onn *MTyd* **129** G1
Llwyn-y-brain
  Carmar **127** C1
Llwyn-y-brain
  Carmar **142** D4
Llwyn-y-groes **142** B2
Llwynypia **129** F3
Llyn Brenig *Conwy*
  LL21 9TT **168** C2
Llyn Llech Owain Country
  Park *Carmar*
  SA14 7NF **128** B1
Llynclys **169** F5
Llynfaes **180** C5
Llysfaen **181** G5
Llyswen **144** A4
Llysworney **129** F5
Llys-y-frân **140** D5
Llywel **143** E4
Load Brook **185** G4
Loandhu **267** F4
Loanend *Aber* **261** H1
Loanhead *Aber* **261** H1
Loanhead *Midlo* **235** G3
Loans **224** B2
Lobb **113** E2
Lobhillcross **99** E2
Loch a Charnain **262** D7
Loch an Eilein Visitor Centre
  & Forest Trail *High*
  PH22 1QT **259** F4
Loch Choire Lodge **273** J5
Loch Eil Outward
  Bound **248** C2
Loch Head *D&G* **206** D2
Loch Head *D&G* **215** F1
Loch Lomond Shores &
  Gateway Centre *WDun*
  G83 8QL **233** E1
Loch Ness Exhibition Centre
  High IV63 6TU **258** C4
Loch Sgioport **254** D1
Lochailort (Ceann Loch
  Ailleart) **247** G1
Lochaline
  (Loch Àlainn) **247** F5
Lochans **214** B5
Locharbriggs **217** D2
Lochawe
  (Loch Obha) **240** D2
Lochboisdale (Loch
  Baghasdail) **254** C3
Lochbuie **239** F2
Lochcarron
  (Loch Carrann) **264** E7
Lochdhu Hotel **275** F4
Lochdon **239** G1
Lochdrum **265** J4

Lochearnhead (Ceann Loch
  Èireann) **242** A2
Lochee **244** B1
Lochend *High* **275** H2
Lochend (Ceann Loch)
  High **258** C1
Locheport
  (Locheuphort) **262** D5
Lochfoot **216** D3
Lochgair **240** B5
Lochgarthside **258** C3
Lochgelly **243** G5
Lochgilphead (Ceann Loch
  Gilb) **231** G1
Lochgoilhead **241** E4
Lochgoyn **233** G5
Lochhill *EAyr* **225** D4
Lochhill *Moray* **267** K5
Lochinch Castle **214** C4
Lochinver
  (Loch an Inbhir) **272** C6
Lochlair **252** D5
Lochlane **242** D2
Lochlea **224** C2
Lochluichart **265** K5
Lochmaben **217** E2
Lochmaddy (Loch na
  Madadh) **262** E5
Lochore **243** G5
Lochore Meadows Country
  Park *Fife*
  KY5 8BA **243** G5
Lochportain **262** E4
Lochranza **232** A4
Lochside *Aber* **253** F3
Lochside *High* **273** G3
Lochside *High* **274** D5
Lochside *High* **275** H2
Lochslin **267** F3
Lochton **215** D2
Lochty **244** D4
Lochuisge **247** G4
Lochurr **216** C2
Lochussie **266** B6
Lochwinnoch **233** E4
Lockengate **97** E3
Lockerbie **217** F2
Lockeridge **118** C1
Lockerley **119** D5
Lockhills **210** B4
Locking **116** A2
Lockington *ERid* **196** B3
Lockington *Leics* **173** F5
Lockleywood **171** D4
Locks Heath **107** E2
Locksbottom **122** D2
Locksgreen **106** D3
Lockton **204** B4
Locomotion: The National
  Railway Museum at
  Shildon *Dur*
  DL4 1PQ **212** B5
Loddington
  Leics **160** C2
Loddington
  N'hants **160** D5
Loddiswell **100** D3
Loddon **165** E2
Lode **150** D1
Loders **104** A3
Lodsworth **121** E5
Lofthouse *NYorks* **202** A5
Lofthouse *WYorks* **194** C5
Loftus **203** F1
Logan *D&G* **206** A2
Logan *EAyr* **225** D3
Loganlea **235** D3
Loggerheads **171** E4
Loggerheads Country Park
  Denb CH7 5LH **169** E1
Loggie
  (An Lagaidh) **265** H2
Logie *Angus* **253** E3
Logie *Angus* **252** B4
Logie *Fife* **244** C3
Logie *Moray* **267** H6
Logie Coldstone **260** C4
Logie Hill **266** E4
Logie Newton **260** E1
Logie Pert **253** E3
Logierait **251** E4
Login **141** E5
Lolworth **150** B1
Lonbain **264** C6
Londesborough **196** A3
London **136** C4
London Apprentice **97** E5
London Aquarium *GtLon*
  SE1 7PD **45** F5
London Ashford
  Airport **111** F1
London Beach **124** A5
London Biggin Hill
  Airport **122** D2
London City
  Airport **136** D4
London Colney **136** A2
London Eye *GtLon*
  SE1 7PB **45** F5
London Gatwick
  Airport **122** B4
London Heathrow
  Airport **135** F5
London Luton
  Airport **149** G5
London Minstead **106** C3
London Southend
  Airport **138** B4
London Stansted
  Airport **150** D5
London Transport Museum
  GtLon WC2E 7BB **45** E3
London Wetland Centre
  GtLon SW13 9WT **11** E6
Londonderry **202** B4
Londonthorpe **175** E4
Londubh **264** E3
Lonemore **266** E3
Long Ashton **131** E5
Long Bank **157** G5
Long Bennington **174** D3
Long Bredy **104** B3
Long Buckby **148** B1
Long Clawson **174** C5
Long Compton
  Staffs **171** F5
Long Compton
  Warks **147** E4

Long Crendon **134** B2
Long Crichel **105** F1
Long Dean **132** A4
Long Downs **95** E3
Long Drax **195** F5
Long Duckmanton **186** B5
Long Eaton **173** F4
Long Gill **193** D2
Long Green
ChesW&C **183** F5
Long Green Essex **152** A5
Long Green Worcs **146** A4
Long Hanborough **133** G1
Long Itchington **147** G1
Long Lane **157** F1
Long Lawford **159** G5
Long Load **116** B5
Long Marston
NYorks **195** E2
Long Marston
Warks **147** D3
Long Marton **210** C5
Long Meadowend **156** D4
Long Melford **151** G2
Long Newnton **132** B3
Long Preston **193** E2
Long Riston **196** D3
Long Stratton **164** C2
Long Street **148** C3
Long Sutton Hants **120** C3
Long Sutton Lincs **176** C5
Long Sutton Som **116** B5
Long Thurlow **152** B1
Long Whatton **173** F5
Long Wittenham **134** A3
Longbenton **212** B1
Longborough **147** D5
Longbridge Plym **100** B2
Longbridge Warks **147** E1
Longbridge WMid **158** C5
Longbridge Deverill **117** F3
Longburgh **209** D1
Longburton **104** C1
Longcliffe **172** D2
Longcombe **101** E2
Longcot **133** E3
Longcroft **234** B2
Longcross Devon **99** E3
Longcross Surr **121** E1
Longden **156** D2
Longdon Staffs **158** C1
Longdon Worcs **146** A4
Longdon Green **158** C1
Longdon upon Tern **157** F1
Longdown **102** B3
Longdrum **261** H3
Longfield **123** F2
Longfield Hill **123** F2
Longford Derbys **172** D4
Longford Glos **146** A5
Longford GtLon **135** F5
Longford Shrop **170** D4
Longford Tel&W **157** G1
Longford WMid **159** F4
Longforgan **244** B2
Longformacus **237** D4
Longframlington **220** D1
Longham Dorset **105** G3
Longham Norf **178** A4
Longhill **269** H5
Longhirst **221** E3
Longhope Glos **131** F1
Longhope Ork **277** C8
Longhorsley **220** D2
Longhoughton **229** G5
Longlands Aber **260** C2
Longlands Cumb **209** F3
Longlands GtLon **136** D5
Longlane Derbys **173** D4
Longlane WBerks **133** G5
Longleat House Wilts
BA12 7NW **117** F3
Longleat Safari Park Wilts
BA12 7NW **117** F3
Longlevens **132** A1
Longley **185** F2
Longley Green **145** G2
Longmanhill **269** F4
Longmorn **267** K6
Longnewton ScBord **227** G3
Longnewton Stock **202** C1
Longney **131** G1
Longniddry **236** B2
Longniddry Bents ELoth
EH32 0PX **236** B2
Longnor Shrop **157** D2
Longnor Staffs **172** B1
Longparish **119** F3
Longridge Lancs **192** C4
Longridge Staffs **158** B1
Longridge WLoth **235** D3
Longridge End **146** A5
Longridge Towers **237** G4
Longriggend **234** C2
Longrock **94** C3
Longsdon **171** G3
Longshaw **183** G2
Longside **269** J6
Longslow **171** D4
Longsowerby **209** G1
Longstanton **150** C1
Longstock **119** E4
Longstone **94** C3
Longstowe **150** B2
Longstreet **118** C2
Longthorpe **161** G3
Longton Lancs **192** A5
Longton Stoke **171** G3
Longtown Cumb **218** B5
Longtown Here **144** C5
Longville in the
Dale **157** E3
Longwell Green **131** F5
Longwick **134** C2
Longwitton **220** C3
Longworth **133** F3
Longyester **236** C3
Lonmay **269** J5
Lonmore **263** H7
Look Out Discovery Park,
Bracknell BrackF
RG12 7QW **121** D1
Loose **123** G3
Loosebeare **102** A2

Loosegate **176** B5
Loosley Row **134** D2
Lopcombe Corner **119** D4
Lopen **104** A1
Loppington **170** B5
Lorbottle **220** C1
Lorbottle Hall **220** C1
Lordington **107** G2
Lord's Cricket Ground &
Museum GtLon
NW8 8QN **10** A1
Lord's Hill **106** C1
Lorgill **263** G7
Lorn **233** E1
Lornty **251** G5
Loscoe **173** F3
Loscombe **104** A3
Losgaintir **263** F2
Lossiemouth **267** K4
Lossit **230** A4
Lost Gardens of Heligan
Corn PL26 6EN **97** D5
Lostock Gralam **184** A5
Lostock Green **184** A5
Lostock
Junction **184** A2
Lostwithiel **97** F4
Loth **276** F2
Lothbeg **274** E7
Lothersdale **193** F3
Lothmore **274** E7
Loudwater **135** E3
Loughborough **160** A1
Loughor **128** B3
Loughton Essex **136** D3
Loughton MK **148** D4
Loughton Shrop **157** F4
Louis Tussaud's Waxworks
FY1 5AA **64** Blackpool
Lound Lincs **161** F1
Lound Notts **187** D4
Lound Suff **165** G2
Lount **159** F1
Lour **252** C5
Louth **188** D4
Love Clough **193** E5
Lovedean **107** F1
Lover **106** B1
Loversall **186** C3
Loves Green **137** F2
Lovesome Hill **202** C3
Loveston **127** D2
Lovington **116** C4
Low Ackworth **186** B1
Low Angerton **220** C3
Low Ballevain **222** B3
Low Barlay **215** G5
Low Barlings **188** A5
Low Bentham (Lower
Bentham) **192** C1
Low Bolton **201** F3
Low Bradfield **185** G3
Low Bradley
(Bradley) **193** G3
Low Braithwaite **210** A3
Low Brunton **220** B4
Low Burnham **187** E2
Low Burton **202** B4
Low Buston **221** E1
Low Catton **195** G2
Low Coniscliffe **202** B1
Low Craighead **224** A5
Low Dinsdale **202** C1
Low Ellington **202** B4
Low Entercommon **202** C2
Low Etherley **212** A5
Low Fell **212** B2
Low Gate **211** F1
Low Grantley **202** B5
Low Green **151** G1
Low Habberley **158** A5
Low Ham **116** B5
Low Hawsker **204** C2
Low Haygarth **200** B3
Low Hesket **210** A3
Low Hesleyhurst **220** C2
Low Hutton **195** G1
Low Kingthorpe **204** B4
Low Laithe **194** A1
Low Langton **188** B5
Low Leighton **185** E4
Low Lorton **209** E4
Low Marishes **204** B5
Low Marnham **174** D1
Low Middleton **229** F3
Low Mill **203** F3
Low Moor Lancs **192** D3
Low Moor WYorks **194** A5
Low Moorsley **212** C3
Low Moresby **208** C4
Low Newton-by-
the-Sea **229** G4
Low Row Cumb **210** B1
Low Row NYorks **201** E3
Low Stillaig **232** A3
Low Street **178** B5
Low Tharston **164** C3
Low Torry **235** E1
Low Town **220** D1
Low Toynton **188** C5
Low Wood **199** E4
Low Worsall **202** C2
Lowbands **145** G4
Lowdham **174** B3
Lowe **170** C5
Lowe Hill **171** G2
Lower Achachenna **240** C2
Lower Aisholt **115** F4
Lower Apperley **146** A5
Lower Arncott **134** B1
Lower Ashtead **121** G2
Lower Ashton **102** B4
Lower Assendon **134** C4
Lower Auchalick **232** A2
Lower Ballam **191** G4
Lower Barewood **144** C2
Lower Bartle **192** A4
Lower Bayble
(Pabail larach) **271** H4
Lower Beeding **109** E1
Lower Benefield **161** E4
Lower Bentham (Low
Bentham) **192** C1
Lower Bentley **146** B1
Lower Berry Hill **131** E1

Lower Birchwood **173** F2
Lower Boddington **147** G2
Lower Boscaswell **94** A3
Lower Bourne **120** D3
Lower Brailes **147** F4
Lower Breakish **256** C2
Lower Bredbury **184** D3
Lower Broadheath **146** A2
Lower Brynamman **128** D1
Lower Bullingham **145** E4
Lower Bullington **119** F3
Lower Burgate **106** A1
Lower Burrow **116** B5
Lower Burton **144** D2
Lower Caldecote **149** G3
Lower Cam **131** G2
Lower Cambourne **150** B2
Lower Camster **275** H4
Lower Chapel **143** G4
Lower Cheriton **103** E2
Lower Chicksgrove **118** A4
Lower Chute **119** E2
Lower Clent **158** B4
Lower Creedy **102** B2
Lower
Cumberworth **185** G2
Lower Darwen **192** C5
Lower Dean **149** F1
Lower Diabaig **264** D5
Lower Dicker **110** A2
Lower Dinchope **157** D4
Lower Down **156** C4
Lower Drift **94** B4
Lower Dunsforth **194** D1
Lower Earley **134** C5
Lower Edmonton **136** C3
Lower Elkstone **172** B2
Lower End Bucks **134** B2
Lower End MK **149** E4
Lower End N'hants **149** D1
Lower Everleigh **118** C2
Lower Eythorne **125** E4
Lower Failand **131** E5
Lower Farringdon **120** C4
Lower Fittleworth **108** C2
Lower Foxdale **190** A4
Lower Freystrop **126** C1
Lower Froyle **120** C3
Lower Gabwell **101** F1
Lower Gledfield **266** C2
Lower Godney **116** B3
Lower Gravenhurst **149** G4
Lower Green Essex **150** C4
Lower Green Herts **149** G5
Lower Green Kent **123** E5
Lower Green Norf **178** A2
Lower Green Staffs **158** B2
Lower Green Bank **192** B2
Lower Halstock
Leigh **104** B2
Lower Halstow **124** A2
Lower Hardres **124** D3
Lower Harpton **144** B1
Lower Hartshay **173** E2
Lower Hartwell **134** C1
Lower Hawthwaite **198** D4
Lower Haysden **123** E4
Lower Hayton **157** E4
Lower Heath **171** F1
Lower Hergest **144** B2
Lower Heyford **147** G5
Lower Higham **137** G5
Lower Holbrook **152** C4
Lower Hopton **185** G1
Lower Hordley **170** A5
Lower Horncroft **108** C2
Lower Horsebridge **110** A2
Lower Houses **185** F1
Lower Howsell **145** G3
Lower Kersal **184** C2
Lower Kilchattan **238** C5
Lower Kilcott **131** G4
Lower Killeyan **230** A5
Lower Kingcombe **104** B3
Lower Kingswood **122** B3
Lower Kinnerton **170** A1
Lower Langford **116** B1
Lower Largo **244** C4
Lower Leigh **172** B4
Lower Lemington **147** E4
Lower Lovacott **113** F3
Lower Loxhore **113** G2
Lower Lye **144** D1
Lower Lybrook **131** E1
Lower Lydbrook **131** E1
Lower Machen **130** B4
Lower Maes-coed **144** C4
Lower Mannington **105** G2
Lower Middleton
Cheney **148** A3
Lower Milton **116** C3
Lower Moor **146** B3
Lower Morton **131** F3
Lower Nash **126** D2
Lower Nazeing **136** C2
Lower Netchwood **157** F3
Lower Nyland **117** E5
Lower Oddington **147** E5
Lower Ollach **256** B1
Lower Penarth **130** A5
Lower Penn **158** A3
Lower Pennington **106** C3
Lower Peover **184** B5
Lower Pollicott **134** C1
Lower Quinton **147** D3
Lower Race **130** B2
Lower Rainham **124** A2
Lower Roadwater **114** D4
Lower Sapey **145** F1
Lower Seagry **132** B4
Lower Shelton **149** E3
Lower Shiplake **134** C5
Lower Shuckburgh **147** G1
Lower Slaughter **147** D5
Lower Soothill **194** B5
Lower Stanton
St. Quintin **132** B4
Lower Stoke **124** A1
Lower Stondon **149** G4
Lower Stone **131** F3
Lower Stonnall **158** C2
Lower Stow Bedon **164** A2
Lower Street Dorset **105** E3
Lower Street ESuss **110** C2
Lower Street Norf **179** D2
Lower Street Norf **179** E2
Lower Street Suff **152** C2
Lower Stretton **184** A4
Lower Sundon **149** F5

Lower Swanwick **107** D2
Lower Swell **147** D5
Lower Tadmarton **147** G4
Lower Tale **103** D2
Lower Tean **172** B4
Lower Thurlton **165** F2
Lower Thurnham **192** A2
Lower Town Corn **95** D4
Lower Town Devon **102** A5
Lower Town IoS **96** B1
Lower Town Pembs **140** C4
Lower Trebullett **98** D3
Lower Tysoe **147** F3
Lower Upcott **102** B4
Lower Upnor **137** G5
Lower Vexford **115** E4
Lower Wallop **156** C1
Lower Walton **184** A4
Lower Waterhay **132** C3
Lower Weald **148** C4
Lower Wear **102** C4
Lower Weare **116** B2
Lower Welson **144** B2
Lower Whatley **117** E2
Lower Whitley **184** A5
Lower Wick **146** A3
Lower Wield **120** B3
Lower Winchendon (Nether
Winchendon) **134** C1
Lower Withington **171** F1
Lower Woodend **134** D4
Lower Woodford **118** C4
Lower Wyche **145** G3
Lowerhouse **193** E4
Lowesby **160** C2
Lowestoft **165** G2
Loweswater **209** E4
Lowfield Heath **122** B4
Lowgill Cumb **200** B3
Lowgill Lancs **192** C1
Lowick N'hants **161** E4
Lowick N'umb **229** E3
Lowick Green **199** D4
Lownie Moor **252** C5
Lowry, The GtMan
M50 3AZ **24** D3
Lowsonford **147** D1
Lowther **210** B5
Lowther Castle **210** B5
Lowthorpe **196** C1
Lowton Devon **113** G5
Lowton GtMan **184** A3
Lowton Som **103** E1
Lowton Common **184** A3
Loxbeare **102** C1
Loxhill **121** F4
Loxhore **113** G2
Loxley Kent **147** E2
Loxley Green **172** B4
Loxton **116** A2
Loxwood **121** F4
Lubachoinnich **266** B2
Lubcroy **265** K1
Lubenham **160** C4
Lubfearn **265** K4
Lubmore **265** G6
Lubreoch **249** G5
Luccombe **114** C3
Luccombe Village **107** E4
Lucker **229** F3
Luckett **99** D3
Luckington **132** A4
Lucklawhill **244** C2
Luckwell Bridge **114** C4
Lucton **144** D1
Lucy Cross **202** B1
Ludag **254** C3
Ludborough **188** C3
Ludbrook **100** C2
Ludchurch **127** E1
Luddenden **193** G5
Luddenden Foot **193** G5
Luddenham Court **124** B2
Luddesdown **123** F2
Luddington in the
Brook **161** G4
Ludford Lincs **188** B4
Ludford Shrop **157** E5
Ludgershall Bucks **134** B1
Ludgershall Wilts **119** D2
Ludgvan **94** C3
Ludham **179** E4
Ludlow **157** E5
Ludney **189** D3
Ludstock **145** F4
Ludstone **158** A3
Ludwell **118** A5
Ludworth **212** C3
Luffincott **98** D2
Lufton **104** B1
Lugar **225** D3
Luggate **236** C2
Luggate Burn **236** D2
Luggiebank **234** B2
Lugton **233** F4
Lugwardine **145** E3
Luib **256** B2
Luibeilt **249** E3
Luing **239** G3
Lulham **144** D3
Lullington Derbys **159** E1
Lullington Som **117** E2
Lulsgate Bottom **116** C1
Lulsley **145** G2
Lulworth Cove & Heritage
Centre Dorset
BH20 5RQ **105** E5
Lumb Lancs **193** E5
Lumb WYorks **193** G5
Lumbutts **193** F5
Lumby **195** D4
Lumphanan **260** D4
Lumphinnans **243** G5
Lumsdaine **237** F3
Lumsdale **173** E1
Lumsden **260** C2
Lunan **253** E4
Lunanhead **252** C4
Luncarty **243** F2
Lund ERid **196** B3

Lund NYorks **195** F4
Lund Shet **278** E2
Lundale **270** D4
Lundavra **248** C3
Lunderston Bay Invcly
PA16 0DN **232** D2
Lunderton **269** K6
Lundie Angus **244** A1
Lundie High **257** H3
Lundin Links **244** C4
Lundwood **186** A2
Lundy **112** B1
Lunga **240** A4
Lunna **279** D6
Lunning **279** E6
Lunnon **128** B4
Lunsford's Cross **110** C2
Lunt **183** E2
Luntley **144** C2
Lupin **199** G4
Luppitt **103** E2
Lupset **186** A1
Lupton **199** G4
Lurgashall **121** E5
Lurignich **248** B4
Lusby **176** B1
Luss **241** F5
Lussagiven **231** E1
Lusta **263** H6
Lustleigh **102** A4
Luston **145** D1
Luthermuir **253** E3
Luthrie **244** B3
Luton Devon **103** D2
Luton Devon **103** D2
Luton Luton **149** F5
Luton Airport **149** G5
Lutterworth **160** A4
Lutton Devon **100** B2
Lutton Dorset **105** F4
Lutton Lincs **176** C5
Lutton N'hants **161** G4
Luxborough **114** C4
Luxulyan **97** E4
Lybster High **275** F2
Lybster High **275** H5
Lydacott **113** E5
Lydbury North **156** C4
Lydcott **113** G2
Lydd **111** F1
Lydden **125** E4
Lyddington **161** D3
Lydd-on-Sea **111** F1
Lyde **131** F5
Lydeard
St. Lawrence **115** E4
Lydford **99** F2
Lydford-on-Fosse **116** C4
Lydgate GtMan **185** D1
Lydgate GtMan **185** D2
Lydgate WYorks **193** F5
Lydham **156** C3
Lydiard Millicent **132** C4
Lydiard Tregoze **132** D4
Lydiate **183** E2
Lydiate Ash **158** B5
Lydlinch **104** D1
Lydney **131** F2
Lydstep **127** D3
Lye **158** B4
Lye Cross **116** B1
Lye Green Bucks **135** E2
Lye Green ESuss **123** E5
Lye Green Warks **147** D1
Lye's Green **117** F3
Lymbridge Green **124** D4
Lyme Regis **103** G3
Lymekilns **234** A4
Lyminge **125** D4
Lymington **106** C3
Lyminster **108** C3
Lymm **184** A4
Lymore **106** B4
Lympne **124** D5
Lympsham **116** A2
Lympstone **102** C4
Lynaberack **258** E5
Lynch **114** B3
Lynch Green **178** C5
Lynchat **258** E4
Lyndale House **263** J6
Lyndhurst **106** B2
Lyndon **161** E2
Lyne Aber **261** F4
Lyne ScBord **235** G5
Lyne Surr **121** F1
Lyne Down **145** F4
Lyne of Gorthleck **258** C2
Lyne of Skene **261** F3
Lyne Station **235** G5
Lyneal **170** B5
Lynegar **275** H3
Lyneham Oxon **147** E5
Lyneham Wilts **132** C5
Lyneholmeford **218** D4
Lynemore High **259** H2
Lynemore Moray **259** J1
Lynemouth **221** E2
Lyness **277** C8
Lynford **163** G4
Lyng **178** B4
Lyngate **179** E3
Lynmouth **114** A3
Lynn **157** G1
Lynsted **124** B2
Lynstone **112** C5
Lynton **114** A3
Lynton & Lynmouth Cliff
Railway Devon
EX35 6EP **114** A3
Lyon's Gate **104** C2
Lyonshall **144** C2
Lyrabus **230** A3
Lytchett Matravers **105** F3
Lytchett Minster **105** F3
Lyth **275** H2
Lytham **191** G5
Lytham St. Anne's **191** G5
Lythe **204** B1
Lythe Hill **121** E4
Lythes **277** D9
Lythmore **275** F2

M

M.V. Princess Pocahontas
Kent DA11 0BS **137** G5
Mabe Burnthouse **95** E3
Mabie **217** D3

Lund NYorks **195** F4
Lund Shet **278** E2
Mablethorpe **189** F4
Macclesfield **184** D5
Macclesfield Forest **185** D5
Macduff **269** F4
Macedonia **244** A4
Machan **244** A4
Machany **243** D3
Macharioch **222** C5
Machen **130** B4
Machrie A&B **230** A3
Machrie A&B **230** B5
Machrie NAyr **223** H2
Machrihanish **222** B3
Machrins **238** C5
Machynlleth **154** D2
McInroy's Point **232** D2
Mackerye End **136** A1
Mackworth **173** E4
Macmerry **236** B2
Macterry **269** F6
Madame Tussauds GtLon
NW1 5LR **12** A4
Madderty **243** E2
Maddiston **234** D2
Madehurst **108** B2
Madeley Staffs **171** E3
Madeley Tel&W **157** G2
Madeley Heath **171** E3
Maders **98** D3
Madford **103** E1
Madingley **150** B1
Madjeston **117** F5
Madley **144** D4
Madresfield **146** A3
Madron **94** B3
Maenaddwyn **180** C4
Maenclochog **141** D5
Maendy Cardiff **130** A5
Maendy VGlam **129** G5
Maenporth **95** E4
Maentwrog **167** F3
Maen-y-groes **141** G2
Maer Corn **112** C5
Maer Staffs **171** E4
Maerdy Carmar **142** C5
Maerdy Carmar **142** C5
Maerdy Conwy **168** D3
Maerdy RCT **129** F3
Maesbrook **169** F5
Maesbury Marsh **170** A5
Maes-glas **130** B4
Maesgwynne **141** F5
Maeshafn **169** F1
Maesllyn **141** G3
Maesmynis **143** G3
Maesteg **129** E3
Maes-Treylow **144** B1
Maesybont **128** B1
Maesycrugiau **142** A3
Maesycwmmer **130** A3
Magdalen Laver **137** E2
Maggieknockater **268** B6
Maggots End **150** C5
Magham Down **110** B2
Maghull **183** E2
Magna Centre, Rotherham
SYorks S60 1DX **21** C1
Magna Park **160** A4
Magor **130** D4
Magpie Green **164** B4
Maiden Bradley **117** E4
Maiden Head **116** C1
Maiden Law **212** A3
Maiden Newton **104** B3
Maiden Wells **126** C3
Maidencombe **101** F1
Maidenhayne **103** F3
Maidenhead **135** E4
Maidens **224** A5
Maiden's Green **135** D5
Maidensgrove **134** C4
Maidenwell Corn **97** F2
Maidenwell Lincs **188** D5
Maidford **148** B2
Maids' Moreton **148** C4
Maidstone **123** G3
Maidwell **160** C5
Mail **279** D10
Maindee **130** C4
Mainland Ork **277** B6
Mainland Shet **279** C7
Mains of Ardestie **244** D1
Mains of Balgavies **252** D4
Mains of Ballindarg **252** D3
Mains of Balhall **252** D3
Mains of Burgie **267** H6
Mains of Culsh **269** G6
Mains of Dillavaird **253** F1
Mains of Drum **261** G4
Mains of Dudwick **261** H1
Mains of Faillie **258** E1
Mains of Fedderate **269** G6
Mains of Glack **261** F2
Mains of Glassaugh **268** D4
Mains of
Glenbuchat **260** B3
Mains of Linton **261** F3
Mains of Melgund **252** D4
Mains of Pitfour **269** H6
Mains of Pittrichie **261** G2
Mains of Sluie **267** H6
Mains of Tannachy **268** B4
Mains of Thornton **253** E2
Mains of Tig **214** C2
Mains of Watten **275** H3
Mainsriddle **216** D5
Mainstone **156** B4
Maisemore **146** A5
Major's Green **158** D5
Makendon **220** A1
Makeney **173** E3
Makerstoun **228** A3
Malacleit **262** C4
Malborough **100** D4
Malden Rushett **121** G1
Maldon **138** B2
Malham **193** F1
Maligar **263** K5
Malin Bridge **186** A4
Mallaig (Malaig) **256** C5
Mallaigmore **256** C5
Mallaigvaig **256** C5
Malleny Mills **235** F3
Mallows Green **150** C5
Malltraeth **166** D1

Mallwyd **155** E1
Malmesbury **132** B4
Malmsmead **114** A3
Malpas ChesW&C **170** B3
Malpas Corn **96** C5
Malpas Newport **130** C3
Maltby Lincs **188** D4
Maltby Stock **203** D1
Maltby SYorks **186** C3
Maltby le Marsh **189** E4
Malting End **151** F2
Malting Green **138** C1
Maltman's Hill **124** A4
Malton **203** G5
Malvern Link **145** G3
Malvern Wells **145** G3
Mambeg **232** D1
Mamble **157** F5
Mamhead **102** C4
Mamhilad **130** C2
Manaccan **95** E4
Manadon **100** A2
Manafon **156** A2
Manaton **102** A4
Manby **189** D4
Mancetter **159** F3
Manchester **184** C3
Manchester Airport **184** C4
Manchester Apollo GtMan
M12 6AP **47** G5
Manchester Art Gallery
GtMan M3 3JL **47** E4
Manchester Central GtMan
M2 3GX **46** D5
Manchester Craft & Design
Centre GtMan
M4 5JD **47** F3
Manchester Museum
GtMan M13 9PL **47** F7
Manchester United Museum
& Stadium Tour Centre
GtMan M16 0RA **24** D3
Mancot Royal **170** A1
Mandally
(Manndalaidh) **257** J4
Manea **162** C4
Maneight **242** D5
Manfield **202** B1
Mangaster **278** C5
Mangerton **104** A3
Mangotsfield **131** F5
Mangrove Green **149** G5
Mangurstadh **270** C4
Manish (Manais) **263** G3
Mankinholes **193** F5
Manley **183** G5
Manmoel **130** A2
Mannal **246** A2
Manningford
Abbots **118** C2
Manningford
Bohune **118** C2
Manningford Bruce **118** C2
Manningham **194** A4
Mannings Amusement Park
Suff IP11 2DW **153** D4
Mannings Heath **109** E1
Mannington **105** G2
Manningtree **152** C4
Mannofield **261** H4
Manor Farm Country Park
Hants SO30 2ER **4** D3
Manor Park **135** E4
Manorbier **127** E4
Manorbier Newton **126** D2
Manordeifi **141** F3
Manordeilo **142** C5
Manorowen **140** C4
Mansell Gamage **144** C3
Mansell Lacy **144** D3
Mansergh **200** B4
Manside **173** G2
Mansfield
Woodhouse **173** G1
Manson Green **178** B5
Mansriggs **199** D4
Manston Dorset **105** E1
Manston Kent **125** F2
Manston WYorks **194** C4
Manswood **105** F2
Manthorpe Lincs **161** F1
Manthorpe Lincs **175** E4
Manton NLincs **187** G2
Manton Notts **186** C5
Manton Rut **161** D2
Manton Wilts **118** C1
Manuden **150** C5
Maolachy **240** A2
Maperton **117** D5
Maple Cross **135** F3
Maplebeck **174** C1
Mapledurham **134** B5
Mapledurwell **120** B2
Maplehurst **121** G5
Maplescombe **123** F2
Mapleton **172** C3
Mapperley Derbys **173** F3
Mapperley Notts **173** G3
Mapperton Dorset **104** B3
Mapperton Dorset **105** F3
Mappleborough
Green **146** C1
Mappleton **197** E3
Mapplewell **186** A2
Mappowder **104** D2
Mar Lodge **259** H5
Maraig (Maaruig) **270** E7
Marazion **94** C3
Marbhig **271** G6
Marbury **170** C3
Marbury Country Park
ChesW&C
CW9 6AT **184** A5
March **162** C4
Marcham **133** G3
Marchamley **170** C5
Marchamley Wood **170** C4
Marchington **172** C4
Marchington
Woodlands **172** C5
Marchwiel **170** A3
Marchwood **106** C1
Marcross **114** C1
Marcus **252** D4
Marden Here **145** E3
Marden Kent **123** G4
Marden T&W **221** F4

Marden Wilts 118 B2
Marden Ash 137 E2
Marden Beech 123 G4
Marden Thorn 123 G4
Marden's Hill 123 D5
Mardon 228 D3
Mardy 130 C1
Mare Green 116 A5
Marefield 160 C2
Mareham le Fen 176 A1
Mareham on the Hill 176 A1
Maresfield 109 G1
Marfleet 196 D4
Marford 170 A2
Margam 129 D4
Margam Country Park NPT SA13 2TJ 129 E4
Margaret Marsh 105 E1
Margaret Roding 137 E1
Margaretting 137 F2
Margaretting Tye 137 F2
Margate 125 F1
Margnaheglish 223 F2
Margreig 216 C3
Margrove Park 203 F1
Marham 163 F2
Marhamchurch 112 C5
Marholm 161 G2
Marian Cwm 182 B5
Mariandyrys 181 E4
Marian-glas 180 D4
Mariansleigh 114 A5
Marine Town 124 B1
Marishader 263 K5
Maristow House 100 A1
Mark 116 A3
Mark Causeway 116 A3
Mark Cross 123 E5
Markbeech 123 D4
Markby 189 E5
Markdhu 214 C3
Markeaton 173 E4
Markeaton Park Craft Village Derby DE22 3BG 18 A3
Market Bosworth 159 G2
Market Bosworth Country Park Leics CV13 0LP 159 G2
Market Deeping 161 G1
Market Drayton 171 D4
Market Harborough 160 C4
Market Lavington 118 B2
Market Overton 161 D1
Market Rasen 188 B4
Market Stainton 188 C5
Market Street 179 D3
Market Warsop 173 G1
Market Weighton 196 A3
Market Weston 164 A4
Markethill 244 A1
Markfield 159 G1
Markham 130 A2
Markham Moor 187 E5
Markinch 244 A4
Markington 194 B1
Marks Gate 137 D3
Marks Tey 152 A5
Marksbury 117 D1
Markwell 99 D5
Markyate 135 F1
Marl Bank 145 G3
Marland 184 C1
Marlborough 118 C1
Marlbrook 158 B5
Marlcliff 146 C2
Marldon 101 E1
Marle Green 110 A2
Marlesford 153 E2
Marley Green 170 C3
Marley Hill 212 B2
Marlingford 178 C5
Marloes 126 A2
Marlow Bucks 135 D4
Marlow Here 156 D5
Marlpit Hill 122 D4
Marlpool 173 F3
Marnhull 105 D1
Marnoch 268 D5
Marple 185 D4
Marple Bridge 185 D4
Marr 186 C2
Marrel 275 F7
Marrick 201 F3
Marrister 279 E6
Marros 127 F2
Marsden T&W 212 C1
Marsden WYorks 185 E1
Marsett 201 E4
Marsh 103 F1
Marsh Baldon 134 A3
Marsh Benham 119 F1
Marsh Farm Country Park Essex CM3 5WP 138 B3
Marsh Gibbon 148 B5
Marsh Green Devon 102 D3
Marsh Green GtMan 183 G2
Marsh Green Kent 122 D4
Marsh Green Tel&W 157 F1
Marsh Lane 186 B5
Marsh Street 114 C3
Marshall Meadows 237 G4
Marshalsea 103 G2
Marshalswick 136 A2
Marsham 178 C3
Marshaw 192 B2
Marshborough 125 F3
Marshbrook 156 D4
Marshchapel 189 D3
Marshfield Newport 130 B4
Marshfield SGlos 131 G5
Marshgate 98 B1
Marshland St. James 162 D2
Marshside 183 E1
Marshwood 103 G3
Marske 202 A2
Marske-by-the-Sea 213 F5
Marsland Green 184 A3
Marston ChesW&C 184 A5
Marston Here 144 C2
Marston Lincs 175 D3
Marston Oxon 134 A2
Marston Staffs 171 G5
Marston Staffs 158 A1
Marston Warks 159 E3
Marston Wilts 118 A2
Marston Doles 147 G2
Marston Green 159 D4
Marston Magna 116 C5
Marston Meysey 132 D3
Marston Montgomery 172 C4
Marston Moretaine 149 E3
Marston on Dove 172 D5
Marston St. Lawrence 148 A3
Marston Stannett 145 E2
Marston Trussell 160 B4
Marston Vale Millennium Country Park CenBeds MK43 0PR 149 F3
Marstow 131 E1
Marsworth 135 E1
Marten 119 D1
Marthall 184 B5
Martham 179 F4
Martin Hants 105 G1
Martin Lincs 175 G2
Martin Lincs 176 A1
Martin Drove End 118 B5
Martin Hussingtree 146 A1
Martin Mere Lancs L40 0TA 183 F1
Martinhoe 113 G1
Martinscroft 184 A4
Martinstown 104 C4
Martlesham 152 D3
Martlesham Heath 152 D3
Martletwy 126 D1
Martley 145 G1
Martock 104 A1
Marton ChesE 171 F1
Marton Cumb 198 D5
Marton ERid 197 D4
Marton ERid 197 E1
Marton Lincs 187 F4
Marton Middl 203 E1
Marton NYorks 194 D1
Marton NYorks 203 G4
Marton Shrop 156 B2
Marton Shrop 170 B5
Marton Warks 147 G1
Marton Abbey 195 E1
Marton-in-the-Forest 195 E1
Marton-le-Moor 202 C5
Martyr Worthy 119 G4
Martyr's Green 121 F2
Marwell Zoo Hants SO21 1JH 4 D1
Marwick 276 B5
Marwood 113 F2
Mary Rose PO1 3LX 82 Portsmouth
Mary Tavy 99 F3
Marybank (An Lagaidh) High 266 B6
Marybank Na H-ESiar 271 G4
Maryburgh (Baile Mairi) 266 C6
Maryfield Corn 100 A2
Maryfield Shet 279 D8
Marygold 237 F4
Maryhill Aber 269 G6
Maryhill Glas 233 G3
Marykirk 253 E3
Marylebone GtLon 136 B4
Marylebone GtMan 183 G2
Marypark 259 J1
Maryport Cumb 208 D3
Maryport D&G 206 B3
Marystow 99 E2
Maryton 253 E4
Marywell Aber 261 H5
Marywell Aber 260 D5
Marywell Angus 253 E5
Masham 202 B4
Mashbury 137 F1
Masongill 200 B5
Mastin Moor 186 B5
Mastrick 261 H4
Matchborough 146 C1
Matching 137 E1
Matching Green 137 E1
Matching Tye 137 E1
Matfen 220 C4
Matfield 123 F4
Mathern 131 E3
Mathon 145 G3
Mathry 140 B4
Matlaske 178 C2
Matlock 173 E1
Matlock Bank 173 E1
Matlock Bath 173 D2
Matson 132 A1
Matterdale End 209 G4
Mattersey 187 D4
Mattersey Thorpe 187 D4
Mattingley 120 C2
Mattishall 178 B4
Mattishall Burgh 178 B4
Mauchline 224 C3
Maud 269 H6
Maufant 100 C5
Maugersbury 147 D5
Maughold 190 C2
Mauld 257 K1
Maulden 149 F4
Maulds Meaburn 200 B1
Maunby 202 C4
Maund Bryan 145 E2
Maundown 115 D5
Mautby 179 F4
Mavesyn Ridware 158 C1
Mavis Enderby 176 B1
Maw Green 171 E2
Mawbray 209 D2
Mawdesley 183 F1
Mawdlam 129 E4
Mawgan 95 E4
Mawgan Porth 96 C3
Mawla 96 B5
Mawnan 95 E4
Mawnan Smith 95 E4
Mawsley 160 D5
Mawthorpe 189 E5
Maxey 161 G2
Maxstoke 159 E4
Maxted Street 124 D4
Maxton Kent 125 F4
Maxton ScBord 228 A3
Maxwellheugh 228 B3
Maxwelltown 217 D3
Maxworthy 98 C1
May Hill 145 G5
Mayals 128 C3
Maybole 224 B5
Maybury 121 F2
Mayen 268 D6
Mayfair 136 B4
Mayfield ESuss 110 A1
Mayfield Midlo 236 A3
Mayfield Staffs 172 C3
Mayford 121 E2
Mayland 138 C2
Maylandsea 138 C2
Maynard's Green 110 A2
Maypole IoS 96 B1
Maypole Kent 125 D2
Maypole Mon 131 D1
Maypole Green Essex 152 A5
Maypole Green Norf 165 F2
Maypole Green Suff 153 D1
Maypole Green Suff 152 A2
May's Green NSom 116 A1
Mays Green Oxon 134 C4
Maywick 279 C10
Mead 112 C4
Mead End 118 B5
Meadgate 117 D2
Meadle 134 D2
Meadow Green 145 G2
Meadowhall 186 A3
Meadowmill 236 B2
Meadowtown 156 C2
Meadwell 99 E2
Meaford 171 F4
Meal Bank 199 G3
Mealasta 270 B5
Meals 189 E3
Mealsgate 209 F2
Meanley 192 D3
Meanwood 194 B4
Mearbeck 193 E1
Meare 116 B3
Meare Green 115 F5
Mearns 233 G4
Mears Ashby 148 D1
Measham 159 F1
Meathop 199 F4
Meavy 100 B1
Medbourne 160 D3
Meddon 112 C4
Meden Vale 173 G1
Medlar 192 A4
Medmenham 134 D4
Medomsley 212 A2
Medstead 120 B4
Meer Common 144 C2
Meer End 159 E5
Meerbrook 171 G1
Meesden 150 C4
Meeson 171 D5
Meeth 113 F5
Meeting House Hill 179 E3
Meggethead 226 C3
Meidrim 141 F5
Meifod Denb 168 D2
Meifod Powys 156 A1
Meigle 252 A5
Meikle Earnock 234 B4
Meikle Grenach 232 B3
Meikle Kilmory 232 B3
Meikle Rahane 232 D1
Meikle Strath 253 E2
Meikle Tarty 261 H2
Meikle Wartle 261 F1
Meikleour 243 G1
Meikleyard 224 D2
Meinciau 128 A1
Meir 171 G3
Meirheath 171 G3
Melbost 271 G4
Melbost Borve (Mealabost) 271 G2
Melbourn 150 B3
Melbourne Derbys 173 E5
Melbourne ERid 195 G3
Melbury 113 D4
Melbury Abbas 105 E1
Melbury Bubb 104 B2
Melbury Osmond 104 B2
Melbury Sampford 104 B2
Melby 279 A7
Melchbourne 149 F1
Melcombe Bingham 105 D2
Melcombe Regis 104 C4
Meldon Devon 99 F1
Meldon N'umb 220 D3
Meldreth 150 B3
Meledor 96 D4
Melfort 240 A3
Melgarve 258 B5
Melgum 260 C4
Meliden (Gallt Melyd) 182 B4
Melincourt 129 E2
Melin-y-coed 168 B1
Melin-y-ddol 155 G2
Melin-y-grug 155 G2
Melin-y-Wig 168 D3
Melkinthorpe 210 B5
Melkridge 210 D1
Melksham 118 A1
Melksham Forest 118 A1
Melldalloch 232 A2
Melling Lancs 199 G5
Melling Mersey 183 E2
Melling Mount 183 F2
Mellis 164 B4
Mellon Charles 264 E2
Mellon Udrigle 264 E2
Mellor GtMan 185 D4
Mellor Lancs 192 C4
Mellor Brook 192 C4
Mells 117 E3
Melmerby Cumb 210 C4
Melmerby NYorks 201 F4
Melmerby NYorks 202 C5
Melplash 104 A3
Melrose Aber 269 F4
Melrose ScBord 227 G2
Melsetter 277 B9
Melsonby 202 A2
Meltham 185 E1
Melton ERid 196 B5
Melton Suff 153 D2
Melton Constable 178 B2
Melton Mowbray 160 C1
Melton Ross 188 A1
Meltonby 195 G2
Melvaig 264 D3
Melverley 156 C1
Melverley Green 156 C1
Melvich 274 D2
Membury 103 F2
Memsie 269 H4
Memus 252 C4
Menabilly 97 E4
Menai Bridge (Porthaethwy) 181 D5
Mendham 165 D3
Mendlesham 152 C1
Mendlesham Green 152 B1
Menethorpe 195 G1
Menheniot 97 G3
Menie House 261 H2
Menithwood 145 G1
Mennock 225 G5
Menston 194 A3
Menstrie 242 D5
Mentmore 135 E1
Meoble 247 G1
Meole Brace 157 D1
Meon 107 E2
Meonstoke 107 F1
Meopham 123 F2
Meopham Green 123 F2
Mepal 162 C4
Meppershall 149 G4
Merbach 144 C3
Mercaston 173 D3
Mere ChesE 184 B4
Mere Wilts 117 F4
Mere Brow 183 F1
Mere Green 158 D3
Mere Heath 184 A5
Mereclough 193 E4
Mereside 191 G4
Meretown 171 E5
Mereworth 123 F3
Mergie 253 F1
Meriden 159 E4
Merkadale 255 J1
Merkinch 266 D7
Merkland 216 B3
Merley 105 G3
Merlin's Bridge 126 C1
Merridge 115 F4
Merrifield 101 E3
Merrington 170 B5
Merrion 126 C3
Merriott 104 A1
Merrivale 99 F3
Merrow 121 F2
Merry Hill Herts 136 A3
Merry Hill WMid 158 B4
Merry Hill WMid 158 A3
Merrymeet 97 G3
Mersea Island 138 D1
Mersey Ferries Mersey CH44 6QY 42 A4
Merseyside Maritime Museum Mersey L3 4AQ 42 B5
Mersham 124 C5
Merstham 122 B3
Merston 108 A3
Merstone 107 E4
Merther 96 C5
Merthyr 141 G5
Merthyr Cynog 143 F4
Merthyr Dyfan 115 E1
Merthyr Mawr 129 E5
Merthyr Tydfil 129 G2
Merthyr Vale 129 G3
Merton Devon 113 F4
Merton Norf 164 A2
Merton Oxon 134 A1
Mervinslaw 228 A5
Meshaw 102 A1
Messing 138 C1
Messingham 187 F2
Metcombe 103 D3
Metfield 165 D3
Metherell 100 A1
Metheringham 175 F1
Methil 244 B5
Methlem 166 A4
Methley 194 C5
Methley Junction 194 C5
Methlick 261 G1
Methven 243 F2
Methwold 163 F3
Methwold Hythe 163 F3
MetroCentre 212 B1
Mettingham 165 E3
Metton 178 C2
Mevagissey 97 E5
Mewith Head 192 D1
Mexborough 186 B3
Mey 275 H1
Meysey Hampton 132 D2
Miabhag Na H-ESiar 263 G2
Miabhag Na H-ESiar 270 C7
Mial 264 D4
Miavaig (Miabhaig) 270 C4
Michaelchurch 145 E5
Michaelchurch Escley 144 C4
Michaelchurch-on-Arrow 144 B2
Michaelston-le-Pit 130 A5
Michaelston-super-Ely 130 A5
Michaelston-y-Fedw 130 B4
Michaelstow 97 E2
Michelcombe 100 C1
Micheldever 119 G4
Michelmersh 119 E5
Mickfield 152 C1
Mickle Trafford 170 B1
Micklebring 186 C3
Mickleby 204 B1
Micklefield 194 D4
Micklefield Green 135 F3
Mickleham 121 G2
Micklehurst 185 D2
Mickleover 173 E4
Micklethwaite Cumb 209 F1
Micklethwaite WYorks 193 G3
Mickleton Dur 211 F5
Mickleton Glos 147 D3
Mickletown 194 C5
Mickley Derbys 186 A5
Mickley NYorks 202 B5
Mickley Green 151 G2
Mickley Square 211 G1
Mid Ardlaw 269 H4
Mid Beltie 260 E4
Mid Calder 235 E3
Mid Clyth 275 H5
Mid Hants Railway Hants SO24 9JG 120 B4
Mid Lambrook 104 A1
Mid Lavant 108 A3
Mid Letter 240 C4
Mid Lix 242 A1
Mid Mossdale 200 D3
Mid Yell 278 E3
Midbea 276 D3
Middle Assendon 134 C4
Middle Aston 147 G5
Middle Barton 147 G5
Middle Bickenhill 159 E4
Middle Bockhampton 106 A3
Middle Claydon 148 C5
Middle Drift 97 F3
Middle Drums 253 D4
Middle Duntisbourne 132 B2
Middle Handley 186 B5
Middle Harling 164 A3
Middle Kames 232 A1
Middle Littleton 146 C3
Middle Maes-coed 144 C4
Middle Marwood 113 F2
Middle Mill 140 B5
Middle Quarter 124 A5
Middle Rasen 188 A4
Middle Rigg 243 F4
Middle Salter 192 C1
Middle Sontley 170 A3
Middle Stoford 115 E5
Middle Taphouse 97 F3
Middle Town 96 B1
Middle Tysoe 147 F3
Middle Wallop 119 D4
Middle Winterslow 118 D4
Middle Woodford 118 C4
Middlebie 218 A4
Middlecliff 186 B2
Middlecott 113 E5
Middleham 202 A4
Middlehill Aber 269 G6
Middlehill Corn 97 G3
Middlehope 157 E4
Middlemarsh 104 C2
Middlemoor 99 E3
Middlequarter (Ceathramh Meadhanach) 262 D4
Middlesbrough 213 D5
Middlesceugh 210 A3
Middleshaw 199 G4
Middlesmoor 201 F5
Middlestone 212 B4
Middlestone Moor 212 B4
Middlestown 185 G1
Middleton Aber 261 G3
Middleton Angus 253 D5
Middleton Cumb 200 B4
Middleton Derbys 173 D2
Middleton Derbys 172 C1
Middleton Essex 151 G3
Middleton GtMan 184 C2
Middleton Hants 119 F3
Middleton Here 145 E1
Middleton Lancs 192 A2
Middleton Midlo 236 A4
Middleton N'hants 160 D4
Middleton N'umb 220 C3
Middleton N'umb 229 E3
Middleton Norf 163 E1
Middleton NYorks 203 G4
Middleton P&K 243 G4
Middleton P&K 251 G5
Middleton Shrop 156 B3
Middleton Shrop 157 E5
Middleton Shrop 170 A5
Middleton Suff 153 F1
Middleton Swan 128 A4
Middleton Warks 159 D3
Middleton WYorks 194 A3
Middleton WYorks 194 C5
Middleton Baggot 157 F3
Middleton Bank Top 220 C3
Middleton Cheney 147 G3
Middleton Green 171 G4
Middleton Hall 229 D4
Middleton Moor 153 F1
Middleton of Potterton 261 H3
Middleton on the Hill 145 E1
Middleton One Row 202 C1
Middleton Park 261 H3
Middleton Priors 157 F4
Middleton Quernhow 202 C5
Middleton St. George 202 C1
Middleton Scriven 157 F4
Middleton Stoney 148 A5
Middleton Tyas 202 B2
Middleton-in-Teesdale 211 F5
Middleton-on-Leven 203 D1
Middleton-on-Sea 108 B3
Middleton-on-the-Wolds 196 B3
Middletown Cumb 198 A2
Middletown Powys 156 C1
Middlewich 171 E1
Middlewood ChesE 184 D4
Middlewood SYorks 186 A3
Middlewood Green 152 B1
Middlezoy 116 A4
Middridge 212 B5
Midfield 273 H2
Midford 117 E1
Midge Hall 192 B5
Midgeholme 210 C2
Midgham 119 G1
Midgley WYorks 185 G1
Midgley WYorks 193 G5
Midhopestones 185 G3
Midhurst 121 D5
Midland Railway Centre Derbys DE5 3QZ 173 F2
Midlem 227 G3
Midloe Grange 149 G1
Midpark 232 B4
Midsomer Norton 117 D2
Midthorpe 188 C5
Midtown High 273 H2
Midtown High 264 E3
Midtown of Barras 253 G1
Midville 176 B2
Midway 173 E5
Migdale 266 D2
Migvie 260 C4
Milarrochy 241 G5
Milber 102 B5
Milbethill 268 E5
Milborne Port 104 C1
Milborne St. Andrew 105 D3
Milborne Wick 117 D5
Milbourne N'umb 220 D4
Milbourne Wilts 132 B4
Milburn 210 C5
Milbury Heath 131 F3
Milcombe 147 G4
Milden 152 A3
Mildenhall Suff 163 F5
Mildenhall Wilts 118 D1
Mile Elm 118 A1
Mile End Essex 152 A5
Mile End Glos 131 E1
Mile End Park GtLon E3 4HL 12 D4
Mile Oak 123 F4
Mile Town 124 B1
Milebrook 156 C5
Milebush 123 G4
Mileham 178 A4
Miles Green 171 F3
Miles Hope 145 E1
Milesmark 235 E1
Miles's Green 119 G1
Milfield 228 D3
Milford Derbys 173 E3
Milford Devon 112 C3
Milford Shrop 170 B5
Milford Staffs 171 G5
Milford Surr 121 E3
Milford Haven (Aberdaugleddau) 126 B2
Milford on Sea 106 B3
Milkwall 131 E2
Milky Way Adventure Park Devon EX39 5RY 112 D3
Mill Bank 193 G5
Mill Brow 185 D4
Mill End Bucks 134 C4
Mill End Cambs 151 E2
Mill End Herts 150 B4
Mill End Green 151 E5
Mill Green Cambs 151 E3
Mill Green Essex 137 F2
Mill Green Herts 136 B2
Mill Green Norf 164 C3
Mill Green Shrop 171 D5
Mill Green Staffs 172 B5
Mill Green Suff 153 E1
Mill Green Suff 152 C2
Mill Green Suff 152 A2
Mill Green WMid 158 C2
Mill Hill B'burn 192 C5
Mill Hill Cambs 150 A2
Mill Hill GtLon 136 B3
Mill Houses 192 C1
Mill Lane 120 C2
Mill of Camsail 233 D1
Mill of Colp 269 F6
Mill of Elrick 269 H6
Mill of Fortune 242 C2
Mill of Kingoodie 261 G2
Mill of Monquich 261 G5
Mill of Uras 253 G1
Mill Side 199 F4
Mill Street Kent 123 F3
Mill Street Norf 178 B4
Milland 120 D5
Millbank 269 J6
Millbeck 209 F4
Millbounds 276 E4
Millbreck 269 J6
Millbridge 120 D3
Millbrook CenBeds 149 F4
Millbrook Corn 100 A2
Millbrook Devon 103 G3
Millbrook Soton 106 C1
Millburn Aber 260 D2
Millburn Aber 260 E1
Millcombe 101 E3
Millcorner 110 D1
Milldale 172 C2
Millden 261 H3
Milldens 252 D4
Millearne 243 E3
Millend 147 F5
Millenheath 170 C4
Millennium Seed Bank, Wakehurst Place WSuss RH17 6TN 122 C5
Millerhill 236 A3
Miller's Dale 185 F5
Millers Green Derbys 173 D2
Miller's Green Essex 137 E2
Millgate 193 E5
Millhalf 144 B3
Millhayes Devon 103 E1
Millhayes Devon 103 F2
Millholme 199 G3
Millhouse A&B 232 A2
Millhouse Cumb 209 G3
Millhouse Green 185 G2
Millhousebridge 217 F2
Millikenpark 233 F3
Millin Cross 126 C1
Millington 196 A2
Millington Green 173 D3
Millmeece 171 F4
Millness 257 K1
Millom 198 C4
Millow 150 A3
Millpool 97 F2
Millport 232 C4
Millthorpe 186 A5
Millthrop 200 B3
Milltimber 261 G4
Milltown Aber 259 K4
Milltown Corn 97 F4
Milltown D&G 218 B4
Milltown Derbys 173 E1
Milltown Devon 113 F2
Milltown High 267 G7
Milltown of Aberdalgie 243 F2
Milltown of Auchindoun 260 B1
Milltown of Craigston 269 F5
Milltown of Edinvillie 267 K7
Milltown of Kildrummy 260 C3
Milltown of Rothiemay 268 D6
Milltown of Towie 260 C3
Milnathort 243 G4
Milners Heath 170 B1
Milngavie 233 G2
Milnrow 184 D1
Milnsbridge 185 F1
Milnthorpe 199 F4
Milovaig 263 G6
Milrig 224 D2
Milson 157 F5
Milstead 124 B3
Milston 118 C3
Milton Angus 252 B5
Milton Cambs 150 C1
Milton Cumb 210 B1
Milton D&G 216 C2
Milton D&G 216 C3
Milton D&G 214 D5
Milton Derbys 173 E5
Milton High 265 K6
Milton High 266 E4
Milton High 267 G6
Milton High 264 D7
Milton High 266 C7
Milton High 275 J3
Milton (Baile a' Mhuilinn) High 258 B1
Milton Moray 268 D4
Milton Newport 130 C4
Milton Notts 187 E5
Milton NSom 116 A1
Milton Oxon 147 G4
Milton Oxon 133 G3
Milton P&K 243 E1
Milton Pembs 126 D2
Milton Ports 107 F3
Milton Som 116 B5
Milton Stir 242 A4
Milton Stoke 171 G2
Milton WDun 233 F2
Milton Abbas 105 E2
Milton Abbot 99 E3
Milton Bridge 235 G3
Milton Bryan 149 E4
Milton Clevedon 117 D4
Milton Combe 100 A1
Milton Country Park Cambs CB24 6AZ 150 C1
Milton Damerel 113 D4
Milton End 131 G1
Milton Ernest 149 F2
Milton Green 170 B2
Milton Hill 133 G3
Milton Keynes 149 D4
Milton Keynes Village 149 D4
Milton Lilbourne 118 C1
Milton Malsor 148 C2
Milton Morenish 242 B1
Milton of Auchinhove 260 D4
Milton of Balgonie 244 B4
Milton of Buchanan 241 G5
Milton of Cairnborrow 268 C6
Milton of Callander 242 A4
Milton of Campfield 260 E4
Milton of Campsie 234 A2
Milton of Coldwells 261 H1
Milton of Cullerlie 261 F4
Milton of Cushnie 260 D3
Milton of Dalcapon 251 E4
Milton of Inveramsay 261 F2
Milton of Noth 260 D2
Milton of Tullich 260 B5
Milton on Stour 117 E5
Milton Regis 124 A2
Milton Street 110 A3
Miltonduff 267 J5
Miltonhill 267 H5
Miltonise 214 C3
Milton-Lockhart 234 C5
Milton-under-Wychwood 133 E1
Milverton Som 115 E5
Milverton Warks 147 F1
Milwich 171 G4
Mimbridge 121 E1
Minack Theatre Corn TR19 6JU 94 A4
Minard 240 B5
Minard Castle 240 B5
Minchington 105 F1
Minchinhampton 132 A2
Mindrum 228 C3
Mindrummill 228 C3
Minehead 114 C3
Minera 169 F2
Minety 132 C3
Minety Lower Moor 132 C3
Minffordd Gwyn 154 D1
Minffordd Gwyn 167 E4
Minffordd Gwyn 181 D5
Miningsby 176 B1
Minions 97 G2
Minishant 224 B4
Minley Manor 120 D2
Minllyn 155 E1
Minnes 261 H2

Minngearraidh 254 C2
Minnigaff 215 F4
Minnonie 269 F4
Minskip 194 C1
Minstead 106 B1
Minsted 121 D5
Minster Kent 124 B1
Minster Kent 125 F2
Minster Lovell 133 F1
Minsteracres 211 G2
Minsterley 156 C2
Minsterworth 131 G1
Minterne Magna 104 C2
Minterne Parva 104 C2
Minting 188 B5
Mintlaw 269 J6
Minto 227 G3
Minton 156 D3
Minwear 126 D1
Minworth 159 D3
Miodar 246 B1
Mirbister 277 C6
Mirehouse 208 C5
Mireland 275 J2
Mirfield 194 B5
Miserden 132 B2
Miskin RCT 129 G4
Miskin RCT 129 G3
Misselfore 118 B5
Misson 187 D3
Misterton Leics 160 A4
Misterton Notts 187 E3
Misterton Som 104 A2
Mistley 152 C4
Mitcham 122 B2
Mitchel Troy 131 D1
Mitcheldean 131 F1
Mitchell 96 C4
Mitchelland 199 F3
Mitcheltroy Common 131 D2
Mitford 221 D3
Mithian 96 B4
Mitton 158 A1
Mixbury 148 B4
Mixenden 193 G5
Moar 250 A5
Moat 218 C4
Moats Tye 152 B2
Mobberley ChesE 184 B5
Mobberley Staffs 172 B3
Moccas 144 C3
Mochdre Conwy 181 G5
Mochdre Powys 155 G4
Mochrum 206 D2
Mockbeggar Hants 106 A2
Mockbeggar Kent 123 G4
Mockerkin 209 D4
Modbury 100 C2
Moddershall 171 G4
Modern Art Oxford Oxon OX1 1BP 80 Oxford
Modsarie 273 J2
Moel Famau Country Park Denb LL15 1US 169 E1
Moelfre IoA 180 D4
Moelfre Powys 169 E5
Moffat 226 B5
Mogerhanger 149 G3
Moin'a'choire 230 B3
Moine House 273 H3
Moira 159 F1
Molash 124 C3
Mol-chlach 255 K3
Mold (Yr Wyddgrug) 169 F1
Molehill Green Essex 151 D5
Molehill Green Essex 151 F5
Molescroft 196 C3
Molesden 220 D3
Molesworth 161 F5
Mollance 216 B4
Molland 114 B5
Mollington ChesW&C 183 E5
Mollington Oxon 147 G3
Mollinsburn 234 B2
Monach Islands (Heisker Islands) 262 B5
Monachty 142 B1
Monachyle 241 G3
Monevechadan 241 D4
Monewden 152 D2
Moneydie 243 F2
Moneyrow Green 135 D5
Moniaive 216 B1
Monifieth 244 D1
Monikie 244 D1
Monikie Country Park Angus DD5 3QN 244 C1
Monimail 244 A3
Monington 141 E3
Monk Bretton 186 A2
Monk Fryston 195 E5
Monk Hesleden 213 D4
Monk Sherborne 120 B2
Monk Soham 152 D1
Monk Soham Green 152 D1
Monk Street 151 E5
Monken Hadley 136 B3
Monkerton 102 C3
Monkey Mates W'ham RG41 1JA 134 C5
Monkey World, Wareham Dorset BH20 6HH 105 E4
Monkhide 145 F3
Monkhill 209 G1
Monkhopton 157 F3
Monkland 145 D2
Monkleigh 113 E3
Monknash 129 F5
Monkokehampton 113 F5
Monks Eleigh 152 A3
Monks Eleigh Tye 152 A3
Monk's Gate 109 E1
Monks' Heath 184 C5
Monk's Hill 124 A4
Monks Horton 124 D5
Monks Kirby 159 G4
Monks Risborough 134 D2
Monkscross 99 D3
Monkseaton 221 F4
Monkshill 269 F6
Monksilver 115 D4
Monkstadt 263 J5
Monkswood 130 C2
Monkton Devon 103 E2
Monkton Kent 125 E2
Monkton Pembs 126 C2
Monkton SAyr 224 B3
Monkton T&W 212 C1
Monkton VGlam 129 F5
Monkton Combe 117 E1
Monkton Deverill 117 F4
Monkton Farleigh 117 F1
Monkton Heathfield 115 F5
Monkton Up Wimborne 105 G1
Monkton Wyld 103 G3
Monkwearmouth 212 C2
Monkwood 120 B4
Monmouth (Trefynwy) 131 E1
Monnington Court 144 C4
Monnington on Wye 144 C3
Monreith 207 D2
Montacute 104 B1
Montacute House Som TA15 6XP 104 B1
Monteach 269 G6
Montford 156 D1
Montford Bridge 156 D1
Montgarrie 260 D3
Montgomery (Trefaldwyn) 156 B3
Montgreenan 233 E5
Montpellier Gallery Warks CV37 6EP 85 Stratford-upon-Avon
Montrave 244 B4
Montrose 253 F4
Monxton 119 E3
Monyash 172 C1
Monymusk 260 E3
Monzie 243 D2
Moodiesburn 234 A2
Moons Moat North 146 C1
Moonzie 244 B3
Moor Allerton 194 C4
Moor Cock 192 C1
Moor Crichel 105 F2
Moor End Bed 149 F2
Moor End CenBeds 149 E5
Moor End Cumb 199 G5
Moor End ERid 196 A4
Moor End Lancs 191 G3
Moor End NYorks 195 E4
Moor End WYorks 193 G5
Moor Green Wilts 117 F1
Moor Green WMid 158 C4
Moor Head 194 A4
Moor Monkton 195 E2
Moor Row 208 D5
Moor Side Cumb 198 D5
Moor Side Lancs 192 A4
Moor Side Lancs 192 A4
Moor Side Lincs 176 A2
Moor Street 124 A2
Moorby 176 A1
Moorcot 144 C2
Moordown 105 G3
Moore 183 G4
Moorend 209 G1
Moorends 187 D1
Moorfield 185 E3
Moorgreen 173 F3
Moorhall 186 A5
Moorhampton 144 C3
Moorhouse Cumb 209 G1
Moorhouse Notts 174 C1
Moorland (Northmoor Green) 116 A4
Moorlinch 116 A4
Moors Centre, Danby NYorks YO21 2NB 203 G2
Moors Valley Country Park Dorset BH24 2ET 106 A2
Moors Valley Railway Dorset BH24 2ET 105 G2
Moorsholm 203 F1
Moorside Dorset 105 D1
Moorside GtMan 185 D2
Moorside WYorks 194 B4
Moorthorpe 186 B1
Moortown IoW 106 D4
Moortown Lincs 188 A3
Moortown Tel&W 157 F1
Morangie 266 E3
Morar 256 C5
Morborne 161 G3
Morchard Bishop 102 A2
Morcombelake 104 A3
Morcott 161 E2
Morda 169 F5
Morden Dorset 105 F3
Morden GtLon 122 B2
Morden Hall Park GtLon SM4 5JD 11 F8
Morden Park 122 B2
Mordiford 145 E4
Mordington Holdings 237 G4
Mordon 212 C5
More 156 C3
Morebath 114 C5
Morebattle 228 B4
Morecambe 192 A1
Morefield 265 H2
Moreleigh 101 D2
Morenish 242 B1
Moresby Parks 208 C5
Morestead 119 G5
Moreton Dorset 105 E4
Moreton Essex 137 E2
Moreton Here 145 E1
Moreton Mersey 183 D4
Moreton Oxon 134 B2
Moreton Staffs 172 C4
Moreton Staffs 157 G1
Moreton Corbet 170 C5
Moreton Jeffries 145 F3
Moreton Mill 170 C5
Moreton Morrell 147 F2
Moreton on Lugg 145 E3
Moreton Paddox 147 F2
Moreton Pinkney 148 A3
Moreton Say 170 D4
Moreton Valence 131 G2
Moretonhampstead 102 A4
Moreton-in-Marsh 147 E4
Morfa Carmar 128 B1
Morfa Cere 141 G2
Morfa Bychan 167 E4
Morfa Glas 129 E2
Morfa Nefyn 166 B3
Morgan's Vale 118 C5
Morganstown 130 A4
Mork 131 E2
Morland 210 B5
Morley Derbys 173 E3
Morley Dur 212 A5
Morley WYorks 194 B5
Morley Green 184 C4
Morley St. Botolph 164 B2
Mornick 98 D3
Morningside Edin 235 G2
Morningside NLan 234 C4
Morningthorpe 164 D2
Morpeth 221 E3
Morphie 253 F3
Morrey 158 D1
Morridge Side 172 B2
Morrilow Heath 171 G4
Morriston SAyr 224 A5
Morriston Swan 128 C3
Morristown 130 A5
Morroch 247 F1
Morston 178 B1
Mortehoe 113 E1
Morthen 186 B4
Mortimer 120 B1
Mortimer West End 120 B1
Mortimer's Cross 144 D1
Mortlake 136 B5
Morton Derbys 173 F1
Morton Lincs 175 F5
Morton Lincs 187 F3
Morton Lincs 175 D1
Morton Notts 174 C2
Morton SGlos 131 F3
Morton Shrop 169 F5
Morton Bagot 146 D1
Morton on the Hill 178 C4
Morton Tinmouth 212 A5
Morton-on-Swale 202 C3
Morvah 94 B3
Morval 97 G4
Morvich (A'Mhorhaich) High 257 F2
Morvich High 266 E1
Morvil 140 D4
Morville 157 F3
Morwellham 100 A1
Morwellham Quay Museum Devon PL19 8JL 99 E3
Morwenstow 112 C4
Morwick Hall 221 E1
Mosborough 186 B4
Moscow 233 F5
Mosedale 209 G3
Moselden Height 185 E1
Moseley WMid 158 B3
Moseley Worcs 146 A2
Moses Gate 184 B2
Moss A&B 246 A2
Moss SYorks 186 C1
Moss Wrex 170 A2
Moss Bank 183 G3
Moss Houses 184 C5
Moss Nook 184 C4
Moss of Barmuckity 267 K5
Moss Side GtMan 184 C3
Moss Side Lancs 191 G4
Moss Side Mersey 183 E2
Mossat 260 C3
Mossbank 278 D5
Mossblown 224 C3
Mossburnford 228 A5
Mossdale 216 A3
Mossend 234 B3
Mosser 209 E4
Mossgiel 224 C3
Mosshead 260 D1
Mosside of Ballinshoe 252 C4
Mossley ChesE 171 F1
Mossley GtMan 185 D2
Mossley Hill 183 E4
Mosspaul Hotel 218 B2
Moss-side High 267 F6
Moss-side Moray 268 D5
Mosstodloch 268 B4
Mosston 252 D5
Mossy Lea 183 G1
Mosterton 104 A2
Moston GtMan 184 C2
Moston Shrop 170 C5
Moston Green 171 E1
Mostyn 182 C4
Motcombe 117 F5
Mothecombe 100 C3
Mother Shipton's Cave NYorks HG5 8DD 194 C2
Motherby 210 A5
Motherwell 234 B4
Mottingham 136 D5
Mottisfont 119 E5
Mottisfont Abbey Hants SO51 0LP 119 E5
Mottistone 106 D4
Mottram in Longdendale 185 D3
Mottram St. Andrew 184 C5
Mouldsworth 183 G5
Moulin 251 E4
Moulsecoomb 109 F3
Moulsford 134 A4
Moulsham 137 G2
Moulsoe 149 E3
Moulton ChesW&C 171 D1
Moulton Lincs 176 B5
Moulton N'hants 148 C1
Moulton NYorks 202 B2
Moulton Suff 151 E1
Moulton VGlam 129 G5
Moulton Chapel 162 A1
Moulton St. Mary 179 F5
Moulton Seas End 176 B5
Mounie Castle 261 F2
Mount Corn 96 B4
Mount Corn 97 F3
Mount High 267 G7
Mount Kent 125 D4
Mount WYorks 185 F1
Mount Ambrose 96 B5
Mount Bures 152 A4
Mount Charles 97 E4
Mount Edgcumbe Country Park Corn PL10 1HZ 2 B3
Mount Hawke 96 B5
Mount Manisty 183 E5
Mount Oliphant 224 B4
Mount Pleasant ChesE 171 F2
Mount Pleasant Derbys 173 E3
Mount Pleasant Derbys 159 E1
Mount Pleasant ESuss 109 G2
Mount Pleasant Flints 182 D5
Mount Pleasant GtLon 135 F3
Mount Pleasant Hants 106 C3
Mount Pleasant Norf 164 A2
Mount Pleasant Suff 151 F3
Mount Sorrel 118 B5
Mount Tabor 193 G5
Mountain 193 G4
Mountain Ash (Aberpennar) 129 G3
Mountain Cross 235 F5
Mountain Water 140 C5
Mountbenger 227 E3
Mountblairy 268 E5
Mountblow 233 F2
Mountfield 110 C1
Mountgerald 266 C5
Mountjoy 96 C3
Mountnessing 137 F3
Mounton 131 E3
Mountsorrel 160 A1
Mousa 279 D10
Mousehole 94 B4
Mouswald 217 E3
Mow Cop 171 F2
Mowden 202 B1
Mowhaugh 228 C4
Mowsley 160 B4
Mowtie 253 G1
Moxley 158 B3
Moy High 249 D1
Moy High 249 G1
Moy High 258 E1
Moy House 267 H6
Moygrove 141 E3
Muasdale 231 E5
Much Birch 145 E4
Much Cowarne 145 F3
Much Dewchurch 145 D4
Much Hadham 136 D1
Much Hoole 192 A5
Much Hoole Town 192 A5
Much Marcle 145 F4
Much Wenlock 157 F2
Muchalls 261 H5
Muchelney 116 B5
Muchelney Ham 116 B5
Muchlarnick 97 G4
Muchra 226 D4
Muchrachd 257 J1
Muck 246 D2
Mucking 137 F4
Muckle Roe 279 C6
Muckleford 104 C3
Mucklestone 171 E4
Muckleton 170 C5
Muckletown 260 D2
Muckley 157 F3
Muckley Corner 158 C2
Muckton 189 D4
Mudale 273 H5
Muddiford 113 F2
Muddles Green 110 A2
Muddlesswood 109 E2
Mudeford 106 A3
Mudford 104 B1
Mudgley 116 B3
Mugdock 233 G2
Mugdock Country Park Stir G62 8EL 30 C1
Mugeary 255 K1
Mugginton 173 D3
Muggintonlane End 173 D3
Muggleswick 211 G3
Mugswell 122 B3
Muie 266 D1
Muir 251 F1
Muir of Fowlis 260 D3
Muir of Lochs 268 B4
Muir of Ord (Am Blàr Dubh) 266 C6
Muiravonside Country Park Falk EH49 6LW 235 D2
Muirden 269 F5
Muirdrum 245 D1
Muiredge 244 B5
Muirhead Aber 260 D3
Muirhead Angus 244 B1
Muirhead Fife 244 A4
Muirhead Moray 267 H5
Muirhead NLan 234 A3
Muirhouses 235 E1
Muirkirk 225 E3
Muirmill 234 B1
Muirtack Aber 261 H1
Muirtack Aber 269 G6
Muirton High 266 E5
Muirton P&K 243 E3
Muirton P&K 243 G2
Muirton of Ardblair 251 G5
Muirton of Ballochy 253 E3
Muirtown 267 G6
Muiryfold 269 F5
Muker 201 E3
Mulbarton 178 C5
Mulben 268 B5
Mulhagery 271 F7
Mull 239 E1
Mullach Chàrlabhaigh 270 E3
Mullacott Cross 113 F1
Mullion 95 D5
Mullion Cove 95 D5
Mumby 189 F5
Munderfield Row 145 F2
Munderfield Stocks 145 F2
Mundesley 179 E2
Mundford 163 G3
Mundham 165 E2
Mundon 138 B2
Mundurno 261 H3
Munerigie 257 J4
Mungasdale 265 F2
Mungoswells 236 B2
Mungrisdale 209 G3
Munlochy 266 D6
Munnoch 232 D5
Munsley 145 F3
Munslow 157 E4
Murchington 99 G2
Murcott Oxon 134 A1
Murcott Wilts 132 B3
Murdostoun 234 C4
Murieston 235 E3
Murkle 275 G2
Murlaganmore 242 A1
Murlaggan High 257 G5
Murlaggan High 249 F1
Murra 277 B7
Murrell Green 120 C2
Murroes 244 C1
Murrow 162 B2
Mursley 148 D5
Murston 124 B2
Murthill 252 C4
Murthly 243 F1
Murton Cumb 210 D5
Murton Dur 212 C3
Murton N'umb 237 G5
Murton Swan 128 B4
Murton York 195 F2
Musbury 103 F3
Muscliff 105 G3
Musdale (Musdàl) 240 B2
Museum in Docklands GtLon E14 4AL 12 D4
Museum of Childhood, Edinburgh Edin EH1 1TG 37 G4
Museum of Childhood, London GtLon E2 9PA 12 C4
Museum of Flight ELoth EH39 5LF 236 C2
Museum of Garden History, London GtLon SE1 7LB 45 F7
Museum of London GtLon EC2Y 5HN 45 J2
Museum of Science & Industry, Manchester GtMan M3 4FP 46 C4
Museum of Transport, Glasgow Glas G3 8DP 38 A2
Musselburgh 236 A2
Mustard Hyrn 179 F4
Mustard Shop Norf NR2 1NQ 79 Norwich
Muston Leics 174 D4
Muston NYorks 205 D5
Mustow Green 158 A5
Mutford 165 F3
Muthill 243 D3
Mutley 100 A2
Mutterton 102 D2
Muxton 157 G1
Mybster 275 G3
Myddfai 143 D4
Myddle 170 B5
Myddlewood 170 B5
Mydroilyn 142 A2
Myerscough College 192 A4
Myerscough Smithy 192 C4
Mylor 95 F3
Mylor Bridge 95 F3
Mynachdy 130 A5
Mynachlog-ddu 141 E4
Myndtown 156 C4
Mynydd Llandygai 167 F1
Mynydd Mechell 180 B4
Mynydd-bach Mon 131 D3
Mynydd-bach Swan 128 C3
Mynyddygarreg 128 A2
Mynytho 166 C4
Myrebird 261 F5
Mytchett 121 D2
Mytholm 193 F5
Mytholmroyd 193 G5
Mythop 191 G4
Myton-on-Swale 194 D1
Mytton 156 D1

N

Naast 264 E3
Nab's Head 192 C5
Na-Buirgh 263 F2
Naburn 195 E3
Nackington 125 D3
Nacton 152 D3
Nadderwater 102 B3
Nafferton 196 C2
Nailbridge 131 F1
Nailsbourne 115 F5
Nailsea 131 D5
Nailstone 159 G2
Nailsworth 132 A3
Nairn 267 F6
Nancegollan 94 D3
Nancekuke 96 A5
Nancledra 94 B3
Nanhoron 166 B4
Nannau 168 A5
Nannerch 169 E1
Nanpantan 160 A1
Nanpean 97 D4
Nanstallon 97 E3
Nant Peris 167 F2
Nant-ddu 129 G1
Nanternis 141 G2
Nantgaredig 142 A5
Nantgarw 130 A4
Nant-glas 143 F1
Nantglyn 168 D1
Nantgwyn 155 F5
Nantlle 167 E2
Nantmawr 169 F5
Nantmel 143 G1
Nantmor 167 F3
Nantwich 170 D2
Nantycaws 128 A1
Nant-y-derry 130 C2
Nant-y-dugoed 155 F1
Nantyffyllon 129 E3
Nantyglo 130 A1
Nant-y-Gollen 169 F5
Nant-y-groes 143 G1
Nant-y-moel 129 F3
Nant-y-Pandy 181 E5
Naphill 135 D3
Napley Heath 171 E4
Nappa 193 E2
Napton on the Hill 147 G1
Narberth (Arberth) 127 E1
Narborough Leics 160 A3
Narborough Norf 163 F1
Narkurs 98 D5
Narrachan 240 B3
Nasareth 167 D3
Naseby 160 B5
Nash Bucks 148 C4
Nash Here 144 C1
Nash Newport 130 C4
Nash Shrop 157 F5
Nash VGlam 129 F5
Nash Street 123 F2
Nassington 161 F3
Nasty 150 B5
Nateby Cumb 200 C2
Nateby Lancs 192 A3
Nately Scures 120 C2
National Agricultural Centre, Stoneleigh Warks CV8 2LZ 16 B5
National Army Museum GtLon SW3 4HT 13 A5
National Botanic Garden of Wales Carmar SA32 8HG 128 B1
National Coal Mining Museum for England WYorks WF4 4RH 27 F6
National Exhibition Centre WMid B40 1NT 15 H4
National Fishing Heritage Centre, Grimsby NELincs DN31 1UZ 188 C2
National Gallery GtLon WC2N 5DN 44 D4
National Gallery of Scotland Edin EH2 2EL 37 F4
National Indoor Arena, Birmingham WMid B1 2AA 34 D4
National Marine Aquarium PL4 0LF 81 Plymouth
National Maritime Museum Cornwall Corn TR11 3QY 95 F3
National Maritime Museum, Greenwich GtLon SE10 9NF 13 D5
National Media Museum WYorks BD1 1NQ 65 Bradford
National Memorial Arboretum, Alrewas Staffs DE13 7AR 159 D1
National Motorcycle Museum, Solihull WMid B92 0EJ 159 E4
National Museum Cardiff CF10 3NP 67 Cardiff
National Museum of Scotland Edin EH1 1JF 37 G5
National Portrait Gallery GtLon WC2H 0HE 44 D4
National Railway Museum YO26 4XJ 90 York
National Sea Life Centre, Birmingham WMid B1 2JB 34 D4
National Seal Sanctuary Corn TR12 6UG 95 E4
National Slate Museum, Llanberis Gwyn LL55 4TY 167 E2
National Space Centre, Leicester Leic LE4 5NS 17 C4
National Wallace Monument Stir FK9 5LF 242 D5
National War Museum, Edinburgh Edin EH1 2NG 37 E4
National Waterfront Museum SA1 3RD 86 Swansea
National Wildflower Centre, Liverpool Mersey L16 3NA 22 D3
Natland 199 G4
Natural History Museum at Tring Herts HP23 6AP 135 E1
Natural History Museum, London GtLon SW7 5BD 11 F5
Natureland Seal Sanctuary Lincs PE25 1DB 177 D1
Naughton 152 B3
Naunton Glos 146 D5
Naunton Worcs 146 A4
Naunton Beauchamp 146 B2
Navenby 175 E2
Navestock 137 E3
Navestock Side 137 E3
Navidale 275 F7
Navity 266 E5
Nawton 203 F4
Nayland 152 A4
Nazeing 136 D2
Neacroft 106 A3
Neal's Green 159 F4
Neap 279 E7
Neap House 187 F1
Near Sawrey 199 E3
Nearton End 148 D5
Neasden 136 B4
Neasham 202 C1
Neat Enstone 147 F5
Neath (Castell-nedd) 129 D3
Neatham 120 C3
Neatishead 179 E3
Nebo Cere 142 B1
Nebo Conwy 168 B2
Nebo Gwyn 167 D2
Nebo IoA 180 C3
Necton 163 G2
Nedd 272 D5
Nedderton 221 E3
Nedging 152 A3
Nedging Tye 152 B3
Needham 164 D3
Needham Lake Suff IP6 8NU 152 B2
Needham Market 152 B2
Needham Street 151 F1
Needingworth 162 B5
Needles Pleasure Park IoW PO39 0JD 106 C4
Needwood 172 C5
Neen Savage 157 F5
Neen Sollars 157 F5
Neenton 157 F4
Nefyn 166 C3
Neighbourne 116 D3
Neilston 233 F4
Neithrop 147 G3
Nelson Caerp 130 A3
Nelson Lancs 193 E4
Nelson Village 221 E4
Nemphlar 234 C5
Nempnett Thrubwell 116 C1
Nenthall 211 D3
Nenthead 211 D3
Nenthorn 228 A3
Neopardy 102 A3
Nerabus 230 A4
Nercwys 169 F1
Neriby 230 B3
Nerston 234 A4
Nesbit 229 D3
Nesfield 193 G3
Ness 183 E5
Ness Botanic Gardens ChesW&C CH64 4AY 183 E5
Ness of Tenston 277 B6
Nesscliffe 156 C1
Neston ChesW&C 183 D5
Neston Wilts 117 F1
Nether Alderley 184 C5
Nether Auchendrane 224 B4
Nether Barr 215 F4
Nether Blainslie 236 C5
Nether Broughton 174 B5
Nether Burrow 200 B5
Nether Cerne 104 C3
Nether Compton 104 B1
Nether Crimond 261 G2
Nether Dalgliesh 227 D5
Nether Dallachy 268 B4
Nether Edge 186 A4
Nether End 185 G5
Nether Exe 102 C3
Nether Glasslaw 269 G5
Nether Handwick 252 B5
Nether Haugh 186 B3
Nether Heage 173 E2
Nether Heselden 201 D5
Nether Heyford 148 B2
Nether Kellet 192 B1
Nether Kinmundy 269 J6
Nether Langwith 186 C5
Nether Lenshie 268 E6
Nether Loads 173 E1
Nether Moor 173 E1
Nether Padley 185 G5
Nether Pitforthie 253 G2
Nether Poppleton 195 E2
Nether Silton 203 D3
Nether Skyborry 156 B5
Nether Stowey 115 E4
Nether Urquhart 243 G4
Nether Wallop 119 E4
Nether Wasdale 198 C2
Nether Wellwood 225 E3
Nether Welton 209 G2
Nether Westcote 147 E5
Nether Whitacre 159 E3
Nether Winchendon (Lower Winchendon) 134 C1
Nether Worton 147 G5
Netheravon 118 C3
Netherbrae 269 F5
Netherbrough 277 C6
Netherburn 234 C5
Netherbury 104 A3
Netherby Cumb 218 B4
Netherby NYorks 194 C3
Nethercott 147 G5
Netherfield ESuss 110 C2
Netherfield Notts 174 B3
Netherfield SLan 234 B5
Netherhall 232 D3
Netherhampton 118 C5
Netherhay 104 A2
Netherland Green 172 C4
Netherley 261 G5
Nethermill 217 E2
Nethermuir 269 H6
Netherseal 159 E1
Nethershield 225 D3
Netherstreet 118 A1
Netherthird D&G 216 B5
Netherthird EAyr 225 D4
Netherthong 185 F2
Netherthorpe 186 C4
Netherton Angus 252 D4
Netherton ChesW&C 183 G5
Netherton Devon 102 B5
Netherton Hants 119 E2
Netherton Mersey 183 E2
Netherton N'umb 220 B1
Netherton NLan 234 B4
Netherton Oxon 133 G2
Netherton P&K 251 G4
Netherton SLan 234 D4
Netherton WMid 158 B4
Netherton Worcs 146 B3
Netherton WYorks 185 G1
Netherton WYorks 185 F1
Netherton Burnfoot 220 B1

Netherton
  Northside 220 B1
Netherton Cumb 198 A2
Netherton Ork 275 J1
Nethertown Staffs 158 D1
Netherwitton 220 C2
Netherwood D&G 217 D3
Netherwood EAyr 225 E3
Nethy Bridge 259 H2
Netley Abbey 107 D2
Netley Marsh 106 C1
Nettlebed 134 B4
Nettlebridge 116 D3
Nettlecombe
  Dorset 104 B3
Nettlecombe Som 115 D4
Nettleden 135 F1
Nettleham 188 A5
Nettlestead Kent 123 F3
Nettlestead Suff 152 B3
Nettlestead Green 123 F3
Nettlestone 107 F3
Nettlesworth 212 B3
Nettleton Lincs 188 B2
Nettleton Wilts 132 A5
Nettleton Hill 185 E1
Netton Devon 100 B3
Netton Wilts 118 C4
Neuadd Cere 142 A2
Neuadd IoA 180 B3
Neuadd Powys 143 F3
Nevendon 137 G3
Nevern 141 D4
Nevill Holt 160 D3
New Abbey 217 D4
New Aberdour 269 G4
New Addington 122 C2
New Alresford 119 G4
New Alyth 252 A5
New Arley 159 E3
New Arram 196 C3
New Ash Green 123 F2
New Balderton 174 D2
New Barn 123 F2
New Belses 227 G2
New Bewick 229 E4
New Bolingbroke 176 B2
New Boultham 187 G5
New Bradwell 148 D3
New Brancepeth 212 B3
New Bridge D&G 216 D3
New Bridge
  Devon 102 A5
New Brighton
  Flints 169 F1
New Brighton
  Hants 107 G2
New Brighton
  Mersey 183 E3
New Brighton
  Wrex 169 F2
New Brighton
  WYorks 194 B5
New Brinsley 173 F2
New Broughton 170 A2
New Buckenham 164 B2
New Byth 269 G5
New Cheriton 119 G5
New Cross Cere 154 C5
New Cross GtLon 136 C5
New Cumnock 225 E4
New Deer 269 G6
New Duston 148 C1
New Earswick 195 F2
New Edlington 186 C3
New Elgin 267 K5
New Ellerby 197 D4
New Eltham 136 D5
New End 146 C1
New England 161 G2
New Farnley 194 B4
New Ferry 183 E4
New Galloway 216 A3
New Gilston 244 C4
New Greens 136 A2
New Grimsby 96 A1
New Hartley 221 F4
New Haw 121 F1
New Heaton 228 C3
New Hedges 127 E2
New Herrington 212 C2
New Hinksey 134 A2
New Holland 196 C5
New Houghton
  Derbys 173 G1
New Houghton
  Norf 177 F5
New Houses 200 D5
New Hunwick 212 A4
New Hutton 199 G3
New Hythe 123 G3
New Inn Carmar 142 A4
New Inn Fife 244 A4
New Inn Mon 131 D2
New Inn Torfaen 130 B3
New Invention
  Shrop 156 B5
New Invention
  WMid 158 B2
New Kelso 265 F7
New Lanark 234 C5
New Lanark World Heritage
  Site SLan
  ML11 9DB 234 C5
New Lane 183 F1
New Lane End 184 A3
New Leake 176 C1
New Leeds 269 H5
New Leslie 260 D2
New Lodge 186 A2
New Longton 192 B5
New Luce 214 C4
New Mains 225 G2
New Mains of Ury 253 G1
New Malden 122 B2
New Marske 213 F5
New Marton 170 A4
New Mill Corn 94 B3
New Mill Herts 135 E1
New Mill End 136 A1
New Mill NYorks 203 E1
New Mill NYorks 192 D1
New Mill NYorks 204 D4
New Mill WYorks 185 F2
New Mills Corn 96 C4
New Mills Derbys 185 E4
New Mills Glos 131 F2
New Mills Mon 131 E2
New Mills (Y Felin Newydd)
  Powys 155 G2

New Milton 106 B3
New Mistley 152 C4
New Moat 141 D5
New Ollerton 174 B1
New Orleans 222 C4
New Oscott 158 C3
New Palace &
  Adventureland, New
  Brighton Mersey
  CH45 2JX 22 A2
New Park 97 F1
New Park NYorks 194 B2
New Pitsligo 269 G5
New Polzeath 96 D2
New Quay
  (Ceinewydd) 141 G1
New Rackheath 179 D4
New Radnor
  (Maesyfed) 144 B1
New Rent 210 A4
New Ridley 211 G1
New Road Side 193 F3
New Romney 111 F1
New Rossington 186 D3
New Row Cere 154 D5
New Row Lancs 192 C4
New Sawley 173 F4
New Shoreston 229 F3
New Silksworth 212 C3
New Stevenston 234 B4
New Swannington 159 G1
New Totley 186 A5
New Town CenBeds 149 G3
New Town Cere 141 E3
New Town Dorset 105 F1
New Town Dorset 105 F2
New Town EToth 236 B2
New Town ESuss 109 G1
New Town Glos 146 C4
New Tredegar 130 A2
New Tupton 173 E1
New Ulva 231 F1
New Valley 271 G4
New Village 186 C2
New Walk Museum & Art
  Gallery LE1 7EA
  77 Leicester
New Walsoken 162 C2
New Waltham 188 C2
New Walton Pier Essex
  CO14 8ES 153 D5
New Winton 236 B2
New Yatt 133 F1
New York Lincs 176 A2
New York T&W 221 F4
Newall 194 B3
Newark Ork 276 G3
Newark Peter 162 A2
Newark Castle, Newark-on-
  Trent Notts
  NG24 1BG 174 C2
Newark-on-Trent 174 D2
Newarthill 234 B4
Newball 188 A5
Newbarn 125 D5
Newbarns 198 D5
Newbattle 236 A3
Newbiggin
  Bagpath 132 A3
Newbiggin Cumb 199 E5
Newbiggin Cumb 210 A5
Newbiggin Cumb 210 C5
Newbiggin Cumb 210 B3
Newbiggin Cumb 191 F1
Newbiggin Cumb 198 B3
Newbiggin Dur 211 F5
Newbiggin N'umb 211 F1
Newbiggin NYorks 201 F4
Newbiggin NYorks 201 E3
Newbiggin-by-the-
  Sea 221 F3
Newbigging Aber 261 G5
Newbigging Aber 251 G1
Newbigging Angus 244 C1
Newbigging Angus 244 C1
Newbigging Angus 252 A5
Newbigging SLan 235 F5
Newbiggin-on-Lune 200 C2
Newbold Derbys 186 A5
Newbold Leics 159 G1
Newbold on Avon 159 G5
Newbold on Stour 147 F3
Newbold Pacey 147 E2
Newbold Verdon 159 G2
Newborough
  (Niwbwrch) IoA 166 D1
Newborough Peter 162 A2
Newborough Staffs 172 C5
Newbottle N'hants 148 A4
Newbottle T&W 212 C2
Newbourne 153 D3
Newbridge (Cefn Bychan)
  Caerp 130 B2
Newbridge Corn 94 B3
Newbridge Corn 98 D4
Newbridge Edin 235 F2
Newbridge ESuss 123 D5
Newbridge Hants 106 B1
Newbridge IoW 106 D4
Newbridge NYorks 204 B4
Newbridge Oxon 133 G2
Newbridge Pembs 140 C4
Newbridge Wrex 169 F3
Newbridge Green 146 A4
Newbridge on Wye 143 G2
Newbridge-on-Usk 130 C3
Newbrough 211 E1
Newbuildings 102 A2
Newburgh Aber 269 H5
Newburgh Aber 261 H2
Newburgh Fife 244 A3
Newburgh Lancs 183 F1
Newburgh ScBord 227 E3
Newburn 212 A1
Newbury Som 117 D2
Newbury WBerks 119 F1
Newbury Wilts 117 F3
Newbury Park 136 D4
Newby Cumb 210 B5
Newby Lancs 193 E3
Newby NYorks 203 E1
Newby NYorks 192 D1
Newby NYorks 204 D4
Newby Bridge 199 E4
Newby Cote 200 C5
Newby East 210 A2
Newby Hall NYorks
  HG4 5AE 194 C1
Newby West 209 G1

Newby Wiske 202 C4
Newcastle
  Bridgend 129 E5
Newcastle Mon 130 D1
Newcastle Shrop 156 B4
Newcastle Emlyn (Castell
  Newydd Emlyn) 141 G3
Newcastle International
  Airport 221 D4
Newcastle upon
  Tyne 212 B1
Newcastleton 218 C3
Newcastle-under-
  Lyme 171 F3
Newchapel Pembs 141 F4
Newchapel Staffs 171 F2
Newchapel Surr 122 C4
Newchurch Carmar 141 G5
Newchurch IoW 107 E4
Newchurch Kent 124 C5
Newchurch Lancs 193 E5
Newchurch Lancs 193 E4
Newchurch Mon 131 D3
Newchurch Powys 144 B1
Newchurch Staffs 172 C5
Newcott 103 F2
Newcraighall 236 A2
Newdigate 121 G3
Newell Green 135 D5
Newenden 110 D1
Newent 145 G5
Newerne 131 F2
Newfield Dur 212 B4
Newfield Dur 212 B2
Newfield High 266 E4
Newfound 119 G2
Newgale 140 B5
Newgate 178 B1
Newgate Street 136 C2
Newgord 278 E2
Newhall ChesE 170 D3
Newhall Derbys 173 D5
Newham 229 F4
Newham Hall 229 F4
Newhaven 109 G3
Newhey 184 D1
Newholm 204 B1
Newhouse 234 B3
Newick 109 G1
Newingreen 124 D5
Newington Edin 235 G2
Newington Kent 125 D5
Newington Kent 124 A2
Newington Oxon 134 B3
Newington
  Bagpath 132 A3
Newland Cumb 199 E5
Newland Glos 131 E2
Newland Hull 196 C4
Newland NYorks 195 F5
Newland Oxon 133 F1
Newland Worcs 145 G3
Newlandrig 236 A3
Newlands Cumb 209 G3
Newlands Essex 138 B4
Newlands N'umb 211 G2
Newland's Corner 121 F3
Newlands of Geise 275 F2
Newlands of Tynet 268 B4
Newlyn 94 B4
Newmachar 261 G3
Newmains 234 C4
Newman's End 137 E1
Newman's Green 151 G3
Newmarket Suff 151 E1
Newmarket Na H-ESiar
  271 G4
Newmill Aber 253 F1
Newmill Aber 269 G6
Newmill Aber 261 G2
Newmill Moray 268 C5
Newmill ScBord 227 F4
Newmill of
  Inshewan 252 C3
Newmillerdam 186 A1
Newmillerdam Country Park
  WYorks WF2 6QP 27 H6
Newmills 266 D5
Newmiln P&K 243 F2
Newmiln P&K 243 F2
Newmilns 224 D2
Newney Green 137 F2
Newnham Glos 131 F1
Newnham Hants 120 C2
Newnham Herts 150 A4
Newnham Kent 124 B3
Newnham N'hants 148 A2
Newnham Bridge 145 F1
Newnham Paddox 159 G4
Newnoth 260 D1
Newport Corn 98 D2
Newport Devon 113 F2
Newport ERid 196 A4
Newport Essex 150 D4
Newport Glos 131 F3
Newport High 275 G6
Newport IoW 107 E4
Newport (Casnewydd)
  Newport 130 C4
Newport Norf 179 G4
Newport (Trefdraeth)
  Pembs 141 D4
Newport Tel&W 157 G1
Newport Pagnell 149 D3
Newport-on-Tay 244 C2
Newpound
  Common 121 F5
Newquay 96 C3
Newquay Cornwall
  International Airport 96 C3
Newquay Zoo Corn
  TR7 2LZ 96 C3
Newsbank 171 F1
Newseat 261 F1
Newsells 150 B4
Newsham Lancs 192 B4
Newsham N'umb 221 E4
Newsham NYorks 202 A1
Newsham NYorks 202 C2
Newsholme ERid 195 G5
Newsholme Lancs 193 E2
Newsome 185 F1
Newstead N'umb 229 F4
Newstead Notts 173 G2
Newstead ScBord 227 G2

Newstead Abbey Notts
  NG15 8AN 173 G2
Newthorpe Notts 173 F3
Newthorpe NYorks 195 D4
Newtoft 188 A4
Newton A&B 240 C5
Newton Aber 268 C6
Newton Aber 269 J6
Newton Bridgend 129 E5
Newton Cambs 162 C1
Newton Cambs 150 C3
Newton Cardiff 130 B5
Newton ChesW&C 170 C2
Newton ChesW&C 183 G5
Newton Cumb 198 D5
Newton D&G 217 F1
Newton Derbys 173 F2
Newton GtMan 185 D3
Newton Here 144 C1
Newton Here 145 E3
Newton Here 144 C4
Newton Here 144 C4
Newton High 266 E7
Newton High 266 H3
Newton High 272 E5
Newton High 266 C6
Newton High 266 E6
Newton Lancs 192 C2
Newton Lancs 199 G5
Newton Lancs 191 G3
Newton Lincs 175 F4
Newton Moray 268 B4
Newton N'hants 161 D4
Newton N'umb 211 G1
Newton N'umb 220 B1
Newton NAyr 232 A4
Newton Norf 163 G3
Newton Notts 174 B3
Newton P&K 243 D1
Newton Pembs 140 B5
Newton Pembs 126 C4
Newton ScBord 228 A4
Newton SGlos 131 G3
Newton Shrop 170 B4
Newton SLan 226 A2
Newton Som 115 F4
Newton Staffs 172 B5
Newton Suff 152 A3
Newton Swan 128 C4
Newton Warks 160 A5
Newton Wilts 118 D5
Newton WLoth 235 E2
Newton WYorks 194 D5
Newton Abbot 102 B5
Newton Arlosh 209 F1
Newton Aycliffe 212 B5
Newton Bewley 213 D5
Newton
  Blossomville 149 F2
Newton Bromswold 149 E1
Newton Burgoland 159 F2
Newton by Toft 188 A4
Newton Ferrers 100 B3
Newton Flotman 164 D2
Newton Green 131 E3
Newton Harcourt 160 B3
Newton Kyme 195 D3
Newton Longville 148 D4
Newton Mearns 233 G4
Newton Morrell
  NYorks 202 B2
Newton Morrell
  Oxon 148 B5
Newton Mountain 126 C2
Newton Mulgrave 203 G1
Newton of Affleck 244 C1
Newton of Ardtoe 247 F2
Newton of
  Balcanquhal 243 G3
Newton of Dalvey 267 H6
Newton of Falkland 244 A4
Newton of Leys 258 D1
Newton on the Hill 170 B5
Newton on Trent 187 F5
Newton Poppleford 103 D4
Newton Purcell 148 B4
Newton Regis 159 E2
Newton Reigny 210 A4
Newton St. Cyres 102 B3
Newton St. Faith 178 D4
Newton St. Loe 117 E1
Newton St. Petrock 113 E4
Newton Solney 173 D5
Newton Stacey 119 F3
Newton Stewart 215 F4
Newton Tony 118 D3
Newton Tracey 113 F3
Newton under
  Roseberry 203 E1
Newton
  Underwood 221 D3
Newton upon
  Derwent 195 G3
Newton Valence 120 C4
Newton with
  Scales 192 A4
Newtoncommon 126 C2
Newtongrange 236 A3
Newtonhill 261 H5
Newton-le-Willows
  Mersey 183 G3
Newton-le-Willows
  NYorks 202 B4
Newtonmill 253 E2
Newtonmore (Baile Ùr
  an t-Slèibh) 258 C5
Newton-on-Ouse 195 D2
Newton-on-
  Rawcliffe 204 B3
Newton-on-the-
  Moor 221 D1
Newton Bucks 135 E2
Newtown
  ChesW&C 170 C2
Newtown Corn 97 G2
Newtown Corn 94 C4
Newtown Cumb 210 B1
Newtown Derbys 185 D4
Newtown Devon 114 A5
Newtown Devon 103 D3
Newtown Dorset 104 A2
Newtown Glos 131 F2
Newtown Hants 107 F1
Newtown Hants 119 F5
Newtown Hants 106 B1
Newtown Hants 119 E5

Newtown Hants 107 E1
Newtown Here 145 F3
Newtown Here 145 D2
Newtown High 257 K4
Newtown IoM 190 B4
Newtown IoW 106 D3
Newtown N'umb 220 C1
Newtown N'umb 229 E4
Newtown Oxon 134 C4
Newtown (Y Drenewydd)
  Powys 156 A3
Newtown RCT 129 G3
Newtown Shrop 170 B4
Newtown Som 115 F4
Newtown Som 103 F1
Newtown Staffs 171 G5
Newtown Staffs 172 B1
Newtown Staffs 158 B2
Newtown Wilts 118 A5
Newtown Wilts 119 E1
Newtown Linford 160 A2
Newtown
  St. Boswells 227 G2
Newtown Unthank 159 G2
Newtown-in-Saint-
  Martin 95 E4
Newtyle 252 A5
Newyears Green 135 F4
Neyland 126 C2
Nibley Glos 131 F2
Nibley SGlos 131 G5
Nibley Green 131 G3
Nicholashayne 103 E1
Nicholaston 128 B4
Nidd 194 C1
Nigg Aberdeen 261 H4
Nigg High 267 F4
Nightcott 114 C4
Nilig 168 D2
Nilston Rigg 211 E1
Nimlet 131 G5
Nine Ashes 137 E2
Nine Elms 132 D4
Nine Mile Burn 235 F4
Ninebanks 211 D2
Ninemile Bar
  (Crocketford) 216 C3
Nineveh 145 F1
Ninfield 110 C2
Ningwood 106 D4
Nisbet 228 A4
Nitshill 233 G3
Nizels 123 E3
No Man's Heath
  ChesW&C 170 C3
No Man's Heath
  Warks 159 E2
No Man's Land 97 G4
Noak Hill 137 E3
Noblehill 217 D3
Noblethorpe 185 G2
Nobottle 148 B1
Nocton 175 F1
Noddsdale 232 D3
Nogdam End 179 E5
Noke 134 A1
Nolton 126 B1
Nolton Haven 126 B1
Nomansland
  Devon 102 B1
Nomansland Wilts 106 B1
Noneley 170 B5
Nonington 125 E3
Nook Cumb 218 C4
Nook Cumb 199 G4
Noonsbrough 279 B7
Noranside 252 C3
Norbreck 191 G3
Norbury ChesE 170 C3
Norbury Derbys 172 C3
Norbury GtLon 136 C5
Norbury Shrop 156 C3
Norbury Staffs 171 E5
Norbury Common 170 C3
Norbury Junction 171 E5
Norchard 127 D3
Norcott Brook 184 A4
Nordelph 163 D2
Norden Dorset 105 F4
Norden GtMan 184 C1
Nordley 157 F2
Norham 237 G5
Norland Town 193 G5
Norley 183 G5
Norleywood 106 C3
Norlington 109 G2
Norman Cross 161 G3
Normanby NLincs 187 F1
Normanby NYorks 203 G4
Normanby R&C 203 E1
Normanby by Stow 187 F4
Normanby Hall Country
  Park NLincs
  DN15 9HU 187 F1
Normanby le Wold 188 B3
Normanby-by-
  Spital 188 A4
Normandy 121 E2
Norman's Ruh 246 D5
Norman's Green 103 D2
Normanston 165 G2
Normanton Derby 173 E4
Normanton Leics 174 D3
Normanton Lincs 175 E3
Normanton Notts 174 C2
Normanton Rut 161 E2
Normanton
  WYorks 194 C5
Normanton le
  Heath 159 F1
Normanton on Soar 173 G5
Normanton on
  Trent 174 C1
Normanton-on-the-
  Wolds 173 G4
Normoss 191 G4
Norrington
  Common 117 F1
Norris Green 100 A1
Norris Hill 159 F1
Norristhorpe 194 B5
North Acton 136 B4
North Anston 186 C4

North Ascot 121 E1
North Aston 147 G5
North Baddesley 106 C1
North Ballachulish
  (Baile a' Chaolais a
  Tuath) 248 C3
North Balloch 215 E1
North Barrow 116 D5
North Barsham 178 A2
North Benfleet 137 G4
North Bersted 108 B3
North Berwick 236 C1
North Boarhunt 107 F1
North Bogbain 268 C5
North Bovey 102 A4
North Bradley 117 F2
North Brentor 99 E2
North Brewham 117 E4
North Bridge 121 E4
North Buckland 113 E1
North Burlingham 179 E4
North Cadbury 116 D5
North Cairn 214 A3
North Camp 121 D2
North Carlton
  Lincs 187 G5
North Carlton
  Notts 186 C5
North Cave 196 A4
North Cerney 132 C2
North Chailey 109 F1
North Charford 106 A1
North Charlton 229 F4
North Cheriton 117 D5
North Chideock 104 A3
North Cliffe 196 A4
North Clifton 187 F5
North Cockerington 189 D3
North Coker 104 B1
North Collafirth 278 C4
North Common
  SGlos 131 F5
North Common
  Suff 164 A4
North Commonty 269 G6
North Connel 240 B1
North Coombe 102 B2
North Cornelly 129 E4
North Corner 131 F4
North Cotes 188 D2
North Cove 165 F3
North Cowton 202 B2
North Crawley 149 E3
North Cray 137 D5
North Creake 177 G4
North Curry 116 A5
North Dallens 248 B5
North Dalton 196 B2
North Dawn 277 D7
North Deighton 194 C2
North Dell (Dail Bho
  Thuath) 271 G1
North Duffield 195 F4
North Elkington 188 C3
North Elmham 178 A3
North Elmsall 186 B1
North End Bucks 148 D5
North End Dorset 117 F5
North End ERid 197 D2
North End ERid 197 D3
North End Essex 137 F1
North End Hants 119 G5
North End Hants 106 A1
North End Leics 160 A1
North End N'umb 220 D1
North End NSom 116 B1
North End Ports 107 F2
North End WSuss 108 A3
North End WSuss 108 B3
North Erradale 264 D3
North Essie 269 J5
North Fambridge 138 B3
North Ferriby 196 B5
North Frodingham 196 D2
North Gluss 278 C5
North Gorley 106 A1
North Green Norf 164 D3
North Green Suff 165 E4
North Green Suff 153 E1
North Green Suff 153 E1
North Grimston 196 A1
North Halling 123 G2
North Harby 187 F5
North Hayling 107 G2
North Hazelrigg 229 E3
North Heasley 114 A4
North Heath
  WBerks 133 G5
North Heath
  WSuss 121 F5
North Hill 97 G2
North Hillingdon 135 F4
North Hinksey 133 G2
North Holmwood 121 G3
North Houghton 119 E4
North Huish 100 D2
North Hykeham 175 E1
North Johnston 126 C1
North Kelsey 188 A2
North Kessock 266 D7
North Killingholme 188 B1
North Kilvington 202 D4
North Kilworth 160 B4
North Kingston 106 A2
North Lancing 109 D3
North Lee 134 D2
North Lees 202 C5
North Leigh 133 G1
North Leverton with
  Habblesthorpe 187 E4
North Littleton 146 C3
North Lopham 164 B3
North Luffenham 161 E2
North Marden 108 A2
North Marston 148 C5
North Middleton
  Midlo 236 A4
North Middleton
  N'umb 229 E4
North Millbrex 269 G6
North Molton 114 A5
North Moreton 134 A4

North Mundham 108 A3
North Muskham 174 C2
North Newbald 196 B4
North Newington 147 G4
North Newnton 118 C2
North Nibley 131 G3
North Oakley 119 G2
North Ockendon 137 E4
North Ormesby 203 E1
North Ormsby 188 C3
North Otterington 202 C4
North Owersby 188 A3
North Perrott 104 A2
North Petherton 115 F4
North Petherwin 97 G1
North Pickenham 163 G2
North Piddle 146 B2
North Plain 217 F4
North Pool 101 D3
North Poorton 104 B3
North Quarme 114 C4
North Queensferry 235 F1
North Radworthy 114 A4
North Rauceby 175 F3
North Reston 189 D4
North Riding Forest Park
  NYorks
  YO18 7LT 204 B3
North Rigton 194 B3
North Rode 171 F1
North Roe 278 C4
North Ronaldsay 276 G2
North Ronaldsay
  Airfield 276 G2
North Runcton 163 E1
North Sandwick 278 E3
North Scale 191 E1
North Scarle 175 D1
North Seaton 221 E3
North Shian (Sithean a
  Tuath) 248 B5
North Shields 212 C1
North Shoebury 138 C4
North Side 162 A4
North Skelton 203 F1
North Somercotes 189 E3
North Stainley 202 B5
North Stainmore 200 D1
North Stifford 137 F4
North Stoke
  B&NESom 117 E1
North Stoke Oxon 134 B4
North Stoke WSuss 108 C2
North Stoneham 106 D1
North Street Hants 120 B4
North Street Kent 124 C3
North Street Med 124 A1
North Street
  WBerks 134 B5
North Sunderland 229 G3
North Tamerton 98 D1
North Tarbothill 261 H3
North Tawton 113 G5
North Third 234 B1
North Thoresby 188 C3
North Tidworth 118 D3
North Togston 221 E1
North Town Devon 113 F4
North Town Hants 121 D2
North Town W&M 135 D4
North Tuddenham 178 B4
North Uist (Uibhist a
  Tuath) 262 D4
North Walsham 179 D2
North Waltham 119 G3
North
  Warnborough 120 C2
North Water Bridge 253 E3
North Watten 275 H3
North Weald
  Bassett 137 D2
North Wembley 136 A4
North Wheatley 187 E4
North Whilborough 101 E1
North Wick 116 C1
North Widcombe 116 C2
North Willingham 188 B4
North Wingfield 173 F1
North Witham 175 E5
North Wootton
  Dorset 104 C1
North Wootton
  Norf 177 E5
North Wootton
  Som 116 C3
North Wraxall 132 A5
North Wroughton 132 D4
North Yardhope 220 B1
North Yorkshire Moors
  Railway NYorks
  YO18 7AJ 204 B4
Northacre 164 A2
Northall 149 E5
Northall Green 178 A4
Northallerton 202 C3
Northam Devon 113 E3
Northam Soton 106 D1
Northam Burrows Country
  Park Devon
  EX39 1XR 113 E3
Northampton 148 C1
Northaw 136 B2
Northay Devon 103 F1
Northay Som 103 F1
Northbay 254 C4
Northbeck 175 F3
Northborough 161 G2
Northbourne Kent 125 F3
Northbourne Oxon 134 A4
Northbridge Street 110 C1
Northbrook Hants 119 G4
Northbrook Oxon 147 G5
Northburnhill 269 G6
Northchapel 121 E5
Northchurch 135 E2
Northcote Manor 113 G4
Northcott 98 D1
Northcourt 134 A3
Northdyke 276 B5
Northedge 173 E1
Northend
  B&NESom 117 E1
Northend Bucks 134 C3
Northend Warks 147 F2
Northfield Aber 269 G4

Northfield
  Aberdeen **261** H4
Northfield High **275** J4
Northfield Hull **196** C5
Northfield ScBord **237** G3
Northfield Som **115** F4
Northfield WMid **158** C5
Northfields **161** F2
Northfleet **137** F5
Northhouse **227** F5
Northiam **110** D1
Northill **149** G3
Northington Glos **131** G2
Northington
  Hants **119** G4
Northlands **176** B2
Northleach **132** D1
Northleigh Devon **103** E3
Northleigh Devon **113** G2
Northlew **99** F1
Northmoor **133** G2
Northmoor Green
  (Moorland) **116** A4
Northmuir **252** B4
Northney **107** G2
Northolt **136** A4
Northop
  (Llaneurgain) **169** F1
Northop Hall **169** F1
Northorpe Lincs **176** A4
Northorpe Lincs **188** B3
Northorpe Lincs **161** F1
Northover Som **116** B4
Northover Som **116** B4
Northowram **194** A5
Northport **105** F4
Northpunds **279** D10
Northrepps **178** D2
Northton
  (Taobh Tuath) **262** E3
Northtown **277** D8
Northumberland Dark Sky
  Park N'umb **219** F4
Northumbria Craft Centre,
  Morpeth N'umb
  NE61 1PD **221** E2
Northway Glos **146** B4
Northway Som **115** E5
Northwich **184** A5
Northwick SGlos **131** E4
Northwick Som **116** A3
Northwick Worcs **146** A2
Northwold **163** F3
Northwood GtLon **135** F3
Northwood IoW **106** C4
Northwood Kent **125** F2
Northwood Mersey **183** F3
Northwood Shrop **170** B4
Northwood Green **131** G1
Northwood Hills **136** A3
Norton Glos **146** A5
Norton Halton **183** G4
Norton Herts **150** A4
Norton IoW **106** C4
Norton Mon **144** D5
Norton N'hants **148** B1
Norton Notts **186** C5
Norton NSom **116** A1
Norton NYorks **203** G5
Norton Powys **144** C1
Norton Shrop **157** E2
Norton Shrop **157** G2
Norton Shrop **157** D4
Norton Stock **212** D5
Norton Suff **152** A1
Norton Swan **128** C4
Norton SYorks **186** C1
Norton SYorks **186** A4
Norton VGlam **129** E5
Norton Wilts **132** A4
Norton WMid **158** A4
Norton Worcs **146** A2
Norton Worcs **146** C5
Norton WSuss **108** B3
Norton WSuss **108** A4
Norton Bavant **118** A3
Norton Bridge **171** F4
Norton Canes **158** C2
Norton Canon **144** C3
Norton Disney **175** D2
Norton Ferris **117** F4
Norton Fitzwarren **115** E5
Norton Green
  Herts **150** A4
Norton Green IoW **106** C4
Norton Green
  Stoke **171** G2
Norton Hawkfield **116** C1
Norton Heath **137** F2
Norton in Hales **171** E4
Norton in the
  Moors **171** F2
Norton Lindsey **147** E1
Norton Little Green **152** A1
Norton Malreward **116** D1
Norton Mandeville **137** F2
Norton St. Philip **117** E2
Norton Subcourse **165** F2
Norton Wood **144** C3
Norton Woodseats **186** A4
Norton-Juxta-
  Twycross **159** F2
Norton-le-Clay **202** D5
Norton-sub-
  Hamdon **104** A1
Norwell **174** C1
Norwell Woodhouse **174** C1
Norwich **178** D5
Norwich Castle Museum &
  Art Gallery Norf
  NR1 3JU **79** Norwich
Norwich Cathedral Norf
  NR1 4DH **79** Norwich
Norwich International
  Airport **178** D4
Norwick **278** F1
Norwood End **137** E2
Norwood Green
  GtLon **136** A5
Norwood Green
  WYorks **194** A5
Norwood Hill **122** B4
Norwood Park **116** C4
Noseley **160** C3
Noss Mayo **100** B3
Nosterfield **202** B4
Nosterfield End **151** E3
Nostie **256** E2

Notgrove **146** D5
Nottage **129** E5
Notting Hill **136** B4
Nottingham High **275** H5
Nottingham Nott **173** G3
Nottingham Castle Museum
  & Art Gallery NG1 6EL
  80 Nottingham
Nottington **104** C4
Notton Wilts **118** A1
Notton WYorks **186** A1
Nottswood Hill **131** G1
Noutard's Green **145** G1
Nowton Park Suff
  IP29 5LU **151** G1
Nox **156** D1
Noyadd Trefawr **141** F3
Nuffield **134** B4
Nun Monkton **195** E3
Nunburnholme **196** A3
Nuneaton **159** F3
Nuneham
  Courtenay **134** A3
Nunney **117** E3
Nunnington Here **145** E3
Nunnington
  NYorks **203** F5
Nunnington Park **115** D5
Nunnykirk **220** C2
Nunsthorpe **188** C2
Nunthorpe Middl **203** E1
Nunthorpe York **195** F2
Nunton **118** C5
Nunwick N'umb **220** A4
Nunwick NYorks **202** C5
Nup End **136** B1
Nupend **131** G2
Nursling **106** C1
Nursted **120** C5
Nurton **158** A3
Nutbourne WSuss **108** A4
Nutbourne WSuss **107** G2
Nutfield **122** C3
Nuthall **173** G3
Nuthampstead **150** C4
Nuthurst Warks **159** D5
Nuthurst WSuss **121** G5
Nutley ESuss **109** G1
Nutley Hants **120** B3
Nutwell **186** D2
Nyadd **242** C5
Nybster **275** J2
Nyetimber **108** A4
Nyewood **120** C5
Nymans WSuss
  RH17 6EB **109** E1
Nymet Rowland **102** A2
Nymet Tracey **102** A2
Nympsfield **132** A2
Nynehead **115** E5
Nythe **116** B4
Nyton **108** B3

O

O2, The GtLon
  SE10 0BB **13** E5
Oad Street **124** A2
Oadby **160** B2
Oak Cross **99** F1
Oak Tree **202** C1
Oakamoor **172** B3
Oakbank A&B **239** G1
Oakbank WLoth **235** E3
Oakdale Caerp **130** A3
Oakdale Poole **105** G3
Oake **115** E5
Oaken **158** A2
Oakenclough **192** B3
Oakengates **157** G1
Oakenhead **267** K5
Oakenholt **183** F5
Oakenshaw Dur **212** B4
Oakenshaw
  WYorks **194** A5
Oakerthorpe **173** E2
Oakes **185** F1
Oakfield IoW **107** E4
Oakfield Torfaen **130** B3
Oakford Cere **142** A2
Oakford Devon **114** C5
Oakfordbridge **114** C5
Oakgrove **171** G1
Oakham **161** D2
Oakhanger **120** C4
Oakhill **116** D3
Oakington **150** C1
Oaklands Conwy **168** B2
Oaklands Herts **136** B1
Oakle Street **131** G1
Oakley Bed **149** F2
Oakley Bucks **134** B1
Oakley Fife **235** E1
Oakley Hants **119** G2
Oakley Oxon **134** C2
Oakley Poole **105** G3
Oakley Suff **164** C4
Oakley Green **135** E5
Oakley Park **155** F4
Oakridge Lynch **132** B2
Oaks **156** D2
Oaks Green **172** C4
Oaksey **132** B3
Oakshaw Ford **218** D4
Oakshott **120** C5
Oakthorpe **159** F1
Oaktree Hill **202** C3
Oakwell Hall & Country Park
  WYorks
  WF17 9LG **27** E4
Oakwood Leisure Park
  Pembs
  SA67 8DE **127** D1
Oakwoodhill **121** G4
Oakworth **193** G4
Oare Kent **124** C2
Oare Som **114** B3
Oare Wilts **118** C1
Oasby **175** F4
Oatfield **222** B4
Oath **116** A5
Oathlaw **252** C4
Oatlands **194** C2
Oban
  (An t-Òban) **240** A2
Obley **156** C5
Oborne **104** C1

Obthorpe **161** F1
Occlestone Green **171** D1
Occold **164** C4
Occumster **275** H5
Oceanarium BH2 5AA
  64 Bournemouth
Ochiltree **224** D3
Ochr-y-foel **182** B5
Ochtermuthill **242** D3
Ochtertyre P&K **242** D2
Ochtertyre Stir **242** C5
Ockbrook **173** F4
Ockeridge **145** G1
Ockham **121** F2
Ockle **247** E2
Ockley **121** G4
Octon **204** D5
Odcombe **104** B1
Odd Down **117** E1
Oddendale **200** B1
Oddingley **146** B2
Oddington **134** A1
Odell **149** E2
Odham **113** E5
Odie **276** F5
Odsey **150** A4
Odstock **118** C5
Odstone **159** G1
Offchurch **147** F1
Offenham **146** C3
Offerton **184** D4
Offham ESuss **109** G2
Offham Kent **123** F3
Offham WSuss **108** C3
Offley Hoo **149** G5
Offleymarsh **171** E5
Offord Cluny **150** A1
Offord D'Arcy **150** A1
Offton **152** B3
Offwell **103** E3
Ogbourne Maizey **133** D5
Ogbourne
  St. Andrew **133** D5
Ogbourne
  St. George **133** D5
Ogden Water WYorks
  HX2 8YA **26** A3
Ogil **252** C3
Ogle **220** D4
Oglet **183** F4
Ogmore **129** E5
Ogmore Vale **129** F3
Ogmore-by-Sea **129** E5
Okeford Fitzpaine **105** E1
Oil Terminal **277** C8
Okeford Fitzpaine **105** E1
Okehampton **99** F1
Okehampton Camp **99** F1
Okraquoy **279** D9
Olchard **102** B5
Olchfa **128** C3
Old **160** C5
Old Aberdeen **261** H4
Old Alresford **119** G4
Old Arley **159** E3
Old Basford **173** G3
Old Basing **120** B2
Old Belses **227** G3
Old Bewick **229** E4
Old Blair **251** D3
Old Bolingbroke **176** B1
Old Bramhope **194** B3
Old Brampton **186** A5
Old Bridge of Urr **216** B4
Old Buckenham **164** B2
Old Burdon **212** C2
Old Burghclere **119** F2
Old Byland **203** E4
Old Cassop **212** C4
Old Church Stoke **156** B3
Old Cleeve **114** D3
Old Clipstone **174** B1
Old Colwyn **181** G5
Old Craig **261** H2
Old Craighall **236** A2
Old Crombie **268** D5
Old Dailly **214** D1
Old Dalby **174** B5
Old Dam **185** F5
Old Deer **269** H6
Old Dilton **117** F3
Old Down SGlos **131** F4
Old Down Som **116** D2
Old Edlington **186** C3
Old Eldon **212** B5
Old Ellerby **197** D4
Old Felixstowe **153** E4
Old Fletton **161** G3
Old Ford **136** C4
Old Glossop **185** E3
Old Goginan **154** C4
Old Goole **195** G5
Old Gore **145** F5
Old Grimsby **96** A1
Old Hall **188** C1
Old Hall Green **150** B5
Old Hall Street **179** E2
Old Harlow **137** D1
Old Heath **152** B5
Old Heathfield **110** A1
Old Hill **158** B4
Old Hurst **162** B5
Old Hutton **199** G4
Old Kea **96** C5
Old Kilpatrick **233** F2
Old Kinnernie **261** F4
Old Knebworth **150** A5
Old Leake **176** C2
Old Leslie **260** D2
Old Malton **204** B5
Old Milton **106** B3
Old Milverton **147** E1
Old Montsale **138** D3
Old Netley **107** D1
Old Newton **152** B1
Old Philpstoun **235** E2
Old Poltalloch **240** A4
Old Radnor
  (Pencraig) **144** B2

Old Rattray **269** J5
Old Rayne **260** E2
Old Romney **111** F1
Old Royal Naval College,
  Greenwich GtLon
  SE10 9LW **13** D5
Old Scone **243** G2
Old Shields **234** C2
Old Sodbury **131** G4
Old Somerby **175** E4
Old Stratford **148** C3
Old Sunderlandwick **196** C2
Old Swarland **221** D1
Old Swinford **158** B4
Old Thirsk **202** D4
Old Town Cumb **199** G4
Old Town IoS **96** B1
Old Town Farm **220** A2
Old Tupton **173** E1
Old Warden **149** G3
Old Weston **161** F5
Old Windsor **135** E5
Old Wives Lees **124** C3
Old Woking **121** F2
Old Woodhall **176** A1
Old Woods **170** B5
Oldberrow **146** D1
Oldborough **102** A2
Oldbury Kent **123** E3
Oldbury Shrop **157** G3
Oldbury Warks **159** F3
Oldbury WMid **158** B3
Oldbury Court Estate
  Bristol BS16 2JH **8** D2
Oldbury Naite **131** F3
Oldbury on the Hill **132** A4
Oldbury-on-Severn **131** F3
Oldcastle Bridgend **129** F5
Oldcastle Mon **144** C5
Oldcastle Heath **170** B3
Oldcotes **186** C4
Oldcroft **131** F2
Oldeamere **162** B3
Oldfield **146** A1
Oldford **117** E2
Oldhall Aber **260** C5
Oldhall High **275** H3
Oldham **184** D2
Oldham Edge **184** D2
Oldhamstocks **237** E2
Oldland **131** F5
Oldmeldrum **261** G2
Oldmill **204** D4
Oldpark **157** F2
Oldridge **102** B3
Oldshore Beg **272** E3
Oldshoremore **272** E3
Oldstead **203** E5
Oldtown **266** C3
Oldtown of Aigas **266** B7
Oldtown of Ord **268** E5
Oldwalls **128** A3
Oldways End **114** B5
Oldwhat **269** G5
Oldwich Lane **159** E5
Olgrinmore **275** G3
Oliver **226** C3
Oliver's Battery **119** F5
Ollaberry **278** C4
Ollerton ChesE **184** B5
Ollerton Notts **174** B1
Ollerton Shrop **170** D5
Olmstead Green **151** E3
Olney **149** D2
Olrig House **275** G2
Olton **158** D4
Olveston **131** F4
Olympia GtLon
  W14 8UX **11** A5
Olympic Park GtLon
  E20 1EE **12** D3
Ombersley **146** A1
Ompton **174** B1
Onchan **190** B4
Onecote **172** B2
Onehouse **152** B2
Ongar Hill **177** D5
Ongar Street **144** C1
Onibury **157** D5
Onich
  (Omhanaich) **248** C3
Onllwyn **129** E1
Onneley **171** E3
Onslow Green **137** F1
Onslow Village **121** E3
Opinan High **264** E2
Opinan High **264** D4
Orange Lane **237** E5
Orasaigh **271** F6
Orbliston **268** B5
Orbost **263** H7
Orby **176** D1
Orcadia **232** C3
Orchard **232** C3
Orchard Portman **115** F5
Orcheston **118** B3
Orcop **145** D5
Orcop Hill **145** D5
Ord **256** C3
Ordhead **260** E3
Ordie **260** C4
Ordiequish **268** B5
Ordsall **187** D5
Ore **110** D2
Oreham Common **109** E2
Oreston **100** B2
Oreton **157** F5
Orford Suff **153** F3
Orford Warr **184** A3
Organford **105** F3
Orgreave **158** D1
Orkney Islands **276** D5
Orlestone **124** B5
Orleton Here **145** F1
Orleton Worcs **145** F1
Orleton Common **145** D1
Orlingbury **161** D5
Ormacleit **254** C1
Ormesby **203** E1
Ormesby
  St. Margaret **179** F4
Ormesby
  St. Michael **179** F4
Ormidale **232** B1
Ormiscaig **264** E2

Ormiston **236** B3
Ormlie **275** G2
Ormsaigmore **247** D3
Ormsary **231** F2
Ormskirk **183** F2
Oronsay **230** B1
Orphir **277** C7
Orpington **123** D2
Orrell GtMan **183** G2
Orrell Mersey **183** E3
Orrisdale **190** B2
Orrok House **261** H3
Orroland **208** A2
Orsett **137** F4
Orsett Heath **137** F4
Orslow **158** A1
Orston **174** C3
Orton Cumb **200** B2
Orton N'hants **160** D5
Orton Longueville **161** G3
Orton Rigg **209** G1
Orton Waterville **161** G3
Orton-on-the-Hill **159** F2
Orwell **150** B2
Osbaldeston **192** C4
Osbaldwick **195** F2
Osbaston Leics **159** G2
Osbaston Shrop **170** A5
Osbaston Tel&W **157** E1
Osbaston Hollow **159** G2
Osborne **107** E3
Osborne House IoW
  PO32 6JX **107** E3
Osbournby **175** F4
Oscroft **170** C1
Ose **263** J7
Osgathorpe **159** G1
Osgodby Lincs **188** A3
Osgodby NYorks **195** F4
Osgodby NYorks **205** D4
Oskaig **256** B1
Osleston **173** D4
Osmaston Derby **173** E4
Osmaston Derbys **172** C3
Osmington **104** D4
Osmington Mills **104** D4
Osmondthorpe **194** C4
Osmotherley **203** D3
Osnaburgh (Dairsie) **244** C3
Ospringe **124** C2
Ossett **194** B5
Ossett Street Side **194** B5
Ossington **174** C1
Ostend **138** C2
Osterley **183** G4
Osterley Park & House
  GtLon TW7 4RB **11** B5
Oswaldkirk **203** F5
Oswaldtwistle **192** D5
Oswestry **169** F5
Oteley **170** B4
Otford **123** E3
Otham **123** G3
Othery **116** A4
Otley Suff **152** D2
Otley WYorks **194** B3
Otter **232** A1
Otter Ferry **232** A1
Otterborne **119** F5
Otterburn N'umb **220** A2
Otterburn NYorks **193** F2
Otterburn Camp **220** A2
Otterden Place **124** B3
Otterham **98** B1
Otterham Quay **124** A2
Otterhampton **115** F3
Otternish **262** E4
Ottershaw **121** F1
Otterswick **278** E4
Otterton **103** D4
Otterton Mill Devon
  EX9 7HG **103** D4
Otterwood **106** D2
Ottery St. Mary **103** D3
Ottinge **125** D4
Ottringham **197** E5
Oughterby **209** F1
Oughtershaw **201** D4
Oughterside **209** E2
Oughtibridge **186** A3
Oulston **203** E5
Oulton Cumb **209** F1
Oulton Norf **178** C3
Oulton Staffs **171** G4
Oulton Staffs **171** F5
Oulton Suff **165** G2
Oulton WYorks **194** C5
Oulton Broad **165** G2
Oulton Grange **171** G4
Oulton Street **178** C3
Oultoncross **171** G4
Oundle **161** F4
Our Dynamic Earth Edin
  EH8 8AS **37** J4
Ousby **210** C3
Ousdale **275** F6
Ousden **151** F2
Ousefleet **196** A5
Ouston Dur **212** B2
Ouston N'umb **220** C4
Out Newton **197** F5
Out Rawcliffe **192** A3
Out Skerries
  Airstrip **278** F5
Outcast **199** E5
Outchester **229** F3
Outertown **277** B7
Outgate **199** E3
Outhgill **200** C2
Outlands **171** E5
Outlane **185** E1
Outwell **162** D2
Outwood Surr **122** C4
Outwood WYorks **194** C5
Outwoods **157** G1
Ouzlewell Green **194** C5
Ovenden **193** G5
Over Cambs **162** B5
Over ChesW&C **170** D1
Over Glos **130** G1
Over SGlos **131** E4
Over Burrows **173** D4
Over Compton **104** B1
Over Dinsdale **202** C1
Over End **185** G5
Over Green **159** D3
Over Haddon **172** D1

Over Hulton **184** A2
Over Kellet **192** B1
Over Kiddington **147** G5
Over Monnow **131** D1
Over Norton **147** G5
Over Peover **184** B5
Over Rankeilour **244** B3
Over Silton **203** D3
Over Stowey **115** E4
Over Stratton **104** A1
Over Tabley **184** B4
Over Wallop **119** D4
Over Whitacre **159** E3
Over Winchendon (Upper
  Winchendon) **134** C1
Over Worton **147** G5
Overbister **276** F3
Overbrae **269** G5
Overbury **146** B4
Overcombe **104** C4
Overgreen **186** A5
Overleigh **116** B4
Overpool **183** E5
Overscaig Hotel **273** G6
Overseal **159** F1
Overslade **159** G5
Oversland **124** C3
Oversley Green **146** C2
Overstone **148** D1
Overstrand **178** D1
Overthorpe **147** G3
Overton Aber **261** F3
Overton Aberdeen **261** G3
Overton ChesW&C **183** G5
Overton Hants **119** G3
Overton Lancs **192** A2
Overton NYorks **195** E2
Overton Shrop **157** E5
Overton Swan **128** A4
Overton (Owrtyn)
  Wrex **170** A3
Overton WYorks **185** G1
Overton Bridge **170** A3
Overtown Lancs **200** B5
Overtown NLan **234** C4
Overtown Swin **133** D5
Overy **134** A3
Oving Bucks **148** C5
Oving WSuss **108** B3
Ovingdean **109** F3
Ovingham **211** G1
Ovington Dur **202** A1
Ovington Essex **151** F3
Ovington Hants **119** G4
Ovington N'umb **211** G1
Ovington Norf **178** A5
Ower Hants **106** C1
Ower Hants **107** D1
Owermoigne **105** D4
Owler Bar **185** G5
Owlpen **131** G3
Owl's Green **153** D1
Owlswick **134** C2
Owmby **160** D2
Owmby **188** A2
Owmby-by-Spital **188** A4
Owslebury **119** G5
Owston **160** C2
Owston Ferry **187** F2
Owstwick **197** E4
Owthorpe **174** B4
Oxborough **163** F2
Oxcliffe Hill **192** A1
Oxcombe **188** D5
Oxen End **151** E5
Oxen Park **199** E4
Oxencombe **102** B4
Oxenhall **145** G5
Oxenholme **199** G3
Oxenhope **193** G4
Oxenpill **116** B3 Oxenton
  146 B4
Oxenwood **119** E2
Oxford **134** A2
Oxford Cathedral Oxon
  OX1 1AB **80** Oxford
Oxford Story Oxon
  OX1 3AJ **80** Oxford
Oxford University Museum
  of Natural History
  Oxon OX1 3PW
  80 Oxford
Oxhey **136** A3
Oxhill **147** F3
Oxley **158** B2
Oxley Green **138** C1
Oxley's Green **110** B1
Oxnam **228** B5
Oxnead **178** D3
Oxnop Ghyll **201** E3
Oxshott **121** G1
Oxspring **185** G2
Oxted **122** C3
Oxton Mersey **183** E4
Oxton Notts **174** B2
Oxton ScBord **236** B4
Oxwich **128** A4
Oxwich Green **128** A4
Oxwick **178** A3
Oykel Bridge **265** K1
Oyne **260** E2
Ozleworth **131** G3

P

Pabbay **262** D3
Packington **159** F1
Packwood **159** D5
Padanaram **252** C4
Padarn Country Park
  Gwyn
  LL55 4TY **167** G2
Padbury **148** C4
Paddington **136** B4
Paddlesworth **125** D4
Paddock **124** B3
Paddock Wood **123** F4
Paddockhaugh **267** K6
Paddockhole **218** A3
Paddolgreen **170** C4
Padeswood **169** F1
Padfield **185** E3
Padiham **193** D4
Padside **194** A3
Padstow **96** D2
Padworth **120** B1
Paganhill **132** A2
Pagham **108** A4
Paglesham
  Churchend **138** C3

Paglesham
  Eastend **138** C3
Paible **263** F2
Paignton **101** E1
Paignton & Dartmouth
  Steam Railway
  Torbay
  TQ4 6AF **101** E2
Paignton Pier
  Torbay
  TQ4 6BW **101** E1
Paignton Zoo
  Torbay
  TQ4 7EU **101** E2
Pailton **159** G4
Paine's Corner **110** B1
Painscastle **144** A3
Painshawfield **211** G1
Painswick **132** A2
Pairc **97** E3
Paisley **233** F3
Pakefield **165** G2
Pakenham **152** A1
Palace of Holyroodhouse
  Edin EH8 8DX **37** J4
Palacerigg Country Park
  NLan G67 3HU **234** B2
Pale **168** C4
Palehouse
  Common **109** G2
Palestine **119** D3
Paley Street **135** D5
Palgowan **215** G2
Palgrave **164** C4
Pallinsburn House **228** C3
Palmarsh **124** D5
Palmers Cross **121** F3
Palmers Green **136** C3
Palmerscross **267** K5
Palmerstown **130** A5
Palnackie **216** C5
Palnure **215** F4
Palterton **173** F1
Pamber End **120** B2
Pamber Green **120** B2
Pamber Heath **120** B1
Pamington **146** B4
Pamphill **105** F2
Pampisford **150** C3
Pan **277** C8
Panborough **116** B3
Panbride **245** D1
Pancrasweek **112** C5
Pancross **129** G5
Pandy Gwyn **154** C2
Pandy Mon **144** C5
Pandy Powys **155** F2
Pandy Wrex **169** E4
Pandy Tudur **168** B1
Pandy'r Capel **169** D2
Panfield **151** F5
Pangbourne **134** B5
Pannal **194** C2
Pannal Ash **194** B3
Panshanger **136** B1
Pant **169** F5
Pant Glas **167** D3
Pant Gwyn **168** B5
Pant Mawr **155** E4
Pantasaph **182** C5
Panteg **130** C3
Pantglas **155** D3
Pantgwyn Carmar **142** A3
Pantgwyn Cere **141** F3
Pant-lasau **128** C2
Panton **188** B5
Pantperthog **154** D2
Pant-y-dwr **155** F5
Pantyffordd **169** F2
Pant-y-ffridd **156** A2
Pantyffynnon **128** C1
Pantygasseg **130** B3
Pantygelli **130** C1
Pantymwyn **169** E1
Panxworth **179** E4
Papa Stour **279** A6
Papa Stour Airstrip **279** A6
Papa Westray **276** D2
Papa Westray
  Airfield **276** D2
Papcastle **209** E3
Papil **279** C9
Papple **236** C2
Papplewick **173** G2
Papworth Everard **150** A1
Papworth St. Agnes **150** A1
Par **97** E4
Paradise Park, Newhaven
  ESuss BN9 0DH **109** G3
Paradise Wildlife Park,
  Broxbourne Herts
  EN10 7QA **136** C2
Parbold **183** F1
Parbrook Som **116** C4
Parbrook WSuss **121** F5
Parc **168** B4
Parcllyn **141** F2
Parcrhydderch **142** C2
Parc-Seymour **130** D3
Parc-y-rhôs **142** B2
Pardshaw **209** D4
Parham **153** E1
Parish Holm **225** F2
Park **268** D5
Park Close **193** E3
Park Corner ESuss **123** E5
Park Corner Oxon **134** B4
Park End N'umb **220** A4
Park End Staffs **171** F5
Park End Worcs **157** G5
Park Gate Hants **107** E2
Park Gate Worcs **158** B5
Park Gate WYorks **194** A3
Park Gate WYorks **185** G1
Park Green **152** C1
Park Hill **186** A4
Park Lane **170** B4
Park Langley **122** C2
Park Rose Pottery & Leisure
  Park ERid
  YO15 3QF **196** D1
Park Street **136** A2
Parkend Cumb **209** G3
Parkend Glos **131** F2
Parker's Green **123** F4
Parkeston **152** D4
Parkfield Corn **98** D4

Parkfield *SGlos* **131** F5
Parkfield *WMid* **158** B3
Parkford **252** C4
Parkgate *ChesW&C* **183** D5
Parkgate *D&G* **217** E2
Parkgate *Kent* **124** A5
Parkgate *Surr* **122** B4
Parkgate *SYorks* **186** A6
Parkham **113** D3
Parkham Ash **113** D3
Parkhill *Angus* **253** E5
Parkhill *P&K* **251** G5
Parkhouse **131** D2
Parkmill **128** C2
Parkneuk **253** F2
Parkside **170** A2
Parkstone **105** G3
Parkway **116** C5
Parley Cross **105** G3
Parley Green **106** A3
Parlington **194** D4
Parracombe **113** G1
Parrog **140** D4
Parson Cross **186** A3
Parson Drove **162** B2
Parsonage Green **137** F1
Parsonby **209** E3
Partick **233** G3
Partington **184** B3
Partney **176** C1
Parton *Cumb* **208** C4
Parton *D&G* **216** A3
Partridge Green **109** D2
Parwich **172** C2
Paslow Wood
 Common **137** E2
Passenham **148** C4
Passfield **120** D4
Passingford Bridge **137** E3
Paston **179** E2
Paston Street **179** E2
Pasturefields **171** G5
Patchacott **99** E1
Patcham **109** F3
Patchetts Green **136** A3
Patching **108** C3
Patchole **113** G1
Patchway **131** F4
Pateley Bridge **194** A1
Path of Condie **243** F3
Pathe **116** A4
Pathfinder Village **102** B3
Pathhead *Aber* **253** F3
Pathhead *EAyr* **225** E4
Pathhead *Fife* **244** A5
Pathhead *Midlo* **236** A3
Pathlow **147** D2
Patmore Heath **150** C5
Patna **224** C4
Patney **118** B2
Patrick **190** A4
Patrick Brompton **202** B3
Patrington **197** F5
Patrington Haven **197** F5
Patrishow **144** B5
Patrixbourne **125** D3
Patterdale **209** G5
Pattingham **158** A3
Pattishall **148** B2
Pattiswick **151** G5
Paul **94** B4
Paulerspury **148** C3
Paull **197** D5
Paull Holme **197** D5
Paul's Green **94** D3
Paulton **117** D2
Paultons Park *Hants*
 SO51 6AL **106** C1
Pauperhaugh **220** D1
Pave Lane **157** G1
Pavenham **149** E2
Pavilion Gardens, Buxton
 Derbys
 SK17 6XN **185** E5
Pawlett **116** A3
Pawston **228** C3
Paxford **147** D4
Paxhill Park **109** F1
Paxton **237** G4
Payden Street **124** B3
Payhembury **103** D2
Paythorne **193** E2
Peacehaven **109** G3
Peacemarsh **117** F5
Peachley **146** A2
Peak Dale **185** E5
Peak Forest **185** F5
Peakirk **161** G2
Pean Hill **124** D2
Pear Tree **173** E4
Pearsie **252** B4
Pearson's Green **123** F4
Peartree **136** B1
Peartree Green
 Essex **137** E3
Peartree Green
 Here **145** F4
Pease Pottage **122** B5
Peasedown
 St. John **117** E2
Peasehill **173** F2
Peaseland Green **178** B4
Peasemore **133** G5
Peasenhall **153** E1
Peaslake **121** F3
Peasley Cross **183** G3
Peasmarsh
 ESuss **111** D1
Peasmarsh *Surr* **121** E3
Peaston **236** B3
Peastonbank **236** B3
Peat Inn **244** C4
Peathill **269** H4
Peatling Magna **160** A3
Peatling Parva **160** A4
Peaton **157** E4
Pebble Coombe **122** B3
Pebmarsh **151** G4
Pebworth **146** D3
Pecket Well **193** F5
Peckforton **170** C2
Peckham **136** C5
Peckleton **159** G2
Pedham **179** E4

Pedmore **158** B4
Pedwell **116** B4
Peebles **235** G5
Peel *IoM* **190** A3
Peel *Lancs* **191** G4
Peening Quarter **111** D1
Peggs Green **159** G1
Pegsdon **149** G4
Pegswood **221** E3
Pegwell **125** F2
Peighinn nan
 Aoireann **254** C1
Peinchorran **256** B1
Peinlich **263** K6
Pelaw **212** B1
Pelcomb **126** C1
Pelcomb Bridge **126** C1
Pelcomb Cross **126** C1
Peldon **138** C1
Pellon **193** G5
Pelsall **158** C2
Pelton **212** B2
Pelutho **209** E2
Pelynt **97** G4
Pemberton **183** G2
Pembrey (Pen-bre) **128** A2
Pembrey Country Park
 Carmar
 SA16 0EJ **128** A2
Pembridge **144** C2
Pembroke (Penfro) **126** C2
Pembroke Dock
 (Doc Penfro) **126** C2
Pembury **123** F4
Penallt **131** E1
Penally **127** E3
Penalt **145** E5
Penare **97** D5
Penarran **156** A4
Penarth **130** A5
Pen-bont
 Rhydybeddau **154** C4
Penboyr **141** G4
Penbryn **141** F2
Pencader **142** A4
Pen-cae **142** A2
Pen-cae-cwm **168** C1
Pencaenewydd **166** D3
Pencaitland **236** B3
Pencarnisiog **180** B5
Pencarreg **142** B3
Pencarrow **97** F1
Pencelli **143** G5
Pen-clawdd **128** B3
Pencoed **129** F4
Pencombe **145** E2
Pencoyd **145** E5
Pencraig *Here* **145** E5
Pencraig *Powys* **168** D5
Pendeen **94** A3
Penderyn **129** F2
Pendine
 (Pentywyn) **127** F2
Pendlebury **184** B2
Pendleton **193** D4
Pendock **145** G4
Pendoggett **97** E2
Pendomer **104** B1
Pendoylan **129** G5
Penegoes **155** D2
Pen-ffordd **141** D5
Pengam **130** A3
Penge **136** C5
Pengenffordd **144** A5
Pengorffwysfa **180** C3
Pengover Green **97** G3
Pen-groes-oped **130** C2
Pengwern **182** B5
Penhale **95** D3
Penhallow **96** B4
Penhalvean **95** E3
Penhelig **154** C3
Penhill **133** D4
Penhow **130** D3
Penhurst **110** B2
Peniarth **154** C2
Penicuik **235** G3
Peniel **142** A5
Penifiler **263** K7
Peninver **222** C3
Penisa'r Waun **167** E1
Penisarcwm **155** G1
Penishawain **143** G4
Penistone **185** G2
Penjerrick **95** E3
Penketh **183** G4
Penkill **214** D1
Penkridge **158** B1
Penlean **98** C1
Penley **170** B4
Penllech **166** B4
Penllergaer **128** C3
Pen-llyn *IoA* **180** B4
Penllyn *VGlam* **129** F5
Pen-lôn **166** D1
Penmachno **168** A2
Penmaen **128** B4
Penmaenan **181** F5
Penmaenmawr **181** F5
Penmaenpool (Llyn
 Penmaen) **154** C1
Penmaen-Rhôs **181** G5
Penmark **115** D1
Penmon **181** E4
Penmorfa **167** E3
Penmynydd **180** D5
Penn *Bucks* **135** E3
Penn *WMid* **158** A3
Penn Street **135** E3
Pennal **154** C2
Pennal-isaf **154** D2
Pennan **269** F4
Pennance **96** B5
Pennant *Cere* **142** B3
Pennant *Powys* **155** E3
Pennant Melangell **168** D5
Pennar **126** C2
Pennard **128** B4
Pennerley **156** C3
Penninghame **215** E4
Pennington *Cumb* **199** D5
Pennington *Hants* **106** C3
Pennington Flash Country
 Park *GtMan*
 WN7 3PA **184** A3
Pennington Green **184** A2
Pennorth **144** A5

Pennsylvania **131** G5
Penny Bridge **199** E4
Pennycross **100** A2
Pennyfuir **240** A1
Pennygate **179** E3
Pennyghael **239** E2
Pennyglen **224** A4
Pennygown **247** F5
Pennymoor **102** B1
Penny's Green **164** C2
Pennyvenie **224** C5
Penparc *Cere* **141** F3
Penparc *Pembs* **140** B4
Penparcau **154** B4
Penpedairheol **130** C2
Penpethy **97** E1
Penpillick **97** E4
Penpol **95** F3
Penpoll **97** F4
Penponds **94** D3
Penpont *D&G* **216** C1
Penpont *Powys* **143** F5
Penprysg **129** F4
Penquit **100** C2
Penrherber **141** F4
Penrhiw **141** E3
Penrhiwceiber **129** G3
Penrhiw-llan **141** G3
Penrhiwgoch **128** B1
Penrhiw-pâl **141** G3
Penrhiwtyn **128** D3
Penrhos *Gwyn* **166** C4
Penrhos *IoA* **180** A4
Penrhos *Mon* **130** D1
Penrhos *Powys* **129** E1
Penrhos-garnedd **181** D5
Penrhyn Bay
 (Bae Penrhyn) **181** G4
Penrhyn Castle *Gwyn*
 LL57 4HN **181** E5
Penrhyn-coch **154** C4
Penrhyndeudraeth **167** F4
Penrhyn-side **181** G4
Penrhys **129** G3
Penrice **128** A4
Penrith **210** B5
Penrose *Corn* **96** C2
Penrose *Corn* **97** G1
Penruddock **210** A5
Penryn **95** E3
Pensarn *Carmar* **128** A1
Pensarn *Conwy* **182** A5
Pen-sarn *Gwyn* **167** E5
Pen-sarn *Gwyn* **166** D3
Pensax **145** G1
Pensby **183** D4
Penselwood **117** E4
Pensford **117** D1
Pensham **146** B3
Penshaw **212** C2
Penshurst **123** E4
Pensilva **97** G3
Pensnett **158** B4
Penston **236** B2
Pentewan **97** E5
Pentir **167** E1
Pentire **96** B3
Pentireglaze **96** D2
Pentlepoir **127** E2
Pentlow **151** G3
Pentlow Street **151** G3
Pentney **163** F1
Penton Mewsey **119** E3
Pentonville **136** D5
Pentraeth **180** D5
Pentre *Powys* **169** D5
Pentre *Powys* **155** E4
Pentre *Powys* **144** B1
Pentre *Powys* **156** B3
Pentre *Powys* **156** A4
Pentre *RCT* **129** F3
Pentre *Shrop* **156** C1
Pentre *Shrop* **156** C5
Pentre *Wrex* **169** F3
Pentre *Wrex* **170** A3
Pentre Berw **180** C5
Pentre Ffwrndan **183** D5
Pentre Galar **141** E4
Pentre Gwenlais **128** C1
Pentre Gwynfryn **167** E5
Pentre Halkyn **182** D5
Pentre Isaf **168** B1
Pentre Llanrhaeadr **169** D1
Pentre Maelor **170** A3
Pentre Meyrick **129** F5
Pentre Poeth **128** C3
Pentre Saron **168** D1
Pentre-bach *Cere* **142** B3
Pentre-bach *MTyd* **129** G2
Pentre-bach *Powys* **143** F4
Pentre-bach *RCT* **129** G4
Pentre-bont **168** A2
Pentrebeirdd **156** B1
Pentre-bwlch **169** E3
Pentrecagal **141** G4
Pentre-celyn *Denb* **169** E2
Pentre-celyn
 Powys **155** E2
Pentre-chwyth **128** C3
Pentreclwydau **129** E2
Pentre-cwrt **141** G4
Pentre-Dolau-
 Honddu **143** F3
Pentredwr *Denb* **169** E3
Pentre-dwr *Swan* **128** C3
Pentrefelin *Carmar* **142** B3
Pentrefelin *Cere* **142** C3
Pentrefelin *Conwy* **181** G5
Pentrefelin *Gwyn* **167** E4
Pentrefelin *Powys* **169** E5
Pentrefoelas **168** B2
Pentregat **141** G2
Pentreheyling **156** B3
Pentre-llwyn-
 llŵyd **143** F2
Pentre-llyn **154** C5
Pentre-llyn-
 cymmer **168** C2
Pentre-piod **168** B4
Pentre-poeth **130** B4
Pentre'r beirdd **156** A1
Pentre'r Felin **168** B1
Pentre-r-felin **143** F5
Pentre-tafarn-y-
 fedw **168** A1
Pentre-ty-gwyn **143** E4
Pentrich **173** E2
Pentridge **105** G1

Pentwyn *Caerp* **130** A2
Pen-twyn *Caerp* **130** B2
Pentwyn *Cardiff* **130** B4
Pen-twyn *Mon* **131** D2
Pentwyn-mawr **130** A3
Pentyrch **130** A4
Penuwch **142** B2
Penwithick **97** E4
Penwood **119** F1
Penwortham **192** B5
Penwortham Lane **192** B5
Penwyllt **129** E1
Pen-y-banc **142** C1
Pen-y-bont
 Carmar **143** D4
Pen-y-bont
 Carmar **141** G5
Pen-y-bont *Powys* **155** G1
Pen-y-bont *Powys* **169** F5
Penybont *Powys* **144** A1
Penybontfawr **169** D5
Penybryn *Caerp* **130** A3
Pen-y-bryn *Pembs* **141** E3
Pen-y-bryn *Wrex* **169** F3
Pen-y-cae *Powys* **129** E1
Penycae *Wrex* **169** F3
Pen-y-cae-mawr **130** D3
Pen-y-cefn **182** C5
Pen-y-clawdd **130** D2
Pen-y-coedcae **129** G4
Penycwm **140** B5
Pen-y-Darren **129** G2
Pen-y-fai **129** E4
Pen-y-fan **129** E4
Pengffordd *Powys* **155** G1
Pen-y-ffordd *Flints* **182** C4
Pengffridd **167** E2
Pen-y-gaer **144** A5
Pen-y-garn *Carmar* **142** B4
Pen-y-garn *Cere* **154** C4
Penygarn *Torfaen* **130** B2
Penygarnedd **169** E5
Pen-y-garreg **143** G3
Pen-y-Graig *Gwyn* **166** B4
Pen-y-graig *Gwyn* **167** D2
Penygraig *RCT* **129** G3
Penygroes *Carmar* **128** B1
Pen-y-groes *Gwyn* **167** D2
Pen-y-Gwryd Hotel **167** F2
Pen-y-lan **130** A5
Pen-y-Mynydd
 Carmar **128** A1
Penymynydd
 Flints **170** A1
Pen-y-parc **169** F1
Pen-yr-englyn **129** F3
Pen-yr-heol *Mon* **130** D1
Penyrheol *Swan* **128** C3
Pen y sarn **180** C3
Pen-y-stryt **169** E2
Pen-y-Mynydd
 Carmar **128** A1
Penywaun **129** F2
Penzance **94** B3
Penzance Heliport **94** B3
People's Palace & Winter
 Gardens *Glas*
 G40 1AT **30** H6
Peopleton **146** B2
Peover Heath **184** B5
Peper Harow **121** E3
Peplow **170** D5
Pepper Arden **202** B2
Pepper's Green **137** F1
Perceton **233** E5
Percie **260** D5
Percyhorner **269** H4
Perham Down **119** D3
Periton **114** C3
Perivale **136** A4
Perkhill **260** D4
Perkins Beach **156** C2
Perkin's Village **102** D3
Perlethorpe **186** B5
Perran Downs **94** C3
Perranarworthal **95** E3
Perranporth **96** B4
Perranuthnoe **94** C4
Perranzabuloe **96** B4
Perrott's Brook **132** C2
Perry Barr **158** C3
Perry Crofts **159** E2
Perry Green
 Essex **151** G5
Perry Green *Herts* **136** D1
Perry Green *Wilts* **132** B4
Perry Street **137** E5
Perrymead **117** E1
Pershall **171** F5
Pershore **146** B3
Persie House **251** G3
Pert **253** E3
Pertenhall **149** F1
Perth (Peairt) **243** G2
Perthcelyn **129** G3
Perthy **170** A4
Pestalozzi Children's
 Village **110** C2
Peter Tavy **99** F3
Peterborough **161** G3
Peterburn **264** D3
Peterchurch **144** C4
Peterculter **261** G4
Peterhead **269** K6
Peterlee **212** D3
Peter's Green **136** A1
Peters Marland **113** E4
Peters Port
 (Port Pheadair) **262** D7
Petersfield **120** C5
Petersfinger **118** C5
Peterston
 Wentlooge **130** B4
Peterston-super-
 Ely **129** G5
Peterstow **145** E5
Petham **124** D3
Petrockstowe **113** F5
Pett **111** E1
Pettaugh **152** C2
Petteril Green **210** A3
Pettinain **235** E5
Pettistree **153** D2
Petton *Devon* **114** D5
Petton *Shrop* **170** B5
Petts Wood **122** D2
Petty **261** F1
Pettycur **235** G1

Pettymuick **261** H2
Petworth **121** E5
Pevensey **110** B3
Pevensey Bay **110** B3
Peverell **100** A2
Pewsey **118** C1
Pheasant's Hill **134** C4
Phesdo **253** E2
Philham **112** C3
Philharmonic Hall, Liverpool
 Mersey L1 9BP **43** E5
Philiphaugh **227** F3
Phillack **94** C3
Philleigh **95** F2
Philpstoun **235** E2
Phocle Green **145** F5
Phoenix Green **120** C3
Phones **258** E5
Phorp **267** H6
Photographer's Gallery, The,
 London *GtLon*
 WC2H 7HY **44** E3
Pibsbury **116** B5
Pica **208** C4
Piccadilly Corner **165** D3
Pickering **203** G4
Pickering Nook **212** A2
Picket Piece **119** E3
Picket Post **106** A2
Pickford Green **159** E4
Pickhill **202** C4
Picklescott **156** D3
Pickletillem **244** C2
Pickmere **184** A5
Pickney **115** E5
Pickstock **171** E5
Pickup Bank **192** D5
Pickwell *Devon* **113** E1
Pickwell *Leics* **160** C1
Pickworth *Lincs* **175** F4
Pickworth *Rut* **161** E1
Picton *ChesW&C* **183** F5
Picton *NYorks* **202** D2
Piddinghoe **109** G3
Piddington *Bucks* **134** D3
Piddington *N'hants* **148** D2
Piddington *Oxon* **134** B1
Piddlehinton **104** D3
Piddletrenthide **104** D3
Pidley **162** B3
Piece Hall, Halifax *WYorks*
 HX1 1RE **26** B4
Piercebridge **202** B1
Pierowall **276** D3
Pigdon **221** D2
Pike Hill **193** E4
Pikehall **172** C2
Pikeshill **106** B2
Pilgrims Hatch **137** E3
Pilham **187** F3
Pill **131** E5
Pillaton *Corn* **99** D4
Pillaton *Staffs* **158** B1
Pillerton Hersey **147** E3
Pillerton Priors **147** E3
Pilleth **144** B1
Pilley *Hants* **106** C3
Pilley *SYorks* **186** A2
Pilling **192** A3
Pilling Lane **191** G3
Pillowell **131** F2
Pilning **131** E4
Pilsbury **172** C1
Pilsdon **104** A3
Pilsgate **161** F2
Pilsley *Derbys* **173** F1
Pilsley *Derbys* **185** G5
Pilson Green **179** E4
Piltdown **109** G1
Pilton *Devon* **113** F2
Pilton *N'hants* **161** F4
Pilton *Rut* **161** E2
Pilton *Som* **116** C3
Pilton *Swan* **128** A4
Pilton Green **128** A4
Pimhole **184** C1
Pimlico **135** F2
Pimperne **105** F2
Pin Mill **152** D4
Pinchbeck **176** A5
Pinchbeck Bars **176** A5
Pinchbeck West **176** A5
Pincheon Green **187** D1
Pinchinthorpe **203** E1
Pindon End **148** C3
Pinehurst **132** D4
Pinfold **183** E1
Pinged **128** A2
Pinhay **103** G3
Pinhoe **102** C3
Pinkneys Green **135** D4
Pinley Green **147** E1
Pinminnoch **214** C1
Pinmore **214** C1
Pinn **103** E4
Pinner **136** A4
Pinner Green **136** A3
Pinvin **146** B2
Pinwherry **214** C2
Pinxton **173** F1
Pipe & Lyde **145** E3
Pipe Gate **171** E4
Pipe Ridware **158** C1
Pipehill **158** C2
Piperhall **232** B4
Piperhill **267** F6
Pipers Pool **97** G1
Pipewell **160** D4
Pippacott **113** F2
Pipton **144** A4
Pirbright **121** E2
Pirnmill **231** G5
Pirton *Herts* **149** G4
Pirton *Worcs* **146** A3
Pisgah **242** C4
Pishill **134** C4
Pistyll **166** C3
Pitagowan **250** D3
Pitblae **269** H5
Pitcairngreen **243** F2
Pitcairns **243** F3
Pitcaple **261** F2
Pitch Green **134** C2
Pitch Place *Surr* **121** E3
Pitch Place *Surr* **121** D4
Pitchcombe **132** A2

Pitchcott **148** C5
Pitchford **157** E2
Pitcombe **117** D4
Pitcot **129** E5
Pitcox **236** D2
Pitcur **244** A1
Pitfichie **260** E3
Pitgrudy **266** E2
Pitinnan **261** F1
Pitkennedy **252** D4
Pitkevy **244** A4
Pitlessie **244** B4
Pitlochry **251** E4
Pitman's Corner **152** C1
Pitmedden **261** G2
Pitminster **103** F1
Pitmuies **253** D4
Pitmunie **260** E3
Pitnacree **251** E4
Pitney **116** B5
Pitroddie **244** A2
Pitscottie **244** C3
Pitsea **137** G4
Pitsford **148** C1
Pitsford Hill **115** D4
Pitstone **135** E1
Pitt *Devon* **102** D1
Pitt *Hants* **119** F5
Pitt Rivers Museum *Oxon*
 OX1 3PP **80** Oxford
Pittendreich **267** J5
Pittentrail **266** E1
Pittenweem **244** D4
Pitteuchar **244** A5
Pittington **212** C3
Pittodrie House **260** E2
Pitton *Swan* **128** A4
Pitton *Wilts* **118** D5
Pittulie **269** H4
Pittville **146** B5
Pity Me **212** B3
Pityme **96** D2
Pixey Green **164** D4
Pixley **145** F4
Place Newton **204** B5
Plaidy **269** F5
Plain Dealings **127** D1
Plainfield **220** B1
Plains **234** B3
Plainsfield **115** E4
Plaish **157** E3
Plaistow *GtLon* **136** C4
Plaistow *WSuss* **121** F4
Plaitford **106** B1
Plaitford Green **119** D5
Plas **142** A5
Plas Gwynant **167** F2
Plas Isaf **169** D3
Plas Llwyd **182** A5
Plas Llwyngwern **155** D2
Plas Llysyn **155** F3
Plas Nantyr **169** E4
Plas-rhiw-Saeson **155** F2
Plastow Green **119** G1
Plas-yn-Cefn **182** B5
Platt **123** F3
Platt Bridge **184** A2
Platt Lane **170** C4
Platt's Heath **124** A3
Plawsworth **212** B3
Plaxtol **123** F3
Play Hatch **134** C5
Playden **111** E1
Playford **152** D3
Playing Place **96** C5
Playley Green **145** G4
Plealey **156** D2
Plean **234** C1
Pleasance **244** A3
Pleasant Valley **150** D4
Pleasington **192** C5
Pleasley **173** G1
Pleasleyhill **173** G1
Pleasure Beach, Great
 Yarmouth *Norf*
 NR30 3EH **179** G4
Pleasure Island Theme Park
 NELincs
 DN35 0PL **188** D2
Pleasurewood Hills Theme
 Park *Suff*
 NR32 5DZ **165** G2
Pleck *Dorset* **104** D1
Pleck *WMid* **158** B3
Pledgdon Green **151** D5
Pledwick **186** A1
Plemstall **183** F5
Plenmeller **210** D1
Pleshey **137** F1
Plessey Woods Country
 Park *N'umb*
 NE22 6AN **221** E3
Plockton (Am Ploc) **256** E1
Plocrapol **263** G2
Plomer's Hill **135** D3
Plot Gate **116** C4
Plough Hill **159** F3
Plowden **156** C4
Ploxgreen **156** C2
Pluckley **124** B4
Pluckley Thorne **124** B4
Plucks Gutter **125** E2
Plumbland **209** E3
Plumbley **186** B4
Plumley **184** B5
Plumpton *Cumb* **210** A4
Plumpton *ESuss* **109** F2
Plumpton *N'hants* **148** B3
Plumpton Green **109** F2
Plumpton Head **210** B4
Plumstead *GtLon* **137** D5
Plumstead *Norf* **178** C2
Plumtree **174** B4
Plungar **174** C4
Plush **104** D2
Plusha **97** G1
Plushabridge **98** D3
Plwmp **141** G2
Plym Bridge **100** B2
Plymouth **100** A2
Plymouth City
 Airport **100** B2
Plymouth Pavilions
 Plymouth
 PL1 3LF **81** Plymouth
Plympton **100** B2
Plymstock **100** B2

Plymtree **103** D2
Pockley **203** F4
Pocklington **196** A3
Pockthorpe **178** B3
Pocombe Bridge **102** B3
Pode Hole **176** A5
Podimore **116** C5
Podington **149** E1
Podmore **171** E4
Podsmead **132** A1
Poffley End **133** F2
Point Clear **139** D1
Pointon **175** G4
Polanach **248** B4
Polapit Tamar **98** D2
Polbae **215** D3
Polbain **272** B7
Polbathic **98** D4
Polbeth **235** E3
Poldean **217** F1
Pole Moor **185** E1
Polebrook **161** F4
Polegate **110** A3
Poles **266** E2
Polesden Lacey *Surr*
 RH5 6BD **121** G2
Polesworth **159** E2
Polglass **265** G1
Polgooth **97** D4
Polgown **225** F5
Poling **108** C3
Poling Corner **108** C3
Polkemmet Country Park
 WLoth
 EH47 0AD **234** D3
Polkerris **97** E4
Poll a' Charra **254** C3
Polla **273** F3
Pollardras **94** D3
Polldubh **248** D3
Pollie **274** C7
Pollington **186** D1
Polloch **247** G3
Pollok **233** G3
Pollokshaws **233** G3
Pollokshields **233** G3
Polmassick **97** D5
Polmont **234** D2
Polnoon **233** G4
Polperro **97** G4
Polruan **97** F4
Polsham **116** C3
Polstead **152** A4
Polstead Heath **152** A3
Poltalloch **240** A5
Poltimore **102** C3
Polton **235** G3
Polwarth **237** E3
Polyphant **97** G1
Polzeath **96** C2
Pomphlett **100** B2
Pond Street **150** C4
Ponders End **136** C3
Pondersbridge **162** A3
Ponsanooth **95** E3
Ponsonby **198** B2
Ponsongath **95** E5
Ponsworthy **102** A5
Pont Aber **142** D5
Pont Aberglaslyn **167** E3
Pont ar Hydfer **143** E5
Pont Crugnant **155** E3
Pont Cyfung **168** A1
Pont Dolgarrog **168** A1
Pont Pen-y-benglog **167** F1
Pont Rhyd-sarn **168** B5
Pont Rhyd-y-cyff **129** E4
Pont Walby **129** E2
Pont yr Alwen **168** C2
Pontamman **128** C1
Pontantwn **128** A1
Pontardawe **128** C2
Pontarddulais **128** B2
Pontargothi **142** B5
Pont-ar-llechau **142** D5
Pontarsais **142** A5
Pontblyddyn **169** F1
Pontben Llwyd **129** F2
Pontefract **195** D5
Ponteland **221** D4
Ponterwyd **154** D4
Pontesbury **156** D2
Pontesbury Hill **156** C2
Pontesford **156** D2
Pontfadog **169** F4
Pontfaen *Pembs* **140** D4
Pont-faen *Powys* **143** F4
Pontgarreg **141** G2
Pont-Henri **128** A2
Ponthir **130** C3
Ponthirwaun **141** F3
Pontllanfraith **130** A3
Pontlliw **128** C2
Pontllyfni **166** D2
Pontlottyn **130** A2
Pontneddfechan **129** F2
Pontrhydfendigaid **142** D1
Pontrhydyfen **129** D3
Pont-rhyd-y-groes **154** D5
Pontrhydyrun **130** B3
Pontrilas **144** C5
Pont-robert **156** A1
Pont-rug **167** E1
Ponts Green **110** B2
Pontshill **145** F5
Pont-siân **142** A3
Pontsticill **129** G1
Pontwelly **142** A4
Pontyates
 (Pont-iets) **128** A2
Pontyberem **128** B1
Pont-y-blew **170** A4
Pontybodkin **169** F2
Pontyclun **129** F4
Pontycymer **129** F3
Pontygwaith **129** G3
Pontymister **130** B3
Pontymoel **130** B2
Pont-y-pant **168** A2
Pontypool **130** B2
Pontypridd **129** G3
Pont-y-rhyl **129** F4
Pontywaun **130** B3
Pooksgreen **106** C1
Pool *Corn* **96** A5
Pool *WYorks* **194** B3
Pool Bank **199** F4
Pool Green **158** C2

Pool Head 145 E2
Pool of Muckhart 243 F4
Pool Quay 156 B1
Pool Street 151 F4
Poole 105 G3
Poole Keynes 132 B3
Poole Pottery *Poole*
BH15 1HJ 3 B4
Poolend 171 G2
Poolewe 264 E3
Pooley Bridge 210 A5
Pooley Street 164 B3
Poolfold 171 F2
Poolhill 145 G5
Poolsbrook 186 B5
Poolthorne Farm 188 A2
Pope Hill 126 C1
Popeswood 120 D1
Popham 119 G3
Poplar 136 C4
Porchfield 106 D3
Porin 265 K6
Poringland 179 D5
Porlock 114 B3
Porlock Weir 114 B3
Port Allen 244 A2
Port Appin (Port na
h-Apainn) 248 B5
Port Askaig 230 C3
Port Bannatyne 232 B3
Port Carlisle 218 A4
Port Charlotte 230 A4
Port Clarence 213 E5
Port Driseach 232 A2
Port e Vullen 190 C2
Port Ellen 230 B5
Port Elphinstone 261 F3
Port Erin 190 A5
Port Erroll 261 J1
Port Eynon 128 A4
Port Gaverne 97 E1
Port Glasgow 233 E2
Port Henderson 264 D4
Port Isaac 97 E1
Port Logan 206 A2
*Port Lumpne Wild Animal
Park Kent
CT21 4PD 124 D5*
Port Mòr 246 D2
Port Mulgrave 203 G1
Port na Craig 251 E4
Port nan Long 262 D4
Port of Menteith 242 A4
Port o' Ness
(Port Nis) 271 H1
Port o'Warren 216 C5
Port Penrhyn 181 D5
Port Quin 97 D1
Port Ramsay 248 A5
Port St. Mary 190 A5
Port Solent 107 F2
Port Sunlight 183 E4
Port Talbot 129 D4
Port Wemyss 230 A4
Port William 206 D2
Portachoillan 231 F4
Portavadie 232 A2
Portbury 131 E5
Portchester 107 F2
Portencross 232 C5
Portesham 104 C4
Portessie 268 C4
Port of Ness
Portfield *A&B* 239 G2
Portfield *WSuss* 108 A3
Portfield Gate 126 C1
Portgate 99 E2
Portgordon 268 B4
Portgower 275 F7
Porth *Corn* 96 C3
Porth *RCT* 129 G3
Porth Colmon 166 A4
Porth Navas 95 E4
Porthallow *Corn* 95 E4
Porthallow *Corn* 97 G4
Porthcawl 129 E5
Porthcothan 96 C2
Porthcurno 94 A4
Porthgain 140 B4
Porthill 171 F3
Porthkerry 115 D1
*Porthkerry Country Park
VGlam
CF62 3BY 115 D1*
Porthleven 94 D4
Porthmadog 167 E4
Porthmeor 94 B3
Portholland 97 D5
Porthoustock 95 F4
Porthpean 97 E4
Porthtowan 96 A5
Porthyrhyd
Carmar 142 D4
Porthyrhyd
Carmar 128 B1
Porth-y-waen 169 F5
Portincaple 241 E5
Portington 195 G4
Portinnisherrich 240 B3
Portinscale 209 F4
Portishead 131 D5
Portknockie 268 C4
*Portland Basin Museum
GtMan
OL7 0QA 25 H3*
Portlethen 261 H5
Portlethen Village 261 H5
Portloe 95 G3
Portlooe 97 G4
Portmahomack 267 G3
Portmeirion 167 E4
*Portmeirion Village Gwyn
LL48 6ET 167 E4*
Portmellon 97 E5
Portmore 106 C3
Port-na-Con 273 G2
Portnacroish
(Port na Croise) 248 B5
Portnaguran (Port nan
Giùran) 271 H4
Portnahaven 230 A4
Portnaluchaig 247 F1
Portobello 236 A2
Porton 118 C4
Portpatrick 214 B5
Portreath 96 A5

Portree (Port Righ) 263 K7
Portscatho 95 F3
Portsea 107 F2
Portskerra 274 D2
Portskewett 131 E4
Portslade 109 E3
Portslade-by-Sea 109 E3
Portslogan 214 A5
Portsmouth 107 F3
*Portsmouth Guildhall
82 Portsmouth
PO1 2AB*
*Portsmouth Historic
Dockyard PO1 3LJ
82 Portsmouth*
Portsonachan 240 C2
Portsoy 268 D4
Portuairk 246 D3
Portvoller 271 H4
Portway *Here* 144 C3
Portway *Here* 145 D3
Portway *Here* 145 D4
Portway *Worcs* 158 C5
Portwrinkle 99 D5
Portyerrock 207 E3
Posenhall 157 F2
Poslingford 151 F3
Postbridge 99 G3
Postcombe 134 C3
Postling 124 D5
Postwick 179 D5
Potarch 260 E5
Potsgrove 149 E5
Pott Row 177 F5
Pott Shrigley 184 D5
Potten End 135 F2
Potter Brompton 204 C5
Potter Heigham 179 F4
Potter Street 137 D2
Pottergate Street 164 C2
Potterhanworth 175 F1
*Potterhanworth
Booths 175 F1*
*Potteries Museum & Art
Gallery ST1 3DW
85 Stoke-on-Trent*
Potterne 118 A2
Potterne Wick 118 B2
Potternewton 194 C4
Potters Bar 136 B2
Potters Crouch 136 A2
Potter's Green 159 F4
Potters Marston 159 G3
Potterspury 148 C3
Potterton *Aber* 261 H3
Potterton *WYorks* 194 C4
Pottle Street 117 F3
Potto 203 D2
Potton 150 A3
Pott's Green 152 A5
Poughill *Corn* 112 C5
Poughill *Devon* 102 B2
Poulshot 118 A2
Poulton 132 D2
Poulton-le-Fylde 191 G4
Pound Bank 145 G3
Pound Green *ESuss* 110 A1
Pound Green *Suff* 151 F2
Pound Green
Worcs 157 G5
Pound Hill 122 B5
Pound Street 119 F1
Poundbury 104 C3
Poundffald 128 B3
Poundfield 123 E5
Poundgate 109 G1
Poundland 214 C2
Poundon 148 B5
Poundsbridge 123 E4
Poundsgate 102 A5
Poundstock 98 C1
Povey Cross 122 B4
Pow Green 145 G3
Powburn 229 E5
Powderham 102 C4
*Powderham Castle Devon
EX6 8JQ 102 C4*
Powerstock 104 B3
Powfoot 217 F3
Powick 146 A2
*Powis Castle & Garden
Powys
SY21 8RG 156 B2*
Powler's Piece 113 D4
Powmill 243 F5
Poxwell 104 D4
Poyle 135 F5
Poynings 109 E2
Poyntington 117 D5
Poynton *ChesE* 184 D4
Poynton *Tel&W* 157 E1
Poynton Green 157 E1
Poyntzfield 266 E5
Poys Street 165 E4
Poyston 126 C1
Poyston Cross 126 C1
Poystreet Green 152 A2
Praa Sands 94 C4
Pratis 244 B4
Pratt's Bottom 123 D2
Praze-an-Beeble 94 D3
Predannack Wollas 95 D5
Prees 170 C4
Prees Green 170 C4
Prees Heath 170 C4
Prees Higher Heath 170 C4
Prees Lower Heath 170 C4
Preesall 191 G3
Preesgweene 169 F4
Prenbrigog 169 F1
Prendergast 126 C1
Prendwick 229 E5
Pren-gwyn 142 A3
Prenteg 167 E3
Prenton 183 E4
Prescot 183 F3
Prescott *Devon* 103 D1
Prescott *Shrop* 170 B5
Presley 267 H6
Pressen 228 C3
Prestatyn 182 B4
Prestbury *ChesE* 184 D5
Prestbury *Glos* 146 B5
Presteigne
(Llanandras) 144 C1
Presthope 157 E3
Prestleigh 116 D3
Prestolee 184 B2

Preston *B&H* 109 F3
Preston *Devon* 102 B5
Preston *Dorset* 104 D4
Preston *ELoth* 236 C2
Preston *ERid* 197 E4
Preston *Glos* 145 F4
Preston *Glos* 132 C2
Preston *Herts* 149 G5
Preston *Kent* 124 C2
Preston *Kent* 125 E2
Preston *Lancs* 192 B5
Preston *N'umb* 229 F4
Preston *Rut* 161 D2
Preston *ScBord* 237 E5
Preston *Shrop* 157 E1
Preston *Som* 115 D4
Preston *Suff* 152 A2
Preston *Torbay* 101 E1
Preston *Wilts* 132 C4
Preston Bagot 147 D1
Preston Bissett 148 B4
Preston Bowyer 115 E5
Preston Brockhurst 170 C5
Preston Brook 183 G4
Preston Candover 120 B3
Preston Capes 148 A2
Preston Deanery 148 C2
Preston Gubbals 157 D1
*Preston Guildhall Lancs
PR1 1HT 192 B5*
Preston on Stour 147 E2
Preston on the Hill 183 G4
Preston on Wye 144 C3
Preston Plucknett 104 B1
Preston upon the Weald
Moors 157 F1
Preston Wynne 145 E3
Preston-le-Skerne 212 C5
Prestonpans 236 A2
Preston-under-Scar 201 F3
Prestwich 184 C2
Prestwick *N'umb* 221 D4
Prestwick *SAyr* 224 B3
Prestwold 173 G5
Prestwood *Bucks* 135 D2
Prestwood *Staffs* 172 C3
Price Town 129 F3
*Prickly Ball Farm &
Hedgehog Hospital
Devon
TQ12 6BZ 101 E1*
Prickwillow 163 D4
Priddy 116 C2
Priest Hill 192 C4
Priest Hutton 199 G5
Priest Weston 156 B3
Priestcliffe 185 F5
Priestland 225 F2
Priestwood 123 F2
Primethorpe 160 A3
Primrose Green 178 B4
Primrose Hill 136 B4
Princes End 158 B3
Princes Gate 127 E1
Princes Risborough 134 D2
Princethorpe 159 G5
Princetown *Caerp* 130 A1
Princetown *Devon* 99 F3
Prior Muir 244 D3
Prior's Frome 145 E4
Priors Halton 157 D5
Priors Hardwick 147 G2
Priors Marston 147 G2
Prior's Norton 146 A5
Priors Park 146 A4
Priorslee 157 G1
*Priory Country Park Bed
MK41 9SH 149 F2*
Priory Wood 144 B3
Priston 117 D1
Pristow Green 164 C3
Prittlewell 138 B4
Privett 120 B5
Prixford 113 F2
Proaig 230 C4
Probus 96 C5
Protstonhill 269 G4
*Provand's Lordship Glas
G4 0RH 39 H3*
Prudhoe 211 G1
Prussia Cove 94 C4
Pubil 249 G5
Publow 116 D1
Puckeridge 150 B5
Puckington 103 G1
Pucklechurch 131 F5
Pucknall 119 E5
Puckrup 146 A4
Puddinglake 171 E1
Puddington
ChesW&C 183 E5
Puddington
Devon 102 B1
Puddlebrook 131 F1
Puddledock 164 B2
Puddletown 105 D3
Pudleston 145 E2
Pudsey 194 B4
*Pugneys Country Park
WYorks
WF2 7EQ 27 G6*
Pulborough 108 C2
*Pulborough Brooks RSPB
Nature Reserve WSuss
RH20 2EL 108 C2*
Puldagon 275 J4
Puleston 171 E5
Pulford 170 A2
Pulham 104 D2
Pulham Market 164 C3
Pulham St. Mary 164 D3
Pulley 157 D2
Pulloxhill 149 F4
Pulrossie 266 E3
Pulverbatch 156 D2
Pumpherston 235 E3
Pumsaint 142 C3
Puncheston 140 D5
Puncknowle 104 B4
Punnett's Town 110 B1
Purbrook 107 F2
Purewell 106 A3
Purfleet 137 E5
Puriton 116 A3
Purleigh 138 B2
Purley 122 C2
Purley on Thames 134 B5
Purlogue 156 B5

Purlpit 117 F1
Purls Bridge 162 C4
Purse Caundle 104 C1
Purslow 156 C4
Purston Jaglin 186 B1
Purtington 103 G2
Purton *Glos* 131 F2
Purton *Glos* 131 F2
Purton *Wilts* 132 C4
Purton Stoke 132 C3
Pury End 148 C3
Pusey 133 F3
Putley 145 F4
Putley Green 145 F4
Putney 136 B5
Putsborough 113 E1
Puttenham *Herts* 135 D1
Puttenham *Surr* 121 E3
Puttock End 151 G3
Putts Corner 103 E3
Puxton 116 B1
Pwll 128 A2
Pwllcrochan 126 C2
Pwlldefaid 166 A5
Pwll-glas 169 E2
Pwllgloyw 143 G4
Pwllheli 166 C4
Pwll-Mawr 130 B5
Pwllmeyric 131 E3
Pwll-trap 127 F1
Pwll-y-glaw 129 D3
Pye Corner *Herts* 137 D1
Pye Corner *Kent* 124 C4
Pye Corner
Newport 130 C4
Pye Green 158 B1
Pyecombe 109 E2
Pyle *Bridgend* 129 E4
Pyle *IoW* 107 E5
Pylle 116 D4
Pymoor (Pymore) 162 C4
Pymore (Pymoor)
Cambs 162 C4
Pymore *Dorset* 104 A3
Pyrford 121 F2
Pyrford Green 121 F2
Pyrton 134 B3
Pytchley 161 D5
Pyworthy 112 D5

Q

Quabbs 156 B4
Quadring 176 A4
Quadring Eaudike 176 A4
Quainton 148 C5
Quarff 279 D9
Quarley 119 D3
Quarndon 173 E3
Quarr Hill 107 E3
Quarrier's Village 233 E3
Quarrington 175 F3
Quarrington Hill 212 C4
Quarry Bank 158 B4
*Quarry Bank Mill & Styal
Estate ChesE
SK9 4LA 184 C4*
Quarrybank 170 C1
Quarrywood 267 J5
Quarter 234 B2
Quatford 157 G3
Quatt 157 G4
Quebec 212 A3
Quedgeley 132 A1
Queen Adelaide 163 D4
Queen Camel 116 C5
Queen Charlton 116 D1
Queen Dart 102 B1
*Queen Elizabeth Country
Park, Petersfield Hants
PO8 0QE 107 G2*
*Queen Elizabeth Forest Park
Stir FK8 3SX 241 G5*
*Queen Elizabeth II
Conference Centre GtLon
SW1P 3EE 44 D6*
*Queen Elizabeth II Country
Park, Ashington N'umb
NE63 9YF 221 E3*
Queen Oak 117 E4
Queen Street 235 E3
Queenborough 124 C1
Queen's Bower 107 E4
*Queen's Gallery,
Buckingham Palace
GtLon SW1A 1AA 44 B4*
*Queen's Hall, Edinburgh
Edin EH8 9JG 37 H6*
Queen's Head 170 A5
*Queen's View Centre P&K
PH16 5NR 251 E3*
Queensbury *GtLon* 136 A4
Queensbury
WYorks 194 A4
Queensferry (South
Queensferry)
Edin 235 F2
Queensferry 170 A1
*Queenswood Country Park
Here HR6 0PY 145 D2*
Queenzieburn 234 A2
Quemerford 118 B1
Quendale 279 F9
Quendon 150 D4
Queniborough 160 B1
Quenington 132 D2
Quernmore 192 B1
Queslett 158 C3
Quethiock 98 D4
Quholm 277 B6
Quick's Green 134 A5
Quidenham 164 B3
Quidhampton 119 G2
Quidinish
(Cuidhtinis) 263 F3
Quilquox 261 H1
Quina Brook 170 C4
Quindry 277 D8
Quine's Hill 190 B4
Quinhill 231 F4
Quinton *N'hants* 148 C2
Quinton *WMid* 158 B4
Quinton Green 148 C2
Quintrell Downs 96 C3
Quixhill 172 C3

Quoditch 99 E1
Quoig 242 D2
Quoiggs House 242 D4
Quoisley 170 C3
Quorn (Quorndon) 160 A1
Quorndon (Quorn) 160 A1
Quothquan 226 A2
Quoyloo 276 B5
Quoys 278 F1
Quoys of Reiss 275 J3

R

*R.A.F. Museum, Cosford
Shrop TF11 8UP 157 G2*
*R.A.F. Museum, Hendon
GtLon
NW9 5LL 10 D1*
*R.H.S. Garden Harlow Carr
NYorks
HG3 1QB 194 B2*
*R.H.S. Garden Hyde Hall
Essex
CM3 8ET 137 G3*
*R.H.S. Garden Rosemoor
Devon EX38 8PH 113 F4*
*R.H.S. Garden Wisley Surr
GU23 6QB 121 F2*
Raasay 264 B7
Raby 183 E5
Rachan 226 C2
Rachub 167 F1
Rackenford 102 B1
Rackham 108 C2
Rackheath 179 D4
Rackwick *Ork* 277 B8
Rackwick *Ork* 276 D3
Radbourne 173 D4
Radcliffe *GtMan* 184 B2
Radcliffe *N'umb* 221 E5
Radcliffe on Trent 174 B4
Radclive 148 B4
Radcot 133 E3
Raddington 114 D5
Radernie 244 C4
Radford *B&NESom* 117 D2
Radford *Nott* 173 G3
Radford *Oxon* 147 G5
Radford *WMid* 159 F5
Radford Semele 147 F1
Radipole 104 C4
Radlett 136 A2
Radley 134 A3
Radley Green 137 F2
Radmore Green 170 C2
Radnage 134 C3
Radstock 117 D2
Radstone 148 A3
Radway 147 F3
Radway Green 171 E2
Radwell *Bed* 149 F2
Radwell *Herts* 150 A4
Radwinter 151 E4
Radyr 130 A4
Raechester 220 B3
Raemoir House 260 E5
Raffin 272 C5
Rafford 267 H6
Ragdale 160 B1
Ragged Appleshaw 119 E3
Raglan 130 D2
Ragnall 187 F5
Rahoy 247 F4
Rainford 183 F2
Rainham *GtLon* 137 E4
Rainham *Med* 124 A2
Rainhill 183 F3
Rainhill Stoops 183 G3
Rainow 185 D5
Rainsough 184 B2
Rainton 202 C5
Rainworth 173 G2
Raisbeck 200 B2
Raise 210 D3
Rait 244 A2
Raithby *Lincs* 176 B1
Raithby *Lincs* 188 D4
Rake 120 D5
Raleigh's Cross 114 D4
Ram 142 B3
Ram Alley 118 D1
Ram Lane 124 B4
Ramasaig 263 G7
Rame *Corn* 95 E3
Rame *Corn* 100 A3
Rampisham 104 B2
Rampside 191 F1
Rampton *Cambs* 150 C1
Rampton *Notts* 187 F5
Ramsbottom 184 B1
Ramsbury 133 E5
Ramscraigs 275 G6
Ramsdean 120 C5
Ramsdell 119 G2
Ramsden 133 F1
Ramsden Bellhouse 137 G3
Ramsden Heath 137 G3
Ramsey *Cambs* 162 A4
Ramsey *Essex* 152 D4
Ramsey *IoM* 190 C2
Ramsey Forty Foot 162 B4
Ramsey Heights 162 A4
Ramsey Island
Essex 138 C2
Ramsey Island
Pembs 140 A5
Ramsey Mereside 162 A4
Ramsey St. Mary's 162 A4
Ramsgate 125 F2
Ramsgate Street 178 B2
Ramsgill 202 A5
Ramsholt 153 E3
Ramshorn 172 B3
Ramsnest Common 121 E4
Ranachan 247 G3
Ranby *Lincs* 188 C5
Ranby *Notts* 187 D4
Rand 188 B5
*Rand Farm Park Lincs
LN8 5NJ 188 B5*
Randwick 132 A2
Rangemore 172 C5
Rangeworthy 131 F4
Ranish (Ranais) 271 G5
Rankinston 224 C4
Rank's Green 137 G1
Ranmoor 186 A4

Rannoch School 250 A4
Ranochan 248 A1
Ranscombe 114 C3
Ranskill 187 D4
Ranton 171 F5
Ranton Green 171 F5
Ranworth 179 E4
Rapness 276 E3
Rapps 103 G1
Rascarrel 208 A2
Rash 200 B4
Rashwood 146 B1
Raskelf 203 D5
Rassau 130 A1
Rastrick 194 A5
Ratagan 257 F3
Ratby 160 A2
Ratcliffe Culey 159 F3
Ratcliffe on Soar 173 F5
Ratcliffe on the
Wreake 160 B1
Ratford Bridge 126 B1
Ratfyn 118 C3
Rathen 269 H4
Rathillet 244 B2
Rathliesbeag 249 E1
Rathmell 193 E1
Ratho 235 F2
Ratho Station 235 F2
Rathven 268 C4
Ratley 147 F3
Ratling 125 E3
Ratlinghope 156 D3
Ratsloe 102 C3
Rattar 275 H1
Ratten Row *Cumb* 209 G2
Ratten Row *Lancs* 192 A3
Rattery 100 D1
Rattlesden 152 A2
Rattray 251 G5
Raughton Head 209 G2
Raunds 161 E5
Ravenfield 186 B3
Ravenglass 198 B3
*Ravenglass & Eskdale
Railway Cumb
CA18 1SW 198 C3*
Ravenhills Green 152 C5
Raven's Green 152 C5
Raveningham 165 E2
Ravenscar 204 D3
Ravensdale 190 B2
Ravensden 149 F2
Ravenshall 193 F3
Ravenshayes 102 C3
Ravenshead 173 G2
Ravensmoor 170 D2
Ravensthorpe
N'hants 160 B5
Ravensthorpe
WYorks 194 B5
Ravenstone *Leics* 159 G1
Ravenstone *MK* 149 D2
Ravenstonedale 200 C2
Ravenstruther 234 D5
Ravensworth 202 A2
Raw 204 C2
Rawcliffe *ERid* 195 F5
Rawcliffe *York* 195 E3
Rawcliffe Bridge 195 F5
Rawdon 194 B4
Rawmarsh 186 B3
Rawnsley 158 C1
Rawreth 137 G3
Rawridge 103 F2
Rawson Green 173 E3
Rawtenstall 193 E5
Rawyards 234 B3
Raxton 261 G1
Raydon 152 B4
Raylees 220 B2
Rayleigh 138 B3
Raymond's Hill 103 G3
Rayne 151 F5
Rayners Lane 136 A4
Raynes Park 122 B2
Reach 151 D1
Read 193 D4
Reading 134 C5
Reading Green 164 C4
Reading Street 124 B5
Reagill 200 B1
*Real Mary King's Close, The
Edin EH1 1PG 37 H6*
Rearquhar 266 E2
Rearsby 160 B1
Rease Heath 170 D2
Reaster 275 H2
Reaveley 229 E5
Reawick 279 C8
Reay 274 E2
Reculver 125 E2
Red Ball 103 D1
Red Bull 171 F2
Red Dial 209 F2
Red Hill *Hants* 107 G1
Red Hill *Warks* 146 D2
Red Lodge 163 E5
Red Oaks Hill 151 D4
Red Point 264 D5
Red Post *Corn* 112 C5
Red Post *Devon* 101 E1
Red Rail 145 E5
Red Rock 183 G2
Red Roses 127 F1
Red Row 221 E2
Red Street 171 F2
*Red Wharf Bay
(Traeth Coch) 180 D4*
Redberth 127 D2
Redbourn 136 A1
Redbourne 188 A3
Redbrook *Glos* 131 E1
Redbrook *Wrex* 170 C3
Redbrook Street 124 B5
Redburn *High* 266 C5
Redburn *High* 267 G7
Redburn *N'umb* 211 D1
Redcar 213 F5
Redcastle *Angus* 253 E4
Redcastle *High* 266 C7
Redcliff Bay 130 D5
Redcloak 253 G1
Reddingmuirhead 234 D2
Reddish 184 C3
Redditch 146 C1
Rede 151 G2
Redenhall 165 D3
Redesdale Camp 220 A2

Redesmouth 220 A3
Redford *Aber* 253 F2
Redford *Angus* 253 D5
Redford *Dur* 211 G4
Redford *WSuss* 121 D5
Redgrave 164 B4
Redheugh 252 C3
Redhill *Aber* 260 E1
Redhill *Aber* 261 F4
Redhill *Moray* 268 C5
Redhill *Notts* 173 G3
Redhill *NSom* 116 B1
Redhill *Surr* 122 B3
*Redhill Aerodrome &
Heliport 122 B4*
Redhouse *A&B* 231 G3
Redhouse *Aber* 260 D2
Redhouses 230 B3
Redisham 165 F3
Redland *Bristol* 131 E5
Redland *Ork* 276 C5
Redlingfield 164 C4
Redlynch *Som* 117 E4
Redlynch *Wilts* 118 D5
Redmarley D'Abitot 145 G4
Redmarshall 212 C5
Redmile 174 C4
Redmire 201 F3
Redmoor 97 E3
Rednal 170 A5
Redpath 227 G2
Redruth 96 A5
Redscarhead 235 G5
Redshaw 225 G3
Redstone Bank 127 E1
Redwick *Newport* 130 D4
Redwick *SGlos* 131 E4
Redworth 212 B5
Reed 150 B4
Reed End 150 B4
Reedham 179 F5
Reedley 193 E4
Reedness 195 G5
Reef (Riof) 270 D4
Reepham *Lincs* 188 A5
Reepham *Norf* 178 B3
Reeth 201 F3
Regaby 190 C2
Regil 116 C1
Regoul 267 F6
Reiff 272 B7
Reigate 122 B3
Reighton 205 E5
Reisgill 275 H5
Reiss 275 J3
Rejerrah 96 C4
Releath 95 D3
Relubbus 94 C3
Relugas 267 G7
Remenham 134 C4
Remenham Hill 134 C4
Remony 250 C5
Rempstone 173 G5
Rendcomb 132 C1
Rendham 153 E1
Rendlesham 153 E2
Renfrew 233 G3
Renhold 149 F2
Renishaw 186 B5
Rennington 229 G5
Renton 233 E2
Renwick 210 B3
Repps 179 F4
Repton 173 E5
Rescobie 252 D4
Rescorla 97 E4
Resipole 247 G3
Resolfen 129 E2
Resolis 266 D5
Resolven 129 E2
Resourie 248 A2
Resipryn 97 F3
Reston 237 F3
Restormel 97 F3
Reswallie 252 D4
Reterth 96 D3
Retew 96 D4
Retford
(East Retford) 187 E4
Rettendon 137 G3
Rettendon Place 137 G3
Retyn 96 C4
Revesby 176 A1
Revesby Bridge 176 B1
Rew 102 A5
Rew Street 107 D3
Rewe *Devon* 102 C3
Rewe *Devon* 102 B3
Reybridge 118 A1
Reydon 165 F4
Reydon Smear 165 G4
Reymerston 178 B5
Reynalton 127 D2
Reynoldston 128 A4
Rezare 99 D3
Rhadyr 130 C2
Rhandirmwyn 143 D3
Rhaoine 266 D1
Rhayader
(Rhaeadr Gwy) 143 F1
Rhedyn 166 B4
*Rheged - the Village in the
Hill Cumb
CA11 0DQ 210 A5*
Rhegreanoch 272 C7
Rheindown 266 C7
Rhelonie 266 C2
Rhemore 247 E4
Rhenigidale
(Reinigeadal) 270 E7
Rheola 129 E2
Rhes-y-cae 169 E1
Rhewl *Denb* 169 E3
Rhewl *Denb* 169 E1
Rhewl *Shrop* 170 A4
Rhian 273 H7
Rhicarn 272 C6
Rhiconich 272 E3
Rhicullen 266 D4
Rhidorroch 265 H2
Rhifail 274 C3
Rhigos 129 F2
Rhilochan 266 E1
Rhinduie 266 C7
Rhireavach 265 G2
Rhiroy 265 H3
Rhiston 156 B3
Rhiw 166 B5
Rhiwargor 168 C5

Rhiwbina 130 A4
Rhiwbryfdir 167 F3
Rhiwderin 130 B4
Rhiwinder 129 G4
Rhiwlas Gwyn 167 E1
Rhiwlas Gwyn 168 C4
Rhiwlas Powys 169 F4
Rhode 115 F4
Rhodes Minnis 124 D4
Rhodesia 186 C5
Rhodiad-y-brenin 140 A5
Rhodmad 154 B5
Rhonadale 222 C2
Rhonehouse
(Kelton Hill) 216 B5
Rhoose 115 D1
Rhos Carmar 141 G4
Rhos NPT 128 D2
Rhos Common 156 B1
Rhosaman 128 D1
Rhoscolyn 180 A5
Rhoscrowther 126 C2
Rhosesmor 169 F1
Rhos-fawr 166 C4
Rhosgadfan 167 E2
Rhos-goch IoA 180 C4
Rhosgoch Powys 144 A3
Rhos-hill 141 E3
Rhoshirwaun 166 A5
Rhoslan 167 D3
Rhoslefain 154 B2
Rhosllanerchrugog 169 F3
Rhoslligwy 180 C4
Rhosmaen 142 C5
Rhosmeirch 180 C5
Rhosneigr 180 B5
Rhosnesni 170 A2
Rhôs-on-Sea 181 G4
Rhossili 128 A4
Rhosson 140 A5
Rhostrehwfa 180 C5
Rhostryfan 167 D2
Rhostyllen 170 A3
Rhos-y-bol 180 C4
Rhos-y-brithdir 169 E5
Rhosycaerau 140 C4
Rhos-y-garth 154 C5
Rhos-y-gwaliau 168 C4
Rhos-y-llan 166 B4
Rhos-y-mawn 168 B1
Rhos-y-Meirch 144 B1
Rhu 233 D1
Rhuallt 182 B5
Rhubodach 232 B2
Rhuddall Heath 170 C1
Rhuddlan 182 B5
Rhue 265 H2
Rhulen 144 A3
Rhumach 247 F1
Rhunahaorine 231 F5
Rhyd Gwyn 167 F3
Rhyd Powys 155 F2
Rhydargaeau 142 A5
Rhydcymerau 142 B4
Rhyd-Ddu 167 E2
Rhydding 128 D3
Rhydgaled 168 C1
Rhydlanfair 168 B2
Rhydlewis 141 G3
Rhydlios 166 A4
Rhydlydan Conwy 168 B2
Rhydlydan Powys 155 G3
Rhydolion 166 B5
Rhydowen 142 A3
Rhyd-Rosser 142 B1
Rhydspence 144 B3
Rhydtalog 169 F2
Rhyd-uchaf 168 B4
Rhyd-wen 168 C5
Rhyd-wyn 180 B4
Rhyd-y-ceirw 169 F2
Rhyd-y-clafdy 166 C4
Rhydycroesau 169 F4
Rhydyfelin Cere 154 B5
Rhydyfelin RCT 129 G4
Rhyd-y-foel 182 A5
Rhyd-y-fro 128 D2
Rhyd-y-groes 167 E1
Rhydymain 168 B5
Rhydymwyn 169 F1
Rhyd-yr-onnen 154 C2
Rhyd-y-sarn 167 F3
Rhydywrach 127 E1
Rhyl 182 B4
Rhyl Sun Centre Denb
LL18 3AQ 182 B4
Rhymney 130 A2
Rhyn 170 A4
Rhynd 243 G2
Rhynie Aber 260 C2
Rhynie High 267 F4
Ribbesford 157 G5
Ribchester 192 C4
Ribigill 273 H3
Riby 188 B2
Riccall 195 F4
Riccarton 224 C2
Richards Castle 145 D1
Richings Park 135 F5
Richmond GtLon 136 A5
Richmond NYorks 202 A2
Richmond SYorks 186 B4
Rich's Holford 115 E4
Rickarton 253 G1
Rickerscote 171 G5
Rickford 116 B2
Rickinghall 164 B4
Rickleton 212 B2
Rickling 150 C4
Rickling Green 150 D5
Rickmansworth 135 F3
Riddell 227 G3
Riddings 173 F2
Riddlecombe 113 G4
Riddlesden 193 G3
Ridge Dorset 105 F4
Ridge Herts 136 B2
Ridge Wilts 118 A4
Ridge Green 122 C4
Ridge Lane 159 E3
Ridgebourne 143 G1
Ridgeway 186 B4
Ridgeway Cross 145 G3
Ridgeway Moor 186 B4
Ridgewell 151 F3
Ridgewood 109 G1
Ridgmont 149 E4
Ridham Dock 124 B2
Riding Gate 117 E5
Riding Mill 211 G1
Ridley 123 F2
Ridleywood 170 A2
Ridlington Norf 179 E2
Ridlington Rut 160 D2
Ridsdale 220 B3
Riechip 251 F5
Rievaulx 203 E4
Rift House 213 D4
Rigg D&G 218 A5
Rigg High 264 B6
Riggend 234 B3
Rigifa 275 J1
Rigmaden Park 200 B4
Rigsby 189 E5
Rigside 225 G2
Riley Green 192 C5
Rileyhill 158 D1
Rilla Mill 97 G2
Rillaton 97 G2
Rillington 204 B5
Rimington 193 E3
Rimpton 116 D5
Rimswell 197 F5
Rinaston 140 C5
Ring o' Bells 183 F1
Ringford 216 A5
Ringinglow 185 G4
Ringland 178 C4
Ringles Cross 109 G1
Ringmer 109 G2
Ringmore Devon 100 C3
Ringmore Devon 102 C5
Ringorm 267 K7
Ring's End 162 B2
Ringsfield 165 F3
Ringsfield Corner 165 F3
Ringshall Herts 135 E1
Ringshall Suff 152 B2
Ringshall Stocks 152 B2
Ringstead N'hants 161 E5
Ringstead Norf 177 F3
Ringwood 106 A2
Ringwould 125 F4
Rinloan 259 K4
Rinmore 260 C3
Rinnigill 277 C8
Rinsey 94 C4
Ripe 110 A3
Ripley Derbys 173 E2
Ripley Hants 106 A3
Ripley NYorks 194 B1
Ripley Surr 121 F2
Riplingham 196 B4
Ripon 202 C5
Rippingale 175 G5
Ripple Kent 125 F4
Ripple Worcs 146 A4
Ripponden 185 E1
Risabus 230 B5
Risbury 145 E2
Risby ERid 196 C4
Risby Suff 151 F1
Risca 130 B3
Rise 197 D3
Riseden 123 G5
Risegate 176 A5
Riseholme 187 G5
Riseley Bed 149 F1
Riseley W'ham 120 C1
Rishangles 152 C1
Rishton 192 D4
Rishworth 185 E1
Risinghurst 134 A2
Risley Derbys 173 F4
Risley Warr 184 A3
Risplith 194 B1
Rispond 273 G2
Rivar 119 E1
Rivenhall 138 B1
Rivenhall End 138 B1
River Kent 125 F4
River WSuss 121 E5
River Bank 150 D1
River Bridge 116 A3
River Link Boat Cruises
Devon TQ6 9AJ 101 E3
Riverford Bridge 101 D1
Riverhead 123 E3
Riverside 130 A5
Riverside Country Park Med
ME7 2XH 124 A2
Riverside Museum &
Tall Ship Glenlee
Glas G3 8RS 30 C3
Riverton 113 G2
Riverview Park 137 F5
Riviera International Centre
Torbay TQ2 5LZ
87 Torquay
Rivington 184 A1
Roa Island 191 F1
Roach Bridge 192 B5
Road Green 165 D2
Road Weedon 148 B2
Roade 148 C2
Roadhead 218 D4
Roadside High 275 G2
Roadside Ork 276 F3
Roadside of Kinneff 253 G2
Roadwater 114 D4
Roag 263 H7
Roast Green 150 C4
Roath 130 A5
Robert Burns Birthplace
Museum SAyr
KA7 4PQ 224 B4
Roberton ScBord 227 F4
Roberton SLan 226 A3
Robertsbridge 110 C1
Robertstown
Moray 267 K7
Robertstown RCT 129 G2
Roberttown 194 A5
Robeston Cross 126 B2
Robeston Wathen 127 D1
Robeston West 126 B2
Robin Hill Countryside
Adventure Park IoW
PO30 2NU 107 E4
Robin Hood
Derbys 185 G5
Robin Hood Lancs 183 G1
Robin Hood WYorks 194 C5
Robin Hood Doncaster
Sheffield Airport 187 D3
Robin Hood's Bay 204 C2
Robinhood End 151 F4
Robins 120 D5
Robinswood Hill Country
Park Glos
GL4 6SX 132 A1
Roborough Devon 113 F4
Roborough Plym 100 B1
Roby 183 F3
Roby Mill 183 G2
Rocester 172 C4
Roch 140 B5
Roch Bridge 140 B5
Roch Gate 140 B5
Rochallie 251 G4
Rochdale 184 C1
Roche 97 D3
Rochester Med 123 G2
Rochester N'umb 220 A2
Rochester Cathedral Med
ME1 1SX 123 G2
Rochford Essex 138 B3
Rochford Worcs 145 F1
Rock Corn 96 D2
Rock N'umb 229 G5
Rock Worcs 157 G5
Rock Ferry 183 E4
Rockbeare 102 D3
Rockbourne 106 A1
Rockcliffe Cumb 218 B5
Rockcliffe D&G 216 C5
Rockcliffe Cross 218 B5
Rockfield A&B 231 G4
Rockfield High 267 G3
Rockfield Mon 131 D1
Rockford 106 A2
Rockhampton 131 F3
Rockhead 97 E1
Rockingham 161 D3
Rockland All Saints 164 A2
Rockland St. Mary 179 E5
Rockland St. Peter 164 A2
Rockley 133 D5
Rockside 230 A3
Rockwell End 134 C4
Rockwell Green 103 E1
Rodborough 132 A2
Rodbourne 132 B4
Rodbridge Corner 151 G3
Rodd 144 C1
Roddam 229 E4
Rodden 104 C4
Rode 117 F2
Rode Heath 171 F2
Rodeheath 171 F1
Rodel (Roghadal) 263 F3
Roden 157 E1
Rodhuish 114 D4
Rodington 157 E1
Rodington Heath 157 E1
Rodley 131 G1
Rodmarton 132 B3
Rodmell 109 G3
Rodmersham 124 B2
Rodmersham Green 124 B2
Rodney Stoke 116 B2
Rodsley 172 D3
Rodway 115 F3
Roe Cross 185 D3
Roe Green 150 B4
Roecliffe 194 C1
Roehampton 136 B5
Roesound 279 C6
Roffey 121 G4
Rogart 266 E1
Rogate 120 D5
Rogerstone 130 B4
Rogiet 131 D4
Rokemarsh 134 B3
Roker 212 D2
Rollesby 179 F4
Rolleston Leics 160 C2
Rolleston Notts 174 C2
Rollestone 118 B3
Rolleston-on-Dove 172 D5
Rolston 197 E3
Rolstone 116 A1
Rolvenden 124 A5
Rolvenden Layne 124 A5
Romaldkirk 211 F5
Roman Baths & Pump Room
B&NESom BA1 1LZ
63 Bath
Romanby 202 C3
Romanno Bridge 235 F5
Romansleigh 114 A5
Romesdal 263 K6
Romford Dorset 105 G2
Romford GtLon 137 E4
Romiley 184 D3
Romney, Hythe &
Dymchurch Railway
Kent TN28 8PL 124 D5
Romney Street 123 E2
Romsey 119 E5
Romsley Shrop 157 G4
Romsley Worcs 158 B5
Rona 264 C6
Ronachan 231 F4
Ronague 190 A4
Ronnachmore 230 B4
Rood End 158 C4
Rookhope 211 F3
Rookley 107 E4
Rookley Green 107 E4
Rooks Bridge 116 A2
Rook's Nest 115 D4
Rookwith 202 B4
Roos 197 E4
Roose 191 F1
Roosebeck 191 F1
Roosecote 191 F1
Rootham's Green 149 F2
Rootpark 235 D4
Ropley 120 B4
Ropley Dean 120 B4
Ropley Soke 120 B4
Ropsley 175 E4
Rora 269 J5
Rorandle 260 E3
Rorrington 156 C2
Rosarie 268 B6
Rose 96 B4
Rose Ash 114 A5
Rose Green Essex 152 A5
Rose Green WSuss 108 B4
Rose Hill 109 G2
Roseacre Kent 123 G3
Roseacre Lancs 192 A4
Rosebank 234 C5
Rosebrough 229 F4
Rosebush 141 D5
Rosecare 98 B1
Rosecliston 96 C4
Rosedale Abbey 203 G3
Roseden 229 E4
Rosehall 266 B1
Rosehearty 269 H4
Rosehill Aber 260 D5
Rosehill Shrop 157 D1
Roseisle 267 J5
Roselands 110 B3
Rosemarket 126 C2
Rosemarkie 266 E6
Rosemary Lane 103 E1
Rosemount P&K 251 G5
Rosemount SAyr 224 B3
Rosenannon 97 D3
Rosenithon 95 F4
Rosepool 126 B1
Rosevean 97 E4
Roseville 158 B3
Rosewell 235 G3
Roseworth 212 D5
Rosgill 199 G1
Roshven 247 G2
Roskhill 263 H7
Roskorwell 95 E4
Rosley 209 G2
Roslin 235 G3
Rosliston 159 E1
Rosliston Forestry Centre
Derbys
DE12 8JX 159 E1
Rosneath 233 D1
Ross D&G 207 G2
Ross N'umb 229 F3
Ross P&K 242 C2
Ross Priory 233 F1
Rossdhu House 233 E1
Rossett 170 A2
Rossett Green 194 C2
Rosside 199 D5
Rossie Farm School 253 E4
Rossie Ochill 243 F3
Rossie Priory 244 A1
Rossington 186 D3
Rosskeen 266 D5
Rosslyn Chapel Midlo
EH25 9PU 32 D4
Rossmore 105 G3
Ross-on-Wye 145 F5
Roster 275 H5
Rostherne 184 B4
Rosthwaite Cumb 209 F5
Rosthwaite Cumb 198 D4
Roston 172 C3
Rosudgeon 94 C4
Rosyth 235 F1
Rothbury 220 C1
Rother Valley Country Park
SYorks S26 5PQ 21 E3
Rotherby 160 B1
Rotherfield 123 E5
Rotherfield Greys 134 C4
Rotherfield Peppard 134 C4
Rotherham 186 B3
Rothersthorpe 148 C2
Rotherwick 120 C2
Rothes 267 K7
Rothesay 232 B3
Rothiebrisbane 261 F1
Rothiemurchus High
PH22 1QH 259 G4
Rothienorman 261 F1
Rothiesholm 276 F5
Rothley Leics 160 A1
Rothley N'umb 220 C3
Rothney 260 E2
Rothwell Lincs 188 B3
Rothwell N'hants 160 D4
Rothwell WYorks 194 C5
Rotsea 196 C2
Rottal 252 B3
Rotten Row Bucks 134 C4
Rotten Row WMid 159 D5
Rottingdean 109 F3
Rottington 208 C5
Roud 107 E4
Roudham 164 A3
Rough Close 171 G4
Rough Common 124 D3
Rougham Norf 177 G5
Rougham Suff 152 A1
Rougham Green 152 A1
Roughburn 249 F1
Roughlee 193 E3
Roughley 158 D3
Roughton Lincs 176 A1
Roughton Norf 178 D2
Roughton Shrop 157 G3
Round Bush 136 A3
Roundbush Green 137 E1
Roundham 104 A2
Roundhay 194 C4
Roundstreet
Common 121 F5
Roundway 118 B1
Rous Lench 146 C2
Rousay 276 D4
Rousdon 103 F3
Rousham 147 G5
Rousham Gap 147 G5
Routenburn 232 C3
Routh 196 C3
Rout's Green 134 C3
Row Corn 97 E2
Row Cumb 199 F4
Row Cumb 210 C4
Row Heath 139 E1
Row Town 121 F1
Rowanburn 218 C4
Rowardennan
Lodge 241 F5
Rowarth 185 E4
Rowbarton 115 F5
Rowberrow 116 B2
Rowchoish 241 F4
Rowde 118 A1
Rowden 99 G1
Rowen 181 F5
Rowfields 172 C3
Rowfoot 210 C1
Rowhedge 152 B5
Rowhook 121 G4
Rowington 147 E1
Rowland 185 G5
Rowland's Castle 107 G1
Rowlands Gill 212 A2
Rowledge 120 D3
Rowlestone 144 C5
Rowley Devon 102 A1
Rowley Dur 211 G3
Rowley Shrop 156 C2
Rowley Park 171 G5
Rowley Regis 158 B4
Rowly 121 F3
Rowner 107 E2
Rowney Green 158 C5
Rownhams 106 C1
Rowrah 209 D5
Rowsham 135 D1
Rowsley 173 D1
Rowstock 133 G4
Rowston 175 F2
Rowthorne 173 F1
Rowton
ChesW&C 170 B1
Rowton Shrop 156 C1
Rowton Tel&W 157 F1
Roxburgh 228 B3
Roxby NLincs 187 G1
Roxby NYorks 203 G1
Roxton 149 G2
Roxwell 137 F2
Royal Academy of Arts
GtLon W1J 0BD 44 C4
Royal Albert Hall GtLon
SW7 2AP 11 F5
Royal Albert Memorial
Museum & Art Gallery
Devon EX4 3RX
72 Exeter
Royal Armouries Museum,
Leeds WYorks
LS10 1LT 41 G5
Royal Artillery Barracks
GtLon SE18 5DP 13 F5
Royal Bath & West
Showground Som
BA4 6QN 116 D4
Royal Botanic Garden,
Edinburgh Edin
EH3 5LR 36 D1
Royal Botanic Gardens,
Kew GtLon
TW9 3AB 11 C6
Royal British Legion
Village 123 G3
Royal Centre NG1 5ND
80 Nottingham
Royal Cornwall Museum
Corn TR1 2SJ 96 C5
Royal Festival Hall GtLon
SE1 8XX 45 F5
Royal Highland Showground
Edin EH28 8NB 32 A2
Royal Horticultural Halls
GtLon SW1P 2PB 44 D7
Royal Hospital Chelsea
GtLon SW3 4SR 13 A5
Royal Leamington
Spa 147 F1
Royal Mews, Buckingham
Palace GtLon
SW1W 0QH 44 B6
Royal Naval Museum
PO1 3NH
82 Portsmouth
Royal Oak 183 F2
Royal Observatory
Greenwich GtLon
SE10 8XJ 13 D5
Royal Opera House GtLon
WC2E 9DD 45 E3
Royal Pavilion B&H
BN1 1EE 65 Brighton
Royal Scots Regimental
Museum, The Edin
EH1 2YT 37 E5
Royal Scottish Academy
Edin EH2 2EL 37 F4
Royal Tunbridge
Wells 123 E5
Royal Victoria Country Park
Hants SO31 5GA 4 C4
Royal Welch Fusiliers
Regimental Museum
Gwyn
LL55 2AY 167 D1
Royal Wootton
Bassett 132 C4
Royal Yacht Britannia
Edin EH6 6JJ 32 C1
Roybridge (Drochaid
Ruaidh) 249 E1
Roydon Essex 136 D1
Roydon Norf 164 B3
Roydon Norf 177 F5
Roydon Hamlet 136 D2
Royston Herts 150 B3
Royston SYorks 186 A1
Royton 184 D2
Rozel 100 C5
Ruabon (Rhiwabon) 170 A3
Ruaig 246 B2
Ruan Lanihorne 96 C5
Ruan Major 95 D5
Ruan Minor 95 E5
Ruanaich 238 B2
Ruardean 131 F1
Ruardean Hill 131 F1
Ruardean Woodside 131 F1
Rubery 158 B5
Ruckcroft 210 B3
Ruckinge 124 C5
Ruckland 188 D5
Rucklers Lane 135 F2
Ruckley 157 E2
Rudbaxton 140 C5
Rudby 203 D2
Rudchester 212 A1
Ruddington 173 G4
Ruddlemoor 97 E4
Rudford 145 G5
Rudge 117 F2
Rudgeway 131 F4
Rudgwick 121 F4
Rudhall 145 F5
Rudheath 184 A5
Rudley Green 138 B2
Rudloe 117 F1
Rudry 130 A4
Rudston 196 C1
Rudyard 171 G2
Rudyard Lake Staffs
ST13 8RT 171 G2
Rufford 183 F1
Rufford Country Park Notts
NG22 9DF 174 B1
Rufforth 195 E2
Ruffside 211 F2
Rugby 160 A5
Rugby Football Union,
Twickenham GtLon
TW1 1DZ 11 B6
Rugeley 158 C1
Ruilick 266 C7
Ruishton 115 F5
Ruisigearraidh 262 E3
Ruislip 135 F4
Ruislip Gardens 135 F4
Ruislip Manor 136 A4
Rum 255 J5
Rumbling Bridge 243 F5
Rumburgh 165 E3
Rumford 96 C2
Rumleigh 100 A1
Rumney 130 B5
Rumwell 115 E5
Runacraig 242 A3
Runcorn 183 G4
Runcton 108 A3
Runcton Holme 163 E2
Rundlestone 99 F3
Runfold 121 D3
Runhall 178 B5
Runham Norf 179 F4
Runham Norf 179 G5
Runnington 115 E5
Runsell Green 137 G2
Runshaw Moor 183 G1
Runswick Bay 204 B1
Runtaleave 252 A3
Runwell 137 G3
Ruscombe Glos 132 A2
Ruscombe
W'ham 134 C5
Rush Green
GtLon 137 E4
Rush Green Herts 150 A5
Rushall Here 145 F4
Rushall Norf 164 C3
Rushall Wilts 118 C2
Rushall WMid 158 C2
Rushbrooke 151 G1
Rushbury 157 E3
Rushden Herts 150 B4
Rushden N'hants 149 E1
Rushford Devon 99 E3
Rushford Norf 164 A3
Rushgreen 184 A4
Rushlake Green 110 B2
Rushmere 165 F3
Rushmere
St. Andrew 152 D3
Rushmoor 121 D3
Rushock 158 A5
Rusholme 184 C3
Rushton ChesW&C
170 C1
Rushton N'hants 160 D4
Rushton Shrop 157 F2
Rushton Spencer 171 G1
Rushwick 146 A2
Rushy Green 109 G2
Rushyford 212 B5
Ruskie 242 B4
Ruskington 175 F2
Rusko 215 G5
Rusland 199 E4
Rusper 122 B5
Ruspidge 131 F1
Russ Hill 122 B4
Russel 264 E7
Russell Green 137 G1
Russell's Green 110 C2
Russell's Water 134 C3
Russel's Green 165 D4
Rusthall 123 E5
Rustington 108 C3
Ruston 204 C4
Ruston Parva 196 C1
Ruswarp 204 B2
Rutherend 234 A4
Rutherford 228 A3
Rutherglen 234 A3
Ruthernbridge 97 E3
Ruthers of Howe 275 J2
Ruthin (Rhuthun)
Denb 169 E2
Ruthin VGlam 129 F5
Ruthrieston 261 H4
Ruthven Aber 268 D6
Ruthven Angus 252 A5
Ruthven High 259 F1
Ruthven High 258 E5
Ruthvoes 96 D3
Ruthwaite 209 F3
Ruthwell 217 E4
Rutland Water Rut
LE15 8QL 161 D2
Ruyton-XI-Towns 170 A5
Ryal 220 C4
Ryal Fold 192 C5
Ryall Dorset 104 A3
Ryall Worcs 146 A3
Ryarsh 123 F3
Rydal 199 E2
Ryde 107 E3
Rydon 112 D5
Rye 111 E1
Rye Foreign 111 D1
Rye Harbour 111 E2
Rye Park 136 C2
Rye Street 145 G4
Ryebank 170 C4
Ryeford 145 F5
Ryehill Aber 260 E2
Ryehill ERid 197 E5
Ryhall 161 F1
Ryhill 186 A1
Ryhope 212 D2
Rylands 173 G4
Rylstone 193 F2
Ryme Intrinseca 104 B1
Ryther 195 E4
Ryton Glos 145 G4
Ryton NYorks 203 G5
Ryton Shrop 157 G2
Ryton T&W 212 A1
Ryton-on-
Dunsmore 159 F5

S

S.S. Great Britain Bristol
BS1 6TY 8 B3
Saasaig 256 C4
Sabden 193 D4
Sabden Fold 193 E4
Sackers Green 152 A4
Sacombe 136 C1
Sacombe Green 136 C1
Sacriston 212 B3
Sadberge 202 C1
Saddell 222 C2
Saddington 160 B3
Saddle Bow 163 E1
Sadgill 199 F2
Saffron Walden 150 D4
Sageston 127 D2
Saham Hills 178 A5
Saham Toney 163 G2
Saighdinis 262 D5
Saighton 170 B1
St. Abbs 237 G3
St. Agnes 96 B4
St. Aidan's Winery N'umb
TD15 2RX 229 F2
St. Albans 136 A2
St. Albans Cathedral Herts
AL1 1BY 136 A2
St. Allen 96 C4
St. Andrews 244 D3
St. Andrew's & Blackfriars
Halls Norf NR3 1AU
79 Norwich
St. Andrews Major 130 A5
St. Anne 101 G4
St. Anne's 191 G5
St. Ann's 217 E1
St. Ann's Chapel
Corn 99 E3
St. Ann's Chapel
Devon 100 C3
St. Anthony 95 F3
St. Anthony-in-
Meneage 95 E4
St. Anthony's Hill 110 B3
St. Arvans 131 E3
St. Asaph
(Llanelwy) 182 B5
St. Athan 114 D1
St. Aubin 100 C5
St. Audries 115 E3
St. Austell 97 E4
St. Bees 208 C5
St. Blazey 97 E4
St. Blazey Gate 97 E4
St. Boswells 227 G2
St. Botolph's Church, Boston
Lincs PE21 6NP 176 B3
St. Brelade 100 B5
St. Breock 97 D2
St. Breward 97 E2
St. Briavels 131 E2
St. Brides 126 B1
St. Brides Major 129 E5
St. Bride's
Netherwent 130 D4
St. Brides
Wentlooge 130 B4
St. Bride's-super-
Ely 129 G5
St. Budeaux 100 A2
St. Buryan 94 B4
St. Catherine 117 E1
St. Catherines 240 D4
St. Clears (Sanclêr) 127 F1
St. Cleer 97 G3
St. Clement Chanl 100 C5
St. Clement Corn 96 C5
St. Clether 97 G1
St. Colmac 232 B3
St. Columb Major 96 D3
St. Columb Minor 96 C3
St. Columb Road 96 D4
St. Combs 269 J4
St. Cross South
Elmham 165 D3
St. Cyrus 253 F3
St. Davids Fife 235 F1
St. David's P&K 243 E2
St. David's (Tyddewi)
Pembs 140 A5
St. David's Hall CF10 1AH
67 Cardiff
St. Day 96 B5
St. Decumans 115 D3
St. Dennis 97 D4
St. Denys 106 D1
St. Dogmaels
(Llandudoch) 141 E3
St. Dogwells 140 C5
St. Dominick 100 A1
St. Donats 114 C1
St. Edith's Marsh 118 A1
St. Endellion 97 D2
St. Enoder 96 C4
St. Erme 96 C5
St. Erney 99 D5
St. Erth 94 C3
St. Erth Praze 94 C3
St. Ervan 96 C2
St. Eval 96 C3
St. Ewe 97 D5
St. Fagans 130 A5
St. Fagans National History
Museum Cardiff
CF5 6XB 7 A4
St. Fergus 269 J5
St. Fillans 242 B2
St. Florence 127 D2
St. Gennys 98 B1
St. George Bristol 131 F5
St. George Conwy 182 A5
St. Georges NSom 116 A1
St. George's Tel&W 157 G1
St. George's
VGlam 129 G5
St. George's Hall, Liverpool
Mersey L1 1JJ 42 D3
St. Germans 99 D5
St. Giles' Cathedral,
Edinburgh Edin
EH1 1RE 37 F4
St. Giles in the
Wood 113 F4
St. Giles on the
Heath 99 D1
St. Harmon 155 F5

St. Helen Auckland **212** A5
St. Helena **178** C4
St. Helen's *ESuss* **110** D2
St. Helens *IoW* **107** F4
St. Helens *Mersey* **183** G3
St. Helier *Chanl* **100** C5
St. Helier *GtLon* **122** B2
St. Hilary *Corn* **94** C3
St. Hilary *VGlam* **129** G5
St. Hill **122** C5
St. Illtyd **130** B2
St. Ippolitts **149** G5
St. Ishmael **127** G2
St. Ishmael's **126** B2
St. Issey **96** D2
St. Ive **98** D4
St. Ives *Cambs* **162** B5
St. Ives *Corn* **94** C2
St. Ives *Dorset* **106** A2
St. James South
  Elmham **165** E3
St. John *Chanl* **100** C4
St. John *Corn* **100** A2
St. John the Baptist Church,
  Cirencester *Glos*
  GL7 2NX **132** C2
St. John's *GtLon* **136** C5
St. John's *IoM* **190** A3
St. John's *Surr* **121** E2
St. John's *Worcs* **146** A2
St. John's Chapel
  Devon **113** F3
St. John's Chapel
  Dur **211** E4
St. John's Fen End **162** D1
St. John's Hall **211** G4
St. John's Highway **162** D1
St. John's Kirk **226** D1
St. John's Town of
  Dalry **216** A2
St. Judes **190** B2
St. Just **94** A3
St. Just in Roseland **95** F3
St. Katherines **261** F1
St. Keverne **95** E4
St. Kew **97** E2
St. Kew Highway **97** E2
St. Keyne **97** G3
St. Lawrence *Corn* **97** E3
St. Lawrence *Essex* **138** C1
St. Lawrence *IoW* **107** E5
St. Lawrence's Church,
  Eyam *Derbys*
  S32 5QH **185** G5
St. Leonards
  Bucks **135** E2
St. Leonards
  Dorset **106** A2
St. Leonards
  ESuss **110** D3
St. Leonards
  Grange **106** D3
St. Leonard's Street **123** F3
St. Levan **94** A4
St. Lythans **130** A5
St. Mabyn **97** E2
St. Madoes **243** G2
St. Margaret South
  Elmham **165** E3
St. Margarets
  Here **144** C4
St. Margarets
  Herts **136** C1
St. Margarets
  Wilts **118** D1
St. Margaret's at
  Cliffe **125** F3
St. Margaret's Hope **277** D8
St. Mark's **190** A4
St. Martin *Chanl* **101** F5
St. Martin *Chanl* **100** C5
St. Martin *Corn* **97** G4
St. Martin *Corn* **95** E4
St. Martin-in-the-Fields
  Church *GtLon*
  WC2N 4JH **44** E4
St. Martins *P&K* **243** G1
St. Martin's *Shrop* **170** A4
St. Mary **100** C5
St. Mary Bourne **119** F2
St. Mary Church **129** G5
St. Mary Cray **123** D2
St. Mary Hill **129** F5
St. Mary Hoo **137** G5
St. Mary in the
  Marsh **111** F1
St. Mary Magdalene Chapel,
  Sandringham *Norf*
  PE35 6EH **177** E5
St. Mary the Virgin Church,
  Holy Island *N'umb*
  TD15 2RX **229** F2
St. Mary the Virgin Church,
  Oxford *Oxon*
  OX1 4AH **134** A2
St. Mary the Virgin Church,
  Rye *ESuss*
  TN31 7HE **111** E2
St. Marychurch **207** F1
St. Mary's *IoS* **96** B1
St. Mary's *Ork* **277** D7
St. Mary's Airport **96** B1
St. Mary's Bay **111** F1
St. Mary's Church, Whitby
  NYorks
  YO22 4JT **204** D1
St. Mary's Grove **116** B1
St. Maughans
  Green **131** D1
St. Mawes **95** F3
St. Mawgan **96** C3
St. Mellion **99** D4
St. Mellons **130** B4
St. Merryn **96** C2
St. Mewan **97** D4
St. Michael Caerhays **97** D5
St. Michael Church **116** A4
St. Michael Penkevil **96** C4
St. Michael South
  Elmham **165** E3
St. Michaels *Fife* **244** C2
St. Michaels *Kent* **124** A5
St. Michaels *Worcs* **145** E1
St. Michael's Church,
  Hathersage *Derbys*
  S32 1AJ **185** G4

St. Michael's Mount *Corn*
  TR17 0HT **94** C3
St. Michael's on
  Wyre **192** A3
St. Mildred's Church,
  Whippingham *IoW*
  PO32 6LP **107** E3
St. Minver **97** D2
St. Monans **244** D4
St. Mungo Museum of
  Religious Life & Art
  Glas G4 0RH **39** H3
St. Mungo's Cathedral,
  Glasgow *Glas*
  G4 0QZ **39** J3
St. Neot **97** E3
St. Neots **149** G1
St. Newlyn East **96** C4
St. Nicholas *Pembs* **140** C4
St. Nicholas *VGlam* **129** G5
St. Nicholas at
  Wade **125** E2
St. Ninians **242** C5
St. Osyth **139** E1
St. Ouen **100** B5
St. Owen's Cross **145** E5
St. Paul's Cathedral,
  London *GtLon*
  EC4M 8AD **45** J3
St. Paul's Cray **123** D2
St. Paul's Walden **149** G5
St. Peter **100** C5
St. Peter Port **101** F5
St. Peter's **125** F2
St. Petrox **126** C3
St. Pinnock **97** G3
St. Quivox **224** B3
St. Ruan **95** E5
St. Sampson **101** F4
St. Saviour *Chanl* **101** E5
St. Saviour *Chanl* **100** C5
St. Stephen **96** D4
St. Stephens *Corn* **100** A2
St. Stephens *Corn* **98** D2
St. Stephens *Herts* **136** A2
St. Teath **97** E1
St. Thomas **102** C3
St. Tudy **97** E2
St. Twynnells **126** C3
St. Veep **97** F4
St. Vigeans **253** E5
St. Wenn **97** D3
St. Weonards **145** D5
St. Winnow **97** F4
St. Winwaloe's Church,
  Gunwalloe *Corn*
  TR12 7QE **95** D4
Saintbury **146** C4
Salachail **248** C4
Salcombe **100** D4
Salcombe Regis **103** E4
Salcott **138** C1
Sale **184** B3
Sale Green **146** B2
Saleby **189** E5
Salehurst **110** C1
Salem *Carmar* **142** C5
Salem *Cere* **154** C4
Salem *Gwyn* **167** E2
Salen *A&B* **247** E5
Salen *High* **247** F3
Salendine Nook **185** F1
Salesbury **192** C4
Saleway **146** B2
Salford *CenBeds* **149** E4
Salford *GtMan* **184** C3
Salford *Oxon* **147** E5
Salford Priors **146** C2
Salfords **122** B4
Salhouse **179** E4
Saline **243** F5
Salisbury **118** C5
Salisbury Cathedral
  Wilts SP1 2EF
  83 Salisbury
Salkeld Dykes **210** B4
Sallachan **248** B3
Sallachry **240** C3
Sallachy *High* **266** C1
Sallachy *High* **257** F1
Salle **178** C3
Sally Lunn's House
  B&NESom BA1 1NX
  63 Bath
Salmonby **188** D5
Salmond's Muir **245** D1
Salperton **146** C5
Salph End **149** F2
Salsburgh **234** C3
Salt **171** G5
Salt Hill **135** E4
Salt Holme **213** D5
Saltaire **194** A4
Saltash **100** A2
Saltburn **266** E4
Saltburn-by-the-
  Sea **213** F5
Saltburn's Inclined
  Tramway *R&C*
  TS12 1DP **213** F5
Saltby **174** D5
Saltcoats *Cumb* **198** B3
Saltcoats *NAyr* **232** D5
Saltcotes **191** G5
Saltdean **109** F3
Salterbeck **208** C4
Salterforth **193** E3
Saltergate **204** B3
Salterhill **267** K5
Salterswall **170** D1
Saltfleet **189** E3
Saltfleetby All
  Saints **189** E3
Saltfleetby
  St. Clements **189** E3
Saltfleetby St. Peter **189** E4
Saltford **117** D1
Salthaugh Grange **197** E5
Salthouse **178** B1
Saltley **158** C4
Saltmarshe **195** G5
Saltness **277** B8
Saltney **170** A1
Salton **203** G4
Saltrens **113** E3
Saltwell Park, Gateshead
  T&W NE9 5AX **28** B3
Saltwick **221** D4

Saltwood **125** D5
Salum **246** B2
Salvington **108** D3
Salwarpe **146** A1
Salwayash **104** A3
Sambrook **171** E5
Samhla **262** C5
Samlesbury **192** C4
Sampford Arundel **103** E1
Sampford Brett **115** D3
Sampford
  Courtenay **113** G5
Sampford Moor **103** E1
Sampford Peverell **102** D1
Sampford Spiney **99** F3
Samuelston **236** B2
Sanaigmore **230** A2
Sancton **196** B4
Sand *Shet* **279** C8
Sand *Som* **116** B3
Sandaig *A&B* **246** A2
Sandaig *High* **256** D4
Sandaig *High* **256** D3
Sandal Magna **186** A1
Sanday **276** F3
Sanday Airfield **276** F3
Sandbach **171** E1
Sandbank **232** C1
Sandbanks **105** G4
Sandend **268** D4
Sanderstead **122** C2
Sandford *Cumb* **200** C1
Sandford *Devon* **102** B2
Sandford *Dorset* **105** F4
Sandford *IoW* **107** E4
Sandford *NSom* **116** B2
Sandford *Shrop* **170** C4
Sandford *Shrop* **170** A5
Sandford *SLan* **234** B5
Sandford Orcas **116** C5
Sandford St. Martin **147** G5
Sandfordhill **269** K6
Sandford-on-
  Thames **134** A2
Sandgarth **277** E6
Sandgate **125** E5
Sandgreen **215** G5
Sandhaven **269** H4
Sandhead **214** B5
Sandhills *Dorset* **104** C1
Sandhills *Dorset* **104** B2
Sandhills *Surr* **121** E4
Sandhills *WYorks* **194** C4
Sandhoe **211** F1
Sandholme *ERid* **196** A4
Sandholme *Lincs* **176** B4
Sandhurst *BrackF* **120** D1
Sandhurst *Glos* **146** A5
Sandhurst *Kent* **110** C1
Sandhurst Cross **110** C1
Sandhutton **202** C4
Sandiacre **173** F4
Sandilands **189** F4
Sandiway **184** A5
Sandleheath **106** A1
Sandleigh **133** G2
Sandling **123** G2
Sandlow Green **171** E1
Sandness **279** A7
Sandon *Essex* **137** G2
Sandon *Herts* **150** B4
Sandon *Staffs* **171** G5
Sandown **107** F4
Sandplace **97** G4
Sandquoy **276** G3
Sandridge *Devon* **101** E2
Sandridge *Herts* **136** A1
Sandridge *Wilts* **118** A1
Sandringham **177** E5
Sandrocks **109** F1
Sandsend **204** B1
Sandside **199** F4
Sandside House **274** E2
Sandsound **279** C8
Sandtoft **187** E2
Sanduck **102** A4
Sandway **124** A3
Sandwell **158** C4
Sandwell Park Farm *WMid*
  B71 4BG **54** C4
Sandwell Valley Country
  Park *WMid*
  B71 4BG **14** D2
Sandwich **125** F3
Sandwick *Cumb* **199** F1
Sandwick *Shet* **279** D10
Sandwick (Sanndabhaig)
  Na H-ESiar **271** G4
Sandwith **208** C5
Sandy *Carmar* **128** A2
Sandy *CenBeds* **149** G3
Sandy Bank **176** A2
Sandy Haven **126** B2
Sandy Lane *Wilts* **118** A1
Sandy Lane *Wrex* **170** B3
Sandy Lane
  WYorks **194** A4
Sandy Way **107** D4
Sandycroft **170** A1
Sandygate *Devon* **102** B5
Sandygate *IoM* **190** B2
Sandyhills **216** C5
Sandylands **192** A1
Sandypark **102** A4
Sandyway **145** D5
Sangobeg **273** G2
Sankyn's Green **145** G1
Sanna **247** D3
Sannaig **230** B3
Sannox **232** B5
Sanquhar **225** F5
Santon Bridge **198** C2
Santon Downham **163** G4
Sant-y-Nyll **129** G5
Sapcote **159** G3
Sapey Common **145** G1
Sapiston **164** A4
Sapperton *Derbys* **172** C4
Sapperton *Glos* **132** B2
Sapperton *Lincs* **175** F4
Saracen's Head **176** B5
Sarclet **275** J4
Sardis **126** C2
Sarisbury **107** E2
Sark **101** G5

Sark Dark Sky Island **101** G5
Sarn *Bridgend* **129** F4
Sarn *Powys* **156** B3
Sarn Bach **166** C5
Sarn Meyllteyrn **166** B4
Sarnau *Carmar* **127** G1
Sarnau *Cere* **141** G2
Sarnau *Powys* **156** B1
Sarnau *Powys* **143** G4
Sarnesfield **144** C2
Saron *Carmar* **128** C1
Saron *Carmar* **141** G3
Saron *Gwyn* **167** E1
Saron *Gwyn* **167** D2
Sarratt **135** F3
Sarre **125** E2
Sarsden **147** E5
Sarsgrum **273** F2
Sartfield **190** B2
Satley **212** A3
Satron **201** E3
Satterleigh **113** G3
Satterthwaite **199** E3
Sauchen **260** E3
Saucher **243** G1
Sauchie **243** D5
Sauchieburn **253** E3
Saughall **183** E5
Saughall Massie **183** D4
Saughtree **219** D2
Saul **131** G2
Saundby **187** E4
Saundersfoot **127** E2
Saunderton **134** C2
Saunton **113** E2
Sausthorpe **176** B1
Saval **266** C1
Savalbeg **266** C1
Saverley Green **171** G4
Savile Town **194** B5
Sawbridge **148** A1
Sawbridgeworth **137** D1
Sawdon **204** C4
Sawley *Derbys* **173** F4
Sawley *Lancs* **193** D3
Sawley *NYorks* **194** B1
Sawston **150** C3
Sawtry **161** G4
Saxby *Leics* **160** D1
Saxby *Lincs* **188** A4
Saxby All Saints **187** G1
Saxelbye **174** B5
Saxham Street **152** B1
Saxilby **187** F5
Saxlingham **178** B2
Saxlingham Green **164** D2
Saxlingham
  Nethergate **164** D2
Saxlingham Thorpe **164** D2
Saxmundham **153** E1
Saxon Street **151** E2
Saxondale **174** B4
Saxtead **153** D1
Saxtead Green **153** D1
Saxtead Little
  Green **153** D1
Saxthorpe **178** C2
Saxton **195** D4
Sayers Common **109** E2
Scackleton **203** F5
Scadabhagh **263** G2
Scaftworth **187** D3
Scagglethorpe **204** B5
Scaitcliffe **193** D5
Scalasaig **238** C5
Scalby *ERid* **196** A5
Scalby *NYorks* **204** D3
Scaldwell **160** C5
Scale Houses **210** B3
Scaleby **210** A1
Scalebyhill **210** A1
Scales *Cumb* **209** G4
Scales *Cumb* **199** D5
Scalford **174** C5
Scaling **203** G1
Scallasaig **256** E3
Scallastle **239** G1
Scalloway **279** C9
Scalpay (Eilean
  Scalpaigh) **263** H2
Scamblesby **188** C5
Scammadale **240** A2
Scamodale **248** A2
Scampston **204** B5
Scampton **187** G5
Scaniport **261** F3
Scapa **277** D7
Scapegoat Hill **185** E1
Scar **276** F3
Scarborough **204** D4
Scarborough Sea Life &
  Marine Sanctuary
  NYorks
  YO12 6RP **204** D3
Scarcewater **96** D4
Scarcliffe **173** F1
Scarcroft **194** C3
Scardroy **265** J6
Scarff **278** B4
Scarfskerry **275** H1
Scargill **201** F2
Scarinish **246** B2
Scarisbrick **183** E1
Scarning **178** A4
Scarrington **174** C3
Scarrowhill **210** B2
Scarth Hill **183** F2
Scarthingwell **195** D4
Scartho **188** C2
Scarwell **276** B5
Scatraig **258** E1
Scaur (Kippford)
  D&G **216** C5
Scaur *D&G* **216** C3
Scawby **187** G2
Scawby Brook **187** G2
Scawton **203** E4
Scayne's Hill **109** F1
Scealascro **270** D5
Scethrog **144** A5
Schaw **224** C3
Scholar Green **171** F2
Scholes *SYorks* **186** A3
Scholes *WYorks* **194** C4
Scholes *WYorks* **185** F2
Scholes *WYorks* **194** A5

School Green **170** D1
School House **103** E1
Schoose **208** D4
Sciberscross **266** D1
Science Museum *GtLon*
  SW7 2DD **11** F5
Scilly Isles
  (Isles of Scilly) **96** B1
Scissett **185** G1
Sco Ruston **179** D3
Scofton **186** D4
Scole **164** C4
Scolpaig **262** C4
Scone **243** G2
Scones Lethendy **243** G2
Sconser **256** B1
Scoor **238** D3
Scopwick **175** F2
Scorborough **196** C3
Scorrier **96** B5
Scorriton **100** D1
Scorton *Lancs* **192** B3
Scorton *NYorks* **202** B2
Scot Hay **171** E3
Scotby **210** A2
Scotch Corner **202** B2
Scotch Whisky Heritage
  Centre *Edin*
  EH1 2NE **37** F4
Scotforth **192** A2
Scothern **188** A5
Scotland **175** F4
Scotland End **147** F4
Scotland Street **152** A4
Scotland Street School
  Museum of Education
  Glas G5 8QB **38** C7
Scotlandwell **243** G4
Scotnish **231** F1
Scots' Gap **220** C3
Scotston *Aber* **253** F2
Scotston *P&K* **251** E5
Scotstoun **233** G3
Scotstown **248** A3
Scott Willoughby **175** F4
Scotter **187** F2
Scotterthorpe **187** F2
Scottish Exhibition &
  Conference Centre
  (S.E.C.C.) *Glas*
  G3 8YW **38** B4
Scottish National Gallery
  of Modern Art *Edin*
  EH4 3DR **36** B4
Scottish National Portrait
  Gallery *Edin*
  EH2 1JD **37** F3
Scottish Parliament *Edin*
  EH99 1SP **37** H4
Scottish Seabird Centre,
  North Berwick *ELoth*
  EH39 4SS **236** C1
Scottish Wool Centre,
  Aberfoyle *Stir*
  FK8 3UQ **242** A4
Scottlethorpe **175** F5
Scotton *Lincs* **187** F3
Scotton *NYorks* **202** A3
Scotton *NYorks* **194** C2
Scottow **179** D3
Scoughall **236** D1
Scoulton **178** A5
Scounslow Green **172** B5
Scourie **272** D4
Scourie More **272** D4
Scousburgh **279** F9
Scouthead **185** D2
Scrabster **275** G1
Scrafield **176** B1
Scrainwood **220** B5
Scrane End **176** B3
Scraptoft **160** B2
Scratby **179** G4
Scrayingham **195** G2
Scredington **175** F3
Scremby **176** C1
Scremerston **229** E2
Screveton **174** C3
Scriven **194** C2
Scronkey **192** A3
Scrooby **187** D3
Scropton **172** C4
Scrub Hill **176** A2
Scruton **202** C3
Sculthorpe **177** G4
Scunthorpe **187** F1
Scurlage **128** A4
Sea **103** G1
Sea Life Centre, Blackpool
  FY1 **64** Blackpool
Sea Life Centre, Brighton
  B&H BN2 1TB
  65 Brighton
Sea Life Centre, Great
  Yarmouth *Norf*
  NR30 3AH **179** G5
Sea Life Sanctuary,
  Hunstanton *Norf*
  PE36 5BH **177** E3
Sea Mills **131** E5
Sea Palling **179** F3
Seabank **248** B5
Seaborough **104** A2
Seaburn **212** D1
Seacombe **183** E3
Seacroft *Lincs* **177** D1
Seacroft *WYorks* **194** C4
Seadyke **176** B4
Seafield *A&B* **231** G2
Seafield *SAyr* **224** B3
Seafield *WLoth* **235** E3
Seaford **109** G4
Seaforth **183** E3
Seagrave **160** B1
Seagry Heath **132** C4
Seaham **212** D2
Seaham Grange **212** D2
Seahouses **229** G3
Seal **123** E3
Sealand **170** A1
Seale **121** E3
Sea-Life Adventure,
  Southend-on-Sea *S'end*
  SS1 2ER **138** B4

Sealyham **140** C5
Seamer *NYorks* **203** D1
Seamer *NYorks* **204** D4
Seamill **232** C5
SeaQuarium, Rhyl *Denb*
  LL18 3AF **182** B4
Searby **188** A2
Seasalter **124** C2
Seascale **198** B2
Seathorne **177** D1
Seathwaite *Cumb* **209** F5
Seathwaite *Cumb* **198** D3
Seatle **199** E4
Seatoller **209** F5
Seaton *Corn* **98** D5
Seaton *Cumb* **208** D3
Seaton *Devon* **103** F3
Seaton *Dur* **212** C2
Seaton *ERid* **197** D3
Seaton *N'umb* **221** F4
Seaton *Rut* **161** E3
Seaton Burn **221** E4
Seaton Carew **213** E5
Seaton Delaval **221** F4
Seaton Junction **103** F3
Seaton Ross **195** G3
Seaton Sluice **221** F4
Seaton Tramway *Devon*
  EX12 2NQ **103** F3
Seatown *Aber* **269** J5
Seatown *Dorset* **104** A3
Seatown *Moray* **268** D4
Seave Green **203** E2
Seaview **107** F3
Seaville **209** E1
Seavington
  St. Mary **104** A1
Seavington
  St. Michael **104** A1
Seawick **139** E1
Sebastopol **130** B3
Sebergham **209** G2
Seckington **159** E2
Second Coast **265** F2
Sedbergh **200** B3
Sedbury **131** E3
Sedbusk **201** D3
Seddington **149** G3
Sedgeberrow **146** C4
Sedgebrook **175** D4
Sedgefield **212** C5
Sedgeford **177** F4
Sedgehill **117** F5
Sedgemere **159** E5
Sedgley **158** B3
Sedgwick **199** G4
Sedlescombe **110** C2
Sedlescombe
  Street **110** C2
Seend **118** A1
Seend Cleeve **118** A1
Seer Green **135** E3
Seething **165** E2
Sefton **183** E2
Seghill **221** E4
Seifton **157** D4
Seighford **171** F5
Seil **239** G3
Seilebost **263** F2
Seion **167** E1
Seisdon **158** A3
Seisiadar **271** H4
Selattyn **169** F4
Selborne **120** C4
Selby **195** F4
Selham **121** E5
Selhurst **122** C2
Selkirk **227** F3
Sellack **145** E5
Sellafield **198** B2
Sellafield Visitors Centre
  Cumb
  CA20 1PG **198** B2
Sellafirth **278** E3
Sellindge **124** D5
Selling **124** C3
Selly Oak **158** C4
Selmeston **110** A3
Selsdon **122** C2
Selsey **108** A4
Selsfield Common **122** C5
Selside *Cumb* **199** G3
Selside *NYorks* **200** C5
Selsley **132** A2
Selstead **125** E4
Selston **173** F2
Selworthy **114** C3
Semblister **279** C7
Semer **152** A3
Semington **117** F1
Semley **117** F5
Send **121** F2
Send Marsh **121** F2
Senghenydd **130** A3
Sennen **94** A4
Sennen Cove **94** A4
Sennybridge **143** F5
Senwick **207** G2
Sequer's Bridge **100** C2
Serby **186** D4
Serpentine Gallery *GtLon*
  W2 3XA **11** F5
Serrington **118** B4
Sessay **203** D5
Setchey **163** E1
Setley **106** C3
Setter *Shet* **279** E8
Setter *Shet* **279** C7
Settiscarth **277** C6
Settle **193** E1
Settrington **204** B5
Seven Ash **115** E4
Seven Bridges **132** D3
Seven Kings **137** D4
Seven Sisters **129** E2
Seven Springs **132** B1
Sevenhampton
  Glos **146** C5
Sevenhampton
  Swin **133** E3
Sevenoaks **123** E3
Sevenoaks Weald **123** E3
Severn Beach **131** E4

Severn Stoke **146** A3
Severn Valley Railway
  Shrop
  DY12 1BG **157** G4
Sevick End **149** F2
Sevington **124** C4
Sewards End **151** D4
Sewardstone **136** C3
Sewerby **197** D1
Sewerby Hall & Gardens
  ERid
  YO15 1EA **197** E1
Seworgan **95** E3
Sewstern **175** D5
Seymour Villas **113** E1
Sezincote **147** D4
Sgarasta Mhòr **263** F2
Sgiogarstaigh **271** H1
Sgodachail **266** B2
Shabbington **134** B2
Shackerley **158** A2
Shackerstone **159** F2
Shackleford **121** E3
Shadfen **221** E3
Shadforth **212** C3
Shadingfield **165** F3
Shadoxhurst **124** B5
Shadsworth **192** D5
Shadwell *Norf* **164** A3
Shadwell *WYorks* **194** C3
Shaftenhoe End **150** C4
Shaftesbury **117** F5
Shafton **186** A1
Shakespeare's Birthplace
  Warks CV37 6QW
  85 Stratford-upon-Avon
Shakespeare's Globe Theatre
  GtLon SE1 9DT **45** J4
Shalbourne **119** E1
Shalcombe **106** C4
Shalden **120** B3
Shalden Green **120** C3
Shaldon **102** C5
Shalfleet **106** D4
Shalford *Essex* **151** F5
Shalford *Surr* **121** F3
Shalford Green **151** F5
Shallowford *Devon* **114** A3
Shallowford *Staffs* **171** F5
Shalmsford Street **124** C3
Shalmstry **275** G2
Shalstone **148** B4
Shalunt **232** B2
Shambellie **217** D4
Shamley Green **121** F3
Shandon **233** D1
Shandwick **267** F4
Shangton **160** C3
Shankend **227** G5
Shankhouse **221** E4
Shanklin **107** E4
Shanklin Chine *IoW*
  PO37 6BW **107** E4
Shannochie **223** E3
Shantron **233** E1
Shantullich **266** D6
Shanzie **252** A4
Shap **199** G1
Shapinsay **277** E6
Shapwick *Dorset* **105** F2
Shapwick *Som* **116** B4
Sharcott **118** C2
Shard End **159** D4
Shardlow **173** F4
Shareshill **158** B2
Sharlston **186** A1
Sharlston Common **186** A1
Sharnal Street **137** G5
Sharnbrook **149** E2
Sharneyford **193** E5
Sharnford **159** G3
Sharnhill Green **104** D2
Sharow **202** C5
Sharp Street **179** E3
Sharpenhoe **149** F4
Sharperton **220** B4
Sharpham House **101** E2
Sharpness **131** F2
Sharpthorne **122** C5
Sharrington **178** B2
Shatterford **157** G4
Shattering **125** E3
Shaugh Prior **100** B1
Shave Cross **104** A3
Shavington **171** E2
Shaw *GtMan* **184** D2
Shaw *Swin* **132** C4
Shaw *WBerks* **119** F1
Shaw *Wilts* **117** F1
Shaw Green *Herts* **150** A4
Shaw Green *NYorks* **194** B2
Shaw Mills **194** B1
Shaw Side **184** D2
Shawbost
  (Siabost) **270** E3
Shawbury **170** C5
Shawell **160** A4
Shawfield *GtMan* **184** C1
Shawfield *Staffs* **172** B1
Shawford **119** F5
Shawforth **193** E5
Shawhead **216** C3
Shawtonhill **234** A5
Sheanachie **222** C4
Sheandow **259** K1
Shearington **217** E4
Shearsby **160** B3
Shebbear **113** E5
Shebdon **171** E5
Shebster **275** F2
Shedfield **107** E1
Sheen **172** C1
Sheepridge **185** F1
Sheepscombe **132** A1
Sheepstor **100** B1
Sheepwash *Devon* **113** E5
Sheepwash *N'umb* **221** E3
Sheepway **131** D5
Sheepy Magna **159** F2
Sheepy Parva **159** F2
Sheering **137** E1
Sheerness **124** B1
Sheet **120** C5
Sheffield **186** A4
Sheffield Botanic Gardens
  SYorks S10 2LN **21** B3
Sheffield Bottom **120** B1
Sheffield Green **109** G1

Sheffield Park Garden
 ESuss
 TN22 3QX **109** G1
Shefford **149** G4
Shefford Woodlands **133** F5
Sheigra **272** D2
Shelderton **156** D5
Sheldon *Derbys* **172** C1
Sheldon *Devon* **103** E2
Sheldon *WMid* **158** D4
Sheldwich **124** C3
Sheldwich Lees **124** C3
Shelf *Bridgend* **129** F4
Shelf *WYorks* **194** A5
Shelfanger **164** C3
Shelfield *Warks* **146** D1
Shelfield *WMid* **158** C2
Shelfield Green **146** D1
Shelford **174** C3
Shellachan *A&B* **240** C2
Shellachan *A&B* **240** C2
Shellbrook **159** F1
Shellbrook Hill **170** A3
Shelley *Essex* **137** E2
Shelley *Suff* **152** B4
Shelley *WYorks* **185** G1
Shellingford **133** F3
Shellow Bowells **137** F2
Shelsley
 Beauchamp **145** G1
Shelsley Walsh **145** G1
Shelswell **148** B4
Shelthorpe **160** A1
Shelton *Bed* **149** F1
Shelton *Norf* **164** D2
Shelton *Notts* **174** C3
Shelton *Shrop* **157** D1
Shelve **156** C3
Shelwick **145** E3
Shelwick Green **145** E3
Shenfield **137** F3
Shenington **147** F3
Shenley **136** A2
Shenley Brook End **148** D4
Shenley Church End **148** D4
Shenleybury **136** A2
Shenmore **144** C4
Shennanton **215** E4
Shenstone *Staffs* **158** D2
Shenstone *Worcs* **158** A5
Shenstone
 Woodend **158** D2
Shenton **159** F2
Shenval **259** K2
Shepeau Stow **162** B1
Shephall **150** A5
Shepherd's Bush **136** B5
Shepherd's Green **134** C4
Shepherd's Patch **131** G2
Shepherdswell
 (Sibertswold) **125** E4
Shepley **185** F2
Sheppardstown **275** H5
Shepperdine **131** F3
Shepperton **121** F1
Shepreth **150** B3
Shepreth Wildlife Park
 Cambs SG8 6PZ **150** B3
Shepshed **159** G1
Shepton
 Beauchamp **104** A1
Shepton Mallet **116** B3
Shepton Montague **117** D4
Shepway **123** G3
Sheraton **212** D4
Sherborne *Dorset* **104** C1
Sherborne St. John **120** B2
Sherborne **147** E1
Sherborne Street **152** A3
Sherburn *Dur* **212** C3
Sherburn *NYorks* **204** C5
Sherburn Hill **212** C3
Sherburn in Elmet **195** D4
Shere **121** F3
Shereford **177** G5
Sherfield English **119** D5
Sherfield on
 oddon **120** B2
Sherford *Devon* **101** D3
Sherford *Som* **115** F5
Sheriff Hutton **195** F1
Sheriffhales **157** G1
Sheringham **178** C1
Sheringham Park *Norf*
 NR26 8TL **178** C1
Sherington **149** D3
Shernal Green **146** B1
Shernborne **177** F4
Sherramore **258** C2
Sherrington **118** A4
Sherston **132** A4
Sherwood **173** G3
Sherwood Forest Country
 Park *Notts*
 NG21 9HN **174** B1
Sherwood Forest Fun Park
 Notts
 NG21 9QA **174** B1
Sherwood Green **113** F3
Sherwood Pines Forest
 Park *Notts*
 NG21 9JL **174** B1
Shetland Islands **279** B7
Shevington **183** G2
Shevington Moor **183** G1
Sheviock **99** D5
Shide **107** E4
Shiel Bridge
 (Drochaid Sheile) **257** F3
Shieldaig *High* **264** E6
Shieldaig *High* **264** E4
Shieldhill **234** C2
Shielfoot **247** F2
Shielhill **252** C4
Shiels **260** E4
Shifford **133** F2
Shifnal **157** G2
Shilbottle **221** D1
Shildon **212** B5
Shillingford
 Devon **104** C5
Shillingford *Oxon* **134** A3
Shillingford Abbot **102** C4
Shillingford
 St. George **102** C4
Shillingstone **105** E1

Shillington **149** G4
Shillmoor **220** A1
Shilstone **113** F5
Shilton *Oxon* **133** E2
Shilton *Warks* **159** G4
Shimpling *Norf* **164** D3
Shimpling *Suff* **151** G2
Shimpling Street **151** G2
Shincliffe **212** B3
Shiney Row **212** C2
Shinfield **120** C1
Shingay **150** B3
Shingham **163** F2
Shingle Street **153** E3
Shinness Lodge **273** H7
Shipbourne **123** E3
Shipbrookhill **184** A5
Shipdham **178** A5
Shipham **116** B2
Shiphay **101** E1
Shiplake **134** C5
Shiplake Row **134** C5
Shipley *N'umb* **229** F5
Shipley *Shrop* **158** A3
Shipley *WSuss* **121** G5
Shipley *WYorks* **194** A4
Shipley Bridge
 Devon **100** C2
Shipley Bridge *Surr* **122** C4
Shipley Common **173** F3
Shipley Country Park
 Derbys DE75 7GX **18** D2
Shipmeadow **165** E2
Shippea Hill **163** E4
Shippon **133** G3
Shipston on Stour **147** E3
Shipton *Glos* **132** C1
Shipton *NYorks* **195** E2
Shipton *Shrop* **157** E3
Shipton Bellinger **118** D3
Shipton Green **108** A3
Shipton Moyne **132** A4
Shipton Oliffe **132** C1
Shipton Solers **132** C1
Shipton-on-
 Cherwell **133** G1
Shiptonthorpe **196** A3
Shipton-under-
 Wychwood **133** E1
Shira **241** D3
Shirburn **134** B3
Shirdley Hill **183** E1
Shire Hall Gallery, Stafford
 Staffs ST16 2LD **171** G5
Shire Oak **158** C2
Shirebrook **173** G1
Shirecliffe **186** A3
Shiregreen **186** A3
Shirehampton **131** E5
Shiremoor **221** F4
Shirenewton **131** D3
Shiroaks **186** C4
Shirl Heath **144** D2
Shirley *Derbys* **172** D3
Shirley *GtLon* **122** C2
Shirley *Hants* **106** A3
Shirley *Soton* **106** D1
Shirley *WMid* **158** D5
Shirley Heath **158** D5
Shirley Warren **106** C1
Shirleywich **171** G5
Shirrell Heath **107** E1
Shirwell **113** F2
Shirwell Cross **113** F2
Shiskine **223** E3
Shittlehope **211** G4
Shobdon **144** C1
Shobley **106** A2
Shobrooke **102** B2
Shocklach **170** B3
Shocklach Green **170** B3
Shoeburyness **138** C4
Sholden **125** F3
Sholing **107** D1
Shoot Hill **156** D1
Shooter's Hill **136** D5
Shop *Corn* **96** C2
Shop *Corn* **112** C4
Shop Corner **152** D4
Shopnoller **115** E4
Shore **184** D1
Shoreditch **136** C4
Shoreham **123** E2
Shoreham Airport **109** D3
Shoreham-by-Sea **109** E3
Shoremill **266** E5
Shoresdean **237** G5
Shoreswood **237** G5
Shoreton **266** D5
Shorley **119** G5
Shorncote **132** C3
Shorne **137** F5
Shorne Ridgeway **137** F5
Short Cross **156** B2
Short Green **164** B3
Short Heath *Derbys* **159** F1
Short Heath *WMid* **158** C3
Shortacombe **99** F2
Shortbridge **109** G1
Shortfield Common **120** D3
Shortgate **109** G2
Shortgrove **150** D4
Shorthampton **147** F5
Shortlands **122** C2
Shortlanesend **96** C5
Shorton **101** E1
Shorwell **107** D4
Shoscombe **117** E2
Shotatton **170** A5
Shotesham **164** D2
Shotgate **137** D3
Shotley *N'hants* **161** E3
Shotley *Suff* **152** D4
Shotley Bridge **211** G2
Shotley Gate **152** D4
Shotleyfield **211** G2
Shottenden **124** C3
Shottermill **121** D4
Shottery **147** D2
Shotteswell **147** G3
Shottisham **153** E3
Shottle **173** E2
Shottlegate **173** E3
Shotton *Dur* **212** D4
Shotton *Dur* **212** C5
Shotton *Flints* **170** A1

Shotton *N'umb* **221** E4
Shotton Colliery **212** C3
Shotts **234** C3
Shotwick **183** E5
Shouldham **163** E2
Shouldham Thorpe **163** E2
Shoulton **146** A2
Shover's Green **123** F5
Shraleybrook **171** F3
Shrawardine **156** C1
Shrawley **146** A1
Shreding Green **135** F4
Shrewley **147** E1
Shrewsbury **157** D1
Shrewton **118** B3
Shri Venkateswara (Balaji)
 Temple of the United
 Kingdom *WMid*
 B69 3DU **14** C3
Shrine of Our Lady of
 Walsingham (Anglican)
 Norf NR22 6EF **178** A2
Shripney **108** B3
Shrivenham **133** E4
Shropham **164** A2
Shroton (Iwerne
 Courtney) **105** E1
Shrub End **152** A5
Shucknall **145** E3
Shudy Camps **151** E3
Shugborough Estate *Staffs*
 ST17 0XB **171** G5
Shurdington **132** B1
Shurlock Row **134** D5
Shurnock **146** C1
Shurrery **275** F3
Shurrery Lodge **275** F3
Shurton **115** F3
Shustoke **159** E3
Shute *Devon* **103** F2
Shute *Devon* **102** B2
Shutford **147** F3
Shuthonger **146** A4
Shutlanger **148** C3
Shutt Green **158** A2
Shuttington **159** E2
Shuttlewood **186** B5
Shuttleworth **184** B1
Siabost Bho Dheas **270** E3
Siabost Bho Thuath **270** E3
Siadar Iarach **271** F2
Siadar Uarach **271** F2
Sibbaldbie **217** F2
Sibdon Carwood **156** D4
Sibertswold
 (Shepherdswell) **125** E4
Sibford Ferris **147** F4
Sibford Gower **147** F4
Sible Hedingham **151** F4
Sibley's Green **151** E4
Sibsey **176** B2
Sibson *Cambs* **161** F3
Sibson *Leics* **159** F2
Sibster **275** J3
Sibthorpe **174** C3
Sibton **153** E1
Sibton Green **165** E4
Sicklesmere **151** G1
Sicklinghall **194** C3
Sidbury *Devon* **103** E3
Sidbury *Shrop* **157** F4
Sidcot **116** B2
Sidcup **137** D5
Siddal **194** A5
Siddington *ChesE* **184** C5
Siddington *Glos* **132** C3
Sidemoor **158** B5
Sidestrand **179** D2
Sidford **103** E3
Sidlesham **108** A4
Sidley **110** C3
Sidlow **122** B4
Sidmouth **103** E4
Sigford **102** A5
Sigglesthorne **197** D3
Sigingstone **129** F5
Signet **133** E1
Silchester **120** B1
Sildinis **270** E6
Sileby **160** B1
Silecroft **198** C4
Silfield **164** C2
Silian **142** B2
Silk Willoughby **175** F3
Silkstead **119** F5
Silkstone **185** G2
Silkstone Common **185** G2
Sill Field **199** G4
Sills **220** A1
Sillyearn **268** D5
Silpho **204** C3
Silsden **193** G3
Silsoe **149** F4
Silver End *CenBeds* **149** G3
Silver End *Essex* **151** G5
Silver Green **165** D2
Silver Street *Kent* **124** A3
Silver Street *Som* **116** C4
Silverburn **235** G3
Silvercraigs **231** G1
Silverdale *Lancs* **199** F5
Silverdale *Staffs* **171** F3
Silvergate **178** C3
Silverhill **110** C2
Silverlace Green **153** E2
Silverley's Green **165** D4
Silvermoss **261** G1
Silverstone **148** B3
Silverton **102** C2
Silvington **157** F5
Silwick **279** B8
Simister **184** C2
Simmondley **185** E3
Simonburn **220** A4
Simonsbath **114** A4
Simonside **212** C1
Simonstone
 Bridgend **129** F4
Simonstone
 Lancs **193** D4
Simprim **237** F5
Simpson **149** D4
Sinclair's Hill **237** F4
Sinclairston **224** C4
Sinderby **202** C4
Sinderhope **211** E2

Sindlesham **120** C1
Sinfin **173** E4
Singdean **227** G5
Singleton *Lancs* **191** G4
Singleton *WSuss* **108** A2
Singlewell **137** F5
Sinkhurst Green **124** A4
Sinnahard **260** C3
Sinnington **203** G4
Sinton Green **146** A1
Sipson **135** F5
Sirhowy **130** A1
Sirhowy Valley Country
 Park *Caerp*
 NP11 7BD **130** A3
Sisland **165** E2
Sissinghurst **123** G5
Sissinghurst Castle Garden
 Kent TN17 2AB **124** A5
Siston **131** F5
Sithney **94** D4
Sittingbourne **124** B2
Siulaisiadar **271** H4
Six Ashes **157** G4
Six Mile Bottom **151** D2
Six Hills **174** B5
Six Roads End **172** C5
Sixhills **188** B4
Sixmile **124** D4
Sixpenny Handley **105** G1
Sizewell **153** F1
Skail **274** C4
Skaill *Ork* **277** B6
Skaill *Ork* **277** E7
Skares *Aber* **260** E1
Skares *EAyr* **224** D4
Skarpigarth **279** A7
Skateraw **237** E2
Skaw **279** E6
Skeabost **263** K7
Skeabrae **276** B5
Skeeby **202** B2
Skeffington **160** C2
Skeffling **189** D1
Skegby **173** G1
Skegness **177** D1
Skegness Water Leisure
 Park *Lincs*
 PE25 1JF **177** D1
Skelberry *Shet* **279** F9
Skelberry *Shet* **279** D6
Skelbo **266** E2
Skelbo Street **266** E2
Skelbrooke **186** C1
Skeld (Easter Skeld)
 279 C8
Skeldon **224** B4
Skeldyke **176** B2
Skellingthorpe **187** G5
Skellister **279** D7
Skellow **186** C1
Skelmanthorpe **185** G1
Skelmersdale **183** F2
Skelmonae **261** G1
Skelmorlie **232** C3
Skelmuir **269** H6
Skelpick **274** C3
Skelton *Cumb* **210** A4
Skelton *ERid* **195** G5
Skelton *NYorks* **201** F2
Skelton (Skelton-in-
 Cleveland) *R&C* **203** F1
Skelton *York* **195** E2
Skelton-in-Cleveland
 (Skelton) **203** F1
Skelton-on-Ure **194** C1
Skelwick **276** D3
Skelwith Bridge **199** E2
Skendleby **176** C1
Skendleby Psalter **189** E5
Skenfrith **145** D5
Skerne **196** C2
Skeroblingarry **222** C3
Skerray **273** J2
Skerton **192** A1
Sketchley **159** F3
Sketty **128** C3
Skewen **128** D3
Skewkwel **128** D7
Skewsby **203** F5
Skeyton **179** D3
Skeyton Corner **179** D3
Skidbrooke **189** E3
Skidbrooke North
 End **189** E3
Skidby **196** C4
Skilgate **114** C5
Skillington **175** D5
Skinburness **209** E1
Skinflats **234** D1
Skinidin **263** H7
Skinnet **275** G2
Skinningrove **203** G1
Skipness **231** G4
Skippool **191** G3
Skipsea **197** D2
Skipsea Brough **197** D2
Skipton **193** F2
Skipton Castle *NYorks*
 BD23 1AW **193** F2
Skipton-on-Swale **202** C4
Skipwith **195** F4
Skirbeck **176** B3
Skirbeck Quarter **176** B3
Skirethorns **193** F1
Skirlaugh **196** D4
Skirling **226** B2
Skirmett **134** C4
Skirpenbeck **195** G2
Skirwith *Cumb* **210** C4
Skirwith *NYorks* **200** C5
Skirza **275** J2
Skittle Green **134** C2
Skomer Island **126** A2
Skulamus **256** C2
Skullomie **273** J2
Skyborry Green **156** B5
Skye **255** K1
Skye Green **151** G5
Skye of Curr **259** G2
Skyreholme **193** G1
Slack *Aber* **260** D1
Slack *Derbys* **173** D1
Slack *WYorks* **193** F5
Slackhall **185** E4
Slackhead **268** C4
Slad **132** A2

Slade *Devon* **113** F1
Slade *Devon* **103** E2
Slade *Pembs* **126** C1
Slade *Swan* **128** A4
Slade Green **137** E5
Slade Hooton **186** C4
Sladesbridge **97** E2
Slaggyford **210** C2
Slaidburn **192** D2
Slaithwaite **185** E1
Slaley **211** F2
Slamannan **234** C2
Slapton *Bucks* **149** E5
Slapton *Devon* **101** E3
Slapton *N'hants* **148** B3
Slate Haugh **268** C4
Slatepit Dale **173** E1
Slattadale **264** E4
Slaugham **109** E1
Slaughden **153** F2
Slaughterford **132** A5
Slawston **160** C3
Sleaford *Hants* **120** D4
Sleaford *Lincs* **175** F3
Sleagill **199** G1
Sledge Green **146** A4
Sledmere **196** B1
Sleights **204** B2
Slepe **105** F3
Slerra **112** D3
Slickly **275** H2
Sliddery **223** E3
Sliemore **259** H2
Sligachan **255** K2
Slimbridge **131** G2
Slimbridge Wildfowl &
 Wetlands Trust *Glos*
 GL2 7BT **131** G2
Slindon *Staffs* **171** F4
Slindon *WSuss* **108** B3
Slinfold **121** G5
Sling **131** E1
Slingsby **203** F5
Slioch **260** D1
Slip End *CenBeds* **135** F1
Slip End *Herts* **150** A4
Slipper Chapel, Houghton
 St. Giles *Norf*
 NR22 6AL **178** A2
Slipton **161** E5
Slitting Mill **158** C1
Slochd **259** F2
Slockavullin **240** A5
Slogarie **216** A4
Sloley **179** D3
Slongaber **216** C3
Sloothby **189** E5
Slough **135** F4
Slough Green
 Som **115** F5
Slough Green
 WSuss **109** E1
Sluggan **259** F2
Slyne **192** A1
Smailholm **228** A3
Small Dole **109** E3
Small Hythe **124** A5
Smallbridge **184** D1
Smallbrook **102** B3
Smallburgh **179** E3
Smallburn *Aber* **269** J6
Smallburn *EAyr* **225** E3
Smalldale **185** E5
Smalley **173** F3
Smallfield **122** C4
Smallford **136** A2
Smallridge **103** F2
Smallthorne **171** F2
Smallworth **164** B3
Smannell **119** E3
Smardale **200** C2
Smarden **124** A4
Smeatharpe **103** E1
Smeeth **124** C5
Smeeton
 Westerby **160** B3
Smercilet **254** C3
Smerral **275** G5
Smestow **158** A3
Smethcott **157** D3
Smethwick **158** C4
Smethwick Green **171** F1
Smirisary **247** F2
Smisby **159** F5
Smith End Green **145** G2
Smithfield **210** A1
Smithies **186** A1
Smithincott **103** D1
Smith's End **150** B4
Smith's Green
 Essex **151** D5
Smith's Green
 Essex **151** E3
Smithstown **264** D4
Smithton **266** E7
Smithy Green **184** B5
Smockington **159** F4
Smugglers Adventure
 ESuss TN34 3HY
 75 Hastings
Smyrton **214** C2
Smythe's Green **138** C1
Snailbeach **156** C2
Snailwell **151** E1
Snainton **204** C4
Snaith **195** F5
Snape *NYorks* **202** B4
Snape *Suff* **153** E2
Snape Green **183** E1
Snape Watering **153** E2
Snarestone **159** F2
Snarford **188** A4
Snargate **111** E1
Snave **111** F1
Sneachill **146** B2
Snead **156** C3
Snead's Green **146** A1
Sneaton **204** B2
Sneatonthorpe **204** C2
Snelland **188** A4
Snellings **198** A2
Snelston **172** C3
Snetterton **164** A2
Snettisham **177** E4
Snipeshill **124** B2

Snishival
 (Sniseabhal) **254** C1
Snitter **220** C1
Snitterby **187** G3
Snitterfield **147** E2
Snitterton **173** D1
Snittlegarth **209** F3
Snitton **157** E5
Snodhill **144** C3
Snodland **123** G2
Snow End **150** C4
Snow Street **164** B3
Snowden Hill **185** G2
Snowdon Mountain Railway
 Gwyn
 LL55 4TY **167** E2
Snowshill **146** C4
Snowshill Manor *Glos*
 WR12 7JU **146** C4
Soar *Cardiff* **129** G4
Soar *Carmar* **142** C5
Soar *Devon* **100** D4
Soay **255** K3
Soberton **107** F1
Soberton Heath **107** F1
Sockbridge **210** B5
Sockburn **202** C2
Sodom **182** B5
Sodylt Bank **170** A4
Softley **211** G5
Soham **163** D5
Soham Cotes **163** D5
Soldon **112** D4
Soldon Cross **112** D4
Soldridge **120** B4
Sole Street *Kent* **124** C4
Sole Street *Kent* **123** F2
Soleburn **214** B4
Solihull **159** D5
Solihull Lodge **158** C5
Sollas (Solas) **262** D4
Sollers Dilwyn **144** D2
Sollers Hope **145** F4
Sollom **183** F1
Solomon's Tump **131** G1
Solsgirth **243** E5
Solva **140** A5
Solwaybank **218** A4
Somerby *Leics* **160** C1
Somerby *Lincs* **188** A2
Somercotes **173** F2
Somerford **158** B2
Somerford Keynes **132** C3
Somerley **108** A4
Somerleyton **165** F2
Somersal Herbert **172** C4
Somersby **188** D5
Somerset House *GtLon*
 WC2R 1LA **45** F3
Somersham
 Cambs **162** B5
Somersham *Suff* **152** B3
Somerton *Newport* **130** C4
Somerton *Oxon* **147** G5
Somerton *Som* **116** B5
Somerton *Suff* **151** G2
Sompting **109** D3
Sompting Abbotts **109** D3
Sonning **134** C5
Sonning Common **134** C4
Sonning Eye **134** C5
Sontley **170** A3
Sookholme **173** G1
Sopley **106** A3
Sopworth **132** A4
Sorbie **207** E2
Sordale **275** G2
Sorisdale **246** B3
Sorn **225** D3
Sornhill **224** D2
Soroba **240** A2
Sortat **275** H2
Sotby **188** C5
Sots Hole **175** G1
Sotterley **165** F3
Soudley **171** E5
Soughton **169** F1
Soulbury **149** D5
Soulby **200** C1
Souldern **148** A4
Souldrop **149** E1
Sound *ChesE* **170** D3
Sound *Shet* **279** D8
Sound *Shet* **279** D8
Sourhope **228** C4
Sourin **276** D4
Sourton **99** F1
Soutergate **198** D4
South Acre **163** G1
South Acton **136** A5
South Alkham **125** E4
South Allington **101** D4
South Alloa **243** D5
South Ambersham **121** E5
South Anston **186** C4
South Ascot **121** E1
South Baddesley **106** C3
South Ballachulish (Baile a'
 Chaolais a Deas) **248** C4
South Balloch **215** E2
South Bank **213** E5
South Barrow **116** C5
South Bellsdyke **234** D1
South Benfleet **137** G4
South Bersted **108** B3
South Blackbog **261** F1
South
 Bockhampton **106** A3
South Bowood **104** A3
South Brent **100** C1
South Brentor **99** E2
South Brewham **117** E4
South Broomhill **221** E2
South Burlingham **179** E5
South Cadbury **116** D5
South Cairn **214** A4
South Carlton **187** G5
South Cave **196** B4
South Cerney **132** C3
South Charlton **229** F4
South Cheriton **117** D5
South Church **212** B5
South Cliffe **196** A4
South Clifton **187** F5
South Cockerington **189** D4
South Collafirth **278** C4
South Common **109** F2

South Cornelly **129** E4
South Corriegills **223** F2
South Cove **165** F3
South Creagan **248** B5
South Creake **177** G4
South Crosland **185** F1
South Croxton **160** B1
South Dalton **196** B3
South Darenth **137** E5
South Dell
 (Dail Bho Dheas) **271** G1
South Duffield **195** F4
South Elkington **188** C4
South Elmsall **186** B1
South End *Bucks* **149** D5
South End *Cumb* **191** F1
South End *Hants* **106** A1
South End *NLincs* **196** D5
South Erradale **264** D4
South Fambridge **138** B3
South Fawley **133** F4
South Ferriby **196** B5
South Field **196** C5
South Flobbets **261** F1
South Garth **278** E3
South Godstone **122** C4
South Gorley **106** A1
South Green *Essex* **137** F3
South Green *Essex* **138** D1
South Green *Norf* **178** B4
South Green *Suff* **164** C5
South Gyle **235** F2
South Hall **232** B2
South Hanningfield **137** G3
South Harefield **135** F4
South Harting **107** G1
South Hayling **107** G3
South Hazelrigg **229** E3
South Heath **135** E2
South Heighton **109** G3
South Hetton **212** C3
South Hiendley **186** A1
South Hill **98** D3
South Hinksey **134** A2
South Hole **112** C4
South Holme **203** F5
South Holmwood **121** G3
South Hornchurch **137** E4
South Hourat **233** D4
South Huish **100** C3
South Hykeham **175** E1
South Hylton **212** C2
South Kelsey **188** A3
South Kirkton **261** F4
South Knighton **102** B5
South Kyme **175** G3
South Lakes Wild Animal
 Park *Cumb*
 LA15 8JR **198** D5
South Lancing **109** D3
South Ledaig **240** B1
South Leigh **133** F2
South Leverton **187** E4
South Littleton **146** C3
South Lopham **164** B3
South Luffenham **161** E2
South Malling **109** G2
South Marston **133** D4
South Middleton **229** D4
South Milford **195** D4
South Milton **100** C3
South Mimms **136** B2
South Molton **114** A5
South Moor **212** A2
South Moreton **134** A4
South Mundham **108** A3
South Muskham **174** C2
South Newbald **196** B4
South Newington **147** G4
South Newton **118** B4
South Normanton **173** F2
South Norwood **122** C2
South Nutfield **122** C4
South Ockendon **137** E4
South Ormsby **189** D5
South Ossett **185** G1
South Otterington **202** C4
South Owersby **188** A3
South Oxhey **136** A3
South Park **122** B4
South Parks **244** A4
South Perrott **104** A2
South Petherton **104** A1
South Petherwin **98** D2
South Pickenham **163** G2
South Pool **101** D3
South Queensferry
 (Queensferry) **235** F2
South Radworthy **114** A4
South Rauceby **175** F3
South Raynham **177** G5
South Redbriggs **269** F6
South Reston **189** E4
South Ronaldsay **277** D9
South Ruislip **136** A4
South Runcton **163** E2
South Scarle **174** C1
South Shian
 (Sithean a Deas) **248** B5
South Shields **212** C1
South Shields Museum &
 Art Gallery *T&W*
 NE33 2JA **28** D2
South Somercotes **189** E3
South Somercotes Fen
 Houses **189** E3
South Stainley **194** C1
South Stoke
 B&NESom **117** E1
South Stoke *Oxon* **134** B4
South Stoke *WSuss* **108** C3
South Street *ESuss* **109** F2
South Street
 GtLon **122** D3
South Street *Kent* **123** E4
South Street *Kent* **124** D2
South Street *Kent* **124** C3
South Tawton **99** G1
South Thoresby **189** E5
South Tidworth **118** D3
South Tottenham **136** C4

South Town Devon 102 C4
South Town Hants 120 B4
South Uist (Uibhist a Deas) 254 C1
South Upper Barrack 269 H6
South View 120 B2
South Walsham 179 E4
South Warnborough 120 C3
South Weald 137 E3
South Weston 134 C3
South Wheatley Corn 98 C1
South Wheatley Notts 187 E4
South Whiteness 279 C8
South Wigston 160 A3
South Willingham 188 B4
South Wingfield 173 E2
South Witham 161 E1
South Wonston 119 F4
South Woodham Ferrers 138 B3
South Wootton 177 E5
South Wraxall 117 F1
South Yardle 158 D4
South Zeal 99 G1
Southall 136 A4
Southam Glos 146 B5
Southam Warks 147 G1
Southampton 106 D1
Southampton Airport 107 D1
Southbar 233 F3
Southborough GtLon 122 D2
Southborough Kent 123 E4
Southbourne Bourne 106 A3
Southbourne WSuss 107 G2
Southbrook 102 D3
Southburgh 178 B5
Southburn 196 B2
Southchurch 138 C4
Southcott Devon 99 F1
Southcott Wilts 118 C2
Southcourt 134 D1
Southdean 219 E1
Southdene 183 F3
Southease 109 G3
Southend A&B 222 B5
Southend Aber 269 F6
Southend Bucks 134 C4
Southend (Bradfield Southend) WBerks 134 A5
Southend Wilts 133 D5
Southend Airport 138 B4
Southend Pier S'end SS1 1EE 138 B4
Southend-on-Sea 138 B4
Southerfield 209 E2
Southerly 99 F2
Southern Green 150 B4
Southerndown 129 E5
Southerness 217 D5
Southery 163 E3
Southfield 244 A5
Southfields 136 B5
Southfleet 137 F5
Southgate Cere 154 B4
Southgate GtLon 136 C3
Southgate Norf 178 C3
Southgate Norf 177 E4
Southgate Swan 128 B4
Southill 149 G3
Southington 119 G3
Southleigh 103 F3
Southmarsh 117 E4
Southminster 138 C3
Southmoor 133 F3
Southmuir 252 B4
Southoe 149 G1
Southolt 152 C1
Southorpe 161 F2
Southowram 194 A5
Southport 183 E1
Southport Pier Mersey PR8 1QX 183 E1
Southrepps 179 D2
Southrey 175 G1
Southrop 133 D2
Southrope 120 B3
Southsea Ports 107 F3
Southsea Wrex 169 F2
Southtown Norf 179 G5
Southtown Ork 277 D8
Southwaite Cumb 200 C2
Southwaite Cumb 210 A3
Southwark Cathedral GtLon SE1 9DA 12 B4
Southwater 121 G5
Southwater Street 121 G5
Southway 116 C3
Southwell Dorset 104 C5
Southwell Notts 174 B2
Southwell Minster Notts NG25 0HD 174 C2
Southwick D&G 216 D5
Southwick Hants 107 F2
Southwick N'hants 161 F3
Southwick Som 116 A3
Southwick T&W 212 C2
Southwick Wilts 117 F2
Southwick WSuss 109 E3
Southwold 165 G4
Southwood 116 C4
Sowden 102 C4
Sower Carr 191 G3
Sowerby NYorks 202 D4
Sowerby WYorks 193 G5
Sowerby Bridge 193 G5
Sowerby Row 209 G2
Sowerhill 114 B5
Sowley Green 151 F2
Sowood 185 E1
Sowton 102 C3
Soyal 266 C2
Spa Common 179 D2
Spa Complex NYorks YO11 2HD 83 Scarborough
Spadeadam 219 D4
Spalding 176 A5
Spaldington 195 G4
Spaldwick 161 G5
Spalefield 245 D4
Spalford 174 D1
Spanby 175 F4
Sparham 178 B4
Spark Bridge 199 E4
Sparkford 116 D5
Sparkhill 158 C4
Sparkwell 100 B2
Sparrow Green 178 A4
Sparrowpit 185 E4
Sparrow's Green 123 F5
Sparsholt Hants 119 F4
Sparsholt Oxon 133 F4
Spartylea 211 E3
Spath 172 B4
Spaunton 203 G4
Spaxton 115 F4
Spean Bridge (Drochaid an Aonachain) 249 E1
Spean Bridge Woollen Mill High PH34 4EP 249 E1
Spear Hill 108 D2
Speddoch 216 C2
Speedwell 131 F5
Speen Bucks 134 D2
Speen WBerks 119 F1
Speeton 205 E5
Speke 183 F4
Speldhurst 123 E4
Spellbrook 137 D1
Spelsbury 147 F5
Spen Green 171 F1
Spencers Wood 120 C1
Spennithorne 202 A4
Spennymoor 212 B4
Spernall 146 C1
Spetchley 146 A2
Spetisbury 105 F2
Spexhall 165 E3
Spey Bay 268 B4
Speybridge 259 H2
Speyview 267 K7
Spilsby 176 B1
Spindlestone 229 F3
Spinkhill 186 B5
Spinnaker Tower PO1 3TN 82 Portsmouth
Spinningdale 266 D3
Spirthill 132 B5
Spital High 275 G3
Spital W&M 135 E5
Spital in the Street 187 G3
Spitalbrook 136 C2
Spitfire & Hurricane Memorial, R.A.F. Manston Kent CT12 5DF 125 F2
Spithurst 109 G2
Spittal D&G 215 F4
Spittal D&G 215 E5
Spittal ELoth 236 B2
Spittal N'umb 229 E1
Spittal Pembs 140 C5
Spittal of Glenmuick 252 B1
Spittal of Glenshee 251 G3
Spittalfield 251 G5
Spixworth 178 D4
Splayne's Green 109 G1
Splott 130 B5
Spofforth 194 C2
Spondon 173 F4
Spooner Row 164 B2
Spooneley 171 D4
Sporle 163 G1
Sportsman's Arms 168 C2
Spott 237 D2
Spratton 160 C5
Spreakley 120 D3
Spreyton 99 G1
Spriddlestone 100 B2
Spridlington 188 A4
Spring Grove 136 A5
Spring Vale 107 F3
Springburn 234 A3
Springfield A&B 232 B2
Springfield D&G 218 B5
Springfield Fife 244 B3
Springfield Moray 267 H6
Springfield P&K 243 G1
Springfield WMid 158 C4
Springhill Staffs 158 C2
Springhill Staffs 158 B2
Springholm 216 C4
Springkell 218 A4
Springleys 261 F1
Springside 224 B2
Springthorpe 187 F4
Springwell 212 B2
Sproatley 197 D4
Sproston Green 171 E1
Sprotbrough 186 C2
Sproughton 152 C3
Sprouston 228 B3
Sprowston 178 D4
Sproxton Leics 175 D5
Sproxton NYorks 203 F4
Sprytown 99 E2
Spurlands End 135 D3
Spurstow 170 C2
Spyway 104 B3
Square Point 216 B3
Squires Gate 191 G4
Srondoire 231 G2
Sronphadruig Lodge 250 C2
Stableford Shrop 157 G3
Stableford Staffs 171 F4
Stacey Bank 185 G3
Stackhouse 193 E1
Stackpole 126 C3
Stacksteads 193 E5
Staddiscombe 100 B2
Staddlethorpe 196 A5
Staden 185 E5
Stadhampton 134 B3
Staffield 210 B3
Staffin 263 K5
Stafford 171 G5
Stagden Cross 137 F1
Stagsden 149 E3
Stagshaw Bank 211 F1
Stain 275 J2
Stainburn Cumb 208 D4
Stainburn NYorks 194 B3
Stainby 175 E5
Staincross 186 A1
Staindrop 212 A5
Staines-upon-Thames 135 F5
Stainfield Lincs 175 F5
Stainfield Lincs 188 B5
Stainforth NYorks 193 E1
Stainforth SYorks 186 D1
Staining 191 G4
Stainland 185 E1
Stainsacre 204 C2
Stainsby Derbys 173 F1
Stainsby Lincs 188 D5
Stainton Cumb 199 G4
Stainton Cumb 210 A5
Stainton Dur 201 F1
Stainton Middl 203 D1
Stainton NYorks 202 A3
Stainton SYorks 186 C3
Stainton by Langworth 188 A5
Stainton le Vale 188 B3
Stainton with Adgarley 198 D5
Staintondale 204 C3
Stair Cumb 209 F4
Stair EAyr 224 C3
Stairfoot 186 A2
Staithes 203 G1
Stake Pool 192 A3
Stakeford 221 E3
Stakes 107 F2
Stalbridge 104 D1
Stalbridge Weston 104 D1
Stalham 179 E3
Stalham Green 179 E3
Stalisfield Green 124 B3
Stalling Busk 201 E4
Stallingborough 188 B1
Stallington 171 G4
Stalmine 191 G3
Stalybridge 185 D3
Stambourne 151 F4
Stamford Lincs 161 F2
Stamford N'umb 229 G5
Stamford Bridge ChesW&C 170 B1
Stamford Bridge ERid 195 G2
Stamfordham 220 C4
Stanah 191 G3
Stanborough 136 B1
Stanborough Park Herts AL8 6XF 136 B1
Stanbridge CenBeds 149 E5
Stanbridge Dorset 105 G2
Stanbridge Earls 119 E5
Stanbury 193 G4
Stand 234 B3
Standalone Farm, Letchworth Garden City Herts SG6 4JN 150 A4
Standburn 234 D2
Standedge Tunnel & Visitor Centre WYorks HD7 6NQ 185 E1
Standeford 158 B2
Standen 124 A5
Standen Street 124 A5
Standerwick 117 F2
Standford 120 D4
Standford Bridge 171 E5
Standish Glos 132 A2
Standish GtMan 183 G1
Standlake 133 F2
Standon Hants 119 F5
Standon Herts 150 B5
Standon Staffs 171 F4
Standon Green End 136 C1
Stane 234 C4
Stanecastle 224 B2
Stanfield 178 A3
Stanford CenBeds 149 G3
Stanford Kent 124 D5
Stanford Shrop 156 C1
Stanford Bishop 145 F2
Stanford Bridge 145 G1
Stanford Dingley 134 A5
Stanford End 120 C1
Stanford in the Vale 133 F3
Stanford on Avon 160 A5
Stanford on Soar 173 G5
Stanford on Teme 145 G1
Stanford Rivers 137 E2
Stanford-le-Hope 137 F4
Stanfree 186 B5
Stanghow 203 F1
Stanground 162 A3
Stanhoe 177 G4
Stanhope Dur 211 F4
Stanhope ScBord 226 C3
Stanion 161 E4
Stanklyn 158 A5
Stanley Derbys 173 F3
Stanley Dur 212 A2
Stanley Notts 173 F1
Stanley P&K 243 G1
Stanley Staffs 171 G2
Stanley Wilts 132 B5
Stanley WYorks 194 C5
Stanley Common 173 F3
Stanley Crook 212 A4
Stanley Gate 183 F2
Stanley Hill 145 F3
Stanleygreen 170 C4
Stanlow ChesW&C 183 F5
Stanlow Shrop 157 G3
Stanmer 109 F2
Stanmore GtLon 136 A3
Stanmore WBerks 133 G5
Stannersburn 219 F3
Stanningfield 151 G2
Stannington N'umb 221 E4
Stannington SYorks 186 A4
Stansbatch 144 C1
Stansfield 151 F2
Stanshope 172 C2
Stanstead 151 G3
Stanstead Abbotts 136 C1
Stansted 123 F2
Stansted Airport 150 D5
Stansted Mountfitchet 150 D5
Stanton Derbys 159 E1
Stanton Glos 146 C4
Stanton N'umb 220 D2
Stanton Staffs 172 C3
Stanton Suff 164 A4
Stanton by Bridge 173 E5
Stanton by Dale 173 F4
Stanton Drew 116 C1
Stanton Fitzwarren 133 D3
Stanton Harcourt 133 G2
Stanton Hill 173 F1
Stanton in Peak 172 D1
Stanton Lacy 157 D5
Stanton Lees 173 D1
Stanton Long 157 E3
Stanton Prior 117 D1
Stanton St. Bernard 118 B1
Stanton St. John 134 A2
Stanton St. Quintin 132 B5
Stanton Street 152 A1
Stanton under Bardon 159 G1
Stanton upon Hine Heath 170 C5
Stanton Wick 116 D1
Stanton-on-the-Wolds 174 B4
Stanwardine in the Fields 170 B5
Stanwardine in the Wood 170 B5
Stanway Essex 152 A5
Stanway Glos 146 C4
Stanway Green Essex 152 A5
Stanway Green Suff 164 D4
Stanwell 135 F5
Stanwell Moor 135 F5
Stanwick 161 E5
Stanwix 210 A2
Stanydale 279 B7
Staoinebrig 254 C1
Stapeley 171 D3
Stapenhill 173 D5
Staple Kent 125 E3
Staple Som 115 E3
Staple Cross 114 D5
Staple Fitzpaine 103 F1
Staplecross 110 C1
Staplefield 109 E1
Stapleford Cambs 150 C2
Stapleford Herts 136 C1
Stapleford Leics 160 D1
Stapleford Lincs 175 D2
Stapleford Notts 173 F4
Stapleford Wilts 118 B4
Stapleford Abbotts 137 D3
Stapleford Tawney 137 E3
Staplegrove 115 F5
Staplehay 115 F5
Staplehurst 123 G4
Staplers 107 E4
Staplestreet 124 C2
Stapleton Cumb 218 D4
Stapleton Here 144 C1
Stapleton Leics 159 G3
Stapleton NYorks 202 B1
Stapleton Shrop 157 D2
Stapleton Som 116 B5
Stapley 103 E1
Staploe 149 G1
Staplow 145 F3
Star Fife 244 B4
Star Pembs 141 F4
Star Som 116 B2
Starbotton 201 E5
Starcross 102 C4
Stareton 159 F5
Starkholmes 173 E2
Starling 184 B1
Starling's Green 150 C4
Starr 215 F1
Starston 164 D3
Startforth 201 F1
Startley 132 B4
Statham 184 A4
Stathe 116 A5
Stathern 174 C4
Station Town 212 D4
Staughton Green 149 G1
Staughton Highway 149 G1
Staunton Glos 131 E1
Staunton Glos 145 G5
Staunton Harold Hall 173 E5
Staunton Harold Reservoir Derbys DE73 8DN 173 E5
Staunton in the Vale 174 D3
Staunton on Arrow 144 C1
Staunton on Wye 144 C3
Staveley Cumb 199 F3
Staveley Derbys 186 B5
Staveley NYorks 194 C1
Staveley-in-Cartmel 199 E4
Staverton Devon 101 D1
Staverton Glos 146 A5
Staverton N'hants 148 A1
Staverton Wilts 117 F1
Staverton Bridge 146 A5
Stawell 116 A4
Stawley 115 D5
Staxigoe 275 J3
Staxton 204 D5
Staylittle (Penffordd-las) 155 E3
Staynall 191 G3
Staythorpe 174 C2
Stean 201 F5
Steane 148 A4
Stearsby 203 F5
Steart 115 F3
Stebbing 151 E5
Stebbing Green 151 E5
Stechford 158 D4
Stedham 121 D5
Steel Cross 123 E5
Steel Green 198 C5
Steele Road 218 D2
Steen's Bridge 145 E2
Steep 120 C5
Steep Marsh 120 C5
Steeple Dorset 105 F4
Steeple Essex 138 C2
Steeple Ashton 118 A2
Steeple Aston 147 G5
Steeple Barton 147 G5
Steeple Bumpstead 151 E3
Steeple Claydon 148 B5
Steeple Gidding 161 G4
Steeple Langford 118 B4
Steeple Morden 150 A3
Steeraway 157 F2
Steeton 193 G3
Stein 263 H6
Steinis 271 G4
Steinmanhill 269 F6
Stella 212 A1
Stelling Minnis 124 D4
Stembridge 116 B5
Stemster High 275 G2
Stemster High 275 G4
Stemster House 275 G2
Stenalees 97 E4
Stenhill 103 D1
Stenhousemuir 234 C1
Stenigot 188 C4
Stenness 278 B5
Stenscholl 263 K5
Stenson 173 E5
Stenton ELoth 236 D2
Stenton P&K 251 F5
Stepaside Pembs 127 E2
Stepaside Powys 155 G4
Stepney 136 C4
Steppingley 149 F4
Stepps 234 A3
Sternfield 153 E1
Sterridge 113 F1
Stert 118 B2
Stetchworth 151 E2
Stevenage 150 A5
Stevenston 233 D5
Steventon Hants 119 G3
Steventon Oxon 133 G3
Steventon End 151 E3
Stevington 149 E2
Stewart Park, Middlesbrough Middl TS7 8AR 29 C4
Stewartby 149 F3
Stewarton D&G 207 E2
Stewarton EAyr 233 F5
Stewkley 149 D5
Stewley 103 G1
Stewton 189 D4
Steyning 109 D2
Steynton 126 C2
Stibb 112 C4
Stibb Cross 113 E4
Stibb Green 118 D1
Stibbard 178 A3
Stibbington 161 F3
Stichill 228 B3
Sticker 97 D4
Stickford 176 B1
Sticklepath Devon 99 G1
Sticklepath Som 103 G1
Stickling Green 150 C4
Stickney 176 B2
Stiff Street 124 A2
Stiffkey 178 A1
Stifford's Bridge 145 G3
Stileway 116 B3
Stilligarry (Stadhlaigearraidh) 254 C1
Stillingfleet 195 E3
Stillington NYorks 195 E1
Stillington Stock 212 C5
Stilton 161 G4
Stinchcombe 131 G3
Stinsford 104 D3
Stirchley Tel&W 157 G2
Stirchley WMid 158 C4
Stirkoke House 275 J3
Stirling Aber 269 K6
Stirling (Sruighlea) Stir 242 C5
Stirling Castle Stir FK8 1EJ 242 C5
Stirling Visitor Centre Stir FK8 1EH 242 C5
Stirton 193 F2
Stisted 151 G5
Stitchcombe 118 D1
Stithians 95 E3
Stittenham 266 D4
Stivichall 159 F5
Stix 250 C5
Stixwould 175 G1
Stoak 183 F5
Stobo 226 C2
Stoborough 105 F4
Stoborough Green 105 F4
Stobwood 235 D4
Stock 137 F3
Stock Green 146 B2
Stock Lane 133 E5
Stock Wood 146 C2
Stockbridge Hants 119 E4
Stockbridge Stir 242 C4
Stockbridge WSuss 108 A3
Stockbury 124 A2
Stockcross 119 F1
Stockdale 95 E3
Stockdalewath 209 G2
Stockerston 160 D3
Stockgrove Country Park CenBeds LU7 0BA 149 E5
Stocking Green Essex 151 D4
Stocking Green MK 148 D3
Stocking Pelham 150 C5
Stockingford 159 F3
Stockinish (Stocinis) 263 G2
Stockland Cardiff 130 A5
Stockland Devon 103 F2
Stockland Bristol 115 F3
Stockleigh English 102 B2
Stockleigh Pomeroy 102 B2
Stockley 118 B1
Stocklinch 103 G1
Stockport 184 C3
Stocksbridge 185 G3
Stocksfield 211 G1
Stockton Here 145 E1
Stockton Norf 165 E2
Stockton Shrop 157 G3
Stockton Shrop 156 B2
Stockton Tel&W 157 G1
Stockton Warks 147 G1
Stockton Wilts 118 A4
Stockton Heath 184 A4
Stockton on Teme 145 G1
Stockton on the Forest 195 F2
Stockton-on-Tees 202 D1
Stockwell 132 B1
Stockwell Heath 172 B5
Stockwood Bristol 116 D1
Stockwood Dorset 104 B2
Stodday 192 A2
Stodmarsh 125 E2
Stody 178 B2
Stoer 272 C6
Stoford Som 104 B1
Stoford Wilts 118 B4
Stogumber 115 D4
Stogursey 115 F3
Stoke Devon 112 C3
Stoke Hants 119 F2
Stoke Hants 107 G2
Stoke Med 124 A1
Stoke Plym 100 A2
Stoke WMid 159 F5
Stoke Abbott 104 A2
Stoke Albany 160 D4
Stoke Ash 164 C4
Stoke Bardolph 174 B3
Stoke Bishop 131 E5
Stoke Bliss 145 F1
Stoke Bruerne 148 C2
Stoke by Clare 151 F3
Stoke Canon 102 C3
Stoke Charity 119 F4
Stoke Climsland 99 D3
Stoke D'Abernon 121 G2
Stoke Doyle 161 F4
Stoke Dry 161 D3
Stoke Edith 145 F3
Stoke Farthing 118 B5
Stoke Ferry 163 F3
Stoke Fleming 101 E3
Stoke Gabriel 101 E2
Stoke Gifford 131 F5
Stoke Golding 159 F3
Stoke Goldington 148 D3
Stoke Green 135 E4
Stoke Hammond 149 D5
Stoke Heath Shrop 171 D5
Stoke Heath Worcs 146 B1
Stoke Holy Cross 178 D5
Stoke Lacy 145 F3
Stoke Lyne 148 A5
Stoke Mandeville 134 D1
Stoke Newington 136 C4
Stoke on Tern 170 D5
Stoke Orchard 146 B5
Stoke Pero 114 B3
Stoke Poges 135 E4
Stoke Pound 146 B1
Stoke Prior Here 145 E2
Stoke Prior Worcs 146 B1
Stoke Rivers 113 G2
Stoke Rochford 175 E5
Stoke Row 134 B4
Stoke St. Gregory 116 A5
Stoke St. Mary 115 F5
Stoke St. Michael 117 D3
Stoke St. Milborough 157 E4
Stoke sub Hamdon 104 A1
Stoke Talmage 134 B3
Stoke Trister 117 E5
Stoke Villice 116 C1
Stoke Wake 105 D2
Stoke-by-Nayland 152 A4
Stokeford 105 E4
Stokeham 187 E5
Stokeinteignhead 102 C5
Stokenchurch 134 C3
Stokenham 101 E3
Stoke-on-Trent 171 F3
Stokesay 156 D4
Stokesby 179 F4
Stokesley 203 E2
Stolford 115 F3
Ston Easton 116 D2
Stonar Cut 125 F2
Stondon Massey 137 E2
Stone Bucks 134 C1
Stone Glos 131 F3
Stone Kent 137 E5
Stone Kent 111 E1
Stone Som 116 C4
Stone Staffs 171 G4
Stone SYorks 186 C4
Stone Worcs 158 A5
Stone Allerton 116 B2
Stone Cross Dur 201 F1
Stone Cross ESuss 110 B3
Stone Cross ESuss 110 A1
Stone Cross Kent 124 C5
Stone Cross Kent 123 E5
Stone House 200 C4
Stone Street Kent 123 E3
Stone Street Suff 165 E3
Stone Street Suff 152 A4
Stonea 162 C3
Stonebridge ESuss 110 A1
Stonebridge NSom 116 A2
Stonebridge Warks 159 E4
Stonebroom 173 F2
Stonecross Green 151 G2
Stonefield A&B 231 G2
Stonefield Staffs 171 G4
Stonegate ESuss 110 B1
Stonegate NYorks 203 G2
Stonegrave 203 F5
Stonehaugh 219 F4
Stonehaven 253 G1
Stonehenge Wilts SP4 7DE 118 C3
Stonehill 121 E1
Stonehouse ChesW&C 183 G5
Stonehouse D&G 216 C4
Stonehouse Glos 132 A2
Stonehouse N'umb 210 C2
Stonehouse Plym 100 A2
Stonehouse SLan 234 B5
Stoneleigh Surr 122 B2
Stoneleigh Warks 159 F5
Stoneley Green 170 D2
Stonely 149 G1
Stoner Hill 120 C5
Stones 193 F5
Stones Green 152 C5
Stonesby 174 D5
Stonesfield 133 F1
Stonestreet Green 124 C5
Stonethwaite 209 F5
Stoney Cross 106 B1
Stoney Middleton 185 G5
Stoney Stanton 159 G3
Stoney Stoke 117 E4
Stoney Stratton 117 D4
Stoney Stretton 156 C2
Stoneyburn 235 D3
Stoneyford 103 D4
Stoneygate 160 B2
Stoneyhills 138 C3
Stoneykirk 214 B5
Stoneywood 261 G3
Stonganess 278 E2
Stonham Aspal 152 C2
Stonham Barns Suff IP14 6AT 152 C2
Stonnall 158 C2
Stonor 134 C4
Stonton Wyville 160 C3
Stony Houghton 173 F1
Stony Stratford 148 C3
Stonybreck 278 A1
Stoodleigh Devon 102 C1
Stoodleigh Devon 113 G2
Stopham 108 C2
Stopsley 149 G5
Stoptide 96 D2
Storeton 183 E4
Stormontfield 243 G2
Stornoway (Steornabhagh) 271 G4
Stornoway Airport 271 G4
Storridge 145 G3
Storrington 108 C2
Storrs 185 G4
Storth 199 F4
Storwood 195 G3
Storybook Glen Aber AB12 5FT 261 G5
Stotfield 267 K4
Stotfold 150 A4
Stottesdon 157 F4
Stoughton Leics 160 B2
Stoughton Surr 121 E2
Stoughton WSuss 107 G1
Stoughton Cross 116 B3
Stoul 256 D5
Stoulton 146 B3
Stour Provost 117 E5
Stour Row 117 F5
Stourbridge 158 A4
Stourhead Wilts BA12 6QD 117 E4
Stourpaine 105 E2
Stourport-on-Severn 158 A5
Stourton Staffs 158 A4
Stourton Warks 147 E4
Stourton Wilts 117 E4
Stourton Caundle 104 D1
Stove 276 F4
Stoven 165 F3
Stow Lincs 187 F4
Stow ScBord 236 B5
Stow Bardolph 163 E2
Stow Bedon 164 A2
Stow cum Quy 150 D1
Stow Longa 161 G5
Stow Maries 138 B3
Stow Pasture 187 F4
Stowbridge 163 D2
Stowe Glos 131 E2
Stowe Shrop 156 C5
Stowe Staffs 158 D1
Stowe Landscape Gardens Bucks MK18 5DQ 148 B4
Stowe-by-Chartley 172 B5
Stowehill 148 B2
Stowell Glos 132 C1
Stowell Som 117 D5
Stowey 116 C2
Stowford Devon 99 E2
Stowford Devon 113 G3
Stowford Devon 103 E4
Stowlangtoft 152 A1
Stowmarket 152 B2
Stow-on-the-Wold 147 D5
Stowting 124 D4
Stowupland 152 B2
Straad 232 B3
Stracathro 253 E3
Strachan 260 E5
Strachur (Clachan Strachur) 240 C4
Stradbroke 164 D4
Stradishall 151 F2
Stradsett 163 E2
Stragglethorpe 175 E2
Straight Soley 133 F5
Straiton Edin 235 G3
Straiton SAyr 224 B5
Straloch Aber 261 G2
Straloch P&K 251 F3
Stramshall 172 B4
Strands 198 C4
Strang 190 B4
Strangford 145 E5
Strannda 263 F3
Stranraer 214 B4
Strata Florida 142 D1
Stratfield Mortimer 120 B1
Stratfield Saye 120 B1
Stratfield Turgis 120 B2
Stratford CenBeds 149 G3
Stratford Glos 146 A4
Stratford GtLon 136 C4
Stratford St. Andrew 153 E2
Stratford St. Mary 152 B4
Stratford sub Castle 118 C4
Stratford Tony 118 B5
Stratford-upon-Avon 147 E2
Stratford-upon-Avon Butterfly Farm Warks CV37 7LS 85 Stratford-upon-Avon
Strath 275 H3
Strathan High 272 C6
Strathan High 257 F5
Strathaven 234 B5
Strathblane 233 G2
Strathcanaird 265 H1
Strathcarron 265 F7
Strathclyde Country Park NLan ML1 3ED 31 G5
Strathdon 260 B3
Strathgirnock 260 B5
Strathkinness 244 C3
Strathmiglo 244 A3

Strathpeffer (Strath Pheofhair) 266 B6
Strathrannoch 265 K4
Strathtay 251 E4
Strathwhillan 223 F2
Strathy 266 D2
Strathyre 242 A3
Stratton Corn 112 C5
Stratton Dorset 104 C3
Stratton Glos 132 C2
Stratton Audley 148 B5
Stratton Hall 152 D4
Stratton St. Margaret 133 D4
Stratton St. Michael 164 D2
Stratton Strawless 178 D3
Stratton-on-the-Fosse 117 D2
Stravanan 232 B4
Stravithie 244 D3
Strawberry Hill 136 A5
Stream 115 D4
Streat 109 F2
Streatham 136 B5
Streatham Ice and Leisure Centre GtLon
SW16 6HX 13 B7
Streatham Vale 136 B5
Streatley CenBeds 149 F5
Streatley WBerks 134 A4
Street Devon 103 F1
Street Lancs 192 B2
Street NYorks 203 G2
Street Som 116 B4
Street Som 103 G2
Street Ashton 159 G4
Street Dinas 170 A4
Street End 108 A4
Street Gate 212 B2
Street Houses 195 E3
Street Lane 173 E3
Street on the Fosse 116 D4
Streethay 158 D1
Streethouse 194 C5
Streetlam 202 C3
Streetly 158 C3
Streetly End 151 E3
Strefford 156 D4
Strelley 173 G3
Strensall 195 F1
Strensham 146 B3
Stretcholt 115 F3
Strete 101 E3
Stretford GtMan 184 B3
Stretford Here 144 D2
Stretford Here 145 E2
Strethall 150 C4
Stretham 162 D5
Strettington 108 A3
Stretton ChesW&C 170 B2
Stretton Derbys 173 E1
Stretton Rut 161 E1
Stretton Staffs 158 A1
Stretton Staffs 173 D5
Stretton Warr 184 A4
Stretton en le Field 159 F1
Stretton Grandison 145 F3
Stretton Heath 156 C1
Stretton Sugwas 145 D3
Stretton under Fosse 159 G4
Stretton Westwood 157 E3
Stretton-on-Dunsmore 159 G5
Stretton-on-Fosse 147 E4
Stribers 199 E4
Strichen 269 H5
Strines 185 D4
Strinesdale Countryside Area GtMan
OL4 2JJ 25 H1
Stringston 115 E3
Strixton 149 E1
Stroat 131 E3
Stromeferry 256 E1
Stromemore 256 E1
Stromness 277 B7
Stronaba 249 E1
Stronachlachar 241 G3
Strone A&B 232 C1
Strone High 258 C2
Strone High 248 D2
Strone Stir 241 G3
Stronechrubie 272 E7
Stronlonag 232 C1
Stronmilchan (Sròn nam Mialchon) 241 D2
Stronsay 276 F5
Stronsay Airfield 276 F5
Strontian (Sròn an t-Sithein) 248 A3
Strontoiller 240 B2
Stronvar 242 A2
Strood 123 G2
Strood Green Surr 122 B4
Strood Green WSuss 121 F5
Strood Green WSuss 121 G4
Stroquhan 216 C2
Stroud Glos 132 A2
Stroud Hants 120 C5
Stroud Common 121 F3
Stroud Green Essex 138 B3
Stroud Green Glos 132 A2
Stroude 121 F1
Stroul 131 D1
Stroxton 175 E4
Struan High 255 J1
Struan P&K 250 C3
Strubby Lincs 189 E4
Strubby Lincs 188 B5
Strumpshaw 179 E5
Struthers 244 B4
Struy 258 B1
Stryd y Facsen 180 B4
Stryt-cae-rhedyn 169 F1
Stryt-issa 169 F2

Stubhampton 105 F1
Stubley 186 A5
Stubshaw Cross 183 G2
Stubton 175 D3
Stuck A&B 232 B3
Stuck A&B 240 D5
Stuckbeg 241 E5
Stuckgowan 241 F4
Stuckindroin 241 F3
Stuckreoch 240 C5
Stuckton 106 A1
Stud Green 135 D5
Studdon 211 E2
Studfold 200 D5
Studham 135 F1
Studholme 209 F1
Studland 105 G4
Studland & Godlingston Heath NNR Dorset
BH19 3AX 105 G4
Studley Warks 146 C1
Studley Wilts 132 B5
Studley Common 146 C1
Studley Green 134 C3
Studley Roger 202 B5
Studley Royal Park & ruins of Fountains Abbey NYorks
HG4 3DY 194 B1
Stuggadhoo 190 B4
Stump Cross Essex 150 D3
Stump Cross Lancs 192 B4
Stuntney 163 D5
Stunts Green 110 B2
Sturbridge 171 F4
Sturgate 187 F4
Sturmer 151 E3
Sturminster Common 105 D1
Sturminster Marshall 105 F2
Sturminster Newton 105 D1
Sturry 125 D2
Sturton by Stow 187 F4
Sturton le Steeple 187 E4
Stuston 164 C4
Stutton NYorks 195 D3
Stutton Suff 152 D4
Styal 184 C4
Styrrup 186 D3
Suardail 271 G4
Succoth A&B 241 E4
Succoth Aber 260 C1
Succothmore 240 D4
Suckley 145 G2
Suckley Green 145 G2
Suckley Knowl 145 G2
Sudborough 161 E4
Sudbourne 153 F2
Sudbrook Lincs 175 E3
Sudbrook Mon 131 E4
Sudbrooke 188 A5
Sudbury Derbys 172 C4
Sudbury GtLon 136 A4
Sudbury Suff 151 G3
Sudbury Hall Derbys
DE6 5HT 172 C4
Sudden 184 C1
Sudgrove 132 B2
Suffield Norf 178 D2
Suffield NYorks 204 C3
Sugarloaf 124 C5
Sugnall 171 E4
Sugwas Pool 145 D3
Suie Lodge Hotel 241 G2
Suisnish 256 B1
Sulby IoM 190 B2
Sulby IoM 190 B4
Sulgrave 148 A3
Sulham 134 B5
Sulhamstead 120 B1
Sullington 108 C2
Sullom 278 C5
Sullom Voe Oil Terminal 278 C5
Sully 115 E1
Sumburgh 279 F10
Sumburgh Airport 279 F9
Summer Bridge 194 B1
Summer Isles 265 F1
Summer Lodge 201 E3
Summercourt 96 C4
Summerfield Norf 177 F4
Summerfield Worcs 158 A5
Summerhill 170 A2
Summerhouse 202 B1
Summerlands 199 G4
Summerleaze 130 D4
Summertown 134 A2
Summit 184 D1
Sun Green 185 D3
Sunadale 231 G5
Sunbiggin 200 B3
Sunbury 121 G1
Sundaywell 216 C2
Sunderland Cumb 209 E3
Sunderland Lancs 192 A2
Sunderland T&W 212 C2
Sunderland Bridge 212 B4
Sunderland Museum & Winter Gardens
T&W SR1 1PP 86 Sunderland
Sundhope 227 E3
Sundon Park 149 F5
Sundown Adventure Land Notts
DN22 0HX 187 E5
Sundridge 123 D3
Sundrum Mains 224 C3
Sunhill 132 D2
Sunipol 246 C4
Sunk Island 188 C1
Sunningdale 121 E1
Sunninghill 121 E1
Sunningwell 133 G2
Sunniside Dur 212 A4
Sunniside T&W 212 B2
Sunny Bank 199 D3
Sunny Brow 212 A4
Sunnylaw 242 C5
Sunnyside Aber 261 G5
Sunnyside N'umb 211 E1
Sunnyside SYorks 186 B3
Sunnyside WSuss 122 C5
Sunton 118 D2
Sunwick 237 F4
Surbiton 121 G1

Surfleet 176 A5
Surfleet Seas End 176 A5
Surlingham 179 E5
Sustead 178 C2
Susworth 187 F2
Sutcombe 112 D4
Sutcombemill 112 D4
Suton 164 B2
Sutors of Cromarty 267 F5
Sutterby 189 D5
Sutterton 176 A4
Sutton Cambs 162 C5
Sutton CenBeds 150 A3
Sutton Devon 102 A2
Sutton Devon 100 D3
Sutton GtLon 122 B2
Sutton Kent 125 F4
Sutton Lincs 175 D2
Sutton Norf 179 E3
Sutton Notts 174 C4
Sutton Notts 187 D4
Sutton Oxon 133 G2
Sutton Pembs 126 C1
Sutton Peter 161 F3
Sutton Shrop 157 G4
Sutton Shrop 171 D4
Sutton Shrop 157 E1
Sutton Shrop 170 A5
Sutton Staffs 171 E5
Sutton Suff 153 E3
Sutton SYorks 186 C1
Sutton WSuss 108 B2
Sutton Abinger 121 G3
Sutton at Hone 137 E5
Sutton Bassett 160 C4
Sutton Benger 132 B5
Sutton Bingham 104 B1
Sutton Bonington 173 G5
Sutton Bridge 176 C5
Sutton Cheney 159 G2
Sutton Coldfield 158 D3
Sutton Courtenay 134 A3
Sutton Crosses 176 C5
Sutton Grange 202 B5
Sutton Green Oxon 133 G2
Sutton Green Surr 121 F2
Sutton Green Wrex 170 B3
Sutton Holms 106 A2
Sutton Howgrave 202 C5
Sutton in Ashfield 173 F2
Sutton in the Elms 160 A3
Sutton Ings 196 D4
Sutton Lane Ends 184 D5
Sutton le Marsh 189 F4
Sutton Leach 183 G3
Sutton Maddock 157 G2
Sutton Mallet 116 A4
Sutton Mandeville 118 A5
Sutton Montis 116 D5
Sutton on Sea 189 F4
Sutton on the Hill 172 D4
Sutton on Trent 174 C1
Sutton Poyntz 104 D4
Sutton St. Edmund 162 B1
Sutton St. James 162 C1
Sutton St. Nicholas 145 E3
Sutton Scarsdale 173 F1
Sutton Scotney 119 F4
Sutton upon Derwent 195 G3
Sutton Valence 124 A4
Sutton Veny 117 F3
Sutton Waldron 105 E1
Sutton Weaver 183 G5
Sutton Wick B&NESom 116 C2
Sutton Wick Oxon 133 G3
Sutton-in-Craven 193 G3
Sutton-on-Hull 196 D4
Sutton-on-the-Forest 195 E1
Sutton-under-Brailes 147 F4
Sutton-under-Whitestonecliffe 203 D4
Swaby 189 D5
Swadlincote 159 F1
Swaffham 163 F2
Swaffham Bulbeck 151 D1
Swaffham Prior 151 D1
Swafield 179 D2
Swainbost (Suainebost) 271 H1
Swainby 203 D2
Swainshill 145 D3
Swainsthorpe 178 D5
Swainswick 117 E1
Swalcliffe 147 F4
Swalecliffe 124 D2
Swallow 188 B2
Swallow Beck 175 E1
Swallow Falls Conwy
LL24 0DW 168 A2
Swallowcliffe 118 A5
Swallowfield 120 C1
Swallows Cross 137 F3
Swampton 119 F2
Swan Green ChesW&C 184 B5
Swan Green Suff 165 D4
Swan Street 151 G5
Swanage 105 G5
Swanage Railway Dorset
BH19 1HB 105 G5
Swanbach 171 D3
Swanbourne 148 D5
Swanbridge 115 E1
Swancote 157 G3
Swanland 196 B5
Swanlaws 228 B5
Swanley 123 E2
Swanley Village 123 E2
Swanmore Hants 107 E1
Swanmore IoW 107 E3
Swannington Leics 159 G1
Swannington Norf 178 C4
Swanscombe 137 F5
Swansea (Abertawe) 128 C3
Swansea Museum SA1 1SN
86 Swansea
Swanston 235 G2
Swanton Abbot 179 D3
Swanton Morley 178 B4
Swanton Novers 178 B2

Swanton Street 124 A3
Swanwick Derbys 173 F2
Swanwick Hants 107 E2
Swanwick Green 170 C3
Swarby 175 F3
Swardeston 178 D5
Swarkestone 173 E5
Swarland 221 D1
Swarraton 119 G4
Swarthmoor 199 D5
Swaton 175 G4
Swavesey 150 B1
Sway 106 B3
Swayfield 175 E5
Swaythling 106 D1
Swaythorpe 196 C1
Sweetham 102 B3
Sweethay 115 F5
Sweetshouse 97 E3
Swefling 153 E1
Swell 116 A5
Swepstone 159 F1
Swerford 147 F4
Swettenham 171 F1
Swffryd 130 B3
Swift's Green 124 A4
Swiftsden 110 C1
Swilland 152 C2
Swillington 194 C4
Swimbridge 113 G3
Swimbridge Newland 113 F2
Swinbrook 133 E1
Swincliffe 194 B2
Swincombe 113 G1
Swinden 175 D1
Swinderby 175 D1
Swindon Staffs 158 A3
Swindon Swin 133 D4
Swindon Village 146 B5
Swine 196 D4
Swinefleet 195 G5
Swineford 117 D1
Swineshead Bed 149 F1
Swineshead Lincs 176 A3
Swineshead Bridge 176 A3
Swineside 201 F4
Swiney 275 H5
Swinford Leics 160 A5
Swinford Oxon 133 G2
Swingate 173 G3
Swingfield Minnis 125 E4
Swingleton Green 152 A3
Swinhoe 229 G4
Swinhope 188 C3
Swining 279 D6
Swinithwaite 201 F4
Swinscoe 172 C3
Swinside Hall 228 B5
Swinstead 175 F5
Swinton GtMan 184 B2
Swinton NYorks 203 G5
Swinton NYorks 202 B5
Swinton ScBord 237 F5
Swinton SYorks 186 B3
Swinton Quarter 237 F5
Swintonmill 237 F5
Swithland 160 A1
Swordale 266 C5
Swordland 247 E2
Swordle 247 E2
Swordly 274 C2
Sworton Heath 184 A4
Swyddffynnon 142 C1
Swyncombe 134 B3
Swynnerton 171 F4
Swyre 104 B4
Sychnant 155 F5
Syde 132 B1
Sydenham GtLon 136 C5
Sydenham Devon 99 E3
Sydenham Damerel 99 E3
Sydling St. Nicholas 104 C3
Sydmonton 119 F2
Sydney 171 E2
Syerston 174 C3
Sykehouse 186 D1
Sykes 192 C2
Sylen 128 C2
Symbister 279 E6
Symington SAyr 224 B2
Symington SLan 226 A2
Symonds Yat 131 E1
Symondsbury 104 A3
Synod Inn (Post-mawr) 142 A2
Syre 273 J4
Syreford 146 C5
Syresham 148 B3
Syston Leics 160 B1
Syston Lincs 175 E3
Sytchampton 146 A1
Sywell 148 D1
Sywell Country Park N'hants
NN6 0QX 148 D1

T

Taagan 265 G5
Tableyhill 184 B5
Tabost 271 F6
Tachbrook Mallory 147 F1
Tacher 275 G4
Tackley 147 G5
Tacolneston 164 C2
Tadcaster 195 D3
Tadden 105 F2
Taddiport Derbys 185 F5
Taddington Glos 146 C4
Taddiport 113 E4
Tadley 120 B1
Tadlow 150 A3
Tadmarton 147 F4
Tadpole Bridge 133 F2
Tadworth 122 B3
Tafarnaubach 130 A1
Tafarn-y-bwlch 141 D4
Tafarn-y-Gelyn 169 E1
Taff Merthyr Garden Village 130 A3
Taff's Well (Ffynnon Taf) 130 A4
Tafolwern 155 E2
Taibach NPT 129 D4
Tai-bach Powys 169 E5
Taicynhaeaf 154 C1
Tain High 275 H2
Tain High 266 E3

Tai'n Lôn 166 D3
Tai'r Bull 143 F5
Tairgwaith 128 D1
Tai'r-heol 130 A3
Tairlaw 224 C5
Tai'r-ysgol 128 C3
Takeley 151 E5
Takeley Street 150 D5
Talachddu 143 G4
Talacre 182 C4
Talardd 168 B5
Talaton 103 D3
Talbenny 126 B1
Talbot Green 129 G4
Talbot Village 105 G3
Talerddig 155 F2
Talgarreg 142 A2
Talgarth 144 A4
Taliesin 154 C3
Talisker 255 J1
Talke 171 F2
Talke Pits 171 F2
Talkin 210 B2
Talkin Tarn Country Park Cumb
CA8 1HN 210 B2
Talla Linnfoots 226 C3
Talladale 265 F4
Talladh-a-Bheithe 250 A4
Talland 97 G3
Tallarn Green 170 B3
Tallentire 209 E3
Talley (Talyllychau) 142 C4
Tallington 161 F2
Talmine 273 H2
Talog 142 A5
Tal-sarn 142 B2
Talsarnau 167 F4
Talskiddy 96 C3
Talwrn IoA 180 C5
Talwrn Wrex 169 F2
Talwrn Wrex 170 A2
Talybont Cere 154 C4
Tal-y-bont Conwy 168 A1
Tal-y-bont Gwyn 167 E5
Tal-y-bont Gwyn 181 E5
Talybont-on-Usk 144 A5
Tal-y-Cae 167 F1
Tal-y-cafn 181 F5
Tal-y-coed 130 D1
Talygarn 129 G4
Talyllyn Gwyn 154 D2
Talyllyn Powys 144 A5
Talysarn 167 D2
Tal-y-wern 155 E2
Tamavoid 242 A5
Tamerton Foliot 100 A1
Tamworth 159 E2
Tamworth Green 176 B3
Tan Office Green 151 F2
Tan-lan 167 F3
Tandem 185 F1
Tandridge 122 C3
Tanerdy 142 A5
Tanfield 212 A2
Tanfield Lea 212 A2
Tang 194 B2
Tang Hall 195 F2
Tangiers 126 C1
Tanglandford 261 G1
Tangley 119 E2
Tangmere 108 B3
Tangwick 278 B5
Tangy 222 B3
Tank Museum, Bovington Dorset
BH20 6JG 105 E4
Tankerness 277 E7
Tankersley 186 A2
Tankerton 124 D2
Tannach 275 J4
Tannachy 266 E1
Tannadice 252 C4
Tannington 152 D1
Tannochside 234 A3
Tansley 173 E2
Tansley Knoll 173 E2
Tansor 161 F2
Tantobie 212 A2
Tanton 203 E1
Tanworth in Arden 158 D5
Tan-y-fron 168 C1
Tan-y-graig 166 C4
Tanygrisiau 167 F3
Tan-y-groes 141 F3
Tan-yr-allt 167 D2
Taobh a' Deas Loch Baghasdail 254 C3
Taobh Siar 270 D7
Tapeley 113 E3
Taplow 135 E4
Tapton Grove 186 B5
Taransay (Tarasaigh) 270 C7
Taraphocain 248 C5
Tarbat House 266 E4
Tarbert A&B 231 E4
Tarbert A&B 231 E1
Tarbert A&B 231 E3
Tarbert High 247 F3
Tarbert (Tairbeart) Na H-ESiar 270 D7
Tarbet (An Tairbeart) A&B 241 F4
Tarbet High 256 D5
Tarbet High 272 D5
Tarbock Green 183 F4
Tarbolton 224 C3
Tarbrax 235 E4
Tardebigge 146 B1
Tardy Gate 192 B5
Tarfside 252 C2
Tarland 260 C4
Tarleton 192 A5
Tarlscough 183 F1
Tarlton 132 B3
Tarnbrook 192 B2
Tarnock 116 A2
Tarporley 170 C1
Tarr 115 E4
Tarrant Crawford 105 F2
Tarrant Gunville 105 F1
Tarrant Hinton 105 F1
Tarrant Keyneston 105 F2
Tarrant Launceston 105 F2
Tarrant Monkton 105 F2
Tarrant Rawston 105 F2

Tarrant Rushton 105 F2
Tarrel 267 F3
Tarring Neville 109 G3
Tarrington 145 F3
Tarnacraig 223 E2
Tarsappie 243 G2
Tarskavaig 256 B4
Tarves 261 G1
Tarvie (Tairbhidh) High 266 B6
Tarvie P&K 251 F3
Tarvin 170 B1
Tarvin Sands 170 B1
Tasburgh 164 D2
Tasley 157 F2
Taston 147 F5
Tate Britain GtLon
SW1P 4RG 13 B5
Tate Liverpool Mersey L3 4BB 42 B5
Tate Modern GtLon
SE1 9TG 45 H4
Tate St. Ives Corn
TR26 1TG 94 C2
Tatenhill 172 D5
Tathall End 148 D3
Tatham 192 C1
Tathwell 188 D4
Tatsfield 122 D3
Tattenhall 170 B2
Tattenhoe 148 D4
Tatterford 177 G5
Tattersett 177 G4
Tattershall 176 A2
Tattershall Bridge 175 G2
Tattershall Thorpe 176 A2
Tattingstone 152 D3
Tatton Park ChesE
WA16 6QN 184 B4
Tatworth 103 G2
Tauchers 268 B6
Taunton 115 F5
Tavelty 261 F3
Taverham 178 C4
Tavernspite 127 E1
Tavistock 99 E3
Taw Bridge 113 G5
Taw Green 99 G1
Tawstock 113 F3
Taxal 185 E5
Tayburn 233 G5
Taychreggan 240 C2
Tayinloan 231 E5
Taylors Cross 112 C5
Taynafead 240 C4
Taynish 231 F1
Taynton Glos 145 G5
Taynton Oxon 133 E1
Taynuilt (Taigh an Uillt) 240 C1
Tayock 253 E4
Tayovullin 230 A2
Tayport 244 C2
Tayvallich 231 F1
Tea Green 149 G5
Tealby 188 B3
Tealing 244 C1
Team Valley 212 B1
Teanamachar 262 C5
Teangue 256 C4
Teasses 244 C4
Tebay 200 B2
Tebworth 149 E5
Techniquest, Cardiff Cardiff
CF10 5BW 7 B4
Tedburn St. Mary 102 B3
Teddington Glos 146 B4
Teddington GtLon 136 A5
Tedstone Delamere 145 F2
Tedstone Wafre 145 F2
Teeton 160 B5
Teffont Evias 118 A4
Teffont Magna 118 A4
Tegryn 141 F4
Tehidy Country Park Corn
TR14 0HA 96 A5
Teigh 161 D1
Teigncombe 102 A4
Teigngrace 102 B5
Teignmouth 102 C5
Telford 157 F2
Telford Wonderland Tel&W
TF3 4AY 157 G2
Telham 110 C2
Tellisford 117 F2
Telscombe 109 G3
Telscombe Cliffs 109 G3
Tempar 250 B4
Templand 217 E2
Temple Corn 97 F2
Temple Midlo 236 A4
Temple Balsall 159 E5
Temple Bar 142 B2
Temple Cloud 116 D2
Temple End 151 E2
Temple Ewell 125 E4
Temple Grafton 146 D2
Temple Guiting 146 C5
Temple Herdewyke 147 F2
Temple Hirst 195 F5
Temple Normanton 173 F1
Temple Sowerby 210 C5
Templecombe 117 E5
Templeton Devon 102 B1
Templeton Pembs 127 E1
Templeton Bridge 102 B1
Templewood 253 E3
Tempsford 149 G2
Ten Mile Bank 163 E3
Tenbury Wells 145 F1
Tenby (Dinbych-y-pysgod) 127 E2
Tendring 152 C5
Tendring Green 152 C5
Tenga 167 E5
Tenterden 124 A5
Tepersie Castle 260 D2
Terally 206 B2
Terling 137 G2
Tern 157 F1
Ternhill 170 D4
Terregles 216 D3
Terriers 135 D3
Terrington 203 F5
Terrington St. Clement 177 D5

Terrington St. John 162 D1
Terry's Green 158 D5
Tervieside 259 K1
Teston 123 G3
Testwood 106 C1
Tetbury 132 A3
Tetbury Upton 132 A3
Tetchill 170 A4
Tetcott 98 D1
Tetford 188 D5
Tetney 188 D2
Tetney Lock 188 D2
Tetsworth 134 B2
Tettenhall 158 A2
Tettenhall Wood 158 A3
Tetworth 150 A2
Teuchan 261 J1
Teversal 173 F1
Teversham 150 C2
Teviot Water Gardens ScBord TD5 8LE 228 B4
Teviothead 227 F5
Tewel 253 G1
Tewin 136 B1
Tewkesbury 146 A4
Tewkesbury Abbey Glos
GL20 5RZ 146 A4
Teynham 124 B2
Thackley 194 A4
Thainston 253 E2
Thainstone 261 F3
Thakeham 108 D2
Thame 134 C2
Thames Ditton 121 G1
Thames Haven 137 G4
Thamesmead 137 D4
Thanington 124 D3
Thankerton 226 A2
Tharston 164 C2
Thatcham 119 G1
Thatto Heath 183 G3
Thaxted 151 E4
The Apes Hall 163 D3
The Bage 144 B3
The Balloch 242 B3
The Banking 261 F1
The Bar 121 G5
The Birks 261 F4
The Bog 156 C3
The Bourne 120 D3
The Bratch 158 A3
The Broad 145 D1
The Bryn 130 C2
The Burf 146 A1
The Burn 253 D2
The Butts 117 E3
The Camp 132 B2
The Chequer 170 B3
The City Bucks 134 C3
The City Suff 165 E3
The Common Wilts 118 D4
The Common Wilts 132 C4
The Craigs 266 B2
The Cronk 190 B2
The Delves 158 C3
The Den 233 E4
The Dicker 110 A3
The Down 157 F3
The Drums 252 B3
The Eaves 131 F2
The Flatt 219 D4
The Folly 136 A1
The Forge 144 C2
The Forstal ESuss 123 E5
The Forstal Kent 124 C5
The Grange Lincs 189 F5
The Grange Shrop 170 A4
The Grange Surr 122 C4
The Green A&B 246 C4
The Green Cumb 198 C4
The Green Essex 137 G1
The Green Flints 169 F1
The Green Wilts 117 F4
The Grove 146 A4
The Haven 121 F4
The Headland 213 E4
The Heath 172 B4
The Herberts 129 F5
The Hermitage 122 B3
The Hill 198 C4
The Howe 190 A5
The Isle 157 D1
The Laurels 165 E2
The Leacon 124 B5
The Lee 135 D2
The Lhen 190 B1
The Lodge 241 D5
The Marsh 156 C4
The Moor ESuss 110 D2
The Moor Kent 110 C1
The Mumbles 128 C4
The Murray 234 A4
The Mythe 146 A4
The Narth 131 E2
The Neuk 261 F5
The Node 136 B1
The Oval 117 E1
The Polchar 259 G4
The Quarter 124 A4
The Reddings 146 B5
The Rhos 126 D1
The Rookery 171 F2
The Rowe 171 F4
The Sale 159 D1
The Sands 121 D3
The Shoe 132 A5
The Slade 134 A5
The Smithies 157 F2
The Stocks 111 E1
The Swillett 135 F3
The Thrift 150 B4
The Vauld 145 E3
The Wern 169 F2
The Wyke 157 G2
Theakston 202 C4
Thealby 187 F1
Theale Som 116 B3
Theale WBerks 134 B5
Thearne 196 C4
Theberton 153 F1
Thedden Grange 120 B4
Theddingworth 160 B4
Theddlethorpe All Saints 189 E4
Theddlethorpe St. Helen 189 E4

Thelbridge Barton 102 A1
Thelbridge Cross 102 A1
Thelnetham 164 B4
Thelveton 164 C3
Thelwall 184 A4
Themelthorpe 178 B3
Thenford 148 A3
Therfield 150 B4
Thermae Bath Spa B&NESom BA1 1SJ 63 Bath
Thetford Lincs 161 G1
Thetford Norf 163 G4
Thetford Forest Park Norf IP27 0TJ 163 G4
Thethwaite 209 G2
Theydon Bois 136 D3
Theydon Garnon 137 D3
Theydon Mount 137 D3
Thickwood 132 A5
Thimbleby Lincs 176 A1
Thimbleby NYorks 202 B4
Thingley 117 F1
Thirkleby 203 D5
Thirlby 203 D4
Thirlestane 236 C5
Thirn 202 B4
Thirsk 202 D4
Thirston New Houses 221 D2
Thirtleby 197 D4
Thistleton Lancs 192 A4
Thistleton Rut 161 E1
Thistley Green 163 E5
Thixendale 196 A1
Thockrington 220 B4
Tholomas Drove 162 B2
Tholthorpe 195 D1
Thomas Chapel 127 E2
Thomas Close 210 A3
Thomastown 260 D1
Thompson 164 A2
Thomshill 267 K6
Thong 137 F5
Thongsbridge 185 F2
Thoralby 201 F4
Thoresby 186 D5
Thoresthorpe 189 E5
Thoresway 188 B3
Thorganby Lincs 188 C3
Thorganby NYorks 195 F3
Thorgill 203 G3
Thorington 165 F4
Thorington Street 152 B4
Thorley 137 D1
Thorley Houses 150 C5
Thorley Street Herts 137 D1
Thorley Street IoW 106 C4
Thormanby 203 D5
Thornaby-on-Tees 203 D1
Thornage 178 B2
Thornborough Bucks 148 C4
Thornborough NYorks 202 B5
Thornbury Devon 113 D5
Thornbury Here 145 F2
Thornbury SGlos 131 F3
Thornbury WYorks 194 A4
Thornby 160 B5
Thorncliff 185 G1
Thorncliffe 172 B2
Thorncombe 103 G2
Thorncombe Street 121 F3
Thorncote Green 149 G3
Thorncross 106 D4
Thorndon 152 C4
Thorndon Country Park Essex CM13 3RZ 137 F3
Thorndon Cross 99 F1
Thorne 187 D1
Thorne St. Margaret 115 D5
Thorner 194 C4
Thorney Bucks 135 F5
Thorney Notts 187 F5
Thorney Peter 162 A2
Thorney Som 116 B5
Thorney Close 212 C2
Thorney Hill 106 B3
Thornfalcon 115 F5
Thornford 104 C1
Thorngrafton 211 D1
Thorngrove 116 A4
Thorngumbald 197 E5
Thornham 177 F3
Thornham Magna 164 C4
Thornham Parva 164 C4
Thornhaugh 161 F2
Thornhill Cardiff 130 A4
Thornhill Cumb 198 D3
Thornhill D&G 216 C1
Thornhill Derbys 185 F4
Thornhill Soton 107 D1
Thornhill Stir 242 B4
Thornhill WYorks 185 G1
Thornhill Lees 185 G1
Thrigby Hall Wildlife Gardens Norf NR29 3DR 179 F4
Thornholme 196 D1
Thornicombe 105 E2
Thornley Dur 212 D4
Thornley Dur 212 A4
Thornley Gate 211 E2
Thornliebank 233 G4
Thornroan 261 G1
Thorns 151 F2
Thorns Green 184 B4
Thornsett 185 E4
Thornthwaite Cumb 209 F4
Thornthwaite NYorks 194 A2
Thornton Angus 252 B5
Thornton Bucks 148 C4
Thornton ERid 195 G3
Thornton Fife 244 A5
Thornton Lancs 192 A3
Thornton Leics 159 G2
Thornton Lincs 176 A1
Thornton Mersey 183 E2
Thornton Middl 203 D1
Thornton N'umb 237 G5
Thornton P&K 251 F5
Thornton Pembs 126 C2
Thornton WYorks 194 A4
Thornton Bridge 202 D5
Thornton Curtis 188 A1
Thornton Heath 122 C2
Thornton Hough 183 E4
Thornton in Lonsdale 200 B5
Thornton le Moor 188 A3
Thornton Park 237 G5
Thornton Rust 201 E4

Thornton Steward 202 A4
Thornton Watlass 202 A4
Thorntonhall 233 G4
Thornton-in-Craven 193 F3
Thornton-le-Beans 202 C3
Thornton-le-Clay 195 F1
Thornton-le-Dale 204 B4
Thornton-le-Moor 202 C4
Thornton-le-Moors 183 F5
Thornton-le-Street 202 D4
Thorntonloch 237 E2
Thornwood 137 D2
Thornyhill 253 E2
Thornylee 227 F2
Thoroton 174 C3
Thorp Arch 194 D3
Thorpe Derbys 172 C2
Thorpe ERid 196 B3
Thorpe Lincs 189 E4
Thorpe Norf 165 F2
Thorpe Notts 174 C2
Thorpe NYorks 193 G1
Thorpe Surr 121 F1
Thorpe Abbotts 164 C3
Thorpe Acre 173 G5
Thorpe Arnold 174 C5
Thorpe Audlin 186 B1
Thorpe Bassett 204 B5
Thorpe Bay 138 C4
Thorpe by Water 161 D3
Thorpe Constantine 159 E2
Thorpe Culvert 176 C1
Thorpe End 179 D4
Thorpe Green Essex 152 C5
Thorpe Green Lancs 192 B5
Thorpe Green Suff 152 A2
Thorpe Hall 203 E5
Thorpe Hesley 186 A3
Thorpe in Balne 186 C1
Thorpe in the Fallows 187 G4
Thorpe Langton 160 C3
Thorpe Larches 212 C5
Thorpe le Street 196 A3
Thorpe Malsor 160 D5
Thorpe Mandeville 148 A3
Thorpe Market 178 D2
Thorpe Morieux 152 A2
Thorpe on the Hill Lincs 175 E1
Thorpe on the Hill WYorks 194 C5
Thorpe Park Surr KT16 8PN 121 F1
Thorpe Row 178 A5
Thorpe St. Andrew 179 D5
Thorpe St. Peter 176 C1
Thorpe Salvin 186 C4
Thorpe Satchville 160 C1
Thorpe Street 164 B4
Thorpe Thewles 212 C5
Thorpe Tilney Dales 175 G2
Thorpe Underwood N'hants 160 C5
Thorpe Underwood NYorks 195 D2
Thorpe Waterville 161 F4
Thorpe Willoughby 195 E4
Thorpefield 202 D5
Thorpe-le-Soken 152 C5
Thorpeness 153 F1
Thorpland 163 E2
Thorrington 152 B5
Thorverton 102 C2
Thrandeston 164 C4
Thrapston 161 E4
Threapland 193 F1
Threapwood 170 B3
Threapwood Head 172 B3
Three Ashes 117 D3
Three Bridges 122 B5
Three Burrows 96 B5
Three Chimneys 124 A5
Three Cocks (Aberllynfi) 144 A4
Three Counties Showground Worcs WR13 6NW 145 G3
Three Crosses 128 B3
Three Cups Corner 110 B1
Three Hammers 97 G1
Three Holes 162 D2
Three Leg Cross 123 F5
Three Legged Cross 105 G2
Three Mile Cross 120 C1
Three Oaks 110 D2
Threehammer Common 179 E4
Threekingham 175 F4
Threemilestone 96 B5
Threlkeld 209 G4
Threshfield 193 F1
Threxton Hill 163 G2
Thriepley 244 B1
Thrigby 179 F4
Thringarth 211 F5
Thringstone 159 G1
Thrintoft 202 C3
Thriplow 150 C3
Throapham 186 C4
Throckenholt 162 B2
Throcking 150 B4
Throckley 212 A1
Throckmorton 146 B3
Throop 105 E3
Throphill 220 D3
Thropton 220 C1
Througham 132 B2
Throwleigh 99 G1
Throwley 124 B3
Throws 151 E4
Thrumpton Notts 173 G4
Thrumpton Notts 187 E5
Thrumster 275 J4
Thrunton 229 E5
Thrupp Glos 132 B2
Thrupp Oxon 133 G1
Thrupp Oxon 133 E3
Thruscross 194 A2
Thrushelton 99 E2
Thrussington 160 B1
Thruxton Hants 119 D3
Thruxton Here 144 D4
Thrybergh 186 B3
Thrybergh Country Park SYorks S65 4NU 186 B3
Thulston 173 F4
Thunder Bridge 185 F1

Thundergay 231 G5
Thundersley 138 B4
Thunderton 269 J6
Thundridge 136 C1
Thurcaston 160 A1
Thurcroft 186 B4
Thurdistoft 275 H2
Thurdon 112 C4
Thurgarton Norf 178 C2
Thurgarton Notts 174 B3
Thurgoland 185 G2
Thurlaston Leics 160 A3
Thurlaston Warks 159 G5
Thurlbear 115 F5
Thurlby Lincs 161 G1
Thurlby Lincs 175 E5
Thurlby Lincs 189 E5
Thurleigh 149 F2
Thurlestone 100 C3
Thurloxton 115 F4
Thurlstone 185 G2
Thurlton 165 F2
Thurlwood 171 F2
Thurmaston 160 B2
Thurnby 160 B2
Thurne 179 F4
Thurnham 148 A3
Thurning N'hants 161 F4
Thurning Norf 178 B3
Thurnscoe 186 B2
Thursby 209 G1
Thursden 193 F4
Thursford 178 A2
Thursford Collection Norf NR21 0AS 178 A2
Thursley 121 E4
Thurso (Inbhir Theòrsa) 275 G2
Thurstaston 182 D4
Thurston 152 A1
Thurston Clough 185 D2
Thurstonfield 209 G1
Thurstonland 185 F1
Thurton 179 E5
Thurvaston Derbys 172 D4
Thurvaston Derbys 172 C4
Thuster 275 H3
Thuxton 178 B5
Thwaite NYorks 201 D3
Thwaite Suff 152 C1
Thwaite Head 199 E3
Thwaite St. Mary 165 E2
Thwaites 193 G3
Thwaites Brow 193 G3
Thwing 196 D5
Tibbermore 243 F2
Tibberton Glos 145 G5
Tibberton Tel&W 171 D5
Tibberton Worcs 146 B2
Tibbie Shiels Inn 226 D3
Tibenham 164 C2
Tibertich 240 A4
Tibshelf 173 F1
Tibthorpe 196 B2
Ticehurst 123 F5
Tichborne 119 G4
Tickencote 161 E2
Tickenham 131 D5
Tickford End 149 D3
Tickhill 186 C3
Ticklerton 157 D3
Ticknall 173 E5
Tickton 196 C3
Tidbury Green 158 D5
Tidcombe 119 D2
Tiddington Oxon 134 B2
Tiddington Warks 147 E2
Tiddleywink 132 A5
Tidebrook 110 B1
Tideford 98 D5
Tideford Cross 98 D4
Tidenham 131 E3
Tidenham Chase 131 E3
Tideswell 185 F5
Tidmarsh 134 B5
Tidmington 147 E4
Tidpit 105 G1
Tidworth 118 D3
Tiers Cross 126 C1
Tiffield 148 B2
Tifty 269 F6
Tigh a' Gearraidh 262 C4
Tighachnoic 247 F5
Tighnablair 242 D3
Tighnabruaich 232 A2
Tighnacomaire 248 B3
Tigley 101 D1
Tilbrook 149 F1
Tilbury 137 F5
Tilbury Green 151 E4
Tile Hill 159 E5
Tilehurst 134 B5
Tilford 121 D3
Tilgate 122 B5
Tilgate Forest Row 122 B5
Tilgate Park WSuss RH10 5PQ 122 B5
Tillathrowie 260 C1
Tillers' Green 145 F4
Tillery 261 H2
Tilley 170 C5
Tillicoultry 243 E5
Tillietudlem 225 G1
Tillingham 138 C2
Tillington Here 145 D3
Tillington WSuss 121 E5
Tillington Common 145 D3
Tillyarblet 252 D3
Tillybirloch 260 E4
Tillycairn Castle 260 E3
Tillycorthie 261 H2
Tillydrine 260 E5
Tillyfar 260 E3
Tillyfour 260 D3
Tillyfourie 260 E3
Tillygreig 261 G2
Tillypronie 260 C4

Tilsworth 149 E5
Tilton on the Hill 160 C2
Tiltups End 132 A3
Timberland 175 G2
Timberland Dales 175 G1
Timbersbrook 171 F1
Timberscombe 114 C3
Timble 194 A2
Timewell 114 C5
Timperley 184 B4
Timsbury B&NESom 117 D2
Timsbury Hants 119 E5
Timsgearraidh 270 C4
Timworth 151 G1
Timworth Green 151 G1
Tincleton 105 D3
Tindale 210 C2
Tindon End 151 E4
Tingewick 148 B4
Tingley 194 B5
Tingrith 149 F4
Tingwall 279 D8
Tingwall (Lerwick) Airport 279 D8
Tinhay 99 D2
Tinney 98 C1
Tinshill 194 B4
Tinsley 186 B3
Tinsley Green 122 B5
Tintagel 97 E1
Tintagel Castle Corn PL34 0HE 97 E1
Tintern Parva 131 E2
Tintinhull 104 A1
Tintwistle 185 E3
Tinwald 217 E2
Tinwell 161 F2
Tippacott 114 A3
Tipperty Aber 253 F1
Tipperty Aber 261 H2
Tipps End 162 C3
Tiptoe 106 B3
Tipton 158 B3
Tipton St. John 103 D3
Tiptree 138 C1
Tiptree Heath 138 B1
Tiptree Museum Essex CO5 0RF 138 C1
Tirabad 143 E3
Tiree 246 A2
Tiree Airport 246 A2
Tirindrish 249 E1
Tirley 146 A5
Tirphil 130 A2
Tirril 210 B5
Tir-y-dail 128 C1
Tisbury 118 A5
Tisman's Common 121 F4
Tissington 172 C2
Tister 275 G2
Titchberry 112 C3
Titchfield 107 E2
Titchmarsh 161 F4
Titchwell 177 F3
Titchwell Marsh Norf PE31 8BB 177 F3
Titley 144 C1
Titlington 229 F5
Titmore Green 150 A5
Titsey 122 D3
Titson 112 C5
Tittensor 171 F4
Tittesworth Reservoir & Visitor Centre Staffs ST13 8TQ 171 G2
Tittleshall 177 G5
Tiverton ChesW&C 170 C1
Tiverton Devon 102 C1
Tivetshall St. Margaret 164 C3
Tivetshall St. Mary 164 C3
Tivington 114 C3
Tixall 171 G5
Tixover 161 E2
Toab Ork 277 E7
Toab Shet 279 F9
Tobermory 247 E4
Toberonochy 239 G4
Tobson 270 D4
Tocher 260 E1
Tockenham 132 C5
Tockenham Wick 132 C4
Tockholes 192 C5
Tockington 131 F4
Tockwith 195 D2
Todber 117 E5
Toddington CenBeds 149 F5
Toddington Glos 146 C4
Todenham 147 E4
Todhills Angus 244 C1
Todhills Cumb 218 B5
Todlachie 260 E3
Todmorden 193 F5
Todwick 186 B4
Toft Cambs 150 B2
Toft Lincs 161 G1
Toft Shet 279 D5
Toft Hill 212 A5
Toft Monks 165 F2
Toft next Newton 188 A4
Toftcarl 275 J4
Toftrees 177 G5
Toftwood 178 A4
Togston 221 E1
Tokavaig 256 C3
Tokers Green 134 B5
Tolastadh a' Chaolais 270 D4
Tolastadh Ùr 271 H3
Toll Bar 186 C2
Toll of Birness 261 J1
Tolland 115 E4
Tollard Farnham 105 F1
Tollard Royal 105 F1
Tollcross 234 A3
Toller Down Gate 104 B2
Toller Fratrum 104 B3
Toller Porcorum 104 B3
Toller Whelme 104 B3
Tollerton Notts 174 B4
Tollerton NYorks 195 E1
Tollesbury 138 C1
Tollesby 203 E1
Tolleshunt D'Arcy 138 C1
Tolleshunt Knights 138 C1

Tolleshunt Major 138 B1
Tolmachan 270 C7
Tolpuddle 105 D3
Tolvah 259 F5
Tolworth 121 G1
Tom an Fhuadain 271 F6
Tomatin 259 F2
Tombreck 258 D1
Tomchrasky (Tom Chrasgaidh) 257 J3
Tomdoun 257 H4
Tomdow 267 H7
Tomich High 257 K2
Tomich High 266 D4
Tomich High 266 D1
Tomintoul 259 J3
Tomnacross 266 C7
Tomnamoon 267 H6
Tomnaven 260 C1
Tomnavoulin 259 K2
Tomvaich 259 H1
Ton Pentre 129 F3
Tonbridge 123 E4
Tondu 129 E4
Tonedale 115 E5
Tonfanau 154 B2
Tong Kent 124 A4
Tong Shrop 157 G2
Tong WYorks 194 B4
Tong Norton 157 G2
Tong Street 194 A4
Tonge 173 F5
Tongham 121 D3
Tongland 216 A5
Tongue 273 H3
Tongue House 273 H3
Tongwynlais 130 A4
Tonmawr 129 E3
Tonna 129 D3
Tonwell 136 C1
Tonypandy 129 F3
Tonyrefail 129 G4
Toot Baldon 134 A2
Toot Hill 137 E2
Toothill Hants 106 C1
Toothill Swin 132 D4
Tooting Graveney 136 B5
Top End 149 F1
Top of Hebers 184 C2
Topcliffe 202 D5
Topcroft 165 D2
Topcroft Street 165 D2
Toppesfield 151 F4
Toppings 184 B1
Toprow 164 C2
Topsham 102 C4
Topsham Bridge 100 D3
Torastan 246 B3
Torbain 259 J3
Torbeg Aber 260 B5
Torbeg NAyr 223 E3
Torbothie 234 C4
Torbryan 101 E1
Torcastle 248 D2
Torcross 101 E3
Tordarroch 258 D1
Toredutt 267 J5
Toremore High 259 J1
Toremore High 275 G5
Torfrey 97 F4
Torgyle 257 K3
Torksey 187 F5
Torlum 262 C6
Torlundy (Tòrr Lunndaidh) 248 D2
Tormarton 131 G5
Tormisdale 230 A4
Tormore 223 D2
Tormsdale 275 G3
Tornagrain 266 E6
Tornahaish 259 K4
Tornaveen 260 E4
Torness 258 C2
Toronto 212 A4
Torpenhow 209 F3
Torphichen 235 D2
Torphins 260 E4
Torpoint 100 A2
Torquay 101 F1
Torquhan 236 B5
Torr 100 B2
Torran A&B 240 A4
Torran High 266 E4
Torran High 264 B7
Torrance 234 A2
Torrance House 234 A4
Torrancroy 260 B3
Torre Som 114 D3
Torre Torbay 101 F1
Torridon 264 E6
Torrin 256 B2
Torrisdale A&B 222 C2
Torrisdale High 273 J2
Torrish 274 E7
Torrisholme 192 A1
Torroble 266 C1
Torry Aber 268 C6
Torry Aberdeen 261 H4
Torryburn 235 E1
Torsonce 236 B5
Torterston 269 J6
Torthorwald 217 E3
Tortington 108 B3
Torton 158 A5
Tortworth 131 G3
Torvaig 263 K7
Torver 199 D3
Torwood 234 C1
Torworth 187 D4
Tosberry 112 C3
Toscaig 256 D1
Toseland 150 A1
Tosside 193 D2
Tostarie 246 C5
Tostock 152 A1
Totaig 263 G6
Totamore 246 A4
Tote 263 K7
Tote Hill 121 D5
Totegan 274 D2
Totford 119 G4
Totham Hill 138 B1
Tothill 189 E4
Totland 106 C4
Totley 186 A5
Totnes 101 E1

Toton 173 G4
Totronald 246 A4
Totscore 263 J5
Tottenham 136 C3
Tottenhill 163 E1
Tottenhill Row 163 E1
Totteridge Bucks 135 D3
Totteridge GtLon 136 B3
Totternhoe 149 E5
Tottington GtMan 184 B1
Tottington Norf 163 G3
Totton 106 C1
Toulton 115 E4
Toulvaddie 267 F4
Tournaig 264 E3
Toux 269 H5
Tovil 123 G3
Tow Law 212 A4
Towan Cross 96 B5
Toward 232 B2
Towcester 148 B3
Towednack 94 B3
Tower Bridge Exhibition GtLon SE1 2UP 12 C4
Tower End 163 E1
Tower of London GtLon EC3N 4AB 12 C4
Towersey 134 C2
Towie Aber 269 G4
Towie Aber 260 D2
Towie Aber 260 C3
Towiemore 268 B6
Town End Cambs 162 C3
Town End Cumb 199 F4
Town End Mersey 183 F4
Town Green Lancs 183 F2
Town Green Norf 179 E4
Town of Lowton 184 A3
Town Row 123 E5
Town Street 163 F4
Town Yetholm 228 C4
Townend 232 D2
Townfield 211 F3
Townhead D&G 207 G2
Townhead SYorks 185 F2
Townhead of Greenlaw 216 B4
Townhill Fife 235 F1
Townhill Swan 128 C3
Towns End 119 G2
Towns Green 170 D1
Townshend 94 C3
Towthorpe ERid 196 B1
Towthorpe York 195 F2
Towton 195 D4
Towyn 182 A5
Toynton All Saints 176 B1
Toynton Fen Side 176 B1
Toynton St. Peter 176 B1
Toy's Hill 123 D3
Trabboch 224 C3
Traboe 95 E4
Tradespark High 267 F6
Tradespark Ork 277 D7
Trafford Centre 184 B3
Trafford Park 184 B3
Trago Mills, Newton Abbot Devon TQ12 6JD 102 B5
Trallong 143 F5
Trallwn 128 C3
Tram Inn 145 D4
Tranent 236 B2
Tranmere 183 E4
Trantlebeg 274 D3
Trantlemore 274 D3
Tranwell 221 D3
Trap 128 C1
Trap Street 171 F1
Traprain 236 C2
Trap's Green 146 D1
Traquair 227 E2
Trawden 193 F4
Trawscoed (Crosswood) 154 C5
Trawsfynydd 168 A3
Trealaw 129 G3
Treales 192 A4
Trearddur 180 A5
Treaslane 263 J6
Tre-Aubrey 129 G5
Trebanog 129 G3
Trebanos 128 D2
Trebarrow 98 C1
Trebartha 97 G2
Trebarvah 95 E3
Trebarwith 97 E1
Trebeath 97 G1
Trebetherick 96 D2
Treborough 114 D4
Trebudannon 96 C3
Trebullett 98 D3
Treburley 98 D3
Treburrick 96 C2
Trebyan 97 E3
Trecastle 143 E5
Trecott 113 G5
Trecrogo 98 D2
Trecwn 140 C4
Trecynon 129 F2
Tredaule 97 G1
Tredavoe 94 B4
Treddiog 140 B5
Tredegar 130 A2
Tredington Glos 146 B5
Tredington Warks 147 E3
Tredinnick Corn 96 D3
Tredinnick Corn 97 G4
Tredogan 115 D2
Tredomen 144 A4
Tredrissi 141 D3
Tredunnock 130 C3
Tredustan 144 A4
Treen Corn 94 A4
Treen Corn 94 B3
Treesmill 97 E4
Treeton 186 B4
Trefasser 140 B4
Trefdraeth 180 C5
Trefecca 144 A4
Trefechan 129 G2
Trefeglwys 155 F3
Trefenter 142 C1

Treffgarne 140 C5
Treffynnon 140 B5
Trefgarn Owen 140 B5
Trefil 130 A1
Treflan 142 B2
Trefin 140 B4
Treflach 169 F5
Trefnanney 156 B1
Trefnant 182 B5
Trefonen 169 F5
Trefor Gwyn 166 C3
Trefor IoA 180 B4
Treforest 129 G4
Treforest Industrial Estate 130 A4
Trefriw 168 A1
Tregadillett 97 G1
Tregaian 180 C5
Tregare 130 D1
Tregarland 97 G4
Tregarne 95 E4
Tregaron 142 C2
Tregarth 167 F1
Tregaswith 96 C3
Tregavethan 96 B5
Tregear 96 C4
Tregeare 97 G1
Tregeiriog 169 E4
Tregele 180 B3
Tregidden 95 E4
Tregiskey 97 E5
Treglemais 140 B5
Tregolds 96 C2
Tregole 98 B1
Tregonetha 97 D3
Tregony 96 D5
Tregoodwell 97 F1
Tregoss 97 D3
Tregowris 95 E4
Tregoyd 144 A4
Tregrehan Mills 97 E4
Tre-groes 142 A3
Treguff 129 G5
Tregullon 97 E3
Tregunnon 97 G1
Tregurrian 96 C3
Tregynon 155 G3
Trehafod 129 G3
Trehan 100 A2
Treharris 129 G3
Treherbert 129 F3
Tre-hill 129 G5
Trekenner 98 D3
Treknow 97 E1
Trelan 95 E5
Trelash 98 B1
Trelassick 96 C4
Trelawnyd 182 B5
Trelech 141 F4
Treleddyd-fawr 140 A5
Trelewis 130 A3
Treligga 97 E1
Trelights 97 D2
Trelill 97 E2
Trelissick 95 F3
Trelissick Corn TR3 6QL 95 F3
Trelleck 131 E2
Trelleck Grange 131 D2
Trelogan 182 C4
Trelowla 97 G4
Trelystan 156 B2
Tremadog 167 E3
Tremail 97 F1
Tremain 141 F3
Tremaine 97 G1
Tremar 97 G3
Trematon 99 D5
Tremeirchion 182 B5
Tremethick Cross 94 B3
Tremore 97 E3
Trenance Corn 96 C3
Trenance Corn 96 D2
Trenarren 97 E5
Trench Tel&W 157 F1
Trench Wrex 170 A4
Trencreek 96 C3
Trenear 95 D3
Treneglos 97 G1
Trenewan 97 F4
Trengune 98 B1
Trent 104 B1
Trent Port 187 F4
Trent Vale 171 F3
Trentham 171 F3
Trentishoe 113 G1
Trenwheal 94 C3
Treoes 129 F5
Treorchy 129 F3
Treowen 130 B3
Tre'r-ddol 154 C3
Trerhyngyll 129 G5
Tre-Rhys 141 E3
Trerulefoot 98 D5
Tresaith 141 F2
Tresco 96 A1
Trescott 158 A3
Trescowe 94 C3
Tresean 96 B4
Tresham 131 G3
Treshnish 246 C5
Tresillian 96 C5
Tresinney 97 F1
Tresinwen 140 B3
Treskinnick Cross 98 C1
Treslea 97 F3
Tresmeer 97 G1
Tresowes Green 94 D4
Tresparrett 98 B1
Tresparrett Posts 98 B1
Tressait 251 D3
Tresta Shet 278 F3
Tresta Shet 279 C7
Treswell 187 E4
Trethewey 94 A4
Trethomas 130 A4
Trethurgy 97 E4
Tretio 140 A5
Tretire 145 E5
Tretower 144 A5
Treuddyn 169 F2
Trevadlock 97 G2
Trevalga 98 A1
Trevalyn 170 A2
Trevanson 97 D2
Trevarnon 94 C3
Trevarrack 94 B3

Trevarren **96** D3
Trevarrian **96** C3
Trevarrick **97** D5
Tre-vaughan *Carmar* **141** G5
Tre-vaughan *Carmar* **127** E1
Treveighan **97** E2
Trevellas **96** B4
Trevelmond **97** G3
Trevenen **95** D4
Treverva **95** E3
Trevescan **94** A4
Trevethin **98** D4
Trevine **240** C2
Treviscoe **96** D4
Trevivian **97** F1
Trevone **96** C2
Trevor **169** F3
Trewalder **97** E1
Trewarmett **97** E1
Trewarthenick **96** D5
Trewassa **97** F1
Trewellard **94** A3
Trewen *Corn* **97** G1
Trewen *Here* **131** E1
Trewennack **95** D4
Trewent **126** D3
Trewern **156** B1
Trewethern **97** G4
Trewidland **97** G4
Trewilym **141** E3
Trewint *Corn* **98** B1
Trewint *Corn* **97** G1
Trewithian **95** F3
Trewoon **97** D5
Treworga **96** C5
Treworlas **97** F3
Trewornan **97** D2
Treworthal **95** F3
Tre-wyn **144** C5
Treyarnon **96** C2
Treyford **108** A2
Trezaise **97** D4
Triangle **193** G5
Trickett's Cross **105** G2
Triermain **210** B1
Trimdon **212** C4
Trimdon Colliery **212** C4
Trimdon Grange **212** C4
Trimingham **179** D2
Trimley Lower Street **153** D4
Trimley St. Martin **153** D4
Trimley St. Mary **153** D4
Trimpley **157** G5
Trimsaran **128** A2
Trimstone **113** E1
Trinafour **250** C3
Trinant **130** B3
Tring **135** E1
Trinity *Angus* **253** E3
Trinity *Chanl* **100** C5
Trinity *Edin* **235** G2
Trisant **154** D5
Triscombe *Som* **114** C4
Triscombe *Som* **115** E4
Trislaig **248** C2
Trispen **96** C4
Tritlington **221** E2
Trochry **243** E1
Troedyraur **141** G3
Troedyrhiw **129** G2
Trofarth **181** G5
Trondavoe **278** C5
Troon *Corn* **95** D3
Troon *SAyr* **224** B2
Tropical Butterfly House,
  Wildlife & Falconry Centre
  SYorks S25 4EQ **21** F3
Tropical World, Roundhay
  WYorks LS8 2ER **27** G1
Trosaraidh **254** C3
Troston **163** G5
Troswell **98** C1
Trottick **244** C1
Trottiscliffe **123** F2
Trotton **120** D5
Trough Gate **193** E5
Troughend **220** A2
Troustan **232** B2
Troutbeck *Cumb* **199** F2
Troutbeck *Cumb* **209** G4
Troutbeck Bridge **199** F2
Trow Green **131** F2
Troway **186** A5
Trowbridge *Cardiff* **130** B4
Trowbridge *Wilts* **117** F2
Trowell **173** F4
Trowle Common **117** F2
Trowley Bottom **135** F1
Trows **228** A3
Trowse Newton **178** D5
Troy **194** B4
Trudernish **230** C4
Trudoxhill **117** E3
Trull **115** F5
Trumaisgearraidh **262** D4
Trumpan **263** H5
Trumpet **145** F4
Trumpington **150** C2
Trumps Green **121** E1
Trunch **179** D2
Trunnah **191** G3
Truro **96** C5
Truro Cathedral *Corn*
  TR1 2AF **96** C5
Truscott **98** D2
Trusham **102** B4
Trusley **173** E4
Trusthorpe **189** F4
Truthan **96** C4
Trysull **158** A3
Tubney **133** G3
Tuckenhay **101** E2
Tuckhill **157** G4
Tuckingmill **96** A5
Tuddenham *Suff* **152** C3
Tuddenham *Suff* **163** F5
Tudeley **123** F4
Tudeley Hale **123** F4
Tudhoe **212** B4
Tudweiliog **166** B4
Tuesley **121** E3
Tuffley **132** A1
Tufton *Hants* **119** F3
Tufton *Pembs* **140** D5
Tugby **160** C2
Tugford **157** E4
Tughall **229** G4

Tulchan **243** E2
Tulleys Farm *WSuss*
  RH10 4PE **122** C5
Tullibardine Distillery *P&K*
  PH4 1QG **243** E4
Tullibody **243** D5
Tullich *A&B* **240** C3
Tullich *A&B* **240** A3
Tullich *High* **267** F4
Tullich *High* **258** D2
Tullich *Moray* **268** B6
Tullich *Stir* **242** A1
Tullich Muir **266** E4
Tulliemet **251** F4
Tulloch *Aber* **261** G1
Tulloch *High* **266** D2
Tulloch *Moray* **267** H6
Tullochgorm **240** B1
Tullochgribban High **259** G2
Tullochvenus **260** D4
Tulloes **252** D4
Tullybannocher **242** C2
Tullybelton **243** F1
Tullyfergus **252** A5
Tullymurdoch **251** G4
Tullynessle **260** D3
Tulse Hill **136** C5
Tumble (Y Tymbl) **128** B1
Tumby **176** A1
Tumby Woodside **176** A2
Tummel Bridge **250** C4
Tunbridge Wells **123** E5
Tundergarth Mains **217** F2
Tunga **271** G4
Tungate **179** D3
Tunley **117** D2
Tunstall *ERid* **197** F4
Tunstall *Kent* **124** A2
Tunstall *Lancs* **200** B5
Tunstall *Norf* **179** F5
Tunstall *NYorks* **202** B3
Tunstall *Stoke* **171** F2
Tunstall *Suff* **153** E2
Tunstall *T&W* **212** C2
Tunstead *GtMan* **185** E2
Tunstead *Norf* **179** D3
Tunstead Milton **185** E4
Tunworth **120** B3
Tupholme **175** G1
Tupsley **145** E4
Tupton **173** E1
Tur Langton **160** C3
Turbiskill **231** F1
Turcossie **269** G5
Turgis Green **120** B2
Turin **252** D4
Turkdean **132** D1
Turleigh **117** F1
Turn **184** C1
Turnastone **144** C4
Turnberry **224** A5
Turnchapel **100** A2
Turnditch **173** D3
Turner's Green **147** D1
Turners Hill **122** C5
Turners Puddle **105** E3
Turnford **136** C2
Turnworth **105** E2
Turret Bridge **257** K5
Turriff **269** F6
Turton Bottoms **184** B1
Turvey **149** E2
Turville **134** C3
Turville Heath **134** C3
Turweston **148** B4
Tutankhamun Exhibition,
  Dorchester *Dorset*
  DT1 1UW **104** C3
Tutbury **172** D5
Tutbury Castle *Staffs* DE13
  9JF **172** D5
Tutnall **158** B5
Tutshill **131** E3
Tuttington **178** D3
Tutts Clump **134** A5
Tutwell **99** D3
Tuxford **187** E5
Twatt *Ork* **276** B5
Twatt *Shet* **279** C7
Twechar **234** B2
Tweedmouth **237** G4
Tweedsmuir **226** B3
Twelve Oaks **110** B1
Twelveheads **96** B5
Twemlow Green **171** E1
Twenty **175** E5
Twickenham **136** A5
Twigworth **146** A5
Twineham **109** E1
Twineham Green **109** E1
Twinhoe **117** E2
Twinstead **151** G4
Twiss Green **184** A3
Twiston **193** E3
Twitchen *Devon* **114** A4
Twitchen *Shrop* **156** C5
Twitton **123** E3
Twizell House **229** F4
Two Bridges *Devon* **99** G3
Two Bridges *Glos* **131** F2
Two Dales **173** D1
Two Gates **159** E2
Two Mills **183** E5
Twycross **159** F2
Twycross Zoo *Leics*
  CV9 3PX **159** F2
Twyford *Bucks* **148** B5
Twyford *Derbys* **173** E5
Twyford *Dorset* **105** E1
Twyford *Hants* **119** F5
Twyford *Leics* **160** C1
Twyford *Oxon* **147** G4
Twyford *W'ham* **120** C4
Twyford Common **145** E4
Twyn Shôn-Ifan **130** A3
Twyning **146** A4
Twynllanan **143** D3
Twyn-yr-odyn **130** A5
Twyn-y-Sheriff **130** D2
Twywell **161** E5
Ty Croes **180** B5
Tycroes **128** C1

Tycrwyn **156** A1
Tydd Gote **162** C1
Tydd St. Giles **162** C1
Tydd St. Mary **162** C1
Tye Common **137** F3
Tye Green *Essex* **151** F5
Tye Green *Essex* **150** D3
Tye Green *Essex* **137** F1
Tye Green *Essex* **136** D2
Tyersal **194** A4
Ty-hen **166** A4
Tyldesley **184** A2
Tyler Hill **124** D2
Tylers Green *Bucks* **135** E3
Tyler's Green *Essex* **137** E2
Tylorstown **129** G3
Tylwch **155** F5
Ty-Mawr *Conwy* **168** C3
Ty-mawr *Denb* **169** E3
Ty-nant *Conwy* **168** C3
Ty-nant *Gwyn* **168** C5
Tyndrum
  (Taigh an Droma) **241** F1
Tyne Green Country Park
  N'umb NE46 3RY **211** F1
Tyneham **236** A4
Tynehead **236** A4
Tynemouth **212** C1
Tynewydd **129** F3
Tyninghame **236** D2
Tynron **216** C1
Tyntesfield **131** E5
Tyn-y-cefn **169** E4
Ty'n-y-coedcae **130** A4
Tyn-y-cwm **155** E4
Ty'n-y-ffridd **169** E4
Ty'n-y-garn **129** E4
Tyn-y-gongl **180** D4
Tynygraig *Cere* **142** C1
Tyn-y-graig
  Powys **143** G3
Ty'n-y-groes **181** F5
Tyrie **269** H4
Tyringham **149** D3
Tyseley **158** D4
Tythegston **129** E5
Tytherington *ChesE* **184** D5
Tytherington *SGlos* **131** F4
Tytherington *Som* **117** E3
Tytherleigh **103** G1
Ytherton Lucas **132** B5
Tyttenhanger **136** A2
Ty-uchaf **168** C5
Tywardreath **97** E4
Tywardreath Highway **97** E4
Tywyn **154** B2

U

Uachdar **262** D6
Uags **256** D1
Ubberley **171** G3
Ubbeston Green **165** E4
Ubley **116** C2
Uckerby **202** B2
Uckfield **109** G1
Uckinghall **146** A4
Uckington **146** B5
Uddingston **234** A3
Uddington **225** G2
Udimore **111** D2
Udley **116** B1
Udny Green **261** G2
Udny Station **261** G2
Udston **234** B4
Udstonhead **234** B5
Uffcott **132** D5
Uffculme **103** D1
Uffington *Lincs* **161** F2
Uffington *Oxon* **133** F4
Uffington *Shrop* **157** E1
Ufford *Peter* **161** F2
Ufford *Suff* **153** D2
Ufton **147** F1
Ufton Green **120** B1
Ufton Nervet **120** B1
Ugborough **100** C2
Ugford **118** B4
Uggeshall **165** F3
Ugglebarnby **204** B2
Ugley **150** D5
Ugley Green **150** D5
Ugthorpe **203** G1
Uidh **254** B5
Uig *A&B* **246** A4
Uig *A&B* **232** B1
Uig (Uige) *High* **263** J5
Uigen **270** C4
Uiginish **263** H7
Uigshader **263** K7
Uisken **238** C3
Uiskevagh
  (Uisgebhagh) **262** D6
Ulbster **275** J4
Ulcat Row **210** A5
Ulceby *Lincs* **189** E5
Ulceby *NLincs* **188** B1
Ulceby Cross **189** E5
Ulceby Skitter **188** B1
Ulcombe **124** A4
Uldale **209** F3
Uldale House **200** C3
Uley **131** G3
Ulgham **221** E2
Ullapool (Ullapul) **265** H2
Ullenhall **146** D1
Ullenwood **132** B1
Ulleskelf **195** E4
Ullesthorpe **160** A4
Ulley **186** B5
Ullingswick **145** E3
Ullinish **255** J1
Ullock **209** D4
Ulpha *Cumb* **198** C3
Ulpha *Cumb* **199** F4
Ulrome **197** D2
Ulsta **278** D4
Ulting **138** B2
Uluvalt **239** E1
Ulva **238** D1
Ulverston **199** D5
Ulwell **105** G4
Ulzieside **225** F5

Umberleigh **113** G3
Unapool **272** E5
Underbarrow **199** F3
Undercliffe **194** A4
Underhill **136** B3
Underhoull **278** E2
Underling Green **123** G4
Underriver **123** E3
Underwood *Newport* **130** C4
Underwood *Notts* **173** F2
Underwood *Plym* **100** B2
Undley **163** E4
Undy **130** D4
Ungisiadar **270** D5
Unifirth **279** B7
Union Croft **261** G5
Union Mills **190** B4
Union Street **123** G5
University of Glasgow Visitor
  Centre *Glas*
  G12 8QQ **38** B1
Unst **278** F1
Unst Airport **278** F2
Unstone **186** A5
Unstone Green **186** A5
Unsworth **184** C1
Unthank *Cumb* **210** A4
Unthank *Derbys* **186** A5
Up Cerne **104** C2
Up Exe **102** C2
Up Hatherley **146** B5
Up Holland **183** G2
Up Marden **107** G1
Up Mudford **104** B1
Up Nately **120** B2
Up Somborne **119** E4
Up Sydling **104** C2
Upavon **118** C2
Upchurch **124** A2
Upcott *Devon* **99** E1
Upcott *Devon* **113** F3
Upcott *Here* **144** C2
Upcott *Som* **114** C5
Upend **151** E2
Upgate **178** C4
Upgate Street *Norf* **164** B2
Upgate Street *Norf* **165** D2
Uphall *Dorset* **104** B2
Uphall *WLoth* **235** E2
Uphall Station **235** E3
Upham *Devon* **102** B2
Upham *Hants* **119** G5
Uphampton *Here* **144** C1
Uphampton *Worcs* **146** A1
Uphempston **101** E1
Uphill **116** A2
Uplands *Glos* **132** A2
Uplands *Swan* **128** C3
Uplawmoor **233** F4
Upleadon **145** G5
Upleatham **203** F1
Uplees **124** C2
Uplowman **102** D1
Uplyme **103** G3
Upminster **137** E4
Upottery **103** F2
Upper Affcot **156** D4
Upper Ardroscadale **232** B3
Upper Arley **157** G4
Upper Arncott **134** B1
Upper Astley **157** E1
Upper Aston **158** A3
Upper Astrop **148** A4
Upper Bayble
  (Pabail Uarach) **271** H4
Upper Beeding **109** D2
Upper Benefield **161** E4
Upper Bentley **146** B1
Upper Berwick **157** D1
Upper Bighouse **274** D3
Upper Boat **130** A4
Upper Boddam **260** E1
Upper Boddington **147** G2
Upper Borth **154** C4
Upper Boyndlie **269** H4
Upper Brailes **147** F4
Upper Breakish **256** C2
Upper Breinton **145** D3
Upper Broadheath **146** A2
Upper Broughton **174** B5
Upper Brynamman **128** D1
Upper Bucklebury **119** G1
Upper Burgate **106** A1
Upper Burnhaugh **261** G5
Upper Caldecote **149** G3
Upper Camster **275** H4
Upper Canada **116** A2
Upper Catesby **147** G2
Upper Catshill **158** B5
Upper Chapel **143** G3
Upper Cheddon **115** F5
Upper Chicksgrove **118** A4
Upper Chute **119** D2
Upper Clatford **119** E3
Upper Coberley **132** B1
Upper Colwall **145** G3
Upper Cotton **172** B3
Upper Cound **157** E2
Upper Cumberworth **185** G2
Upper Cwmbran **130** B3
Upper Dallachy **268** B4
Upper Dean **149** F1
Upper Denby **185** G2
Upper Denton **210** C1
Upper Derraid **259** H1
Upper Derwent Reservoirs
  Derbys S33 0AQ **185** F4
Upper Diabaig **264** D5
Upper Dicker **110** A2
Upper Dovercourt **152** D4
Upper Dunsforth **194** D1
Upper Dunsley **135** E1
Upper Eastern Green **159** E4
Upper Eathie **266** E5
Upper Egleton **145** F3
Upper Elkstone **172** B2
Upper End **185** E5
Upper Enham **119** E3
Upper Farmcote **157** G3
Upper Farmilode **131** G1
Upper Froyle **120** C3
Upper Gills **175** J1
Upper Glendessarry **257** F5
Upper Godney **116** B3
Upper Gornal **158** B3

Upper Gravenhurst **149** G4
Upper Green *Essex* **150** C4
Upper Green *Essex* **151** D3
Upper Green *Mon* **130** C1
Upper Green *WBerks* **119** E1
Upper Grove Common **145** E5
Upper Gylen **240** A2
Upper Hackney **173** D1
Upper Halliford **121** F1
Upper Halling **123** F2
Upper Hambleton **161** G2
Upper Harbledown **124** D3
Upper Hardres Court **125** D3
Upper Hartfield **123** D5
Upper Hatton **171** F4
Upper Hayesden **123** E4
Upper Hayton **157** E4
Upper Heath **157** E4
Upper Heaton **185** F1
Upper Hellesdon **178** D4
Upper Helmsley **195** F2
Upper Hengoed **169** F4
Upper Hergest **144** B3
Upper Heyford
  N'hants **148** B2
Upper Heyford
  Oxon **147** G5
Upper Hill *Here* **145** D2
Upper Hill *SGlos* **131** F3
Upper Horsebridge **110** A2
Upper Howsell **145** G3
Upper Hulme **172** B1
Upper Inglesham **133** E3
Upper Kilchattan **238** C5
Upper Killay **128** B3
Upper Knockando **267** J7
Upper Lambourn **133** F4
Upper Langford **116** B2
Upper Langwith **173** G1
Upper Largo **244** C4
Upper Leigh **172** B4
Upper Ley **131** G1
Upper Loads **173** E1
Upper Lochton **260** E5
Upper Longdon **158** C1
Upper Longwood **157** F2
Upper Ludstone **158** A3
Upper Lybster **275** H5
Upper Lydbrook **131** F1
Upper Lyde **145** D3
Upper Lye **144** C1
Upper Maes-coed **144** C4
Upper Midhope **185** G3
Upper Milovaig **263** G7
Upper Milton **133** E1
Upper Minety **132** C3
Upper Moor **146** B3
Upper Morton **131** F3
Upper Muirskie **261** G5
Upper Nash **126** D2
Upper Newbold **186** A5
Upper North Dean **135** D3
Upper Norwood **136** C5
Upper Obney **243** F1
Upper Oddington **147** E5
Upper Ollach **256** B1
Upper Padley **185** G5
Upper Pennington **106** B3
Upper Pollicott **134** C1
Upper Poppleton **195** E2
Upper Quinton **147** D3
Upper Ratley **119** E5
Upper Ridinghill **269** J5
Upper Rissington **147** E5
Upper Rochford **145** F1
Upper Sanday **277** E7
Upper Scolton **140** C5
Upper Seagry **132** B4
Upper Shelton **149** E3
Upper Sheringham **178** C1
Upper Shuckburgh **147** G1
Upper Siddington **132** C3
Upper Skelmorlie **232** D3
Upper Slaughter **147** D5
Upper Sonachan **240** C2
Upper Soudley **131** F1
Upper Staploe **149** G2
Upper Stoke **179** D5
Upper Stondon **149** G4
Upper Stowe **148** B2
Upper Street *Hants* **106** A1
Upper Street *Norf* **179** E4
Upper Street *Norf* **164** C4
Upper Street *Suff* **152** C2
Upper Street *Suff* **152** C2
Upper Strensham **146** B4
Upper Sundon **149** F5
Upper Swanmore **107** E1
Upper Swell **147** D5
Upper Tean **172** B4
Upper Thurnham **192** A2
Upper Tillyrie **243** G4
Upper Tooting **136** B5
Upper Town *Derbys* **172** D1
Upper Town *Derbys* **173** D2
Upper Town *Derbys* **172** D2
Upper Town *Here* **145** E3
Upper Town *NSom* **116** C1
Upper Tysoe **147** F3
Upper Upham **133** E5
Upper Upnor **137** G5
Upper Victoria **244** D1
Upper Vobster **117** E3
Upper Wardington **147** G3
Upper Waterhay **132** C3
Upper Weald **148** B3
Upper Weedon **148** B2
Upper Welson **144** B3
Upper Weston **117** E1
Upper Whiston **186** B4
Upper Wick **146** A2
Upper Wield **120** B4
Upper Winchendon (Over
  Winchendon) **134** C1
Upper Witton **158** C3
Upper Woodford **118** C4
Upper Woolhampton **119** G1
Upper Wootton **119** G2
Upper Wraxall **132** A5
Upper Wyche **145** G3
Upperby **210** A2
Uppermill **185** E2
Upperthong **185** F2
Upperton **121** E5
Uppertown *Derbys* **173** E1
Uppertown *Ork* **275** J1

Uppingham **161** D2
Uppington **157** E2
Upsall **203** D4
Upsettlington **237** F5
Upshire **136** D2
Upstreet **125** E2
Upthorpe **164** A4
Upton *Bucks* **134** C1
Upton *Cambs* **161** G5
Upton *ChesW&C* **170** B1
Upton *Corn* **97** G2
Upton *Corn* **112** C5
Upton *Devon* **103** D2
Upton *Devon* **100** D3
Upton *Dorset* **105** F3
Upton *Dorset* **104** D4
Upton *ERid* **196** D2
Upton *Hants* **119** E2
Upton *Hants* **106** C1
Upton *Leics* **159** F3
Upton *Lincs* **187** F4
Upton *Mersey* **183** D4
Upton *N'hants* **148** C3
Upton *Norf* **179** E4
Upton *Notts* **187** E5
Upton *Notts* **174** C2
Upton *Oxon* **134** A4
Upton *Oxon* **133** E1
Upton *Pembs* **126** D2
Upton *Peter* **161** G2
Upton *Slo* **135** E5
Upton *Som* **114** C5
Upton *Som* **116** B5
Upton *Wilts* **117** F3
Upton *WYorks* **186** B1
Upton Bishop **145** F5
Upton Country Park *Poole*
  BH17 7BJ **3** A3
Upton Cressett **157** F3
Upton Crews **145** F5
Upton Cross **97** G2
Upton End **149** G4
Upton Grey **120** B3
Upton Hellions **102** B2
Upton Lovell **118** A3
Upton Magna **157** E1
Upton Noble **117** E4
Upton Park **136** D4
Upton Pyne **102** C3
Upton St. Leonards **132** A1
Upton Scudamore **117** F3
Upton Snodsbury **146** B2
Upton upon Severn **146** A3
Upton Warren **146** B1
Upwaltham **108** B2
Upware **162** D5
Upwell **162** D2
Upwey **104** L4
Upwick Green **150** C5
Upwood **162** A4
Uradale **279** D9
Urafirth **278** C5
Urchany **267** F7
Urchfont **118** B2
Urdimarsh **145** E3
Ure **278** B5
Urgha **263** G2
Urlay Nook **202** D1
Urmston **184** B3
Urpeth **212** B2
Urquhart *High* **266** C6
Urquhart *Moray* **267** K5
Urquhart Castle *High*
  IV63 6XJ **258** C2
Urra **203** E2
Urray **266** C6
Ushaw Moor **212** B3
Usher Hall, Edinburgh *Edin*
  EH1 2EA **36** C5
Usk (Brynbuga) **130** C2
Usselby **188** A3
Usworth **212** C2
Utley **193** G3
Uton **102** B3
Utterby **188** D3
Uttoxeter **172** B4
Uwchmynydd **166** A5
Uxbridge **135** F4
Uyeasound **278** E2
Uzmaston **126** C1

V

Valley (Y Fali) **180** A5
Valley Truckle **97** F1
Valleyfield *D&G* **216** A5
Valleyfield *Fife* **235** E1
Valsgarth **278** F1
Vange **137** G4
Vardre **128** C2
Varteg **130** B2
Vatersay (Bhatarsaigh)
  254 B5
Vatsetter **278** E4
Vatten **263** H7
Vaul **246** B2
Vaynor **129** G1
Vaynor Park **156** A2
Veaullt **144** A2
Veensgarth **279** D8
Velindre *Pembs* **141** D4
Velindre *Powys* **144** A4
Vellow **115** D4
Veness **276** E5
Venn **100** D3
Venn Ottery **103** D3
Venngreen **113** D4
Vennington **156** C2
Venny Tedburn **102** B3
Venterdon **99** D3
Ventnor **107** E5
Ventnor Botanic Gardens *IoW*
  PO38 1UL **107** E5
Venton **100** B2
Venue Cymru, Llandudno
  Conwy LL30 1BB **181** F4
Vernham Dean **119** E2
Vernham Street **119** E2
Vernolds Common **157** D4
Verwood **105** G2
Veryan **95** G3
Veryan Green **96** D5
Vickerstown **191** E1
Victoria **97** D3
Victoria & Albert Museum
  GtLon SW7 2RL **11** F5

W

Victoria Art Gallery *B&NESom*
  BA2 4AT **63** Bath
Vidlin **279** D6
Viewfield **275** F2
Viewpark **234** B3
Vigo **158** C2
Vigo Village **123** F2
Villavin **113** F4
Vinehall Street **110** C1
Vine's Cross **110** A2
Viney Hill **131** F2
Virginia Water **121** E1
Virginstow **99** D1
Virley **138** C1
Vobster **117** E3
Voe *Shet* **279** D6
Voe *Shet* **278** C4
Vogrie Country Park *Midlo*
  EH23 4NU **32** D4
Voirrey Embroidery *Mersey*
  CH63 6JA **22** D3
Volks Electric Railway *B&H*
  BN2 1EN **109** F3
Vowchurch **144** C4
Voy **277** B6
Vron Gate **156** C2

W.R. Outhwaite & Son
  Ropemakers *NYorks*
  DL8 3NT **201** D4
Waberthwaite **198** C3
Wackerfield **212** A5
Wacton **164** C2
Wadborough **279** D8
Wadborough **146** B3
Waddesdon **134** C1
Waddesdon Manor *Bucks*
  HP18 0JH **134** C1
Waddeton **101** E2
Waddicar **183** E3
Waddingham **187** G3
Waddington *Lancs* **192** D3
Waddington *Lincs* **175** E1
Waddingworth **188** B5
Waddon *Devon* **102** B5
Waddon *GtLon* **122** C2
Wadebridge **97** D3
Wadeford **103** G1
Wadenhoe **161** F4
Wadesmill **136** C1
Wadhurst **123** F5
Wadshelf **186** A5
Wadworth **186** C3
Wadworth Hill **197** E5
Waen *Denb* **169** E1
Waen *Denb* **168** C1
Waen Aberwheeler **169** D1
Waen-fâch **156** B1
Waen-wen **167** E1
Wag **275** F6
Wainfleet All Saints **176** C2
Wainfleet Bank **176** C2
Wainfleet St. Mary **176** C2
Wainford **165** E2
Waingroves **173** F3
Wainhouse Corner **98** B1
Wainscott **137** G5
Wainstalls **193** G5
Waitby **200** C2
Wakefield **194** C5
Wakehurst Place *WSuss*
  RH17 6TN **122** C5
Wakerley **161** E3
Wakes Colne **151** G5
Walberswick **165** F4
Walberton **108** B3
Walbottle **212** A1
Walcot *Lincs* **175** F4
Walcot *NLincs* **196** A5
Walcot *Shrop* **156** C4
Walcot *Tel&W* **157** E1
Walcot Green **164** C2
Walcote *Leics* **160** A4
Walcote *Warks* **146** D2
Walcott **179** E2
Walcott Dales **175** G2
Walden **201** E4
Walden Head **201** E4
Walden Stubbs **186** C1
Walderslade **123** G2
Walderton **107** G1
Walditch **104** A3
Waldley **172** C4
Waldridge **212** B3
Waldringfield **153** D3
Waldron **110** A2
Wales **186** B4
Wales Millennium Centre,
  Cardiff *Cardiff*
  CF10 5AL **130** A5
Walesby *Lincs* **188** B3
Walesby *Notts* **187** D5
Waleswood **186** B4
Walford *Here* **156** C5
Walford *Here* **145** E5
Walford *Shrop* **170** B5
Walford *Staffs* **171** F4
Walford Heath **156** D1
Walgherton **171** D3
Walgrave **160** D5
Walhampton **106** C3
Walk Mill **193** E4
Walkden **184** B2
Walker **212** B1
Walker Art Gallery, Liverpool
  Mersey L3 8EL **42** D3
Walker Fold **192** C3
Walkerburn **227** E2
Walkeringham **187** E3
Walkerith **187** E3
Walkern **150** A5
Walker's Green **145** E3
Walkford **106** B3
Walkhampton **100** B1
Walkington Hill **194** C1
Walkington **196** B4
Walkwood **146** C1
Wall *Corn* **94** D3
Wall *N'umb* **211** E1
Wall *Staffs* **158** D2
Wall End **198** D4
Wall Heath **158** A4
Wall Houses **211** E1
Wall under Heywood **157** E3
Wallace Collection, London
  GtLon W1U 3BN **44** A2

Wallacehall 218 A4
Wallacetown 224 A5
Wallasey 183 D3
Wallaston Green 126 C2
Wallend 124 A1
Waller's Green 145 F4
Wallingford 134 B4
Wallington GtLon 122 B2
Wallington Hants 107 E2
Wallington Herts 150 A4
Wallingwells 186 C4
Wallis 140 D5
Wallisdown 105 G3
Walliswood 121 G4
Walls 279 B8
Wallsend 212 C1
Wallyford 236 A2
Walmer 125 F3
Walmer Bridge 192 A5
Walmersley 184 C1
Walmsgate 189 D5
Walpole 165 E4
Walpole Cross Keys 162 D1
Walpole Highway 162 D1
Walpole Marsh 162 C1
Walpole St. Andrew 162 D1
Walpole St. Peter 162 D1
Walrond's Park 116 A5
Walrow 116 A3
Walsall 158 C3
Walsall Wood 158 C2
Walsgrave on Sowe 159 F4
Walsham le Willows 164 B4
Walshford 194 D2
Walsoken 162 C1
Walston 235 E5
Walsworth 149 G4
Walter's Ash 134 D3
Walterston 129 G5
Walterstone 144 C5
Waltham Kent 124 D4
Waltham NELincs 188 C2
Waltham Abbey 136 C2
Waltham Chase 107 E1
Waltham Cross 136 C2
Waltham on the
    Wolds 174 C5
Waltham
    St. Lawrence 134 D5
Walthamstow 136 C4
Walton Bucks 134 D1
Walton Cumb 210 B1
Walton Derbys 173 E1
Walton Leics 160 A4
Walton Mersey 183 E3
Walton MK 149 D4
Walton Peter 161 G2
Walton Powys 144 B2
Walton Shrop 157 D5
Walton Som 116 B4
Walton Staffs 171 F4
Walton Suff 153 E4
Walton Tel&W 157 E1
Walton Warks 147 E2
Walton WYorks 186 A1
Walton WYorks 194 D3
Walton Cardiff 146 B4
Walton East 140 D4
Walton Elm 105 D1
Walton Hall Gardens Warr
    WA4 6SN 23 H4
Walton Highway 162 C1
Walton Lower Street 153 D4
Walton on the Hill 122 B3
Walton on the Naze 139 F1
Walton on the Wolds 160 A1
Walton Park D&G 216 B3
Walton Park NSom 130 D3
Walton West 126 B1
Walton-in-Gordano 130 D3
Walton-le-Dale 192 B5
Walton-on-Thames 121 G1
Walton-on-the-hill 171 G5
Walton-on-Trent 159 E2
Walwen Flints 182 C5
Walwen Flints 182 D5
Walwick 220 B4
Walworth 202 B1
Walworth Gate 212 B5
Walwyn's Castle 126 B1
Wambrook 103 F2
Wanborough Surr 121 E3
Wanborough Swin 133 E4
Wandel 226 A3
Wandon 229 E4
Wandon End 149 G5
Wandsworth 136 B5
Wandylaw 229 F4
Wangford Suff 165 F4
Wangford Suff 163 F4
Wanlip 160 A1
Wanlockhead 225 G4
Wannock 110 A3
Wansbeck Riverside Park
    N'umb NE63 8TX 221 E3
Wansford ERid 196 C2
Wansford Peter 161 F3
Wanshurst Green 123 G4
Wanstrow 117 E3
Wanswell 131 F2
Wantage 133 F4
Wapley 131 G5
Wappenbury 147 F1
Wappenham 148 B3
Warblebank 209 F2
Warbleton 110 B2
Warblington 107 G2
Warborough 134 A3
Warboys 162 B4
Warbreck 191 G4
Warbstow 98 C1
Warburton 184 A4
Warcop 200 C1
Ward End 158 D4
Warden Kent 124 C1
Warden N'umb 211 F1
Warden Hill 146 B5
Warden Street 149 G3
Wardhouse 260 D1
Wardington 147 G3
Wardle ChesE 170 D2

Wardle GtMan 184 D1
Wardley GtMan 184 B2
Wardley Rut 160 D2
Wardley T&W 212 C1
Wardlow 185 F5
Wardsend 184 D4
Wardy Hill 162 C4
Ware Herts 136 C1
Ware Kent 125 E2
Wareham 106 B3
Warehorne 124 B5
Waren Mill 229 F3
Warenford 229 F4
Warenton 229 F3
Wareside 136 C1
Waresley Cambs 150 A2
Waresley Worcs 158 A5
Warfield 135 D5
Wargrave Mersey 183 G3
Wargrave W'ham 134 C5
Warham Here 145 D4
Warham Norf 178 A1
Wark N'umb 220 A4
Wark N'umb 228 C3
Warkleigh 113 G3
Warkton 161 D5
Warkworth N'hants 147 G3
Warkworth N'umb 221 E1
Warland 193 F5
Warleggan 97 F3
Warley Essex 137 E3
Warley WMid 158 C4
Warley Town 193 G5
Warlingham 122 C3
Warmfield 194 C5
Warmingham 171 E1
Warminghurst 108 D2
Warmington N'hants 161 F3
Warmington Warks 147 G3
Warminster 117 F3
Warmlake 124 A4
Warmley 131 F5
Warmley Hill 131 F5
Warmsworth 186 C2
Warmwell 105 D4
Warndon 146 A2
Warners End 135 F2
Warnford 120 B5
Warnham 121 G4
Warningcamp 108 C3
Warninglid 109 E1
Warren ChesE 184 C5
Warren Pembs 126 C3
Warren House 99 G2
Warren Row 134 D4
Warren Street 124 B3
Warrenby 213 E5
Warren's Green 150 A5
Warrington MK 149 D2
Warrington Warr 184 A4
Warroch 243 F4
Warsash 107 D2
Warslow 172 B2
Warsop Vale 173 G1
Warter 196 A2
Warthill 195 F2
Wartle 260 D4
Wartling 110 B3
Wartnaby 174 C5
Warton Lancs 199 G5
Warton Lancs 192 A5
Warton N'umb 220 C1
Warton Warks 159 E2
Warton Bank 192 A5
Warwick 147 E1
Warwick Bridge 210 A2
Warwick Castle Warks
    CV34 4QU 16 A6
Warwick Wold 122 C3
Warwick-on-Eden 210 A2
Wasbister 276 C4
Wasdale Head 198 C2
Waseley Hills Country Park
    Worcs B45 9AT 14 C1
Wash 185 E4
Wash Common 119 F1
Washall Green 150 C4
Washaway 97 E3
Washbourne 101 D2
Washbrook 116 B3
Washfield 102 C1
Washfold 201 F2
Washford Som 114 D3
Washford Worcs 146 C1
Washford Pyne 102 B1
Washingborough 188 A5
Washington T&W 212 C2
Washington WSuss 108 D2
Washmere Green 152 A3
Wasing 119 G1
Waskerley 211 G3
Wasperton 147 E2
Wasps Nest 175 F1
Wass 203 E5
Wat Tyler Country Park Essex
    SS16 4UH 137 G4
Watchet 115 D3
Watchfield Oxon 133 E3
Watchfield Som 116 A3
Watchgate 199 G3
Watcombe 101 F1
Watendlath 209 F5
Water 193 E5
Water Eaton MK 149 D4
Water Eaton Oxon 134 A1
Water End Bed 149 F4
Water End CenBeds 149 F4
Water End ERid 195 G4
Water End Essex 151 D3
Water End Herts 136 B2
Water End Herts 135 F1
Water Newton 161 G3
Water Orton 159 D3
Water Stratford 148 B4
Water Yeat 199 D4
Waterbeach 150 C1
Waterbeck 218 A4
Watercombe 105 D4
Waterend 134 C3
Waterfall 172 B2
Waterfoot ERenf 233 G4
Waterfoot Lancs 193 E5
Waterford 136 C1
Watergate 97 F1
Waterhead Cumb 199 E2
Waterhead D&G 216 B2
Waterheath 165 F2
Waterhill of Bruxie 269 H6

Waterhouses Dur 212 A3
Waterhouses Staffs 172 B2
Wateringbury 123 F3
Waterlane 132 B2
Waterloo Aber 261 J1
Waterloo Derbys 173 F1
Waterloo GtMan 184 D1
Waterloo High 256 C2
Waterloo Mersey 183 E3
Waterloo NLan 234 C4
Waterloo Norf 178 D4
Waterloo P&K 243 F1
Waterloo Pembs 126 C2
Waterloo Poole 105 G3
Waterloo Cross 103 D1
Waterloo Port 167 D1
Waterlooville 107 F1
Watermead Country Park
    Leics LE7 4PF 17 C3
Watermeetings 226 A4
Watermillock 210 A5
Waterperry Oxon
    OX33 1JZ 134 B2
Waterperry Oxon 134 B2
Waterrow 115 D5
Waters Upton 157 F1
Watersfield 108 C2
Watershed Mill Visitor Centre,
    Settle NYorks
    BD24 9LR 193 E1
Watersheddings 184 D2
Waterside Aber 261 H1
Waterside Aber 261 J2
Waterside B'burn 192 D5
Waterside Bucks 135 E2
Waterside EAyr 224 C5
Waterside EAyr 233 F5
Waterside EDun 234 A2
Watersmeet House Devon
    EX35 6NT 114 A3
Waterstock 134 B2
Waterston 126 C2
Waterthorpe 186 B4
Waterworld, Hanley ST1 5PU
    85 Stoke-on-Trent
Watford Herts 136 A3
Watford N'hants 148 B1
Watford Park 130 A4
Wath NYorks 202 C5
Wath NYorks 194 A1
Wath Brow 208 D5
Wath upon Dearne 186 B2
Watley's End 131 F4
Watlington Norf 163 D1
Watlington Oxon 134 B3
Watnall 173 G3
Watten 275 H3
Wattisfield 164 B4
Wattisham 152 B2
Watton Dorset 104 A3
Watton ERid 196 C3
Watton Norf 178 A5
Watton at Stone 136 C1
Wattston 234 B3
Watton's Green 137 E3
Wattstown 129 G3
Wattsville 130 B3
Waughtonhill 269 H5
Waun Fawr 154 C4
Waun y Clyn 128 A2
Waunarlwydd 128 C3
Waunclunda 142 C4
Waunfawr 167 E2
Waun-Lwyd 130 A2
Wavendon 149 E4
Waverbridge 209 F2
Waverton ChesW&C 170 B1
Waverton Cumb 209 F2
Wavertree 183 E4
Wawne 196 C4
Waxham 179 F3
Waxholme 197 F5
Way Gill 193 F1
Way Village 102 B3
Way Wick 116 A1
Wayford 104 A2
Waytown 104 A3
Weachyburn 268 E5
Weacombe 115 E3
Weald 133 F2
Weald & Downland Open Air
    Museum WSuss
    PO18 0EU 16 B6
Weald Country Park Essex
    CM14 5QS 137 E3
Wealdstone 136 A3
Weardley 194 B3
Weare 116 B2
Weare Giffard 113 E3
Wearhead 211 E4
Wearne 116 B5
Weasenham
    All Saints 177 G5
Weasenham St. Peter 177 G5
Weathercote 200 C5
Weatheroak Hill 158 C5
Weaverham 184 A5
Weaverthorpe 204 C5
Webheath 146 C1
Webton 144 D4
Wedderlairs 261 G1
Weddington 159 F3
Wedhampton 118 B2
Wedmore 116 B3
Wednesbury 158 B3
Wednesfield 158 B3
Weedon 135 D1
Weedon Bec 148 B2
Weedon Lois 148 B3
Weeford 158 D2
Week Devon 102 A1
Week Devon 101 D1
Week Som 114 C4
Week Orchard 112 C5
Week St. Mary 98 C1
Weeke 161 D4
Weekley 161 D4
Weel 196 C4
Weeley 152 C5
Weeley Heath 152 C5
Weem 250 D4
Weeping Cross 171 G5
Weethley 146 C2
Weeting 163 F4
Weeton ERid 197 F5

Weeton Lancs 191 G4
Weeton NYorks 194 B3
Weetwood 194 B4
Weir Essex 138 C4
Weir Lancs 193 E5
Weir Quay 100 A1
Weirbrook 170 A5
Weisdale 279 C7
Welbeck Abbey 186 C5
Welborne 178 B5
Welbourn 175 E2
Welburn NYorks 195 G1
Welburn NYorks 203 F5
Welbury 202 C2
Welby 175 D4
Welches Dam 162 C4
Welcombe 112 C4
Weldon 161 E4
Welford N'hants 160 B4
Welford WBerks 133 G5
Welford-on-Avon 146 D2
Welham Leics 160 C3
Welham Notts 187 E4
Welham Green 136 B2
Well Hants 120 C5
Well Lincs 189 E5
Well NYorks 202 B4
Well End Bucks 135 D4
Well End Herts 136 B3
Well Hill 123 D2
Well Street 123 F3
Well Town 102 C2
Welland 145 G3
Wellbank 244 C1
Wellbank 234 C3
Wellesbourne 147 E2
Wellhill 267 G5
Wellhouse WBerks 134 A5
Wellhouse WYorks 185 E1
Welling 137 D5
Wellingborough 149 D1
Wellingham 177 G5
Wellingore 175 E2
Wellington Cumb 198 B2
Wellington Here 145 D3
Wellington Som 115 E5
Wellington Tel&W 157 F1
Wellington Heath 145 G3
Wellington Marsh 145 D3
Wellow B&NESom 117 E2
Wellow IoW 106 C4
Wellow Notts 174 B1
Wells 116 C3
Wells Cathedral Som
    BA5 2UE 116 C3
Wells Green 158 D4
Wellsborough 159 F2
Wells-next-the-Sea 178 A1
Wellstye Green 137 F1
Wellwood 235 E1
Welney 162 D3
Welsh Bicknor 131 E1
Welsh End 170 C4
Welsh Frankton 170 A4
Welsh Hook 140 C5
Welsh Mountain Zoo Conwy
    LL28 5UY 181 G5
Welsh Newton 131 D1
Welsh St. Donats 129 G5
Welshampton 170 B4
Welshpool
    (Y Trallwng) 156 B2
Welton B&NESom 117 D2
Welton Cumb 209 G2
Welton ERid 196 B5
Welton Lincs 188 A4
Welton N'hants 148 A1
Welton le Marsh 176 C1
Welton le Wold 188 C4
Welwick 197 F5
Welwyn 136 B1
Welwyn Garden City 136 B1
Wem 170 C5
Wembdon 115 F4
Wembley 136 A4
Wembley GtLon
    HA9 0WS 10 C3
Wembley Park 136 A4
Wembury 100 B3
Wembworthy 113 G4
Wemyss Bay 232 C3
Wenallt Cere 154 C5
Wenallt Gwyn 168 C3
Wendens Ambo 150 D4
Wendlebury 148 A1
Wendling 178 A4
Wendover 135 D2
Wendron 95 D3
Wendy 150 B3
Wenfordbridge 97 E2
Wenhaston 165 F4
Wenlli 168 B2
Wennington Cambs 162 A5
Wennington GtLon 137 E4
Wennington Lancs 200 B5
Wensley Derbys 173 D1
Wensley NYorks 201 F4
Wensleydale Cheese Visitor
    Centre, Hawes NYorks
    DL8 3RN 201 D4
Wentbridge 186 B1
Wentnor 156 C3
Wentworth Cambs 162 C5
Wentworth SYorks 186 A3
Wenvoe 130 A5
Weobley 144 D2
Weobley Marsh 144 D2
Weoley Castle 158 C4
Wepham 108 C3
Wepre 169 F1
Wepre Country Park Flints
    CH5 4HL 169 F1
Wereham 163 E2
Wergs 158 A2
Wern Gwyn 167 E4
Wern Powys 156 B1
Wern Powys 130 A1
Wern Shrop 169 F4
Wernffrwd 128 B3
Wernrheolydd 130 C2
Wern-y-cwrt 130 C2
Werrington Corn 98 D2
Werrington Peter 161 G2
Werrington Staffs 171 G3
Wervil Grange 141 G2
Wervin 183 F5
Wesham 192 A4

Wessington 173 E2
West Aberthaw 114 D1
West Acre 163 F1
West Acton 136 A4
West Allerdean 237 G5
West Alvington 100 D3
West Amesbury 118 C3
West Anstey 114 B5
West Ashby 188 C5
West Ashford 113 F2
West Ashling 108 A3
West Ashton 117 F2
West Auckland 212 A5
West Ayton 204 C4
West Bagborough 115 E4
West Barkwith 188 B4
West Barnham 108 B3
West Barns 237 D2
West Barsham 178 A2
West Bay 104 A3
West Beckham 178 C2
West Benhar 234 C3
West Bergholt 152 A5
West Bexington 104 B4
West Bilney 163 F1
West Blatchington 109 E3
West Boldon 212 C1
West Bourton 117 E5
West Bowling 194 A4
West Brabourne 124 C4
West Bradford 192 D3
West Bradley 116 C4
West Bretton 185 G1
West Bridgford 173 G4
West Bromwich 158 C3
West Buckland
    Devon 113 G2
West Buckland Som 115 E5
West Burrafirth 279 B7
West Burton NYorks 201 F4
West Burton WSuss 108 B2
West Butsfield 211 G3
West Butterwick 187 F2
West Byfleet 121 F1
West Cairncake 269 G6
West Caister 179 G4
West Calder 235 E3
West Camel 116 C5
West Carbeth 233 G2
West Carr Houses 187 E2
West Cauldcoats 234 A5
West Chaldon 105 D4
West Challow 133 F4
West Charleton 101 D3
West Chevington 221 E2
West Chiltington 108 C2
West Chiltington
    Common 108 C2
West Chinnock 104 A1
West Chisenbury 118 C2
West Clandon 121 F2
West Cliffe 125 F4
West Clyne 267 F1
West Coker 104 B1
West Compton
    Dorset 104 B3
West Compton Som 116 C3
West Cowick 195 F5
West Cross 128 C4
West Crudwell 132 B3
West Curry 96 D1
West Curthwaite 209 G2
West Dean Wilts 119 D5
West Dean WSuss 108 A2
West Deeping 161 G2
West Derby 183 E3
West Dereham 163 E2
West Ditchburn 229 F4
West Down 113 F1
West Drayton GtLon 135 F5
West Drayton Notts 187 E5
West Dullater 242 A4
West Dunnet 275 H1
West Edington 221 D3
West Ella 196 C5
West End Bed 149 E2
West End BrackF 135 E5
West End Caerp 130 B3
West End Cambs 162 C3
West End ERid 196 C1
West End Hants 107 D1
West End Herts 136 B2
West End Kent 125 D2
West End Lancs 192 A1
West End Lincs 189 D3
West End Norf 179 F4
West End Norf 178 A5
West End NSom 116 B1
West End NYorks 194 A2
West End Oxon 133 G2
West End Oxon 134 A4
West End SLan 235 D5
West End Suff 165 F3
West End Surr 121 G1
West End Surr 121 E1
West End Wilts 132 B5
West End Wilts 118 A5
West End Wilts 118 A5
West End Green 120 B1
West Farleigh 123 G3
West Farndon 148 A2
West Felton 170 A5
West Firle 109 G3
West Fleetham 229 F4
West Flotmanby 205 D5
West Garforth 194 C4
West Ginge 133 G4
West Green 120 C5
West Green Hants 120 C2
West Grimstead 118 D5
West Grinstead 121 G5
West Haddlesey 195 E5
West Haddon 160 B5
West Hagbourne 134 A4
West Hagley 158 B4
West Hall 210 B1
West Hallam 173 F3
West Halton 196 B5
West Ham 136 C4
West Handley 186 A5
West Hanney 133 G3
West Hanningfield 137 G3
West Hardwick 186 B1
West Harnham 118 C5
West Harptree 116 C2
West Harrow 136 A4

West Harting 120 C5
West Hatch Som 115 F5
West Hatch Wilts 118 A5
West Head 163 D2
West Heath ChesE 171 F1
West Heath GtLon 137 D5
West Heath Hants 121 D2
West Heath Hants 119 F1
West Heath WMid 158 C5
West Helmsdale 275 F7
West Hendon 136 B4
West Hendred 133 G4
West Heslerton 204 B5
West Hewish 116 A1
West Hill Devon 103 D3
West Hill ERid 197 D1
West Hill NSom 131 D5
West Hoathly 122 C5
West Holme 105 E4
West Horndon 137 F4
West Horrington 116 C3
West Horsley 121 F2
West Horton 229 E3
West Hougham 125 E5
West Howe 105 G3
West Howetown 114 C4
West Huntspill 116 A3
West Hyde 135 F3
West Hythe 124 D5
West Ilsley 133 G4
West Itchenor 107 G2
West Keal 176 B1
West Kennett 118 C1
West Kilbride 232 D5
West Kingsdown 123 E2
West Kington 132 A5
West Kington Wick 132 A5
West Kirby 182 D4
West Knapton 204 B5
West Knighton 104 D4
West Knoyle 117 F4
West Kyloe 229 E2
West Lambrook 104 A1
West Langdon 125 F4
West Langwell 266 D1
West Lavington
    Wilts 118 B2
West Lavington
    WSuss 121 D5
West Layton 202 A2
West Leake 173 G5
West Learmouth 228 C3
West Lees 203 D2
West Leigh Devon 113 G5
West Leigh Devon 101 D2
West Leigh Som 115 E4
West Leith 135 E1
West Lexham 163 G1
West Lilling 195 F1
West Lingo 244 C4
West Linton 235 F4
West Liss 120 C5
West Littleton 131 G5
West Lockinge 133 G4
West Looe 97 G4
West Lulworth 105 E4
West Lutton 196 B1
West Lydford 116 C4
West Lyn 114 A3
West Lyng 116 A5
West Lynn 163 E1
West Mains 229 E2
West Malling 123 F3
West Malvern 145 G3
West Marden 107 G1
West Markham 187 E5
West Marsh 188 C2
West Marton 193 E2
West Melbury 117 F5
West Melton 186 B2
West Meon 120 B5
West Meon Hut 120 B5
West Mersea 138 D1
West Milton 104 A3
West Minster 124 B1
West Molesey 121 G1
West Monkton 115 F5
West Moors 105 G2
West Morden 105 F3
West Morriston 236 D5
West Morton 193 G3
West Mostard 200 C3
West Mudford 116 C5
West Muir 253 D2
West Ness 203 F5
West Newbiggin 202 C1
West Newton ERid 197 D4
West Newton Norf 177 D5
West Norwood 136 C5
West Ogwell 101 E1
West Orchard 105 E1
West Overton 118 C1
West Panson 98 D1
West Park Aber 261 F5
West Park Mersey 183 G3
West Parley 105 G3
West Peckham 123 F3
West Pelton 212 B2
West Pennard 116 C4
West Pentire 96 B3
West Perry 149 G1
West Porlock 114 B3
West Prawle 101 D4
West Preston 108 C3
West Pulham 104 D2
West Putford 113 D4
West Quantoxhead 115 E3
West Raddon 102 B2
West Rainton 212 C3
West Rasen 188 A4
West Raynham 177 G4
West Retford 187 D4
West Rounton 202 D2
West Row 163 E5
West Rudham 177 G4
West Runton 178 C1
West Saltoun 236 B3
West Sandford 102 B2
West Sandwick 278 D4
West Scrafton 201 F4
West Shepton 116 D3
West Shinness
    Lodge 273 H7
West Somerset Railway Som
    TA24 5BG 115 E4

West Somerton 179 F4
West Stafford 104 D4
West Stockwith 187 E3
West Stoke 108 A3
West Stonesdale 201 D2
West Stoughton 116 B3
West Stour 117 E5
West Stourmouth 125 E2
West Stow 163 G4
West Stow Country Park Suff
    IP28 6HG 163 F5
West Stowell 118 C1
West Stratton 119 G3
West Street Kent 124 B3
West Street Med 137 G5
West Street Suff 164 A4
West Tanfield 202 B5
West Taphouse 97 F3
West Tarbert 231 G3
West Tarring 108 D3
West Thirston 221 D2
West Thorney 107 G2
West Thurrock 137 E5
West Tilbury 137 F5
West Tisted 120 B5
West Tofts Norf 163 G3
West Tofts P&K 243 G1
West Torrington 188 B4
West Town B&NESom 116 C1
West Town Hants 107 G3
West Town NSom 116 B1
West Town Som 116 C4
West Tytherley 119 D5
West Walton 162 C1
West Wellow 106 B1
West Wemyss 244 B5
West Wick 116 A1
West Wickham
    Cambs 151 E3
West Wickham GtLon 122 C2
West Williamston 126 D2
West Winch 163 E1
West Wintersow 118 D4
West Wittering 107 G3
West Witton 201 F4
West Woodburn 220 A3
West Woodhay 119 E1
West Woodlands 117 E3
West Worldham 120 C4
West Worlington 102 A1
West Worthing 108 D3
West Wratting 151 E2
West Wycombe 134 D3
West Yatton 132 A5
West Yell 278 D4
West Youlstone 112 C4
Westbere 125 D2
Westborough 174 D3
Westbourne Bourne 105 G3
Westbourne WSuss 107 G2
Westbourne Green 136 B4
Westbrook Kent 125 F1
Westbrook WBerks 133 G5
Westbrook Wilts 118 A1
Westbury Bucks 148 B4
Westbury Shrop 156 C2
Westbury Wilts 117 F2
Westbury Leigh 117 F2
Westbury on Trym 131 E5
Westbury-on-Severn 131 G1
Westbury-sub-Mendip 116 C3
Westby Lancs 191 G4
Westby Lincs 175 E5
Westcliff-on-Sea 138 B4
Westcombe 117 D4
Westcot 133 F4
Westcott Bucks 134 C1
Westcott Devon 102 D2
Westcott Surr 121 G3
Westcott Barton 147 G5
Westcourt 118 C1
Westcroft 148 D4
Westdean ESuss 110 A4
Westdowns 97 E1
Westend Town 131 G5
Wester Aberchalder 258 C2
Wester Badentyre 269 F5
Wester Balgedie 243 G4
Wester Culbeuchly 268 E4
Wester Dechmont 235 E2
Wester Fintray 261 G3
Wester Foffarty 252 C5
Wester Greenskares 269 F4
Wester Gruinards 266 C2
Wester Hailes 235 G3
Wester Lealty 266 D4
Wester Lonvine 266 D3
Wester Newburn 244 C4
Wester Ord 261 G4
Wester Quarff 279 D9
Wester Skeld 279 B8
Westerdale NYorks 203 F2
Westerdale High 275 G3
Westerfield ESuss 110 D2
Westerfield Suff 152 C3
Westergate 108 B3
Westerham 122 D3
Westerhope 212 A1
Westerleigh 131 F5
Westerloch 275 J3
Westerton Aber 261 F5
Westerton Angus 253 E4
Westerton Dur 212 B4
Westerton P&K 243 D2
Westerwick 279 B8
Westfield Cumb 208 C4
Westfield ESuss 110 D2
Westfield High 275 G2
Westfield NLan 234 B2
Westfield Norf 178 A5
Westfield WLoth 234 D2
Westfield WYorks 194 B5
Westfield Sole 123 G2
Westgate Dur 211 F4
Westgate N'umb 220 B4
Westgate NLincs 187 E2
Westgate Norf 178 A1
Westgate Hill 194 B5
Westgate on Sea 125 F1
Westhall Aber 260 E2
Westhall Suff 165 F3
Westham Dorset 104 C5
Westham ESuss 110 B3
Westham Som 116 B3
Westhampnett 108 A3
Westhay Devon 103 G2
Westhay Som 116 B3

Westhead 183 F2
Westhide 145 E3
Westhill Aber 261 G4
Westhill High 266 E7
Westhope Here 145 D2
Westhope Shrop 157 D4
Westhorp 148 A2
Westhorpe Lincs 176 A4
Westhorpe Notts 174 B2
Westhorpe Suff 152 B1
Westhoughton 184 A2
Westhouse 200 B5
Westhouses 173 F2
Westhumble 121 G2
Westing 278 E2
Westlake 100 C2
Westlands 171 F3
Westlea 132 D4
Westleigh Devon 113 E3
Westleigh Devon 103 D1
Westleigh GtMan 184 A2
Westleton 153 F1
Westley Shrop 156 C2
Westley Suff 151 G1
Westley Heights 137 F4
Westley Waterless 151 E2
Westlington 134 C1
Westlinton 218 B5
Westloch 235 G4
Westmancote 146 B4
Westmarsh 125 E2
Westmeston 109 F2
Westmill 150 B5
Westminster 136 B5
Westminster Abbey GtLon SW1P 3PA 44 E6
Westminster Abbey - Chapter House & Pyx Chamber GtLon SW1P 3PA 44 E6
Westminster Cathedral GtLon SW1P 2QW 44 C7
Westmuir 252 B4
Westness 276 C5
Westnewton Cumb 209 E2
Westnewton N'umb 228 D3
Westoe 212 C1
Weston B&NESom 117 E1
Weston ChesE 171 E2
Weston Devon 103 E4
Weston Devon 103 E2
Weston Dorset 104 C5
Weston Halton 183 G4
Weston Hants 120 C5
Weston Here 144 C2
Weston Herts 150 A4
Weston Lincs 176 A5
Weston Moray 268 C4
Weston N'hants 148 A3
Weston Notts 174 C1
Weston NYorks 194 A3
Weston Shrop 170 C5
Weston Shrop 157 E3
Weston Shrop 156 C5
Weston Soton 107 D1
Weston Staffs 171 G5
Weston WBerks 133 G5
Weston Bampfylde 116 D5
Weston Beggard 145 E3
Weston by Welland 160 C3
Weston Colville 151 E2
Weston Corbett 120 B3
Weston Coyney 171 G3
Weston Favell 148 C1
Weston Green Cambs 151 E2
Weston Green Norf 178 C4
Weston Heath 157 G1
Weston Hills 176 A5
Weston in Arden 159 F4
Weston Jones 171 E5
Weston Longville 178 C4
Weston Lullingfields 170 B5
Weston Park Staffs TF11 8LE 158 A1
Weston Patrick 120 B3
Weston Point 183 F4
Weston Rhyn 169 F4
Weston Subedge 146 D3
Weston Town 117 E3
Weston Turville 135 D1
Weston under Penyard 145 F5
Weston under Wetherley 147 F1
Weston Underwood Derbys 173 D3
Weston Underwood MK 149 D2
Westonbirt 132 A4
Westonbirt - The National Arboretum Glos GL8 8QS 132 A4
Westoning 149 F4
Weston-in-Gordano 131 D5
Weston-on-Avon 147 D2
Weston-on-the-Green 134 A1
Weston-on-Trent 173 F5
Weston-super-Mare 116 A1
Weston-under-Lizard 158 A1
Westonzoyland 116 A4
Westow 195 G1
Westpoint Arena, Clyst St. Mary Devon EX5 1DJ 102 C3
Westport A&B 222 B3
Westport Som 116 A5
Westra 130 A5
Westray 276 D3
Westray Airfield 276 D2
Westridge Green 134 A5
Westrigg 234 D3
Westruther 236 D5
Westry 162 B3
Westside 261 G5
Westvale 183 F3
Westville 173 G3
Westward 209 F2
Westward Ho! 113 E3
Westwell Kent 124 B4
Westwell Oxon 133 E2
Westwell Leacon 124 B4
Westwick Cambs 150 C1
Westwick Dur 201 F1
Westwick Norf 179 D3
Westwick NYorks 194 C1
Westwood Devon 102 D3
Westwood Peter 161 G3
Westwood SLan 234 A4
Westwood Wilts 117 F2
Westwood Heath 159 E5
Westwoodside 187 E3
Wetham Green 124 A2
Wetheral 210 A2
Wetherby 194 D3
Wetherden 152 B1
Wetherden Upper Town 152 B1
Wetheringsett 152 C1
Wethersfield 151 F4
Wethersta 279 C6
Wetherup Street 152 C1
Wetley Abbey 171 G3
Wetley Rocks 171 G3
Wettenhall 170 D1
Wettenhall Green 170 D1
Wetton 172 C2
Wetwang 196 B2
Wetwood 171 E4
Wexcombe 119 D2
Wexham Street 135 E4
Weybourne Norf 178 C1
Weybourne Surr 121 D3
Weybread 164 D3
Weybread Street 165 D4
Weybridge 121 F1
Weycroft 103 G2
Weydale 275 G2
Weyhill 119 E3
Weymouth 104 C5
Weymouth Sea Life Adventure Park & Marine Sanctuary Dorset DT4 7SX 104 C4
Whaddon Bucks 148 D4
Whaddon Cambs 150 B3
Whaddon Glos 132 A1
Whaddon Glos 146 B5
Whaddon Wilts 118 C5
Whaddon Wilts 117 F1
Whaddon Gap 150 B3
Whale 210 B5
Whaley 186 C5
Whaley Bridge 185 E4
Whaley Thorns 186 C5
Whaligoe 275 J4
Whalley 192 D4
Whalsay 279 E6
Whalsay Airport 279 E6
Whalton 220 D3
Wham 193 D1
Whaplode 176 B5
Whaplode Drove 162 B1
Whaplode St. Catherine 162 B1
Wharfe 193 D1
Wharles 192 A4
Wharley End 149 E3
Wharncliffe Side 185 G3
Wharram le Street 196 A1
Wharram Percy 196 A1
Wharton ChesW&C 171 D1
Wharton Here 145 E2
Whashton 202 A2
Whatcote 147 F3
Whateley 159 E3
Whatfield 152 B3
Whatley 117 E3
Whatlington 110 C2
Whatsole Street 124 D4
Whatstandwell 173 E2
Whatton 174 C4
Whauphill 207 E2
Whaw 201 E2
Wheatacre 165 F2
Wheatcroft 173 E2
Wheatenhurst 131 G2
Wheatfield 134 B3
Wheathampstead 136 A1
Wheathill Shrop 157 F4
Wheathill Som 116 C4
Wheatley Hants 120 C4
Wheatley Oxon 134 B2
Wheatley WYorks 193 G5
Wheatley Hill 212 C4
Wheatley Lane 193 E4
Wheatley Park 186 C2
Wheaton Aston 158 A1
Wheddon Cross 114 C4
Wheedlemont 260 C2
Wheelerstreet 121 E3
Wheelock 171 E2
Wheelock Heath 171 E2
Wheelton 192 C5
Wheen 252 B2
Wheldale 195 D5
Wheldrake 195 F3
Whelford 133 D3
Whelley 183 G2
Whelpley Hill 135 E2
Whelpo 209 G3
Whelston 182 D5
Whenby 195 F1
Whepstead 151 G2
Wherstead 152 C3
Wherwell 119 E3
Wheston 185 F5
Whetley Cross 104 A2
Whetsted 123 F4
Whetstone GtLon 136 B3
Whetstone Leics 160 A3
Whicham 198 C4
Whichford 147 F4
Whickham 212 B1
Whiddon 113 E5
Whiddon Down 99 G1
Whifflet 234 B3
Whigstreet 252 C5
Whilton 148 B1
Whim 235 G4
Whimble 112 D5
Whimple 102 D3
Whimpwell Green 179 E3
Whin Lane End 191 G3
Whinburgh 178 B5
Whinlatter Forest Cumb CA12 5TW 209 E4
Whinny Hill 202 C1
Whinnyfold 261 J1
Whippingham 107 E3
Whipsnade 135 F1
Whipsnade Zoo CenBeds LU6 2LF 135 F1
Whipton 102 C3
Whirlow 186 A4
Whisby 175 E1
Whissendine 160 D1
Whissonsett 178 A3
Whisterfield 184 C5
Whistley Green 134 C5
Whiston Mersey 183 F3
Whiston N'hants 148 D1
Whiston Staffs 172 B3
Whiston Staffs 158 A1
Whiston SYorks 186 B3
Whiston Cross 157 G2
Whiston Eaves 172 B3
Whitacre Fields 159 E3
Whitacre Heath 159 E3
Whitbeck 198 C4
Whitbourne 145 G2
Whitburn T&W 212 D1
Whitburn WLoth 234 D3
Whitby ChesW&C 183 E5
Whitby NYorks 204 B1
Whitby Abbey NYorks YO22 4JT 204 C1
Whitby Lifeboat Museum NYorks YO21 3PU 204 B1
Whitbyheath 183 E5
Whitchurch B&NESom 116 D1
Whitchurch Bucks 148 D5
Whitchurch Cardiff 130 A4
Whitchurch Devon 99 E3
Whitchurch Hants 119 F3
Whitchurch Here 131 E1
Whitchurch Pembs 140 A5
Whitchurch Shrop 170 C3
Whitchurch Warks 147 E3
Whitchurch Canonicorum 103 G3
Whitchurch Hill 134 B5
Whitchurch-on-Thames 134 B5
Whitcombe 104 D4
Whitcott Keysett 156 B4
White Ball 103 D1
White Colne 151 G5
White Coppice 184 A1
White Cross Corn 96 C4
White Cross Devon 102 D3
White Cross Here 145 D3
White Cross Wilts 117 E4
White Cube GtLon N1 6PB 12 C4
White End 146 A5
White Hill 117 F4
White Houses 187 E5
White Kirkley 211 G4
White Lackington 104 D3
White Ladies Aston 146 B2
White Lund 192 A1
White Mill 142 A5
White Moor 173 E3
White Notley 137 G1
White Ox Mead 117 E2
White Pit 189 D5
White Post Farm Centre, Farnsfield Notts NG22 8HL 174 B2
White Rocks 144 D5
White Roding 137 E1
White Waltham 134 D5
Whiteacen 267 K7
Whiteash Green 151 F4
Whitebirk 192 D5
Whitebog 269 H5
Whitebridge High 275 H1
Whitebridge (An Drochaid Bhàn) High 258 B3
Whitebrook 131 E2
Whiteburn 236 C5
Whitecairn 214 D5
Whitecairns 261 H3
Whitecastle 235 E5
Whitechapel 192 B3
Whitechurch 141 E4
Whitecote 194 B4
Whitecraig 236 A2
Whitecroft 131 F2
Whitecrook 214 C5
Whitecross Corn 94 C3
Whitecross Corn 97 D2
Whitecross Dorset 104 A3
Whitecross Falk 235 D2
Whiteface 266 E3
Whitefield Aber 261 F2
Whitefield Devon 114 A4
Whitefield Dorset 105 F3
Whitefield GtMan 184 C2
Whitefield High 258 C2
Whitefield High 275 H3
Whitefield P&K 243 G1
Whiteford 261 F2
Whitegate 170 D1
Whitehall Devon 103 E1
Whitehall Hants 120 C2
Whitehall Ork 276 F5
Whitehall WSuss 121 G5
Whitehaven 208 C5
Whitehill Aber 269 H5
Whitehill Hants 120 C4
Whitehill Kent 124 B3
Whitehill Midlo 236 A3
Whitehill NAyr 233 D4
Whitehills 268 E4
Whitehouse A&B 231 G3
Whitehouse Aber 260 E3
Whitehouse Common 158 D3
Whitekirk 236 C1
Whitelackington 103 G1
Whitelaw 237 F4
Whiteleen 275 J4
Whitelees 224 B2
Whiteley 107 E2
Whiteley Bank 107 E4
Whiteley Green 184 D5
Whiteley Village 121 F1
Whiteleys 214 B5
Whitemans Green 109 F1
Whitemire 267 G6
Whitemoor 97 D4
Whiteness 279 C8
Whiteoak Green 133 F1
Whiteparish 118 D5
Whiterashes 261 G2
Whiterow 275 J4
Whiteshill 132 A2
Whiteside N'umb 210 D1
Whiteside WLoth 235 D3
Whitesmith 110 A2
Whitestaunton 103 F1
Whitestone A&B 222 C2
Whitestone Aber 260 E5
Whitestone Devon 102 B3
Whitestreet Green 152 A4
Whitestripe 269 H5
Whiteway 132 B1
Whitewell Aber 269 H4
Whitewell Lancs 192 C3
Whitewell Wrex 170 B3
Whiteworks 99 G3
Whitewreath 267 K6
Whitfield Here 144 D4
Whitfield Kent 125 F4
Whitfield N'hants 148 B4
Whitfield N'umb 211 D2
Whitfield SGlos 131 F3
Whitford Devon 103 F3
Whitford (Chwitffordd) Flints 182 C5
Whitgift 196 A5
Whitgreave 171 F5
Whithorn 207 E2
Whiting Bay 223 F3
Whitkirk 194 C4
Whitlam 261 G2
Whitland (Hendy-Gwyn) 127 F1
Whitland Abbey 127 F1
Whitleigh 100 A1
Whitletts 224 B3
Whitley NYorks 195 E5
Whitley Read 120 C1
Whitley Wilts 117 F1
Whitley WMid 159 F5
Whitley Bay 221 F4
Whitley Chapel 211 F2
Whitley Heath 171 F5
Whitley Lower 185 G1
Whitley Row 123 D3
Whitlock's End 158 D5
Whitminster 131 G2
Whitmore Dorset 105 G2
Whitmore Staffs 171 F3
Whitnage 102 D1
Whitnash 147 F1
Whitnell 115 F3
Whitney-on-Wye 144 B3
Whitrigg Cumb 209 F1
Whitrigg Cumb 209 F3
Whitsbury 106 A1
Whitsome 237 F4
Whitson 130 C4
Whitstable 124 D2
Whitstone 98 C1
Whittingham 229 E5
Whittingslow 156 D4
Whittington Derbys 186 A5
Whittington Glos 146 C5
Whittington Lancs 200 B5
Whittington Norf 163 F3
Whittington Shrop 170 A4
Whittington Staffs 158 A4
Whittington Staffs 159 D2
Whittington Worcs 146 A2
Whittlebury 148 B3
Whittle-le-Woods 192 B5
Whittlesey 162 A3
Whittlesford 150 C3
Whittlestone Head 184 B1
Whitton GtLon 136 A5
Whitton N'umb 220 C1
Whitton NLincs 196 B5
Whitton Powys 144 B1
Whitton Shrop 157 E5
Whitton Stock 212 C5
Whitton Suff 152 C3
Whittonditch 133 E5
Whittonstall 211 G2
Whitway 119 F2
Whitwell Derbys 186 C5
Whitwell Herts 149 G5
Whitwell IoW 107 E5
Whitwell NYorks 202 B3
Whitwell Rut 161 E2
Whitwell Street 178 C3
Whitwell-on-the-Hill 195 G1
Whitwick 159 G1
Whitwood 194 D5
Whitworth 184 C1
Whitworth Art Gallery, Manchester GtMan M15 6ER 25 E4
Whixall 170 C4
Whixley 194 D2
Whorlton Dur 202 A1
Whorlton NYorks 203 D2
Whygate 219 F4
Whyle 145 E1
Whyteleafe 122 C3
Wibdon 131 E3
Wibsey 194 A4
Wibtoft 159 G4
Wichenford 145 G1
Wichling 124 B3
Wick Bourne 106 A3
Wick Devon 103 E2
Wick (Inbhir Ùige) High 275 J3
Wick SGlos 131 G5
Wick Som 115 F3
Wick Som 116 C4
Wick VGlam 129 F5
Wick Wilts 118 C5
Wick Worcs 146 B3
Wick WSuss 108 C3
Wick Airport 275 J3
Wick Hill Kent 124 A4
Wick Hill W'ham 120 C1
Wick St. Lawrence 116 A1
Wicken Cambs 163 D5
Wicken N'hants 148 C4
Wicken Bonhunt 150 C4
Wickenby 188 A4
Wicker Street Green 152 A3
Wickerslack 200 B1
Wickersley 186 B3
Wicketwood Hill 174 B3
Wickford 137 G3
Wickham Hants 107 E1
Wickham WBerks 133 F5
Wickham Bishops 138 B1
Wickham Heath 119 F1
Wickham Market 153 E2
Wickham St. Paul 151 G4
Wickham Skeith 152 B1
Wickham Street Suff 151 F2
Wickham Street Suff 152 B1
Wickhambreaux 125 E3
Wickhambrook 151 F2
Wickhamford 146 C3
Wickhampton 179 F5
Wicklewood 178 B5
Wickmere 178 C2
Wicksteed Park N'hants NN15 6NJ 161 D5
Wickstreet 110 A3
Wickwar 131 G4
Widcombe 117 E1
Widdington 150 D4
Widdop 193 F4
Widdrington 221 E2
Widdrington Station 221 E2
Wide Open 221 E4
Widecombe in the Moor 102 A5
Widegates 97 G4
Widemouth Bay 112 C5
Widewall 277 D8
Widford Essex 137 F2
Widford Herts 136 D1
Widford Oxon 133 E1
Widgham Green 151 E2
Widmer End 135 D3
Widmerpool 174 B5
Widnes 183 G4
Widworthy 103 F3
Wigan 183 G2
Wigan Pier GtMan WN3 4EU 183 G2
Wiganthorpe 203 F5
Wigborough 104 A1
Wiggaton 103 E3
Wiggenhall St. Germans 163 D1
Wiggenhall St. Mary Magdalen 163 D1
Wiggenhall St. Mary the Virgin 163 D1
Wiggenhall St. Peter 163 E1
Wiggens Green 151 E3
Wigginton Herts 135 E1
Wigginton Oxon 147 F4
Wigginton Shrop 170 A4
Wigginton Staffs 159 E2
Wigginton York 195 F2
Wigglesworth 193 E2
Wiggonby 209 G1
Wiggonholt 108 C2
Wighill 195 D3
Wighton 178 A2
Wightwizzle 185 G3
Wigley 106 C1
Wigmore Here 144 D1
Wigmore Med 124 A2
Wigsley 187 F5
Wigsthorpe 161 F4
Wigston 160 B3
Wigston Parva 159 G4
Wigthorpe 186 C4
Wigtoft 176 A4
Wigton 209 F2
Wigtown 215 F5
Wike 194 C3
Wilbarston 160 D4
Wilberfoss 195 G2
Wilburton 162 C5
Wilby N'hants 149 D1
Wilby Norf 164 B2
Wilby Suff 164 D4
Wilcot 118 C1
Wilcott 156 C1
Wilcrick 130 D4
Wilday Green 186 A5
Wildboarclough 171 G1
Wilde Street 163 F5
Wilden Bed 149 F2
Wilden Worcs 158 A5
Wildhern 119 E2
Wildhill 136 B2
Wildmoor 158 B5
Wildsworth 187 F3
Wilford 173 G4
Wilkesley 170 D3
Wilkhaven 267 G3
Wilkieston 235 F3
Wilksby 176 A1
Willand Devon 102 D1
Willand Som 103 E1
Willaston ChesE 171 D2
Willaston ChesW&C 183 E5
Willaston Shrop 170 C4
Willen 149 D3
Willen Lakeside Park MK MK15 9HQ 9 D2
Willenhall WMid 158 B3
Willenhall WMid 159 F5
Willerby ERid 196 C5
Willerby NYorks 204 D5
Willersey 146 D4
Willersley 144 C3
Willesborough 124 C4
Willesborough Lees 124 C4
Willesden 136 B4
Willesleigh 113 F2
Willesley 132 A4
Willett 115 E4
Willey Shrop 157 F3
Willey Warks 159 G4
Willey Green 121 E2
William's Green 152 A3
Williamscot 147 G3
Williamson Park, Lancaster Lancs LA1 1UX 192 A1
Williamthorpe 173 F1
Willian 150 A4
Willimontswick 211 D1
Willingale 137 E2
Willingdon 110 A3
Willingham 162 C5
Willingham by Stow 187 F4
Willingham Green 151 E2
Willington Bed 149 G2
Willington Derbys 173 D5
Willington Dur 212 A4
Willington Kent 123 G3
Willington T&W 212 C1
Willington Warks 147 E4
Willington Corner 170 C1
Willisham 152 B2
Willitoft 195 G4
Williton 115 D3
Willoughbridge 171 E3
Willoughby Lincs 189 E5
Willoughby Warks 148 A1
Willoughby Waterleys 160 A3
Willoughby-on-the-Wolds 174 B5
Willoughton 187 G3
Willow Green 184 A5
Willows Farm Village Herts AL2 1BB 136 A2
Willows Green 137 G1
Willsbridge 131 F5
Willslock 172 B4
Willsworthy 99 F2
Willtown 116 A5
Wilmcote 147 D2
Wilmington B&NESom 117 D1
Wilmington Devon 103 F2
Wilmington ESuss 110 A3
Wilmington Kent 137 E5
Wilmslow 184 C4
Wilnecote 159 E2
Wilney Green 164 B3
Wilpshire 192 C4
Wilsden 193 G4
Wilsford Lincs 175 F3
Wilsford Wilts 118 C4
Wilsford Wilts 118 C2
Wilsham 114 A3
Wilshaw 185 F2
Wilsill 194 A1
Wilsley Green 123 G5
Wilsley Pound 123 G5
Wilson 173 F5
Wilstead 149 F3
Wilsthorpe ERid 197 D1
Wilsthorpe Lincs 161 F1
Wilstone 135 E1
Wilton Cumb 208 D5
Wilton Here 145 E5
Wilton NYorks 204 B4
Wilton R&C 203 E1
Wilton ScBord 227 F4
Wilton Wilts 119 D1
Wilton Wilts 118 B4
Wilton House Wilts SP2 0BJ 118 B4
Wiltown 103 E1
Wimbish 151 D4
Wimbish Green 151 E4
Wimblebury 158 C1
Wimbledon 136 B5
Wimbledon All England Lawn Tennis & Croquet Club GtLon SW19 5AG 11 E7
Wimblington 162 C3
Wimborne Minster 105 G2
Wimborne Minster Dorset BH21 1HT 3 B2
Wimborne St. Giles 105 G1
Wimbotsham 163 E2
Wimpole 150 B2
Wimpole Home Farm Cambs SG8 0DW 150 B3
Wimpole Lodge 150 B3
Wimpstone 147 E3
Wincanton 117 E5
Winceby 176 B1
Wincham 184 A5
Winchburgh 235 E2
Winchcombe 146 C5
Winchelsea 111 E2
Winchelsea Beach 111 E2
Winchester 119 F5
Winchester Cathedral Hants SO23 9LS 89 Winchester
Winchet Hill 123 G4
Winchfield 120 C2
Winchmore Hill Bucks 135 E3
Winchmore Hill GtLon 136 C3
Wincle 171 G1
Wincobank 186 A3
Windermere 199 F3
Windermere Lake Cruises Cumb LA12 8AS 199 E3
Winderton 147 F3
Windhill 266 C7
Windle Hill 183 E5
Windlehurst 185 D4
Windlesham 121 E1
Windley 173 E3
Windmill 185 F5
Windmill Hill ESuss 110 B2
Windmill Hill Som 103 G1
Windmill Hill Worcs 146 B3
Windrush 133 D1
Windsor 135 E5
Windsor Castle W&M SL4 1NJ 89 Windsor
Windsor Green 151 G2
Windy Nook 212 B1
Windygates 244 B4
Windy-Yett 233 F4
Wineham 109 E1
Winestead 197 E5
Winewall 193 F4
Winfarthing 164 C3
Winford IoW 107 E4
Winford NSom 116 C1
Winforton 144 B3
Winfrith Newburgh 105 E4
Wing Bucks 149 D5
Wing Rut 161 D2
Wingate 212 C4
Wingates GtMan 184 A2
Wingates N'umb 220 C2
Wingerworth 173 E1
Wingfield CenBeds 149 F5
Wingfield Suff 164 D4
Wingfield Wilts 117 F2
Wingfield Green 164 D4
Wingham 125 E3
Wingham Well 125 E3
Wingmore 125 D4
Wingrave 135 D1
Winkburn 174 C2
Winkfield 135 E5
Winkfield Row 135 D5
Winkhill 172 B2
Winkleigh 113 G5
Winksley 202 B5
Winkton 106 A3
Winlaton 212 A1
Winlaton Mill 212 A1
Winless 275 J3
Winmarleigh 192 A3
Winnard's Perch 96 D3
Winnersh 134 C5
Winnington 184 A5
Winscombe 116 B2
Winsford ChesW&C 171 D1
Winsford Som 114 C4
Winsham Devon 113 E2
Winsham Som 103 G2
Winshill 173 D5
Winsh-wen 128 C3
Winskill 210 B4
Winslade 120 B3
Winsley 117 F1
Winslow 148 C5
Winson 132 C2
Winsor 106 C1
Winster Cumb 199 F3
Winster Derbys 172 D1
Winston Dur 202 A1
Winston Suff 152 C1
Winston Green 152 C1
Winstone 132 B2
Winswell 113 E4
Winter Gardens FY1 1HW 64 Blackpool
Winter Gardens NSom BS23 1AJ 88 Weston-super-Mare
Winterborne Came 104 D4
Winterborne Clenston 105 E2
Winterborne Herringston 104 C4
Winterborne Houghton 105 E2
Winterborne Kingston 105 E3
Winterborne Monkton 104 C4
Winterborne Stickland 105 E2
Winterborne Whitechurch 105 E2
Winterborne Zelston 105 E3
Winterbourne SGlos 131 F4
Winterbourne WBerks 133 G5
Winterbourne Abbas 104 C3
Winterbourne Bassett 132 D5
Winterbourne Dauntsey 118 C4
Winterbourne Earls 118 C4
Winterbourne Gunner 118 C4
Winterbourne Monkton 132 D5
Winterbourne Steepleton 104 C4
Winterbourne Stoke 118 B3
Winterbrook 134 B4
Winterburn 193 F2
Wintercleugh 226 A4
Winteringham 196 B5
Winterley 171 E2
Wintersett 186 A1
Wintershill 107 E1
Winterslow 118 D4
Winterton 187 G1
Winterton-on-Sea 179 F4
Winthorpe Lincs 177 D1
Winthorpe Notts 174 D2
Winton Bourne 105 G3
Winton Cumb 200 C1
Wintringham 204 B5
Winwick Cambs 161 G4
Winwick N'hants 160 B5
Winwick Warr 184 A3
Wirksworth 173 D2
Wirksworth Moor 173 E2
Wirral Country Park Mersey CH61 0HN 182 D4
Wirswall 170 C3
Wisbech 162 C2
Wisbech St. Mary 162 C2
Wisborough Green 121 F5
Wiseton 187 E4
Wishaw NLan 234 B4
Wishaw Warks 159 D3
Wisley 121 F2
Wispington 188 C5
Wissett 165 E4
Wissington 152 A4
Wistanstow 156 D4
Wistanswick 171 D5
Wistaston 171 D2
Wiston Pembs 126 D1
Wiston SLan 226 A2
Wiston WSuss 108 D2
Wistow Cambs 162 A4
Wistow NYorks 195 E4
Wiswell 192 D4
Witcham 162 C5
Witchampton 105 F2
Witchburn 222 C3
Witchford 162 D5
Witcombe 116 B5
Witham 138 B1
Witham Friary 117 E3
Witham on the Hill 161 F1
Withcall 188 C4
Withcote 160 C2
Withdean 109 F3
Witherenden Hill 110 B1
Witherhurst 110 B1
Witheridge 102 B1
Witherley 159 F3
Withern 189 E4
Withernsea 197 F5
Withernwick 197 D3
Withersdale Street 165 D3
Withersfield 151 E3
Witherslack 199 F4
Witherslack Hall 199 F4
Withiel 97 D3
Withiel Florey 114 C4
Withielgoose 97 E3
Withington Glos 132 C1
Withington GtMan 184 C3
Withington Here 145 E3
Withington Shrop 157 E1
Withington Staffs 172 B4
Withington Green 184 C5
Withington Marsh 145 E3
Withleigh 102 C1
Withnell 192 C5
Withnell Fold 192 C5
Withybrook Som 117 D3
Withybrook Warks 159 G4
Withycombe 114 D3
Withycombe Raleigh 102 D4
Withyham 123 D5
Withypool 114 B4
Witley 121 E4
Witnesham 152 C2
Witney 133 F2
Wittering 161 F2
Wittersham 111 D1
Witton Angus 253 D2

Witton Norf 179 E5
Witton Worcs 146 A1
Witton Bridge 179 E2
Witton Gilbert 212 B3
Witton Park 212 A4
Witton-le-Wear 212 A4
Wiveliscombe 115 D5
Wivelsfield 109 F1
Wivelsfield Green 109 F2
Wivenhoe 152 B5
Wiveton 178 B1
Wix 152 C5
Wixford 146 C2
Wixhill 170 C5
Wixoe 151 F3
Woburn 149 E4
Woburn Safari Park CenBeds MK17 9QN 9 F3
Woburn Sands 149 E4
Wokefield Park 120 B1
Woking 121 F2
Wokingham 120 D1
Wolborough 102 B5
Wold Newton ERid 204 D5
Wold Newton NELincs 188 C3
Woldingham 122 C3
Wolds Village, Bainton ERid YO25 9EF 196 B2
Wolfelee 227 G5
Wolferlow 145 F1
Wolferton 177 E5
Wolfhampcote 148 A1
Wolfhill 243 G1
Wolfpits 144 B2
Wolf's Castle 140 C5
Wolfsdale 140 C5
Woll 227 F3
Wollaston N'hants 149 E1
Wollaston Shrop 156 C1
Wollaston WMid 158 A4
Wollerton 170 D5
Wollescote 158 B4
Wolsingham 211 G4
Wolston 159 G5
Wolsty 209 E1
Wolvercote 134 A2
Wolverhampton 158 B3
Wolverhampton Art Gallery WMid WV1 1DU 14 A1
Wolverley Shrop 170 B4
Wolverley Worcs 158 A5
Wolvers Hill 116 A1
Wolverton Hants 119 G2
Wolverton MK 148 D3
Wolverton Warks 147 E1
Wolverton Wilts 117 E4
Wolverton Common 119 G2
Wolvesnewton 131 D3
Wolvey 159 G4
Wolvey Heath 159 G4
Wolviston 213 D5
Womaston 144 B1
Wombleton 203 F4
Wombourne 158 A3
Wombwell 186 A2
Womenswold 125 E3
Womersley 186 C1
Wonastow 131 D1
Wonersh 121 F3
Wonford 102 C3
Wonson 99 G2
Wonston 119 F4
Wooburn 135 E4
Wooburn Green 135 E4
Wood Bevington 146 C2
Wood Burcote 148 B3
Wood Dalling 178 B3
Wood Eaton 158 A1
Wood End Bed 149 F3
Wood End Bed 149 F1
Wood End Bucks 148 C4
Wood End Herts 150 B5
Wood End Warks 159 E3
Wood End Warks 158 D5
Wood End Warks 159 E4
Wood End WMid 158 B4
Wood Enderby 176 A1
Wood Green GtLon 136 C3
Wood Green Norf 164 D2
Wood Green Animal Shelter, Godmanchester Cambs PE29 2NH 150 A1
Wood Lane 170 B4
Wood Norton 178 B3
Wood Seats 186 A3
Wood Stanway 146 C4
Wood Street 179 E3
Wood Street Village 121 E2
Woodacott 113 D5
Woodale 201 F5
Woodall 186 B4
Woodbastwick 179 E4
Woodbeck 187 E5
Woodborough Notts 174 B3
Woodborough Wilts 118 C2
Woodbridge Devon 103 D3
Woodbridge Dorset 104 D1
Woodbridge Suff 153 D3
Woodbury Devon 102 D4
Woodbury Som 116 C3
Woodbury Salterton 102 D4
Woodchester 132 A2
Woodchurch Kent 124 B5
Woodchurch Mersey 183 D4
Woodcombe 114 C3
Woodcote Oxon 134 B4
Woodcote Tel&W 157 G1
Woodcote Green 158 B5
Woodcott 119 F2
Woodcroft 131 E3
Woodcutts 105 F1
Woodditton 151 E2
Woodeaton 134 A1
Woodend Aber 260 E3
Woodend Cumb 198 C3
Woodend High 258 E2
Woodend High 247 G3
Woodend N'hants 148 B3
Woodend P&K 250 C5
Woodend WSuss 108 A3
Woodend Green 151 D5
Woodfalls 118 C5
Woodfield Oxon 148 A5
Woodfield SAyr 224 B3
Woodfoot 200 B1
Woodford Corn 112 C4
Woodford Devon 101 D3

Woodford Glos 131 F3
Woodford GtLon 136 D3
Woodford GtMan 184 C4
Woodford N'hants 161 E5
Woodford Som 115 D4
Woodford Bridge 136 D3
Woodford Green 136 D3
Woodford Halse 148 A2
Woodgate Devon 103 E1
Woodgate Norf 178 B4
Woodgate WMid 158 B4
Woodgate Worcs 146 B1
Woodgate WSuss 108 B3
Woodgreen 106 A1
Wuudhall Invcly 233 E2
Woodhall NYorks 201 E3
Woodhall Hills 194 A4
Woodhall Spa 175 G1
Woodham Bucks 134 B1
Woodham Dur 212 B5
Woodham Surr 121 F1
Woodham Ferrers 137 G3
Woodham Mortimer 138 B2
Woodham Walter 138 B2
Woodhaven 244 C2
Woodhead Aber 261 F1
Woodhead Staffs 172 B3
Woodhey 183 E4
Woodhey Green 170 C2
Woodhill Shrop 157 G4
Woodhill Som 116 A5
Woodhorn 221 E3
Woodhouse Cumb 199 G4
Woodhouse Leics 160 A1
Woodhouse SYorks 186 B4
Woodhouse WYorks 194 B4
Woodhouse WYorks 194 C5
Woodhouse WYorks 194 A5
Woodhouse Down 131 F4
Woodhouse Eaves 160 A1
Woodhouse Green 171 G1
Woodhouses GtMan 184 C2
Woodhouses Staffs 159 D1
Woodhouses Staffs 158 C2
Woodhuish 101 F2
Woodingdean 109 F3
Woodington 119 E5
Woodland Devon 101 D1
Woodland Dur 211 G5
Woodland Kent 124 D4
Woodland Head 102 A3
Woodlands Dorset 105 G2
Woodlands Hants 106 C1
Woodlands NYorks 194 C2
Woodlands Shrop 157 G4
Woodlands Som 115 E3
Woodlands Leisure Park, Dartmouth Devon TQ9 7DQ 101 D2
Woodlands Park 135 D5
Woodlands St. Mary 133 F5
Woodlane 172 C5
Woodleigh 100 D3
Woodlesford 194 C5
Woodley GtMan 184 D4
Woodley W'ham 134 C5
Woodmancote Glos 132 C2
Woodmancote Glos 146 B5
Woodmancote Glos 131 G3
Woodmancote WSuss 109 E2
Woodmancote WSuss 107 G2
Woodmancott 119 G3
Woodmansey 196 C4
Woodmansterne 122 B3
Woodmanton 102 D4
Woodmill 172 C5
Woodminton 118 B5
Woodmoor 156 B2
Woodnesborough 125 F3
Woodnewton 161 F3
Woodperry 134 A1
Woodplumpton 192 B4
Woodrising 178 A5
Woodrow 105 D1
Wood's Corner 110 B2
Woods Eaves 144 B3
Wood's Green 123 F5
Woodseaves Shrop 171 D4
Woodseaves Staffs 171 E5
Woodsend 133 E5
Woodsetts 186 C4
Woodsford 105 D3
Woodside Aberdeen 261 H4
Woodside BrackF 135 E5
Woodside CenBeds 135 F1
Woodside Cumb 208 D3
Woodside D&G 217 E3
Woodside Fife 244 C4
Woodside Fife 244 A4
Woodside GtLon 122 C2
Woodside Hants 106 C3
Woodside Herts 136 B2
Woodside NAyr 233 E4
Woodside P&K 243 G1
Woodside Shrop 156 C4
Woodside WMid 158 B4
Woodside Animal Farm & Leisure Park CenBeds LU1 4DG 135 F1
Woodside Green 124 B3
Woodstock Oxon 133 G1
Woodstock Pembs 140 D5
Woodthorpe Derbys 186 B5
Woodthorpe Leics 160 A1
Woodthorpe Lincs 189 E4
Woodthorpe SYorks 186 A4
Woodthorpe York 195 E3
Woodton 165 D2
Woodtown 113 E3
Woodvale 183 E1
Woodville 159 F1
Woodwall Green 171 E4
Woodwalton 162 A4
Woodwick 276 C5
Woodworth Green 170 C2
Woodyates 105 G1
Wookey 116 C3
Wookey Hole 116 C3
Wookey Hole Caves & Papermill Som BA5 1BB 116 C3
Wool 105 E4
Woolacombe 113 E1
Woolage Green 125 E4
Woolage Village 125 E3
Woolaston 131 E2

Woolaston Slade 131 E2
Woolavington 116 A3
Woolbeding 121 D5
Woolcotts 114 C4
Wooldale 185 F2
Woolfardisworthy Devon 102 A2
Woolfardisworthy Devon 112 D3
Woolfold 184 B1
Woolfords Cottages 235 E4
Woolgarston 105 F4
Woolgreaves 186 A1
Woolhampton 119 G1
Woolhope 145 F4
Woolland 105 D2
Woollard 116 D1
Woollaton 113 E4
Woollensbrook 136 C2
Woolley B&NESom 117 E1
Woolley Cambs 161 G5
Woolley Corn 112 C4
Woolley Derbys 173 E1
Woolley WYorks 186 A1
Woolley Green W&M 135 D5
Woolley Green Wilts 117 F1
Woolmer Green 136 B1
Woolmere Green 146 B1
Woolmersdon 115 F4
Woolpit 152 A1
Woolpit Green 152 A1
Woolscott 147 G1
Woolsgrove 102 A2
Woolstaston 157 D3
Woolsthorpe 174 D4
Woolsthorpe by Colsterworth 175 E5
Woolston Devon 100 D3
Woolston Shrop 170 A5
Woolston Shrop 156 D4
Woolston Soton 106 D1
Woolston Warr 184 A4
Woolston Green 101 D1
Woolstone Glos 146 B4
Woolstone MK 149 E2
Woolstone Oxon 133 E4
Woolton 183 F4
Woolton Hill 119 F1
Woolverstone 152 C4
Woolverton 117 E2
Woolwich 136 D5
Woonton 144 C2
Wooperton 229 E5
Woore 171 E3
Wootten Green 164 D4
Wootton Bed 149 F3
Wootton Hants 106 B3
Wootton IoW 107 E3
Wootton Kent 125 E4
Wootton N'hants 148 C2
Wootton NLincs 188 A1
Wootton Oxon 133 G1
Wootton Oxon 133 G2
Wootton Shrop 157 D5
Wootton Shrop 170 A5
Wootton Staffs 171 F5
Wootton Staffs 172 C3
Wootton Bassett 132 C4
Wootton Bridge 107 E3
Wootton Common 107 E3
Wootton Courtenay 114 C3
Wootton Fitzpaine 103 G3
Wootton Green 149 F3
Wootton Rivers 118 C1
Wootton St. Lawrence 119 G2
Wootton Wawen 147 D1
Worcester 146 A2
Worcester Cathedral Worcs WR1 2LH 90 Worcester
Worcester Park 122 B2
Worcester Woods Country Park Worcs WR5 2LG 146 A2
Wordsley 158 A4
Wordwell 163 G5
Worfield 157 G3
Worgret 105 F4
Work 277 D6
Workhouse End 149 G2
Workington 208 D4
Worksop 186 C5
Worlaby Lincs 188 D5
Worlaby NLincs 188 A1
World Museum Liverpool Mersey L3 8EN 42 D3
World of Beatrix Potter Attraction Cumb LA23 3BX 199 F3
World of James Herriot, Thirsk NYorks YO7 1PL 202 D1
World's End Bucks 135 D2
Worlds End Hants 107 F1
World's End WBerks 133 G5
Worlds End WMid 158 D4
Worle 116 A1
Worleston 171 D2
Worlingham 165 F3
Worlington 163 E5
Worlingworth 152 D1
Wormald Green 194 C1
Wormbridge 144 D4
Wormegay 163 E1
Wormelow Tump 145 D4
Wormhill 185 F5
Worminghall 134 B2
Wormingford 152 A4
Wormington 146 C4
Worminster 116 C3
Wormiston 245 E4
Wormit 244 B2
Wormleighton 147 G2
Wormley Herts 136 C2
Wormley Surr 121 E4
Wormley West End 136 C2
Wormshill 124 A3
Wormsley 144 D3
Worplesdon 121 E2
Worrall 186 A3
Worsbrough 186 A2
Worsley 184 B2
Worstead 179 E3
Worsted Lodge 150 D2
Worston 193 D3
Worswell 100 B3
Worth Kent 125 F3
Worth WSuss 122 B5

Worth Matravers 105 F5
Wortham 164 B4
Worthen 156 C2
Worthenbury 170 B3
Worthing Norf 178 A4
Worthing WSuss 108 D3
Worthington 173 F5
Worting 120 B3
Wortley Glos 131 G3
Wortley SYorks 186 A3
Wortley WYorks 194 B4
Worton NYorks 201 E4
Worton Wilts 118 A2
Wortwell 165 D3
Wothersome 194 D3
Wotherton 156 B2
Wotter 100 B1
Wotton 120 A1
Wotton Underwood 134 B1
Wotton-under-Edge 131 G3
Woughton on the Green 149 D4
Wouldham 123 G2
Wrabness 152 C4
Wrae 269 F5
Wrafton 113 E2
Wragby 188 B5
Wragholme 189 D3
Wramplingham 178 C5
Wrangaton 100 C2
Wrangham 260 E1
Wrangle 176 C1
Wrangle Lowgate 176 C2
Wrangway 103 E1
Wrantage 116 A5
Wrawby 188 A2
Wraxall NSom 131 D5
Wraxall Som 116 D4
Wray 192 C1
Wray Castle 199 E2
Wrays 122 B4
Wraysbury 135 F5
Wrayton 200 B5
Wrea Green 191 G4
Wreay Cumb 210 A5
Wreay Cumb 210 A3
Wrecclesham 120 D3
Wrekenton 212 B2
Wrelton 203 G4
Wrenbury 170 C3
Wrench Green 204 C4
Wreningham 164 C2
Wrentham 165 F3
Wrenthorpe 194 C5
Wrentnall 156 D2
Wressle ERid 195 G4
Wressle NLincs 187 G2
Wrestlingworth 150 A3
Wretham 164 A2
Wretton 163 E2
Wrexham (Wrecsam) 170 A3
Wrexham Arts Centre Wrex LL11 1AU 170 A2
Wrexham Industrial Estate 170 A3
Wribbenhall 157 G5
Wrightington Bar 183 G1
Wrightpark 242 B5
Wright's Green 137 E1
Wrinehill 171 E3
Wrington 116 B1
Writhlington 117 D2
Writtle 137 F2
Wrockwardine 157 F1
Wroot 187 E2
Wrose 194 A4
Wrotham 123 F3
Wrotham Heath 123 F3
Wrotham Hill Park 123 F2
Wrottesley 158 A2
Wroughton 132 D4
Wroxall IoW 107 E5
Wroxall Warks 159 E5
Wroxeter 157 E2
Wroxham 179 E4
Wroxham Barns Norf NR12 8QU 179 E3
Wroxton 147 G3
Wstrws 141 G3
Wyaston 172 C3
Wyberton 176 B3
Wyboston 149 G2
Wybunbury 171 D3
Wych Cross 122 D5
Wychbold 146 B1
Wychnor 159 D1
Wychnor Bridges 159 D1
Wyck 120 C4
Wyck Rissington 147 D5
Wycliffe 202 A1
Wycoller 193 F4
Wycoller Country Park Lancs BB8 8SY 193 F4
Wycomb 174 C5
Wycombe Marsh 135 D3
Wyddial 150 B4
Wye 124 C4
Wyesham 131 E1
Wyfordby 160 C1
Wyke Devon 102 B3
Wyke Dorset 117 E5
Wyke Shrop 157 F2
Wyke Surr 121 E2
Wyke WYorks 194 A5
Wyke Champflower 117 D4
Wyke Regis 104 C5
Wykeham NYorks 204 C4
Wykeham NYorks 204 B5
Wyken Shrop 157 G3
Wyken WMid 159 F4
Wykey 170 A5
Wylam 212 A1
Wylde Green 158 D3
Wyllie 130 A3
Wylye 118 B4
Wymering 107 F2
Wymeswold 174 B5
Wymington 149 E1
Wymondham Leics 161 D1
Wymondham Norf 178 C5
Wyndham 129 F3
Wynford Eagle 104 B3
Wynnstay Park 170 A3
Wynyard 212 D5
Wynyard Woodland Park Stock TS21 3JG 212 D5
Wyre Forest Worcs DY14 9XQ 157 G5

Wyre Piddle 146 B3
Wyresdale Tower 192 C2
Wysall 174 B5
Wyson 145 E1
Wytham 133 G2
Wythburn 209 G5
Wythenshawe 184 C4
Wyton Cambs 162 A5
Wyton ERid 197 D4
Wyverstone 152 B1
Wyverstone Street 152 B1
Wyville 175 D5
Wyvis Lodge 266 B3

X

Xscape Castleford WYorks WF10 4DA 194 D5

Y

Y Bryn 168 B5
Y Fan 155 F4
Y Felinheli 167 E1
Y Ffôr 166 C4
Y Fron (Upper Llandwrog) 167 E2
Yaddlethorpe 187 F2
Yafford 106 D4
Yafforth 202 C3
Yalberton 101 E2
Yalding 123 F4
Yanley 116 C1
Yanwath 210 B5
Yanworth 132 C1
Yapham 195 G2
Yapton 108 B3
Yarburgh 188 D3
Yarcombe 103 F2
Yardley 158 D4
Yardley Gobion 148 C3
Yardley Hastings 149 D2
Yardro 144 B2
Yarford 115 F5
Yarkhill 145 F3
Yarlet 171 G5
Yarley 116 C3
Yarlington 117 D5
Yarm 202 D1
Yarmouth 106 C4
Yarnacott 113 G2
Yarnbrook 117 F2
Yarnfield 171 F4
Yarnscombe 113 F3
Yarnton 133 G1
Yarpole 145 D1
Yarrow ScBord 227 E3
Yarrow Som 116 A3
Yarrow Feus 227 E3
Yarrowford 227 F3
Yarsop 144 D3
Yarwell 161 F2
Yate 131 G4
Yatehouse Green 171 E1
Yateley 120 D1
Yatesbury 132 C5
Yattendon 134 A5
Yatton Here 144 D1
Yatton NSom 116 B1
Yatton Keynell 132 A5
Yaverland 107 F4
Yawl 103 G3
Yaxham 178 B4
Yaxley Cambs 161 G3
Yaxley Suff 164 C4
Yazor 144 D3
Ye Olde Pork Pie Shoppe, Melton Mowbray Leics LE13 1NW 160 C1
Yeabridge 104 A1
Yeading 136 A4
Yeadon 194 B4
Yealand Conyers 199 G5
Yealand Redmayne 199 G5
Yealand Storrs 199 G5
Yealmbridge 100 B2
Yealmpton 100 B2
Yearby 213 E5
Yearsley 203 E5
Yeaton 156 D1
Yeaveley 172 C3
Yeavering 228 C3
Yedingham 204 B5
Yelford 133 F2
Yell 278 D4
Yelland Devon 113 E2
Yelland Devon 99 F1
Yelling 150 A1
Yellowcraig ELoth EH39 5DS 236 C1
Yelvertoft 160 A5
Yelverton Devon 100 B1
Yelverton Norf 179 D5
Yenston 117 E5
Yeo Mill 114 B5
Yeo Vale 113 E3
Yeoford 102 A3
Yeolmbridge 98 D2
Yeomadon 112 D5
Yeovil 104 B1
Yeovil Country Park Som BA20 1QZ 104 B1
Yeovil Marsh 104 B1
Yeovilton 116 C5
Yerbeston 127 D2
Yesnaby 277 B6
Yesterday's World, Battle ESuss TN33 0AQ 110 C2
Yetholm Mains 228 C4
Yetlington 229 E5
Yetminster 104 B1
Yettington 103 D4
Yetts o'Muckhart 243 F4
Yew Green 147 E1
Yielden 149 F1
Yieldshields 234 C4
Ynys 167 E2
Ynys Tachwedd 154 C3
Ynysboeth 129 G3
Ynysddu 130 A3
Ynyshir 129 G3
Ynyslas 154 C3
Ynysmaerdy 129 G4
Ynystawe 128 C2
Ynyswen 127 F3
Ynysybwl 129 G3
Yockenthwaite 201 E5

Yockleton 156 C1
Yokefleet 196 A5
Yoker 233 G3
Yonder Bognie 268 E6
York 195 F2
York Castle Museum YO1 9SA 90 York
York Dungeon YO1 9RD 90 York
York Minster YO1 7HH 90 York
Yorkletts 124 C2
Yorkley 131 F2
Yorkshire Museum YO1 7FR 90 York
Yorkshire Sculpture Park WYorks WF4 4LG 185 G1
Yorton 170 C5
Yorton Heath 170 C5
Youldon 112 D5
Youldonmoor Cross 112 D5
Youlgreave 172 D1
Youlthorpe 195 G2
Youlton 195 D1
Young's End 137 G2
Yoxall 158 D1
Yoxford 153 E1
Ysbyty Cynfyn 155 D5
Ysbyty Ifan 168 B3
Ysbyty Ystwyth 154 D5
Ysceifiog 182 C5
Ysgubor-y-coed 154 C3
Ystalyfera 129 D2
Ystrad 129 F3
Ystrad Aeron 142 B2
Ystrad Meurig 142 D1
Ystrad Mynach 130 A3
Ystradfellte 129 F1
Ystradgynlais 129 D1
Ystradowen Carmar 128 D1
Ystradowen VGlam 129 G5
Ystumtuen 154 D1
Ythanwells 260 E1
Ythsie 261 G1

Z

Zeal Monachorum 102 A2
Zeals 117 E4
Zelah 96 C4
Zennor 94 B3
Zouch 173 G5
ZSL London Zoo GtLon NW1 4RY 12 A3

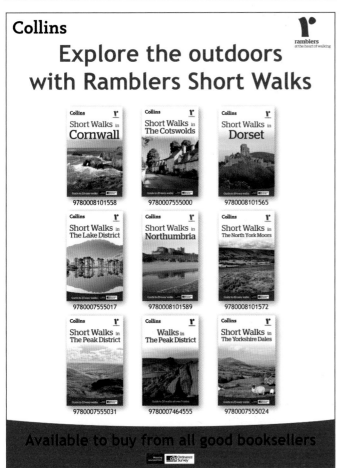